WINCHESTER'S
SCREEN
ENCYCLOPEDIA

EDITED BY
MAUD M. MILLER

*Sixteen illustrations in colour and
sixty-four in monochrome*

WINCHESTER PUBLICATIONS LIMITED
16 MADDOX STREET LONDON W.1

First published in mcmxlviii by
Winchester Publications Limited,
16 Maddox Street, London, W.1

MADE AND PRINTED IN GREAT BRITAIN BY L. T. A. ROBINSON, LTD., LONDON, S.W.9

WINCHESTER'S
SCREEN ENCYCLOPEDIA

SIR LAURENCE AND LADY OLIVIER (VIVIEN LEIGH)

INTRODUCTORY NOTE

SOME years before the war it was my interesting and sometimes adventurous fortune to be closely occupied on what might be called the fringe of the film world (i.e. the journalistic fringe) in Great Britain and in Hollywood. Part of my responsibility was the editing of a number of specialized film publications—including *The World Film Encyclopedia* (Amalgamated Press Ltd., 1933)—which happily enjoyed a success in the industry itself and also in the larger entertainment world which the industry serves.

The industry has always been a much maligned industry—sometimes wrongly so and sometimes rightly ; but since the days to which I refer there have been marked changes and developments, many of which have revealed a new and fresh outlook that has been welcome. Many more marked changes and developments are yet to come, some of them quite revolutionary. It was to record the changes and developments over the years and to present what is also a new and fresh outlook on matters pertaining to the screen world that this volume was planned, with Maud M. Miller as its editor.

A further purpose is to provide a volume of reference value to any one who, in any way, is interested in what is both an industrious and a romantic craft ; thus it is designed to appeal not only to the industry itself but also to the vast public that supports the craft of film making, which is a very multifarious business as this volume so adequately reveals. The makers of films serve the world of entertainment, education, science, natural history, and contribute to the welfare of many other branches of human activity ; and if their first consideration has been and must be that of entertainment, who shall gainsay that such a consideration is not without worthiness—if the best brains in the craft are always striving " to go one better " ?

So here is the volume, with its objects outlined, and the discriminating reader will soon judge whether or not those objects have been achieved.

My appreciative thanks are due to the distinguished contributors who have helped to make this publication possible, to those who have helped anonymously in making difficult compilations, and not least to Maud M. Miller for her zeal and enthusiasm as editor.

CLARENCE WINCHESTER

16 *Maddox Street,*
*London, W.*1.

CONTENTS

CONTENTS—*continued*

LIST OF ILLUSTRATIONS

Colour Plates

In monochrome

AS I LOOK BACK

Cecil M. Hepworth

Hon. F.R.P.S., Hon. M.B.K.S., Hon. Member of the British Film Academy

ONCE I wrote a book. There is nothing remarkable about that, except that the book appeared to embrace the whole art and science of the cinematograph in one small volume, and that it was written and published in 1897—more than half a century ago ! It was almost certainly the first book on the subject ever written.* It was quite certainly the worst. Two distinctions which can never be wrested from me.

Now I am called upon to contribute a Foreword to the, at present, latest and, I hope, the best of such books. " Foreword " is in the singular and should, I imagine, consist of a single word. But I can think of only one single word which would meet my predicament and, as that is unsuitable, I must of necessity fall into the regrettable modern practice of adding unnecessary further words to those which already are there in such great abundance. I stand appalled at the courage which could aspire to the making of this Encyclopedia, for the work involved must certainly have been prodigious. To contemplate it now from the point of view of the author of that funny little book of fifty years ago is like looking at modern films with the eyes of a " fifty-footer ". For that in the beginning was the greatest length of any film.

The first " Living Photographs " ever to be seen in public in this country were those of the famous Frenchman, Louis Lumière, who opened an exhibition with that title in a small hall in Upper Regent Street, London. Each of his film subjects was fifty feet in length and occupied fifty seconds of time. The date of that first public showing was February 26, 1896, and that date has come to be regarded as the birthday of the films in England. It is interesting to note that several of the first films contained the seeds of most of the pictures of the present day : comic, scenic, news, adventure, family life, and so on. At first these films attracted very little attention— then the Press took it up and the enthusiasm started. I toured the country the following year with a little show of my own—half a dozen one-minute films and a lot of lantern slides. There was no lack of enthusiasm among the people who now saw living pictures for the first time. They stood up and *yelled*. The first film I took myself was of the Boat Race of 1898 ; and the year after that saw the opening of the enterprise at Walton-on-Thames which afterwards became famous as the birthplace of a long stream of Hepworth films. The first seventy or so were fifty-footers, then there were occasional longer ones and gradually, very gradually, they came to be measured in hundreds, then thousands of feet. Where do we go from here ? When I was making films—I don't mean the fifty-footers, but in the later stages—I used to believe that the production staff had to do only half the job and the audience did the other half. We deliberately left a great deal to the imagination. Nowadays everything is shown, everything is told : nothing is left for the people to do. They are getting like the old man on the stile : Sometimes they sits and thinks, more often they just sits. They are apt to soak up what they see and hear but to contribute nothing, for nothing is required of them. They are apt to be easily bored. To combat this, the producers fling in ever greater grandeur, more palatial palaces, bigger staircases, more sound and fury, more brilliant colours, more ferocious fighting and even greater length.

I find these films a little tiring. I would like them rather shorter, a little more simple. Does that mean that I have still got a fifty-foot mind ? I wonder !

Animated Photography—The A.B.C. of the Cinematograph.

CECIL M. HEPWORTH
(*Photo : National Film Library*)

ADOLPH ZUKOR.

FORTY YEARS IN FILMS

Adolph Zukor

I AM happy to write a foreword for this book. I have been deeply impressed with the progress made by the British motion picture industry despite the arduous problems of the war and post-war years. There is always room for good pictures, and real progress made in one country benefits the whole international structure of our industry, from both the artistic and business angles. Free healthy competition is the lifeblood of any industry, especially ours.

Naturally I have noted many changes during the nearly forty years which I have devoted to films, and virtually all of them are for the better. Since I brought *Queen Elizabeth*, starring Sarah Bernhardt, to the American screen in 1912, the first full-length feature film to be shown in our country, feature pictures of substantially greater length, many *too* long, have become a commonplace. Sound, colour, and many other technical advancements in the screen art, which once seemed so revolutionary, have become accepted ingredients of motion pictures. The industry is looking forward to new scientific worlds to conquer, including three-dimensional films that can be seen and heard without the use of special apparatus by the audiences.

On the artistic side also the world motion picture has decidedly improved. Better educated in general, and accustomed to progressively better pictures, the world public has become more discriminating, and an ever-inspiring challenge to the picture-maker to increase the merits of his product. So long as we have free competition this challenge will of necessity be met.

As always, the story, in my opinion, is the most important element in picture-making, and from my observation the world public agrees with me. Unless the audience is really interested in the story which the film is telling, the film is a failure, no matter what stars are in it or how skilfully the director and the technical staffs have laboured. A popular star, a gifted director and surpassing ingenuity by the studio " back lot " cannot turn a " sow's ear " of a bad story into the " silk purse " of a good and successful motion picture. Whether the story be modern or costume, it must ring true with the audience. It must be about people with whom the spectator can identify himself. In America we say, " There must be somebody in the film whom they can cheer, and somebody whom they can hiss." The audience must be interested enough to follow every foot of film and have their basic emotions really stirred.

People became very well acquainted with their basic emotions during the late war. They will not accept today fraudulent attempts to stimulate those emotions on the screen. Even the broadest comedies must have a solid, valid basis, otherwise they will be dismissed as " just silly ". Likewise the modern audience will not cry over the old-fashioned artificial " tear-jerker ". Strong, honest stories are the answer. Unfortunately there are not enough of them available, despite the fact that today, unlike the early days, the world's best authors have become interested in writing for pictures.

Naturally stars are still important. Fortunately, like the writers, good artists from every walk of entertainment, including the stage, today recognize the motion picture as a highly desirable medium for their talents. And fortunately also, potential untrained stars are still being "discovered" direct for films and being developed more carefully and intelligently than ever. The field for the artist has substantially broadened with the more adult tastes of the picturegoer. No longer are surpassing " good looks " in a conventional mould the chief requirement of a star. The era of the beautiful baby-faced blonde and the almost too handsome " great lover " is over. Today the requirement, as to photographic quality, is for the artist who projects a unique, arresting and colourful personality from the screen, no matter what his or her " looks " may be. Many of our present-day outstanding screen personalities are far from " good-looking " on the Venus-Apollo standard. Stars must, indubitably, be able to act, and to act well. Among other modern advantages, this enables us to film good and unusual stories that would have been ineligible for the screen even ten years ago.

The greater and more adult skill of the artists, producers, directors, writers and technical staffs ; the broadening of the audiences' tastes ; the willingness of the film makers to journey to locations all over the world, aided by the increasing use of air transport, in order to film their product ; the growing world competition among the studios ; all these, and many other modern developments, forecast a brilliant future for the entertainment film.

Another branch of film-making which I have watched with interest, namely the educational film, received tremendous impetus from the war, when the wide use of training films by all branches of the war services showed the ability of the screen to teach quickly and decisively. The tremendous increase of the use of the film as a major adjunct to books in schools and colleges, of the documentary picture to acquaint the world with itself and its problems, and of the sub-standard size film in the home, are bound to be mighty future developments. The cinema today seems, on the face of it, to have come a long way from the early concept of the motion picture, and provides a fascinating album of memories for any pioneer to study in his leisure moments.

As Mr. Irving Berlin says in his song, " There's no business like show business." To me, the most important, vital, and exciting branch of show business is the motion picture, past, present and future. I only wish that I were thirty years younger !

FILMS IN GREAT BRITAIN

SIR RALPH RICHARDSON
(*London Film Productions*)

Sir Alexander Korda

THE FUTURE AND THE FILM

TO the generation trained in the school of H. G. Wells the imagination lights first on technical and mechanical progress. So in films one must first think of what technical developments are likely to be achieved, and then how these technical achievements will contribute to the film.

The more mature film-maker of today has grown up with the cinema. There are many still actively engaged in the production of films who were among the pioneers of fifty years ago. Indeed the span of time between past and present is not very great—almost as though a man could stretch out with one arm and touch the shadow that was yesterday's moving picture, while the other hand reaches the framework for tomorrow's design.

In my own professional life I have seen most of the technical developments which have taken place in the last thirty years, ever since I entered the film world to write sub-titles after having written a newspaper article on the " new moving pictures " which were then spreading into central Europe from France, Italy and Germany. During those thirty years there has been tremendous technical progress in the development of the moving picture camera, in the quality of the raw stock, in the laboratories and in the studios.

But, even taking into account the immensely important minor inventions in the field of studio equipment, such as lighting, laboratory equipment and film sensitivity, and a hundred other branches of film production, I think there has been only one invention that has really altered the substance of film-making, and that is sound.

Before the coming of sound the film was rather like the dummy of a ventriloquist—the wooden model of what has now become a recognized part of films. Just as the dummy's words are put into its mouth by the man who pulls the strings to make it move at the same time, so the shadows on the screen were the " puppets " of the director and his team of technicians. With the coming of sound, however, the shadows became substance, the dummy came to life, moving and talking of its own volition.

Whatever lovers of silent films may say, silent films came to an end. Without sound I do not believe that films would have remained, much less that they would have developed into the tremendously popular thing they are today in the world of entertainment.

SIR ALEXANDER KORDA *is chairman of London Film Productions Ltd., and was knighted in* 1942 *for his services to the film industry.*

It is really the application of sound which has made films grow up ; or—let us put it this way—it is sound which has given films the possibility of growing up.

When sound arrived, everybody went crazy about it as so often happens with a new fashion. For a while everything appearing on the screen that could have a noise attached to it, promptly became vocal ; it was a little time before sound was fitted into its appropriate place in the structure of a film.

It is worth noting here that H. G. Wells was one of the first people outside the film industry to evaluate the use of sound in films. When he came into the studios and worked on the production of his own story *The Shape of Things to Come*, he had already realized the possibilities of sound development. He had sensed at once that the modern sound film should be a musical composition as well as a narrative and visual composition. With this conviction he worked in close collaboration with Arthur Bliss, the composer, in planning the musical and emotional sequences. That incredible, prophetic mind of H. G. Wells visualized music in films as an integral part of the film, not as an incidental introduced merely for effect. He was over sixty years at that time, yet he not only recognized the power of the sound film, but in the work of the trick cameras used in this particular film he saw the counterpart of his early scientific romances. As he described it, he " saw himself talking to the world again with all the wisdom of experience, expressed with the force and novelty of his first youth."

Have we reached perfection in sound ? By no means. But the use of silence as the counterpoint to sound is becoming more frequent. In scenes where at one time noise would have been used to indicate an emotional climax, it has been realized that the use of silence, discreetly timed, has a greater dramatic value. This is good. This is progress.

In the field of technical development, the most important step in twenty years is noiseless recording, by means of which background noises can be eliminated. At the other end of the sound-track—in the cinema—audiences take for granted the amplification and synchronization of sound which comes from the screen. This sound, however, comes from one fixed spot behind, and in the centre of, the screen, no matter where the actor speaking the dialogue is situated on the screen. There will come a time, surely, when the voice of the actor will be projected accurately from his position on the screen. Or it could be that the scientists will discover a way to project separate sound-tracks for each ear of each member of the audience. This suggests the use of ear-phones—which is obviously absurd—so we can assume that bi-aural reception in the cinema is not likely to be achieved until such clumsy apparatus can be eliminated from our calculations.

Colour is another important development of the future. I would not rate this as high as some. There was a time some years ago when it was anticipated that every film would be made in colour, but technical research on the application of colour was very considerably restricted by the exigencies of war. In the use of colour on the screen we have a long road to travel before we attain perfection. When colour was introduced much the same thing happened as with sound. Colour rioted all over the screen, and still does, quite frequently. There is too much emphasis still on the primary colours, too little emphasis on the more subtle values of light and shade. Perhaps it is because the colour cameras are not yet sufficiently selective—perhaps it is because the film world is still too dazed with the idea of brilliance to appreciate the values of half-tones and the natural delicacy with which Nature paints the landscape. A common belief among psychologists is that pictures of trees and of water help to provide a restful atmosphere. A copse in which there are trees of half a hundred varying shades always conveys a sense of restful colour harmony. Until we can reproduce this sense of harmony when photographing a film in colour, we cannot truthfully claim to have made any real progress in film technique.

Many people blame colour and sound when they criticize films generally, but colour and sound are both only instruments. They can no more be blamed for a colour and sound film being bad than a good piano can be blamed for the bad playing of a pianist.

What will be the next invention ? The three-dimensional film ? It will obviously come, and already stereoscopy, to give it the more popular name, is well advanced in the U.S.S.R.

Stereoscopic films were produced in Moscow before the war, and were very successful in a specially designed cinema there. Making a stereoscopic film is quite simple. In order to photograph the effect of depth in a film the cameras are fitted with mirrors which record two pictures, one for the right eye and one for the left. It is in the projection of the stereoscopic film that the real secret lies.

The first screens were made of very fine copper wires strung in different directions to conform to certain scientific calculations. In a newer form the screen is made of plastic material, and in place of the copper wires there are thousands of minute lenses, between four and eight microns thick, which reflect the rays from the projector at the back of the theatre, and give the audience the illusion of seeing an image that has not only a frontal surface but sides and depth as well.

A special studio devoted to the making and development of stereoscopic films is now functioning in Moscow, and at least twenty cinemas in various cities have been planned for the showing of three-dimensional films. The high cost of the special screens for such theatres is one of the main factors in the apparent delay of universal production of stereoscopic films, but they will obviously come, if not in our generation, certainly in the next.

Sooner or later, too, television will become a corporate part of the cinema. Televised newsreels and sporting events will become part of cinema entertainment, and television will become the great diffuser of films. Evolutionary as these things may sound, I do not believe that progress will be confined to developments of a technical nature. True, such things as new lamps and new studios, new cameras and new ways of using them will be discovered, and it is in photography particularly that we may expect to develop one of the most progressive methods of film-making. I mean, of course, the development of back projection.

Experiments which have already taken place suggest that back projection will develop to the pitch where exterior backgrounds as well as interior sets can be built and filmed in such a manner that producers will be able to eliminate expensive location trips to, say, Timbuctoo, and to " shoot " their stars in the home studios in a much shorter period of time than a journey to Timbuctoo, with all the paraphernalia of transport, equipment and so forth, necessitates.

Although entirely revolutionary methods of film-making may yet be discovered, I firmly believe that the future development of films lies entirely in the *spirit* in which films are made. Any real revolution will come through the makers of films, through the inspirations which motivate their ideas and their ideals. Today films are already so highly developed on the technical side that I think we can safely disregard the technique of film-making in their future artistic development, almost as much as the writer disregards the technical development of the printing machine. While I would not like to be taken too literally in this, still I feel that the most important development of films *will* be on the artistic side— in the way in which stories are told, in the way in which they will be chosen for the screen, in the growing up of non-fictional films and, too, in the growing up of fictional films.

The non-fictional film has been making great progress in the past ten years or so, and as a result of this progress newer uses for the film are being found ; the scope of the non-fictional film is widening all the time, particularly so in schools where visual education, supplementary to " live " teaching, is on the way to becoming an accomplished fact.

Another development more particularly concerns the audience, which is after all the most important component in the recipe—for without the appreciation of the audience the film is as though it had never been conceived.

I consider that audiences should have every opportunity to see any one film for as long as they like. Under the conditions which now govern the exhibition of films this is difficult. Normally a film is shown for a week only, or in many places for only three days of a week. Because exhibitors' booking is done on long-term contracts, each film, no matter how successful, has to be taken off at the end of its stipulated period to make way for another, even though the newcomer may be of inferior quality and less entertainment value. The day will come, I hope, when we shall see a change in this system, and a good film drawing a steady audience will be allowed to remain in one theatre until there are signs that the public is no longer interested in it.

I believe that in the future certain types of entertainment films will come to be regarded in the same sympathetic manner as stage successes, and allowed to run as long as the public wishes to see them. Moreover, I foresee a healthy spirit of competition coming back again in modern guise. Instead of three, four, or five cinemas in the same district showing the same film for one week only, and for the same week (as so often happens today), cinema proprietors would have the opportunity for the initiative and showmanship which is the birthright of anyone in the entertainment business. It should be up to the individual showman to get the best goods to put in his shop window and so attract the customers.

On the surface this may seem a very materialistic outlook ; but if the cinema of the future is to flourish and be capable of further artistic development, then material problems cannot be ignored. Artists must live, and although many creative artists have produced their best work in poverty or hardship—sometimes even in desperate need— we moderns can hardly regard such states as healthy for film-making. For the film today is a necessity of our existence, and, as I have pointed out, the entertainment film is only one side of it.

Proof that the man in the street will always appreciate a good film has been given by the enthusiasm which greeted the re-appearance of many older films in British cinemas when American producers stopped sending their films here because of the seventy-five per cent *ad valorem* tax. The change I advocate in film exhibition, therefore, is only reasonable : for when genuine creative activity has produced a film—no less than when it has produced a picture, a beautiful frock, or even a beautiful meal— people should be allowed to enjoy it at their leisure and not have their pleasure curtailed by the dictates of others.

I believe, as I have always believed, that film frontiers will in due course disappear ; that films will become international in appeal. The men and women who were abroad so much during the war have returned to their homes with a wider vision of the world, with an appetite for knowledge as well as for entertainment in their cinemas. On both sides of the Atlantic audiences have a keener perception than they had before the war.

In Britain, where there has long been great interest in the foreign language film, the interest is increasing. But in the United States the home product, before the war, provided adequate entertainment. Since then, however, men from Omaha, Memphis and Wichita, from Iowa, Wisconsin and Arkansas have acquired an interest in the people of other lands—people with whom they lived and with whom they shared a common danger. Today these men and women of the United States are " conditioned " to life as it is lived in other countries besides their own. Reports from America indicate that more and more " specialized " cinemas for the showing of foreign language films have been opened, where French, Russian, Italian, and other European films are finding ever-increasing audiences.

It has always been my belief that sound and colour are in reality only "trimmings", but that the five essentials remain the same. A good story, a good script, good photography, good cast, good direction. I still believe it—but if the film is to progress, we must have *better* stories, *better* scripts, the *best* photography, the *best* cast and the *best* direction we can find. We cannot move backwards in inspiration, or technical achievement will outstrip human endeavour and, like Frankenstein's monster, destroy its creator.

And then . . . we should have to begin all over again.

PATRICIA ROC
(*Gainsborough*)

Margaret Stewart

THE RANK "EMPIRE"

TRADE, it used to be said, follows the flag. If J. Arthur Rank gets his way, it will follow the film. Rank has only one aim and object in life—to put British films on the map, and to make it possible for every film fan from Detroit to Delhi, Moscow to Melbourne, Chicago to Chungking, to see Stewart Granger and Patricia Roc. And already, to many people the world over, the words "Rank" and "British films" are synonymous.

It took three hundred years of patient pioneering for countless explorers, traders and adventurers to fling the British flag far and wide over the seven seas. Rank's cinema empire is a one-man show; he is seeking to build it in a decade and against time in a fast-moving competitive world. Yet the serious financial position of his production enterprises and the criticisms that came to a head over the Odeon deal in December 1947 have led many people to wonder "Is the Rank Empire tottering?"

Rank certainly does not mean to be deflected from his Empire-building. He has given an assurance that he has no intention of "in any way withdrawing from his effort for the British film industry" and has promised the Government to continue both to produce and to export as many films as possible.

His 1948 programme includes the production of thirty-eight feature films, for which he will require at least two million pounds in new capital. But it will not include any more expensive "prestige" films, like *Caesar and Cleopatra*, which were mainly responsible for the heavy financial losses reported to the General Cinema Finance shareholders. In the year which ended on September 28, 1946, there was a loss on film production of £1,667,070, as compared with losses of £378,293 in 1945 and £179,412 in 1944.

It was in order to provide the two million pounds necessary for the new production programme that Odeon Theatres, the exhibiting organization, acquired General Cinema Finance, the producing organization.

The announcement of the proposed acquisition was criticized mainly because of the secrecy which surrounded the deal. Odeon shareholders, commented the City, were being asked to buy a pig in the poke.

Rank's defence was that the deal merely represented the consolidation of two interests, one dealing with distribution and the other with production, both of which were in any case

MARGARET STEWART *is Industrial Correspondent of "The Economist", and a contributor to the "News Chronicle".*

controlled by himself. He argued the advantages of giving the exhibiting side a bigger stake in production, and expressed the hope that it would lead to an expansion of British film production at a time when fewer foreign films could reach the country because of the seventy-five per cent import duty.

When it came to a vote at an extraordinary general meeting of the Odeon shareholders, the deal was unanimously approved.

The controversy, which hit the headlines of the press, involves more than the city editors and the Odeon shareholders. The whole of the film-going public has an interest in the ownership of the industry, and if as a result of the incident more information is made public about film finances, a good purpose will have been served.

It is appropriate, therefore, to examine the background, present position and prospects of the Rank Empire.

It was not until the eve of World War II that Rank entered the film industry in a big way. True, he had to face inevitable wartime obstacles of shortage of labour and materials, and Government control, but on the whole he was helped by the war. A film-hungry public, with bulging pockets and little opportunity for spending money, cut off from Continental films and with fewer new American movies, presented a good opportunity for Rank to develop and consolidate his business.

Today the Rank Organisation controls more than sixty per cent of the cinemas of Britain, and over half the film production. It only stopped expanding because people began to get alarmed at what was officially described as "the trend towards monopoly in the film industry". The Government appointed a special committee of investigation—or, to use the official phraseology, "following upon representations by the Cinematograph Films Council, the President of the Board of Trade in a letter dated 6th December, 1943, invited the Council to give him their advice on what further practical measures, if any, are necessary to check the development of monopoly in the film industry." That report generally referred to as the "Monopoly Report"—was delivered on August 1, 1944, and the Government, having accepted the conclusion of the committee that there was a danger of a Rank monopoly, said to Rank, "Thus far, and no farther."

J. Arthur Rank was quite happy to comply, and to stop acquiring new circuits and cinemas. Nobody suggested that he should give up any of those he already had, and, what was more important to him, no limitations were placed on the overseas expansion of his organization. Far from it: the Government swiftly recognized the export potential of British films, their education value and their dollar-earning capacity at a time when the nation was in debt to practically the whole world. So Rank was given every possible encouragement to build up his overseas contacts and to develop an international network of distributing agencies and picture houses in the United States, the Dominions, Europe and the Middle East. Indeed, so good have been the relations between this millionaire monopolist and the British Labour Government that many eyebrows have been raised, sceptically, at what is regarded as a strange alliance of opposites.

The Rank Organisation, however, has never sought any financial help from the state. Money, it seemed at one time, was no object to Rank, who was prepared to finance such lavish Technicolor productions as *Caesar and Cleopatra* (hotly criticized for costing £1,300,000), *Men of Two Worlds*, which took two years to make, and the Wesley Ruggles production *London Town*, which cost nearly £1,000,000. Rank's answer to the criticisms of the expense of these productions was that if they succeeded in bringing in dollars and raising British prestige with American audiences, the money would have been well spent. In actual fact, *Caesar and Cleopatra* did not, according to reports, turn out to be a box-office draw in the United States ; and *Men of Two Worlds*, dealing with the colour problem, was from the first a non-starter there.

It all started about 1931, when J. Arthur Rank, finding that the flour mill business he inherited from his father did not occupy all his restless energies, conceived the idea that the cinema would be a good medium for combating godlessness. Methodism was in his blood, and, having been a regular chapelgoer all his life, he was determined to arrest the materialistic trend of a generation growing up in the dismal and depressed 'thirties. His first ventures were failures—a film about St. Francis of Assissi, starring Donald Wolfit, and a Temperance film called *The Seven Men of Preston*. In 1935 he produced a documentary about Yorkshire fishermen, *The Turn of the Tide*, which won third place at the International Film Exhibition at Venice, but failed to arouse any enthusiasm among distributors.

Nettled by their attitude, Rank decided to go into the business properly—to produce his own films in his own studios, and to show them in his own theatres. Together with the late C. M. Woolf of Gaumont British Pictures (who became managing director), he set up General Film Distributors. Over the next few years the two men collaborated in building up the great distribution and production organization. After having bought the Odeon, Leicester-square, London, in 1936, Rank went into three smaller circuits, and in 1937 reached an agreement with the Gaumont British Picture Corporation which gave him joint production with Gainsborough Pictures, distribution

of the G.B. Newsreel, and the Shepherd's Bush Laboratories. Thus, from small beginnings, were laid the foundations of the mammoth combine, the J. Arthur Rank Organisation Limited, which dominates the British—if not the world—film scene today.

The Rank Organisation is a giant vertical trust, a world within a world, comprising more than eighty companies engaged in the production, distribution and exhibition of films, and the manufacture of cinema equipment. It employs well over 30,000 people in its various branches, and has a highly efficient research department. Here, successful experiments in the development of the back projection process known as the " independent frame " were carried out in 1947. This may well revolutionize film production by cutting down the time a film unit requires inside a studio to make a film, with consequent economy in the cost of production.

The total value of the Organisation has been put at anything from fifty to sixty million pounds. But actually the capitalization of the parent firm which controls the Organisation—Manorfield Investments Limited—is only one hundred pounds.

Rank made his first major purchase in the early days of the war, when he bought the Odeon cinema circuit established by the late Oscar Deutsch. Then, after some pretty hard bargaining, he bought the Gaumont British chain of cinemas. His films are also shown in a West of England circuit of seventeen theatres, in which he is a partner, and at the Leicester-square Theatre, London. The production side of the Rank Organisation has been developed on an equally ambitious scale. Rank's first studio, Pinewood, was acquired before the war. Later he acquired from Alexander Korda and the Prudential Assurance Company the new studio at Denham. Studios at Shepherd's Bush, Islington and Highbury (used for research, the grooming of junior starlets and, latterly, for the production of second feature films) were later added, followed by a studio at Elstree where religious films are now made. The corner-stone of G.B. Animation was laid in 1945, when David Hand, an ex-colleague of Disney, came to Britain, and in an old manor house at Cookham, Berks, gathered the nucleus of a cartoon studio.

The production of films is distributed among a number of different companies within the combine. Gainsborough Pictures, which includes films made at Shepherd's Bush and Islington, are directly dependent. So also are Two Cities. Independent Producers (1942) are financially dependent, but have creative freedom. Under this collective title are Archers, Cineguild, Individual, and Wessex Films. A number of other producers operate within the Organisation—Sydney Box Productions, Highbury, and some smaller companies.

A separate company, Production Facilities (Films) Limited, was formed in 1945 to handle technical and commercial matters for the film production companies, and there is a large advertising business as well. The Rank Organisation controls two newsreels, Universal and Gaumont British, and has developed a subsidiary for Instructional films, producing shorts, education and industrial films. One of the latest developments, started in 1946, is *This Modern Age*, British rival to *The March of Time*. Each film runs for about twenty minutes and costs about £30,000 to make. The plan for the children's clubs, showing specially made feature films, as well as serials, cartoons, instructional films and short features, is well advanced, under the guidance of Mary Field and her Advisory Council of other child experts.

Rank saw that the ownership of actual film studios and circuits was not enough if his Organisation was to be self-sufficient, and started to collect ancillary interests. He bought out Gaumont British Kalee, and thus became his own producer of equipment and screens. G.B. Kalee not only produces for the home market, where it supplies over sixty per cent of British cinemas with equipment, but it has considerable export potential; and the group has agents operating in China, India, Australia and South America, as well as on the continent of Europe, with the ultimate object of creating an organization equivalent to the United States Western Electric Company, or the pre-war German Zeiss-Ikon Company. By acquiring an interest in Taylor, Taylor & Hobson, in 1946, Rank assured his supply of lenses. In the same year, rights for the manufacture of Bell & Howell equipment in the United Kingdom were obtained. From British Acoustics he secures sound equipment machinery. 1947 saw the formation of a special company, with a £150,000 capital, to manufacture cinema seats, and also the formation of a cosmetics company, for the exclusive use of his stars.

In 1947 Rank announced his scheme for building a chain of television stations throughout the country to transmit news events and feature films in hundreds of cinemas. Nor is this the limit of his interests. The Rank Organisation also owns twenty-five music-halls, the General Theatre Corporation, and two repertory theatres, and recently acquired the Winter Garden Theatre in the West End of London.

The process of control has been completed by the much-criticized deal, referred to above, whereby Rank's Odeon Theatres Corporation acquired the issued shares of the General Cinema Finance Corporation. This has a controlling interest in Gaumont British Picture Corporation Limited, and holds investments in other cinema and studio-owning companies. At the time of the deal its assets—just over eight million pounds, of which only £193,000 was in cash—exceeded liabilities by £1,300,000. This acquisition, as Rank pointed out, represented a consolidation of major film interests.

So much for the domestic set-up. Abroad, the Organisation's main company is Eagle-Lion Distributors, which distributes British films all over the world. After Rank's visit to America in 1945 United World Pictures was formed, and later the Eagle-Lion company of the U.S., and Prestige Pictures. In 1946 Rank acquired a controlling interest in Universal Pictures, Hollywood. The company now known as Universal-International was formed in 1947, absorbing United World Pictures. By this move a major Hollywood producing company, with supplementary distribution machinery in the United States and Latin America, was added to the Rank Empire.

The Organisation is well established in Canada. British films are distributed through the Eagle-Lion company, and Rank owns the Odeon circuit of one hundred and ten theatres. In Australia he is a partner in the Rydge circuit of eighty-two theatres, and in New Zealand in the hundred and twenty Kerridge theatres. In 1947 Rank brought off a successful deal with the South African film magnates, John and Max Schlesinger, for the showing of British films in four hundred cinemas south of the equator. A super cinema was built in Cairo, and Rank also secured control over the majority of cinemas in Jamaica by the simple process of acquiring majority interests in the Palace Amusement Company. Cinemas were also purchased in Eire in 1947, and there is an extensive system of distribution in India, China and the Middle East.

The following summary table shows the extent of Rank exhibiting interests overseas, 1947 :

Australia	115 cinemas
Canada	138 ,,
Ceylon	19 ,,
Egypt	3 ,,
Eire	16 ,,
Holland	12 ,,
Italy	130 ,,
Jamaica	16 ,,
Malaya	3 ,,
New Zealand	143 ,,
South Africa	130 ,,

In South America British films have had a great success. The Rank experts recognize that the Latin American countries represent a large, virtually untapped market which, with publicity and exploitation, could develop rapidly. In less than eight months, in 1946-7, British films took over £800,000. Rank has an agreement with the U.S.S.R. for reciprocal showings of films, and, after long negotiations, a similar reciprocal agreement was reached with France in 1946. Czechoslovakia agreed to show British features and *This Modern Age* documentaries for two years.

Amid all this world-wide activity Rank is mainly interested in the American market. He hopes to take the battle right into Hollywood, and ultimately to beat the Americans at their own game, despite any setbacks resulting from the dollar crisis of August 1947. The reported success of such British films as *Henry V, Brief Encounter, The Seventh Veil, Odd Man Out* and, above all, *Great Expectations*, has encouraged his hopes for the future. But no information has been made available about the financial results of these enterprises ; and the high dollar expenditure for exploitation must be set against the final returns of all films sent to America.

In the main it is a friendly battle. It could hardly be much else, with the degree of integration of interests between the Rank and American companies, such as RKO Radio, 20th Century-Fox, United Artists and Universal, with all of whom he has production or distribution agreements —as well as studio interests in the Pagewood Studios in Australia, and with South African studios in Johannesburg.

Months of persistent and patient negotiations culminated in the agreement, signed in June 1947 after Rank's tour of the United States, for British films to be shown in 3000 American cinemas. These 3000 represent some sixty per cent of all North American cinemas, and the deal was widely hailed as the first really effective breach of the U.S. market, the consolidation of earlier-established bridgeheads. But because of the British Governments imposition of an *ad valorem* tax of seventy-five per cent on foreign films and the general dollar crisis, Anglo-American film relations are very much in the melting-pot. At the end of 1947, negotiations were still proceeding between the British Treasury and the representative in Britain of the American Motion Picture Association, but no agreement had been reached.

Equally uncertain is the actual or potential dollar-earning capacity of Rank's films in the United States. American films in Britain cost an average of seventeen million pounds in each of the three years, 1944, 1945 and 1946. No precise estimate of the earnings of British films has been given, and in view of the colossal expenditure on advertising and exploitation, and the payment, in dollars, for American films imported to Britain, the net gain must be small. Rank is clearly viewing the matter as a long-term policy and taking a stupendous gamble. Given more production facilities and more studio space at home, he has estimated that he could make eighty to a hundred and ten feature films a year, instead of the present thirty to forty, which might earn for Britain as much as eighteen to twenty million dollars a year. This is very hypothetical. Indeed, there is not even any secure ground for confidence that the vast dollar expenditure could be offset by the takings from British films, especially if a film war intervenes.

* * *

J. Arthur Rank is the epitome of mid-Victorian business men. Unlike most of them, however, he was not a self-made man, but inherited millions from his miller father and married an heiress, the daughter of Lord Marshall, of Horace Marshall & Son, wholesale newsagents. Money and mills were not all he got from old Joseph Rank. He inherited business acumen. He has never forgotten his father's advice, " Arthur, my boy, never

under-estimate your competitors, they are always smarter than you ! "

Rank once said that his guiding motto in life was " Get all you can ; give all you can ; and save all you can." He has certainly got what he could, and he certainly gives generously to charity. As for saving—well, only a small proportion of his personal wealth goes to finance his films, and he lives modestly and temperately.

J. Arthur Rank combines temperance with tolerance. He allows the maximum freedom of action to his producers and directors. It has been said of him that all he wants to know about a film project are the right answers to the two questions, " Will it be box-office ? " and " How much will it cost ? "

This alleged attitude once caused him to be severely taken to task by one of Britain's most famous stars, James Mason. " Arthur Rank," the hero of *Odd Man Out* was reported as saying, " is the worst thing that has happened to the British film industry." The reasons for this criticism were that Rank had too much money and completely mishandled and misunderstood his creative artists. The quarrel was later made up, but similar criticisms have been levelled at the Rank Organisation by others.

The trouble is that like any medieval prince or oriental potentate who is in a position to distribute patronage and largesse, Arthur Rank is the target of sycophants and intriguers. His intimate friends are few—apart from his wife, who shares all his business enterprises as well as such private life as he has. He works sixteen and sometimes twenty hours a day, takes only a fortnight off every year, and has little time or energy to spare for his favourite relaxations of golf and shooting. Rank's waking and sleeping hours are filled with films, but he still devotes one day each week to his milling business.

In some ways Rank is a medievalist in a moneyed age. He feels himself inspired by a crusade to show British films and to further the Christian faith. " I am doing this work for God and my country," he once said.

The question of whether on balance Rank's influence has been good or bad for the British film industry cannot be answered hastily. His critics, who are many, will not hesitate to condemn him. Obviously it is dangerous that one man should have so much power to influence public opinion through the medium of the film. And obviously, in a young industry like films, competition is healthy and monopoly can be stifling in effect. But the situation is paradoxical. It seems clear that, without Rank, British film production might never have advanced to its present state, and his organization presents a potentially important source of foreign currency at a time of financial crisis. Whatever the academic arguments against monopoly in the industry, the quality of many of the films produced under the Rank regime has been a good advertisement for Britain.

THE STRUCTURE OF
THE J. ARTHUR RANK ORGANISATION

Parent Company :
Manorfield Investments Ltd.

Finance and Holding Companies :
British & Dominions Film Corporation Ltd.
Denham & Pinewood Holdings Ltd.
General Cinema Finance Corporation Ltd.
General Theatre Corporation (Canada) .
Metropolis & Bradford Trust Company Ltd.
Odeon Cinema Holdings Ltd.
Odeon Holdings (New Zealand) Ltd.
Odeon Holdings (South Africa) Pty. Ltd.
Overseas Cinematograph Theatres Ltd.

Studio, Laboratory and Production Companies :
British Pictorial Productions Ltd.
D. & P. Studios Ltd.
Denham Laboratories Ltd.
Film Laboratories Ltd.
Gainsborough Pictures (1928) Ltd.
G. B. Animation Ltd.
G. B. Instructional Ltd.
G.H.W. Productions Ltd.
Independent Producers Ltd.
Production Facilities (Films) Ltd.
This Modern Age Ltd.
Two Cities Films Ltd.

Distribution Companies :
British Distributors (India) Ltd.
Eagle-Lion Distributors (Greece) Ltd.
Eagle-Lion Distributors Ltd. (Branches in Austria, Singapore, Hong Kong, China, Manila)
Eagle-Lion Distributors (Middle East) Ltd.
Eagle-Lion Film A/S (Denmark)
Eagle-Lion Films of Canada Ltd.
Eagle-Lion Films S.A. (Italy)
Eagle-Lion France S.A.
Eagle-Lion Maatschappij N.V. (Holland)
Film A.B. Eagle-Lion (Sweden)
Gaumont British Distributors Ltd.
General Film Distributors Ltd.
J. Arthur Rank Organisation Inc. (U.S.A.)
Universal Pictures Ltd.

Exhibiting Companies :
Albany Ward Theatres Ltd.
Associated Provincial Picture Houses Ltd.
Denman (London) Cinemas Ltd.
Denman Picture Houses Ltd.
Gaumont British Picture Corporation Ltd.
Gaumont Super Cinemas Ltd.
General Theatre Corporation Ltd.
Odeon (Alexandria) Ltd.
Odeon Associated Theatres Ltd.
Odeon (Cairo) Ltd.

Odeon (Ireland) Ltd.
Odeon Properties Ltd.
Odeon Theatres Ltd.
Odeon Theatres of Canada Ltd.
Overture Theatre Ltd.
Provincial Cinematograph Theatres Ltd.
Soc. Anglo-Portugesa de Cinemas S.A.R.L.

Miscellaneous Companies—Equipment, Research, Sub-Standard
Bell & Howell Company Ltd.
British Acoustic Films Ltd.
Bush Radio Ltd.
Cinema-Television Ltd.
Gaumont Kalee (Seating) Ltd.
G.B. Equipments Ltd.
G.B. Screen Services Ltd.
Taylor, Taylor & Hobson Ltd.

ASSOCIATED COMPANIES
Studio, Laboratory and Production Companies :
Alliance Productions Ltd.
G. B. Kalee Ltd.
Universal Pictures Company Inc.

Distribution Companies :
African Consolidated Films Ltd.
British Empire Films (Pty.) Ltd. (Australia)
Gaumont Eagle-Lion S.A. (Belgium)

MICHAEL WILDING
(*Herbert Wilcox*)

THE STORY OF THE
ASSOCIATED BRITISH
PICTURE CORPORATION

TO many filmgoers the name "Elstree" is synonymous with British International Pictures—or B.I.P. as the company was affectionately known for many years before re-organization took place in October 1933 and the familiar name was changed to Associated British Pictures.

The first "big" studios in Britain were begun at Elstree in 1926. These studios play an important part in film history, for they are linked with the names of at least three international film pioneers—Friese-Greene, Pathé and the Warner brothers.

William Friese-Greene, an Englishman, patented the first moving picture camera on June 21, 1889. His son Claude carried on his father's experimental work, largely in the field of colour photography, while he was working as one of B.I.P.'s ace cameramen.

The Frenchman Charles Pathé started film-making on his own about the turn of the century, and later produced the newsreel which is now affiliated, with the Pathe distributing agency, to the Associated British Picture Corporation.

The story of the studios themselves began when Herbert Wilcox, the British producer and director, met an American, J. D. Williams, a cinema owner with properties in the United States and Australia, who was visiting Britain in 1926 to study the possibilities of extending his film interests.

When the two men first met, Wilcox had just completed *Nell Gwyn*, starring Dorothy Gish. As a result of this expensive film Wilcox was penniless and had no idea when or where his next meal would be. The salesman instinct for which Wilcox is celebrated asserted itself when he met the American, and before the two men parted Wilcox had sold *Nell Gwyn* outright for £35,000. Williams arranged distribution of the film in the U.S.A., and, partly out of his profits, built studios at Boreham Wood, called them British National Studios, and invited Wilcox to become one of the company's directors.

At about the same time, Pathé's London company was going through a process of evolution. In the early 'twenties Lord Beaverbrook held certain financial interests in the company. These he disposed of in 1926 to the American company, First National—then a subsidiary of Warner Brothers.

The following year Warners absorbed First National, and resold their Pathé interests to a Scottish lawyer, John Maxwell. Recognizing the potentialities of the cinema, Maxwell had begun buying halls throughout Britain, and was also developing—in London—a distributing agency known as Wardour Films, which had evolved from a Scottish company, Waverly Films.

Maxwell also entered into an association with J. D. Williams at Elstree to produce films. Through Williams' American and Australian holdings, a certain amount of overseas distribution was thus made possible.

Then Wilcox decided to build his own studios there, and resigned from the original J. D. Williams' British National Studios in 1927 to devote his whole time to his own productions.

In keeping with their transatlantic interests the Maxwell-Williams studios were then renamed "British International Pictures".* The name of Pathé came to be associated with Elstree through the distributing agency, " Pathé Pictures ".

Another studio was begun at Welwyn in 1926. Here, a subsidiary of the Maxwell group called British Instructional Films produced *Secrets of Nature* and a number of educational films under the direction of H. Bruce Woolfe, Percy Smith and Mary Field. This unit was afterwards acquired by Gaumont British, and became Gaumont British Instructional. The Welwyn Studios were turned over to feature production.

In 1927 B.I.P. began expansion of their studios, which had consisted originally of only two stages. Before these plans were fully carried out, however, J. D. Williams left the company and his interests were taken over by John Maxwell.

B.I.P. Studios were enlarged to three blocks, containing nine stages. While Alfred Hitchcock was filming *Blackmail* there it was decided to halt production, wire the studios for sound, and re-make the film as a " talkie "—Britain's first.

By 1929 B.I.P. had become the largest film-producing unit in Britain. The earliest bi-lingual (*Atlantic*) and tri-lingual (*Two Worlds*) films were made in its studios. Two of George Bernard

---

* The company now known under the name " British National " was formed in 1935 by J. Arthur Rank, John Corfield, and Lady Yule. Later, Rank severed his connection with the company. In 1939 Lady Yule acquired studios at Elstree built originally by Ludwig Blattner and enlarged by Joe Rock.

Shaw's plays were filmed there—*Arms and the Man* and *How He Lied to Her Husband*. Stars whose names are now part of film history first faced the cameras on its stages. Technicians who are now equally world famous learned their craft there. For ten years B.I.P. produced an average of fifteen films a year, and their distribution was assured in the A.B.C. chain of theatres which Maxwell had founded. Maxwell also entered into a distribution agreement with certain American companies—among them Metro-Goldwyn-Mayer and Warner Brothers.

The film slump of 1937-8 affected B.I.P. as adversely as it did any other studio, and what little production was maintained was financed from the profits of the A.B.C. chain of cinemas.

On the outbreak of war the studios were requisitioned for use as an Army ordnance depot, and were not freed until early in 1946. Production during this period was carried on at Welwyn Studios.

By this time a strong American interest had been taken in Associated British. After the death of John Maxwell in 1940, the Warner brothers acquired fifty per cent of the Maxwell holdings of the share capital, the balance remaining in the hands of his widow and her family under certain trusts.

During the war certain adjustments were made. Since 1945 Warners have held two million A.B.P. ordinary shares—or thirty-seven and a half per cent of the Corporation's shares. Max Milder, managing director of Warner Brothers' London office was appointed managing director of Associated British in 1941.

In 1946 Mr. Milder announced a million-pound scheme for rebuilding Elstree Studios, and the smaller Warner-British studios at Teddington, which had been badly damaged by enemy action. Reconstruction work included a complete re-survey of Elstree, and the building of a new administration block and four additional stages, making a total of thirteen stages.

Making this announcement Mr. Milder said : " The new studios will be equipped with the technical efficiency of Warner Brothers' huge plant in Burbank, California. The British studios will embody the Burbank plan of dressing-rooms, wardrobes, crafts departments and engineering shops. Import licences have been granted for complete photographic, lighting and sound recording installations selected by the Corporation experts during their American inspections."

In 1946, Pathé revived its educational and instructional department under the old name of British Instructional Films. Pathé Newsreel and Pathé Pictorial were completely re-organized under the direction of Howard Thomas.

The Pathé Gazette (now Pathé News) was born in Paris in March 1909, when Charles Pathé told his colleagues of a plan to show the world a new kind of film. " It will take the audience round the world in five minutes," he said, " and we shall call it the newsreel." His colleagues thought he was mad, but it was " madness " with a touch of genius. It was Charles Pathé who persuaded the High Command during World War I to allow his news cameramen to accompany the troops into the battlefields, and through his news-reels he created a bond of experience between the fighting men and their families, by showing not only the generals and the parades, but also the daily lives of the men in the trenches.

In twenty years the wheel has turned full circle. B.I.P. grew from the inspiration of an American pioneer, J. D. Williams, and is now linked again to American interests—those of the Warner Brothers. The A.B.C. circuit, with more than 450 cinemas, ensures distribution of films in Britain. Through the Warner machinery in the United States, films made at the new Elstree Studios have been promised overseas distribution.

Twenty years after, the name of British National is once more allied to the group. By an agreement signed in 1947, all films produced at Lady Yule's studios are today released through the Pathé distributing organization. Since 1937 Pathé has been the distributing agency in Britain of films made by the Monogram and Producers' Releasing Corporation group of the U.S.A.

The story of B.I.P. and Elstree would not be complete without mention of Joe Grossman, one of the more picturesque veterans of British films. Appointed studio manager in July 1927, he has lived at Elstree through the glories and the hazards, the fires and the bombs, and is as much a part of its history as the stones of which the studios were built.

In World War I " Joe " was awarded the special diploma of the Grand Order of St. John of Jerusalem for services in connection with the transport of the wounded. During his career at B.I.P. he has conducted kings, queens, statesmen, and visiting celebrities of all nations round the studios. As an executive in the Red Cross he has been present at every Royal Premiere—and many more Royal occasions. As chief of the local fire brigade, whose headquarters were for years inside the studio grounds, he has attended every fire within a twenty-mile radius.

Nor is the story complete without record of his remark to the King of the Hellenes whom he was escorting round the studios, explaining the mystery of film-making : " . . . of course it's quite simple to us, though I daresay it's all Greek to you, Your Majesty ! "

Sir Henry L. French, G.B.E., K.C.B.

QUOTA LEGISLATION

THE Cinematograph Films Acts of 1927 and 1938 have played an immensely important part in the development of the British film industry. These Acts are generally spoken of as " Quota " Acts. It is an ugly un-English word, but it has the great advantage of being short. I propose therefore to use it throughout this article.

What does Quota really mean ? What is its value to the industry ? What is its future to be ? These are the questions which this article will discuss.

Film quotas were first made obligatory in this country by the Act of 1927. Their form, but not their purpose, was slightly changed by the Act of 1938. This Act expires in 1948. It is this last fact which explains why the subject of Quota has attracted so much attention during the past two years, in both the general and trade Press.

The Act of 1927 imposed certain quota obligations on both film renters and film exhibitors. The renter is the man who in the industry acts as a wholesaler or distributor ; he occupies a midway position between the producer of the film and the exhibitor—or cinema owner— who shows it to the public.

Why did Parliament in 1927 decide to put certain statutory obligations upon renters and exhibitors ? The reason was that the large, experienced and efficient American film industry had at that time what may be fairly described as a stranglehold on the film industry of this country. Parliament decided therefore to pass an Act the purpose of which was to give the British industry a chance of surviving and expanding.

The Act of 1927 may be regarded as an experiment. Its supporters were neither very satisfied nor very disappointed with the way it worked. When it came to an end in 1938, Parliament had no serious doubt about renewing it, and an effort was then made to close some of the gaps which the previous ten years had shown to exist in its provisions.

Unfortunately, the Act of 1938 had scarcely been brought into operation before war broke out in September, 1939, and it is true to say that the Act of 1938 has never been given a fair chance of justifying itself.

At present about eighty per cent of screen time in Great Britain is being devoted to the exhibition of American films. Among renters in this country about the same proportion (that is, eighty per cent) represents American interests. When the Act of 1927 was in course of preparation, exhibitors

Sir Henry French *has been Director General of the British Film Producers Association since* 1946.

urged that, if they were going to be required to show a certain proportion of British films in their cinemas, a similar obligation should apply to renters. In fact, Parliament went further and made the renters' quota throughout the ten years covered by the Act of 1938 slightly higher than the exhibitors' quota so as to give exhibitors a choice of films among those available from renters.

In no respect was the Act of 1927 more experimental than in the provisions dealing with renters' quota. Whatever the theoretical case for the renters' quota might have been, practice proved very different from theory. Ways and means were found by many distributors for ensuring that the showing of American films and the revenues to be derived from them were both affected as little as possible by the obligations placed upon renters. Everyone in the industry has heard of " Quota Quickies ", the admitted purpose of which was to enable American renters to comply with their quota obligations by acquiring cheaply made British films while interfering as little as possible with their main task which, of course, was to distribute and collect revenue for imported films.

If war had not come in 1939 the Act of 1938 might have proved more efficient than its predecessor. The fact however is that the improved renters' quota provisions of 1938 in the form in which they were placed on the Statute Book have never been put to the test. Therefore, we have no experience how far the 1938 statutory provisions respecting renters' quota would be effective if they were put into operation.

Instead of renters being required, as the Act laid down, to acquire British long films in 1947 equal to thirty per cent of the total of all films they distribute, this obligation has been reduced by a Board of Trade Order and renters are actually obliged to acquire a minimum of one British film of 7000 feet or more out of a total of 100,000 feet of film ; in other words, their thirty per cent obligation has been reduced to seven per cent, while the exhibitors' obligation has been reduced from twenty-five per cent to twenty per cent. The important point about these figures is that, whereas Parliament thought it necessary to place the renters' quota at a higher level than the exhibitors' quota so as to ensure that the latter's requirements would be fully covered when renting films from distributors, the position today is quite different—the renters' quota is considerably less than one half of the exhibitors' quota.

The question of renters' quota is one of the points about which there is much controversy. The exhibitor still urges that the renter should be placed under some statutory obligation, and considers that if this is not done he (the exhibitor) will unquestionably find his own quota more onerous than it otherwise would be. It is difficult to understand this attitude when consideration is given to the present position of exhibitors' and renters' quotas, but undoubtedly many exhibitors hold tenaciously to the same objective that they fought for in 1927 and again in 1938.

The position of British film producers is different. Their attitude on renters' quota is clear-cut. They say that the renters' quota is of little or no value to the exhibitor. On the other hand, it is extremely harmful to film producers in this country. Largely owing to war conditions, the production facilities in British studios are restricted and likely to remain so for some time. Stages, timber, plaster, technicians and labour are all scarce. The British producer therefore says, " Why should an American company be forced by statute to arrange for some part of these limited facilities to be devoted to the making of a film which it really does not want, but which it will have to have if the renters' quota is re-enacted ? "

This is not merely a difference of opinion between exhibitors and producers. The taxpayer has a very real interest in the issue. If the stages at a British studio are being used for production by a British company, the profits which may be earned will be ploughed back into the British film industry. The film may also be sent overseas and become an important export earning foreign currency, including dollars. On the other hand, if those stages are producing a film for an American company, the profits earned in this country may go to the United States to swell the already large sum payable every year for the use in this country of American-produced films. In addition, if this film produced in a British studio is sent overseas, the money which it earns may not come back to Britain but will probably be sent to America. Therefore in January 1947 the producers recommended unanimously and strongly that no statutory obligation should be placed upon renters to acquire British films.

Now to turn to the exhibitors' quota. For all practical purposes there is no controversy about the fundamental issue that there must for another ten years at least be an exhibitors' quota. There is, nevertheless, a wide difference of opinion as to the form in which the statutory obligation should be placed upon exhibitors. The producers recommended that there should be two separate quotas, one applied to what is called the first feature, that is, the principal film in the programme, and a second quota at a lower level for the "supporting programme". The exhibitors have made representations to the effect that an arrangement of the kind recommended by the producers would be unworkable. Nevertheless, British producers consider this part of their recommendations as absolutely essential if the new Act is to be a real improvement on the two preceding Acts. Moreover, producers can see no serious administrative difficulty in the adoption of the modification which they recommend.

The chief point at issue is not so much the *form* of the exhibitors' quota, but the *level* of the quota. There is general agreement that Parliament should not be invited to fix the quota year by year as it has done in the previous Acts for a period of ten years, but that the Board of Trade should be entrusted with the responsibility of determining the level of the quota to be periodically imposed on exhibitors. The Board of Trade should, it is recommended, be required to take into account the quantity of British films which will be available.

There is also general agreement about another important aspect of exhibitors' quota. It is universally recognized that some cinemas find it more difficult than others to fulfil their obligations. It is, therefore, widely agreed that there should not be a uniform quota applicable to all cinemas, but that it should vary according to the ability of the exhibitor to fulfil his obligations.

There is one further matter on which there is general agreement. No reasonable person wants to exclude American films from this country. No one wants to keep any good film, wherever it is produced, out of this country. No one wants to reduce the total number of films available in this country to such an extent as would require a number of cinemas to close their doors or to reduce the number of performances per week.

Producers have recommended that the minimum proportion of British films to be shown at what may be called the normal cinema should be six out of twenty-six first features and four out of twenty-six films in supporting programmes. There would of course be cinemas which, owing to their particular circumstances, would be given an individual quota less than six and four respectively.

Exhibitors consider that the producers have asked for too much. Fortunately, the decision will not rest with either producers or exhibitors. It will be for Parliament to determine the issue.

PRODUCTION, DISTRIBUTION AND EXHIBITION
IN GREAT BRITAIN

PRODUCTION COMPANIES

ALLIANCE FILM STUDIOS LTD.
(Comprising Coronet, Diadem, Gloria, Holbein, Kenilworth and Tudor Films)
Riverside Studios, Crisp-road, Hammersmith, London W.6
Telephone : RIVERSIDE 3012
Dirs. : James A. Carter, N. Bronsten, Walter Forde (production executives), M. Rubens.

ALLIANCE PRODUCTIONS LTD.
(RKO Radio British films, made in association with the Rank Organisation)
Dean House, 2 Dean-street, London W.1.
Telephone : GERRARD 5640

APOLLO FILMS LTD.
127-133 Wardour-street, London W.1
Telephone : GERRARD 7311
Dirs. : W. J. Fullerton (chmn.), F. H. Bentley, C. R. Delliston, Sir Granville Gibson, C. E. Tidswell.

ARCHERS FILM PRODUCTIONS LTD., THE
Empire House, 117-9 Regent-street, London W.1
Telephone : REGENT 0621
Dirs. : Michael Powell, Emeric Pressburger.

ARGYLE BRITISH PRODUCTIONS LTD.
59 Shaftesbury-avenue, London W.C.2
Telephone : GERRARD 4081
Dirs. : John F. Argyle, F. H. Argyle.

ASSOCIATED BRITISH PICTURE CORPORATION LTD.
30 Golden-square, London W.1
Telephone : GERRARD 7887
Chmn. : Sir Philip Warter ; managing dir. : Max Milder ; dirs. : Robert Clark, Edward Maloney ; exec. prod. (Welwyn Studios) : Warwick Ward.

JOHN BAXTER PRODUCTIONS LTD.
10 Eccleston-place, London S.W.1
Telephone : SLOANE 8791
Managing dir. and exec. i/c production : John Baxter.

BRITISH AVIATION PICTURES LTD.
The Manor, Davies-street, London W.1
Telephone : MAYFAIR 4016
Dirs. : George King, John Stafford, C. King (production executives).

BRITISH NATIONAL FILMS LTD.
National Studios, Boreham Wood, Elstree, Herts
Telephone : ELSTREE 1644
Dirs. : Sir Henry Richardson (chmn.), Louis H. Jackson (managing dir. and exec. i/c production), Lady Yule, G. M. Yule.

BRYANSTON FILMS LTD.
20 Brown-street, Bryanston-square, London W.1
Dir. : Leslie Arliss (production executive).

BUTCHER'S FILM SERVICE LTD.
175 Wardour-street, London W.1
Telephone : GERRARD 7282
I/c production : F. W. Baker.

CHARTER FILM PRODUCTIONS LTD.
Colquhoun House, Broadwick-street, London W.1
Telephone : GERRARD 8646
Dirs. : John Boulting, Roy Boulting.

CHILDREN'S ENTERTAINMENT FILMS, G.B.
Instructional Ltd.
17 Oxendon-street, Haymarket, London S.W.1
Telephone : WHITEHALL 2826
Dirs. : J. Arthur Rank (chmn.), L. W. Farrow, Mark Ostrer, I. H. Cremieu-Javal, H. Bruce Woolfe, Mary Field (director of production), Donald F. Carter.
  C.E.F. is not a "producing unit" in the accepted sense. Stories and ideas are submitted and it is the work of the scenario department to read and select them. An approved story is then offered to a suitable producing company, which contracts to make it. The production manager of C.E.F. advises on casting and watches the making of each film from its initial stages to the final print.

CINEGUILD LTD.
Pinewood Studios, Iver Heath, Bucks
Telephone : IVER 700
Dirs. : Anthony Havelock-Allan, David Lean, Ronald Neame.

COLUMBIA (BRITISH) PRODUCTIONS LTD.
13 Wigmore-street, London W.1
Telephone : LANGHAM 4571
Managing dir. : Joseph Friedman ; exec. prod. : Ivan Lassgallner.

CONQUEROR FILMS LTD.
Moorgate Hall, Moorgate, London E.C.2
Telephone : MONARCH 9481
Nettlefold Studios, Walton-on-Thames, Surrey.
Dirs. : Paul Soskin (production executive), R. C. Sheen, A. E. Baker, L. A. Mordern.

JOHN CORFIELD PRODUCTIONS LTD.
Panton House, 25 Haymarket, London S.W.1
Telephone : ABBEY 6044
Managing dir. and exec. i/c production : John Corfield.

EALING STUDIOS LTD.
Ealing Green, London W.5
Telephone : EALING 6761.
Managing dir. : Reginald P. Baker ; dir. : Michael Balcon (exec. i/c production).

EXCELSIOR FILM PRODUCTIONS LTD.
4 Tilney-street, Park-lane, London W.1
Telephone : GROSVENOR 2446
Dirs. : Marcel Hellman (exec. i/c production), H. Alan Hawes, Harold French.

21

GAINSBOROUGH PICTURES (1928) LTD.
Lime Grove Studios, Shepherd's Bush, London W.12
Telephone : SHEPHERD'S BUSH 1210
Dirs. : J. Arthur Rank (chmn.), Sydney Box (managing dir. and exec. i/c production), L. W. Farrow, John Davis, Stephen J. Gordon.

GRAND NATIONAL PICTURES LTD.
Wallace House, 113-117 Wardour-street, London W.1
Telephone : GERRARD 6543
Managing dir. : Maurice J. Wilson.

HOLYROOD FILM PRODUCTIONS LTD.
49 Old Bond-street, London W.1
Telephone : REGENT 2114
Dirs. : Clarence Elder, Karl Grune.

IMPERADIO PICTURES LTD.
18 Berkeley-street, London W.1
Telephone : MAYFAIR 6555
Dirs. : Herbert Wilcox (exec. i/c production), A. Wilcox.

INDIVIDUAL PICTURES LTD.
Empire House, 117-119 Regent Street, London W.1
Telephone : REGENT 0621
Dirs. : Sidney Gilliat, Frank Launder.

INTERNATIONAL SCREENPLAYS LTD.
45 Clarges-street, London S.W.1
Telephone : GROSVENOR 3312
Dirs. : Anatole de Grunwald, Anthony Asquith, Terence Rattigan.

ANTHONY KIMMINS PRODUCTIONS LTD.
146 Piccadilly, London W.1
Telephone : MAYFAIR 8272
Dir. : Anthony Kimmins (production executive).

KING, GEORGE.
The Manor, Davies-street, London W.1
Telephone : MAYFAIR 4016
Exec. prod. : Embassy Pictures (Associated) Ltd., Pennant Picture Productions Ltd. (See also British Aviation Pictures.)

LONDON FILM PRODUCTIONS LTD.
146 Piccadilly, London W.1
Telephone : MAYFAIR 8272
Chmn. : Sir Alexander Korda ; joint managing dirs. : Harold Boxall, Sir David Cunyngname, Bt. ; dirs. : Vincent Korda, Zoltan Korda.

MANCUNIAN FILM CORPORATION LTD.
3 The Parsonage, Manchester 3
Telephone : BLACKFRIARS 1023
Managing dir. : John E. Blakeley

METRO-GOLDWYN-MAYER BRITISH STUDIOS LTD.
1 Belgrave-piace, London S.W.1
Telephone : SLOANE 0746
Studios : Elstree, Herts
Dirs. : Ben Goetz (chmn., managing dir. and exec. i/c production), H. Sydney Wright, Sam Eckman, Jr., G. R. Webb, J. C. Squier.

ORTUS FILMS LTD.
Piccadilly House, Jermyn-street, London S.W.1
Telephone : REGENT 4724
Dir. : John Sutro.

PARAMOUNT BRITISH PRODUCTIONS LTD.
162-170 Wardour-street, London W.1
Telephone : GERRARD 7700
Managing dir. and exec. i/c production : Frank Farley.

PEAK FILMS LTD.
10 Bury-street, St. James's, London S.W.1
Telephone : WHITEHALL 5288
Dir. : Ivor McLaren.

PENDENNIS PICTURE CORPORATION LTD.
Ford House, 90 Regent-street, London W.1
Telephone : REGENT 5548
Dir. : Steven Pallos.

PILGRIM PICTURES LTD.
1 Hanover-square, London W.1
Telephone : MAYFAIR 8361
Dirs. : Filippo del Giudice, Alan Jarvis.

PREMIER PRODUCTIONS LTD.
27 Princes-gate, London S.W.7
Telephone : KENSINGTON 2491
Dirs. : I. Ostrer, Maurice Ostrer (production executive).

REED FILM PRODUCTIONS LTD.
Africa House, Kingsway, London W.C.2
Telephone : MAYFAIR 1421
Dir. : Carol Reed.

RKO RADIO BRITISH PRODUCTIONS LTD.
2-4 Dean-street, London W.1
Telephone : GERRARD 5640
Managing dir. : Robert S. Wolff.

TWENTIETH CENTURY PRODUCTIONS LTD.
Twentieth Century House, Soho-square, London W.1
Telephone : GERRARD 7766
Managing dir. : William J. Kupper.

WESLEY RUGGLES PRODUCTIONS LTD.
9 Cavendish-square, London W.1
Telephone : LANGHAM 3777
Dirs. : J. Arthur Rank, G. I. Woodham Smith, Barrington C. Gain ; exec. prod. : Wesley Ruggles.

TWO CITIES FILMS LTD.
15 Hanover-square, London W.1
Telephone : MAYFAIR 9242
Dirs. : J. Arthur Rank, Josef Somlo (exec. i/c production), L. W. Farrow, Barrington C. Gain, Alexander Galperson, J. H. Keeling.

WARNER BROS. (BRITISH) PICTURES LTD.
Warner House, 135 Wardour-street, London W.1
Telephone : GERRARD 5600
Studios : Teddington, Middx
Chmn. and managing dir. : Max Milder.

WESSEX FILM PRODUCTIONS LTD.
Pinewood Studios, Iver Heath, Bucks
Telephone Iver 700
Dirs. : Ian Dalrymple, W. Rosser-James, Jack Lee, J. M. Dalrymple.

Newsreel Producers

BRITISH MOVIETONEWS LTD.
22 Soho-square, London, W.1.
Telephone : GERRARD 7811.
Dirs. : Lord Rothermere, Spyros P. Skouras, G. F. Sanger, Sir Gordon Craig, W. J. Kupper (managing dir.) ; editor : Gerald F. Sanger ; news editor : Edwin Adams ; make-up editor : T. F. Scales ; production manager : Jack Ramsden ; cameramen include : Paul Wyand, Richard Harris, Martin Gray, Alec Tozer ; chief sound recordist : Patrick Sunderland ; commentator : Lionel Gamlin.

BRITISH PARAMOUNT NEWS
10 School-road, London, N.W.10
Telephone : ELGAR 4030.
Dirs. : J. E. Perking, E. Ayres, P. D. Cornwall ; editor : G. T. Cummins ; news editor : E. J. H. Wright ; cameramen include : A. W. Farmer, J. F. Gemmell, E. H. Hawkins, R. L. Read ; sound recordist : A. Smith ; commentator : John C. Stagg.

ANNA NEAGLE
(*Herbert Wilcox*)

B

GAUMONT BRITISH NEWS
142 Wardour-street, London, W.1
Telephone : GERRARD 9292
Cutting-rooms : Lime Grove Studios, Shepherd's
Bush, London, W.12
Telephone : SHEPHERD'S BUSH 1210
Dirs.: J. Arthur Rank (chmn.), L. W. Farrow,
Mark Ostrer, David Ostrer ; producer and gen.
manager : Castleton Knight ; editor : R. S. Howard ;
production manager : H. W. Bishop ; cameramen
include : F. R. G. Bonnett, E. A. Candy, P. Cannon,
H. J. Morley, J. Turner, A. W. Prentice, A. R.
Edmonds ; commentator : Robert Robinson.

PATHE NEWS
103-9 Wardour-street, London, W.1
Telephone : GERRARD 5701

Chmn.: Sir Philip Warter ; managing dir.: W.
Moffatt ; producer-in-chief : Howard Thomas ;
editor ; G. Clement Cave ; associate editor (technical) :
J. Rogerson ; cameramen include : Jock Gemmell, Ken
Gordon, J. Rudkin, W. Jordan, K. Richard, G Baynes,
W. McComville ; commentator : Bob Danvers Walker.

UNIVERSAL NEWS
127 Wardour-street, London, W.1
Telephone : GERRARD 3265.
Dirs.: J. Arthur Rank (chmn.), John Davis, John
Woolf, Clifford W. Jeapes (producer and editor) ;
assistant editor : Leslie Murray ; news editor : Cecil R.
Snape ; cameramen include : R. Noble, D. Towler,
J. R. Cotter, R. Holton, S. Mumford, G. Oswald,
F. Purnell, F. Wilson ; sound recordist : F. R.
Crockett ; commentator : Peter Watson.

FILM DISTRIBUTORS

AMBASSADOR FILMS LTD.
179 Wardour-street, London, W.1
Telephone : GERRARD 3872

ANGLO-AMERICAN FILM CORPORATION LTD.
123 Wardour-street, London, W.1
Telephone : GERRARD 4177

ANGLO-CANADIAN DISTRIBUTORS LTD.
76 Wardour-street, London, W.1
Telephone : GERRARD 2882

ANIMA FILM COMPANY
76 Wardour-street, London, W.1
Telephone : GERRARD 2882

BRITISH LION FILM CORPORATION
76 Wardour-street, London, W.1
Telephone : GERRARD 2882

BUTCHER'S FILM SERVICE LTD.
175 Wardour-street, London, W.1
Telephone : GERRARD 7282

CAVENDISH PICTURES LTD.
27 St. Anne's Court, Wardour-street, London, W.1
Telephone : GERRARD 2208

COLUMBIA PICTURES
139 Wardour-street, London, W.1
Telephone : GERRARD 4321

EAGLE-LION DISTRIBUTORS LTD.
169 Oxford-street, London, W.1
Telephone : GERRARD 9777

EALING DISTRIBUTION LTD.
199-71 Oxford-street, London, W.1
Telephone : GERRARD 2644

EROS FILMS LTD.
119 Wardour-street, London, W.1
Telephone : GERRARD 3202

EQUITY BRITISH FILMS LTD.
26 St. Anne's Court, Wardour-street, London, W.1
Telephone : GERRARD 2208

EXCLUSIVE FILMS LTD.
National House, 60-6 Wardour-street, London, W.1
Telephone : GERRARD 2309

FEDERATED FILM CORPORATION
60 Wardour-street, London, W.1
Telephone : GERRARD 6704

GAUMONT BRITISH DISTRIBUTORS LTD.
Film House, Wardour-street, London, W.1
Telephone : GERRARD 9292

GENERAL FILM DISTRIBUTORS LTD.
127-33 Wardour-street, London, W.1
Telephone : GERRARD 7311

GRAND NATIONAL PICTURES LTD.
113-17 Wardour-street, London, W.1
Telephone : GERRARD 6543

INDEPENDENT FILM DISTRIBUTORS LTD.
111a Wardour-street, London, W.1
Telephone : GERRARD 3743

INTERNATIONAL FILM RENTERS LTD.
167 Wardour-street, London, W.1
Telephone : GERRARD 3257

METRO-GOLDWYN-MAYER LTD.
19 Tower-street, London, W.C.2
Telephone : TEMPLE BAR 8444

MONARCH FILMS LTD.
National House, 60-6 Wardour-street, London, W.1
Telephone : GERRARD 8368

NEW REALM PICTURES LTD.
Queens House, Leicester-square, London, W.C.2
Telephone : GERRARD 6302

OMNIA FILMS LTD.
90 Regent-street, London, W.1
Telephone : REGENT 5546

PARAMOUNT FILM SERVICE LTD.
166 Wardour-street, London, W.1
Telephone : GERRARD 7000

PATHE PICTURES LTD.
Film House, Wardour-street, London, W.1
Telephone : GERRARD 4314

PREMIER DISTRIBUTORS LTD.
Piccadilly House, Piccadilly Circus, London, W.1
Telephone : REGENT 4724

RKO RADIO PICTURES LTD.
2-4 Dean-street, London, W.1
Telephone : GERRARD 5640

RENOWN PICTURES CORPORATION LTD.
Independent House, Wardour-street, London, W.1
Telephone : GERRARD 4403

SELZNICK STUDIO RELEASING DIVISION LTD.
15 Great Cumberland-place, London, W.1
Telephone : PADDINGTON 6661

SHERWOOD FILMS LTD.
26 D'Arblay-street, London, W.1
Telephone : GERRARD 4148

STANDARD FILM AGENCY
26 St. Anne's Court, Wardour-street, London, W.1
Telephone : GERRARD 2208

20th CENTURY-FOX FILM CORPORATION
31-2 Soho-square, London, W.1
Telephone : GERRARD 7766

UNITED ARTISTS CORPORATION LTD.
Film House, Wardour-street, London, W.1
Telephone : GERRARD 5084

WARNER BROS. PICTURES LTD.
Warner House, 135 Wardour-street, London, W.1
Telephone : GERRARD 5600

FILM EXHIBITORS

CIRCUITS OF SIX CINEMAS AND OVER

ASSOCIATED BRITISH CINEMAS LTD.
30-31 Golden-square, London, W.1
Telephone : GERRARD 7887
This circuit comprises 453 cinemas, of which 28 are not in operation owing to war damage. Number operating as at December 1947 was 425.

ODEON THEATRES LTD.
Albion House, 59 New Oxford-street, London, W.C.1
Telephone : TEMPLE BAR 4333.
This circuit comprises 313 cinemas, of which 9 are not in operation owing to war damage. Number operating as at December 1947 was 304.

GAUMONT BRITISH PICTURE CORPORATION LTD.
142-50 Wardour-street, London, W.1
Telephone : GERRARD 9292.
This circuit comprises 297 cinemas, of which 53 are not in operation owing to war damage or use for purposes other than the showing of films. Number operating as at December 1947 was 244.

ATKINSON PICTURES LTD. 7
9 North-road, St. Andrews, Bristol 6
Telephone : BRISTOL 44190.

BAILEY, W. H. 16
Hippodrome, Workington, Cumberland
Telephone : WORKINGTON 194.

BANCROFT, H. 10
Empire Theatre, Wisbech, Cambs
Telephone : WISBECH 116.

BAYLISS, H. S. 18
Chesterton, Bridgnorth, Salop
Telephone : LLANDRINDOD WELLS 2128.

BEDFORD CINEMAS (1928) LTD. ... 6
J. F. Wood, 19 Castle-street, Liverpool 2
Telephone : CENTRAL 1544.

BOSTOCK CINEMA CIRCUIT 21
45 Chevallier-street, Ipswich
Telephone : IPSWICH 4036.

BRADLEY, H. E. 6
Northern Operators Ltd., Pentridge Buildings, Holme-street, Burnley
Telephone : BURNLEY 3048.

BRANFORD, ALAN V. 7
Gaiety Cinema, Whitehaven, Cumberland
Telephone : WHITEHAVEN 312.

BRENNAN, JAMES 16
107 Duke-street, Barrow-in-Furness
Telephone : BARROW 990.

CALEDONIAN ASSOCIATED CINEMAS LTD. 49
Royal Bank Buildings, Drummond-street, Inverness
Telephone : INVERNESS 1.

CANSFIELD, L. 7
Palace Cinema, Lowtown, Pudsey, Yorks
Telephone : PUDSEY 3453.

CAPITAL & PROVINCIAL NEWS THEATRES 20
100 Baker-street, London, W.1
Telephone : WELBECK 0081.

CHESHIRE COUNTY CINEMAS LTD. ... 7
Empress Theatre, Runcorn, Cheshire
Telephone : RUNCORN 2291.

CLAVERING & ROSE 7
199 Piccadilly, London, W.1
Telephone : REGENT 1146.

CLAYTON, E. C. 6
Bank Chambers, 70 The Moor, Sheffield 1
Telephone : SHEFFIELD 24673.

CLIFTON CINEMA CIRCUIT 34
Princes Chambers, 6 Corporation-street, Birmingham 2
Telephone : NORTHERN 0806.

CONSETT CINEMAS LTD. 6
45 Heaton-road, Newcastle-on-Tyne 6
Telephone : NEWCASTLE 56080.

CORNE, MAX 6
7 St. John-square, Cardiff
Telephone : CARDIFF 355.

JACK DAVIS CIRCUIT 10
147 Wardour-street, London, W.1
Telephone : GERRARD 1416.

CHAS. K. DEEMING CIRCUIT 6
Grand Cinema, Coalville, Leics
Telephone : COALVILLE 56.

DEESIDE ENTERPRISE CINEMAS LTD. ... 8
Bridge House, Queensferry, Chester
Telephone : CONNAH'S QUAY 49.

EAGLE PICTUREDROMES LTD. 11
County Playhouse, King-street, Wigan
Telephone : WIGAN 3476.

ECKART CIRCUIT 41
New Star Cinema, Castleford, Yorks
Telephone : CASTLEFORD 2618.

ELTON, HERBERT 11
Commerce Chambers, Elite Buildings, Nottingham
Telephone : NOTTINGHAM 2273.

J. F. EMERY CINEMA CIRCUIT 33
Midland Bank House, 26 Cross-street, Manchester
Telephone : BLACKFRIARS 7876.

BRINLEY EVANS CIRCUIT 14
Criterion Theatre, George-street, Hull
Telephone : HULL 33752.

FILER CINEMA CIRCUIT 6
129 Victoria-road North, Southsea
Telephone : PORTSMOUTH 5113

GRAHAM, SAM 23
Oxford House, Oxford-street, Nottingham
Telephone : NOTTINGHAM 40326.

GRANADA THEATRES LTD. (including LONDON & DISTRICT CINEMAS LTD.) ... 47
36 Golden-square, London, W.1
Telephone : GERRARD 3554.

S. A. GRATTON & SON 6
9 McFarlane-street, Glasgow, C.4
Telephone : BELL 2214.

GRAVES CINEMAS LTD. 9
Athenaeum Buildings, Maryport, Cumberland
Telephone : MARYPORT 16.

GEORGE GREEN LTD. 17
11 Renfrew-street, Glasgow, C
Telephone : DOUGLAS 5481.

IVOR R. GROVE CIRCUIT 7
Regal Theatre, North Bridge-street, Bathgate,
W. Lothian
Telephone : BATHGATE 315.

H. & G. ENTERPRISES (LONDON) LTD. ... 9
Broadmead House, 21 Panton-street, Hay-
market, London, S.W.1
Telephone : WHITEHALL 1992.

HANMER, PHILIP M. 11
51a Rodney-street, Liverpool
Telephone : ROYAL 4452.

V. E. HARRISON CIRCUIT 6
45 Dereham-road, Norwich
Telephone : NORWICH 24894.

R. C. HILL CIRCUIT 6
Palace Theatre, Truro, Cornwall
Telephone : TRURO 2167.

E. J. HINGE CIRCUIT 22
147-9 Northumberland-street, Newcastle-on-
Tyne
Telephone : NEWCASTLE-ON-TYNE 20317.

HYDE, A. S. 12
Glenroyal, Briggate, Shipley, Yorks.
Telephone : SHIPLEY 2974.

ISAACS, C. 7
2 Southcourt-road, Cardiff
Telephone : BRIDGEND 101

**ISLE OF WIGHT THEATRES LTD. &
ASSOCIATED COMPANIES** 13
V. Badman, Theatre Royal, Ryde, I.O.W.
Telephone : RYDE 2387.

J. H. L. THEATRES LTD. 11
Wallace House, 113-7 Wardour-street, London,
W.1
Telephone : GERRARD 1363.

ARTHUR JACOBS CINEMA CIRCUIT ... 6
Alhambra, Shotton, Flints.
Telephone : CONNAH'S QUAY 121.

JOSEPH, C. S. 9
38 John Bright-street, Birmingham 1
Telephone : MIDLAND 1933.

KING, SIR ALEXANDER B. 48
190 West Regent-street, Glasgow, C.2
Telephone : DOUGLAS 1195.

ALFRED LEVY CIRCUIT 8
9 Ranelagh-street, Liverpool 1
Telephone : ROYAL 5675.

LONDON & PROVINCIAL CINEMAS LTD. 18
150 Southampton Row, London, W.C.1
Telephone : TERMINUS 5155.

MARKS CIRCUIT CINEMAS 17
326 Cheetham Hill-road, Manchester 8
Telephone : COLLYHURST 2133.

MARSHALL & IVES CIRCUIT 7
178 Westgate-road, Newcastle-on-Tyne
Telephone : NEWCASTLE 27451.

MAYFAIR CIRCUIT 10
G. Elcock, 64 Park-street, London, W.1
Telephone : MAYFAIR 8262.

J. J. McCRACKEN CIRCUIT 19
Newgate Chambers, Rochdale, Lancs
Telephone : ROCHDALE 4451.

MEDWAY CINEMAS LTD. 7
Walmar House, 288 Regent-street, London, W.1
Telephone : LANGHAM 2677.

MIDLAND SUPER CINEMAS LTD. ... 9
2 Denman-street, London, W.1
Telephone : GERRARD 2832.

MILNE, J. B. 19
Bannerman House, 27 South Tay-street,
Dundee
Telephone : DUNDEE 4019.

MOORHOUSE, H. D. 43
Imperial Buildings, 7 Oxford-road,
Manchester 1
Telephone : ARDWICK 2226.

MORRIS, LOUIS 16
52 Shaftesbury-avenue, London, W.1
Telephone : GERRARD 1668.

NORTHERN THEATRES COMPANY LTD. 9
5 Rawson-street, Halifax
Telephone : HALIFAX 2267.

**NORTH-WESTERN FILM BOOKING
AGENCY** 11
Kensington Cinema, Kensington, Liverpool 7
Telephone : ANFIELD 863.

PALMER, GEORGE 13
149 West George-street, Glasgow
Telephone : CENTRAL 1621.

PEARCE, J. E. 7
Eros House, 31 Regent-street, London, S.W.1
Telephone : REGENT 1560.

PORTSMOUTH TOWN CINEMAS LTD. ... 8
Shaftesbury Cinema, Kingston-road,
Portsmouth
Telephone : PORTSMOUTH 4976.

RICHARDS, RANDOLPH E. 7
Picturedrome, Eastbourne
Telephone : EASTBOURNE 1441.

S. M. SUPER CINEMAS LTD. 59
37-8 Golden-square, London, W.1
Telephone : GERRARD 4556.

SCARBOROUGH, G. H. 17
"Ashfield", Elmfield-avenue, Leicester
Telephone : LEICESTER 78009.

SEGELMAN, G. (Lincoln area) 12
Mutual House, 23 Albion-place, Leeds 1
Telephone : LINCOLN 525.

SHIPMAN & KING 31
Wellington House, 125-30 Strand, London,
W.C.2
Telephone : TEMPLE BAR 5077.

SNAPE & WARD CIRCUIT 10
Equitable Buildings, 14 John Dalton-street,
Manchester
Telephone : DEANSGATE 3542.

SPEAKMAN, W. J. 15
126 Bold-street, Liverpool 1
Telephone : ROYAL 2272.

SPECKMAN, SOL 30
Norwich Union Chambers, 42 Westgate-road,
Newcastle-on-Tyne 1
Telephone : NEWCASTLE 28082.

SPRING, FRANK E. 6
3 The Parsonage, Manchester
Telephone : BLACKFRIARS 7905.

M. STODDART & SON 15
12 Lesbury-terrace, Chopwell, Newcastle-on-
Tyne
Telephone : CHOPWELL 210.

STROSS, RAYMOND 8
Astoria House, 62 Shaftesbury-avenue,
London, W.1
Telephone : GERRARD 2474.

E. TAYLOR CINEMA CIRCUIT 6
Castle Cinema, Builth Wells, Brecon
Telephone : BUILTH WELLS 291.

GEORGE TAYLOR CIRCUIT 7
27 Merkland-street, Partick, Glasgow, W.1
Telephone : WESTERN 2766.

THOS. THOMPSON CIRCUIT 19
4 Palladium Buildings, Eastbourne-road,
Middlesbrough
Telephone : LINTHORPE 88156.

TYNE PICTURE HOUSES LTD. 10
2 Saville-place, Newcastle-on-Tyne
Telephone : NEWCASTLE-ON-TYNE 20544.

UNITED ENTERTAINMENTS LTD. 20
Fred A. Prior, General Buildings, Bridlesmith-
gate, Nottingham
Telephone : NOTTINGHAM 44584.

WALLAW PICTURES LTD. 9
Wallaw Buildings, Ashington, Northumberland
Telephone : ASHINGTON 31.

WATTS, A. B. 13
12 Museum-place, Cardiff
Telephone : CARDIFF 2900.

WHINCUP, C. H. 14
54 New Briggate, Leeds
Telephone : LEEDS 20972.

WILLIS, W. E. 14
Globe Cinema, Albany-road, Penylan, Cardiff
Telephone : CARDIFF 3072.

JACKSON WITHERS CIRCUIT 30
17 Park-place, Cardiff
Telephone : CARDIFF 4502.

There are also 2450 individually owned cinemas in Great Britain.

FILM LABORATORIES

BRENT LABORATORIES LTD.
North Circular-road, Cricklewood, London, W.2.
Telephone : GLADSTONE 4271-2

CINIT LTD.
Cinit House, 283 Lonsdale-road, Barnes, London, S.W.13.
Telephone : PROSPECT 1073-4

DENHAM LABORATORIES LTD.
Denham, Uxbridge, Mddx.
Telephone : DENHAM 2323

HENDERSON FILM LABORATORIES LTD.
18-20 St. Dunstan's-road, South Norwood, London, S.E.25.
Telephone : LIVINGSTONE 2255-6-7

GEORGE HUMPHRIES & CO., LTD.
71-7 Whitfield-street, London, W.1.
10 North Court, Chitty-street, Tottenham Court-road, London, W.1.
Telephone : Museum 3636

THE KAY FILM PRINTING COMPANY LTD.
Oxford-road, Finsbury Park, London, N.4
Telephone : ARCHWAY 3050-1-2-3

KAY (WEST END) LABORATORIES LTD.
22 Soho-square, London, W.1.
Telephone : GERRARD 7811

OLYMPIC KINEMATOGRAPH LABORATORIES LTD.
School-road, Willesden, London, N.W.10.
Telephone : ELGAR 7831-2-3-4

TECHNICOLOR LTD.
Bath-road, Harmondsworth, West Drayton, Mddx.
Telephone : WEST DRAYTON 2211

TOPICAL FILM COMPANY LTD.
North Circular-road, Cricklewood, London, N.W.2.
Telephone : GLADSTONE 4271-2

SYDNEY WAKE LTD.
83 Wardour-street, London, W.1.
Telephone : GERRARD 5716, 6489

STEWART GRANGER
(Gainsborough)

A DIRECTORY OF
TRADE AND TECHNICAL ORGANIZATIONS

AMUSEMENT CATERERS' ORGANIZATION (NORTHERN IRELAND)
White Cinema Club, Belfast. Pres.: F. I. Keogh; hon. sec.: F. A. Spiers, 27 Garfield-street, Belfast, (Tel. Belfast 20724).
Aims: *For social and charity purposes.*

ASSOCIATED FILM CARRIERS OF GREAT BRITAIN LTD.
82 Victoria-street, London, S.W.1 (Tel. Victoria 5069). Pres.: A. G. Dolphin; sec.: G. Dickinson.
Aims: *To promote, protect and develop the general interests of the film transport industry and persons and bodies engaged in, or concerned with, the supply and transport of cinematograph films and accessories by road.*

ASSOCIATION OF CINEMATOGRAPH AND ALLIED TECHNICIANS
2 Soho-square, London, W.1 (Tel. Gerrard 8506). Pres.: The Hon. Anthony Asquith; gen. sec.: G. H. Elvin, F.C.I.S.
Affiliated to the T.U.C. and Labour Party, and caters for film technicians and other employees of all departments and grades, including—camera, sound, editing and cutting, art, still photography, floor and production staff, scenario, laboratory, television, radio equipment, newsreel, raw stock manufacture, cartoon, diagram and still strips.
Aims: *Negotiation on behalf of all members in all matters pertaining to salaries, hours and other conditions of employment. Establishment and maintenance of professional status. Employment bureau with accurate records of disengaged technicians of all departments and grades. Consultation with authorities on employment of foreign technicians. Publication of the "Cine Technician" (six issues per annum). Educational facilities including lectures and film shows. Social activities. Co-operation with kindred organizations in Great Britain and abroad.*

ASSOCIATION OF SPECIALISED FILM PRODUCERS
3 Portman Chambers, 7-9 Baker-street, London, W.1 (Tel. Welbeck 5711). Hon. Pres.: H. Bruce Woolfe; chmn.: F. A. Hoare; sec.: L. G. Parker.
Formed as an official body to represent the short film industry in Great Britain, and to advise Government departments and other official bodies on all questions relating to short films.
Aims: *To promote and develop the use of short films generally, and to maintain liaison with other film trade organizations concerned in the promotion of the British film industry*

ASSOCIATION OF THEATRE ORGANISTS
Chmn.: Thomas Dando; hon. sec.: Jack Courtnay, F.T.C.L., 77 Westbourne-grove, London, W.2.

BRITISH ACTORS' EQUITY ASSOCIATION
(incorporating the Stage Guild)
Imperial Buildings, 56 Kingsway, London, W.C.2 (Tel. Chancery 6924). Pres.: Beatrix Lehmann; gen. sec.: Gordon Sandison.
Aims: *To act as the actors' union in every way, safeguarding rates of pay, conditions of work, and so on.*

BRITISH BOARD OF FILM CENSORS
113-117 Wardour-street, London, W.1 (Tel. Gerrard 4851). Pres.: Sir Sidney West Harris; sec.: J. Brooke Wilkinson.
An organization established to protect the public and the trade against the exhibition of films considered unsuitable for this country.

BRITISH FILM ACADEMY
7 Deanery-street, Park-lane, London, W.1 (Tel. Grosvenor 4296). Chmn.: David Lean; sec.: Roger Manvell, Ph.D.
An organization for the advancement of the film. Only those working on the making of films or on professional research into the cinema are eligible for ordinary membership. For further information see page 219.

BRITISH FILM INSTITUTE
164 Shaftesbury-avenue, London, W.C.2 (Tel. Temple Bar 1642). Pres.: Duke of Sutherland, K.T.; dir.: Oliver Bell, M.A., J.P.; sec.: R. W. Dickinson, M.A.
Aims: *The main object of the Institute is to encourage the use and development of the cinematograph as a means of entertainment and instruction.*

BRITISH FILM PRODUCERS' ASSOCIATION
Seymour House, 17 Waterloo-place, London, S.W.1 (Tel. Whitehall 1986). Dir. gen.: Sir Henry L. French, G.B.E., K.C.B.; gen. sec.: E. W. Wingrove, A.C.I.S.
Deals with all matters pertaining to British film production. Acts as a negotiating body with the Board of Trade, and as a public relations organization for the British film industry as a whole.

BRITISH KINEMATOGRAPH SOCIETY
Dean House, 2 Dean-street, London, W.1 (Tel. Gerrard 1154). Pres.: I. D. Wratten; hon. sec.: E. Oram.
The scientific and technical society of the industry; corporate or associate membership is open to any technician engaged in the industry. Student membership is open to persons under 21 years taking an approved course in kinematography. The Society arranges lectures and demonstrations, and publishes a journal, " British Kinematography ".

BRITISH POSTER ADVERTISING ASSOCIATION
48 Russell-square, London, W.C.1 (Tel. Museum 3234-5).
An organization for the general protection of the poster trade.

BRITISH SHORT FILM MAKERS' SOCIETY LTD.
Hon. sec. and treas.: F. T. Lenton, F.A.I.A., 26-7 D'Arblay-street, London, W.1 (Tel. Gerrard 4148).
Aims: *To promote and protect by all legal means the interests of persons, firms and corporations engaged in the trade or business of making short cinematograph films, and to express and represent the opinions of its members to Government departments and others. To encourage and extend the use of short cinematograph films, and to provide members and others with such advisory services as may be thought fit.*

29

CHRISTIAN CINEMA AND RELIGIOUS FILM SOCIETY

6 Eaton-gate, London, S.W.1 (Tel. Sloane 2143). Pres. : Archbishop of Canterbury ; actg. gen. sec. : Captain P. N. Corry, I.A. (retired).

An organization for religious uses of films.

CINEMA CLUB, Glasgow

Fdr. and first pres. : Prince Bendon ; hon. pres. : Sir Alexander B. King, C.B.E., J.P. ; pres. : Jack G. Breckenbridge ; hon. sec. : William Kempsell, 163 Hope-street, Glasgow, C.2 (Tel. Central 3114). Organizers of the Annual Cinema Ball since 1919.

Aims : *To promote social intercourse among members and to co-operate with and assist all schemes which have for their aim the advancement, welfare and success of the cinematograph trade in all its branches.*

CINEMATOGRAPH EXHIBITORS' ASSOCIATION

164 Shaftesbury-avenue, London, W.C.2 (Tel. Temple Bar 7864). Pres. : B. T. Davis, A.S.A.A. ; gen. sec. : W. R. Fuller.

Aims : *To promote goodwill and a good understanding between all proprietors of cinemas and other places of entertainment, and between them and such persons as work for them, and between them and the manufacturers and renters of films. To act as an organization safeguarding the interests of the members in every way.*

CINEMATOGRAPH FILMS COUNCIL

Sec. : Miss E. R. Ward, Board of Trade, Millbank, London, S.W.1.

Appointed under the provisions of the Cinematograph Films Act, 1938.

CINEMATOGRAPH TRADE BENEVOLENT FUND

Patron : H.M. the King ; pres. : Reginald C. Bromhead, F.C.A. ; sec. : Reginald C. O. Viveash, Queen's House, Leicester-square, London, W.C.2 (Tel. Gerrard 4104).

An organization to alleviate distress among members of the cinematograph trade.

CINEMATOGRAPH TRADE PROVIDENT INSTITUTION

Pres. : Reginald C. Bromhead, F.C.A. ; sec. : Reginald C. O. Viveash, Queen's House, Leicester-square, London, W.C.2 (Tel. Gerrard 4104).

A Friendly Society providing various health and unemployment benefits, maternity and death allowances, and the like, to subscribers.

CINEMA VETERANS

Pres. : J. C. Squier ; hon. sec. : Thomas France, 59 Woodland-rise, Muswell-hill, London, N.10 (Tel. Tudor 2132).

A society for cinema veterans. (" A cinema veteran is one who was actively employed in the cinema industry in or before 1903, and remained therein for a reasonable period.") There is no entrance fee or subscription but all applicants must submit their record of service to the committee before acceptance, and only those whose record is approved and confirmed are entitled to wear the Association's badge.

ELECTRICAL TRADES UNION

Gen. Office : Hayes-court, Hayes, Kent ; London Area Office : 324 Gray's Inn-road, London, W.C.1 (Tel. Terminus 5115-6-7). Asst. gen. sec. : W. C. Stevens.

Affiliated to the T.U.C. and Labour Party.

FEDERATED BRITISH FILM AND STAGE ASSOCIATION AND UNIVERSAL FILM-GOERS' LEAGUE

32 Amesbury-avenue, Streatham-hill, London, S.W.2 (Tel. Tulse Hill 4858). Pres. : Charles Boyer ; music

pres. : (Great Britain) Jack Hylton, (overseas) Jose Iturbi ; sec. : Miss K. Costello.

Aims : *To support all the best British and American films, plays and players, and to link up the audiences of cinemas and theatres everywhere for this object. To act as the voice of the filmgoer and support his interests.*

FEDERATION OF CINEMATOGRAPH SOCIETIES

Chmn. : T. S. Lutas, A.R.P.S. ; hon. sec. : Dr. H. Mandiwall, F.R.P.S., 234 Staines-road, Hounslow, Middlesex.

In alliance with the Royal Photographic Society of Great Britain. The Federation caters in general for amateur film societies (there is one professional member—the Association of Cinematograph and Allied Technicians).

FILM INDUSTRY EMPLOYEES' COUNCIL

2 Soho-square, London, W.1 (Tel. Gerrard 8506). Pres. : W. Stevens ; gen. sec. : G. H. Elvin, F.C.I.S.

A federated trade union body embracing all film production workers. Constituent unions : Association of Cinematograph and Allied Technicians ; British Actors' Equity Association ; Electrical Trades Union ; Film Artistes' Association ; Musicians' Union ; National Association of Theatrical and Kine Employees.

FILM INDUSTRY PUBLICITY CIRCLE

8-9 Long Acre, London, W.C.2 (Tel. Temple Bar 3068). Pres. : Mervyn McPherson ; hon. sec. : J. Pole.

The Circle was formed to combine the responsible publicity directors and managers of producing, exhibiting and renting companies into an association designed to represent and protect the film industry as a whole in its public and press relations.

Aims : *To counteract propaganda hostile to the film industry. To cultivate and promote close and cordial relations with the Critics' Circle and with editorial and advertising representatives of the press, and to assist the industry as a whole in its relations with the press and the public. To promote greater cohesion and unity of purpose and method between the three main branches of the industry, so that it may be possible to achieve overall publicity campaigns for films throughout production, distribution and exhibition. To incorporate the Central Clearing House, organizer of press show arrangements.*

FILM STRIPPERS' ASSOCIATION LTD.

6 Broad Street-place, London, E.C.2, and 57 Buckland-road, London, E.10 (Tel. Leytonstone 1694). Chmn. : F. J. Thurston Moon ; hon. sec. : W. T. Collins.

An organization for the protection of the trade of film stripper.

INCORPORATED ASSOCIATION OF KINEMATO-GRAPH MANUFACTURERS LTD.

51 Lincoln's Inn Fields, London, W.C.2 (Tel. Holborn 2683). Chmn. : Tom Davies, J.P. ; sec. : J. Brooke Wilkinson. Equipment section—chmn : E. E. Blake ; sec. : Leslie Wakefield.

Aims : *To promote the consideration and discussion of all questions affecting the interests of manufacturers, publishers and sellers of cinematograph films, and generally to watch over, protect and advance those interests. To promote economy and efficiency, and to co-operate with the various branches of the trade for the promotion of mutual interests.*

INDEPENDENT FILM RENTERS' POOL ASSOCIATION, THE

26-7 D'Arblay-street, London, W.1 (Tel. Gerrard 4148). Chmn.: F. T. Lenton, F.A.I.A.; sec.: N. T. Wood, A.L.A.A.

Aims: *To pool surplus allocation under the Cinematograph Film (Control) Order, 1943.*

INSTITUTE OF AMATEUR CINEMATOGRAPHERS LTD.

8 West-street, Epsom, Surrey. Sec.: Leslie M. Froude, F.C.A.

Aims: *To promote the general advance of amateur cinematography, moving pictures, sound on film, sound records and their applications, and secure for such amateurs a recognized amateur status; and to raise the standard of cinematic art generally.*

KINEMA PROJECTIONISTS' AND ENGINEERS' ASSOCIATION (incorporated in the National Association of Theatrical and Kine Employees). Estd. 1890

71 South End-road, London, N.W.3 (Tel. Hampstead 7671). Pres.: L. A. Wilson; gen. sec.: T. O'Brien, M.P.

Affiliated to the English and Scottish T.U.C.s, and the National Federation of Professional Workers and Trades Councils.

KINEMATOGRAPH RENTERS' SOCIETY, LTD.

30 Old Compton-street, London, W.1 (Tel. Gerrard 4383). Pres.: D. E. Griffiths, O.B.E.; sec.: Frank Hill, M.V.O., F.C.I.S.

Aims: *To promote and protect in every possible way the interests, financial welfare and success of the film renting trade, and to devise means to promote co-operation amongst those engaged in the film industry for the protection of their mutual interest. To watch and keep records for reference and comparison of all matters in any way concerning the industry, and to deal with any contingency affecting the trade or the members of the Society that may arise. To procure information for members as to the standing and responsibility of parties with whom they propose to transact business. To give legal advice to all members.*

LANCASHIRE CINEMA OLD BOYS' ASSOCIATION

Pres.: F. Collinson, 107 Dickens-lane, Poynton, Ches. (Tel. Poynton 2327); hon. sec.: J. M. Howe, Palace Cinema, Bolton-road, Pendlebury, Manchester (Tel. Swinton 1805).

LONDON POSTER ADVERTISING ASSOCIATION LTD., THE

48 Russell-square, London, W.C.1 (Tel. Museum 3234).

An organization for the protection of the trade.

LONDON SCIENTIFIC FILM SOCIETY

34 Soho-square, London, W.1 (Tel. Gerrard 1620). Hon. sec.: Francis Gysin.

A society for the promotion of the use and study of scientific films. Publishers of the journal "The Scientific Film".

MOTION PICTURE PRODUCERS AND DISTRIBUTORS OF AMERICA INC.

28 West 44th-street, New York City, U.S.A. Pres.: Eric A. Johnston; sec.: Carl E. Milliken. London rep.: Fayette W. Allport, 15-16 New Burlington-street, London, W.1 (Tel. Regent 3811).

Deals with all matters pertaining to the film industry as a whole, notably censorship in the U.S.A., the Production Code, and foreign relations.

MUSICIANS' UNION

7 Sicilian-avenue, London, W.C.1 (Tel. Holborn 1238). Gen. sec.: F. Dambman.

This organization is a trade union composed mainly of members of symphony, theatre, cinema and music-hall orchestras, and dance bands.

NATIONAL ASSOCIATION OF THEATRICAL AND KINEMATOGRAPH EMPLOYEES

71 South End-road, London, N.W.3 (Tel. Hampstead 7671). Gen. pres.: J. Smith; gen. sec.: T. O'Brien, M.P.

The only union exclusively engaged in the organization of workers in the entertainment industry, and the only union nationally recognized by the Cinematograph Exhibitors' Association of Great Britain and Northern Ireland and the Theatre Proprietors' Associations as the trade union for the purpose of negotiating wages and conditions for all cinema and theatre employees.

THE NEWS AND SPECIALISED THEATRE ASSOCIATION OF GREAT BRITAIN AND NORTHERN IRELAND

31 Dover-street, London, W.1 (Tel. Regent 2787). Chmn.: Dixon Scott; gen. sec.: Miss D. M. Vaughan, B.A., F.C.A. Registered under the Trades Union Act.

Aims: *To promote goodwill and understanding between the members, secure legislation for their benefit, and oppose measures detrimental to their mutual interests. To ensure that the members shall maintain a high standard of service to the public—the minimum requirements to be determined by the council from time to time. To take steps to secure news films for presentation to the public which shall be free from censorship, political bias or propaganda, bearing in mind that in times of extreme national crisis, censorship from within or without the industry may be necessary in the interests of the State. To encourage the production and circulation of short British and foreign films which have an entertainment or educational value, and to investigate and encourage the development of scientific research which is calculated to assist the members in the course of their business.*

NEWSREEL ASSOCIATION OF GREAT BRITAIN AND IRELAND LTD.

Queens House, Leicester-place, Leicester-square, London, W.C.2 (Tel. Gerrard 3177 and 7766). Sec.: E. Long-Maddox.

Aims: *To promote and protect the interests, welfare and business of associates engaged in the production and distribution of cinematograph films depicting current events, known as newsreels, and to bring about and maintain co-operation between them.*

PERFORMING RIGHT SOCIETY

33 Margaret-street, London, W.1 (Tel. Langham 3864).

An association of composers, authors, and publishers of copyright musical works, established to issue licences for the public performances of such work. The Society is not concerned with plays, sketches or other works of a non-musical character, nor with operas, musical plays or other dramatico-musical works performed in their entirety and by living persons on the stage; but it is concerned, *inter alia*, with performances of music in conjunction with cinematograph films. Any person desiring to perform copyright music in public should apply to the society for a licence.

PHONOGRAPHIC PERFORMANCE LTD.

144 Wigmore-street, London, W.1 (Tel. Welbeck 2231, 2240). Dirs.: Sir Ernest Fisk, B. E. G. Mittell, J. F. Axtmann, E. R. Lewis, Brian Bramall; gen. manager: H. M. Lemoine.

A company founded by the British Phonographic Society to control the rights of the leading manufacturers of gramophone records and to issue licences for the public performances of all records bearing the names of the leading firms.

ROYAL PHOTOGRAPHIC SOCIETY

16 Princes-gate, London, S.W.7 (Tel. Kensington 3334).

Patron: H.M. the King; pres.: F. J. Tritton, B.Sc., F.R.I.C., F.R.P.S.; hon. sec.: J. Dudley Johnston, Hon. F.R.P.S.; sec.: L. E. Hallett, F.C.I.S. Kinematograph Section—chmn.: Stanley Schofield, F.R.P.S.; hon. sec.: T. S. Lutas, F.R.P.S.

A society for the general advancement of photographic science and its applications.

SCIENTIFIC FILM ASSOCIATION, THE

34 Soho-square, London, W.1, and 2 Newton-place, Glasgow, C.3. Pres.: Basil Wright; hon. sec.: Jeanne Urquhart.

Aims: *To promote the use and study of scientific films in every way.*

SCIENTIFIC FILMS COMMITTEE OF THE ASSOCIATION OF SCIENTIFIC WORKERS

15 Half Moon-street, London, W.1 (Tel. Grosvenor 4761). Pres.: J. D. Bernal, F.R.S.

This Committee has operated for some years as an information centre for scientific film societies and others interested in the scientific film, for getting science represented as truthfully and as widely as possible on the screen.

SCREENWRITERS' ASSOCIATION

7 Deanery-street, London, W.1 Pres.: Frank Launder; vice-pres.: J. B. Williams; hon. sec.: Guy Morgan.

Affiliated to the Incorporated Society of Authors, Playwrights and Composers, and the League of British Dramatists.

SOCIETY OF CINEMA MANAGERS OF GREAT BRITAIN AND IRELAND

164 Shaftesbury-avenue, London, W.C.2 (Tel. Temple Bar 7864). National chmn.: Leslie C. Holderness; national sec.: S. Butchart, F.S.C.

Aims: *To organize managers, house managers, relief managers, assistant managers and trainee managers, and to encourage the highest standard of management with a view to attaining, upholding and maintaining a dignity and respect consistent with the status of the profession.*

SOCIETY OF CINEMATURIANS

Pres.: E. J. Hinge; sec.: William Miller, Regal Cinema, Oxford-road, Manchester 1.

Aims: *To promote social and benevolent activities.*

THEATRE ORGANISTS' BENEVOLENT FUND

Pres.: Major S. J. Wright; hon. sec.: Jack Courtnay, F.T.C.L., 77 Westbourne-grove, London, W.2.

VARIETY ARTISTES' FEDERATION

18 Charing Cross-road, London, W.C.2 (Tel. Temple Bar 6950). Hon. chmn.: Dave O'Gorman; gen. sec.: Lewis Lee. A trade union.

Government Departments Dealing with the Film Industry

BOARD OF TRADE (Films Branch)

Horseferry House, Horseferry-road, London, S.W.1 (Tel. Victoria 6800).

Registration of films for Quota purposes.

BONDED FILM STORES LTD.

33-5 Endell-street, London, W.C.2 (Tel. Temple Bar 3887).

CENTRAL OFFICE OF INFORMATION (Films Division)

Norgeby House, 83 Baker-street, London, W.1 (Tel. Welbeck 4420). Dir.: R. E. Tritton.

GOVERNMENT CINEMATOGRAPH ADVISER

J. G. Hughes-Roberts, M.V.O., H. M. Stationery Office, 65 Whitehall, London, S.W.1 (Tel. Whitehall 8855-9), and Room 0028, The War Office, Whitehall, London, S.W.1 (Tel. Whitehall 9400, ext. 326).

H.M. CUSTOMS AND EXCISE

The Films Officer, Strand 5th Station (Films), Third Floor, 133-5 Oxford-street, London, W.1 (Tel. Gerrard 2189).

WHO'S WHO IN FILMS

CLARK GABLE
(*Metro-Goldwyn-Mayer*)

ABBOTT, Bud. Real name William Abbott. Born Atlantic City, New Jersey, U.S.A., Oct. 2, 1895. Ht. 5 ft. 11 in. ; wt. 150 lb. Brown hair, blue eyes. Mother and father in circus troupe. Left school at age of 15 to become sailor ; then box-office cashier at burlesque theatre and actor in burlesque, where he met Lou Costello. They formed act together, and played for seven years ; also on radio in Kate Smith's programme. Appeared on Broadway in " Streets of Paris," signed by Universal for first film : *One Night in the Tropics* (1940). Other films include—1941 : *Buck Privates* (Univ), *In the Navy* (Univ), *Hold that Ghost* (Univ), *Keep 'Em Flying* (Univ) ; 1942 : *Ride 'Em Cowboy* (Univ), *Rio Rita* (MGM), *Pardon My Sarong* (Univ), *Who Done It ?* (Univ) ; 1943 : *It Ain't Hay* (Univ), *Hit the Ice* (Univ) ; 1944 : *Lost in a Harem* (MGM), *In Society* (Univ) ; 1945 : *Here Come the Co-Eds* (Univ), *The Naughty Nineties* (Univ), *Abbott and Costello In Hollywood* (Univ) ; 1946 : *The Little Giant* (Univ), *The Time of Their Lives* (Univ) ; 1947 : *Rookies Come Home* (UI), *The Wistful Widow of Wagon Gap* (UI).

ACKLAND, Rodney. Writer, director, stage actor. Born London, May 18, 1908. Studied for stage at the Central School of Speech Training and Dramatic Art, London. Debut on London stage at Gate Theatre in 1924. Began screen writing in 1938, collaborating in story and scenario of *Bank Holiday*. In 1942, wrote and directed *Thursday's Child*. Screenplays include : *Yellow Sands, Keep Smiling, 49th Parallel, Hatter's Castle, George and Margaret, Uncensored, Love Story.*

ADAMS, Robert. Born Georgetown, British Guiana. Educ. Mico Teachers' Training College, Jamaica (hons. grad.). Has been headmaster in British Guiana, master on staff of Trinidad College, artist's model, journalist, professional boxer and wrestler, and singer. Is qualified engineering draughtsman. Gave up teaching to come to Britain with threefold ambition— to be a barrister, an opera singer and an actor. Arrived in London penniless. To earn money, took to wrestling and travelled all over Europe, at the same time studying law. First application for admission to the Inner Temple was turned down. Then had his voice trained and became singer. In 1935 made first stage appearance, with Paul Robeson, in " Stevedore " at the Embassy Theatre, London. Shortly after was given lead in " All God's Chillun " and "Emperor Jones " on stage, radio and television. Began film career in 1935 in *Midshipman Easy* (Ealing). Served in A.R.P. for a year from outbreak of war, then worked for a time in a factory. In 1946 was admitted to the Middle Temple. Other films include : *King Solomon's Mines, Sanders of the River.* 1946 : *Caesar and Cleopatra* (Pascal), *Men of Two Worlds* (Two Cities).

ADDINSELL, Richard. Composer. Born London, 1904. Studied law at Hertford College, Oxford. Began to compose at 21. First musical score was for the theatre, to "Adam's Opera " by Clemence Dane, 1928. Went to New York in 1933 to write and supervise music for stage presentation of " Alice in Wonderland". Went on to Hollywood, where he spent six months at RKO-Radio Studios composing background music. In 1936 wrote his first complete film score for British films, *The Amateur Gentleman.* Other feature film music includes : *Fire over England, South Riding, Farewell Again, Dark Journey, Vessel of Wrath, Goodbye Mr. Chips !, The Lion Has Wings, Contraband, Gaslight, Love on the Dole, Dangerous Moonlight* (for which, in 1941, he composed the " Warsaw Concerto "), *Blithe Spirit.* During the war years he wrote a great deal of music for documentaries, notably, *Men of the Lightship, The Siege of Tobruk, Diary for Timothy.*

AHERNE, Brian. Born King's Norton, Worcs., May 2, 1902. Ht. 6 ft. 3 in. Fair hair, blue eyes. Educ. Edgbaston, Birmingham ; Malvern College, Worcs. Trained as a child at Italia Conti's School, London, and made stage debut at age of 9 in Birmingham. Appeared in London in " Where the Rainbow Ends " at age of 11. Studied architecture for a time but returned to acting in 1923 in revival of " Paddy the Next Best Thing " at the Savoy Theatre, London. Started film career in 1924. First American stage appearance 1931 in " The Barretts of Wimpole Street." Pilots own aeroplane and has owned an interest in a flying school. Films include : *Song of Songs, The Constant Nymph* (G.B. 1933), *What Every Woman Knows, Beloved Enemy, Juarez.* 1940 : *My Son, My Son* (UA) ; 1942 : *My Sister Eileen* (Col) ; 1943 : *Forever and a Day* (RKO), *What a Woman* (Col), *First Comes Courage* (Col) ; 1946 : *The Locket* (RKO); 1948 : *The Queen's Necklace* (Benedict Bogeaus—UA).

ALBERT, Eddie. Real name Eddie Albert Heimberger. Born Rock Island, Illinois, U.S.A., Apr. 22, 1908. Ht. 5 ft. 11½ in. ; wt. 170 lb. Educ. Central High School, Minneapolis ; University of Minnesota. During school years, worked in drugstore and made local reputation as amateur actor and radio singer. Went to New York, sang in night-clubs, at political rallies, holiday celebrations. After several broadcasts, won regular radio work on N.B.C. in programme " Honeymooners". Had walk-on stage part in " O, Evening Star", acted in repertory, made hit in farce " Brother Rat". Film offer followed. Also on stage in " Room Service", " The Boys from Syracuse". First film : *Brother Rat* (Warn) 1938. War service : U.S. Navy, 1940-46. Other films include : *Four Wives.* 1940 : *An Angel from Texas* (Warn), *A Dispatch from Reuter's* (Warn) ; 1941 : *The Wagons Roll at Night* (Warn), *Out of the Fog* (Warn) ; 1942 : *Eagle Squadron* (Univ) ; 1943 : *Ladies' Day* (RKO), *Bombardier* (RKO) ; 1947 : *A Woman Destroyed* (UI), *Time Out of Mind* (UI).

ALBERTSON, Frank. Former screen name James Cruze. Born Fergus Falls, Minnesota, U.S.A., Feb. 2, 1909. Ht. 5 ft. 9 in. ; wt. 145 lb. Brown hair, blue eyes. Educ. Puyallup, Washington ; Hollywood high schools. Made film debut 1922. One of first important roles was in *Prep and Pep* (1928). Other films include : *The Cohens and the Kellys in Hollywood,*

Ah Wilderness, The Plainsman. 1942 : *Wake Island* (Para), *Underground Agent* (Col) ; 1943 : *Keep 'Em Slugging* (Univ) ; 1944 : *And the Angels Sing* (Para), *I Love a Soldier* (Para) ; 1945 : *Arson Squad* (PRC), *How Do You Do* (PRC) ; 1946 : *They Made Me a Killer* (Para), *Gay Blades* (Rep) ; 1947 : *Ginger* (Mono).

ALDA, Robert. Real name Alphonso D'Abruzzo. Born New York City, Feb. 26, 1914. Ht. 5 ft. 10 in. ; wt. 165 lb. Black hair, brown eyes. Educ. Stuyvesant High School ; New York University. Was draughtsman in New York firm, then department store clerk. Won singing contest in 1932 which led to radio and night-club appearances ; in 1935, soloist and " feed " to comics in full-time vaudeville. Teamed with Hank Henry, 1938 ; toured Buffalo, Detroit, Toronto, Chicago ; appeared with summer repertory companies in New York ; played camps in " Fun for Your Money", 1942. Sent to Hollywood for test. Being unknown, he fitted requirements for actor to play role of George Gershwin in *Rhapsody in Blue* (Warn), 1945. Other films include—1946 : *Cinderella Jones* (Warn), *The Man I Love* (Warn), *Cloak and Dagger* (Warn) ; 1947 : *Nora Prentiss* (Warn) ; 1948 : *April Showers* (Warn).

ALEKAN. Director of photography. Born France, 1909. Camera operator and lighting expert. Recent French films include : *Le Diable Souffle, Les Modis, Bataille du Rail, La Belle et la Bête.* Also did exterior work in France for American film *Arch of Triumph.* Came to Britain in 1947 to direct photography for *Anna Karenina.*

ALERME, André. Born Dieppe, France, Sept. 9, 1877. Intended for medical career, but after military service, took to the stage and in the 1890's appeared in operetta and musical comedy until World War I. After the war, returned to Paris stage, appearing with Lucien and Sacha Guitry. Made first film appearance in *Le Blanc et le Noir,* with Raimu. Other films include : *Mam'zelle Nitouche, Son Altesse l'Amour, Pension Mimosa, Tovarich, Arènes Joyeuses, La Kermesse Héroïque, Coup de Tête, Les Malheurs de Sophie, Trente et Quarante, Le Cavalier Noir, Une Fille à Papir, Pour une Nuit d'Amour, L'Arche de Noé, Le Voleur de Porte-Bien, Par la Fenêtre.*

ALEXANDROV, C. V. Born 1903. At 10 began work as theatre electrician and property master in theatre at Sverdlovsk. After the revolution he joined the " Prolekult ". Assisted Eisenstein in the production of *The Strike, Potemkin, October, Old and New, The General Line.* In 1929, with Eisenstein and Tisse, he went to the U.S.A., to prepare for a film on Mexico. Has also acted in films. First independent work : *Jazz Comedy,* 1934, which received an award that year in the International Film Festival at Venice. Other films include: *The Circus* (1936), *Volga-Volga* (1938), *The Bright Path* (1941).

ALLBRITTON, Louise. Born Oklahoma, U.S.A., July 3, 1920. Ht. 5 ft. 7½ in. ; wt. 124 lb. Blonde hair, green eyes. Educ. High School, Wichita Falls ; University of Oklahoma. Early dramatic training at Pasadena Playhouse, then got a small part in a film at Universal. Films include—1942 : *Parachute Nurse* (Col), *Who Done It ?* (Univ), *Danger in the Pacific* (Univ) ; 1943 : *It Comes up Love* (Univ), *Good Morning Judge* (Univ), *Fired Wife* (Univ) ; 1944 : *Follow the Boys* (Univ), *Her Primitive Man* (Univ), *Bowery to Broadway* (Univ), *This Is the Life* (Univ), *San Diego, I Love You* (Univ) ; 1945 : *Men in Her Diary* (Univ), *That Night with You* (Univ) ; 1946 : *Tangier* (Univ) ; 1947 : *The Egg and I* (Univ).

ALLEN, Adrianne. Born Manchester, Feb. 7, 1907. Ht. 5 ft. 4 in. ; wt. 115 lb. Fair hair, grey eyes. Educ. London, Paris, Switzerland, Belgium. Entered Royal Academy of Dramatic Art at 17, and started stage career in 1925 with Basil Dean's company. Made film debut in *Loose Ends* (BIP) 1930, one of the most discussed early British talkies, followed by *The Stronger Sex, The Woman Between, Black Coffee.* Went to America for stage play " Cynara " in New York, and attracted attention of Paramount who gave her a contract. First Hollywood film : *The Night of June 13,* with Clive Brook. During World War II served in London W.V.S. and toured with Emlyn Williams for ENSA. Early films include : *Merrily We Go to Hell, The Morals of Marcus.* Returned to the screen after the war. 1947 : *The October Man* (Two Cities) ; 1948 : *Bond Street* (World Screen).

ALLGOOD, Sara. Born Dublin, Oct. 31, 1883. Educ. Marlborough-street Training College, Dublin. Joined Irish National Theatre Society, Dublin. Made debut with them in 1904 in Dublin. First London appearance same year. Long career with Abbey Theatre Players. Entered films in 1929 with *Blackmail* (BIP), the first British talkie. Other films include : *The Passing of the Third Floor Back, It's Love Again. Kathleen Mavourneen, Storm in a Teacup.* 1941 : *Lady Hamilton* (Korda-Hollywood), *How Green Was My Valley* (20th) ; 1942 : *The War Against Mrs. Hadley* (MGM) ; 1943 : *City Without Men* (Col) ; 1944 : *The Lodger* (20th), *Between Two Worlds* (Warn), *Jane Eyre* (20th), *The Keys of the Kingdom* (20th), *The Strange Affair of Uncle Harry* (Univ) ; 1946 : *The Spiral Staircase* (RKO), *Kitty* (Para), *Cluny Brown* (20th) ; 1947 : *Ivy* (UI), *The Fabulous Dorseys* (Charles R. Rogers—UA), *Mourning Becomes Electra* (RKO) ; 1948 : *My Wild Irish Rose* (Warn).

ALLYSON, June. Real name Jan Allyson. Born Westchester Co., New York, Oct. 7. Ht. 5 ft. 1 in. ; wt. 99 lb. Blonde hair, blue eyes. Took up swimming and dancing to prevent permanent paralysis after leg accident at the age of 9. Modelled her dance style on Astaire-Rogers films ; saw *Gay Divorce* eighteen times. Became chorus girl at 16 in Broadway musical " Very Warm for May ". Returned to high school to graduate. Decided to become doctor, and returned to chorus to earn money for medical training. She won a feature role in musical " Best Foot Forward ", and was signed by MGM for the screen version, in which she made her film debut in 1943. Films include— 1943 : *Girl Crazy* (MGM), *Thousands Cheer* (MGM), *Meet the People* (MGM) ; 1944 : *Two Girls and a Sailor* (MGM), *Music for Millions* (MGM) ; 1945 : *Her Highness and the Bellboy* (MGM), *The Sailor Takes a Wife* (MGM), *Two Sisters from Boston* (MGM) ; 1946 : *Till the Clouds Roll By* (MGM), *The Secret Heart* (MGM) ; 1947 : *High Barbaree* (MGM), *The Pirate* (MGM), *Good News* (MGM) ; 1948 : *Love Bites Man* (MGM).

ALWYN, William. Composer. Born Northampton, 1905. Achieved great distinction in music before going into films in 1936. His compositions include concertos, string quartets and songs. In 1937-40 held the Colland Fellowship of the Worshipful Company of Musicians and afterwards became an Honorary Freeman of the Company. Has composed music for many feature and documentary films, including *The Future's in the Air* (1936), *Penn of Pennsylvania*, *Squadron Leader X*, *Desert Victory*, *Tunisian Victory*, *The Way Ahead*, *The Rake's Progress*, *Odd Man Out*, *Green for Danger*, *Take My Life*, *Captain Boycott*, *The October Man*, *So Evil My Love*, and the Manchester civic film *A City Speaks*.

AMBLER, Eric. Writer, producer. Born Blackheath, London, 1909. Educ. Colf's School, Blackheath. Refused London University science scholarship; entered advertising business and in spare office moments wrote first novel, later filmed in U.S.A.: *The Mask of Dimitrios*. Other works filmed include: *Journey into Fear*, *Background to Danger*, *Hotel Reserve* (adapted from his novel " Epitaph for a Spy "). During World War II, was in charge of production of over 200 Army training films. Specially released from duties in 1944 to write script of *The Way Ahead* (Two Cities). Joined the Rank Organisation in 1947, and wrote and produced *The October Man* (Two Cities).

AMECHE, Don. Real name Dominico Felix Amici. Born Kenosha, Wisconsin, U.S.A., 1908. Ht. 6 ft ; wt. 170 lb. Dark hair, dark eyes. Educ. Columbia ; University of Wisconsin. Studied law for a time until he played lead in " The Devil's Disciple " for the Drama Club of Wisconsin, and then decided on acting career. Went to New York, but had difficulty in getting stage work and for a time was in a motor-car factory, a mattress factory, and with a road gang. With repertory companies and in vaudeville until he won a radio audition in Chicago and remained there for six years. Failed first film test ; after second test made debut in *Sins of Man* (20th) 1936. Other films include : *Ladies in Love*, *Ramona*, *You Can't Have Everything*, *In Old Chicago*, *Alexander's Ragtime Band*, *Josette*, *Gateway*, *Happy Landing*. 1940 : *Four Sons* (20th), *Down Argentine Way* (20th) ; 1941 : *That Night in Rio* (20th), *Moon over Miami* (20th), *Kiss the Boys Goodbye* (Para)'; 1942 : *The Magnificent Dope* (20th), *Girl Trouble* (20th) ; 1943 : *Something to Shout About* (Col), *Heaven Can Wait* (20th) ; 1944 : *Greenwich Village* (20th), *A Wing and a Prayer* (20th); 1945 : *Guest Wife* (UA), *It's in the Bag* (UA), *Genius in the Family* (Univ). ; 1946: *So Goes My Love*, (Univ); 1947; *Will Tomorrow Ever Come* (Rep) ; 1948: *Sleep, My Love* (Triangle-UA).

AMES, Leon. Real name Leon Wycoff. Born Portland, Indiana, U.S.A., Jan. 20, 1903. Ht. 5 ft. 11 in. ; wt. 175 lb. Brown hair, blue eyes. Educ. grammar and high schools, Delphi, Indiana. Made stage debut in " The Cat and the Canary ". First film : *Murders in the Rue Morgue* (Univ) 1932. Supporting player in more than sixty films. Recent films include—1940 : *East Side Kids* (Mono) ; 1941 : *Ellery Queen and the Murder Ring* (Col), *No Greater Sin* (University Film) ; 1943 : *Crime Doctor* (Col), *The Iron Major* (RKO) ; 1944 : *Meet Me in St. Louis* (MGM), *Thirty Seconds over Tokyo* (MGM), *The Thin Man Goes Home* (MGM), *Between Two Women* (MGM) *Son of Lassie* (MGM), *Anchors Aweigh* (MGM) ; 1945 : *Weekend at the Waldorf* (MGM), *Yolanda and the Thief* (MGM), *They Were Expendable* (MGM), *The Postman Always Rings Twice* (MGM), *The Great Morgan* (MGM) *No Leave, No Love* (MGM) ; 1946 : *The Show-Off* (MGM), *Mr. Griggs Returns* (MGM), *The Beginning or the End?* (MGM), *Lady in the Lake* (MGM), *Undercover Girl* (MGM) ; 1947: *Song of the Thin Man* (MGM), *Merton of the Movies* (MGM).

ANDERSON, Dusty. Real name Ruth Anderson. Born Toledo, Ohio, U.S.A., Dec. 17, 1918. Ht. 5 ft. 7 in. ; wt. 118 lb. Dark brown hair, blue eyes. Educ. Toledo High School ; University of Toledo ; Toledo Art School. Wanted to act, paint and decorate; won £100 prize at Toledo cinema " bank night " which covered expenses of New York trip ; became popular model for magazine covers and monopolist of bathing suit poses, as she did not quibble at winter posing on beaches. First film role as a model in *Cover Girl* (Col) 1944. Other films include : *Memory for Two* (Col) ; 1945 : *One Way to Love* (Col), *The Crime Doctor's Warning* (Col) ; 1946 : *The Gentleman Misbehaves* (Col), *Gallant Journey* (Col) ; 1947 : *Down to Earth* (Col).

ANDERSON, Judith. Born Adelaide, Australia, Feb. 10, 1898. Ht. 5 ft. 4 in. ; wt. 118 lb. Brown hair, blue eyes. When young studied for the opera. Made stage debut in 1915 in Sydney in " Royal Divorce", and abandoned singing for acting. Went to Hollywood in 1918 with a letter of introduction to Cecil B. De Mille, but considered unsuitable for films so went on stage in New York. Then to Chicago where achieved first major success in " Cobra " (1924). First film : *Blood Money* (UA) 1933. Then to stage, making London debut in 1937 as Lady Macbeth with Laurence Olivier. Played in two Royal Command performances. Returned to screen in *Rebecca* (UA) 1940. Other films include—1942 : *King's Row* (Warn); 1944 : *Laura* (20th) ; 1945 : *And Then There Were None* (20th) ; 1946 : *Spectre of the Rose* (Rep) ; 1947 : *The Red House* (Sol Lesser–UA), *Pursued* (Warn).

ANDREWS, Dana. Born Collins, Missouri, U.S.A., Jan. 1, 1912. Ht. 6 ft. ; wt. 168 lb. Brown hair, brown eyes. Educ. Sam Houston College, Huntsville, Texas. Ambition—to be a lawyer or a singer ; worked as accountant in Texas till 1931. Hitch-hiked to Hollywood : became garage-hand, then joined Pasadena Playhouse as extra, rising to feature parts in two years. Seen by talent scout. First film : *The Westerner* (UA) 1939. Other films include— 1940 : *Lucky Cisco Kid* (20th), *Sailor's Lady* (20th), *Kit Carson* (UA) ; 1941 : *Tobacco Road* (20th), *Belle Starr* (20th), *Swamp Water* (20th) ; 1942 : *Ball of Fire* (RKO), *Berlin Correspondent* (RKO), *The Man Who Came Back* (20th) ; 1943 : *Strange Incident* (20th), *Crash Dive* (20th), *North Star* (RKO-Goldwyn) ; 1944 : *Purple Heart* (20th), *A Wing and a Prayer* (20th), *Up in Arms* (Goldwyn-RKO), *Laura* (20th) ; 1945 : *Fallen Angel* (20th), *State Fair* (20th) ; 1946 : *A Walk in the Sun* (20th), *Canyon Passage* (Univ), *The Best Years of Our Lives* (Goldwyn-RKO) ; 1947: *Boomerang* (20th); 1948: *Night Song* (RKO), *Daisy Kenyon* (20th).

ANKERS, Evelyn. Born Valparaiso, Chile, of English parents. Blonde hair. Educ. Latymer School ; Godolphyn School ; Royal Academy of Dramatic Art, London. Made her first stage appearance in Chile at the age of 10. Brought to Britain by her parents, appeared on London stage in " Bats in the Belfry " with Vivien Leigh. After making several British films, went to New York where she appeared on stage in " Ladies in Retirement". Films (all Univ to 1945) include : *Murder in the Family*, *The Petersville Diamond* ; 1941 : *Hold that Ghost*, *Ghost of Frankenstein*, *Eagle Squadron*, *Great Impersonation*, *Sherlock Holmes and the Voice of Terror* ; 1943 : *You're a Lucky Fellow, Mr. Smith*, *Hers to Hold*, *All by Myself*, *His Butler's Sister*, *Son of Dracula*; 1944 : *Ladies Courageous*,

Jungle Woman, Follow the Boys, Weird Woman, Invisible Man's Revenge, Pardon My Rhythm, Pearl of Death, Bowery to Broadway; 1945: *The French Key* (Rep), *Queen of Burlesque* (Mono); 1946: *Black Beauty* (20th).

ANNAKIN, Ken. Director. Born Yorkshire, 1915. Left desk job in 1932 to travel the world; became gold-prospector in New Zealand; in Australia, cycled from Perth to Brisbane; grew bananas; became radio writer, newspaperman, civil servant, variety artist. Served in R.A.F., becoming film camera assistant. When invalided out, joined producer Sydney Box at Riverside Studios, London, as camera assistant. Within a year was directing documentaries for War Office, Ministry of Information, and British Council, including: *London 1942, Make Fruitful the Land, Pacific Thrust, We of the West Riding, British Justice.* In 1947, directed first feature film: *Holiday Camp* (Gains). Also directed *Broken Journey, Miranda.*

ARDEN, Eve. Real name Eunice Quedens. Born Mill Valley, California, U.S.A., Apr. 30. Ht. 5 ft. 7 in.; wt. 129 lb. Blonde hair, green eyes. Educ. Mill Valley Grammar School. Went to work in mercantile establishment, San Francisco. Joined Alcazar theatre repertory company, San Francisco, for eighteen months; then started Bandbox Repertory Theatre with three troupers, playing in hotel lobbies. Later made hit at Pasadena Playhouse in musical "Lo and Behold". Signed by Lee Schubert for New York stage—"Ziegfeld Follies of 1936"; also in "Ziegfeld Follies of 1938", "Let's Face It". First film: *Stage Door* (RKO), 1937. Other films include: *Oh Doctor, Cocoanut Grove, Having Wonderful Time, Forgotten Woman, A Child Is Born, Slightly Honorable,* 1940: *No, No, Nanette* (RKO); 1941: *Whistling in the Dark* (MGM), *Sing for Your Supper* (Col); 1943: *Let's Face It* (Para); 1944: *Cover Girl* (Col), *The Doughgirls* (Warn); 1945: *Patrick the Great* (Univ), *Pan-Americana* (RKO), *Earl Carroll Vanities* (Rep), *Mildred Pierce* (Warn); 1946: *Kid from Brooklyn* (RKO); 1947: *The Arnelo Affair* (MGM); 1948: *The Voice of the Turtle* (Warn).

ARLETTY. Real name Arlette Bathiat. Born Courbevoie, Auvergne, France, Mar. 15. Brown hair, brown eyes. Became shorthand-typist, mannequin and artist's model before debut as singer at the Capucines, Paris, followed by lead in operetta "Yes". First film was *Chien Qui Rapporte,* followed by *Je te Confie ma Femme.* Then alternated between screen and stage until she made film hit in *Hôtel du Nord;* after that, made succession of films, including: *Le Jour Se Lève, Fric-Frac, Circonstances Atténuantes, Tempête sur Paris, Madame Sans-Gêne, Les Visiteurs du Soir, Les Enfants du Paradis, L'Ile des Enfants Perdus.*

ARLISS, Leslie. Director, writer. Born London, 1901. Educ. Tonbridge School, Kent. Spent seven years as journalist in London and film and dramatic critic on the "Johannesburg Star", in South Africa. Entered film industry as writer for British International Pictures, Elstree, 1930. In 1932, for Gaumont British, collaborated on screen plays: *Orders Is Orders, Jack Ahoy, Rhodes of Africa.* In 1937-9, worked for Goldwyn and 20th Century-Fox in Hollywood; 1940-2, collaborated on screen plays: *Pastor Hall, For Freedom, The Foreman Went to France.* Co-director of *The Farmer's Wife.* Films he has directed include: *The Night Has Eyes* (in which he gave leading part to the "unknown" James Mason), *The Man in Grey, Love Story, The Wicked Lady, A Man About the House, Idol of Paris.*

ARNOLD, Edward. Real name Guenther Schneider. Born New York, Feb. 18, 1890. Ht. 5 ft. 11 in.; wt. 206 lb. Brown hair, grey eyes. Educ. East Side Settlement House. At 10, an orphan living in a New York tenement, he got jobs in meat market and jewellery store until sent to school, where he had his first experience of acting, in "The Merchant of Venice." Worked in upholstery shop, oiled engines, sold papers; later was page-boy, insurance salesman, grocery assistant before becoming actor. Stage appearances included "The Jazz Singer", "The Nervous Wreck", and "Whistling in the Dark". First film: *The Penalty of Fame* (Univ) 1932. Has appeared in over a hundred films including: *Rasputin the Mad Monk, The White Sister, I'm No Angel, Roman Scandals, Cardinal Richelieu, Biography of a Bachelor Girl, The Glass Key, Diamond Jim, Crime and Punishment, Sutter's Gold, Come and Get It, You Can't Take It with You, The Crowd Roars, Idiot's Delight, The Earl of Chicago, Mr. Smith Goes to Washington.* 1940: *Lillian Russell* (20th); 1942: *Johnny Eager* (MGM), *The War Against Mrs. Hadley* (MGM); 1943: *The Youngest Profession* (MGM); 1944: *Kismet* (MGM), *Janie* (Warn), *Standing Room Only* (Para), *Mrs. Parkington* (MGM); 1945: *Main Street after Dark* (MGM), *Weekend at the Waldorf* (MGM), *The Hidden Eye* (MGM), *No Leave, No Love* (MGM); 1946: *Janie Gets Married* (Warn), *Three Wise Fools* (MGM), *The Mighty McGurk* (MGM), *My Brother Talks to Horses* (MGM), *Cynthia's Secret*; 1947: *Dear Ruth* (Para), *The Hucksters* (MGM), *Polly Fulton* (MGM).

ARTHUR, Jean. Real name Gladys Green. Born New York City, Oct. 17, 1905. Ht. 5 ft. 4 in.; wt. 110 lb. Blonde hair, grey-green eyes. Educ. New York public schools. Intended to become a teacher, but while at school worked as photographer's model and was shortly given screen test. In Hollywood, 1923, began in a series of two-reelers, at her own request, in order to gain experience. Remained in films steadily till 1931, when she made her stage debut in New York in "Foreign Affairs". Since then has appeared in many stage and screen successes, and has recently spent four years entirely in the theatre. First feature film *Warming Up* (Para) 1928. Other films include: *The Canary Murder Case, Brotherly Love, The Green Murder Case, Here Comes the Band Wagon, Mysterious Dr. Fu Manchu, Saturday Night Kid, Sins of the Fathers, Stairs of Sand, Halfway to Heaven, Paramount on Parade, Return of Dr. Fu Manchu, Street of Chance, Young Eagles, The Past of Mary Holmes, Whirlpool, The Defence Rests, Most Precious Thing in Life, The Whole Town's Talking, Party Wire, Public Hero No. 1, Diamond Jim, If You Could Only Cook, Mr. Deeds Goes to Town, The Ex-Mrs. Bradford, Adventure in Manhattan, More Than a Secretary, The Plainsman, History is Made at Night, Easy Living, You Can't Take it With You, Mr. Smith Goes to Washington.* 1940: *Too Many Husbands* (Col), *Arizona* (Col); 1942: *The Talk of the Town* (Col); 1943: *The More the Merrier* (Col), *The Lady Takes a Chance* (RKO); 1944: *The Impatient Years* (Col); 1948: *A Foreign Affair* (Para).

ASHERSON, Renee. Born London, May 19, 1915. Ht. 5 ft. 3 in. Fair hair, blue eyes. Educ. Gerrards Cross; France, Switzerland. Theatrical training at Webber-Douglas Dramatic School. Stage debut, in a "walking-on" role, in "Romeo and Juliet" at the New Theatre, London, 1935. Later joined the Birmingham Repertory Company, and afterwards the

Old Vic. Made screen debut in 1944 in *The Way Ahead* (Two Cities), and achieved outstanding success as Princess Katharine in *Henry V* (Two Cities) 1945. Other films include ; 1945 *The Way to the Stars* (Two Cities) ; 1946 : *Caesar and Cleopatra* (Pascal).

ASQUITH, Anthony. Director. Born London, 1902. Educ. Winchester ; Balliol College, Oxford. After leaving Oxford, joined Bruce Woolfe at the Surbiton Studios, where, in the late 'twenties, British Instructional Films were making " reconstruction " films of World War I and other documentary films. After having assisted in production of *Boadicea*, Asquith made his first two films, *Shooting Stars* (1928), and *Underground* (1929), a new kind of realistic thriller, making use of scenes shot in London's Underground. Is president of the Association of Cine Technicians. In 1946 formed International Screenplays Ltd., in association with Terence Rattigan and Anatole de Grunwald. Films directed include : *Dance Little Lady, Cottage on Dartmoor, Tell England, The Window Cleaner, Marry Me, Moscow Nights, Pygmalion* (co-directed with Leslie Howard ; Pascal, 1938), *French without Tears, Cottage to Let, Uncensored, Freedom Radio, Quiet Wedding, We Dive at Dawn, Demi-Paradise, Fanny by Gaslight, The Way to the Stars, While the Sun Shines, The Winslow Boy.*

ASTAIRE, Fred. Real name Frederick Austerlitz. Born Omaha, Nebraska, U.S.A., May 10, 1900. Ht. 5 ft. 9 in. ; wt. 140 lb. Brown hair, brown eyes. Educ. privately. Accompanied sister Adele to dancing classes at age of 4. Made stage debut in variety a year later. First appearance in New York at age of 11. Toured United States for several years. First Broadway production : " Over the Top " (1917). Seen in London for first time, May 30, 1923, at Shaftesbury Theatre in " Stop Flirting ". Began films in 1933 with *Dancing Lady* (GMG). Others include: *Flying Down to Rio, The Gay Divorce, Roberta, Top Hat, Follow the Fleet, Swing Time, Shall We Dance, Carefree, The Story of Vernon and Irene Castle.* 1940 : *Broadway Melody of 1940* (MGM) ; 1942 : *Holiday Inn* (Para) ; 1943 : *The Sky's the Limit* (RKO) ; 1945 : *Yolanda and the Thief* (MGM) ; 1946 : *Ziegfeld Follies of 1946* (MGM), *Blue Skies* (Para) ; 1948 : *Easter Parade* (MGM).

ASTOR, Mary. Real name Lucille Langhanke. Born Quincy, Illinois, U.S.A., May 3, 1906. Ht. 5 ft. 5½ in. ; wt. 120 lb. Auburn hair, brown eyes. Educ. Kenwood Loring School, Chicago. First appeared on screen in two-reelers from 1920. Later became widely popular in silent films—*Don Juan, Beau Brummel, Dry Martini*, and many others. Went on stage, then returned to screen in 1930. Early films include: *Ladies Love Brutes, Behind Office Doors, Smart Women, The Lost Squadron, Jennie Gerhardt, Easy to Love, The Man with Two Faces, Return of the Terror, Page Miss Glory, And So They Were Married, Dodsworth, The Prisoner of Zenda, The Hurricane, There's Always a Woman, Woman Against Woman, Listen Darling, Midnight.* 1940 : *Turnabout* (UA), *Brigham Young* (20th) ; 1941 : *The Great Lie* (Warn), *The Maltese Falcon* (Warn) ; 1942 : *The Palm Beach Story* (Para), *Across the Pacific* (Warn) ; 1943 : *Thousands Cheer* (MGM), *Young Ideas* (MGM) ; 1944 : *Meet Me in St. Louis* (MGM), *Blonde Fever* (MGM) ; 1946 : *Claudia and David* (20th), *Desert Fury* (Para) ; 1947 : *The Rich Full Life* (MGM), *Fiesta* (MGM), *Cass Timberlane* (MGM).

ATTENBOROUGH, Richard. Born Cambridge, Aug. 29, 1923. Ht. 5 ft. 8 in. ; wt. 137 lb. Fair hair, blue eyes. Educ. Wyggeston Grammar School, Leics ; Royal Academy of Dramatic Art (Leverhulme Scholarship). Always wanted to be an actor ; appeared in " Ah, Wilderness ", " Cottage to Let ", " The Little Foxes ", " Brighton Rock " and other plays. First film appearance was as the young stoker who deserted his post at the height of battle in the Two Cities (Noel Coward) production of *In Which We Serve* (1942). During World War II, was attached to the Film Unit of the R.A.F. as an air gunner-cameraman. Other films include—1943 : *Journey Together* (R.A.F. Film Unit) ; 1946 : *School for Secrets* (Two Cities) ; 1947 : *The Man Within* (Box), *Dancing with Crime* (Alliance) ; 1948 : *Brighton Rock* (Boultings–ABPC), *London Belongs to Me* (Individ).

AUER, Mischa. Born St. Petersburg (now Leningrad), Russia, Nov. 17, 1905. Ht. 6 ft. 2 in. ; wt. 165 lb. Brown hair, brown eyes. Educ. St. Petersburg ; New York City ; specializing in literature and the arts. Went to America as orphan at age of 12 to join grandfather. Playing in " Magda " with stage company in Los Angeles, when offered small part in *Something Always Happens* (Para), 1928. Among other early films were *The Lives of a Bengal Lancer, Clive of India, Tough Guy.* In 1936 was cast in first comic role in *My Man Godfrey.* Has played comics ever since. Other films include : *Winterset, Three Smart Girls, One Hundred Men and a Girl, You Can't Take It With You.* 1943 : *Around the World* (RKO) ; 1944 : *Up in Mabel's Room* (UA), *Lady in the Dark* (Para) ; 1945 : *A Royal Scandal* (20th), *Brewster's Millions* (UA), *And Then There Were None*—British title, *Ten Little Niggers* (20th) ; 1946 : *Sentimental Journey* (20th).

AUMONT, Jean-Pierre. Born Paris, Jan. 5, 1909. Ht. 6 ft. ; wt. 165 lb. Fair hair, blue eyes. Educ. privately and at Paris public schools. Studied acting at the Conservatoire of Drama, Paris. Stage debut at age of 16 in " Romance ". Starred in French adaptations of " Outward Bound ", " Her Cardboard Lover ", " White Cargo ", " Design for Living ", " The Infernal Machine ". Film debut in *Jean de la Lune ;* later appeared in many other French films, notably with Simone Simon, Annabella, Jean Gabin, Danielle Darrieux. After service with the French army in 1940 (Croix de Guerre), went via Canada, where he appeared in variety, to U.S.A. Later played opposite Katharine Cornell on Broadway in " Rose Burke ". Seen on stage by talent scout, was signed for two American films, *Assignment in Brittany* (MGM) 1943, and *Cross of Lorraine* (MGM) 1943. Returned to France to serve with the Free French Army, and after the liberation appeared on Paris stage in " La Grande Fille Toute Simple " and made *Le Déserteur*, before returning to Hollywood in 1946 for *Heartbeat* (RKO), a re-make of *Battement de Cœur.* Appeared in *Song of Scheherazade* (Univ) 1946. Came to Britain to appear at the first Royal Command Film Performance, Nov. 1, 1946. 1948 : *Atlantis* (Seymour Nebenzal-UA), *The First Gentleman* (Col) made in Britain.

AURIC, Georges. Composer. Born France, 1899. Began composing at age of 15, and later was one of the group of French composers known as " Les Six". Compositions include many ballets including " Les Facheaux ", produced by the Ballets Russes in 1924. French film music includes : *Le Sang d'un Poète,*

JUNE ALLYSON
(*Metro-Goldwyn-Mayer*)

L'Eternel Retour, A Nous la Liberté, Torrents, La Belle et la Bête. British films include : Dead of Night, Caesar and Cleopatra, Hue and Cry, It Always Rains on Sundays.

AUTRY, Gene. Actor, song writer. Born Tioga, Texas, U.S.A., Sept. 29, 1907. Ht. 5 ft. 11 in. ; wt. 170 lb. Sandy brown hair, blue eyes. Educ. Tioga High School. Worked on ranch in Oklahoma, then for San Francisco Railroad Company. In 1928 became radio singer and recording artist, specializing in Western songs. First film, In Old Santa Fé (1934). As singing star of Westerns, one of world's top box-office successes. Writes songs for his films. Served four years in U.S.A.A.F., returning to Republic Studios in 1946. Other films include : Tumbling Tumbleweeds, Coming Round the Mountains, The Singing Cowboy, Boots and Saddles, Springtime in the Rockies, Gold Mine in the Sky, Rhythm of the Saddle, Western Jamboree, Shooting High (his last film before going into the army). 1946 : Saddle Pals, Twilight on the Rio Grande, Robin Hood of Texas ; 1947 : The Last Round-Up (Col).

AYLMER, Felix. Born Corsham, Wilts, Feb. 21, 1889. Educ. Magdalen College School and Exeter College, Oxford. Studied for the stage with Rosina Filippo. First stage appearance at the London Coliseum, in " Cook's Man ", 1911. Has appeared in more than 300 plays and about 100 films since his screen debut in The Temporary Widow, made in Germany by UFA. Other films—all British—include: The Improper Duchess, The Wandering Jew, Seven Sinners, Tudor Rose, As You Like It, Victoria the Great, Action for Slander, South Riding, The Citadel, Dreaming Lips, Sixty Glorious Years, Official Secret, Mill on the Floss, Young Man's Fancy, Bank Holiday. 1943 : Demi-Paradise (Two Cities) ; 1944 : Mr. Emmanuel (Two Cities) ; 1945 : The Way to the Stars (Two Cities), The Wicked Lady (Gains) ; 1946 : Caesar and Cleopatra (Pascal), The Years Between (Sydney Box), Laughing Lady (Brit Nat) ; 1947 : The Man Within (Gains), Green Fingers (Brit Nat), The October Man (Two Cities), A Man About the House (LFP), The Ghosts of Berkeley Square (Brit Nat) ; 1948 : Broken Journey (Gains), Hamlet (Two Cities), The Calendar (Gains), Escape (20th) made in Britain.

AYRES, Lew. Born Minneapolis, Minnesota, U.S.A., Dec. 28, 1908. Ht. 5 ft. 9 in. ; wt. 150 lb. Dark brown hair, brown eyes. Educ. high school, Minneapolis ; Arizona University. Orchestral musician before starting film career. Made film debut in Compromised (Pathe) 1931. Appeared as the youthful lover with Greta Garbo in The Kiss, and as Paul in All Quiet on the Western Front. Made Dr. Kildare series (MGM) 1940-41. Served in U.S. Army Medical Corps for four years. Early films include : Common Clay, Shakedown, Holiday, Broadway Serenade. 1945 : State Fair (20th), The Dark Mirror (Univ) ; 1947 : The Unfaithful (Warn) ; 1948 : Johnny Belinda (Warn).

BACALL, Lauren. Real name Betty Joan Perske. Born New York City, Sept. 16, 1924. Ht. 5 ft. 6½ in.; wt. 119 lb. Tawny-blonde hair, blue-green eyes. Educ. private school ; Julia Richman High School. Inspired by acting of Bette Davis, she trained at American Academy of Dramatic Art, and appeared in short-lived plays, " Johnny Two-by-Four " and " Franklin Street ". Fashion model for " Harper's Bazaar ". Director Howard Hawks, after having seen her photograph in magazine, tested her, and

produced and directed her first film : To Have and To Have Not (Warn) 1944. Other films include—1945 : Confidential Agent (Warn) ; 1946 : The Big Sleep (Warn) ; 1947 : The Dark Passage (Warn).

BADDELEY, Hermione. Born Broseley, Salop, Nov. 13, 1906. Trained Margaret Morris School of Dancing, toured with the Arts League of Service, and made London stage debut, 1918 at Court Theatre, in " La Boite à Joujou". Has had a long and distinguished stage career, notably in " The Likes Of 'Er ", " Tobias and the Angel ", " The Greeks had a Word for It ", and many revues, including, " Rise Above It". Created role of Ida Arnold in the play " Brighton Rock ", and later repeated her role on the screen. Films include ; 1947 : Brighton Rock (Boultings-ABPC) ; 1948 : It Always Rains on Sunday (Ealing).

BAINTER, Fay. Born Los Angeles, California, Dec. 7, 1891. Ht. 5 ft. 5 in. ; wt. 112 lbs. Always wanted to be an actress from high school days, and began stage career with Belasco Stock Company in Los Angeles. Appeared in many Broadway successes. First film This Side of Heaven (MGM), 1934. Other films include : Quality Street, The Soldier and the Lady, Make Way for Tomorrow, Jezebel, White Banners, Mother Carey's Chickens, Yes My Darling Daughter, Daughters Courageous. 1940 : Young Tom Edison (MGM), Bill of Divorcement, (RKO), Our Town (UA) ; 1941 : Love Crazy (MGM) ; 1942 : The War Against Mrs. Hadley (MGM), Mrs. Wiggs of the Cabbage Patch (Para) ; 1943 : The Human Comedy (MGM), Salute to the Marines (MGM), Presenting Lily Mars (MGM), Cry Havoc (MGM), The Heavenly Body (MGM) ; 1944 : Dark Waters (UA), Three Is a Family (UA) ; 1945 : State Fair (20th), The Virginian (Para) ; 1947 : Deep Valley (Warn), The Secret Life of Walter Mitty (Goldwyn-RKO).

BAKER, Roy. Director. Born London, 1917. Educ. City of London School ; Lycée Corneille, Rouen, France. Formerly assistant director to Alfred Hitchcock and Carol Reed. War service with Army Kinematograph Unit as director of training films. First major film as director : The October Man (Two Cities) 1947.

BALCON, Jill. Born Westminster, London, Jan. 3, 1925. Hr. 5 ft. 6 in. ; wt. 121 lb. Black hair, green-grey eyes. Educ. Roedean. Youthful ambition: to be an actress. Won gold medal and Clifford Bax Cup for verse-reading at Central School of Speech and Drama, London. After touring experience, including work for ENSA, became B.B.C. announcer. On suggestion of film director Cavalcanti, was given first film role in Nicholas Nickleby (Ealing) 1947. 1948 : Good Time Girl (Ealing), Saraband for Dead Lovers (Ealing).

BALCON, Sir Michael. Executive producer. Born Birmingham, 1896. Educ. King Edward's School. In 1920, with Victor Saville as partner, became director of Victory Motion Picture Company, making advertising films in Birmingham. Then in London formed Gainsborough Pictures, making screen history in 1922 with his first production Woman to Woman, for which he brought Betty Compson from America at £1000 a week to play opposite Clive Brook. Took over Famous Players studio at Islington, a converted power station, and produced both silent and talking films, including The Rat, The Lodger, Downhill, the Squibs series (starring Betty Balfour), Easy Virtue, The Constant Nymph, Journey's End, The Ringer, Jack's the Boy, Sunshine Susie, Michael and Mary. In 1932 was appointed to the rebuilt Gaumont studio at Shepherd's Bush, London, and became director of production for both Gaumont British and Gainsborough Pictures. His first Gaumont British production *Rome Express* established wide prestige for British film industry. Productions 1932-36 include : *Man of Aran, Friday the 13th, The Good Companions, I Was a Spy, Evergreen, The Iron Duke, The Tunnel, The 39 Steps, King of the Damned, Secret Agent, First a Girl, Sabotage, O.H.M.S., Tudor Rose, The Passing of the Third Floor Back, Rhodes of Africa.* In January 1937 joined MGM British, visited Hollywood and returned to produce *A Yank at Oxford* at Denham Studios. Later in 1937 became executive producer at Ealing Studios. During World War II, Balcon produced many outstanding feature-documentaries of topical interest, among them, *Ships with Wings, The Foreman Went to France, Next of Kin, San Demetrio London.* In sending a small unit, headed by Harry Watt, to Australia in 1945 to make *The Overlanders*, he showed himself the first British producer to take advantage of the potentialities of film-making there. Other recent productions include : *Johnny Frenchman, Champagne Charlie, Painted Boats, The Captive Heart, Halfway House, Dead of Night, Hue and Cry, Nicholas Nickleby, The Loves of Joanna Godden, Frieda, It Always Rains on Sunday, Saraband for Dead Lovers, Against the Wind, Eureka Stockade* (1947-8) in Australia, *Scott of the Antarctic.*

BALL, Lucille. Born Butte, Montana, U.S.A., Aug. 6, 1911. Ht. 5 ft. 6 in. ; wt. 120 lb. Educ. public schools Jamestown, New York State, Chautauqua Institute for Music. Tried drama school, but was told she was wasting her time. Became showgirl in road show " Rio Rita ", then drug store assistant, then fashion designer's model. Lost three years of career through car accident but returned to modelling and advertisement fame as "The Chesterfield Girl". Became film extra, 1934, and appeared in *Roman Scandals, Bottoms Up, Bulldog Drummond, Moulin Rouge, Kid Millions*, and other films. First major success, *Roberta* (1935). After having appeared on Broadway in " Hey Diddle Diddle " (1936) returned to Hollywood for *Stage Door* (1937). During next five years made *Room Service, Having Wonderful Time, Next Time I Marry, Two Crowded Hours, Panama Lady*, and other films, all with RKO. 1940 : *The Marines Fly High* (RKO), *Dance, Girl, Dance* (RKO), *You Can't Fool Your Wife* (RKO), *Too Many Girls* (RKO) ; 1941 : *The Navy Steps Out* (RKO), *Look Who's Laughing* (RKO) ; 1942 : *The Valley of the Sun* (RKO), *The Big Street* (RKO), *Seven Days' Leave* (RKO) ; 1943 : *Dubarry Was a Lady* (MGM), *Best Foot Forward* (MGM), *Thousands Cheer* (MGM) ; 1944 *Ziegfeld Follies* (MGM) ; 1945 : *Without Love* (MGM), *Easy to Wed* (MGM), *Two Smart People* (MGM) ; 1946 : *The Dark Corner* (20th) ; 1947 : *Lover Come Back* (Univ), *Her Husband's Affairs* (Col), *Personal Column* (Hunt Stromberg-UA).

BANJO. Dog star. Born Canada, 1940. English setter. Black and white with dark red spots. Three times winner as the best breed in Canadian national dog shows. First film : *Banjo* (RKO) 1947.

BARI, Lynn. Real name Marjorie Bitzer. Born Roanoke, Virginia, U.S.A., Dec. 18. Ht. 5 ft. 6 in. ; wt. 122 lb. Dark brown hair, hazel eyes. Educ. private schools in Roanoke, Boston, New Hampshire. Ambition was to be a film star, so studied at Hollywood drama school. Answered MGM advertisement for

chorus girls in Joan Crawford film. First film appearance : *Dancing Lady* (MGM) 1933. Early films include : *Stand Up and Cheer, I'll Give a Million, The Baroness and the Butler, Walking Down Broadway, Battle of Broadway, Mr. Moto's Gamble, Josette, Always Good-bye, Speed to Burn, Meet the Girls, Sharpshooters, Pardon Our Nerve, Chasing Danger, Return of the Cisco Kid, News Is Made at Night, Hotel for Women, We're in the Army Now, Charlie Chan in City of Darkness, City of Chance.* 1940 : *Kit Carson* (UA), *Lillian Russell* (20th), *Earthbound* (20th), *Free, Blonde and 21* (20th), *Charter Pilot* (20th), *Pier 13* (20th) ; 1941 : *Sleepers West* (20th), *Blood and Sand* (20th), *Sun Valley Serenade* (20th), *Perfect Snob* (20th) ; 1942 : *China Girl* (20th), *The Magnificent Dope* (20th), *Orchestra Wives* (20th), *Secret Agent of Japan* (20th) ; 1943 : *Hello, Frisco, Hello* (20th) ; 1944 : *The Bridge of San Luis Rey* (UA), *Tampico* (20th), *Sweet and Lowdown* (20th) ; 1945 : *Captain Eddie* (20th) ; 1946 : *Shock* (20th), *Home Sweet Homicide* (20th) *Nocturne* (RKO) ; 1947 : *Margie* (20th), *Nocturne*, (RKO).

BARKAS, Geoffrey. Producer. Born Richmond, Surrey, Aug. 27, 1896. Educ. City of London School. Entered film industry in 1921 as assistant cameraman Universal City, Hollywood. Returned to Britain as cameraman with Gaumont British, Samuelson and Ideal. In 1923-24 was producer, director, writer and photographer for the *Secrets of Nature* series (British Instructional) ; in 1925 was official cameraman on the Prince of Wales's tours in Africa and South America. Became director in 1926, with feature made in northern Nigeria, *Palaver ;* then co-director of films reconstructing World War I—*The Somme, Q Ships, Tell England.* From 1933 to 1936 was co-director for Gaumont British, organizing and directing flight scenes in India for *Wings over Everest ;* and later, as director and associate producer, supervised exterior scenes in Africa for *King Solomon's Mines, Rhodes of Africa*, and *The Camels are Coming*, in India for *Soldiers Three* and in Canadian Rockies for *The Great Barrier.* 1939-45, in H.M. Forces. 1947, produced the children's films *The Little Ballerina, Dusty Bates.*

BARNES, Barry K. Real name Nelson Barry Mackintosh Barnes. Born Chelsea, London, Dec. 27, 1906. Ht. 6 ft. Brown hair, blue eyes. Educ. City of London School ; Dollar Academy. Left school to work in drawing-office of his father's store-fitting business. Won scholarship to Royal Academy of Dramatic Art and made stage debut in 1927 at Court Theatre, London, in " Paul I ". Played in repertory at Hull, Edinburgh, Newcastle-on-Tyne. Outstanding success as Robert Browning in " The Barretts of Wimpole Street " in London and on Australian tour ; many other stage successes since. First film : *The Return of the Scarlet Pimpernel* (LFP), 1937. Other films include : *Who Goes Next ? This Man is News, This Man in Paris, Prison Without Bars, The Ware Case ;* 1940 : *The Midas Touch* (Warn Brit), *Girl in the News* (20th-Brit) ; 1946 : *Bedelia* (Corfield) ; 1947 : *Dancing With Crime* (Alliance).

BARNES, Binnie. Real name Gertrude Maud Barnes. Born London, Mar. 25, 1906. Ht. 5 ft. 5 in. Red hair, green eyes, Educ. Sevenoaks, Kent ; Paris. Worked on farm and then as probationer nurse before making first stage appearance in 1924 as one of the Tiller Girls. Appeared with them in France and Germany, then returned to London as exhibition ballroom dancer. Then joined Tex McLeod, learnt rope-spinning, and toured with him in South Africa and Australia. Returned to Britain and took part in Charlot's Revue, 1928. Later became famous as the blues singer in " Cavalcade". Screen debut in 1939, when she made three shorts for Gainsborough between stage appearances. First important film part in *Night in Montmartre*, 1931. Her playing of Catherine Howard in *The Private Life of Henry VIII* (1933) brought her a U.S. contract. Recent films include—1941 : *This Thing Called Love* (Col), *Angels with Broken Wings* (Rep) ; 1942 : *Call out the Marines* (RKO), *I Married an Angel* (MGM) ; 1943 : *The Man from Down Under* (MGM) ; 1944 : *The Hour Before the Dawn* (Para), *Up in Mabel's Room* (UA), *Barbary Coast Gent* (MGM) ; 1945 : *It's in the Bag* (UA), *The Spanish Main* (RKO) ; 1946 : *The Time of Their Lives* (Univ) ; 1948 : *If Winter Comes* (MGM), *My Own True Love* (Para).

BARNET, B. Producer (U.S.S.R.). A pupil of film producer Leon Kuleshov, Barnet was first an actor appearing in *The Adventures of Mr. West* (1924) and other films. At the same time worked as a producer, and in 1927 made the adventure film *Miss Mend*, in which he also played one of the principal parts. Later made *The House on the Trubnaya, Moscow in the October* (dedicated to the tenth anniversary of the October Revolution), *The Girl with the Box* (comedy), *The Breaking of the Ice*. His first talking picture was *The Suburb*. He has also produced a number of cultural and educational films.

BARRAULT, Jean-Louis. Born Vésinet, France, Sept. 8, 1910. Brown eyes, brown hair. Educ. Chaptal College. Worked in Paris markets, in an office, and as nightwatchman at Atelier Theatre, Paris, before joining repertory company at that theatre. Made stage debut in " Volpone". Became actor, director, scenic designer, dancer and pantomimist for Comédie Française. Director Marc Allegret saw him on stage and gave him first film role in *Les Beaux Jours*. Other films include : *Sous les Yeux d'Occident, Prison de Velours*. Helped to conceive story of *Les Enfants du Paradis*, in which he played the clown, Baptiste Deburau.

BARRYMORE, Ethel. Born Philadelphia, U.S.A., Aug. 15, 1879. Educ. Convent of Notre Dame, Philadelphia. Sister of Lionel and the late John Barrymore. At 15 acted in " The Rivals " at Academy of Music, Montreal. Professional debut: "That Impudent Young Couple ", Empire, New York, 1896. First New York starring role in " Captain Jinks of the Horse Marines ", 1901 ; became one of America's greatest stage actresses. Began silent film career with *The Nightingale*, 1914. In 1932 appeared with her brothers in *Rasputin and the Empress* (MGM). Recent films include—1944 : *None but the Lonely Heart* (RKO) ; 1945 : *The Spiral Staircase* (RKO) ; 1947 : *The Farmer's Daughter* (RKO), *Moss Rose* (20th) 1948 : *Night Song* (RKO), *The Paradine Case* (Selznick).

BARRYMORE, Lionel. Born Philadelphia, U.S.A., Apr. 28, 1878. Ht. 6 ft. ; wt. 195 lb. White hair, blue eyes. Educ. privately, New York. On stage at the age of 5 with his parents Maurice Barrymore and Georgia Drew. At 18 on New York stage with his grandmother Louisa Drew in " The Rivals ". Studied art in Paris, became illustrator ; then acted in " Peter Ibbetson ", " The Copperhead ", " The Claw ", " Laugh, Clown, Laugh ". Silent films from 1909 include *The Barrier, The Temptress, West of Zanzibar*. Directed early talkies : *Madame X, The Rogue Song,*

Ten Cents a Dance. Films 1930-39 (all MGM) include : *The Yellow Passport, Arsène Lupin, Mata Hari, Grand Hotel, Rasputin the Mad Monk, Dinner at Eight, This Side of Heaven, Treasure Island, David Copperfield, Ah Wilderness, Camille, Captains Courageous, A Yank at Oxford, Test Pilot, On Borrowed Time.* 1940 : *Dr. Kildare's Strange Case,* (MGM), *Dr. Kildare Goes Home* (MGM), *Dr. Kildare's Crisis* (MGM) ; 1941 : *Two-Gun Cupid* (MGM), *The Penalty* (MGM), *My Life Is Yours* (MGM), *Lady be Good* (MGM), *Mary Names the Day* (MGM), *The Doctor and the Debutante* (MGM) ; 1942 : *Calling Dr. Gillespie* (MGM), *The Man on America's Conscience* (MGM— not shown in U.K. till 1946), *Dr. Gillespie's New Assistant* (MGM) ; 1943 : *Crazy to Kill* (MGM), *A Guy Named Joe* (MGM) ; 1944 : *Three Men in White* (MGM), *Since You Went Away* (UA) ; 1945 : *Between Two Women* (MGM), *The Valley of Decision* (MGM) ; 1946 : *Duel in the Sun* (Selznick), *Three Wise Fools* (MGM), *It's a Wonderful Life* (RKO), *The Secret Heart* (MGM), *Cynthia's Secret* (MGM).

BARTHOLOMEW, Freddie. Born London, Mar. 28, 1924. Ht. 5 ft. 11 in. ; wt. 150 lb. Brown hair, brown eyes. Received his education from his aunt, Millicent Bartholomew, in Warminster. Recited and acted from age of 3 ; appeared in one of Madeleine Carroll's early films at Elstree, *Fascination*, and in small parts on the London stage. Laws governing the use of children in British studios prevented him from adopting a film career in Britain, but in 1934 he went to America " for a holiday " while MGM were testing applicants for the title part in *David Copperfield*, which he secured. Other films include : *Anna Karenina, Professional Soldier, Lloyds of London, Little Lord Fauntleroy, The Devil Takes the Count, Captains Courageous, Kidnapped, The Boy from Barnardo's, Listen Darling.* 1940 : *Swiss Family Robinson* (RKO), *Tom Brown's Schooldays* (RKO) ; 1941 : *Naval Academy* (Col) ; 1942 : *A Yank at Eton* (MGM) ; 1943 : *Junior Army* (Col) ; 1944 : *The Town Went Wild.*

BASSERMAN, Albert. Born Mannheim, Germany, Sept. 7, 1867. One of the most distinguished actors on German stage ; on Hitler's accession to power in 1933, went to Austria ; after the Anschluss in 1938, went to Hollywood. Made American screen debut in *Dr. Erhlich's Magic Bullet* (Warn) 1940. Other films include—1940 : *A Dispatch from Reuter's* (Warn), *Foreign Correspondent* (UA), *Escape* (MGM) re-issued 1947 as *When the Door Opened*; 1941 : *New Wine* (UA) ; 1942 : *Invisible Agent* (Univ), *The Moon and Sixpence* (UA), *Once Upon a Honeymoon* (RKO), *Reunion in France* (MGM) ; 1943 : *Madame Curie* (MGM) ; 1944 : *Since You Went Away* (UA) ; 1945 : *Rhapsody in Blue* (Warn). Visited Britain to appear in *Red Shoes* (Archers) 1948.

BATES, Herbert Ernest. Author. Born May 16, 1905. Educ. Grammar School, Kettering. Worked as provincial journalist ; at 20, published first novel. In World War II served in R.A.F., and wrote stories under pseudonym " Flying Officer X ", one of which, " It's just the way it is ", was filmed. Other works, written under his own name, include " The Two Sisters ", " The Poacher ", " Fair Stood the Wind for France ", " The Bride Comes to Evensford " which has been filmed, and many short stories. Has written numerous film scripts including that for *The Loves of Joanna Godden.*

43

BAX, Sir Arnold. Composer. Born London, 1883. Displayed great skill in composition while still a student at the Royal Academy of Music. He was knighted in 1937, and became Master of the King's Musick in 1942. In that year he wrote his first film score, the music to *Malta G.C.*

BAXTER, Anne. Born Michigan City, Indiana, U.S.A., May 7, 1923. Blonde hair, hazel eyes. Educ. Theodore Ervine School of Drama. On stage since she was 12 years old. To Hollywood in 1939 to undergo tests for lead in *Rebecca;* but production was shelved, and she returned to New York stage. Then to Hollywood again ; this time was signed for *The Great Profile* (20th) 1940, with the late John Barrymore. Other films include—1941 : *Charley's American Aunt* (20th) ; 1942 : *The Pied Piper* (20th), *The Magnificent Ambersons* (RKO) ; 1943 : *Crash Dive* (20th), *Five Graves to Cairo* (Para), *North Star* (Goldwyn-RKO) ; 1944 : *The Sullivans* (20th), *The Eve of St. Mark* (20th), *Sunday Dinner for a Soldier* (20th), *Guest in the House* (UA) ; 1945 : *A Royal Scandal*—British title *Czarina* (20th) ; 1946 : *Angel on My Shoulder* (UA), *Smoky* (20th) ; 1947 : *The Razor's Edge* (20th), *Blaze of Noon* (Para).

BAXTER, Beryl. Born Birmingham, April, 9 1926. Ht. 5 ft. 5½ in. ; wt. 112 lb. Black hair, blue eyes. Educ. Brighton and Hove High School. Left school at 14 to begin dramatic training. First professional role with Stratford-on-Avon Festival Company, 1943. In repertory at Altrincham and in London, 1943-5. Understudy to Patricia Burke in " Stage Door ", 1946, but after only two weeks was chosen for a role in " Fifty-Fifty " at the Strand Theatre, London. Is one of the first players being " groomed for stardom " by Maurice Ostrer, who gave her a leading part, opposite Michael Rennie, in her first film *Idol of Paris* (Premier) 1948.

BAXTER, John. Director. Born Sidcup, Kent, 1897. Playing small parts in touring theatrical companies ; sang with the D'Oyley Carte Opera Company; later became a touring theatrical manager. Entered film industry, 1932, as casting director at Sound City Studios, Shepperton. Associate director to Ivar Campbell on *Reunion.* The first two films he directed, *Doss House* and *Song of the Plough,* both made in 1932, are still regarded as classics of " down to earth " films. Other films include : *Lest We Forget, Music Hall, Say It with Flowers, Kentucky Minstrels, Flood Tide, The Small Man, A Real Bloke, Hearts of Humanity, Men of Yesterday, Song of the Road, Jimmy Boy, Sunshine Ahead, Birds of a Feather, Old Mother Riley in Society, Crooks Tour, Old Mother Riley in Business, Love on the Dole, Old Mother Riley's Ghost, The Common Touch, Let the People Sing, We'll Smile Again, When We Are Married, Theatre Royal, The Shipbuilders, Dreaming, Here Comes the Sun, The Grand Escapade, When You Come Home, Nothing Venture, Fortune Lane.*

BAXTER, Warner. Born Columbus, Ohio, U.S.A., Mar. 29, 1893. Ht. 5 ft. 11 in. Brown hair, brown eyes. Educ. Polytechnic High School. San Francisco. Lost possessions in San Francisco earthquake, 1906. Returned to Columbus, 1908, became office boy, then commercial traveller. First stage experience as stand-in for dancing partner in local vaudeville. Later resumed business as insurance salesman, but returned to stage as juvenile lead in local repertory and had long career in repertory and on Broadway. Made first film appearance with Ethel Clayton in *Her*

Own Money, 1923. Made many other silent films. Achieved sudden stardom in *The Cisco Kid,* 1931. Other films include : *Six Hours to Live, Paddy the Next Best Thing, 42nd Street, Stand Up and Cheer, King of Burlesque, Slave Ship, Kidnapped, The Return of the Cisco Kid.* 1940 : *Earthbound* (20th) ; 1941 : *Adam Had Four Sons* (Col) ; 1943 : *The Crime Doctor* (Col), (first of the series) ; 1944 : *Lady in the Dark* (Para).

BEATON, Cecil. Art adviser. Born Jan. 14, 1904, Educ. Harrow and Cambridge. Hobbies : painting and photography. Started photographing his two sisters and reached the top of his profession when he became official photographer to the Royal Family. World-famous for his photographs of beautiful women. Debut as stage designer in 1936 for Cochran. Set designer and consultant for *Beware of Pity* ; designed costumes for *The Young Mr. Pitt, An Ideal Husband, Anna Karenina.*

BEATTY, Robert. Born Hamilton, Ontario, Canada, Oct. 19, 1909. Ht. 6 ft. ; wt. 160 lb. Dark brown hair, dark brown eyes. Educ. Delta College, Hamilton, University of Toronto (B.A.). Cashier and salesman in Hamilton ; four years in amateur drama. To London, 1937, to study at Royal Academy of Dramatic Art. 1938, understudy to Raymond Massey in " Idiot's Delight " ; 1939, at Criterion Theatre in " Grouse in June " ; 1940-3, B.B.C. Empire news reader, narrator Radio Newsreel. Began screen career as stand-in for Raymond Massey in British studios. First film appearance : *Murder in Soho* (ABPC), 1938. Other films include—1941 : *Dangerous Moonlight* (RKO) ; 1942 : *Suspected Person* (ABPC), *49th Parallel* (Ortus), *One of Our Aircraft is Missing* (Brit Nat) ; 1943 : *San Demetrio, London* (Ealing), *It Happened One Sunday* (ABPC) ; 1946 : *Appointment With Crime* (Brit Nat) ; 1947 : *Odd Man Out* (Two Cities), *Green Fingers* (Brit Nat), ; 1948 : *Against the Wind* (Ealing), *So Died a Rat* (Brit Nat).

BECKETT, Scotty. Born Oakland, California, U.S.A., Oct. 4, 1929. Began film career as child in *Our Gang* comedies. Other films include : *Gallant Lady, Stand Up and Cheer, George White's Scandals, Pursuit, The Case Against Mrs. Ames, Anthony Adverse, The Charge of the Light Brigade, Marie Antoinette, Listen Darling* ; 1940 : *Blue Bird* (20th), *My Son, My Son* (UA) ; 1941 : *Father's Son* (Warn) ; 1942 : *It Happened in Flatbush* (20th) ; 1944 : *The Climax* (Univ) ; 1945 : *Junior Miss, Circumstantial Evidence* (20th) ; 1946 : *My Reputation* (Warn), *Her Adventurous Night* (Univ), *The Jolson Story* (Col) ; 1947 : *White Tie and Tails* (UI).

BEERY, Noah, Jr. Born New York, Aug. 10. 1916. Ht. 5 ft. 10 in. ; wt. 178 lb. Black hair, brown eyes. Educ. Hollywood Military Academy ; North Hollywood High School. As a small boy appeared in silent film, *The Mark of Zorro.* First stage part as adult was in local Hollywood theatre, where he was seen by a talent scout and was signed up to play in three Western serials. Remained in Westerns until 1940 when he had his first big success in *Of Mice and Men* (UA). 1941 : *Sergeant York* (Warn) ; 1943 : *Gung Ho !* (Univ), *Top Man* (Univ), *Frontier Badman* (Univ), *Corvette K-225* (Univ), *We've Never Been Licked* (Univ) ; 1944 : *Hi, Beautiful !* (Univ), *Weekend Pass* (Univ) ; 1945 : *Crimson Canary* (Univ), *Beautiful Cheat* (Univ), *See My Lawyer* (Univ), *Her Lucky Night* (Univ), *Under Western Skies* (Univ) ; 1946 : *What a Woman* (Univ) ; 1947 : *The Cat Creeps* (UI).

LAUREN BACALL
(*Warner*)

BEERY, Wallace. Born Kansas City, U.S.A., Apr. 1, 1889. Ht. 6 ft. 1 in.; wt. 225 lb. Brown hair, brown eyes. Educ. Kansas City High School; Chase School, Kansas City. In Ringling's Circus at age of 16, sang in Henry Savage's musicals, New York, played in repertory in Kansas City. His first films were made with the Essanay Company, in Chicago from 1913. Later, with Keystone and Universal, made two-reel comedies with Raymond Hatton. After World War I, became prominent as screen villian in silent films; under contract to MGM since 1928. Early films include: *The Four Horsemen of the Apocalypse, Robin Hood, Chinatown Nights, Behind the Door, The Devil's Cargo, The Big House, Billy the Kid, Min and Bill* (with Marie Dressler, 1930), *The Champ, Hell Divers, Grand Hotel, Tugboat Annie, Dinner at Eight, Viva Villa, Treasure Island, China Seas, Bad Man of Brimstone, Port of Seven Seas, Stablemates, Stand Up and Fight, Thunder Afloat.* 1940: *Arouse and Beware, Twenty-Mule Team, Bad Man of Wyoming*; 1941: *Two-Gun Cupid, Barnacle Bill, The Bugle Sounds*; 1942: *Jackass Mail*; 1943: *Salute to the Marines*; 1944: *Rationing, Barbary Coast Gent, This Man's Navy*; 1945: *Bad Bascomb*; 1946: *The Mighty McGurk.* 1948: *Alias the Gentleman, Date with Judy.*

BELITA. Real name Gladys Lyne Jepson Turner. Born Garlogs, Nether Wallop, Hants, 1925. Fair hair, blue eyes. Appeared before she was 2 at a London bazaar as a Christmas-tree doll. Began skating at 4 and made several public appearances as ballet dancer. At 14, starred in " Opera on Ice " in London. Went to the United States a year later as exhibition skater. Star of " Ice-Capades " in New York for two years. Signed for films by Pathe Monogram. Films include—1942: *Silver Skates;* 1944: *Lady Let's Dance;* 1946: *Suspense;* 1947: *The Gangster.*

BEL GEDDES, Barbara. Real name Barbara Geddes Shreuer. Born New York, Oct. 31, 1922. Ht. 5 ft. 3½ in.; wt. 112 lb. Mid-blonde hair, hazel eyes. Educ. Buxton Country Day School, Milburn, New Jersey; Putney School, Putney, Vermont; André Brook School, Terrytown, New York. Daughter of stage designer Norman Bel Geddes. Began her career in the theatre; after a great success in " Deep Are the Roots " on Broadway, was signed up for Hollywood. First film: *The Long Night* (RKO) 1947, a re-make of the French classic *Le Jour Se Lève.* 1948: *I Remember Mama* (RKO).

BELL, Marie. Born Bordeaux, France, Dec. 23, 1905. Auburn hair, green eyes. Educ. Bordeaux Conservatoire. Studied dancing and appeared as dancer at London Pavilion. Trained for stage career in Paris and became member of Comédie Française. Made silent film debut in *La Valse de L'Adieu,* and talking debut in *La Nuit Est à Nous.* Other films include: *L'Homme Qui Assassina, L'Homme a l'Hispano, La Folle Aventure, Le Grand Jeu, Fédora, Poliche, La Garçonne, Ceux du Ciel, Le Roman d'un Jeune Homme Pauvre, La Tentation, Un Carnet de Bal, Vie Privée, Le Colonel Chabert.*

BELLAMY, Ralph. Born Chicago, U.S.A., June 17, 1905. Ht. 6 ft. 1½ in.; wt. 191 lb. Brown hair, blue eyes. Has been in more than a hundred films since his first appearance at the age of 13 in a silent film, *Wings of the Morning* (Fox). While at school, organized small theatre in Chicago; then much stage work on tour and in New York. Broadway success

in " Roadside " brought him film contract for *The Secret Six* (MGM), 1931; later films include: *The Magnificent Lie, Rebecca of Sunnybrook Farm, Destination Unknown, Once to Every Woman, The Awful Truth, The Crime of Dr. Hallett, Boy Meets Girl, Carefree, Girls' School, Trade Winds, Smashing the Spy Ring.* 1941: *Affectionately Yours* (FN), *Dive Bomber* (Warn); 1942: *Men of Texas* (Univ); 1943: *Eyes of the Underworld* (Univ), *The Great Impersonation* (Univ); 1944: *Guest in the House* (UA); 1945: *Delightfully Dangerous* (UA), *Lady on a Train* (Univ).

BENDIX, William. Born East Side, New York, Jan. 14, 1906. Educ. New York Public School No. 5; Townsend Harris Preparatory School. Youthful ambition: to be a baseball player. Worked as amateur actor and as M.C. in cabaret and clubs; became manager of large grocery store in Orange, New Jersey. Depression of 1935 led him to become actor with New Jersey Federal Theatre Project for two years, and with New York Theatre Guild until 1941. Made his debut on the screen in *Woman of the Year* (MGM) 1942. Other films include—1942: *The Brooklyn Orchid* (UA), *The Glass Key* (Para), *Wake Island* (Para); 1943: *The Crystal Ball* (UA), *China* (Para), *Star Spangled Rhythm* (Para), *Guadalcanal Diary* (20th), *The Hairy Ape* (UA), *Hostages* (Para); 1944: *Greenwich Village* (20th), *Abroad with Two Yanks* (UA), *Lifeboat* (20th); 1945: *It's in the Bag* (UA), *Don Juan Quilligan* (20th), *A Bell for Adano* (20th), *Two Years Before the Mast* (Para); 1946: *The Blue Dahlia* (Para), *The Dark Corner* (20th), *Calcutta* (Para), *Sentimental Journey* (20th); 1947: *Blaze of Noon* (Para), *White Tie and Tails* (UI), *Where There's Life* (Para), *The Web* (UI), *Variety Girl* (Para); 1948: *The Time of Your Life* (Cagney-UA), *A Connecticut Yankee* (Para).

BENJAMIN, Arthur. Composer. Born Sydney, Australia, 1893. Came to Britain to study at Royal College of Music, and returned to Australia to teach at Sydney Conservatoire. Later joined teaching staff of Royal College of Music, London. Notable film scores include: *The Man Who Knew Too Much, The Scarlet Pimpernel, Turn of the Tide, Under the Red Robe,* and, more recently, *Master of Bankdam.* Since 1937 has lived mainly in Canada.

BENNETT, Bruce. Real name Herman Brix. Born Tacoma, Washington, U.S.A., May 19, 1909. Ht. 6 ft. 2 in.; wt. 185 lb. Light brown hair, blue eyes. Educ. grade and high schools, Tacoma; University of Washington (B.A.). Prominent athlete; member of American Olympic team, Amsterdam, 1928. Worked on lumber camp sawmill, oil well equipment company; insurance salesman. Worked season with Max Reinhardt, appearing in " Too Many Husbands ". Introduced to films by the late Douglas Fairbanks, Sr., and played Tarzan in film made in Gautemala. Recent films include—1940: *Lone Wolf Keeps a Date* (Col); 1942: *Atlantic Convoy* (Col), *Sabotage Squad* (Col), *Underground Agent* (Col); 1943: *The More the Merrier* (Col), *Sahara* (Col); 1944: *I'm from Arkansas, Danger Signal*; 1945: *Mildred Pierce* (Warn); 1946: *The Man I Love* (Warn), *A Stolen Life* (Warn); 1947: *Nora Prentiss* (Warn), *Cheyenne* (Warn), *The Dark Passage*; 1948: *Treasure of the Sierra Madre* (Warn).

BENNETT, Compton. Director. Born London. As a young man embarked on watch repairing and then electrical engineering. Served in the Army in World War I. Afterwards ran a dance band and worked as a clerk before discovering that he had a talent for drawing. Joined the film industry as a cutter, editing films at Denham. Films directed : *Men of Rochdale, The Seventh Veil, The Years Between, Daybreak.* After the success of *The Seventh Veil* in 1946, went to Hollywood, where he studied production methods and directed *My Own True Love* before returning to Britain.

BENNETT, Constance. Actress, producer. Born New York City, Oct. 22 1906. Ht. 5 ft. 4 in. ; wt. 102 lb. Fair hair, blue eyes. Educ. Miss Shandor's school, New York City ; Miss Merrill's School, Mamaronek, New York ; Mme. Balsan, Paris. Her father, the actor Richard Bennett, offered her a stage career, but she preferred films, making debut in *Cytharea* (Goldwyn) 1920. After making nine silent films in nine months, she left Hollywood for four years and travelled in Europe, returning in 1929 to make her first talkie, *Rich People* (RKO), 1930. Other films include : *Sin Takes a Holiday, Born to Love, Bought, Everything is Thunder* (for GB, in Britain), *The Goose Hangs High, Sally, Irene and Mary, This Thing Called Love, Three Faces East, Our Betters, Topper.* 1942 : *Wild Bill Hickok Rides* (Warn), *Madame Spy* (Univ). Formed her own company, 1944. Appeared in and produced *Madame Pimpernel* (Constance Bennett-UA), 1945. 1946: appeared in *Centennial Summer* (20th) ; 1947: *The Unsuspected* (Warn).

BENNETT, Joan. Born Palisades, New Jersey, U.S.A., Feb. 27, 1910. Ht. 5 ft. 3 in, ; wt. 110 lb. Fair hair, blue eyes. Educ. privately, and at boarding schools in Connecticut, France and London. A daughter of Richard Bennett, she wanted to become an interior decorator. When this fell through, she accepted her father's offer to appear with him in " Jarnegan ". She was immediately noticed by Hollywood, and offered a role in Ronald Colman's *Bulldog Drummond* (UA) 1929, followed by a leading part in *Three Live Ghosts.* Other films include : *Mississippi Gambler, Disraeli, Crazy That Way, Putting on the Ritz, Maybe It's Love, Moby Dick, Careless Lady, She Wanted a Millionaire, The Trial of Vivian Ware, Weekends Only, Me and my Gal, Wild Girl, Arizona to Broadway, Little Women, The Pursuit of Happiness, The Man Who Reclaimed His Head, Mississippi, Private Worlds, Two for Tonight, She Couldn't Take It, The Man Who Broke the Bank at Monte Carlo, 13 Hours by Air, Big Brown Eyes, Wedding Present, Two in a Crowd, Vogues of 1938, I Met My Love Again, Trade Winds, The Texans, Artistes and Models Abroad.* 1941 : *Man Hunt* (20th) ; 1942 : *Twin Beds* (UA), *Girl Trouble* (20th) ; 1943 : *Margin for Error* (20th) ; 1944 : *The Woman in the Window* (RKO) ; 1945 : *Nob Hill* (20th), *Scarlet Street* (Univ) ; 1946 : *Col. Effingham's Raid* (20th), *The Man of the Hour* (20th) ; 1947 : *The Macomber Affair* (Benedict Bogeaus-UA): 1948 : *The Secret Beyond the Door* (UI), *Woman on the Beach* (RKO).

BENNY, Jack. Real name Joseph Kubelsky. Born Waukegan, Illinois, U.S.A., Feb. 14. Ht. 5 ft. 9 in. ; wt. 150 lb. Greying brown hair, blue eyes. Educ. Grade School, High School, Waukegan. Worked in father's haberdashery business. Has been violinist, doorman and property man. While acting as vaudeville M.C. in Los Angeles, was seen by film executive. First film appearance : *The Hollywood Revue of 1929* (MGM). Other films include : *Chasing Rainbows, The Medicine Man, Bright Moments, The Song-Writers' Revue, Mr. Broadway, Transatlantic Merry-Go-Round, Broadway Melody of 1936, It's in the . Air, Big Broadcast of 1937, College Holiday, Artists and Models, Artists and Models Abroad, Man*

About Town. 1940 : *Buck Benny Rides Again* (Para) ; *Love Thy Neighbour* (Para) : 1941 : *Charley's American Aunt* (20th) ; 1942 : *George Washington Slept Here* (Warn), *To Be or Not. To Be* (UA) ; 1943 : *The Meanest Man in the World* (20th) ; 1944 : *Hollywood Canteen* (Warn) ; 1945 : *The Horn Blows at Midnight* (Warn) , *It's in the Bag* (UA).

BENSON, George. Born Cardiff, Jan. 11, 1911. Ht. 5 ft. 8 in. ; wt. 140 lb. Fair hair, blue eyes. Educ. Blundell's School, Devon. Student at Royal Academy of Dramatic Art for two years, winning Silver Medal in 1930. Began stage career in " Charlot's Masquerade ", 1930, at Cambridge Theatre, London. Then many theatrical roles, and a few minor parts in films including *The Man from Toronto* and *Keep Fit.* Served in the Army during the war. Returned to stage in April 1946 with Beatrice Lillie in " Better Late" at the Garrick Theatre, London. Was seen there by Eric Ambler and offered his first important film role in *October Man* (Two Cities) 1947.

BERGMAN, Ingrid. Born Stockholm, Sweden, 1917. Ht. 5 ft. 7½ in. ; wt. 127 lb. Ash-blonde hair, hazel eyes. Educ. Lyceum for Flickor (where she wrote, directed and appeared in school play, 1932) and Royal Dramatic Theatre School, Stockholm. Before the end of her first term, was selected by Svensk Film Industry for small part in film *Munkbrogreven.* During next two years, appeared in eleven more films, starring in nine. Performance in *Intermezzo* led to her appearing in American version (Selznick-UA, 1939 : British title, *Escape to Happiness*). On Broadway stage, 1940-1, in " Liliom " ; in 1942, on stage in Hollywood and elsewhere in " Anna Christie ". Other films include—1941 : *Adam had Four Sons* (Col), *Rage in Heaven* (MGM), *Dr. Jekyll and Mr. Hyde* (MGM) ; 1942 : *En Enda Natt* (*Only One Night*) made in Sweden, *Casablanca* (Warn), *Saratoga Trunk* (Warn : not released until 1946) ; 1943 : *For Whom the Bell Tolls* (Para) ; 1944 : *The Murder in Thornton Square* (MGM) ; 1945 : *Spellbound* (UA) ; 1946 : *The Bells of St. Mary's* (RKO) ; 1947 : *Notorious* (RKO), *Arch of Triumph* (Enterprise-MGM) ; 1948 : *Joan* (Wanger)

BERKELEY, Lennox. Composer. Born Boar's Hill, Oxford, 1903. General education at Oxford, musical education largely in Paris. His major works include the oratorio " Jonah ", performed at the Leeds Festival, 1937 ; and music for the ballet, " The Judgment of Paris ", performed at Sadler's Wells in 1938. Entered films in 1942, when he wrote the music for a religious short, *The Sword of the Spirit.* He also scored *Hotel Reserve, Out of Chaos, The First Gentleman.*

BERLIN, Irving. Composer. Real name Isidore Baline. Born South Russia, May 11, 1888. Parents emigrated to New York in 1893. Had no formal music education. First jobs included leading a beggar through cafés in Bowery and working as a singing waiter. First song published 1907 ; found fame with " Alexander's Ragtime Band ". Since World War I, has been one of America's foremost songwriters, with such hits as " Always ", " Remember ", " What'll I Do ? ", " Blue Skies ", " All Alone ". Films for which he has written music and lyrics include : *Top Hat, Follow the Fleet, On the Avenue, Carefree, Alexander's Ragtime Band, Second Fiddle, Louisiana Purchase, Holiday Inn, This is the Army, Blue Skies, Easter Parade.*

BERNSTEIN, Sidney. Born Ilford, Essex, 1888. Gave up engineering apprenticeship at 19 to become clerk in film distributor's office. In his early twenties became interested in the theatre, largely through influence of Komisarjevsky and Arnold Bennett. Junior manager of Empire, Edmonton, London, 1922. In 1925 toured Russia to study films, studios, and theatres. Built Phœnix Theatre, London; also associated with productions at Court Theatre. Founded Granada chain of cinemas (so called because the name " Granada " attracted him on a walking tour in Spain), for which Frank Dobson and Komisarjevsky were later engaged as designers. In 1927 introduced Saturday morning matinees for children at the ten cinemas he then owned in London suburbs ; in same year instituted the now famous Bernstein Questionnaire. In this, half a million copies of twelve questions are distributed to film audiences, and the answers are then used in planning future programmes. A Junior Questionnaire was instituted in 1947. In 1940, joined M.O.I. Films Division as Honorary Adviser ; later appointed head of the Film Section of Pyschological Warfare Division of S.H.A.E.F., and made responsible for supply of films to liberated countries. In 1945, formed Transatlantic Films for production of films in Britain and U.S.A.

BERRY, Jules. Born Poitiers, France. Educ. Buffon School, Paris. Joined the Beaux-Arts with intention of becoming architect, but attended stage audition for *Le Dépit Amoureux,* and later acted in *La Duchesse des Folies-Bergère.* Fourteen years on Brussels stage. Appeared in silent films, but disliked the work. Returned to screen in sound film *Quick.* Other films include : *Le Roi des Palaces, Arlette et Ses Papas, Une Femme Chipée, Un Petit Trou pas Cher, Le Crime de Monsieur Pégotte, Jeunes Filles à Marier, Touche-à-Tout, La Fille du Puisatier* (shown in Britain as *The Well-Digger's Daughter*).

BEY, Turhan. Real name Turhan Selahettine Sahultavy Bey. Born Vienna, Austria, March 30. Ht. 6 ft. 1 in. ; wt. 170 lb. Black hair, brown eyes. Came to Hollywood, 1941, attended dramatic school, where film talent scout saw him. First film : *Footsteps in the Dark* (Warn) 1941. Other films include : 1941 : *Burma Convoy* (Univ), *Bombay Clipper* (Univ), *Drums of the Congo* (Univ), *Destination Unknown* (Univ), *Arabian Nights* (Univ) ; 1943 : *White Savage* (Univ) ; 1944 : *Dragon Seed* (MGM), *Bowery to Broadway* (Univ), *The Climax* (Univ) ; 1945 : *Sudan* (Univ) : 1946 : *A Night in Paradise* ; 1947 : *Out of the Blue* (Eagle Lion-Hollywood).

BICKFORD, Charles. Born Cambridge, Massachusetts, U.S.A., Jan. 1, 1891. Ht. 6 ft. 1½ in. Red hair, blue eyes. Educ. Foster School, Somerville, Mass. ; Everett (Mass.) High School ; Massachusetts Institute of Technology—studying engineering. Army engineer in World War I. Then became stage actor. Screen debut in *Dynamite* (Pathé), 1929. Early films include : *Scandal for Sale, Thunder Below, Anna Christie, Hell's Heroes, A Notorious Gentleman, Little Miss Marker, Under Pressure, The Farmer Takes a Wife, Red Waggon* (BIP, Britain, 1933), *Rose of the Rancho, The Plainsman, Valley of Giants, Stand Up and Fight, Mutiny in the Big House, One Hour to Live, Thou Shalt Not Kill, Of Mice and Men.* 1940 : *Girl from God's Country* (Rep) ; 1941 : *Burma Convoy* (Univ) ; 1942 : *Reap the Wild Wind* (Para) ; 1943 : *Song of Bernadette* (20th), *Mr. Lucky* (RKO) ; 1944 : *Wing and a Prayer* (20th) ; 1945 : *Captain Eddie*

(20th), *Fallen Angel* (20th) ; 1946 : *The Woman on the Beach* ; 1947 : *Duel in the Sun* (Selznick), *The Farmer's Daughter* (RKO), *Brute Force* (UI) ; 1948 : *Johnny Belinda* (Warn), *Woman on the Beach* (RKO).

BLACK, Edward. Producer. Born Birmingham, 1900. Brother of the late George Black of London Palladium fame, and son of George Black, Sr., pioneer British film exhibitor. Worked with his brother as exhibitor until 1930, when he joined the Gaumont British Studios at Shepherd's Bush first as studio manager, then as producer. Has produced over sixty feature films including : *Tudor Rose, Owd Bob, Bank Holiday, The Lady Vanishes, Night Train to Munich, Kipps, The Young Mr. Pitt, Waterloo Road, Fanny by Gaslight, The Man in Grey ;* and has made stars of Margaret Lockwood, Phyllis Calvert, Michael Redgrave and Stewart Granger. Joined MGM British Studios Ltd. in 1944. Lent in 1946 to London Film Productions for whom he produced : *Man About the House, Bonnie Prince Charlie.*

BLAINE, Vivian. Real name Vivian Stapleton. Born Newark, New Jersey, U.S.A., Nov. 21, 1921. Ht. 5 ft. 2 ins. ; wt. 114 lb. Blonde hair, blue eyes. Educ. Weequahic and Southside High Schools, Newark. Youthful ambition to be teacher or secretary. Studied singing ; was successful dance band vocalist at 17 ; sang in hotels and night clubs. First film : *It Happened in Flatbush* (20th) 1942. Other films (all 20th) include : *Through Different Eyes ;* 1943 : *He Hired the Boss, Girl Trouble, Jitterbugs ;* 1944 : *Greenwich Village, Something for the Boys, Nob Hill* 1945 : *State Fair ;* 1946 : *Come Back to Me, If I'm Lucky, Three Little Girls in Blue.*

BLAIR, Barbara. Born New York City. Ht. 5 ft. 3 in. Blonde hair, blue eyes. Educ. New York convent school. Began work at age of 14 as child model in department store. As chorus girl in " Nelly Kelly", took leading role on opening night when principal fell ill. Played in vaudeville and created the popular character, " Snooney", a kind of female Charles Chaplin ; took part in radio programmes with Rudy Vallee. Appeared on Broadway in 1930 in " George White's Scandals", and at the Palace Theatre, London, in 1937 in her own production " Take It Easy". British films include : *Star of the Circus, Hold My Hand, Luck to Me, The Outsider, I Killed the Count.* 1946 : *Bedelia* (Corfield) ; 1947 : *While the Sun Shines* (Internat Screenplays).

BLAIR, Janet. Real name Martha Janet Lafferty. Born Blair, Pennsylvania, U.S.A. Ht. 5 ft. 4 in. ; wt. 116 lb. Fair hair, blue eyes. Educ. high school. Sang and danced at local club and church entertainments ; trained for ballet ; decided to become singer and joined Hal Kemp's band ; was later given film contract by Columbia. First film : *Three Girls about Town* (Col) 1941. Other films include—1942 : *Blondie Goes to College* (Col), *Two Yanks in Trinidad* (Col), *Broadway* (Univ), *My Sister Eileen* (Col) ; 1943 : *Something to Shout About* (Col), *Once Upon a Time* (Col) ; 1945 : *Tonight and Every Night* (Col) ; 1946 : *Tars and Spars* (Col) ; 1947 : *Gallant Journey* (Col), *The Fabulous Dorseys* (Charles Rogers-UA), *I Love Trouble* (Col) ; 1948 : *The Black Arrow* (Col).

BLANCHAR, Pierre. Born near Algiers. Dark hair, grey-blue eyes. Trained as merchant seaman. Wounded and gassed in World War I. Studied for stage at Paris Conservatoire, and made professional debut with fellow-pupil Charles Boyer in " La Dolores ".

48

Appeared frequently with Boyer on Paris stage and became a leading French actor. As film actor achieved notable success in the war film *Les Croix du Bois*, as the student in *Crime and Punishment*, and as the epileptic doctor in *Un Carnet de Bal*. Came to Britain to play Napoleon opposite Ruth Chatterton in *A Royal Divorce* (Wilcox) 1939. During World War II, worked with French underground movement and assisted in production of film of the liberation of Paris. Recent films include: *Bataillon du Ciel, Symphonie Pastorale*, prize-winning film at the Cannes Film Festival in 1946.

BLISS, Arthur. Composer. Born London, 1891. Educ. Rugby ; Pembroke College, Oxford ; Cambridge (where he took music degrees). In 1933, went to California, returning in 1925. Film career began in 1935 when, in collaboration with H. G. Wells, he wrote the score for *Things to Come*, recorded by Muir Mathieson and the London Symphony Orchestra. Other films for which he has written scores include : *Defeat of the Germans near Moscow* (U.S.S.R.—English presentation), *Présence au Combat* (France) and *Men of Two Worlds* (Britain). His music for the British feature-documentary *Conquest of the Air* was performed as an orchestral suite in 1938, but the film in its originally planned form never reached the screen.

BLONDELL, Joan. Born New York Aug. 30, 1909. Ht. 5 ft. 4 in., wt. 120 lb. Fair hair, grey eyes. Came from stage family and toured the world as child actress with them. Remained in Australia until she was 18 then returned to America. After spell on New York stage, made film debut in *Sinner's Holiday* (Warn) 1929. Is proficient swimmer, and saved two boys from drowning at Malibu Beach in 1932. Recent films include—1940 : *Two Girls on Broadway* (MGM) ; 1941 : *Model Wife* (Univ), *Three Girls about Town* (Col) ; 1942 : *Lady for a Night* (Rep) ; 1944 : *Cry Havoc* (MGM) ; 1945 : *Don Juan Quilligan, Tree Grows in Brooklyn* (20th) ; 1946 : *Adventure* (MGM) ; 1947 : *Christmas Eve* (Benedict Bogeaus-UA) ; *Nightmare Alley* (20th).

BLYTH, Ann. Born Mt. Kisco, New York, Aug. 16, 1928. Ht. 5 ft. 2 in. ; wt. 103 lb. Brown hair, blue eyes. Educ. St. Stephen's and St. Patrick's Schools, Manhattan. First professional appearance was a broadcast at the age of 5. While still at school joined San Carlos Opera Company and sang for three seasons at the Center Theatre. Broadway debut in " Watch on the Rhine " brought her a film contract. First film : *Chip off the Old Block* (Univ) 1944. Other films include— 1944 : *Babes on Swing Street* (Univ), *The Merry Monahans* (Univ), *Bowery to Broadway* (Univ) ; 1945 : *Mildred Pierce* (Warn). Shortly after having made this film she was badly injured in a sleighing accident in Snow Valley, California, and was unable to work for nearly two years. Returned to the screen in 1947 with : *Swell Guy* (UI), *Brute Force* (UI), *Killer McCoy* (MGM). 1948 : *A Woman's Vengeance* (UI), *Another Part of the Forest* (UI).

BOGARDE, Dirk. Real name Van Den Bogaerd. Ht. 5 ft. 10½ in. ; wt. 162 lb. Dark brown hair, brown eyes. Educ. Scotland and on the continent. Trained for the diplomatic service, but later became artist. Worked in several London theatres at various jobs from call boy to scene painter ; then took lead at short notice in J. B. Priestley's play " When We Are Married ". Other London successes followed. He served in Europe and Far East during World War II

and was chief English announcer for Java radio network 1945-6. Two of his D-Day landing sketches are in the British Museum, and he has lectured on military subjects. First film *Esther Waters* (Wessex) 1948.

BOGART, Humphrey. Born New York City, Dec. 25, 1900. Ht. 5 ft. 10 in. ; wt. 170 lb. Dark brown hair, brown eyes. Educ. Trinity School ; Phillips Andover Academy. Served in U.S. Navy in World War I. Later worked in Wall-street office before becoming actor in New York. His many stage appearances include. " Saturday's Children ", and " It's a Wise Child ". Appeared in films from 1932, concurrently with stage work, but the insistence of the late Leslie Howard that he should play gangster in *The Petrified Forest* (Warn) 1936, gave him his real start in films and made him a Warner contract star. Early films include : *The Devil with Women, Two Against the World, Bullets or Ballots, China Clipper, Isle of Fury, The Great O'Malley, The Black Legion, Marked Woman, St. Quentin, Kid Galahad, Dead End, Stand-In, Swing Your Lady, Men are Such Fools, Crime School, The Amazing Dr. Clitterhouse, Racket Busters, Angels with Dirty Faces, King of the Underworld, You Can't Get Away with Murder, Arizona Kid.* 1940 : *They Drive By Night ;* 1941 : *The Maltese Falcon, High Sierra ;* 1942 : *Across the Pacific, The Big Shot ;* 1943 : *Action in the North Atlantic, Thank Your Lucky Stars, Casablanca ;* 1944 : *Passage to Marseilles, To Have and Have Not ;* 1945 : *Conflict ;* 1946 : *The Big Sleep ;* 1947 : *Dead Reckoning* (Col), *The Two Mrs. Carrolls, The Dark Passage ;* 1948 : *Treasure of the Sierra Madre.*

BOND, Derek. Born Glasgow, Jan. 26, 1920. Ht. 6 ft. 2½ in. ; wt. 178 lb. Dark brown hair, blue eyes. Educ. Haberdashers' School. Youthful ambition : to be actor or journalist. Attempted journalism and banking before making television debut in " R.U.R.", followed by stage debut on tour in " As Husbands Go ". Army service in World War II interrupted career at Colchester Repertory. Met Michael Balcon and was given contract to take effect on Army release. P.o.W. in Italy. First film : *The Captive Heart* (Ealing) 1945. Other films include : 1947 : *Nicholas Nickleby* (Ealing), *The Loves of Joanna Godden* (Ealing), *Uncle Silas* (Two Cities) ; 1948 : *Broken Journey* (Gains), *Scott of the Antarctic* (Ealing).

BONDI, Beulah. Born Chicago, May 3, 1892. Ht. 5 ft. 4 in. ; wt. 125 lb. Brown hair, brown eyes. Educ. Convent of the Holy Name of Jesus and Mary, Montreal ; Valparaiso University. Studied for stage under mother's tuition. First stage appearance at 11, in Indiana, as Cedric Errol, in " Little Lord Fauntleroy ". Afterwards worked in repertory and later for some years on New York stage. Made film debut in *The Stranger's Return* (MGM) 1933. Since then has played many character parts. Recent films include—1940 : *Our Town* (UA) ; 1942 : *One Foot in Heaven* (Warn) ; 1943 : *Watch on the Rhine* (Warn) ; 1944 : *And Now Tomorrow, I Love a Soldier, Our Hearts Were Young and Gay* (Para), *She's a Soldier Too* (Col), *The Very Thought of You* (Warn) ; 1945 : *Back to Bataan* (RKO), *The Southerner* (UA) ; 1946 : *Sister Kenny, It's a Wonderful Life* (RKO).

BORRADAILE, Osmond. Director of photography. Born Canada. Is regarded as Britain's leading photographer of exteriors, and has specialized for years on this branch of camera-work in all parts of the world. Films in which he was responsible for outdoor photography include : *Sanders of the River, Elephant Boy, The Drum, The Four Feathers, The Thief of Bagdad, The Lion Has Wings,* 49th Parallel—U.S. title, *The Invaders.* During World War II, helped to develop Army Film Unit in Middle East. Took part in Abyssinian campaign and siege of Tobruk, and photographed Syrian campaign ; flew with South African Air Force. In 1945 went in Harry Watts' unit to Australia to film *The Overlanders.* Recent productions include : *Bonnie Prince Charlie, Scott of the Antarctic.*

BORZAGE, Frank. Director. Born Salt Lake City, Utah, U.S.A., 1894. At 13 decided to be an actor, and worked in a coal mine until he had enough money for theatrical training. Later joined touring company, and eventually reached Hollywood where he became a film extra, and then a featured player, in Thomas Ince's productions. Ran his own company and played lead in number of Westerns. Became director in 1920, when he made the first version of *Humoresque.* Other films include : *Seventh Heaven, The River, Street Angel, True Heaven, Lucky Star, They Had to See Paris, Song of My Heart, Devil with the Women, Liliom, Doctors' Wives, Young as You Feel, Bad Girl, After Tomorrow, Young America, We Humans, Farewell to Arms, Secrets, No Greater Glory, A Man's Castle, Flirtation Walk, Little Man What Now ?, Living on Velvet, Shipmates Forever, Stranded, Green Light, History is Made at Night, Big City, Mannequin, Three Comrades, The Shining Hour, Disputed Passage, Strange Cargo, The Mortal Storm, Flight Command, Stage Door Canteen, His Butler's Sister, Till We Meet Again, The Spanish Main, I've Always Loved You, Magnificent Doll, Will Tomorrow Ever Come ?*

BOULTING, John. Producer, director. Twin brother of Roy Boulting. Born Bray, Berks, Nov. 1913. Educ. Reading School, where he became captain of Rugby. While at school, assisted brother Roy to form cine and dramatic societies. Began film career at 15s. a week as general factotum in a Wardour-street distributor's office. Graduated to sales work and shortly afterwards was transferred to studio production. Ambulance driver for Republican forces in Spanish Civil War. Returned to U.K., and with brother Roy formed Charter Film Productions, in 1937. Made several successful feature films on a small budget : *Consider Your Verdict* (1938), costing only £1800, created sensation in film world. Other early films include : *Inquest, Trunk Crime, Pastor Hall* (first British film to expose Nazi concentration camps). In World War II, served in R.A.F., first as A.C.2 Flight Mechanic, and then, after a special leave in 1942 with brother to produce *Thunder Rock,* as Flight Lieutenant in R.A.F. Film Unit, for which he directed *Journey Together* (1945). Since 1946, he and his brother have worked together, each producing and directing alternately. Produced *Fame Is the Spur,* directed *Brighton Rock.*

BOULTING, Roy. Producer, director. Twin brother of John Boulting. Born Bray, Berks, Nov. 1913. Educ. Reading School, where he founded the first cine society at any English public school. Then worked in Canada at a number of jobs : wrote dialogue for a film produced at Trenton Studios, Ontario. In 1933, worked his passage back to this country to begin serious film career ; first job was as assistant to assistant director at Marylebone studios, near Edgware-road, London. In 1937, formed Charter Film

Productions with brother John. Films include : *Consider Your Verdict, Inquest, Trunk Crime, Pastor Hall.* Army service during World War II, first as Trooper, and then, after special leave in 1942 with brother to direct *Thunder Rock,* as Captain in Army Film Unit. Directed *Desert Victory* and *Burma Victory.* Since 1946 he and his brother, as a team, have each directed and produced alternately. Directed *Fame Is The Spur,* produced *Brighton Rock.*

BOWEN, Marjorie. Novelist. Real name Margaret Gabrielle Long. Also writes under pseudonyms of " George R. Preedy " and " Joseph Shearing ". Born Hayling Island, Hants, 1888. Of her many stories, those filmed include : *Moss Rose, Blanche Fury, Mark of Cain, So Evil My Love.*

BOWER, Dallas. Production executive. Born London, 1907. Educ. Hurstpierpoint College. Originally trained as an engineer, and edited a technical journal, but always wanted to join film industry. Experience with Marconi Company and British Thomson-Houston led him to begin film career as sound recordist 1927, then film editor and scenario writer before becoming director with *The Path of Glory.* Directed long documentary on the development of science during the reign of George V, for Jubilee celebrations. Also worked on development of television ; B.B.C. Director of Television 1936-9. 1940-2, Production Supervisor with Ministry of Information Films Division; joined Olivier as associate producer for *Henry V,* 1947 : preparatory work for *Christopher Columbus.*

BOWMAN, Lee. Born Cincinnati, Ohio, U.S.A. Dec. 28, 1914. Ht. 6.ft. 1 in. ; wt. 175 lb. Brown hair, hazel eyes. Educ. University of Cincinnati. Was to have been a lawyer, but followed his sister on to the stage. Semi-professional singer while at university ; then studied at American Academy of Dramatic Art ; afterwards entered repertory as actor and then as part owner. Seen in Britain in " The Old Lady Shows Her Medals ". Performance on Broadway in Carnegie Players' production " Berkeley Square " led to first film part : *Men in White,* (MGM) 1936. Other films include : *Last Train from Madrid, I Met Him in Paris, Sophie Lang Goes West, This Way Please, Having Wonderful Time, First Hundred Years, Tarnished Angel, Man to Remember, Next Time I Marry, Love Affair, Lady and the Mob, Society Lawyer, Stronger than Desire, Miracles for Sale, Fast and Furious, Another Thin Man, Dancing Co-Ed.* 1940 : *The Great Victor Herbert* (Para), *Florian* (MGM), *Gold Rush Maisie* (MGM), *Wyoming* (MGM), *Third Finger Left Hand* (MGM) ; 1941 : *Buck Privates* (Univ), *Washington Melodrama* (MGM), *Model Wife* (Univ), *Married Bachelor* (MGM), *Design for Scandal* (MGM), *We Were Dancing* (MGM), *Kid Glove Killer* (MGM) ; 1942 : *Pacific Rendezvous* (MGM), *Tish* (MGM), *Three Hearts for Julia* (MGM) ; 1943 : *Bataan* (MGM), *Cover Girl* (Col) ; 1944 : *The Impatient Years* (Col), 1945 : *Tonight and Every Night* (Col) ; 1946 : *She Wouldn't Say Yes* (Col), *The Walls Come Tumbling Down* (Col) ; 1947 : *A Woman Destroyed* (UI), *Desert Fury* (Para).

BOX, Betty E. Producer. Born Beckenham, Kent, 1919. Educ. Beckenham County School. Sister of Sydney Box. Produced plays for children, trained in commercial art at Bournemouth Art School. Production department assistant of Verity Films for a number of years, making shorts and training films during World War II. Joined Sydney Box at Riverside Studios in

1942 as personal assistant, and worked on feature films, including : *Acacia Avenue, The Seventh Veil, The Years Between, Girl in a Million, Daybreak*. Associate producer, *The Upturned Glass*. Appointed executive producer at Gainsborough (Islington) Studios in 1946. In 1947 produced : *Dear Murderer, When the Bough Breaks, Miranda, Blind Goddess*.

BOX, Muriel. Production executive. Born New Malden, Surrey, 1905. Acted in silent films at Stoll Studios. Later joined script department of British Instructional Films and worked in all production departments. In 1933 married Sydney Box, with whom she had written more than sixty-five one-act plays. In World War II directed documentary shorts for British Council and M.O.I. In 1942 with Sydney Box formed independent producing unit at Riverside Studios, Hammersmith (films include : *The Seventh Veil, The Years Between, Girl in a Million*), collaborating with him in script writing. In 1945 her play " Love in These Days " was produced at " Q " Theatre, London. In 1946 became scenario editor, Gainsborough Pictures.

BOX, Sydney. Producer. Born Beckenham, Kent, 1907. Won scholarship to Beckenham Secondary School, helped family finances by delivering newspapers and goods, and during last two years at school contributed weekly sports column to " Kentish Times ". Later became full-time reporter, eventually on " Evening Standard " and " Daily Sketch ". One of the founders of Beckenham Little Theatre movement. In collaboration with his wife, Muriel Box, has written more than sixty-five one-act plays, and through her became interested in film production. Their first joint script was *Alibi Inn*. Began film production by making shorts : in 1940 formed Verity Films which during World War II made more than 120 films for M.O.I. and other Government departments. He also produced the feature films *On Approval, English without Tears, The Flemish Farm*, and *Don't Take It To Heart* before becoming independent producer in 1942 at Riverside Studios, Hammersmith. First important feature there was *The Seventh Veil* ; later productions include : *The Years Between, Girl in a Million, Daybreak, The Upturned Glass*. In 1946 appointed Executive Producer at Gainsborough Pictures. His recent productions include *The Man Within, The Brothers, Holiday Camp, Jassy, Good Time Girl, Broken Journey, Snowbound, The Calendar, Easy Money, The Bad Lord Byron*.

BOXER, John. Born London, Apr. 25, 1909. Ht. 5 ft. 9 in. Dark hair, brown eyes. Educ. Grocers' Company School, Royal Academy of Dramatic Art, 1928-30. Then joined Embassy Repertory Theatre, Swiss Cottage, London. Later plays in London included " Escape Me Never " and " Strife ". In 1933 to New York, where performance of role of Claud in " George and Margaret " led later to film debut in same role : *George and Margaret* (Warn Brit) 1940. Played small film parts during leaves from British Army, 1940-5. Films include : 1940 : *Convoy* (Ealing) ; 1941 : *Flying Fortress* (Warn Brit) ; 1942 : *In Which We Serve* (Two Cities), *The Foreman Went to France* (Ealing) ; 1943 : *Demi-Paradise* (Two Cities), *Millions Like Us* (Gains), *The Flemish Farm* (Two Cities), *Adventures of Tartu* (MGM Brit) ; 1945 : *Waterloo Road* (Gains) ; 1947 : *The October Man* (Two Cities).

BOYER, Charles. Born Figeac, France, Aug. 8, 1899. Ht. 5 ft. 9 in. ; wt. 150 lb. Educ. College Champollion, Figeac ; the Sorbonne (Phil.D) ; Paris

Conservatoire of Drama. After leaving the Conservatoire became famous on the stage, notably in " Melo " —from which the film *Traümende Munde* (*Dreaming Lips*) was adapted—" Mayerling ", and " Le Bonheur ". Appeared in French silent films including *La Ronde Infernale, Le Capitaine Fracasse, Le Grillon du Foyer, L'Homme du Large*. First sound film, *Barcarolle d'Amour* (UFA, Germany) 1930. Went to Hollywood to make French versions of *The Trial of Mary Dugan, The Man from Yesterday* and *Red-Headed Woman*. In Berlin made French versions of *Tumultes, F.P.I Does Not Answer, The Empress and Me* ; in Paris made *L'Epervier, La Bataille, Liliom, Mayerling*. Returned to Hollywood, 1934, to make English-speaking films, including : *Caravan, Private Worlds, Break of Hearts, Shanghai, The Garden of Allah, History is Made at Night, Tovarich, Marie Walewska*—U.S. title *Conquest, Algiers, Love Affair*. Served with French Army 1939-40, until the collapse of France, when he returned to America. Films since then include— 1940 : *All This and Heaven Too* (Warn) ; 1941 : *Back Street* (Univ), *Hold Back the Dawn* (Para) ; 1942 : *Tales of Manhattan* (20th) ; 1943 : *Flesh and Fantasy* (Univ), *The Constant Nymph* (Warn), *Heart of a Nation*—completed version of *Untel Père et Fils*, smuggled out of France in sections during the German occupation ; 1944 : *Together Again* (Col), 1945 : *Confidential Agent* (Warn) ; 1946 : *Cluny Brown* (20th) ; 1948 : *Arch of Triumph* (Enterprise-MGM), *A Woman's Vengeance* (UI).

BRACKEN, Eddie. Born Astoria, Long Island, U.S.A., Feb. 7, 1920. Ht. 5 ft. 10½ in ; wt. 165 lb. Brown hair, blue eyes. Educ. Professional Children's School, New York. Was child entertainer in Long Island, then in *Our Gang* at Hal Roach studios. First Broadway stage role at 13 in " The Lottery ", followed by three years of other successes. Then hitch-hiked to Hollywood, but failed to secure film work and returned to New York. In 1939, overnight success in the Broadway stage show " Too Many Girls " brought offers from every major Hollywood studio. In 1940, appeared in film version *Too Many Girls* (RKO), followed by— 1941 : *Reaching for the Sun* (Para), *Caught in the Draft* (Para), *Life With Henry* (Para) ; 1942 : *The Fleet's In* (Para), *Sweater Girl* (Para) ; 1943 : *Happy-Go-Lucky* (Para), *Star Spangled Rhythm* (Para), *Young and Willing* (UA) ; 1944 : *Hail the Conquering Hero* (Para), *The Miracle of Morgan's Creek* (Para), *Rainbow Island* (Para) ; 1945 : *Bring on the Girls* (Para), *Hold That Blonde* (Para) ; 1946 : *Ladies' Man* (Para), *Duffy's Tavern* (Para), *Out of This World* (Para) ; 1947 : *Fun on a Week-end* (UA).

BRACKETT, Charles. Producer, writer. Born Saratoga Springs, New York, Nov. 26, 1892. Educ. Harvard Law School ; Williams College. Served in A.E.F. during World War I. Wrote story " War ", which he brought home and sold to " Saturday Evening Post ". Became regular contributor to " Saturday Evening Post " and " Collier's " ; 1926-29, dramatic critic of " The New Yorker ". Wrote two novels, " American Colony " (1929), " Entirely Surrounded " (1932) ; went to Hollywood as writer in 1934. Scripts include : *Enter Madame* (in collaboration), *Secrets of a Secretary, Piccadilly Jim* (in collaboration), *Live, Love and Learn*. Joint scripts with Billy Wilder include : *Bluebeard's Eighth Wife, Midnight, What a Life, Rhythm on the River, Arise My Love, Ball of Fire, Ninotchka, Hold Back the Dawn, The Major and the Minor, Five Graves to Cairo* (also producer). Became Paramount producer,

PHYLLIS CALVERT
(*Gainsborough*)

1944, with *The Uninvited*. Has since produced and collaborated on screenplay of *Double Indemnity*, *The Lost Weekend*, *To Each His Own*, *The Emperor Waltz*, *A Foreign Affair*.

BRASSEUR, Pierre. Actor, playwright. Born Paris, Dec. 22, 1905. Son of an actor and well known on Paris stage. Has appeared in his own plays including " Un Ange Passe " (1946). Became playwright and script writer because he was unable to convince film producers that he could play roles other than gangsters. Films include : *Claudine à l'Ecole*, *Café de Paris*, *Quai des Brumes*, *Dernière Jeunesse*, *L'Honorable Léonard*, *Lunière d'Eté*, *Le Pays sans Etoiles*, *La Femme Fatale*, *Jericho*, *Les Portes de la Nuit*, *L'Amour autour de la Maison*, *L'Arche de Noé*, *Rocambole*, *Petrus*, *Les Enfants du Paradis* (in which he played role of the dramatic actor Frédérick Lemaître), *Croisière pour l'Inconnu*.

BRAZZI, Rossano. Born Bologna, Italy, 1915. Films include : *Kean*, *Tosca*, *Rigoletto*, *I Due Foscari*, *Noi Vivi*. 1944 : *Le Baruffe Chiozzotte* (Cervinia), *I Due Comandamenti* (Film Religiosi) ; 1945 : *Malia* (Titanus Amato) ; 1946 : *Aquila Nera* (CDI), *Eleonora Duse* (S. Giorgio), *Furia* (AGIC), *La Grande Aurora* (Scalera) ; 1947 : *Il Passatore* (GFI).

BREMER, Lucille. Born Amsterdam, New York, Feb. 21. Ht. 5 ft. 4 in. ; wt. 111 lb. Auburn hair, blue eyes. Took dancing lessons when she was 7 and became ballet dancer in Philadelphia Opera Company. At 16 was one of " The Rockettes ", famous New York precision dancers. Became model and cabaret and stage dancer. Seen at Club Versailles, New York by producer Arthur Freed, and given film contract. First film : *Meet Me in St. Louis* (MGM) 1944. Other films (all MGM) include : *Ziegfeld Follies* ; 1945 : *Yolanda and the Thief* ; 1946 : *Till the Clouds Roll By* ; 1947 : *Cynthia's Secret*, *Adventures of Casanova* (Eagle Lion-Hollywood).

BRENNAN, Walter. Born Swampscott, Massachusetts, U.S.A. Fair hair, blue eyes. Educ. Rindge Technical College, Cambridge, Massachusetts. Played small film parts for ten years, and at one time was stand-in for Slim Summerville. When his real estate business failed, he turned to films as a career in 1935. Films include : *Barbary Coast*, *Come and Get It*, *Banjo on my Knee*, *The Buccaneer*, *Wild and Woolly*, *Kentucky*, *The Adventures of Tom Sawyer*, *Stanley and Livingstone*. 1940 : *North-West Passage* (MGM), *Maryland* (20th) ; 1941 : *Meet John Doe* (Warn), *Sergeant York* (Warn), *Rise and Shine* (20th) ; 1942 : *Pride of the Yanks* (RKO), *Stand by for Action* (MGM) ; 1943 : *Slightly Dangerous* (MGM), *Hangmen Also Die* (UA), *North Star* (RKO) ; 1944 : *Home in Indiana* (20th), *The Princess and The Pirate* (RKO) ; 1945 : *To Have and Have Not* (Warn), *Dakota* (Rep) ; 1946 : *Centennial Summer* (20th), *My Darling Clementine* (20th).

BRENT, George. Born Shannonbridge, Ireland, Mar. 15, 1904. Ht. 6 ft. 0½ in. ; wt. 180 lb. Black hair, hazel eyes. Educ. two-room schoolhouse in Ireland ; American high school ; Dublin University. Appeared on American repertory stage and in many silent films. Success on Broadway stage led to sound film debut in : *The Rich are Always with Us* (Warn) 1932. Other films include : *Lily Turner*, *42nd Street*, *Bureau of Missing Persons*, *The Painted Veil*, *Stranded*, *Special Agent*, *Front Page Woman*, *The Case Against*

Mrs. Ames, *God's Country and the Woman*, *Mountain Justice*, *Jezebel*, *Dark Victory*. 1940 : *Till We Meet Again* (Warn), *South of Suez*, *Adventure in Diamonds* (Para) ; 1942 : *In This Our Life* (Warn), *Twin Beds* (UA), *You Can't Escape for Ever* (Warn), *Silver Queen* (UA) ; 1944 : *Experiment Perilous* (RKO) ; 1945 : *The Spiral Staircase* (RKO), *The Affairs of Susan* (Para) ; 1946 : *My Reputation* (Warn), *Tomorrow is Forever* (RKO) ; 1947 : *Temptation* (UI), *Lover Come Back* (UI), *Slave Girl* (UI), *Christmas Eve* (Benedict Bogeaus-UA), *The Corpse Came C.O.D.* (Col), *Out of the Blue* (Eagle Lion-Hollywood).

BRITTEN, Benjamin. Composer. Born Lowestoft, 1913. Studied composition at Royal College of music 1930-33. Became known through his unaccompanied choral work " A Boy Was Born ". His opera " Peter Grimes " put him in the forefront of British composers. Entered films in 1936 with the score of the G.P.O. documentary, *Coal Face*, and in the same year wrote the music for *Night Mail*. His first feature film was *Love from a Stranger*. In 1946 wrote " A Young Person's Guide to the Orchestra—Variations on a Theme of Purcell " as the score for the documentary, *Instruments of the Orchestra*, directed by Muir Mathieson.

BRITTON, Barbara. Real name Barbara Brantingham. Born Long Beach, California, U.S.A., Sept. 20. Ht. 5 ft. 5 in. ; wt. 110 lb. Blonde hair, blue eyes. Educ. Lincoln Grammar School ; Long Beach Junior College. Her photograph in local paper while at college attracted Hollywood agent, who brought talent scout to see her college play. First film : *Secret of the Wastelands* (Para) 1941. Appeared in small parts until, when Maureen O'Hara fell ill, she took over the lead, opposite Ray Milland, in *Till We Meet Again* (Para) 1944. Other films include— 1941 : *Louisiana Purchase* (Para) ; 1942 : *The Fleet's In* (Para), *Wake Island* (Para), *Mrs. Wiggs of the Cabbage Patch* (Para), *Reap the Wild Wind* (Para) ; 1943 : *Star Spangled Rhythm* (Para), *Young and Willing* (UA), *So Proudly We Hail* (Para) ; 1944 : *The Story of Dr. Wassell* (Para), *Showboat Serenade* (Para short) ; 1945 : *The Great John L.* (UA), *Captain Kidd* (UA) ; 1946 : *They Made Me a Killer* (Para), *The Virginian* (Para), *The Assassin* (Col) ; 1947 : *The Fabulous Suzanne* (Rep), *Return of Monte Cristo* (Col).

BRODZSKY, Nicholas. Composer. Born Odessa, Russia, 1905. Received musical education in Russia and later in Vienna, Rome and Budapest. Wrote his first film score for film made in Vienna in 1930 starring Richard Tauber ; after writing music for several other continental films came to Britain in 1936. Wrote music of Cochran's Coronation revue " Home and Beauty ". Has written the music for more than sixty films, including *French Without Tears*, *Freedom Radio*, *Quiet Wedding*, *The Way to the Stars*, *Carnival*, *Beware of Pity*, *While the Sun Shines*, *A Man about the House*, *The Turners of Prospect Road*.

BROOKS, Leslie. Born Lincoln, Nebraska, U.S.A., July 13, 1922. Ht. 5 ft. 6 in. ; wt. 114 lb. Brown hair, blue eyes. Educ. high schools, Omaha and Hollywood. Sang in church choir ; became model for covers of " thriller " magazines, then first entered films as showgirl. Films include : 1941 : *Ziegfeld Girl* (MGM), *Navy Blues* (Warn) ; 1942 : *Yankee Doodle Dandy* (Warn) ; 1944 : *Cover Girl* (Col), *Nine Girls* (Col) ; 1946 : *Memory for Two* (Col).

BROWN, Clarence. Director. Born Clinton, Massachusetts, U.S.A., May 10, 1890. Educ. Tennessee University. Served in U.S. Air Force in World War I, and for a time was an automobile engineer. Entered films as assistant to director Maurice Tourneur on *Trilby* ; did not return to films till 1921, when he directed *The Great Redeemer*, starring John Gilbert. Joined MGM in 1924 and launched Garbo in *The Flesh and the Devil*. His other films include : *The Trail of '98*, *A Woman of Affairs*, *Navy Blues*, *Anna Christie*, *Romance*, *The Eagle*, *Kiki*, *A Free Soul*, *Possessed* (MGM) 1931, *Inspiration*, *Emma*, *Letty Lynton*, *The Son-Daughter*, *Service*, *Night Flight*, *Sadie Mckee*, *Chained*, *Anna Karenina* (MGM) 1935, *Ah Wilderness*, *Wife versus Secretary*, *The Gorgeous Hussy*, *Maria Walewska*, *Of Human Hearts*, *Idiot's Delight*, *The Rains Came*, *Edison the Man*, *Come Live with Me*, *They Met in Bombay*, *The Human Comedy*, *The White Cliffs of Dover*, *National Velvet*, *The Yearling*, *Song of Love*.

BROWN, Vanessa. Real name Smylla Brind. Born Vienna, Austria, Mar. 24. Ht. 5 ft. 5 in. ; wt. 120 lb. Chestnut hair, blue eyes. Educ. Jean Jaurès School, Paris ; Joan of Arc Junior High School, New York. Lived in Paris 1934-37, where father was scriptwriter for Fox (Europe). On New York stage for two and a half years in " Watch on the Rhine ". In radio programme " Quiz Kids ", which resulted in film offer. Had previously dubbed voice for film *Prisoner of Shark Island*. First film : *Youth Runs Wild* (RKO) 1944. Other films include—1947 : *Margie* (20th) *The Late George Apley* (20th), *Mother Wore Tights* (20th), *The Foxes of Harrow* (20th).

BRUCE, Nigel. Born San Diego, California, U.S.A., Feb. 4, 1895. Son of Sir William Waller Bruce, Bt. Educ. The Grange, Stevenage ; Abingdon, Berks. Stage debut at Comedy Theatre, London, in " Why Marry ? " 1920. His long list of stage successes in London and New York includes the part of Johnny Tellwell in " Springtime for Henry ", which he later played on the screen. First British film was *The Squeaker* (Brit. Lion) 1930. Early British films include : *The Calendar*, *Escape*, *Red Aces*, *I Was a Spy*, *The Scarlet Pimpernel*. First American film : *Treasure Island* (MGM) 1934. Also in 1934 : *Springtime for Henry* (20th). Other films include : *Becky Sharp*, *The Trail of the Lonesome Pine*, *The Charge of the Light Brigade*, *The Last of Mrs. Cheyney*, *Hound of the Baskervilles*, *The Rains Came*. 1940 : *The Adventures of Sherlock Holmes*, *Rebecca* (UA), *Susan and God* (MGM) ; 1941 : *The Chocolate Soldier* (MGM) ; 1942 : *This Above All* (20th), *Journey for Margaret* (MGM) ; 1943 : *Lassie, Come Home* (MGM) ; 1944 : *The Scarlet Claw* (Univ), *Frenchman's Creek* (Para), *The Pearl of Death* (Univ) ; 1945 : *Son of Lassie* (MGM), *The House of Fear* (Univ), *The Corn Is Green* (Warn), *Pursuit to Algiers* (Univ), *The Woman in Green* (Univ) ; 1946 : *Terror by Night* (Univ), *Dressed to Kill* (Univ), *Sherlock Holmes and the Secret Code* (Univ) ; 1947 : *The Two Mrs. Carrolls* (Warn), *The Exile* (UI).

BURDEN, Hugh. Actor, playwright. Born Colombo, Ceylon, Apr. 3, 1913. Ht. 5 ft. 10½ in. ; wt. 154 lb. Brown hair, brown eyes. Studied at Royal Academy of Dramatic Art before going on stage. Author of " The Young and Lively ". Served in Army during World War II. After discharge appeared on London stage in " The Duke in Darkness ". Film debut, 1941, in *Ships with Wings* (Ealing). Other films include : *The Way Ahead* (Two Cities) 1944, and *Fame Is The Spur* (Two Cities) 1947, in which he made a notable success as Arnold Ryerson.

BURKE, Billie. Born Washington, U.S.A., Aug, 7, 1885. Came to Britain as a child. Toured Austria, Germany, Russia, France, 1898-99. Made debut in English music-hall at age of 15. Went to America in 1907, scoring immediate hit in " My Wife " at New York. Has been in films since early silent days, making first screen appearance in *Peggy*, 1916. Others include : *Bill of Divorcement* (RKO), 1932 ; *Christopher Strong*, *Dinner at Eight*, *Finishing School*, *Forsaking All Others*, *Society Doctor*, *Becky Sharp*, *Piccadilly Jim*, *Craig's Wife*, *Parnell*, *Topper*, *The Young in Heart*, *Topper Takes a Trip*, *The Wizard of Oz*. 1940 : *The Captain Is a Lady* (MGM) ; 1942 : *The Man Who Came to Dinner* (Warn), *In This Our Life* (Warn), *They All Kissed The Bride* (Col), *Girl Trouble* (20th) ; 1943: *Hi Diddle Diddle* (UA), *Gildersleeve on Broadway* (RKO) ; 1944 : *Laramie Trail* (Rep) ; 1945 : *Swing Out, Sister* (Univ), *The Cheaters* (Rep) ; 1946 : *Breakfast in Hollywood* (UA) ; 1947 : *Bachelor Girls* (Andrew Stone-UA).

BUSHELL, Anthony. Born Westerham, Kent, May 19, 1904. Ht. 6 ft. ; wt. 150 lb. Fair hair, blue eyes. Educ. Magdalen College School ; Hertford College, Oxford. Trained for stage at Royal Academy of Dramatic Art ; stage debut, 1924, with Gladys Cooper and Sir Gerald du Maurier in " Diplomacy ", Adelphi Theatre, London. Played with Gladys Cooper, Ivor Novello, Henry Ainley in England ; in 1927, to New York, where he appeared in " Her Cardboard Lover ", " The Sacred Flame ", " Disraeli ". Made film debut in Hollywood in *Disraeli* (Warn) 1929. Films made during next three years in Hollywood include : *The Show of Shows*, *Green Stockings*, *Three Faces East*, *Expensive Women*, *Lovin' the Ladies*, *The Queen's Husband*, *Journey's End*, *Chances*, *Five Star Final*, *The Shop Angel*, *Vanity Fair*, *Escapade*, *Born to Love*, *A Woman Commands*. British films include : *The Flirting Widow*, *The Silver Greyhound*, *I Was a Spy*, *Soldiers of the King*, *The Ghoul*, *Crime on the Hill*, *Red Waggon*, *Channel Crossing*, *Love at Second Sight*, *Lilies of the Field*, *Forbidden Territory*, *Admirals All*, *The Scarlet Pimpernel*, *Dark Journey*, *Farewell Again*, *The Return of the Scarlet Pimpernel*, *The Lion Has Wings*. 1940-5, in H.M. Forces. 1947 : associate producer, with Laurence Olivier, of *Hamlet*.

BUZZELL, Edward. Director. Born Brooklyn, New York, Nov. 13, 1897. Was musical comedy star ; then in 1929 entered films as actor, played in *Little Johnny Jones*, *Keeping Company*, and others. In 1932 became director with *The Big Timer* (Col). Other films directed include : *Virtue, Hollywood Speaks*, *Child of Manhattan*, *Ann Carver's Profession*, *Love Honour and Oh Baby*, *Cross-Country Cruise*, *The Human Side*, *False Witness*, *The Girl Friend*, *Three Married Men*, *The Luckiest Girl in the World*, *As Good as Married*, *Romance for Three*, *Fast Company*, *Honolulu*, *Marx Brothers at the Circus*, *Marx Brothers Go West*, *The Get-Away*, *Married Bachelor*, *Ship Ahoy*, *The Omaha Trail*, *The Youngest Profession*, *Best Foot Forward*, *Keep Your Powder Dry*, *Easy to Wed*, *Three Wise Fools*, *Song of the Thin Man*.

BYINGTON, Spring. Born Colorado Springs, Colorado, U.S.A., Oct. 17, 1898. Ht. 5 ft. 3in. ; wt. 123 lb. Blonde hair, blue eyes. Appeared in

JAMES MASON
(*Two Cities*)

DEBORAH KERR
(*Archers*)

repertory at Denver, Colorado and toured U.S.A. and South America from 1915. New York debut in 1924 in " Beggar on Horseback ". Successful stage career led to first film : *Little Women* (RKO), 1933. Other films include : *The Jones Family* series, *Mutiny on the Bounty, Ah Wilderness, Dodsworth, The Charge of the Light Brigade, Theodora Goes Wild, Penrod and Sam, A Family Affair, Jezebel, You Can't Take It with You, The Blue Bird.* 1940 : *Young As You Feel* (20th), *My Love Came Back* (Warn), *On Their Own* (20th), *Lucky Partners* (RKO), *Laddie* (RKO), *Arkansas Judge* (Rep), *Meet John Doe* (Warn) ; 1941 : *When Ladies Meet* (MGM), *The Devil and Miss Jones* (RKO), *The Vanishing Virginian* (MGM), *Ellery Queen and the Perfect Crime* (Col) ; 1942 : *Roxie Hart* (20th), *Rings on Her Fingers* (20th), *Once Upon a Thursday* (MGM), *The War Against Mrs. Hadley* (MGM), *Presenting Lily Mars* (MGM) ; 1943 : *Heaven Can Wait* (20th), *The Heavenly Body* (MGM) ; 1944 : *I'll Be Seeing You* (UA), *Thrill of a Romance* (MGM), *Salty O'Rourke* (Para), *The Enchanted Cottage* (RKO), *Captain Eddie* (20th), *Dragonwyck* (20th), *A Letter for Evie* (MGM), *Meet Me on Broadway* (Col) ; 1946 : *Little Mister Jim* (MGM), *Faithful in My Fashion* (MGM), *My Brother Talks to Horses* (MGM), *Living in a Big Way* (MGM) ; 1947 : *The Rich, Full Life* (MGM) ; 1948 : *It Had to Be You* (Col), *Polly Fulton* (MGM).

BYRD, Bretton. Real name James Thomas Byrd. Composer and music director. Born Ramsgate, 1904. Started musical career with concert party in Pokesdown, Bournemouth. In 1930 joined music staff at Gainsborough studios after an introduction to Louis Levy. Composed for and orchestrated *Love on Wheels*, and has since worked on over a hundred British films, among them : *Keep Smiling* featuring Gracie Fields ; most of Jessie Matthews' films including *Gangway, Head Over Heels, First a Girl, Evergreen* ; also *The Magic Bow*, in which he collaborated with Yehudi Menuhin, who recorded the music for the part of Paganini acted by Stewart Granger.

CAGNEY, James. Born New York City, July 17, 1904. Ht. 5 ft. 8½ in. ; wt. 160 lb. Red hair, brown eyes. Educ. Stuyvesant High School ; Columbia University ; but gave up higher education in order to support his family. After a few months in the chorus of " Pitter-Patter " in New York, was soft-shoe dancer in vaudeville at 17. Spotted by a Warner Bros. talent scout and went to Hollywood, where his first film was *Sinners' Holiday* (Warn) 1930. Often described as " the screen's number one tough guy ". With his brother William, formed his own company, Cagney Productions, 1942. Other films include : *Doorway to Hell, Steel Highway, Blonde Crazy, The Crowd Roars, Taxi, Winner Take All, Hard to Handle, Picture Snatcher, Mayor of Hell, Footlight Parade, Lady-Killer, Here Comes the Navy, Jimmy the Gent, He Was Her Man, St. Louis Kid, Devil Dogs of the Air, A Midsummer Night's Dream, Frisco Kid, The Irish in Us, " G " Men, Ceiling Zero, Great Guy, Something to Sing About, Boy Meets Girl, Angels with Dirty Faces, Each Dawn I Die.* 1941 : *Strawberry Blonde* (Warn) ; 1942 : *Yankee Doodle Dandy* (Warn ; for which he won the Academy Award) ; 1943 : *Johnny Come Lately* (Cagney-UA) ; 1945 : *Blood on the Sun* (Cagney-UA) ; 1946 : 13 *Rue Madeleine* (20th) ; 1947 : *The Stray Lamb* (Cagney-UA) ; 1948 : *The Time of Your Life* (Cagney-UA).

CALAMAI, Clara. Born 1919. Films include— 1944 : *Le Sorelle Materassi* (Universalcine), *La Resa di Titi* (Annua), *Ossessione* (ICI) ; 1945 : *Il Mondo Vuole Cosi* (Aurea), *Due Lettere Anonime* (Lux Ninfa), *Adulterà* (G.F.I.), *L'Ultimo Amore* (Pau Eric), *Il Tirannodi Padova* (Scalera).

CALDWELL, Betty. Born Mason City, Iowa, U.S.A., Jan. 9, 1926. Ht. 5 ft. 6 in. ; wt. 120 lb. Brown hair, blue eyes. Educ. primary and high schools, Mason City ; College of St. Teresa, Winona, Massachusetts. Appeared in " Call It a Day " at high school ; left college to join Mason City Players as actress, producer, scene-shifter, box-office clerk. Went to Hollywood, became model ; at South Californian Industrial Exposition, was selected as " Girl of the Future ". Producer Hunt Stromberg saw her picture in local paper, which led to screen test and seven-year contract. First film : *Young Widow* (Hunt-Stromberg-UA) 1947. 1948 : *A Miracle Can Happen* (Benedict Bogeaus-UA).

CALLEIA, Joseph. Real name Joseph Spurin-Calleia. Born Malta. Ht. 5 ft. 11 in. ; wt. 160 lb. Black hair, black eyes. Educ. St. Julian's and St. Aloysius' Colleges, Malta. Theatrical debut in musical show in Malta. Afterwards sent to Britain to study engineering, but instead went on stage, singing Scottish ballads in Harry Lauder style. After success in London went to U.S.A. 1918, but not warmly received on Broadway, so became furnace-man and later tram repair man. Eventually entered chorus of musical comedy " Have a Heart ", and later, as member of Otis Skinner company, appeared on Broadway and toured in Britain. Studied singing and toured Europe as concert singer ; then in New York turned to drama as actor and stage manager. Then turned to films. First film appearance in *Public Hero No. 1* (MGM), 1935. Other films include : *Tough Guy, Robin Hood of El Dorado, His Brother's Wife, After the Thin Man, Marie Antoinette, Algiers.* 1940 : *Wyoming* (MGM) ; 1941 : *The Monster and the Girl* (Para) ; 1942 : *Jungle Book* (Para), *The Glass Key* (Para) ; 1943 : *For Whom the Bell Tolls* (Para) ; 1944 : *The Cross of Lorraine* (MGM), *The Conspirators* (Warn) ; 1946 : *Gilda* (Col) ; 1947 : *The Beginning or the End ?* (MGM).

CALVERT, Phyllis. Born Chelsea, London, Feb. 18, 1918. Ht. 5 ft. 5 in. ; wt. 126 lb. Auburn hair, grey eyes. Studied dancing from age of 7, but gave up original ambition to be dancing teacher in favour of stage career. Appeared at 10 with Ellen Terry in " Crossings " at Lyric Theatre, Hammersmith, London. Later, toured in musical " She Shall Have Music " ; one year as student with Malvern Theatre Players ; then in repertory at Coventry and York. Success in first London appearance, " A Woman's Privilege ", 1939. Later seen by talent scout and given first film part in *They Came By Night* (Gains-20th) 1940. Served as London Air Raid Warden during the war. Films include : 1940 : *Charley's (Big Hearted) Aunt* (Gains), *Let George Do It* (Ealing), *Inspector Horn-leigh Goes To It* (Gains-20th), *Neutral Port* (Gains) ; 1941 : *Kipps* (20th-Brit) ; 1942 : *The Young Mr. Pitt* (20th-Brit), *Uncensored* (Gains) ; 1943 : *The Man in Grey* (Gains), *Fanny By Gaslight* (Gains), *2000 Women* (Gains) ; 1944 : *Madonna of the Seven Moons* (Gains) ; 1945 : *They Were Sisters* (Gains) ; 1946 : *Men of Two Worlds* (Two Cities), *The Magic Bow* (Gains) ; 1947 : *The*

Root of All Evil (Gains). Went to Hollywood to appear in *Time Out of Mind* (UI) 1947. Returned to Britain for *Broken Journey* (Gains), 1948, then made another trip to Hollywood to star in *My Own True Love* (Para), 1948.

CALVET, Corinne. Born France, 1927, daughter of American mother, French father. Dark hair, green eyes. Left school to study sculpture. Turned to stage career, working with Charles Dullin, and later joined film-acting school. Played small roles in four films, including *La Part de l'Ombre, Nous ne Sommes pas Mariés*, and made hit with *Petrus* (1946), followed by *Le Chateau de la Dernière Chance*. Went to Hollywood, 1947.

CAMERON, Rod. Real name Roderick Cox. Born Calgary, Canada, Dec. 7, 1910. Ht. 6 ft. 4 in. ; wt. 198 lb. Brown hair, brown eyes. On account of childhood injury, failed to pass medical test for " Mounties ", so to prove he was in good health worked as labourer on the Hudson River tunnel, New York, then under construction. Then to Hollywood, hoping to play in Westerns ; while waiting for a chance, worked as construction labourer and later as engineer. Finally secured a small part in *The Old Maid*, but his scenes were cut from the finished film. Then as stand-in for Fred MacMurray developed taste for light comedy. First screen appearance, in *Christmas in July* (Para), 1940. Other films include— 1940 : *The Quarterdeck* (Para), *North-West Mounted Police* (Para) ; 1941 : *The Monster and the Girl* (Para), *Henry Aldrich for President* (Para) ; 1942 : *The Remarkable Andrew* (Para), *True to the Army* (Para), *Priorities on Parade* (Para), *Wake Island* (Para), *The Forest Rangers* (Para) ; 1943 : *Gung Ho* (Univ) ; 1944 : *Mrs. Parkington* (MGM), *Boss of Boomtown* (Univ), *Trigger Trail* (Univ), *Riders of the Santa Fé* (Univ) ; 1945 : *Salome, Where She Danced* (Univ), *Frontier Gal* (Univ) ; 1946 : *The Runaround* (Univ), *Bank Robbery* (Univ), *Mile A Minute* (Univ), *The Bride Wasn't Willing* (Univ) ; 1947 : *The Pirates of Monterey* (UI) ; 1948 : *River Lady* (UI).

CAMPANINI, Carlo. Born Torino, Italy, 1907. Films include : *Addio Giovinezza, Dora Nelson, Catene Invisibili* ; 1945 : *Le Miserie del Signor Travet* (Pao-Lux) ; 1946 : *Albergo Luna* (Lux), *Il Bandito* (Lux), *La Primula Bianca* (Lux).

CAMPBELL, Beatrice. Born County Down, Northern Ireland, July 31, 1924. Ht. 5 ft. 5½ in. ; wt. 122 lb. Fair hair, blue eyes. Educ. Daughter of the Cross Convent, County Tyrone, and Holy Child Convent, Harrogate. Studied medicine for a year in Belfast, then turned to stage. Played in repertory at Belfast Opera House. War service in the W.A.A.F. as driver ; later, as ENSA artist, spotted by director Frank Launder. First film, *Wanted for Murder* (Excelsior-20th), 1946. Also in *My Brother Jonathan* (ABPC) 1948.

CAPRA, Frank. Producer, director. Born Palermo, Italy, May 29, 1897. Educ. Manual Arts High School, Los Angeles ; California Institute of Technology. Joined Western Pipe & Steel Company. Won 500 dollar scholarship and toured U.S.A., studying art and music. Served in Army, World War I. Became tutor, then writer. Entered film industry, 1921, as director *Screen Snap Shots* series (Col). Became assistant director, Paul Gerson Company (San Francisco) ; gag-man for Hal Roach *Our Gang*

comedies ; directed Harry Langdon comedies (FN) ; then directed for Columbia until 1941. Co-produced : *Meet John Doe* (Warn). Films which he has directed include : *That Certain Thing, Submarine, Ladies of Leisure, The Bitter Tea of General Yen, Lady for a Day, It Happened One Night, Mr. Deeds Goes to Town* (1936 Academy Award as director), *The Lost Horizon, You Can't Take It with You, Mr. Smith Goes to Washington*. 1941-5 : war service as chief of production, U.S. Army Pictorial Service. In 1945, with Samuel Briskin, formed production company, Liberty Films Inc., Hollywood. Recent films (directed) : *Arsenic and Old Lace, It's a Wonderful Life*. Produced and directed *The World and His Wife*.

CARDIFF, Jack. Director of photography. Born 1914. For ten years was a child actor on stage, appearing in small parts with Dorothy and Lillian Gish. Entered film industry as clapper-boy and later joined the Technicolor company. In 1937 collaborated on photography of first British colour film, *Wings of the Morning* (New World), and in 1939 filmed some of the exteriors in *The Four Feathers* (LFP) ; is now a leading Technicolor photographer. During the war he worked on documentaries and propaganda films, including *Western Approaches*. Recent films in which he has worked include : *Caesar and Cleopatra* (exteriors), *A Matter of Life and Death, Black Narcissus, Red Shoes.*

CAREY, Joyce. Daughter of Lilian Braithwaite. Born Mar. 30, 1898. Brown hair, brown eyes. Educ. Westgate-on-sea ; London. Studied for stage under Kate Rorke at the Florence Etlinger Dramatic School. First stage appearance at age of 15, with her mother in " Mr. Wu ". Notable in " The Young Person in Pink " (1920—several times revived). " Sweet Aloes ", the play which she wrote under the name of Jay Mallory and in which she acted, was later filmed in Hollywood, under the title *Give Me Your Heart*. Appeared in several silent films including *God and the Man, Because, The Newcomes*, but then returned to the stage. Recent films include—1942 : *In Which We Serve* (Two Cities) ; 1945 : *Blithe Spirit* (Cineguild), *The Way to the Stars* (Two Cities) ; 1946 : *Brief Encounter* (Cineguild) ; 1947 : *The October Man* (Two Cities), *London Belongs To Me* (Individ).

CAREY, Macdonald. Born Sioux City, Iowa, U.S.A., Mar. 15, 1913. Ht. 6 ft. ; wt. 170 lb. Brown hair, brown eyes. Educ. Sioux Central High School ; University of Wisconsin ; University of Iowa (B.A.). Youthful ambition : to be a journalist. Left college, 1936, to join Shakespearean company. Later, radio actor in Chicago and New York until Moss Hart gave him Broadway role opposite Gertrude Lawrence in " Lady in the Dark ". Then made his first film : *Dr. Broadway* (Para), 1942. Served in U.S. Marine Corps, 1943-45. Other films include—1942 : *Take a Letter, Darling* (Para), *Wake Island* (Para) ; 1943 : *Shadow of a Doubt* (Univ), *Salute for Three* (Para) ; 1946 : *Suddenly It's Spring* (Para) ; 1947 : guest star in *Variety Girl* (Para).

CARLSON, Richard. Born Minneapolis, Minnesota, U.S.A., Apr. 29, 1912. Ht. 5 ft. 11 in. ; wt. 168 lb. Brown hair, blue eyes. Educ. University of Minnesota (M.A.). Wrote plays at school and became actor, writer and producer in his university drama group ; afterwards, stage career in Minneapolis, Pasadena and New York. Signed by David Selznick as actor, writer, director. First film: *The Young in Heart* (UA), 1938. Served in U.S. Navy, 1943-6. Other films include : *Duke of West Point, Dancing Co-ed, These Glamour Girls, Little Accident.* 1940 : *The Ghost Breakers* (Para), *Beyond Tomorrow* (RKO), *Too Many Girls* (RKO), *No, No, Nanette* (RKO), *The Howards of Virginia* (Col) ; 1941 : *Back Street* (Univ), *Hold That Ghost* (Univ), *West Point Widow* (Para), *The Little Foxes* (RKO) ; 1942 : *Fly by Night* (Para), *Once Upon a Thursday* (MGM), *White Cargo* (MGM), *Highway by Night* (RKO), *My Heart Belongs to Daddy* (Para), *Presenting Lily Mars* (MGM), *Young Ideas ;* 1947. *So Well Remembered* (RKO), made in Britain.

CARMICHAEL, Hoagy. Composer, band leader, actor. Real name Hoagland Howard Carmichael. Born Bloomington, Indiana, U.S.A., Nov. 22. Ht. 5 ft. 8 in. ; wt. 140 lb. Brown hair, brown eyes. Educ. Indiana University (LL.B.). Wrote songs while an undergraduate and formed first band at 18 to finance his education. Spent two years as lawyer, then formed another band and toured America before settling down as song writer. Most famous composition, " Stardust ", of which 15,000,000 records and 1,000,000 copies of sheet music were sold. Under contract to Paramount as song writer when he made first film appearance in *Topper* (MGM), 1937. First major screen part was as philosophical pianist in *To Have and To Have Not* (Warn), 1944, for which he also wrote theme song, " How Little We Know ". Has also appeared in—1945 : *Johnny Angel* (RKO) ; 1946 : *Canyon Passage* (Univ) ; 1947 : *The Best Years of Our Lives* (Goldwyn) ; 1948 : *Night Song* (RKO).

CARMINATI, Tullio. Real name Count Tullio Carminati di Brambilla. Born Zara, Dalmatia, Sept. 21, 1894. Ht. 5 ft. 11 in. ; black hair, blue eyes. Ran away from home at 15 and joined theatrical company at £1 a month. Brought home by his father, ran away again, and was disinherited. Played in repertory throughout Italy. In 1922 appeared with Eleanore Duse, and directed many of her plays. Film debut 1914, in Italy. Then made films in Germany before going to U.S.A. to star in *The Bat* (UA), 1926. Other silent films include *The Duchess of Buffalo, Three Sinners.* With the arrival of sound films, suffered temporary eclipse until it was realized that his foreign accent was an asset : then found new success opposite the late Grace Moore, in *One Night of Love* (Col), 1934. Visited Britain to make *The Three Maxims* and *The Street Singer*—U.S. title *London Melody.* Interned in U.S.A. when Italy entered World War II. After the war, returned to Italy, where he resumed his stage and screen career. In 1947 made *When in Rome* (Vicandro).

CARNE, Marcel. Director. Established reputation as one of France's leading film directors with *Le Quai des Brumes* (1937), *Hôtel du Nord* (1938), *Le Jour se Lève* (1939). Continued his work during German occupation of France with *Les Visiteurs du Soir,* a fantasy of medieval legend, and *Les Enfants du Paradis.* For this film he is said to have engaged hundreds of his countrymen to save them from being sent to Germany as slave labour. The film, dealing with Paris theatrical life in the early nineteenth century, is considered a masterpiece and runs for nearly four hours. Recent films : *Les Portes de la Nuit, L'Ile des Enfants Perdus.*

CARROLL, John. Real name Julien La Faye. Born New Orleans, Louisiana, U.S.A., July 17. At 10 left home for Houston, Texas. Became newspaper seller, steel riveter, dock labourer, ranch hand, merchant seaman, shop assistant, racing car driver in Chicago, steeple-painter. Resumed his education, then studied singing, first in New Orleans and later in Milan, Paris, and Berlin. In Paris became taxi driver, then café singer ; returned to U.S.A. as deep sea diver. To Hollywood as actor and singer. First film : *Hi Gaucho* (RKO), 1935. Other films include : *Muss 'Em Up, Murder on the Bridle Path, We Who are about to Die, Rose of the Rio Grande, I am a Criminal, Only Angels have Wings, Wolf Call.* 1940 : *Congo Maisie* (MGM), *Phantom Riders* (MGM), *Susan and God* (MGM), *Go West* (MGM), 1941 : *Lady be Good* (MGM), *Hired Wife* (Univ), *This Woman is Mine* (Univ), *Sunny* (RKO) ; 1942 : *Rio Rita* (MGM), *Pierre of the Plains* (RKO), *Flying Tigers* (Rep) ; 1943 : *The Youngest Profession* (MGM), *Hit Parade of 1943* (Rep). 1943-5, served in U.S. Army. 1945 : *A Letter for Evie* (MGM); 1947 : *Fiesta* (MGM).

CARROLL, Madeleine. Born West Bromwich, Staffs, Feb. 26, 1906. Ht 5 ft. 5 in. ; wt. 115 lb. Fair hair, blue eyes. Educ. Birmingham University (B.A. Hons., French). Taught French for one term at girls' school in Hove, saved £20 and came to London to become actress. Nearly starved before she secured job with a touring company ; modelled hats between engagements. Chosen from 150 applicants for leading role in *The Guns of Loos* (Stoll) 1928. Early British films include : *The American Prisoner, Atlantic, Young Woodley, The " W " Plan, Escape, Mme. Guillotine, Kissing Cup's Race, Fascination, First-Born, School for Scandal, Sleeping Car, I Was a Spy.* Went to Hollywood to appear in *The World Moves On* (20th), 1934. Returned to Britain, 1935 ; appeared in *Loves of a Dictator, The Thirty-Nine Steps, Secret Agent.* Later Hollywood films include : *The Case Against Mrs. Ames, The General Died at Dawn, Lloyds of London, On the Avenue, It's All Yours, The Prisoner of Zenda, Blockade, Café Society.* 1941 : *One Night in Lisbon* (Para) ; 1942 : *My Favourite Blonde* (Para). Spent four war years with the Red Cross in France, and made member of Légion d'Honneur. 1947 : *White Cradle Inn* (Peak).

CARSON, Jack. Born Carmen, Manitoba, Canada, Oct. 27, 1910. Ht. 6 ft. 1 in. ; wt. 202 lb. Brown hair, blue eyes. Educ. Hartford Avenue School, Milwaukee ; St. John's Military Academy Delafield, Wisconsin ; Carleton College, Northfield, Minnesota. Vaudeville actor at 19 on tour and in New York. Then M.C. in Middle West vaudeville ; also worked as salesman, and railway construction labourer. Went to Hollywood to appear in *Stage Door* (RKO) 1937. Other films include : *Stand in, The Saint in New York, Vivacious Lady, Carefree, Destry Rides Again.* 1940 : *Enemy Agent* (Univ), *Alias the Deacon* (Univ), *Love Thy Neighbour* (Para) ; 1941 : *Strawberry Blonde* (Warn), *The Bride Came C.O.D.* (Warn) ; 1942 : *The Male Animal* (Warn), *Larceny, Inc.* (Warn), *The Hard Way* (Warn), *Gentleman Jim* (Warn) ; 1943 : *Princess O'Rourke* (Warn), *Thank Your Lucky Stars* (Warn) ; 1944 : *Shine On, Harvest Moon* (Warn), *Make Your Own Bed* (Warn), *Arsenic and Old Lace* (Warn), *The Doughgirls* (Warn), *Hollywood Canteen* (Warn) ; 1945 : *Mildred Pierce* (Warn) ; 1946 : *One More Tomorrow* (Warn) ; 1947 : *The Time, the Place and the Girl* (Warn), *Royal Flush* (Warn), *Love and Learn* (Warn) ; 1948 : *April Showers* (Warn).

CARSTAIRS, John Paddy. Director, writer. Son of the late Nelson Keys, actor. Born London, 1910. Educ. Repton School ; Clare College, Cambridge. interested in film-making while still at school, and is credited with having produced the first full-length film ever made at a school. Author of twenty successful humorous and romantic novels (including " Vinegar and Brown Paper ", and " Curried Pineapple ") and " Bunch," the story of his father's life. Entered films, 1927, as assistant cameraman on *Dawn* (Herbert Wilcox) and spent three years with B & D as script clerk, camera operator, assistant director, film editor. Later, scenario writer with major British companies, and in Hollywood with MGM, Columbia, Paramount and Al Christie. Author of screenplays *Falling in Love, Hope of His Side, Two's Company, It's a Boy* and others. Since 1936 has directed many features, including *Paris Plane, Holidays End, Double Exposure, Night Ride, The Saint in London, Spare a Copper, Meet Maxwell Archer*. From 1939, served with R.N.V.R., and directed many shorts for M.O.I. and for R.N. Film Unit. Resumed feature-film direction, 1947, with *Dancing With Crime*.

CARTER, James. Producer. Born England, 1902. After training at Royal Academy of Music and Royal School of Art, entered films in 1923 as art director, first at Worton Hall Studios, and then in 1928 for the late Julius Hagen at Twickenham Studios, where he learnt economy of production by working on " Quota quickies ". Then art direction of *The Stars Look Down, Under Your Hat, You Will Remember*. During World War II made training films for the three services. Art director of *Acacia Avenue, The Seventh Veil, Girl in a Million*. In 1946 joined board of newly-formed Alliance Film Studios, which acquired Twickenham, Southall, and Riverside (Hammersmith) Studios for making " independent " films. Productions include : *They Made Me a Fugitive*—U.S. title, *I Became a Criminal, Dancing With Crime, Daughter of Darkness, Things Happen at Night, The Brass Monkey, No Orchids for Miss Blandish, Just William's Luck* (first of the new *Just William* series).

CARTER, Janis. Real name Janis Dremann. Born Cleveland, Ohio, U.S.A., Ht. 5 ft. 7 in. ; wt. 125 lb. Fair hair, blue eyes. Educ. grade and high schools, East Cleveland ; Western Reserve University (B.A. Mus. Bac.). Studied singing from age of 8. Played lead in college productions of Gilbert and Sullivan and Noel Coward comedies. Went to New York, and sang solos in church choirs ; sang with Grace Moore on radio and wrote radio comedy scripts ; also became model, posing for " Vogue and Harpers Bazaar ". Spent a year touring in " Du Barry was a Lady " ; also in " I Married An Angel " ; made Broadway hit in " Panama Hattie ". First film : *Cadet Girl* (20th) 1941. Leading lady in *The Whistler* series (Col), which began in 1944 with *The Mark of the Whistler*. Other films include—1942 : *Girl Trouble* (20th), *That Other Woman* (20th) ; 1943 : *Lady of Burlesque* (UA) ; 1944 : *Swing out the Blues* (Col), *Girl in the Case* (Col), *Together Again* (Col) ; 1945 : *The Missing Juror* (Col), *The Fighting Guardsman* (Col) ; 1946 *One Way to Love* (Col), *Notorious Lone Wolf* (Col), *The Trespasser* (Col) ; 1947 : *Paula* (Col), *I Love Trouble* (Col) ; 1948 : *The Eternal Melody* (Rabinovitch-Col) made in Italy with Jan Kiepura and Martha Eggerth.

CAULFIELD, Joan. Born Orange, New Jersey, U.S.A., June 1, 1922. Ht. 5 ft. 5 in. ; wt. 100 lb. Educ. Theodore Roosevelt Junior High School, Miss Beard's School, Orange ; Columbia University. Youthful ambition : to be an actress. Well known as magazine model before leaving college. In Broadway musicals " Beat the Band " (1942) and " Kiss and Tell ". Star in her first film, *Miss Susie Slagle's* (Para) 1945. Other films include—1946 : *Blue Skies* (Para), *Monsieur Beaucaire* (Para), *Welcome Stranger* (Para) ; 1947 : *Dear Ruth* (Para), guest star in *Variety Girl* (Para), *The Unsuspected* (Warn).

CAVALCANTI, Alberto. Director. Born Rio de Janeiro, Brazil, Feb. 6, 1897. Educ. Geneva Fine Arts School. Started in films in Paris as art director, then became director. Later produced many films there, including outstanding documentary *Rien que les Heures*. Came to Britain and joined G.P.O. Film Unit ; films include : *North Sea, The First Days, Squadron 992, Men of the Lightship*. In 1941 became an associate producer at Ealing. Feature films directed include : *The Foreman Went to France, Halfway House, Went The Day Well?, Champagne Charlie*, the " Constance Kent " and " Ventriloquist's dummy " sequences in *Dead of Night, Nicholas Nickleby, They Made Me a Fugitive, The First Gentleman*.

CERVI, Gino. Born Bologna, Italy, 1905. Films include : *Ettore Fieramosca, Salvator Rosa ;* 1942 : *I Promessi Sposi* (Lux) ; 1944 : *La Locandiera* (Cines), *Quartetto Pazzo* (Safic) ; 1945 : *Umanità* (Luce Nuova), *Un Uomo Ritorna* (Zeus), *Malia* (Titanus Amato), *Le Miserie del Signor Travet* (Pao-Lux), *Lo Sbaglio di Essere Vivo* (Fauno) ; 1946 : *L'Angelo e il Diavolo* (Lore) *Aquila Nera* (CDI), *Cronaca Nera* (Aurea), *Daniele Cortis* (Universalia), *Furia* (AGIC) ; 1947 : *I Miserabili* (Lux) ; 1948 : *Anna Karenina* (LFP).

CHANEY, Lon, Jr. Real name Creighton Chaney. Born Oklahoma City, Oklahoma, U.S.A., Feb. 10, 1915. Ht. 6 ft. 3 in. ; wt. 205 lb. Dark brown hair, hazel eyes. Son of late Lon Chaney, famous star of silent films. Educ. Los Feliz Grammar School ; Hollywood High School ; Commercial Experts Training Institute, Los Angeles. Was news-boy, butcher boy, ice-man, clothing salesman and model until, on death of his father, made first film *Girl Crazy* (RKO) 1932. Other films include : *The Bird of Paradise, Son of the Border, Captain Hurricane, Accent on Youth, Wife, Doctor and Nurse, Jesse James, Union Pacific, Of Mice and Men* (in which he scored notable success in role of Lenny). 1940 : *North-West Mounted Police* (Para) ; 1941 : *Too Many Blondes* (Univ), *Billy the Kid* (MGM) ; 1942 : *North to the Klondike* (Univ), *Ghost of Frankenstein* (Univ) ; 1944 : *The Ghost Catchers* (Univ), *Weird Woman* (Univ) ; 1945 : *Here Come the Co-eds* (Univ), *House of Frankenstein* (Univ), *The Mummy's Curse* (Univ, *The Frozen Ghost* (Univ), *The Daltons Ride Again* (Univ), *The House of Dracula* (Univ), *Pillow of Death* (Univ) ; 1946 : *Strange Confession* (Univ) ; 1947 : *My Favourite Brunette* (Para).

CHAPLIN, Charles Spencer. Born Kennington, London, April 16, 1889. Ht. 5 ft. 6½ in. ; wt. 126 lb. White hair, blue eyes. Educ. St. Mary-the-Less School, Kennington. Son of professional actors.

BING CROSBY
(*Paramount*)

Made actual film debut at 8 by joining in a march of the Scots Guards through St. James's Park which was being filmed. Skill at imitations and clog-dancing brought him position in juvenile stage troupe "The Eight Lancashire Lads". Appeared 1905 as Billy the page-boy in "The Painful Predicament of Sherlock Holmes" with Irene Vanbrugh. Success with impersonations in "Casey's Court" led to one year's engagement at 45s. per week. Joined Fred Karno's "Mumming Birds", and went with them to U.S.A., 1910. While with Karno, invited to make films for the old Keystone Company; appeared in "The Kid Auto Races", 1913. Made hundreds of two-reelers for Keystone, Essanay and Mutual. With Douglas Fairbanks, Sr., Mary Pickford and D. W. Griffith founded United Artists, 1919. Among his famous early films were *Tillie's Punctured Romance* (1914) with the late Marie Dressler; *Shoulder Arms* (1917) often regarded as one of the best examples of his work; *The Kid* (1920) introducing Jackie Coogan; *The Idle Class* (1921) in which he played a dual role; *The Gold Rush* (1925: re-issued with sound 1942) *The Circus* (1929). The screen's greatest artist in mime, Chaplin was reluctant to give voice to his characters when talkies arrived: *City Lights* (1931) and *Modern Times* (1936) had sound and music, but no dialogue. Two years before World War II he began the satirical film *The Great Dictator* (shown 1940) when his voice was heard for the first time. After a long interval his next film, *Monsieur Verdoux*, was completed and shown in 1947. He invariably directs, and writes the story and the music for, the films in which he stars.

CHAPMAN, Edward. Born Harrogate, Oct. 13, 1901. Ht. 5 ft. 8½ in. Brown hair, brown eyes. Educ. Ardingley College; City of London School. Bank clerk at Harrogate for six years, acting local amateur dramatic society. Then at Repertory Theatre, Nottingham, and on tour. Launched on film career by Alfred Hitchcock in 1929 as the "Paycock" in *Juno and the Paycock* (BIP). Served for five years in R.A.F. Fighter Command in World War II. Other films include: *Murder, Skin Game, Tilly of Bloomsbury, The Flying Squad, Happy Ever After, Blossom Time, The Divine Spark, Things to Come, The Man Who Could Work Miracles, Rembrandt, April Romance, I've Got a Horse, The Citadel, Who Killed John Savage? The Nursemaid Who Disappeared, Marigold, Four Just Men, There Ain't No Justice, Poison Pen, Inspector Hornleigh on Holiday.* 1940: *The Proud Valley* (Ealing), *Briggs Family* (Warn-Brit), *Jeannie* (Hellman), *Inspector Hornleigh Goes to It* (Gains-20th); 1941: *Ships with Wings* (Ealing); 1942: *They Flew Alone* (Wilcox-RKO); 1947: *The October Man* (Two Cities), *It Always Rains on Sunday* (Ealing).

CHAPMAN, Marguerite. Born Chatham, New York, Mar. 9. Educ. High School, Chatham. Studied millinery designing; became New York model. Producer Howard Hughes suggested screen career. First film: *On Their Own* (20th), 1940. Other films include: *Charlie Chan at the Wax Museum* (20th), *Four Sons* (20th); 1941: *A Girl, a Guy and a Sailor* (RKO), *Navy Blues* (Warn), *The Body Disappears* (Warn), *You're in the Army Now* (Warn); 1942: (all Col): *Submarine Raider, Meet the Stewarts, Parachute Nurse, Spirit of Stanford, Daring Young Man, A Man's World*; 1943 (all Col): *One Dangerous Night, Murder in Times Square, Appointment in Berlin, Destroyer, My Kingdom for a Cook*; 1944: *Strange Affair* (Col); 1945 (all Col): *Counter Attack, One*

Way to Love, Pardon My Past; 1946: (all Col): *The Walls Came Tumbling Down, Mr. District Attorney;* 1947: *Relentless* (Col); 1948: *At the Sign of the Ram* (Col).

CHARISSE, Cyd. Real name Tula Finklea. Born Amarillo, Texas, U.S.A., Mar. 8. Ht. 5 ft. 6 ins.; Wt. 115 lb. Dark brown hair, brown eyes. Her father's enthusiasm for ballet was cause of her taking dancing lessons. Joined Colonel de Basil's Ballet Russe. Married Nico Charisse, ballet instructor, and opened dance school in Hollywood. Appeared in two small film roles before achieving success as ballerina in *Ziegfeld Follies* (MGM) 1944. First film: *Something to Shout About* (Col) 1943. Other films include—1943: *Mission to Moscow* (Warn); 1945: *The Harvey Girls* (MGM); 1946: *Three Wise Fools* (MGM), *Till the Clouds Roll By* (MGM); 1947: *Fiesta* (MGM), *The Unfinished Dance* (MGM); 1948: *On an Island with You* (MGM).

CHECCHI, Andrea. Born Florence, Italy, 1915. Films include: *Grandi Magazzini, Catene Invisibili, Via delle Cinque Lune, La Contessa Castiglione;* 1942: *Avanti c'è Pasto* (Amato), *Malambra* (Lux); 1944: *Lettere al Sottotenente* (Scalera); 1945: *L'Ultimo Amore* (Pau Eric), *Le Vie del Peccato* (RE.CI.TE.), *Un Americano in Vacanza* (Lex); 1946: *Due Lettere Anonime* (Lux-Ninfa), *Albergo Luna* (Lux), *Biraghin* (Excelsa), *Cronaca Nera* (Aurea), *Eleonora Duse* (S. Giorgio), *La Notte Porta Consiglio* (Pao), *La Primula Bianca* (Lux); 1947: *I Fratelli Karamazof, Caccia Tragica* (ANPI).

CHESTER, Charlie. Born Eastbourne, Sussex. Entered entertainment world, 1938, in non-stop revue, Prince of Wales Theatre, London; toured in variety. In 1939, first civilian entertainer of troops in Maginot Line. Joined Royal Irish Fusiliers, 1940. Chosen to test security of military camps by entering them in various guises. Toured Britain entertaining troops on gun-sites; first British entertainer to appear before General Eisenhower, Garrison Theatre, Tidworth. After D-Day, entertained Allied troops. Learnt Dutch from interpreter and became popular artist in Holland. During Army career wrote scripts of over eighty "Stars in Battledress" shows. In 1946, achieved great success as comedian with B.B.C. programme "Stand Easy". Producer Sydney Box engaged him as variety comedian in: *Holiday Camp* (Gains) 1947.

CHEVALIER, Maurice. Born Menilmontant, Paris, Sept. 12, 1889. Ht. 5 ft. 11½ in.; wt. 165 lb. Brown hair, blue eyes. Went to work at 10 to help his mother. Became assistant, in turn, to electrician, painter of toy dolls and merchant, but hankered after stage. Made unsuccessful debut at age of 12 in concert. Later earned twelve francs a week at Tourelles Casino. Became acrobat with brother Paul, but found his real vocation as song-and-dance artist. Toured in France then appeared in Paris at Eldorado, Folies-Bergère, La Cigale. Wounded in World War I, spent twenty-six months as P.O.W.; awarded Croix de Guerre. Resumed career in 1920 at Montparnasse Casino, followed by partnership with Mistinguette in Parisian revues. Also became famous in London, South America, and elsewhere. During his three years as top star of Casino de Paris, was seen by Jesse Lasky and went to Hollywood for film debut in *Innocents of Paris* (1929). American films include: *The Love Parade, The Big Pond, Paramount on Parade, Playboy* of Paris, One Hour with You, Little Café, The Smiling Lieutenant, Love Me Tonight, A Bedtime Story, The Way to Love, The Merry Widow, The Man from the Folies-Bergère. British Films : The Beloved Vagabond, Break the News. In 1946 resumed film career, in Paris, with Le Silence et d'Or, French and English versions ; shown in U.S.A., 1947 as Man About Town (RKO).

CHIAURELLI, M. Producer. Born Tbilisi (Tiflis), Caucasus, 1894. Began his career on the stage, in 1916, and entered Soviet films in 1921, as actor. In 1928 produced his first feature film, First Cornet Streshniv. Other films include : Saba (1931), Habarda (1932), The Last Masquerade (1934), Arsene (1935), The Great Flame (Sunset) (1936), Georgi Saakadze—in two series (1937-9), The Vow (1945-6), The Last Days of Berlin, a feature documentary (1947-8).

CHRISTIANS, Mady. Real name Marguerita Maria Christians. Born Vienna, Jan. 19, 1900. Educ. privately. Went to New York at 12 and made stage debut at German Theatre, Irving Place, then under her father's management. In 1917 returned to Vienna and studied under Max Reinhardt. Achieved fame in classical roles in Europe and America. Before resuming her stage career in America, in 1931, made films on the continent, including : Glass of Water, Finances of the Archduke, Cinderella, Waltz Dream, Queen Louise, Duel (made in Britain) Priscilla's Fortnight, Meet My Sister, The Black Hussar, Ich und die Kaiserin, and The House of Dora Green ; and many tri-lingual films. First American film : One Year Later (Allied Pictures) 1931. Others include : Wicked Woman, Come and Get It, Seventh Heaven (20th) 1937, The Woman I Love, Heidi. 1938-44, on American stage, notably in "Henry IV" and "Hamlet" with Maurice Evans. Appeared in Address Unknown (Col) 1944, then returned to New York where she appeared for two years in John Van Druten's play "I Remember Mama". 1948 : Letters from an Unknown Woman (UI), All My Sons (UI). Came to Britain to star in and direct the London stage production "I Remember Mama", 1948.

CHURCHILL, Sarah. Born London, Oct. 7, 1918. Ht. 5 ft. 5 in. ; wt. 112 lb. Auburn hair, hazel eyes. Educ. Notting Hill High School ; North Foreland Lodge, Broadstairs. Studied ballet for two years before deciding to become actress. Stage debut in chorus of "Follow the Sun", 1936. Four years with touring and repertory companies. Served in W.A.A.F. during World War II. Film debut in He Found a Star (Corfield) 1942. Also appeared in Spring Meeting (ABPC) 1944. Offered Hollywood contract 1946, but refused. To Italy to appear in When in Rome (Vicandro). While there, acted in Daniele Cortis (Universalia) 1947. In this she was the only player to speak her lines in English, her part being dubbed on the sound-track in Italian ; in the English-language version all voices were dubbed but hers.

CLAIR, René. Producer, director. Real name René Chomette. Born Southern France, 1899. As reporter on "L'Intransigeant", Paris, in his early twenties, came into touch with film studios. Became film actor under name of René Clair, then assistant director in 1922. In 1923, wrote, produced and directed first film, Paris qui Dort, scoring immediate success. About this time wrote novel, "Adams", under real name, but publishers insisted he was now more famous as "Clair". Wrote and directed many interesting experimental films, including Entr'acte, Le Chapeau de

Paille d'Italia (The Italian Straw Hat). With arrival of sound, won wide fame with : Sous les Toits de Paris, Le Million, A Nous la Liberté, Le Quatorze Juillet. In Britain—1936: The Ghost Goes West; 1937 : Break the News. Was making Air Pur in France when war broke out. To America in August, 1940. U.S. films : Flame of New Orleans, I Married a Witch, Forever and a Day, It Happened Tomorrow, And Then There Were None. Returned to France, 1946, and directed Man About Town (in French and English versions) with Maurice Chevalier.

CLARE, Mary. Born London, July 17, 1894. Worked in an office, borrowed £50 for dramatic training, made stage debut on tour, 1910. First London appearance, 1913, in "Turandot" at St. James's Theatre. Outstanding plays include : "The Skin Game", "The Likes of 'Er", "White Cargo", "The Ghost Train", "The Constant Nymph". In 1931, made stage history as Jane Marryot in "Cavalcade", the play which Noel Coward wrote specially for her. Appeared in silent films. First sound film : Hindle Wakes (Gaumont), 1931. Other films include : Many Waters, Gypsy Blood, The Skin Game, Keepers of Youth, The Constant Nymph (silent version and first sound version GB) 1933, Jew Süss—U.S. title Power, Lorna Doone, The Clairvoyant, The Passing of the Third Floor Back, Young and Innocent, Say It with Flowers, Night Club Queen, The Challenge, The Lady Vanishes, The Citadel, There Ain't No Justice, A Girl Must Live, On the Night of the Fire, The Briggs Family. 1940 : Old Bill and Son (Somlo), Mrs. Pym of Scotland Yard (Argyle), The Patient Vanishes (ABPC) ; 1941 : Next of Kin (Ealing), One Exciting Night (Col-Brit) ; 1943 : The Hundred Pound Window (Warn-Brit) ; 1944 : Fiddlers Three (Ealing) ; 1946 : London Town (Wesley Ruggles) ; 1948 : Three Weird Sisters (Brit-Nat), Oliver Twist (Cineguild), Esther Waters (Wessex).

CLARK, Dane. Born New York City, Feb. 18, 1914. Ht. 5 ft. 9 in. ; wt. 160 lb. Educ. Cornell University, Johns Hopkins University. Studied law ; was professional baseball player, and middle-weight fighter. Anonymous voice in radio serials for two years. Joined Theatre Union and Mercury Theatre ; Broadway appearances in "Of Mice and Men", "Dead End" and other plays. First film, Tennessee Johnson —British title The Man on America's Conscience (MGM) 1942. Other films include—1942 : The Glass Key (Para), Sunday Punch (MGM) ; 1943 : Action in North Atlantic (Warn) ; 1944 : Destination Tokyo (Warn), Hollywood Canteen (Warn), The Very Thought of You (Warn) ; 1945 : Forever in Love (Warn), God is My Co-pilot ; 1946 : A Stolen Life (Warn), Her Kind of Man (Warn) ; 1947 : That Way with Women, The Dark Passage, Deep Valley (Warn) ; 1948 : Whiplash (Warn).

CLARK, Petula. Born West Ewell, Surrey, Nov. 15, 1932. Ht. 4 ft. 10 in. ; wt. 87 lbs. Light brown hair, blue eyes. Educ. privately and Romonoff School, Surbiton. At 7 saw Flora Robson at Streatham Hill Theatre, London, and decided to become an actress. At 9 had won five talent contests. At 10 made notable success as singer in B.B.C. Children's Hour show "It's All Yours". Has appeared at Albert Hall five times ; gave more than five hundred shows to troops during World War II ; also television star. Played only small parts in films until director Wesley Ruggles saw her at Albert Hall concert and gave her featured role in London Town. First film Medal for the General (Brit-Nat) 1944. Other films include—

1945 : *I Know Where I'm Going* (Archers) ; 1946 : *Trouble at Townsend* (GBI), *Strawberry Roan* (Brit-Nat), *London Town* (Wesley Ruggles) ; 1948 : *Vice Versa* (Two Cities), *Easy Money* (Gains).

CLAYTON, Jan. Born Alomongordo, New Mexico, Aug. 28. Ht. 5 ft. 2 in. ; wt. 100 lb. Red-blonde hair, blue eyes. Won a scholarship in music and dramatics. Voted " the most talented girl " at college, and given a screen test after a New York talent contest. Became singer in Hollywood night club ; on stage in " Meet the People", " Can't Get You Down", " Sailor Beware". Began screen career in Hopalong Cassidy films. First film : *In Old Mexico* (Para) 1938. Other films include : *Sunset Trail, The Llano Kid* ; 1940 : *The Showdown* (Para), *Flight Angels* (Warner), *Father Is a Prince* (Warner) ; 1946 : *This Man's Navy* (MGM).

CLEMENTS, John. Born London, Apr. 25, 1910. Ht. 5 ft. 11½ in. Brown hair, brown eyes. Educ. St. Paul's School ; St. John's College, Cambridge. After leaving university joined first Nigel Playfair's and later Ben Greet's Shakespearean company. Formed the " Intimate Theatre " at Palmers Green, 1935, as a combined repertory and try-out theatre. Film debut : *Ticket of Leave* (Para Brit) 1935. Other films include : *Things to Come, Rembrandt, Knight without Armour, South Riding, Star of the Circus, The Housemaster, The Four Feathers.* 1940 : *Convoy* (Ealing) ; 1941 : *This England* (Brit-Nat), *Ships with Wings* (Ealing) ; 1942 : *Undercover* (Ealing) ; 1945 : *They Came to a City* (Ealing) ; 1947 : directed and starred in *Call of the Blood* (Pendennis-Stafford).

CLIFFORD, Hubert. Composer. Born Bairnsdale, Australia, 1904. Studied at the Royal College of Music in London, and was B.B.C. Empire music supervisor 1941-4. First film score in 1943 for *Power on the Land.* Music for other documentaries includes : *The Battle of Britain, Left of the Line.* In 1946 was appointed music director to London Film Productions.

COBB, Lee J. Born New York City, Dec. 8, 1911. Educ. City College, New York. Had to abandon music as career ; studied aeronautical engineering at college, but became interested in theatre. At 18 was marked for character roles with Group Theatre ; at 21 lost his hair and remained a character actor. Played twenty-two stage roles before appearing on screen in *North of the Rio Grande* (Para) 1937. Other films include : *Rustler's Valley, Danger on the Air, Golden Boy.* 1940 : *This Thing Called Love* (Col) ; 1941 : *Men of Boys' Town* (MGM) ; 1943 : *The Moon Is Down* (20th), *Tonight We Raid Calais* (20th), *The Song of Bernadette* (20th) ; 1944 : *Winged Victory* (20th) ; 1946 : *Anna and the King of Siam* (20th), 1947 : *Johnny O'Clock* (Col), *Boomerang* (20th), *Carnival in Costa Rica* (20th) ; 1948 : *Captain from Castille* (20th).

COBURN, Charles. Born Macon, Georgia, U.S.A., June 19, 1877. At 14 was programme seller and usher at Savannah Theatre, Georgia, becoming manager five years later. Was department store packer, usher and professional bicycle racer before organizing Coburn Players in 1906 with his wife Ivah Wills. Long stage career. In 1935 established Mohawk Drama Festival at Union College, Schenectady, New York. When wife died in 1938, went to Hollywood to begin new career. Early films include : *Of Human Hearts, Vivacious Lady, Idiot's Delight, Story of Alexander Graham Bell, Stanley and Livingstone, Road to Singapore, Edison the Man, The Captain Is a Lady.* 1941 : *The Devil and Miss Jones* (RKO), *H. M. Pulham, Esq.* (MGM) ; 1942 : *In This Our Life* (Warn), *The More the Merrier* (Col), *The Constant Nymph* (Warn), *Heaven Can Wait* (20th), *Princess O'Rourke* (Warn) ; *My Kingdom for a Cook* (Col) ; 1944 : *Knickerbocker Holiday* (UA), *Wilson* (20th), *The Impatient Years* (Col), *Together Again* (Col) ; 1945 : *A Royal Scandal* (20th), *Colonel Effingham's Raid, Shady Lady* (Univ), *Over 21* (Col) ; 1946 : *The Green Years* (MGM), *The Man of the Hour* (20th) ; 1947 : *The Paradine Case* (Selznick) ; 1948 : *Personal Column* (Hunt Stromberg-UA).

COLBERT, Claudette. Real name Claudette Chauchoin. Born Paris, Sept. 13, 1905. Ht. 5 ft. 4½ in. ; wt. 108 lb. Brown hair, hazel eyes. Educ. public schools, Paris and New York. Youthful ambition, to be an actress. At 4 came to New York for stage training ; with help of Cornelia Otis Skinner, made Broadway debut 1923 in " Then Wild Westcotts ". Gained title of " the girl with the most beautiful legs on Broadway ". Appeared on London stage in " The Barker ", 1928. First film *For the Love of Mike* (FN) 1927 ; but considered herself unsuitable for films. In her first talkie, *The Hole in the Wall* (Para) 1929, won success by her voice. Nearly fifty films since then, including : *The Smiling Lieutenant, The Sign of The Cross, I Cover the Waterfront, Three-Cornered Moon, It Happened one Night, Four Frightened People, Cleopatra, Under Two Flags, I Met Him in Paris, Zaza, Midnight.* 1940 : *Boom Town* (MGM), *Arise My Love* (Para), *Skylark* (Para) ; 1941 : *Remember the Day* (20th) ; 1942 : *The Palm Beach Story* (Para) ; 1943 : *No Time for Love* (Para), *So Proudly We Hail* (Para) ; 1944 : *Since You Went Away* (UA), *Practically Yours* (Para) ; 1945 : *Guest Wife* (UA) ; 1946 : *Tomorrow is Forever* (RKO), *Without Reservations* (RKO) ; 1947 : *The Egg and I* (UI) ; 1948 : *Sleep My Love* (Triangle-UA).

COLEMAN, Nancy. Born Everett, Washington, U.S.A., Dec. 30, 1917. Went to San Francisco to become an actress ; found no one would employ an amateur, so took job as a lift attendant until she managed to secure a broadcasting audition and was engaged for radio serials. Saved a thousand dollars and went to New York, where she gained an important part in " Susan and God " starring Gertrude Lawrence. Performance in another play, " Liberty Jones ", led to film debut opposite John Garfield in *Dangerously They Live* (Warn) 1942. Other films include—1942 : *King's Row* (Warn), *Gay Sisters* (Warn), *Desperate Journey* (Warn) ; 1943 : *Edge of Darkness* (Warn) ; 1944 : *In Our Time* (Warn) ; 1945 : *Devotion* (Warn) ; 1947 : *Violence* (Mono).

COLLEANO, Bonar. Real name Bonar William Sullivan. Born New York City, Mar. 14, 1924. Ht. 5 ft. 11 in. ; wt. 165 lb. Black hair, brown eyes. Educ. Professional Children's School, New York ; Streatham Grammar School and Cannock House, Eltham, in England. One of famous Colleano Circus Family. Began career at 5 at Palace Theatre, New York, partnering father and mother. Toured America, Europe, went to school in England 1936-8, toured Britain in variety with " The Five Colleanos ", appeared in " Sweet and Low " revue, London, 1942. Offered first film role as Lieutenant Joe Frizelli in *The Way to the Stars* (Two Cities) 1945. Other films include—1946 : *Wanted for Murder* (20th Brit), *A Matter of Life and Death* (Archers) ; 1947 : *While the Sun Shines* (Internat Screen) ; 1948 : *Good Time Girl* (Gains), *One Night With You* (Two Cities).

COLLIER, Constance. Born Windsor, Berks, Jan. 22, 1878. First stage appearance at 4 as Peaseblossom in " A Midsummer Night's Dream". One of her early successes on London stage was in " The Gaiety Girl ", 1894. To New York in 1908 to appear in "Samson" —the first of many appearances there. She is also a successful playwright and has published an autobiography, " Harlequinade ". Films include : *Shadow of a Doubt, Peter Ibbetson, Professional Soldier, Girls' Dormitory, Little Lord Fauntleroy, Thunder in the City, Wee Willie Winkie, Stage Door, A Damsel in Distress, Zaza.* 1940 : *Susan and God* (MGM) ; 1945 : *Kitty* (Para) ; 1946 : *Monsieur Beaucaire* (Para) ; 1947 : *The Perils of Pauline* (Para). In 1947 came to Britain to appear in *An Ideal Husband* (LFP).

COLLINS, Anthony. Composer, music director. Born Hastings, 1903. Had a wide musical education before becoming orchestral player with Covent Garden and London Symphony Orchestras. Has been associated with Herbert Wilcox for many years. Was composer and conductor for *Victoria the Great,* and wrote music of *Sixty Glorious Years, Nurse Edith Cavell, A Royal Divorce.* Went to Hollywood in 1939 where he wrote music for *Irene, No No Nanette, Sunny, Forever and a Day, Tom Brown's Schooldays.* Returned to London in 1945 to score the films *I Live in Grosvenor Square, Piccadilly Incident, The Courtneys of Curzon Street.*

COLMAN, Ronald. Born Richmond, Surrey, Feb. 9, 1891. Grey-brown hair, brown eyes. Educ. Hadley School, Littlehampton. At 16 became London Office boy at 15s. per week ; after five years became clerk. Joined London Scottish Regiment, 1914 ; injured at Messines. Small parts on London stage from 1916 in "The Maharani of Arakan", "The Misleading Lady"; lead in " Damaged Goods ", "The Little Brother ", and others. Appeared in British silent films from 1917 ; debut in two-reel comedy for Geo. Dewhurst. Also with Cecil M. Hepworth and the old Broadwest Company. To America, 1920. Toured in " East Is West " ; later, George Arliss gave him part in New York in " The Green Goddess ". Hollywood film debut : *The White Sister* (Metro) 1922. Silent films include : *Lady Windermere's Fan, The Dark Angel, Beau Geste, Stella Dallas, The Winning of Barbara Worth, The Rescue, Two Lovers.* Sound films include : *Bulldog Drummond, Condemned, Raffles, Devil to Pay, Arrowsmith, Cynara, The Masquerader, Clive of India. A Tale of Two Cities, Under Two Flags, The Lost Horizon, The Prisoner of Zenda, If I Were King, The Light That Failed.* 1941 : *My Life with Caroline* (RKO) ; 1942 : *Talk of the Town* (Col), *Random Harvest* (MGM) ; 1944 : *Kismet* (MGM) ; 1947 : *The Late George Apley* (20th) ; 1948 : *A Double Life* (UI).

COMFORT, Lance. Director. Born London, 1908. Educ. Harrow County School. Entered films, 1926. as cameraman on medical research, 1928, cameraman at Ealing Studios ; afterwards at Islington and Gaumont Studios. 1932 to Stoll Studios as sound recordist. Began career as director with documentaries in 1938 ; associate director *Love on the Dole* 1940 ; directed his first feature film, *Penn of Pensylvania,* 1941.

Other films directed : *Those Kids from Town, When We Are Married, Hatter's Castle, Hotel Reserve, The Great Day, Escape to Danger, Squadron Leader " X ", Bedelia, Temptation Harbour, Daughter of Darkness.*

COMPTON, Fay. Born London, Sept. 18, 1894. Ht. 5 ft. 5 in. ; wt. 120 lb. Educ. Leatherhead Court, Surrey ; Paris. Daughter of theatrical parents, made first stage appearance at the Albert Hall in 1906 in Christmas fantasy. Made professional stage debut with " Pelissier's Follies " at the Apollo Theatre, London, 1911, and shortly afterwards married Pelissier. Began her film career in silent days in *One Summer's Day* (1917) in Britain. While visiting America made her first talkie, in Hollywood, *Fashions in Love* (Para) 1929, opposite Adolphe Menjou. Early British films include *A Woman of No Importance, Bill of Divorcement* (Ideal, 1922), *This Freedom, Loves of Mary Queen of Scots, Claude Duval, The Eleventh Commandment, The Happy Ending*—silent version, also talkie (GB 1928), *Settled Out of Court, Somehow Good, Zero, London Love, Tell England, Cape Forlorn, Uneasy Virtue, Autumn Crocus, Waltzes from Vienna, Phantom Light, The Mill on the Floss, So This is London.* During 1940-5 worked mainly in the theatre in London, and touring abroad for the British Council. 1942 : *The Prime Minister* (Warn-Brit) ; 1947 : *Odd Man Out* (Two Cities), *Nicholas Nickleby* (Ealing) ; 1948 : *London Belongs To Me* (Individ), *Esther Waters* (Wessex).

CONNORS, Katherine. Born Brooklyn, New York, Apr. 8, 1921. Ht. 5 ft. 7 in. ; wt. 125 lb. Black hair, blue eyes. Educ. Public School 185, Brooklyn ; St. Angela Hall. Left Brooklyn for Hollywood, 1942 ; appeared with Victory Players and made hit in " Mr. and Mrs. North ". Films include : *Rendezvous 24* (20th), 1946, *Caribbean Mystery* (20th), 1946.

CONTE, Richard. Real name Nicholas Peter Conte. Born Jersey City, U.S.A., Mar. 24, 1914. Ht. 5 ft. 10½ in. ; wt. 160 lb. Dark hair, brown eyes. Educ. Public School 32, Jersey City ; Dickinson High School, New Jersey. Became Wall-street messenger, truck driver, pianist, waiter, barber. Then while dance partner at club, took part in musical show there, and was given New York stage chance. Performance in " The Family ", 1943, led to film debut in *Guadalcanal Diary* (20th) 1943. War service in U.S. Army. Other films (all 20th) include—1944 : *The Purple Heart* ; 1945 : *A Bell for Adano, Captain Eddie, The Spider* ; 1946 : *A Walk in the Sun, Somewhere in the Night,* 13 *Rue Madeleine* ; 1947 : *The Other Love* (Enterprise-MGM) ; 1948 : *Call Northside 777* (20th).

CONWAY, Jack. Director. Born Graceville, Minnesota, U.S.A., July 17, 1887. Educ. Durham preparatory school. Became leading stage actor, then played lead in one of the first Hollywood films, *Her Indian Hero,* 1909, which was made in two days. D. W. Griffith launched him as director, 1912, with *The Old Armchair.* Became director for Selig, Bosworth, Universal, Reliance and other companies then joined MGM. Other films include : *Untamed, They Learned About Women, New Moon, The Unholy Three, The Easiest Way, The Dancing Partner, Arsène Lupin, Red-headed Woman, But the Flesh Is Weak, Hell Below, Accidents Wanted, The Solitaire Man, Viva Villa, 100% Pure, The Gay Bride, The Trunk Mystery, A Tale of Two Cities, Libelled Lady, Saratoga, A Yank at Oxford* (for MGM in Britain, 1938), *Too*

Hot to Handle, Let Freedom Ring, Lady of the Tropics, Boom Town, Love Crazy, Honky Tonk, Crossroads, Assignment in Brittany, Dragon Seed, High Barbaree, The Hucksters.

CONWAY, Tom. Real name Thomas Charles Sanders. Born St. Petersburg (now Leningrad), Sept. 15, 1904. Ht. 6 ft. 1 in. ; wt. 180 lb. Brown hair, brown eyes. Came to Britain with his brother, George Sanders, and was educated at Brighton College. Went to South Africa, where he worked on a cattle ranch, and in gold, asbestos and copper mines, and also drove a taxi. Returned to Britain and joined the Manchester Repertory Company. Then seen by Hollywood talent scout. Film debut : *Sky Murder* (MGM) 1940. Other films include—1941 : *The Trial of Mary Dugan* (MGM), *Free and Easy* (MGM), *Bad Man* (MGM), *Lady Be Good* (MGM) ; 1942 : *Rio Rita* (MGM), *Grand Central Murder* (MGM). Also in 1942 made his first appearance in the *Falcon* series. 1945 : *One Exciting Night* (Para) ; 1946 : *Whistle Stop* (UA) ; 1947 : *Lost Honeymoon* (Eagle Lion-Hollywood), *Repeat Performance* (Eagle Lion-Hollywood).

COOPER, Gary. Real name Frank J. Cooper. Born Helena, Montana, U.S.A., May 7, 1901. Ht. 6 ft. 2 in. ; wt. 180 lb. Brown hair, blue eyes. Educ. Dunstable School, England ; Iowa College, U.S.A. Spent part of his boyhood in Britain, returning to Helena at 13. Sent to a ranch to recuperate after car smash, he learnt to be a cowboy before going to College. First job was a newspaper cartoonist. Went to Los Angeles to develop artistic activities, but was unsuccessful ; for some months was an advertising agent's salesman. Then for eighteen months he worked as film extra, till in 1925 a producer of two-reel Westerns picked him from the crowd for a featured part. First important film part was in *The Winning of Barbara Worth* (Para) 1926. Other films include : *Wings, It, Nevada, Beau Sabreur, Lilac Time, Shopworn Angel, The Virginian, Seven Days Leave, The Texan, Paramount on Parade, The Spoilers, Morocco, City Streets, I Take This Woman, The Devil and the Deep, A Farewell to Arms, If I Had a Million, One Sunday Afternoon, Design for Living, Alice in Wonderland, Now and Forever, The Lives of a Bengal Lancer, Her Wedding Night, Peter Ibbetson, Desire, Mr. Deeds Goes to Town, The General Died at Dawn, The Plainsman, Souls at Sea, Adventures of Marco Polo, Bluebeard's Eighth Wife, The Cowboy and the Lady, Beau Geste.* 1940 : *The Westerner* (UA), *North-West Mounted Police* (Para) ; 1941 : *Meet John Doe* (Warn), *Sergeant York* (Warn) ; 1942 : *Ball of Fire* (Goldwyn), *Saratoga Trunk* (Warn) shown in Britain 1946 ; 1943 : *For Whom The Bell Tolls* (Para), *Pride of the Yankees* (Goldwyn) ; 1944 : *The Story of Dr. Wassell* (Para), *Casanova Brown* (Goldwyn) ; 1945 : *Along Came Jones* (Goldwyn) ; 1946 : *Unconquered* (Para) ; 1947 : *Cloak and Dagger* (Warn), guest star in *Variety Girl* (Para).

COOPER, Gladys. Born Lewisham, London, Dec. 18, 1888. Ht. 5 ft. 5 in. ; wt. 118 lb. Blonde hair, blue eyes. Stage debut Dec. 18, 1905 at Theatre Royal, Colchester in title role in " Bluebell in Fairyland ". Became chorus girl at Daly's and Gaiety Theatres for George Edwardes. Later one of the most famous actresses of the English stage, appearing in " The Yellow Ticket ", " The Last of Mrs. Cheyney ", " The Letter ", " The Sacred Flame ", " Cynara ", " The Rats of Norway ", and other plays. First New York

appearance, " The Shining Hour ", Booth Theatre, 1934. Entered silent films in 1920's, early films include : *Dandy Donovan, The Eleventh Commandment, Bonnie Prince Charlie, The Bohemian Girl, The Iron Duke* (1934). In 1939 starred for fourteen months on Broadway in " Spring Meeting ". Asked by director Alfred Hitchcock to make her first Hollywood film : *Rebecca* (UA) 1940. Other films include—1940 : *Kitty Foyle* (RKO) ; 1941 : *The Gay Falcon* (RKO), *Lady Hamilton,* (Korda-Hollywood), *The Black Cat* (Univ) ; 1942 : *This Above All* (20th), *Now, Voyager* (Warn), *Eagle Squadron* (Univ) ; 1943 : *Forever and A Day* (RKO), *Mr. Lucky* (RKO), *Princess O' Rourke* (Warn), *The Song of Bernadette* (20th) ; 1944 : *The White Cliffs of Dover* (MGM), *Mrs. Parkington* (MGM) ; 1945 : *The Valley of Decision* (MGM), *Love Letters* (Para), *The Green Years* (MGM) ; 1946 : *Beware of Pity* (Two Cities) in Britain, *Mr. Griggs Returns* (MGM) ; 1947 : *Green Dolphin Street* (MGM), *The Pirate* (MGM); 1948 : *Homecoming* (MGM).

COOPER, Jackie. Born Los Angeles, U.S.A., Sept. 15, 1922. Ht. 5 ft. 9 in. ; wt. 145 lb. Educ. privately. Nephew of director Norman Taurog who gave him his first film role at age of 4, in a film starring Lloyd Hamilton. *Our Gang* series in 1930. Early films include : *Skippy, Donovan's Kid, Sooky, The Champ, Divorce in the Family, When a Feller Needs a Friend, The Bowery, Lone Cowboy, Treasure Island, Peck's Bad Boy, Dinky, O'Shaughnessy's Boy, Tough Guy, The Devil Takes the Count, Boy of the Streets, White Banners, That Certain Age, Scouts to the Rescue, Gangster's Boy, Spirit of Culver.* 1940 : *Seventeen* (Para) ; 1942 : *Syncopation* (RKO) ; 1944 : *Where Are Your Children ?* (Mono). 1944-6, served in U.S. Navy ; 1947 : *Stork Bites Man* (Comet-UA).

COREY, Wendell. Born Dracutt, Massachusetts. Dec. 20, 1914. Ht. 6 ft. 2 in. ; wt. 120 lb. Brown hair, blue eyes. Youthful ambitions included law, journalism and professional tennis. Began career selling refrigerators and washing machines. Appeared as amateur for a year in the Springfield Little Theatre, Massachusetts. Toured with the Federal Theatre Group and appeared in several New York stage productions. Had just been turned down for a role in " The Rugged Path " by Robert E. Sherwood, with Spencer Tracy, and was considering return to the refrigerator business when he received leading role in " Dream Girl " in which he was seen by film producer Hal Wallis. Visited Britain, 1947, to appear in " The Voice of the Turtle ". Made his screen debut in *Desert Fury* (Hal Wallis-Para) 1947. Also in 1947 made *I Walk Alone* (Hal Wallis-Para). Went to Switzerland to appear in *Children Without Names* (Wechsler-MGM), 1948.

CORFIELD, John. Producer. Born Liverpool, 1893. Educ. Liverpool College ; Liverpool University. Began career in Liverpool solicitor's office ; 1917-19, with British Embassy in Washington ; then sales manager for Coventry motor firm. Entered film industry, 1929, with own company, producing "quota" films ; in 1935, in partnership with Lady Yule and J. Arthur Rank, formed British National Films Ltd. First production, adapted from Leo Walmsley story of Yorkshire fisher-folk, *Turn of the Tide.* Until 1940, manager, producer and director for Brit Nat. Then formed John Corfield Productions. Productions include : *What Would You Do, Chums ?, Laugh It Off, Old Mother Riley Joins Up, Spies of the Air, Dead*

PEGGY CUMMINS
(20th Century-Fox)

Men Tell No Tales, Contraband, Old Mother Riley in Society, Gaslight, Crook's Tour, Old Mother Riley in Business, This England, Night Journey, He Found a Star, Headline, Bedelia, The White Unicorn, High Pavement.

CORRIGAN, Lloyd. Born San Francisco, Oct. 16, 1900. Educ. San Francisco ; Hollywood High School ; University of California. On stage at 7 ; during university days, appeared in repertory at Phoenix, Arizona ; screen debut in silent films with Bebe Daniels, 1924. Joined Paramount as writer for nine years, writing originals for Clara Bow, Bebe Daniels ; also *Dr. Fu Manchu, Anybody's Woman, Return of Fu Manchu,* and others. Became director from 1930 with *Along Came Ruth ;* also directed *Follow Through, No One Man, Daughter of the Dragon, Beloved Bachelor, The Broken Wing, He Learned about Women, La Cucaracha* (first film made in three-colour Technicolor), *Murder on a Honeymoon, Dancing Pirate, Night Key, Lady Behave.* Returned to screen acting in *High School* (20th), 1939. Other films include—1940 : *Young Tom Edison* (MGM), Elsa Maxwell's *Public Deb. No. 1* (20th), *Two Girls on Broadway* (20th) ; 1941 : *A Girl, a Guy and a Gob* (RKO), *Men of Boys' Town* (MGM) ; 1942 : *Bombay Clipper* (Univ), *North of the Klondyke* (Univ), *Treat 'Em Rough* (Univ), *The Great Man's Lady* (Para) ; *The Wife Takes a Flyer* (Col), *The Mystery of Marie Roget* (Univ), *Maisie Gets Her Man* (MGM), *Lucky Jordan* (Para) ; 1943 : *Hitler's Children* (RKO), *Secrets of the Underworld* (Rep), *King of the Cowboys* (Rep) ; 1944 : *Song of Nevada* (Rep), *Goodnight, Sweetheart* (Rep), *The Fighting Guardsman, The Thin Man Goes Home* (MGM), *Lake Placid Serenade* (Rep), *Since You Went Away* (UA) ; 1945 : *Crime Doctor's Courage* (Col) ; 1946 : *Bandit of Sherwood Forest* (Col).

COSTELLO, Lou. Real name Louis Francis Cristello. Born Paterson, New Jersey, Mar. 6, 1908. Ht. 5 ft. 4 in. ; wt. 180 lb. Black hair, brown eyes. Educ. New Jersey High School. Became prize fighter, drug-store attendant, hat shop salesman. Bought a car, drove to Hollywood, hired by MGM as studio labourer. Became stunt man, then comedian in burlesque, where he met Bud Abbott. They formed act, played for seven years, won fame on radio in Kate Smith programme. Appeared on Broadway in " Streets of Paris", signed by Universal for first film : *One Night in the Tropics* (1940). Other films (all Univ) include—1941 : *Buck Privates, In the Navy, Hold That Ghost, Keep 'Em Flying ;* 1942 : *Ride 'Em Cowboy, Rio Rita* (MGM), *Pardon My Sarong, Who Done It ;* 1943 : *It Ain't Hay, Hit the Ice ;* 1944 : *Lost in a Harem* (MGM), *In Society ;* 1945 : *Here Come the Co-Eds, The Naughty Nineties, In Hollywood ;* 1946 : *The Little Giant, The Time of their Lives ;* 1947 : *Rookies Come Home* (UI), *The Wistful Widow of Wagon Gap* (UI).

COTTEN, Joseph. Born Petersburg, Virginia, May 15, 1905. Ht. 6 ft. Fair hair, blue eyes. Youthful ambition : to be an actor. Became professional footballer, salesman, clerk and postman to earn money for dramatic training. Entered theatre life as drama critic, then actor on Broadway, 1930-40, in " Absent Father", " Accent on Youth", " The Postman Always Rings Twice", " The Philadelphia Story". Broadcast in series with Martha Scott in Orson Welles programme. Welles gave him first film part in *Citizen Kane* (RKO) 1940. Other films include—1941 : *Lydia* (Korda-Hollywood) ; 1942 : *The Magnificent Ambersons* (RKO), *Journey into Fear* (RKO) ; 1943 :

Shadow of a Doubt (Univ), *Hers to Hold,* (Univ) ; 1944 : *The Murder in Thornton Square* (MGM), *Since You Went Away* (UA) ; 1945 : *I'll Be Seeing You* (UA), *Love Letters* (Para) ; 1946 : *Duel in the Sun* (Selznick) ; 1947 : *The Farmer's Daughter* (RKO) ; 1948 : *Portrait of Jennie* (Selznick).

COURT, Hazel. Born Birmingham, Feb. 10, 1926. Ht. 5 ft. 4 in. ; wt. 110 lb. Auburn hair, green eyes. Studied at Birmingham School of Languages. Then decided on acting career : attended Birmingham School of Drama, and played with Birmingham Repertory Theatre while still a student. Film debut in *Champagne Charlie* (Ealing) 1945. Other films include —1946 : *Carnival* (Two Cities), *Gaiety George* (King) ; 1947 : *The Root of All Evil* (Gains), *Meet Me at Dawn* (Excelsior 20th), *Dear Murderer* (Gains), *Holiday Camp* (Gains) ; 1948 : *High Pavement* (Corfield).

COWARD, Noel. Actor, author, producer. Born Teddington, Middlesex, Dec. 16, 1899. As a boy-actor appeared in " Where the Rainbow Ends " and other successes. First film appearance was with Lillian Gish in scenes made in Britain by D. W. Griffith, for *Hearts of the World* (1918). Very early in his career achieved outstanding fame on the London stage as writer and actor in plays and revues. With Mary Clare in mind for the central character, Coward wrote and produced " Cavalcade ", filmed by Fox in 1932. To ensure accuracy in the Hollywood production a camera unit filmed an entire performance at Drury Lane Theatre, London. While appearing on the New York stage in 1933, Coward made *The Scoundrel* at Paramount's Long Island Studios. In the film *In Which We Serve,* he wrote the story, co-directed, and played the part of the ship's captain. Other works filmed include : *The Vortex, Bitter Sweet, Design for Living, Strange Interval, This Happy Breed, Blithe Spirit, Brief Encounter.*

COX, Jack. Director of photography. Born London, July 26, 1896. Educ. Worthing, Sussex. Entered films, 1912, as assistant director in converted tram-shed studio, Walthamstow. Borrowed £90 to screen a story he had found ; exteriors of this film, *Her Pony's Love,* were photographed by him at Bognor, Sussex. Later, worked with Director Maurice Elvey at Stoll Studios ; photographed fourteen films starring Matheson Lang. Also worked at Gaumont Studio and for British International Pictures, Elstree, photographing some of the first British talkies, including : *Blackmail, Murder, The Farmer's Wife, Champagne, The Ring* and *Juno and the Paycock.* Other films include : *The Skin Game, No. 17, Mimi, O.K. for Sound, Owd Bob, Crackerjack, Blighty, A Girl Must Live, The Lady Vanishes, They Came by Night, Charley's Big-Hearted Aunt, Neutral Port, The Ghost Train, Cottage to Let, We Dive at Dawn, 2000 Women, Madonna of the Seven Moons, They Were Sisters, The Wicked Lady, The Magic Bow, Holiday Camp, Idol of Paris.*

CRABBE, Buster. Real name Clarence Linden Crabbe. Born Oakland, California, U.S.A. Ht. 6 ft. 1 in. ; wt. 188 lb. Brown eyes, brown hair. Educ. University of Southern California. Became expert swimmer during boyhood at Hawaii. Made film debut in 1933 in jungle thrillers. Has appeared in many " Tarzan " films. Films include : *Wanderer of the Wasteland, Desert Gold, The Arizona Raiders, Murder Goes to College, Forlorn River, Thrill of a Lifetime, Hunted Men.* 1942-43 : *Billy the Kid* series (Pathé) ; 1946 : *Swamp Fire* (Para).

CRABTREE, Arthur. Director. Born Shipley, Yorks, Nov. 29, 1900. Became interested in photography as a boy and exhibited at London Salon of Photography and Royal Photographic Society, 1923-28. Entered film industry in 1929 as camera assistant with Alfred Hitchcock. Cameraman to Gaumont British in 1932. As director of photography, first film was *Wedding Group*, 1935 ; then director of photography on *Said O'Reilly to McNab, Bank Holiday, Convict 99, Alf's Button Afloat, Old Bones of the River, Where's That Fire, Frozen Limits, Kipps, Uncensored, The Man in Grey, Fanny by Gaslight, Dear Octopus, Waterloo Road*. Since 1944 has directed films, including : *Madonna of the Seven Moons, They Were Sisters, Caravan, Dear Murderer, The Calendar*.

CRAIG, James. Real name James H. Meador. Born Nashville, Tennessee, U.S.A., Feb. 4, 1912. Ht. 6 ft. 2½ in. ; wt. 190 lb. Black hair, brown eyes. Educ. grade and high schools, Nashville ; Rice University, Texas. During school days was news-boy, telegraph-boy, time-keeper, assistant to carpenters and electricians, farmhand, lorry driver. Went to Hollywood on holiday and secured film test, but was told to study acting. Spent year with Little Theatre, returned to Hollywood and made successful test. Has also appeared on Broadway ; gained screen recognition as Mark in *Kitty Foyle* (RKO) 1940. First film : *Thunder Trail* (Para) 1937. Other films include : *The Buccaneer, Big Broadcast of 1938, Born to the West, Pride of the West, Behind Prison Gates, North of Shanghai, The Taming of the West, The Man They Could Not Hang.* 1940 : *Zanzibar* (Univ), *Seven Sinners* (Univ), *South to Karanga* (Univ), *I'm Nobody's Sweetheart Now* (Univ), *Law and Order* (Univ) ; 1941 : *All That Money Can Buy* (RKO), *Unexpected Uncle* (RKO), *Valley of the Sun* (RKO), *Friendly Enemies* (UA) ; 1942 : *The Omaha Trail* (MGM), *Seven Miles from Alcatraz* (RKO), *North-West Rangers* (MGM) ; 1943 : *The Human Comedy* (MGM), *The Girl in Overalls* (MGM), *Lost Angel* (MGM), *The Heavenly Body ;* 1944 : *Kismet* (MGM), *Marriage Is a Private Affair* (MGM), *Gentle Annie* (MGM) ; 1945 : *Our Vines Have Tender Grapes* (MGM), *Dangerous Partners* (MGM), *She Went to the Races* (MGM), *Boy's Ranch ;* 1946 : *Little Mister Jim* (MGM) ; 1947 : *Cynthia's Secret* (MGM).

CRAIN, Jeanne. Born Barstow, California, U.S.A., May 25, 1925. Ht. 5 ft. 4½ in. ; wt. 114 lb. Light brown hair, hazel eyes. Educ. St. Mary's Academy ; Inglewood High School ; Los Angeles University. Played lead in school productions. In 1941 posed for magazine covers ; was " Miss Long Beach of 1941". Failed screen test for Orson Welles owing to nervousness. Later, made successful test for 20th-Fox. Films (all 20th)—1944 : *Home in Indiana, In the Meantime Darling ;* 1945 : *Winged Victory, State Fair, Leave Her to Heaven ;* 1946 : *Centennial Summer ;* 1947 : *Margie*.

CRAVEN, Frank. Born Boston, Massachusetts, U.S.A., 1878. Parents were members of famous Boston Stock Company. Made debut with them at age of 3 in " The Silver King". Played child roles with parents until 9 years old, then attended school in Reading, Pennsylvania. Became runner for a bank ; worked in insurance business ; returned to stage at 17, this time as an old man in " The Silver King". Began successful career in 1911 with three-year run in " Bought and Paid For", followed by " Too Many Cooks". Starred on Broadway for many years and is a veteran touring company player, known throughout every important city in U.S.A. Author of plays : " The New Year", " New Brooms", " Too Many Cooks", " The 19th Hole" ; successful stage producer, screen writer, musical comedy librettist, song lyric writer. First began his film career as writer ; sold his play " The First Year " to Fox and wrote script. Then acted in *The Very Idea* (RKO) 1929. Other films include : *Barbary Coast, Small Town Girl, Penrod and Sam, Miracles for Sale, Our Neighbours the Carters*. 1940 : *Our Town* (UA) (repeated stage success as narrator) ; *City for Conquest* (Warn) ; 1941 : *Lady from Cheyenne* (Univ), *Richest Man in Town* (Col). Visited Britain with stage tour of " Our Town" 1945-6.

CRAWFORD, Andrew. Born Glasgow, Oct. 24, 1917. Ht. 5 ft. 11½ in. ; wt. 180 lb. Brown hair, hazel eyes. Educ. Queen's Park, Glasgow. Youthful ambition : to be an artist. After Glasgow Art School and publicity job with local branch of Fox Films, became repertory actor in Glasgow, Ilkley, Leeds, Worcester. Served in World War II in air-crew, Bomber Command. Film producer Sydney Box added him to his Company of Youth on seeing him in " And No Birds Sing", Comedy Theatre, London, 1946. First film : *The Brothers* (Gains) 1946. 1947 : *Dear Murderer* (Gains), *Jassy* (Gains) ; 1948 : *Miranda* (Gains), *Broken Journey* (Gains), *London Belongs To Me* (Individ).

CRAWFORD, Anne. Real name Imelda Crawford. Born Haifa, Palestine, Nov. 22, 1920. Ht. 5 ft. 6 in. Fair hair, green eyes. Educ. St. Margaret's Convent, Edinburgh. At 10, wrote and produced play " The Witch and the Dream Fairies". First intended to become a barrister, but won elocution prizes and decided on stage. Trained at Royal Academy of Dramatic Art ; joined Manchester and York repertory companies, appearing in " Spring Meeting", " Outward Bound", " Rebecca", " The Insect Play", and other plays. Herbert Wilcox gave her first screen role in : *They Flew Alone*, 1942. Later films include—1942 : *The Peterville Diamond* (Warn Brit), *The Dark Tower* (Warn Brit) ; 1943 : *Night Invader* (Warn Brit), *The Hundred Pound Window* (Warn Brit), *Headline* (Corfield) *Millions Like Us* (Gains) ; 1944 : *2000 Women* (Gains) ; 1945 : *They Were Sisters*. Also in 1945 toured camps in France, Holland and Belgium for ENSA in " Love in a Mist ". 1946 : *Caravan* (Gains), *Bedelia* (Corfield) ; 1947 : *Master of Bankdam* (Holbein), *Night Beat* (LFP) ; 1948 : *Daughter of Darkness* (Alliance), *The Blind Goddess* (Gains).

CRAWFORD, Broderick. Son of Helen Broderick. Born Philadelphia, U.S.A., Dec. 9. Ht. 6 ft. 1 in. ; wt. 190 lb. After stage experience, made screen debut in *The Woman's Touch*, 1937. Films include : *Submarine D-1, Ambush, Undercover Doctor, The Real Glory, Eternally Yours*. 1940 : *Slightly Honourable* (UA), *I Can't Give You Anything but Love, Baby* (Univ), *When the Daltons Rode* (Univ) ; 1942 : *Butch Minds the Baby* (Univ), *Broadway* (Univ), *Sin Town* (Univ) ; 1946 : *The Runaround* (Univ), *Black Angel* (Univ) ; 1947 : *Slave Girl* (UI) ; 1948 : *The Time of Your Life* (Cagney-UA).

CRAWFORD, Joan. Real name Lucille LeSueur. Born San Antonio, Texas, U.S.A., Mar. 23, 1908. Ht. 5 ft. 4 in. ; wt. 110 lb. Red-brown hair, blue eyes. Educ. Kansas City (private schools) ; Stevens College. Columbia, Missouri. Youthful ambition : to be a dancer. Worked her way through college by serving as waitress in college dining-hall. Studied dancing in spare time. Became shop-girl in Kansas City ; then chorus girl for two weeks at Springfield, Massachusetts. Returned to store and saved enough money for second stage attempt. Became café revue dancer in Chicago, and within three months was in chorus of J. J. Shubert's " Innocent Eyes " in Chicago, followed by Broadway success. Was signed on long-term contract by MGM. First film : *Pretty Ladies*, 1925. Outstanding films include : *Sally Irene and Mary, West Point, Dancing Daughters, Our Blushing Brides, Dance Fools Dance, Paid, Laughing Sinners, This Modern Age, Possessed, Rain, Letty Lynton, Dancing Lady, Today We Live, Forsaking All Others, No More Ladies, I Live My Life, The Gorgeous Hussy, Love on the Run, The Last of Mrs. Cheyney, The Bride Wore Red, Mannequin, The Shining Hour, Ice Follies of 1939.* 1940 : *Susan and God* (MGM), *A Woman's Face* (MGM), *When Ladies Meet* (MGM) ; 1942 : *They All Kissed the Bride* (MGM) ; 1943 : *Reunion in France* (MGM), *Above Suspicion* (MGM), *Hollywood Canteen* (Warn) ; 1945 : *Mildred Pierce* (Warn) ; 1947 : *Humoresque* (Warn), *Possessed* (Warn) ; 1948 : *Daisy Kenyon* (20th).

CRICHTON, Charles. Director. Born New Brighton, Ches., 1911. Educ. Oxford University. After having been gold-prospector in Canada returned to Britain. Became interested in film production when Leontine Sagan and Zoltan Korda made Oxford exteriors for *Men of Tomorrow*. Entered films as cutting-room assistant at Denham Studios ; then film editor on *Things to Come, Elephant Boy, Prison without Bars, The Thief of Bagdad*, and others. Joined Ealing Studios as film editor ; then became director First film : *Find, Fix and Strike* (Ealing documentary) 1944, followed by other documentaries : *For Those in Peril* (story-documentary on men of the Air Sea Rescue branch of R.A.F.), *Painted Boats.* Also directed golfing sequence in *Dead of Night, Hue and Cry, Against the Wind.*

CRISP, Donald. Actor, director. Born London. Educ. Oxford University. Served in Army in Boer War, in British Secret Service in World War I, and in Intelligence branch of American Army in World War II. Went to America in 1906. Played in Grand Opera for a year, then stage director. Began film career in 1908 when he appeared in *The French Maid* for Biograph. Was Biograph stock player for two years, then for many years was director. Later, established studios in London, Paris and Berlin for the Famous Players company. During this period directed and starred in several films at Islington Studios (established by Famous Players) now owned by Gainsborough. Directed Douglas Fairbanks, Sr., in *The Mark of Zorro* and *Don Q*, and John Barrymore in *Svengali*. Later devoted whole time to acting. Films include : *The Little Minister, Mutiny on the Bounty, Laddie, The Charge of the Light Brigade, Mary of Scotland, The Life of Emile Zola, Jezebel, The Sisters, Dawn Patrol, Wuthering Heights.* 1940 : *The Sea Hawk* (Warn) ; 1941 : *Shining Victory* (Warn), *How Green Was My Valley* (20th) ; 1942 : *The Gay Sisters* (Warn) ; 1943 : *Forever and a Day* (RKO), *Lassie Come Home* (MGM) ; 1944 : *The Adventures of Mark Twain* (Warn), *The Uninvited* (Para) ; 1945 : *Son of Lassie, The Valley of Decision* (MGM) ; 1947 : *Ramrod* (Enterprise-MGM) ; 1948 : *Master of Lassie* (MGM).

CROMWELL, John. Director. Born Toledo, Ohio, Dec. 23, 1888. Educ. Howe School, Indiana. Began

his career in the theatre, first as actor, later also as stage manager. Became stage producer, 1923, but four years later returned to acting. While appearing in " The Rocket " in Los Angeles in 1928 he was given a Hollywood contract and made his screen debut in one of the first sound films there, *The Dummy* (Para) 1929. In same year directed his first film : *Close Harmony* (Para). Other films directed include : *Burlesque, Dance of Life, Tom Sawyer, For the Defence, The Texan, Street of Chance, Scandal Sheet, Seven Days' Leave, The Mighty, Unfaithful, Vice Squad, Rich Man's Folly, The World and the Flesh, Hell's Highway* (co-directed), *The Silver Cord, Double Harness, Ann Vickers, Sweepings, Spitfire* (RKO 1934). *Of Human Bondage* (RKO 1934), *The Fountain, Jalna, Village Tale, I Dream Too Much, Little Lord Fauntleroy, Banjo on my Knee, To Mary—With Love, Prisoner of Zenda* (UA 1937), *Algiers, Abe Lincoln in Illinois, So Ends Our Night, Son of Fury, Since You Went Away, The Enchanted Cottage, Anna and the King of Siam, Dead Reckoning, Night Song* (produced).

CRONIN, Archibald Joseph, M.D., M.R.C.P. Author. Born July 19, 1896. Educ. Glasgow University. Served in World War I as surgeon in R.N.V.R. Worked as a doctor until 1930. First novel : " Hatter's Castle " (1931). Works filmed : *The Citadel, Hatter's Castle, The Stars Look Down, The Keys of the Kingdom, The Green Years.*

CRONYN, Hume. Born London, Ontario, Canada, July 18. Ht. 5 ft. 7½ in. ; wt. 145 lb. Brown hair, blue eyes. Educ. Bishop Ridley College ; McGill University. Travelled Europe, East Indies, then became student at American Academy of Dramatic Art, later teaching there for four years. Played old mountaineer in " Mountain Ivy " and thereafter specialized in " old man " roles. On Broadway stage in " Three Men on a Horse ", " Room Service ", " Mr. Big ", " Three Sisters ", and other plays. Hitchcock gave him first film part in *Shadow of a Doubt* (Univ) 1943. Other films include—1943 : *Phantom of the Opera* (Univ), *The Cross of Lorraine* (MGM) *Lifeboat* (20th) ; 1944 : *The Seventh Cross* (MGM), *Main Street after Dark* (MGM) ; 1945 : *A Letter for Evie* (MGM), *The Postman Always Rings Twice* (MGM); 1946 : *The Sailor Takes a Wife* (MGM), *The Green Years* (MGM) ; 1947 : *The Beginning or the End ?* (MGM), *Brute Force* (UI) ; 1948 : *Love Bites Man.* (MGM).

CROSBY, Bing. Real name Harry Lillis Crosby. Born Tacoma, Washington, U.S.A., May 2, 1904. Ht. 5 ft. 9 in. ; wt. 165 lb. Brown hair, blue eyes. Educ. Webster School, Spokane ; Ganzaga University (which later bestowed on him the honorary degree of Mus. Doc.). Youthful ambition was the law, but became a drummer in a Spokane dance band, then singer in a trio with Paul Whiteman. Made film shorts for Mack Sennett, also recordings. Became famous as radio and stage crooner. First film : *The Big Broadcast of 1932* (Para). Films include : *College Humour, The Big Broadcast of 1936, Anything Goes, Going Hollywood, Rhythm on the Range, Too Much Harmony, Pennies from Heaven, We're Not Dressing, Waikiki Wedding, She Loves Me Not, Double or Nothing, Here Is My Heart, Doctor Rhythm, Mississippi, Sing You Sinners, East Side of Heaven, Paris Honeymoon, The Star Maker.* 1940 : 1940 : *Road to Singapore* (Para), *If I Had My Way* (Univ), *Rhythm on the River* (Para) ; 1941 : *Road to Zanzibar* (Para), *Birth of the Blues* (Para) ; 1942 : *Road to Morocco* (Para), *Holiday Inn*

(Para) ; 1943 : *Dixie* (Para), *Star Spangled Rhythm* (Para) ; 1944 : *Here Come the Waves* (Para), *Going My Way* (Para) ; 1945 : *The Bells of St. Mary's* (RKO), *Duffy's Tavern* (Para), *Road to Utopia* (Para) ; 1946 : *Blue Skies* (Para) ; 1947 : *Welcome Stranger* (Para), guest star in *Variety Girl* (Para), *Road to Rio* ; 1948 : *The Emperor Waltz* (Para), *A Connecticut Yankee* (Para).

CRUICKSHANK, Andrew. Born Aberdeen, Dec. 25, 1907. Ht. 5 ft. 11 in. Brown hair, green eyes. Educ. Aberdeen Grammar School. Trained for civil engineering, but after amateur appearances with Aberdeen Lyric Opera Society decided to become actor. Appeared in touring and repertory companies ; London debut at Savoy Theatre, 1930 in " Othello " with Paul Robeson. In New York, 1934, in " Richard of Bordeaux". 1937-9, with Old Vic Company in London and on their tours of Europe and Egypt. Served in army 1940-5, then resumed acting career. Author of plays, " Lysistrata " and " Adults Only". Entered films in 1938 with *Auld Lang Syne*. 1948 : *Idol of Paris* (Premier), *Mark of Cain* (Two Cities).

CUGAT, Xavier. Born Barcelona, Spain, Jan. 1. Ht. 5 ft. 8 in. Brown hair, blue eyes. As a youth was violinist with Enrico Caruso, who also taught him to draw. Well-known both as fifteen-minute caricaturist and as leader of Latin-American band. Film debut, 1936, in *Go West Young Man* (Para). Later films include : 1942 : *You Were Never Lovelier* (Col) ; 1943 : *Stage Door Canteen* (UA), *Tropicana* (Col) ; 1944 : *Two Girls and a Sailor* (MGM), *Bathing Beauty* (MGM) ; 1945 : *Weekend at the Waldorf* (MGM), *No Leave, No Love* (MGM) ; 1946 : *This Time for Keeps* (MGM), *Holiday in Mexico* (MGM) ; 1947 : *On an Island with You.*

CUKOR, George. Director. Born New York City. After service in student Army Training Corps, 1917-18, became assistant stage manager of Chicago company performing " The Better 'Ole ". Became Broadway stage manager ; created George Cukor Stock Company ; was first to introduce guest stars into touring companies. Produced Broadway plays including " Her Cardboard Lover", " The Constant Wife". To Hollywood, 1929. Co-director of *River of Romance* (Para) 1929 ; wrote dialogue for *All Quiet on the Western Front* ; co-directed *Grumpy, Virtuous Sin, The Royal Family* ; became sole director with *Tarnished Lady.* Is renowned for skill in directing women stars. Other films include : *Girls About Town, One Hour with You, Rockabye, What Price Hollywood, Bill of Divorcement* (RKO) 1932, *Dinner at Eight, Little Women, David Copperfield, Sylvia Scarlett, Romeo and Juliet, Camille, Holiday, Zaza, The Women, Susan and God, The Philadelphia Story, A Woman's Face, Two-Faced Woman, Her Cardboard Lover, Keeper of the Flame, The Murder in Thornton Square, Winged Victory, Desire Me, A Double Life.*

CULVER, Roland. Born London, Aug. 31, 1900. Educ. Highgate College. Trained at Royal Academy of Dramatic Art. London plays include : " Old Bachelor", " The Average Man", " Fortune", " French without Tears", " An Ideal Husband". Made screen debut in early British sound film : *77, Park Lane.* Films include : *Love on Wheels, Accused, French Without Tears* (1939, in which he made hit as naval commander). 1940 : *Night Train to Munich* (Gains), *Old Bill and Son* (Somlo) ; 1941 : *Quiet Wedding* (Soskin-Para Brit), *This England* (Brit Nat) ; 1942 :

The Day Will Dawn (Soskin), *Talk About Jacqueline* (Hellman), *Secret Mission* (Hellman) ; 1943 : *The First of the Few*—U.S. title, *Spitfire* (Leslie Howard) ; 1944 : *On Approval* (Clive Brook), *English Without Tears* (Two Cities), *Give Us the Moon* (Gains), *The Life and Death of Colonel Blimp* (Archers), *Dear Octopus* (Soskin) ; 1945 : *Dead of Night* (Ealing), *Perfect Strangers* (MGM-London). Went to Hollywood to appear in *To Each His Own* (Para) 1946. Since then he has made films in both Britain and U.S.A., including—1946 : *The Emperor Waltz* (Para), *Down to Earth* (Col) ; 1947 : *Wanted for Murder* (Excelsior), *Singapore* (Para).

CUMMINGS, Irving. Director. Born New York City, Oct. 9, 1888. Educ. New York. Left high school at age of 15, became messenger boy and spent free time frequenting theatres and agencies. Joined Proctor Stock Company as leading man. Entered films, 1909, at Mount Vernon, New York, playing lead in one-reeler *At the Window* (Pat Powers) and in five-reeler *The Last Volunteer* (Pathé). Became director for Fox. Films include : *Romance of the Underworld, Dressed to Kill, Behind That Curtain, In Old Arizona, Not Quite Decent, A Devil with Women, Holy Terror, The Mad Game, Grand Canary, It's a Small World, Curly Top, Poor Little Rich Girl, Little Miss Broadway, Just Around the Corner, Hollywood Cavalcade, Everything Happens at Night, Lillian Russell, Down Argentine Way, That Night in Rio, Belle Starr, My Girl Sal, Springtime in the Rockies, Sweet Rosie O'Grady, What a Woman, The Impatient Years, The Dolly Sisters.*

CUMMINGS, Robert. Real name Charles Clarence Robert Orville Cummings. Born Joplin, Missouri, U.S.A., June 9. Ht. 6 ft. 1 in. ; wt. 179 lb. Brown hair, blue eyes. Educ. Joplin High School ; Pittsburgh University. Youthful ambition to be an airman. When British play boom hit Broadway, he cycled round England to acquire accent ; returned to New York and made debut as " English " actor, Blade Stanhope Conway, in Galsworthy's " The Roof". In Texan role as lead in King Vidor's *So Red the Rose* (Para) 1935. Made about twenty films for Paramount and was planning return to Broadway when made new success in *Three Smart Girls Grow Up* (Univ), 1939. War service in U.S.A.A.F. Other films include : *Virginia Judge, Millions in the Air, Desert Gold, Border Flight, Three Cheers for Love, Forgotten Faces, Hollywood Boulevard, Hideway Girl, The Accusing Finger, Arizona Mahoney, Souls at Sea, Last Train from Madrid, Sophie Lang Goes West, Wells Fargo, College Swing, You and Me, Touchdown Army, I Stand Accused, The Under-Pup, Rio, Charlie McCarthy, Detective, Everything Happens at Night.* 1940 : *And One Was Beautiful* (MGM), *One Night in the Tropics* (Univ), *Spring Parade* (Univ) ; 1941 : *Moon over Miami* (20th), *Free and Easy* (MGM), *The Devil and Miss Jones* (RKO), *It Started with Eve* (Univ) ; 1942 : *Saboteur* (Univ), *Between Us Girls* (Univ), *King's Row* (Warn) ; 1943 : *Princess O'Rourke* (Warn), *Forever and a Day* (RKO) ; 1945 : *You Came Along* (Para) ; 1946 : *The Bride Wore Boots* (Para), *The Chase* (Seymour Nebenzal-UA); 1947 : *Heaven Only Knows* (Seymour Nebenzal-UA), *The Lost Moment* (Wanger) ; 1948 : *Sleep My Love* (Triangle-UA).

CUMMINS, Peggy. Born Prestatyn, North Wales, Dec. 8, 1925. Ht. 5 ft. 1 in. ; wt. 98 lb. Light blonde hair, blue-green eyes. Educ. Alexander School, Dublin. Childhood spent in Killiney, Dublin ; learned to dance at Abbey School of Ballet. Appeared at 7 in

" The Duchess of Malfi". Came to London, 1938, appeared in Gate Theatre productions, revue " Let's Pretend", and radio programmes. Seen by 20th-Fox scout while playing " Alice in Wonderland", and went to U.S.A. in 1946 for title role in *Forever Amber*, but she did not appear in the part. First film : *Dr. O'Dowd* (Warn Brit) 1939. Later films include : 1942 : *Salute John Citizen* (Brit Nat) ; 1943 : *English without Tears* (Two Cities), *Welcome Mr. Washington* (Brit Nat) ; 1947 : *The Late George Apley* (20th-Fox : her first American film), *Moss Rose* (20th). Returned to Britain, 1947, to appear in *Escape* (20th Brit).

CURTIS, Alan. Born Chicago, Illinois, U.S.A., July 24, 1909. Ht. 6 ft. ; wt, 180 lb. Black hair, hazel eyes. Educ. Senn High School, Chicago. Worked as model for John Powers Agency, New York ; also with agencies in Paris. Made French film short, advertising cars, which was seen by American producer who offered Hollywood contract. First film : *Winterset* (RKO) 1936. Later films include : *China Passage, Yellow Jack, Shopworn Angel, Duke of West Point, Hollywood Cavalcade.* 1940 : *Four Sons* (20th), *High Sierra* (20th) ; 1941 : *We Go Fast* (20th) ; 1943 : *Gung Ho* (Univ), *Hitler's Madmen* (MGM), *Two Tickets to London* (Univ) ; 1944 : *Follow the Boys* (Univ), *Invisible Man's Revenge* (Univ), *Phantom Lady* (Univ) ; 1945 : *See My Lawyer* (Univ), *The Naughty Nineties* (Univ), *Shady Lady* (Univ), *The Daltons Ride Again* (Univ).

CUSACK, Cyril. Born Durban, South Africa, 1910. Educ. New Bridge College, County Kildare ; University College, Dublin. Family tradition to go on the stage. In 1932 he joined the Abbey Theatre, Dublin, as actor and producer, where he remained for fourteen years, with occasional appearances on the London stage, notably in Eugene O'Neill's " Ah, Wilderness", and " Bride for the Unicorn", and opposite Vivien Leigh in " The Doctor's Dilemma". Made his film debut as Pat the driver in *Odd Man Out* (Two Cities) 1947. Other films—1948 : *Escape* (20th Brit), *Oliver Twist* (Cineguild), *Esther Waters* (Wessex).

DAILEY, Dan, Jr. Born New York City, Dec. 14. Ht. 6 ft. 1 in. ; wt. 185 lb. Fair hair. Brought up in theatrical colony at Baldwin, Long Island, and appeared in local stage productions when a child. Became dancer in vaudeville and cabaret ; has also been grocer's assistant, waiter, caddy, shoe salesman. In cast of stage show " Babes in Arms", then returned to business before becoming free-lance entertainer. Juvenile lead in " I Married an Angel". While playing in Hollywood, seen by film scout. First film : *The Mortal Storm* (MGM) 1940. Other films include— 1940 : *The Captain Is a Lady* (MGM), *Dulcy* (MGM), *Hullabaloo* (MGM), *Keeping Company* (MGM) ; 1941 : *Wild Man of Borneo* (MGM), *Ziegfeld Girl* (MGM), *Washington Melodrama* (MGM), *The Getaway* (MGM), *Moon Over Her Shoulder* (20th), *Down in San Diego* (MGM), *Lady Be Good* (MGM) ; 1942 : *Panama Hattie* (MGM), *Mokey* (MGM), *Sunday Punch* (MGM), *Give Out, Sisters* (Univ). 1942-6, on war service. 1947 : *Mother Wore Tights* (20th).

DALEY, Cass. Real name Katharine Daley. Born Philadelphia, July 17, 1915. Worked for several years from age of 14 as stocking trimmer in hosiery mill. Became comedy singer in New York Clubs, was featured in " Ziegfeld Follies", toured America and Britain (1938) in vaudeville. Was playing five shows a day in Cleveland when she was signed to appear in *The Fleet's In* (Para) 1942. Later films include—1943 : *Riding High* (Para), *Star Spangled Rhythm* (Para), *Crazy House* (Univ) ; 1945 : *Out of This World* (Para), *Duffy's Tavern* (Para) ; 1946 : *Ladies' Man* (Para).

DALL, John. Born Manhattan, New York City, May 26, 1918. Ht. 6 ft. 1 in. ; wt. 165 lb. Brown hair, blue-grey eyes. Educ. high school ; Columbia University. Left college to train as actor. Joined Clare Tree Major's Children's Theatre ; success on Broadway. Had small part in *For the Love of Mary*, 1939. First important role in *The Corn Is Green* (Warn) 1945. In 1947 made : *Something in the Wind* (UI) ; 1948 : *Another Part of the Forest* (UI).

DALRYMPLE, Ian. Producer, director. Born in the Transvaal, South Africa, Aug. 26, 1903. Educ. Rugby School ; Trinity College, Cambridge. Entered films in silent days, started in editing and cutting departments, working on such films as *The Constant Nymph* and *Taxi for Two*. Later films, as supervising editor, include : *Rome Express, The Good Companions, I Was a Spy, Little Friend, Evergreen, The Man Who Knew Too Much, Jew Süss*. Worked as writer on : *South Riding, Action for Slander, Storm in a Teacup, The Divorce of Lady X, The Citadel*. Scenario writer and producer of *The Lion Has Wings*— Britain's first propaganda film of World War II. Was Producer-in-Chief of Crown Film Unit during the war. Producer of : *London Can Take It, Listen To Britain, Ferry Pilot, Target for Tonight, Close Quarters, Coastal Command, Western Approaches*. In 1946 formed Wessex Film Productions ; co-produced *The Woman in the Hall ;* co-produced and co-directed *Esther Waters*.

DALY, Mark. Born Edinburgh, Aug. 23, 1887. Educ. George Heriot School, Edinburgh. Stage debut, Court Theatre, Swansea, Sept. 1906, in " The Woman from Gaol". Played in provincial concert parties and pantomime till 1912, when he appeared at Shaftesbury Theatre, London, in " Princess Caprice". After service in World War I, toured as principal comedian with Fred Karno's companies ; played in Australia 1922-5 ; returned to England to appear in variety, pantomime and West-End plays. Screen debut in 1930. Films include : *The Private Life of Henry VIII, The Ghost Goes West, Lilac Time, Knight without Armour, Command Performance, Ten Days in Paris, Next of Kin, The Big Blockade*. In 1946 was teamed with Graham Moffat for Children's Entertainment Films : has appeared in six episodes of *The Voyage of Peter Joe*, and *Stage Fright*.

DANE, Clemence. Dramatist and novelist. Real name Winifred Ashton. Born Blackheath, London. Formerly artist and actress under the name of Diana Portis. Plays include : " A Bill of Divorcement", " Will Shakespeare", " The Happy Hypocrite " (based on story by Max Beerbohm). Novels include : " Broome Stages " (a novel about a stage family), " The Nelson Touch," " Perfect Strangers". Filmed : *A Bill of Divorcement ; Perfect Strangers*, in which she also collaborated on screenplay. Has also written many film scripts.

DANE, Patricia. Born Jacksonville, Florida. Ht. 5 ft. 4 in. ; wt. 112 lb. Made first public appearance at 10 when she won amateur dancing contest. Left University of Alabama to be fashion designer in New York. Then went to Hollywood for holiday and stayed there. Film debut in *Ziegfeld Girl* (MGM)

YVONNE DE CARLO
(*Universal-International*)

1941. Later films include—1941: *I'll Wait for You* (MGM), *Life Begins for Andy Hardy* (MGM), *Johnny Eager* (MGM); 1942: *Rio Rita* (MGM), *Grand Central Murder* (MGM), *Somewhere I'll Find You* (MGM), *Northwest Rangers* (MGM); 1943: *I Dood It* (MGM).

DANTINE, Helmut. Born Vienna, Austria, Oct. 7, 1918. Ht. 6 ft.; wt. 160 lb. Brown hair, grey eyes. Educ. Europe; University of California. Trained for Austrian diplomatic service; army officer when Hitler invaded Austria. After brief internment, was given freedom on condition he left country. Joined American relatives in California, who sent him to University, intending him for business career in Middle West. Instead joined Pasadena Community Playhouse and opened two petrol stations to earn money while studying acting. Seen in play and signed for first film: *International Squadron* (Warn 1941). Other films include—1942: *Mrs. Miniver* (MGM), in which he attracted attention as wounded German airman, *Casablanca* (Warn); 1943 (all Warner): *Edge of Darkness, Northern Pursuit, Mission to Moscow*; 1944: *Passage to Marseille, Hollywood Canteen, Mask of Dimitrios*; 1945: *Hotel Berlin, Escape in the Desert*; 1946; *Shadow of a Woman*.

DARNELL, Linda. Born Dallas, Texas, Oct. 16. Ht. 5 ft. 4¾ in; wt. 109 lb. Brown hair, brown eyes. Educ. Sunset High School, Dallas. On Dallas stage with Cathedral Players of St. Matthew's Church; Civic Theatre; New Theatre League. Tested for films in 1938, considered too young, but later won contract with 20th-Fox. First film: *Hotel for Women* 1939. Other films include: *Daytime Wife*; 1940: *Stardust* (20th), *Brigham Young* (20th), *Mark of Zorro* (20th), *Chad Hanna* (20th); 1941: *Blood and Sand* (20th), *Rise and Shine* (20th); 1942: *The Loves of Edgar Allan Poe* (20th); 1944: *Buffalo Bill* (20th), *It Happened Tomorrow* (UA), *Summer Storm* (UA), *Sweet and Lowdown* (20th); 1945: *The Great John L.* (UA), *Fallen Angel* (20th), *Hangover Square* (20th); 1946: *Anna and the King of Siam* (20th), *Centennial Summer* (20th), *My Darling Clementine* (20th); 1947: *Forever Amber* (20th); 1948: *The Walls of Jericho* (20th).

DA SILVA, Howard. Born Cleveland, Ohio, May 4, 1909. Ht. 6 ft.; wt. 170 lb. Educ. Carnegie Institute. Played in student theatricals; paid for course at Carnegie Technical School of Drama by working in steel mills. Joined apprentice acting group in New York; then on tour for four years. Directed and acted on Broadway and in Cleveland. Film debut in *Once in a Blue Moon* (Para) 1936. Other films include—1940: *Abe Lincoln in Illinois* (RKO), *I'm Still Alive* (RKO); 1941: *Strange Alibi* (Warn), *The Sea Wolf* (Warn), *Nine Lives Are Not Enough* (Warn), *Bad Men of Missouri* (Warn), *Sergeant York* (Warn); 1942: *Juke Girl* (Warn), *Reunion in France* (MGM), *Omaha Trail* (MGM), *Keeper of the Flame* (MGM); 1943: *Tonight We Raid Calais* (20th), *Duffy's Tavern* (Para), *The Lost Weekend* (Para); 1945: *Two Years Before the Mast*; 1946: *The Blue Dahlia* (Para); 1947: *Unconquered* (Para), *Blaze of Noon* (Para), *Your Red Wagon* (RKO).

DAVENPORT, Harry. One of the " grand old men " of films. Born New York, Jan. 19, 1866. Child actor from age of 6. Began film career as a director with Vitagraph Company in 1912. More than twenty years later made debut as a film actor with

Noel Coward in *The Scoundrel* (Para), 1935. Has played hundreds of character roles since then, among them Doctor Meade in *Gone With The Wind*, 1939. Recent films include—1943: *Jack London* (UA), *Princess O'Rourke* (Warn), *Strange Incident* (20th); 1944: *Meet Me in St. Louis* (MGM), *Music for Millions* (MGM); 1945: *This Love of Ours* (Univ), *Pardon My Past* (Col), *Too Young to Know* (Warn); 1946: *Adventure* (MGM), *Enchanted Forest* (Pathé); 1947: *Bachelor Knight* (RKO).

DAVIES, John Howard. Born London, Mar. 9, 1939. Fair hair, blue eyes. Educ. The Hall School, Hampstead. Unexpectedly won title-role in *Oliver Twist* (Cineguild) 1948, through meeting film agent who was a friend of his father. Although below legal age, was allowed to appear in this film after hundreds of older children had been tested without success.

DAVIS, Bette. Real name Ruth Elizabeth Davis. Born Lowell, Massachusetts, U.S.A., Apr. 5, 1908. Ht. 5 ft. 3 in.; wt. 112 lb. Fair hair, blue eyes. Educ. Cushing Academy, Ashburnham, Massachusetts. Left school 1926; kept house at home for one year; joined John Murray Dramatic School, New York. Stage debut, Chicago, 1928, with George Cukor Stock Company on Broadway. Later appeared in New York in " The Earth Between ", Ibsen's " The Wild Duck ", and other plays. To Hollywood to appear in *Bad Sister* (Univ) 1931; but developed inferiority complex before cameras, and contract was not renewed at end of year. George Arliss gave her fresh chance in *The Man Who Played God* (Warn) 1932, and, later, fame came to her with *Of Human Bondage* (RKO) 1934. Her other films include: *Bureau of Missing Persons, Waterloo Bridge* (Univ) 1931, *Parachute Jumper, Other People's Business, The Working Man, The Big Shakedown, The Dark Horse, The Rich Are Always with Us, Jimmy the Gent, Fog over 'Frisco, So Big, Cabin in the Cotton, Housewife, Three on a Match, 20,000 Years in Sing-Sing, Bordertown, Ex-Lady, The Girl from 10th Avenue, Fashion Follies of 1934, Front Page Woman, Special Agent, Dangerous, The Petrified Forest, Satan Met a Lady, The Golden Arrow, Marked Woman, Kid Galahad, It's Love I'm After, Jezebel, The Sisters, Dark Victory, Juarez, The Old Maid, The Private Lives of Elizabeth and Essex.* 1940 (all Warner): *All This and Heaven Too, The Letter*; 1941: *The Great Lie, The Bride Came C.O.D., The Man Who Came to Dinner, The Little Foxes* (RKO); 1942: *In This Our Life, Now Voyager*; 1943: *Watch on the Rhine, Old Acquaintance, Thank Your Lucky Stars*; 1944: *Mr. Skeffington, Hollywood Canteen*; 1945: *The Corn Is Green*; 1946: *Stolen Life, Deception*, 1948: *Winter Meeting*.

DAY, Josette. Born Paris. At 9 was a dancer at the Opéra; at 15 made screen debut in a Henri Fescourt production. Her films include: *Serments* (made in Sweden), *Sœur d'Armes* and *L'Homme du Jour* with Maurice Chevalier, *Monsieur Bretonneau* with Raimu, *La Fille du Puisatier* (*The Well-Digger's Daughter*), *Arlette et l'Amour, La Belle et la Bête.*

DAY, Laraine. Real name Laraine Johnson. Born Roosevelt, Utah, Oct. 13, 1920. Ht. 5 ft. 5 in.; wt. 112 lb. Light brown hair, blue eyes. Educ. Long Beach High School, California. Took part in family plays as a child. Studied acting under Elias Day, whose name she adopted professionally. Acted in local theatre and spotted there by Hollywood agent taking refuge from storm. First screen appearance in soda fountain scene of *Stella Dallas* (UA) 1937 ; then in several Westerns. Other films include *Scandal Sheet, Sergeant Madden* and the *Dr. Kildare* series, in one of which she had to be " killed off " so she could leave series and make other films. Later films include —1940 : *My Son, My Son* (UA), *Foreign Correspondent* (UA) ; 1941 : *The Trial of Mary Dugan* (MGM), *Unholy Partners* (MGM), *Kathleen* (MGM) ; 1942 : *Fingers at the Window* (MGM), *Journey for Margaret* (MGM) ; 1943 : *Mr. Lucky* (RKO), *The Story of Dr. Wassell* (Para), *Bride by Mistake* (RKO) ; 1945 : *Those Endearing Young Charms* (RKO), *Keep Your Powder Dry* (MGM) ; 1946 : *The Locket* (RKO) ; 1947 : *Tycoon* (RKO).

DEARDEN, Basil. Director. Born Westcliff-on-Sea, Essex, Jan. 1, 1911. Brother of Peter Dearing, actor-producer, and Peggy Dear, stage manager. Worked as London office boy, and in holidays took " walking-on " parts in Ben Greet Shakespearean productions. Became assistant stage manager Grand Theatre, Fulham, London, for one year ; then joined Ben Greet Company and toured America in one-night stands. Returned to London and became stage production manager to Basil Dean for five years. Wrote and produced " Under Suspicion", Playhouse, London. Became assistant to Basil Dean at Ealing Studios, and there from 1937 worked under Michael Balcon as associate producer, writer and (from 1940) director. After having worked on George Formby and Will Hay comedies, he directed *The Bells Go Down, The Halfway House, They Came to a City*, and the " bus " sequence and linking story of *Dead of Night*. Co-directed *The Captive Heart*, and directed *Frieda, Saraband for Dead Lovers*.

DE CAMP, Rosemary. Born Prescott, Arizona, Nov. 14. Ht. 5 ft. 2 in. ; wt. 112 lb. Black hair, hazel eyes. Educ. Prescott Grammar School ; Mills College (M.A., Drama). At 14 was in Little Theatre productions in Phoenix, Arizona ; at 21 was retained at college as drama teacher. Played in repertory and on tour. In New York understudied in " Merrily We Roll Along " ; was drama critic for the " Morning Telegraph " ; played in repertory and radio drama. Martha Scott sponsored her for role in first film : *Cheers for Miss Bishop* (UA) 1941. Other films include—1942 : *Eyes in the Night* (MGM), *Jungle Book* (UA), *Smith of Minnesota* (Col) ; 1943 : *Yankee Doodle Dandy* (Warn), *This Is the Army* (Warn). 1944 : *The Merry Monahans* (Univ), *Practically Yours* (Para) ; 1945 : *Rhapsody in Blue* (Warn), *Danger Signal* (Warn), *Too Young to Know* (Warn), *Blood on the Sun* (UA), *Forever in Love* (Warn) ; 1946 : *From This Day Forward* (RKO) ; 1947 : *Royal Flush* (Warn).

DE CARLO, Yvonne. Born Vancouver, B.C., Sept. 1, 1924. Real name Peggy Yvonne Middleton. Ht. 5 ft. 4¼ in. ; wt. 117 lb. Dark brown hair, blue-grey eyes. Educ. King Edward's High School ; Vancouver, Studied dancing June Roper School, Vancouver ; appeared at Vancouver Little Theatre ; became featured dancer at local theatres. From 1937 to 1941 paid yearly visits to Hollywood for training ; and appeared in her own numbers at Hollywood night clubs and theatres. Nearly took over " sarong " roles from Dorothy Lamour, but instead played only small parts. In 1944 her cousin and twenty of his fellow flyers of the R.C.A.F. submitted her photo in Walter Wanger's search for " the most beautiful girl in the world ". As a result won lead in *Salome, Where She Danced*. First film : *This Gun for Hire* (Para) 1942. Later films include : *Harvard Here I Come* (Col), *Youth on Parade* (Rep), *Road to Morocco* (Para) ; 1944 : *Story of Dr. Wassell* (Para) ; 1945 : *Salome, Where She Danced* (Univ), *Frontier Gal* (Univ) ; 1946 : *The Bride Wasn't Willing* (Univ), *Song of Scheherazade* (Univ) ; 1947 : *Brute Force* (UI), *Slave Girl* (UI) ; 1948 : *River Lady* (UI), *Adventures of Black Bart* (UI), *Casbah* (UI).

DE CORDOVA, Arturo. Real name Arturo Garcia. Born Merida, Yucatan, Mexico, May 8, 1908. Ht. 5 ft. 11½ in. ; wt. 155 lb. Dark brown hair, brown eyes. Educ. New York Public Schools ; Buenos Ayres ; and in dairy-farming at the Cavin Institute, Lausanne, Switzerland. First was sports writer for the United Press ; later on Mexican radio, then made his first film, *Jealousy*, produced by a Russian theatrical producer, Arcady Boytler, in Mexico City in 1934. When he saw himself on the screen decided to remain in radio, but was persuaded to try again, in another Mexican film, *Ceilito Lindo*, followed by *La Zandunga, La Noche de los Mayas, Son's Command* (Spanish version, in Hollywood), *Refugiados en Madrid, The Miracle of Main Street* (Spanish version, in Hollywood). 1940 : *Mientras Mexico Duerme, The Count of Monte Cristo, Alexandra*, all in Mexico. Went to Hollywood 1942. First film there, 1943 : *For Whom the Bell Tolls* (Para). Also 1943, *Hostages* (Para). 1944 : *Frenchman's Creek* (Para), *Incendiary Blonde* (Para), *A Medal for Benny* (Para), *Twilight* (Casa-Mexico) ; 1945 : *Masquerade in Mexico* (Para) ; 1946 : *The Flame* (Para) ; 1947 : *New Orleans* (Jules Levy-UA).

DE FILIPPO, Edoardo—known as " E'Duardo". Born Naples, 1900. Began professional career as a writer of plays for the legitimate theatre, in the Neapolitan dialect ; later became actor. Wrote and appeared in " Napoli Milionara", " Questi Fantasmi", " Filumena Marturano". Has also starred in a number of films, including : *Tre Uomini in Frak, Il Marchese Rabolit, A Che Servono Questi Quattrini, Ma l'Amor Mio Non Muore*.

DE FILIPPO, Peppino. Brother of " E'Duardo". Born Naples, 1906. Like many leading players in the Italian cinema, comes from the theatre, where he has a high reputation as a comedy actor, specializing in dialects, which is considered an outstanding qualification today. Films include : *Il Cappello A Tre Punte, Ma l'Amor Mio Non Muore, Notte di Forunna, Il Sogno di Tutti, A Che Servono Questi Quattrini, Campo de' Fiori* (Amato) 1942.

DEFORE, Don. Born Cedar Rapids, Iowa, Aug. 25, 1917. Ht. 6 ft. 2 in. ; wt. 190 lb. Brown hair, green eyes. Educ. Washington High School, Cedar Rapids ; University of Iowa. Joined Cedar Rapids Community Players, then won scholarship to Pasadena Playhouse, California. Stage plays include, on Broadway ; " The Male Animal", " Sailor Beware", and " The Hasty Heart". Film debut : *We Go Fast* (20th) 1941. Later films include—1941 : *The Male Animal* (Warn) ; 1943 : *City without Men* (Col), *The Human Comedy* (MGM) ; 1944 : *A Guy Named Joe* (MGM), *Thirty Seconds Over Tokyo* (MGM) ; 1945 : *The Affairs of Susan* (Para), *You Came Along* (Para), *The Stork Club* (Para) ; 1946 : *Without Reservations* (RKO) ; 1947 : *It Happened on Fifth Avenue* (Mono), *Ramrod* (Enterprise-MGM) ; 1948 : *Romance in High C* (Warn).

DE GRUNWALD, Anatole. Writer, producer. Born St. Petersburg (now Leningrad), 1910. Educ. Paris ; Cambridge University (Modern Languages). Entered films as a scriptwriter, on *French without Tears* (Two Cities) 1939. Also wrote scripts for : *Freedom Radio, Major Barbara, Quiet Wedding, Pimpernel Smith, Jeannie, The First of the Few, English without Tears, Unpublished Story, Tomorrow We Live.* Produced : *The Demi-Paradise, The Way to the Stars,* which won the "Daily Mail" Film Award for 1945. In association with Anthony Asquith and Terence Rattigan formed International Screenplays Ltd., 1946, and its subsidiary company World Screenplays Ltd., 1947. Produced *While the Sun Shines, Bond Street, The Winslow Boy, Queen of Spades.*

DE HAVEN, Gloria. Born Los Angeles, California, July 23. Blonde hair, blue eyes. Ht. 5 ft. 2½ in.; wt. 112 lb. Trained for stage with Edward Clark's Little Theatre and sang with Bob Crosby and Jan Savitt bands. Screen debut in : *Susan and God* (MGM) 1940. Other films include—1940 : *When Ladies Meet* (MGM), *Keeping Company* (MGM) ; 1941 : *The Great Dictator* (UA), *The Penalty* (MGM) ; 1943 : *Best Foot Forward* (MGM), *Thousands Cheer* (MGM), *Broadway Rhythm* (MGM) ; 1944 : *Two Girls and a Sailor* (MGM), *Step Lively* (RKO), *The Thin Man Goes Home* (MGM) ; 1945 : *Between Two Women* (MGM) ; 1947 : *Summer Holiday* (MGM).

DE HAVEN, Robert. Born San Diego, California, Jan 13, 1922. Educ. North Hollywood High School Washington and Lee University, Virginia. Left engineering studies for war service in U.S.A.A.F. As schoolboy, had sold magazines at main entrance to Columbia Pictures Studio. Returned there, 1946, to renew acquaintance with studio gateman ; was seen by executive, tested and signed up all in one day. First film : *Gallant Journey* (Col) 1947.

DE HAVILLAND, Olivia. Born Tokio, Japan, July 1, 1916. Sister of Joan Fontaine. Ht. 5 ft. 3 in. Brown hair, brown eyes. Educ. Notre Dame Convent; Belmont High School, Saratoga, California. Intended to become teacher ; saved money for college career by teaching Latin and working in library. Understudy in Max Reinhardt's stage production of "A Midsummer Night's Dream", and made her screen debut as Hermia in the film version, 1935. Other films include : *Anthony Adverse, The Great Garrick, Four's a Crowd, Dodge City, Gone with the Wind, Captain Blood.* 1940 : *Santa Fe Trail* (FN) ; 1941 : *Strawberry Blonde* (FN), *Hold Back the Dawn* (Para) ; 1942 : *The Male Animal* (Warn), *In This Our Life* (Warn) ; 1943 : *Devotion* (Warn), *Government Girl* (RKO), *Princess O'Rourke* (Warn), *Thank Your Lucky Stars* (Warn) ; 1945 : *The Dark Mirror* (Univ), *To Each His Own* (Para), *The Well-Groomed Bride* (Para) ; 1947 : *Ivy* (UI) ; 1948 : *The Snake Pit* (20th).

DEL GIUDICE, Filippo. Producer. Born Trani, Southern Italy, Mar. 26, 1892. Educ. University of Rome (LL.D.). Began career as attorney. Came to Britain, 1933, as legal expert on cases of domicile and nationality. In association with Toeplitz, Sassoon and Crosfield, founded nucleus of Two Cities Films Ltd., first as legal adviser. Began producing, 1939, with *French without Tears* and *Freedom Radio.* Interned in Isle of Man, 1939-40. On release, became managing director of Two Cities Films. Films he produced include : *Unpublished Story, In Which We Serve, The Gentle Sex, Henry V, Tawny Pipit, The Way Ahead,*

This Happy Breed, The Flemish Farm, The Demi-Paradise, English Without Tears, Blithe Spirit, The Way to the Stars, Carnival, School for Secrets, Men of Two Worlds, Beware of Pity. 1947, formed his own company, Pilgrim Pictures Ltd.

DEL POGGIO, Carla. Actress. Born Naples, 1924. Films include : *Maddalena, Zero in Condotta, La Bocca Sulla Strada, La Scuola dei Timidi, Violette Nei Capelli, C'è Sempre Una Sua, Uno Garibaldino al Convento.* 1945 : *Umanità* (Luce Nuova) ; 1946 : *Il Bandito* (Lux), *L'Angelo e il Diavolo* (Lore) ; 1947 : *Caccia Tragica* (ANPC).

DEMAREST, William. Born St. Paul, Minnesota, Feb. 27, 1892. On stage in vaudeville, 1905, then in repertory ; 'cellist in dance band ; professional boxer ; in carnival act. 1930-3, on New York stage. Screen debut : *Fingerprints* (Warn) 1927. Returned to screen in *Diamond Jim* (Univ) 1935. Became talent scout for a year, discovering Ellen Drew and Jane Wyman. Resumed films with *Wedding Present* (Para) 1936. Films include : *Love on the Run, Big City, Rebecca of Sunnybrook Farm, Mr. Smith Goes to Washington.* 1940 : *The Great McGinty* (Para) ; 1941 : *Sullivan's Travels* (Para) ; 1942 : *Pardon My Sarong* (Univ), *The Palm Beach Story* (Para) ; 1943 : *True to Life* (Para), *Dangerous Blondes* (Col), *The Great Moment ;* 1944 : *The Miracle of Morgan's Creek* (Para), *Hail the Conquering Hero* (Para), *Nine Girls* (Col), *Once Upon a Time* (Col) ; 1945 : *Pardon My Past* (Col : his hundredth featured film role), *Salty O'Rourke* (Para), *Duffy's Tavern* (Para), *Along Came Jones* (RKO) ; 1946 : *The Jolson Story* (Col) ; 1947 : *The Perils of Pauline* (Col), *Variety Girl* (Para).

DE MARNEY, Derrick. Actor, producer. Born London, Sept. 21, 1906. Dark hair, grey eyes. Stage debut in 1923 at Theatre Royal, Bury St. Edmunds, Suffolk, in "The Admiral's Lady" ; London debut, 1926, in "All The King's Horses", Globe Theatre. Between 1926 and 1930, appeared in "Romance", "Young Woodley", and other plays in London. In 1930 to New York, where his plays included "Young Mr. Disraeli". On the screen since 1936. Films include : *Things to Come, Windfall, Café Mascot, Land without Music, Pearls of the Crown* (French production with Sacha Guitry), *Young and Innocent, Victoria the Great, The Blonde Cheat* (for RKO in Hollywood, 1938), *Sixty Glorious Years, The Spider, The Lion Has Wings.* 1940 : *Three Silent Men* (Butcher), *Dangerous Moonlight* (RKO Brit) ; 1942 : *The First of the Few* (Leslie Howard Productions). In 1940 formed Concanen Films and became producer and director of many short films for British M.O.I. and Polish Government during next five years. Film on immunization against diphtheria was chosen by UNESCO Festival in Paris as best educational documentary. In 1943 produced feature film *The Gentle Sex* (Concanen-Two Cities) ; 1946, co-produced and acted in *Latin Quarter* (Brit Nat) ; 1947 : *Uncle Silas* (Two Cities).

DE MILLE, Cecil Blount. Producer. Born Ashfield, Massachusetts, U.S.A., Aug. 12, 1881. Educ. Pennsylvania Military College. Comes of play-writing family; with brother William wrote "The Stampede", "The Royal Mounted", and, with David Belasco, "The Return of Peter Grimm". Trained at American Academy of Dramatic Art, became actor in New York. Entered film industry, 1913, in association with Jesse L. Lasky : directed *The Squaw Man* and thereafter became a leader in the American film industry and " father " of the spectacular film. Directed many films for Lasky's company and its successors : in 1925 joined Producers' Distributing Corporation as producer and director ; subsequently produced for MGM and Paramount. Silent films include : *The Ten Commandments, King of Kings, Carmen, Joan the Woman, The Woman God Forgot, The Volga Boatman, Male and Female, Manslaughter, Don't Change Your Husband, Old Wives for New*. Most lavish spectacle, *The Sign of the Cross* (Para) 1933. Later films include : *Cleopatra, The Plainsman, Union Pacific, North-West Mounted Police, Reap the Wild Wind, Story of Dr. Wassell, Unconquered*. In preparation, 1948, *Samson and Delilah*.

DENIS, Maria. Born Buenos Aires, 1910. One of Italy's best-known stars. Films include : *Seconda B, La Contessa di Parma, Belle o Brutte si Sposan Tutte, I due Misantropi, Napoli d'Altri Tempe, Partire, Le Due Madri, L'Assedio dell'Alcazar, Addio Giovinezza, Sissignora, La Maestrina*. 1944 : *La Bohème* (Scalera), *Nessuno Torna Indietro* (Artisti Associati) ; 1945 : *Malia* (Amato) ; 1946 : *Cronaca Nera* (Aurea), *La Danza della Morte* (Ardea-Alcine).

DENISON, Michael. Born 1917. Ht. 6 ft. ; wt. 154 lb. Dark hair, blue eyes. Educ. Oxford, where he appeared with Oxford University Dramatic Society. Professional stage debut with Vivien Leigh in John Gielgud's production of " Richard II", later in " As You Like It " with Nova Pilbeam. Later trained at Webber-Douglas School of Dramatics. First London appearance in " Troilus and Cressida " at the Westminster Theatre ; then in " Dangerous Corner". Film debut in *Tilly of Bloomsbury* (Gains) 1939. During World War II, served in Army. 1947 : *Hungry Hill* (Two Cities) ; 1948 : *My Brother Jonathan* (ABPC), *Blind Goddess* (Gains).

DENNING, Richard. Real name Louis A. Denninger. Born Poughkeepsie, New York, Mar. 27. Ht. 6 ft 2 in. ; wt. 185 lb. Fair hair, blue eyes. Educ. Manual Arts College ; Woodbury Business College, Los Angeles. Originally planned to become doctor, but went into business and rose from mail boy to vice-president. Joined night school drama classes and was seen in play by talent scout. First film : *Hold 'Em Navy !* (Para) 1937. In five years appeared in about fifty films, playing opposite Dorothy Lamour in *Beyond the Blue Horizon* (Para) 1942. Films include : *Big Broadcast of 1938, The Buccaneer, College Swing, Daughter of Shanghai, Her Jungle Love, The Texans, Give Me a Sailor, Touchdown, Zaza, King of Alcatraz, Illegal Traffic, Arkansas Traveller, Say It in French, King of Chinatown, Ambush, Persons in Hiding, I'm from Missouri, Federal Offence, Grand Jury Secrets, Sudden Money, Union Pacific, Some Like It Hot, Gracie Allen Murder Case, Star Maker, Hotel Imperial, Geronimo, Million Dollar Legs, Disputed Passage, Television Spy, Our Neighbours the Carters, Undercover Doctor*. 1940 (all Para) : *Seventeen, Parole Fixer, Emergency Squad, The Farmer's Daughter, Those Were the Days, Touchdown, Golden Gloves, Queen of the Mob, North-West Mounted Police, Love Thy Neighbour;* 1941 : *Adam Had Four Sons* (Col), *West Point Widow* (Para) ; 1942 : *Ice-Capades of 1942* (Rep), *The Glass Key* (Para), *Star Spangled Rhythm* (Para), *Beyond the Blue Horizon* (Para). 1942-5, war service in U.S. Navy. 1946 : *Seven Were Saved* (Para), *Black Beauty* (20th).

DE SICA, Vittoria. Actor, director. Born Sara (Frosinone), Italy, 1905. Films include : *La Segretaria per Tutti, Il Signore Max, Rose Scarlatte, Maddalena Zero in Condotta, L'Avventuriera del Piano di Sopra, Se io fossi Onesto* ; 1944 : *L'Ippocampo* (Arno), *Nessuno Torna Indietro* (Artisti Associati) ; 1945 : *Lo Sbaglio di Essere Vivo* (Fauno), *Il Mondo Vuolo Cos* (Aurea) ; 1946 : *La Notte Porta Consiglio* (Pao), *Lo Sconosciuto di San Marino* (Gamma). In 1947 directed *Sciuscia* (*Shoe-Shine*).

DICK, Douglas. Born Charleston, Virginia, Nov. 20, 1920. Ht. 6 ft. ; wt. 148 lb. Brown hair, blue-green eyes. Educ. Belles Military School, Jacksonville, Florida ; University of Kentucky ; University of Arizona. While at college appeared with Hilltop Theatre Group, Baltimore and at summer theatre at Hampton, Long Island. Studied acting with Benne Schneider. 1941-5, served in U.S. Coastguard and Naval Air Corps. On discharge appeared with Tucson, Arizona, Community Theatre and toured in U.S. First film : *The Searching Wind* (Para) 1946. 1947 : *Saigon* (Para) ; 1948 : *Casbah* (UI).

DICKINSON, Desmond. Director of photography. Born London, May 5, 1902. Entered film industry, 1919, as film laboratory assistant with Clarendon Film Company, Croydon. During World War II, was Director of Documentaries for Strand Film Company, in conjunction with War office. Recent films include : *The Arsenal Stadium Mystery, Men of Two Worlds* (East African exteriors), *Hungry Hill*.

DICKINSON, Thorold. Director. Born Bristol, Nov. 16, 1903. Educ. Clifton College ; Oxford University. Entered films 1925, as assistant to director George Pearson, on *Mr. Preedy and the Countess*, and *The Little People*, both made in France. During 1926 was stage director to Lena Ashwell's repertory company, Notting Hill Gate, London. 1927-36, worked as film editor for British and Dominions, Gainsborough, Stoll, and Ealing Studios. At Ealing, produced *Midshipman Easy* and directed *The High Command*, 1936. In 1938 he went to Spain to make documentaries for Republicans. Directed : *The Arsenal Stadium Mystery, Gaslight* (re-made in Hollywood as *The Murder in Thornton Square*), *The Prime Minister*. 1941-43, with Army Kinematograph Service, when he directed *Next of Kin* at Ealing Studios, primarily as lesson in security precautions for the Forces, but afterwards shown publicly. Also organized production of army training films at Wembley Studios. After demobilization, 1944, went to Tanganyika to make exteriors for *Men of Two Worlds*, which he completed in Britain, 1945.

DIETERLE, William. Born Ludwigshaven, Germany, July 15, 1893. Educ. Mannheim. Studied under Max Reinhardt from 1919 and became established actor ; roles included Brutus in " Julius Cæsar". In 1924, owned a Berlin theatre as producer-actor ; later turned to films as director-actor. To Hollywood, 1930, for intended two-months' stay to direct German version of American film. Signed by Warner for five years. Became American citizen, 1937. Films include : *The Last Night, Her Majesty Love, Man Wanted, The Jewel Robbery, Lawyer Man, Scarlet Dawn, The Crash, Grand Slam, Adorable, Devils in Love, Six Hours to Live, Madame Du Barry, The Firebird, Concealment, A Midsummer Night's Dream, Dr. Socrates, The Story of Louis Pasteur, Satan Met a Lady, The White Angel, The Making of O'Malley,*

OLIVIA DE HAVILLAND
(*Universal-International*)

Another Dawn, The Life of Emile Zola, Blockade, Juarez, The Hunchback of Notre Dame, Dr. Ehrlich's Magic Bullet, A Dispatch from Reuter's. Produced and directed : *All That Money Can Buy, Syncopation.* Also directed : *The Man on America's Conscience, Kismet, I'll Be Seeing You, This Love of Ours, Love Letters, The Searching Wind.*

DIETRICH, Marlene. Real name Mary Magdalene von Losch. Born Berlin, Dec. 27, 1902. Ht. 5 ft. 5 in. ; wt. 120 lb. Red-gold hair, blue eyes. Educ. privately at Weimar ; Musical Academy, Berlin. Intended musical career, studied violin ; but injured wrist in accident, so turned to stage and trained with Max Reinhardt. Stage debut in " The Taming of the Shrew" ; also appeared in musical comedies in Berlin. First entered films as extra. Most important German film was *The Blue Angel* 1930, directed by Joseph Von Sternberg, in which she appeared opposite Emil Jannings. Went to Hollywood to star in *Morocco* with Gary Cooper in 1931. Films there include : *Dishonoured, Shanghai Express, Blonde Venus, Song of Songs, Scarlet Empress, The Devil Is a Woman, Desire, The Garden of Allah.* Came to Britain in 1936, to appear with Robert Donat in *Knight without Armour.* Became American citizen in 1937. In Hollywood made : *Angel, Destry Rides Again.* 1940 : *Seven Sinners* (Univ) ; 1941 : *Flame of New Orleans* (Univ), *Manpower* (Warn) ; 1942 : *The Lady Is Willing* (Col), *The Spoilers* (Univ), *Pittsburgh* (Univ) ; 1944 : *Follow the Boys* (Univ), *Kismet* (MGM). Toured extensively with U.S.A. Camp Shows in U.S., Europe and Africa during World War II. In France, 1946 : *Martin Roumagnac* (with Jean Gabin). 1947 (in U.S.A.) : *Golden Earrings* (Para) ; 1948 : *A Foreign Affair* (Para).

DISNEY, Walt. Artist, producer. Born Chicago, Dec. 5, 1901. Educ. McKinley High School, Chicago. Wanted to be actor ; as a boy won numerous talent competitions for impersonations at local theatres. Served with American Red Cross in World War I ; studied drawing and photography ; became commercial artist in Chicago, Kansas City, 1919-22. Became cartoonist for Kansas City slide firm ; from 1923-26 produced " Alice " comedies (a combination of live actors and cartoons) for Winkler Pictures. 1927, created and produced first twenty-six Oswald cartoons ; in May 1928, began making *Mickey Mouse* cartoons in sound ; from 1930, also *Silly Symphonies.* Films released through Columbia 1930-2, through UA 1932-6. Signed by RKO, 1936. Feature films include : *Snow White and the Seven Dwarfs,* 1937 (his first full-length feature, made in colour). 1940 : *Pinnochio, Fantasia ;* 1941 : *The Reluctant Dragon, Dumbo ;* 1942 : *Bambi, Saludos Amigos ;* 1943 : *Victory Through Air Power ;* 1944 : *The Three Caballeros* (combined live action and cartoon) ; 1946 : *Make Mine Music, Song of the South.* Throughout World War II devoted himself largely to the production of training and educational films. Visited Britain and Eire, 1947, to study backgrounds for film about leprechauns, *The Little People.* 1947 : *Fun and Fancy Free.* In production 1947-8 : *How Dear to My Heart, Alice in Wonderland.*

DIX, Richard. Real name Ernest Carlton Brimmer. Born St. Paul, Minnesota, July 18, 1895. Ht. 6 ft. ; wt. 180 lb. Brown hair, brown eyes. Educ. Grammar and high school, St. Paul ; University of Minnesota. Worked in bank, then in architect's office. Joined School of Drama at Northwestern University. Played

in touring companies and on Broadway in " The Hawk". Stage success led to long and outstanding career as silent star. First film : *Not Guilty* (First National) 1921. Silent films include : *The Vanishing American, The Quarterback, Womanhandled, Paradise for Two, Redskin.* Outstanding sound films include : *Cimarron, Nothing But the Truth, Seven Keys to Baldpate, Roar of the Dragon, West of the Pecos, The Arizonian, The Tunnel* (GB, made in Britain), *Man of Conquest, Devil's Playground, The Devil Is Driving.* 1942 : *Tombstone* (Para), *The Kansan* (UA) ; 1943 : *Buckskin Frontier* (UA), *The Ghost Ship* (RKO). In 1944 made *The Mark of the Whistler,* first of *The Whistler* series, in which he now appears regularly.

DMYTRYK, Edward. Director. Born Grand Forks, British Columbia, Canada. Educ. Hollywood High School ; California Institute of Technology, where he studied mathematical physics, training to become scientist. From 1923 worked after school at Paramount as handy man to film cutters and editors. Became film editor, 1930 ; director, 1939. Films include : *Television Spy, Golden Gloves, The Devil Commands, Confessions of Boston Blackie, Counter Espionage, Hitler's Children, The Falcon Strikes Back, Behind the Rising Sun, Farewell My Lovely, Tender Comrade, The Invisible Army, Back to Bataan, Cornered, Till the End of Time, So Well Remembered* (first Rank-RKO film to be made in Britain) ; 1947 : *Crossfire.*

DONALDSON, Ted. Born New York City, Aug. 20, 1933. Ht. 4 ft. 1½ in. ; wt. 87 lb. Red-blond hair, hazel eyes. Educ. Professional Children's School, New York. On radio from age of 4, including television. On Broadway stage, 1940, as Harlan in " Life with Father " ; in 1943 in " Sons and Soldiers". Made notable screen debut as trainer of dancing caterpillar in *Once Upon a Time* (Col) 1944. Other films include : *Mr Winkle Goes to War* (Col), *The Fighting Guardsman ;* 1945 : *A Tree Grows in Brooklyn* (20th), *A Guy, a Gal and a Pal* (Col). From 1946 appeared in *Rusty* series (Col) about boy and dog.

DONAT, Robert. Born Withington, Manchester, Mar. 18, 1905. Ht. 6 ft. ; wt. 151 lb. Chestnut-brown hair, brown eyes. Educ. Elementary school, Rusholme ; Central High School for Boys, Manchester. Film enthusiast in childhood ; then developed stage ambition and studied elocution with James Bernard. The famous Shakespearean Henry Baynton gave him first stage role, Lucius in " Julius Cæsar", Prince of Wales Theatre, Birmingham, July 5, 1921. Then for two years did non-theatrical work. During 1924-28 joined Sir Frank Benson's company and played repertory at Manchester, Wakefield, Huddersfield. 1928-30 with Liverpool Repertory Theatre ; Festival Theatre Company, Cambridge. West-End debut 1930 in " Knave and Queen " at Ambassador's Theatre : show closed after week's run. 1930-2, appeared at Embassy Theatre, Swiss Cottage, London; with Birmingham Repertory Company at Malvern Festival ; on West End stage in " St. Joan", "Salome", " Precious Bane". In 1933 found himself famous with hit at Piccadilly Theatre in " The Sleeping Clergyman". 1943-6, ran Westminster Theatre, London ; presented Christmas play " The Glass Slipper", St. James's Theatre, 1944, and Westminster Theatre, 1945. Screen debut 1932 playing Oxford undergraduate in *Men of Tomorrow* (LFP). In 1931, declined offer of film lead opposite Norma Shearer in " Smilin' Through ". Early films : *That Night in London, Cash, The Private Life of Henry VIII, The*

Count of Monte Cristo (made in Hollywood for Small-UA, 1934) *The 39 Steps, The Ghost Goes West, Knight without Armour, The Citadel, Goodbye Mr. Chips !* 1942 : *The Young Mr. Pitt* (20th Brit) ; 1943 : *The Adventures of Tartu* (MGM Brit) ; 1945 : *Perfect Strangers*—U.S. title *Vacation from Marriage* (MGM-London) ; 1947 : guest star as Parnell in *Captain Boycott* (Individ). 1948 : *The Winslow Boy* (LFP).

DONATH, Ludwig. Born Vienna, Mar. 5, 1905. Ht. 5 ft. 11 in. ; wt. 154 lb. Brown hair, blue eyes. Stage and radio actor, and teacher of acting in Europe. Played anti-Nazi roles on Viennese stage ; when Nazis invaded Austria in 1947, escaped arrest and went to America. First American film : *Ellery Queen* (Col) 1942. Other films include : *The Lady from Chungking* (PDC) ; 1943 : *Hangmen Also Die* (UA), *The Strange Death of Adolf Hitler* (Univ) ; 1944 : *The Seventh Cross* (MGM), *The Hitler Gang* (Para), *Story of Dr. Wassell* (Para), *The Master Race* (RKO) ; 1945 : *Counter-Attack* (Col) ; 1946 : *The Jolson Story* (Col) ; 1947 : *Assigned to Treasury* (Col).

DONLEVY, Brian. Born Portadown, Ireland, Feb. 9, 1890. Ht. 5 ft 11 in.. ; wt. 190 lb. Brown hair, blue eyes. Taken to U.S.A. when 10 months old. Educ. Cleveland, Ohio ; St. John's Military Academy, Delafield, Wisconsin. Airman in World War I. Became advertisement model. First stage role as corporal in " What Price Glory". Twelve years on Broadway. Film debut, 1929. Films include : *Mary Burns Fugitive, Barbary Coast, High Tension, Crack-up, Born Reckless, In Old Chicago, We're Going to Be Rich* (20th-Fox ; made in Britain, 1938), *Jesse James, Battle of Broadway, Union Pacific, Beau Geste, Destry Rides Again*. 1940 : *The Great McGinty* (Para), *When the Daltons Rode* (Univ), *Brigham Young* (20th), *I Wanted Wings* (Para), *The Great Man's Lady* (Para) ; 1941 : *South of Tahiti* (Univ), *A Gentleman After Dark* (UA), *Billy the Kid* (MGM), *The Birth of the Blues* (Para), *The Remarkable Andrew* (Para), *Two Yanks in Trinidad* (Col) ; 1942 : *Wake Island* (Para), *The Glass Key* (Para), *Cargo of Innocents* (MGM), *Nightmare* (Univ) ; 1943 : *Hangmen Also Die* (UA), *The Miracle of Morgan's Creek* (Para) ; 1944 : *An American Romance* (MGM), *Two Years Before the Mast* (Para) ; 1945 : *The Virginian* (Para), *Duffy's Tavern* (Para), *Our Hearts Were Growing Up* (Para) ; 1946 : *The Trouble with Women* (Para), *Canyon Passage* (Univ), *Song of Sheherazade* (Univ) ; 1947 : *The Beginning or the End* ? (MGM), *Killer McCoy* (MGM), *Heaven Only Knows* (Seymour Nebenzal-UA), *Kiss of Death* (20th).

DONOHUE, Steve. Stunt artist. Born Ireland, 1919. A leading British film stunt man, partner with ex-boxer Dave Crowley and Pat Ryan in firm specializing in film stunts. Formerly actor at the Abbey Theatre, Dublin, and other Irish theatres, navvy, book-keeper, dance-hall chucker-out, amateur boxer and wrestler. Soldier in Spanish civil war, physical training instructor to Commandos during World War II. Entered films after demobilization ; received his first scar through battle scenes in *Cæsar and Cleopatra*, in which he also dropped sixteen feet into two feet of water. His recent films include : *Caravan* (a leap of sixteen feet), *Night Beat* (broke leg leaping from Thames Embankment), *Anna Karenina* (fall beneath express train).

DORN, Philip. Real name, Fritz van Dungen. Born Scheveningen, Holland, Sept. 30. Ht. 6 ft. 2 in. ;

wt. 175 lb. Brown hair, blue eyes. Educ. Academy of Fine Arts and Architecture, The Hague. Became boat builder, then stage star in Holland. Spent four years on tour, Africa, Dutch East Indies and India, where he also made several scientific films. Made several feature films in Holland, notably *De Kribbebyter*, directed by Henry Koster. Later, in Hollywood, Koster invited him to play leading role in *Ski Patrol* (Univ) 1940. Films include : *Enemy Agent* (Univ), *Escape* (MGM), reissued 1947 as *When the Door Opened ;* 1941 : *Ziegfeld Girl* (MGM), *Underground* (Warn), *Tarzan's Secret Treasure* (MGM) ; 1942 : *Calling Dr. Gillespie* (MGM), *Random Harvest* (MGM) ; 1943 : *Reunion in France* (MGM), *Chetniks* (20th), *Paris After Dark* (20th) ; 1944 : *Passage to Marseille* (Warn), *Blonde Fever* (MGM) ; 1945 : *Escape in the Desert* (Warn) ; 1946 : *Concerto* (Rep) ; 1948 : *I Remember Mama* (RKO).

DOUGLAS, Kirk. Born Amsterdam, New York, Dec. 9, 1916. Ht. 6 ft. ; wt. 170 lb. Fair hair, green eyes. Educ. Amsterdam public schools ; St. Lawrence University. Studied acting at American Academy of Dramatic Arts, paying his way by becoming bell-hop, punch-press operator, parking attendant, waiter, usher, wrestler. First New York stage role was as singing messenger boy in " Spring Again". Became understudy and stage-manager in Katharine Cornell production " Three Sisters" ; then juvenile lead in " Kiss and Tell " with Joan Caulfield. Served in World War II in U.S. Navy. Resumed career with stage and radio roles, including " The Wind Is Ninety " which led to screen test. First film *The Strange Love of Martha Ivers* (Para) 1946. Other films include : 1947 : *I Walk Alone* (Para), *Build My Gallows High* (RKO), *Mourning Becomes Electra* (RKO).

DOUGLAS, Melvyn. Real name Melvyn Hesselberg. Born Macon, Georgia, Apr. 5, 1901. Ht. 6 ft. 2 in. ; wt. 185 lb. Brown hair, hazel eyes. Educ. Toronto Conservatory of Music. Had ambitions as writer, but found this not enough to live on, so worked as lift operator, farm labourer, newspaper reporter, salesman. Was given chance to play Bassanio in repertory production " Merchant of Venice". Founded own company at Madison, Wisconsin ; later appeared on Broadway in " A Free Soul". " No More Ladies", and other plays. First film : *Tonight or Never* (UA) 1931. Early films include : *As You Desire Me, The Old Dark House, She Married Her Boss, Annie Oakley, The Gorgeous Hussy, Theodora Goes Wild, I Met Him in Paris, Fast Company, The Shining Hour, Ninotchka.* 1940 : *My Two Husbands* (Col), *He Stayed to Breakfast* (Col), *Third Finger Left Hand* (MGM), *Married but Single* (Col) ; 1941 : *That Uncertain Feeling* (UA), *A Woman's Face* (MGM), *Our Wife* (Col), *Two-Faced Woman* (MGM), *We Were Dancing* (MGM) ; 1942 : *They All Kissed the Bride* (Col), *Three Hearts for Julia* (MGM). 1942-6, war service in U.S. Army. 1947 : *The Sea of Grass* (MGM), *The Guilt of Janet Ames* (Col), *My Own True Love* (Para) ; 1948 : *The Pittsburgh Escapade* (RKO).

DOUGLAS, Robert. Born Bletchley, Bucks, Nov. 9, 1909. Ht. 5 ft. 10½ in.. ; wt. 150 lb. Fair hair, blue eyes. Trained at Royal Academy of Dramatic Art ; stage debut in " The Best People", Theatre Royal, Bournemouth, 1927. Began film career, 1931, in *Josser* series, starring Ernie Lotinga (BIF). Other films include : *The Blarney Stone, Many Waters, The Street Singer*—U.S. title *London Melody, Our Fighting Navy, The Challenge, Over the Moon*. In

World War II served in R.A.F. and later in Air Branch, Royal Navy. Returned to stage, 1945, and was acting in Frederick Lonsdale's " But for the Grace of God " at St. James's Theatre, London, when seen by Hollywood scout. Made, in Britain, *The End of the River* (Archers) 1947, and shortly afterwards left for Hollywood. 1948: *Christopher Blake* (Warn), *The Adventures of Don Juan* (Warn).

DOVZHENKO, Alexander. Writer, director, producer. Born Sosnitsi, Ukraine, 1894. Educ. public schools ; Teachers' Institute. Trained in natural science, economics, athletics. In 1921 worked on rebuilding of Kharkov. Later in Warsaw, Berlin, and elsewhere as Soviet diplomat. In 1923, was cartoonist for Kharkov newspapers and periodicals. Entered films, 1925, as scenario writer for *Vasya the Reformer*. 1926, wrote and directed his first film, a short slapstick comedy, *Love's Berries*. 1927 : *The Diplomatic Pouch* (directed) ; 1928 : *Zvenigora* (directed) ; 1929 : *Arsenal* (wrote and directed) ; 1930 : *Earth*—U.S. title, *Soil* (wrote and directed) ; 1932 : *Ivan*—U.S. title, *Frontier* (wrote and directed) ; 1935 : *Aerograd* (wrote and directed) ; 1939 : *Shors* (wrote and directed) ; 1940 : *Liberation* (directed) ; 1943 : *Battle for the Ukraine* (produced) ; 1945 : *Ukraine in Flames* (produced) ; 1947 : *Life in Blossom*, biography of Michurin, in Agfacolor (directed).

DOWLING, Joan. Born Hayes, Middlesex, 1931. Ht. 5 ft. 1 in. ; wt. 116 lb. Fair hair, blue eyes. Educ. local council school. At 10 won local singing competition. While still at school, attended elocution classes and played in Shakespeare at Regent's Park (London) Open Air Theatre. Entertained troops, played in pantomime. Did war work in soap factory. Afterwards, when playing in " No Room at the Inn ", was seen by film talent scout. First film : *Hue and Cry* (Ealing) 1947.

DOWNS, Cathy. Born Jefferson, Long Island, U.S.A., Mar. 3. Ht. 5 ft. 6 in. ; wt. 122 lb. Brown hair, blue eyes. Educ. Bay Avenue Grammar School ; Patchogue High School, Long Island. Became model in New York and elsewhere. First film : *Diamond Horseshoe* (20th) 1944. Other films (all 20th) include— 1945 : *The Dolly Sisters ;* 1946 : *The Dark Corner, My Darling Clementine.*

DRAKE, Charles. Real name Charles Ruppert. Born Bayside, Long Island, U.S.A. Ht. 6 ft. 3 in. ; wt. 190 lb. Educ. high school, Nichols College, Dudley, Massachussetts. As young man worked in New York Department store while trying for stage job. In 1939 became Hollywood extra and had to augment earnings by working after hours in a car park. Hitchhiked back to New York. Won a radio audition contest there ; returned to Hollywood. 1943-5, served with U.S. Army. Films include—1941 : *Dive Bomber* (Warn), *The Maltese Falcon* (Warn) ; 1942 (all Warn) : *Now Voyager, The Man Who Came to Dinner, Dangerously They Live, The Male Animal, Yankee Doodle Dandy, The Gay Sisters ;* 1943 : *Air Force* (Warn) ; 1945 : *You Came Along* (Para), *Conflict* (Warn) ; 1946 : *A Night in Casablanca, Whistle Stop* (UA) ; 1947 : *Winter Wonderland* (Rep).

DRAKE, Tom. Real name Alfred Alderdice. Born New York, Aug. 5. Ht. 6 ft. ; wt. 165 lb. Brown hair, brown eyes. Educ. Mercersburg Academy, Pennsylvania. At 18 was in summer theatre, thence to New York stage in 1938. First film : *Two Girls and a Sailor* (MGM) 1944. Other films (all MGM) include : *Marriage Is a Private Affair, You Can't Do That to Me, Mrs. Parkington, Meet Me in St. Louis, This Man's Navy.* 1945 : *Courage of Lassie ;* 1946 : *Faithful in My Fashion, The Green Years ;* 1947 : *The Beginning or the End ?, I'll Be Yours* (Univ), *Cass Timberlane ;* 1948 : *Alias the Gentleman, Master of Lassie.*

DRAYTON, Alfred. Real name Alfred Varick. Born Brighton, Nov. 1, 1881. In amateur theatricals at 19. Eight years later became a professional for 25*s.* a week in " The Beloved Vagabond " at the New Theatre, Cardiff. Comedy partnership with Robertson Hare began 1936, with play " Aren't Men Beasts?". Has combined films with stage since early days of talkies. Early films include : *The Calendar, Lord Babs, Jack Ahoy, The Little Damozel, Friday the Thirteenth, Loves of a Dictator, Aren't Men Beasts !, The Crimson Circle, First a Girl, So This Is London? Tropical Trouble, A Spot of Bother.* 1942 : *The Big Blockade* (Ealing) ; 1944 : *Don't Take It to Heart* (Two Cities), *They Knew Mr. Knight* (G. H. W. Production, shown publicly 1946) ; 1945 : *Halfway House* (Ealing) ; 1947 : *Nicholas Nickleby* (Ealing), *Things Happen at Night* (Alliance).

DRESDEL, Sonia. Real name Lois Obee. Born Hull, May 5, 1913. Ht. 5 ft. 4½ in. ; wt. 116 lb. Brown hair, grey-blue eyes. Educ. High School for Girls, Aberdeen. Acted in repertory and on provincial tours before appearing on London dramatic stage. After great success in " This Was a Woman", appeared in her original role on the screen. 1947 : *While I Live* (Dryhurst) ; 1948 : *This Was a Woman* (Hellman).

DREW, Ellen. Born Kansas City, Nov. 23, 1915. Ht. 5 ft. 3½ in. ; wt. 110 lb. Brown hair, grey eyes. Worked as shop assistant, took stage training. Won beauty contest ; worked three years in Hollywood snack-bar before agent spotted her. Trained at Paramount acting school. Played small parts until Wesley Ruggles gave her lead with Bing Crosby and Fred MacMurray in *Sing You Sinners* (Para) 1938. Came to Britain, 1939, to make *French without Tears*. Films include : *If I Were King, The Lady from Kentucky, Gracie Allen Murder Case, Geronimo.* 1940 : *Women Without Names* (Para), *Buck Benny Rides Again* (Para), *Christmas in July* (Para), *Texas Rangers Ride Again* (Para) ; 1941 : *The Mad Doctor* (Para), *The Monster and The Girl* (Para), *Reaching for the Sun* (Para), *The Parson of Panamint* (Para), *Night of January 16th* (Para), *Our Wife* (Col) ; 1942 : *The Remarkable Andrew* (Para), *My Favourite Spy* (RKO) ; 1943 : *Night Plane from Chungking* (Para), *The Imposter* (Univ) ; 1944 : *Dark Mountain* (Para) ; 1945 : *China Sky* (RKO), *Isle of the Dead* (RKO), *Man Alive* (RKO) ; 1946 : *Sing while you Dance* (Col), *Crime Doctor's Manhunt* (Col) ; 1947 : *Johnny O'Clock* (Col), *The Swordsman* (Col); 1948 : *The Man from Colorado* (Col).

DUANE, Michael. Born Dunkirk, Indiana, U.S.A., Apr. 12, 1914. Ht. 6 ft. ; wt. 164 lb. Brown hair, hazel eyes. Educ. Harrisburg Academy, Pennsylvania; High School, Indianapolis ; Culver Military Academy. Studied art and scenic designing, John Harron Art School, Indianapolis ; spent three years acting and designing with John Goodman Theatre, Chicago. Stage debut, carrying a spear, 1928. Opened designing business in Manhattan, spent his summers acting. Broadway debut, 1942, in " Walk into My Parlour";

other roles on stage and radio. 1944-6, on war service. Film debut : *City without Men* (Col) 1943. Films (all Col) include—1943 : *Redhead from Manhattan, Dangerous Blondes ;* 1946 : *The Devil's Mask, Keeper of the Bees.*

DU MAURIER, Daphne. Novelist, dramatist. Daughter of the late Sir Gerald du Maurier. Born London, May, 13 1907. Educ. privately in London and Paris. Her first novel appeared in 1931, and she has also written, " Gerald : A Portrait " (biography of her father) and " The Du Mauriers " (family biography). Her plays include " Rebecca ", adapted from her own novel, and " The Years Between ". Filmed : (novels) *Jamaica Inn, Rebecca, Frenchman's Creek, Hungry Hill ;* (play) *The Years Between.* In preparation : *The King's General.*

DUNNE, Irene. Born Louisville, Kentucky, Dec. 20, 1904. Ht. 5 ft. 5 in. ; wt. 115 lb. Red-brown hair, grey eyes. Educ. Loretta Academy, Louisville ; convent, St. Louis ; Chicago College of Music. Left college for chorus of " The Beggar's Opera " in New York. Understudied Peggy Wood and sang lead one night in " The Clinging Vine " ; made hit and starred in touring company of show. Returned to Broadway to sing leads in " Sweetheart Time ", " Irene ", " Lollipops ", " The City Chap ", and Ziegfeld's production of " Show Boat". First film : *Present Arms* (RKO-Radio) 1930. Made sensational success in her next film : *Cimarron* (RKO) 1930. Other films include : *Married in Haste, The Great Lover, Bachelor Apartment, Melody of Life, 13 Women, Consolation Marriage, Back Street, The Secret of Madame Blanche, The Silver Cord, Ann Vickers, No Other Woman, Behold We Live, This Man Is Mine, Stingaree, Age of Innocence, Roberta, Sweet Adeline, Magnificent Obsession.* Her black-faced song in *Show Boat* (Univ) 1936 revealed talents as comedienne which were made better use of in : *Theodora Goes Wild, High Wide and Handsome, The Awful Truth, Joy of Living, Love Affair, Invitation to Happiness, When Tomorrow Comes.* 1940 : *My Favourite Wife* (RKO) ; 1941 : *Penny Serenade* (Col), *Unfinished Business* (Univ) ; 1942 : *Lady in a Jam* (Univ) ; 1943: *A Guy Named Joe* (MGM) ; 1944 : *The White Cliffs of Dover* (MGM), *Together Again* (Col) ; 1945 : *Over 21* (Col) ; 1946 : *Anna and the King of Siam* (20th) ; 1947 : *Life with Father* (Warn) ; 1948 : *I Remember Mama* (RKO).

DURANTE, Jimmy. Born New York, Feb. 19, 1893. Ht. 5 ft. 7½ in. ; wt. 155 lb. Brown hair, blue eyes. Educ. New York public schools. Son of an East Side barber, became father's lather boy, then photo-engraver, dance pianist, dance-band organizer. Formed entertainment trio, Clayton, Jackson and Durante, which appeared in *Roadhouse Nights* (Para) 1929. On Broadway, 1928, in Ziegfeld's " Show Girl", and in 1931, in " The New Yorkers". To Hollywood in 1931. Films include : *New Adventures of Get-Rich-Quick Wallingford, The Cuban Love Song, The Passionate Plumber, Speak Easily, The Phantom President, Blondie of the Follies, Hell Below, What—No Beer ?, Ring Up the Curtain, Meet the Baron.* 1934, returned to Broadway with " Strike Me Pink". Resumed films with : *Palooka, Students' Tour, Strictly Dynamite, George White's Scandals, She Learned About Sailors, Carnival Nights, Land without Music.* Continued stage, radio and night club appearances. Recent films include—1940 : *Melody Ranch* (Rep) ; 1941 : *You're in the Army now* (Warn), *The Man Who Came*

to Dinner (Warn) ; 1942 : *This Time for Keeps* (MGM) ; 1944 : *Two Girls and a Sailor* (MGM), *Music for Millions* (MGM) ; 1945 : *Two Sisters from Boston* (MGM) ; 1946 : *This Time for Keeps* (MGM), *It Happened in Brooklyn* (MGM) ; 1947 : *On an Island with You* (MGM) ; 1948 : *You're Beautiful !* (MGM).

DURBIN, Deanna. Real name Edna May Durbin, Born Winnipeg, Canada, Dec. 4, 1921. Ht. 5 ft. 5 in. ; wt. 113 lb. Brown hair, blue eyes. Educ. grammar school, Bret Hart Junior High School, Los Angeles, Took part in school dramatics, sang at church socials. Appeared in Eddie Cantor's radio show. Was signed by MGM to represent the opera star Ernestine Schumann-Heink as a child, for film based on this singer's life ; but film was cancelled when this singer suddenly died. Only film for MGM was short with Judy Garland, *Every Sunday Afternoon* (1935) ; several months later was signed by Universal for *Three Smart Girls* (1936), and became the screen's outstanding juvenile singing star at 14. Other films include : *100 Men and a Girl, Mad About Music, That Certain Age, Three Smart Girls Grow Up, First Love.* 1940 (all Univ) : *It's a Date, Spring Parade ;* 1941 : *Nice Girl ?, It Started with Eve ;* 1943 : *The Amazing Mrs. Holliday, Hers to Hold, His Butler's Sister ;* 1944 : *Christmas Holiday, Can't Help Singing ;* 1945 : *Lady on a Train ;* 1946 : *Because of Him ;* 1947 : *I'll Be Yours* (UI), *Something in the Wind* (UI). 1948 : *Up in Central Park* (UI).

DURYEA, Dan. Born White Plains, New York, Jan. 23, 1907. Ht. 6 ft. 1 in. ; wt. 160 lb. Fair hair, brown eyes. Educ. White Plains High School ; Cornell University. Took active part in college drama. Entered advertising business, but later became actor. First stage appearance as a G-Man on Broadway in " Dead End". In Lillian Hellman's play, " The Little Foxes", and brought to Hollywood to play original role. First film : *The Little Foxes* (RKO) 1941. Other films include : 1942 : *Ball of Fire* (RKO) ; 1943 : *Pride of the Yankees* (RKO), *Sahara* (Col) ; 1944 : *Ministry of Fear* (Para), *Mrs. Parkington* (MGM) ; *None but the Lonely Heart* (RKO) ; 1945 : *The Great Flamarion* (Rep), *Valley of Decision* (MGM), *Main Street After Dark* (MGM), *Lady on a Train* (Univ), *Scarlet Street* (Univ) ; 1946 : *Along Came Jones* (RKO), *White Tie and Tails, Woman in the Window* (RKO), *Black Angel* (UI) ; 1948 : *River Lady* (UI), *Adventure of Black Bart* (UI), *Another Part of the Forest* (UI).

DUVIVIER, Julien. Director. Born Lille, Oct. 8, 1896. Began his career in France as actor. First film, 1919, was financed by a mustard manufacturer and cost only £300. Made thirty silent films and then the talkies for which he has become famous, including *Poil de Carotte, Pépé le Moko, Un Carnet de Bal.* Went to Hollywood and re-made *Un Carnet de Bal* as *Lydia.* Other Hollywood films include : *The Great Waltz, Tales of Manhattan, Flesh and Fantasy.* Returned to France in 1946 and made *Panique.* Came to Britain in 1947 and made *Anna Karenina.*

DYALL, Valentine. Born Chelsea, London. Educ. Harrow ; Christ Church, Oxford. While playing in Oxford University Dramatic Society, was seen by John Gielgud and began professional career. Many appearances in stage and radio plays, including part as " The Man in Black " in B.B.C. series " Appointment with Fear". Made film debut in *The Life and Death of Colonel Blimp* (Archers) 1945. Other films include—

1944 : *Henry V* (Two Cities) ; 1945 : *Silver Fleet* (Archers) ; 1946 : *I Know Where I'm Going* (Archers), *Brief Encounter* (Cineguild), *Caesar and Cleopatra* (Pascal), *Pink String and Sealing Wax* (Ealing) ; 1947 : *The White Unicorn* (Corfield).

EASDALE, Brian. Composer. Born Manchester, 1909. Studied under Gordon Jacob and Armstrong Gibbs at Royal College of Music. Wrote his first opera, " Rapunzel", at 17. His tone poem, " Sixth Day", was played by Malcolm Sargent and the London Philharmonic Orchestra in 1935. In that year he became Music Director for the Group Theatre, London ; theatrical scores include that for "Mourning Becomes Electra". Composed a number of scores for G.P.O. Film Unit documentaries. Later wrote music for war documentary, *Ferry Pilot*. War service, first with R.A. and later with Directorate of Public Relations Film Unit in India, where he wrote the music for *Dagger Division* and *Johnny Ghurka*. Also composed the music for feature films *Black Narcissus* and *Red Shoes*.

EASTON, Jock. Real name John Easton. Actor and stunt man. Born Falkirk, Scotland, Apr. 27, 1912. Ht. 6 ft. 1½ in. ; wt. 174 lb. Brown hair, blue-grey eyes. Educ. Comely Park School, Falkirk. Youthful ambition, to be a soldier. Left home at 15 to join fun-fair in England. Joined army at 18 ; parachutist (M.C.) during World War II. Took film crowd work while waiting for passage to South America, making debut in *This Man Is Mine* (Col Brit) 1946 as Canadian soldier. Conducted fight scenes in *Good Time Girl*, *They Made Me a Fugitive*, *They Walk Alone*. In 1947, formed, with others, special film stunt unit.

ECK, Nikola. Producer, film scenario writer, playwright. Born 1902. Studied under Meyerhold at U.S.S.R. State Experimental Theatrical School, then worked for five years in Meyerhold's Theatre as actor and stage manager. Attended the State Cinematograph School, graduating in 1928. First film : *How It Should and How It Should Not Be Done ;* then followed sound film *The Road to Life* (1931). Has written film scenarios and plays for workers' clubs. In 1935 he made the first Russian full-length coloured film, *The Nightingale*.

EISENSTEIN, Sergei. Producer, director. Born Riga, 1898. Began his career as a poster artist in 1920. Studied Japanese, worked in the Japanese section of the Academy of Russian General Staff. Entered films, 1924, formed group with cameramen Tisse and Nielsen and producers Alexandrov and Gomorov. His first film, *The Strike*, 1924, revolutionized production methods by using masses of ordinary people instead of trained actors—a method which he is generally recognized to have perfected in *Battleship Potemkin* (1925-6). With Alexandrov, made *October* (*Ten Days that Shook the World*). In 1929, with Alexandrov and Tisse, Eisenstein went to America where he made a film about Mexico. On his return to U.S.S.R., was engaged as a lecturer at the State Institute of Cinematography. Other outstanding films include : *The General Line* (1929), *Alexander Nevski* (1939), *The Magic Seed* (1941), *Ivan the Terrible* (1944).

ELVEY, Maurice. Director. Born Yorkshire, Nov. 11, 1887. Became film director in 1913 ; has directed about 200 films, more than any other British director.

Has produced and directed in Hollywood, Berlin and London. Films include : *Hound of the Baskervilles*, *When Knights Were Bold*, *Wreck of the Birkenhead*, *Mademoiselle from Armentières*, *Quinneys*, *School for Scandal*, *High Treason*, *Water Gypsies*, *The Lost Chord*, *The Wandering Jew*, *The Clairvoyant*, *The Tunnel*, *Man in the Mirror*, *This Week of Grace*, *The Lodger*, *Sally in Our Alley*, *Soldiers of the King*, *Melody and Romance*, *Who Goes Next ?*, *The Return of the Frog*, *Sons of the Sea*, *Lost on the Western Front*, *For Freedom*, *The Battle of the River Plate*, *Room for Two*, *Under Your Hat*, *The Lamp Still Burns*, *Salute John Citizen*. Go-directed : *The Gentle Sex* ; directed (and was associate producer) : *Medal for the General*, *Strawberry Roan* ; directed and co-produced : *Beware of Pity*.

EMERSON, Faye. Born Elizabeth, Louisiana, July 8, 1917. Educ. San Diego State College. Stage experience with St. James's Repertory Theatre, Carmel, California, and in touring company. First film : *The Nurse's Secret* (Warner) 1941. Other films (all Warn) include—1941 : *Bad Men of Missouri*, *Nine Lives Are Not Enough*, *Manpower*, *Blues in the Night*, *Wild Bill Hickok Rides* ; 1942 : *Juke Girl*, *Murder in the Big House*, *Lady Gangster*, *The Hard Way*, *Secret Enemies* ; 1943 : *The Desert Song*, *Destination Tokyo* ; 1944 : *The Very Thought of You*, *Between Two Worlds*, *Mask of Dimitrios*, *Uncertain Glory*, *Crime by Night* ; 1945 : *Hotel Berlin*, *Danger Signal* ; 1946 : *Her Kind of Man*, *Nobody Lives Forever*.

ERMINA, Macario. Actor. Born Urin, Italy, 1904. Famous stage clown ; specializes in parts with Piedmontese dialect. Films include : *Imputato Alzatevi*, *Aria di Paese*, *Lo Vedi Come Sei ?*, *Il Pirata Sono Io !*, *Non Me Lo Dire*, *Il Vagabondo*, *Il Chiromante*. 1945 : *L'Innocente Casimiro* (Lux) ; 1947 : *Come Persi la Guerra* (Lux).

ERMLER, F. Producer. Born Rezhitsa, Russia, 1898. The son of a cabinet-maker he studied at the U.S.S.R. Institute of Screen Art, and later became a producer at the Leningrad film studios. In 1926 he produced his first film, *Kitty the Pippin*. Other films include : *Children of Storm*, *The House in the Snowdrift*, *Parisian Cobbler*, *A Chip of the Empire*, *The Counter-Plan*, *Peasants*, *The Great Citizen*, *No Greater Love* —U.S.S.R. title : *She Defends Her Country*, *The Turning-Point* (1946), *Diplomats* (1948).

EVANS, Dale. Real name Frances Butts. Born Uvalde, Texas, Oct. 31, 1918. Brown hair, grey-green eyes. Ht. 5 ft. 3 in. ; wt. 110 lb. Educ. business college. Was a singer on Texas radio and in Chicago night-club till film debut in *Here Comes Elmer* (Republic) 1943. Has been leading lady to Roy Rogers in numerous Westerns. Recent outstanding films (all Republic) include : *The Side Kids*, *Hoosier Holiday*, *In Old Oklahoma*, *Casanova in Burlesque*, *The Cowboy and the Senorita*, *Yellow Rose of Texas*, *San Fernando Valley*, *Song of Nevada*, *The Big Show-off*, *Hitch-hike to Happiness*, *Sunset in El Dorado*, *Bells of Rosarito*, *Man from Oklahoma*, *Don't Fence Me In*, *Along the Navajo Trail*, *Song of Arizona*, *Rainbow Over Texas*, *My Pal Trigger*, *Roll on, Texas Moon*, *Out California Way*, *Helldorado*, *Under Nevada Skies*, *Home in Oklahoma*.

EYTHE, William. Real name William John Joseph Eythe. Born Mars, Pennsylvania, Apr. 7, 1918. Ht. 5 ft. 11 in. ; wt. 170 lb. Dark brown hair, brown eyes. Educ. Mars High School, Carnegie Technical

DOUGLAS FAIRBANKS, Jr.
(*Universal-International*)

Institute. Singer and dancer in amateur theatricals ; played in summer theatres. Wrote and directed radio plays for small local station. Has lectured on astronomy and worked in dairy. In 1941 joined professional touring company ; on New York stage in Steinbeck's " The Moon Is Down ". Films (all 20th) include—1942 : *Strange Incident ;* 1943 : *The Song of Bernadette, The Eve of St. Mark ;* 1944 : *Wilson, A Wing and a Prayer ;* 1945 : *A Royal Scandal, The House on 92nd Street ;* 1946 : *Man of the Hour, Centennial Summer ;* 1947 : *Meet Me at Dawn* (Excelsior-20th Brit).

FABRIZI, Aldo. Born Rome, 1897. One of Italy's leading film stars. His performance as the priest in *Open City* has been acclaimed on both sides of the Atlantic as a major event in the re-birth of the Italian cinema since World War II. Films include—1942 : *Avanti c'e Posto* (Amato), *Campo de' Fiori* (Amato). 1945 : *Città Aperta—Open City* (Excelsa), first shown in Britain 1947 ; 1946 : *Mio Figlio Professore* (Lux) ; 1947 : *Vivere in Pace—To Live in Peace* (Lux), also shown in Britain 1947 ; *Pensione California* (Pao-Lux).

FAIRBANKS, Douglas, Jr., Born New York City, Dec. 9, 1909. Ht. 6 ft. 1 in. ; wt. 180 lb. Light brown hair, blue eyes. Educ. Pasadena Polytechnic School ; Harvard Military Academy, Los Angeles ; New York Collegiate Sch. ; London. Studied art in Paris. As a child appeared occasionally in films with his famous father. Debut as silent film actor in *Stephen Steps Out* (Para) 1923. Returned to Paris, resumed films, 1925 : *Wild Horse Mesa, The Air Mail, Stella Dallas.* 1929, on Hollywood stage : " Young Woodley ", " Saturday's Children ". First sound film : *The Barker* (FN) 1928, with Milton Sills and Dorothy Mackaill. In Britain, 1934, acted in Manchester in " The Winding Journey ". 1935-7, became associate producer and star in English films. 1941-6, war service U.S.N.R. (decorations include Legion of Honour, Croix de Guerre). Films include : *The Dawn Patrol, The Power of the Press, Outward Bound, Captured, Morning Glory, The Amateur Gentleman* (British), *Catherine the Great* (British), *Accused* (British), *Prisoner of Zenda* (UA) 1937, *Having Wonderful Time, Gunga Din, The Sun Never Sets, Rulers of the Sea.* 1940 : *Green Hell* (Univ), *Angels Over Broadway* (Col) ; 1941 : *The Corsican Brothers* (UA) ; 1947 : *Sinbad the Sailor* (RKO), produced and appeared in *The Exile* (UI).

FARR, Derek. Born London, Feb. 7, 1912. Ht. 6 ft.; wt. 158 lb. Brown hair, blue eyes. Educ. Cranbrook School, Kent ; Royal Academy of Dramatic Art. Schoolmaster at preparatory school in Littlehampton, Sussex, before taking up stage. Played as amateur in Sevenoaks Repertory Company. During World War II served in British Army ; invalided out, 1945, after much active service. Films include—1940 : *Freedom Radio* (Col Brit), *The Outsider* (ABPC), *Black Eyes* (ABPC) ; 1941 : *Quiet Wedding* (Soskin-Para) ; 1946 : *Quiet Weekend* (ABPC), *Wanted for Murder* (Excelsior-20th Brit) ; 1947 : *Teheran* (Pendennis-Stafford) ; 1948 : *Bond Street* (World Screen).

FARRAR, David. Born London, Aug. 21, 1908. Ht. 5 ft. 11 in. ; wt. 161 lb. Brown hair, grey eyes. Youthful ambition, to be a journalist. Joined newspaper as " copy boy " when 14 ; two years later became junior reporter. Studied at night school for degree ; and took part in amateur theatricals. At twenty-four had secured his B.A. and also written a text-book on journalism. Then decided to become a professional actor. Joined touring company. First film test not entirely satisfactory, so remained in theatre, taking over the Grafton Theatre, Tottenham Court-road, London, with his own company in 1939. When this was put out of action by bombing, made a second and successful attempt at a film career. Films include—1943 : *Night Invader* (Warn Brit) ; 1945 : *The Lisbon Story* (Brit Nat), *The Echo Murders* (Brit Nat) ; 1946 : *The Trojan Brothers* (Brit Nat) ; 1947 : *Black Narcissus* (Archers), *Frieda* (Ealing).

FARROW, John Villiers. Director, author. Born Sydney, Australia, 1904. Educ. privately, Australia, England. Gained early renown as member of scientific expeditions ; decorated for research into national histories of Spain, France, Rumania. Author of " Damien the Leper " (1937), " The Pageant of the Popes " (1942). Created Knight of the Holy Sepulchre by Pius XI (1937) ; awarded Grand Cross of same order by Pius XII (1940) ; is also Chevalier of Tunis, LL.D. (Loyola University, California), officer of the Orders of St. John of Jerusalem and Crown of Rumania. Entered film industry as writer : *Ladies of the Mob, Wolf Song, Sailor's Sweetheart, Seven Days' Leave,* and others. Became director-writer, in 1937, with : *War Lord* (Warn). Films include : *She Loved a Fireman, Without Warning, Little Miss Thoroughbred, My Bill, Broadway Musketeers, Code of the Streets, The Saint Strikes Back, Sorority House, Five Came Back, Full Confession, Reno, Married and in Love, A Bill of Divorcement.* 1940-41 and 1943, war service in Royal Navy and Royal Canadian Navy. Directed *Wake Island,* which received New York Critics' Circle Award. Latest films : *Commandos Strike at Dawn, China, The Hitler Gang, Two Years Before the Mast, Calcutta, Easy Come Easy Go, California, Blaze of Noon, The Big Clock, The Night Has a Thousand Eyes.*

FAYE, Alice. Real name Alice Seppert. Born New York City, May 5, 1915. Ht. 5 ft. 5 in. ; wt. 112 lb. Light gold hair, deep blue eyes. Studied dancing ; at 13 tried Ziegfeld Follies, but too young ; at 14 in chorus of " Scandals " ; then vocalist with Rudy Vallee orchestra, with which she appeared in first film : *George White's Scandals* (20th) 1934. Other films include : *When New York Sleeps, She Learned About Sailors, 365 Nights in Hollywood, Music Is Magic, King of Burlesque, Poor Little Rich Girl, Sing Baby Sing, Stowaway, On the Avenue, Every Night at Eight, Wake Up and Live, In Old Chicago, You Can't Have Everything, Sally Irene and Mary, Alexander's Ragtime Band, Tailspin, Rose of Washington Square, Hollywood Cavalcade, Barricade.* 1940 (all 20th) : *Lillian Russell, Tin Pan Alley ;* 1941 : *That Night in Rio, Great American Broadcast, Weekend in Havana ;* 1943 : *Hello Frisco Hello, The Gang's All Here ;* 1945 : *The Girls He Left Behind, Fallen Angel.* Has recently been devoting herself to radio work.

FERBER, Edna. Playwright, novelist. Born Kalamazoo, Michigan, Aug. 15, 1887. Educ. Appleton, Wisconsin. At 17 became reporter on local newspaper. Plays include : " Minick ", " The Royal Family ", " Dinner at Eight ", " The Land is Bright " (all with George S. Kaufman). Novels include : " So Big ", " Showboat ", " Cimarron ", " Come and Get It ". Works filmed include : *Showboat, Cimarron, The Royal Family of Broadway, Dinner at Eight, So Big, Come and Get It, Saratoga Trunk.*

FERNANDEL. Real name Fernand Contandin. Born Marseilles, May 8, 1903. Had sung in public from age of 6. Worked at various jobs, then, after French military service in 1925, developed as comedian. Later, toured French provinces as singer. Made Paris debut in 1928 and in 1930 was seen by film director Marc Allegret. First film : *Josette.* Appeared in *Le Blanc et le Noir* with Sacha Guitry, *Paris-Béguin*, and numerous short films before making hit as male May Queen in *Le Rosier de Mme. Husson.* Other films include : *Pas de Femmes, Un Homme sans Nom, Les Gaietés de l'Escadron, Le Jugement de Minuit, Le Coq du Régiment, L'Ordonnance, Lidoire, D'Amour et d'Eau Fraîche, Adémaï Aviateur, Nuit de Folie, La Garnison Amoureuse, L'Hotel du Libre Echange, Le Train de 8 heures 47, Angèle, Les Bleus de la Marine, Le Cavalier Lafleur, Ferdinand le Noceur, Jim la Houlette, Les Gaietés de la Finance, Ignace, Ernest le Rebelle, Les Cinq Sous de Lavarede, Le Club des Soupirants, Le Schpountz, Raphael le Tatoue, Le Cavalcade des Heures, Fric-Frac, Les Mystères de St. Val, Nais, Les Gueux au Paradis, Affaire de Cœur, Petrus.*

FERREIRA, Bibi. Real name Abigail Izquierdo Ferreira. Born Rio de Janeiro, June 1, 1922. Ht. 5 ft. 2 in. ; wt. 112 lb. Black hair, brown eyes. Educ. British-American School, Rio de Janeiro. Speaks five languages fluently. First appeared on stage as an infant in her father's theatrical company. By the time she was 7, had toured all the major theatres of Latin America with her parents. For a time was ballerina at the Brazilian Opera House, Rio. At 21 as star, producer and business manager, opened her own theatre company at the Phoenix, one of the largest theatres in Rio. Also wrote, produced and starred in her own weekly radio programme, " My Diary ". Came to Britain to appear in *End of the River* (Archers) 1947.

FEUILLERE, Edwige. Born Vésoul, France, Oct. 29, 1907. Spent early life in Italy and Switzerland, returning to France in 1918. Educ. Dijon. Studied singing and acting at Paris Conservatoire in 1928 and made debut in 1931 in *La Parisienne.* Became well known on Paris stage and in 1947 appeared at the Hébertot Theatre in Jean Cocteau's " The Eagle Has Two Heads ". Film debut in *Le Cordon Bleu.* Other films include : *Monsieur Albert, Une Petite Femme dans le Train, Maquillage, Topaze, Le Roi Pausole, Matricule 33, Toi que j'Adore, Ces Messieurs de la Santé, Le Miroir aux Alouettes, Golgotha, Barcarolle, Stradivarius, Sans Lendemain, L'Emigrante, Sarajevo, J'Etais une Aventurière, La Dame de Malacca, La Duchesse de Langeais, Mademoiselle Bonaparte, Mister Flow, Feu, Marthe-Richard, Lucrèce, La Part de l'Ombre, Tant que je Vivrai, L'Idiot, Il Suffit d'une Fois.*

FIELD, Mary. Born Wimbledon, Surrey, 1896. Educ. The Study, Wimbledon ; Surbiton High School ; Bedford College for Women, University of London (M.A., London, with distinction in Imperial History). Was a teacher for some years, specializing in history, before returning to the University for historical research. Entered films, 1926, under H. Bruce Woolfe at British Instructional. Was script girl, film editor and scriptwriter in the early days of Welwyn Studios, with Anthony Asquith, the late Arthur Woods, and J. O. C. Orton. Achieved notice with *Secrets of Nature* and *Secrets of Life* series in silent days. Was one of the first British documentary directors, with *King's English*, and *The Changing Year.* Directed one

feature comedy, *Strictly Business*, with Jacqueline Logan, in 1931, for B.I.P. Has directed and produced hundreds of instructional and documentary films for British Instructional Ltd. and later for G.B. Instructional Ltd. In 1944 was appointed Director of Rank's " Children's Entertainment Films ". Is a well-known lecturer and writer on " Children and Films " and author of " Secrets of Nature ", with F. Percy Smith, " Cine-Biology " with F. Percy Smith and J. V. Durden, and " The Boys' and Girls' Film Book " with Maud M. Miller.

FIELD, Sid. Born Birmingham, Apr. 1, 1904. Ht. 5 ft. 10¾ in. Brown hair, blue eyes. Began his career at 8 by giving impersonations of Charlie Chaplin in the streets of Birmingham. First public appearance was at mothers' meeting in the local church hall, first professional appearance in " 14 Kino Juveniles ", at the Empire Theatre, Bristol. Appeared as a comedian in 1929 for the first time. Made his London debut in 1943 in " Strike a New Note ". First film was *London Town* (Wesley Ruggles) 1946. Appeared in the first Royal Command Film Performance at the Empire Theatre, London, Nov. 1, 1946.

FIELD, Virginia. Real name Margaret Cynthia Field. Born London. Educ. England, Paris, Vienna. On New York stage in many successes, notably " Victoria Regina ". Began screen career in 1934 in *The Lady Is Willing*, with the late Leslie Howard, (made in Britain for Columbia). Other films include : *Little Lord Fauntleroy, Ladies in Love, Lloyds of London.* 1941 : *Singapore Woman* (Warn) ; 1942 : *Atlantic Convoy* (Col) ; 1943 : *The Crystal Ball* (UA) ; 1946 : *The Perfect Marriage* (Para), guest artist in *Variety Girl* (Para), *Repeat Performance* (Eagle Lion–Hollywood); 1947 : *Christmas Eve* (Benedict Bogeaus-UA) ; 1948 : *Dream Girl* (Para).

FIELDING, Marjorie. Born Gloucester, 1892. Russet hair, blue eyes. Educ. Cheltenham Ladies' College. Stage debut, 1913, in " His House in Order ". In 1938 created stage role of Mildred Royde in " Quiet Wedding ", a part she played more than two thousand times. Played in London and with ENSA in " Quiet Weekend ". Repeated her role in the film *Quiet Wedding* (Soskin-Para) 1941. Other recent films include—1942 : *The Demi-Paradise* (Two Cities) ; 1943 : *The Yellow Canary* (Wilcox-RKO) ; 1946 : *Quiet Weekend* (ABPC) ; 1947 : *Fame Is the Spur* (Boultings-Two Cities).

FITZGERALD, Barry. Real name William Joseph Shields. Born Dublin, Mar. 1, 1888. Ht. 5 ft. 3 in. Grey hair, blue eyes. Educ. Merchant Taylors' School ; Skerry's College. Became junior administrative officer in Board of Trade, Dublin. Paid visits back-stage to Abbey Theatre, Dublin, and decided to become actor. Joined Abbey Theatre, appeared in Dublin, also London, provinces, and U.S.A. Director John Ford asked him to play his stage role in the film version of *The Plough and the Stars* (RKO) 1937. Other films include : *Ebb Tide, Bringing Up Baby, Pacific Liner, Dawn Patrol, Four Men and a Prayer, The Saint Strikes Back, Full Confession.* 1940 : *The Long Voyage Home* (UA), *San Francisco Docks* (Univ) ; 1941 : *The Sea Wolf* (Warn), *How Green Was My Valley* (20th), *The Amazing Mrs. Holliday* (Univ), *Corvette K-225* (Univ), *Two Tickets to London* (Univ) ; 1944 : *Going My Way* (Para), *I Love a Soldier* (Para), *Incendiary Blonde* (Para) ; 1945 : *Two Years Before the*

Mast (Para), *The Stork Club* (Para), *Duffy's Tavern* (Para) ; 1946 : *California* (Para), *Easy Come Easy Go* (Para), *Welcome Stranger* (Para) ; 1948 : *The Naked City* (UI).

FITZGERALD, Geraldine. Born Dublin, Nov. 24, 1914. Ht. 5 ft. 3 in. ; wt. 112 lb. Auburn hair, hazel eyes. Educ. Dublin School of Art. Gave up art for stage, trained Dublin Gate Theatre. Visited London on holiday and was given a small part in a " quota quickie ". Was given the lead in *Turn of the Tide* (Brit Nat) 1935. Later apeared in *The Mill on the Floss*, then went to New York, to appear on stage in " Heartbreak House ". Her performance in this brought her a Hollywood contract, and she appeared with Bette Davis in *Dark Victory* (Warn) 1939. Other films include : *Wuthering Heights*. 1941 : *Flight from Destiny* (Warn) ; 1942 : *Gay Sisters* (Warn) ; 1943 : *Watch on the Rhine* (Warn) ; 1944 : *Till We Meet Again* (Para), *Ladies Courageous* (Univ) ; 1945 : *Wilson* (20th), *The Strange Affair of Uncle Harry* (Univ) ; 1946 : *Three Strangers* (Warn), *O.S.S.* (Para), *Nobody Lives Forever* (Warn). Came to Britain, 1947, to make *So Evil My Love* (Hal Wallis-Para).

FLAHERTY, Robert J. Director. Born Iron Mountain, Michigan. Educ. Michigan College of Mines. One of the pioneers of the documentary film. Spent several years as explorer ; headed four expeditions through Hudson Bay and Baffin's Land. In 1920-21, he made a sub-Arctic expedition, financed by the New York fur company, Revillon Frères, to film Eskimo life for his famous *Nanook of the North*, which was re-issued with synchronized background music and a spoken commentary in 1947. Spent a year in the Samoan Isles making *Moana* ; co-directed *Tabu* ; in 1934 was assigned by Michael Balcon to produce, direct and photograph *Man of Aran*, for which he spent two years on Isle of Aran, off west coast of Ireland. In 1937, co-directed *Elephant Boy* (LFP) ; 1942 : produced and directed *The Land* (for U.S. Department of Agriculture).

FLEMING, Victor. Director. Born Pasadena, California. Educ. public schools, Los Angeles. Began his film career in early silent days as cameraman in the old American Studios at Santa Barbara. Served in World War I in U.S. Intelligence Department, and accompanied President Wilson to Europe as Chief Photographer. Returned to Hollywood 1919 and began career as director with *Women's Place* (First National). Other silent films include : *Red Hot Romance, The Lane That Had No Turnings, Anna Ascends, Dark Secrets, Law of the Lawless, To the Last Man, Call of the Canyon, Empty Hands, Gods of the Sea, Son of His Father, Adventure* (Para) 1925, *The Devil's Cargo, The Blind Goddess, Man Trap, The Rough Riders, The Way of All Flesh, Hula*. Sound films include : *Abie's Irish Rose, The Virginian, Wolf Song, Around the World in 80 Minutes, The Wet Parade, Red Dust, White Sister, Blonde Bombshell, Treasure Island, Reckless, The Farmer Takes a Wife, Captains Courageous, Test Pilot, The Wizard of Oz, Gone With the Wind, Dr. Jekyll and Mr. Hyde, Tortilla Flat, A Guy Named Joe, Adventure* (MGM) 1945. *Joan.*

FLEMYNG, Robert. Born Liverpool, Jan. 3, 1912. Ht. 5 ft. 11 in. ; wt. 170 lb. Brown hair, grey eyes. Educ. Haileybury School. After short period of medical training, made stage debut at Truro, Cornwall,

in 1931 in " Rope " ; later in same year " walked-on " at Westminster Theatre, London, in " The Anatomist ". Spent three years with Liverpool Repertory Company ; later made first big hit in " French Without Tears ", 1937. Screen debut opposite Jessie Matthews in *Gangway* (GB) 1937. In September 1939 was appearing on New York stage in " No Time for Comedy " ; immediately returned to Britain and joined R.A.M.C. Awarded M.C., O.B.E. (Military). After demobilization, 1945, returned to London stage in " The Guinea Pig ", and to films in *Bond Street* (World Screen) 1948.

FLETCHER, Cyril. Born Watford, Herts, June 25, 1913. Ht. 6 ft. ; wt. 168 lb. Dark brown hair and eyes. Youthful ambition : to be a straight actor. Studied acting at Guildhall School of Music and Drama, followed by five years in insurance business, five years with Fol-de-Rols concert party ; since 1940 in revue and own radio shows. Now fully occupied with road shows, summer seaside shows and dog breeding. Director Herbert Wilcox asked him to play as himself in first film *The Yellow Canary* (Wilcox-RKO), 1943. Also appeared in *Nicholas Nickleby* (Ealing) 1947.

FLYNN, Errol. Born Tasmania, June 20, 1909. Ht. 6 ft. ; wt. 175 lb. Brown hair, brown eyes. Educ. schools in Ireland, France, Australia. Went to New Guinea ; became policeman, coconut plantation overseer, seaman for two years. Then struck lucky in New Guinea gold fields, sold valuable claim, went on sailing trip in ketch with three friends. Has narrated this in book, " Beam Ends ". Served as guide to Dr. H. Erben, explorer, in New Guinea head-hunters' country ; appeared in film record of this trip, and was offered role in Australian film *In the Wake of the Bounty*. Appeared on English stage in several plays, including John Drinkwater's " A Man's House". Played small roles at Warners' Teddington Studio before going to Hollywood, where his first film was *Don't Bet on Blondes* (Warn) 1934. Other films include : *The Case of the Curious Bride, Captain Blood, The Charge of the Light Brigade, The Green Light, The Prince and the Pauper, Another Dawn, The Perfect Specimen, The Adventures of Robin Hood, Four's a Crowd, The Sisters, Dawn Patrol, Dodge City, Private Lives of Elizabeth and Essex.* Since then (all Warn)—1940: *Santa Fe Trail* ; 1941 : *Dive Bomber* ; 1942 : *Desperate Journey, Gentleman Jim* ; 1943 : *Edge of Darkness, Northern Pursuit, Thank Your Lucky Stars !* ; 1944 : *Uncertain Glory* ; 1945 : *Objective Burma* (withdrawn from British cinemas after public protest), *San Antonio* ; 1946 : *Never Say Good-bye* ; 1947 : *Silver River, Cry Wolf* ; 1948 : *The Adventures of Don Juan.*

FOCH, Nina. Born Leyden, Holland, Apr. 20, 1924. Educ. New York. Spent early childhood travelling in Europe ; then taken to America. In early teens, gave piano recital at Aeolian Hall, New York. Trained at Art Students' League ; became shop window dresser, New York ; spent several years studying in Little Theatres. Toured in small parts ; then on Broadway in " Life Is Like That " and " No One of Importance ". Seen by talent scout on stage and given contract. First film : *The Return of the Vampire* (Col) 1943. Other films (all Col) include 1943 : *Nine Girls* ; 1944 : *Cry of the Werewolf, She's a Soldier Too, Shadows in the Night, She's a Sweetheart, Strange Affair* ; 1945 : *A Song to Remember, I Love a Mystery, Prison Ship* ; 1946 : *Blackie's Rendezvous, My Name is Julia Ross* ; 1947 : *Johnny O'Clock.*

FONDA. Henry. Born Grand Island, Nebraska, May 16, 1908. Ht. 6 ft. 1 in ; wt. 165 lb. Dark brown hair, blue eyes. Educ. Dundee Grade School, Central High School, University of Minnesota. Ambition was to be a newspaper reporter, but failed, so became ice-man, garage hand, window dresser, telephone man. Joined Omaha Community Playhouse and later other Little Theatres as designer and actor : then became extra and understudy with New York Theatre Guild. Made hit in " The Swan". First film : *The Farmer Takes a Wife* (Fox) 1935. Other films include : *Way Down East, I Dream Too Much, Trail of the Lonesome Pine, The Moon's Our Home, Spendthrift, Wings of the Morning* (20th Brit, 1936), *You Only Live Once, Slim, That Certain Woman, I Met My Love Again, Jezebel, Blockade, Spawn of the North, Mad Miss Manton, Jesse James, Let Us Live, Story of Alexander Graham Bell, Young Mr. Lincoln, Drums Along the Mohawk, The Grapes of Wrath.* 1940 : *Lillian Russell* (20th), *The Return of Frank James* (20th), *Chad Hanna* (20th), *The Lady Eve* (Para) ; 1941 : *Wild Geese Calling* (20th), *You Belong to Me* (Col), *The Male Animal* (Warn) ; 1942 : *The Big Street* (RKO), *Rings on Her Fingers* (20th), *Tales of Manhattan* (20th), *The Magnificent Dope* (20th), *The Immortal Sergeant* (20th), *The Ox-bow Incident*—British title *Strange Incident* (20th).1942-5, served in U.S. Navy. 1946 : *My Darling Clementine* (20th) ; 1947 : appeared in, directed and produced *The Long Night* (RKO).

FONTAINE, Joan. Real name Joan de Havilland (sister of Olivia). Born Tokio, Japan, Oct. 22, 1917. Ht. 5 ft. 4 in. ; wt. 108 lb. Blonde hair, blue eyes. Spent childhood in San Francisco ; studied art in Saratoga, California. On stage in "Call it a Day" in Los Angeles, and offered long-term film contract. First film : *Quality Street* (RKO) 1937. Other films include : *The Man Who Found Himself, You Can't Beat Love, Music for Madame, A Damsel in Distress, Maid's Night Out, Blonde Cheat, Sky Giant, Duke of West Point, Gunga Din, Man of Conquest, The Women.* 1940 : *Rebecca* (UA) ; 1941 : *Suspicion* (RKO) ; 1942 : *This Above All* (20th) ; 1943 : *The Constant Nymph* (Warn) ; 1944 : *Jane Eyre* (20th), *Frenchman's Creek* (Para) ; 1945 : *The Affairs of Susan ;* 1946 : *From This Day Forward* (RKO) ; 1947 : *Ivy* (Univ), *The Walls of Jericho, The Emperor Waltz* (Para) ; 1948 : *Letters from an Unknown Woman* (UI).

FORD, Glenn. Real name Gwyllyn Ford. Born Quebec, Canada, May 1. Ht. 6 ft. 1 in. Educ. Santa Monica High School. At age of 4, had converted family barn into theatre and presented "Tom Thumb's Wedding", "King Arthur and His Knights". Left school 1934 and, with no stage training, played in touring company. Spent four years with the Players, a Santa Monica Little Theatre group, and later appeared with Francis Lederer in "Golden Boy". First film : *Heaven with a Barbed Wire Fence* (20th) 1939. Other films (all Col) include —1940 : *My Son Is Guilty, Convicted Woman, Men without Souls, The Lady in Question, Blondie Plays Cupid, Babies for Sale.* 1941 : *So Ends Our Night* (UA) in which he achieved great success, *Texas, Go West Young Lady ;* 1942 : *Adventures of Martin Eden, Flight Lieutenant ;* 1943 : *Desperadoes, Destroyer ;* 1943-5, served in U.S. Marines. 1946 : *A Stolen Life* (Warn), *Gilda ;* 1947 : *Gallant Journey ;* 1948 : *The Man from Colorado.*

FORD, John. Real name Scan O'Fearna. Director, writer. Born Cape Elizabeth, Maine, Feb. 1, 1895.

Educ. University of Maine. Began directing two-reelers from 1917. Silent films directed include : *The Iron Horse, Three Bad Men, Four Sons, Blue Eagle, Riley the Cop, Mother Machree, Upstream, Strong Boy, Salute, Born Reckless, Up the River,* and *Men Without Women* (which he also wrote). Sound films include : *The Brat, Arrowsmith, Flesh, Airmail, Pilgrimage, Dr. Bull, The World Moves On, The Lost Patrol, Steamboat Round the Bend, The Informer* (RKO ; 1935 Academy Award for direction), *The Whole Town's Talking, Prisoner of Shark Island, Mary of Scotland, The Plough and the Stars, The Hurricane, Wee Willie Winkie, Four Men and a Prayer, Submarine Patrol, Stagecoach* (also produced), *Young Mr. Lincoln, Drums Along the Mohawk, Grapes of Wrath, The Long Voyage Home, Tobacco Road, How Green Was My Valley, The Battle of Midway* (for U.S. War Activities Committee), *They Were Expendable.* Also photographed, edited, and wrote additional dialogue for British War documentary *We Sail at Midnight.* Recent films : *My Darling Clementine, The Fugitive* (directed and produced).

FORDE, Culley. Born London. Educ. convent school. Wife of director Walter Forde. Entered films as continuity girl and editor with Ideal Films, Elstree. Had considerable experience as film editor in early British films ; re-cut *King of Kings, Volga Boatman.* Assistant and co-producer of all husband's films.

FORDE, Walter. Director. Born London, 1897. Early career as knockabout comedian and pianist in vaudeville and revue. In 1923-5 directed and starred in one-reel and two-reel comedies for Universal, Hollywood. In Britain starred in series of successful feature-length comedies for Nettlefold : *Wait and See, You'd Be Surprised, Would You Believe It ?* Directed many silent films, including *The Silent House,* and early talkies : *Lord Richard in the Pantry, The Last Hour, Bed and Breakfast, Third Time Lucky, The Ringer, The Ghost Train, Splinters in the Navy, Jack O'Lantern, Lord Babs, Jack's the Boy.* In 1932 made *Rome Express,* first film at rebuilt Gaumont British studios. Later films include : *Orders Is Orders, Jack Ahoy, For Ever England, Chu Chin Chow, Bulldog Jack, King of the Damned, Land without Music, Kicking the Moon Around, The Gaunt Stranger, Let's Be Famous !, The Four Just Men, Cheer Boys Cheer, Inspector Hornleigh on Holiday, Saloon Bar, Sailors Three, Inspector Hornleigh Goes to It, The Ghost Train, Atlantic Ferry, Flying Fortress, Jewel Robbery, It's That Man Again, Time Flies, One Exciting Night, Master of Bankdam.*

FOSTER, Preston. Born Ocean City, New Jersey, Aug. 24, 1902. Ht. 6 ft. 2 in. ; wt. 200 lb. Brown hair, blue eyes. Educ. High School, Pitman, New Jersey. Left school 1918. Sang with Pennsylvania Opera Company for two seasons. In 1928 became Broadway actor, appearing as deaf-and-dumb Chinese in " New Moon ", and later joined Lionel Atwill's company. The play " Two Seconds " (1931), in which he made hit, was seen by director Mervyn LeRoy who took him with the play to Hollywood, 1932. Had previously appeared as extra and small part player at Long Island Studios, New York, making screen debut in Richard Dix's *Nothing But the Truth* (Para) 1930. Other films include : *Life Begins, Doctor X, 'Two Seconds, Elmer the Great, Dangerous Crossroads, Heat Lightning, Wharf Angel, The Informer, The Arizonian, Last Days of Pompeii, Annie Oakley, We Who Are About to Die, Love Before Breakfast, The Plough and the Stars, Sea Devils, First Lady, The Storm, The Last*

HUMPHREY BOGART
(*Warner*)

JOAN CAULFIELD
(*Paramount*)

Warning, News Is Made at Night, Geronimo, Café Hostess. 1940 : *Moon Over Burma* (Para), *North West Mounted Police* (Para) ; 1941 : *Unfinished Business* (Univ) ; 1942 : *Secret Agent of Japan* (20th), *Gentleman After Dark* (UA), *Night in New Orleans* (Para), *Little Tokyo, U.S.A.* (20th), *Thunder Birds* (20th), *American Empire* (UA) ; 1943 : *My Friend Flicka* (20th), *Guadalcanal Diary* (20th) ; 1944 : *Bermuda Mystery* (20th) ; 1945 : *Valley of Decision* (MGM), *Twice Blessed* (MGM), *Thunderhead Son of Flicka* (20th), *The Last Gangster* (20th) ; 1946 : *The Harvey Girls* (MGM), *The Strange Triangle* (20th), *Tangier* (Univ) ; 1947 : *Ramrod* (Enterprise-MGM) ; 1948 : *Green Grass of Wyoming.*

FOSTER, Susanna. Real name Suzanne DeLee Flanders Larson. Born Chicago, Illinois, Dec. 6, 1924. Ht. 5 ft. 7 in. ; wt. 120 lb. Blonde hair, blue eyes. Trained as a singer. First attracted major attention in *The Phantom of the Opera.* First film : *The Great Victor Herbert* (Para) 1941. Other films include—1941 : *The Hard-Boiled Canary* (Para), *There's Magic In Music* (Para) ; 1943 : *The Phantom of the Opera* (Univ), *Top Man* (Univ) ; 1944 : *The Climax* (Univ), *Bowery to Broadway* (Univ), *San Diego I Love You* (Univ), *Follow the Boys* (Univ), *This Is the Life* (Univ) ; 1945 : *Frisco Sal* (Univ), *That Night with You* (Univ).

FRANKEL, Benjamin. Composer, musical director. Born London, 1906. Studied music at the Guildhall School of Music, and Trinity College. Also in Cologne and Berlin. Professor of Composition, Guildhall School of Music. Has been associated with film-music scoring for many years, specializing first in jazz and dance music. Later went over to more serious music. Films include : *Radio Parade of 1935, Public Nuisance Number One, Love in Exile, The Singing Cop, Music Hath Charms, No Monkey Business.* During the war composed for documentaries, and the British Council films *Macbeth* and *Julius Cæsar.* Recent feature films on which he has worked include : *He Found a Star, They Met in the Dark, Flight from Folly, The Seventh Veil, The Years Between, Girl in a Million, Dear Murderer, Night Beat, Dancing with Crime, Mine Own Executioner.*

FRENCH, Harold. Director. Born London, Apr. 23, 1897. Educ. Edge Hill College, Wimbledon. Made acting debut, 1912, in " The Winter's Tale " at the Savoy Theatre, London. 1912-13 in repertory at Liverpool and Manchester ; 1916-17 with Birmingham Repertory Company. 1917-19, in British Army. Appeared in " Cyrano de Bergerac ", 1919, and later in revue and musical comedy ; has also been stage producer. Debut as film actor in *East Lynne on the Western Front,* 1931. Appeared in : *The Officers' Mess, The Star Reporter, Yes Madame, Night of the Garter, The Umbrella, Mannequin, Faces, Murder at the Inn, How's Chances?, I Adore You.* Became film director, with Paramount-British, 1936. Has since directed : *Cavalier of the Streets, House of the Arrow, Dead Men Are Dangerous, Jeannie, Unpublished Story, The Day Will Dawn*—U.S. title *The Avengers, Secret Mission, Dear Octopus, English without Tears, Mr. Emmanuel, Quiet Weekend, White Cradle Inn, My Brother Jonathan, The Blind Goddess.*

FREND, Charles. Director. Born Pulborough, Sussex, Nov. 21, 1909. Educ. King's School, Canterbury ; Trinity College, Oxford. At Oxford became film critic of " The Isis ". Introduced to film industry through the late Donald Calthrop, actor, and began as cutting room assistant in British International Studios, Elstree, 1931. Joined Gaumont British as editor on Hitchcock's *Waltzes from Vienna,* 1933 ; until 1937, edited Hitchcock's films : *Sabotage, Secret Agent, Young and Innocent.* 1937-9, film editor on MGM—British productions : *A Yank at Oxford, The Citadel, Goodbye Mr. Chips !* Also *Major Barbara.* Began directing with *The Big Blockade* (1941). Has since directed : *The Foreman Went to France, San Demetrio London, Return of the Vikings, Johnny Frenchman, The Loves of Joanna Godden, Scott of the Antarctic.*

FURSE, Judith. Born Deepcut Camp, Camberley, Mar. 4, 1912. Ht. 5 ft. 10 in. Brown hair, brown eyes. Educ. St. Paul's Girls' School, travelled round the world with soldier father ; then returned to London to join Old Vic as student. While in stage play " Goodness, How Sad" at the Vaudeville, London, was spotted and offered film role. Made screen debut in *Goodbye Mr. Chips !,* 1939. Recent films include— 1944 : *A Canterbury Tale* (Archers) ; 1945 : *Johnny Frenchman* (Ealing) ; 1946 : *Quiet Weekend* (ABPC) ; 1947 : *Black Narcissus* (Archers).

FURSE, Roger. Costume and set designer. Born Ightham, Kent, 1903. Educ. St. George's Choir School, Windsor ; Eton. Studied art at Slade School and in Paris. Has also studied and worked in America. In Britain, has designed for the Old Vic and many West End productions. Designed maps and other materials for *The True Glory* and *Burma Victory,* costumes for *Henry V,* decor for *Odd Man Out.*

GABIN, Jean. Real name Jean Moncorge. Born Paris, May 17, 1904. Ht. 5 ft. 10 in. ; wt. 170 lb. Fair hair, green eyes. Educ. Meriel School ; Agricultural Institute. At first did not wish to follow the family profession on stage and worked in iron foundry for six years. Later became extra at Folies-Bergère ; singer in cafes, music halls, operetta. Three years' service in French Marines in World War I. Then in operetta " Trois Jeunes Filles Nues" ; made music-hall reputation with help of Mistinguett ; toured South America ; starred in Paris. First film : *Chacun sa Chance,* 1930. With success of early films, transferred from comedy to drama. French films include: *Paris-Béguin, Gloria, Cœur de Lilas, Les Gaietés de l'Escadron, La Belle Mariniere, La Foule Hurle, L'Etoile de Valencia, Adieu les Beaux Jours, Tunnel, Maria Chapdelaine, Variétés, La Bandera, La Belle Equipe, Pépé le Moko, Les Bas Fonds, La Grande Illusion* (film which brought him world fame), *La Bête Humaine, Le Quai des Brumes, Remorque.* 1939- 40, war service on French minesweeper. To Hollywood, 1941. First American film : *Moontide* (20th : a re-make of *Le Quai des Brumes*). 1944 : *The Impostor* (Univ). Returned to France after liberation of Paris. 1945 : *Mimoir* ; 1946 : *Martin Roumagnac* (with Marlene Dietrich).

GABLE, Clark. Real name William Clark Gable. Born Cadiz, Ohio, Feb. 1, 1901. Ht. 6 ft. 1 in. ; wt. 190 lb. Brown hair, grey eyes. At 15 worked in an Akron rubber factory. Joined local theatre as call-boy. Then worked with father in Oklahoma oil field. At 19 returned to stage with touring company in Kansas City. Was stage actor for ten years till a talent scout saw his performance in " The Last Mile", which won him a part in *The Painted Desert* (RKO) 1930. Served with U.S.A.A.F. 1942-4 ; while stationed in Britain produced a special film made largely during bombing

JOAN FONTAINE
(*Universal-International*)

operations, for training air gunners. Other films include : *Dance Fools Dance, The Easiest Way, Finger Points, The Secret Six, Laughing Sinners, Night Nurse, Rise of Helga, A Free Soul, Sporting Blood, Possessed* (MGM) 1931, *Hell's Divers, Polly of the Circus, Red Dust, Strange Interval, No Man of Her Own, The White Sister, Hold Your Man, Night Flight, Dancing Lady, It Happened One Night, Men in White, Manhattan Melodrama, Chained, After Office Hours, Forsaking All Others, Call of the Wild, China Seas, Mutiny on the Bounty, Wife Versus Secretary, Cain and Mabel, San Francisco, Love on the Run, Parnell, Saratoga, Test Pilot, Too Hot to Handle, Idiot's Delight, Gone with the Wind* (Selznick) 1939, first shown in Britain in 1940, generally released in 1942, and re-issued in 1944 and 1947. 1940 : *Strange Cargo* (MGM), *Boom Town* (MGM), *Comrade X* (MGM) ; 1941 : *They Met in Bombay* (MGM), *Honky Tonk* (MGM) ; 1942 : *Somewhere I'll Find You* (MGM) ; 1945 : *Adventure* (MGM) ; 1947 : *The Hucksters* (MGM) ; 1948 : *Homecoming* (MGM).

GARDINER, Reginald. Real name William Reginald Gardiner. Born Wimbledon, Feb. 27, 1903. Ht. 5 ft. 10½ in. ; wt. 150 lb. Reddish-brown hair, brown eyes. Educ. Shrewsbury School. Became architectural student, but left for Royal Academy of Dramatic Art. Appeared in London and provincial stage in " The Rat ", " Blackmail ", " The Lure ", and many other plays, and in British films. In 1938 in Broadway shows and then to Hollywood. First film : *How's Chances ?* (20th-Brit), 1934. Others include : *Born to Dance, Everybody Sing, Marie Antoinette, Sweethearts, Heaven on a Shoe String, Flying Deuces.* 1940 : *The Doctor Takes A Wife* (Col), *Dulcy* (MGM), *The Great Dictator* (UA) ; 1941 : *My Life with Caroline* (RKO), *A Yank in the RAF* (20th), *Sundown* (Wanger) ; 1942 : *The Man Who Came to Dinner* (Warn), *Captain of the Clouds* (Warn) ; 1943 : *Immortal Sergeant* (20th), *Claudia* (20th) ; 1944 : *Sweet Rosie O'Grady* (20th), *Molly and Me* (20th) ; 1945 : *Christmas in Connecticut* (Warn), *Dolly Sisters* (20th), *Horn Blows at Midnight* (Warn) ; 1946 : *Do You Love Me ?* (20th), *Cluny Brown* (20th) ; 1947 : *I Wonder Who's Kissing Her Now ?* (20th).

GARDNER, Ava. Born Smithfield, North Carolina, Dec. 24. Ht. 5 ft. 6 in. ; wt. 120 lb. On first film test her Carolina drawl was so thick as to be almost incomprehensible ; but after course of voice training made another test and won contract. Films—1941 : *Highway to Freedom* (MGM) ; 1942 : *We Were Dancing* (MGM), *This Time for Keeps* (MGM), *Kid Glove Killer* (MGM), *Pilot No. 5* (MGM) ; 1943 : *Hitler's Madman,* (MGM), *Swing Fever* (MGM), *Young Ideas* (MGM), *Ghosts on the Loose* (Mono), *Lost Angel* (MGM) ; 1944 : *Two Girls and a Sailor* (MGM), *Three Men in White* (MGM), *You Can't Do That to Me* (MGM) ; 1945 : *She Went to the Races* (MGM) ; 1946 : *Whistle Stop* (UA), *The Killers* (Univ) ; 1947 : *The Hucksters* (MGM), *Singapore* (UI) ; 1948 : *Upward to the Stars* (MGM).

GARFIELD, John. Born New York, Mar. 4, 1913. Ht. 5 ft. 8 in. ; wt. 165 lb. Educ. Theodore Roosevelt School, New York. Won scholarship to Maria Ouspenskaya Drama School and at 15 made stage debut in New York. Outstanding stage successes include " Counsellor-at-Law " and " Golden Boy ", 1937. While appearing in this play was spotted by film talent scout. First film : *Four Daughters* (Warn) 1938. Other films include : *Blackwell's Island, They*

Made Me a Criminal, Juarez, Dust Be my Destiny. 1940 : *Saturday's Children* (Warn) ; 1941 : *The Sea Wolf* (Warn) ; 1942 : *Tortilla Flat* (MGM) ; 1943 : *Air Force* (Warn), *Thank Your Lucky Stars* (Warn) ; 1944 : *Between Two Worlds* (Warn), *Destination Tokyo* (Warn), *Hollywood Canteen* (Warn) ; 1946 : *Nobody Lives Forever* (Warn) ; 1947 : *Humoresque* (Warn), *Body and Soul* (MGM) ; 1948 : *Gentlemen's Agreement* (20th).

GARLAND, Judy. Real name Frances Gumm. Born Grand Rapids, Michigan, June 10, 1922. Ht. 5 ft. 3 in. ; wt. 115 lb. Auburn hair, brown eyes. Educ. Los Angeles High School. At 3 sang " Jingle Bells " at local theatre ; later joined parents and two sisters in stage act, then with sisters in close harmony trio. First film, a short with Deanna Durbin : *Every Sunday Afternoon* (MGM) 1935. Became established as juvenile singing star in *Broadway Melody of 1938* (MGM). Other films (all MGM) include : *Thoroughbreds Don't Cry, Everybody Sing, Love Finds Andy Hardy, Listen Darling, The Wizard of Oz, Babes in Arms.* 1940 : *Andy Hardy Meets Debutante, Strike Up the Band, Little Nellie Kelly ;* 1941 : *Ziegfeld Girl, Life Begins for Andy Hardy, Babes on Broadway ;* 1942 : *For Me and My Gal, Presenting Lily Mars ;* 1943 : *Girl Crazy, Thousands Cheer ;* 1944 : *Meet Me in St. Louis, Ziegfeld Follies, Under the Clock ;* 1945 : *The Harvey Girls ;* 1946 : *Till the Clouds Roll By ;* 1947 : *The Pirate ;* 1948 : *Easter Parade* (MGM).

GARNER, Peggy Ann. Born Canton, Ohio, Feb. 3, 1932. Blonde hair, hazel eyes. Became New York child model. Went to Hollywood, 1938, and secured first screen rôle : *Little Miss Thoroughbred* (Warn) 1938. Other films include : *In Name Only* (RKO). 1940 : *Blondie Brings up Baby* (Col), *Abe Lincoln in Illinois* (RKO) ; 1942 : *Eagle Squadron* (Univ) ; 1943 : *The Pied Piper* (20th), *Jane Eyre* (20th) ; 1944 : *The Keys of the Kingdom* (20th), *A Tree Grows in Brooklyn* (20th) ; 1945 : *Junior Miss* (20th), *Nob Hill* (20th) ; 1946 : *Home Sweet Homicide* (20th) ; 1947 : *Bob, Son of Battle* (20th).

GARSON, Greer. Born County Down, N. Ireland, Sept. 29. Ht. 5 ft. 6 in. ; wt. 112 lb. Red hair, blue-green eyes. Educ. London University (B.A.), Grenoble University. Originally intended to teach, but joined London advertising firm, then made debut with Birmingham Repertory Theatre in " Street Scene ", 1932. From 1934-38 on London stage : " Golden Arrow ", " Accent on Youth ", " Old Music ", and other plays. Louis B. Mayer saw her in " Old Music " and personally offered her a contract. Spent year idle in Hollywood, then made first film, in Britain : *Goodbye Mr. Chips !* (MGM-Brit) 1939. Films (all MGM) include—1939 : *Remember ;* 1940 : *Pride and Prejudice ;* 1942 : *Blossoms in the Dust, When Ladies Meet ;* 1942 : *Mrs. Miniver, Random Harvest ;* 1943 : *The Youngest Profession, Madame Curie ;* 1944 : *Mrs. Parkington ;* 1945 : *The Valley of Decision, Adventure ;* 1947 : *Desire Me ;* 1948 : *Julia Misbehaves.*

GENN, Leo. Actor, barrister. Born London, Aug. 9, 1905. Ht. 5 ft. 11½ in. ; wt. 172 lb. Dark hair, brown eyes. Educ. City of London School ; St. Catherine's College, Cambridge ; Middle Temple. Practised as barrister for four years before going on stage. After amateur experience made professional debut at Eastbourne in 1930 in " A Marriage Has Been Disarranged ". London debut a month later in same part. Entered films in 1936. Made many broadcasts and was narrator of the B.B.C. series "Shadow of the Swastika" 1939-40. In World War II served in Royal Artillery. Was a member of the No. 1 War Crimes Investigation Team, and Assistant Prosecutor at the Belsen Trial. Films include—*Jump for Glory, Cavalier of the Streets, The Rat, The Drum, Kate Plus Ten.* 1944: *Henry V* (UA); 1946. *Caesar and Cleopatra* (Pascal); 1947: *Green for Danger* (Individ).

GERAY, Steve. Born Uzhorod, Czechoslovakia, Nov. 10, 1904. Educ. preparatory school and University of Technology, Budapest. Tried to be violinist, then painter; but found success as actor, with debut in "Brothers Karamazov", Budapest, receiving honour of membership of the Hungarian National Theatre. Also appeared on London stage in revue and musical comedy. Has appeared in more than fifty Continental and British films. In 1939 went to America as M.C. of "Folies-Bergère", and then made his American debut in *Man at Large* (20th) 1941. Other films include—1941: *Blue White and Perfect* (20th); 1942: *Eyes in the Night* (MGM), *The Moon and Sixpence* (UA); 1943: *Phantom of the Opera* (Univ), *Hostages* (Para), *Pilot No. 5* (MGM), *Night Plane from Chungking* (Para); 1944: *Meet the People* (MGM), *The Seventh Cross* (MGM), *The Mask of Dimitrios* (Warn), *The Conspirators* (Warn); 1945: *Hotel Berlin* (Warn), *Mexicana* (Rep), *The Crimson Canary* (Univ), *Spellbound* (UA), *Cornered* (RKO); 1946: *Monte Cristo's Revenge* (Col), *So Dark the Night* (Col), *The Assassin* (Col).

GIACHETTI, Fosco. Born Sesto Fiorentino, Florence, 1902. Films include: *Guiseppe Verdi, L'Assedio dell' Alcazar, Nozze di Sangue, Farinella Nebbia.* 1945: *Noi Vivi* (Scalera): 1944: *L'Abito Nero da Spoza* (Vi. Va), *Il Sole di Montecassino* (Arno); 1945: *Notte di Tempesta* (Pau Lux), *La Vita Ricomincia* (Excelsa); 1946: *Addio Mia Bella Napoli* (Ideal).

GIFFORD, Frances. Born Long Beach, California, Dec. 7, 1922. Ht. 5 ft. 6 in.; wt. 120 lb. Auburn hair, blue eyes. Educ. Woodrow Wilson High School; University of California. Studied law, was fashion model during holidays. During a sight-seeing trip round film studio was asked to make test, and signed contract same day. First film: *Fugitive from Justice* (Warn) 1940. Other films include: *Mercy Plane, Hold That Woman.* 1941: *Border Vigilantes* (Para), *The Reluctant Dragon* (RKO), *West Point Widow* (Para), *The Remarkable Andrew* (Para); 1942: *Beyond the Blue Horizon* (Para), *The Glass Key* (Para), *Tombstone* (Para), *My Son Alone* (UA), *My Heart Belongs to Daddy* (Para); 1943: *Henry Aldrich Gets Glamour* (Para), *Tarzan Triumphs* (RKO), *Cry Havoc* (MGM); 1944: *Marriage Is a Private Affair* (MGM), *Thrill of a Romance* (MGM); 1945: *Our Vines Have Tender Grapes* (MGM), *She Went to the Races* (MGM); 1946: *Little Mister Jim* (MGM); 1947: *The Arnelo Affair* (MGM); 1948: *Luxury Liner* (MGM).

GILCHRIST, Connie. Real name Rose Gilchrist. Born Brooklyn Heights, New York, Feb. 2. Ht. 5 ft. 6 in.; wt. 140 lb. Blonde hair, blue eyes. Educ. Assumption Academy. Daughter of actress Martha Daniels, made stage debut in London at 16. Toured France in repertory, managed theatrical companies in America and acted on Broadway. Seen with Helen Hayes in "Ladies and Gentlemen", was given screen test. First film: *Hullabaloo* (MGM) 1940. Films (all MGM except where stated) include—1941: *The*

Wild Man of Borneo, A Woman's Face, Whistling in the Dark, We Were Dancing, Billy the Kid, Johnny Eager, Barnacle Bill; 1942: *This Time for Keeps, Tortilla Flat, Sunday Punch, Grand Central Murder, The War Against Mrs. Hadley, Apache Trail, Presenting Lily Mars*; 1943: *Cry Havoc, The Heavenly Body, Thousands Cheer, The Girl in Overalls*; 1945: *Junior Miss* (20th), *The Valley of Decision, Young Widow* (UA), *Bad Bascomb*; 1946: *Tenth Avenue Angel, Merton of the Movies*; 1947: *Song of the Thin Man.*

GILLIATT, Sydney. Writer, director, producer. Born Cheshire, 1908. Educ. London University. Began as assistant in scenario department of British International Pictures. Later at Gaumont British worked on script of *Rome Express.* Research for this film made him an expert on Continental railway timetables, which has since become one of his hobbies. Working on the same film was Frank Launder, with whom he collaborated in the writing of many other screenplays, which included *A Yank at Oxford* for MGM British, and later *The Lady Vanishes, They Came by Night, Night Train to Munich, Girl in the News, Kipps* and *The Young Mr. Pitt.* They also wrote "The Body Was Well Nourished" presented by Jack Buchanan in 1940 at the Lyric Theatre, London. In 1943 Maurice Ostrer assigned them to write, direct and produce *Millions Like Us,* 2000 *Women, Waterloo Road.* In 1945 they formed independent unit, Individual Pictures Ltd., to write, direct and produce their own films: *The Rake's Progress, I See a Dark Stranger, Green for Danger, Captain Boycott, London Belongs to Me, The Blue Lagoon.*

GILMORE, Virginia. Real name Sherman Poole. Born Del Monte, California, July 26, 1919. Ht. 5 ft. 4 in.; wt. 110 lb. Blonde hair, brown eyes. Educ. Immaculate Heart Convent, Hollywood; Burlingame High School, California; San Mateo Junior College; University of California. First job was as shop assistant; then appeared in "Of Mice and Men" at San Francisco Green Room Theatre and worked on radio in San Francisco. First film: *Manhattan Heartbeat* (20th) 1940. Other films include: *Laddie* (RKO). 1941: *Jennie* (20th); 1942: *Western Union* (20th), *Berlin Correspondent* (20th), *Pride of the Yankees* (RKO), *Tall, Dark and Handsome* (20th); 1943: *Loves of Edgar Allen Poe* (20th), *Orchestra Wives* (20th), *That Other Woman* (20th); 1944: *Sundown Jim* (20th), *Chetniks* (20th); 1946: *Wonder Man* (RKO).

GIOI, Vivi. Born Leghorn, Italy, 1913. Films include: *Dopo Divorzieremo,* 100 *Lettere d'Amore, Giungla, Primo Amore, Bengasi*; 1944: *Tutta la Città Canta* (Littoria), *La Casa Senza Tempo* (Bolognesi); 1946: *Il Marito Povero* (Di Pinto); 1947: *Caccia Tragica* (ANPI).

GIROTTI, Massimo. Born Marte (Macerata), Italy, 1914. Films include: *La Corona de Ferro, Le Due Tigri, Un Pilota Ritorna.* 1944: *La Carne e l'Anima* (Titanus), *Ossessione* (ICI); 1945: *Desiderio* (Fuiana), *Un Giorno Nella Vita* (Arbia); 1946: *Fatalità* (Universalcine); 1947: *Preludio d'Amore* (Altatros).

GISH, Lilian. Born Springfield, Ohio, Oct. 14, 1896. Sister of Dorothy Gish. Fair hair, blue eyes. Ht. 5 ft. 4 in.; wt. 110 lb. Educ. Dayton and Baltimore. Stage debut at six with sister in melodrama "In Convict's Stripes" at Rising Sun, Ohio. New York stage debut, 1913, with Mary Pickford in Belasco's "A Good Little

Devil " and screen debut same year with Mary Pickford in *The Unseen Enemy* (D. W. Griffith). Her famous films include : *Birth of a Nation* (1915), *Intolerance* (1916), *Souls Triumphant* (1917), *Heart of the World* (made in Europe), *The Great Love* (1918), *Broken Blossoms*, *Way Down East*, *Orphans of the Storm ; The White Sister* and *Romola* both made in Italy, 1924-5 ; *The Scarlet Letter*, *La Bohème*, *Annie Laurie*, *The Enemy*, *Wind*, *One Romantic Night*, *His Double Life*. Returned to stage, 1930, and has appeared in " Uncle Vanya ", " The Old Maid " (Glasgow, 1936), " Hamlet ", " Dear Octopus ", " Life with Father " (Chicago). Resumed films, 1946, with *Miss Susie Slagle's* (Para) ; 1947 : *Duel in the Sun* (Selznick) ; 1948 : *Portrait of Jennie* (Selznick).

GLEASON, James. Born New York City, May 23, 1886. Ht. 5 ft. 10 in. ; wt. 140 lb. Light brown hair, blue eyes. On stage at 2 months ; at 5 starred in " Stricken Blind ". At 16 joined Army as trumpeter. On New York stage in : " The Fall Guy ", " The Shannons on Broadway ". Author of " The Fall Guy ", " Is Zat So ? " Has had a long career as a feature player. Made two silent films, New York. First sound film : *A Free Soul* (MGM) 1930. Other films include : *The Big Gamble*, *The Suicide Fleet*, *Hoopla*, *Orders Is Orders* (GB, in Britain) 1933, *Murder on a Honeymoon*, *West Point of the Air*, *The Ex-Mrs. Bradford*, *The Big Game*, *Yours for the Asking*, *Manhattan Merry-go-round*, *The Higgins Family*, *Should Husbands Work*, *On Your Toes* ; 1940 : *Grandpa Goes to Town* (Rep), *Earl of Puddlestone* (Rep) ; 1941 : *Meet John Doe* (Warn), *Affectionately Yours* (Warn), *Here Comes Mr. Jordan* (Col), *Nine Lives Are Not Enough* (Warn), *Thanks a Million* (Roach-UA), *Hayfoot* (Roach-UA), *Arsenic and Old Lace* (Warn), *A Date with the Falcon* (RKO), *The Falcon Takes Over* (RKO) ; 1942 : *My Gal Sal* (20th), *Footlight Serenade* (20th), *Manila Calling* (20th) ; 1943 : *Crash Dive* (20th) ; 1944 : *Keys of the Kingdom* (20th), *A Guy Named Joe* (MGM), *Once Upon a Time* (Col), *Airship Squadron 4X ;* 1945 : *A Tree Grows in Brooklyn* (20th), *This Man's Navy* (MGM), *The Clock* (MGM), *Captain Eddie* (20th) ; 1946 : *Home Sweet Homicide* (20th) ; 1947 : *Down to Earth* (Col).

GLYN, Patricia. Real name Bettine Glyn. Born London, June 30, 1925. Ht. 5 ft. 2 in. ; wt. 126 lb. Fair hair, blue-grey eyes. Educ. private boarding school. Started stage career at 17 as assistant stage manager with repertory company at £1 per week. Then toured. London stage debut in " Quiet Weekend ", in which she also travelled for ENSA on the Continent. First film : *Millions Like Us* (Gainsborough) 1943. 1947 : *Uncle Silas* (Two Cities).

GLYNNE, Maureen. Born Streatham, London, Aug. 18, 1928. Fair hair, blue eyes. Educ. St. Andrew's Convent, Coventry Hall, Streatham ; St. Mary's Convent, Hampstead. At 3 appeared with mother's musical act, " The Glynne Sisters ", in Capetown, S. Africa ; at 7 in children's variety show, Ambassador's Theatre, London. Became child cabaret entertainer in London night clubs ; appeared in plays and pantomime, including boy parts. London stage plays include " The Intruder ", " Janie ", " Watch on the Rhine ". Much radio experience, after debut 1938 in B.B.C.'s " In Town Tonight " feature, including leads in radio versions of Hollywood musicals " Babes in Arms ", " Babes on Broadway ". Made film debut 1935, in Clapham and Dwyer comedy. Other films include : *John Halifax, Gentleman* (with Roddy

McDowall), *The Life Story of Chopin*, *The Outsider* (with Harold Huth and George Sanders), *A Royal Divorce* (with Ruth Chatterton), *Sixty Glorious Years*, *The Nursemaid Who Disappeared*. 1942 : *Gert and Daisy's Weekend* (Butcher) ; 1944 : *A Medal for the General* (Brit Nat) ; 1946 : *The Turners of Prospect Road* (Grand Nat).

GODDARD, Paulette. Born Whitestone, Long Island, U.S.A., June 3, 1911. Ht. 5 ft. 4 in. ; wt. 110 lb. Dark brown hair, blue eyes. At 11, combined lessons with first stage job in chorus of Ziegfeld's " Rio Rita ". Became member of Hal Roach's studio staff company, but left when she discovered only her legs were seen on the screen. Appeared in close-up in *The Kid from Spain* (UA) 1932. Films include : *The Young in Heart*, *Dramatic School*, *The Cat and the Canary*, *The Women*. 1940 : *The Great Dictator*, *The Ghost Breakers*, *North West Mounted Police* (Para), *Second Chorus* (Para) ; 1941 : *Pot o' Gold* (UA), *Nothing But the Truth* (Para), *Hold Back the Dawn* (Para) ; 1942 : *Reap the Wild Wind* (Para), *The Lady Has Plans* (Para), *The Forest Rangers* (Para) ; 1943 : *Star Spangled Rhythm* (Para), *The Crystal Ball* (UA), *So Proudly We Hail* (Para) ; 1944 : *Standing Room Only* (Para), *I Love a Soldier* (Para) ; 1945 : *Kitty* (Para), *Duffy's Tavern* (Para), *Diary of a Chambermaid ;* 1946 : *Suddenly It's Spring* (Para), *The Unconquered* (Para), *My Favourite Brunette* (Para) ; 1947 : *An Ideal Husband* (LFP), made in Britain ; 1948 : *Hazard* (Para), *A Miracle Can Happen* (Benedict Bogeaus-UA).

GOETZ, Ben. Producer. Born New York City, June 2, 1891. Originally studied law but forsook this for work in film laboratory. Joined Erbograph Laboratories, New York City, and later became Vice-President of Consolidated Film Laboratories. Then became production executive with MGM, and in 1937 came to Britain as Chairman and Managing Director of Metro-Goldwyn-Mayer British Studios Ltd. This company made *A Yank at Oxford*, *Goodbye Mr. Chips !*, *Busman's Honeymoon*, *The Citadel*, *Perfect Strangers*, and in 1947 opened the new studios at Boreham Wood, Elstree, Herts.

GOLDWYN, Samuel. Real name Samuel Goldfish. Born Warsaw, 1884. As a young man worked in the glove trade. With Jesse Lasky, founded the Lasky Company in 1910 ; their first major film was *The Squaw Man*, 1913, directed by Cecil B. De Mille. In 1917 Goldwyn brought about a merger between Famous Players and Lasky ; in 1918 with Arch and Edgar Selwyn formed Goldwyn Pictures Corporation, which he sold to Metro in 1924. In 1927 became owner-member of United Artists ; in 1940 became an independent producer again. Is regarded as the greatest discoverer of " glamour " in the film industry : " I know it when I see it, but I can't put it into words ". Has made stars of Ronald Colman, Gary Cooper, Anna Sten, Vilma Banky, and in recent years, Danny Kaye, Teresa Wright, Virginia Mayo and Cathy O'Donnell. Had never won Academy Award until his *The Best Years of Our Lives* won nine in 1946. To Goldwyn went the most coveted of these, the Irving Thalberg Award presented to the producer who achieves in his own personally produced film the standards set by the late Irving Thalberg, MGM producer, who worked consistently to raise the cultural standard of U.S. films.

GORCEY, Leo. Born New York City, June 3, 1919. On New York stage, 1935, in " Dead End " ; repeated role in film version (UA) 1937. Other films include: *Crime School, Dress Parade, Angels with Dirty Faces, Hell's Kitchen, Battle of City Hall.* 1941 : *Angels with Broken Wings* (Rep) ; 1942 : *Born to Sing* (MGM) ; 1943 : *Destroyer* (Col), *Mr. Muggs Steps Out* (Mono) ; 1944 : *Block Busters* (Mono), *Follow the Leader* (Mono), *Million Dollar Kid* (Mono), *Bowery Champs* (Mono) ; 1945 : *Muggs Rides Again* (Mono), *Docks of New York* (Mono), *Come Out Fighting* (Mono) ; 1946 : *Live Wires* (Mono), *Midnight Manhunt* (Para) ; 1947 : *Bowery Bombshell* (Mono), *Spook Busters* (Mono), *Pride of the Bowery* (Mono).

GORING, Marius. Born Newport, Isle of Wight. Ht. 5 ft. 10 in. ; wt. 162 lb. Light brown hair, blue eyes. Educ. Perse School, Cambridge, Universities of Paris, Munich, Frankfurt, Vienna. Trained for stage with Old Vic dramatic school ; joined company in Shakespeare and classics. West End debut, 1934, in " The Voysey Inheritance ". Toured France and Switzerland with " Compagnie des Quinze ". London plays include : " Mary Tudor ", " The Happy Hypocrite ", " The Doll's House ". War service 1939-46, first in army, then conducting anti-Nazi radio propaganda for Foreign Office under name Charles Richardson. First film : *Consider Your Verdict* (Charter) 1936. Other films include : *Rembrandt, Dead Men Tell No Tales, Flying Fifty-Five, Spy in Black, The Case of the Frightened Lady.* 1941 : *The Big Blockade* (Ealing), *The Night Raider* ; 1946 : *A Matter of Life and Death* (Archers) ; 1947 : *Take My Life* (Cineguild) ; 1948 : *Red Shoes* (Archers).

GOULDING, Edmund. Director, writer. Born London, Mar. 20, 1891. Made London acting debut in 1909 at Holborn Empire in sketch " Gentleman, the King ". Stage actor and producer, author of plays " Out of the Fog ", " God Save the King ". With Edgar Selwyn wrote New York play " Dancing Mothers ". Joined MGM in 1925 as writer and was responsible for *Love*, early Garbo success. Conducted original experimental tests for sound films, wrote scenario for first big talkie : *The Broadway Melody.* Films include : *Riptide* (also author), *The Flame Within* (also author), *Grand Hotel* (also producer), *Maytime* (also wrote screenplay), *Dawn Patrol, Dark Victory, Sally Irene and Mary, The Old Maid, We Are not Alone, Till We Meet Again, The Great Lie, Claudia, Of Human Bondage, The Razor's Edge, Nightmare Alley.*

GRABLE, Betty. Born St. Louis, Missouri, Dec. 18, 1916. Ht. 5 ft. 3½ in. ; wt. 112 lb. Golden-blonde hair, blue eyes. Educ. Mary Institute, St. Louis ; Hollywood Professional School. On radio at 7 ; studied singing, dancing in Hollywood. Made early films as chorus girl and speciality dancer. Joined Ted Fio-Rito's band as singer ; danced and sang with Jay Whidden's Band ; 1935, vaudeville with Jackie Coogan ; 1937, New York stage : " Du Barry Was a Lady ". First film appearance (as dancer) : *Let's Go Places* (20th) 1930. Films include : *Whoopee, Kiki, Hold 'Em Yale !, The Gay Divorcee, What Price Innocence, The Nitwits, Old Man Rhythm, Collegiate, Follow the Fleet, Don't Turn 'Em Loose, Pigskin Parade, This Way Please, Thrill of a Lifetime, College Swing, Million Dollar Legs, Give Me a Sailor.* (All 20th) 1940 : *Down Argentine Way, Tin Pan Alley* ; 1941 : *Moon Over Miami, A Yank in the R.A.F., Hot Spot, Song of the Islands* ; 1942 : *Coney Island, Sweet Rosie O'Grady, Pin Up Girl* ; 1945 : *Diamond Horseshoe, The Dolly Sisters* ; 1947 : *The Shocking Miss Pilgrim, Mother Wore Tights.*

GRAHAM, William. Born Darlington, Co. Durham, 1932. Red hair. Learnt to dance at 4 by improvising steps whilst listening to radio and gramophone ; won local prizes for dancing. In 1946 he appeared at Darlington Hippodrome in Carroll Levis Discoveries show, and toured Britain 1946-7 as member of Levis's troupe. Chosen from 1000 applicants for role of " William ", tousle-headed " bad boy " of Richmal Crompton books. Film debut in *Just William's Luck* (Alliance) 1947, and under long-term contract for continuation of " William " series.

GRAHAME, Gloria. Real name Gloria Hallward. Born Los Angeles, California, Nov. 28. Ht. 5 ft. 5½ in. Blonde hair, green eyes. Educ. Hollywood High School ; Pasadena High School. Daughter of English actress ; was prominent in school plays. Seen by stage producer and given professional role in " Good Night Ladies ", in Chicago. On Broadway, understudied Miriam Hopkins in " Skin of Our Teeth ", and appeared in " Stardust " and other shows. First film *Blonde Fever* (MGM) 1944. Other films include— 1945 : *Without Love* (MGM) ; 1946 : *It's a Wonderful Life* (RKO), *It Happened in Brooklyn* (MGM) ; 1947 : *Song of the Thin Man* (MGM), *Merton of the Movies* (MGM), *Crossfire* (RKO) ; 1948 : *Roughshod* (RKO).

GRAHAME, Margot. Born Canterbury, Kent, Feb. 20, 1911. Ht. 5 ft. 4½ in. ; wt. 118 lb. Red hair, green eyes. At 3 went to South Africa ; made first stage appearance at His Majesty's Theatre, Johannesburg, early in 1926 in " The Scarlet Pimpernel ". Returned to London in 1926, appearing in several stage plays including two Aldwych farces " A Cup of Kindness " and " A Night Like This ". Film debut in *Rookery Nook* (1929), one of Britain's first talkies, with Tom Walls. Other British films include : *The Love Habit, Sorrell and Son, Yes Mr. Brown, Illegal, I Adore You, Glamour, Creeping Shadows.* Went to America in 1934. First Hollywood film : *The Informer*, for which she won an Academy Award for her performance as Katie Madden. Other Hollywood films include : *The Arizonian, Criminal Lawyer, Fight for Your Lady, The Three Musketeers, Two in the Dark, Michael Strogoff, The Buccaneer.* Then on American stage ; played lead in " Heart of a City ", war story of Windmill Theatre, London. Returned to Hollywood in 1945 and made *The Fabulous Joe* (Hal Roach-UA) and *Forever Amber* (20th), 1947. Came back to Britain in 1947 and appeared in *Broken Journey* (Gains) ; 1948 : *Cagliostro* (Small), made in Italy.

GRANGER, Farley. Real name Farley Earle Granger. Born San Jose, California, July 1, 1925. Educ. North Hollywood High School. Youthful ambition : to be a veterinary surgeon. At school designed settings for school plays, but did not act. Was shop assistant for a time. Only acting experience was one week on the stage of a 175-seat theatre in Hollywood when at the age of 17, while still at school, saw newspaper advertisement for romantic juvenile lead to play opposite Anne Baxter. His application led to long-term contract. Film debut in *The North Star* (RKO) 1943. Served in Armed Forces, 1944-6. Films include—1944 : *The Purple Heart* (20th) ; 1947 : *Your Red Wagon* (RKO).

GRANGER, Stewart. Real name James Stewart. Born London, May 6, 1913. Ht. 6 ft. 2 in. ; wt. 196 lb. Black hair, brown eyes. Educ. Epsom College. Youthful ambition : to become nerve specialist ; went to medical school. Left at 17 for business job. Then trained at Webber-Douglas School of Dramatic Art and entered repertory at Hull and Birmingham, 1934-6. On London stage from 1937 ; was with Vivien Leigh in " Serena Blandish ", with Flora Robson in " Autumn ", with Lilian Braithwaite in " The House in the Square ". Two and a half years' war service with British Army ; invalided out 1942. Resumed stage career with Robert Donat in " To Dream Again ", then played lead in " Rebecca ". First film *So This Is London* (20th) 1938. Films include—1940 : *Convoy* (Ealing) ; 1943 : *Thursday's Child* (ABPC), *The Man in Grey* (Gains), *The Lamp Still Burns* (Two Cities), *Fanny By Gaslight* (Gains) ; 1944 : *Waterloo Road* (Gains), *Love Story* (Gains), *Madonna of the Seven Moons* (Gains) ; 1946 : *Caesar and Cleopatra* (Pascal), *Caravan* (Gains), *The Magic Bow* (Gains) ; 1947 : *Captain Boycott* (Individ) ; 1948 : *Blanche Fury* (Cineguild), *Saraband for Dead Lovers* (Ealing).

GRANT, Cary. Real name Archibald Leach. Born Bristol, Jan. 18, 1904. Ht. 6 ft. 1 in. ; wt. 172 lb. Educ. Fairfield Academy, Bristol. Ran away from home to become acrobat. As knockabout comedian appeared for two years at New York Hippodrome. Returned to England to appear in repertory ; then to New York in " Die Fledermaus " and Broadway musicals. First film : *This Is the Night* (Para) 1932. Other films include : *Sinners in the Sun, Hot Saturday, Merrily We Go to Hell, The Devil and the Deep, Madame Butterfly, Blonde Venus, The Woman Accused, Terror Abroad, She Done Him Wrong, The Eagle and the Hawk, Gambling Ship, I'm No Angel, Alice in Wonderland, Born to Be Bad, Thirty Day Princess, Kiss and Make Up, Ladies Should Listen, Enter Madame, Wings in the Dark, The Last Outpost, Sylvia Scarlett, Big Brown Eyes, Wedding Present, Suzy, The Amazing Quest of Mr. Ernest Bliss* (in Britain), *When You're in Love, The Awful Truth, Topper, The Toast of New York, Bringing Up Baby, Holiday, Gunga Din, Only Angels Have Wings, In Name Only ;* 1940 : *The Howards of Virginia* (Col) ; 1941 : *The Philadelphia Story* (MGM), *Penny Serenade* (Col), *Suspicion* (RKO) ; 1942 : *Talk of the Town, Once Upon a Honeymoon* (RKO) ; 1943 : *Destination Tokyo* (Warn) ; 1944 : *Mr. Lucky* (RKO), *Once Upon a Time* (Col), *None but the Lonely Heart* (RKO), *Arsenic and Old Lace* (Warn) ; 1946 : *Night and Day ;* 1947 : *Notorious* (RKO), *Bachelor Knight* (RKO).

GRANVILLE, Bonita. Born Chicago, Illinois, Feb. 2, 1923. Fair hair, grey eyes. Educ. Hollywood High School. At 3, joined parents' vaudeville act. Through resemblance to Ann Harding, won part of daughter in *Westward Passage* (RKO) 1932. Gained fame as vicious schoolgirl in *These Three* (Warn) 1936. Other films include : *Silver Dollar, Cavalcade* (Fox) 1933, *Cradle Song, Ah Wilderness, Song and Saddle, The Plough and the Stars, Angels Wash Their Faces, Those Were the Days, Call It a Day, Maid of Salem, The Life of Emile Zola, Gentleman After Midnight ;* 1940 (all MGM) : *Forty Little Mothers, The Mortal Storm, Third Finger Left Hand, Gallant Sons, Escape*, re-issued 1947 as *When the Door Opened ;* 1941 : *The People v. Dr. Kildare* (MGM), *Wild Men of Borneo* (MGM), *Down in San Diego* (MGM) ; 1942 : *H. M. Pulham, Esq.* (MGM), *Syncopation* (RKO), *Now, Voyager* (Warn), *The Glass Key* (Para) ; 1943 : *Seven Miles from Alcatraz* (RKO), *Hitler's Children* (RKO) ; 1944 : *Youth Runs Wild* (RKO), *Song of the Open Road* (UA) ; 1945 : *The Beautiful Cheat* (Univ), *Señorita from the West* (Univ) ; 1946 : *What a Woman* (Univ), *Love Laughs at Handy Hardy* (MGM), *Suspense* (Pathé).

GRAVES, Peter. Born London, Oct. 21, 1911. Ht. 6 ft. ; wt. 172 lb. Brown hair, blue eyes. Educ. Harrow School. Worked for estate agents, then for insurance firm before stage debut in Cochran's revue " Streamline ". Appeared in London in several Ivor Novello productions, including " Glamorous Night ", " Careless Rapture ", " The Dancing Years ", and other successes. First film : *Kipps* (20th-Brit) 1941. Other films include—1941 : *Ships with Wings* (Ealing) ; 1942 : *King Arthur Was a Gentleman* (Gains) ; 1943 : *Miss London, Ltd.* (Gains), *Give Us the Moon* (Gains) ; 1944 : *Bees in Paradise* (Gains) ; 1945 : *I'll Be Your Sweetheart* (Gains), *Waltz Time* (Brit Nat), *Gaiety George* (King) ; 1947 : *Spring Song* (Brit Nat), *Mrs. Fitzherbert* (Brit Nat) ; 1948 : *Spring in Park Lane* (Wilcox-Brit Lion).

GRAVET, Fernand. Real name Fernand Mertens Graavey. Born Brussels, Dec. 25, 1905. Ht. 5 ft. 11 in. ; wt. 145 lb. Educ. St. Paul's School, London. Began acting career on the London stage as a child, rising to stardom in Paris. Early French films include : *Paradis Perdu, Touche-à-Tout, Fanfare d'Amour, La Guerre des Valses, Le Dernier Tournant, Coiffeur pour Dames, Sept Hommes—Une Femme, Mister Flow.* In Britain appeared with Anna Neagle in *Bitter Sweet* and *The Queen's Affair.* In Germany made French and English versions *Early to Bed* (UFA-Gaumont). Went to Hollywood and made *The King and the Chorus Girl* (Warn) 1937 and *The Great Waltz* (MGM) 1939. Returned to Paris, where his films include : *Le Mensonge de Nina Petrovna, Histoire de Rire, La Nuit Fantastique, Romance à Trois, Le Capitaine Fracasse, Domino, La Rabouilleuse, Pamela, Il Suffit d'une Fois, N'Ecrivez Jamais !, La Nuit Fantastique.*

GRAY, Allan. Composer. Born Poland. Was musical director to Max Reinhardt. Has scored most of the films made in recent years by Michael Powell of the Archers Film Company. These include : *The Life and Death of Colonel Blimp, A Canterbury Tale, I Know Where I'm Going, A Matter of Life and Death.*

GRAY, Dulcie. Born Kuala Lumpur, Malaya, Nov. 20, 1919. Ht. 5 ft. 5 in., wt. 116 lb. Fair hair, blue eyes. Brought to England at 3. Educ. schools at Wallingford, Wokingham, Swanage. In order to earn money to go to Dramatic School, she became fashion model. Started acting with small parts in repertory in Aberdeen. Made a name for herself in " The Little Foxes ", 1942 ; in 1943 played Rose in " Brighton Rock " and was offered film contract. Films include—1944 : *Madonna of the Seven Moons* (Gains), *A Place of One's Own* (Gains) ; 1945 : *They Were Sisters* (Gains) ; 1946 : *Wanted for Murder* (20th-Brit) ; 1947 : *A Man About the House* (LFP), *Mine Own Executioner* (Kimmins) ; 1948 : *My Brother Jonathan* (ABPC).

GRAY, Sally. Born Holloway, London, Feb. 14, 1918. Ht. 5 ft. 4½ in. ; wt. 112 lb. Blonde hair, hazel eyes. Youthful ambition : to be an actress. Grandmother was a principal boy ; mother a ballerina. At 13, trained at Fay Compton School of Dramatic Art, and the next year was in chorus of " Bow Bells", London Hippodrome ; later lead in " Over She Goes ". First important film role was with George Sanders in *The Saint in London* (RKO) 1938. Previously, had played small parts, beginning with *Cheer Up*. Other films include : *Lambeth Walk,*

CARY GRANT
(*Warner*)

Widow in London, Saint's Vacation. 1940 : *Dangerous Moonlight* (RKO) ; 1946 : *Carnival* (Two Cities) ; 1947 : *Green for Danger* (Individ) ; *They Made Me a Fugitive* (Alliance), *The Mark of Cain* (Two Cities).

GRAYSON, Kathryn. Real name Zelma Hedrick. Born Winston-Salem, North Carolina, Feb. 9. Ht. 5 ft. 3 in. ; wt. 120 lb. Brown hair, hazel eyes. Educ. private and public schools St. Louis ; Manual Arts High School, Hollywood. Overheard singing on deserted stage of St. Louis Municipal Opera House one day by Frances Marshall, of Chicago Civic Opera Company, who then coached her. First film : *Andy Hardy's Private Secretary* (MGM) 1941. Other films (all MGM) include : *The Vanishing Virginian ;* 1942 : *Rio Rita, Seven Sweethearts ;* 1943 : *Thousands Cheer ;* 1944 : *Anchors Aweigh ;* 1945 : *Two Sisters from Boston ;* 1946 : *Ziegfeld Follies of 1946, Till the Clouds Roll By, It Happened in Brooklyn ;* 1948 : *The Kissing Bandit, This Summer is Yours.*

GREEN, F. L. Novelist. Born Portsmouth, Hants. Educ. Salesian College, Farnborough. Works include: " Julius Penton ", " Give Us the World ", " Music in the Park ", " A Song for the Angels ", " On the Edge of the Sea ". Filmed : *On the Night of the Fire ; Odd Man Out,* in which he also collaborated on screenplay.

GREENE, Max. Director of photography. Born Germany, 1897. Entered film industry in Berlin with his father Julius Greenbaum who before 1914 made " talkies " by synchronizing gramophone records with films. Deputised for cameramen and worked on early films starring Albert Basserman. Began British career in 1930 with Michael Balcon, producer for Gaumont British and Gainsborough, and photographed: *It's a Boy, The Constant Nymph, Bulldog Jack, Car of Dreams, The Guv'nor, Strangers on Honeymoon, Non-Stop New York* and others. Since 1940 responsible for photography of: *Pastor Hall, The Stars Look Down, This England, Under Your Hat, Hatter's Castle, Thunder Rock, Ships with Wings, They Flew Alone, Yellow Canary, I Lived in Grosvenor Square, Piccadilly Incident, The Courtneys of Curzon Street, Spring in Park Lane ;* co-directed : *Hotel Reserve, Escape to Danger ;* directed : *The Man from Morocco.*

GREENE, Richard. Born Plymouth, Aug. 25, 1919. Ht. 6 ft. ; wt. 170 lb. Dark-brown hair, grey-blue eyes. Educ. Cardinal Vaughan School, London. To realize ambition to be actor, earned money as photographer's model. Made debut at 19 as spear-carrier in " Julius Cæsar ", Old Vic, London ; later in repertory. Performance in " French without Tears " brought him seven-year Hollywood contract. First film : *Four Men and a Prayer,* 1938. In British Armed Forces 1939-44. U.S. Films (all 20th) include : *My Lucky Star, Submarine Patrol, Kentucky, The Little Princess, Hound of the Baskervilles, Stanley and Livingstone, Here I Am a Stranger, Little Old New York, I Was an Adventuress.* In Britain made— 1941 : *Unpublished Story* (Two Cities) ; 1942 : *Flying Fortress* (Warn) ; 1943 : *Yellow Canary* (Wilcox) ; 1944 : *Don't Take It to Heart* (Two Cities) ; 1947 : *Gaiety George* (King). In Hollywood, 1947: *Forever Amber* (20th).

GREENSTREET, Sidney. Born Sandwich, Kent, Dec. 27, 1879. Ht. 5 ft. 10½ in. ; wt. 280 lb. Brown hair, hazel eyes. Educ. Dane Hill School, Margate. Youthful ambition : to be an actor. Apart from brief period as Ceylon tea-planter, spent all 1900-41 on stage. Began with Ben Greet Players and toured England in Shakespearean plays ; American debut in 1905 ; has toured as actor all over the world. Was asked many times to make films. First film : *The Maltese Falcon* (Warn) 1941. Other films (all Warn until 1947) include—1942 : *They Died with Their Boots On, Across the Pacific, Casablanca ;* 1944 : *Passage to Marseilles, Between Two Worlds, The Conspirators, The Mask of Dimitrios ;* 1945 : *Devotion, Conflict, Pillow to Post ;* 1946 : *Three Strangers, The Verdict ;* 1947 : *That Way with Women* (Warn), *The Hucksters* (MGM). Also in 1947 made : *The Woman in White* (Warn).

GREENWOOD, Joan. Born Chelsea, London, Mar. 4, 1921. Ht. 5 ft. 2 in. ; wt. 98 lb. Fair hair, green-grey eyes. Educ. St. Catherine's School, Bramley, Surrey. Left school at 15 for Royal Academy of Dramatic Art. Two years later was on London stage in Molière's " Le Malade Imaginaire ". Appeared in other London plays and in repertory at Playhouse, Oxford. Seen in " The Women ", was introduced to Leslie Howard and given first film role as A.T.S. girl in *The Gentle Sex* (Concanen-Two Cities) 1942. Other films include—1944 : *They Knew Mr. Knight* (G.W.H. Productions : shown publicly 1946) ; 1946 : *Latin Quarter* (Brit Nat), *Girl in a Million* (Box) ; 1947 : *The Man Within* (Gains), *The October Man* (Two Cities), *White Unicorn* (Corfield) ; 1948 : *Saraband for Dead Lovers* (Ealing).

GREENWOOD, John. Composer. Born London, 1899. Educ. Royal College of Music. Has conducted many of his works with the B.B.C. Symphony and London Symphony Orchestras. Has written the music for : *The Constant Nymph, A.1 at Lloyd's, Pimpernel Smith, Wavell's 30,000* (documentary), *The Lamp Still Burns, Nine Men, San Demetrio London, Hungry Hill, Frieda.*

GREENWOOD, Walter. Novelist, dramatist. Born Salford, Lancashire, Dec. 17, 1903. Educ. Langworthy Road Council School, Salford. At 12, began part-time work as milk roundsman's boy and pawnbroker's clerk. Left school at 13, became office boy, stage assistant at a millionaire's private theatre, clerk, packing-case maker, signwriter. " On the dole " several times. Never earned more than 35s. a week until employed in automobile factory. Wrote his first novel, " Love on the Dole ", in 1933. Others include : " His Worship the Mayor ", " Standing Room Only ", " The Secret Kingdom ", " How the Other Man Lives ", " Something in My Heart ". His plays include : " Love on the Dole " (in collaboration with Ronald Gow), " My Son's My Son ", " Give Us This Day ", " Only Mugs Work ", " The Cure for Love", " So Brief the Spring ". Filmed : *Love on the Dole.* Has written and collaborated on very many screenplays, among them the Manchester civic film, *A City Speaks.* In 1947 visited Australia, where he collaborated on the story and screenplay of *Eureka Stockade*—the first British screenwriter to work in Australia.

GREER, Jane. Born Washington, D.C., Sept. 9, 1924. Ht. 5 ft. 5 in. ; wt. 115 lb. Dark brown hair, brown eyes. Educ. Western High School, Washington. Left school to sing Latin-American numbers at Washington night club. Posed for " Life " magazine in first uniform issued to W.A.C.S. and was offered screen test. First film : *Pan Americana* (RKO) 1945. Other films (all RKO) include—1945 : *Two O'clock Courage,*

George White's Scandals ; 1946 : *The Falcon's Alibi, Sunset Pass, Splitface, Sinbad the Sailor* ; 1947 : *They Won't Believe Me, Build My Gallows High* ; 1948 : *Stations West,*

GRIERSON, John. Film publicist, director, producer. Born Deanston, nr. Stirling, Scotland, 1889. Educ. Glasgow University. Left University to serve in minesweepers in World War I, but later resumed his studies and graduated in philosophy. Travelled in the U.S.A. 1924-7 on a Rockefeller Foundation Scholarship in social Science. His observations led him to regard the cinema " as a pulpit and to use it as a propagandist ". On his return to Britain became Film Officer to the Empire Marketing Board, for whom he produced and directed *Drifters* (1929), a film of the herring industry in the North Sea. On success of this film—technically, aesthetically and as propaganda—established unit devoted to the making of similar films, and developed British documentary. Coined the word " documentary " (from " documentaire " used by the French to describe travel films) while in America, to describe Robert Flaherty's *Nanook of the North* in a review for the " New York Sun ". When Empire Marketing Board was dissolved in 1933, Grierson became Supervising Producer and head of G.P.O. Film Unit until 1937 ; responsible for such films as 6.30 *Collection, Air Mail, Under the City, Night Mail, North Sea, B.B.C.—the Voice of Britain, We Live in Two Worlds.* In 1937 founded the Film Centre, to act as advisers to Government departments, scientific industrial and social organizations in the making of specialized films. In 1939 he was appointed Canada's first Film Commissioner, to develop Canadian production, and to publicize, through the medium of the film, Canada's achievements and their relation to world affairs ; series *The World in Action* was an outstanding contribution to this. Returned to Britain, 1945. Became Film Liaison Officer and Adviser on Mass Communication to UNESCO.

GUEST, Val. Director, screenwriter. Born England, 1911. At 2 went to California with parents. Became reporter on " Los Angeles Examiner ", then actor, appearing in several films. Later, returned to journalism and became Hollywood correspondent for *Screenplay* and for British magazines ; for a time also worked as columnist with Walter Winchell. Became scriptwriter when he adversely reviewed a Marcel Varnel comedy and was offered a job of writing Varnel's next. Teamed for seven years with Varnel on Gainsborough comedies. His screenplays include : *Oh ! Mr. Porter, Old Bones of the River, All In, Good Morning Boys, Convict 99, Ask a Policeman, Where's That Fire, Inspector Hornleigh Goes to It, King Arthur Was a Gentleman.* 1943, directed and collaborated on story of *Miss London, Ltd.* ; directed *Bees in Paradise, Give Us the Moon* (in which he gave Jean Simmons her first screen role), *I'll Be Your Sweetheart, Just William's Luck.*

GWENN, Edmund. Born London, Sept. 25, 1875. Educ. St. Olave's and King's College, London. Stage debut in 1896 at Public Hall, Tottenham, London, in " Rogues and Vagabonds " and made first West End appearance in " A Jealous Mistake " (1899) at Globe Theatre. On tour in Britain, Australia and New Zealand till 1903. For next ten years, appeared in more than fifty plays in London. Served in the Army in World War I, and returned to theatre in 1919. His stage career occupies five columns in John Parker's " Who's Who in the Theatre ". Repeated stage role of

George Redfern in film *Laburnum Grove* (Ealing) 1936. Screen career began with *The Skin Game*, 1920 ; and talkie debut in *How She Lied to Her Husband* (BIP) 1930. Other early films include : *Money for Nothing, Condemned to Death, Frail Women, Tell Me Tonight, Hindle Wakes, Love on Wheels, The Admiral's Secret, I Was a Spy, Early to Bed, The Good Companions* (GB, 1933 ; achieved notable success as " Jess Oakroyd "), *Channel Crossing, Friday the 13th, Waltzes from Vienna, Java Head.* In 1934 made first Hollywood film : *The Bishop's Misadventures* (MGM). Returned to Britain for : *Passing Shadows, Father and Son, Warn London, Laburnum Grove.* U.S. films from 1935 : *Sylvia Scarlett, Mad Holiday, Anthony Adverse, The Country Bumpkin, The Walking Dead, Parnell.* In Britain from 1937 : *A Yank at Oxford, South Riding, Penny Paradise, Cheer Boys Cheer, An Englishman's Home.* U.S. films from 1940 : *The Earl of Chicago* (MGM), *The Farmer Takes a Wife* (20th), *Pride and Prejudice* (MGM), *Foreign Correspondent* (UA), *The Devil and Miss Jones* (RKO) ; 1941 : *Scotland Yard* (20th), *Cheers for Miss Bishop* (UA), *One Night in Lisbon* (Para), *Charley's American Aunt* (20th) ; 1942 : *A Yank at Eton* (MGM), *Meanest Man in the World* (20th), *Forever and a Day* (RKO) ; 1943 : *Lassie Come Home* (MGM), *Between Two Worlds* (Warn) ; 1944 : *Keys of the Kingdom* (20th), *Of Human Bondage* (Warn) ; 1945 : *Bewitched* (MGM), *Dangerous Partners* (MGM), *She Went to the Races* (MGM) ; 1946 : *Undercurrent* (MGM), *Bob, Son of Battle* (20th) ; 1947 : *Green Dolphin Street* (MGM), *The Big Heart* (20th), *Life With Father* (Warn).

GYNT, Greta. Real name Greta Woxholt. Born Oslo, 1917. Ht. 5 ft. 6 in. ; wt. 112 lb. Fair hair, blue eyes. Educ. convent schools, Norway, England. Entered Ambla Noess's revue at Chat Noir, Oslo, after having been in concert party, and became successful revue artist. Impresario Sydney Carroll brought her to London, 1936, as leading dancer in " A Midsummer Night's Dream ", Open Air Theatre, Regent's Park. Stage and screen roles followed. First film was for the Svenska Film Industry, Sweden, 1935. British films include—1944 : *Mr. Emmanuel* (Two Cities) ; 1946 : *London Town* (Wesley Ruggles) ; 1947 : *Take My Life* (Cineguild), *Dear Murderer* (Gains) ; 1948 : *The Calendar* (Gains), *Easy Money* (Gains).

HAFFENDEN, Elizabeth. Dress designer. Born London, Apr. 18, 1906. Trained Croydon Art School ; Modern School of Embroidery ; Royal College of Art. Originally intended to become teacher, but became fabric designer, then entered films at Sound City Studio as dress designer. Worked on *Colonel Blood, The Thief of Bagdad* (assistant to Oliver Messel), *The Four Feathers, The Return of the Scarlet Pimpernel* (assistant to René Hubert), *The Spy in Black.* Joined Gainsborough Studios, 1939, and worked on *Girl in the News, Night Train to Munich, The Young Mr. Pitt* (assistant to Cecil Beaton), *The Man in Grey, Fanny by Gaslight, Bedelia, Jassy, Uncle Silas.*

HALE, Alan. Real name Rufus Alan McKahan. Born Washington D.C., Feb. 10, 1892. Educ. University of Pennsylvania. Wrote obituaries for Philadelphia paper, then turned to stage and screen. Began long silent film career, 1911, with Lubin Company, Philadelphia, in *The Cowboy and the Lady.* Other silent films include : *Robin Hood, The Covered Wagon, The Four Horsemen.* Directed films 1925-8, 1930. Has appeared in about eighty films, including :

Little Man What Now?, It Happened One Night, A Message to Garcia, Stella Dallas, Adventures of Robin Hood (Warn) 1938, (repeated silent role of " Little John "), *Algiers, The Sisters, Dodge City.* Recent films (all Warn) include—1941 : *Strawberry Blonde, Footsteps in the Dark, Manpower* ; 1942 : *Captains of the Clouds, Juke Girl, Desperate Journey, Gentleman Jim* ; 1943 : *Action in the North Atlantic, Thank Your Lucky Stars, This Is the Army !* ; 1944 : *The Adventures of Mark Twain, Destination Tokyo, Make Your Own Bed* ; 1945 : *Roughly Speaking, Janie, Hotel Berlin, God Is My Co-Pilot, Escape to the Desert* ; 1946 : *The Time, the Place and the Girl* ; 1947 : *My Wild Irish Rose, Pursued* ; 1948 : *The Adventures of Don Juan.*

HALE, Barbara. Born DeKalb, Illinois, Apr. 18, 1922. Ht. 5 ft. 5 in. ; wt. 115 lb. Brown hair, hazel eyes. Educ. Chicago Academy of Fine Arts. Youthful ambition : to become reporter. Studied dancing and acting as child ; won several beauty contests. For two years trained in commercial art ; became Chicago model and then won a long-term contract. First film : *Gildersleeve's Bad Day* (RKO) 1943. Other films (all RKO) include—1943 : *Higher and Higher* ; 1944 : *The Falcon Out West, The Falcon in Hollywood, Goin' To Town, Heavenly Days* ; 1945 : *First Yank into Tokyo* ; 1946 : *West of the Pecos, Belle of the Yukon, Lady Luck* ; 1947 : *A Likely Story.*

HALL, Jon. Real name Charles Locher. Born Fresno, California, Feb. 26. Ht. 6 ft. 2 in. ; wt. 196 lb. Brown hair, brown eyes. Educ. Tahiti, England, Switzerland. Swimming champion of Tahiti. Some stage experience. Went to Hollywood in 1937 where his ability as a surf swimmer won him the leading role in *The Hurricane* (UA), adapted from the book by his cousin, James Nordoff Hall. Served in World War II with U.S. Army. Other films include : *Sailors' Lady, South of Pago-Pago, Kit Carson.* 1942 : *The Tuttles of Tahiti* (RKO), *Eagle Squadron* (Univ), *Invisible Agent* (Univ), *Arabian Nights* (Univ) ; 1943 : *White Savage* (Univ) ; 1944 : *Cobra Woman* (Univ), *The Invisible Man's Revenge* (Univ), *Gypsy Wildcat* (Univ), *Ali Baba and the Forty Thieves* (Univ), *San Diego I Love You !* (Univ), *Lady in the Dark* (Para) ; 1945 : *Sudan* (Univ), *Men in Her Diary* (Univ) ; 1946 : *The Michigan Kid* (Univ) ; 1947 : *The Vigilantes Return* (UI).

HAMMOND, Kay. Real name Dorothy Katherine Standing. Born London, 1909. Ht. 5 ft. 5 in. Brown hair, grey eyes. Studied at Royal Academy of Dramatic Art. Made stage debut in London at Regent Theatre in " Tilly of Bloomsbury ", 1927. Made several films in Germany before appearing in *A Night in Montmartre* (Gains) 1931. Other early films include : *Two on a Doorstep, Children of Chance, Out of the Blue, Fascination, Nine Till Six, The Third String, Almost a Divorce, Chance of a Night-time, Money Means Nothing, Sally Bishop, Double Harness, Sleeping Car, Britannia of Billingsgate, Bitter Sweet.* Among her successful plays was " Blithe Spirit " 1941-4, in which she played Elvira ; later appeared in same role on screen. 1942 : *Jeannie* (Marcel Hellman) ; 1945 : *Blithe Spirit* (Cineguild) ; 1947 : *Call of the Blood* (Pendennis).

HANLEY, Jimmy. Born Norwich, Oct. 22, 1918. Ht. 6 ft. ; wt. 182 lb. Fair hair, blue eyes. Educ. Downhills Park. Always wanted to be film actor. At 5 won seaside talent contest. Joined Italia Conti's School ; made stage debut as John in " Peter Pan ", London Palladium, 1930. Screen debut as circus rider in *Red Wagon* (BIP) 1933. Combined films and stage until 1938 ; has also been part-owner of garage. Active service in British Army in World War II ; invalided out 1944. Other films include : *Little Friend, Forever England, The Tunnel, Boys Will Be Boys, Cotton Queen, For You Alone, Landslide, Night Ride, The Housemaster, Coming of Age, There Ain't No Justice.* 1940 : *Gaslight* (Brit Nat) ; 1942 : *Salute John Citizen* (Brit Nat) ; 1943 : *The Gentle Sex* (Concanen-Two Cities), 1944 : *The Way Ahead* (Two Cities), *Henry V* (Two Cities) ; 1945 : *Acacia Avenue* (Box), *Kiss the Bride Goodbye* (Butcher), *Murder in Reverse* (Brit Nat) ; 1946 : *The Captive Heart* (Ealing) ; 1947 : *Master of Bankdam* (Holbein), *Holiday Camp* (Gains), *It Always Rains on Sunday* (Ealing).

HARDING, Ann. Real name Anna Gatley. Born Fort Sam Houston, Texas, Aug. 7, 1902. Ht. 5 ft. 2 in. ; wt. 106 lb. Ash-blonde hair, blue-grey eyes. Educ. Montclair, New Jersey ; Bryn Mawr College. During childhood travelled round Texas, where her father, a U.S. Army Officer, was stationed, and became expert rider and steeplechaser. Made first stage appearance as Shylock in school production of " The Merchant of Venice ". Began career after leaving college as clerk in an insurance office, then joined a small repertory company. Was touring California in " Candida " when she had a breakdown, and while recuperating was approached by three studios with offers of contracts. Made her screen debut in *Paris Bound* (Pathé) 1929. Other films include : *Her Private Affair, War and Women, Holiday, Condemned, Girl of the Golden West, East Lynne, Devotion* (Pathé 1931), *Prestige, The Greater Love, Westward Passage, Just a Woman, The Conquerors, Animal Kingdom, Double Harness, The Right to Romance, When Ladies Meet, Gallant Lady, The Life of Vergie Winters, The Fountain, Biography of a Bachelor Girl, The Flame Within, Enchanted April, Peter Ibbetson, The Lady Consents, The Witness Chair, Love from a Stranger* (made in Britain 1937). 1942 : *Eyes in the Night* (MGM) ; 1943 : *Mission to Moscow* (Warn), *North Star* (Goldwyn) ; 1944 : *Nine Girls* (Col), *Janie* (Warn) ; 1945 : *Those Endearing Young Charms* (RKO) ; 1946 : *Cinderella Jones* (Warn) ; 1947 : *It Happened on Fifth Avenue* (Mono), *Christmas Eve* (Benedict Bogeaus-UA).

HARDWICKE, Sir Cedric. Born Lye, Stourbridge, Worcs., Feb. 13, 1893. Educ. Bridgnorth School. Won beauty competition at 1 ; was producing amateur Shakespeare at 12. Trained at Royal Academy of Dramatic Art, and made debut as Brother John in " The Monk and the Woman ", Lyceum Theatre, London, 1913. Joined Frank Benson Company, 1913 ; toured South Africa ; served as infantry officer in World War I ; joined Birmingham Repertory Company 1922 ; made stage name in " The Farmer's Wife " (1924). Other outstanding plays include : " Yellow Sands ", " The Late Christopher Bean ", " The Barretts of Wimpole Street ", " The Amazing Dr. Clitterhouse ". Played in New York, 1936. Knighted 1934. First film : *Dreyfus,* 1931. British films include : *Rome Express, Orders Is Orders, The Ghoul, The Lady Is Willing, Bella Donna, Nell Gwyn, Jew Süss*—U.S. title *Power, Tudor Rose.* To Hollywood, 1934. American films include : *Becky Sharp, Les Miserables, Green Light, On Borrowed Time, Stanley and Livingstone, The Hunchback of Notre Dame* ; 1940 : *The Invisible Man Returns* (Univ), *Tom Brown's School-*

days (RKO), *The Howards of Virginia* (Col) ; 1941 : *Victory* (Para), *Sundown* (UA), *Suspicion* (RKO) ; 1942 : *Valley of the Sun* (RKO), *The Ghost of Frankenstein* (Univ), *Invisible Agent* (Univ) ; 1943 : *Commandos Strike at Dawn* (Col), *The Moon Is Down* (20th), *Forever and a Day* (RKO), *The Cross of Lorraine* (MGM) ; 1944 : *The Lodger* (20th), *A Wing and a Prayer* (20th), *Wilson* (20th), *Keys of the Kingdom* (20th) ; 1945 : *The Picture of Dorian Gray* (MGM) ; 1946 : *Sentimental Journey* (20th), *Mrs. Loring's Secret.* In Britain made : *Beware of Pity* (Two Cities) 1946, *Nicholas Nickleby* (Ealing) 1947. Also in 1947 made, in U.S.A. : *Tragic Symphony* (Mono), *Ivy* (UI); 1948 : *A Woman's Vengeance, A Connecticut Yankee* (Para), *Personal Column* (Benedict Bogeaus-UA).

HARDY, Oliver. Real name Oliver Norvelle Hardy. Born Atlanta, Georgia, Jan. 18, 1892. Ht. 6 ft. 1 in.; wt. 308 lb. Black hair, brown eyes. Educ. public schools, Harlem and Atlanta ; Georgia Military Academy. Left after first year as law student at Georgia University to join a minstrel show. While singing with troupe in Jacksonville, Florida, made film debut, 1915, for Lubin Film Company who were searching for a fat comedian ; then was featured comedian for them in Hollywood in many films before Laurel-Hardy partnership began. Made over 170 films with Laurel, mostly two-reel comedies, the best known of which include : *The Rogue Song, Night Owls, Below Zero, Hay Wire, Pack Up Your Troubles, Hollywood Party, Bonnie Scotland, The Bohemian Girl, Blockheads.* 1940 : *A Chump at Oxford, Saps at Sea* (UA) ; 1941 : *Great Guns* (20th) ; 1942 : *A-Haunting We Will Go* (20th) ; 1943 : *Air Raid Wardens* (MGM), *Jitterbugs* (20th), *The Dancing Masters* (20th) ; 1944 : *Nothing But Trouble* (MGM), *Big Noise* (20th), *The Bullfighters* (20th). In 1947 came to Britain with Laurel for stage tour.

HARE, Robertson. Born London, Dec. 17, 1891. Ht. 5 ft. 5½ in. Brown hair. Began stage career in 1911, touring English provinces in "The Bear Leaders." Became established comedian, playing typical British hen-pecked husband, in Ben Travers farces at Aldwych Theatre, London 1924-33. With stage partners Tom Walls and Ralph Lynn, has repeated most of his stage successes on the screen. First film : *Rookery Nook* (B and D) 1929. Other films include : *On Approval, Tons of Money, Thark, A Night Like This, Just My Luck, It's a Boy, Friday the 13th, Turkey Time, A Cup of Kindness, Are You a Mason ?, Dirty Work, Oh Daddy !, Fighting Stock, Stormy Weather, Car of Dreams, Foreign Affaires, Jack of All Trades, Aren't Men Beasts ?, Spot of Bother, So This Is London.* From 1940 : *Spotted Dick* (ABPC), *Women Aren't Angels* (ABPC) ; 1941 : *Banana Ridge* (ABPC) ; 1945 : *He Snoops to Conquer* (Col-Brit) ; 1948 : *Things Happen at Night* (Alliance).

HARKER, Gordon. Born London, Aug. 7, 1885. Ht. 5 ft. 9 in. ; wt. 147 lb. Brown hair, hazel eyes. Educ. Ramsey Grammar School, Isle of Man. Began stage career, 1902, on tour as "walk-on" and prompter to Fred Terry in "Sweet Nell of Old Drury". First appeared in London, 1903, playing small parts in Shakespeare with Ellen Terry. Joined Oscar Asche's company in London ; world tours from 1904-13. Served in World War I, invalided out in 1919 and resumed London career as Batouch the Arab in "The Garden of Allah". Played many varied roles till he successfuly portrayed a Cockney in now

famous curtain-raiser "Five Birds in a Cage". Noticed by Edgar Wallace as Cockney in "Tunnel Trench", and scored sensational success in 1926, as Sam Hackitt in Wallace's "The Ringer". Seen in this by Alfred Hitchcock and given film role in : *The Ring* (Gainsborough) 1927. Films include : *The Farmer's Wife, Champagne, The Crooked Billet, Return of the Rat, Taxi for Two, Sport of Kings, Shadows, The W Plan, Escape, Third Time Lucky, Professional Guest, The Calendar* (1931), *Two White Arms, The Ringer, The Squeaker, The Stronger Sex, The Man They Couldn't Arrest, Condemned to Death, The Frightened Lady, Love on Wheels, Rome Express, The Lucky Number, Britannia of Billingsgate, This Is The Life, Friday the 13th, My Old Dutch, Dirty Work, Road House, The Phantom Light, The Lad, Admirals All, Squibs* (talkie), *Boys Will Be Boys, Hyde Park Corner, The Amateur Gentleman, Two's Company, Millions, Beauty and the Barge, Return of the Frog, Blondes for Danger, Lightning Conductor, Inspector Hornleigh, Inspector Hornleigh Goes To It* (Gains), *Saloon Bar* (Ealing), *Once a Crook* (20th Brit) ; 1943 : *Warn That Man* (ABPC) ; 1945 : *Acacia Avenue* (Box-Col) ; 1948 : *Things Happen at Night* (Alliance).

HARLOW, John. Director. Born Ross-on-Wye, 1896. Served. during whole of World War I, then took up concert-party, music hall and dramatic work. Adapted "Wanted for Murder" for the stage and wrote play, "Haven't We Met Before ?". Entered films, 1927, as assistant director. Films directed include : *One Company, Headline, Candles at Nine, This Was Paris, The Dark Tower, The Agitator, Green Fingers.*

HARRISON, Joan. Writer, producer. Born Guildford, Surrey, June 21, 1911. Educ. Sorbonne, Paris ; Oxford University (B.A.). Became advertisement copywriter in London. Took secretarial course, worked for various writers for two and half years. Entered films as assistant and script-writer to Alfred Hitchcock. To Hollywood, 1939, to write screenplay *Rebecca.* Worked as writer on three Hitchcock films : *Foreign Correspondent, Suspicion, Saboteur.* Became producer with *Phantom Lady* (Univ) 1944. Recent films : *Dark Waters, Nocturne, Strange Affair of Uncle Harry, They Won't Believe Me, Ride The Pink Horse.*

HARRISON, Kathleen. Born Blackburn, Lancs, Feb. 23, 1898. Educ. Clapham High School. After a year at the Royal Academy of Dramatic Art, London, and eight years abroad, made stage debut, 1926, at the Pier Theatre, Eastbourne in "The Constant Flirt". Other stage appearances include the role of Mrs. Terence in "Night Must Fall" (1935), which she later repeated in the Hollywood film version (MGM 1937). Film debut in *Hobson's Choice* (BIP 1931). Other films include : *Aren't We All ?, The Man from Toronto, The Ghoul, The Great Defender, Line Engaged, Broken Blossoms, The Tenth Man, Aren't Men Beasts ?, Wanted, Bank Holiday, Lover's Knot, Convict 99, A Girl Must Live, I've Got a Horse, Home from Home, The Outsider ;* 1940 : *Girl in the News* (20th Brit) ; 1941 : *The Ghost Train* (Gains), *Major Barbara* (Pascal), *Kipps* (20th Brit) ; 1942 : *In Which We Serve* (Two Cities) ; 1943 : *Dear Octopus* (Gains) ; 1945 : *Great Day* (RKO Brit) ; 1946 : *Carnival* (Two Cities) ; 1947 : *Temptation Harbour* (ABPC), *Holiday Camp* (Gains) ; 1948 : *Bond Street* (World Screen), *Oliver Twist* (Cineguild).

REX HARRISON
(20th Century-Fox)

HARRISON, Rex. Born Huyton, Cheshire, Mar. 5, 1908. Ht. 6 ft. 1 in. Brown hair, brown eyes. Educ. Uppingham School. Joined Liverpool Repertory Company at 16 ; toured in " Charley's Aunt " and other plays. Performance in " French without Tears", in New York, 1936, brought him wide fame. First major film part was leading man to Miriam Hopkins when she came to Britain in 1936 to appear in *Men Are Not Gods* (LFP). Served in Radar Section, R.A.F., 1940-4. Other films include : *The Great Game, Get Your Man, All at Sea, Storm in a Teacup, School for Husbands, Over the Moon, St. Martin's Lane, The Citadel, Night Train to Munich.* 1940 : *Major Barbara* (Pascal) ; 1945 : *I Lived in Grosvenor Square* (Wilcox-ABPC), *Blithe Spirit* (Cineguild) ; 1946 : *The Rake's Progress*—U.S. title *Notorious Gentleman* (Individ). In Hollywood, 1946 : *Anna and the King of Siam* (20th) ; 1947 : *The Ghost and Mrs. Muir* (20th), *The Foxes of Harrow* (20th) In Britain, 1948 : *Escape* (20th).

HART, Richard. Born Providence, Rhode Island, Apr. 14. Ht. 6 ft. ; wt. 170 lb. Brown hair, blue eyes. Educ. Brown University. Intended to be journalist, but became salesman. Visited parents on Rhode Island farm, 1940, and was given lead in local company " The Shoestring Players ", and decided to become actor. After two years training appeared on New York stage in " It's Up to You ", " The Cardboard Lover " and other plays. First film : *Desire Me* (MGM) 1946. Other films include : *Green Dolphin Street* (MGM).

HARTNELL, William. Born Seaton, Devon. Ran away from school to join Sir Frank Benson's Shakespearean Company. Experience with numerous touring and repertory companies, and as understudy ; toured Canada, 1928. After crowd work played the comedy lead in *I'm an Explosive !* During World War II served with Royal Armoured Corps ; invalided out. In 1943 appeared in " Brighton Rock " at Garrick Theatre, London. Films include : *Follow the Lady, Seeing Is Believing, Farewell Again, Too Dangerous to Live.* 1940 : *They Came by Night* (20th-Brit), *Murder Will Out, The Peterville Diamond* (Warn-Brit) ; 1942 : *Flying Fortress* (Warn-Brit), *Sabotage at Sea* (Brit Nat) ; 1943 : *The Dark Tower* (Warn-Brit), *The Bells Go Down* (Ealing) ; 1944 : *The Way Ahead* (Two Cities), *The Agitator* (Brit Nat) ; 1945 : *Murder in Reverse* (Brit Nat) ; 1946 : *Strawberry Roan* (Brit Nat), *Appointment with Crime* (Brit Nat) ; 1947 : *Odd Man Out* (Two Cities), *Temptation Harbour* (ABPC) ; 1948 : *Brighton Rock* (Boultings-ABPC), *Escape* (20th-Brit).

HASSO, Signe. Real name Signe Larssen. Born Stockholm, Aug. 15. Red hair, grey-green eyes. Ht. 5 ft. 4 in. ; wt. 115 lb. Stage debut at 12 in Molière at Royal Dramatic Theatre, Stockholm ; later joined theatre school. At 15, toured Netherlands; at 18, played lead in Schiller's " Mary Queen of Scots ". Gained government scholarship to Royal Academy School ; established herself as a leading Swedish stage star, winning award for best performance of the year for work in " Mädchen in Uniform ". Starred at Blanche Theatre, Stockholm, and appeared in classical plays in Scandinavia, Germany, Austria and England. Began screen career in silent films, and appeared in fourteen Swedish sound films before going to U.S.A. in 1940. Appeared on New York stage in " Golden Wings " and made American screen debut in *Journey for Margaret* (MGM) 1942. Other films include—

1943 : *Assignment in Brittany* (MGM), *Heaven Can Wait* (20th) ; 1944 : *Story of Dr Wassell* (Para), *The Seventh Cross* (MGM) ; 1945 : *Dangerous Partners* (MGM), *Johnny Angel* (RKO), *The House on 92nd Street* (20th) ; 1946 : *Scandal in Paris* (Pressburger-UA), *Strange Triangle* (20th) ; 1947 : *Where There's Life* (Para) ; 1948 : *To the Ends of the Earth* (Col), *A Double Life* (Col).

HATCHER, Mary: Born Haines City, Florida, June 6, 1929. Ht. 5 ft. 2 in. ; wt. 108 lb. Brown hair, brown eyes. Educ. Gorrie Grammar School and Woodrow Wilson Junior High School, Tampa, Florida; Gardner School for Girls, New York. Sang and danced in local talent shows at Tampa and on local Tampa radio. Studied music in New York, then on holiday in Hollywood met screen vocal coach : test and contract followed. First film : *Our Hearts Were Growing Up* (Para) 1944. Chosen by Theatre Guild to tour U.S.A. as Laurey in " Oklahoma " 1945-6. Returned to films with *Variety Girl* (Para) 1947.

HATFIELD, Hurd. Born New York, Dec. 7. Ht. 6 ft. ; wt. 140 lb. Brown hair, brown eyes. Educ. Columbia University. Appeared in University production of Shakespeare's " Cymbeline ", then offered scholarship to Michael Chekhov's drama school in Devonshire. Returned to America to join Chekhov Theatre Group. Appeared on Broadway. Toured in " King Lear ", " Twelfth Night ", and other plays. Given film test while on holiday in Hollywood. First film : *Dragon Seed* (MGM) 1944. Other films include : *The Picture of Dorian Gray* (MGM) ; 1945 : *Diary of a Chambermaid* (UA) ; 1947 : *The Beginning or the End?* (MGM), *Torrents of Spring* (Ortus, made in France), *The Unsuspected* (Warn).

HATHAWAY, Henry. Director. Born Sacramento, California, Mar. 13, 1900. Educ. Venice High School, California ; St. Ignatius, San Francisco. At 7 played in one-reelers for American Film Company ; joined Universal, 1914, first as prop boy, then in juvenile roles. After U.S. Army service 1918, and a year in business, resumed films with Goldwyn Company ; then made Westerns for Paramount, first as actor and then in 1932 as director with *Wild Horse Mesa.* Later films directed include : *Heritage of the Desert, Sunset Pass, Under the Tonto Rim, To the Last Man, Thundering Herd, Man of the Forest, The Last Round-Up, Come on Marines !, The Witching Hour, Now and Forever, The Lives of a Bengal Lancer, Peter Ibbetson, Trail of the Lonesome Pine, Go West Young Man, Souls at Sea, Spawn of the North, The Real Glory, Johnny Apollo, Brigham Young, Shepherd of the Hills, Sundown, Ten Gentlemen from West Point, China Girl, Strange Incident, A Wing and a Prayer, Home in Indiana, Nob Hill, The House on 92nd Street, The Dark Corner, 13 Rue Madeleine, Kiss of Death.*

HAVELOCK-ALLAN, Anthony. Producer, director. Born Darlington, Co. Durham, Feb. 28, 1905. Educ. Charterhouse and Switzerland. Destined for army career but became artists' and recording manager, Brunswick Gramophone Company, London. Entered films, 1935, as producer, and made more than twenty quota films for Paramount. In 1938, joined Pinebrook Ltd., as producer at Pinewood Studios. Associate producer to Noel Coward on *In Which We Serve* (Two Cities) 1942. With David Lean and Ronald Neame, formed Cineguild Ltd., 1943. Other films include : *This Man Is News, Lightning Conductor, The Lambeth Walk* (associate producer), *Stolen Life, This Man in*

Paris, Silent Battle, Escape in the Dark, Lovely Tomorrow (also directed), From the Four Corners, Unpublished Story (associate producer). Produced This Happy Breed, Blithe Spirit, Brief Encounter, Great Expectations, Blanche Fury, Oliver Twist.

HAVER, June. Born Rock Island, Illinois, June 10, 1926. Ht. 5 ft. 2 in. ; wt. 102 lb. Golden-blonde hair, blue eyes. Educ. Beverly Hills High School. Youthful ambition ; to be film star. Stage debut at 8 ; M.C., director, pianist and singer in radio show " Stars of Tomorrow " at 11. Sang with Dick Jurgens and Ted Fio-Rito orchestras ; appeared in school play " Ever Since Eve". First film : Home in Indiana, (20th), 1944. Other films include—1944 : Irish Eyes Are Smiling (20th) ; 1945 : Where Do We Go From Here ? (20th), The Dolly Sisters (20th) ; 1946 : Three Little Girls in Blue (20th) ; 1947 : I Wonder Who's Kissing Her Now ? (20th), Summer Lightning (20th).

HAYDEN, Sterling. Born Montclair, New Jersey. Ht. 6 ft. 5 in. ; wt. 212 lb. Educ. Browne and Nichols School, Cambridge, Massachusetts. Spent boyhood sailing American Atlantic Coast, rejected suggestions of film career ; sailed to all parts of the world as mate of schooner, captained millionaire's yacht. Then became part-owner of schooner, lost all his money, and so accepted offer of screen test. First film : Virginia (Para) 1941. After Bahama Passage (Para) 1941, returned to sea. In World War II, served in U.S. Marine Corps. Resumed films with Blaze of Noon (Para) 1947.

HAYES, George " Gabby". Born Wellsville, New York State, May 7, 1885. One of the great old-timers of Westerns. Appeared in silent films and in talkies, including The Rainbow Man and Mr. Deeds Goes to Town, before joining Roy Rogers' team, with which he has now appeared regularly for several years.

HAYMES, Dick. Born Buenos Aires, Argentine, Sept. 13, Ht. 6 ft. ; wt. 160 lb. Light brown hair, blue eyes. Educ. Lausanne ; Paris ; Preparatory School, Tarrytown, New York State ; Peekskill Military School. Debut as singer at 15 ; became singer with Harry James's, Tommy Dorsey's and Benny Goodman's bands. Had been extra in Westerns, but it was his radio voice that won him seven-year film contract. First featured film : Four Jills and a Jeep (20th) 1944. Other films include—1944 : Irish Eyes Are Smiling (20th) ; 1945 : Diamond Horseshoe (20th), State Fair (20th) ; 1946 : Do You Love Me ? (20th) ; 1947 : The Shocking Miss Pilgrim (20th), Carnival in Costa Rica (20th) ; 1948 : Up in Central Park (UI).

HAYWARD, Louis. Real name Seafield Grant. Born Johannesburg, Mar. 19, 1909. Ht. 5 ft. 11 in. ; wt. 160 lb. Brown hair, blue eyes. Educ. South Africa ; St. Saveur School, Redon, France ; England. Nearly joined his uncle in timber firm, but decided to train for English stage career. Later, founded touring company with money borrowed from his mother, and made successful venture as actor-manager in " East Lynne". Toured in " Beau Geste " and " Dracula", made London debut in " The Bread-winner". Appeared on Broadway in " Point Valaine". First appeared on screen in Sorrell and Son (B & D) 1934. First American film : The Flame Within (MGM) 1935. Other films include : A Feather in Her Hat, Anthony Adverse, Absolute Quiet, Trouble for Two, The Luckiest Girl in the World, Midnight Intruder, Rage of Paris, Condemned Woman, The Woman I Love, The Saint in New York, Duke of West Point, The Man in the Iron Mask. 1940 : My Son, My Son (Small-UA), Son of Monte Cristo (Small-UA), Dance, Girl, Dance (RKO) ; 1941 : Ladies in Retirement (Col). 1942-5, served in U.S. Marine Corps. 1947 : Young Widow (Hunt Stromberg-UA), Strange Woman (Hunt Stromberg-UA), Repeat Performance (Eagle Lion-Hollywood) ; 1948 : The Black Arrow (Col).

HAYWARD, Susan. Real name Edythe Marrener Barker. Born Brooklyn, New York, June 30. Ht. 5 ft. 3 in. ; wt. 108 lb. Educ. Public School 81, Brooklyn ; Brooklyn Commercial School. Won school art prize and used money for stage tuition at night school ; was also fashion model. Tested for part of Scarlett O'Hara in Gone with the Wind, but considered too inexperienced. After training in film technique, was given small parts in Girls on Probation (Warn) 1938, Adam Had Four Sons (Col) 1941. Starred with Fred MacMurray and Paulette Goddard in The Forest Rangers (Para) 1942. Other films include : Beau Geste, Our Leading Citizen, $1000 a Touchdown. 1941 : Sis Hopkins (Rep), Among the Living (Para) ; 1942 : Reap the Wild Wind (Para), The Forest Rangers (Para), I Married A Witch (UA) ; 1943 : Young and Willing (UA), Hit Parade of 1943 (Rep), Star Spangled Rhythm (Para), The Hairy Ape (UA), Jack London (UA) ; 1944 : The Fighting Sea-Bees (Rep), And Now Tomorrow (Para) ; 1945 : Murder He Says (Para), Canyon Passage (Univ) ; 1946 : Deadline at Dawn (RKO) ; 1947 : A Woman Destroyed (UI), They Won't Believe Me (RKO), The Lost Moment (UI).

HAYWORTH, Rita. Real name Marguerite Cansino. Born Manhattan, Oct. 17, 1918. Ht. 5 ft. 4 in. ; wt. 118 lb. Auburn hair, blue eyes. Educ. New York. At 6 made stage debut with father in dancing act, and at 14 joined act professionally. Played dancer in Dante's Inferno (20th) 1935, and a number of small roles in such films as Under the Pampas Moon, Charlie Chan in Egypt, before making her first real success in Only Angels Have Wings (Col) 1939. Other films include — 1941 : Strawberry Blonde (Warn), Blood and Sand (20th), You'll Never Get Rich (Col) ; 1942 : My Gal Sal (20th), Tales of Manhattan (20th), You Were Never Lovelier (Col) ; 1944 : Cover Girl (Col) ; 1945 : To-night and Every Night (Col), Gilda (Col) ; 1947 : Down to Earth (Col) ; The Lady from Shanghai (Col) ; 1948 : Born Yesterday (Col).

HEFLIN, Van. Real name Emmett Evan Heflin, Jr. Born Walters, Oklahoma, Dec. 13, 1910. Ht. 6 ft. 1 in. ; wt. 150 lb. Fair hair, grey eyes. Educ. Polytechnic High School, Long Beach, California ; Oklahoma University. During school holidays went to sea. In 1928 sailed via Panama for New York where he met director Richard Boleslavski who gave him first stage role in " Mr. Money Penny". After three years more at sea, finished university education, then became touring actor ; one year at Yale Dramatic School, season in Denver, Colorado, understudy on Broadway in " Sailor Beware". Later played lead in " The Philadelphia Story " and other plays. First film : A Woman Rebels (RKO) 1936. Other films include : Outcasts of Poker Flat, Flight from Glory, Salute to Romance, Saturday's Heroes. 1940 : Sante Fé Trail (Warn) ; 1941 (all MGM) : The Feminine Touch, Johnny Eager, H. M. Pulham, Esq. ; 1942 (all MGM) : Kid Glove Killer, Grand Central

Murder, Seven Sweethearts, Tennessee Johnson—British title, *The Man on America's Conscience, Presenting Lily Mars.* 1942-45, served in U.S. Army. 1946 : *The Strange Love of Martha Ivers* (Para), *Till the Clouds Roll By* (MGM), *Possessed* (Warn) ; 1947 : *Green Dolphin Street* (MGM) ; 1948 : *Polly Fulton* (MGM), *Upward to the Stars* (MGM), *Green Dolphin Street* (MGM).

HELLER, Otto. Director of photography. Born Prague, Mar. 9, 1896. Educ. Prague. Has been a chief cameraman and lighting expert for twenty-five years, with more than 250 films to his credit. Entered films, 1912, as cinema projectionist, then worked in film laboratories and turned to photography in 1920. In Europe worked for : A.B. Film-Prague Barrandov Studios ; Sascha Film, Vienna ; UFA and Ondra-Lamac Films, Berlin ; Pathé, Gaumont and Paramount in Paris ; Cineton-Studios, Amsterdam. British films include : *High Command, Mademoiselle Docteur, The Amazing Quest of Mr. Ernest Bliss, Alibi, Tomorrow We Live, The Night Invader, The Hundred Pound Window, The Dark Tower, They Met in the Dark, Candlelight in Algeria, One Exciting Night, Mr. Emmanuel, Gaiety George, Flight from Folly, Night Boat to Dublin, Temptation Harbour, They Made Me a Fugitive, Sunshine Susie* (French-German version). During World War II, served in R.A.F.

HELPMANN, Robert. Born Mount Gambier, South Australia, Apr. 9, 1911. Educ. Prince Alfred's College, Adelaide. First appeared as solo dancer at Theatre Royal, Adelaide, 1923. For five years was principal dancer for J. C. Williamson Ltd. ; also appeared as actor in " This Year of Grace ", " The Barretts of Wimpole Street ", " The Insect Play ", " Hamlet ", and many other plays. Came to Britain to train with Sadler's Wells Ballet School and made first appearance at that theatre in 1931 as " Satan " in ballet " Job ". 1932-46, with Sadler's Wells Ballet as principal dancer and as choreographer of " Comus ", " Hamlet ", " The Birds ", " Miracle in the Gorbals ", " Adam Zero ". First film appearance : *One of Our Aircraft Is Missing* (Brit Nat) 1942. Other films include—1945 : *Henry V* (Two Cities) ; 1946 : *Caravan* (Gains) ; 1948 : *Red Shoes* (Archers).

HEMINGWAY, Ernest. Author. Born Oak Park, Illinois, July 21, 1896. Ran away from school at 15, returned to high school, then became cub reporter on " Kansas City Star ". In World War I, went overseas as an ambulance driver, then joined Italian army as infantryman. In the 1920's was Paris correspondent for " Toronto Daily Star ". Became author with " The Sun Also Rises " (1926), " A Farewell to Arms " (1929). Big game hunter and deep sea fisherman in Africa, Europe, America. Correspondent on Republicans' side in Spanish Civil War for " New York Times ", and from his experiences produced two books, " The Fifth Column " and " For Whom the Bell Tolls ". Other works include : " Green Hills of Africa ", " To Have and Have Not " and many short stories. Filmed : *A Farewell to Arms, For Whom the Bell Tolls, To Have and Have Not, The Macomber Affair.*

HENLEY, David. Film executive. Born London, Dec. 25, 1894. Served in army in World War I. Joined D'Oyley Carte Opera Company as singer ; later in S. Rhodesia in diamond buying, tobacco growing, dance band management ; frequently returned to Africa during subsequent stage career. During

theatre slump of 1931, was instrumental in helping form British Equity (actors' association) and worked as organizer for five years. From 1936 as London representative for Myron Selznick, was business agent for Laurence Olivier, Vivien Leigh, Noel Coward, Rex Harrison, Lilli Palmer, Ann Todd, and others. Joined J. Arthur Rank Organization, 1945, as director of players : drew up " Company of Youth " scheme (whereby contract players are trained at Worthing Repertory Theatre) and is responsible for contracts and the building-up of players.

HENREID, Paul. Real name Paul von Hernreid. Born Trieste, Jan. 10, 1908. Ht. 6 ft. 3 in. ; wt. 170 lb. Educ. Theresienrische Akademie, and Graphic Akademie, Vienna. Trained at Actors' Conservatoire, Vienna ; appeared there in many plays and films before coming to Britain, 1935, to appear in anti-Nazi play " The Madman of Europe ". In Britain made—*Night Train to Munich* (20th Brit) 1939, and *Goodbye Mr. Chips !* (MGM Brit) 1940. Went to America to play in " Flight to the West ". American films include—1942 : *Joan of Paris* (RKO), *Now, Voyager* (Warn) ; 1943 : *Casablanca* (Warn) ; 1944 : *In Our Time* (Warn), *Between Two Worlds* (Warn), *The Conspirators* (Warn) ; 1945 : *Devotion* (Warn), *The Spanish Main* (RKO) ; 1946 : *Of Human Bondage* (Warn), *Deception* (Warn) ; 1947 : *Song of Love* (MGM).

HEPBURN, Katharine. Born Hartford, Connecticut, Nov. 8, 1909. Ht. 5 ft. 7 in. ; wt. 110 lb. Brown hair, blue eyes. Educ. Hartford High School ; Bryn Mawr College (Psych. D.). Joined Edwin Knopf's repertory company, Baltimore ; studied voice training and ballet in New York ; won early Broadway reputation in " The Big Pond ", " Death Takes a Holiday ", " The Warrior's Husband ". Success in last play brought film contract. First film : *A Bill of Divorcement* (RKO) 1932. Has since played stage and screen concurrently. Repeated Broadway role in " The Philadelphia Story " in film version. Films include : *Morning Glory, Little Women, Spitfire, Break of Hearts, Sylvia Scarlett, Mary of Scotland, A Woman Rebels, Quality Street, Stage Door, Bringing Up Baby, Free to Live.* 1940 : *The Philadelphia Story* (MGM) ; 1942 : *Woman of the Year* (MGM), *Keeper of the Flame* (MGM) ; 1943 : *Stage Door Canteen* (UA) ; 1944 : *Dragon Seed* (MGM) ; 1945 : *Without Love* (MGM) ; 1946 : *Undercurrent* (MGM) ; 1947 : *The Sea of Grass* (MGM), *Song of Love* (MGM) ; 1948 : *The World and His Wife* (MGM).

HERBERT, Hugh. Born Binghampton, New York State, Aug. 10, 1887. Ht. 5 ft. 8 in. ; wt. 170 lb. Educ. Cornell University. Best known as whimsical (" woo-woo ") comedian, but has had long career as stage writer, actor and producer : has written 150 plays, sketches, vaudeville acts. First theatrical job was as " voice behind the screen " ; reading lines of male characters in silent films. Went to Hollywood to collaborate with Murray Roth on script of first all-talking film : *The Lights of New York* (Warn) 1928. Wrote script of *The Great Gabbo*, starring Eric von Stroheim, then became writer-director-comedian. Early films include : *Mind Your Own Business, Goodbye Again, Bureau of Missing Persons, Footlight Parade, College Coach, From Headquarters, She Had to Say Yes, Convention City.* 1940 : *La Conga Nights* (Univ), *Private Affairs* (Univ), *Slightly Tempted* (Univ), *A Little Bit of Heaven* (Univ), *The Villain Still Pursued Her* (RKO). Collaborated on screen-play and appeared in

Hit Parade of 1941 (Rep). 1941 : *Meet the Chump* (Univ), *The Black Cat* (Univ), *Hello Sucker !* (Univ), *Badlands of Dakota* (Univ), *Hellzapoppin* (Univ), *Nobody's Fool* (Univ), *Don't Get Personal* (Univ), *Temporarily Yours* (Univ) ; 1942 : *Mrs. Wiggs of the Cabbage Patch* (Para) ; 1943 : *Ever Since Eve* (Univ) ; 1944 : collaborated on screen-play and appeared in : *Kismet* (MGM) ; 1945 : *Men in Her Diary* (Univ), *One Way to Love* (Col) ; 1946 : *Carnegie Hall* (Federal-UA).

HERLIE, Eileen. Born Glasgow, Mar. 8, 1920. Ht. 5 ft. 5 in. Brown hair, brown eyes. Educ. Shawlands Academy. To gain stage experience began in amateur theatricals, while working as short-hand typist. Professional debut with Scottish National Players, at Lyric, Glasgow, in 1938. Failed in early attempts to appear on London stage ; first important role, " Mrs. de Winter " in " Rebecca ", on tour and in London. Notable London success as the Queen in " The Eagle has Two Heads ", 1946, led to British film contract and offer to play title role in *Salome* opposite Orson Welles. Film debut in *Hungry Hill* (Two Cities) 1947 ; 1948 : *Hamlet* (Two Cities).

HILDYARD, Jack. Director of photography. Born Richmond, Surrey, 1912. First sold shirts, then joined British International Pictures. Became camera operator, working in association with Robert Krasker, and, later, director of photography : *The Lamp Still Burns, Henry V, School for Secrets, While the Sun Shines, Vice Versa, The First Gentleman.*

HILLIER, Erwin. Director of photography. Born Austria, Sept. 2, 1911. Educ. Academy of Arts, Berlin. Entered German films, but with decline of production, came to Britain, 1929. Gained first opportunity to show his style in *The Lady from Lisbon* (1940). Films include : *The Silver Fleet, Rhythm Serenade, A Canterbury Tale, They Knew Mr. Knight, The Great Day, I Know Where I'm Going, London Town, The October Man.*

HILTON, James. Author. Born England, Sept. 9, 1900. Educ. Leys School, Cambridge ; Christ's College, Cambridge. Prolific writer of screen material. Works filmed : *Goodbye Mr. Chips!, Knight without Armour, We Are Not Alone, Mrs. Miniver, Random Harvest.* Collaborated in writing : *Story of Dr. Wassell, So Well Remembered.*

HITCHCOCK, Alfred. Director. Born London, Aug. 13, 1899. Educ. St. Ignatius' College, London. Trained as engineer, specializing in mechanical drawing, then became clerk and artist in advertising agency at 15s. a week. To supplement income wrote captions for silent films. In 1920 joined Famous Players-Lasky at Islington Studios ; later entered script department. Assistant scenarist to Graham Cutts on *Woman to Woman*, for which he also wrote script, designed the sets and managed production. Directed his first film, *The Pleasure Garden*, for Michael Balcon at Gainsborough, 1925. Early films include : *The Lodger, Downhill, Easy Virtue, Blackmail* (BIP, the first British sound film), *Murder, The Ring, Juno and the Paycock, The Manxman, The Farmer's Wife, Rich and Strange, Number 17, Champagne, The Skin Game, The Case of Lady Camber.* Joined Gaumont British, 1933, and directed *Waltzes from Vienna, The Man Who Knew Too Much, The 39 Steps, Secret Agent, Sabotage, Young and Innocent, The Lady Vanishes.* After making *Jamaica Inn* for Mayflower Productions

went to U.S.A., 1939, and made *Rebecca, Foreign Correspondent, Mr. and Mrs. Smith, Suspicion, Saboteur, Shadow of a Doubt, Lifeboat.* In 1943-4 visited Britain to direct foreign language shorts for M.O.I. Recent films : *Spellbound, Notorious, The Paradine Case.* Since 1945 has been associated with Sidney Bernstein in Transatlantic Film Productions.

HOBSON, Valerie. Born Larne, N. Ireland, 1918. Ht. 5 ft. 5 in. ; wt. 112 lb. Light brown hair, grey eyes. Educ. St. Augustine's ; Priory Convent School, London. Studied ballet with Espinosa ; trained also at Royal Academy of Dramatic Art. On London stage at 14 in " Orders Is Orders " ; " Ball at the Savoy"; " The Path of Glory " ; " Conversation Piece". Repeated stage role in first film, *The Path of Glory*, 1934, followed by *Badger's Green.* In 1936 went to U.S.A. and made : *Strange Wives, The Mystery of Edwin Drood, The Bride of Frankenstein, The Were-Wolf of London, Chinatown Squad, The Great Impersonation, August Week-end, Tugboat Princess, Rendezvous at Midnight.* Returned to Britain, 1937, and made : *The Eunuch of Stamboul, Jump for Glory, The Drum, This Man Is News, Spy in Black, Q Planes, The Silent Battle, This Man in Paris.* 1940 : *Contra-band* (Brit Nat), *Atlantic Ferry* (Warn-Brit) : 1941 : *Unpublished Story* (Two Cities) ; 1943 : *The Adventures of Tartu* (MGM Brit) ; 1946 : *The Years Between* (Box), *Great Expectations* (Cineguild) ; 1948 : *Blanche Fury* (Cineguild).

HODIAK, John. Born Pittsburgh, Pennyslvania, Apr. 16. Ht. 6 ft. ; wt. 180 lb. Brown hair, hazel eyes. Educ. Holbrook Grammar School ; Hamtrach High School, Michigan. Became radio announcer and radio actor ; and worked in business office. Spotted by film talent scouts in radio play " Li'l Abner". First film : *A Stranger in Town* (MGM) 1943. Other films include :—1943 : *By Hook or By Crook* (MGM), *Song of Russia* (MGM), *Lifeboat* (20th) ; 1944 : *Marriage Is a Private Affair* (MGM), *You Can't Do That to Me* (MGM), *Sunday Dinner for a Soldier* (20th) ; 1945 : *A Bell for Adano* (20th), *The Harvey Girls* (MGM), *Two Smart People* (MGM) ; 1946 : *Somewhere in the Night* (20th) ; 1947 : *The Arnelo Affair* (MGM), *Desert Fury* (Para).

HOLDEN, Fay. Real name Fay Hammerton. Born Birmingham, Sept. 20, 1895. Auburn hair, brown eyes. Ht. 5 ft. 3½ in. ; wt. 124 lb. Appeared in stage dancing troupe at 9 ; played her first dramatic part at 10 under name of Gaby Fay, became established as comedy actress in England, Canada, and U.S.A., first appeared on New York stage with Mrs. Patrick Campbell. Went to Hollywood in 1935 ; scouts found her playing character role in " Hollywood Holiday " at Pasadena Playhouse. First film : *I Married a Doctor* (Warn) 1936. Early films include : *Polo Joe, Wives Never Know, Bulldog Drummond Escapes, You Can't Take Money, Florence Nightingale, King of Gamblers, Souls at Sea, Double or Nothing, Exclusive, You're Only Young Once* (MGM 1938—her first Mrs. Hardy role), *Judge Hardy's Children, Test Pilot, Love Is a Headache, The Battle of Broadway, Love Finds Andy Hardy, Hold That Kiss, Out West with the Hardys, Sweethearts, Sergeant Madden, The Hardys Ride High, Andy Hardy Gets Spring Fever, Judge Hardy and Son.* 1940 : *Andy Hardy Meets Debutante* (MGM) ; 1941 : *Bitter Sweet* (MGM) ; 1941 : *Ziegfeld Girl* (MGM), *Andy Hardy's Private Secretary* (MGM), *Washington Melodrama* (MGM), *Blossoms in the Dust* (MGM), *I'll Wait for You* (MGM), *Life*

Begins for Andy Hardy (MGM), H. M. Pulham, Esq. (MGM) ; 1942 : The Courtship of Andy Hardy (MGM), Andy Hardy's Double Life (MGM) ; 1944 : Andy Hardy's Blonde Trouble (MGM) ; 1946 : Love Laughs at Andy Hardy (MGM), The Baxter Millions (UA), Little Miss Big (Univ), Canyon Passage (Univ).

HOLDEN, William. Real name William Beedle. Born O'Fallon, Illinois, Apr. 17, 1918. Ht. 6 ft. ; wt. 165 lb. Brown hair, blue eyes. Educ. South Pasadena Junior College. Took part in radio plays while at high school and college. Seen by talent scout at Pasadena Playhouse. First film : Golden Boy (Col) 1939. Other films include—1940 : Invisible Stripes, Those Were the Days (Para), Our Town (UA), Arizona (Col) ; 1941 : I Wanted Wings (Para), Texas (Col) ; 1942 : The Remarkable Andrew (Para), The Fleet's In ! (Para), Meet the Stewarts (Col), Young and Willing (UA). Served in Armed Forces, 1943-6. 1947 : Blaze of Noon (Para), Dear Ruth (Para) ; 1948 : The Man from Colorado.

HOLLINGSWORTH, John. Music director. Born London, 1916. Educ. Bradfield College ; Guildhall School of Music. Joined the R.A.F. in 1940 and became associate conductor of R.A.F. Symphony Orchestra. Toured this country and America, and studied Hollywood methods of recording film music. First film work, 1942, conducting R.A.F. Orchestra for background music to Target for To-night. Started work on feature films, 1945, as assistant musical director to Muir Mathieson, with whom he collaborated in the arrangement of Rachmaninoff's music for Brief Encounter.

HOLLOWAY, Stanley. Born London, Oct. 1, 1890. Ht. 5 ft. 10½ in. ; wt. 164 lb. Brown hair, grey eyes. Began his career as a boy singer, studied singing in Milan. After war service 1915-18 became established in London musical comedy and variety. One of the original members of the Co-Optimists : appeared with them 1921-7, and has also appeared in two of their revivals. Made his first broadcast in 1924. At Noel Coward's suggestion made his first film, as juvenile lead in The Rotters in 1921. Since then he has appeared on both stage and screen, but recently has confined himself almost exclusively to films. Many of his early films were shorts based on his music-hall monologues, such as " Albert and the Lion ". Feature films include : Sleeping Car (GB) 1932, Lily of Killarney, The Girl from Maxim's, Love at Second Sight, Sing as We Go (with Gracie Fields), Road House, John Peel, Squibs (talkie version), In Town To-night, Play Up the Band !, Cotton Queen, Vicar of Bray, The Blacksmith. 1940 : Major Barbara (Pascal) ; 1942 : Salute John Citizen (Brit Nat) ; 1944 : This Happy Breed (Cineguild), The Way Ahead (Two Cities), Champagne Charlie (Ealing) ; 1946 : Caesar and Cleopatra (Pascal), Brief Encounter (Cineguild), Carnival (Two Cities) ; 1947 : Nicholas Nickleby (Ealing), Meet Me at Dawn (Excelsior-20th), Snowbound (Gains) ; 1948 : One Night With You (Two Cities), Hamlet (Two Cities).

HOLM, Celeste. Fair hair, blue eyes. Educ. France. Studied ballet at 3. On stage for Theatre Guild in " Time of Your Life ", " Bloomer Girl ", and other shows. Was the original Annie in " Oklahoma ! ". First film : Three Little Girls in Blue (20th) 1946. 1947 : Carnival in Costa Rica (20th) ; 1948 : Gentlemen's Agreement.

HOLT, Patrick. (Former stage name Patrick Parsons.) Born Cheltenham, Jan. 31, 1912. Ht. 6 ft. Auburn hair, grey eyes. Educ. Christ's Hospital. When 18, worked in a Burmese rice mill, but returned to Britain to take up acting. First stage appearance at the " Q " Theatre, London, was followed by two years with Hull Repertory Company. In two Gordon Harker thrillers in London, then with Sally Gray in Sword of Honour. During World War II, served in British Army ; took part in many troop shows in India. Resumed film career with Hungry Hill (Two Cities) 1947. Also in 1947 made : Frieda (Ealing), The October Man (Two Cities), Master of Bankdam (Holbein), When the Bough Breaks (Gains) ; 1948 : Mark of Cain (Two Cities), High Pavement (Corfield-Huth).

HOLT, Tim. Real name Charles John Holt. Born Beverly Hills, California, Feb. 5, 1918. Ht. 5 ft. 11 in.; wt. 165 lb. Brown hair, brown eyes. Educ. Culver Military Academy, Indiana ; University of California. Son of Jack Holt ; decided to follow father's career. First film : History Is Made at Night (Wanger) 1937. Other films include : Stella Dallas, I Met My Love Again, Gold Is Where You Find It, Renegade Ranger, Sons of the Legion, The Law West of Tombstone, Stagecoach, Spirit of Culver, The Girl and the Gambler, Fifth Avenue Girl. 1940 : Swiss Family Robinson (RKO), Laddie (RKO), Wagon Train (RKO), The Fargo Kid (RKO) ; 1941 : Along the Rio Grande (RKO), Back Street (Univ) ; 1942 : The Magnificent Ambersons (RKO), Hitler's Children (RKO). Served in U.S.A.A.F. 1942-6 (D.F.C.). 1946 : My Darling Clementine (20th) ; 1947 : Thunder Mountain (RKO), Under the Tonto Rim (RKO), Treasure of the Sierra Madre (Warn).

HONEGGER, Arthur. Composer. Born Le Havre, 1892, of Swiss parents. Studied in Switzerland and France. Came into prominence as a member of " Les Six ", group of French modernist composers. Has worked for French and British films, including : Les Misérables, Crime et Châtiment, Mademoiselle Docteur, Mayerling, Pygmalion.

HOPE, Bob. Real name Leslie Townes Hope. Born Eltham, May 29, 1904. Ht. 6 ft. ; wt. 180 lb. Brown hair, brown eyes. During childhood, migrated with family to Cleveland, Ohio. Learnt tap-dancing while at high school ; developed wise-cracking technique entertaining business colleagues. Fatty Arbuckle helped him get first stage job as black-face turn in road show. After years of song-and-dance work in small theatres and clubs, appeared eventually on Broadway in " Roberta ", " Ziegfeld Follies " and other shows ; also on radio. Failed film test, 1928. First film : The Big Broadcast of 1938 (Para) ; made hit singing " Thanks for the Memory " with Shirley Ross. Other films (all Para) include : College Swing, Give Me a Sailor, Thanks for the Memory, Never Say Die, Some Like It Hot, The Cat and the Canary. 1940 : Road to Singapore, The Ghost Breakers ; 1941 : Road to Zanzibar, Caught in the Draft, Nothing But the Truth, Louisiana Purchase ; 1942 : My Favourite Blonde, Road to Morocco ; 1943 : They Got Me Covered (RKO) Let's Face It, Star Spangled Rhythm ; 1945 : Duffy's Tavern, Road to Utopia ; 1946 : The Princess and the Pirate, Monsieur Beaucaire ; 1947 : My Favourite Brunette, guest star in Variety Girl, Where There's Life, Road to Rio, Paleface.

HOPKINS, Joan. Born London, Aug. 31, 1915. Fair hair, blue eyes. Educ. local elementary school and Royal Academy of Dramatic Art, where she won grants to enable her study. First important stage role was in " Ladies in Retirement " at St. Martin's Theatre, London, 1941. Film debut in *We Dive at Dawn* (Gains) 1943. Other films include—1943 : *Alibi* (Brit Lion) ; 1944 : *Squadron Leader X* (RKO Brit) ; 1947 : *Temptation Harbour* (ABPC) ; 1948 : *The First Gentleman* (Col-Brit).

HORNE. Lena. Born Brooklyn, New York, June 30. Black hair, brown eyes. Educ. New York public schools. In chorus of Cotton Club ; then achieved fame as singer in " Blackbirds of 1940 ". Became star of radio and floor shows. Singing in Hollywood night club, led to her first film role : *Panama Hattie* (MGM) 1943. Other films include : *Cabin in the Sky* (MGM) ; 1943 : *By Hook or By Crook* (MGM), *Stormy Weather* (20th), *Thousands Cheer* (MGM), *Swing Fever* (MGM), *Broadway Rhythm* (MGM) ; 1944 : *Two Girls and a Sailor* (MGM), *Ziegfeld Follies* (MGM) ; 1946 : *Till the Clouds Roll By* (MGM). Visited Britain for stage appearances 1947.

HORTON, Edward Everett. Born Brooklyn, New York, Mar. 18, 1888. Educ. Columbia University. Began his career in the chorus of a Gilbert and Sullivan Opera Company in Staten Island, New York, 1908. Appeared in many stage successes, notably " Lilac Time ", " Smilin' Through " and " Private Lives ". Began his film career in early silent films, among them, *Too Much Business* and the first version of *Ruggles of Red Gap* (Essanay) 1918. Appeared in *The Terror* (Warn) 1928, the first sound film shown in Britain. Also many of the early Vitaphone sound shorts made in New York. Early feature films include : *Holiday, Once a Gentleman, Kiss Me Again, Toast of the Legion, Reaching for the Moon, Lonely Wives, The Front Page, Six Cylinder Love, The Age for Love, A Bedtime Story, The Way to Love, Design for Living, Alice in Wonderland, It's a Boy* (GB, in Britain, 1934), *The Poor Rich, Uncertain Lady, Easy to Love, Smarty, The Merry Widow, Kiss and Make Up, Ladies Should Listen, Sing and Like It, Success at Any Price, The Woman in Command* (GB, in Britain, 1935), *The Night is Young, Biography of a Bachelor Girl, All the King's Horses, The Devil is a Woman, Ten-Dollar Raise, In Caliente, Little Big-Shot, Going Highbrow, Top Hat, The Private Secretary* (Julius Hagen, in Britain, 1936), *His Night Out, Your Uncle Dudley, Her Master's Voice, The Singing Kid, Hearts Divided, The Man in the Mirror* (Julius Hagen, in Britain, 1937), *Nobody's Fool, Lost Horizon, Let's Make a Million, Angel, Wild Money, The King and the Chorus Girl, The Perfect Specimen, The Great Garrick, Oh Doctor !, Shall We Dance, Hitting a New High, Danger—Love at Work !, College Swing, Bluebeard's Eighth Wife, Paris Honeymoon, Holiday* (Para, 1938), *Little Tough Guys in Society.* 1940 : *You're the One* (Para) ; 1941 : *Sunny* (RKO), *Ziegfeld Girl* (MGM), *Bachelor Daddy* (Univ), *Weekend for Three* (RKO), *Here Comes Mr. Jordan* (Col), *The Body Disappears* (Warn) ; 1942 : *I Married an Angel* (MGM), *The Magnificent Dope* (20th), *Springtime in the Rockies* (20th) ; 1943 : *Forever and a Day* (RKO), *Thank Your Lucky Stars* (Warn), *The Gang's All Here* (20th) ; 1944 : *Summer Storm* (UA), *Brazil* (Rep), *San Diego I Love You* (RKO), *The Town Went Wild* (PRC), *Arsenic and Old Lace* (Warn) ; 1945 : *Lady on a Train* (Univ), *Strange Confession* (RKO), *Steppin' in Society* (Rep) ; 1946 : *Cinderella Jones* (RKO), *Faithful in My Fashion*

(MGM), *Earl Carroll Sketchbook* (Rep) ; 1947 : *Down to Earth* (Col), *Her Husband's Affairs* (Col).

HOWARD, Ronald. Born Anerley, Surrey, 1918. Ht. 6 ft. Fair hair, blue eyes. Educ. Tonbridge School, Kent ; Jesus College, Cambridge. Son of the late Leslie Howard, whom he closely resembles. Contributed as writer to university magazine ; later on joined London " Sunday Chronicle ", 1939, first as reporter, then film critic. Served 1939-46 in R.N.V.R. On demobilization, persuaded to make film test. Had previously " walked on " in *Romeo and Juliet* (in Hollywood) and in *Pimpernel Smith* (at Denham), in which films his father starred. First major appearance, in *While the Sun Shines* (Internat Screen) 1947 ; Other films include—1947 : *Night Beat* (LFP) ; 1948 : *My Brother Jonathan* (ABPC), *Bond Street* (World Screen).

HOWARD, Trevor. Born Cliftonville, Kent, Sept. 29, 1916. Ht. 5 ft. 11 in. ; wt. 154 lb. Light brown hair, light blue eyes. Educ. Brantford, Ontario ; Clifton College. Youthful ambition, to play cricket for England. Travelled the world during childhood. All-round sportsman at school. Won scholarship to Royal Academy of Dramatic Art, 1933, and appeared on London stage, in repertory and in Shakespeare at Stratford-on-Avon. Served in Army 1940-3, then returned to stage. First film : *The Way Ahead* (Two Cities) 1943. Other films include—1945 : *The Way to the Stars* (Two Cities), *Brief Encounter* (Cineguild) ; 1946 : *I See a Dark Stranger* (Individ) ; 1947 : *Green for Danger* (Individ), *They Made Me a Fugitive*, (Alliance), *So Well Remembered* (RKO).

HOWES, Sally Ann. Born England, July 30, 1930. Daughter of Bobby Howes. Youthful ambition : to become veterinary surgeon. In 1943, chosen from 200 applicants to play role of child heroine in first film : *Thursday's Child* (ABPC). Other films include—1944 : *Halfway House* (Ealing), *Dead of Night* (Ealing) ; 1945 : *Pink String and Sealing Wax* (Ealing) ; 1947 : *Nicholas Nickleby* (Ealing) ; 1948 : *Anna Karenina* (LFP), *High Pavement* (Corfield-Huth).

HUGHES, Howard. Producer. Born Houston, Texas, Dec. 25, 1905. Educ. Fessenden School, Boston ; Californian Institute of Technology ; Rice Institute, Houston. At 18 inherited his father's share in a tool manufacturing company ; though a minor and therefore not legally permitted to assume control, he took the matter to court and proved his ability to carry out his father's wishes. Owns the biggest brewery in Texas. Is a notable flyer and aircraft designer : designed the Hughes Flying Boat, under construction, 1946-8, the largest in the world ; awarded Harmon Trophy for record round-the-world flight with a crew of four, 1938 ; owns large holdings in Trans-World Airlines ; has made more than 25,000 flights, and has been injured, sometimes gravely, on test flights. Produced his first film, *Two Arabian Knights* (UA) 1926. Other outstanding productions include : *The Rocket, Everybody's Acting, The Mating Call, Hell's Angels* (which he also directed), *The Front Page, Scarface, Sky Devils, The Outlaw* (made in 1943 and held up owing to objections from censor till 1946), *Mad Wednesday, Vendetta.*

HUGHES, Peggy. Stunt artist. Born Kensington, London, Sept. 22, 1923. Educ. Westbourne Park High School. Early ambition to be actress, but after war service in Women's Land Army, turned stunt

RITA HAYWORTH
(Columbia)

girl and made film debut in fight scene in *Fame is the Spur*, 1947. Films include: *Good Time Girl* (fight scene), *Three Weird Sisters* (fall from balcony), *This Was a Woman* (fall on stairs), *Safety First* (fall from moving car).

HULBERT, Claude. Real name Claude Noël Hulbert. Brother of Jack Hulbert. Born London Dec. 25, 1900. Ht. 5 ft. 10 in.; wt. 145 lb. Fair hair, blue eyes. Educ. privately, and Caius College, Cambridge. Youthful ambition: to be fireman. At 3 had first lesson in acrobatic dancing, after visit to circus. Joined concert party with Ernest Crampton after leaving Cambridge. In acrobatic comedy parts in musical comedy. Radio comedian since early B.B.C. days in double act with wife, Enid Trevor. Tried for two years to enter films before Tom Walls gave him role in Aldwych farce *A Night Like This* (B & D) 1929. In N.F.S. 1939-45. Worked for ENSA in Britain, France, Holland, West and East Africa. Early films include several Aldwych farces. Collaborated on music and lyrics for his brother's film *Jack Ahoy*; appeared in *Bulldog Jack*. Also made: *Interrupted Honeymoon, The Vulture, It Isn't Cricket, Ship's Concert, Hail and Farewell, His Lordship Regrets, Many Tanks Mr. Atkins*. 1943: *Sailors Three* (Ealing). 1944: *My Learned Friend* (Ealing); 1946: *London Town* (Wesley Ruggles); 1947: *No Nightingales* (Brit Nat).

HUNT, Marsha. Real name Marcia Hunt. Born Chicago, Oct. 17, 1917. Ht. 5 ft. 5 ins. Brown hair. Educ. New York public schools. Joined Irvine School of Dramatics, was part-time model. Originally did not want to enter films. First film: *Virginia Judge* (Para) 1935. Spent three years playing *ingénue* roles: *Hollywood Boulevard, College Holiday, Star Reporter, The Hardys Ride High* and many more. Was about to try Broadway when given role in *These Glamour Girls* (1939). Other films include:—1940: *Pride and Prejudice* (MGM), *Irene* (RKO); 1941: *Flight Command* (MGM), *Cheers for Miss Bishop* (UA), *Blossoms in the Dust* (MGM), *Unholy Partners* (MGM), *The Trial of Mary Dugan* (MGM), *The Penalty* (MGM), *I'll Wait for You* (MGM); 1942: *Joe Smith, American* (MGM), *Kid Glove Killer* (MGM), *Affairs of Martha* (MGM), *Panama Hattie* (MGM), *Seven Sweethearts* (MGM); 1943: *Human Comedy* (MGM), *Pilot No. 5* (MGM), *Lost Angel* (MGM), *Thousands Cheer* (MGM); 1944: *Cry Havoc* (MGM), *Bride by Mistake* (RKO), *None Shall Escape* (Col); 1945: *Valley of Decision* (MGM), *Music for Millions* (MGM), *A Letter for Evie* (MGM); 1947: *A Woman Destroyed* (UI), *Carnegie Hall* (Federal-UA).

HUNTER, Ian. Born Capetown, South Africa, June 13, 1900. Ht. 6 ft. 1 in.; wt. 188 lb. Brown hair, blue-grey eyes. Educ. St. Andrew's College, Grahamstown, Cape Colony. Came to Britain, 1917; served in Army in World War I. Then in "walking-on" part in London play "Jack o' Jingles". Appeared in many silent films at the Stoll studios, including: *The Ring, Downhill, Easy Virtue, His House in Order*. Sound films include: *Sally in Our Alley* (with Gracie Fields), *The Water Gypsies, The Sign of Four, There Goes the Bride* (with Jessie Matthews), *The Man from Toronto* (with Jessie Matthews), *Orders Is Orders, The Night of the Party, Something Always Happens, No Escape, Death at Broadcasting House, The Morals of Marcus, The Phantom Light*. Went to Hollywood 1934; in 1942 came home and served three years in R.N.V.R. U.S.

films include: *A Midsummer Night's Dream, Men on Her Mind, I Found Stella Parrish, Jalna, The White Angel, The Devil Takes the Count, To Mary—with Love, Stolen Holiday, Call it a Day, Confession, That Certain Woman, Another Dawn, 52nd Street, Adventures of Robin Hood, Always Good-bye, Secrets of an Actress, The Sisters, Comet Over Broadway, Yes My Darling Daughter, Little Princess, Serenade, Tarzan Finds a Son, Maisie, Bad Little Angel, Tower of London*. 1940: *Strange Cargo* (MGM), *Broadway Melody of 1940* (MGM), *The Long Voyage Home* (UA), *Dulcy* (MGM), *Gallant Sons* (MGM), *Bitter Sweet* (MGM); 1941: *Come Live with Me* (MGM), *Ziegfeld Girl* (MGM), *Billy the Kid* (MGM), *Andy Hardy's Private Secretary* (MGM), *A Yank at Eton* (MGM), *Forever and a Day* (RKO). In Britain, 1946: *Bedelia* (Corfield); 1947: *White Cradle Inn* (Peak), *The White Unicorn* (Corfield).

HUNTER, Kim. Real name Janet Cole. Born Detroit, Michigan, Nov. 12, 1922. Ht. 5 ft. 3 in.; wt. 113 lb. Mid-brown hair, hazel eyes. Educ. Detroit and Miami High Schools. Youthful ambitions: to join Navy, be a dress designer, pianist, actress. Chose stage in 1940 after success in school plays, played lead for three years in small companies. Seen by David Selznick at Pasadena Playhouse in "Arsenic and Old Lace". First film: *The Seventh Victim* (RKO) 1943, followed by *Tender Comrade* (RKO) 1944. Chosen by Michael Powell and Emeric Pressburger as typical American girl for role of WAAC stationed in England, in *A Matter of Life and Death* (Archers) 1946. Resumed stage career, 1947.

HUNTLEY, Raymond. Born Birmingham, Apr. 23, 1904. Ht. 6 ft. Brown hair, grey eyes. Educ. King Edward's School, Birmingham. At 18 spent two years with Birmingham Repertory Company, then toured in America. Films include: *Rembrandt, Knight without Armour, Night Train to Munich, Pimpernel Smith*. 1940: *Freedom Radio* (Zampi-Col); 1944: *They Came to a City* (Ealing), *The Way Ahead* (Two Cities); 1945: *I see a Dark Stranger* (Individ); 1946: *School for Secrets* (Two Cities); 1948: *So Evil My Love* (Hal Wallis-Para) made in Britain, *Broken Journey* (Gains).

HURST, Brian Desmond. Director. Born Castle Reagh, Ireland. Educ. Académie Julienne; Académie de la Grande Chaumière, Paris. Enlisted at 15 in World War 1. Studied art in Paris, then went to Hollywood and worked with John Ford. Attracted attention in Britain in 1934 with his direction of *The Tell-Tale Heart*, from the Edgar Allan Poe short story. Films include: *Ourselves Alone* (collaborated), *The Tenth Man, Sensation, Glamorous Night, Prison without Bars, Riders of the Sea, The Lion has Wings* (collaborated), *On the Night of the Fire, Dangerous Moonlight, Alibi, The Hundred Pound Window, Theirs Is the Glory* (documentary of Battle of Arnhem), *Hungry Hill, Mark of Cain*.

HUSTON, John. Director, writer. Son of Walter Huston. Born in an American hamlet won in a poker game by his grandfather. Educ. Lincoln High School, Los Angeles. Tried professional boxing, then acting at Greenwich Village, New York. Spent two years as cavalry officer with Mexican Army and, at 21, turned short-story writer for "American Mercury". Wrote "Frankie and Johnnie", a book in play form, which was bought by Goldwyn. Went to Hollywood to study film script technique; worked with William

Wyler on *House Divided*. Also wrote in Britain for Gaumont British and studied art in Paris. Wrote story "Three Strangers", took it to Hollywood and sold it to Warner, who engaged him as scriptwriter, 1938. Collaborated on : *The Amazing Dr. Clitterhouse, Juarez, Dr. Ehrlich's Magic Bullet, Jezebel, High Sierra, Sergeant York*. In 1941, turned director with his own script of *The Maltese Falcon*, followed by *In This Our Life* (directed and wrote screenplay). Also directed *Across the Pacific*. Served in U.S. Army 1943-6 ; during war service, directed shorts and documentaries. Directed and wrote screenplay of *Treasure of the Sierra Madre*.

HUSTON, Walter. Born Toronto, Ontario, Apr. 6, 1884. Brown hair, hazel eyes. Ht. 6 ft. ; wt. 180 lb. Trained as mechanical engineer and helped on father's building projects during holidays. Experience with college dramatics prompted him to join Toronto road show, 1902. Appeared in New York, 1905, in "The Convict's Stripes", then toured in "The Sign of the Cross". Left stage for civil engineering, but resumed theatrical career with vaudeville in 1909, scored great success at Shubert Theatre, 1934-5, in "Dodsworth". Made first films at Paramount Long Island Studio in 1928 : *Gentleman of the Press* and *The Lady Lies*. Other films include : *The Virginian, The Bad Man, Abraham Lincoln, Criminal Code, Star Witness, The Ruling Voice, A Woman from Monte Carlo, A House Divided, Law and Order, Beast of the City, Wet Parade, American Madness, Rain, Night Court, Congo, Hell Below, Gabriel Over the White House, Storm at Daybreak, The Prizefighter and the Lady, Ann Vickers, Keep 'em Rolling!* Came to Britain, 1936, to play title role in *Rhodes of Africa* (GB). 1937, repeated stage role of Samuel Dodsworth in *Dodsworth* (UA). Also made *Of Human Hearts ;* 1940 : *The Light That Failed* (Para) ; 1941 : *All That Money Can Buy* (RKO), *Swamp Water* (20th) ; 1942 : *Shanghai Gesture* (UA), *Always in My Heart* (Warn) ; 1943 : *Edge of Darkness* (Warn), *Mission to Moscow* (Warn), *North Star* (Goldwyn), *Yankee Doodle Dandy* (Warn), *The Outlaw* (Howard Hughes—not released till 1946) ; 1944 : *Dragon Seed* (MGM) ; 1945 : *Ten Little Niggers* —U.S. title *And Then There Were None* (20th) ; 1946 : *Dragonwyck* (20th), *Duel in the Sun* (Selznick) ; 1947 : *Summer Holiday* (MGM) ; 1948 : *Treasure of the Sierra Madre* (Warn).

HUTCHESON, David. Born Craigmore, Isle of Bute, Scotland, June 14, 1905. Ht. 6 ft. 2½ in. ; wt. 180 lb. Brown hair, blue eyes. Educ. Shrubbington House, Farnham ; Tonbridge School, Kent. In 1921-6 roamed Canada, U.S.A., Central and South America as dance-band drummer, cabaret vocalist, rum-runner, beach life-saver. Then after stage experience in London and New York made film debut, 1930, as English peer in *The Best People*, made at Paramount's Long Island studios. First British film : *Romance in Rhythm* (Stoll) 1934. Other films include : *The Sky's the Limit, The Middle Watch, This'll Make You Whistle*. Served in R.A.F. and Army, 1940-5. During service leaves, appeared in—1942 : *Sabotage at Sea* (Brit Nat) ; 1943 : *Next of Kin* (Ealing) ; 1944 : *The Life and Death of Colonel Blimp* (Archers). In 1944-5 raised ENSA company, taking first full-length musical comedy, "No, No, Nanette", to Middle East troops. Returned to screen, 1946 with *School for Secrets* (Two Cities). 1948 : *Vice Versa* (Two Cities), *Mark of Cain* (Two Cities).

HUTCHINSON, U. Phillips. Make-up artist. President, British Make-up Men's Association. Born Grimsby. Wanted to be jockey ; worked in Sir John Robinson's stables, Worksop. Then spent five years with Doncaster hairdresser's shop ; ran own business ; won top award at British Hairdressers' Academy. Then in India as hairdresser to Viceroy's staff and to ruling princes ; later learnt Hindustani and became guide in Kashmir. Returned to hairdressing in England ; joined Elstree Studios, 1931, then Denham Studios.

HUTTON, Betty. Born Battle Creek, Michigan, Feb. 26, 1921. Ht. 5 ft. 4 in. ; wt. 112 lb. Platinum blonde hair, blue eyes. At 16, singer with Vincent Lopez' orchestra in Detroit. One day, thinking she was a failure, yelled with anger, punched the air, jumped on the piano—thus by accident hitting on the technique that was the basis of her new career. Became cabaret and vaudeville star in New York, 1938, then appeared in musicals including "Panama Hattie" : the owner of this show, B. G. De Sylva, was also film production chief and signed her for first film *The Fleet's In* (Para) 1942. Other films (all Para) include— 1943 : *Happy Go Lucky, Star Spangled Rhythm, Let's Face It, The Miracle of Morgan's Creek, And the Angels Sing ;* 1944 : *Incendiary Blonde, Here Come the Waves ;* 1945 : *Duffy's Tavern, The Stork Club ;* 1946, *Cross My Heart ;* 1947 : *The Perils of Pauline ;* 1948 : *Dream Girl* (Para).

HUTTON, Robert. Real name Robert Bruce Winne. Born Kingston, New York State, June 11, 1920. Ht. 6 ft. 2 in. ; wt. 160 lb. Light brown hair, blue eyes. Educ. Blair Academy, New York. In 1940 tried but failed to secure Hollywood job. Joined the Woodstock Players at Kingston for several seasons and was discovered there by Warner scout, 1943. First film : *Destination Tokyo* (Warn) 1943. Films (all Warn) include—1944 : *Janie, Hollywood Canteen;* 1945 : *Roughly Speaking, Too Young to Know ;* 1946 : *Janie Gets Married ;* 1947 : *Time Out of Mind* (UI), *Love and Learn ;* 1948 : *Need for Each Other* (Warn).

IRELAND, John. Actor. Born Victoria, British Columbia, Canada, Jan. 30, 1914. Ht. 6 ft. 2 in. wt. 175 lb. Dark brown hair, blue eyes. Educ. Grammar School, San Francisco ; San Pedro Commerce High School, New York. Worked in water carnival ; took part in five-mile marathon swim in Toronto, 1935. Played ten years Broadway stage ; was also in Irish Repertory. Appeared in *My Darling Clementine* (20th) 1946, *Wake Up and Dream* (20th) 1947.

IRELAND, John. Composer. Born Bowdon, Cheshire, Aug. 13, 1879. Educ. Leeds Grammar School ; privately ; and at Royal College of Music, where he is now Professor of Composition. Mus.D. (Hon.), University of Durham. The great variety of his compositions did not include any film music until he wrote the score for *The Overlanders* in 1946.

IRVING, Ernest. Composer, music director. Born Godalming, Surrey, 1878. One of the pioneers of British film music ; has composed and conducted every kind of music. Member of the Honorary Committee of Management of the Royal Philharmonic Society. Since 1936 has been musical director at Ealing Studios, where Gracie Fields made many of her greatest film recordings under his direction.

IRVING, Laurence. Designer, producer. Born London, Apr. 11, 1897. Son of actor-manager H. B. Irving, grandson of Sir Henry Irving. Educ. Wellington School. Served in World War I in Royal Naval Air Service ; Croix de Guerre. In 1919-20 studied at Byam Shaw School of Art and Royal Academy Schools, and became book illustrator. Illustrated John Masefield's " Philip The King " ; Joseph Conrad's " Mirror of the Sea " ; Hakluyt's " Voyages " ; wrote and illustrated " Windmills and Waterways ". Several years as stage designer, then entered films, 1928, in Hollywood as designer : *The Man in the Iron Mask*, *The Taming of the Shrew* (for Douglas Fairbanks, Sr.). In England from 1930 : 77 *Park Lane, Colonel Blood, Moonlight Sonata, Pygmalion*. 1939-45, war service as Senior Intelligence Officer Photographic Wing, R.A.F.; awarded O.B.E. 1946, resumed film work as co-producer with *Uncle Silas*.

IRWIN, Margaret. Novelist. Educ. Clifton and Oxford. Her novels include : " Still She Wished For Company ", "Royal Flush ", " The Proud Servant ", " The Stranger Prince ", " The Gay Galliard " " Young Bess ". Films in preparation, 1947: *Gay Galliard, Young Bess*.

ITURBI, Jose. Born Valencia, Spain, Nov. 28. Ht. 5 ft. 10½ in. ; wt. 160 lb. Brown hair, brown eyes. Educ. Valencia Conservatory ; Barcelona ; Paris Conservatory. An infant prodigy, taught piano at 7. Later head of piano faculty, Geneva Conservatory, for four years. As pianist gave 303 concerts in Europe in three years. Made American concert debut, 1929. Debut as conductor, Mexico City, 1933. Musical director and permanent conductor Rochester Philharmonic Orchestra, 1936-44. First film : *Thousands Cheer* (MGM) 1943. Other films (all MGM) include : 1944 : *Two Girls and a Sailor, Music for Millions, Anchors Aweigh ;* 1945 : *Holiday in Mexico*. Toured Britain and Europe, autumn 1947. 1948 : *The Birds and the Bees, Triumph of Music*.

JACKSON, Gordon. Real name, Gordon Cameron Jackson. Born Glasgow, Dec. 19, 1923. Ht. 5 ft. 11 in. Fair hair, blue eyes. Educ. Hillhead High School, Glasgow. Youthful ambition : to be a journalist. A Scottish radio producer, remembering his " Children's Hour " broadcasts while at school, recommended him for films. Obtained leave from apprenticeship as draughtsman in Glasgow to make first film, *The Foreman Went to France* (Ealing) 1942. Other films include : 1943 ; *Millions Like Us* (Gains), *Nine Men* (Ealing) ; 1944 : *San Demetrio, London* (Ealing) ; 1945 : *Pink String and Sealing Wax* (Ealing), 1946 : *The Captive Heart* (Ealing) ; 1947 : *Against the Wind* (Ealing). Went to Australia to make *Eureka Stockade* (Ealing), 1948.

JAGGER, Dean. Born Lima, Ohio, Nov. 7, 1903. Ht. 6 ft. 2 in. ; 198 lb. Brown hair, brown eyes. Educ. Wabash College, Crawfordsville, Indiana. Was a country schoolmaster at 16. Then studied drama at Lyceum Arts Conservatory, Chicago, and played in repertory and vaudeville ; appeared on Broadway in " Missouri Legend ", " They Shall Not Die ". First film : *The Woman From Hell* (Fox), 1929. Other films include : *College Rhythm, Home on the Range, Car 99, Woman Trap, 13 Hours By Air, Woman In Distress, Escape By Night* ; 1940 : *Brigham Young* (20th) ; 1941 : *Western Union* (20th) ; 1942 : *Valley of the Sun* (RKO), *Omaha Trail* (MGM) ; 1943 : *I Escaped from the Gestapo* (Mono), *North Star* (RKO);

1944 : *Alaska* (Mono), *When Strangers Marry* (Mono) ; 1945 : *I Lived in Grosvenor Square* (Wilcox-ABPC, in Britain) ; 1946 : *Sister Kenny* (RKO).

JAMES, Harry. Born Albany, Georgia, Mar. 15, 1916. Ht. 6 ft. 1 in. ; wt. 175 lb. Brown hair, blue eyes. Educ. privately ; public school, Beaumont, Texas. Was child contortionist in circus. At 8 began to learn trumpet, later joining Ben Pollack's Band. His trumpet solo " Deep Elm " brought him a contract with Benny Goodman. After two years formed own band. First film appearance with band : *Syncopation* (RKO), 1941. Other films include : 1942 ; *Private Buckeroo* (Univ), *Springtime in the Rockies* (20th) ; 1943 : *Best Foot Forward* (MGM) 1944 : *Two Girls and a Sailor* (MGM). *Bathing Beauty* (MGM) ; 1945 : *Do You Love Me ?* (20th) ; 1946 : *If I'm Lucky* (20th) ; 1947 : *Carnegie Hall* (Federal-UA).

JARMAN, Claude, Jr. Born Nashville, Tennessee, Sept. 27, 1934. Ht. 4 ft. 10 in ; wt. 89 lb. Fair hair, blue eyes. Educ. Eakin Elementary School, Nashville. After 12,000 boys had been interviewed for film role, director Clarence Brown, posing as school building inspector, found him in a Nashville classroom ; and, attracted by his Southern accent and love of animals, took him away from his home town for first time to appear in *The Yearling* (MGM), 1946. Other films include : 1947 : *High Barbaree* (MGM); 1948 : *A Family for Jock* (MGM).

JEANS, Ursula. Born Simla, India, May 5, 1906. Ht. 5 ft. 6 in. Fair hair, blue eyes. Came to England 1919 ; studied at Royal Academy of Dramatic Art : toured in 1925 with Owen Nares : London debut as *ingénue* with Ivor Novello in " Firebrand ", 1926, followed by many other stage successes. In 1939, with Old Vic. In 1946, toured Near and Far East for ENSA in " It Depends What You Mean " and " The Barretts of Wimpole St." On screen since 1931 : *The Love Habit, The Flying Fool, The Crooked Lady, Cavalcade* (Fox, in Hollywood, 1933), *I Lived With You, Friday the Thirteenth, The Man in the Mirror, Dark Journey, Storm in a Teacup, Over the Moon*. 1943 : *The Life and Death of Colonel Blimp* (Archers) ; 1944 : *Mr. Emmanuel* (Two Cities) ; 1947 : *The Woman in the Hall* (Wessex).

JEFFREYS, Anne. Born Goldsboro, North Carolina, Jan. 28. Ht. 5 ft. 5 in. ; wt. 120 lb. Blonde hair, blue eyes. Educ. Anderson College, North Carolina. Studied voice training in New York ; made professional debut on radio programmes ; was also photographer's model. On holiday in Hollywood was spotted by talent scout. First film : *I Married an Angel* (MGM), 1942. Other films include : *Billy the Kid Trapped* (PRC), *The Old Homestead* (Rep), *X Marks the Spot* (Rep) ; 1944 : *Step Lively* (RKO), *Outlaw Busters* ; 1945 : *Dillinger* (Mono), *Zombies on Broadway* (RKO), *Dick Tracy* (RKO), *Vacation in Reno* (RKO) ; 1946 : *Splitface* (RKO), *Genius at Work* (RKO), *The Amazing Mr. Hammer* (RKO), *Step by Step* (RKO).

JENKINS, Jackie " Butch". Born Los Angeles, California, Aug. 19, 1938. Fair hair, brown eyes. Discovered on the beach by Director Clarence Brown, who was looking for a boy to play younger brother to Mickey Rooney. " Butch " was not then interested in films, being only 5 and having seen only a cartoon. Made successful debut in *The Human Comedy* (MGM) 1943. Other films (all MGM) include :— 1944 : *An*

American Romance, National Velvet; 1945: *Our Vines Have Tender Grapes, Boys' Ranch*; 1946: *Little Mister Jim*; 1947: *My Brother Talks to Horses, Summer Holiday*; 1948: *Love Bites Man*.

JENKINS, Megs. Born Birkenhead, Cheshire, Apr. 31, 1917. Ht. 5 ft. 4½ in.; wt. 168 lb. Dark brown hair, grey eyes. At 16 was seen in a dramatic school performance by William Armstrong of the Liverpool Repertory Company: joined the company for four years. First major film: *Millions Like Us* (Gains) 1943. Is noted for her mimicry of accents. Served at Admiralty Photostat Department during the war—Other films include:—1943: *The Lamp Still Burns* (Two Cities); 1945: *Acacia Avenue* (Box-Col); 1947: *Green for Danger* (Individ). Went to Australia for stage tour. Returned to Britain to appear in *Saraband for Dead Lovers* (Ealing) 1948.

JERGENS, Adele. Born Brooklyn, New York. Ht. 5 ft. 6½ in.; wt. 128 lb. Brown hair, brown eyes. Educ. Rockville Centre High School. Youthful ambition: to be a reporter. Trained as dancer at Albertina Rasch Studios. While at school, made stage debut at 15 in Brooklyn musical. Became one of New York's best-known models and leading show-girl. Appeared in night clubs and hotel shows in Le Touquet, London, Biarritz, Rio de Janeiro. Seen by Columbia scout when deputizing for Gypsy Rose Lee in New York stage show " Star and Garter". First film: *Tonight and Every Night* (Col) 1945. Other films include:—1946: *She Wouldn't Say Yes* (Col). 1947: *Down to Earth* (Col), *The Corpse Came C.O.D.* (Col).

JOHN, Rosamund. Real name Nora Rosamund Jones. Born Tottenham, North London, Oct. 19, 1913. Ht. 5 ft. 6½ in.; wt. 126 lb. Honey-blonde hair, green-grey eyes. Educ. Tottenham Drapers' College. Youthful ambition: to be actress or author. After a year in France at 19, returned to London, was introduced by former history mistress to Milton Rosmer and chosen for film role of Scots girl in *The Secret of the Loch* (Ealing) 1934. Gained stage experience in Shakespeare, repertory, as Cochran " young lady " and with Robert Donat in " The Devil's Disciple " before resuming films. 1942: with Leslie Howard in *The First of the Few*. Other films include—1943: *The Gentle Sex* (Concanen-Two Cities), *The Lamp Still Burns* (Two Cities); 1944: *Tawny Pipit* (Two Cities); 1945: *The Way to the Stars* (Two Cities); 1947: *Green for Danger* (Individ), *The Upturned Glass* (Box), *Fame is the Spur* (Boultings-Two Cities); 1948: *When the Bough Breaks* (Gains).

JOHNS, Glynis. Born Pretoria, South Africa, Oct. 5, 1923. Daughter of Mervyn Johns. Ht. 5 ft. 3¼ in.; wt. 108 lb. Fair hair, grey-blue eyes. Educ. Clifton High School, Bristol; Hampstead High School, London. Trained for ballet and made stage debut at 13 as solo dancer in " Bucky's Bears", Garrick Theatre, London. Was still only 13 when she made great impression in first film, *South Riding* (Victor Saville Productions) 1936. In 1937 starred in " A Kiss for Cinderella", Phoenix Theatre, London. 1939-46, on London stage in " Quiet Wedding", " Quiet Week-end", " I'll See You Again ", " Fools Rush In". Films include: *Murder in the Family, Prison Without Bars, Briggs Family*. 1940: *On the Night of the Fire* (Somlo), *The Prime Minister* (Warn-Brit); 1943: *Adventures of Tartu* (MGM-Brit),

Halfway House (Ealing); 1945: *Perfect Strangers* (MGM-London); 1946: *This Man is Mine* (Col); 1947: *Frieda* (Ealing), *An Ideal Husband* (LFP), *Mine Own Executioner* (LFP), *Miranda* (Gains).

JOHNS, Mervyn. Born Pembroke, Wales, Feb. 18, 1899. Ht. 5 ft. 7 in.; wt. 148 lb. Brown hair, blue eyes. Educ. Llandovery. Youthful ambition: to be actor. Left school 1916 to serve as pilot in R.F.C.; then studied medicine at London Hospital, but left for Royal Academy of Dramatic Art. Two years in repertory, one year with concert parties; London debut 1923. Ben Travers gave him first film part as journalist in *Lady in Danger* (1934). Favourite role —the spy in *Next of Kin*. In World War II served in Administrative Branch, R.A.F. Films include: *The Guv'nor, Foreign Affairs, Pot Luck, Cutie, In the Soup, Everything is Thunder, Dishonour Bright, Finale, Storm in a Teacup, The Blacksmith, Night Ride, The Last Curtain, Sweet Racket, Almost a Gentleman, Jamaica Inn, The Midas Touch*. 1940: *Saloon Bar* (Ealing), *Convoy* (Ealing); 1941: *Girl in the News* (Gains); 1942: *The Foreman Went to France* (Ealing), *Next of Kin* (Ealing), *Went the Day Well?* (Ealing), *The Bells Go Down* (Ealing); 1943: *The Halfway House* (Ealing); 1944: *My Learned Friend* (Ealing), *San Demetrio, London* (Ealing), *They Knew Mr. Knight* (GHW), shown publicly 1946; 1945: *Twilight Hour* (Brit Nat), *Dead of Night* (Ealing); *Pink String and Sealing Wax* (Ealing); 1946: *The Captive Heart* (Ealing). 1947: *Captain Boycott* (Individ); 1948: *So Died a Rat* (Brit Nat), *Easy Money* (Gains).

JOHNSON, Celia. Born Richmond, Surrey, Dec. 18, 1908. Educ. St. Paul's Girls School, and in France. Trained at Royal Academy of Dramatic Art, London; made debut at Theatre Royal, Huddersfield in " Major Barbara " 1928; scored success in London in " The Artist and the Shadow" at Kingsway Theatre, 1930. Plays include " Rebecca ", " Wind and the Rain ", " Pride and Prejudice ". Played Ophelia in " Hamlet ", at Broadhurst Theatre, New York, 1931. Made first screen appearance in *A Letter From Home* (MOI short), 1942. Other films include: 1942: *In Which We Serve* (Two Cities), *Dear Octopus* (Gains); 1944: *This Happy Breed* (Cineguild); 1946: *Brief Encounter*.

JOHNSON, Van. Born Newport, Rhode Island, Aug. 25. Ht. 6 ft. 2 in.; wt. 185 lb. Red-blonde hair, blue eyes. Educ. Newport public schools. Sang and danced in school shows. Became clerk in father's estate-agent business, but hankered after stage career. Attended rehearsal of " New Faces of 1937 " at Vanderbilt Theatre, New York, given job in chorus. Went into vaudeville, became one of " Eight Men of Manhattan " with Mary Martin at famous Rainbow Room in New York; After 9 months in " Pal Joey ", 1941, left for Hollywood to make first film: *Murder in the Big House* (Warner), 1941. Other films (all MGM) include—1942: *Somewhere I'll find You, The War Against Mrs. Hadley, Pilot No. 5, Dr. Gillespie's New Assistant*; 1943: *The Human Comedy, Crazy to Kill, Madame Curie, A Guy Named Joe*; 1944: *The White Cliffs of Dover, Two Girls and a Sailor, Three Men in White, Thirty Seconds Over Tokyo*; 1945: *Between Two Women, Thrill of a Romance, Weekend at the Waldorf, Easy to Wed, No Leave No Love*; 1946: *Till the Clouds Roll by*; 1947: *High Barbaree, The Romance of Rosy Ridge*; 1948: *Love Bites Man, The World and His Wife*.

JOHNSTON, Margaret. Born Sydney, Australia, Aug. 10, 1917. Ht. 5 ft. 7 in. Dark ash-blonde hair, blue eyes. Educ. Sydney. Came to London to study at the Royal Academy of Dramatic Art. Joined repertory companies, first at Worthing, later at Coventry : then as understudy, notably for Elizabeth Allan in " Quiet Wedding " at Wyndham's Theatre, London. Played in " Murder Without Crime " at the " Q " Theatre, and also in " The Last of Summer ". Film debut in *The Rake's Progress* (Individ) 1946 ; 1947 : *A Man About the House* (LFP).

JONES, Emrys. Born Manchester, Sept. 22, 1915. Ht. 5 ft. 10 in. ; wt. 141 lb. Fair hair, blue eyes. Worked in provincial repertory and touring companies before appearing in London with John Gielgud's company. Spotted for films while playing in " The Hasty Heart " at the Aldwych Theatre, London, 1945. Film debut in *The Wicked Lady* (Gains) 1945. Other films include—1946 : *Beware of Pity* (Two Cities) ; 1947 : *Holiday Camp* (Gains) ; 1948 : *This Was a Woman* (Excelsior).

JONES, Griffith. Born London, Nov. 19, 1910. Ht. 6 ft. 2 in. Brown hair. Educ. Polytechnic Secondary School, Shepherds Bush, London ; University College, London. Abandoned law studies for training at Royal Academy of Dramatic Art, winning gold medal, 1932. Whilst student, made stage debut in " Carpet Slippers ", Embassy Theatre, London 30. Made hit as Caryl Sanger in " Escape me Never " with Elizabeth Bergner, 1933 ; repeated role at Shubert Theatre, New York, 1935. Visited Gainsborough Studios to read dialogue for a friend's film test and asked by Victor Saville to return next day. Made film debut as art critic in *The Faithful Heart* (Gains 1932). Other films include : *Money Talks, Catherine the Great, Leave It To Blanche, Escape Me Never, First a Girl, The Wife of General Ling, The Mill on the Floss, A Yank at Oxford, The Four Just Men, A Young Man's Fancy.* 1940 : *Atlantic Ferry* (Warn) ; 1942 : *This Was Paris* (Warn), *The Day Will Dawn* (Soskin), *Uncensored* (Gains). 1942-4, served with H.M. Forces. 1945 : *Henry V* (Two Cities) ; *The Wicked Lady* (Gains) : 1946 : *The Rake's Progress* (Individ), 1947 : *They Made Me a Fugitive* (Alliance) in which he made an outstanding success as a " spiv " ; 1948 : *Good-time Girl* (Gains), *Miranda* (Gains).

JONES, Jennifer. Real name Phylis Isley. Born Tulsa, Oklahoma, 1919. Ht. 5 ft. 5 in. ; wt. 115 lb. Brown hair, brown eyes. Educ. Monte Cassino Junior College, Tulsa, and, on scholarship, at Northwestern University, Chicago. Toured with her parents' theatrical company as a child, but did not take any part in their shows ; then her father formed the Mansfield Players, in order to give her dramatic training. Later she studied at American Academy of Dramatic Art New York, broadcasting in annual vacations from a Tulsa station. She then joined a " Little Theatre " in New York, then began her film career in Westerns in Hollywood. After having seen *Claudia* five times, she persuaded David Selznick's New York office to give her film test. She was trained by Selznick for more than a year, then lent to 20th-Fox for *Song of Bernadette*, for which she won the 1943 Academy Award. Other films : 1944 : *Since You Went Away*, (Selznick) ; 1945 : *Love Letters* (Para) ; 1946 : *Cluny Brown* (20th) ; 1947 : *Duel in the Sun* (Selznick) ; 1948 : *Portrait of Jennie* (Selznick).

JOSLYN, Allyn. Real name Allyn Morgan Joslin. Born Milford, Pennsylvania, July 21, 1905. Ht. 6 ft. 1½ in. ; wt. 175 lb. Dark brown hair, blue-green eyes. Educ. New York public schools ; Philadelphia High School. Became office boy, then chorus boy in " Toot, Toot ", singer in musicals, stage manager ; spent nine years on radio. Was in the successful George Abbott's stage show " Boy Meets Girl " which resulted in first film role in *They Won't Forget* (Warner) 1937. Films include : *Expensive Husbands, Hollywood Hotel, Cafe Society, Only Angels Have Wings, Fast and Furious.* 1940 : *If I Had My Way* (Univ), *Spring Parade* (Univ), *The Great McGinty* (Para), *No Time For Comedy* (Warn) ; 1941 : *This Thing Called Love* (Col), *Bed Time Story* (Col) ; 1942 : *The Wife Takes a Flyer* (Col), *The Affairs of Martha* (MGM), *My Sister Eileen* (Col) ; 1943 : *Immortal Sergeant* (20th), *Heaven Can Wait* (20th), *Young Ideas* (MGM), *Dangerous Blondes* (Col) ; 1944 : *The Imposter* (Univ), *Sweet and Lowdown* (20th), *Bride By Mistake* (RKO), *Strange Affair* (Col) ; 1945 : *The Horn Blows At Midnight* (Warn), *Junior Miss* (20th) ; 1946 : *Colonel Effingham's Raid* (20th), *It Shouldn't Happen To A Dog* (20th), *The Thrill of Brazil* (Col).

JOURDAN, Louis. Born Marseilles, 1922. Dark hair. Ht. 6 ft. ; wt. 160 lb. In 1939 studied acting at René Simon's dramatic school in Paris, was seen by a film scout and given first screen part in *Le Corsair*, starring Charles Boyer. War stopped production, but during German occupation of France the Nazis permitted him to appear in non-political films. 1941 : *First Appointment, L'Arlésienne* ; 1942 : *La Belle Aventure, Félicie Nanteuil, La Vie de Bohème.* Refused German request for him to appear in pro-Nazi films ; joined underground movement and helped print and distribute secret newspaper. After the war, Selznick's European talent scout recommended him for Hollywood. First American films : *The Paradine Case* (Selznick), 1948 ; *Letters from an Unknown Woman* (UI), 1948.

JOUVET, Louis. Born Crozon, Finisterre, France, Dec. 24, 1887. Brown hair, brown eyes. Educ. Brive ; Lyons ; Paris. Began his career as a chemist's assistant, but appeared on the Paris stage, under Jacques Copeau's direction, 1922, at the Théâtre de Vieux Colombier. After a short stay in America, where he studied film production, he returned to France, where he has since appeared in many stage and screen successes. Became director of the Comédie de Champs-Elysées, 1924. Has been director of the Athenée Theatre since 1934. Is also professor at Paris Conservatoire. Films include : *Topaze, Knock, La Kermesse Héroïque, Les Bas Fonds, Forfaiture, L'Alibi, Mademoiselle Docteur* (French version), *Drôle de Drama, Carnet de Bal, La Marseillaise, Le Drame de Shanghai, La Fin du Jour, Entrée des Artistes, Hotel du Nord, La Charette Fantôme, Sérénade, Volpone, Untel Père et Fils* (Heart of a Nation), *Ramuntcho, L'Ecole des Femmes, La Maison du Maltais, Bataillon du Ciel, Copie Conforme*—British title *Monsieur Alibi*.

JOYCE, Brenda. Real name Betty Leabo. Born Excelsior Springs Missouri, Feb. 25, 1918. Ht. 5 ft. 4 in. ; wt. 112 lb. Blonde hair, brown eyes. Educ. Los Angeles High School ; University of California. Left school to become fashion model at department store. Tom Moore, veteran screen star, arranged screen test. First film : *The Rains Came* (20th) 1939. Other films include : *Little Old New*

BOB HOPE
(*Paramount*)

York, Here am I a Stranger ; 1940 : *Maryland* (20th) ; 1941 : *Private Nurse* (20th), *Marry the Boss's Daughter* (20th) ; 1942 : *Right to The Heart* (20th), *Whispering Ghosts* (20th), *The Postman Didn't Ring* (20th), *Little Tokyo, USA* (20th) ; 1944 : *I'll Tell the World* (Univ) ; 1945 : *Strange Confession* (Univ), *Tarzan and The Amazons* (RKO), *The Enchanted Forest* (PRC) ; 1946 : *Danger Woman* (Univ), *Tarzan and The Leopard Woman* (RKO), *Enchanted Forest* (Pathé), *I'll Tell the World* (Univ), *Pillow of Death* (Univ) ; 1947 : *Tarzan and the Huntress* (RKO), *Stepchild* (PRC) ; 1948 : *Tarzan and the Mermaid* (RKO).

JUSTIN, John. Born London, 1917. Educ. Bryanston School, and in Germany. During early childhood lived in Argentina, to which he returned for a year's visit later. Joined first the Plymouth then the Liverpool Repertory Company ; also studied at the Royal Academy of Dramatic Art. Was seen by Korda while in a performance of " Dear Octopus " and signed for *The Thief of Bagdad* (LFP) 1940. Learned to fly when a boy of 12, and in May 1940 joined the R.A.F. ; later became test pilot. Released to appear in *The Gentle Sex* (Two Cities) 1942, and in 1945 for *Journey Together* (RAF Film Unit) ; 1947 : *Call of the Blood* (Pendennis).

KAYE, Danny. Born Brooklyn, New York, Jan. 18, 1913. Ht. 6 ft. ; wt. 160 lb. Red hair, blue eyes. Educ. public school, Brooklyn. Worked for insurance company, then entertainer in summer camps and on dramatic stage. In New York in " Lady in The Dark ", " Let's Face It ". Seen by Sam Goldwyn, who introduced him to the screen, in *Up in Arms* (1944). Other films include—1945 : *Wonder Man* (Goldwyn) ; 1946 : *The Kid From Brooklyn* (Goldwyn) ; 1947 : *The Secret Life of Walter Mitty* (Goldwyn), *That's Life* (Goldwyn).

KELLY, Gene. Actor, dancer. Real name Eugene Kelly. Born Pittsburgh, Pennsylvania, Aug. 23, 1912. Ht. 5 ft. 9 in. ; wt. 115 lb. Black hair, brown eyes. Educ. Pennsylvania State College, University of Pittsburgh. Financed his own education by becoming bricklayer, concrete mixer, drug-store attendant and dance instructor. Enrolled at law school, but left to join his family in running a dance school at Pittsburgh. Appeared on Broadway in " Leave It To Me ", " One for the Money " and " Pal Joey " where a Hollywood talent scout saw him ; teamed with Judy Garland in first film *For Me and My Gal* (MGM) 1942. Other films include—1942 : *Pilot No. 5* (MGM) ; 1943 : *Du Barry Was A Lady* (MGM), *Thousands Cheer* (MGM), *Cover Girl* (Col), *The Cross of Lorraine* (MGM) ; 1944 : *Christmas Holiday* (Univ), *Ziegfeld Follies* (MGM), *Anchors Aweigh* (MGM). War service with U.S. Navy, 1944-6. 1946 : *Living In A Big Way* (MGM) ; 1947 : *The Big Pirate* (MGM), *On an Island with You* (MGM) ; 1948 : *The Three Musketeers* (MGM).

KEMPSON, Rachel. Born Dartmouth, Devon, May 28, 1910. Educ. St. Agnes School, East Grindstead, Sussex, and Oakleigh, Buckhurst Hill. Trained at Royal Academy of Dramatic Art and made debut at Stratford Memorial Theatre, 1933, in " Much Ado About Nothing ". First appeared in London, 1933, at Westminster Theatre in " The Lady From Alfaqueque ". Returned to Stratford in 1934 ; then with Liverpool Repertory Company. 1935-6, with Old Vic. Appeared in several London plays. Films

include : 1946 : *The Captive Heart* (Ealing). Went to Hollywood and appeared in *A Woman's Vengeance* (UI) 1948.

KENDALL, Kay. Born Withernsea, Yorks, June 29, 1921. Ht. 5 ft. 9 in. ; wt. 110 lb. Fair hair, blue eyes. At 12 studied ballet for six years under Lydia Kyasht. In World War II, with ENSA. Played small parts in four films—1944 : *Champagne Charlie* (Ealing), *Dreaming* (Gains), *Fiddlers Three* (Ealing) ; 1945 : *Waltz Time* (Brit Nat). Originally chosen as one of Wesley Ruggles' " Dozen-and-One " girls but won leading role opposite Sid Field in *London Town* (Wesley Ruggles) 1946.

KENT, Jean. Real name Joan Summerfield. Born London, June 29, 1921. Ht. 5 ft. 5 in. ; wt. 112 lb. Red hair, hazel eyes. Educ. London convent. Studied dancing as a child ; stage debut at Theatre Royal, Bath, in 1933, deputizing for her mother, a ballet star. Chorus girl and soubrette at the Windmill Theatre, London, for three years. First film *It's That Man Again !* with Tommy Handley (Gains) 1943. Other films include—1943 : *Miss London Ltd.*, (Gains) ; 1944 : *Bees In Paradise* (Gains), *Fanny By Gaslight* (Gains), *2000 Women* (Gains) ; 1945 : *Waterloo Road* (Gains), *Madonna of the Seven Moons* (Gains) ; 1946 : *The Rake's Progress* (Individ), *Carnival* (Two Cities), *Caravan* (Gains), *The Magic Bow* (Gains) ; 1947 : *The Man Within* (Box), *The Loves of Joanna Godden* (Ealing) ; 1948 : *Good Time Girl* (Gains), *Bond Street* (World Screen).

KERR, Deborah. Real name Deborah Jane Kerr-Trimmer. Born Helensburgh, Scotland, Sep. 30, 1921. Ht. 5 ft. 7 in. ; wt. 127 lb. Red-gold hair, blue-green eyes. Educ. Northumberland House School, Bristol. Trained as a ballet dancer from 1936, first with her aunt, Phyllis Smale, at Bristol, later at Sadlers Wells Ballet School. Stage debut in a " walking-on " role in Shakespeare at the Open Air Theatre, Regent's Park, London, 1939. Then went to Oxford Repertory Company. Given a small part in *Major Barbara* (Pascal), 1940, as the Salvation Army lass who got slapped by Robert Newton. On London stage with Robert Donat in " Heartbreak House " 1943. Toured with ENSA on the Continent, 1945. Films include—1940 : *Love on the Dole* (Brit Nat) ; 1941 : *Penn of Pensylvania* (Brit Nat), *Hatters Castle* (Para-Brit) ; 1942 : *The Day Will Dawn*—U.S. title *The Avengers* (Soskin), *The Life and Death of Colonel Blimp* (Archers) ; 1944 : *Perfect Strangers*—U.S. title *Vacation from Marriage* (MGM-London) ; 1945 : *I See a Dark Stranger* (Individ) ; 1947 : *Black Narcissus* (Archers). After completing this film left for Hollywood on a " straight " seven-year contract, with no " options ". First film there, 1947 : *The Hucksters* (MGM) ; 1948 : *If Winter Comes* (MGM).

KERRIDGE, Mary. Born London. Ht. 5 ft. 7 in. Fair hair, blue-grey eyes. Before deciding on stage career was hotel receptionist, Bank of England clerk, secretary, mannequin, photographer's model. Stage experience included repertory at Margate, Southsea and Windsor. Played opposite Ivor Novello in " I Lived with You ", toured with Donald Wolfit in 1944. While playing title role in " Anna Christie " at Windsor was spotted by a talent scout and given contract. First film *Anna Karenina* (LFP) 1947.

KEYES, Evelyn. Born Port Arthur, Texas. Ht. 5 ft. 4 in. ; wt. 115 lb. Blonde hair, blue eyes. Educ.

High School, Atlanta, Georgia. Became tap dancer in night clubs in Atlanta and elsewhere in the south. Given a screen test (1935), but no offer resulted ; so worked till she had money enough to make Hollywood trip. Met constant rebuffs because of Southern accent, so tried to lose it—but found it was required for first film role : *The Buccaneer* (Para), 1938. Other films include : *Sons of the Legion* (Para) ; *Gone With the Wind, Sudden Money, Union Pacific* ; 1940 : *Slightly Honorable* (Wanger-UA), *The Lady in Question* (Col), *Before I Hang* (Col) ; 1941 : *The Face Behind the Mask* (Col), *Here Comes Mr. Jordan* (Col) which brought first real recognition, *Ladies in Retirement* (Col) ; 1942 : *Adventures of Martin Eden* (Col), *Flight Lieutenant* (Col) ; 1943 : *The Desperadoes* (Col), *Dangerous Blondes* (Col) ; 1944 : *Nine Girls* (Col), *Strange Affair* (Col) ; 1945 : *1001 Nights* (Col) ; 1946 : *The Jolson Story* (Col), *Renegades* (Col), *Thrill of Brazil* (Col) ; 1947 : *Johnny O'Clock*.

KILBRIDE, Percy. Born San Francisco, July 16, 1888. Ht. 5 ft. 6½ in. ; wt. 125 lb. Red-brown hair, blue-green eyes. First a call-boy at Central Theatre, San Francisco, then actor in " A Tale of Two Cities ". Made Broadway debut, 1928, in " Those We Love ". Has appeared in more than 800 stage roles. In his first film, *George Washington Slept Here*, played role he had acted on stage. Other films include—1942 : *Keeper of the Flame* (MGM) ; 1945 : *State Fair* (20th) ; 1946 : *Welcome Stranger* (Para) ; 1947 : *The Egg and I* (UI) ; 1948 : *The Adventures of Black Bart* (UI).

KILBURN, Terry. Born Ilford, Essex, Nov. 25, 1926. Educ. St. Helen's College. Appeared in children's concerts, was taught acting at Italia Conti's School, London. Seen here by Roger Marchetti, Hollywood lawyer and film agent. Went to Hollywood, appeared with Eddie Cantor in radio programme, made film debut as Lancashire boy in *Lord Jeff* (MGM) 1938. Other films include : *A Christmas Carol* (MGM), *Sweethearts* (MGM) ; 1939 : *Goodbye Mr. Chips !* (MGM-British), *Andy Hardy Gets Spring Fever* (MGM), *They Shall Have Music* (UA-Goldwyn), *Adventures of Sherlock Holmes* (20th) ; 1942 : *A Yank at Eton* (MGM) ; 1944 : *National Velvet* (MGM) ; 1947 : *Bulldog Drummond at Bay* (Col).

KIMMINS, Anthony. Director, writer. Born Harrow, Middlesex, Nov. 10, 1901. Educ. Osborne and Dartmouth Naval Colleges. Joined the Royal Navy, becoming Lieutenant-Commander and one of the first Fleet Air Arm pilots. Wrote and produced theatrical shows for the Fleet, and during convalescence from an accident, wrote first stage comedy " While Parents Sleep ", 1932, which ran for 826 performances at the Royalty, London. Also author of " Night-Club Queen ", and " Chase the Ace ". Retired from Navy, with ambitions to become film director. Became screen actor in *How's Chances ?* (1934). Directed *A Friend Like You* (1934). Then author variously on screenplay, dialogue and story *Midshipman Easy, Queen of Hearts, Laburnum Grove, Keep Your Seats Please, The Show Goes On, Good Morning Boys, Talk of the Devil, While Parents Sleep, Come on George.* Directed and wrote screenplay of *All at Sea, Keep Fit, I See Ice, It's In The Air, Trouble Brewing.* As Royal Naval Reservist, was called up for special duties with Naval Intelligence in August, 1939. Became well known during war as leading radio commentator on Naval matters. Later became Chief of Naval Information in the Pacific. Demobilized in May, 1946 and, in association with Alexander Korda, is now writer,

producer and director of his own unit. First production : *Mine Own Executioner*, 1947. Also co-directed *Bonnie Prince Charlie* (LFP).

KING, Andrea. Born Paris, Feb. 1. Ht. 5 ft. 5 in. ; wt. 120 lb. Blonde hair, green eyes. Educ. Edgewood School, Greenwich, Connecticut. Appeared in school plays ; then secured role as tomboy in Broadway production of " Growing Pains " ; later in " Girls in Uniform ", " Life With Father " and other plays. Through resemblance to Ida Lupino, was picked for part of sister in *The Very Thought of You* (Warner), 1944 ; retained in cast though Ida Lupino was later withdrawn. Other films (all Warner) include—1944 : *Hollywood Canteen* ; 1945 : *Roughly Speaking, God is My Co-Pilot, Hotel Berlin* ; 1946 : *Shadow of A Woman, The Man I Love* ; 1947 : *My Wild Irish Rose* ; 1948 : *Ride a Pink Horse* (UI).

KING, George. Director, producer. Born London, 1900. Began his film career as an assistant director in 1922. Later worked for a time as publicist and exploiter on the London sales staff of an American film company. Began directing in 1928. During 1928-38, directed some sixty films, many of them being " quota quickies " for American companies in Britain. Early films include *John Halifax Gentleman, Ticket of Leave, Case of the Frightened Lady*. Also produced several Tod Slaughter old-style melodramas, notably *Murder in the Red Barn* and *The Demon Barber of Fleet Street*. Formed his own company, George King Productions, 1941. Recent productions include: *Tomorrow We Live, Candlelight in Algeria, Gaiety George, The Shop at Sly Corner*.

KING, Henry. Director. Born Christiansburg, Virginia, Jan. 24, 1896. Educ. Public Schools at Riverside and Roanoke, Va. Intended for the ministry, but after spell on Norfolk and Western railroad, entered show business, touring in drama, vaudeville, burlesque, circuses. Entered films as actor, writer, and finally became director with *Tol'able David*, 1921, starring Ernest Torrence and David Barthelmess. Other films include : *Fury, The White Sister, Stella Dallas, The Winning of Barbara Worth, Lightnin', Over the Hill, State Fair, Way Down East, The Country Doctor, Ramona, Lloyd's of London, Seventh Heaven, In Old Chicago, Alexander's Ragtime Band, Jesse James, Stanley and Livingstone, Little Old New York, Chad Hanna, A Yank in the R.A.F., Remember The Day, The Black Swan, The Song of Bernadette, Wilson, A Bell for Adano, Margie, Captain from Castile*.

KJELLIN, Alf (pronounced *Shelleen*). Born Lund, Sweden, Feb. 28, 1920. Ht. 6 ft. Fair hair, blue eyes. Educ. public schools at Karlstad and Stockholm. Decided to become an actor while still at school ; hitch-hiked to Stockholm twice a week in order to meet theatre producers. At 16, Royal Dramatic Theatre turned him down as being too young, but Swedish Film Studios offered him pupil-contract. Spent three days a week learning film acting, the other three doing stage crowd scenes. After a tour with a theatrical troupe, began to play more important parts. Military service interrupted his career, but in ten years he has played in twenty-six films. In August, 1947, Selznick signed him for Hollywood.

KNIGHT, Esmond. Born East Sheen, Surrey, May 4, 1906. Ht. 5 ft. 9 in. ; wt. 154 lb. Dark brown hair, blue eyes. Educ. Westminster School. While at school, trained for stage at Pax Roberts Salon, Chelsea ; made debut with Old Vic 1925 in " The Merchant of Venice". Spent a year in Birmingham Repertory Co. ; appeared in Paris, 1929, in " Maya " and in many London successes. Cast as a gypsy in first film : *Romany Love* (1931). Other films include : *The Ringer, Pagliacci, The Arsenal Stadium Mystery, Dandy Dick, Waltzes From Vienna,· What Men Live By, Black Roses* (made in Germany). 1940 : *Contraband* (Brit Nat), *This England* (Brit Nat). 1940-3, served in R.N.V.R. Blinded when serving in H.M.S. " Prince of Wales " in action against the " Bismarck", May, 1941. Learned Braille same year ; then on radio as narrator of true Service stories. In 1942, resumed film career as Nazi officer in *The Silver Fleet* (Archers) ; also wrote story of Bismarck action for *Blackwood's Magazine* and autobiography " Seeking the Bubble". Was operated on in Nov. 1942, in attempt to restore sight of one eye. While taking part in *Halfway House* (Ealing) 1943, began to see dimly ; sight has since steadily improved. Recent films —1943 : *A Canterbury Tale* (Archers) ; 1945 : *Henry V* (Two Cities) ; 1947 : *Black Narcissus* (Two Cities), *Uncle Silas* (Two Cities), *Holiday Camp* (Gains), *The End of the River* (Archers), *Hamlet* (Two Cities).

KNOWLES, Bernard. Director. Born Manchester' 1900. Educ. Hawkesyard School, Staffordshire. At the end of World War I was training in R.A.F. On demobilization, went to U.S.A. and spent a year as press photographer ; returned to Britain, 1921, and joined Islington Studio as second cameraman on *Flames of Passion*, starring Mae Marsh. Became director of photography on *Mumsie* at Islington, starring Pauline Frederick and Herbert Marshall. Other films as director of photography include : *This Marriage Business, The Silver King, Rookery Nook, The Hounds of the Baskervilles, The Good Companions, Jew Süss, The 39 Steps, Sabotage, Rhodes of Africa, Secret Agent, The Mikado, East Meets West, King of The Damned, Young and Innocent, French Without Tears, Gaslight, Freedom Radio, Quiet Wedding, Unpublished Story, The Demi-Paradise, The Lamp Still Burns, Love Story*. Made debut as director with *A Place of One's Own*, 1944. Also directed *The Magic Bow, The Man Within, Jassy, The White Unicorn, Easy Money*.

KNOWLES, Patric. Real name Reginald Lawrence Knowles. Born Horsforth, Yorkshire, Nov. 11, 1911. Ht. 6 ft. ; wt. 180 lb. Brown hair, hazel eyes. Went into father's theatre-programme publishing firm, made stage debut Oxford Playhouse, played in repertory companies and on London stage in " By Appointment". First film : *Irish Hearts* (Clifton Hurst) 1934. British films include : *Abdul the Damned, Royal Jubilee, Honours Easy, The Guv'nor*. Went to Hollywood in 1936. War service in Royal Canadian Air Force and as civilian instructor, U.S.A.A.F. American films include : *Charge of the Light Brigade, Adventures of Robin Hood, Give Me Your Heart, Storm Over Bengal, Married and In Love*. 1940 : *Bill of Divorcement* (RKO) *Anne of Windy Poplars* (RKO) *Women in War* (Rep) ; 1941 : *How Green Was My Valley* (20th), *The Wolf Man* (Univ) ; 1942 : *The Mystery of Marie Roget* (Univ), *Lady in a Jam* (Univ), *Sin Town* (Univ), *Eyes of the Underworld* (Univ), *Who Done It ?* (Univ) ; 1943 : *Frankenstein Meets the Wolf Man* (Univ) ; 1944 : *Pardon My Rhythm* (Univ), *Kitty* (Para) ; 1946 : *Of Human Bondage* (Warn), *Masquerade in Mexico* (Para), *Bride Wore Boots* (Para), *Monsieur Beaucaire* (Para), *O.S.S.* (Para) ; 1947 : *Ivy* (UI) ; 1948 : *A Connecticut Yankee* (Para).

KNOX, Alexander. Born Strathroy, Ontario, Canada, Jan 16, 1907. Ht. 5 ft. 10½ in. ; wt. 150 lb. Dark brown hair, blue eyes. Educ. Grammar and high schools in London, Ontario ; University of Western Ontario. Distinguished himself at university as writer and actor, spent holidays as reporter. In 1929, joined Boston Repertory Co. ; also worked for Boston Post. Saved money for trip to Britain, 1931, debut on London stage in Edgar Wallace's " Smoky Cell", followed by series of American roles. Made London hit in " The King of Nowhere". Author of novel " Bride of Quietness " and several mystery stories. Made film debut in Britain : *The Gaunt Stranger* (Ealing), 1938. American films include :—1940 : *The Sea Wolf* (Warn) ; 1941 : *This Above All* (20th) ; 1943 : *None Shall Escape* (Col) ; 1944 : *Wilson* (20th); 1945 : *Over 21* (Col) ; 1946 : *Sister Kenny* (RKO) ; 1947 : *Indian Summer* (RKO) ; 1948 : *Sign of the Ram* (Col).

KNUDSEN, Peggy. Born Duluth, Minnesota, Apr. 27, 1923. Ht. 5 ft. 6 in. ; wt. 114 lb. Light brown hair. Became New York model and canteen hostess. On New York stage in title role of " My Sister Eileen" ; also as Susan in " Susan and God". Seen by Hollywood scout and signed up for *Shadow of a Woman* (Warn) 1946. Other films include—1946 : *Never Say Goodbye* (Warn) ; 1947 : *Stallion Road* (Warn).

KORDA, Sir Alexander. Born Hungary, Sept. 16, 1893. Educ. Reformist College and Royal University of Budapest. Eldest of Korda brothers. At 20 joined Budapest paper " Fuggetlen Magyororszag". Began film career by hiring a ramshackle shed on the outskirts of Budapest, where he wrote, directed, photographed and cut his own films. As director for Sascha Films, Vienna, made a hit with his first film *The Prince and the Pauper*. In Berlin directed Maria Corda in a number of pictures, including *A Modern Du Barry*. Then in Hollywood made *In the Night Watch, The Woman from Monte Carlo, The Private Life of Helen of Troy, The Princess and the Plumber* and *Women Everywhere*. Back in Europe, founded Pallas Films, and directed European versions of Paramount Films in Paris. Later came for Paramount to London where he made *Service for Ladies*. In February 1932 formed London Film Productions, and made *The Private Life of Henry VIII* (1934) starring Charles Laughton. Built Denham Studios (completed 1936) ; became owner-producer in United Artists, 1935. Other films made under his auspices include : *Catherine the Great, Don Juan, The Scarlet Pimpernel, Sanders of the River, Things to Come, The Man Who Could Work Miracles, The Ghost Goes West, Rembrandt, Fire Over England, Elephant Boy, The Drum, Four Feathers, The Lion Has Wings*. Sold United Artists holdings and in 1940 formed Alexander Korda Film Productions, operating in Hollywood. Films made there include : *The Thief of Bagdad* (begun in Britain), *Lady Hamilton, Lydia, The Jungle Book*. Knighted for his services to films in 1942. In 1943 amalgamated London Film Productions with MGM-British Studios Ltd., becoming chairman, managing director and production supervisor ; and during this period produced and directed *Perfect Strangers*—U.S. title, *Vacation from Marriage*. In 1945 severed connection with MGM and once again became head of London Film Productions Ltd. In 1946 acquired British Lion Film Corporation Ltd., and two studios—Sound City, at Shepperton, and Worton Hall, at Isleworth—known now as London Film Studios, Shepperton, and London Film Studios, Isleworth. In 1947 produced and directed *An Ideal Husband*.

KORDA, Vincent. Art director. Youngest of Korda brothers. Born Hungary. Well-known artist : many exhibitions of his paintings have been held in this country and on the Continent. Has been Art Director-in-Chief of London Film Productions since its formation, 1932. Art direction includes: *The Girl from Maxims, The Private Life of Henry VIII, Catherine the Great, The Scarlet Pimpernel, The Ghost Goes West, Things to Come, Rembrandt, The Thief of Bagdad, Lady Hamilton, Perfect Strangers*—U.S. title *Vacation from Marriage, An Ideal Husband.*

KORDA, Zoltan. Director. Born Hungary, May 4, 1895. Studied camera work and direction in Budapest and directed two successful films for Vita Film Co. With UFA Films in Berlin for four years. Went to Hollywood as a writer for Fox, returned to London to join his producer brother Alexander in 1932. Supervised *Men of Tomorrow ;* directed *Cash.* Went to Africa in 1934 to direct *Sanders of the River.* Other films include: *Forget Me Not, Elephant Boy* (co-directed). Directed: *The Drum, Four Feathers, Thief of Bagdad* (also associate producer), *The Jungle Book, Sahara, Counter-Attack, The Macomber Affair, A Woman's Vengeance.*

KORNGOLD, Erich Wolfgang. Composer, music director. Born Brünn (now Brno, Czechoslovakia) 1897. A child prodigy, his early compositions created a sensation. Conducted many of his own works in Europe before going to Hollywood in 1935, at the invitation of Max Reinhardt, to work on the music of *A Midsummer Night's Dream.* Remained in Hollywood. Has also written the music for *Anthony Adverse* (Academy Award, 1936), *The Prince and The Pauper, The Adventures of Robin Hood* (Academy Award, 1938), *Elizabeth and Essex, King's Row, The Sea Hawk, Green Pastures, Between Two Worlds, Of Human Bondage, The Constant Nymph, Devotion, Deception.*

KORVIN, Charles. Born Pestyen, Czechoslovakia, Nov. 21, 1907. Ht. 6 ft. ; wt. 175 lb. Dark hair, hazel eyes. Educ. Sorbonne, Paris. Paid for tuition by taking " walking-on " parts in Paris Opéra. Became guide-lecturer at the Louvre Museum, news photographer in several parts of Europe. Joined Barter Theatre Stock Company, Abington, Virginia, U.S.A. for three summers ; appeared on Broadway in "Winter Soldiers", " Dark Eyes". First film : *Enter Arsène Lupin* (Univ), 1944. Other films include ; 1945 : *This Love of Ours* (Univ). 1947 : *Temptation* (UI).

KOSTER, Henry. Director. Born Berlin, May 1, 1905. Educ. Academy of Arts and Sciences, Berlin., Became cartoonist and reporter on Berlin newspaper ; then script writer for UFA, for whom he wrote more than fifty screenplays. Debut as director with *Marie Bashkirtseff* (UFA) : worked as writer and director in other Continental studios ; in 1935 won gold medal, Moscow International Exposition of Motion Picture Arts, for direction of *Peter,* a comedy made in Budapest. Went to Hollywood, 1936, where he directed Deanna Durbin's first films : *Three Smart Girls, 100 Men and a Girl, The Rage of Paris, Three Smart Girls Grow Up.* Other films include : *Spring Parade, It Started with Eve, Between Us Girls, Music for Millions, Two Sisters from Boston, The Unfinished Dance.*

KOZINTZEV, Grigori. Producer. Originally a painter, he turned to the Soviet theatre in 1920, in partnership with L. Trauberg, and two years later they joined forces with U. Yutkevich and G. Kryzhinsky to organize the " Theatre of the Eccentric Actor ", known as " FEX ". Early FEX productions include " The Trick " and " Marriage " by Gogol. In 1924 Kozintsev entered the film industry and produced *The Adventures of an October Child* and *The Devil's Wheel.* Other films include : *The Cloak*—from a story by Gogol (1925), *Little Brother* (1926), *The Union of the Great Case*—U.S.S.R. title *S.V.D.* (1927), *New Babylon* (1928-9), *Alone* (1932). The following year he began the Maxim Gorki trilogy *The Youth of Maxim, The Return of Maxim* and *Vjborg Side,* completed in 1939. Also made *Ordinary People* (1945-6) ; *Pirogov,* a biography of the great Soviet surgeon (1947-8).

KRASKER, Robert. Director of Photography. Born Perth, Australia, Aug. 21, 1913. Educ. Australia and art schools in Paris. Trained as cameraman 1931, at Deutsche Photohändlerschule in Dresden and with Paramount in Paris. Came to London as assistant and interpreter to Georges Perinal, and worked with him on Korda's *Private Life of Henry VIII* and *The Shape of Things to Come.* Illness of Perinal during *Dangerous Moonlight* (RKO) 1941 gave him opportunity to complete the photography on his own. His films, as director of photography, include : *The Gentle Sex, The Lamp Still Burns, Henry V, Caesar and Cleopatra* (co-director of photography), *Brief Encounter, Odd Man Out.*

KULESHOV, L. Producer. Born 1899. A painter in early youth, he entered Soviet films in 1916. First independent work was *Engineer Pright's Project.* Spent the greater part of 1918 and 1919 at various fronts during the Civil War in Russia. In 1920 he formed a group of cinema artists and film producers, among them Pudovkin, Komarov, Khoklova and Barnet. In the same year he produced one of the first Soviet artistic films, *On the Red Front.* In 1921 became a teacher in the Moscow Film Institute, here showing his worth as a true pioneer of the Russian cinema by teaching Pudovkin and many others who later became great. 1947, became Professor at U.S.S.R. State Institute of Cinematography. Produced *The Adventures of Mr. West, The Death Ray, Forty Hearts, Horizon, Expiation, By the Law, An Acquaintance of Yours, The Happy Canary, The Great Consoler, Dochunda, It Happened on a Volcano, Timur's Vow, We From The Urals* (1946).

LA CAVA, Gregory. Director. Born Towanda, Pennsylvania, Mar. 10, 1892. Educ. Towanda and Rochester, New York State. Trained at Art Institute Chicago and Art Students' League, New York. From 1911 to 1916 was cartoonist on New York papers ; in the early days of movie cartoons worked on animation of " Mutt and Jeff " ; for several years was in charge of cartoon animation for William Randolph Hearst. Entered film production 1922, first as co-writer of *Torchy* stories for Johnny Hines ; then directed *Womanhandled* (Para) 1926. Films include : *Let's Get Married, Say It Again, Running Wild, So's Your Old Man, The Gay Defender, Feel My Pulse, Half a Bride, Saturday's Children, Big News, His First Command, Laugh and Grow Rich, Smart Woman, Symphony of Six Million, Age of Consent, Half-Naked Truth, Gabriel Over The White House, Bed of Roses, Gallant Lady, The Affairs of Cellini, Private Worlds, She Married Her Boss, What Every Woman Knows*

My Man Godfrey, Stage Door, Fifth Avenue Girl. Produced, directed and collaborated on screen plays of *Primrose Path* and *Unfinished Business ;* directed *Lady in a Jam ;* directed and wrote original story of *Living in a Big Way.*

LACEY, Catherine. Born London, England, May 6, 1904. Educ. Burlington House, London, and The Girdlers, Herne Bay, Kent. Made first stage appearance at West Pier, Brighton, 1925, with Mrs. Patrick Campbell in " The Thirteenth Chair " ; first West-End appearance in " Cock o' the Roost ", Garrick, 1926 ; first American appearance in " The Venetian ", Masque Theatre, New York, 1931. Consistently on the stage ever since. First film : *The Lady Vanishes* (Gains), 1939. Other films include : *Poison Pen ;* 1941 : *Cottage To Let* (Gains) ; 1945 : *Pink String and Sealing Wax* (Ealing), *I Know Where I'm Going* (Archers) ; 1946 : *Carnival* (Two Cities) ; 1947 : *The October Man* (Two Cities).

LADD, Alan. Born Hot Springs, Arkansas, Sept. 3, 1913. Ht. 5 ft. 10 in. ; wt. 150 lb. Fair hair, blue eyes. Educ. North Hollywood High School. Began his career as an actor training at Universal, but was not successful. Became newspaperman, salesman, café proprietor, then rigger in film studio, fixing high scaffolding for lamps. Was then advised to try acting, so saved hard for dramatic tuition, but still could not manage to enter films, so became Los Angeles radio actor for two years. Voice heard by an actors' agent, who signed him, and endeavoured to interest film producers, and who, later, married him. First film, *Rulers of the Sea* (Para 1939). Continued playing radio roles, and had small parts in more than thirty films, till his performance in *Joan of Paris* won him chance of stardom in *This Gun for Hire.* War service, 1943, in U.S. Army Corps. Early films include : *Goose Step, Beasts of Berlin, Light of The Western Stars, In Old Missouri, Meet the Missus, Captain Caution, The Black Cat, Her First Romance, Petticoat Politics, Paper Bullets.* 1942 : *Joan of Paris* (RKO), *This Gun for Hire* (Para), *The Glass Key* (Para), *Lucky Jordan* (Para) ; 1943 : *Star Spangled Rhythm* (Para), *China* (Para) ; 1944 : *And Now Tomorrow* (Para) ; 1945 : *Two Years Before the Mast* (Para), *Salty O'Rourke* (Para), *Duffy's Tavern* (Para) ; 1946 : *The Blue Dahlia* (Para), *Calcutta* (Para), *O.S.S.* (Para) ; 1947 : *Wild Harvest* (Para), *Saigon* (Para) ; 1947 : *Whispering Smith* (Para), *The Long Grey Line* (Para).

LAIRD, Jenny. Actress, author. Born Manchester, Feb. 13, 1917. Ht. 5 ft. 3½ in. ; wt. 112 lb. Light Auburn hair, green eyes. Educ. Maidstone High School ; London University. Joined Herne Bay Repertory Company at thirty shillings a week, then had private theatrical tuition and made London stage debut in " People At Sea", 1937. Tried for several years to get into films ; appeared in semi-documentary *Painted Boats* (Ealing) 1945. Then retired to Scottish island and wrote a novel. With her husband, John Fernald, collaborated in writing a play, " And No Birds Sing". Films include : 1943 : *The Lamp Still Burns* (Two Cities) ; 1946 : *Wanted For Murder* (20th-Brit) ; 1947 : *Black Narcissus* (Archers).

LAKE, Arthur. Real name Arthur Silverlake. Born Corbin, Kentucky, Apr. 17. Ht. 6 ft. ; wt. 160 lb. Brown hair, blue eyes. Educ. privately, and at public school and Warner High School, Nashville, Tennessee. Appeared at 3 in " Uncle Tom's Cabin " in parent's touring repertory company ; later played child roles and toured in vaudeville skit with sister. Made silent film debut as boy in Western with Franklyn Farnum : *When Love Is Young* (Univ), 1924. Spent five years with Universal, appearing in many " Sweet Sixteen " comedies. First sound film : *Air Circus* (Fox) 1928, followed by portrayal of comic strip hero in *Harold Teen.* Films include : *On With The Show, Cradle Snatchers, Dance Hall, Tanned Legs, Cheer Up and Smile, She's My Weakness, Indiscreet, Midshipman Jack, Orchids to You, Tommy, 23½ Hours Leave, Annapolis Salute, Topper, Exiled To Shanghai, Everybody's Doing It, Double Danger, There Goes My Heart.* In *Blondie* (Col), 1938, made his first appearance as Dagwood Bumstead, in the film version of Chic Young's comic strip. The twenty-first of the *Blondie* series was made in October, 1947. Other recent films include—1944 : *Sailor's Holiday* (Col), *Three Is a Family* (UA) ; 1945 : *The Big Show-Off* (Rep).

LAKE, Veronica. Real name Constance Ockelman. Born Brooklyn, New York, Nov. 14, 1919. Ht. 5 ft. 2 in ; wt. 98 lb. Blonde hair, blue eyes. Educ. Villa Maria School, Montreal ; McGill University. Youthful ambition : to be surgeon. Given small schoolgirl part in *Sorority House* (RKO), 1939, under name " Connie Keane ". Studied acting at Bliss-Hayden School, worked nine months in school plays : then secured small parts in a *Jones Family* film, in *The Wrong Room* (RKO), and in *All Women Have Secrets* (Para). Wore her hair combed up until *Forty Little Mothers* (MGM), after which her " peek-a-boo " style secured major part for her, under new name Veronica Lake, in *I Wanted Wings* (Para), 1941 ; in this she secured overnight success. Other films include :—1941 : *Sullivan's Travels* (Para) ; 1942 : *This Gun for Hire* (Para), *The Glass Key* (Para), *I Married a Witch* (UA) ; 1943 : *Star Spangled Rhythm* (Para), *So Proudly We Hail* (Para) ; 1944 : *The Hour Before the Dawn* (Para), *Bring on the Girls* (Para) ; 1945 : *Out of This World* (Para), *Miss Susie Slagle's* (Para), *Duffy's Tavern* (Para), *Hold That Blonde* (Para) ; 1946 : *The Blue Dahlia* (Para), *Saigon* (Para) ; 1947 : *Ramrod* (Enterprise-MGM). Guest star in *Variety Girl* (Para).

LAMARR, Hedy. Real name Hedy Kiesler. Born Vienna, Nov. 9. Ht. 5 ft. 6 in. ; wt. 120 lb. Dark brown hair, blue eyes. As first step towards realizing ambition to be film actress, ran away from school at 15 and became script clerk in a small Viennese studio. Applied for small acting part and made screen debut in *Storm in a Water Glass.* For a time studied acting under Max Reinhardt in Berlin. Returned to the screen in *Extase.* First film in America was *Algiers* (UA) 1938. Other films include : *Lady of the Tropics* (MGM), *I Take This Woman* (MGM). 1940 : *Boom Town* (MGM), *Comrade X* (MGM) ; 1941 : *Come Live with Me* (MGM), *Ziegfeld Girl* (MGM), *H. M. Pulham, Esq.* (MGM) ; 1942 : *Tortilla Flat* (MGM), *Crossroads* (MGM), *White Cargo* (MGM) ; 1943 : *The Heavenly Body ;* 1944 : *The Conspirators* (Warn), *Experiment Perilous* (RKO) ; 1945 : *Her Highness and the Bellboy* (MGM) ; 1946 : *The Strange Woman* (Hunt Stromberg-UA) ; 1947 : *Dishonoured Lady* (Hunt Stromberg-UA).

LAMBERT, Constant. Composer, conductor. Born London, 1905. Has been largely associated with ballet. Wrote the foreword for Kurt London's book " Film Music", 1936. His score for *Merchant Seamen* was

ALAN LADD
(*Paramount*)

given its first performance as a concert suite by the London Philharmonic Orchestra in 1943. He appeared in *Battle for Music*, conducting the London Philharmonic Orchestra.

LAMBERT, Jack. Born Ardrossan, Ayrshire, Dec. 29, 1899. Ht. 5 ft. 11½ in.; wt. 172 lb. Educ. Ardrossan Academy, Royal Technical College, Glasgow. Served as a boy in the R.N.V.R. in World War I. Began his career as a sanitary inspector; appeared in amateur stage productions for ten years before becoming a professional. Went as amateur to New York, to participate in Play Tournament at Frolic Theatre, 1929, in the role of Kenneth Dowey in "The Old Lady Shows Her Medals". On his return, played same part at the Lyric Theatre, Hammersmith, London, which brought an offer to appear professionally in "A Song of Sixpence", at Daly's Theatre, 1930. Has since appeared in many stage successes. Made film debut in *Honeymoon Adventure* (ARP) 1931, but was not impressed by sight of himself on screen, and returned to stage. Served in Army, 1939-45 (at various times Commandant of a Battle School and of a Training School for Snow and Mountain Warfare). Was given leave to appear in *Nine Men* (Ealing) 1943. Films include: 1946: *The Captive Heart* (Ealing); 1947: *Hue and Cry* (Ealing). Went to Australia to appear in *Eureka Stockade* (Ealing), 1948.

LAMOUR, Dorothy. Born New Orleans, Dec. 10, 1914. Ht. 5 ft. 5 in.; wt. 117 lb. Brown hair, blue eyes. Educ. Beauregard Grammar School; John McDonough High School; Spence's Business College, New Orleans. Was "Miss New Orleans" in 1931. Became lift operator in Chicago department store. Persuaded to enter a singing contest, offered job as vocalist by band-leader Herbie Kay, became famous for sultry radio voice. Photo in radio magazine led to film job. First film: *The Jungle Princess* (Para), 1936. Other films include: *Swing High, Swing Low, College Holiday, Last Train from Madrid, High Wide and Handsome, Thrill of a Lifetime, Big Broadcast of 1938, The Hurricane, Jungle Love, Tropic Holiday, Spawn of the North, St. Louis Blues, Man about Town, Disputed Passage;* 1940: *Johnny Apollo* (20th), *Typhoon* (Para), *Road to Singapore* (Para), *Moon Over Burma* (Para), *Chad Hanna* (20th); 1941 (all Para): *Road to Zanzibar, Caught in the Draft, Aloma of the South Seas;* 1942 (all Para): *The Fleet's In, Beyond the Blue Horizon, The Road to Morocco;* 1943: *Star Spangled Rhythm* (Para), *They Got Me Covered* (RKO), *Dixie* (Para), *Riding High* (Para); 1944 (all Para): *And the Angels Sing, Rainbow Island;* 1945 (all Para): *A Medal For Benny, Duffy's Tavern, Road to Utopia;* 1946: *Masquerade in Mexico* (Para); 1947 (all Para); *Wild Harvest, My Favourite Brunette, Road to Rio;* guest star in *Variety Girl*.

LANCASTER, Burt. Real name Burton Stephen Lancaster. Born New York, Nov. 2, 1913. Ht. 6 ft. 2 in.; wt. 185 lb. Light brown hair, blue eyes. Educ. Public School 83, New York; DeWitt Clinton High School; New York University. At 18 joined circus as acrobat; spent five years in circuses with partner Nick Cravat; later appeared in vaudeville, fairs, nightclubs and hotels in Middle West. In 1941 became shopwalker, then salesman, at Chicago department store; occasionally turned cartwheels to relieve boredom and to startle customers. Then after other jobs joined Columbia Broadcasting Company in New York, managing programmes. War service

1942-5 in Europe and Africa; acted in and directed soldier shows. Returned to New York, 1945. Secured role in Harry Brown's play "A Sound of Hunting", in which he was seen by film producer Hal Wallis. First film: *The Killers* (Univ) 1946. Other films include:—1947: *I Walk Alone* (Hal Wallis-Para), *Brute Force* (UI), *Desert Fury* (Hal Wallis-Para); 1948: *All My Sons* (UI).

LANDIS, Carole. Real name Frances Lillian Mary Ridste. Born Fairchild, Wisconsin, Jan. 1, 1919. Ht. 5 ft. 6 in.; wt. 118 lb. Blonde hair, blue eyes. Worked as shop assistant, cinema usherette, waitress; became film chorus girl and appeared on stage in "Roberta", starring Bob Hope. First film appearance: *Varsity Show* (Warn) 1937. Other films include: *A Day at the Races, The Emperor's Candlesticks, Adventurous Blonde, Gold Diggers of Paris, Four's a Crowd, Three Texas Steers, Cowboys from Texas.* 1940: *One Million B.C.* (Roach-UA), *Turnabout* (Roach-UA), *Mysterious Sea Raider* (Para); 1941: *Road Show* (Roach-UA), *Moon Over Miami* (20th), *Topper Returns* (Roach-UA), *Dance Hall* (20th), *Hot Spot* (20th), *Cadet Girl* (20th); 1942: *A Gentleman at Heart* (20th), *My Girl Sal* (20th), *It Happened in Flatbush* (20th), *Orchestra Wives* (20th), *Manila Calling* (20th), *The Powers Girl* (UA); 1943: *Wintertime* (20th); 1944: *Having Wonderful Crime* (RKO); 1946: *Behind Green Lights* (20th), *It Shouldn't Happen to a Dog* (20th), *Scandal in Paris* (UA); 1947: *Out of the Blue* (Eagle Lion-Hollywood). Came to Britain to appear in *The Brass Monkey* (Alliance), 1948.

LANE, Priscilla. Real name Priscilla Mullican. Youngest of five "Lane Sisters". Born Indianola, Iowa, June 12, 1917. Ht. 5 ft. 2½ in.; wt. 102 lb. Fair hair, blue eyes. Educ. Fagin School of Dramatic Arts, New York. Made stage debut at a Des Moines theatre by singing at premiere of film featuring her sister, Lola Lane. Joined "The Pennsylvanians" as singer at 14. Made first film with them, *Varsity Show* (Warn) 1937. Other films include: *Love, Honour and Behave, Men Are Such Fools, Cowboy From Brooklyn, Four Daughters, Yes, My Darling Daughter, Daughters Couageous, Dust be My Destiny, Roaring Twenties, Four Wives.* 1940: *Brother Rat* (Warn), *Three Cheers for the Irish* (Warn), *Four Mothers* (Warn); 1941: *Million Dollar Baby* (Warn), *Blues in the Night* (Warn); 1942: *Saboteur* (Univ), *Silver Queen* (Sherman-UA); 1943: *Meanest Man in the World* (20th); 1944: *Arsenic and Old Lace* (Warn); 1947: *Fun on a Weekend* (Andrew Stone-UA).

LANFIELD, Sydney. Director. Born Chicago, Apr. 20, 1900. Educ. public schools; University of Chicago. Went into vaudeville, first at College Inn, Chicago, then New York and on tour. In New York became member of first jazz band ever organized, the "Dixieland Jazz Band". Al Jolson persuaded manager of restaurant where they first appeared that this new type of entertainment was worth retaining; band soon became famous. While in vaudeville in Hollywood, 1926, was engaged by Fox to write gags. Became assistant director; then, in 1930, writer, with *Cheer Up and Smile, Three Girls Lost, Hush Money.* In 1932 became director with: *Dance Team* (Fox). Other films directed include: *Society Girl, Hat-check Girl, Broadway Bad, Moulin Rouge, The Last Gentleman, Hold 'Em, Yale!, King of Burlesque, One in A Million, Wake Up and Live, Love and Hisses, Always Good-bye, The Hound of the Baskervilles, Second Fiddle, Swanee River, You'll Never Get Rich, The Lady Has Plans,*

My Favourite Blonde, The Meanest Man in the World, Let's Face It, Standing Room Only, Bring On The Girls, The Well-Groomed Bride, Trouble With Women, Where There's Life, Stations West.

LANG, Fritz. Director. Born Vienna, 1890. Educ. Realschule, College of Technical Sciences, and Academy of Dramatic Arts, Vienna. Also studied art in Paris and Munich. In Austrian army in World War I. Engaged as script writer in Berlin, 1919 by Erich Pommer. Became director with *Doctor Mabuse* (1922) made for Decla, one of the first German films to be shown in Britain after World War I. Outstanding early films include : *Metropolis* (UFA) 1926. and " *M* " (Nero) 1931. Advised that he was on Hitler's black list, escaped to Paris, and afterwards went to America, where his first film was *Fury* (MGM) 1936. Other films include : *Liliom, You Only Live Once, You and Me, The Return of Frank James, Western Union, Man Hunt, Hangmen Also Die, Ministry of Fear, The Woman In the Window, Scarlet Street, Cloak and Dagger, Secret Beyond the Door.*

LANG, Walter. Director. Born Memphis, Tennessee, Aug. 10, 1896. Educ. Memphis Grammar and High Schools, and University of Tennessee. Youthful ambition, to be painter and illustrator. Made sketching tours to every country in the world except India and Russia. Spent his early years abroad directing and appearing in plays. Went to Hollywood in 1925, where his breadth of experience helped him to become a director. Films include : *The Earth Woman, College Hero, Elegy, Shadows of the Past, Night Flyer, Sally of our Alley, Spirit of Youth, Big Fight, Cock of the Walk, Hello Sister !, Brothers, Costello Case, Women go on Forever, Hell Bound, Command Performance, No More Orchids, Warrior's Husband, Meet the Baron, The Party's Over, Whom The Gods Destroy, The Mighty Barnum, Carnival, Hooray for Love !, Love Before Breakfast, Wife Doctor and Nurse, Second Honeymoon, The Baroness and the Butler, I'll Give a Million, Little Princess, The Blue Bird, Star Dust, The Great Profile, Tin Pan Alley, Moon Over Miami, Weekend In Havana, Song of the Islands, The Magnificent Dope, Coney Island, Greenwich Village, State Fair, Sentimental Journey, Claudia and David, Mother Wore Tights.*

LANGFORD, Frances. Born Lakeland, Florida, Apr. 4. Ht. 5 ft. 3 in. ; wt. 108 lb. Blonde hair, brown eyes. Educ. Southern College, Florida. Active in dramatics and glee club at college ; studied singing ; later invited by Rudy Vallee to be guest star at New Orleans. Became singer in vaudeville, nightclubs, radio. First film : *Every Night At Eight* (Para) 1935. Other films include : *Collegiate, Broadway Melody of 1936, Palm Springs, Born to Dance, The Hit Parade, Hollywood Hotel ;* 1940 : *Dreaming Out Loud* (RKO), *Too Many Girls* (RKO) ; 1941 : *Hit Parade of 1941* (Rep), *All American Co-Ed* (UA), *Swing It Soldier* (Univ), *Mississippi Gambler* (Univ) ; 1942 : *Yankee Doodle Dandy* (Warn) ; 1943 : *This Is the Army* (Warn), *Career Girl ;* 1944 : *Girl Rush* (RKO), *Dixie Jamboree ;* 1945 : *Bamboo Blonde* (RKO), *People Are Funny* (Para), *Radio Stars on Parade* (RKO) ; 1946 : *Beat the Band* (RKO).

LANGLEY, Noel. Writer. Born Durban, South Africa, Dec. 25, 1911. Educ. Durban High School ; Natal University. Began his career with South Africa Broadcasting Corporation, then came to Britain and worked for some years in the scenario department of Gaumont-British. Wrote his first play, " For Ever "

1934. Other early plays include " No Regrets " and " Cage Me a Peacock ". Author of many short stories and the novel " There's a Porpoise Close Behind Us ". Went to Hollywood 1937, and joined the scenario department of MGM. Wrote screen adaptations *Maytime, The Wizard of Oz.* Collaborated on very many others, including *Florian* and *The Unexpected Uncle.* Served with Royal Canadian Navy during World War II. After demobilization returned to Britain where he wrote the screenplay *They Made Me A Fugitive.*

LANSBURY, Angela. Born London, Oct. 16, 1926. Ht. 5 ft. 7 in. ; wt. 130 lb. Blonde hair, blue eyes. Educ. South Hampstead School for Girls, London. Granddaughter of the late George Lansbury. Was studying acting in London when war began, and was evacuated to U.S.A. in August 1940. Continued drama studies at Fagan School, New York ; made cabaret appearances in Canada. Coached by mother, actress Moyna MacGill, for film test 1944. First picture : *Murder in Thornton Square* (MGM), 1944. Other films include : 1944 : *National Velvet* (MGM), *The Picture of Dorian Gray* (MGM) ; 1945 : *The Harvey Girls* (MGM), *The Hoodlum Saint* (MGM) ; 1946 : *Till The Clouds Roll By* (MGM) ; 1947 : *Tenth Avenue Angel* (MGM), *The Private Affairs of Bel Ami* (Loew-Lewin) ; 1948 : *If Winter Comes* (MGM), *The World and His Wife* (MGM).

LASSIE. Dog star. Real name ' Pal '. Born North Hollywood, California, June 8, 1940. Male collie. Golden brown, black and white hair, brown eyes. Owner : Rudd Weatherwax. First film : *Lassie Come Home* (MGM) 1943. Films (all MGM) include— 1944 : *Son of Lassie ;* 1945 : *Courage of Lassie ;* 1948 : *A Family for Jock* (MGM).

LAUGHTON, Charles. Born Scarborough, July 1, 1899. Ht. 5 ft. 10 in. ; wt. 185 lb. Brown hair, grey eyes. Educ. Stonyhurst College, Lancashire. In 1915, studied for the hotel business at Claridge's Hotel, London, then became cashier's clerk. In World War I, served in Army, and was gassed 1918. On recovery, took over his family's hotel in Scarborough for four years, but gave it up to his brother and joined Scarborough Players. After a season, entered Royal Academy of Dramatic Art, winning highest acting award, the Bancroft Gold Medal. Made professional debut, Barnes Theatre, London, 1926, in " The Government Inspector ". Established strong reputation on London stage with : " The Cherry Orchard ", " Liliom ", " Alibi ", " On the Spot ", " Payment Deferred ", and other plays. Also appeared in New York. Made first film in Britain in 1928 : *Piccadilly* (BIP). First American film : *The Sign of the Cross* (Para), 1932. That year he also made, in U.S.A., *If I Had a Million, Payment Deferred, White Woman, The Island of Lost Souls ;* then returned to Britain and made *The Private Life of Henry VIII* (LFP) 1933. Other films include : *The Devil and the Deep, The Barretts of Wimpole Street, Les Misérables, Ruggles of Red Gap, Mutiny on the Bounty.* In Britain 1936-9 made *Rembrandt ;* with Erich Pommer formed Mayflower Pictures and made *Vessel of Wrath, St. Martin's Lane, The Beachcomber, Jamaica Inn ;* returned to Hollywood and made *The Hunchback of Notre Dame.* 1940 : *They Knew What They Wanted* (RKO) ; 1941 : *It Started With Eve* (Univ) ; 1942 : *The Tuttles of Tahiti* (RKO), *Tales of Manhattan* (20th), *Stand by for Action* (MGM) ; 1943 : *Forever and a Day* (RKO), *This Land Is Mine* (RKO), *The Man from*

Down Under (MGM), *The Canterville Ghost* (MGM), *The Suspect* (Univ) ; 1945 : *Captain Kidd* (Univ) ; 1946 : *Because of Him* (Univ) ; 1948 : *The Paradine Case* (Selznick), *The Big Clock* (Para), *A Miracle Can Happen* (Benedict Bogeaus-UA), *The Queen's Necklace* (Benedict Bogeaus-UA).

LAUNDER, Frank. Writer, director, producer. Born Hitchin, Herts, 1907. Educ. Brighton. Worked in Official Receiver's office, Brighton, at the same time appearing in classical plays with Brighton Repertory Company. The first play he wrote, " There Was No Signpost ", attracted the attention of the late John Maxwell, of British International Pictures, who gave him a post as screenwriter at Elstree Studios in 1930. Wrote one of the earliest " talkie " scripts in Britain, from Thomas Hardy's " Under The Greenwood Tree." Later joined Gaumont British, where he wrote and collaborated on many productions, including *Rome Express, Friday the 13th.* Was scenario editor at Warner's British studios, 1936-8. Collaborated on script of *A Yank at Oxford* for MGM-British. At Gainsborough studios with his former G.B. colleague, Sidney Gilliatt, collaborated on screenplays of *The Lady Vanishes, They Came by Night, Night Train to Munich, Girl in the News, Kipps, The Young Mr. Pitt.* In 1940 their first stage play together, " The Body Was Well Nourished ", was presented by Jack Buchanan. In 1943 Maurice Ostrer, then Producer-in-Chief at Gainsborough, assigned them as a team to write and direct their own films *Millions Like Us, 2000 Women, Waterloo Road.* With Gilliatt, in 1945, formed Individual Pictures, to write, direct and produce their own films : *The Rake's Progress, I See a Dark Stranger, Green for Danger, Captain Boycott, London Belongs to Me, The Blue Lagoon.*

LAUREL, Stanley. Real name Arthur Stanley Jefferson. Born Ulverston, Lancs, June 16, 1895. Ht. 5 ft. 9 in. ; wt. 150 lb. Auburn hair, blue eyes. Educ. King James School, Bishop Auckland ; Queen's Park School, Glasgow. First stage appearance at 7 in the drama " Lights of London ". Joined variety troupe as song and dance man when fifteen. In 1910 went to America with Fred Karno's troupe " The London Comedians ", which included Charlie Chaplin, whom he understudied for a time. Began screen career with Hal Roach in 1917. Made about fifty comedies. For a time was producer and director. In 1924 was cast with Oliver Hardy in *Home from the Honeymoon,* which marked beginning of long comedy screen partnership. They have made more than 170 films together, including : *Pardon Us, Helpmates, Pack Up Your Troubles, Babes in Toyland, Bonnie Scotland, The Bohemian Girl, Our Relations, Way Out West, Swiss Miss, Blockheads ;* 1940 : *A Chump at Oxford* (UA), *Saps at Sea* (UA) ; 1941 : *Great Guns* (20th) ; 1942 : *A-Haunting We Will Go* (20th) ; 1943 : *The Air Raid Wardens* (MGM), *Jitterbugs* (20th), *The Dancing Masters* (20th) ; 1944 : *Nothing But Trouble* (MGM), *Big Noise* (20th) ; 1945 : *The Bullfighters* (20th). Came to Britain with Hardy in 1947 for extensive stage tour.

LAURIE, John. Born Dumfries, March 25, 1897. Educ. Dumfries Academy. In 1916-18 in army. Then trained for career as architect, but took to stage, studying at Central School of Speech Training, London. Made professional debut, 1921, in " What Every Woman Knows ", Theatre Royal, Dumfries. In Shakespeare 1922-25 with Old Vic and at Stratford-on-

Avon ; has played almost every leading role in Shakespeare's plays. Director Alfred Hitchcock gave him first film role as Johnny Boyle in *Juno and The Paycock* (BIP), 1930. Has become one of Britain's leading character actors, playing in many films especially in Scottish parts. Films include : *Red Ensign, The 39 Steps, Tudor Rose, As You Like It, East Meets West, Edge of The World, Jericho, Farewell Again, The Ware Case, Royal Divorce, Q Planes, Laugh It Off.* 1940 : *Convoy* (Ealing), *Sailors Three* (Ealing), *The Ghost of St. Michael's* (Ealing), *Dangerous Moonlight* (RKO-Brit) ; 1941 : *Ships With Wings* (Ealing), *Mother Riley Cleans Up* (Butcher) ; 1943 : *The Gentle Sex* (Concanen-Two Cities), *The Lamp Still Burns* (Two Cities), *Fanny By Gaslight* (Gains) ; 1944 : *The Way Ahead* (Two Cities), *The Life and Death of Colonel Blimp* (Archers), *The Agitator* (Brit Nat), *Medal for the General* (Brit Nat) ; 1945 : *Henry V* (Two Cities), *Perfect Strangers* (MGM-London), *I Know Where I'm Going* (Archers) ; 1946 : *Caesar and Cleopatra* (Pascal), *School for Secrets* (Two Cities) ; 1947 : *The Brothers* (Gains), *Jassy* (Gains), *Uncle Silas* (Two Cities), *Mine Own Executioner* (Kimmins) ; 1948 : *Bonnie Prince Charlie* (LFP), *Hamlet* (Two Cities).

LAWFORD, Peter. Born London, Sept. 7, 1923. Ht. 6 ft. ; wt. 160 lb. Brown hair, blue eyes. Screen debut as child in British film, *Poor Old Bill* (BIP), 1931. Travelled extensively with parents. Before beginning screen career in earnest was car park attendant in Florida and theatre usher in California. First American film, *The Boy From Barnardo's* (MGM) 1938. Other films include—1942 : *A Yank at Eton* (MGM), *Thunder Birds* (20th), *Eagle Squadron* (Univ), *Mrs. Miniver* (MGM), *The Immortal Sergeant* (20th) ; 1943 : *Someone to Remember* (Rep), *The Night is Ending* (20th), *The Man From Down Under* (MGM), *The Purple V* (Rep), *West Side Kid* (Rep) ; 1944 : *The White Cliffs of Dover* (MGM), *The Canterville Ghost* (MGM), *Mrs. Parkington* (MGM), *The Picture of Dorian Gray* (MGM), *Son of Lassie* (MGM) ; 1945 : *Two Sisters from Boston* (MGM), *Cluny Brown* (20th) ; 1946 : *My Brother Talks to Horses* (MGM), *It Happened in Brooklyn* (MGM) ; 1947 : *On an Island With You* (MGM), *Good News* (MGM) ; 1948 : *Easter Parade* (MGM).

LAWRENCE, Michael. Born Dublin, 1919. Dark hair, blue eyes. Educ. University College, Dublin (B.A.). Intended to become a barrister but while appearing with the University Dramatic Society decided on stage career. Joined Abbey Theatre as designer and actor. Then joined Gate Theatre and between seasons played vaudeville in Dublin. On way to Newcastle to take up repertory contract as juvenile lead, stopped in London and made screen test, leading to first film role in *I See a Dark Stranger* (Individ), 1945. Fulfilled Newcastle contract while making subsequent films, which include—1946 : *Carnival* (Two Cities), *Piccadilly Incident* (Wilcox-ABPC) ; 1947 : *The Root of All Evil* (Gains).

LEAN, David. Director. Born Croydon, Surrey, 1908. Educ. Leighton Park. Entered films 1928, at Gainsborough Studios, London, as " clapper boy ". Became assistant director, film editor on Gaumont-British News, and editor of feature films including *Escape Me Never, Pygmalion, One of Our Aircraft is Missing, French Without Tears, Major Barbara, 49th Parallel*—U.S. title, *The Invaders.* In 1942, co-directed, with Noel Coward, *In Which We Serve.*

Since then has directed *This Happy Breed, Blithe Spirit, Brief Encounter, Great Expectations, Oliver Twist*. In association with Ronald Neame and Anthony Havelock-Allan formed Cineguild Productions, 1943.

LEE, Jack. Director. Born Slad Valley, Gloucestershire. Worked first in a local factory before trying to get into films. Advised by Paul Rotha to take technical film course at the Polytechnic, Regent Street, and worked his way up. First film job was as Junior Producer to the G.P.O. Film Unit, for twenty-five shillings a week ; later, with Crown Film Unit, co-directed *Ordinary People* and *Coastal Command ;* directed : *The Pilot is Safe, By Sea and Land, The Eighth Plague, Close Quarters, Children on Trial.* First feature film as director, *The Woman in the Hall* (Wessex) 1947.

LEFAUR, André. Born Paris, July 21, 1879. Educ. Rollin College. Made stage debut on tour with Coquelin and spent 40 years in the French theatre. Made screen debut in silent films : *Chouchou Poids Plume* and *Monsieur Lebidois, Propriétaire*. His first sound film was *Le Bal*. Recent pictures include : *Le Bois Sacré, L'Habit Vert, Madame La Présidente, Le Club des Aristocrats, Ma Sœur Anne, Le Baron Fontaine, Les Petites Filles du Quai aux Fleurs*.

LEHMANN, Carla. Born Winnipeg, Feb. 26, 1917. Ht. 5 ft. 6 in. ; wt. 122 lb. Fair hair, blue eyes. Educ. Riverbend School, Winnipeg. Started as an amateur at 15 with local theatre in Winnipeg. Toured in " He Who Gets Slapped " with the New York Jewish Art Theatre. Came to Britain, 1934 for course at the Royal Academy of Dramatic Art, then joined the Croydon Repertory Company for a year. Film debut in *So This Is London* (20th-Brit) 1939. Other films include : *Once A Crook ;* 1941 : *Cottage to Let* (Gains) ; 1942 : *Flying Fortress* (Warn-Brit) ; 1944 : *Candlelight in Algeria* (George King) ; 1945 : *Acacia Avenue* (Box-Col) ; 1947 : *Fame Is The Spur* (Boultings-Two Cities).

LEIGH, Vivien. Real name Vivian Mary Hartley. Born Darjeeling, India, Nov. 23, 1913. Ht. 5 ft. 3 in.; wt. 106 lb. Brown hair, green eyes. Educ. Sacred Heart Convent, Roehampton, London, and on the Continent. Studied drama in Paris with one of the teachers of the Comédie Française, and continued her training in Italy and Austria before returning to Britain, where she became a pupil at the Royal Academy of Dramatic Art. While still a student made her first film appearance in a schoolgirl role in *Things Are Looking Up* (GB) 1934. Other early films were *The Village Squire, Gentleman's Agreement,* and *Look Up and Laugh !* Made her London stage debut in " The Green Sash " at the " Q " Theatre 1935. A few months later in the same year was an overnight sensation as Henriette in " The Mask of Virtue ", and was immediately signed up on long-term film contract. Her first starring role was in *Fire Over England* (LFP) 1936, followed by *Dark Journey, Storm In A Teacup, First and Last, A Yank at Oxford* and *St. Martin's Lane*. With the Old Vic Company she went to Elsinore, in 1937, where she played Ophelia to Laurence Olivier's Hamlet, at Kronberg Castle, Shakespeare's own setting for " Hamlet ". While visiting America in 1938 secured leading role in *Gone With the Wind*, after exhaustive tests as Scarlett O'Hara in three stages of her career ; this performance won her an Academy Award in 1939. Also in Hollywood appeared in *Waterloo Bridge* (MGM) 1940, and *Lady Hamilton*

(Korda-Hollywood) 1941. Afterwards appeared on the London stage in " The Doctor's Dilemma " and " Skin of our Teeth ", 1945. Toured in North Africa for ENSA, 1943. 1946 : *Caesar and Cleopatra*, (Pascal) ; 1947 : *Anna Karenina* (LFP).

LEIGHTON, Margaret. Born Birmingham, 1922. Ht. 5 ft. 8 in. Blonde hair, blue eyes. Determined to act from childhood ; joined school dramatic society. First engagement with Birmingham Repertory Company as comic maid, at thirty shillings a week : after a few weeks her salary was withdrawn and she became student, assistant stage manager and general help. Soon after abandoned repertory for tour, playing the bear in " Noah ". Returned to Birmingham, where she secured her first important part as Rosalind in " As You Like It ". While there, received contract from Old Vic. During second season with them was given a film test. Had given up idea of film career, and was with Old Vic Company in Paris in 1945, when she was persuaded to sign seven-film contract. Made her film debut as Flora MacDonald in *Bonnie Prince Charlie* (LFP), 1948.

LEISEN, Mitchell. Director. Born Menominee, Michigan, Oct. 1898. Educ. primary schools at St. Louis and Kansas City ; Western Military Academy and Soldan High School, St. Louis. Decided to study architecture at Washington University, but preferred sculpture. Worked in the advertising department of the " Chicago Tribune ", as a draughtsman. Entered films and became De Mille's costume and set designer, an association which lasted twelve years. Became director with *Cradle Song*, starring Dorothy Wieck, (Para) 1933. Other films include : *Death Takes a Holiday, Murder at the Vanities, Behold My Wife, Four Hours to Kill, Hands Across the Table, Thirteen Hours by Air, Big Broadcast of 1937, Swing High, Swing Low, Easy Living, Big Broadcast of 1938, Artists and Models Abroad, Remember the Night, Midnight, Arise My Love, I Wanted Wings, Take a Letter Darling !, No Time For Love, Lady In The Dark, Frenchman's Creek* (produced and directed), *Practically Yours, Masquerade in Mexico, Kitty, To Each His Own, Suddenly It's Spring, Golden Earrings*.

LEONARD, Robert Z. Director. Born Chicago, Oct. 7, 1889. Educ. University of Colorado. Began career as actor and singer, 1904. Played several seasons of repertory, Los Angeles ; began screen career as hero in Selig-Pariscope's *Courtship of Miles Standish*, 1910. Became director, 1915 ; gave Rudolph Valentino his first start, set Joan Crawford on road to success, introduced Clark Gable to stardom with Garbo in *Rise of Helga*. Other films include : *The Waning Sex, Little Journey, Time The Comedian, Cheaper to Marry, Baby Mine, Adam and Evil, Tea for Three, Lady of Chance, Her Cardboard Lover, Marianne, The Divorcée, Gay Madrid, Let Us Be Gay, The Bachelor Father, It's A Wise Child, Five and Ten, Lovers Courageous, Strange Interlude, Peg O' My Heart, Dancing Lady, Outcast Lady, The Great Ziegfeld, Piccadilly Jim, After Office Hours, Escapade, Maytime, The Firefly.* Produced and directed : *Broadway Seranade, New Moon ;* directed *Pride and Prejudice, Third Finger, Left Hand, Ziegfeld Girl ;* associate producer and director, *When Ladies Meet ;* directed *We Were Dancing ;* produced and directed *Stand By for Action, The Man From Down Under ;* directed *Marriage is a Private Affair, Week-end at the Waldorf, The Secret Heart, The Rich Full Life*.

LEROY, Mervyn. Producer, director. Born San Francisco, 1900. Associated with show business since the age of 11. Was in variety before he entered films as " prop boy". Was wardrobe man, camera assistant, extra, actor and scenarist, before becoming a director in silent films, 1927. Films include : *No Place to Go, Oh Kay ! Hot Stuff, Little Johnny Jones, Numbered Men, Top Speed, Show Girl in Hollywood, Playing Around, Broken Dishes, Little Caesar, Gentleman's Fate, Too Young to Marry, Broadminded, Five Star Final, Local Boy Makes Good, Tonight or Never, Three on a Match, Heart of New York, High Pressure, Two Seconds, Big City Blues, I am a Fugitive From A Chain Gang, Hard to Handle, Tugboat Annie, Elmer the Great, Gold-diggers of 1933, The World Changes, Hi Nellie ! Heat Lightning, Happiness Ahead, Sweet Adeline, Oil For the Lamps of China, Page Miss Glory, I Found Stella Parrish, Anthony Adverse, Three Men On A Horse, The Great Garrick* (produced), *Mr. Dodd Takes The Air* (produced), *Romance Is Sacred, They Won't Forget, Fools For Scandal, Dramatic School* (produced), *Stand Up And Fight* (produced) *Marx Brothers At the Circus* (produced), *The Wizard of Oz* (produced), *Waterloo Bridge, Escape, Blossoms In The Dust, Unholy Partners, Johnny Eager, Random Harvest, Madame Curie, Thirty Seconds Over Tokyo, Without Reservations, Homecoming.*

LESLIE, Joan. Real name Joan Brodel. Born Detroit, Michigan, Jan. 26, 1925. Ht. 5 ft. 4 in. ; wt. 118 lb. Auburn hair, hazel eyes. Educ. St. Benedict's School, Detroit ; Our Lady of Lourdes, Toronto ; Immaculate Heart High School, Los Angeles. Born in theatrical family, sang on stage at 2 and for the next thirteen years took part in vaudeville with parents and sisters. Then in New York became photographer's model, singer on radio and in night clubs, where she was seen in sister act by film talent scout. First film : *Camille* (MGM) 1937. Films include — 1940 : *Military Academy* (Col), *Foreign Correspondent* (UA), *Laddie* (RKO) ; 1941 : *High Sierra* (Warn), *The Waggons Roll At Night* (Warn), *Thieves Fall Out* (Warn), *Sergeant York* (Warn) ; 1942 : *The Male Animal* (Warn) ; 1943 : *Yankee Doodle Dandy* (Warn), *The Hard Way* (Warn), *The Sky's The Limit* (RKO), *This Is The Army* (Warn), *Thank Your Lucky Stars* (Warn) ; 1944 : *Hollywood Canteen* (Warn) ; 1945 : *Rhapsody in Blue* (Warn), *Where Do We Go From Here ?* (20th), *Too Young To Know* (Warn) ; 1946 : *Cinderella Jones* (Warn), *Janie Gets Married* (Warn) ; 1947 : *Royal Flush* (Warn), *Repeat Performance* (Eagle Lion-Hollywood).

LESSER, Sol. Producer. Born Spokane, Washington, Feb. 17, 1890. Educ. public schools, San Francisco. Entered the film industry as an exhibitor ; founder of West Coast Theatres Incorporated. Later became producer in Hollywood, where he made many of the early Jackie Coogan films ; later specialized in travel and scientific films. In 1933 produced *Thunder Over Mexico*. Other productions include : *Tarzan the Fearless, Peck's Bad Boy, Return of Chandu, When a Man's a Man, The Dude Ranger, Cowboy Millionaire, Hard Luck Harrigan, Thunder Mountain, Whispering Smith Speaks, O'Malley of the Mounted, Border Patrolman, King of the Royal Mounted, Wild Brian Kent, Let's Sing Again, Rainbow on the River, The Californian, Secret Valley, Western Gold, Hawaii Calls, Breaking the Ice, Peck's Bad Boy with the Circus, Fisherman's Wharf, Our Town, The Tuttles of Tahiti, Stage Door Canteen*, the *Tarzan* series (RKO), *Three's a Family, The Red House.*

LEVANT, Oscar. Pianist, author, composer, actor. Born Pittsburgh, Pennsylvania, Dec. 26, 1906. Appeared as actor in number of films, including *Dance of Life* (Para) 1929. In 1934 collaborated on screenplay of *Orient Express* ; wrote music and lyrics for film *In Person*, 1935 ; *Kiss The Boys Goodbye* (Para) 1941 ; in 1945 appeared in and recorded Gershwin's music for *Rhapsody in Blue* (Warn). 1947: *Humoresque* (Warn) ; 1948 : *Romance in High " C "* (Warn).

LEVIS, Carroll. Born Toronto, Mar. 15, 1910. Ht. 5 ft. 9 in. ; wt. 196 lb. White hair, blue eyes. Educ. David Livingstone School, Vancouver. Youthful ambitions : to be engine-driver, explorer, author, reporter. Started work at 13 in his local cinema ; then apprenticed to an advertising agency. Became publicity and advance agent for a hypnotist, two circuses and several road shows. Was also a feature-writer. Came to Britain in 1935 ; well-known broadcaster. Played himself in *Discoveries* (Grand Nat) 1939. Two years' ENSA work during war. 1948 : *The Brass Monkey* (Alliance).

LEVY, Louis. Musical director. Born London, Nov. 30, 1893. Worked as a tailor's apprentice to earn money for musical tuition ; then after nine months appeared in music halls. Won a scholarship to study violin under Papini in Italy. Joined Montague Pike's circuit, playing violin in " picture palaces " (as they were then called). Has been associated with the film industry in Britain since its pioneer days. Became director of music at the New Gallery Cinema, Regent Street, London, in 1916, and was largely responsible for British development of the " theme song " in films, dating back to silent era. Among his pioneer achievements was the fitting of music to Robert Flaherty's *Nanook of the North*, 1922. In 1928, with the Gaumont Company, synchronized music to one of the early British sound films, *High Treason*. Was music director for Gaumont and Gainsborough till October 1947, when he resigned ; he was associated with more than eighty major films for G.B., including all the Jessie Matthews and Jack Hulbert musicals. Organized a casting bureau for composers. Famous as the man who introduced outside broadcasts, with his Orchestra, from the Shepherd's Bush Pavilion, in 1924, and radio feature, " Music from the Movies ", 1936. Was lent to MGM for *The Citadel*, to Pascal for *Pygmalion*, and acted as associate producer on *I'll Be Your Sweetheart*, based on the story of Charing Cross Road's " Tin Pan Alley ".

LEWIS, Sinclair. Writer. Born Sauk Center, Minnesota, Feb. 7, 1885. Educ. Yale University. Awarded the 1930 Nobel prize for literature. Publications filmed include : *Main Street, Arrowsmith, Newly Rich, Ann Vickers, Babbitt, I Married a Doctor, Mantrap, Dodsworth, Untamed, Cass Timberlane.*

LIEVEN, Albert. Born Hohenstein, Germany, June 23, 1906. Ht. 6 ft. Fair hair, grey eyes. Educ. Koenigsberg ; Berlin University. Intended to become a scientist, but at 22 turned to the stage. Began at the Little Court Theatre in Gera, Thuringia, at £3. 10s. a month. Played as extra in opera, juvenile leads in Shakespeare. After seven years, was given a contract with the State Theatre in Berlin. Also appeared in many German films. Left Germany when the Nazis came to power. Came to Britain 1936 and a year later made his London debut in " Victoria Regina " at the Lyric Theatre. Other plays include " Get A Load of This " and " The Lisbon Story ". With the B.B.C.

European Propaganda Service, 1940-5. British films include—1940 : *Jeannie* (Hellman) ; 1942 : *The Young Mr. Pitt* (20th-Brit) ; 1943 : *The Yellow Canary* (Wilcox-RKO) ; 1944 : *English Without Tears* (Two Cities) ; 1945 : *The Seventh Veil* (Ortus-Box) ; 1946 : *Beware of Pity* (Two Cities) ; 1947 : *Frieda* (Ealing).

LINDFORS, Viceca. Born Uppsala, Sweden, Dec. 29, 1920. Ht. 5 ft. 5 in.; wt. 120 lb. Brown hair, deep blue eyes. Educ. schools in Sweden. Youthful ambition to be a dramatic dancer. Began her career at becoming a telephone operator at the age of 16, in her father's publishing house, then trained at Royal Dramatic Training School, Stockholm, for three years. Had great success in school plays. In 1940 formed an acting club with fellow students, and played " French Without Tears " for three months in Stockholm. Then toured in " Gentle People ". Professional debut 1941 at the Royal Dramatic Theatre, Stockholm, in " The Corn Is Green ". First film 1940, when she made *In Paradise*, for a Swedish company. After having seen her in several films, the local Warner representative sent a copy of one to Jack Warner in Hollywood, in 1945, which resulted in a contract without any further test. U.S. films include—1948 : *To the Victor* (Warn), *Night Upon Night* (Warn), *The Adventures of Don Juan* (Warn).

LINDSAY, Margaret. Real name Margaret Kies. Born Dubuque, Iowa, Sept. 19, 1910. Ht. 5 ft. 5 in. ; wt. 98 lb. Dark brown hair, hazel eyes. Educ. National Park Seminary, Washington. Trained at American Academy of Dramatic Art ; came to Britain and appeared in several plays. On her return to U.S.A. her acquired " English accent " deceived William H. Mooring, English writer, who was checking " all-British " cast for *Cavalcade* (Fox), 1932 ; she obtained role and was regarded for long period as English actress. Films include : *Private Detective 62, House on 56th Street, Dangerous, Isle of Fury, Law in Her Hand, Garden of the Moon, Three Girls on Broadway, Green Light, Slim, Gold Is Where You Find It, West of Singapore, Bordertown, The Case of the Curious Bride, The Lady Consents, Jezebel.* 1940 : *The House of Seven Gables* (Univ), *Double Alibi* (Univ) ; 1942 : *A Close Call for Ellery Queen* (Col) ; 1943 : *Let's Have Fun* (Col) ; 1944 : *Alaska* (Mono) ; 1945 : *Club Havana* (PRC) ; 1946 : *The Adventures of Rusty* (Univ), *Her Sister's Secret* (PRC) ; *Scarlet Street* (Univ) ; 1947 : *The Vigilantes Return* (Univ), *Seven Keys to Baldpate* (RKO), *Cass Timberlane* (MGM), *Louisiana* (Mono).

LIPSCOMB, W. P. Writer, producer. Born Merton, Surrey, 1887. Educ. King's College, London. On London stage as actor before serving in World War I, during which he contributed humorous articles to " Punch ". On demobilization, became commercial traveller ; went to U.S.A. Entered films, 1928, as script writer. Has also written a number of stage plays including " Clive of India " and " Thank You, Mr. Pepys ". His British films (variously as original author, adapter, collaborator) include : *Splinters* (first British talkie script), *French Leave, Plunder, Canaries Sometimes Sing, On Approval, The Speckled Band, There Goes the Bride, The Sign of Four, I Was a Spy, The Good Companions, Soldiers of the King, Colonel Blood* (also directed). In Hollywood, 1933-43, as script writer on : *Clive of India, Les Miserables, Tale of Two Cities, Cardinal Richelieu, Under Two Flags, Lloyds of London, Garden of Allah, Moon Over Burma, Pygmalion, Pacific Blackout.* During World

War II served with Ministry of Aircraft Production in Washington. Resumed film career 1946, and produced *Beware of Pity, Mark of Cain.*

LIPTON, Celia. Born Edinburgh, Dec. 25, 1923. Ht. 5 ft. 4½ in. ; wt. 116 lb. Blonde hair, blue eyes. Educ. St. Joseph's Convent, Hendon, and Park Lodge, Surbiton. Attended the Royal Academy of Dramatic Art immediately on leaving school ; made her stage debut when only sixteen, with her father Sydney Lipton's band. She was also a broadcasting star at sixteen, taking Judy Garland's roles in radio versions of " Babes In Arms ", " Strike Up the Band " and " The Wizard of Oz ". Was first tested for films by Marcel Hellman in 1939, but was considered too immature for the part. So spent the next seven years getting experience before attempting to enter films again. In 1947 Hellman gave her another test, and signed her for an important role in *This Was A Woman* (Excelsior).

LITVAK, Anatole. Director. Born Kiev, Russia, May, 1902. Established reputation in Europe as director of Jan Kiepura musical *Tell Me Tonight.* In France directed *Mayerling, L'Equipage* ; in Britain *Sleeping Car.* U.S. films directed include : *The Woman I Love, Tovarich* (also produced), *The Amazing Dr. Clitterhouse, The Sisters. All This and Heaven Too, Castle on the Hudson, City for Conquest, Out of the Fog, Blues in the Night, This Above All.* 1942-6, served with U.S. armed forces. Directed *The Long Night* (RKO).

LIVESEY, Roger. Born Barry, South Wales, June 25, 1906. Red hair, blue eyes. Educ. Westminster City School. Trained by Italia Conti. First stage appearance at 11 at St. James's Theatre, London, in 1917, as office boy in " Loyalty ". Screen debut in *Lorna Doone* (1935). Films include : *Rembrandt, The Drum, Keep Smiling, Spies of the Air, The Girl in the News* ; 1942 : *49th Parallel* (Ortus) ; 1943 : *The Life and Death of Colonel Blimp* (Archers) ; 1945 : *I Know Where I'm Going* (Archers) ; 1946 : *A Matter of Life and Death* (Archers) ; 1948 : *Vice Versa* (Two Cities).

LLEWELLYN, Richard. Novelist. Real name Richard David Vivian Llewellyn Lloyd. Born Wales. Educ. St. David's, Cardiff, and London. Studied coal mining, and hotel management in Italy. His works include the play " Noose ". Novels filmed : *How Green Was My Valley, None but the Lonely Heart.*

LLOYD, Frank. Producer, director. Born Glasgow, Feb. 1889. From 1904, on English stage in musicals light opera and repertory ; then in Canada first as actor then as telephone wireman. Went to Hollywood, 1913, where he played small parts in Lois Weber productions. In 1914, began directing one-reelers for Universal ; feature director for Morosco-Pallas, Fox, Goldwyn, Schenck, Sol Lesser, First National. Won wider recognition, 1922, as director of *Oliver Twist* (F.N.) and in 1924 with *The Sea Hawk* (F.N.). Other films directed include : *Adoration, Dark Streets, The Divine Lady, Drag* (made in first year of sound), *Sons of the Gods, Sin Flood, The Right of Way, Adios, Passport to Hell, Cavalcade* (Fox 1933), *Berkeley Square, Hoop-la, East Lynne, Servants' Entrance, The Lash, Way of All Men, Age of Love, Mutiny on the Bounty, Under Two Flags, Maid of Salem, Wells Fargo ;* produced and directed *If I Were King ;* directed *Rulers of the Sea ;* produced and directed *The Howards*

HEDY LAMARR
(*Hunt Stromberg*)

of Virginia, *The Lady From Cheyenne*; produced and directed *This Woman is Mine*; produced *The Spoilers, Invisible Agent, Forever and a Day*; directed *Blood on the Sun*.

LLOYD, Harold. Born Burchard, Nebraska, Apr. 20, 1893. Ht. 5 ft. 10 in. Brown hair, brown eyes. Educ. Denver and San Diego High Schools; John Lane Connor Dramatic School. Began his theatrical career at age of 12, when he appeared with the Burwood Stock Company, Omaha, in " Tess of the D'Urbervilles". Entered films as an extra, and became famous in his early one- and two-reel comedies made in the silent days, especially for his horn-rimmed " prop " spectacles. Made the first full-length comedy, *Grandma's Boy*, 1922, and later produced and starred in many successful comedies both silent and with sound. Films include : (silent) *Dr. Jack, Safety Last, Why Worry ?, The Freshman, Girl Shy, The Kid Brother, For Heaven's Sake, Speedy, Welcome Danger*; (sound) *Feet First, Movie Crazy, The Cat's Paw, The Milky Way, Professor Beware*. Produced *A Girl, a Guy and a Gob* and *My Favourite Spy*. Returned to the screen 1947 as a comedian in *Mad Wednesday* (Howard Hughes).

LOCKHART, Gene. Actor, author. Real name Eugene Lockhart. Born Ontario, Canada, July 25, 1892. Ht. 5 ft. 8 in. ; wt. 180 lb. Fair hair, blue eyes. Educ. St. Michael's School, Toronto ; De la Salle Institute and Brompton Oratory, London. Began professional career at age of 6 as Highland dancer with " Kilties Band" of Canada. When fifteen appeared in sketches with Beatrice Lillie. Has written songs, over 200 radio scripts, written and produced revues, taught classes at the Julliard Musical Foundation. Went to Hollywood in 1934 to make screen debut in *By Your Leave* (Univ). Has appeared in over forty films, including *Captain Hurricane, Storm over the Andes, Career Woman, Mama Steps Out, Too Many Wives, Something to Sing About, A Christmas Carol, Sweethearts, Algiers, One Foot in Heaven, They Died with their Boots On, Steel Against the Sky* (Warn), *International Lady* (Small-UA) ; 1942 : *Juke Girl* (Warn), *The Gay Sisters, You Can't Escape Forever* (Warn) ; 1943 : *Forever and a Day* (RKO), *Hangmen Also Die* (RKO), *Mission to Moscow* (Warn), *The Desert Song* (Warn), *Madame Curie* (MGM) ; 1944 : *The White Cliffs of Dover* (MGM), *Going My Way* (Para), *Action in Arabia* (RKO) ; 1945 : *The House on 92nd Street* (20th), *Leave Her to Heaven* (20th), *That's the Spirit* (Univ) ; 1946 : *Meet Me on Broadway* (Col), *A Scandal in Paris* (UA), *Strange Woman* (Hunt Stromberg-UA) ; 1947 : *The Shocking Miss Pilgrim* (20th), *The Rich Full Life* (MGM), *The Big Heart* (20th), *The Foxes of Harrow* (20th) ; 1948 : *Joan* (Wanger).

LOCKWOOD, Margaret. Born Karachi, India, Sept. 15, 1916. Ht. 5. ft. 5½ in. ; wt. 114 lb. Educ. Sydenham High School, England. While studying at the Italia Conti School appeared at Holborn Empire as fairy in " A Midsummer Night's Dream", 1928. Had a walking-on part in " Cavalcade", 1932. During a course at the Royal Academy of Dramatic Art she was chosen for the title role in " Hannele", in the Leontine Sagan production at the Haymarket Theatre, London ; later given part in " House on Fire" and " Family Affairs". Made her film debut in *The Case of Gabriel Perry* (Brit Lion), 1934. Went to Hollywood, 1939, for two films. In both 1946 and 1947 won the " Daily Mail " Film Award as the most popular British star. Has one daughter, Margaret Julia, who occasionally appears in her films, under the name of " Toots " Lockwood. Films include— in U.S.A. : *Rulers of the Sea, Susannah of the Mounties* ; in Britain : *Lorna Doone, Midshipman Easy, Beloved Vagabond, Dr. Syn, Bank Holiday, The Lady Vanishes, Night Train to Munich* ; 1940 : *The Stars Look Down* (Grafton-Grand Nat), *A Girl Must Live* (Gains), *Gestapo* (Gains) ; 1941 : *Quiet Wedding* (Soskin-Para), *Girl in the News* (Gains) ; 1943 : *Alibi* (Brit Lion), *Give Us The Moon* (Gains), *Dear Octopus* (Gains), *The Man in Grey* (Gains) ; 1944 : *A Place of One's Own* (Gains), *Love Story* (Gains) ; 1945 : *I'll Be Your Sweetheart* (Gains), *The Wicked Lady* (Gains) ; 1946 : *Bedelia* (Corfield) ; 1947 : *Hungry Hill* (Two Cities), *Jassy* (Gains), *The White Unicorn* (Corfield).

LODER, John. Real name John Lowe. Born London, Jan. 3, 1898. Ht. 6 ft. 3 in. ; wt. 170 lb. Educ. Eton, Sandhurst. Prisoner in Germany during World War I. Then entered films, making screen debut in UFA studios in 1927. Has since appeared in many films in Britain and U.S.A. First film in Britain : *The First Born* (Gains) 1929. Other films include : *The Doctor's Secret, Sunset Pass, Racketeer, Lilies of the Field, Sweethearts and Wives, Her Private Affair, Wedding Rehearsal, Money Means Nothing, Java Head*. 1941 : *Scotland Yard* (20th), *How Green Was My Valley* (20th), *Confirm or Deny* (20th), *One Night in Lisbon* (Para) ; 1942 : *Maxwell Archer, Detective* (Mono), *Now Voyager* (Warn), *Gentleman Jim* (Warn), *Continental Express* (Mono), *Eagle Squadron* (Univ), *Gorilla Man* (Warn) ; 1943 : *Mysterious Doctor* (Warn), *Old Acquaintance* (Warn) ; 1944 : *Passage to Marseille* (Warn), *The Hairy Ape* (UA), *Abroad With Two Yanks* (UA) ; 1945 : *Jealousy* (Rep), *The Woman Who Came Back* (Rep), *Brighton Strangler* (RKO-Radio), *The Fighting Guardsman* (Col) ; 1946 : *The Wife of Monte Cristo* (Pathé), *One More Tomorrow* (Warn) ; 1947 : *Dishonoured Lady* (Hunt Stromberg-UA).

LOM, Herbert. Born Prague, 1917. Educ. Prague University. On stage and screen in Prague from 1937 ; on London stage and screen in 1939. Made British film debut in *Mein Kampf—My Crimes* (ABPC) 1940. Other films include—1942 : *Tomorrow We Live* (King), *Secret Mission* (Hellman), *The Young Mr. Pitt* (20th-Brit) ; 1943 : *The Dark Tower* (Warn-Brit) ; 1944 : *Hotel Reserve* (RKO-Brit) ; 1945 : *The Seventh Veil* (Ortus-Box) ; 1946 : *Night Boat to Dublin* (ABPC), *Appointment With Crime* (Brit Nat) ; 1947 : *Dual Alibi* (Brit Nat) ; 1948 : *Good Time Girl* (Gains), *Snowbound* (Gains), *The Brass Monkey* (Alliance).

LONG, Richard. Born Chicago, Dec. 17, 1927. Ht. 6 ft. ; wt. 160 lb. Brown hair, blue eyes. Educ. high schools Chicago, Evanston Township. First film : *Tomorrow is Forever* (RKO) 1946. Other films include—1946 : *The Dark Mirror* (Univ), *The Stranger* (RKO) ; 1947 : *The Egg and I* (UI), *Good Time Girl* (Gains).

LORRE, Peter. Ht. 5 ft. 5 in. ; wt. 135 lb. Brown hair, brown eyes. Born Rosenberg, Hungary, June 26, 1904. Educ. Vienna. Ran away from home at 17 and improvised own theatre, acting, play writing, scene painting. Became bank clerk, 1922, to finance stage activities. In 1924, played small part with Breslau company ; went to Zurich, attracted attention in

Galsworthy's "Society"; spent 2 years in Vienna; first leading role was in "Pioniere in Ingolstadt", Berlin, 1928. Seen by Fritz Lang who gave him his first screen part, in "M" (Nero), 1931. Achieved immediate fame in this, as murderer of children—a part based on the exploits of a real-life Düsseldorf killer. Appeared in two British Hitchcock thrillers before going to Hollywood, 1935. Films include: *Thirteen Trunks of Mr. O. F., White Demon, De Haute à Bas* (Paris), *The Man Who Knew Too Much* (GB), *Secret Agent* (GB), *Mad Love* (MGM: his first American film), *Crime and Punishment, Crack Up, Nancy Steele is Missing, Lancer Spy* and the *Mr. Moto* series. 1940: *Strange Cargo* (MGM), *I Was an Adventuress* (20th), *Island of Doomed Men* (Col), *Stranger on the Third Floor* (RKO), *You'll Find Out* (RKO); 1941: *The Face Behind the Mask* (Col), *Mr. District Attorney* (Rep), *They Met in Bombay* (MGM), *The Maltese Falcon* (Warn), *All Through the Night* (Warn); 1942: *Invisible Agent* (Univ), *The Boogie Man Will Get You!* (Col), *Casablanca* (Warn); 1943: *The Constant Nymph* (Warn), *Background to Danger* (Warn); 1944: *The Cross of Lorraine* (MGM), *Passage to Marseilles* (Warn), *The Mask of Dimitrios* (Warn), *The Conspirators* (Warn), *Arsenic and Old Lace* (Warn); 1945: *Hotel Berlin* (Warn), *Confidential Agent* (Warn); 1946: *Three Strangers* (Warn), *The Verdict* (Warn), *The Chase* (Seymour Nebenzal-UA); 1947: *My Favourite Brunette* (Para), *Black Angel* (UI); 1948: *The Beast With Five Fingers* (Warn), *Casbah* (UI).

LORRING, Joan. Real name Magdalen Ellis. Born Hong-Kong, Apr. 17, 1926. Ht. 5 ft. 2 in.; wt. 103 lb. Chestnut hair. Educ. English schools, Hong-Kong; University High School, Los Angeles. In America from 1939. Appeared in "Quiet Wedding" at the Pasadena Playhouse, and in other "Little Theatre" productions, also on radio programmes. First film: *Song of Russia* (MGM), 1944. Other films include— 1945: *The Corn Is Green* (Warn); 1946: *Three Strangers* (Warn), *The Verdict*; 1947: *The Other Love* (Enterprise-MGM), *The Gangster* (Mono), *The Lost Moment* (Wanger).

LOTTI, Mariella. Born Milan, 1921. Films (Italian) include: *Il Corsaro Nero : Il Cavaliere senza Nome, Il Mariti, Turbamento, La Gorgona*; 1944: *Il Fiore sotto gli Occhi* (Icar), *La Freccia nel Fianco* (Inx), *Nessun Torna Indietro* (Artisti Associati); 1945: *Canto ma Sottovoce* (Italfilm), *Un Giorno nella Vita* (Arbis); 1946: *Oltreggio all'Amore* (O.F.S.), *Il Cavaliere del Sogno* (C.B. Seita).

LOUISE, Anita. Real name Anita Louise Fremault. Born New York, Jan. 9, 1915. Fair hair, blue eyes. Educ. Professional Children's School, New York; Greenwood School for Girls, Hollywood. On New York stage at seven in "Peter Ibbetson"; also in "Gloss of Youth", "The Greatest Thing in The World". Silent screen debut in *The Sixth Commandment*, 1924. Other films include *Millie, Swansong, The Most Precious Thing in the World, The Floradora Girl, Wonder of Woman, What a Man, The Marriage Playground, Madame DuBarry, Midsummer Night's Dream, Lady Tubbs, Story of Louis Pasteur, The Firebird, Anthony Adverse, Green Light, Call It a Day, First Lady, Tovarich, Marie Antoinette, My Bill, The Sisters, These Glamour Girls, Reno*. 1940: *Glamour For Sale* (Col); 1941: *Two in a Taxi* (Col), *Harmon of Michigan* (Col); 1943: *Dangerous Blondes* (Col); 1944: *Nine Girls* (Col), *Casanova Brown* (RKO), *The Fighting Guardsman;* 1945: *Love Letters* (Para); 1946: *The Bandit of Sherwood Forest* (Col), *The Devil's Mask* (Col); 1947: *Personality Kid* (Col), *Shadowed* (Col).

LOVELL, Raymond. Born Montreal, Apr. 13, 1900. Ht. 6 ft.; wt. 211 lb. Fair hair, blue eyes. Educ. Cheltenham; Pembroke College, Cambridge. Made his stage debut in "East Lynne" in Dundalk, Ireland, 1924, and toured in "Charley's Aunt" before organizing his own repertory companies in Leeds, Bradford, Bournemouth and Southampton. Has appeared in many London stage successes, notably "John Bull's Other Island", "Mr. Bolfry", and "Laura". Began his film career in *Love, Life and Laughter*, (ARP) 1933. Other films include: *Warn London, Crime Unlimited, Secret Lives, Mademoiselle Docteur* (English version), *Glamorous Night*. 1940: *Contraband* (Brit Nat); 1941: *The Common Touch* (Brit Nat); 1942: *Uncensored* (Gains), *The Young Mr. Pitt* (20th-Brit), *49th Parallel*—U.S. title, *The Invaders* (Ortus); 1943: *The Goose Steps Out* (Ealing), *Alibi* (Brit-Lion), *The Man in Grey* (Gains); 1944: *The Way Ahead* (Two Cities), *Candlelight in Algeria* (King), *Hotel Reserve* (RKO-Brit); 1946: *Caesar and Cleopatra* (Pascal), *Appointment With Crime* (Brit Nat), *Night Boat to Dublin* (ABPC); 1947: *The End of the River* (Archers), *Three Weird Sisters* (Brit Nat); 1948: *So Evil My Love* (Hal Wallis-Para) made in Britain, *The Calendar* (Gains), *Blind Goddess* (Gains), *Easy Money* (Gains).

LOWE, Edmund. Born San Jose, California, Mar. 3, 1892. Ht. 6 ft. Dark brown hair, blue eyes. Educ. San Jose High School and Santa Clara University (M.A.). Taught English Literature at Santa Clara. Then studied law for two years, but turned to stage, 1911. Screen debut in 1918 in *Vive La France!* (Para). Appeared 1919 in *Eyes of Youth*, in which Rudolph Valentino had small part. First major success in *What Price Glory?* (Fox) 1926, as "Quirt". As "Quirt" he also played in *The Cockeyed World, Women of All Nations* and *Hot Pepper*. Other early films include *East Lynne, Is Zat So?, In Old Arizona, The 'Cisco Kid, Attorney for the Defence, Guilty as Charged, Chandu the Magician, Under Pressure, The Great Hotel Murder, Black Sheep, Thunder in the Night, King Solomon of Broadway, Grand Exit, The Great Impersonation*. Came to Britain in 1936 to appear in *The Wrecker* (GB). Recent films include—1943: *Dangerous Blonde* (Col); 1944: *The Girl in the Case* (Col), *Oh What a Night* (Mono); 1945: *Dillinger* (Mono); 1946: *The Enchanted Forest* (Pathé), *The Strange Mr. Gregory* (Pathé).

LOWERY, Robert. Real name Robert Lowery Hanke. Born Kansas City, Missouri. Ht. 6 ft. 1 in. Dark hair, brown eyes. Educ. Paseo High School, Kansas City. Started singing with dance orchestras, then appeared on the stage in "Little Theatre" plays. Served in U.S. Forces in World War II. First film *Wake Up and Live* (20th) 1936. Other films include: *Life Begins in College, Passport Husband, Submarine Control, Young Mr. Lincoln, Charlie Chan in Reno, Drums Along the Mohawk*; 1940 (all 20th): *City of Chance, Free Blonde and Twenty-One, Shooting High, Star Dust, Charlie Chan's Murder Cruise, Maryland, Mark of Zorro, Murder Over New York*; 1941 (all 20th): *Ride on Vaquero, Private Nurse, Cadet Girl*; 1942 *Who is Hope Shuyler?* (20th); 1943: *The Immortal Sergeant* (20th); 1944: *The Navy Way* (Para); *Dark Mountain* (Para), *Road to Alcatraz* (Rep), *Dangerous Passage* (Para), *Hot Rhythm*; 1945: *Fashion Model, Danger Signal* (Para), *Big Town* (Para),

Prison Ship (Col), *Jungle Flight* (Para), *Lady Chaser* (Pathé) ; 1946 : *They Made Me a Killer* (Para), *Sensation Hunters* (Mono), *House of Horrors* (Univ), *Gas House Kids* (PRC).

LOY, Myrna. Real name Myrna Williams. Born Helena, Montana, Aug. 2 1905. Ht. 5 ft. 5 in. ; wt. 120 lb. Red hair, blue-green eyes. Educ. Westlake School for Girls, Los Angeles. Left school to become teacher of dancing in Culver City ; later obtained work as film cutter in Horsley studio. First appeared on screen as " fallen woman " in the early version of *Ben Hur*, 1924. " Vamp " type in early films : *Pretty Ladies, Midnight Taxi, Noah's Ark, King of the Kyber Rifles, The Desert Song, Rogue of the Rio Grande, Cock of the Walk*. First important role in *Renegades*, 1930, followed by *Last of the Duanes, Hush Money, Transatlantic, The Devil to Pay, Arrowsmith, Vanity Fair, The Woman in Room 13, The Mask of Fu Manchu, A Night in Cairo, Crooks in Clover, Men in White, Manhattan Melodrama, The Thin Man* (MGM, 1934 : first of the series), *Whipsaw, Wife Versus Secretary, The Great Ziegfeld, Libelled Lady, After the Thin Man, Parnell, Man-Proof, Test Pilot, Too Hot to Handle, The Rains Came, Another Thin Man ;* 1940 : *I Love You Again* (MGM) ; *Third Finger, Left Hand* (MGM) ; 1941 : *Love Crazy* (MGM), *Shadow of the Thin Man* (MGM) ; 1944 : *The Thin Man Goes Home* (MGM) ; 1945 : *A Genius in the Family* (Univ) ; 1946 : *The Best Years of Our Lives* (Goldwyn-RKO) ; 1947 : *Song of the Thin Man* (MGM), *Bachelor Knight* (RKO) ; 1948 : *The Red Pony* (Col).

LUGUET, André. Born Fontenay-sous-Bois, France, May. 15, 1892. Grey hair, brown eyes. Educ. Paris. Studied English in London, trained for stage at Paris Conservatoire, wounded in World War I while in French Air Force. Began stage career with four years at the Comédie Française. First feature film, *Les Cinq Gentlemen Maudits* (1920) ; had previously made shorts for Gaumont (France) and made films in America, England and Germany. His most notable pictures are : *Jeunes Filles en Détresse, A Nous Deux, Madame La Vie, Le Dernier des Six, Bolero, Signe Illisible, Mademoiselle Béatrice, Métier des Femmes, L'Honorable Cathérine, A Tout Cœur, Farandole, Curieuse Histoire, Au Petit Bonheur, Six Heures à Perdre*.

LUND, John. Born Rochester, New York State, Feb. 6, 1913. Ht. 6 ft. 1½ in. ; wt. 175 lb. Light brown hair, blue eyes. Educ. Rochester. Became ditch-digger, drug. store attendant, carpenter, time keeper ; amateur role at Rochester in " Waiting For Lefty " led to jobs in small professional company. This company failed, so he joined New York advertising agency then in " Railroads on Parade " pageant at New York Fair in 1939. On Broadway stage in " As You Like It " ; subsequently in " New Faces ", " Early To Bed ", " The Hasty Heart " ; at the same time on radio as actor, announcer, script writer. Performance in " The Hasty Heart " won film contract. First film : *To Each His Own* (Para), 1946. Other films include : 1947 : *The Perils of Pauline* (Para), guest star in *Variety Girl* (Para) ; 1948 : *A Foreign Affair* (Para), *Night Has a Thousand Eyes* (Para).

LUPI, Roldano. Born 1911. Films include—*Gelosia;* 1944 : *Il Cappello da Prete* (Universalcine), *La Porta del Cielo* (Arbis), *Nessun Torna Indietro* (Artisti Associati), *La Freccia nel Fianco* (Lux) ; 1945 : *Il*

Testimone (Arbis), *Verso la Luce* (Pax), *Adulterà* (G. F. Iutes) ; 1946 : *Pian delle Stelle* (A.N.P.I.) ; 1947 : *Pensione California* (Pao Lux).

LUPINO, Ida. Born London, Feb. 4, 1918. Ht. 5 ft. 3 in. ; wt. 105 lb. Blonde hair, blue eyes. Daughter of the late Stanley Lupino. Became film extra at 13 and in following year was given a leading role in *Her First Affair* (Sterling) 1932. British films include : *Money For Speed, High Finance, The Ghost Camera, Prince of Arcadia, I Lived With You*. Went to Hollywood, 1934. Her U.S. films include : *The Search For Beauty, Come On Marines, Ready for Love, Paris in Spring, Smart Girl, Peter Ibbetson, Anything Goes, Yours for the Asking, One Rainy Afternoon, The Gay Desperado, Sea Devils, The Lady and the Mob*. 1940 : *The Light That Failed* (Para), *They Drive By Night* (Warn) ; 1941 : *High Sierra* (Warn), *Out of the Fog* (Warn), *Ladies in Retirement* (Col) ; 1942 : *Moontide* (20th), *Life Begins at 8.30* (20th) ; 1943 : *The Hard Way* (Warn), *Forever and a Day* (RKO), *Thank Your Lucky Stars* (Warn) ; 1944 : *In Our Time* (Warn) ; 1945 : *Devotion* (Warn), *Pillow to Post* (Warn) ; 1946 : *The Man I Love* (Warn), *Escape Me Never* (Warn) ; 1947 : *Deep Valley* (Warn) ; 1948 : *The Queen's Necklace* (Benedict Bogeaus-UA).

LYNN, Diana. Real name Dolores Loehr. Born Los Angeles, Oct. 26, 1927. Ht. 5 ft. 3½ in. ; wt. 105 lb. Blonde hair, blue eyes. Educ. Miss Grace's Private School, Los Angeles. Played as pianist with Los Angeles Junior Symphony Orchestra at 11. Accompanied a violinist at a studio audition and was invited for audition herself. Given important role in first film : *Magic in Music* (Para) 1940. Other films (all Para) include—1942 : *The Major and the Minor ;* 1943 : *Henry Aldrich Gets Glamour, The Miracle of Morgan's Creek, And the Angels Sing ;* 1944 : *Our Hearts Were Young and Gay ;* 1945 : *Out of This World, Our Hearts Were Growing Up ;* 1946 : *Duffy's Tavern, The Bride Wore Boots ;* 1947 : *Easy Come, Easy Go ;* guest star in *Variety Girl*.

LYNN, Jeffrey. Real name Ragnar Godfrey Lind. Born Auburn, Massachusetts, 1910. Educ. Bates College. Began as schoolmaster in local high school ; became New York shop assistant, commissionaire for a Broadway cinema, telephone company worker. Then joined touring theatrical companies ; given screen test while playing in " Brother Rat " in Los Angeles, but forgotten. Bette Davis's previous recommendation of him reminded studio of his existence ; made success in *Four Daughters* (Warn), 1938. First film, a Vitaphone short, 1938. Served in U.S. Army 1942-6. Other films (all Warn) include : *Cowboy from Brooklyn, Four Daughters, Romance and Rhythm, When Were You Born ?, Yes My Darling Daughter, Daughters Courageous, Espionage Agent, Roaring Twenties, Four Wives, A Child is Born ;* 1940 : *The Fighting 69th, It All Came True, All This and Heaven Too, My Love Came Back, Money and The Woman, Flight From Destiny, Four Mothers ;* 1941 : *Million Dollar Baby, Underground, Law of the Tropics, The Body Disappears*. 1948 : *Whiplash, The Adventures of Black Bart* (UI).

MCALLISTER, Lon. Born Los Angeles, Apr. 17, 1923. Ht. 5 ft. 6 in. ; wt. 130 lb. Brown hair, blue eyes. Educ. Mar-Ken High School ; Chapman College. Ambition : to travel the world in his own boat, and write novels. Has worked in Jack Benny's and other radio shows. For six years played small parts in films, including *Babes in Arms, Romeo and*

Juliet, Souls At Sea, Joe and.Ethel Turp, Henry Aldrich, Gentleman Jim. First major role in *Stage Door Canteen* (Goldwyn) 1943. War service with U.S. Army Air Force. Recent films include : 1944 : *Home in Indiana* (20th) ; 1947 : *Bob, Son of Battle* (20th), *The Red House* (Sol Lesser-UA) ; *Summer Lightning* (20th).

MᶜCALLUM, John. Born Brisbane, Australia, 1918. Ht. 6 ft. 1 in. Dark brown hair, blue eyes. Educ. Australia, and in Harrogate, Yorks. Began his stage career in repertory at Tonbridge, then at Stratford-on-Avon and with the Old Vic. Returned to Australia at the outbreak of World War II to join army. Made film debut in a Government short, *Jo Goes Back*, while still serving with the army in the Pacific. Also appeared in *Australia is Like This*, and *A Son is Born.* During this period he met Jesse Lasky Jr. who suggested that he should go to Hollywood. Exodus of " G.I. Brides " from Australia made it impossible to get a passage, so sailed to Britain. While awaiting transport to U.S.A., secured film test for a small part, but test result was so good that he was given a leading role in *The Root of All Evil* (Gains) 1947, which in turn led to long-term contract with J. Arthur Rank Organisation. Other films include : 1947 : *The Loves of Joanna Godden* (Ealing), *It Always Rains on Sundays ;* 1948 : *Miranda* (Gains), *The Calendar* (Gains).

MᶜCRACKEN, Esther Helen. Playwright. Born Newcastle-on-Tyne, June 25, 1902. Educ. Central Newcastle High School. From 1929 to 1937 acted in Newcastle Repertory Company. Her plays include : " The Willing Spirit ", " Counter Attractions ", " White Elephants ", " Living Room ", " No Medals ". Plays filmed : *Quiet Wedding, Quiet Weekend.*

MᶜCREA, Joel. Born Los Angeles, Nov. 5, 1905. Brown hair, blue eyes. Ht. 6 ft. 2 in. ; wt. 170 lb. Educ. Hollywood High School ; University of Southern California. Took part in amateur dramatics and community theatre plays, playing lead in " The Patsy ", " Laff That Off ", " The Little Journey " and other plays. Two years a film extra ; first leading role, *The Jazz Age* (RKO), 1929. Other films include : *Five O'Clock Girl, Dynamite, So This Is College, The Single Standard, Lightnin', The Silver Horde, Once A Sinner, Kept Husbands, Born To Love, The Lost Squadron, Bird of Paradise, Most Dangerous Game, Rockabye, The Sport Parade, Our Betters, Bed of Roses, The Silver Cord, One Man's Journey, Chance At Heaven, Gambling Lady, Half a Sinner, Richest Girl in the World, Private Worlds, Our Little Girl, Woman Wanted, Barbary Coast, Splendor, These Three, Come and Get It, Two In a Crowd, Adventure in Manhattan, Banjo On My Knee, Internes Can't Take Money, Wells Fargo, Woman Chases Man, Dead End, Three Blind Mice, Youth Takes A Fling, Union Pacific, They Shall Have Music, Espionage Gent.* 1940 : *He Married his Wife* (20th), *Primrose Path* (RKO), *Foreign Correspondent* (UA) ; 1941 : *Reaching for The Sun* (Para), *Sullivan's Travels* (Para) ; 1942 : *The Great Man's Lady* (Para), *The Palm Beach Story* (Para) ; 1943 : *The More the Merrier* (Col) ; 1944 : *Buffalo Bill* (20th), *The Great Moment* (Para) ; 1945 : *The Unseen* (Para) ; 1946 : *The Virginian* (Para) ; 1947 : *Ramrod* (Enterprise-MGM).

MACDONALD, David. Director. Born Helensburgh, Scotland, May 9, 1904. Worked for a time on rubber plantation in Malaya. In 1929 went to Hollywood as assistant director to Cecil B. de Mille. Returned to Britain 1936 as assistant director to Raoul Walsh on *O.H.M.S.* (GB) 1937. Since then directed many

feature films including *Dead Men Tell No Tales, Meet Mr. Penny, This Man is News, Spies of the Air, The Midas Touch, This England.* Joined the Army in 1940. Became head of Army Film Unit. War documentaries include *Desert Victory* and *Burma Victory.* Since demobilization has directed *The Brothers, Good Time Girl, Snowbound, The Bad Lord Byron.*

McDONALD, Marie. Real name Marie Frye. Born Burgin, Kentucky, Aug. 3. Ht. 5 ft. 6 in. Began her career as New York model. On the stage in George White's " Scandals " and later as singer with Tommy Dorsey's band. Film debut 1941 : *It Started With Eve* (Univ), *You're Telling Me* (Univ) ; 1942 : *Pardon My Sarong* (Para), *Lucky Jordan* (Para) ; 1943 : *Tornado* (Para), *Riding High* (Para) ; 1944 : *I Love a Soldier* (Para), *Standing Room Only* (Para), *Guest In The House* (UA) ; 1945 : *It's a Pleasure* (RKO) *Getting Gertie's Garter* (UA) ; 1947 : *Living in a Big Way* (MGM).

McDONALD, Ray. Born Boston, Massachusetts, June 27. Ht. 5 ft. 11 in. ; wt. 145 lb. Brown hair, blue eyes. In vaudeville act with sister at 11. Broadway debut in " Babes in Arms ". Featured as dancing star ; in Broadway musical " Park Avenue ", 1947. First film *Down in San Diego* (MGM), 1941. Other films include—1941 : *Life Begins for Andy Hardy* (MGM), *Babes on Broadway* (MGM) ; 1942 : *Born to Sing* (MGM), *Presenting Lily Mars* (MGM). 1942-6, served in U.S. Army. 1944 : *Winged Victory* (20th). 1946 : *Till The Clouds Roll By* (MGM).

McDOWALL, Roddy. Born Herne Hill, London, Sept. 17, 1928. Brown hair, brown eyes. Educ. St. Joseph's College, Highgate. Trained in drama and elocution at Hanover Academy, London. Appeared in small parts in British films before being evacuated to America, 1940, where he secured role of Huw in *How Green Was My Valley* (20th) 1941. First British film : *Murder in the Family* (Fox-Brit), 1936 ; others include : *You Will Remember, The Outsider, John Halifax Gentleman, Just William, Hey Hey U.S.A., This England.* In U.S.A., 1941 : *Man Hunt* (20th), *Confirm or Deny* (20th) ; 1942 : *On the Sunny Side* (20th), *The Pied Piper* (20th), *Son of Fury* (20th) ; 1943 : *My Friend Flicka* (20th), *Lassie Come Home* (MGM) ; 1944 : *The White Cliffs of Dover* (MGM), *The Keys of the Kingdom* (20th) ; 1945 : *Thunderhead, Son of Flicka* (20th), *Molly and Me* (20th), *Holiday in Mexico* (MGM) ; 1947 : *Macbeth* (Rep) ; 1948 : *Green Grass of Wyoming* (20th).

McGUIRE, Dorothy. Born Omaha, Nebraska, June 14, 1919. Ht. 5 ft. 6 in. ; wt. 120 lb. Blonde hair, blue eyes. Educ. Ladywood Convent, Indianapolis ; Pine Manor Junior College, Wellesley, Mass. In 1932 appeared in " A Kiss for Cinderella " at local theatre. New York stage appearances include : " Bachelor Born ", " Our Town ", " My Dear Children ", " Swinging The Dream ", " Midsummer Night's Dream ". Outstanding stage success in title-role of " Claudia " led to her entering films in the same role : *Claudia* (20th) 1943. Other films include : 1944 : *A Tree Grows in Brooklyn* (20th) ; 1945 : *The Enchanted Cottage* (RKO), *The Spiral Staircase* (RKO) ; 1946 : *Claudia and David* (20th), *Till the End of Time* (RKO) ; 1948 : *Gentlemen's Agreement* (20th).

McKENNA, Siobhan (Erse for " Susan " ; pronounced *Shuvawn*). Born Belfast, May 24, 1923. Ht. 5 ft. 5 in.

Brown hair, hazel eyes. Educ. Irish National University. Produced and acted at University's all-Gaelic Theatre ; became member of Dublin's Gate and Abbey Theatres. Won recognition with 3-minute cameo role in first film : *Hungry Hill* (Two Cities), 1947. 1948 : *Daughter of Darkness* (Alliance).

McMANUS, Sharon. Born Norfolk, Nebraska, June 10, 1938. Brown hair, brown eyes. Developed a remarkable memory when very young. At 3 appeared in children's concert at the famous " Boys' Town ", near Omaha, Nebraska, and later recommended by Father Flanagan (technical adviser for film *Boys' Town*) for screen test. First film appearances were in three shorts, *A Great Day is Coming, Little White Lie, Amber Returns.* First feature film : *Anchors Aweigh* (MGM) 1944, in which she made hit in Mexican dance with Gene Kelly. Other films include : 1945 : *Bewitched* (MGM), *Boys' Ranch* (MGM) ; 1946 : *Little Mister Jim* (MGM), *This Time for Keeps* (MGM).

MACMURRAY, Fred. Born Kankakee, Illinois, Aug. 30, 1908. Ht. 6 ft. 3 in. ; wt. 185 lb. Black hair, blue eyes. Educ. Beaver Dam High School ; Carroll College, Waukesha, Wisconsin. Could play violin at 5 ; worked in canning factory during school holidays to earn money to buy saxophone. Played in dance orchestra while at College, then worked in bands in Chicago for a year. Also worked as clerk and salesman. To Hollywood 1928 : became film extra, and between films worked as saxophonist and singer. Joined " Californian Collegians " as saxophonist, singer and clown, and appeared with them on Broadway in " Three's a Crowd ", and " Roberta ". During " Roberta ", was given film contract, but was kept idle in Hollywood for six months before being chosen as leading man to Claudette Colbert in *The Gilded Lily* (Para) 1935. Other films include : *Grand Old Girl, Car 99, Men Without Names, Alice Adams, Hands Across the Table, The Bride Comes Home, Trail of the Lonesome Pine, 13 Hours by Air, The Princess Comes Across, Texas Rangers, Champagne Waltz, Maid of Salem, Swing High Swing Low, Exclusive, True Confession, Cocoanut Grove, Men With Wings, Sing You Sinners !, Café Society, Invitation to Happiness, Honeymoon in Bali, Remember the Night ;* 1940 : *Little Old New York* (20th), *Too Many Husbands* (Col), *Rangers of Fortune* (Para) ; 1941 : *Virginia* (Para), *One Night in Lisbon* (Para), *Dive Bomber* (Warn), *New York Town* (Para) ; 1942 : *The Lady is Willing* (Col) ; *Take A Letter Darling* (Para), *Forest Rangers* (Para) ; 1943 : *No Time for Love* (Para), *Above Suspicion* (MGM), *Star Spangled Rhythm* (Para), *And the Angels Sing* (Para) ; 1944 : *Standing Room Only* (Para), *Double Indemnity* (Para), *Practically Yours* (Para), *Murder, He Says !,* 1945 : *A Tree Grows in Brooklyn* (20th), *Pardon my Past* (Col), *Where Do We Go From Here ?* (20th), *Captain Eddie.* (20th) ; 1946 : *Suddenly It's Spring* (Para), *Smoky* (20th) ; 1947 : *The Egg and I* (UI), *Singapore* (UI) ; 1948 : *Miracle of the Bells* (RKO), *A Miracle Can Happen* (Benedict Bogeaus-UA).

MACPHAIL, Angus. Story supervisor. Born London, Apr. 8, 1903. Educ. Westminster School, London ; Trinity Hall, Cambridge. Whilst at University, edited " The Granta " with Ian Dalrymple. Entered film industry, 1926, as film editor and title writer at Islington Studios for Michael Balcon, becoming script writer 1927. Continued to work for Balcon at Gaumont-British Studios, 1931-37, as story supervisor, associate producer and Balcon's personal assistant. In 1939,

went with Balcon to Ealing Studios as story supervisor. His Ealing screen-play credits include : *Next of Kin, Dead of Night, The Captive Heart, Frieda, The Loves of Joanna Godden.*

MADISON, Guy. Born Bakersfield, California, Jan. 19, 1922. Ht. 6 ft. ; wt. 180 lb. Fair hair, hazel eyes. Educ. Bakersfield High School. Youthful ambition : to sail the Pacific. Ill-health sent him at 8 to mountain resort, where he learned to swim and hunt ; worked in orchards. Left school to work as telephone linesman and to save money to buy commercial fishing boat. 1942-4, served in U.S. Navy. In 1944, hitch-hiked to Hollywood, met talent scout. First film : *Till the End of Time* (RKO) 1946 ; 1947 : *Two Men and a Girl* (RKO).

MAGNANI, Anna. Born Alexandria, Egypt, 1910. Originally was a comedy actress in Hermione Gingold style. Given dramatic role as young widow by director Roberto Rosselini in *Open City* (Excelsa), 1945, in which part she achieved widespread fame. Other films include : *Quartetto Pazzo, Campo de'Fiori, L'Ultima Carrozzella ;* 1945 : *Abbasso la Miseria* (Damus), *Un Uomo Ritorna* (Zeus Film) ; 1946 : *Abbasso la Ricchezza* (Ora Film Lux), *Lo Sconosciuto di S. Marino* (Gamma film), *Avanti a Lui Tremava Tutta Roma* (Excelsa) ; 1947 : *L'Onorevole Angelina* (Lux).

MAIN, Marjorie. Real name Mary Tomlinson. Born Acton, Indiana, Feb. 4. Ht. 5 ft. 5 in. ; wt. 136lb. Brown hair, blue eyes. Specialized in amateur recitation work ; became dramatic instructor at girls' school, Bourbon College, Paris, Kentucky. Finding teaching monotonous, joined Shakespearean touring company ; later appeared in vaudeville, and in Broadway plays and musicals. First film : *Take a Chance* (Para), 1933. Played small parts till she found her mark in series opposite Wallace Beery. Films include : *Music in the Air, Crime Without Passion, Dead End, Love in a Bungalow, Stella Dallas, The Man Who Cried Wolf, The Wrong Road, Boy of the Streets, The Shadow, Test Pilot, Prison Farm, Romance of the Limberlost, Penitentiary, Little Tough Guy, Under the Big Top, Girls' School, Too Hot to Handle, Angels Wash Their Faces, Lucky Night, Melody of Youth, Another Thin Man, I Take This Woman, The Women.* 1940 : *Women Without Names* (Para), *The Captain is a Lady* (MGM), *Bad Man of Wyoming* (MGM) ; 1941 : *The Trial of Mary Dugan* (MGM), *The Wild Man of Borneo* (MGM), *A Woman's Face* (MGM), *Shepherd of the Hills* (Para), *Barnacle Bill* (MGM), *Honky Tonk* (MGM), *The Bugle Sounds ;* 1942 : *Once Upon a Thursday* (MGM), *Jackass Mail* (MGM), *Tish* (MGM), *The Man on America's Conscience* (MGM), *We Were Dancing* (MGM) ; 1943 : *Heaven Can Wait* (20th), *Johnny Vagabond* (UA) ; 1944 : *Rationing* (MGM), *Meet Me in St. Louis* (MGM), *Murder, He Says !* (Para), *Gentle Annie* (MGM) ; 1945 : *The Harvey Girls* (MGM), *Bad Boscomb* ; 1946 : *The Show-Off* (MGM), *Undercurrent* (MGM) ; 1947 : *The Egg and I* (UI), *The Wistful Widow of Wagon Gap* (UI).

MALONE, Dorothy. Real name Dorothy Maloney. Born Chicago, Jan. 30, 1925. Ht. 5 ft. 7 in. ; wt. 124 lb. Dark brown hair, blue-green eyes. Educ. Ursuline Convent and Highland Park High School, Dallas : Hockaday Junior College ; Southern Methodist University. A college production of " Starbound " brought a film offer, but she stayed at school. Later went to Hollywood to study dancing and diction for a

DOROTHY MALONE
(*Warner*)

year. Seen by talent scout in amateur play " Ladies Unmasked ". First film : *The Big Sleep* (Warn), 1946. Other films include : 1946 : *Night and Day* (Warn), *Janie Gets Married* (Warn).

MAMOULIAN, Rouben. Director. Born Tiflis, Caucasus, 1898. Educ. Paris and University of Moscow, specializing in law. At same time studied acting, stage-writing and directing and later abandoned law for the theatre. Came to Britain, 1920 and produced plays for Russian Repertory Company ; was also language lecturer at King's College, London. Went to New York to direct American Opera Company. On Broadway produced " Porgy ", folk play with all-negro cast. Entered films 1928. Directed : *Applause, City Streets, Dr. Jekyll and Mr. Hyde, Love Me Tonight, Song of Songs, Queen Christina, We Live Again, Becky Sharp, The Gay Desperado, High Wide and Handsome, Golden Boy, The Mark of Zorro, Blood and Sand* (Academy Award for best colour production of 1941), *Rings on Her Fingers, Summer Holiday.*

MANKIEWICZ, Joseph. Producer, writer. Born Wilkes-Barre, Pennsylvania, Feb. 11, 1909. Educ. Columbia University. Youthful ambition : to be actor and playwright. Went to Germany and worked for " Chicago Tribune " as assistant correspondent, then in UFA Studios translating films into English. In 1929 he returned to U.S.A. and joined Paramount for whom he wrote the screenplays of " Skippy ", " If I Had a Million " and " Million Dollar Legs ". In 1934 he joined MGM as writer and producer. Productions include : *Three Godfathers, The Gorgeous Hussy, Double Wedding, The Bride Wore Red, Mannequin, Three Comrades, Shopworn Angel, A Christmas Carol, Adventures of Huckleberry Fin, Strange Cargo, The Philadelphia Story, The Feminine Touch, Woman of the Year, Reunion in France, Keys of the Kingdom, Somewhere in the Night.* Directed *The Ghost and Mrs. Muir, The Late George Apley, Dragonwyck, Escape.*

MARAIS, Jean. Born Cherbourg, France, Dec. 11, 1913. Made stage reputation in " Les Parents Terribles " and in Cocteau's " The Eagle Has Two Heads ". Film debut : *Le Scandale.* Other films include : *L'Eperiret, Les Hommes Nouveaux, Le Pavilion Brule, Le Voyage sans Retour, Le Lit à Colonnes, L'Eternel Retour, La Belle et la Bête, Les Chouans.*

MARCH, Fredric. Real name Frederick McIntyre Bickel. Born Racine, Wisconsin, Aug. 31, 1897. Ht. 6 ft. ; wt. 170 lb. Dark hair, dark eyes. Educ. University of Wisconsin. Was bank clerk before making New York stage debut, 1920, in " Deburau ". Notable stage appearances include " Arms and The Man ", " Liliom ", " Saturday's Children ", " The Royal Family ", " A Bell For Adano ". First film : *The Dummy,* 1929. Other films include : *Jealousy, Paris Bound, Sarah and Son, The Royal Family of Broadway, Dr. Jekyll and Mr. Hyde, The Sign of the Cross, Smilin' Through, Design for Living, Death Takes a Holiday, The Affairs of Cellini, The Barretts of Wimpole Street, Les Misérables, The Dark Angel, Anna Karenina, Mary of Scotland, Anthony Adverse, Trade Winds ;* 1940 : *Susan and God* (MGM) ; 1944 : *Adventures of Mark Twain* (Warn), *Tomorrow the World* (UA) ; 1946 : *The Best Years of Our Lives* (Goldwyn) ; 1948 : *Another Part of the Forest* (UI).

MARRIOTT, Moore. Real name George Thomas Moore Maryott. Born West Drayton, Middlesex,

Sept. 14, 1885. Ht. 5 ft. 6 in. ; wt. 164 lb. White hair, brown eyes. Educ. William Ellis School, Hampstead. Youthful ambition : to be an architect. Born of theatrical family, was on stage at age of five, then in London repertory companies ; was a provincial star at 19. In 1908 met Cecil M. Hepworth, for whom he made great many silent films. After serving in World War I, resumed screen career. Has played in over 300 films. First major film : *Dick Turpin* (British and Colonial), 1908 ; made his first sound film, *Mr. Smith Wakes Up,* at Wembley Studios in 1928. From 1936, created famous screen character of the old man in Gainsborough series of Will Hay comedies. Three of his best in this series are *Oh ! Mr. Porter, Windbag the Sailor, Where's That Fire ?* Recent films include : 1942 : *Back Room Boys* (Gains), *Balloonatics* (Gains), *Hi Gang* (Gains) ; 1944 : *The Agitator* (Brit Nat) ; 1947 : *Green For Danger* (Individ), *The Root of All Evil* (Gains), *Green Fingers* (Brit Nat), *The Hills of Donegal* (Butcher).

MARLY, Florence. Born Czechoslovakia. Ht. 5 ft. 5½ in. ; wt. 115 lb. Auburn hair, green eyes. Began her career in Czechoslovak theatre. French films include *Les Maudits,* prize-winning film at the Cannes 1947 Film Festival. Has also made several Spanish-language films, and the French-English versions of *The Mayor of Casterbridge* in Paris, 1947. Seen by a talent scout in Paris, signed up for Hollywood, and given leading role opposite Ray Milland in first American film, *The Sealed Verdict* (Para) 1948.

MARSH, Carol. Real name Norma Simpson. Born Southgate, London, 1920. Ht. 5 ft. 4½ in. ; wt. 110 lb. Light brown hair, blue eyes. Trained for stage at drama section, Royal Academy of Music ; made stage debut, 1946, with Worthing Repertory Company, Sussex. Chosen from 3000 applicants as leading lady to Richard Attenborough in her first film : *Brighton Rock* (Boultings-ABPC) 1948.

MARSH, Garry. Born St. Margaret's, Richmond, Surrey, May 21, 1902. Educ. Richmond. Began stage career 1919, at King's Theatre, Southsea, in music-hall sketch " The Dowry " with John Lawson's Company. First film : *Night Birds,* 1930. Appeared in casts of almost all early British films. Films include : *Josser, Uneasy Virtue, Third Time Lucky, Keepers of Youth, Stamboul, Dreyfus, After Office Hours, No. 17, The Maid of the Mountains, Falling For You, The Love Nest, Ask Beccles, Warn London, The Green Pack, Full Circle, Night Mail, Bargain Basement, Scrooge, When Knights Were Bold, The Amazing Quest of Mr. Ernest Bliss, The Man in the Mirror, Bank Holiday, Convict 99, Break the News, I See Ice, It's In The Air, This Man Is News, Trouble Brewing, The Four Just Men, This Man in Paris, Hoots Mon !, Lost on the Western Front, Goodbye to Yesterday, Let George Do It.* 1940-5, served in R.A.F. and became chief of mobile recording unit. 1945 : *I'll Be Your Sweetheart* (Gains). 1946 : *The Rake's Progress* (Individ) ; 1947 : *While The Sun Shines* (Internat Screen), *Dancing with Crime* (Alliance), *Just William's Luck* (Alliance), the first of new " William " series ; 1948 : *Things Happen at Night* (Alliance).

MARSHALL, George. Director. Born Chicago, Dec. 29, 1891. Educ. St. John's Military Academy ; University of Chicago. First job was as photograph salesman ; then became professional baseball player, jeweller's assistant, student engineer on U.S. railway ; newspaper reporter ; entered films as extra, 1912.

Appeared in Wallace Reid films, serials, Al Christie comedies ; then became prop boy, make-up man, editor, assistant director to Harry Carey. Directed Carey in three-reel Westerns until 1917. Served in U.S. Army in World War I. In 1919 made Ruth Roland serials for Pathé. Made Tom Mix westerns for Fox ; in 1925 became supervising director of all Fox shorts. For Warners wrote and directed Bobby Jones *How to Golf* shorts ; made Laurel and Hardy comedies for Hal Roach ; comedies for Mack Sennett. Became associate producer for Fox, 1934. Recently with Paramount. Feature films include : *Ever Since Eve, She Learned About Sailors, Life Begins At Forty, Music Is Magic, A Message to Garcia, Can This Be Dixie !, Wild Gold, 365 Nights In Hollywood, Ten Dollar Raise, Love Under Fire, Show Them No Mercy, The Crime of Dr. Forbes, Nancy Steele Is Missing, Battle of Broadway, Hold That Co-Ed !, In Old Kentucky, The Goldwyn Follies, You Can't Cheat An Honest Man, Destry Rides Again, The Ghost Breakers, When The Daltons Rode, Pot O'Gold, Texas, Valley of the Sun, The Forest Rangers, Girls' Town, True To Life, Star Spangled Rhythm, Melody Inn, And The Angels Sing, Incendiary Blonde, Murder He Says !, Hold That Blonde, Monsieur Beaucaire, The Blue Dahlia, The Perils of Pauline, Variety Girl.*

MARSHALL, Herbert. Actor. Born London, May 23, 1890. Ht. 6 ft. ; wt. 175 lb. Dark brown hair, blue eyes. Educ. St. Mary's, Harlow, Essex. Youthful ambition : to become an artist. Left school to become clerk in London firm of chartered accountants. In 1911, made stage debut as servant in " The Adventures of Lady Ursula ", Opera House, Buxton. Toured U.S.A. and Canada with Cyril Maude in " Grumpy " ; served in army in World War I, and lost a leg. Toured Canada and U.S.A., 1921-2. Screen debut in British silent film *Mumsie* (Gains) 1927. Early British films include : *Dawn, Murder, The Calendar, The Faithful Heart, Michael and Mary, I Was a Spy.* U.S. films include : *Secrets of a Secretary, The Blonde Venus, Trouble in Paradise, Evenings For Sale, Solitaire Man, Four Frightened People, The Painted Veil, Riptide, The Good Fairy, The Flame Within, Accent on Youth, The Dark Angel, If You Could Only Cook, The Lady Consents, A Woman Rebels, Breakfast For Two ;* 1940 : *The Letter* (Warn), *Till We Meet Again* (Warn), *A Bill of Divorcement* (RKO), *Foreign Correspondent* (UA) ; 1941 : *Adventure in Washington* (Col), *The Little Foxes* (RKO), *When Ladies Meet* (MGM), *Kathleen* (MGM) ; 1942 : *The Moon and Sixpence* (UA) ; 1943 : *Flight for Freedom* (RKO), *Forever and a Day* (RKO), *Young Ideas* (MGM) ; 1944 : *Andy Hardy's Blonde Trouble* (MGM) ; *The Unseen* (Para), *The Enchanted Cottage* (RKO) ; 1946 : *Crack-Up* (RKO), *Duel In the Sun* (Selznick), *The Razor's Edge* (20th) ; 1947 : *Ivy* (UI) ; 1948 : *The High Wall* (MGM).

MARSHALL, Herbert P. J. Producer, director, writer. Born London, Jan. 20, 1906. Educ. elementary school, London, and Higher Academy of Cinema, Moscow. Entered films 1929 as editor of documentary films for British Empire Marketing Board under John Grierson, then made his own documentary films. In 1930, on invitation of Pudovkin, went to study under Eisenstein and Pudovkin in Directors' Faculty, Higher Academy of Cinema, Moscow ; graduated 1935. Assistant Director Soviet Theatres, producer for Soviet radio. From assistant director to co-director *Song of Heroes* (U.S.S.R.). Returned to Britain 1937. Co-founder Unity Theatre, London. First producer of a Clifford Odets' play in Britain—" Plant In The Sun ",

with Paul Robeson. 1939, co-author, with his wife Fredda Brilliant, and also associate producer, of *The Proud Valley* (Ealing). 1940-1, founder of the Neighbourhood Theatre ; managed, designed and produced " Thunder Rock ". Producer, Old Vic and Sadlers' Wells. 1941-2, produced, edited, directed and dubbed Soviet films for British distribution, including *One Day in Soviet Russia, Our Russian Allies, In The Rear of the Enemy, Red Flyer, Alexander Nevsky.* In 1947 formed independent unit, Citizen Films, and with Fredda Brilliant made in Czechoslovakia and Poland two Children's Entertainment Films about those countries in the *Magic Globe* series. Made English version Soviet children's film *The Elephant and the Skipping Rope.* Author of : " Mayakovsky and his Poetry ", " Theory and Practice of Theatre Production " ; editor " International Library of Theatre and Cinema ", co-editor, with Ivor Montagu, " Soviet Life and Letters ", co-editor, with John Allen, " Anthology of the Actor's Art ".

MARTINS, Orlando. Born Lagos, Nigeria, 1901. Ht. 6 ft. 1 in. Worked for French firms as a clerk before coming to Britain when eighteen, by bribing his way over on a boat. On arrival, joined the Merchant Navy and served on the old s.s. *Mauretania.* After leaving Merchant Navy was wrestler for a time while trying to get work as an actor. Got his first chance as an extra with Diaghileff. For a time travelled as a snake charmer in Sanger's Circus. First stage role in " They Shall Not Die ", in America. Later appeared with Paul Robeson in " Toussaint L'Ouverture " and subsequently was in almost every film made by Robeson in this country. Worked in an aircraft factory during World War II and was also civil defence worker for two years. Recent films include—1946 : *Men of Two Worlds* (Two Cities) ; 1947 : *The End of the River* (Archers).

MARX Brothers.

Groucho. Real name Julius Marx. Born New York, Oct. 21, 1895. Ht. 5 ft. 7½ in. ; wt. 155 lb. Brown hair, brown eyes.

Harpo. Real name Arthur Marx. Born New York, Nov. 23, 1893. Ht. 5 ft. 7½ in. ; wt. 140 lb. Brown hair, brown eyes.

Chico. Real name Leonard Marx. Born New York, Mar. 22, 1891. Ht. 5 ft. 6 in. ; wt. 150 lb. Brown hair, brown eyes.

According to them, their success is due to their mother (the daughter of a stage magician and his harpist wife) who trained her four sons for stage. Chico was pianist, Harpo also played piano but preferred harp, Groucho was singer and tap-dancer. She found engagements for all her sons in turn, until after World War I, the four brothers together—Groucho, Harpo, Chico and Zeppo—" arrived " with " I'll Say She Is " which ran in New York for two years. This was followed by " The Coconuts " and " Animal Crackers". Paramount engaged them to make a film version of *The Coconuts* in 1929. Their next film was *Animal Crackers* (1930). *Monkey Business* (1931) was their first original for the screen ; then came *Horse Feathers* (1932) and *Duck Soup* (1932). At this stage Zeppo retired from the quartet, leaving Groucho, Harpo and Chico to make *A Night at the Opera* (1935), *A Day at the Races* (1937), *Room Service* (1938), *At the Circus* (1939), *Marx Brothers Go West* (1940), *The Big Store* (1941). Groucho appeared solo with Carmen Miranda, in *Copacabana* (Alfred E. Green-UA) 1947.

MASON, James. Born Huddersfield, May 15, 1909. Ht. 6 ft. Black hair, brown eyes. Educ. Marlborough School ; Peterhouse College, Cambridge (B.A. Architecture ; M.A.). Played in several university stage productions, and gave up training as architect for stage career. Debut with touring company in " Rasputin, the Rascal Monk ", Aldershot, 1931. Appeared with various repertory companies, and from Croydon Repertory Company went on to London debut in " Gallows Glorious ", Shaftesbury Theatre, 1933. Joined Old Vic and later played season at Dublin Gate Theatre. In 1937 collaborated with Pamela Kellino in writing stage play " Flying Blind ", in which both also appeared. First film : *Late Extra* (Fox) 1935. Won the " Daily Mail " Award as the most popular British male star, 1946 and 1947. Other films include : *Troubled Waters, Twice Branded, Prison Breakers, Blind Man's Buff, Secret of Stamboul, Fire Over England, Mill on the Floss, The High Command, Catch-As-Catch-Can, The Return of the Scarlet Pimpernel, I Met a Murderer* (collaborated on screenplay), *This Man Is Dangerous.* 1941 : *Hatter's Castle* (Para-Brit), *The Patient Vanishes* (ABPC) ; 1942 : *Secret Mission* (Hellman), *Thunder Rock* (Charter) ; 1943 : *Alibi* (Brit Lion), *The Bells Go Down* (Ealing), *Fanny by Gaslight* (Gains), *The Man in Grey* (Gains), *They Met in the Dark* (Hellman) ; 1944 : *Candlelight in Algeria* (George King), *Hotel Reserve* (RKO-Brit), *A Place of One's Own* (Gains) ; 1945 : *They Were Sisters* (Gains), *The Wicked Lady* (Gains), *The Seventh Veil* (Box-Ortus) ; 1947 : *Odd Man Out* (Two Cities), *The Upturned Glass* (Box). Went to the U.S.A. in 1947 and with Pamela Kellino, John Monahan and Roy Kellino, formed producer-unit, Gamma Films of America, October, 1947.

MASSEY, Raymond. Born Toronto, Canada, Aug, 30, 1896. Ht. 6 ft. 2 in. ; wt. 162 lb. Brown hair brown eyes. Educ. Appleby School, Oakville, Canada Oxford University. Served in Canadian army in World War I ; later served in Siberia. Took part in drama at Oxford, and made his first professional appearance at Everyman Theatre, Hampstead, London in " In The Zone ", 1922. Later participated in the ownership and management of this theatre. Has had a long and distinguished career in the theatre, notably in plays by Bernard Shaw. Co-producer with Gladys Cooper of several London successes. Made his American stage debut in " Hamlet " in 1931, and in 1938-40 gave outstanding performance in the title role of " Abe Lincoln in Illinois " a role he later portrayed for the screen. Served in World War II with the Canadian Artillery, attached to the Adjutant General's Office, Canada. Appeared in several early British films, including *The Speckled Band,* and *The Face at the Window,* before making his Hollywood debut in *The Old Dark House* (Univ) 1932. Other films include : (in Britain) *The Scarlet Pimpernel, Things To Come ;* in U.S.A. : *The Prisoner of Zenda.* 1940 : *Abe Lincoln in Illinois* (RKO), *Santa Fé Trail* (Warn) ; 1942 : *49th Parallel*—U.S. title *The Invaders* (Ortus), *Reap The Wild Wind* (Para), *Desperate Journey* (Warn) ; 1943 : *Action in the North Atlantic* (Warn) ; 1944 : *Arsenic and Old Lace* (Warn), *The Woman in the Window* (RKO) ; 1945 : *Hotel Berlin* (Warn), *God is my Co-Pilot* (Warn) ; 1946 : *A Matter of Life and Death*—U.S. title *Stairway to Heaven* (Archers) ; 1947 : *Possessed* (Warn), *Mourning Becomes Electra* (RKO).

MATHIESON, Muir. Musical director. Born Stirling, Scotland, 1911. At 13 founded the Stirling Boys' Orchestra and made his debut as a conductor and pianist. Later studied at Royal College of Music, London, but began professional career conducting ballet in Toronto and Montreal, in 1931. Has made many broadcasts conducting London Symphony Orchestra. Entered films as assistant musical director to London Film Productions in 1932, and has been associated with nearly all films made at Denham Studios since they were built in 1935. Since 1942 has been Musical Director to J. Arthur Rank Organization. During the war was musical adviser to Ministry of Information, Army and R.A.F. Film Units. Has directed music for more than 200 films. In 1946 directed film *Instruments of the Orchestra,* a documentary, featuring the London Symphony Orchestra under Sir Malcolm Sargent, and with music specially written by Benjamin Britten.

MATTHEWS, Jessie. Born Soho, London, Mar. 11 1907. Ht. 5 ft. 5 in. ; wt. 116 lb. Brown hair, brown eyes. Educ. Pulteney Girls' School, Soho. As a small child showed a talent for dancing, fostered by her elder sister Rosie ; at school produced Christmas ballets ; then studied dancing with Elise Clare, and at 11 appeared in " Bluebell in Fairyland ". Made professional debut at 14 as " Little Red Riding Hood " in suburban pantomime. When 15, entered chorus of C. B. Cochran's " Music Box Revue ", and had one solo song, " Down on the Farm ". In Charlot's " Revue of 1924 ", New York, was chorus girl and understudy to Gertrude Lawrence ; when Gertrude Lawrence fell ill she took over for seven weeks and scored outstanding success. First starring role in London was in " The Charlot Show of 1926 " followed by three years in Cochran productions including " This Year of Grace ", "Wake up and Dream ! " and " Ever Green ", later adapted for the screen. Appeared in two small dancing roles in *The Beloved Vagabond* and *Straws in the Wind,* 1923, and made her talkie debut in *Out of the Blue* (BIP) 1931. Became one of Britain's most popular screen personalities during the next seven years, with Gaumont-British. Gave up theatre entirely until 1939, when she returned to it. Films include : *There Goes The Bride, The Man From Toronto, The Midshipmaid, The Good Companions* (shown in February 1933 at the first " talkie " premiere attended by King George V), *Friday The Thirteenth, Waltzes from Vienna, Evergreen* (1934), *First a Girl, It's Love Again, Head over Heels, Gangway, Sailing Along, Climbing High.*

MATTHEWS, Pamela. Born Caterham, Surrey Aug. 5, 1922. Ht. 5 ft. 8 in. ; wt. 126 lb. Dark brown hair, amber eyes. Educ. St. Paul's Girls' School. Studied stage design, and was then secretary to two novelists before deciding on a stage career, which was postponed for four years while she worked during World War II in Government office, and with the Red Cross. Made her stage debut with Worthing Repertory Company in " A Soldier For Christmas " in 1945. While acting as stand-in for Rosalyn Boulter at Denham Studios was spotted by director Peter Ustinov, who gave her a small part in *School For Secrets* (Two Cities) 1946. Also appeared in *A Matter of Life and Death* (Archers) 1946.

MATURE, Victor. Born Louisville, Kentucky, Jan. 29, 1915. Ht. 6 ft. 2½ in. ; wt. 198 lb. Brown hair, brown eyes. Educ. parochial schools ; Kentucky Military Institute. Began in father's refrigerator company, later owned restaurant, but decided on stage career. Trained Pasadena Playhouse, California ;

had appeared in some sixty plays when Hal Roach saw him in " To Quito and Back ", and suggested screen career. First film : *The Housekeeper's Daughter* (UA) 1939. Films include—1940 : *One Million B.C.* (Roach-UA), *Captain Caution* (Roach-UA), *No, No, Nanette* (RKO) ; 1941 : *Hot Spot* (20th), *The Shanghai Gesture* (Pressburger-UA) ; 1942 : *Song of the Islands* (20th), *My Gal Sal* (20th), *Footlight Serenade* (20th) *Seven Days Leave* (RKO) ; 1942-6, served in U.S. Navy. 1946 : *My Darling Clementine* (20th) ; 1947 : *Moss Rose* (20th), *Kiss of Death* (20th).

MAUGHAM, W. Somerset. Writer. Born Paris, Jan. 25, 1874. Educ. King's School, Canterbury ; Heidelberg University, St. Thomas's Hospital, London. M.R.C.S., L.R.C.P. Author of plays, novels, very many short stories, and critical works. Plays filmed : *Our Betters*, *The Letter* (twice). Novels filmed : *Of Human Bondage* (twice) ; "Ashenden"—filmed as *Secret Agent* ; *The Moon and Sixpence*, *Rain*, *Land of Promise*, *Strictly Unconventional*, *The Razor's Edge*, *Neil MacAdam*. Under the omnibus title *Quintet* (Gains), 1948, the following five short stories have been filmed, with an introduction by the author : " Alien Corn ", " The Colonel's Lady ", " The Sanatorium ", " The Kite ", " The Facts of Life ".

MAXWELL, Lois. Born Kitchener, Ontario, Feb. 14, 1927. Ht. 5 ft. 7½ in. ; wt. 119 lb. Auburn hair, green-blue eyes. Educ. Lawrence Park Collegiate Institute ; Royal Academy of Music, Canada. Professional dancer at 10, took part in college productions, played juvenile leads on radio at 14. At 16 came to Britain with group of artists entertaining Canadian Army. Shortly after D-Day, landed on continent as troops' entertainer, but authorities discovered she was only 17 and sent her back to Britain, where she resumed dramatic training. Won first Lady Louis Mountbatten Scholarship at Royal Academy of Dramatic Art. Joined London and District Theatre. Toured in play " Fit For Heroes ". Given part in *A Matter of Life and Death* (Archers), 1946, but scenes in which she appeared were cut out. Went back on tour, then appeared in " Our Betters ". Was spotted while acting as " feed " in film test in Britain to another young actor, and given Hollywood contract. First film : *Mary Hagen* (Warn) 1947. 1948 : *Christopher Blake* (Warn).

MAXWELL, Marilyn. Real name Marvel Maxwell. Born Clarinda, Iowa, Aug. 3. Ht. 5 ft. 6 in. ; wt. 125 lb. Blonde hair, hazel eyes. Educ. Central High School, Fort Wayne, Indiana ; Washington Grammar School. At 16 was singing on amateur radio show, Des Moines, Iowa. Later sang with Buddy Rogers' and Ted Weems' orchestras. Declined films for two years because she thought she had not enough talent. Was featured radio singer for seven years, and appeared regularly on Bing Crosby's radio programme. First film : *Cargo of Innocents* (MGM) 1942. Other films (all MGM) include—1942 : *Presenting Lily Mars* ; 1943 : *Salute the Marines*, *Thousands Cheer*, *Crazy to Kill*, *Swing Fever* ; 1944 : *Three Men in White*, *Lost in a Harem*, *Between Two Women* ; 1946 : *The Show-Off*, *High Barbaree* ; 1947 : *Summer Holiday*.

MAY, Hans. Musical director and composer. Born Vienna, 1891. At 8 had composed a sonata. Came to Britain in early days of sound, and composed musical score for one of the first British talkies, *Piccadilly* (B.I.P. 1929). Has since written scores for about a hundred films in France, Germany and Britain. Outstanding film scores include those for *Mayerling*, *Lilac Domino*, *Viennese Waltz*, *Southern Roses*, *I Killed the Count*, *Pastor Hall*, *The Stars Look Down*, *Thunder Rock*, *Itma*, *Madonna of the Seven Moons*, 2000 *Women*, *The Wicked Lady*, *Waltz Time*, *The Lisbon Story*, *Bedelia*. The song " Starlight Serenade " was taken from a background theme in *The Stars Look Down*.

MAYO, Virginia. Real name Virginia Jones. Born St. Louis, Missouri, Nov. 30. Ht. 5 ft. 4 in. ; wt. 115 lb. Ash-blonde hair, hazel eyes. Educ. St. Louis Dramatic School. Left school to join floor show in local hotel and eventually appeared in Billy Rose's Diamond Horseshoe night-club in New York, where she was seen by Goldwyn, who signed her for " glamour grooming ". Films include—1943 : *Salute to the Marines* (MGM), *Jack London* (UA) ; 1944 : *Lady in the Death House*, *Lost in a Harem* (MGM), *The Princess and The Pirate* (RKO), *Three Men in White* (MGM), *Seven Days Ashore* (RKO), *Up in Arms* (RKO) ; 1945 : *Wonder Man* (RKO) ; 1946 : *The Kid From Brooklyn* (RKO), *The Best Years of Our Lives* (Goldwyn) ; 1947 : *Out of the Blue* (Eagle Lion-Hollywood), *The Secret Life of Walter Mitty* (Goldwyn).

MEADOWS, Jayne. Real name Jayne Cotter. Born Wu Chang, China, Sept. 27. Ht. 5 ft. 6 in. ; wt. 135 lb. Titian hair, black eyes. Was already well-known on Broadway stage before accepting her screen test while on holiday in Southern California. First film : *Undercurrent* (MGM) 1946. Others include : *Lady in the Lake* (MGM), *Cynthia's Secret* (MGM) ; 1947 : *Song of the Thin Man* (MGM).

MEDINA, Patricia. Born Liverpool. Black hair, dark brown eyes. Educ. London. Youthful ambition: to become doctor. Travelled extensively and became good linguist, which enabled her to take roles in series of French plays in London, 1938. Seen on stage by British National talent scout and tested. First film : *Simply Terrific* (Warn-Brit) 1938. Films include : *Double or Quits*, *Secret Journey* ; 1942 : *The Day Will Dawn*—U.S. title *The Avengers* (Soskin) ; 1943 : *They Met in the Dark* (Hellman) ; 1944 : *Hotel Reserve* (RKO-Brit), *Kiss the Bride Good-bye* (Butcher), *Don't Take It To Heart* (Two Cities) ; 1945 : *Waltz Time* (Brit Nat). In U.S., 1946 : *The Secret Heart* (MGM), *The Beginning or The End?* (MGM) ; 1947 : *Moss Rose* (20th), *The Foxes of Harrow*.

MELCHIOR, Lauritz. Singer. Born Copenhagen, Mar. 20, 1890. Ht. 6 ft. 4 in. ; wt. 250 lb. White hair, blue eyes. One of the world's greatest Wagnerian tenors. Began as clerk in Copenhagen music publishing firm, and studied singing and dramatics. After eight years achieved first contract Copenhagen Royal Opera. Fame came when singing Wagnerian roles at Covent Garden Opera House, London, 1919. American debut, Metropolitan Opera House, 1926. Now an outstanding figure in U.S. musical life. Since 1920 has sung in over 1000 operatic performances. First film : *Thrill of a Romance* (MGM) 1945. Other films include :—1945 : *Two Sisters From Boston* (MGM) ; 1946 : *This Time For Keeps* (MGM), *The Red Mill* (MGM).

MENJOU, Adolphe. Born Pittsburgh, Pennsylvania, Feb. 18, 1890. Educ. Culver Military Academy ; Cornell University. Took part in college theatricals with the idea of becoming an actor. Served in World

War I, then with U.S. army of occupation in East Prussia ; returned to New York 1920. Appeared in vaudeville and on New York stage. Appeared in early silent films, *The Sheik* and *The Three Musketeers* and became established as portrayer of world-weary cosmopolites in Chaplin's film *A Woman of Paris* (1923). Has made films on the Continent as well as in America. In France, he appeared in the early sound film *La Route est Belle*, and was also in the first French film to have an English version, *Mon Gosse de Père*. Other films include : *The Marriage Circle, The Grand Duchess and the Waiter, Serenade, The Amazons, The Valentine Girl, The Kiss, Ten Months, His Private Life, The Tiger Lady, Marquis Preferred, The King on Main Street, Are Parents People, Gentleman of Paris, Fashions in Love, The Social Celebrity, Blonde or Brunette ?, Forbidden, The Front Page, Friends and Lovers, Two White Arms, Bachelor's Affairs, Night Club Lady, Blame the Woman, The Circus Queen Murder, Morning Glory, A Farewell to Arms, Worst Woman in Paris, Convention City, The Trumpet Blows, Little Miss Marker, Easy to Love, Journal of a Crime, The Human Side, The Mighty Barnum, Gold-Diggers of 1935, Broadway Gondolier, The Milky Way, Wives Never Know, Sing Baby Sing, Café Metropole, 100 Men and a Girl, Stage Door, Goldwyn Follies, Thanks for Everything, A Letter of Introduction.* 1940 : *A Bill of Divorcement* (RKO), *Turnabout* (UA) ; 1941 : *Roadshow* (UA), *Father Takes a Wife* (RKO) ; 1942 : *Roxie Hart* (20th), *Syncopation* (RKO), *You Were Never Lovelier* (Col) ; 1943 : *Sweet Rosie O'Grady* (20th), *Hi Diddle Diddle* (UA) ; 1944 : *Step Lively* (RKO). 1943-4, entertained troops overseas. 1945 : *Man Alive* (RKO) ; 1947 : *Heartbeat* (RKO), *Bachelor Girls* (Andrew-Stone-UA), *I'll Be Yours* (UI), *The Hucksters* (MGM).

MEREDITH, Burgess. Born Cleveland, Ohio, Nov. 16, 1909. Ht. 5 ft. 7 in. ; wt. 135 lb. Sandy hair, hazel eyes. Educ. Amherst College. Became reporter, shop assistant, vacuum cleaner salesman, merchant seaman. Eve Le Gallienne gave him first stage role in her Civic Repertory Company, New York, as Peter in " Romeo and Juliet", 1929. After his success in " Winterset" was invited to play his original role in film *Winterset* (RKO) 1936. 1942-45, served in U.S. Army. Other films include : *Idiot's Delight.* 1940 : *Of Mice and Men* (UA) ; 1941 : *Second Chorus* (Para), *That Uncertain Feeling* (UA), *Tom, Dick and Harry* (RKO) ; 1942 : *Street of Chance* (Para) ; 1945 : *The Story of G.I. Joe* (UA), *Diary of a Chambermaid* (UA) ; 1947 : *Magnificent Doll* (UI), *Mine Own Executioner* (Kimmins) in Britain ; 1948 : *A Miracle Can Happen* (Benedict Bogeaus-UA).

MERRICK, Lynn. Born Fort Worth, Texas. Ht. 5 ft. 5 in. ; wt. 118 lb. Fair hair, blue eyes. Educ. Westlake School for Girls, Beverley Hills, California. At 8 won amateur dramatic contest at the Pallas Theatre, Dallas, Texas, was spotted by film talent scout while appearing in a local " Little Theatre", and given a film contract. Film debut in *Night Flight* (Warn) 1938. Later made twenty-four Westerns without a break. Recent films include : 1941 : *Youth on Parade* (Col) ; *Stagecoach Express* (Rep), *Jesse James, Jr.* (Rep), *Mountain Rhythm* (Rep), *Doughboys in Ireland* (Col) ; 1943 : *Swing Out the Blues* (Col), *Dangerous Blondes* (Col), *Nine Girls* (Col), *Stars on Parade* (Col) ; 1944 : *Meet Miss Bobbysocks* (Col) ; 1945 : *A Guy, a Gal and a Pal* (Col), *Blonde from Brooklyn.* Also in 1945 made *Booked on*

Suspicion, the first of the *Boston Blackie* series, in which she appears regularly. 1946 : *The Voice of the Whistler* (Col), *Lady of Mystery* (Col), *Dangerous Business* (Col); 1947 : *Down to Earth* (Col), *I Love Trouble* (Col).

MESSEL, Oliver. Artist. Born London, Jan. 13, 1905. Educ. Eton. First attracted attention by designing masks ; later designed for Cochran's revues and other stage productions. Went to Hollywood 1932 where he designed settings for *Romeo and Juliet*. In Britain, designed costumes for *The Scarlet Pimpernel, The Thief of Bagdad*. Also responsible for *décor* and costumes in *Caesar and Cleopatra*.

MIDDLETON, Guy. Born Hove, Sussex, Dec. 14, 1907. Ht. 6 ft. Brown hair, grey eyes. Educ. Harrow School. Worked on London Stock Exchange for three years before stage debut in 1928 at Palace Theatre, Salisbury, in " The Crooked Billet ". Made first London appearance in 1929 at Daly's Theatre in " The Lady of the Rose ". Scored a great success as the villain in "Young England", 1934, intended by its author as serious drama, but treated by audiences as old-time melodrama. First film : *A Woman Alone* (Garrett-Klement), 1935. Other films include : *Under Proof, Fame, Gay Adventure, Keep Fit, Break the News, French Without Tears.* From 1940 : *For Freedom* (Gains), *Dangerous Moonlight* (RKO-Brit) ; 1942 : *Talk About Jacqueline* (Hellman) ; 1945 : *The Demi-Paradise* (Two Cities), *The Half-Way House* (Ealing) ; 1944 : *Champagne Charlie* (Ealing). 1939-44, served in Army. 1945 : *The Rake's Progress* (Individ) ; 1946 : *Night Boat to Dublin* (ABPC) ; 1947 : *A Man About the House* (LFP) ; 1948 : *Snowbound* (Gains), *One Night With You* (Two Cities).

MILDER, Max. Born Zonesville, Ohio. Entered film industry 1920. Came to London, 1931, in charge of all Warner interests in Britain. Managing director Warner Brothers' London Office : Managing Director Warners' Teddington Studios, Middlesex. Appointed Managing Director, Associated British Picture Corporation, 1941. Also Managing Director, Associated British Cinemas.

MILES, Bernard. Born Hillingdon, Middlesex, Sept. 27, 1907. Ht. 6 ft. 1 in. ; wt. 185 lb. Dark hair, dark eyes. Educ. Uxbridge County School ; Pembroke College, Oxford. Country upbringing gave him natural gift for authentic dialect ; appeared as rustic in London intimate revue. Was schoolmaster for a year, then repertory and West End actor, making film debut in crowd in *Channel Crossing* (GB) 1932. Later played village policeman in *Quiet Wedding*, the role which brought him screen fame. 1939-45 : served in Home Guard, National Fire Service and ENSA. Films include : *Pastor Hall;* 1941 : *Quiet Wedding* (Soskin-Para), *One of our Aircraft is Missing* (Brit Nat) ; 1942 : *The Big Blockade* (Ealing), *First of the Few*—U.S. title *Spitfire* (Leslie Howard), *In Which We Serve* (Two Cities) ; 1944 : *Tawny Pipit* (Two Cities) ; 1946 : *Carnival* (Two Cities) ; 1947 : *Great Expectations* (Cineguild), *Nicholas Nickelby* (Ealing), *Fame Is the Spur* (Boultings-Two Cities).

MILLAND, Ray. Real name Reginald Truscott-Jones. Born Neath, South Wales, Jan. 3, 1908. Ht. 6 ft. 1½ in. ; wt. 175 lb. Dark brown hair, blue eyes. Educ. King's College, Cardiff. Worked on a potato boat, spent four years in Household Cavalry, travelled Europe, became extra in British films. First film : *The Plaything.* Toured Britain in stage play " The

RAY MILLAND
(*Paramount*)

Woman in Room 13 ". Took lead in film *The Flying Scotsman* when Cyril McLaglen fell ill. Sent by talent scout to Hollywood where he appeared in *Polly of the Circus* (MGM) 1932. Made several trips between London and Hollywood, appearing in minor film roles, till, after *Bolero*, Paramount put him under contract in 1934. Films include : *Bought, Ambassador Bill, Larceny Lane, The Man Who Played God, Payment Deferred, This is the Life, Orders Is Orders, Bolero, Many Happy Returns, Menace, We're Not Dressing, The Glass Key, Millions in the Air, One Hour Late, The Gilded Lily, Four Hours to Kill, Alias Mary Dow, Big Broadcast of 1937, The Jungle Princess, Next Time We Love, Return of Sophie Lang, Bulldog Drummond Escapes, Easy Living, Ebb Tide, Three Smart Girls, Wings Over Honolulu, Wise Girl, Her Jungle Love, Men With Wings, Say It in French, Tropic Holiday, Everything Happens at Night, Hotel Imperial, Beau Geste, French Without Tears* (made in Britain). 1941 : *Irene* (RKO), *Arise My Love* (Para), *Untamed* (Para) , *Doctor Takes a Wife* (Col) ; 1941 : *I Wanted Wings* (Para), *Skylark* (Para) ; 1942 : *Are Husbands Necessary !* (Para), *The Lady Has Plans* (Para), *The Major and the Minor* (Para), *Reap the Wild Wind* (Para), *Star Spangled Rhythm* (Para) ; 1943 : *The Crystal Ball* (UA), *Forever and a Day* (RKO), *Lady in the Dark* (Para) ; 1944 : *Ministry of Fear* (Para), *The Uninvited* (Para), *Till We Meet Again* (Para) ; 1945 : *The Lost Weekend* (Para), *Kitty* (Para) ; 1946 : *The Trouble with Women* (Para), *The Well-Groomed Bride* (Para), *Mrs. Loring's Secret* (Para), *California* (Para) ; 1947 : guest star in *Variety Girl* (Para), *Golden Earrings* (Para) ; 1948 : *So Evil My Love* (Hal Wallis : made in Britain), *The Big Clock* (Para), *The Sealed Verdict* (Para).

MILLAR, Ronald. Writer, actor. Born Reading, Nov. 12, 1919. Educ. Charterhouse ; King's College, Cambridge. Stage debut at Ambassador's Theatre, London, in " Swinging The Gate ", 1940. Served in World War II in Royal Navy, where he wrote first play " Murder From Memory ", produced at the Ambassador's Theatre, 1942. Invalided out, appeared on London stage in " War and Peace ", " Mr. Bolfry ", " Zero Hour ", " The Sacred Flame ". Debut as film actor in *We Dive at Dawn* (Gains) 1943. Author of other plays " Zero Hour ", " The Other Side ", " Frieda ". Filmed : *Frieda*.

MILLER, Ann. Born Houston, Texas, Apr. 12, 1919. Ht. 5 ft. 5½ in. ; wt. 120 lb. Dark hair, blue eyes. Began dancing lessons at 3, took stage fright at local dance recital, and for a time studied piano and violin instead. Resumed dancing later, creating own numbers. At 12 went to Hollywood and appeared as tap-dancer at Orpheum Theatre, Los Angeles. Seen as stage dancer in San Francisco and given film test. First film : *New Faces of 1937* (RKO). Other films include : *Stage Door, Life of the Party, Radio City Revels, Having Wonderful Time, Room Service, Tarnished Angel, You Can't Take It With You.* 1940 : *Too Many Girls* (RKO), *Hit Parade of 1941* (Rep), *Melody Ranch* (Rep) ; 1941 : *Time Out For Rhythm* (Col), *Go West Young Lady* (Col) ; 1942 : *True to the Army* (Para), *Priorities on Parade* (Para) ; 1943 : *Reveille With Beverley* (Col), *What's Buzzin' Cousin ?* (Col) ; 1944 : *Hey Rookie !* (Col), *Jam Session* (Col), *Carolina Blues* (Col) ; 1945 : *Eadie Was a Lady* (Col), *Eve Knew Her Apples* (Col) ; 1946 : *Thrill of Brazil* (Col) ; 1947 : *The Petty Girl* (Col).

MILLER, Kristine. Real name Jacqueline Olivia Eskeson. Born Buenos Aires, 1925. Blonde hair, blue eyes. Educ. Copenhagen. Awarded the title " The Viking Girl " by a group of Royal Danish Illustrators, as a compliment to her looks and athletic accomplishments. With her family escaped from Denmark at the time of the Nazi invasion, and settled in San Francisco, where she began her acting career in the Little Theatre. Seen by Hal Wallis while appearing in " The Doll's House ", and given a small part in *Desert Fury* (Hal Wallis) 1947. Also in *I Walk Alone* (Hal Wallis) 1947.

MILLS, John. Born Suffolk, Feb. 22, 1908. Ht. 5 ft. 8½ in. ; wt. 146 lb. Brown hair, blue eyes. Educ. Norwich. Made early unsuccessful attempt at London stage ; became office worker, commercial traveller, then in chorus of " The Five O'Clock Girl" at the London Hippodrome, 1929. Performance as Lieutenant Raleigh in Indian tour of " Journey's End", 1930, led Noel Coward, who saw it in Bombay, to recommend him to C. B. Cochran. Achieved reputation in musicals in 1930's, but later fulfilled his desire to become known as straight actor. First film role in *The Midshipmaid* (GB), 1933. Served in Army in World War II. On London dramatic stage in " Men in Shadow " (1943), " Duet for Two Hands " (1945). Films include : *Britannia of Billingsgate, The Ghost's Camera, The River Wolves, A Political Party, Forever England, Car of Dreams, First Offence, O.H.M.S., Good-bye Mr. Chips !;* 1940 : *Green Cockatoo* (Fox) ; 1941 : *Old Bill and Son* (Somlo), *Cottage to Let* (Gains) ; 1942 : *Black Sheep of Whitehall* (Ealing), *The Big Blockade* (Ealing), *The Young Mr. Pitt* (20th-Brit), *In Which We Serve* (Two Cities) ; 1943 : *We Dive at Dawn* (Gains) ; 1944 : *This Happy Breed* (Cineguild), *Waterloo Road* (Gains) ; 1945 : *The Way to the Stars* (Two Cities) ; 1946 : *Great Expectations* (Cineguild) ; 1947 : *So Well Remembered* (RKO-Brit), *The October Man* (Two Cities) ; 1948 : *Scott of the Antarctic* (Ealing).

MINASSION, George. Technicolor technician. Born London, 1915. Educ. Chester College. Childhood spent in Istanbul. Was intended for tea trade and became tea-taster. Entered film industry, 1936, in Denham Laboratories on negative cutting and sensametric control. In 1938, joined Technicolor as negative cutter. 1940-2 : war service with R.A.F. In 1942, re-joined Technicolor ; became Technicolor camera assistant on *Life and Death of Colonel Blimp*. 1944, Technicolor technician on *This Happy Breed, Henry V, Blithe Spirit ;* and exteriors of *Caesar and Cleopatra, Men of Two Worlds.*

MINELLI, Vincente. Director. Born Chicago. Began touring at 3 with family stage troupe. Directed stage presentations for New York cinemas ; art director Radio City Music Hall for three and a half years ; then stage producer with " At Home Abroad", " Ziegfeld Follies ", " Very Warm for May ", " The Show Is On", " Hooray for What". Went to Hollywood, 1940, where he spent two years on script work, as ideas man, and as director of special scenes in major musicals. Became film director in : *Cabin in the Sky* (MGM) 1943. Also directed *I Dood It, Meet Me in St. Louis, Under the Clock, Yolanda and the Thief, Undercurrent.*

MIRANDA, Carmen. Real name Maria de Carmo da Cunha. Born Portugal, Feb. 1914. Ht. 5 ft. ; wt. 98 lb. Black hair, brown eyes. Educ. Convent of Santa Teresinha, Rio, Brazil. Was model in department store. Sang on radio, appeared in South American night clubs, made 400 recordings. Seen by Lee Shubert with a samba band in Rio, was booked for New York musical " The Streets of Paris". Made instantaneous hit, and was offered film contract. Frequently in her films wears platform shoes eight inches high to make her look taller. First film: *Down Argentine Way* (20th) 1940. Films include: 1941 : *That Night in Rio* (20th), *Weekend in Havana* (20th) ; 1942 : *Springtime In The Rockies* (20th) ; 1943 : *The Gang's All Here !* (20th) ; 1944 : *Greenwich Village* (20th), *Four Jills In a Jeep* (20th), *Something For The Boys* (20th) ; 1946 : *Doll Face* (20th), *Come Back To Me* (20th), *If I'm Lucky* (20th) ; 1947 : *Copacabana* (Alfred E. Green-UA).

MIRANDA, Isa. Born Milan, 1912. Films include: *Come le Foglie, Passaporto Rosso, Scipione l'Africano, Nina Petrovna, Senza Cielo, E' Caduta una Donna, Documento Z 3, Malombra, Zaza.* 1944 : *La Carne e l'Anima* (Titanus) ; 1945 : *Lo Sbaglio di Essere Vivo* (Fanno Film).

MITCHELL, Cameron. Born Dallastown, Pennsylvania, Nov. 4. Ht. 6 ft. ; wt. 173 lb. Brown hair, brown eyes. Stage-trained, was with Alfred Lunt-Lynn Fontanne repertory company and on Broadway in " Taming of the Shrew ". Director Richard Whorf, former stage colleague, arranged screen test for him after he had left U.S. army, 1943. Appeared in a number of shorts. First feature film : *The Hidden Eye* (MGM) 1945. Other films (all MGM) include—1945: *They Were Expendable, What Next Corporal Hargrove?* 1946 : *The Mighty McGurk, Tenth Avenue Angel ;* 1947 : *High Barbaree.*

MITCHELL, Thomas. Born Elizabeth, New Jersey, July 11, 1895. Educ. Elizabeth High School, New Jersey. Became cub reporter, then wrote vaudeville sketch which led to introduction and appearance with stock companies. Played in and directed several Broadway plays ; collaborated on screenplays in Hollywood. First film appearance : *Craig's Wife* (Col) 1936. Other films include : *Adventures in Manhattan, Theodora Goes Wild, Man of the People, When You're in Love, The Lost Horizon, I Promise to Pay, Make Way for Tomorrow, The Hurricane, Love Honour and Behave, Stagecoach, Only Angels Have Wings, Mr. Smith Goes to Washington, Swiss Family Robinson, The Hunchback of Notre Dame, Gone With the Wind.* 1940 : *Three Cheers for the Irish* (Warn), *Our Time* (UA), *The Long Voyage Home* (UA), *Angels Over Broadway* (Col), *Flight From Destiny* (Warn) ; 1941 : *Out of the Fog* (Warn) ; 1942 : *Joan of Paris* (RKO), *Song of the Islands* (20th), *This Above All* (20th), *Moontide* (Warn), *Tales of Manhattan* (20th), *The Black Swan* (20th) ; 1943 : *The Immortal Sergeant* (20th), *The Outlaw* (Howard Hughes-UA ; held up by the U.S. censors until 1946), *Bataan* (MGM), *Flesh and Fantasy* (Univ) ; 1944 : *The Sullivans* (20th), *Wilson* (20th), *Buffalo Bill* (20th), *Dark Waters* (UA) ; 1945 : *The Keys of the Kingdom* (20th), *The Dark Mirror* (Univ), *It's a Wonderful Life* (RKO) ; 1946 : *Adventure* (MGM) ; 1947 : *High Barbaree* (MGM), *Romance of Rosy Ridge* (MGM), *Silver River* (Warn).

MITCHUM, Robert. Born Bridgeport, Connecticut, Aug. 6, 1917. Ht. 6 ft. 1 in. ; wt. 180 lb. Light brown hair, hazel eyes. Educ. Duke University, Durham, North Carolina. In song-and-dance act with sister at age of 8. Went by cargo-boat to S. America when he was 16. Worked on war plant at Lockheed

Aircraft factory, then joined the U.S. Army when America entered the war. Began films by replacing an actor killed in a *Hopalong Cassidy* Western. Other films include—1943 : *We've Never Been Licked* (Univ), *Corvettes in Action, Gung Ho* (Univ) ; 1944 : *Girl Rush* (RKO), *Nevada* (RKO) ; 1945 : *Thirty Seconds Over Tokyo* (MGM), *Story of G.I. Joe* (UA) ; 1946 : *Undercurrent* (MGM), *Till The End of Time* (RKO), *The Locket* (RKO) ; 1947 : *Pursued* (Warn), *West of the Pecos* (RKO), *Build My Gallows High* (RKO), *Desire Me* (MGM), *Crossfire* (RKO).

MOFFATT, Graham. Born Shepherd's Bush, London, Dec. 6, 1919. Ht. 5 ft. 10 in. ; wt. 168 lb. Educ. Shepherd's Bush. Began his career as page-boy at Gaumont-British Studios. Tom Walls noticed him one day, and put him into cassock and surplice for first film role as choir-boy in *A Cup of Kindness* (G.B) 1934. As "fat boy " he made swift film success in series of British comedies with Will Hay and Moore Marriott. In World War II served with the R.A.F. Has also appeared on variety stage. Films include : *Where There's A Will, Gangway, Dr. Syn, Owd Bob, Oh ! Mr. Porter, Windbag the Sailor, Convict 99, Old Bones of the River, Ask a Policeman, Where's That Fire ?* 1941 : *I Thank You* (Gains) ; 1945 : *I Know Where I'm Going* (Archers) ; 1946-7 : teamed with Mark Daly in new comedy team for Children's Entertainment Films : *The Voyage of Peter Joe* Series.

MOLLISON, Henry. Born Dundee, Feb. 21, 1905. Son of the late William Mollison, theatrical producer. Ht. 6 ft. Brown hair, brown eyes. Educ. St. Paul's School, London ; Caen University, France. Appeared on the stage with his father at the age of 3 ; began his professional career in 1924 with Frank Benson's company. First London appearance, in " Young Woodley ", 1928. Has also appeared on U.S. stage. Played in a number of early British films, including *Third Time Lucky* (1931), *Letting in the Sunshine, Drake of England, McGlusky the Sea Rover.* U.S. films include : *Manhattan Moon, The Lone Wolf Returns, The Music Goes Round, The Devil's Squadron, They Met in a Taxi, Secret Patrol, Find the Witness, A Bride for Henry, Youth Takes a Fling.* Was on his way to Britain to join up in 1939 when his ship was captured, and spent five years as a German P.o.W. Produced 56 shows during 43 months in P.o.W. camp. Resumed stage and screen career on his return to Britain. 1947 : *Hungry Hill* (Two Cities), *The Loves of Joanna Godden* (Ealing).

MONTALBAN, Ricardo. Born Mexico City. Ht. 5 ft. 11 in. ; wt. 170 lb. Brown hair, brown eyes. Educ. Fairfax High School, California. Appeared in high school plays, and was offered screen test ; worked as singer and then won role with Tallulah Bankhead in " Her Cardboard Lover " on Broadway. Some time later his mother's illness recalled him to Mexico where he appeared in small part as bullfighter in Mexican film, which led to nine other films. Became popular star in Mexico and on completing *Los Nosotros* was signed by MGM in 1947 to appear with Esther Williams in *Fiesta.* 1948 : *On An Island With You* (MGM), *His Only Son* (MGM).

MONTAND, Yves. Born Venice, Oct. 1921. Educ. Marseilles, to which his family moved in 1923. Began his career at 11 as delivery boy ; next became hairdresser's apprentice in his sister's business, and in 1936 worked in a metal factory. On Sundays went round local cafés as singer in Maurice Chevalier style.

During the war worked as a docker in Marseilles for a time, but in 1940 went to Paris ; his first professional appearance there, in check jacket and tie, was received with derisive applause, but next day he left off the jacket and tie and found himself successful. While appearing at the Moulin Rouge met French stage star Piaf ; first she considered him "a vulgar boy from Marseilles", but after having studied his performance realized his ability and herself taught him much about singing for the music-halls. Film director Marcel Carné heard him in Paris theatre and gave him leading role in *Les Portes de la Nuit*. Later was seen by U.S. producer Jack Warner, then visiting Europe, for whom he signed a contract in his dressing-room, without any preliminary test ; left for U.S.A., 1947.

MONTEZ, Maria. Real name Maria de Santo Silas. Born Barahona, Dominican Republic, June 6. 1920. Ht. 5 ft. 7 in. ; wt. 120 lb. Red-brown hair, brown eyes. Educ. Sacred Heart Convent, Santa Cruz de Teverite, Canary Islands. Travelled in Europe in her 'teens, appeared on the stage in Belfast. Became model in New York. First film : *The Invisible Woman* (Univ) 1941. Others include—1941 : *Boss o, Bullion City* (Univ), *South of Tahiti* (Univ), *Raiders of the Desert* (Univ), *That Night in Rio* (20th) ; 1942 : *Bombay Clipper* (Univ), *Moonlight in Hawaii* (Univ), *Mystery of Marie Roget* (Univ), *Arabian Nights* (Univ) ; 1943 : *White Savage* (Univ) ; 1944 : *Follow the Boys* (Univ), *Cobra Woman* (Univ), *Ali Baba and the 40 Thieves* (Univ), *Gypsy Wildcat* (Univ) ; 1945 : *Sudan* (Univ) ; 1946 : *Tangier* (Univ) ; 1947 : *Pirates of Monterey* (UI) ; 1948 : *The Exile* (UI), *Atlantis* (Seymour Nebenzal-UA).

MONTGOMERY, Doreen. Writer. Born Glasgow, Apr. 12. 1916. Educ. Edinburgh University (M.A.). Joined "The Scotsman", Edinburgh ; then with London advertising firm. Screen writer since 1936, with interval as London newspaper reporter, 1940-2. Screenplays include : *Room 13*, *Dead Men Tell No Tales*, *Lassie From Lancashire*, *At The Villa Rose*, *The House of The Arrow*, *Poison Pen*, *Just William*, *Bulldog Sees It Through*, *The Flying Squad*, *The Man in Grey*, *Fanny By Gaslight*, *Love Story*, *This Man is Mine*, *She Died Young*, *Bonnie Prince Charlie*.

MONTGOMERY, Douglass. Real name Robert Douglas Montgomery. Born Canada, Oct. 29, 1912. Ht. 6 ft. ; wt. 180 lb. Fair hair, green eyes. Educ. Los Angeles High School ; Robinson Duff Institute, New York. Youthful ambition, to swim for Canada in the Olympic Games. First stage role as son to character played by Lionel Barrymore at Pasadena Playhouse, California. During the next few years continued his schooling while appearing in juvenile leads on the New York stage. First screen appearance in *Paid* (MGM) 1931. Served with Canadian Army during the war, released to appear in *The Way to the Stars*. Settled in Britain after demobilization. Has broadcast in Britain many times, notably in the series "An American in Britain" and "A Yank at the Court of King Arthur". Films include : *Five and Ten*, *Waterloo Bridge* (Univ). 1931 : *A House Divided*, *Little Women*, *Eight Girls in a Boat*, *Little Man, What Now ?*, *Music in the Air*, *Mystery of Edwin Drood*, *Lady Tubbs*, *Harmony Lane*, *Everything is Thunder* (GB) made in Britain, *Life Begins With Love*, *Counsel for Crime*. 1945 : *The Way to the Stars* (Two Cities) ; 1947 : *Woman to Woman* (Brit Nat) ; *When in Rome* (Vicandro), made in Italy.

MONTGOMERY, George. Real name George Montgomery Letz. Born Brady, Montana, Aug. 29, 1916. Ht. 6 ft. 2 in. ; wt. 195 lb. Dark blond hair, blue eyes. Educ. Montana Grade Schools, Great Falls High School, University of Montana. Always wanted to be actor ; began in school plays and local companies. Became stunt man for Westerns before 20th Century Fox signed him for *Cisco Kid and the Lady* 1946. Served with the U.S. armed forces during World War II. Films include :—1940 : *Stardust, Young People* ; 1941 : *Charter Pilot, Jennie, Cowboy and the Blonde* ; 1942 : *Accent on Love, Last of the Duanes, Riders of the Purple Sage, Cadet Girl* ; 1943 : *Roxie Hart, 10 Gentlemen from West Point, Orchestra Wives* ; 1944 : *China Girl, Coney Island, Bombers' Moon* 1946 : *Three Little Girls in Blue* ; 1947 : *The High Window*.

MONTGOMERY, Robert. Actor, director. Born Beacon, New York, May 21, 1904. Ht. 6 ft. ; wt. 160 lb. Brown hair, blue eyes. Educ. Pawling School for Boys. At 16 was an engine-wiper in a railway machine shop, then became deckhand in oil tanker. Became interested in theatre, played small part in "Mask and the Face", joined repertory company in Rochester, New York State, and appeared in seventy plays in eighteen months. Broadway plays include : "Dawn", "Arleen O'Dare", "One of the Family", "Possession". First film : *So This Is College* (MGM) 1929. Other films include : *Untamed, Three Live Ghosts, Their Own Desire, War Nurse, Our Blushing Brides, The Divorcee, Free and Easy, The Big House, Love in the Rough, The Richest Man in the World, The Easiest Way, Inspiration, Strangers May Kiss, Shipmates, The Man in Possession, Private Lives, Lovers Courageous, But the Flesh is Weak, Letty Lynton, Blondie of the Follies, Faithless, Hell Below, The Man I Made, When Ladies Meet, Night Flight, Another Language, Fugitive Lovers, Riptide, Mystery of Mr "X", Hideout, Forsaking All Others, Vanessa, No More Ladies, Biography of a Bachelor Girl, Petticoat Fever, Suicide Club, Piccadilly Jim, The Last of Mrs. Cheyney, Ever Since Eve, Night Must Fall, Live Love and Learn, The First Hundred Years, Yellow Jack, Three Loves has Nancy, Fast and Loose, The Earl of Chicago*. 1940 : *Busman's Honeymoon* (MGM-Brit), *Mr. and Mrs. Smith* (RKO) ; 1941 : *Rage in Heaven* (MGM), *Here Comes Mr. Jordan* (Col), *Unfinished Business* (Univ). War service with the U.S. Navy 1941-4. 1945 : *They Were Expendable* (MGM) ; 1946 : *Lady in the Lake* (MGM ; also directed) ; 1947 : *Upward to the Stars* (MGM ; also directed), *Ride the Pink Horse* (UI ; also directed).

MOORE, Kieron. Real name Kieron O'Hanrahan. Born Skibbereen, Co. Cork, Oct. 5, 1925. Ht. 6 ft. 1 in. ; wt. 160 lb. Dark brown hair, brown eyes. Educ. St. Mary's College, Dublin. Was training for a medical career but became interested in the theatre. Formed a Gaelic theatre from Dublin schools, put on and acted in two plays at the little Peacock Theatre in Dublin. Won male lead in a Gaelic play at the Abbey Theatre, where he spent two years. At 19 came to London and appeared in "Desert Rats" (which made an overnight success) and "Roses for Me". Film debut in *The Voice Within* (Grand Nat) 1944. In 1946 London Films signed him up for seven years without even a screen test. 1947 : *A Man About the House* (LFP), *Mine Own Executioner* (Kimmins) ; 1948 : *Anna Karenina* (LFP).

MOORE, Tom. Born County Meath, Eire, 1885. Some stage experience before going to Hollywood. Began screen career in 1922 with Kalem Company. One of earliest films was *The Cowboy and the Lady* (Para) 1922. Among his many other films were : *A Kiss for Cinderella, Big Brother, One Night in Rome, Mr. Broadway, Bombay Mail, Reunion.* Then dropped acting and for more than ten years was dramatic coach for 20th Century-Fox. In early 1947 decided to return to screen and was offered more parts than he could take. Films in 1947 include : *Moss Rose* (20th), *Forever Amber* (20th), *Summer Lightning* (20th).

MOORE, Victor. Born Hammonton, New Jersey, Feb. 24, 1876. Educ. Hammonton and Boston public schools. Entered films in 1916, with Jesse Lasky; made 41 one-reel comedies for Klever Company. More recently in one-reel comedies for Warner-Vitaphone. Recent feature films include : *Dangerous Dan McGrew, Gold-diggers of 1937, Meet the Missus, Make Way for Tomorrow ;* 1941 : *Louisiana Purchase* (Para) ; 1943 : *Star Spangled Rhythm, Riding High, True to Life* (Para), *The Heat's On* (Col) ; 1944 : *Carolina Blues* (Col) ; 1945 : *It's In The Bag* (UA), *Duffy's Tavern* (Para). In 1947 made notable hit in *It Happened on Fifth Avenue* (Mono).

MOOREHEAD, Agnes. Born Boston, Massachusetts, Dec. 6. Ht. 5 ft. 6 in. ; wt. 115 lb. Dark red hair, deep blue eyes. Educ. Public Schools, Ohio, and University of Wisconsin. Directed dramatics at Central High School in Soldiers Grove, Wisconsin. Studied at American Academy of Dramatic Art, and later in plays on Broadway. Joined Orson Welles' Mercury Players on radio, and went with them to Hollywood, where she made her film debut in Welles' *Citizen Kane* (RKO), 1941. Other films include— 1942 : *The Magnificent Ambersons* (RKO), *The Big Street* (RKO) ; 1943 : *Journey Into Fear* (RKO), *The Youngest Profession* (MGM), *Government Girl* (RKO) ; 1944 : *The Seventh Cross* (MGM), *Jane Eyre* (20th), *Dragon Seed* (MGM), *Since You Went Away* (UA), *Mrs. Parkington* (MGM), *Tomorrow the World* (UA) ; 1945 : *Keep Your Powder Dry* (MGM), *Our Vines Have Tender Grapes* (MGM), *Her Highness and the Bellboy* (MGM) ; 1947 : *The Dark Passage* (Warn) ; 1948 : *Tisa* (Warn), *The Lost Moment* (Wanger), *Johnny Belinda* (Warn), *Stations West* (RKO).

MORENO, Marguerite. Born Paris, Sept. 15, 1891. Film debut : *Le Chateau de Quatre Obèses.* Her outstanding films include : *La Nuit Blanche, Secrets, Douce, La Collection Ménard, Les Malheurs de Sophie, La vie d'un Autre, Ex-Citoyen d'Honneur, L'Idiot, Un Revenant, Rendez-vous à Paris, L'Ile des Mirages.*

MORGAN, Dennis. Real name Stanley Morner. Born Prentice, Wisconsin, Dec. 20, 1910. Ht. 6 ft. 2 in. ; wt. 195 lb. Brown hair, blue eyes. Educ. Marshfield High School ; Wisconsin University ; Carroll College, Wisconsin. Worked in father's lumber camp in school holidays. Toured Middle West as one of five singers doing potted version of " Faust ". Worked on radio and newspaper in Milwaukee. Appeared in Chicago production of " Carmen " starring Mary Garden, who recommended him to MGM. First film : *Suzy* (MGM), 1936. Other films include : *Fighting 69th, Cheers for the Irish, Flight Angels, Tear Gas Squad, River's End.* 1940 : *Kitty Foyle* (RKO) ; 1941 (all Warn) : *Affectionately Yours, Bad Men of Missouri, Kisses for*

Breakfast ; 1942 (all Warn) : *Captains of the Clouds, In This Our Life, Wings for the Eagle ;* 1943 : *The Hard Way* (Warn) ; 1944 (all Warn) : *Thank Your Lucky Stars, The Desert Song, Shine on Harvest Moon, The Very Thought of You ;* 1945 (all Warn) : *God Is My Co-Pilot, Indiscretion, Christmas in Connecticut ;* 1946 : *One More Tomorrow* (Warn) ; 1947 (all Warn) : *The Time The Place and the Girl, Royal Flush, Cheyenne, My Wild Irish Rose ;* 1948 : *To the Victor* (Warn).

MORGAN, Frank. Real name Frank Wupperman. Born New York, June 1, 1890. Ht. 6 ft. ; wt. 180 lb. Grey hair, brown eyes. Educ. Cornell University. Was first a cowboy, then vaudeville performer. Since his debut in silent films in 1917 has made more than eighty films. First talkie, *Dangerous Nan McGrew* (Para) 1930. Other films include : *Reunion in Vienna, When Ladies Meet, The Affairs of Cellini, Naughty Marietta, The Great Ziegfeld, The Last of Mrs. Cheyney, Saratoga, The Crowd Roars, The Wizard of Oz.* 1940 (all MGM) : *The Shop Around the Corner, The Ghost Comes Home, Broadway Melody of 1940, The Mortal Storm, Hullabaloo, Keeping Company, Boom Town ;* 1941 (all MGM) : *The Wild Man of Borneo, Washington Melodrama, Honky Tonk, The Vanishing Virginian ;* 1942 (all MGM) : *Tortilla Flat, White Cargo, The Human Comedy, A Stranger in Town, Thousands Cheer ;* 1943 : *The White Cliffs of Dover* (MGM), *Casanova Brown* (RKO) ; 1945 : *Yolanda and the Thief* (MGM), *Courage of Lassie* (MGM) ; 1946 : *The Great Morgan* (MGM), *Lady Luck* (RKO), *Mr. Griggs Returns* (MGM), *Summer Holiday* (MGM) ; 1947 : *Green Dolphin Street* (MGM).

MORGAN, Michele. Real name Simone Roussel. Born Paris, Feb. 29, 1920. Ht. 5 ft. 4 in. ; wt. 120 lb. Fair hair, blue eyes. Educ. elementary schools, Paris. Studied drama at École René Simon. Made her film debut while still at drama school, in 1937, opposite Charles Boyer, in *Gribouille.* Other French films include : *L'Orage, Quai des Brumes, Remorque, La Loi du Nord.* American showings of her films brought a flood of Hollywood offers. Left Paris when it fell into German hands in 1940, and travelled via Marseilles and Spain to Lisbon where she caught a ship to U.S.A. First Hollywood film : *Joan of Paris* (RKO) 1942. 1943 : *Higher and Higher* (RKO), *Two Tickets to London* (Univ) ; 1944 : *Passage to Marseilles* (Warn). After making *The Chase* (Seymour Nebenzal-UA) 1946 returned to France and made *Symphonie Pastorale,* prize-winning film at the Cannes Film Festival, 1946. Signed long-term contract with London Film Productions and came to Britain, 1947, to appear in *The Lost Illusion* (Carol Reed).

MORISON, Patricia. Born New York City, March 19, 1919. Ht. 5 ft. 5 in. ; wt. 118 lb. Dark brown hair, blue eyes. Educ. Washington Irving High School, New York. Wanted to become designer, and won scholarship to the Metropolitan Museum of Art. Asked to understudy Margaret Sullavan. On stage in : " Growing Pains ", " The Two Bouquets " ; understudied Helen Hayes in " Victoria Regina ". Talent scout saw her in " The Two Bouquets ", and shortly afterwards she went to Hollywood. First film : *Persons in Hiding* (Para) 1939. Other films include : *I'm From Missouri, The Magnificent Fraud ;* 1940 : *The Untamed* (Para), *Rangers of Fortune* (Para) ; 1941 : *Romance of the Rio Grande* (20th), *The Round-Up* (Para) ; 1941 : *One Night in Lisbon* (Para) ; 1942 : *Beyond the Blue Horizon* (Para), *Night in New Orleans* (Para), *Are Husbands Really Necessary ?* (Para) :

1943 : *Silver Skates* (Mono), *Where are Your Children ?* (Mono), *Hitler's Madmen* (MGM), *The Fallen Sparrow* (RKO), *Calling Dr. Death* (Univ) ; 1945 : *Without Love* (MGM) ; 1946 : *Danger Woman* (Univ) ; 1947 : *Tarzan and the Huntress* (RKO), *Kiss of Death*.

MORLAY, Gaby. Born Angers, France, June 8, 1893. Made first film appearance in 1914 in *La Scandale Rouge*. Her most recent pictures include : *Le Bois Sacré, Service de Nuit, La Cavalcade des Hommes, Farandole, L'Enfant de L'Amour, Paix sur la Terre, Dernier Metro, Un Revenant, Mensonges, Hyménée, Le Village Perdu, Les Amants de Pont St. Jean.*

MORRIS, Chester. Born New York, Feb. 16, 1901. Ht. 5 ft. 9 in. Brown hair, grey-green eyes. Educ. Lincoln School, Mount Vernon, New York. Played truant as child to appear in film for Tannhauser Company in New Rochelle. Toured in vaudeville act with parents for four years. Played in several theatrical companies, making debut in " The Copperhead " with Lionel Barrymore in 1917. On New York stage for about 10 years ; made Broadway sensation as villain in " Crime ". First film : *Alibi* (UA) 1928, one of the first gangster films. Achieved immediate screen success. Early films include : *I Promise to Pay, The Devil's Playground, Big House, Five Came Back, Flight From Glory, Blind Alley.* 1941 : *Meet Boston Blackie* (Col), the first of " Boston Blackie " series in which he has appeared ever since. Also 1941 : *No Hands on The Clock* (Para) ; 1942 : *Canal Zone* (Col), *I Live On Danger* (Para), *Wrecking Crew* (Para) ; 1943 : *Aerial Gunner* (Para), *High Explosive* (Para), *Tornado* (Para), *Thunderbolt* ; 1944 : *Secret Command* (Col), *Derelict Ship, Men of the Deep, Gambler's Choice* (Para), *Double Exposure* (Para) ; 1945 : *One Way to Love* (Col) ; 1946 : *Blind Spot* (Col).

MORRIS, Wayne. Real name Bert de Wayne Morris, Jr. Born Los Angeles, Feb. 17, 1914. Ht. 6 ft. 2 in. ; wt. 190 lb. Educ. Los Angeles High School ; Los Angeles Junior College. Gained thorough knowledge set designing, lighting and play construction during acting career at Pasadena Playhouse, where he was seen by film talent scout and signed on long-term contract. First film : *China Clipper* (Warn) 1936. Served with U.S. Navy 1941-6. Other films include : *Kid Galahad, Love Honour and Behave, Men Are Such Fools, The Kid From Kokomo, Return of Dr. X, Brother Rat and a Baby, An Angel from Texas* ; 1940 : *Double Alibi* (Univ), *The Quarterback* (Para), *Bad Men of Missouri* (Warn), *The Smiling Ghost* (Warn), *Three Sons O'Guns* ; 1947 : *Deep Valley* (Warn), *The Time of Your Life* (Cagney-UA).

MORRISON, Murdo. Born Isle of Lewis, Outer Hebrides. Educ. village school ; Nicholson's Institute ; Edinburgh University. All-round sportsman ; won championship trophy at first post-war Highland Games in Stornoway, 1945. Left his native island to become film actor, but met with little success, except in crowd work. Was seen in repertory by director Michael Powell, who gave him a small role in *I Know Where I'm Going* (Archers) 1945. Also appeared in *The Silver Darlings* (ABPC) 1947.

MORROS, Boris. Producer, music director. Born Russia, Jan. 1, 1895. Educ. University and Imperial Conservatory of St. Petersburg. Musical director and composer with Chauve Souris Company. Director of opera in Russia, France, Italy and Egypt. Went to America to become musical director at Rivoli Theatre, New York. Later became general musical director for Paramount Publix Theatres, producer of stage shows and managing director of Paramount Theatres in New York. In 1939 resigned as musical director to form Boris Morros Productions. In 1943 produced army training films and in 1945 with William le Baron, formed Federal Films. Productions include : *The Flying Deuces, Second Chorus, Tales of Manhattan, Carnegie Hall.*

MOWBRAY, Alan. Born London. Ht. 6 ft. ; wt. 158 lb. Brown hair, grey eyes. Joined provincial touring companies after World War I. Went to America in Shaw's " Apple Cart ". Toured U.S.A. with Theatre Guild and then went to Hollywood. As supporting player has appeared in about 250 films in ten years. Recent films include—1941 : *Lady Hamilton* (Korda-Hollywood), *That Uncertain Feeling* (UA) ; 1942 : *A Yank at Eton* (MGM) ; 1943 : *His Butler's Sister* (Univ), *Holy Matrimony* (20th) ; 1944 : *My Gal Loves Music* (Univ) ; 1945 : *Earl Carroll Vanities* (Rep), *Men in Her Diary* (Univ), *Where do we Go from Here ?* (20th) ; 1946 : *Terror By Night* (Univ), *Phantom of 42nd Street* (Pathé), *Sunbonnet Sue* (Mono), *Tell It to a Star* (Rep) ; 1947 : *Merton of the Movies* (MGM), *Captain from Castile* (20th), *Prince of Thieves* (Col).

MUNI, Paul. Real name Muni Weisenfreund. Born Lemberg, Austria (now Lvov, U.S.S.R.), Sept. 22, 1897. Ht. 5 ft. 10 in. ; wt. 165 lb. Educ. New York, where his family had emigrated when he was very young. Made stage debut at age of 11, when touring with his parents, who were in a theatrical company ; played an old man, as no other actor was available. Afterwards joined the Yiddish Theatre Group, and later played several seasons with the Theatre Guild. Outstanding stage performance was in " Counsellor-at-law ". Film debut in *The Valiant* (Fox) 1928. Other films include : *Seven Faces, Scarface, I Am a Fugitive From a Chain Gang, The World Changes, Hi Nellie !, Bordertown, Black Fury, Dr. Socrates, The Story of Louis Pasteur, The Life of Emile Zola, Juarez, We Are Not Alone.* 1940 : *Hudson's Bay* (20th) ; 1942 : *The Commandos Strike at Dawn* (Col) ; 1945 : *A Song to Remember* (Col), *Counter Attack* (Col) ; 1946 : *Angel on My Shoulder* (UA).

MURPHY, George. Born New Haven, Connecticut, July 4, 1904. Ht. 5 ft. 11½ in. ; wt. 175 lb. Brown hair, blue eyes. Educ. Yale University, where he was noted athlete. Worked in coal-mining in Pennsylvania ; later became mechanic in Ford's works in Detroit. Formed dance act with Juliette Johnson which played first in chop-suey restaurant, then in night-clubs, and became star act in New York, London, Paris. In 1927 starred in New York musicals " Good News ", " Here Comes the Bride ", " Roberta " and others. First film : *Kid Millions* (UA) 1934. Other films include : *After the Dance, Public Menace, Broadway Melody of 1938, Little Miss Broadway, Hold That Girl, The Women Men Marry, Risky Business.* 1940 : *Broadway Melody of 1940* (MGM), *Choose Your Partner* (MGM), *Public Deb. No. 1* (20th), *Little Nelly Kelly* (MGM) : 1941 : *The Navy Steps Out* (RKO), *Tom, Dick and Harry* (RKO), *Cash and Carry* (MGM), *Rise and Shine* (20th) ; 1942 : *The Mayor of 44th Street* (RKO), *For Me and My Gal* (MGM), *The Navy Comes Through* (RKO), *Hello Beautiful* (UA) ; 1943 : *Bataan* (MGM), *This Is the Army* (Warn), *Broadway Rhythm* (MGM) ; 1944 :

Show Business (RKO), Step Lively (RKO); 1945: Having Wonderful Crime (RKO); Up She Goes (MGM); 1947: Tenth Avenue Angel (MGM), The Arnelo Affair (MGM), The Rich Full Life (MGM); 1948: The Big City (MGM).

MURRAY, Stephen. Born Partney, Lincs, Sept. 6, 1912. Ht. 6 ft. Brown hair, blue eyes. Educ. Brentwood. Youthful ambition: to enter Foreign Office. Trained for stage at Royal Academy of Dramatic Art, London; debut, 1933, at Stratford-on-Avon Memorial Theatre in " Much Ado About Nothing ". With Birmingham Repertory Company and Malvern Festivals, 1934-5; then in Old Vic and, 1938-9, at Westminster Theatre, London, where his outstanding performance was in title role of John Drinkwater's " Abraham Lincoln ". Has given many poetry readings for the B.B.C. Served in army 1941-6. First film: The Prime Minister (Warn-Brit) 1941, in which he played Gladstone from twenty to seventy years of age. Other films include: 1942: Next of Kin (Ealing), Undercover (Ealing); 1946: Master of Bankdam (Holbein); 1948: London Belongs To Me (Individ).

NAISH, J. Carrol. Real name Joseph Patrick Carrol Naish. Born New York, Jan. 21, 1900. Ht. 5 ft. 9 in.; wt. 160 lb. Black hair, brown eyes. Educ. St. Cecilia's Academy, New York. Joined the U.S. flying service during World War I. Afterwards tried his hand at every job he came across, and fulfilled ambition to travel all over the world, working his passage wherever he went. Then became actor; appeared in Paris and New York. Performance in " Shanghai Gesture " in Los Angeles brought him film contract. First film The Hatchet Man (Warn) 1932. Other films include: Crack-Up, Think Fast Mr. Moto; 1939: Lives of a Bengal Lancer, Hotel Imperial, Beau Geste; 1940: Typhoon (Para), Down Argentine Way (20th); 1941: Birth of the Blues (Para), That Night in Rio (20th), Blood and Sand (20th), The Corsican Brothers (UA), Forced Landing (Para), Accent on Love (20th), Mr. Dynamite (Univ); 1942: A Gentleman at Heart (20th), The Pied Piper (20th), Dr. Broadway (Para), Tales of Manhattan (20th), The Man in the Trunk (20th), Dr. Renault's Secret (20th); 1943: Sahara (Col), Harrigan's Kid (MGM), Good Morning, Judge (Univ), Behind the Rising Sun (RKO), Gung Ho (Univ), Calling Dr. Death (Univ); 1944: Dragon Seed (MGM), Jungle Woman (Univ), The Monster Maker (PRC), Mark of the Whistler (Col), Two Man Submarine (Col), Voice in the Wind (UA); 1945: Enter Arsène Lupin (Univ), House of Frankenstein (Univ), Getting Gertie's Garter (UA), Strange Confession (UA), A Medal for Benny (Para), The Southerner (UA); 1946: Dr. Renault's Secret (20th), Bad Bascomb (MGM); 1947: Carnival in Costa Rica (20th), Humoresque (Warn), Beast with Five Fingers (Warn), The Kissing Bandit (MGM), The Fugitive (Argosy-RKO).

NATTIER, Nathalie. Real name Nathalie Belaieff. Of Russian origin, was brought up in France. Made her film debut in Seul Dans le Nuit, secured her first important role in L'Etrange Destin, and established herself as a star in L'Idiot. Seen by director Marcel Carné, who gave her leading role (originally intended for Marlene Dietrich) in Les Portes de la Nuit. Also starred in Le Chateau de la Dernière Chance.

NAZZARI, Amedeo. Born Cagliari, Italy, 1909. Films include: Luciano Serra, Pilota, Fedora, La Cena delle Beffe, Bengasi, La Bisbetica Domata;

1944: La Donna della Montagna (Lux); 1945: Un Giorno Nella Vita (Orbis); 1946: Il Bandito (Lux), Il Cavaliere del Sogno, Fatalità (Universalcine); 1947: La Figlia del Capitano (Lux).

NEAGLE, Anna. Real name Marjorie Robertson. Born Forest Gate, London, Oct. 20, 1908. Ht. 5 ft. 5 in.; wt. 110 lb. Fair hair, blue eyes. Educ. St. Alban's High School. Originally intended to become a games mistress, but later studied dancing with Gwladys Dillon and made her stage debut in chorus of Charlot's Revue, 1925. Also appeared in Cochran's cabaret at Trocadero, London, and danced in the chorus of " Rose Marie " and other London shows. Went to New York with the Jack Buchanan production " Wake Up and Dream ". Had done a little crowd work in Elstree studios before she got her first featured role in Should a Doctor Tell? (Brit Lion) 1930. Changed her name to " Anna Neagle " for her next film The Chinese Bungalow. While playing opposite Jack Buchanan in " Stand Up and Sing ! ", was spotted by Herbert Wilcox who starred her, again with Jack Buchanan, in Good Night Vienna ! (B & D) 1932. Other early films: The Flag Lieutenant, The Little Damozel, Bitter Sweet, The Queen's Affair, Nell Gwyn, Peg of Old Drury, Limelight, The Three Maxims, The Street Singer—U.S. title London Melody, Victoria the Great (1937), Sixty Glorious Years (1938). Went to Hollywood in 1939, where she starred in Nurse Edith Cavell (RKO). 1940: No, No, Nanette (RKO); 1941: Sunny (RKO), Irene (RKO); 1942: They Flew Alone (Wilcox-RKO) based on the life of Amy Johnson; 1943: Forever and a Day (RKO), Yellow Canary (Wilcox-RKO); 1945: I Lived in Grosvenor Square (Wilcox-ABPC); 1946: Piccadilly Incident (Wilcox-APBC), which won the " Daily Mail " award as the best film of the year; 1947: The Courtneys of Curzon Street (Wilcox-Brit Lion); 1948: Spring in Park Lane (Wilcox-Brit Lion).

NEAME, Ronald. Director, producer. Son of the late Elwin Neame, photographer, and Ivy Close, star of silent films. Born London, 1911. Educ. University College School, London. Began film career at British International Studios, 1926, as messenger and call boy, then with camera-crew as loader. Was assistant cameraman on first full-length British talkie, Blackmail (B.I.P.) 1929. Worked with the late Claude Friese-Greene for number of years, and became chief cameraman when Friese-Greene was taken ill during Drake of England, 1934. Lighting and photography on about fifty films, including Major Barbara, One of Our Aircraft is Missing, In Which We Serve. In association with David Lean and Anthony Havelock-Allan, formed Cineguild Productions, 1943. For this company photographed This Happy Breed, Blithe Spirit; co-produced Brief Encounter, Great Expectations; directed Take My Life; produced Oliver Twist.

NEBENZAL, Seymour. Producer. Born New York, 1899. Began his film career in Germany, where in 1931 he produced " M ", the film that made a star of the then almost unknown Hungarian actor, Peter Lorre. Other early German productions include: Ariane, Westfront 1918, and The Beggar's Opera. In France produced Mayerling, Betrayal. Returned to America, 1940, where his productions include: We Who Are Young, Prisoner of Japan, Tomorrow We Live, Summer Storm, Whistle Stop, The Chase, Atlantis, Heaven Only Knows.

DAVID NIVEN
(*RKO-Radio*)

NELSON, Barry. Real name Robert Nielson. Born Oakland, California, Apr. 16. Ht. 6 ft. ; wt. 188 lb. Brown hair, blue eyes. Educ. public schools, Oakland ; University of California. Financed his college education by assisting in the production of weekly radio programmes. Directed amateur plays for women's clubs. Appeared as a dozen different characters in pageant " Cavalcade of the Golden West " at San Francisco Exhibition, 1939. While appearing in college production of " Macbeth ", was seen by film talent scout. First film : *Shadow of the Thin Man* (MGM), 1941. Others include—1941 : *The Doctor and The Debutante* (MGM), *Johnny Eager* (MGM) ; 1942 : *China Caravan* (MGM), *Once Upon a Thursday* (MGM), *Rio Rita* (MGM), *Eyes in the Night* (MGM) ; 1943 : *The Human Comedy* (MGM), *Bataan* (MGM), *A Guy Named Joe* (MGM). 1943-6 served in U.S. Army. 1944 : *Winged Victory* (20th) ; 1946 : *The Beginning or The End ?* (MGM), *Undercover Girl.*

NEWLEY, Anthony. Born London Sept. 24, 1931. Educ. Mandeville Secondary School for Boys, Clapton, London. During flying-bomb period in World War II, was evacuated to Morecambe, Lancashire. Left School at 14 and became office boy with London insurance firm, and later, joined advertising department of a London newspaper, Was accepted for dramatic training by Italia Conti School, paying his way by acting as office boy for the school. Made professional debut with Colchester Repertory as Gwyn in " The Wind of Heaven ". First appeared on screen in Children's Entertainment Films *Dusty Bates* and *The Little Ballerina.* In 1947 was chosen for leading role of Dick Bultitude with Roger Livesey in *Vice Versa* (Two Cities), film version of celebrated Anstey fantasy novel in which father and son change bodies.

NEWTON, Robert. Born Shaftesbury, Dorset, June 1, 1905. Began theatrical career at age of 14 on stage staff of Birmingham Repertory Theatre, and later acted in numerous productions there. Toured in South Africa with " Bulldog Drummond " and made his London stage debut in " The Perfect Fit ", 1924. Has also appeared with Nancy Price's " People's National Theatre ", and on the American stage. Spent a year working on a cattle ranch in Canada ; served with the Royal Navy in World War II. Film debut in *Fire Over England* (LEF), 1937. Other films include : *Farewell Again, Dark Journey, Vessel of Wrath—* U.S. title *The Beachcomber, Jamaica Inn, Dead Men are Dangerous, Yellow Sands, Hell's Cargo* ; 1940 : *Major Barbara* (Pascal), *Hatter's Castle* (Para-Brit) ; 1942 : *They Flew Alone* (Wilcox-RKO) ; 1944 : *This Happy Breed* (Cineguild) ; 1945 : *Henry V* (Two Cities) ; 1946 : *Night Boat to Dublin* (ABPC) ; 1947 : *Odd Man Out* (Two Cities), *Temptation Harbour* (ABPC) ; 1948 : *Snowbound* (Gains), *Oliver Twist* (Cineguild).

NEY, Richard. Born New York, Nov. 12. Ht. 6 ft. 3 in. ; wt. 170 lb. Brown hair, blue eyes. Educ. Lakesville High School, Connecticut ; Columbia University (B.A.). Went on tour with " Life With Father " and was offered first screen role during Los Angeles run of the play. First film : *Mrs. Miniver* (MGM), 1942. Also in 1942 made *The War Against Mrs. Hadley* (MGM), before service in U.S. Navy 1942-6. 1946 : *The Late George Apley* (20th) ; 1947 : *Ivy* (UI) ; 1948 : *Joan* (Wanger).

NINCHI, Carlo. Born Bologna, Italy, 1899. Has had a long career in the theatre. Films include :

Il Solitario della Montagna, Marco Visconti, Il Leone di Damasco, Catene Invisibili, Giarabub, La Morte Civile, I Due Foscari. 1944 : *La Signora in Nero, La Vispa Teresa* (Excelsa) *La Porta del Cielo* (Arbis) ; 1945 : *O Sole Mio* (Rinascimento), *Verso la Luce* (Pax), *Le Vie del Peccato, Adultera, Il Canto della Vita* (Excelsa), *Desiderio* (Fincine), *Due Lettere Anonime* (Lux) ; 1946 : *La Primula Bianca* (Lux), *Gli Amanti in Fuga* (Manenti), *Il Carriere di Ferro* (Vic).

NIVEN, David. Born Kirriemuir, Scotland, Mar. 1, 1910. Ht. 6 ft. 1 in. ; wt. 175 lb. Brown hair, blue eyes. Educ. Stowe School. Having failed to pass his entrance examination for Navy at Dartmouth College joined Army instead ; was gazetted 1928 and served in Malta for two years. Returning to Britain he found peacetime soldiering dull, so resigned his commission and worked in Canada on a newspaper, and then on bridge construction. Was also waiter, barman, lumberjack. Later became plantation manager in Cuba. Went to Peru and found a revolution in progress—so joined in the fighting. Then worked in Hollywood as film extra. Eventually signed up by Goldwyn, but given only small parts, until *Dodsworth* (UA) 1937. Left Hollywood in 1939 to rejoin army ; for a time was on General Eisenhower's staff. Released to appear in *The First of the Few*, with the late Leslie Howard, and in *The Way Ahead*, originally planned by the War Office as a counterpart to the naval film *In Which We Serve.* Two films in which he starred —*A Matter of Life and Death* and *The Bishop's Wife*— were chosen for Royal Command Performances, in 1946 and 1947 respectively. Films include : *Without Regret, Rose Marie, Palm Springs, Thank You Jeeves, Dodsworth, Beloved Enemy, Charge of the Light Brigade, We Have Our Moments, Prisoner of Zenda, Dinner at the Ritz* (20th) made in Britain, *Four Men and a Prayer, Three Blind Mice, Dawn Patrol, Bluebeard's Eighth Wife, Wuthering Heights, The Real Glory, Raffles, Bachelor Mother, Eternally Yours.* 1942 : *The First of the Few—* U.S. title *Spitfire* (Leslie Howard), *The Way Ahead* (Two Cities) ; 1946 : *A Matter of Life and Death—* U.S. title *Stairway to Heaven* (Archers) *The Perfect Marriage* (Para) ; 1947 : *Magnificent Doll* (UI), *The Bishop's Wife* (Goldwyn). 1948, in Britain : *Bonnie Prince Charlie* (LFP).

NOLAN, Lloyd. Born San Francisco. Ht. 5 ft. 10½ in. ; wt. 175 lb. Brown hair, brown eyes. Educ. Santa Clara Preparatory School ; Stanford University. Before realizing his ambition to be actor, worked his way round world in tramp steamer. In 1927 joined Pasadena Community Theatre. Went on tour with " The Front Page " ; appeared with Edward Everett Horton in " The Queen's Husband ". Appeared on New York stage in " One Sunday Afternoon ", in which he was seen by a talent scout. First film *Stolen Harmony* (Para) 1935. Other films include : 1935 : *G Men, King of Gamblers, Ebb Tide, Wells Fargo, King of Alcatraz, St. Louis Blues* ; 1940 : *House Across the Bay* (Wanger) ; *Gangs of Chicago* (Republic) ; *Behind the News* (Republic), *The Golden Fleecing* (MGM), *Johnny Apollo* (20th), *Pier 13* (20th), *The Man I Married* (20th), *Charter Pilot* (20th), *Michael Shayne, Private Detective* (20th) ; 1941 : *Mr. Dynamite* (Univ), *Sleepers West* (20th), *Buy Me That Town* (Para), *Dressed to Kill* (20th), *Blues in the Night* (Warn), *Steel Against the Sky* (Warn), *Blue, White and Perfect* (20th); 1942 : *The Man Who Wouldn't Die* (20th), *Manila Calling* (20th) ; 1943 : *Time to Kill* (20th), *Guadalcanal Diary* (20th), *Bataan* (MGM) ; 1944 : *A Tree Grows in*

Brooklyn (20th) ; 1945 : *Circumstantial Evidence* (20th), *The House on 92nd Street* (20th), *Two Smart People* (MGM) ; 1946 : *Somewhere in the Night* (20th), *Two Smart People* (MGM), *Lady in the Lake* (MGM).

NORDEN, Christine. Real name Mary Lydia Thornton. Born Sunderland, Dec. 25, 1924. Ht. 5 ft. 6 in. ; wt. 126 lb. Ash-blonde hair, green eyes. Educ. Sunderland. Wanted to become a reporter, but changed her mind after appearing in several charity shows at the age of 10. As juvenile entertainer for three years to troops in Northern Command gave nearly 600 shows. Featured in radio programme for two years, after which she joined ENSA and was leading lady on tour with revue " Tell The World ". Spotted in a cinema queue by a Hollywood cameraman, then serving with the U.S. Army, who persuaded her to let him take some photographs of her which he sent to Sir Alexander Korda. As a result she was given a test, and put under contract. Made her screen debut in *Night Beat* (LFP) 1947. Also in 1947 : *An Ideal Husband* (LFP), *Mine Own Executioner* (Kimmins) ; 1948 : *Idol of Paris* (Premier), *Bonnie Prince Charlie* (LFP).

NORIS, Assia. Born St. Petersburg (now Leningrad) 1914. Films include : *Batticuore, Grandi Magazzini, Dora Nelson, Una Romantica Avventura*. 1943 : *Un Colpo di Pistola* (Lux), *Margherita Fra i Tre ;* 1944 : *Una Storia d'Amore* (Lux) ; 1945 : *Che Distinta Famiglia* (Enic).

NORTH, " Mike ". Real name Ted North, Jr. Born Topeka, Kansas, Oct. 3, 1918. Ht. 6 ft. 2 in ; wt. 180 lb. Light brown hair, blue eyes. Educ. Highland Park Grammar School, Topeka ; University of Kansas. Toured from early childhood and with parents in stage troupe appeared as " Little Willie " in " East Lynne " at 3. Spent a year at law school, but abandoned his studies to join father's touring company. Appeared in small parts in a number of films from 1940. Served in U.S. Navy, 1943-6. Afterwards, on chance visit to studio, was put on short list for the leading role in *The Unsuspected* and eventually was chosen ; changed his name to " Mike " at the behest of Michael Curtiz, director of the film. First film : *Yesterday's Heroes* (20th) 1940. Other films include :—1940 : *Chad Hanna* (20th) ; 1941 : *The Bride Wore Crutches* (20th), *For Beauty's Sake* (20th), *Charlie Chan in Rio* (20th) ; 1942 : *Roxie Hart* (20th), *To the Shores of Tripoli* (20th), *Syncopation* (RKO), *Manila Calling* (20th), *Girl Trouble* (20th), *Thunder Birds* (20th); 1947 : *The Unsuspected* (Warn).

NUGENT, Elliott. Actor, writer, director. Born Dover, Ohio, Sept. 20, 1900. Educ. Dover High School ; Ohio State University. Member of well-known theatrical family, he began acting at an early age, and collaborated with his father in writing many plays. Has had many Broadway successes, including two years' lead in " The Voice of the Turtle " from 1943. Made his screen debut as an actor in *So This Is College* (MGM) 1929, followed by *Wise Girls, Not So Dumb* and *The Richest Man in the World*. Began directing in 1932, when he co-directed *The Mouthpiece* (Warn) and *Life Begins*. Directed : *Whistling In the Dark, Three-Cornered Moon, If I were Free, Two Alone, Strictly Dynamite, She Loves Me Not, Love in Bloom, College Scandal, Enter Madame, Splendor, Wives Never Know, And So They Were Married, It's All Yours, Professor Beware, Give Me a Sailor, The Cat and*

the Canary, The Male Animal (also collaborated on screenplay), *The Crystal Ball, Up in Arms* (the film that launched Danny Kaye), *Welcome Stranger, The Innocent Years, My Favourite Brunette.*

OBERON, Merle. Real name Estelle O'Brien Merle Thompson. Born Feb. 19, 1911. Ht. 5 ft. 4 in. ; wt. 112 lb. Brown hair, brown eyes. Educ. Martinere College, Calcutta. Joined Calcutta Amateur Theatrical Society at 16. Came to Britain 1928, sold her return ticket to pay her way until she got a job as dance hostess. For some months worked as an extra at Elstree, where she was seen by Alexander Korda, who later signed her up as one of his early film starlets. After appearing in *Service for Ladies, Wedding Rehearsal* and *Men of To-Morrow*, she played the two-minute role as Anne Boleyn in *The Private Lives of Henry VIII*, which established her as a star. Other British films include : *The Private Life of Don Juan, The Battle, The Scarlet Pimpernel*. Went to Hollywood in 1935, where she apppeared in *Folies Bergères, The Dark Angel, These Three* and *Beloved Enemy*. Returning to Britain appeared in *The Divorce of Lady " X ", Over the Moon*. In Hollywood again, made *The Cowboy and The Lady* and *Wuthering Heights*. Appeared in first British propaganda film : *The Lion Has Wings* (LFP) 1939. 1940 : *Till We Meet Again* (Warn) ; 1941 : *Affectionately Yours* (Warn) ; 1943 : *Forever and A Day* (RKO) ; 1944 : *The Lodger* (20th) ; *Dark Waters* (UA) ; 1945 : *Hangover Square* (20th), *A Song to Remember* (Col) ; 1946 : *A Night in Paradise* (Univ), *This Love of Ours* (Univ), *Berlin Express ;* 1947 : *Temptation* (UI) ; 1948 : *Night Song* (RKO).

O'BRIEN, Margaret. Real name Angela O'Brien. Born Los Angeles, California, Jan. 15, 1937. Ht. 3 ft. 8 in. ; wt. 41 lb. Brown hair, hazel eyes. Daughter of stage dancer Gladys Flores. Has acted and recited on radio. Paints, collects toy animals, has cocker spaniel and puppy of Lassie. First film : a U.S. Government short with James Cagney. Became famous with *Babes on Broadway* (MGM) 1941. Other films (all MGM) include : 1942 :—*Journey for Margaret ;* 1943 : *Crazy to Kill, Madame Curie, Jane Eyre* (20th), *Lost Angel, Thousands Cheer ;* 1944 : *The Canterville Ghost, Meet Me in St. Louis, Music for Millions ;* 1945 : *Our Vines Have Tender Grapes, Bad Bascomb ;* 1946 : *Three Wise Fools, Tenth Avenue Angel ;* 1947 : *The Unfinished Dance ;* 1948 : *The Big City.*

O'BRIEN, Pat. Born Milwaukee, Wisconsin, Nov. 11, 1899. Ht. 5 ft. 11 in. ; wt. 175 lb. Brown hair, blue eyes. Educ. Marquette University. Served in U.S. Navy in World War I, then resumed law studies at university. Became song-and-dance man in " Adrienne ", toured in " Way Down East " and " Broadway " ; On New York stage : " A Man's Man " " Coquette ", " The Front Page ". Repeated stage role of Hildy Johnson in film. First film : *The Front Page* (UA) 1932. Other films include : *Flying High, Final Edition, Strange Case of Clara Deane, Air Mail, Destination Unknown, Bureau of Missing Persons, College Coach, Bombshell, Oil for the Lamps of China, Page Miss Glory, Public Enemy's Wife, The Great O'Malley, San Quentin, Boy Meets Girl, Cowboy From Brooklyn, Indianapolis Speedway, Night of Nights.* 1940 : *The Fighting 69th* (Warn), *Till We Meet Again* (Warn), *Torrid Zone* (Warn) ; 1942 : *Two Yanks in Trinidad* (Col), *Broadway* (Univ), *Flight Lieutenant* (Col), *The Navy Comes Through* (RKO) ; 1943 : *Bombardier* (RKO), *The Iron Major* (RKO), *His Butler's*

Sister (Univ) ; 1944 : *Marine Raiders* (RKO), *Secret Command* (Col) ; 1945 : *Having Wonderful Crime* (RKO) ; 1946 : *Crack-Up* (RKO) : 1946 : *The Amazing Mr. Hammer* (RKO), *Man Alive* (RKO) ; 1947 : *Fighting Father Dunne* (RKO).

O'BRIEN, Virginia. Born Los Angeles, California, Apr. 18. Ht. 5 ft. 6½ in. ; wt. 117 lb. Dark brown hair, blue eyes. Her debut as poker-faced singer in stage version of " Meet the People", 1939, led to MGM contract and continuance of career as singer-comedienne. First film : *Hullaballoo* (MGM) 1940. Other films (all MGM) include : *Sky Murder ;* 1941 : *The Big Store, Lady Be Good, Cash and Carry ;* 1942 : *Ship Ahoy, Panama Hattie ;* 1943 : *Du Barry Was a Lady, Thousands Cheer, Meet the People ;* 1944 : *Two Girls and a Sailor, Ziegfeld Follies ;* 1945 : *The Harvey Girls, The Great Morgan ;* 1946 : *The Show-Off, Till the Clouds Roll By ;* 1947 : *Merton of the Movies.*

O'BRYEN, W. J. Born London, 1898. Educ. Ladycross School, Seaford ; The Oratory School, Edgbaston. Joined film and drama department of Curtis Brown Ltd., agents, after World War I, and later became casting director at Gainsborough (Islington) Studios. Film agent, 1930, first on his own, then afterwards with Linnit and Dunfee, artists' agents, specializing in finding stars. Served in army throughout World War II ; joined London Film Productions as talent scout 1945. Post-war film discoveries include Kieron Moore, Margaret Leighton and Eileen Herlie.

O'CONNOR, Donald. Born Chicago, Aug. 30, 1925. Ht. 5 ft. 8 in. ; wt. 137 lb. Brown hair, blue eyes. Son of " Chuck " Connor, famous circus acrobat. At 13 months was in the family act : played vaudeville for several years all over U.S.A. In 1938 was spotted while appearing in charity act in Hollywood, and signed for role of kid brother to character played by Bing Crosby in first film : *Sing You Sinners* (Para) 1938. Other films include : *Men With Wings, Sons of the Legion, Death of a Champion, Million Dollar Legs, Beau Geste, On Your Toes.* 1940-1, returned to vaudeville. 1942 : (all Univ) : *What's Cookin', Private Buckaroo, Give Out Sisters, When Johnny Comes Marching Home, It Comes Up Love ;* 1943 (all Univ) ; *Mister Big, Top Man ;* 1944 (all Univ) : *This Is The Life, Chip Off The Old Block, Follow The Boys, The Merry Monahans, Bowery to Broadway.* Served in U.S. Army Air Force 1944-5. 1945 : *Patrick the Great* (Univ) ; 1947 : *Something in the Wind* (UI) ; 1948 : *Are You With It ?* (UI).

O'CONNOR, Una. Born Belfast, Oct. 23, 1893. Ht. 5 ft. 3 in. ; wt. 104 lb. Dark brown hair, blue-grey eyes. Joined Abbey Theatre Players, Dublin, at 16 ; appeared Court Theatre, London, in " The Magic Glass " ; on New York stage in " The Fake", " Autumn Fire". Returned to London to appear in Noel Coward's " Cavalcade " 1931 ; repeated her role in first U.S. film, *Cavalcade* (Fox) 1933. Had previously in Britain made her film debut in *Dark Red Roses* (Stoll), 1929, and also appeared in *Murder.* Other U.S. films include : *Pleasure Cruise, The Invisible Man, The Poor Rich, The Barretts of Wimpole Street, David Copperfield, The Informer, Rose Marie, Little Lord Fauntleroy, Lloyd's of London, The Plough and The Stars, Call It A Day, Personal Property, Adventures of Robin Hood, We Are Not Alone.* 1940 : *The Sea Hawk* (Warn) *Lillian Russell* (20th), *He Stayed For*

Breakfast (Col) ; 1941 : *Strawberry Blonde* (Warn) ; 1942 : *Always In My Heart* (Warn), *My Favourite Spy* (RKO), *Random Harvest* (MGM) ; 1943 : *This Land is Mine* (RKO), *Forever and A Day* (RKO), *Holy Matrimony* (20th), *Government Girl* (RKO) ; 1944 : *My Pal Wolf* (RKO), *Return of Monte Cristo ;* 1945 : *Whispering Walls, Bells of St. Mary's* (RKO) ; 1946 : *Child of Divorce* (RKO), *Banjo* (RKO), *Cluny Brown* (20th), *Of Human Bondage* (Warn), *Unexpected Guest* (UA).

O'DONNELL, Cathy. Real name Ann Steely. Born Siluria, Alabama. Ht. 5 ft. 4 in. ; wt. 110 lb. Dark hair, brown eyes. Educ. Oklahoma City University. After taking business course was employed at Army Induction Centre, Oklahoma City, for six months before being sacked for taking afternoon off to write poetry. In 1942 returned to Oklahoma City University for a dramatic course, and was allowed to carry on as free student. After brief appearance on the stage decided to try films, so took another office job for six months in order to earn money enough to go to Hollywood. Spotted there two weeks after her arrival by talent scout. Sent by Samuel Goldwyn to New York to study at American Academy of Dramatic Arts, and completed training by touring for a time in " Life With Father " before returning to Hollywood. Made film debut in *The Best Years of Our Lives* (Goldwyn) 1947. Other films include : 1947 : *Bury Me Dead* (Eagle Lion-Hollywood) ; 1948 : *Your Red Wagon* (RKO).

O'DRISCOLL, Martha. Born Tulsa, Oklahoma, March 4, 1922. Ht. 5 ft. 4½ in. ; wt. 118 lb. Blonde hair, hazel eyes. Educ. Creighton Grade School, Phoenix, Arizona. At 5 performed ballet and tap dancing at local amateur shows, then in child roles at Phoenix Little Theatre. Seen in school dancing programme by Hermes Pan, dance director. First film : *Collegiate* (Para) 1935. Other films include : *Champagne Waltz, She's Dangerous, Love Is Young, Mad About Music, Secret of Dr. Kildare, Judge Hardy and Son.* 1940 : *40 Little Mothers* (MGM), *Laddie* (RKO) ; 1941 : *The Lady Eve* (Para), *Henry Aldrich for President* (Para), *Pacific Blackout* (Para), *Her First Beau* (Col) ; 1942 : *Reap The Wild Wind* (Para), *My Heart Belongs to Daddy* (Para), *Youth on Parade* (Rep) ; 1943 : *Young and Willing* (UA), *Weekend Pass* (RKO), *The Fallen Sparrow* (RKO), *Crazy House* (Univ), *The Ghost Catchers* (Univ) ; 1944 : *Hi, Beautiful !* (Univ) ; 1945 : *Under Western Skies* (Univ), *Here Come the Co-Eds* (Univ), *Her Lucky Night* (Univ), *The Daltons Ride Again* (Univ), *Shady Lady* (Univ) ; 1946 : *House of Dracula* (Univ), *Blonde Alibi* (RKO), *Criminal Court* (RKO) ; 1947 : *Carnegie Hall* (Federal-UA).

O'HARA, Maureen. Real name Maureen Fitz-simmons. Born Dublin, Aug. 17, 1920. Ht. 5 ft. 7 in. ; wt. 127 lb. Auburn hair, hazel eyes. Trained at the Abbey Theatre School ; between 14 and 17 won every acting award. First film : *Jamaica Inn* (Mayflower Pictures) 1939. Went to Hollywood in same year. Films include : *The Hunchback of Notre Dame ;* 1940 : *A Bill of Divorcement* (RKO), *Dance, Girls, Dance* (RKO) ; 1941 : *They Met in Argentina* (RKO), *How Green Was My Valley* (20th) ; 1942 : *To The Shores of Tripoli* (20th), *The Gentleman from West Point* (20th), *The Black Swan* (20th) ; 1943 : *This Land is Mine* (RKO), *Immortal Sergeant* (20th), *The Fallen Sparrow* (RKO) ; 1944 : *Buffalo Bill* (20th), *And Now Tomorrow* (Para) ; 1945 : *The Spanish Main* (RKO) ;

1946 : *Do You Love Me ?* (20th), *Sentimental Journey* (20th) ; 1947 : *Sinbad The Sailor* (RKO), *Out of All Time* (RKO), *The Homestretch* (20th), *The Big Heart* (20th), *The Foxes of Harrow* (20th).

O'KEEFE, Denis. Real name Denis Flanagan. Born Fort Madison, Iowa. On the stage in " Once in a Lifetime ", " The Broken Wing ", " Bad Girl ", and other plays. Played small screen roles, then leading man in : *Bad Man of Brimstone* (MGM) 1938. Films include : *Hold That Kiss, The Kid From Texas, Unexpected Father, That's Right You're Wrong.* 1940 : *Alias The Deacon* (Univ), *La Conga Nights* (Univ), *I'm Nobody's Sweetheart Now* (Univ), *Pop Always Pays* (RKO), *You'll Find Out* (RKO), *The Girl From Havana* (Rep), *Arise My Love* (Para) ; 1941 : *Bowery Boy* (Rep), *Mr. District Attorney* (Rep), *Topper Returns* (UA-Roach), *Broadway Ltd.* (UA-Roach), *Lady Scarface* (RKO), *Week-end for Three* (RKO) ; 1942 : *Affairs of Jimmy Valentine* (Rep), *Moonlight Masquerade* (Rep) ; 1943 : *Good Morning Judge* (Univ), *Hangmen Also Die* (UA), *Tahiti Honey* (Rep), *The Leopard Man* (RKO), *Hi Diddle Diddle* (UA) ; 1944 : *The Fighting Seabees* (Rep), *Up in Mabel's Room* (UA), *Abroad with Two Yanks* (UA), *Story of Dr. Wassell* (Para), *Sensations of 1945* (UA) ; 1945 : *The Affairs of Susan* (Para), *Brewster's Millions* (UA), *Earl Carroll Vanities* (Rep) ; 1946 : *Come Back to Me* (20th), *Her Adventurous Night* (Univ) ; 1947 : *Dishonoured Lady* (Hunt Stromberg-UA) ; 1948 : *Atlantis* (Seymour Nebenzal-UA).

OLIVIER, Sir Laurence. Born Dorking, Surrey, May 22, 1907. Ht. 5 ft. 10 in. Brown hair, brown eyes. Educ. St. Edward's School, Oxford. Studied drama with Elsie Fogerty. First stage appearance as Katherine, in " The Taming of the Shrew " in performance by boys at Shakespeare Festival Theatre, Stratford-on-Avon, 1922. Spent several years in repertory, notably at Birmingham, and appeared in several West End productions before making his first big success as Stanhope in " Journey's End ", in 1928. Made film debut in *Too Many Crooks* (King) 1930. Went to Germany to appear in *The Temporary Widow* at the UFA Studios. Later went to Hollywood, where he appeared in *The Yellow Ticket, Westward Passage, Friends and Lovers.* Was leading man to Gloria Swanson in her only British film, *Perfect Understanding* 1932. While with Old Vic, 1937-8, went to Elsinore to play " Hamlet " at Kronberg Castle, Denmark, with Vivien Leigh as Ophelia. War service with Fleet Air Arm. With Ralph Richardson, under the auspices of C.E.M.A. re-established the Old Vic Company at New Theatre, London, after they had been bombed out of their famous theatre on the Southwark side of the Thames. Knighted July 1947. Other films include—in Britain : *No Funny Business, As You Like It, Moscow Nights, Divorce of Lady " X ", Fire Over England, First and Last, " Q " Planes.* Went to Hollywood, 1939. Appeared in *Wuthering Heights* (UA) ; 1940 : *Rebecca* (Selznick) ; 1941 : *Pride and Prejudice* (MGM), *Lady Hamilton* (Korda-Hollywood) ; 1942 : *49th Parallel* (Ortus) ; 1943 : *Demi-Paradise* (Two Cities) ; 1945 : *Henry V* (Two Cities) also produced and co-directed ; 1947 : *Hamlet* (Two Cities) ; also directed and co-produced.

OSBORN, Andrew. Born London, Apr. 9, 1912. Educ. Christ's Hospital, Horsham. Began stage career with Newcastle Repertory Company. Took over Richmond Theatre, Surrey, for four years as actor, manager and producer. Appeared on West End stage, 1939, in " Without the Prince ". War service with Army, 1940-46. Then resumed acting career and also played in television. First film : *Who Goes Next ?* (Fox-Brit) 1939. Shortly after demobilization was put under contract by Maurice Ostrer ; appeared in *Idol of Paris* (Premier) 1947.

OSCAR, Henry. Born Hornsey, London, July 14, 1891. Ht. 5 ft. 9 in. Brown hair, blue eyes. Educ. Enfield Grammar School. Began as insurance clerk. Made his first stage appearance at Stratford-on-Avon Memorial Theatre, with Benson Company, as Snug in " A Midsummer Night's Dream ". Film debut, *After Dark* (Fox-Brit) 1932. Was ENSA producer at Drury Lane Theatre, London, during World War II ; returned to films in 1946. Films include : *I Was a Spy, The Terror, Love in Exile, Seven Sinners, The Case of Gabriel Perry, The Man Who Knew Too Much, The Tunnel, Me and Marlborough, Fire Over England, Dark Journey, The Return of the Scarlet Pimpernel, Black Limelight, The Four Feathers, The Saint in London, On the Night of the Fire.* 1940 : *Atlantic Ferry* (Warn-Brit), *Mein Kampf—My Crimes* (ABPC) ; 1941 : *Penn of Pennsylvania* (Brit Nat), *Hatter's Castle* (Para-Brit) ; 1942 : *The Day Will Dawn*—U.S. title *The Avengers* (Soskin) ; 1943 : *Squadron Leader " X "* (RKO-Brit) ; 1947 : *They Made Me a Fugitive* (Alliance).

O'SHEA, Michael. Real name Francis Patrick Michael James O'Shea. Born Hartford, Connecticut, Mar. 17, 1906. Began his career playing small parts on the stage, and appearing in vaudeville, and in orchestras. Wrote, produced and acted. Achieved notable success in " The Eve of St. Mark" on New York stage, and later repeated his role for the film. Films include :—1941 : *Mr. District Attorney* (Col) ; 1943 : *Strip-Tease Lady* (UA) ; 1944 : *Eve of St. Mark* (20th), *Something for the Boys* (20th), *Man From 'Frisco* (Rep), *Jack London* (UA) ; 1945 : *Circumstantial Evidence* (20th), *It's a Pleasure* (RKO), *Where Do We Go From Here ?* (20th), *Last of the Redskins* (Col) ; 1947 : *Violence* (Mono).

OSTRER, Isidore. Born 1889. Formerly senior partner of Ostrer Bros., Merchant Bankers, and member of London Stock Exchange. Entered British film industry in 1922 when, in association with brothers Mark and Maurice, he acquired Leon Gaumont's holding in the original Gaumont company. Was largely responsible for building up Gaumont-British Picture Corporation Ltd., of which he was Chairman for ten years. Resigned chairmanship in 1931 and was appointed President for term of eight years. In 1937 was appointed Director and Chairman ; resigned from board 1941. In 1946 formed independent production company, Premier Productions Ltd., of which he is Chairman.

OSTRER, Mark. Born 1894. Originally merchant banker. Entered film business in 1922 in association with his brothers Isidore and Maurice, when they acquired the holding of Leon Gaumont in the original Gaumont company. Took prominent part in formation of Gaumont-British Picture Corporation Ltd., of which he was appointed joint Managing Director in April, 1931. In May, 1931, was appointed joint Managing Director, General Theatre Corporation. Is also associated with Provincial Cinematograph Theatres Ltd., and Associated Provincial Picture Theatres Ltd.

WALTER PIDGEON
(Metro-Goldwyn-Mayer)

OSTRER, Maurice. Executive producer. Born 1896. Entered films when in 1922 Leon Gaumont's holding in the original Gaumont company was acquired by Ostrer brothers. In 1928 appointed Director of Gainsborough Pictures Ltd. Has taken active part in film production since 1935, first at the Gainsborough Studios, Islington and later at Shepherd's Bush Studios, controlling both establishments. Executive Producer for Gainsborough Pictures from 1936 to 1946. Has been responsible for taking many British players to the top rank among stars. In 1946 resigned from the J. Arthur Rank Organisation, and, in association with his brother Isidore, formed Premier Productions Ltd., of which he is Managing Director. First production, 1948 : *Idol of Paris.*

OWEN, Reginald, Born Wheathampstead, Herts, Aug. 5, 1887. Ht. 6 ft. ; wt. 170 lb. Brown hair, blue eyes. Trained at Tree's Academy of Dramatic Art. Won the first Bancroft Gold Medal for Acting 1905. Stage debut, same year in " The Tempest " at His Majesty's Theatre, London. Long stage career before making film debut in 1929 in *The Letter.* Under the pseudonym " John Ramsey " is part-author of the famous children's classic " Where The Rainbow Ends". Has appeared in more than a hundred films, notably *Voltaire, Queen Christina, The House of Rothschild, Of Human Bondage* (1934), *Anna Karenina,* (MGM) 1936, *A Tale of Two Cities, The Great Ziegfeld, Marie Walewska, Kidnapped, The Earl of Chicago.* 1940 (all MGM) : *Florian, Hullaballoo, The Ghost Goes Home,* 1941(all MGM): *Blonde Inspiration, Free and Easy, They Met in Bombay, Lady Be Good, Tarzan's Secret Treasure ;* 1942 (all MGM) : *We Were Dancing, Woman of the Year, I Married an Angel, Pierre of the Plains, Mrs. Miniver, Cairo, Somewhere I'll Find You, Random Harvest, White Cargo, Mademoiselle France, Forever and a Day* (RKO), *Three Hearts for Julia ;* 1943 : (all MGM) : *Assignment in Brittany, Salute to the Marines, Madame Curie, Lassie Come Home ;* 1944 : *The Canterville Ghost* (MGM), *Kitty* (Para), *National Velvet* (MGM) ; 1945 : *The Valley of Decision* (MGM), *Captain Kidd* (UA), *Diary of a Chambermaid* (UA), *She Went to the Races* (MGM), *Monsieur Beaucaire* (Para), *The Sailor Takes a Wife* (MGM) ; 1946 : *Cluny Brown* (20th), *Mrs. Loring's Secret* (Para) ; 1947 : *If Winter Comes* (MGM), *Green Dolphin Street* (MGM).

OWEN, William. Real name William Rowbottom : known as " Bill Rowbottom " in his early films. Born Acton, London, Mar. 14, 1914. Ht. 5 ft. 4 in. ; wt. 136 lb. Brown hair, blue eyes. Educ. Beaumont Park Elementary School ; Acton Central School. As a child appeared with acting group of his Sunday School, and later with the Acton Co-operative Society's amateur dramatic section. Began his career as printer's apprentice, but gave it up to sing with local dance band, in which he also played drums. At 18 studied at drama school, drumming and singing in London night clubs to earn money for his fees. In 1938 was Entertainments Manager at Butlin's Dovercourt Holiday Camp. Has written satirical lyrics and musical numbers for Unity Theatre. War service with Army. Film debut in *The Way to the Stars* (Two Cities) 1945. Other films include : 1946 : *School for Secrets* (Two Cities) ; 1947 : *Dancing With Crime* (Alliance), *When The Bough Breaks* (Gains) ; 1948 : *Daybreak* (Box), *Easy Money* (Gains) *Trouble in the Air* (Black-Highbury).

PAGNOL, Marcel. Author, director, producer. Member, Académie Française ; President, Society of French Dramatists. Began as teacher of English and literature in Marseilles high school. Became poet, then playwright. First play produced was " The Merchants of Glory " (1926). Other plays include : " Jazz ", " Topaze ", " Marius ", " Fanny ". Entered films 1936, as producer of *The Loves of Toni.* Directed, produced and wrote story of *Merlusse.* In 1938 wrote play which became basis of American film *Port of Seven Seas.* Directed *Harvest, Battement de Cœur* (later re-made in Hollywood as *Heartbeat*) *Angèle, La Femme du Boulanger* (also wrote screenplay and produced), *The Well-Digger's Daughter* (also wrote screenplay and produced).

PAIGE, Janis. Real name Donna Mae Jaden. Born Tacoma, Washington, Sept. 16, 1922. Ht. 5 ft. 5 in. ; wt. 125 lb. Red-brown hair, green eyes. Educ. Stadium High School, Tacoma. Youthful ambition : to be actress. Became secretary, then receptionist. Two roles in operettas at school and enthusiasm of her music teacher made her decide on singing career. Studio scout saw her working as singing entertainer in Hollywood. First film : *Hollywood Canteen* (Warn) 1944. Other films (all Warn) : 1946 : *Her Kind of Man, Of Human Bondage ;* 1947 : *The Time, the Place and the Girl, Royal Flush, Love and Learn, Cheyenne;* 1948 : *Winter Meeting, Romance in High " C ".*

PAIGE, Robert. Real name John Arthur Paige. Born Indianapolis, Indiana, Dec. 2, 1910. Ht. 6 ft. 2 in. ; wt. 175 lb. Brown hair, blue eyes. Educ. Manual Arts High School ; West Point Military Academy. Left college for radio work, later becoming jack-of-all-trades. Was insurance salesman before making screen debut in *Cain and Mabel* (Warn) 1936. Other films include : *Smart Blonde, Meet the Girl Friend, You Can't Win, There's Always a Woman, The Lady Objects.* 1940 : *Thoroughbred* (Col), *Emergency Squad* (Para), *Parole Fixer* (Para), *Women Without Names* (Para), *Opened by Mistake* (Para), *Golden Gloves* (Para), *Dancing on a Dime* (Para) ; 1941 : *The Monster and the Girl* (Para), *San Antonio Rose* (Univ), *Melody Lane* (Univ), *Hellzapoppin* (Univ) ; 1942 : *Don't Get Personal* (Univ), *Jail House Blues* (Univ), *What's Cookin' ?* (Univ), *Almost Married* (Univ), *Pardon My Sarong* (Univ), *Get Hep to Love* (Univ) ; 1943 : *Hi Buddy !* (Univ), *How's About It ?* (Univ), *Cowboy in Manhattan* (Univ), *Hi Ya Chum* (Univ), *Frontier Badman* (Univ), *Mister Big* (Univ), *Son of Dracula* (Univ), *Sherlock Holmes in Washington* (Univ), *Fired Wife* (Univ) ; 1944 : *Follow the Boys* (Univ), *Her Primitive Man* (Univ), *Can't Help Singing* (Univ), *You Can't Ration Love* (Para) ; 1945 : *Shady Lady* (Univ) ; 1946 : *Tangier.* (Univ).

PALMER, Lilli. Born Vienna, May 24, 1920. Ht. 5 ft. 4½ in. ; wt. 112 lbs. Tawny-blonde hair, blue eyes. Spent childhood in Kent, began career in Paris as cabaret artiste. On London stage in " Road to Gandahar ", " Tree of Eden ", " No Time for Comedy" and other plays. First British film : *Crime Unlimited* (Warn-Brit) 1934. Other films include : *First Offence, Secret Agent, The Great Barrier*—U.S. title *Silent Barrier, Sunset in Vienna, Command Performance, The Man With 100 Faces ;* 1940 : *A Girl Must Live, Door With Seven Locks* (Argyle) ; 1942 : *Thunder Rock* (Charter) ; 1943 : *The Gentle Sex* (Concanen-Two

MARGARET LOCKWOOD
(*Gainsborough*)

DENNIS PRICE
(*Two Cities*)

Cities) ; 1944 : *English Without Tears* (Two Cities) ; 1946 : *The Rake's Progress* (Two Cities), *Beware of Pity* (Two Cities). Went to Hollywood, 1946, where her first film was *Cloak and Dagger* (Warn) 1947 ; 1948 : *Tisa* (Warn), *Body and Soul* (Enterprise-MGM).

PARELY, Mila. Born Paris, 1918. Fair hair, amber eyes. Educ. Paris, U.S.A. Had stage ambitions at 11 : favourite game was to blacken her face with soot and imitate Josephine Baker. Appeared in two French films, *Liliom* and *Cartouches*, before going to U.S.A. in 1933 to complete education. Studied for stage at Paramount Dramatic School and appeared in Broadway revue " Calling All Stars " and in musical " The Red Cat " before returning to Paris in 1935. Resumed screen work with *Valse Royale, Pattes de Mouches, Les Jumeaux de Brighton, Mister Flow* ; in 1939-40, *There Were Twelve Women*. After liberation of Paris, made *Le Cavalier Noir* with Georges Guétary and appeared on French stage. Recent French films : *Rêve d'Amour, Dernier Refuge*. Came to Britain to play role of Italian girl in *Snowbound* (Gains) 1948.

PARKER, Cecil. Born Hastings, Sept. 3, 1897. Ht. 6 ft. Dark brown hair, grey eyes. Educ. Hawkhurst, Kent, and at Jesuit College, Bruges, Belgium. Severe wounds in World War I upset plans to become surgeon. Joined an amateur dramatic society, then offered a job with Charles Doran's touring company, with whom he made his professional debut in " The Merchant of Venice " in 1922. First West End appearance in " The Constant Nymph " with Noel Coward and Edna Best at the New Theatre, 1926. Made first film with Tom Walls, in Aldwych farce, *Cuckoo in the Nest* (GB), 1932. Gave outstanding performance as Britannus, in *Caesar and Cleopatra*, and has been in constant demand in British studios since. Early films include : *Her Last Affaire, Dishonour Bright, Dark Journey, Men of Yesterday, The Man Who Changed His Mind, Storm in a Teacup, The Housemaster, The Lady Vanishes, Old Iron, The Citadel* ; 1946 : *Caesar and Cleopatra* (Pascal), *The Magic Bow* (Gains) ; 1947 : *Hungry Hill* (Two Cities), *Captain Boycott* (Individ), *Woman in the Hall* (Wessex); 1948 : *The First Gentleman* (Col-Brit).

PARKER, Clifton. Composer. Born London, 1905. Turned to film work at the outbreak of war after career as orchestral player, composer and orchestrator. His first score was for *It Started at Midnight*, followed by *The Yellow Canary, Western Approaches, Acacia Avenue, Johnny Frenchman, Perfect Strangers, Children on Trial, The Man Within, The Silver Darlings, When the Bough Breaks*.

PARKER, Eleanor. Born Cedarville, Ohio, June 26, 1922. Ht. 5 ft. 6½ in. ; wt. 118 lb. Educ. High School, Cleveland. Began acting in High School plays, community theatre, and repertory ; finally at Pasadena Community Theatre, where she was seen by studio talent scout. First film was a propaganda short for Warner Bros. and she was then put under contract. Films (all Warn) include :—1941 : *They Died With Their Boots On* ; 1942 : *Buses Roar* ; 1943 : *Mission to Moscow* ; 1944 : *Between Two Worlds, The Very Thought of You, Crime By Night, The Last Ride* ; 1945 : *Forever in Love* ; 1946 : *Of Human Bondage, Never Say Goodbye, Escape Me Never* ; 1947 : *The Woman in White* ; 1948 : *The Voice of the Turtle*.

PARKER, Willard. Real name Worster Van Eps. Born New York, Feb. 5, 1912. Ht. 6 ft. 4 in. ; wt. 200 lb. Fair hair, blue eyes. Educ. Richmond Hill Grammar School, Long Island. Began as meter reader for electrical company ; then became professional tennis player and coach. In Hollywood on teaching staff of tennis professional Ellsworth Vines, met Zeppo Marx who arranged film test. Film debut, 1938, in Columbia Westerns ; also played small part in *A Slight Case of Murder* (Warn) 1938. Then to gain acting experience worked in repertory, appeared on Broadway in " Johnny Belinda " ; returned to Hollywood in stage play with Gertrude Lawrence, and received many film offers. Recent films (all Col) include — 1943 : *What a Woman* ; 1944 : *The Fighting Guardsman* ; 1945 : *One Way to Love* ; 1946 : *Renegades ;* 1948 : *Relentless.*

PARKS, Larry. Born Olathe, Kansas, Dec. 3, 1914. Ht. 5 ft. 11 in. ; wt. 160 lb. Educ. University of Illinois (B.Sc.). Intended to be doctor, but joined amateur troupe of college actors touring Illinois. Became usher at Carnegie Hall, New York, then uniformed guide at Radio City where he met Gregory Peck, also a guide at that time. Appeared on Broadway in " My Heart's In The Highlands ", and " The Pure in Heart ". When father died, worked as Pullman car inspector. With two friends, built and sold a bungalow in Hollywood ; then became stand-in for Barry Fitzgerald. Studio then signed him at nominal salary and put him into " B " pictures at first, grooming him for stardom. Scored sensational success in *The Jolson Story*, 1946. First film : *Mystery Ship* (Col) 1941. Other films (all Col) include : 1941 : *Three Girls About Town, Harmon of Michigan, You Belong to Me, Sing For Your Supper, Harvard Here I Come* ; 1942 : *North of the Rockies, Blondie Goes to College, Canal Zone, Alias Boston Blackie, Hello Annapolis, They All Kissed The Bride, Submarine Raider, Atlantic Convoy, Flight Lieutenant, You Were Never Lovelier, The Boogie Man Will Get You* ; 1943 : *Destroyer, Reveille With Beverley, Redhead From Manhattan, Is Everybody Happy ?, First Comes Courage* ; 1944 : *Hey, Rookie !, The Black Parachute, Stars on Parade, Sergeant Mike* (his first feature-role), *She's a Sweetheart ;* 1945 : *Counter Attack* ; 1946 : *Renegades, The Jolson Story* ; 1947 : *Down to Earth, The Swordsman.*

PAXINOU, Katina. Born Piraeus, Greece. From age of 13 studied singing at Conservatory of Geneva for three years. Won a gold medal here, then continued studies in Berlin and Vienna ; sang in Athens Opera. Toured U.S.A. with Greek theatrical company, 1930. Became a star of Greek Royal Theatre in classical Greek plays as well as modern drama. Appeared London 1939, in " Electra", " Hamlet", " Ghosts". Went to U.S.A., 1932, to aid Greek War Relief. On Broadway in " Hedda Gabler". Screen debut in : *For Whom The Bell Tolls* (Para) 1943. Other films include : 1943 : *Hostages* (Para) ; 1945 : *Confidential Agent* (Warn) ; 1946 : *California* (Para). Came to Britain to appear in *Uncle Silas* (Two Cities) 1947 ; also, 1947 : *Mourning Becomes Electra* (RKO).

PAYNE, John. Real name John Howard Payne. Born Roanoke, Virginia, May 28, 1912. Ht. 6 ft. 3 in. ; wt. 190 lb. Brown hair, hazel eyes. Educ. Elementary schools in Roanoke ; Mercersburg Academy ; University of Virginia ; Columbia University, New York. After having played in repertory and radio, was offered a screen contract. First film : *Dodsworth*

(UA) 1936. In World War II served in the U.S. Army Air Force Corps. Films include : *Fair Warning, Love on Toast, Wings of the Navy, King of the Lumberjacks* ; 1940 : *Star Dust* (20th), *Maryland* (20th), *The Great Profile* (20th), *Tin Pan Alley* (20th) ; 1941 : *The Great American Broadcast* (20th), *Moon Over Miami* (20th), *Sun Valley Serenade* (20th), *Weekend in Havana* (20th), *Remember the Day* (20th) ; 1942 : *To the Shores of Tripoli* (20th), *Footlight Serenade* (20th), *Katina* (20th), *Hello, Frisco, Hello* (20th), *Springtime in the Rockies* (20th) ; 1945 : *The Dolly Sisters* (20th) ; 1946 : *Sentimental Journey* (20th) ; 1947 : *Wake Up and Dream* (20th), *It's Only Human* (20th), *The Big Heart* (20th).

PECK, Gregory. Born La Jolla, California, Apr. 5, 1916. Ht. 6 ft. 2½ in. ; wt. 170 lb. Dark brown hair, brown eyes. Educ. San Diego College ; University of California. Was to have been a doctor, but after having played in college theatricals turned to stage career. Became " barker " at New York World's Fair, guide at Radio City, and then won two-year scholarship to Playhouse School of Dramatics. Made debut with Katherine Cornell in " The Doctor's Dilemma " in 1941. Other plays in which he appeared failed, but his reputation was enhanced and he received many screen offers. First film : *Days of Glory* (RKO) 1943. Other films include :—1944 : *The Keys of the Kingdom* (20th) ; 1945 : *Spellbound* (UA), *The Valley of Decision* (MGM) ; 1947 : *Duel in the Sun* (Selznick), *The Yearling* (MGM), *The Macomber Affair* (Benedict Bogeaus-UA) ; 1948 : *The Paradine Case* (Selznick), *Gentlemen's Agreement* (20th), *The Walls of Jericho* (20th).

PERIER, François. Born Paris, Nov. 2, 1919. Film debut : *L'Entraîneuse*. Other films include : *Le Duel, Premier Bal, Les Jours Heureux, Lettres d'Amour, Bonsoir Mesdames, Mariage d'Amour, La Ferme aux Loups, L'Enfant de L'Amour, Sylvie et le Fantôme, Au Petit Bonheur, La Tentation de Barbizon, Un Revenant, Le Silence est d'Or*.

PERINAL, Georges. Director of photography. Born Paris, 1897. Began his film career photographing documentaries, but soon advanced to feature films. In 1929 photographed the first French talkie, René Clair's *Sous Les Toits de Paris*. Other notable French films include : *Le Million, A Nous la Liberté, 14 Juillet, Le Sang du Poète*. With London Film Productions since 1933 when he photographed *The Private Life of Henry VIII*. Other films include : *Catherine the Great, Things to Come, Don Juan, Rembrandt, Sanders of the River, Escape Me Never, The Drum, The Thief of Bagdad, The Four Feathers, The First of the Few, The Life and Death of Colonel Blimp, Perfect Strangers, A Man About the House, An Ideal Husband*.

PERLBERG, William. Producer. Born New York, Oct. 22, 1899. Educ. High School, St. Louis ; Cornell University. After serving in World War I, joined the William Morris Theatrical Agency in New York ; went to Hollywood in 1928. Became assistant to President of Columbia Pictures, and was later appointed Associate Producer. First film : *The King Steps Out*, 1936. Other films include : *There's Always a Woman, Craig's Wife, Good Girls Go to Paris, The Doctor Takes A Wife, Remember the Day, Son of Fury, The Magnificent Dope, Coney Island, Sweet Rosie O'Grady, Claudia, The Song of Bernadette, The Eve of St. Mark, Diamond Horseshoe, Where Do We Go From Here ?, Junior Miss, State Fair, Claudia and David*.

PETERS, Susan. Real name Suzanne Carnahan. Born Spokane, Washington, July 31, 1921. Ht. 5 ft. 4 in. ; wt. 104 lb. Brown hair, grey eyes. Educ. Flintridge Sacred Heart School ; Hollywood High School. Youthful ambition was to be doctor, but at 18 decided on film career. Signed by Warner Bros. and sent to their dramatic school. First film appearance : *Sante Fe Trail* (Warn), 1940. Other films include : 1941 : *Three Sons O'Guns* (Warn), *Scattergood Pulls the Strings* (RKO) ; 1942 : *Escape from Crime* (Warn), *The Big Shot* (Warn), *Tish* (MGM), *Random Harvest* (MGM), *Dr. Gillespie's New Assistant* (MGM), *Andy Hardy's Double Life* (MGM) ; 1943 : *Assignment in Brittany* (MGM), *Young Ideas* (MGM), *Song of Russia* (MGM) ; 1944 : *Keep Your Powder Dry* (MGM).

PHILIPE, Gérard. Born Cannes, France, Apr. 12, 1922. Light brown hair, green eyes. Considered one of France's leading young actors ; awarded prize for best actor at Brussels 1947 Film Festival. Screen debut in : *Petite du Quai aux Fleurs*. Other films include : *La Boite aux Rêves, Une Grande Fille toute Simple, Le Pays sans Etoiles, L'Idiot, Le Diable au Corps, La Chartreuse de Parme*.

PICKFORD, Mary. Real name Gladys Smith. Born Toronto, Apr. 8, 1893. Ht. 5 ft. Fair hair, blue eyes. Educ. Toronto. Began her acting career at the age of 5 with Valentine Stock Company in Toronto. Film debut in *Her First Biscuits*, 1909, directed by D. W. Griffith, who next starred her in *The Violin Maker of Cremona*. Known in early days as " The Biograph Girl " she was given the name of " Dorothy Nicholson " in Britain by film salesmen, when the public wanted to know the identity of the " little girl with curls ". Shortly after this, became " Mary Pickford ". She was one of the first people whom Griffith built up as a screen star. In a few years she earned the title " The World's Sweetheart " and appeared in hundreds of silent films, notably : *Tess of the Storm Country, Little Annie Rooney, Cinderella, Daddy Longlegs, Pollyanna, Stella Maris, Dorothy Vernon of Haddon Hall, Little Lord Fauntleroy, Rebecca of Sunnybrook Farm, Sparrows*. Her first talkie was *Coquette* (UA) 1929. She also appeared with her husband, the late Douglas Fairbanks, Sr., in *The Taming of the Shrew* (UA) 1929. With Douglas Fairbanks, Charlie Chaplin and D. W. Griffith, she was one of the founder-members of United Artists, in 1919. Formed her own independent unit 1926, Mary Pickford Company. 1936, formed the Pickford-Lasky Producing Company, 1945 ; with Sam Coslow, formed Pickford Productions Inc. Also, in 1945, with Edward J. Paskay, and her husband, Charles " Buddy " Rogers, formed Comet Productions. Is author of several books, including : " Why Not Try God ? ", " My Rendezvous with Life " and a novel, " The Demi-Widow ".

PIDGEON, Walter. Born St. John, New Brunswick, Canada, Sept. 23, 1898. Ht. 6 ft. 3 in. ; wt. 195 lb. Black hair, blue eyes. Educ. New Brunswick University. Became bank runner in Boston in 1919 ; studied singing ; first appeared on stage in " You Never Can Tell ". Partnered Elsie Janis in revue " At Home ", touring America and Britain. Appeared on Broadway in " The Mannequin ", " No More Ladies ", " The Night of January 16th ", " Something Gay " and many more. First film : *Mannequin* (Para), 1926. Other early films include : *Her Private Life, Viennese Nights, A Most Immoral Lady, Lady of the Rose, The Kiss Before the Mirror, Journal of a Crime*. Returned to

Broadway stage 1934. Resumed films 1936 : *Fatal Lady, Big Brown Eyes, Saratoga, Man Proof, My Dear Miss Aldrich, Girl of the Golden West, The Shopworn Angel, Too Hot to Handle, Society Lawyer, Nick Carter, Master Detective.* 1940 : *The House Across the Bay* (UA), *Sky Murder* (MGM), *Dark Command* (Rep), *Phantom Raiders* (MGM), *It's a Date !* (Univ), *Flight Command* (MGM) ; 1941 : *Blossoms in the Dust* (MGM), *Man Hunt* (20th), *Design for Scandal* (MGM), *How Green Was My Valley* (20th) ; 1942 : *Mrs. Miniver* (MGM), *White Cargo* (MGM) ; 1943 : *The Youngest Profession* (MGM), *Madame Curie* (MGM) ; 1944 : *Mrs. Parkington* (MGM) ; 1945 : *Weekend at the Waldorf* (MGM), *Holiday in Mexico* (MGM) ; 1946 : *The Secret Heart* (MGM) ; 1947 : *If Winter Comes* (MGM).

PILBEAM, Nova. Real name Margery Pilbeam. Born Wimbledon, Surrey, Nov. 15, 1919. Ht. 5 ft. 4 in. ; wt. 112 lb. Light brown hair, blue eyes. Educ. The Study, Wimbledon. Trained for the stage with Gertrude Burnett. Having the same Christian name as her mother, she was called " Nova " (after her mother's family association with Nova Scotia) to avoid confusion. First appeared in an amateur play, " Children of Laughter " at Blackheath, 1924. Professional stage debut in " Toad of Toad Hall " 1931. Stage work and radio appearance in the Children's Hour led to her selection as the child star of *Little Friend* (GB) 1934. Other films include : *The Man Who Knew Too Much, Tudor Rose, Young and Innocent* ; 1942 : *Next of Kin* (Ealing) ; 1943 : *The Yellow Canary* (Wilcox-RKO) ; 1944 : *Spring Meeting* (ABPC) ; 1947 : *Green Fingers* (Brit Nat) ; 1948 : *Three Weird Sisters* (Brit Nat), *So Died a Rat* (Brit Nat).

PLESCH, Honoria. Dress designer. Born Budapest, 1919. Educ. Hayes Court School, Kent, L.C.C. Art Schools ; London Theatre Studio. The work of Max Reinhardt led her to consider stage designing, but Joseph von Sternberg suggested film career. Worked as apprentice to Oliver Messel, Vincent Korda, Cecil Beaton, Doris Zinkeisen on films : *Thief of Bagdad, Major Barbara, Dangerous Moonlight* ; on C. B. Cochran stage productions. In 1942 designed first film, *Thunder Rock,* becoming youngest designer in British films. Served in A.T.S., 1943-4, and on release did part-time St. John Ambulance work ; designed costumes and sets for American Red Cross Entertainment Unit. Resumed designing with stage productions : " Madame Louise ", and C. B. Cochran's " Big Ben". Later films: *London Town, Fame Is the Spur.*

PLUNKETT, Patricia. Born Streatham, London, 1928. Ht. 5 ft. 4 in. ; wt. 118 lb. Dark brown hair and eyes. Educ. St. Martin's-in-the-Fields High School, London. Had stage ambitions as child ; used converted box-room at home as " theatre " and produced plays with school friends. During World War II went on evacuation scheme first to Ashford, Kent and then to Wales. In 1945 trained at Royal Academy of Dramatic Art : made stage debut while student in small part " Stage Door ", Saville Theatre, London, 1946. Same year, was offered title role in American juvenile delinquency play " Pick-Up Girl " at New Lindsey Theatre, Notting Hill Gate, London. Retained lead when play was transferred to West End and scored overnight success. Michael Balcon saw her in " Pick-Up Girl ", and gave her first film part in *It Always Rains on Sunday* (Ealing) 1947 ; 1948 : *Bond Street* (World Screen).

POMMER, Erich. Producer. Born Hildesheim, Germany, 1889. Began his film career on business side of French Gaumont company in Berlin ; afterwards became representative of the French Éclair company in Central Europe. In 1923 joined UFA in Neubabelsberg, Germany, as production manager, later becoming producer. Outstanding films for UFA include *Vaudeville, Waltz Dream, Faust, Metropolis, Melody of Hearts, The Blue Angel, Monte Carlo Madness, Congress Dances.* Worked in Hollywood in early 'thirties, and came to Britain in 1936. Producer, *Fire Over England, Troopship.* With Charles Laughton formed Mayflower Productions in 1937 and produced *Vessel of Wrath, St. Martin's Lane, Jamaica Inn.* Returned to Hollywood, 1940. Produced *Dance Girl Dance, They Knew What They Wanted.* Went back to Germany in 1947 to help in post-war reconstruction of German film industry.

PORTER, Cole. Composer. Born Peru, Indiana, U.S.A. June 2, 1892. Educ. Yale University. While a law student wrote songs for college men to sing at football games. Studied music under Vincent d'Indy. Served in France during World War I and returned to New York to begin a song-writing career with the score for " Hitchy Koo ! " 1919. Many of the outstanding stage productions for which he wrote the music have been filmed, including : *The Gay Divorcee, Anything Goes, Du Barry Was a Lady, Panama Hattie, Let's Face It, Something for the Boys.* Has also written music and lyrics for films, including : *Born to Dance, Rosalie, Break the News* (made in Britain, with Jack Buchanan, 1938) *Broadway Melody of* 1940, *Andy Hardy's Private Secretary.* The film *Night and Day* (Warn) 1946, was based on the story of his life, and included some of his best-known compositions, including " My Heart Belongs to Daddy ", sung by Mary Martin to whom the song brought overnight fame when she first sang it on the New York stage. Monty Woolley, at one time a college tutor to Cole Porter, also appeared in the film.

PORTER, Jean. Born Cisco, Texas, Dec. 8. Ht. 5 ft. ; wt. 98 lb. Red hair, brown eyes. Educ. Lawlor Professional School, Hollywood. Followed parents into vaudeville, then settled in Hollywood, where she worked in radio and in small film parts until she obtained featured role in *Bathing Beauty.* First film : *About Face* (UA), 1942. Other films include : *Heart of the Rio Grande* (Rep) ; 1943 : *Fall In !* (UA), *The Youngest Profession* (MGM), *That Nazty Nuisance* (UA), *Calaboose* (UA) ; 1944 : *Bathing Beauty* (MGM), *San Fernando Valley* (Rep), *Andy Hardy's Blonde Trouble* (MGM), *Thrill of a Romance* (MGM) ; 1945 : *Twice Blessed* (MGM), *Abbott and Costello in Hollywood* (MGM), *What next, Corporal Hargrove ?* (MGM) ; 1946 : *Till the End of Time* (RKO), *Betty Co-Ed* (Col) ; 1947 : *Mary Hagen* (Warn).

PORTMAN, Eric. Born Halifax, July 13, 1903. Educ. Rishworth School, Yorks. Became a department store salesman. Played leading roles with Halifax Light Opera Society. Joined Robert Courtneidge's Shakespearean Company when they came to Halifax, and was given chance to prove his acting in " Richard II" at Sunderland, 1924. Made London debut in same year in " Comedy of Errors " ; went to New York, 1938, to appear in " I Have Been Here Before". Made first film appearance as Carlos, a gypsy boy, in old-time thriller, *The Murder in the Red Barn* (George King), 1934, followed by another.

The Crimes of Stephen Hawk. Seen by Hollywood producer on stage in "Bitter Harvest", and went to U.S.A. to appear in *The Prince and The Pauper* (Warn) 1937. Returned to England for *Moonlight Sonata* (Pall Mall), before resuming stage career. Director Michael Powell brought him back to screen for memorable performance as Nazi submarine commander in *49th Parallel*—U.S. title *The Invaders* (Ortus), 1941. Other films include: 1942: *One of Our Aircraft Is Missing* (Brit Nat), *Uncensored* (Gains); 1943: *We Dive at Dawn* (Gains), *Squadron Leader " X "* (RKO Brit); 1944: *A Canterbury Tale* (Archers); 1945: *The Great Day*; 1946: *Men of Two Worlds* (Two Cities), *Wanted for Murder* (20th-Brit); 1947: *Dear Murderer* (Gains). 1948: *Daybreak* (Box), *Mark of Cain* (Two Cities), *Corridor of Mirrors* (Apollo) made in Paris; *Blind Goddess* (Gains).

POWELL, Dick. Real name Richard E. Powell. Born Mount View, Arkansas, Nov. 14, 1904. Ht. 6 ft.; wt. 170 lb. Brown hair, blue eyes. Educ. Little Rock High School; Little Rock College. Was singer in choir, at dances, weddings and other local events. Worked in grocery store, tested gas meters, collected money from telephone boxes. Joined a visiting orchestra as singer and player, making debut at Hotel Louisville, Louisville. Became banjoist in Indianapolis orchestra; later toured as singer and instrumentalist. Became known to wide public through radio and gramophone records. 1930-2 was M.C. stage shows at Stanley Theatre, Pittsburgh; while there spotted by film talent scout. First film: *Blessed Event* (Warn) 1932. Became a light comedy and singing star; 1944, achieved ambition to play straight roles with part of newspaper man in *It Happened Tomorrow*. Films include: *42nd Street, Gold Diggers of 1933, Footlight Parade, College Coach, Convention City, Wonder Bar, 20 Million Sweethearts, Dames, Happiness Ahead, Flirtation Waltz, Gold Diggers of 1935, Midsummer Night's Dream, Broadway Gondolier, Page Miss Glory, Shipmates Forever, Colleen, Thanks a Million, On The Avenue, Hearts Divided, Stage Struck, Gold Diggers of 1937, The Singing Marine, Varsity Show, Hollywood Hotel, Cowboy from Brooklyn, Hard To Please, Going Places, Always Leave Them Laughing*. 1940: *Christmas in July* (Para); 1941: *Model Wife* (Univ); 1943: *Star Spangled Rhythm* (Para), *True To Life* (Para), *Riding High* (Para); 1944: *Meet The People* (MGM), *It Happened Tomorrow* (UA), *Farewell My Lovely* (RKO); 1945: *Cornered* (RKO); 1947: *Johnny O'Clock* (Col); 1948: *To The Ends of The Earth* (Col), *Stations West* (RKO).

POWELL, Jane. Real name Suzanne Burce. Born Portland, Oregon, Apr. 1. Ht. 5 ft.; wt. 95 lb. Dark brown hair, blue eyes. Made radio debut at 7 in Portland with children's talent programme. Became popular local entertainer. On holiday in Hollywood, entered talent contest as singer and received ovation. Appeared on radio with Edgar Bergen and Charlie McCarthy. First film: *Song of the Open Road* (UA) 1944. Other films include: *Delightfully Dangerous* (UA); 1945: *Holiday in Mexico* (MGM); 1947: *The Birds and the Bees* (MGM); 1948: *Luxury Liner* (MGM), *A Date With Judy* (MGM).

POWELL, Michael. Director, producer. Born Canterbury, Sept. 30, 1905. Entered films in 1925 as general assistant to Rex Ingram at Victorine Studios, Nice, France. Progressed through all departments, and became assistant director. In early 1930's directed *The Fire Raisers, The Phantom Light* and *The Night of the Party* for Gaumont-British, London. In 1936, caused wide interest with *The Edge of the World*, written and directed by him and made on the Island of Foula. With Emeric Pressburger, formed a writer-producer-director partnership in 1938. His films include: *The Spy in Black* (1939), *The Thief of Bagdad* (co-directed), *The Lion Has Wings* (co-directed), *Contraband, 49th Parallel*—U.S. title *The Invaders, One of Our Aircraft Is Missing*. In 1941 he and Pressburger formed Archers Film Productions. Joint productions include: *The Life and Death of Colonel Blimp, A Canterbury Tale, The Volunteer, I Know Where I'm Going, A Matter of Life and Death*—U.S. title *Stairway to Heaven, Black Narcissus, The End of the River, Red Shoes*.

POWELL. William. Born Pittsburgh, Pennsylvania, July 29, 1892. Ht. 6 ft.; wt. 160 lb. Brown hair, brown eyes. Educ. Pittsburgh; Central Union High School, Kansas City. Was intended for the law, but acting in "The Rivals" at school gave him stage ambitions. Borrowed money for tuition at American Academy of Dramatic Arts. Appeared in New York in "The Ne'er-do-well", 1912. Toured in "Within the Law", played in repertory at Pittsburgh, followed by 40 weeks of one-night stands. For eight years was on Broadway as actor and singer. In silent films from 1920. Joined MGM, 1934. Early films include: *Under the Red Robe, Romola, Interference, Beau Geste, Canary Murder Case, Shadow of the Law, Street of Chance, Ladies' Man, Lawyer Man, Double Harness, Fashions of 1934, The Key, Manhattan Melodrama, The Thin Man* (1934), *Reckless, Rendezvous, The Great Ziegfeld, Libelled Lady, After the Thin Man, The Emperor's Candlesticks, The Baroness and the Butler, Another Thin Man*. 1940: (all MGM) *I Love You Again*; 1941: *Love Crazy, Shadow of the Thin Man*; 1942: *Crossroads*; 1943: *The Youngest Profession, The Heavenly Body*; 1944: *Ziegfeld Follies*; 1945: *The Thin Man Goes Home*; 1946: *The Hoodlum Saint*; 1947: *Life With Father* (Warn), *Song of the Thin Man*; 1948: *Mr. Ashton Was Indiscreet* (UI).

POWER, Tyrone. Born Cincinnati, Ohio, May 5, 1914. Ht. 6 ft.; wt. 155 lb. Dark brown hair, dark brown eyes. Educ. Sisters of Mercy Academy and High School, Cincinnati. Born of theatrical family, he travelled around with them and took small parts at 7. Gradually worked up to Broadway. First plays included "Romance", "Flowers of the Forest" and "Romeo and Juliet". Given film test while on Broadway. First film: *Girls' Dormitory* (20th) 1936. Served in U.S. Marine Corps, 1942-45. Is under contract to 20th Century-Fox. Films include: *Lloyd's of London, In Old Chicago, Marie Antoinette, Alexander's Ragtime Band, Suez, Rose of Washington Square, The Rains Came*. 1940: *Johnny Apollo, Brigham Young, The Mark of Zorro*; 1941: *Blood and Sand, A Yank in the R.A.F., Son of Fury*; 1942: *This Above All, The Black Swan, Crash Dive*; 1946: *The Razor's Edge*; 1947: *Captain from Castile, Nightmare Alley*.

PREMINGER, Otto Ludwig. Born Vienna, 1906. Educ. University of Vienna. At 17 began his career in the theatre, with Max Reinhardt, first as an actor. Later went to Zurich as actor and stage director. Returned to Vienna and founded a small theatre there before becoming interested in films. After directing several Austrian talkies, was signed by Joseph Schenck as a director for Hollywood in 1936. Directed two U.S. films, *Under Your Spell* and *Danger—Love at Work*;

ERIC PORTMAN
(*Two Cities*)

spent two years producing and directing stage plays, and for a time was also attached to the Drama School at Yale University. Returned to Hollywood in 1941 and directed: *The Pied Piper, Margin for Error, They Got Me Covered, Laura, In the Meantime Darling, A Royal Scandal*—British title *Czarina, Fallen Angel, Centennial Summer, Forever Amber*. Produced and directed *Daisy Kenyon*.

PRESLE, Micheline. Born Paris, France, Aug. 22, 1922. Light brown hair, blue-green eyes. Film debut in *Jeunes Filles en Détresse*. Other films include: *Un Seul Amour, Boule de Suif, Le Diable au Corps, La Nuit Fantastique*.

PRESSBURGER, Emeric. Producer, screenwriter. Born Miskole, Hungary, Dec. 5, 1902. Educ. Universities of Prague and Stuttgart. Was journalist before becoming scriptwriter with UFA in Berlin. Came to Britain in 1935, worked on scripts of *One Rainy Afternoon* and *The Challenge*. Met director Michael Powell whilst both were working for London Film Productions, and in 1939 they collaborated on *The Spy in Black* and *Contraband*. With Powell, co-produced *The Silver Fleet, 49th Parallel*—U.S. title *The Invaders, One of Our Aircraft Is Missing*. He and Powell formed Archers Film Productions in 1941. Joint productions include: *The Life and Death of Colonel Blimp, A Canterbury Tale, I Know Where I'm Going, A Matter of Life and Death*—U.S. title *Stairway to Heaven* (chosen for first Royal Command Film Performance, 1946), *Black Narcissus, The End of the River, Red Shoes*.

PRESTON, Robert. Born Newton Highlands, Massachusetts, June 8. Ht. 6 ft. 1 in.; wt. 175 lb. Brown hair, grey eyes. Educ. Los Angeles public schools; Lincoln High School. At 15, joined repertory; then became car-park attendant at Santa Anita race track Los Angeles, where Pasadena Playhouse students invited him to have an audition. In two years played 42 tough character roles. First film: *King of Alcatraz* (Para) 1938. Other films include: *Illegal Traffic, Disbarred, Union Pacific, Beau Geste*. 1940: *Typhoon* (Para), *Moon Over Burma* (Para), *North West Mounted Police* (Para); 1941: *The Lady From Cheyenne* (Univ), *Parachute Battalion* (RKO), *New York Town* (Para), *Night of January 16th* (Para), *Pacific Blackout* (Para); 1942: *This Gun For Hire* (Para), *Reap the Wild Wind*, (Para), *Wake Island* (Para), *Night Plane from Chungking* (Para); 1942-5, served with U.S. Air Force in Europe; 1947: *The Macomber Affair* (Benedict Bogeaus-UA), *Wild Harvest* (Para); 1948: *Whispering Smith* (Para).

PREVILLE, Gisèle. Born France, 1920. Lived in America 1925-34 where father was employed as buyer for dress-making firm. Returned to Paris and became "Miss Paris of 1936". Was mannequin before beginning screen career in small parts. Became cabaret artist South of France during German occupation. Resumed film career in 1945, and appeared in *Mimoir* with Jean Gabin. Came to Britain to appear in *Against the Wind* (Ealing), 1948.

PRICE, Dennis. Born Twyford, Berks, June 23, 1915. Ht. 6 ft.; wt. 160 lb. Light brown hair, grey-blue eyes. Educ. Radley College; Worcester College, Oxford. Had youthful ideas of entering the Church; family hoped he would follow tradition and enter Army; but experience with Oxford University Dramatic Society made him turn to acting. Made stage debut at Croydon Repertory Theatre in

"Behind Your Back", June, 1937. Appeared with John Gielgud's Company at Queen's Theatre, London, 1937. Played in repertory at Croydon during 1938 and at Oxford 1939-40. War service with Royal Artillery, 1940-2. Toured with Noel Coward in "This Happy Breed", "Present Laughter"; also appeared in these two plays and in "Blithe Spirit", in London, 1943. Was seen by director Michael Powell in "Springtime of Others" at Arts Theatre, London, and given first film role in: *A Canterbury Tale* (Archers) 1944. Other films include: 1945: *The Echo Murders* (Brit Nat), *A Place of One's Own* (Gains); 1946: *The Magic Bow* (Gains), *Caravan* (Gains); 1947: *Hungry Hill* (Two Cities), *Dear Murderer* (Gains), *Jassy* (Gains), *Holiday Camp* (Gains), *Master of Bankdam* (Holbein), *The White Unicorn* (Corfield); 1948: *Good Time Girl* (Gains), *Snowbound* (Gains), *Easy Money* (Gains), *The Bad Lord Byron* (Gains).

PRICE, Vincent. Born St. Louis, Missouri, May 27, 1911. Ht. 6 ft. 3½ in.; wt. 175 lb. Fair hair, hazel eyes. Educ. Yale University; University of London; Nuremberg University. Left Yale to become school teacher and singing coach. Decided that European background would help him succeed in stage career. While studying in London, was given role of American cop in Norman Marshall's production "Chicago", Gate Theatre, 1934. Later made London success as Prince Albert in "Victoria Regina"; also in Gilbert Miller's Broadway version with Helen Hayes, 1935-7. First film: *Service de Luxe* (Univ) 1938. Other films include: *Elizabeth and Essex, Green Hell, Tower of London, The Invisible Man Returns, House of Seven Gables*. 1940: *Brigham Young* (20th), *Hudson's Bay* (20th); 1943: *The Song of Bernadette* (20th); 1944: (all 20th): *The Eve of St. Mark, The Keys of the Kingdom, Laura*; 1945 (all 20th): *Wilson, A Royal Scandal, Leave Her to Heaven*; 1946 (all 20th): *Dragonwyck, Shock*; 1947: *Moss Rose, The Web* (UI), *Jeopardy* (UI), *The Long Night* (RKO); 1948: *Up in Central Park* (UI).

PRIESTLEY, John Boynton. Novelist, dramatist, writer. Born Bradford, Sept. 13, 1894. Educ. Bradford; and Trinity Hall, Cambridge (M.A.). Was originally a schoolmaster. Served in World War I and began writing career in 1918. Is author of nearly 30 plays, including "The Good Companions", (in collaboration with Edward Knoblock), "Dangerous Corner", "Eden End", "Time and the Conways", "People at Sea", "Music at Night", "Johnson Over Jordan", "Desert Highway", "Ever Since Paradise". Books include: "The Good Companions", "Angel Pavement", "Faraway", "The Doomsday Men", "English Journey", "Rain Upon Godshill". Plays filmed: *The Good Companions, Laburnam Grove, When We Are Married, They Came to a City*. Has also written and collaborated on screenplays, including: *Let the People Sing, The Foreman Went to France, Britain at Bay*.

PROUD, Peter. Production designer. Born Glasgow, May 6, 1913. Educ. Glasgow; Queen Elizabeth's Grammar School; Dulwich College. Began in father's art business as child. Trained as engineer at college and entered films 1929 as assistant recordist with British International Pictures, Elstree. Transferred to B.I.P. Art Department, working as junior on early Hitchcock films. Joined Gaumont-British 1933, becoming art director in 1934. 1935-9, head of Warner Bros. (British) art department, also designed London stage productions : " Indoor Fire-works", " Half a Crown", " Hyde Park Corner". 1940-5, served in army on Camouflage and Deception, and later with Political Warfare Branch in Bulgaria. While in Italy, directed and produced *I Grani del Populo*, made by ex-partisan Italians and given premiere in Rome. Resumed British art direction 1945-6 : *Green for Danger, Woman in the Hall*. Co-director and production designer : *Esther Waters*.

PUDOVKIN, Vsevoled. Producer, director. Born Pensa, Russia, 1893. Studied in the Physical Mathe-matical Faculty, Moscow State University, after World War I, with intention of becoming an analytical chemist. Turned to art, then to screen acting ; appeared in *The Days of Struggle*. Co-producer *Hunger, Hunger, Hunger* (1922). Other early silent films include : *The Excitement of Chess* (with Capa-blanca), *The Mechanics of the Brain, Mother, The End of St. Petersburg, Storm over Asia*. His first sound film was *A Simple Case* (1930.) Others include: *Living Well* (1931), *Victory* (1932), *Deserter* (1933), *Minn and Pojaisky* (1938-9), *General Suvorov* (1941), *In the Name of the Motherland* (1943 : from Simonov's play " The Russians "), *Admiral Nikimov* (1946-7).

PURCELL, Noel. Born Dublin, Dec. 24, 1900. Ht. 6 ft. 4 in. ; wt. 182 lb. Dark hair, black eyes. Educ. Christian Brothers School, Dublin. Worked as callboy at Gaiety Theatre, Dublin. Left to become a cabinet maker. Began acting when 28 and later went back to Gaiety Theatre as leading comedian. Ten years later, transferred to the Theatre Royal, Dublin. First major screen role in *Captain Boycott* (Individ) 1947. 1948 : *Blue Lagoon* (Individ).

QUINN, Anthony. Born Mexico. Ht. 6 ft. 2 in. ; wt. 185 lb. Black hair, brown eyes. First film appearance in *Parole* (Univ) 1936. During World War II, served in U.S. Armed Forces. Films include : *The Plainsman, Union Pacific*. 1941 : *Blood and Sand* (20th), *The Perfect Snob* (20th), *Thieves Fall Out* (Warn) ; *Knockout* (Warn), *Bullets for O' Hara* (Warn) : 1942 : *Larceny Inc.* (Warn) ; *Road to Moscow* (Para), *The Black Swan* (20th) ; 1943 : *Strange Incident* (20th), *Guadalcanal Diary* (20th) ; 1944 : *Buffalo Bill* (20th), *Irish Eyes Are Smiling* (20th), *Ladies of Washing-ton* (20th) ; 1945 : *China Sky* (RKO) ; 1946 : *Back to Bataan* (RKO), *Where Do We Go From Here ?* (20th) ; *Black Gold* (Mono).

RADFORD, Basil. Born Chester, June 28, 1897. Served in World War I, 1915-17, then studied at Royal Academy of Dramatic Art. First stage appearance in " Bulldog Drummond", Hastings, 1922. Served in Army in World War II. Appeared in an early British film, *Barnum Was Right*, 1929, and several more, but it was not until he and Naunton Wayne appeared as the two imperturbable Englishmen in *The Lady Vanishes* (Gains) 1938, that he achieved reputation for screen comedy. Other films include : *Let's be Famous, Trouble Brewing, Official Secrets, Jamaica Inn, Just William, Flying Squad, Runaway Romance, Night Train to Munich* (with Naunton Wayne), *Climbing High*. 1940 : *Gestapo* (Gains), *Crooks' Tour*, with Naunton Wayne (Brit Nat), *Room for Two* (Grand Nat) ; 1941 : *Girl in the Mews* (20th-Brit) ; 1942 : *Unpublished Story* (Two Cities) ; 1943 : *Millions Like Us* (Gains) ; 1945 : *The Way to the Stars* (Two Cities), *Dead of Night*, with Naunton Wayne (Ealing) ; 1946 : *The Captive Heart* (Ealing), *Girl in a Million*, with Naunton Wayne (Box).

RAFFERTY, Chips. Real name, John Goffage. Born Broken Hill, New South Wales, March 26, 1909. Ht. 6 ft. 6 in. Educ. Australia. Youthful ambition to become an artist. Was first an engineering apprentice, then worked at cattle-droving, journalism, sheep-shearing, gold and tin mining and boundary patrolling. As amateur was scene designer and comedian, later becoming assistant to magician Claude Leslie. Made his film debut for Australian company in *Ants in His Pants* (Cinesound), 1938. War service in Royal Australian Air Force in New Guinea. Films include : 1939 : *Dan Rudd, M.P.* (Cinesound) ; 1940 : *40,000 Horsemen* (Cinesound) ; 1942 : *Rats of Tobruk* (Cinesound) ; 1946 : *The Overlanders* (Ealing). Came to Britain to complete *The Over-landers*, given contract by Michael Balcon and appeared in *The Loves of Joanna Godden* (Ealing), 1947. Returned to Australia, 1947, for starring role in *Eureka Stockade* (Ealing).

RAFT, George. Born New York, Sept. 17, 1903. Ht. 5 ft. 10 in. ; wt. 155 lb. Black hair, brown eyes. Educ. St. Catherine's, New York. Became professional boxer and baseball player ; turned to dancing, won early fame as " world's fastest Charleston dancer". Has appeared in European capitals in night clubs and theatres. Stage shows include : " No Foolin", " Gay Paree", " Palm Beach Nights", " City Chap", " Manhatters ". In Hollywood specialized in " tough roles." First film : *Quick Millions* (Fox) 1931. Other films include : *Hush Money, Scarface, Dancers in the Dark, Night After Night, Undercover Man, If I Had a Million, The Eagle and The Hawk, Pick Up, Midnight Club, The Bowery, All of Me, Bolero, The Trumpet Blows, Limehouse Blues, Rhumba, Stolen Harmony, The Glass Key, Every Night at Eight, She Couldn't Take It, It Had to Happen, Yours for the Asking, Souls at Sea, You and Me, Spawn of the North, The Lady's from Kentucky, Each Dawn I Die, I Stole a Million*. 1940 : *Invisible Stripes* (Warn), *The House Across the Bay* (Wanger-UA), *They Drive By Night* (Warn) ; 1941 : *Manpower* (Warn) ; 1942 : *Broadway* (Univ) ; 1943 : *Background to Danger* (Warn) ; 1944 : *Follow the Boys* (Univ) ; 1945 : *Nob Hill* (20th), *Johnny Angel* (RKO) ; 1946 : *Mr. Ace* (UA), *Nocturne* (RKO), *Whistle Stop* (UA) ; 1947 : *Race Street* (RKO), *Christmas Eve* (Benedict Bogeaus-UA).

RAINES, Ella. Born Snoqualmie Falls, Washington, Aug. 6, 1921. Ht. 5 ft. 3 in. ; wt. 110 lb. Brown hair, green eyes. Educ. University of Washington. With some " Little Theatre " experience, set out for stage career in New York. There fell ill, but agent's photographs of her won her a Hollywood contract. First film : *Corvette K-225* (Univ), 1943. Other films include : 1944 : *Phantom Lady* (Univ), *Hail the Conquering Hero* (Para), *Cry Havoc* (MGM), *Tall in the Saddle* (RKO), *Enter Arsene Lupin* (Univ) ; 1945 : *The Suspect* (Univ), *The Strange Affair of Uncle Harry* (Univ) ; 1946 : *The Runaround* (Univ) ; 1947 : *Time out of Mind* (UI), *The Web* (UI), *Brute Force* (UI), *White Tie and Tails* (UI) ; 1948 : *Mr. Ashton Was Indiscreet* (UI).

RAINS, Claude. Born London, Nov. 10, 1890. Educ. privately. Became call-boy at His Majesty's Theatre, London, at 10 ; subsequently prompter, business manager, stage manager and small part actor. Played in repertory in England and Australia. Served in Army in World War I. On convalescing from war wounds decided on Army career, but was offered role in new play. After successful English stage career, went to America where he appeared for Theatre Guild in " The Moon in the Yellow River", " They Shall Not Die", " Volpone", " Napoleon's Barber " and other plays. Screen debut in *The Invisible Man* (Univ), 1933, was unusual as his face was not seen until the very end of the film. Other films include : *Crime Without Passion, The Man Who Reclaimed His Head, The Mystery of Edwin Drood, The Clairvoyant* (for Gainsborough in Britain, 1935), *The Last Outpost, Anthony Adverse, Hearts Divided, Stolen Holiday, The Prince and the Pauper, They Won't Forget, Gold is Where You Find It, Robin Hood, White Banners, Four Daughters, They Made Me a Criminal, Juarez, Daughters Courageous, Saturday's Children*. 1940 : *The Sea Hawk* (Warn), *The Lady With Red Hair* (Warn), *Four Mothers* (Warn) ; 1941 : *Here Comes Mr. Jordan* (Col), *The Wolf Man* (Univ), *Riot Squad* (Mono), *Kings Row* (Warn) ; 1942 : *Moontide* (Warn), *Now Voyager* (Warn), *Casablanca* (Warn), *Eyes of the Underworld* (Univ) ; 1943 : *Forever and a Day* (RKO), *Phantom of the Opera* (Univ) ; 1944 : *Passage to Marseilles* (Warn), *Mr. Skeffington* (Warn) ; 1945 : *This Love of Ours* (Univ) ; 1946 : *Caesar and Cleopatra* (Pascal) made in Britain, *Angel on My Shoulder* (UA), *Deception* (Warn) ; 1947 : *Notorious* (RKO), *The Unsuspected* (Warn).

RAISMAN, Y. Director. Born 1903. Entered film industry after graduating in Literature and Art in First Moscow State University in 1924. Gained experience in various branches of production, and then directed *The Convict Camp* (1928), which dealt with Russian convict history. Later made *The Thirsty Earth* (a film about the life of the Soviet East), *The Airmen, The Last Night, The Upturned Soil, Mashkenka, Armistice with Finland, Moscow Skies, From Moscow to the Pacific*.

RALSTON, Vera Hruba. Born Prague, 1922. Ht. 5 ft. 5 in. ; wt. 130 lb. Fair hair, blue eyes. Studied in ballet for eight years. Won Prague skating championship at 13 and held it for four years. In 1936 was runner-up to Sonja Henie at Olympic Games. Toured America and Canada ; featured in winter sports show at Madison Square Garden, New York. In 1940 became featured star in new " Ice-Capades Group". While touring with them signed film contract and made hit. Screen debut in *Ice-Capades* 1941. Other films include : 1944 : *Lady and the Monster* (Rep), *Lake Placid Serenade* (Rep) *Storm Over Lisbon* (Rep) ; 1945 : *Dakota* (Rep) ; 1946 : *Murder in the Music Hall* (Rep) ; 1947 : *The Plainsman and the Lady* (Rep).

RAMSDEN, Frances. Ht. 5 ft. 9 in. ; wt. 125 lb. Dark brown hair, brown eyes. Began her career as model in New York. At first turned down director Preston Sturges' offer of film test, but on further persuasion accepted and appeared as Harold Lloyd's leading lady when he made his return to films in *Mad Wednesday* (Howard Hughes) 1947.

RANDELL, Ron. Born Australia. Made debut as radio actor in Sydney, 1933. Author of several radio plays. His facial resemblance to Sir Charles Kingsford Smith, Australian airman who was lost in 1935 while attempting to break air record, gained him role of Kingsford Smith in *Southern Cross* made for Columbia in Australia. This led to Hollywood contract. First U.S. film, *Bulldog Drummond at Bay* (Col) 1947. Also made, in 1948 : *It Had to be You* (Col), *The Sign of the Ram* (Col).

RANK, Joseph Arthur. Born Hull, December 23. 1888. Educ. Leys School, Cambridge. Left school at 17. His early ambition was to promote interest in religion through the medium of religious films. Entered family flour milling business (Joseph Rank, Ltd.), later becoming manager. In World War I served with Field Ambulance Unit. In 1933 investor in Religious Film Society. In 1935 formed British National Pictures in association with Lady Yule and John Corfield. In conjunction with C. M. Woolf, invested in G.F.D. Bought 25 per cent share in Universal Pictures, agreeing to take over distribution of products in Britain, and production and distribution of newsreel. In 1936 created General Cinema Finance Corporation with Paul Lindenberg, C. M. Woolf, Lord Luke and Leslie Farrow as co-directors. In 1941 acquired control of Gaumont British Picture Corporation and of Odeon Theatres, Ltd. Formed Eagle-Lion Distributors, Ltd. Developed Gaumont British Junior Clubs, Odeon National Cinema Clubs for Boys and Girls, and Children's Entertainment Films. In 1945 acquired half interest in Odeon theatre chain Canada, formed Eagle-Lion Distributors in America. In 1946 formed J. Arthur Rank Organisation Ltd. to co-ordinate his interests. In 1947 made arrangements with RKO Radio, Warners, 20th Century, Paramount, to show British films on the five circuits in U.S.A. controlling 3000 cinemas. In all, is director of over 70 companies, and chairman of 23 of them ; has interests in British film distribution in more than 60 countries besides U.S.A. and Britain. Principal Business Activities : Managing director of Joseph Rank Ltd., Chairman of Odeon Theatres Ltd., London, Gaumont British Picture Corporation, Denham and Pinewood Studios; Two Cities Films Ltd., Gainsborough Pictures Ltd., Independent Producers Ltd., Odeon (Ireland) Ltd., the J. Arthur Rank Organisation Ltd., British Acoustic Films, Ltd. and Taylor, Taylor & Hobson Ltd. Member of the board of directors of Universal Pictures of America. President of British Film Producers' Association.

RATHBONE, Basil. Born Johannesburg, S. Africa, June 13, 1892. Ht. 6 ft. 1 in. ; wt. 189 lb. Black hair, hazel eyes. Educ. Repton School, England. Instead of following father's career as engineer, studied acting under his cousin, Sir Frank Benson, and made his debut in " The Taming of the Shrew ", April 22, 1911, Theatre Royal, Ipswich. Went to U.S.A. in 1912. Served in Army in World War I (M.C.). Made name in Shakespeare and appeared 1923-32 in New York and San Francisco. Returned to Britain where he appeared in " Tonight or Never " and " Diplomacy" in London, and then resumed American stage career. Made first film in Hollywood : *The Masked Bride* (MGM) 1925. Early U.S. pictures include : *Loves of Sunya, Last of Mrs. Cheyney, Flirting Widow, This Mad World, The Bishop Murder Case, Lady of Scandal, Notorious Affair, The High Road, Sin Takes a Holiday, The Lady Surrenders, A Woman Commands*. In Britain, 1932-3, made : *After the Ball, One Precious Year, Loyalties*. In Hollywood : *David Copperfield, Anna Karenina, Last Days of Pompeii, Feather in her Hat, Captain Blood, Romeo and Juliet, Garden of Allah*. In Britain : *Love From a Stranger*. In Hollywood : *Tovarich, Adventures of Marco Polo, Dawn Patrol, If I Were King*. From 1939 has played Sherlock Holmes in film series. Other films include : 1941 : *International Lady* (UA) ; 1942 : *Crossroads* (MGM) ; 1943 : *Above Suspicion* (MGM) ; 1944 : *The Spider Woman* (Univ), *The Scarlet Claw* (Univ), *The Pearl of Death*

(Univ), *Frenchman's Creek* (Para), *Bathing Beauty* (MGM) ; 1945 : *House of Fear* (Univ), *Pursuit to Algiers* (Univ), *The Woman in Green* (Univ) ; 1946 : *Terror By Night* (Univ), *Heartbeat* (RKO).

RATOFF, Gregory. Director. Born Samara, Russia, April 20, 1897. Educ. University of St. Petersburg (now Leningrad). Youthful ambition : To found a theatre of his own. Fought in Russian Army in World War I. Went to Germany where he sang and danced and produced his own plays. While he was appearing in " The Kibitzer " film talent scouts signed him for dramatic role in *Symphony of Six Million* produced by David Selznick. Played in films in Britain and Hollywood, before becoming a director in 1937 with *Lancer Spy* (20th). Other films directed include : *Rose of Washington Square, The Great Profile, Adam Had Four Sons, Men in Her Life, Two Yanks in Trinidad, Footlight Serenade, Something to Shout About, The Heat's On, Song of Russia, Irish Eyes are Smiling, Where do We Go From Here ?, Paris Underground, Do You Love Me ?, Carnival in Costa Rica, Moss Rose, Cagliostro* (made in Italy).

RATTIGAN, Terence. Dramatist, screenwriter. Born London, June 12, 1912. Educ. Harrow School ; Trinity College, Oxford. Began playwriting in 1934, when he wrote " First Episode " a play about under-graduates. Served with the R.A.F. in World War II. Other plays include : " After the Dance ", " Flare Path ", " Love in Idleness ", and the following, which were filmed : *French Without Tears, While the Sun Shines, The Winslow Boy.* Became interested in screen-writing in 1939, and collaborated on screen-plays of his own films ; other screenplays : *Quiet Wedding, The Day Will Dawn*—U.S. title *The Avengers, English Without Tears, Uncensored, The Way to the Stars, Bond Street.* With Anatole de Grunwald and Anthony Asquith formed International Screen-plays Ltd., 1946, and World Screenplays Ltd., 1947.

RAWNSLEY, David. Born Sevenoaks, Kent, June 25, 1909. Educ. Westminster School, London. Trained as architect and engineer. Began film career with British International Pictures in 1927 as art director. Joined Royal Navy, 1939 ; was blown up in minesweeper, and invalided out, 1941. Returned to films as art director for : *49th Parallel, One of Our Aircraft is Missing, They Flew Alone, In Which We Serve, The Way Ahead, The Rake's Progress, I See a Dark Stranger.* Joined the J. Arthur Rank Organisa-tion as director of film research, 1946, to experiment and test new methods of film design and equipment. Has earned a notable place in film history for his development of production system known as the Independent Frame Method. First film produced by this method : *Under the Frozen Falls,* for Children's Entertainment Films, 1947.

RAWSTHORNE, Alan. Composer. Born Hasling-den, Lancs, May 2, 1905. Family opposition to a musical career resulted in his training for the dental profession ; he also studied architecture. Finally attended Royal Manchester College of Music. Spent three and a half years at Dartington Hall, South Devon, studying dance and mime. First film music was score for a documentary, *The City.* While in the Army during the war composed music for three Army training films. First feature film : *Burma Victory.* Other musical scores include : *The Captive Heart, School for Secrets, Broken Dykes, Uncle Silas.*

RAY, Renée. Born London, Sept. 22, 1912. Ht. 5 ft. 4 in. Fair hair, blue eyes. Educ. St. Margaret's Convent, Bolton ; St. Mary's School, Banbury. Began screen career as extra in : *Palais de Danse* (GB), 1929. Made a great hit in a small role in *Young Woodley*, 1930. Other films include : *Keepers of Youth, While London Sleeps, Tiger Bay, The King's Cup, Born Lucky, Street Song, Full Circle, 9.45, Safety First, Rolling in Money, Dance Little Lady, Varsity, Two White Arms, The Passing of the Third Floor Back* (GB), 1935, in which she played memorable role as boarding-house skivvy ; *Beloved Impostor, Crime Over London, His Lordship, Please Teacher, The Green Cockatoo, Farewell Again, The Rat, The Housemaster, Jennifer Hale, Bank Holiday, Return of the Frog, Mountains of Mourne.* Recently on stage in " Claudia " and " The Cure for Love ", also toured for ENSA during World War II. Recent films : *Old Bill and Son* (Gains) ; 1947 : *They Made Me a Fugitive* (Alliance). Went to Hollywood 1947, and appeared in *If Winter Comes* (MGM).

RAYE, Martha. Born Butte, Montana. Known as " the girl with the pillar-box mouth ". At 3 appeared in vaudeville with her parents ; at 13 won first prize for singing at an amateur competition in Chicago. Joined Chicago orchestra as vocalist. While singing in night club at Hollywood made film debut in *Rhythm on the Range* (Para), 1936. Other films include : *The Big Broadcast of 1937, Hideaway Girl, College Holiday, Waikiki Wedding, Mountain Music, Artists and Models, Big Broadcast of 1938, College Swing, Tropic Holiday, Never Say Die* ; 1940 : *The Farmer's Daughter* (Para), *The Boys from Syracuse* (Univ) ; 1941 : *Navy Blues* (Warn), *Keep 'em Flying* (Univ), *Hellzapoppin'* (Univ). Experiences on tour with U.S.O. Camp shows in U.S.A., Europe and Africa, 1942-3, "inspired" *Four Jills in a Jeep* (20th), 1944. Chosen by Chaplin as his leading lady in *Monsieur Verdoux* (UA), 1947.

RAYMOND, Gene. Real name Raymond Guion. Born New York, Aug. 13, 1908. Ht. 5 ft. 10 in. ; wt. 155 lb. Fair hair, blue eyes. Educ. Professional Children's School, New York. Made appearances from age of 5. Appeared in many plays before making film debut in *Personal Maid* (Para), 1931. Other films include : *Ladies of the Big House, Forgotten Commandments, Night of June 13, Ex-Lady, Zoo in Budapest, If I Had a Million, Flying Down to Rio, I Am Suzanne, Behold My Wife, Hooray for Love, Seven Keys to Baldpate, Love on a Bet, The Bride Walks Out, Smartest Girl In Town, Walking on Air, That Girl From Paris, There Goes My Girl, The Life of the Party, She's Got Everything, Stolen Heaven* ; 1940 : *Cross Country Romance* (RKO) ; 1941 : *Mr. and Mrs. Smith* (RKO), *Smilin' Through* (MGM) ; 1941-6, war service with U.S. Army Air Force. Stationed in Britain for 2½ years. Resumed film career in *The Locket* (RKO), 1946.

RAYMOND, Jill. Born West Kensington, London, Apr. 22, 1927. Ht. 5 ft. 3½ in. ; wt. 107 lb. Educ. convent school. Black hair, grey-blue eyes. At age of 8 played the title role in a production of " Alice in Wonderland " at school. Spent two years at Oxford University, studying under C. S. Lewis. Trained for stage at Royal Academy of Dramatic Art ; seen in student show by director Jack Lee and given her first role, as sister to character played by Jean Simmons, in *The Woman in the Hall* (Wessex), 1947.

CHIPS RAFFERTY
(*Ealing*)

RAZUMNY, Alexander. Director. Born Elizavetgrad, 1891. Became stage actor in 1908 and remained in the theatre six years. In 1914 studied at Odessa Art School. Entered films in 1916 as artist and cameraman. Is recognized as one of pioneers of Soviet cinematography. Later directed many Soviet films, including : *The Insurrection, Brigade Commander Ivanoff, The Song of Kamenka.* For the Phoebus Company in Berlin he directed : *Superfluous People, The Queen of Spades, Prince or Clown,* and many others. A pioneer in production of children's films in the Moscow studios. 1947-8 : made *Mikhluha Makhlay,* the story of a Soviet explorer.

REAGAN, Ronald. Born Tampico, Illinois, Feb. 6, 1912. Ht. 6 ft. ; wt. 170 lb. Educ. public schools, Galesbury, Monmouth, Tampico, Dixon ; Eureka College, Illinois (B.A.). Became sports columnist on Des Moines newspaper and radio sports commentator. To gain acting experience, joined touring company ; but it was while he was covering a sports event that film talent scout spotted him. First film : *Love is on the Air* (Warn), 1937. Other films include : *Submarine D.1, Sergeant Murphy, Swing Your Lady, Accidents Will Happen, Cowboy From Brooklyn, Going Places, Dark Victory, Hell's Kitchen, Angels Wash Their Faces ;* 1940 (all Warn) : *Brother Rat & a Baby, An Angel From Texas, Murder in the Air, Knute Rockne—All American, Tugboat Annie Sails Again, Sante Fé Trail ;* 1941 : *The Bad Man* (MGM), *Million Dollar Baby* (Warn), *International Squadron* (Warn), *Nine Lives are Not Enough* (Warn), *Kings Row* (Warn) ; 1942 : *Juke Girl* (Warn), *Desperate Journey* (Warn) ; 1943 : *This is the Army* (Warn). 1942-6, war service in U.S.A.A.F. ; 1947 : *Stallion Road* (Warn), *Night Unto Night* (Warn), *Mary Hagen* (Warn) ; 1948 : *The Voice of the Turtle* (Warn).

REDGRAVE, Michael. Born Bristol, March 20 1908. Ht. 6 ft. 3 in. ; wt. 176 lb. Brown hair, Blue eyes. Educ. Clifton College ; Magdalene College, Cambridge, and in Germany and France, with honours in French, German and English. Made unofficial stage debut at 2, when he was carried on stage by father at Melbourne, Australia. Left Cambridge, 1930, to become languages master at Cranleigh School. Produced school plays, " walked on " at Stratford Festival in holidays. Then spent two years with Liverpool Repertory, and one year with Old Vic Company. Believed himself not to be photogenic, and declined film offers, until satisfactory test for Gainsborough gave him five-year contract with right to spend six months of each year on stage. First film *The Lady Vanishes* (Gains) 1938. Favourite role : ventriloquist in *Dead of Night.* Served in Royal Navy 1941-2. Films include : *Climbing High, Stolen Life, The Stars Look Down* (Grafton-Grand Nat). 1941 : *Kipps* (20th-Brit), *Jeannie* (Hellman) ; 1942 : *Thunder Rock* (Charter) ; 1945 : *The Way to the Stars* (Two Cities), *Dead of Night* (Ealing) ; 1946 : *The Captive Heart* (Ealing), *The Years Between* (Box) ; 1947 : *The Man Within* (Box), *Fame is the Spur* (Boultings-Two Cities). Went to Hollywood, 1947, where he appeared in *Mourning Becomes Electra* (RKO), *The Secret Beyond the Door* (UI).

REED, Carol. Director. Born London, Dec. 30, 1906. Educ. King's School, Canterbury. At 17, worked in Maine logging camp. Became actor with British repertory companies. Appeared in Edgar Wallace's play " The Terror ", London, and remained with Wallace for five years as actor, stage director and right-hand man. Joined Basil Dean at Ealing Studios as dialogue director ; then assistant director, and production manager. Began directing, 1945, with *Midshipman Easy* (Ealing). Also directed : *Laburnam Grove, Talk of the Devil, Bank Holiday, Who's Your Lady Friend ?, The Stars Look Down, Night Train to Munich, The Girl in the News, Kipps, The Young Mr. Pitt, A Letter From England* (a film made for M.O.I., introducing Celia Johnson to the screen). 1942-5, director for Army Film Unit ; with Garson Kanin co-directed *The True Glory ;* directed *The Way Ahead. Odd Man Out.* 1947 : formed independent unit, Carol Reed Productions, for which he made *The Lost Illusion.*

REED, Donna. Real name Donna Mullenger. Born Denison, Iowa, Jan. 27. Ht. 5 ft. $3\frac{1}{2}$ in. ; wt. 115 lb. Brown hair, brown eyes. Educ. Los Angeles City College. Appeared in school plays. Trained as a secretary. Won a beauty contest and given a screen test. First film : *The Get-Away* (MGM), 1941. Other films (all MGM) include—1941 : *Shadow of the Thin Man, The Bugle Sounds ;* 1942 : *Courtship of Andy Hardy, Apache Trail, Calling Dr. Gillespie, Mokey, Eyes in the Night ;* 1943 : *The Human Comedy, Crazy to Kill, Thousands Cheer, The Man from Down Under ;* 1944 : *See Here Private Hargrove, The Picture of Dorian Gray, Gentle Annie ;* 1945 : *They Were Expendable ;* 1946 : *Faithful in My Fashion* (MGM), *It's a Wonderful Life* (RKO) ; 1947 : *Green Dolphin Street* (MGM).

REED, Maxwell. Born Larne, Northern Ireland, 1920. Ht. 6 ft. 3 in. Dark brown hair, grey eyes. Educ. Shrewsbury and Charterhouse schools. At 15 ran away from school and travelled round the world as ship's galley boy ; made two trips to Spain during the Civil War with the famous blockade-runner " Potato Jones ". Then went back to school at Charterhouse and began to take interest in the stage. Had studied for four months at Royal Academy of Dramatic Art, when World War II began : joined the R.A.F. but was discharged on medical grounds in 1941. He then went back to sea but was again discharged in 1943. Next resumed acting career, and joined Scarborough Repertory Company, also with Windsor Repertory Company, Palmer's Green Intimate Theatre, and Old Vic. Then followed small parts in films. First important screen role in *The Brothers* (Gains) 1947. In 1947 also appeared in *Dear Murderer* (Gains), *Night Beat* (LFP) ; 1948 : *Daughter of Darkness* (Alliance), *Daybreak* (Gains).

REED, Phillip. Born Brooklyn, New York, March 25. Ht. 6 ft. 2 in. ; wt. 185 lb. Black hair, hazel eyes. Educ. Erasmus Hall High School. Enrolled at Cornell University but left in his first year to join a New Jersey theatrical company. Appeared in variety and on New York stage in " Grand Hotel ", " Ziegfeld Follies of 1931 ", " Serena Blandish ", and other shows. First film : *Female* (Warn), 1933. Other films include : *The House on 56th Street, Lost Lady, Dr. Monica, Registered Nurse, Bedside, Affairs of a Gentleman, Glamour, The Woman in Red, Accent on Youth, Klondike Annie, The Last of the Mohicans, The Luckiest Girl in the World, Madame X, Merrily We Live, Aloma of the South Seas, Week-end for Three ;* 1942 : *Gentleman After Dark* (UA) ; 1943 : *Old Acquaintance* (Warn). 1943-5 served in U.S. Navy. 1946 : *People Are Funny* (Para), *Big Town* (Para), *Once and for All* (PRC), *Song of Scheherazade* (Univ), *Her Sister's Secret* (PRC), *Pirates of Monterey* (U!) ; 1947 : *Song of the Thin Man* (MGM), *Big Town After Dark* (Para).

RELPH, Michael. Producer, production designer. Born Broadstone, Dorset, 1915. Entered films, 1932, as assistant art director at Gaumont-British studios. Joined Warner-British as art director for more than 30 films, mostly " quickies ". Later joined Ealing studios as art director for *The Half-way House, Dead of Night, Nicholas Nickleby.* Has also done considerable work in stage designing. From 1946 at Ealing Studios has collaborated with director Basil Dearden as associate producer and production designer. His recent films include : *The Captive Heart, Frieda, Saraband For Dead Lovers.*

REMARQUE, Erich Maria. Writer. Born Osnabrück, Germany, 1898. Novels filmed include : *All Quiet on the Western Front, The Road Back, Three Comrades, Arch of Triumph.*

RENAUD, Madeleine. Born Paris, Feb. 21, 1903. Educ. Paris. Trained for stage at Paris Conservatoire and made professional debut at Théâtre Francais, followed by tours throughout Europe. Film debut in *L'Etrange Monsieur Victor.* Her films include : *Jean de la Lune, La Belle Marinière, Mistigri, La Couturière de Lunéville, La Maternelle, Maria Chapdelaine, Les Demi-Vierges, Remorque, Le Ciel Est à Vous.*

RENNIE, Michael. Born Bradford, Aug. 25, 1909. Ht. 6 ft. 3 in. ; wt. 176 lb. Black hair, blue eyes. Educ. Harrogate and Leys School, Cambridge. Worked in worsted spinning factory, in steel and rope works, and later as a car salesman, before deciding to become an actor. Went into Repertory at Windsor and York. Got his first chance in films as stand-in for Robert Young, then playing in *Secret Agent* at Gaumont-British Studios, London, in 1936. Rennie was also given a few speaking lines in this film. Returned to repertory at Wakefield, where he played Professor Higgins in " Pygmalion ". Early films include : *Gangway, Divorce of Lady X, This Man in Paris* ; 1940 : *Dangerous Moonlight,* (RKO-Brit) ; 1941 : *Ships With Wings* (Ealing). Served in R.A.F. 1941-3. 1945 : *I'll Be Your Sweetheart* (Gains), *The Wicked Lady* (Gains) ; 1946 : *Caesar and Cleopatra* (Pascal) ; 1947 : *Root of All Evil* (Gains), *White Cradle Inn* (Peak) ; 1948 : *Idol of Paris* (Premier).

RENOIR, Jean. Writer, director. Born Paris, Sept. 15, 1894. Educ. Baccalaureate High School, Paris. Studied sculpture, but became newspaper and magazine correspondent. Entered films as writer-director of French film : *Nana,* 1929. Other French films include : *The Little Match Girl, Tire Au Flanc, La Chienne, Madame Bovary, Toni, Le Crime de Mr. Lange, Les Bas Fonds, La Marseillaise, La Grande Illusion, La Bête Humaine, La Règle du Jeu, Partie de Campagne.* Went to Hollywood 1940, where he has directed : *Swamp Water, This Land is Mine, The Southerner, Diary of a Chambermaid, Woman on the Beach.*

REVERE, Anne. Born New York City, June 25, 1907. Ht. 5 ft. 6 in. ; wt. 125 lb. Brown hair, grey eyes. Educ. Westfield High School, New Jersey. Wellesley College. Youthful ambition, to be a doctor. On leaving school, first taught languages. Then joined Stuart Walker Stock Company, 1928. Made a hit in " Double Door ", and made screen debut in the same role in *Double Door* (Para) 1934. Other films include : 1940 : *The Howards of Virginia* (Col) ; 1941 : *Men of Boys' Town* (MGM) ; 1942 : *Remember the Day* (20th) ; 1943 : *The Meanest Man in the World* (20th), *The Song of Bernadette* (20th), *Star Spangled Rhythm*

(Para), *Old Acquaintance* (Warn) ; 1944 : *Sunday Dinner for a Soldier* (20th), *National Velvet* (MGM), *Rainbow Island* (Para), *The Thin Man Goes Home* (MGM) ; 1945 (all 20th) : *Keys of the Kingdom, Don Juan Quilligan, Fallen Angel, Dragonwyck* ; 1947 : *The Shocking Miss Pilgrim* (20th), *Body and Soul* (Enterprise-MGM) ; 1948 : *Gentleman's Agreement* (20th), *Secret Beyond the Door* (UI).

REYNOLDS, Gene. Born Cleveland, Ohio, 1927. Educ. MGM Studio School, Culver City ; University of California. On the stage at 6 in " We Think We Can " at Detroit Comedy Theatre. Went to Hollywood to play in " Our Gang " children's comedies, and stayed to make films his career. Has since appeared in *Thank You Jeeves !, Sins of Man, The Californian, Madame " X ", Of Human Hearts, In Old Chicago, The Crowd Roars, Boys Town, Love Finds Andy Hardy, The Flying Irishman, Man's Heritage, Melody of Youth, Bad Little Angel, The Blue Bird.* 1940 : *The Mortal Storm* (MGM), *Edison The Man* (MGM), *Sante Fé Trail* (Warn), *Gallant Sons* (MGM) ; 1941 : *Andy Hardy's Private Secretary* (MGM), *The Penalty* (MGM), *Adventure in Washington* (Col) ; 1942 : *The Tuttles of Tahiti* (RKO), *Eagle Squadron* (Univ).

REYNOLDS, Joyce. Born San Antonio, Texas, Oct. 7, 1924. Ht. 5 ft. 3½ in. ; wt. 110 lb. Brown hair, brown eyes. Educ. University of California. Played title role in " Alice in Wonderland " at University where she was seen by film scout. First film : *Yankee Doodle Dandy* (Warn) 1942. Other films (all Warn) : 1942 : *George Washington Slept Here ;* 1943 : *Thank Your Lucky Stars !, The Constant Nymph ;* 1944 : *The Adventures of Mark Twain, Hollywood Canteen, Janie ;* 1946 : *Janie Gets Married ;* 1947 : *Need for Each Other.*

REYNOLDS, Marjorie. Real name Marjorie Godspeed. Born Buhl, Idaho, Aug. 12, 1921. Ht. 5 ft. 3 in. ; wt. 106 lb. Honey-blonde hair, brown eyes. Educ. Los Angeles High School. Trained as dancer at 4 in Los Angeles ; appeared in plays and in silent films : *Scaramouche, Svengali, Revelation, The Broken Wing.* Made two films as dancer at 16 : *Wine, Women and Song* and *College Humour.* Later was in musicals : *Big Broadcast of 1935, Champagne Waltz, College Holiday.* After having left school, studied drama instead of dancing. Played in forty-two Westerns, then in twenty-five thrillers, also in serials : *Tailspin Tommy, Mr. Wong, Tillie the Toiler.* Then returned as dancer opposite Fred Astaire in *Holiday Inn* (Para) 1942. Recent films include : 1943 : *Star Spangled Rhythm* (Para), *Dixie* (Para) ; 1944 : *Up in Mabel's Room* (UA), *Ministry of Fear* (Para), *Three's a Family* (UA) ; 1945 : *Bring on the Girls* (Para), *Duffy's Tavern ;* 1946 : *Meet Me On Broadway* (Col), *Monsieur Beaucaire* (Para), *The Time of Their Lives* (Univ) ; 1947 : *Heaven Only Knows* (Seymour Nebenzal-UA).

RHODES, Marjorie. Born Hull, Apr. 9, 1902. Ht. 5 ft. 4 in. Brown hair, green-hazel eyes. Ran away from home to go on the stage. Toured with concert party, then played in short season of Shakespeare in provinces. Left stage to be married. Returned after fifteen years to appear with Edna Best in London in " Can We Tell ?", 1938. Made first screen appearance in *Poison Pen* (ABPC) 1939. Other films include—1940 : *Love on the Dole* (Brit Nat) ; 1942 : *World of Plenty* (Rotha), *Escape to Danger*

(RKO-Brit) ; 1943 : *Squadron Leader " X "* (RKO-Radio), *Theatre Royal* (Brit-Nat), *When We Are Married* (Brit Nat) ; 1944 : *It Happened One Sunday* (ABPC) ; 1945 : *Great Day* (RKO-Brit) ; 1946 : *School for Secrets* (Two Cities) ; 1947 : *Uncle Silas* (Two Cities).

RICHARD-WILLM, Pierre. Born Bayonne, Basses Pyrénées, France, Nov. 3, 1895. Fair hair, blue eyes. Educ. Paris : École Alsacienne, and École des Beaux-Arts. Began his career as a sculptor, but interest in the theatre led to stage partnership with Ida Rubenstein. Later played at Théâtre de l'Odéon, Paris, for four years. Made film debut in *Toute sa Vie* and gradually left stage for screen. His films include : *Un Soir du Front, Autour d'une Enquête, Le Petit Bout, Sous le Casque de Cuir, Pergolèse, Kiki, Baby, La Fille du Régiment, Pour Etre Aimé, L'Epervier, Le Grand Jeu, La Maison dans la Dune, Les Nuits Moscovites, Le Prince Jean, Barcarolle, Stradivarius, Carnet de Bal, Tamara, Werther, La Tragédie Impériale, Le Courrier du Sud, Anne-Marie, Les Jours Heureux, La Duchesse de Langeais, La Croisée des Chemins, Le Comte de Monte-Cristo, La Fiancée des Tenèbres, Rêves d'Amour, Le Beau Voyage, La Loi du Nord.*

RICHARDS, Ann. Born Sydney, Australia, 1918. Ht. 5 ft. 5 in. ; wt. 118 lb. Honey-blonde hair, grey eyes. Educ. Ascham College, Sydney. Became secretary, was amateur actress, entered Australian films. First film : *It Isn't Done* (Cinesound) 1937. Other Australian films include : *Tall Timber, Lovers, The Rudd Family, Come Up Smiling, Hundred Thousand Cobbers.* At outbreak of World War II toured troop-training area with repertory. Made her Hollywood debut in short : *The Woman in the House* (MGM). Recent films include :—1944 : *An American Romance* (MGM) ; 1945 : *Love Letters* (Para) ; 1946 : *Badman's Territory* (RKO) ; 1946 : *The Searching Wind* (Para) ; 1947 : *Lost Honeymoon* (Eagle Lion-Hollywood).

RICHARDSON, Sir Ralph. Born Cheltenham, Glos, Dec. 19, 1902. Ht. 6 ft. ; wt. 166 lb. Brown hair, grey eyes. Made his first stage appearance as Lorenzo, in " The Merchant of Venice ", Little Theatre, Brighton, 1922. After touring in the provinces for four years, joined Birmingham Repertory, 1926. Appeared on West End stage in many notable plays, then joined Old Vic in 1930. Film debut in *The Ghoul* (GB) 1933. Early films include : *Friday the Thirteenth, Return of Bulldog Drummond, Bulldog Jack, Things to Come, Man Who Could Work Miracles, Divorce of Lady " X ", South Riding, The Citadel, " Q " Planes, Four Feathers, The Lion Has Wings.* Joined the Fleet Air Arm in 1939, was given special leave to appear in *The Day Will Dawn*—U.S. title *The Avengers* (Soskin, 1942) and *The Silver Fleet* (Archers) 1943. Released from services to re-establish with Laurence Olivier the Old Vic Company, under the auspices of C.E.M.A. Recent films : 1946 : *School for Secrets* (Two Cities). 1947 : *Anna Karenina* (LFP) ; 1948 : *The Lost Illusion* (Carol Reed). Was knighted January, 1947.

RILLA, Walter. Born Neunkirchen, Saar, Germany, Aug. 22, 1895. Educ. University of Koenigsberg ; Breslau ; Berlin. Actor, writer, producer, violinist. Made stage debut at Die Tribune Theater, Berlin, 1921. First film in Britain : *The Scarlet Pimpernel* (LFP) 1934. Returned to Berlin and fell under Nazi suspicion. Escaped to Britain in 1936. 1939, joined B.B.C. European service on broadcasts to Germany, later appointed a feature and drama producer. Films

include : *Victoria the Great, Sixty Glorious Years, Black Eyes, At the Villa Rose.* 1941 : *House of Mystery ;* 1943 : *Adventures of Tartu* (MGM-Brit) ; 1944 : *Candlelight in Algeria* (King), *Mr. Emmanuel* (Two Cities) ; 1946 : *The Lisbon Story* (Brit Nat).

RISKIN, Robert. Writer, director, producer. Born New York. At 17 was writing for Paramount. His stage plays include : " She Couldn't Say No ", " The Mad Turtle ", " The Lady Lies ", and others ; collaborated with Edith Fitzgerald on " Many a Slip " and " Illicit ". Joined Columbia as writer ; his scripts include : *Men in Her Life, Men Are Like That, Miracle Woman, American Madness, The Big Timer, Platinum Blonde, Night Club Lady, Three Wise Girls, Ann Carver's Profession, Lady for a Day, Ex-Lady, Broadway Bill, It Happened One Night* (Academy Award, 1934), *Carnival, The Whole Town's Talking, Lost Horizon, Shopworn, Mr. Deeds Goes to Town, When You're in Love* (also directed), *You Can't Take It with You ;* associate producer, *They Shall Have Music, The Real Glory ;* co-produced *Meet John Doe ;* collaborated on original screenplay, *The Thin Man Goes Home ;* wrote and produced *Magic Town.*

ROBINSON, Edward G. Real name Emanuel Goldenberg. Born Bucharest, Dec. 12, 1893. Ht. 5 ft. 8 in. ; wt. 154 lb. Black hair, brown eyes. Educ. New York public schools ; Columbia University (M.A.). Youthful ambition to become a minister. Appeared in school plays. Served in World War I with U.S. Navy. First appearance on the professional stage was in a vaudeville sketch written by himself, " The Bells of Conscience". Other stage appearances include : " The Man With Red Hair", " The Brothers Karamazov", " Peer Gynt", " The Adding Machine", " The Idle Inn". Made first film, *The Bright Shawl* (First National) in 1923, but concentrated on stage work until coming of sound. Films include : *The Hole in the Wall, The Widow from Chicago, Little Caesar* (Warn) 1932, *Five Star Final, Smart Money, Two Seconds, Silver Dollar, The Little Giant, I Loved a Woman, The Man With Two Faces, The Whole Town's Talking, Barbary Coast, Bullets or Ballots, Thunder in the City, Kid Galahad, The Last Gangster, A Slight Case of Murder, The Amazing Dr. Clitterhouse, I Am the Law, Confessions of a Nazi Spy, Blackmail.* 1940 : *Dr. Ehrlich's Magic Bullet* (Warn), *Brother Orchid* (Warn), *A Dispatch from Reuter's* (Warn) ; 1941 : *The Sea Wolf* (Warn), *Manpower* (Warn), *Unholy Partners* (MGM) ; 1942 : *Larceny Inc.* (Warn), *Tales of Manhattan* (20th) ; 1943 : *Flesh and Fantasy* (Univ), *Destroyer* (Col) ; came to Britain to appear in *Journey Together* (R.A.F. Film Unit), completed 1945 ; 1944 : *Tampico* (20th), *Double Indemnity* (Para), *Mr. Winkle Goes to War* (Col), *The Woman in the Window* (Col) ; 1945 : *Our Vines Have Tender Grapes* (MGM), *Scarlet Street* (Univ), *The Stranger* (RKO) ; 1947 : *The Red House* (Sol Lesser-UA) ; 1948 : *All My Sons* (UI), *Night Has a Thousand Eyes* (Para).

ROBSON, Flora. Real name Flora MacKenzie Robson. Born South Shields, Durham, Mar. 28, 1902. Ht. 5 ft. 8½ in. ; wt. 133 lb. Educ. Palmers Green High School. Trained at Royal Academy of Dramatic Art, where she won Bronze Medal, 1921. Was a factory welfare worker in a food processing factory at Welwyn at one period of her career. First London appearance, was as Queen Margaret in " Will Shakespeare " in 1921. After making film debut in *Dance Pretty Lady !* (BIF) 1931, she played the Empress in *Catherine the Great* (LFP) 1934, and

Queen Elizabeth in *Fire Over England* (LFP) 1937. Has since made films in Hollywood and Britain, including *Wuthering Heights*, *The Lion Has Wings*, *Poison Pen*, *We Are Not Alone*. 1940 : *Invisible Stripes* (Warn), *The Sea Hawk* (Warn) ; 1941 : *Bahama Passage* (Para) ; 1942 : *Saratoga Trunk*—released 1946 (Warn) ; 1944 : *2000 Women* (Gains) ; 1945 : *Great·Day* (RKO-Brit) ; 1946 : *Caesar and Cleopatra* (Pascal), *The Years Between* (Box) ; 1947 : *Black Narcissus* (Archers), *Frieda* (Ealing), *Holiday Camp* (Gains), *Good Time Girl* (Gains) ; 1948 : *Saraband for Dead Lovers* (Ealing).

ROC, Patricia. Real name Felicia Riese. Born Hampstead, London, June 7, 1918. Ht. 5 ft. 4 in. ; wt. 102 lb. Dark hair, blue eyes. Educ. Francis Holland Church of England School, Regent's Park, London ; Bartram Gables School, Broadstairs, Kent ; Paris. As schoolgirl, had several paintings exhibited, and painted fresco in school chapel. Studied at Royal Academy of Dramatic Art and made debut in " Nuts and May ", Ambassadors Theatre, London, 1937. Seen by film scout and given screen test in Paris, followed by first film role with Harry Bauer in Korda's *Rebel Son*—originally *Taras Bulba*, made on the Continent, 1938. Films include : *The Gaunt Stranger*, *A Window in London*, *Doctor O'Dowd*, *The Mind of Mr. Reeder* ; 1940 : *Three Silent Men* (John Baxter) ; 1942 : *The Farmer's Wife* (ABPC), *Let the People Sing* (Brit-Nat) ; 1943 : *Millions Like Us* ; (Gains) ; 1944 : *2000 Women* (Gains), *Love Story* (Gains), *Madonna of the Seven Moons* (Gains) ; 1945 : *The Wicked Lady* (Gains), *Johnny Frenchman* (Ealing), *Canyon Passage* (Univ) made in Hollywood ; 1947 : *The Brothers* (Gains), *So Well Remembered* (RKO), made in Britain, *Jassy* (Gains), *When The Bough Breaks* (Gains). 1948 : *One Night With You* (Two Cities).

ROCHESTER. Real name Eddie Anderson. Born Oakland, California, Sept. 18, 1905. Ht. 5 ft. 7 in. ; wt. 186 lb. In vaudeville and floor shows ; then on radio in Jack Benny broadcasts. Made screen debut in *Transient Lady* (Univ) 1936. Films include : *Rainbow on the River*, *Three Men on a Horse*, *Jezebel*, *You Can't Take It With You*, *Kentucky*, *Thanks for the Memory*, *Honolulu*, *Gone With The Wind*. 1940 : *Buck Benny Rides Again* (Para), *Love Thy Neighbour* (Para) ; 1941 : *Topper Returns* (UA), *Kiss the Boys Goodbye* (Para), *Birth of the Blues* (Para) ; 1942 : *Tales of Manhattan* (20th), *The Meanest Man in the World* (20th), *Star-Spangled Rhythm* (Para), *Cabin in the Sky* (MGM) ; 1943 : *What's Buzzin', Cousin ?* (Col), *Broadway Rhythm* (MGM) ; 1944 : *The Show-Off* (MGM) ; 1945 : *Brewster's Millions* (UA), *I Love a Bandleader* (Col) ; 1946 : *The Sailor Takes a Wife* (MGM), *Memory for Two* (Col).

ROGERS, Ginger. Real name Virginia Katharine McMath. Born Independence, Missouri, July 16, 1911. Ht. 5 ft. 8 in. ; wt. 108 lb. Red hair, blue-green eyes. Champion Charleston dancer of Texas at 14 ; appeared in vaudeville ; sang and danced with Paul Ash band, Chicago Oriental Theatre. Made success in first Broadway show " Top Speed ", followed by triumph in " Girl Crazy ". Made five films at Paramount's Long Island Studio while appearing on stage. Went to Hollywood after " Girl Crazy ", where she played small parts and two-reel comedy roles until she became Fred Astaire's partner in *Flying Down to Rio* (RKO), 1933. Became established as dramatic actress in *Stage Door* (RKO)

1937. First film : *Young Man of Manhattan* (Para) 1930. Early films include : *Queen High*, *The Sap from Syracuse*, *Broadway Bad*, *Don't Bet on Love*, *Gold Diggers of 1933*, *Sitting Pretty*, *The Tip Off*, *Twenty Million Sweethearts*, *The Gay Divorcee*, *Romance in Manhattan*, *Change of Heart*, *Roberta*, *Star of Midnight*, *Top Hat*, *In Person*, *Follow the Fleet*, *Shall We Dance ?*, *Having a Wonderful Time*, *Carefree*, *The Story of Vernon and Irene Castle*, *Bachelor Mother*, *Fifth Avenue Girl*. 1940 : *Primrose Path* (RKO), *Lucky Partners* (RKO), *Kitty Foyle* (RKO), *Tom Dick and Harry* (RKO) ; 1942 : *Roxie Hart* (20th), *Tales of Manhattan* (20th), *Once Upon a Honeymoon* (RKO) ; 1943 : *The Major and the Minor* (Para), *Lady in the Dark* (Para) ; 1944 : *Tender Comrade* (RKO), *I'll Be Seeing You* (UA) ; 1945 : *Weekend at the Waldorf* (MGM) ; 1947 : *Heartbeat* (RKO), *Magnificent Doll* (UI) ; 1948 : *It Had to be You* (Col).

ROGERS, Roy. Real name Leonard Slye. Born in Cincinnati, Ohio, November 5, 1912. Ht. 5 ft. 11 in. ; wt. 160 lb. Light brown hair, blue eyes. Began his film career under name " Dick Weston ". Roy learned to ride on his parents' farm at Duck Run. First job was in a shoe factory ; one of the customers allowed him to ride thoroughbreds on his farm. At 12 learned to play the guitar and memorized many traditional square dances and cowboy songs. In 1929 went to California and worked as truck driver, labourer, and navvy. In early 'thirties was member of several cowboy bands, all of which failed. Later, with Bob Nolan and Tim Spencer, formed " The Sons of the Pioneers " band, which now appears in every Roy Rogers film. Their first recording success, " The Last Round-up " led to a series of radio sketches. The band made its film debut in a two-reel comedy, starring Joan Davis in 1935. Also played in *The Big Show*, a Gene Autry western in 1936. When new cowboy star was required, Rogers played and sang " Tumbling Tumbleweeds " at an audition and got a long-term contract. First starring film was *Under Western Stars*, 1938. Has since made about seventy films for Republic and appeared as " guest star " in others. Recent films include : *Hoosier Holiday*, *In Old Oklahoma*, *Casanova in Burlesque*, *The Cowboy and the Senorita*, *Yellow Rose of Texas*, *San Fernando Valley*, *Song of Nevada*, *Show-Off*, *Hitch-hike to Happiness*, *Sunset in El Dorado*, *Bells of Rosarita*, *Man from Oklahoma*, *Don't Fence Me In !*, *Along the Navajo Trail*, *Song of Arizona*, *Rainbow Over Texas*, *My Pal Trigger*, *Roll on Texas Moon*, *Out California Way*, *Helldorado*, *Under Nevada Skies*, *Home in Oklahoma*, *The Gay Ranchero*, *Springtime in the Sierras*, *Bells of San Angelo*, *Apaché Rose*, *On the Old Spanish Trail*. Also guest appearances in *Hit Parade of 1947*, *Lake Placid Serenade*. Voted the most popular star by young British filmgoers in the first Children's Questionnaire organized by Sidney Bernstein in 1947.

ROLAND, Gilbert. Real name Luis Antonio Damaso De Alonso. Born Juarez, Mexico, Dec. 11, 1905. Ht. 5 ft. 11 in. ; wt. 165 lb. Black hair, brown eyes. Educ. private school, Mexico. Expected by his family to carry on family tradition as bull-fighter for which he received early training, but ran away from home to become actor. Went to Hollywood without any stage experience and made screen debut in *The Plastic Age* (Schulberg) 1925. During World War II, he served three years in the U.S. Army. Outstanding films include : *Camille* (MGM), *Men in Her Life* (Col), *Last Train From Madrid*, *Juarez*. 1940 : *The Sea Hawk* (Warn), *Rangers of Fortune* (Para) ; 1941 :

Angels with Broken Wings (Rep), *My Life With Caroline* (RKO) ; 1942 : *Isle of Missing Men* (Mono) ; 1945 : *Captain Kidd* (UA) ; 1946 : *The Gay Cavalier* (Mono) ; 1947 : *Pirates of Monterey* (Mono) ; *The Other Love* (MGM-Enterprise) ; *South of Monterey* (Mono), *Beauty and the Bandit* (Mono), *Riding the California Trail* (Mono), *High Conquest* (Mono).

ROLFE, Guy. Born Hendon, Middlesex, Dec. 27, 1915. Ht. 6 ft. 4 in. Brown hair, blue eyes. Spent early youth on farm at Great Shefford, Berks. Formed touring team with two young mechanics who, from scrap engines and bodies, built racing cars and motor cycles, which he drove in races. Then at 19 travelled fair grounds as boxer at £4 a week. Later joined touring company of players in Southern Ireland and after two years returned to London and became stand-in for Michael Redgrave in *The Lady Vanishes* (Gains) 1938. In 1945, deciding to enter films, joined repertory as the best short cut to the screen. Was seen by talent scout while appearing at the Connaught Repertory Theatre, Worthing, and was given small part in *Hungry Hill* (Two Cities) 1946. Other films include—1947 : *Odd Man Out* (Two Cities), *Nicholas Nickleby* (Ealing), *Meet Me at Dawn* (Excelsior-20th), *Uncle Silas* (Two Cities) ; 1948 : *Broken Journey* (Gains), *Easy Money* (Gains).

ROMANCE, Viviane. Real name Pauline Ortmans. Born Amiens, France. At age of 14 worked in a factory, making imitation pearls, and later as a seamstress. Then became chorus girl at the Moulin Rouge, can-can dancer at the Bal Tabarin, and partner to dancer Harry Pilcer. Began film career as show-girl extra. Films include : *Liliom, Les Yeux Noirs, Les Deux Gagnants, Marchands d'Amour, Princesse Tam-Tam, Le Club des Aristocrates, La Bandéra, Retour au Paradis, La Belle Equipe, Mademoiselle Docteur* (French version), *L'Ange du Foyer, L'Homme à Abattre, Le Puritain, Naples au Baiser de Feu, Le Joueur, L'Etrange M. Victor, La Maison du Maltais, Gibraltar, Prison de Femmes, L'Esclave Blanche, La Tradition de Minuit, Angélica, La Vénus Aveugle, Une Femme dans la Nuit, Feu Sacré, Cartacalha, Carmen, La Boite aux Rêves, La Route du Bagne, L'Affaire du Collier de la Reine, Panique, La Colère des Dieux, La Maison sous la Mer, Le Carrefour des Passions.*

ROMAY, Lina. Real name Elena Romay. Born New York, Jan. 16. Ht. 5 ft. 3 in. ; wt. 110 lb. Brown hair, brown eyes. Sang at local gathering in Detroit, 1940 : a weekly 15 minute radio programme resulted. When family moved to New York, Xavier Cugat signed her as vocalist for his band, with which she appeared in several films. First important role in *Adventure* (MGM) 1945, led to leading role in *Love Laughs at Andy Hardy* (MGM) 1946. First film appearance : *You Were Never Lovelier* (Col) 1942. Other films include—1943 : *Stage Door Canteen* (UA), *Tropicana* (Col) ; 1944 : *Two Girls and A Sailor* (MGM), *Bathing Beauty* (MGM) ; 1945 : *Weekend at the Waldorf* (MGM), *Adventure* (MGM) ; 1946 : *Honeymoon* (RKO), *Love Laughs at Andy Hardy* (MGM).

ROMERO, Cesar. Born New York, Feb 15, 1907. Ht. 6 ft. 3 in. ; wt. 190 lb. Black hair, dark brown eyes. Educ. Sanford School, Redding Ridge, Connecticut ; Riverdale Country School ; Collegiate School, New York. Early life was spent in luxury until his father's business crashed and he had to earn his own living. Took up dancing and was also given one or two small parts in plays. Engaged as dancer at the Park Central Roof, New York. Later, appeared on Broadway in " Lady Do ! ", " Strictly Dishonourable ", " Stella Brady " and " Social Register ". While playing on Broadway in " All Points West " was given a screen test. First film : *Metropolitan* (20th), 1935. Other films (all 20th) include : *Wee Willie Winkie, Happy Landing, Always Goodbye, The Return of the Cisco Kid*, Served in U.S. Navy during World War II, 1943-46. 1940 : *Viva Cisco Kid, Lucky Cisco Kid, The Gay Caballero, Romance of the Rio Grande* ; 1941 : *Tall, Dark and Handsome, Ride on Vaquero, The Great American Broadcast, Dance Hall, Week-End in Havana, A Gentleman at Heart* ; 1942 : *Tales of Manhattan, Orchestra Wives, Springtime in the Rockies* ; 1943 : *Coney Island, Wintertime* ; 1947 : *Carnival in Costa Rica.*

ROMNEY, Edana. Born Johannesburg, Mar. 15, 1919. Ht. 5 ft. 5½ in. ; wt. 119 lb. Brown hair and eyes. Educ. in a convent ; then studied ballet. Came to England at 14 to finish her education ; won scholarship to Royal Academy of Dramatic Art at 16 ; same year became leading lady to Matheson Lang in Margaret Steen's " Matador ". Played leads in the Open Air Theatre, Regent's Park, London, during the war and was also with the B.B.C. Repertory Company. Film debut in *Alibi* (Brit Lion) 1942. During the filming of *Alibi*, met scriptwriter Rudolph Cartier, with whom she formed Apollo Films, 1946, to write and produce their own films. Their first, *Corridor of Mirrors* (1948), in which she starred, was made at the Buttes-Chaumont studios in Paris.

ROOM, A. Director. Spent many of his early years in the theatre. Began professional career in 1914 as co-director at the Hebrew Philharmonic Theatre, Vilna, Russia. Went to Moscow 1923 and staged A. Faiko's " Lake Lulle " at the " Theatre of the Revolution " in which production he solved certain problems in the use of films in the theatre. Eventually he devoted himself entirely to films. His first film was made for the Moscow Advertising Company in 1924. Other films include : *In Pursuit of Moonshine, The Haven of Death, Bed and Sofa, The Traitor, The Five Year Plan, Invasion.*

ROONEY, Mickey. Real name Joe Yule, Jr., first known on screen as " Mickey McGuire ". Born Brooklyn, Sept. 23, 1922. Ht. 5 ft. 3 in. ; wt. 125 lb. Light brown hair, blue eyes. Began his career at 2 in parents' vaudeville act ; at 5 was touring in dance act. First film : *Not to Be Trusted*, 1926. As " Mickey McGuire " played 1927 in series of comedies based on cartoon character. Returned to vaudeville, as " Mickey Rooney ". Resumed films 1932 with Tom Mix in *My Pal the King* (Univ) and given MGM contract after role in *Hide-Out* (MGM), 1934. Films include : *Riffraff, A Midsummer Night's Dream, Ah Wilderness, Little Lord Fauntleroy, Captains Courageous, A Family Affair* (first of " Hardy Family " films) ; *Thoroughbreds don't Cry, You're Only Young Once, Judge Hardy's Children, The Boy From Barnardo's, Love Finds Andy Hardy, Boys Town, Stablemates, Adventures of Huckleberry Finn, The Hardy's Ride High, Babes in Arms* ; 1940 (all MGM) : *Young Tom Edison, Andy Hardy Meets Debutante, Strike Up the Band* ; 1941 : *Men of Boys Town, Andy Hardy's Private Secretary, Babes on Broadway, Life Begins for Andy Hardy, A Yank at Eton, Andy Hardy's Double Life* ; 1943 : *The Human Comedy, Thousands Cheer, Girl Crazy* ; 1944 : *Andy Hardy's Blonde Trouble, National Velvet.* War service with U.S. Army, 1944-46. 1946 : *Love Laughs at Andy Hardy* ; 1947 : *Summer Holiday, Killer McCoy.*

MICHAEL REDGRAVE
(*Universal-International*)

ROSAY, Francoise. Born Paris. Studied singing at French Conservatoire, at same time playing small stage roles at French National Theatre (Théâtre de l'Odéon). Went to St. Petersburg (now Leningrad), to appear at the Théâtre Michel, and returned to France shortly before World War I. Gave up the theatre when she married Jacques Feyder, French film director. Tested for films but not considered photogenic ; nevertheless played small parts in her husband's films. Scored notable success as an American woman in Feyder's silent film *Gribiche*, and later went to Hollywood with him where she appeared in a number of French-language versions, including *Si l'Empereur Savait Ca !*, and *The Magnificent Lie*. Returned to France, 1929. Among the best known of the films she made there are *La Kermesse Héroïque*, *Le Rosier de Madame Husson*, *Maternité*, *Carnet de Bal*, *Gens du Voyage*, *Ramuntcho*. In World War II broadcast in German to German women, which so infuriated the Nazis that when they occupied Paris they banned all her films. Bombed and machine-gunned while escaping to unoccupied France but finally reached Switzerland. Later went to Tunis, was caught there by German occupation, but escaped and went into hiding, and returned about the same time as the Allied armies. In Britain has appeared in *Halfway House* (Ealing) 1944, *Johnny Frenchman* (Ealing) 1945, *Saraband for Dead Lovers* (Ealing) 1948.

ROSHAL, G. Film producer, teacher. Born 1899. Working in the Soviet theatre in 1922 he stage-managed a series of plays in the " Theatre for the Youth " and in the Yiddish Theatre " Habima ". During this period he lectured on art, and wrote a book on the artistic education of children. Entered films 1925 and produced, among other films, *The Skotinins*, *Salamander*, *Two Women*. In 1933 he produced *A St. Petersburg Night*, one of the first Soviet talkies, which won a prize at the International Cinema Exhibition in Venice the following year. Other films include : *Dawn in Paris* (1937), *The Family Oppenheim* (1938), *In Search of Joy* (1939), *Armontov and Sons* (1941), *Song of Abay* (1943), *Pavlov* (1948)—the story of the great Russian scientist. Wrote the screenplay of *The New Gulliver* (1936). Is also teacher at Institute of Cinematography, Moscow.

ROSS, Hector. Born Thain, Scotland, Feb. 11, 1914. Ht. 6 ft. ; wt. 168 lb. Dark brown hair, brown eyes. Educ. Shrewsbury School. At 17 began six-year spell in repertory ; from Manchester Repertory went to Newcastle in 1938 to become manager of Playhouse Company. Wide experience in radio and television. Served in army 1939-45 ; towards end of his period of service, commanded Central Pool of Artists. Produced and acted in Jack Alldridge's play, " All This is Ended " (specially written for him), first for troops in Italy, then with all-soldier cast at Granville, Walham Green, London, 1946, followed by tour and broadcast. Also appeared on London stage in " Maiden Voyage " and " Drake's Drum ", in which he was seen by talent scout. First film : *Night Beat* (LFP) 1947. 1948 : *Bonnie Prince Charlie* (LFP).

ROTHA, Paul. Writer, documentary producer. Born London, 1907. Educ. London University ; Slade School of Art. Entered films 1928 in Art Department of British International Pictures at Elstree. Later with John Grierson at Empire Marketing Board Film Unit, 1931. Directed first film, *Contact*, for Imperial Airways, 1931-2. Director for Gaumont-British Instructional 1933-5 ; director of productions of Strand Films 1936-7. Visited U.S.A. 1937-8 as adviser to General Education Board of the Rockefeller Foundation, and while there advised and lectured on films in general for the Museum of Modern Art, New York. Joined Film Centre 1938 : started an independent unit, Paul Rotha Productions, 1941, and produced over 80 films for the Ministry of Information during World War II. In 1944 formed Films of Fact Ltd. for the making of documentary and educational films. Author of " The Film Till Now " 1930 ; " Celluloid " 1931 ; " Documentary Film " 1936, new edition 1939 ; " Movie Parade " 1936. Outstanding films include—1930 : *Shipyard* (Orient Line) ; 1935 : *The Face of Britain* (Gaumont-British Instructional) ; 1938 : *New Worlds for Old* (British Gas Council) ; 1939 : *Fourth Estate* (" The Times " newspaper) ; 1942 : *World of Plenty* (Ministry of Information) ; 1945 : *Land of Promise* (Films of Fact) ; 1946 : *A City Speaks* (Manchester City Corporation) ; 1947 : *The World is Rich* (Central Office of Information).

ROWLAND, Roy. Director. Born New York. Educ. University of Southern California. Began film career as a script clerk ; then became assistant director, then director of shorts, including " Cime Does Not Pay " series, Robert Benchley films and Pete Smith shorts. During World War II made Army and Navy training films. In 1942 directed first feature : *A Stranger in Town* (MGM). Other films include : *Lost Angel*, *Our Vines Have Tender Grapes*, *Romance of Rosy Ridge*, *Summer Holiday*, *Killer McCoy*.

ROZSA, Miklos. Composer. Born Budapest, Apr. 18, 1907. Entered Leipzig Conservatory at age of 18. Has composed much symphonic and chamber music. Visited London in 1935 for production of his Hungarian Ballet and stayed to write scores for London Film Productions including, *Knight Without Armour*, *The Squeaker*, *The Four Feathers*, *The Thief of Bagdad*. Went to United States 1941 to score *Lady Hamilton* and *Jungle Book*. Has since written music for many American films, including : *So Proudly We Hail*, *Five Graves to Cairo*, *Double Indemnity*, *Dark Waters*, *Because of Him*, *Blood on the Sun*, *The Lost Weekend*, *Lady on a Train*, *Spellbound*, *A Song to Remember* (incidental music), " The More I Know of Love " in *The Killers*.

RUGGLES, Charles. Born Los Angeles. Ht. 5ft. 6 in. ; wt. 145 lb. Light brown hair, light grey eyes. At parents' request studied chemistry and medicine, but at 15 left home for San Francisco where he was lucky enough to obtain stage work immediately, starting with a small part in " Nathan Hale", 1904. Played in repertory in San Fransisco and Los Angeles, and toured California. Made his screen debut in early talkie, *Gentlemen of the Press* (Para) 1928. Other films include : *The Lady Lies*, *Roadhouse Nights*, *Young Man of Manhattan*, *Queen High*, *Her Wedding Night*, *Charley's Aunt* (Col) 1930, *Trouble in Paradise*, *Evenings for Sale*, *Love Me Tonight*, *70,000 Witnesses*, *Husband's Holiday*, *This Reckless Age*, *Girl Habit*, *The Beloved Bachelor*, *Honour Among Lovers*, *The Smiling Lieutenant*, *One Hour With You*, *This is the Night*, *The Night of June 13*, *Murders in the Zoo*, *Terror Abroad*, *Mama Loves Papa*, *Girl Without a Room*, *Melody Cruise*, *Alice in Wonderland*, *If I Had a Million*, *Melody in Spring*, *Murder in the Private Car*, *Friends of Mr. Sweeney*, *Six of a Kind*,

Pursuit of Happiness, Ruggles of Red Gap, People Will Talk, The Big Broadcast of 1936, No More Ladies, Anything Goes, Early to Bed, Wives Never Know, Mind Your Own Business, Hearts Divided, Turn Off the Moon, Bringing Up Baby, Breaking the Ice, Service de Luxe, His Exciting Night, Yes My Darling Daughter, 1941 : *The Invisible Woman* (Univ), *Model Wife* (Univ), *Honeymoon for Three* (Warn), *The Perfect Snob* (20th), *The Parson of Panamint* (Para) ; 1942 : *Friendly Enemies* (UA) ; 1943 : *Dixie Dugan* (20th) ; 1944 : *Our Hearts Were Young and Gay* (Para), *The Doughgirls* (Warn), *Three is a Family* (UA) ; 1945 : *Incendiary Blonde* (Para), *Bedside Manner* (UA) ; 1946 : *A Stolen Life* (Warn), *Gallant Journey* (Col) ; *The Perfect Marriage* (Para) ; 1947 : *My Brother Talks to Horses* (MGM), *It Happened on Fifth Avenue* (Mono).

RUSSELL, Gail. Born Chicago, Sept. 21, 1925. Ht. 5 ft. 4½ in. ; wt. 111 lb. Educ. Santa Monica High School. Studied commercial art at evening school ; visited by talent scout after recommendation of class-mates who happened to get a lift in film executive's car. First film : *Henry Aldrich Gets Glamour* (Para) 1943. Other films (all Para) include : *Lady in the Dark* ; 1944 : *The Uninvited, Our Hearts Were Young and Gay* ; 1945 : *Her Heart in Her Throat, Salty O'Rourke, Our Hearts Were Growing Up, The Unseen* ; 1946 : *The Virginian, Calcutta* (Para); 1947 : *Bachelor Girls* (Andrew Stone-UA) ; 1948 : *Night has a Thousand Eyes* (Para).

RUSSELL, Jane. Real name Ernestine Jane Geraldine Russell. Born Bemidji, Minnesota. June 21, 1921. Ht. 5 ft. 7 in. ; wt. 122 lb. Dark hair, brown eyes. Educ. Joaquin Miller Grammar School, Burbank ; Van Nuys High School, California. Studied drama with Max Reindhardt and Maria Ouspenskaya. Was also a doctor's receptionist and a photographer's model. Obtained lead in *The Outlaw,* when Hollywood agent sent her picture to producer Howard Hughes. Film was made in 1943, but held by censorship until 1946 in America, and 1947 in Britain. Other films 1947 : *The Young Widow* (Hunt Stromberg-UA) ; 1948 : *Paleface* (Para).

RUSSELL, Rosalind. Born Waterbury, Connecticut, June 4, 1912. Ht. 5 ft. 5 in. ; wt. 120 lb. Black hair, dark brown eyes. Educ. St. Margaret's and Notre Dame, Waterbury ; Marymount College, Tarrytown, New York. At 17, travelled Europe before training at Academy of Dramatic Arts. Stage debut in summer theatre at Lake Placid ; then joined E. E. Clive's " all-English " company in Boston. Made her New York debut in " Garrick Gaieties ". While appearing on Broadway in " The Second Man ", was offered leading role in *Evelyn Prentice,* 1934. Other films include : *The President Vanishes, Forsaking All Others, China Seas, Rendezvous, Under Two Flags, Craig's Wife, Night Must Fall, Man Proof, Four's a Crowd, The Citadel* (MGM-Brit) 1938, *Fast and Loose, The Women* ; 1940 : *His Girl Friday* (Col), *Hired Wife* (Univ), *No Time for Comedy* (Warn), *This Thing Called Love* (Col) ; 1941 : *They Met in Bombay* (MGM), *The Feminine Touch* (MGM), *Design for Scandal* (MGM) ; 1942 : *Take a Letter, Darling* (Para), *My Sister Eileen* (Col) ; 1943 : *Flight For Freedom* (RKO), *What a Woman* (Col) ; 1945 : *Roughly Speaking* (Warn) ; 1946 : *Sister Kenny* (RKO), *She Wouldn't Say Yes* ; 1947 : *The Guilt of Janet Ames* (Col), *Mourning Becomes Electra* (RKO).

RUTHERFORD, Margaret. Born London, May 11, 1892. Educ. Wimbledon Hill School ; Ravenscroft, Eastbourne. Was originally teacher of elocution and pianoforte (A.R.C.M., L.R.A.M.). Studied for stage at Old Vic Theatre, and made debut there, 1925, as " Fairy With The Long Nose " in pantomime " Little Jack Horner ". In repertory at Oxford, Croydon and with Greater London Players ; London debut, 1933, at Vaudeville Theatre in " Wild Justice ". Plays include : " Hervey House ", " Short Story ". First film : *Talk of the Devil* (B and D) 1936. Other films include : *Dusty Ermine, Beauty and the Barge* ; 1943 : *Yellow Canary* (Wilcox-RKO), *The Demi-Paradise* (Two Cities) ; 1944 : *English Without Tears* (Two Cities) ; 1945 : *Blithe Spirit* (Cineguild) in which she gave a memorable performance as the energetic medium. 1947 : *While the Sun Shines* (Internat Screen), *Miranda* (Gains).

RYAN, Kathleen. Born County Dublin, Oct. 6, 1922. Ht. 5 ft. 7 in. ; wt. 125 lb. Red hair, brown eyes. Educ. Mount Annville Convent, Dundrum ; Dublin University (Bachelor of Commerce). Youthful ambition : to go on the stage. After convent schooling went to Europe for further education and then to University to take her B.C. in view of a proposed business career. After having attended drama classes and played in small parts at Gate and Abbey Theatres, finally met director Carol Reed ; then filming exteriors for *Odd Man Out* in Ireland ; when he offered her leading role opposite James Mason, she thought it a joke, and at first turned down the offer but eventually made film debut in *Odd Man Out* (Two Cities), 1947, and afterwards appeared in *Captain Boycott* (Individ) 1947. 1948 : *Esther Waters* (Wessex).

RYAN, Peggy. Real name Margaret Irene Ryan. Born Long Beach, California, Aug. 28, 1924. Ht. 5 ft. 4 in. ; wt. 99 lb. Brown hair, blue eyes. Daughter of stage family, she appeared at clubs and benefit performances at 2½. On stage in " Meet The People ", " They Can't Get You Down." Made her first film appearance at 10. Later danced in second important film with Donald O'Connor, which resulted in long-term contracts for both of them. First film : *Top of the Town* (Univ), 1937. Other films include : *What's Cookin'?, The Women Men Marry, The Flying Irishman, She Married a Cop* ; 1942 : *Girls' Town* (PRC), *Miss Annie Rooney* (UA), *Private Buckaroo* (Univ), *Give Out Sisters* (Univ), *Get Hep to Love* (Univ) ; 1943 : (both Univ) : *When Johnny Comes Marching Home, Top Man* ; 1944 (all Univ) : *The Merry Monahans, Follow the Boys, Babes on Swing Street, Bowery to Broadway, This is the Life!* 1945 (all Univ) : *Patrick the Great, That's the Spirit, Here Come the Co-eds, On Stage Everybody !, Men in her Diary.*

RYAN, Robert. Born Chicago, Nov. 11, 1909. Ht. 6 ft. 3 in. ; wt. 194 lb. Black hair, brown eyes. Educ. Loyola Academy, Chicago (B.A.). Left college 1932, and was in turn seaman, salesman, miner, cowboy, photographer's model, and labourer. A windfall of two thousand dollars enabled him to go to Hollywood, where he studied drama and appeared on stage with Luise Rainer in " A Kiss For Cinderella ", with Tallulah Bankhead in " Clash By Night ". First film appearance : *Name, Age and Occupation,* 1940. Other films include—1940 : *Golden Gloves* (Para), *North West Mounted Police* (Para) ; 1943 (all RKO-Radio) : *Bombadier, The Sky's The Limit, The Iron Major, Behind the Rising Sun, Gangway for Tomorrow, Marine Raiders ;* 1944 : *Tender Comrade ;* 1947 : *Crossfire ;* 1948 : *Woman on the Beach.*

SABU. Real name Sabu Dastagir. Born Mysore, India, Jan. 27, 1924. Ht. 5 ft. 7 in. Black hair, brown eyes. Educ. Beaconsfield, Bucks. Was stable boy for Maharajah of Mysore when at 10 he was noticed by director Robert Flaherty, then filming exteriors in India for *Elephant Boy* (LFP) 1937, and was given role of Toomai of the Elephants in this film. Brought to Britain for studio scenes and sent to school at Beaconsfield, where he quickly learnt English and excelled in sports. Appeared in *The Drum* (LFP) 1938. Was making *The Thief of Bagdad* (LFP) when war broke out ; then, with several others of the cast, went to California, to make the exteriors. Remained in Hollywood and became American citizen. War Service with U.S. Army Air Corps. American films include—1942 : *The Jungle Book* (Korda-Hollywood) ; 1943 : *White Savage* (Univ) ; 1944 : *Cobra Woman* (Univ) ; 1946 : *Tangier* (Univ). In Britain, 1946 : *Black Narcissus* (Archers) ; 1947 : *The End of the River* (Archers).

SAINT-CYR, Renée. Born Beausoleil, near Monte Carlo, France, 1910. Ht. 5 ft. 3 in. ; wt. 100 lb. Made first film in 1934, *Les Deux Orphelines ;* Paris stage debut, 1937, in *L'Opéra de Quat' Sous*. Films include : *Toto, L'Ecole des Cocottes, Arlette et ses Papas, Le Dernier Milliardaire, 27 Rue de la Paix, Les Loups, Entre Eux, Valse Eternelle, Trois Six Neuf, Crackerjack* (in Britain with Tom Walls, 1937), *Les Perles de la Couronne*.

ST. JOHN, Earl. Production executive. Born Baton Rouge, Louisiana. Educ. Louisiana State University. Entered silent films 1913 as salesman, covering Mexico and the southern states of U.S.A. In association with his uncle, Ed Davis, organised the first distribution of British films in Texas and Mexico, 1914. Served in U.S. Army during World War I : was demobilized in Liverpool, and remained in Britain. 1919-39, engaged in film distribution and exhibition. In 1939 appointed personal assistant to John Davis, Odeon Theatres. In Jan. 1947, appointed production adviser to the J. Arthur Rank Organisation. In June 1947 became joint managing director Two Cities Films.

SANDERS, George. Born St. Petersburg (now Leningrad), 1906. Ht. 6 ft. 3 in. ; wt. 215 lb. Brown hair, grey eyes. Educ. Dunhurst ; Bedales ; Brighton College ; Manchester Technical School. First job was selling cigarettes in Patagonia and Chile. Studied singing and appeared in revue. Also understudied Noel Coward in " Conversation Piece ". Film debut in *Strange Cargo* (BIP) 1929. Also appeared in *The Shape of Things to Come, Find the Lady, Dishonour Bright* and *The Outsider*, before going to Hollywood in 1937 to appear in *Lloyds of London*. Other films include : *Love Is News, Slave Ship, The Lady Escapes, Lancer Spy, International Settlement, Four Men and a Prayer, Nurse Edith Cavell, Confessions of a Nazi Spy.* 1940 : *The House of Seven Gables* (Univ), *Rebecca* (Selznick-UA), *Foreign Correspondent* (UA), *This Land is Mine* (RKO) ; 1941 : *Rage in Heaven* (MGM) ; 1942 : *Her Cardboard Lover* (MGM), *Tales of Manhattan,* (20th), *The Moon and Sixpence* (UA) ; 1943 : *Paris After Dark* (20th) ; 1944 : *The Lodger* (20th), *Action in Arabia* (RKO), *Summer Storm,* (UA) ; 1945 : *The Picture of Dorian Gray* (MGM), *Hangover Square* (20th), *The Strange Affair of Uncle Harry* (Univ) ; 1946 : *Scandal in Paris* (UA) ; 1947 : *The Strange Woman* (Hunt Stromberg-UA), *The Ghost and Mrs. Muir* (20th) ; 1948 : *The Private Affairs of Bel Ami* (Loew Lewin - MGM), *Personal Column* (Hunt Stromberg-UA). Also appeared in some of *The Saint* series, and first two of *The Falcon* series in role afterwards continued by his brother Tom Conway.

SAN JUAN, Olga. Born New York, Mar. 16, 1927. Ht. 5 ft. 2 in. ; wt. 110 lb. Black hair, hazel eyes. As a baby went to Puerto Rico from which her parents had originally come, and at 5 returned to New York. Educ. Spanish Neighborhood School, New York. While at school also studied ballet and Spanish music and dancing, and appeared at White House before President Roosevelt. Later appeared at the Copacabana Club, New York. Was seen by a talent scout in her " Brazilian Impressions " act ; made film debut in colour short, *Caribbean Romance* (Para) 1944. Shortly afterwards appeared in the feature film *Rainbow Island* (Para) 1944. Other films include : 1945 : *Out of This World* (Para), *Bombalera*—short (Para) ; 1945 : *Duffy's Tavern* (Para), *Little Witch*—short (Para) ; 1946 : *Blue Skies*—in which she danced with Fred Astaire (Para) ; 1947 : juvenile lead in *Variety Girl* (Para), *Catalina* (Para) ; 1948 : *Are You With It ?* (UI).

SAVILLE, Victor. Producer, director. Born Birmingham, Sept. 25, 1897. Educ. King Edward VI School. Served in army in World War I ; discharged with head wound, 1916. Entered films as salesman with Sol Levy in Birmingham ; handled English marketing of *Birth of a Nation* and *Intolerance*. Later was associated with Herbert Wilcox in film renting in Leeds, and in 1918 became an exhibitor ; with Michael Balcon and Jack Freedman, he continued as renter and importer. Began film production with Balcon at Islington, in 1920, with *Woman to Woman*, for which Betty Compson was brought from U.S.A. Joined Gaumont as production manager in 1926, directed his first feature *The Arcadians*, 1927, followed by *Mademoiselle From Armentières, Roses of Picardy, The Glad Eye*. Formed independent producing company, Burlington Films, and directed *Tesha* and *Kitty*. With advent of sound, went to Hollywood in 1928. Re-made *Kitty* as part-talkie in America ; also made sound version of *Woman to Woman*, with Betty Compson playing her original role. Returned to Britain 1930, and began long run of successful Gaumont-British and Gainsborough productions in association with Michael Balcon. His early GB films include : *The W Plan, A Warm Corner, The Sport of Kings, Hindle Wakes, Michael and Mary, Sunshine Susie, The Faithful Heart, Love on Wheels, The Good Companions, I Was a Spy, Friday the 13th, Evergreen, Evensong, The Iron Duke, Me and Marlborough, First a Girl, It's Love Again*. In 1936, joined London Film Productions as associate producer ; produced and directed *Dark Journey, Storm in a Teacup, Action For Slander, South Riding*. In 1938, joined MGM-British and produced *The Citadel, Goodbye Mr. Chips !* In 1939, went to Hollywood for MGM. Produced *The Earl of Chicago, Bitter Sweet, The Mortal Storm, A Woman's Face, Smilin' Through, The Chocolate Soldier, Dr. Jeykll and Mr. Hyde, White Cargo, Keeper of the Flame, Above Suspicion ;* collaborated on *Forever and a Day ;* directed and produced *Tonight and Every Night ;* produced *The Green Years, Green Dolphin Street ;* directed *If Winter Comes*.

SCHARY, Doré. Writer, producer. Born Newark, New Jersey, Aug. 31, 1905. Educ. Central High School, Newark. Began his career as actor and director in a " Little Theatre " ; also columnist for a Newark newspaper. Author of numerous plays, including " A Man of Ideas", " One Every Minute". Collaborated on numerous screenplays. Won Academy Award for the best original screenplay, with *Boys' Town* (MGM) 1938. Appointed executive producer for MGM 1942, and produced: *Journey for Margaret, The War Against Mrs. Hadley, Lassie Come Home, Bataan.* For UA: *I'll Be Seeing You.* Executive producer RKO since 1945: *The Spiral Staircase, Till the End of Time, The Farmer's Daughter, Bachelor Knight, Crossfire.*

SCHENCK, Joseph M. Production executive. Born Russia, Dec. 25, 1882. Educ. night school. Worked in factory from age of 10; emigrated to U.S.A. with family while still a child. In partnership with his brother Nicholas, ran a drug-store business; also with his brother, 1908, built Paradise Park in Fort George, New York State, one of the earliest amusement parks in America. In 1912 brought the huge Palisades Park at Fort Lee, New Jersey. Marcus Loew leased space in the Park to show " moving pictures "; Schenck invested in the scheme and eventually became major figure in Loew Theatrical Enterprises. In 1935-41, Chairman of 20th Century-Fox Films; appointed Executive Head of Production, 1943. 1938-40: President, Association of Motion Picture Producers. For six years national vice-chairman and California State chairman of the National Foundation for Infantile Paralysis.

SCHNEIDERHOFF, Vladimir. Director, producer. Born St. Petersburg (now Leningrad), 1900. At 18 joined the Red Army. Two years later he transferred to the People's Commissariat of Agriculture, where he organized and controlled a technical school. In 1924 he joined the Proletkino (People's Cinema), studying film technique. Directed *The Great Flight* (*Light of the East*), for which he took part in the air flight from Moscow to Mongolia and China. Later made *Southern China* in Canton, and in 1928 accompanied the Soviet-German mountaineering expedition to the unexplored regions of the Pamir (U.S.S.R.). There he made the full-length film *The Foothills of Death*, and also several short scenic films. In 1929 led film expedition to the Yemen (Arabia). Returning, he became a teacher at the State Institute of Cinematography, and later made *The People of the U.S.S.R.* (1931), *The Gold Lake* (1934) made in the Altai Mountains, *The Valley of Alamas* (1936). Author of books: " Technique of Filming ", " On Top of the World ", " El-Yeman " (The Yemen).

SCOTT, Adrian. Producer. Born Arlington, New Jersey, Feb. 6, 1911. Educ. Amherst College. Began career as free-lance writer; became associate editor stage magazine, then made study of film technique and evolved theories which led to an engagement with MGM, 1938. Collaborated on screenplays of *Keeping Company, Parson of Panamint, We Go Fast, Mr. Lucky.* Joined RKO-Radio as producer 1943. Has since produced: *Farewell My Lovely, My Pal Wolf, Cornered, Deadline at Dawn.* Came to Britain to produce first film made by RKO in association with the J. Arthur Rank Organisation, *So Well Remembered* 1947. Afterwards returned to Hollywood to produce *Crossfire.*

SCOTT, Lizabeth. Born Scranton, Pennsylvania, Sept. 29, 1923. Ht. 5 ft. 6 in.; wt. 115 lb. Tawny-blonde hair, hazel-green eyes. Educ. Central High School, Scranton; Marywood College. Studied at Alviene School of Drama, New York; made stage debut with touring company in " Hellzapoppin". Played repertory in New York and in Virginia. Was playing Sadie Thomson in " Rain " at repertory theatre in New York when she was offered job as understudy to Tallulah Bankhead in " Skin of Our Teeth "; understudied for seven months but went on only once in New York; later played lead for two weeks in Boston. Had at the same time been fashion model; magazine photograph of her led to a screen test and contract. First film: *You Came Along* (Hal Wallis-Para) 1945. Other films include: 1946: *Strange Love of Martha Ivers* (Hal Wallis-Para); 1947: *Dead Reckoning* (Col), *Desert Fury* (Hal Wallis-Para), *I Walk Alone* (Hal Wallis-Para).

SCOTT, Martha. Born Jamesport, Missouri, Sept. 22, 1916. Ht. 5 ft. 4 in.; wt. 105 lb. Brown hair, hazel eyes. Educ. University of Michigan. Intended to become teacher but worked in department store; then appeared in repertory, Detroit Civic Theatre. Later played in New York. Radio part with Orson Welles led to stage role in " Our Town ", which she repeated in first film: *Our Town* (UA), 1940. Other films include: 1940: *Howards of Virginia* (Col); 1941: *Cheers for Miss Bishop* (UA), *They Dare Not Love* (Col); 1942: *One Foot in Heaven* (Warn); 1943: *In Old Oklahoma* (Rep), *Hi Diddle Diddle* (UA). Came to Britain to appear in *So Well Remembered* (RKO) 1947.

SCOTT, Randolph. Born Orange County, Virginia, Jan. 23, 1903. Ht. 6 ft. 2 in.; wt. 190 lb. Light brown hair, hazel eyes. Educ. University of North Carolina. On graduation, toured Europe, then joined father in administrative engineering. Trained for stage at Pasadena Community Playhouse, and spent two years on Hollywood stage, where he was seen by talent scout in play " The Broken Wing". First film: *The Sky Bride* (Para) 1931. Other films include: *Island of Lost Souls, The Lusitania Secret, Heritage of the Desert, Lone Cowboy, Wild Horse Mesa, Hello Everybody !, Murders in the Zoo, Supernatural, Sunset Pass, To the Last Man, Cocktail Hour, Broken Dreams, Last Round-up, Home on the Range, Rocky Mountain Rhythm, Roberta, Village Tale, She, So Red the Rose, Follow the Fleet, And Sudden Death, Go West Young Man, Last of the Mohicans, High Wide and Handsome, Road to Reno, Rebecca of Sunnybrook Farm, The Texans.* 1940: *Virginia City* (Warn), *My Favourite Wife* (Univ), *When the Daltons Rode* (Univ); 1941: *Western Union* (20th), *Belle Starr* (20th); 1942: *Paris Calling* (Univ), *To The Shores of Tripoli* (20th) *The Spoilers* (Univ), *Pittsburgh* (Univ); 1943: *Bombardier* (RKO), *Corvette K-225* (Univ), *Gung Ho!* (Univ), *The Desperadoes* (Col); 1944: *Belle of the Yukon* (RKO), *China Sky* (RKO); 1945: *Captain Kidd* (UA); 1946: *Badman's Territory* (RKO), *Trail Street* (RKO), *Abilene Town* (UA), *Home Sweet Homicide* (20th), *The Assassin* (Col); 1947: *Christmas Eve* (Benedict Bogeaus-UA).

SCOTT, Zachary. Born Austin, Texas, Feb. 24, 1914. Ht. 6 ft. 1 in.; wt. 170 lb. Brown hair, brown eyes. Educ. Austin public schools; University of Texas (B.A.). Interrupted college training to come to Britain for a year and appeared on London stage in " The Outsider ". Began professional career in summer theatres, later appearing on Broadway in " Circle of Chalk ", " The Damask Cheek ", " The Rock " and " Those Endearing Young Charms "; performance in this last led to first film: *The Mask of Dimitrios* (Warn) 1944. Other films include—1945 (all Warn): *San Antonio, Danger Signal, Mildred Pierce, The Southerner* (UA) ; 1946 : *Her Kind of Man* (Warn) ; 1947 : *Stallion Road* (Warn), *Cass Timberlane* (MGM), *The Unfaithful* (Warn) ; 1948 : *Whiplash* (Warn).

SEARL, Jackie. Born Anaheim, California, 1920. Brown hair, blue eyes. Famous as child actor. Began his career at 3, when a radio executive heard him recite and engaged him for " Children's Hour " on a Los Angeles radio station. Made his screen debut shortly afterwards, appearing in children's films as a sneak. First featured role was in *Tom Sawyer* (Para) 1930. Served in the U.S. Army, 1941-6. After demobilization managed his mother's malt shop in Hollywood for 18 months before resuming his film career. Films include : *Finn and Hattie, Forbidden Adventure, Huckleberry Finn, Sooky, Skippy, Hearts of Humanity, Oliver Twist* (Mono) 1933, *High Gear, Dangerous Crossroads, One Year Later, The World Changes, Alice in Wonderland, No Greater Glory, Murder on the Blackboard, Strictly Dynamite, Peck's Bad Boy, A Wicked Woman, Great Expectations* (Univ) 1934, *Unwelcome Stranger, Ginger, Little Lord Fauntleroy, Gentle Julia, Two Wise Maids, Wild and Woolly, Little Tough Guy, That Certain Age, Little Tough Guys in Society.* 1941 : *Glamour Boy* (Para), *Small Town Deb* (20th). 1948 : *Paleface* (Para).

SELZNICK, David. Producer. Born Pittsburgh, Pa, May 10, 1902. Educ. Public Schools, New York ; Columbia University. Son of famous American film pioneer, Lewis T. Selznick, he entered the industry immediately after having left University. Became a scriptwriter, and later associate producer of many early Westerns. Afterwards became chief of scenario department at Paramount ; also associate producer of many early films at these studios, including the 1929 version of *The Four Feathers.* 1931, joined RKO-Radio as an executive producer, where he made such successes as *Lost Squadron, Symphony of Six Million, King Kong* and *Bill of Divorcement* (1932). In 1935 joined MGM where he produced *Dinner at Eight, Dancing Lady, Viva Villa, Manhattan Melodrama, David Copperfield, Reckless, Anna Karenina* (1935), *Tale of Two Cities.* In 1936 formed Selznick International Pictures. Most notable achievement *Gone With the Wind* for which he paid fifty thousand dollars after reading an advance copy of the book by Margaret Mitchell, in 1936. Before Vivien Leigh was cast as Scarlett O'Hara, Selznick interviewed 1400 girls and tested 90. Film took two years to complete, cost £1,000,000 and is the longest film ever shown—3 hours 40 minutes. Since its premiere in Atlanta, setting of the story, in 1939, it has been re-issued all over the world. It took ten Academy Awards in 1939. Other Selznick productions include *Little Lord Fauntleroy, Garden of Allah, A Star is Born, Prisoner of Zenda* (1937), *Nothing Sacred, Adventures of Tom Sawyer, The Young in Heart, Rebecca.* In 1942 formed Vanguard Films Inc. Productions include : *Since You Went Away, I'll Be Seeing You, Spellbound, Duel in the Sun, The Paradine Case, Portrait of Jennie.* Established Selznick Releasing Organisation, 1946, to distribute his own productions.

SEWELL, Vernon. Director. Born London, 1903. Educ. Marlborough College. Trained as a mechanical engineer in Detroit before entering films in Britain as a camera assistant in 1929 at Nettlefold Studios, Walton-on-Thames. Was recordist, assistant art director, cutter, camera operator and technical director

before becoming director in 1937. During World War II served in Royal Navy. Films directed include : *Breakers Ahead, Men Against the Sea, The Silver Fleet, What Men Live By, The World Owes Me a Living, Latin Quarter, Ghosts of Berkeley Square.*

SHARP, Margery. Writer. Born 1905. Educ. Streatham Hill High School ; Bedford College, University of London (B.A.). Plays include " The Nutmeg Tree " ; novels include : " The Flowering Thorn ", " Harlequin House ", " Cluny Brown ", " Britannia Mews ". Filmed : *Cluny Brown, Britannia Mews, Julia Misbehaves* from " The Nutmeg Tree ".

SHAW, George Bernard. Author and dramatist. Born Dublin, July, 26, 1856. First play " Widowers' Houses " was produced at the old Royalty Theatre, London, Dec. 1892, followed by " Arms and the Man ". His plays include " The Philanderer ", " Candida ", " The Devil's Disciple ", " Caesar and Cleopatra ", " Man and Superman ", " Major Barbara ", " The Doctor's Dilemma ", " Androcles and the Lion ", " Pygmalion ", " Back to Methuselah ", " Saint Joan ", " The Apple Cart ", " Too True to be Good ", " The Millionairess ", " Geneva ", " In Good King Charles' Golden Days ", " The Shewing up of Blanco Posnet ". After film versions of *How He Lied to Her Husband* (BIP) 1931 and *Arms and the Man* (BIP) 1932, held out against further screen adaptations until in 1937 Gabriel Pascal, the Hungarian-born producer, prevailed on him to change his mind ; Pascal now holds the film rights of all his works. Other works filmed include : *Pygmalion, Major Barbara, Caesar and Cleopatra.* Scheduled for production by Gabriel Pascal : *The Doctor's Dilemma, The Shewing up of Blanco Posnet, The Devil's Disciple, St. Joan.*

SHAW, Susan. Real name Patsy Sloots. Born West Norwood, London, Aug. 29, 1929. Ht. 5 ft. 4 in. ; wt. 96 lb. Blonde hair, grey eyes. Educ. City of London School. Had no professional stage experience when spotted at London Camera Club demonstration by a film agent, who changed her name to Pat Fanshawe and secured her a test. After a year's " grooming ", was given small part in *The Upturned Glass* (Box) 1947, with her name changed again to Susan Shaw. Also in 1947 made *Holiday Camp* (Gains), *It Always Rains on Sunday* (Ealing) ; 1948 : *London Belongs To Me* (Individ).

SHEARER, Moira. Dancer. Born Dunfermline, Scotland, 1926. Began ballet training under Ethel Lacey while a child in Rhodesia, and continued in London under Flora Fairbairn and Nicholas Legat. Joined Sadler's Wells Ballet School in 1939. Appeared with International Ballet for a year and returned to Sadler's Wells Ballet to make outstanding success in prima ballerina roles, 1946. First film : *Red Shoes* (Archers), 1948.

SHEARER, Norma. Born Montreal, Aug. 10, 1904. Ht. 5 ft. 7 in. ; wt. 118 lb. Brown hair, blue-grey eyes. Educ. Montreal public schools ; Westmount High School. Took part in school plays when 14 and decided to become a film actress. Went to U.S.A. 1920 and made film debut the same year in silent film, *The Stealers.* Other silent films include *The Tower of Lies, He Who Gets Slapped, The Student Prince, Trelawney of the Wells.* Talkies include : *The Trial of Mary Dugan* (1929), *The Last of Mrs. Cheyney, The Hollywood Revue, The Divorcee, Their*

LIZABETH SCOTT
(*Hal Wallis*)

Own Desire, Let's Be Gay, Strangers May Kiss, A Free Soul, Private Lives, Strange Interval, Smilin' Through, Riptide, The Barretts of Wimpole Street, Romeo and Juliet, Marie Antoinette, Idiot's Delight, The Women. In 1940: *Escape* (MGM). Retired from the screen after completing *Her Cardboard Lover* (MGM) 1942, but in 1947 announced that she would resume her film career.

SHEFFIELD, Johnny. Born Pasadena, California, Apr. 11, 1932. Educ. elementary training school of University of California. Son of Reginald Sheffield, once a boy-actor in Britain ; developed as athlete. Stage debut 1938, as " Pud " in " On Borrowed Time " at Santa Barbara, California. Chosen to play the son of Tarzan in the series with Johnny Weissmuller as " Tarzan". First film : *Tarzan Finds a Son* (MGM), 1939. Other films include : *Babes in Arms* (MGM) ; 1940 : *Little Orvie* (RKO).

SHENGELAYA, N. Director. Born Georgia, Russia, 1901. A poet and prominent art worker in Georgia. Assisted in the direction of many Soviet films in early part of his career. Became a director ; made *Eliso* and other films. Regarded as one of the " masters of the silent film ", has played an important part in the development of the Soviet Cinema.

SHERIDAN, Ann. Real name Clara Lou Sheridan. Born Denton, Texas, Feb. 21, 1915. Ht. 5 ft. 6 in. ; wt. 118 lb. Red hair, hazel eyes. Educ. Robert E. Lee Grammar School ; Denton Junior High ,School ; Northeast State Teachers College. Youthful ambition, to be a school teacher. Trained in drama and speech training. Selected by Paramount in " Search-For-Beauty " Contest, 1933. Films include : *Notorious Sophie Lang, Enter Madame, Wagon Wheels, The Glass Key* (Para) 1935, *The Great O'Malley, The Black Legion, San Quentin, Angels with Dirty Faces, A Letter of Introduction, Dodge City, Naughty But Nice.* 1940 (all Warn) : *It All Came True, Castles on the Hudson, Torrid Zone, They Drive By Night, City for Conquest :* 1941 (all Warn) : *Honeymoon for Three, Navy Blues, The Man Who Came to Dinner ;* 1942 (all Warn) : *Kings Row, Juke Girl, George Washington Slept Here ;* 1943 (both Warn) : *Edge of Darkness, Thank Your Lucky Stars ;* 1944 (both Warn) : *Shine on Harvest Moon, The Doughgirls ;* 1946 : *One More Tomorrow* (Warn) ; 1947 (all Warn) ; *Nora Prentiss, Silver River, The Unfaithful.*

SHERWOOD, Robert Emmet. Writer. Born New Rochelle, New York State, Apr. 4, 1896. Educ. Milton Academy ; Harvard University. Served with Canadian Army in World War I. Worked for a time on staff of " Life ", with Dorothy Parker and Robert Benchley. In 1920 introduced a column of film criticism to " Life ", and at the same time was film critic for other U.S. papers. Editor of " Life " 1924-8. Wrote his first play, " The Road to Rome " 1927. With Maxwell Anderson, Elmer Rice and S. N. Behrman founded the Playwright's Company, 1938. In World War II was Chief of the Overseas Branch of the U.S. Office of War Information and director of the American Broadcasting station in Europe—commonly known as " Absie". Plays include : " Tovarich "—adapted from the French, " Acropolis ", " There Shall Be No Night". Plays filmed : *Reunion in Vienna, The Petrified Forest, Tovarich, Idiot's Delight, Abe Lincoln in Illinois, Waterloo Bridge.* Screenplays include : *The Ghost Goes West, The Adventures of Marco Polo, Idiot's*

Delight, Abe Lincoln in Illinois, The Best Years of Our Lives. Collaborated on screenplays : *Thunder in the City, Tovarich, Waterloo Bridge.*

SHUB, Esther. Producer, director. Born 1894. Graduated, Soviet University for Women. In 1918-21 worked in the Soviet Department of Education and with the Art Council of State Circuses. Entered films 1921 remounting foreign films for showing in Russian cinemas. Began directing in 1925 with *Darkness (Two Powers)*, in the same year, *The First Fires* and *The Wings of a Serf (Ivan the Terrible).* In 1926 and 1927 independently produced two historical films, *The Downfall of the Romanov Dynasty* and *The Great Path (10 Years of the October Revolution).* Later made *Russia of Nicholas II* and *Leo Tolstoy* (1929), *Today* (1930), *Communist Youth—the Patron of Electrification* (1932). Visited Turkey in 1934, and in 1935 worked on a sound film for the twentieth anniversary of the October Revolution, and on a film on the life of Pushkin.

SIDNEY, Sylvia. Born New York City, Aug. 8, 1910. Ht. 5 ft. 2 in. ; wt. 104 lb. Brown hair, blue-green eyes. Educ. Washing Irving High School ; New York Theatre Guild School. Made debut at 15 in New York. Made film debut in *Thru' Different Eyes* (Fox) 1929, but was unimpressed by the prospect of film career and returned to New York stage. Returned to Hollywood to appear in *City Streets* (Para), 1931, with Gary Cooper. Another early film was *An American Tragedy*, never shown in Britain, but generally regarded as one of her best. Other films include : *Ladies of the Big House, Street Scene, The Miracle Man, Merrily We Go To Hell, Madame Butterfly, Pick-Up, Jennie Gerhardt, Thirty Day Princess, Behold My Wife !, Accent on Youth, Mary Burns Fugitive, The Trail of the Lonesome Pine, Fury, Sabotage—U.S.* title *A Woman Alone* (made by Hitchcock in Britain, 1937), *You Only Live Once, Dead End, You and Me.* 1941 : *The Wagons Roll at Night* (Warn). Returned to stage for four years. 1945 : *Blood on the Sun* (UA) ; 1946 : *The Searching Wind* (Para), *Mr. Ace* (UA) ; 1947 : *The Stray Lamb* (Cagney-UA).

SIGNORET, Simone. Born Wiesbaden, Germany, 1921. Trained at French cinema drama school ; became film extra, then small part player, also appeared on Paris stage. First film lead in : *Les Démons de L'Aube.* Has since become one of France's leading stars. First British film : *Against the Wind* (Ealing) 1948.

SILVERS, Phil. Born Brooklyn, New York, May 11, 1912. Brown eyes, brown hair. Ht. 5 ft. 11½ in. ; wt. 175 lb. Educ. public and high schools. Sang for pennies on Coney Island beach and eventually entered vaudeville as a boy singer. Later became comedian in burlesque. Recruited by George Abbott to play one of the principals in " Yokel Boy ". While he was playing in this, Garson Kanin cast him as " the good humour man " in *Tom, Dick and Harry* (RKO) 1941. Other films include—1942 : *You're in the Army now* (Warn), *Roxie Hart* (20th), *My Gal Sal* (20th), *Footlight Serenade* (20th), *Just Off Broadway* (20th) ; 1943 : *Coney Island* (20th) ; 1944 : *Four Jills in a Jeep* (20th), *Cover Girl* (Col), *Something for the Boys* (20th) ; 1945 : *Don Juan Quilligan* (20th), *A Thousand and One Nights* (Col), *Diamond Horseshoe* (20th) ; 1946 : *If I'm Lucky* (20th).

SILVI, Lilia. Born Rome, 1922. Films include:
Violette nei Capelli, Scampolo, Barbablù, Scarpe Grosse,
La Bisbetica Domata. 1944: *La Vispa Teresa*
(Excelsa), *Il Diavolo in Collegio* (Excelsa); 1946:
Biragin (Excelsa).

SIM, Alastair. Born Edinburgh, Oct. 9, 1900.
Ht. 5 ft. 11 in.; wt. 164 lb. Grey hair, blue eyes.
Educ. James Gillespie School; Edinburgh University.
For a time was Fulton Lecturer in Elocution at New
College, Edinburgh, then made first stage appearance
at the Savoy Theatre, London, as messenger in
" Othello " 1930. Film debut in *Riverside Murder,*
1934. Other films include: *The Private Secretary,*
Keep Your Seats!, Gangway!, The Squeaker, Alf's
Button Afloat, Climbing High, This Man is News,
Sailing Along, Inspector Hornleigh, This Man in Paris.
1941: *Inspector Hornleigh Investigates* (Gains-20th),
A Cottage to Let (Gains); 1942: *Let the People Sing*
(Brit Nat); 1944: *Waterloo Road* (Gains); 1947:
Green for Danger (Individ), *Hue and Cry* (Ealing),
Captain Boycott (Individ); 1948: *London Belongs to*
Me (Individ).

SIM, Sheila. Real name Sheila Attenborough. Born
Liverpool, June 5, 1922. Ht. 5 ft. 5½ in.; wt. 124 lb.
Light brown hair, blue eyes. Educ. Croydon High
School for Girls; Royal Academy of Dramatic Art.
Always wanted to be actress; while at school visited
local repertory theatre every week. Was a junior
clerk in father's bank in London before going to
R.A.D.A. Repertory experience at Intimate Theatre,
Palmer's Green, London. Served in the Woman's
Land Army, 1940. Toured with Noel Coward's
company in " This Happy Breed "; made first
London appearance with John Gielgud's production
of " Landslide " at Westminster Theatre, 1943. Other
London plays followed. Meeting with Michael Powell
led to offer of a leading role in *A Canterbury Tale*
(Archers) 1944. Later films include—1945: *Great*
Day (RKO-Brit); 1947: *Dancing With Crime*
(Alliance).

SIMMONS, Jean. Born Crouch Hill, London,
Jan. 31, 1929. Ht. 5 ft. 4½ in.; wt. 108 lb. Chestnut
brown hair, hazel eyes. Educ. Orange Hill School for
Girls, Edgware, London. Youthful ambition: to
travel round the world. Was evacuated to Somerset
during the war, but returned to London and began
dramatic studies at the Aida Foster School. After
only two weeks was sent to Gainsborough Studios,
who were looking for child as sister to character played
by Margaret Lockwood. Given the part by director
Val Guest without even being tested. First film:
Give Us the Moon (Gains) 1943. Played lead in
children's film *Sports Day,* 1944. Also brief appearances
in *The Way to the Stars* (Two Cities) 1945, *Kiss the*
Bride Goodbye (Butcher) 1945, *Sexton Blake* (Warn-
Brit) 1945. Played young girl harpist in *Caesar and*
Cleopatra (Pascal) and young Estella in *Great Ex-*
pectations (Cineguild) 1946. Other films—1947:
Hungry Hill (Two Cities), *Black Narcissus* (Archers),
Uncle Silas (Two Cities), *The Woman in the Hall*
(Wessex); 1948: *Hamlet* (Two Cities), *Blue Lagoon*
(Individ).

SIMMS, Ginny. Born San Antonio, Texas, May 25,
1916. Ht. 5 ft. 6 in.; wt. 112 lb. Chestnut hair,
hazel eyes. Educ. William and Mary College, San
Antonio. Brought up on a farm, she sang at age of 8
in local cinema giving sound to character mouthing
" Oh, Suzanna " in silent film *The Covered Wagon.*
Began singing career in small bands; then in Kay

Kyser's band, appearing with him in three films. First
film: *That's Right, You're Wrong* (RKO) 1939. Other
films include—1940: *You'll Find Out* (RKO); 1941:
Playmates (RKO); 1942: *Here We Go Again* (RKO),
Seven Days Leave (RKO); 1943: *Hit the Ice* (Univ);
1944: *Broadway Rhythm* (MGM); 1945: *Shady*
Lady (Univ); 1946: *Night and Day* (Warn).

SIMMS, Larry. Born Santa Monica, California,
Oct. 1, 1934. Began his film career as " Baby
Dumpling ", now known as " Alexander ", in the
Blondie series (Col) and has not missed a film in the
ten years since the series began in 1938. With Arthur
Lake and Penny Singleton, completed twenty-first
episode, *Blondie in the Dough,* in October, 1947.

SIMON, Michel. Born Geneva, April 9, 1895.
Educ. Evangelist School, Geneva. Before World
War I, presented dancing acts on tour, then became
photographer and also opened institute for physical
culture and boxing and became boxing promoter.
After service during World War I with Swiss Army,
resumed photographic business, obtained concession to
photograph Pitoeff's theatre company and later joined
cast. Spent three years with Pitoeff, three with Louis
Jouvet and four with Henry Bernstein. Made screen
debut in silent film *Feu Mathias Pascal.* Sound films
include: *Circonstances Atténuantes, Musiciens du Ciel,*
Rigoletto, La Dame de L'Ouest, La Tosca, Au Bonheur
des Dames, La Fin du Jour, Les Disparus de St. Agil,
Quai des Brumes, Vautrin, Un Ami Viendra ce Soir,
Panique, La Taverne de Poisson Couronné, Non Coupable.

SIMON, Simone. Born Marseilles, Apr. 23, 1914.
Ht. 5 ft. 3 in.; wt. 116 lb. Chestnut hair, blue eyes.
Grew up in Madagascar. Studied art in Paris. Worked
in gramophone shop, then made stage debut at 17 as
maid in " Balthazar ", Apollo Theatre, Paris; in
operettas: " Le Roi Pausole " " Toi c'est Moi ".
Director Tourjansky saw her in " Le Roi Pausole "
and gave her first film role: *Le Chanteur Inconnu*
(1931). As light comedienne, made films in Berlin,
Munich and Paris—*La Petite Chocolatière, Le Roi des*
Palaces, L'Etoile de Valence. Scored hit with Jean-
Pierre Aumont in *Lac-aux-dames.* Other French films:
Les Yeux Noires, Les Beaux Jours, La Bête Humaine
(1939). Went to Hollywood, 1936. American films
include: *Girls' Dormitory, Ladies in Love, Seventh*
Heaven, Love and Hisses, Josette. From 1941: *All*
That Money Can Buy (RKO); 1942: *Cat People*
(RKO); 1943: *Tahiti Honey* (Rep); 1944: *Johnny*
Doesn't Live Here Any More (Mono). Came to Britain
to appear in *Temptation Harbour* (ABPC) 1947.

SIMON, Sylvan S. Director. Born Chicago, March
9, 1910. Educ. University of Michigan (B.A.);
Columbia University. While studying law at Columbia
was given opportunity to direct a New York play, and
thereafter discontinued law studies in favour of stage.
Director of Dramatics, University of Michigan,
1928-32. Talent scout and test director for Warner
Bros., 1935-6. Began directing 1937, *A Girl With*
Ideas. Films include: *Road to Reno, Spring Madness,*
Four Girls in White, The Kid From Texas, These Glamour
Girls, Dancing Co-ed, Two Girls on Broadway, Sporting
Blood, Dulcy, Keeping Company, Washington Melo-
drama, Whistling in the Dark, The Bugle Sounds,
Rio Rita, Grand Central Murder, Whistling in Dixie,
Salute to the Marines, Whistling in Brooklyn, Song of
the Open Road, Son of Lassie, Abbott and Costello in
Hollywood, Bad Bascomb, Mr. Griggs Returns, Thrill
of Brazil, Her Husband's Affairs. Produced and
directed *I Love Trouble.*

SINATRA, Frank, Born Hoboken, New Jersey, Dec. 12, 1918. Ht. 5 ft. 10 in. ; wt. 140 lb. Brown hair, blue eyes. Educ. Demarest High School, Hoboken. Sang with School band and glee club. Delivered newspapers, became copyboy then sports reporter on " Hoboken Observer." After having seen Bing Crosby film, decided to become professional singer. Won radio audition, singing " Night and Day ". Was heard by Harry James and signed as vocalist : later joined Tommy Dorsey's band. His fame as "The Voice" spread via radio and night clubs, his recordings of " I'll Never Smile Again ", " This Love of Mine " broke sales records. Appeared with Tommy Dorsey, in *Las Vegas Nights* (Para), 1941. Other films include—1942 : *Ship Ahoy* (MGM) ; 1943 : *Reveille with Beverley* (Col), *Higher and Higher* (RKO) ; 1944 : *Step Lively* (RKO), *Anchors Aweigh* (MGM) ; 1945 : *The House I Live In* (short subject on tolerance) ; 1946 : *Till the Clouds Roll By* (MGM), *It Happened in Brooklyn* (MGM) ; 1947 : *The Kissing Bandit* (MGM), *Words and Music* (MGM).

SINGLETON, Penny. Real name Dorothy McNulty. Born Philadelphia, Sept. 15. Ht. 5 ft. 4 in. ; wt. 116 lb. Blonde hair, blue-green eyes. Educ. Columbia University. Made stage debut singing and dancing in school show ; studied acrobatic and ballet dancing at Al White's Studio, Philadelphia. Toured in road-show act, seen by J. J. Shubert and signed for a production at the Winter Garden, New York. Made hit as dancing comedienne in " Good News", "Follow Through " ; co-starred with Frank Morgan in " Hey, Nonny, Nonny " ; seen by talent scout while playing in repertory in Iveryton, Connecticut. First film appearance in *After the Thin Man* (MGM) 1936, then played minor parts and was about to return to the stage, given lead in film version of Chic Young's comic strip feature, *Blondie*. The twenty-first episode, *Blondie in the Dough*, was completed in October, 1947, with the original principals, Arthur Lake, Larry Simms and Penny Singleton, still in the cast. Her other films include : *Vogues of 1938*, *Sea Racketeers*, *Swing Your Lady*, *Men are such Fools*, *Boy Meets Girl*, *Garden of the Moon*, *Racket Busters*, *Hard to Get*, *Outside of Paradise* ; 1941 : *Go West Young Lady* (Col) ; 1947 : *Young Widow* (Hunt Stromberg-UA), 1947.

SIODMAK, Robert. Director. Born Memphis, Tenn. Aug. 8, 1900. Educ. Germany. Taken to Europe when a year old. Sight nearly destroyed by a blow from a fellow student. Gave up acting as he was always cast to play old men. Entered banking business then turned to film-making during German currency inflation after World War I. Worked as writer, film editor and assistant director before making first film, *People on Sunday*, from a story by Billy Wilder. Directed *The Tempest* with Emil Jannings. Left Germany for France in 1933, where he directed Charles Boyer, Danielle Darrieux, and other French stars. Returned to America and started at the bottom again ; directed *West Point Widow*, *Someone to Remember*, *Son of Dracula*, *Cobra Woman*, *Phantom Lady*, *Christmas Holiday* and *The Spiral Staircase*, *Time out of Mind*, *Thunder on the Hill*.

SKELTON, Red. Real name Richard Skelton. Born Vincennes, Indiana, July 18. Ht. 6 ft. 2 in. ; wt. 190 lb. Red hair, brown eyes. Father was a star clown with Hagenbeck and Wallace Circus. Boyhood ambition : to be a lion tamer. As a boy worked in a local shop ; became local star comedian. At 12

joined a touring company. Became member of Hittner's " Orange Blossom " troupe on Mississippi show boat ; joined Hagenbeck as circus clown ; also appeared in burlesque, vaudeville and radio. After his first film : *Having Wonderful Time* (RKO-Radio) 1939, signed a contract with MGM, for whom his films include : 1940 : *Flight Command ;* 1941 : *My Life Is Yours, Lady Be Good, Mary Names The Day, Whistling in the Dark ;* 1942 : *Ship Ahoy, She Got Her Man, Whistling in Dixie, Panama Hattie ;* 1943 : *Du Barry Was a Lady, By Hook or By Crook, Thousands Cheer, Whistling in Brooklyn ;* 1944 : *Bathing Beauty.* 1944-5, war service with U.S. Army. 1946 : *Ziegfeld Follies of 1946, The Show-Off ;* 1947 : *Merton of the Movies ;* 1948 : *The Red Mill.*

SKOURAS, Spyros P. Executive. Born Skourchorion, Greece. Educ. Greece, and Jones' Commercial College, St. Louis, Missouri. His early life was spent in Greece with his family. Later they emigrated to America, and he served with the U.S. Air Force in World War I. With his two brothers formed the Skouras Theatres Circuit, and by 1927 controlled 37 theatres. When these were acquired by Warner Bros. he became their general theatre manager. Joined Paramount, 1931, as a theatre executive. In 1942 became President of 20th Century-Fox.

SLEZAK, Walter. Born Vienna, May 3, 1902. Ht. 6 ft. ; wt. 200 lb. Fair hair, blue eyes. Educ. University of Vienna. Youthful ambition : to become a doctor. Son of Leo Slezak, operatic tenor. Met director Michael Curtiz in Vienna, who gave him juvenile lead in film *Sodom and Gomorrah*. Appeared in Berlin on stage and for UFA films. The Shuberts took him to New York, 1930, as musical star for : " Meet My Sister ". Has appeared in many Broadway successes. Director Leo McCarey saw him in " Music in the Air ", offered him first American film role : *Once Upon a Honeymoon* (RKO) 1942. Other films include : 1943 : *This Land Is Mine* (RKO), *The Fallen Sparrow* (RKO) ; 1944 : *Lifeboat* (20th), *Till We Meet Again* (Para), *And Now Tomorrow* (Para), *Step Lively* (RKO), *The Princess and The Pirate* (RKO) ; 1945 : *Salome, Where She Danced* (Univ), *The Spanish Main* (RKO), *Cornered* (RKO) ; 1947 : *Sinbad the Sailor* (RKO) ; 1948 : *The Amazing Mr. Hammer* (RKO), *Deadlier than the Male* (RKO).

SMALL, Edward. Producer. Born Brooklyn, New York, 1891. Began his career as an actor, then became actors' agent. Later, 1925, became screen agent in Hollywood. Joined First National as producer in silent days, where he made many films starring Corinne Griffith. Other silent films include : *McFaddens' Flats, The Cohens and the Kellys* (1926), and *The Gorilla*. In 1932, with Harry Goetz, formed Reliance Pictures. In 1938 formed Edward Small Productions. Notable success was *The Count of Monte Cristo* (1934), for which he signed Robert Donat after seeing him in the comparatively small role of Culpepper in *The Private Life of Henry VIII*. Other productions include : *I Cover the Waterfront, Palooka, Transatlantic Merry-go-round, Let 'Em Have It!, The Melody Lingers On, The Bride Walks Out, We Who Are About to Die, The Last of the Mohicans, Sea Devils, New Faces of 1937, Super Sleuth, The Toast of New York, Duke of West Point, The King of the Turf, Man in the Iron Mask, My Son My Son !, South of Pago Pago, Kit Carson, Sons of Monte Cristo, International Lady, The Corsican Brothers, A Gentleman After Dark, Miss*

Annie Rooney, Friendly Enemies, Twin Beds, Up in Mabel's Room, Abroad with Two Yanks, Brewster's Millions, Getting Gertie's Garter, Temptation, Monte Cristo's Revenge, The Black Arrow, Cagliostro (in Italy) 1948.

SMITH, Alexis. Born Penticton, British Columbia, June 8, 1921. Ht. 5 ft. 7 in. ; wt. 126 lb. Blonde hair, blue eyes. Educ. Hollywood High School ; Los Angeles City College. Received professional offers as singer and dancer at 13, but kept at school by parents. Studied drama at college, and was seen by talent scout in student production of " The Night of January 16 ". After a screen test she was given a long-term contract. First film : *Dive Bomber* (Warn) 1941. Other films (all Warn) include : 1941 : *The Smiling Ghost ;* 1942 : *Gentleman Jim ;* 1943 : *Thank Your Lucky Stars, The Constant Nymph, Conflict, The Adventures of Mark Twain ;* 1944 : *Rhapsody in Blue, The Doughgirls ;* 1945 : *San Antonio ;* 1946 : *Night and Day, One More Tomorrow, Of Human Bondage ;* 1947 : *The Two Mrs. Carrolls, Stallion Road, The Woman in White ;* 1948 : *Whiplash, Christopher Blake.*

SMITH, Sir C. Aubrey. C.B.E. (1938). Knighted 1944. Born London, July 21, 1863. Educ. Charterhouse School ; Cambridge University. Earned cricketing reputation at Cambridge ; later captained Sussex and led English teams in Australia, South Africa. Began professional stage career in A.B. Tapping's Company at Hastings, 1892, in " The Idler ", and made London debut at Garrick Theatre in " The Notorious Mrs. Ebbsmith " in 1895. Toured with Fred Terry and Sir John Hare ; made his first American tour with Hare in 1895. On London and New York stage for many years. Made first screen appearance in American silent film : *Builder of Bridges* (Daniel Frohman) 1915. Also appeared in several British silent films. First talkie : *The Bachelor Father* (MGM) 1931. Since then has spent most of his time in Hollywood, returning to make a few British films, including : *The Tunnel—*U.S. title *Transatlantic Tunnel* (GB) 1936, *Sixty Glorious Years* and *The Four Feathers* (LFP) 1939. His American films include : *Morning Glory, Queen Christina, House of Rothschild, Cleopatra, Clive of India, Lives of a Bengal Lancer, The Crusades, Little Lord Fauntleroy, Romeo and Juliet, Lloyd's of London.* 1940 : *Bill of Divorcement* (RKO), *Rebecca* (UA), *Waterloo Bridge* (MGM) ; 1941 : *Dr. Jekyll and Mr. Hyde* (MGM) ; 1943 : *Forever and a Day* (RKO), *Madame Curie* (MGM) ; 1944 : *White Cliffs of Dover* (MGM), *Secrets of Scotland Yard* (Rep), *Adventures of Mark Twain* (Warn) ; 1945 : *They Shall Have Faith* (Mono), *Scotland Yard Investigator* (Rep), *And Then There Were None—*British title *Ten Little Niggers* (20th). In 1947 visited Britain to see the season's cricket and to appear in *An Ideal Husband* (LFP).

SMITH, Dodie. Dramatist and screenwriter. Born Whitefield, Lancs. Educ. Manchester ; St. Paul's Girls' School, London. Trained at Royal Academy of Dramatic Art ; made debut in musical comedy, 1915. Toured in " Mr. Wu ", appeared at Everyman Theatre, Hampstead 1920-6 and went with the company to Zurich. Spent several years with touring companies, then left stage to become buyer of pictures and toys for London store. Wrote her first play " British Talent " for Three Arts Club, 1924. Scored hit in 1931 with first play on professional stage, " Autumn Crocus ". Other plays include : " Service ", " Touch Wood ", " Bonnet Over The Windmill ", " Lovers and Friends "

in New York, 1943. Has worked on screenplays of American films, including : *The Uninvited, Portrait of a Lady* (from Henry James's novel). Plays filmed include : *Autumn Crocus, Call It a Day, Dear Octopus.*

SMITH, Kent. Born New York, Mar. 19, 1907. Ht. 6 ft. ; wt. 180 lb. Brown hair, brown eyes. Educ. Columbia University ; Phillips-Exeter Academy; Harvard University. Worked in a New York store, as stockroom boy, store clerk, and checker. Later with Henry Fonda, Margaret Sullavan, James Stewart and others formed " The University Players " at West Falmouth, Massachusetts. Appeared on Broadway in " Dodsworth ", " Candida ", " Wingless Victory ", " Old Acquaintance ", and other plays. On Hollywood stage, 1945 in " A Bell for Adano ". First film : *The Cat People* (RKO) 1942. Other films include : *Hitler's Children* (RKO), *Forever and a Day* (RKO), *This Land Is Mine* (RKO), ; 1944 : *Youth Runs Wild* (RKO), *Three Russian Girls* (UA). 1944-5, served in U.S. Army. 1945 : *The Spiral Staircase* (RKO) ; 1947 : *Nora Prentiss* (Warn), *Magic Town* (RKO).

SOLDATI, Mario. Born Turin, 1906. Began his career as art critic and story writer. Went to the United States in 1929, to study at Columbia University. Entered film industry 1931 as assistant director, and later became script-writer. Has since directed a number of outstanding Italian films, including : *Piccolo Mondo Antico, La Trappola, Malombra, Mr. Travet, Daniele Cortis, Eugénie Grandet.*

SOMLO, Josef. Producer. Born Papa, Hungary, 1885. Studied law in Budapest. Entered films 1908, as managing director Projectograph Film Company, Vienna. Became chairman of Film Organization for Austria and Hungary, 1919-21 ; foreign manager for UFA, Berlin. In 1922, formed European production and renting company with Herman Fellner. 1933-36, European representative for Gaumont-British. Came to Britain, 1935 ; formed Victor Saville Productions Ltd. in partnership with director Victor Saville ; produced, for UA distribution, *Storm in a Teacup, Dark Journey, Action For Slander, South Riding.* Continued independent production when partner left for Hollywood : *The Mikado, A Window in London, On The Night of The Fire, The Arsenal Stadium Mystery, Old Bill and Son, The Lady in Distress, Alibi.* Is General Manager British Commonwealth Film Corporation Ltd. In May, 1946, was appointed Assistant Managing Director and producer for Two Cities Films. Co-producer of *Uncle Silas.* 1947, appointed Managing Director and executive producer, Two Cities Films. Productions include : *One Night With You.*

SOTHERN, Ann. Real name Harriette Lake ; direct descendant of Simon Lake, submarine inventor. Born Valley City, North Dakota, Jan 22. Ht. 5 ft. 1 in. wt. 112 lb. Educ. Central High School, Minneapolis ; University of Washington. Appeared in numerous Broadway musicals before going to Hollywood to appear in *Let's Fall in Love* (Col) 1934. Is star of the " Maisie " series (MGM) begun in 1939. Other films include : *The Party's Over, Her Sacrifice, Hell Cat, Melody in Spring, Kid Millions, The Man from the Folies Bergères, Eight Bells, Hooray for Love, Grand Exit, The Girl Friend, Panic on the Air, Hell-Ship Morgan, Walking on Air, My American Wife, Don't Gamble With Love, Smartest Girl in Town, Dangerous*

GALE STORM
(*Monogram*)

Number, There Goes My Girl, Fifty Roads to Town, Super Sleuth, There Goes the Groom, Danger—Love at Work !, She's Got Everything, Trade Winds, Fast and Furious, Hotel for Women, Joe and Ethel Turp Call on the President. 1940 : *Brother Orchid* (Warn), *Dulcy* (MGM) ; 1941 : *Lady be Good !* (MGM) ; 1942 : *Panama Hattie* (MGM), *Three Hearts for Julia* (MGM) ; 1943 : *Thousands Cheer* (MGM), *Cry Havoc* (MGM) ; 1947 : *Indian Summer* (RKO), *April Showers* (Warn).

SPOLIANSKY, Mischa. Composer, musical director. Born Bialystok, Russia, 1898. Went to Berlin where he trained as a violinist, although his real love was the piano and musical composition. Studied in Budapest, Vienna and Italy. First operetta " The Queen of Love ". For some years was associated with producer Joe Pasternak, on the continent, writing music for stage and screen. Has been in Britain since 1933. Wrote music for Cochran's revue, " Home and Beauty " 1937, but now devotes himself almost entirely to music in films. Notable scores are *Sanders of the River* and *King Solomon's Mines,* for both of which he wrote songs for Paul Robeson which have since become famous. Other films for which he has written or directed the music include : *The Lucky Number, Car of Dreams, Tell Me Tonight, My Love for You, The Private Life of Don Juan, The Ghost Goes West, Over the Moon, French Without Tears, Jeannie, Freedom Radio, Secret Mission, Mr. Emmanuel, Don't Take it to Heart, The Forbidden Three, The Man from Morocco, The Demi-Paradise, The Way to the Stars, Beware of Pity, Wanted for Murder, Meet Me at Dawn, Temptation Harbour.*

SPRING, Howard. Author and literary critic. Born Cardiff, 1889. Began full-time work at age of 12 and became butcher's errand boy, office boy, messenger in newspaper office. Educated himself and became reporter till career was interrupted by World War I. Then worked on various newspapers. Books include : " Darkie and Co.", " Shabby Tiger ", " Hard Facts ", " Dunkerley's ", " In the Meantime " (autobiography). Novels filmed : *My Son My Son, Fame Is the Spur.*

STACK, Robert. Born Los Angeles, California, Jan. 13, 1919. Ht. 6 ft. 1 in. ; wt. 175 lb. Fair hair, blue eyes. Educ. Paris ; Los Angeles High School ; University of Southern California. After college, worked in a Lake Tahoe logging camp for year. Saved enough money for drama training in Hollywood and made successful screen test. Film debut in : *First Love* (Univ) 1939. Other films include : 1940 : *The Mortal Storm* (MGM), *A Little Bit of Heaven* (Univ) ; 1941 : *Nice Girl ?* (Univ), *Bad Lands of Dakota* (Univ) ; 1942 : *To Be Or Not To Be ?* (UA), *Eagle Squadron* (Univ), *Men of Texas* (Univ). Served with U.S. Armed Forces, 1943-6.

STAHL, John M. Director. Born New York, Jan. 21, 1886. Educ. New York public schools. Began his career on the stage, at 15, in a Belasco production of " Du Barry " and for fourteen years appeared in many other stage successes. Entered films 1914, when Albert E. Smith gave him chance to direct. Associated with Louis B. Mayer, in the early days of First National (later acquired by Warner Bros) and afterwards at MGM ; also producer-in-chief of Tiffany-Stahl Productions. Outstanding films include : *The Child Thou Gavest Me, Memory Lane, The Gay Decision, A Lady Surrenders, Seed, Strictly Dishonourable, Back Street, Only Yesterday, Imitation of Life, Magnificent Obsession, Parnell, Letter of Introduction, When Tomorrow Comes, Our Wife, Immortal Sergeant, Holy Matrimony, The Eve of St. Mark, The Keys of the Kingdom, Leave Her to Heaven, Foxes of Harrow.*

STANWYCK, Barbara. Real name Ruby Stevens. Born Brooklyn, New York, July 16, 1907. Ht. 5ft. 5 in. ; wt. 115 lb. Auburn hair, deep blue eyes. Educ. Brooklyn public schools. Youthful ambition : to do missionary work in China. Saved money for dancing lessons from her first jobs as parcel wrapper in department store and telephone operator. Became night club dancer : was in " Ziegfeld Follies " at 15, riding an elephant. Became chorus-girl, and obtained small dramatic roles. After first big hit in " Burlesque ", Joe Schenck signed her for pictures. First film *The Locked Door* (UA), 1929. Has appeared in over forty films, including : *Ladies of Leisure, Illicit, So Big, Shopworn, The Bitter Tea of General Yen, Baby Face, Gambling Lady, The Woman in Red, Annie Oakley, A Message to Garcia, The Bride Walks Out, The Plough and the Stars, Stella Dallas, The Mad Miss Manton, Union Pacific, Golden Boy* ; 1940 : *Remember the Night* (Para) ; 1941 : *Meet John Doe* (Warn), *The Lady Eve* (Para), *You Belong to Me* (Col), *Ball of Fire* (RKO) ; 1942 : *The Great Man's Lady* (Para), *The Gay Sisters* (Warn) ; 1943 : *Lady of Burlesque, Flesh and Fantasy* (Univ) ; 1944 : *Double Indemnity* (Para), *Hollywood Canteen* (Warn) ; 1945 : *Christmas in Connecticut* (Warn) ; 1946 : *My Reputation* (Warn), *The Bride Wore Boots* (Para), *California* (Para), *Strange Love of Martha Ivers* (Para) ; 1947 : *Cry Wolf* (Warn), *The Two Mrs. Carrolls* (Warn), guest star in *Variety Girl* (Para), *The Other Love* (Enterprise-MGM).

STARRETT, Charles. Born Athol Massachusetts, Mar. 28. Ht. 6 ft. 2 in. Brown hair, blue eyes. Educ, Mitchell Military Academy, Billerica, Massachusetts ; Worcester Academy ; Dartmouth College. Learned to handle a gun during childhood on grandfather's farm, South China, Maine. Ran away from school at 13, to join a circus as property boy, but father brought him back. For 3 years was football full-back at Dartmouth ; appeared in the Richard Dix film *The Quarterback* (Para), 1926. Decided to become actor. Studied at American Academy of Dramatic Arts ; wrote and presented short play for tired shoppers in New York department store. Made professional debut in " The Goose Hangs High ", Perry, New York State ; on Broadway, 1929, in " Claire Adams ". Film debut in an early talkie made in New York : *Damaged Love,* 1929. In 1930 went to Hollywood where he spent three years appearing in such films as *Fast and Loose, The Viking, Silence, Age For Love, Call It Luck, Transient Love, This Man Is Mine, Stolen Sweets, Sky Bride, Touchdown, Lady and Gent, Mr. Skitch, Three on a Honeymoon, Green Eyes, A Girl Must Live, The Royal Family of Broadway, Desirable, So Red The Rose.* In 1934, was chosen by Columbia as ideal Western hero ; has made on average eight Westerns a year since successful cowboy debut in *Gun Law* (Col), 1934. Hero of *The Durango Kid* series (Col). Contract renewed 1947 for a further seven years.

STEINBECK, John Ernst. Writer. Born Salinas Valley, California, Feb. 27, 1902. Educ. Salinas High School ; Stanford University, California. Won Pulitzer prize for literature, 1940. Has written many plays and novels and short stories dealing with life in and around his native valley in Northern California.

Outstanding works include "Of Mice and Men"—novel and play—and " The Grapes of Wrath " the dramatic and factual story of soil erosion and the trek of the farmers from the " Dust Bowl " of the Middle West. Novels filmed include : *Of Mice and Men, The Grapes of Wrath, The Moon is Down, Tortilla Flat, The Red Pony.* In association with Herbert Kline, wrote, directed and produced *The Forgotten Village* in Mexico. Also, in Mexico, filmed *The Pearl Lopaz.*

STEINER, Max. Composer, music director. Born Vienna. Studied music at Imperial Academy, Vienna. His first important work was the operetta " Beautiful Greek Girl " composed at 14. Came to Britain, 1904, and conducted in London and Blackpool. Went to U.S., 1924, conducting, orchestrating and composing for revue, musical comedy and comic opera. Became musical director to RKO-Pictures, Hollywood, 1929. Joined Warner Bros., 1936, as musical director, and has also composed music for many of their major productions. Has also scored several Selznick productions. Outstanding musical scores include : *Symphony of Six Million, Ann Vickers, The Lost Patrol, Of Human Bondage* (Warn), 1934, *The Informer*—Academy Award 1935, *Break of Hearts, I Dream Too Much, The Charge of the Light Brigade, The Life of Emile Zola, Tovarich, A Star is Born, Jezebel, White Banners, Gone With the Wind, The Sisters, Dawn Patrol, Saratoga Trunk, Now Voyager*—Academy Award 1942, *Since You Went Away*—Academy Award 1944, *A Stolen Life* (Warn) 1946, *Cloak and Dagger, The Big Sleep, Love and Learn, Life With Father, Cheyenne.*

STEPHENS, Ann. Born Golders Green, London, May 21, 1931. Chosen to play " Alice " in recorded version of " Alice in Wonderland ", which she followed with records of " Alice Through the Looking Glass ", " Ann's Nursery Rhymes ", and " Christopher Robin ". Made film debut in *The Young Mr. Pitt* (20th-Brit), 1942 in pillow fight scene with Robert Donat. Other films include : 1942 : *In Which We Serve* (Two-Cities) ; 1943 : *Fanny By Gaslight* (Gains) ; 1944 : *Dear Octopus* (Gains), *They Were Sisters* (Gains), *Alice in Recordland* (short) ; 1947 : *The Upturned Glass* (Box).

STEVENS, Mark. Real name Richard Stevens. Born Cleveland, Ohio, Dec. 13. Ht. 6 ft. ; wt. 170 lb. At 16 he worked for Corona Barn Players in Montreal, and became juvenile lead of Atterbury Players. Worked for radio in the daytime, for theatre in the evening, and as night-club singer and M.C. afterwards. Entered films by playing small parts to gain experience. Major films include—1945 : *Within These Walls* (20th) ; 1946 : *From This Day Forward* (RKO), *The Dark Corner* (20th) ; 1947 : *I Wonder Who's Kissing Her Now ?* (20th).

STEWART, James. Born Indiana, Pennsylvania, May 20, 1909. Ht. 6 ft. 2½ in. ; wt. 165 lb. Brown hair, grey eyes. Educ. Mercersburg Academy ; Princeton University. Intended to become architect, but joined Falmouth Stock Company at Cape Cod and later appeared on New York stage in " Good-bye Again ", " Page Miss Glory ", " Journey At Night " and others. First film : *Murder Man* (MGM) 1935. Joined U.S. Army Air Corps 1941 before U.S.A. entered war ; demobilized 1946, after having been stationed in Britain. Other films include : *Rose Marie, Seventh Heaven, The Last Gangster, Shopworn Angel, You Can't Take It With You, It's A Wonderful World, The Shop Around the Corner, Mr. Smith Goes to Washington, Destry Rides Again.* 1940 : *The*

Mortal Storm (MGM), *The Philadelphia Story* (MGM), *No Time for Comedy* (Warn), *Come Live With Me* (MGM), *Ziegfeld Girl* (MGM), *Pot o' Gold* (Roosevelt-UA) ; 1947 : *It's A Wonderful Life* (RKO), *Magic Town* (RKO) ; 1948 : *Call Northside 777* (20th), *A Miracle Can Happen* (Benedict Bogeaus-UA).

STEWART, Sophie. Born Crieff, Perthshire, Mar. 5, 1908. Ht. 5 ft. 2½ in. ; wt. 112 lb. Dark hair, brown eyes. Educ. Morrison's Academy, Perthshire. At 13 went to London to study Russian ballet. Passed top of her class at 14 years of age, and chosen by Pavlova to appear with her on last world tour. Back in Scotland for short holiday before starting the tour, was run over by lorry, and lost the use of one leg for two years. On recovery, decided on stage career. First film : *The Murder in the Red Barn* (King) 1935. Played title role in film of *Marigold* (BIP) 1938, which she has also played on stage in London and in U.S.A. and Canada, and on radio and television. Films in U.S.A. include : *Nurse Edith Cavell, My Son, My Son* (UA) 1940. Appeared on New York stage in " Twelfth Night ", and toured Canada in " What Every Woman Knows " and " Mary Rose " before returning to stage and screen in Britain. Films include : 1943 : *The Lamp Still Burns* (Two Cities) ; 1945 : *Strawberry Roan* (Brit-Nat) ; 1947 : *Uncle Silas* (Two Cities).

STOCK, Nigel. Born Malta, Sept. 21, 1919. Ht. 5 ft. 11 in. ; wt. 169 lb. Brown hair, blue eyes. Educ. St. Paul's School, London. Has been on the stage since he was 12, when he played small parts at the Grafton Theatre, and also at the Old Vic during school holidays. Later studied at the Royal Academy of Dramatic Art and appeared in several West End productions before World War II. Began his film career in *Break the News* (Jack Buchanan) 1938. Also appeared in *Lancashire Luck, Goodbye Mr. Chips!* Resumed films after six years' war service. 1947 : *Brighton Rock* (Boultings-ABPC), *It Always Rains on Sunday* (Ealing).

STOCKFIELD, Betty. Born Sydney, Australia, Jan. 15, 1905. Came to Britain 1914. Educ. Hertfordshire, and France. Stage debut as chorus girl in revue " London Calling ", Duke of York's Theatre, London, 1924. Has since appeared in London, New York on the stage, and in many French films. In 1947, in London Michael Hickman's production " The Girl Who Couldn't Quite ". Made film debut in Hollywood *What Price Glory ?* (Fox) 1928. British films include : *City of Song* (Sterling), 1930 ; *Captivation, Money for Nothing, Life Goes On, The Impassive Footman, Maid of the Mountains, King of the Ritz, Lord of the Manor, Anne One Hundred, The Man Who Changed His Mind, The Battle, The Lad, The Beloved Vagabond, I See Ice, Dishonour Bright.* 1941 : *Flying Fortress* (Warn-Brit), *Hard Steel* (GHW). Notable French films include : *Club des Femmes, Derrière la Façade, Ils Etaient Neuf Célibataires.*

STOCKWELL, Dean. Born Hollywood, California, Mar. 5, 1936. Brown hair, blue eyes. Educ. Long Island public schools ; Martin Milmore School, Boston. Made radio debut in " Death Valley Days " and " Dr. Christian " with Jean Hersholt. Appeared on stage in Theatre Guild production " Innocent Voyage ", and seen by producer film Joe Pasternak. First film : *Anchors Aweigh* (MGM) 1944. Other films include : 1945 : *The Valley of Decision, The Green Years* ; 1946 : *Home Sweet Homicide* (20th),

SUSAN SHAW
(*Ealing*)

The Mighty McGurk (MGM); 1947: *The Arnelo Affair* (MGM), *The Romance of Rosy Ridge* (MGM), *Song of the Thin Man* (MGM); 1948: *Gentleman's Agreement* (20th).

STOLOFF, Morris. Music director. Born Philadelphia. Studied violin. At 16 made concert tour in United States. Later was youngest member of Los Angeles Philharmonic Orchestra. In 1928 joined Paramount as music teacher. In 1936, music director of Columbia Pictures. Twice an Academy Award winner, for musical direction of *Cover Girl* (Col) 1944 and *The Jolson Story* (Col) 1946. Other films include: *Craig's Wife, Theodora Goes Wild, Lost Horizon, The Awful Truth, You Can't Take It With You, A Song To Remember, The Guilt of Janet Ames, Tonight and Every Night, The Bandit of Sherwood Forest, Gallant Journey, Johnny O'Clock.*

STONE, Lewis. Born Worcester, Massachusetts, Nov. 15, 1879. Ht. 5 ft. 10 in.; wt. 165 lb. White hair, hazel eyes. In vaudeville at age of 17. Served in Spanish-American war. Won fame on Broadway in " Bird of Paradise " and other successes. Recalled to army in World War I, then resumed stage career. In his yacht *Serena* has explored Alaska and other places. Was introduced to screen whilst appearing on stage in Los Angeles. First film: *Honour's Altar* (Ince) 1915. In 1924 joined MGM, for whom he has made more than sixty films. Became one of the most popular leading men in silent films, notably in: *Scaramouche, The Prisoner of Zenda, Milestones, The Patriot, The Lost World.* Sound films include: *Madame X, The Big House, Romance, The Office Wife, The Secret Six, Inspiration, The Lullaby, The Phantom of Paris, Mata Hari, Grand Hotel, Letty Lynton, The White Sister, Bureau of Missing Persons, Queen Christina, Treasure Island, David Copperfield, Vanessa, China Seas, The Unguarded Hour, Outcast, The 13th Chair, Bad Man of Brimstone.* Appeared in: *You're Only Young Once* (MGM) 1937—his first " Judge Hardy " role—and since then in all the " Hardy " series. Other films include: *The Chaser, Yellow Jack, Joe and Ethel Turp call on the President.* 1940: *Sporting Blood;* 1941: *The Bugle Sounds;* 1945: *The Hoodlum Saint;* 1946: *Three Wise Fools,* and the last of the " Hardy " series, *Love Laughs at Andy Hardy.*

STORM, Gale. Real name Josephine Cottle. Born Bloomington, Texas, Apr. 5, 1922. Became interested in dramatics while at school; won acting prize in inter-school competition. Entered Jesse L. Lasky's talent contest " Gateway to Hollywood " in 1939 and won film contract. First screen appearance: *Tom Brown's Schooldays* (RKO) 1940. Films include: *One Crowded Night* (RKO); 1941: *Saddlemates* (Rep), *Gambling Daughters* (PRC). Under contract to Monogram for whom she has made—1942: *Smart Alecks, Foreign Agent, Rhythm Parade, The Lure of the Islands;* 1943: *Cosmo Jones, Crime Smasher, Campus Rhythm;* 1944: *Where Are Your Children?, The Right to Live, Forever Yours!;* 1945: *G.I. Honeymoon, Sunbonnet Sue;* 1946: *Swing Parade of 1946;* 1947: *It Happened on Fifth Avenue.*

STRIDE, April. Born Southsea, Hants, Apr. 21, 1926. Ht. 5 ft. 7 in. Fair hair, blue eyes. Educ. Malta; Byculla School, Southsea. Made first stage appearance at Royal Opera House, Malta. Came to Britain in 1938 to train for ballet, but grew too tall. Studied singing and musical comedy and during World War II appeared in pantomime at Worthing, in

musicals " More New Faces ", " Flying Colours ", " The Love Racket " and in small film parts. Joined ENSA in 1945 and toured Italy and Greece. First important film role was as Sophie Theresa in *Master of Bankdam* (Holbein) 1947. Signed 1947 on long-term contract to Premier Productions, and given leading feminine role in *Idol of Paris,* 1948.

STURGES, Preston. Director, writer. Born Chicago, Aug. 29, 1898. Educ. Chicago; Europe. In early life received without enthusiasm thorough grounding in art and music. 1913-17, assistant stage manager " Oedipus Rex ", in New York, became assistant, then manager of his mother's New York cosmetic business. In U.S. Air Force, 1917-18. Invented kissproof lipstick and ran a cosmetic manufacturing company, 1919-27. Also tried his hand at other inventions. Turned playwright, and (1929) wrote and produced " The Guinea Pig " on Broadway. Also wrote: " Strictly Dishonourable ", " Child of Manhattan ", " Recapture ". Became script writer in Hollywood 1932-39: *The Big Pond, The Power and the Glory, Diamond Jim, One Rainy Afternoon, Port of Seven Seas, Remember the Night.* Sold a script to Paramount with stipulation that he should direct, and achieved first success as writer-director: *The Great McGinty* (Para) 1940. Other films as writer-director: *Christmas in July, Sullivan's Travels, The Lady Eve, The Palm Beach Story, The Great Moment, The Miracle of Morgan's Creek, Hail the Conquering Hero.* With Howard Hughes in 1945 formed California Pictures Corporation, to write and direct series of pictures, including *Mad Wednesday,* in which Harold Lloyd returned to the screen after an absence of seven years.

STURGESS, Ray. Cameraman. Born London, 1909. Sold dog licences for London County Council; became film studio clapper boy; worked on religious shorts. During World War II, became postman; resumed films as clapper boy, became cameraman on *Dangerous Moonlight* (RKO) 1941. Other films include: *The Gentle Sex, The Yellow Canary, Tawny Pipit, Men of Two Worlds, Hungry Hill.*

SULLIVAN, Francis L. Born London, Jan. 6, 1903. Educ. Neuchâtel, Switzerland, and Stonyhurst College, Lancs. Made first stage appearance with Old Vic in " Richard III ", 1921. Subsequently played several parts in Shakespeare and Shaw in London and provinces. Made notable success at St. Martin's Theatre, London, as " Poirot ", Agatha Christie's Belgian detective in " Black Coffee ", 1931. Has also appeared on Broadway in many successful plays. First film: *The Missing Rembrandt* (Twickenham) 1933. Other films include: *Red Wagon, Jew Süss, Chu Chin Chow, The Return of Bulldog Drummond.* In Hollywood 1934-35 made: *Great Expectations* (Univ), *Cheating Cheaters, Strange Wives, The Mystery of Edwin Drood.* Other British films: *Her Last Affaire, Interrupted Honeymoon, Fine Feathers, A Woman Alone, Sabotage, The Limping Man, Non-Stop New York, Action For Slander, Dinner at the Ritz, The First and the Last, The Drum, The Citadel, The Ware Case, The Four Just Men, A Young Man's Fancy* 1941; *Pimpernel Smith* (Brit Nat); 1942: *The Foreman Went to France* (Ealing), *The Day Will Dawn* (Soskin); 1944: *Fiddlers Three* (Ealing); 1946: *Lisbon Story* (Brit Nat), *Caesar and Cleopatra* (Pascal), *Great Expectations* (Cineguild); 1947: *The Man Within* (Box); 1948: *Broken Journey* (Gains), *Oliver Twist* (Cineguild).

SUTHERLAND, Duncan. Art director. Born Perthshire, 1903. Studied at Glasgow School of Architecture. While there produced " potted pantomimes " and revue sketches on semi-professional basis. In 1925 abandoned architecture for the stage, but after four years in concert parties, and a few small parts in films returned to his original career, and was appointed draughtsman at British International Studios, Elstree, in 1929, rising to head of the Art Department in seven months. At B.I.P. he was responsible for most of the art direction during the next ten years. Recent films for which he has designed the settings include : *Thunder Rock, Old Mother Riley Joins Up, Gaslight, Crook's Tour, Undercover, San Demetrio London, Johnny Frenchman, Pink String and Sealing Wax, Bedelia, The Loves of Joanna Godden, It Always Rains on Sunday.*

SUTTON, John. Born Rawalpindi, India, Oct. 22, 1908. Ht. 6 ft. 2 in. ; wt. 170 lb. Dark brown hair, dark brown eyes. Educ. English elementary schools ; Wellington College ; Sandhurst. Youthful ambition to be army officer. Has lived in Africa, China, Malaya and the Philippines, and been veldt rancher and manager of tea plantation. Went to U.S.A. and became technical adviser on films with British backgrounds, then actor. War service 1943-5 in Royal Navy. First film as an actor : *Bulldog Drummond Comes Back* (Para) 1937. Other films include : *Four Men and a Prayer, The Adventures of Robin Hood, Elizabeth and Essex* (Warn) ; 1940 : *The Invisible Man Returns* (Univ), *Sandy is a Lady* (Univ), *I Can't Give You Anything But Love* (Univ), *South to Karanga* (Univ), *Murder Over New York* (20th), *Hudson's Bay* (20th) ; 1941 : *A Very Young Lady* (20th), *A Yank in the R.A.F.* (20th), *Moon Over Her Shoulder* (20th) ; 1942 : *My Gal Sal* (20th), *Ten Gentlemen from West Point* (20th), *Thunder Birds* (20th) ; 1943 : *Jane Eyre* (20th), *The Hour Before Dawn* (Para) ; 1946 : *Claudia and David* (20th).

SYDNEY, Basil. Born St. Osyth, Essex. Apr. 23, 1894. Stage career began 1909. First London appearance, with Matheson Lang, in " Westward Ho ! " at the Palladium, 1913. Served in army in World War I. Appeared in " Romance " in London, 1917, and in the New York presentation, with Doris Keane ; also appeared in the film version, *Romance* (UA) 1920. but returned to the stage until 1932 when he made his first talkie, *The Midshipmaid* (GB). Other films include : *Dirty Work, The Tunnel—U.S. title Transatlantic Tunnel, The Amateur Gentleman, Accused, Crime Over London, Rhodes of Africa, Talk of the Devil, Riverside Murder, Traitors' Gate, Four Just Men.* 1941 : *Ships With Wings* (Ealing) ; 1942 : *The Big Blockade* (Ealing), *Next of Kin* (Ealing), *Went the Day Well ?* (Ealing) ; 1947 : *The Man Within* (Box), *Jassy* (Gains) ; 1948 : *Hamlet* (Two Cities).

TAMIROFF, Akim. Born Baku, Russia, Oct. 29. Ht. 5 ft. 7 in. ; wt. 175 lb. Dark brown hair, grey-blue eyes. Trained for stage at Moscow Art Theatre School. Toured America with theatre group in 1923, and remained there when tour ended, joining " Chauve Souris " company. Later joined the New York Theatre Guild. Was connected with the American Academy of Stage Make-up in New York for a time, before going to Chicago where he appeared in night-clubs. Lost his capital in the great slump in the early 'thirties, and went to Hollywood. His efforts to get into films met with no success until he secured small role in *Sadie McKee* (MGM) 1934. Since then has appeared in more than fifty films, including : *The Great Flirtation, Whom the Gods Destroy, The Lives of a Bengal Lancer, Naughty Marietta, The Winning Ticket, China Seas, Rhumba, Paris in Spring, The Big Broadcast of 1936, The Last Outpost, Two-Fisted, Go Into Your Dance !, Black Fury, The Gay Deception, The Story of Louis Pasteur, Desire, Woman Trap, The General Died at Dawn, Jungle Princess, The Soldier and the Lady, Her Husband Lies, King of the Gamblers, High Wide and Handsome, The Great Gambini, The Buccaneer, Spawn of the North, Ride a Crooked Mile, Paris Honeymoon, Union Pacific.* 1940 : *Geronimo* (Para) in which he was a great success in the title role, *The Way of All Flesh* (Para), *The Great McGinty* (Para) ; 1941 : *The Corsican Brothers* (UA) ; 1942 : *Tortilla Flat* (MGM) ; 1943 : *Five Graves to Cairo* (Para), *For Whom the Bell Tolls* (Para), *His Butler's Sister* (Univ) ; 1944 : *The Bridge of San Luis Rey* (UA), *Dragon Seed* (MGM), *The Miracle of Morgan's Creek* (Para), *Can't Help Singing* (Univ) ; 1946 : *Pardon My Past* (Col), *Scandal in Paris* (Arnold Pressburger-UA) ; 1947 : *Fiesta* (MGM), *Ever the Beginning* (Warn), *The Gangster* (Mono) ; 1948 : *Relentless* (Col).

TANDY, Jessica. Born London, June 7, 1909. Ht. 5 ft. 4 in. ; wt. 120 lb. Brown hair, blue eyes. Educ. Dame Alice Owen's Girls' High School ; Ben Greet Academy of Acting. At 8 decided to become actress. Joined the Birmingham Repertory. Tried London but was first told she was " too plain " ; then played in " Autumn Crocus " and other London productions. Appeared on Broadway in " The White Steed " where a film talent scout offered a part in *The Seventh Cross* (MGM) 1944. Other films include—1944 : *Valley of Decision* (MGM) ; 1945 : *Dragonwyck* (20th) ; 1947 : *The Green Years* (MGM) ; 1947 : *Forever Amber* (20th) ; 1948 : *A Woman's Vengeance* (UI).

TATE, Reginald. Born Garforth, Yorks, Dec. 12, 1896. Ht. 5 ft. 9½ in. ; wt. 147 lb. Dark brown hair, hazel eyes. Educ. York. Youthful ambition : to act. After war service with army and Royal Flying Corps, 1914-18, trained for railway work, but resigned to become teacher and producer at Leeds College of Music and Drama. First London appearance in " Romeo and Juliet ", 1926. Has been almost continuously on London stage since then. Has also produced serial plays, and is frequent broadcaster. Served in R.A.F. 1939-44. Films include : *Whispering Tongues* (Twickenham) 1936 ; *Nursemaid Who Disappeared, Too Dangerous to Live, For Valour, Riverside Murder, Man Behind the Mask, Poison Pen* ; 1942 : *Next of Kin* (Ealing) ; 1943 : *The Life and Death of Colonel Blimp* (Archers) ; 1944 : *The Way Ahead* (Two Cities), *Madonna of the Seven Moons* (Gains) ; 1945 : *The Man From Morocco* (ABPC), *Journey Together* (R.A.F. Film Unit) ; 1946 : *So Well Remembered* (RKO), *Uncle Silas* (Two Cities).

TAUROG, Norman. Director. Born Chicago, Feb. 23, 1899. Educ. New York ; Indianapolis. Was a child actor on the New York stage, and also in films. Later worked as film " property man ". Began his career as director in 1913, making Larry Semon comedies, Lloyd Hamilton comedies and many other silent films. Sound films include : *Lucky Boy, Hot Curves, Troopers Three, Sunny Skies, Follow the Leader, Skippy, Finn and Hattie, Forbidden Adventure, Huckleberry Finn, Sooky, If I Had a Million, Hold 'em Jail, The Phantom President, A Bedtime Story, The Way to Love, We're Not Dressing, Mrs. Wiggs of the Cabbage*

GREGORY PECK
(*Selznick*)

JEAN SIMMONS
(*Two Cities*)

Patch, College Rhythm, Strike me Pink !, Big Broadcast of 1936, Rhythm on the Range, Reunion, Fifty Roads to Town, You Can't Have Everything, Mad About Music, Adventures of Tom Sawyer, Boys' Town, The Girl Downstairs, Lucky Night, Broadway Melody of 1940, Young Tom Edison, Little Nelly Kelly, Are Husbands Necessary?, A Yank at Eton,. Presenting Lily Mars, Girl Crazy, The Hoodlum Saint, The Beginning or the End ?, Love Bites Man.

TAYLOR, Elizabeth. Born London, Feb. 27, 1932. Dark brown hair, blue eyes. In World War II, evacuated to California. Secured first film role, in *Lassie Come Home* (MGM) 1943, after her father on air-raid warden duty in California had met fellow-warden Sam Marx, film producer, who was seeking English girl for the part. Other films include—1943 : *Jane Eyre* (20th) ; 1944 : *The White Cliffs of Dover* (MGM), *National Velvet* (MGM) ; 1945 : *Courage of Lassie* (MGM) ; 1947 : *The Rich Full Life* (MGM), *Killer McCoy* (MGM) ; 1948 : *A Date With Judy* (MGM).

TAYLOR, Robert. Real name Spangler Arlington Brough. Born Filley, Nebraska, Aug. 5, 1911. Ht. 6 ft. ; wt. 175 lb. Dark brown hair, blue eyes. Educ. public schools, Beatrice, Neb. ; Doane College, Crete, Neb. ; Pomona College, Calif. Studied 'cello at school and formed a trio which broadcast while at Doane College. Played lead in university production of " Journey's End ". Play was seen by film talent scout, and after graduation in 1934 studied drama at MGM studios. Made his film debut with late Will Rogers in *Handy Andy* (Fox) 1934. Other films include : *There's Always Tomorrow, A Wicked Woman, Society Doctor, West Point of the Air, Times Square Lady, Murder in The Fleet, Broadway Melody of 1936, Magnificent Obsession, Small Town Girl, The Gorgeous Hussy, Secret Interlude, His Brother's Wife, Camille, His Affair, The Man in Possession, Broadway Melody of 1938, A Yank at Oxford* (MGM-Brit) 1938—which turned his career towards more dramatic roles : *The Crowd Roars, Three Comrades, Stand Up and Fight, Lucky Night, Lady of The Tropics, Remember ?* 1940 : *Waterloo Bridge* (MGM), *Escape* (MGM), *Flight Commander* (MGM) ; 1941 : *Billy the Kid* (MGM), *When Ladies Meet* (MGM), *Johnny Eager* (MGM) ; 1942 : *Her Cardboard Lover* (MGM), *Cargo of Innocents* (MGM), *The Youngest Profession* (MGM), *Bataan* (MGM), *Song of Russia* (MGM). 1943-6, war service with the U.S. Navy. 1946 : *Undercurrent* (MGM) ; 1948 : *High Wall* (MGM).

TCHERINA, Ludmilla. Born 1925. Trained as a ballet dancer under Preobajinska, and later joined the Monte Carlo Ballet. Made her film debut in French film, *Le Revenant*. Appeared as " prima ballerina " in her first British film *Red Shoes* (Archers) 1948.

TEMPLE, Shirley. Born Santa Monica, California, Apr. 23, 1929. The world's most famous child star, now beginning new career as romantic lead. Brown hair, blue eyes. Educ. 20th-Fox Studio School ; Westlake School for Girls, Los Angeles. Was a natural dancer from age of 2, and after her third dancing lesson a talent scout persuaded her mother to allow her to appear in " Baby Burlesks " series (Educational) 1932. Then played small parts in full-length features, *Red Haired Alibi, Out All Night, To The Last Man*. Next appeared in series of shorts, *Frolics of Youth*. Seen in these by composer Jay Gorney, who urged parents to enter her for audition for " Stand Up and Cheer ", which he was scoring. She won small role from 150 other children, made hit with song " Baby Take a Bow ", and gained Fox contract. Had sensational career as child star, but parents took care to organize her life naturally and normally. Films include : *Carolina, Girl in Pawn, When New York Sleeps, Change of Heart, Now I'll Tell, Little Miss Marker, Baby Take a Bow, Now and Forever, Bright Eyes, The Little Colonel, Our Little Girl, Curly Top, The Littlest Rebel, Captain January, Poor Little Rich Girl, Dimples, Stowaway, Wee Willie Winkie, Heidi, Rebecca of Sunnybrook Farm, Little Miss Broadway, Just Around the Corner, The Little Princess, Susannah of the Mounties*. 1940 : *The Blue Bird* (20th), *Young People* (20th) ; 1941 : *Kathleen* (MGM) ; 1942 : *Miss Annie Rooney* (UA) ; 1944 : *Since You Went Away* (UA), *I'll Be Seeing You* (UA) ; 1945 : *Kiss and Tell* (Col), her first adult role ; 1947 : *The Bachelor Knight* (RKO), *Two Men and a Girl* (RKO), *Mary Hagen* (Warn).

THAXTER, Phyllis. Born Portland, Maine, Nov. 20. Ht. 5 ft. 4 in. ; wt. 110 lb. Brown hair, hazel eyes. After leaving school played summer theatre and later joined Montreal Repertory Company. In 1932 had a walking on part in New York production of " What a Life ". Lynne Fontanne gave her role of maid, and understudy to *ingénue*, in " There Shall Be No Night ". Was appearing in " Claudia " in San Francisco when MGM sent for her, as result of previous test. First film : *Thirty Seconds over Tokyo* (MGM), 1944. Other films (all MGM) include— 1945 : *Bewitched, Weekend at the Waldorf* ; 1946 : *Tenth Avenue Angel* ; 1947 : *Sea of Grass, Living in a Big Way*.

THOMPSON, Marshall. Born Peoria, Illinois, Nov. 27. Ht. 6 ft. 1 in. ; wt. 155 lb. Fair hair, blue eyes. Educ. Occidental College, Los Angeles. Seen by talent scout in high school plays, but film test was unsuccessful. Joined an amateur group, Westwood Village Players as writer and actor ; appeared in small role in *Reckless Age* (Univ) 1944. Director Richard Whorf, seeing preview of this film, decided he was potential star. Other films (all MGM) include— 1944 : *Blonde Fever, Under the Clock* ; 1945 : *The Valley of Decision, Twice Blessed, They Were Expendable, Bad Bascomb* ; 1946 : *Mrs. Griggs Returns, Gallant Bess, The Secret Heart, The Romance of Rosy Ridge* ; 1947 : *The Show-Off* ; 1948 : *Homecoming, Polly Fulton*.

THOMPSON, Russell. Director of photography. Born London, 1911. Began his career in laboratories of Gaumont Studios in 1925 : became camera assistant in 1930, worked on early Gaumont sound films : *Down River, Hindle Wakes, The Happy Ending* ; 1932 became cameraman at British Lion Studios, Beaconsfield. In 1939, became photographer with Royal Navy, Fleet Air Arm ; transferred to Naval Film Unit, to make gunnery and training films ; lent to Army to direct 2 training films. 1944, cameraman on staff of Chief of Naval Intelligence ; filmed Japanese war, including surrender of Hong Kong, for British newsreels. Demobilized in 1946. Recent films include : *Odd Man Out, Escape*.

THORN, " V.C." Dog star. Alsatian. Born 1941. Won the Dickin Medal, known as the " Dogs' V.C." for rescue work during the bombing of London. Led a team responsible for tracing over 100 human casualties. His owner-trainer, Malcolm Russell, was awarded the B.E.M. for courageous rescues of buried victims which his dog located. Thorn has also done much experimental work for the R.A.F., in mountain rescues of crashed aircraft and personnel ; also trained in mine detecting for land clearance after the war. Has appeared in several recent films, including : *The End of the River, They Walk Alone, Daughter of Darkness.*

TIERNEY, Gene. Full name Gene Eliza Tierney. Born Brooklyn, New York, Nov. 20, 1920. Ht. 5 ft. 5½ in. ; wt. 118 lb. Reddish-brown hair, green eyes. Educ. Grade School, Connecticut, St. Margaret's Connecticut ; Lausanne, Switzerland. After having completed education, lived society life for a few months but then decided to fulfil ambition to act, and secured role in George Abbott's stage production of " Mrs. O'Brien Entertains ". While she was playing in " The Male Animal ", Darryl F. Zanuck saw her and cast her for role in *The Return of Frank James* (20th), 1940. Other films (all 20th) include—1941 : *Tobacco Road, Hudson's Bay, Belle Starr, Sundown* ; 1942 : *The Shanghai Gesture* (UA), *Son of Fury, Rings on her Fingers, Thunder Birds* ; 1943 : *China Girl* ; 1944 : *Heaven Can Wait, Laura* ; 1945 : *A Bell for Adano, Leave Her to Heaven* ; 1946 : *Dragonwyck* ; 1947 : *The Ghost and Mrs. Muir, The Razor's Edge.*

TIERNEY, Lawrence. Born New York, Mar. 15, 1919. Ht. 6 ft. ; wt. 175 lb. Brown hair, grey-green eyes. Educ. Manhattan College. Was field engineer, locomotive builder and accountant before training for the stage with the New Rochelle Players. Seen by talent scout in American-Irish Theatre, and went to Hollywood to appear in *The Ghost Ship* (RKO) 1943. Other films (all RKO) include :—1943 : *The Falcon Out West* ; 1944 : *Youth Runs Wild* ; 1945 : *Those Endearing Young Charms, Dillinger, Back to Bataan, Mama Loves Papa* ; 1946 : *Badman's Territory, Step by Step, San Quentin* ; 1947 : *Born to Kill, The Devil Thumbs a Ride.*

TISSIER, Jean. Born Paris, Apr. 1, 1896. Dark hair, blue eyes. Educ. Janson. Tried journalism, then the stage, making debut in " Madame Sans-Gêne ". Other stage plays include : " La Puce à l'Oreille ", " L'Homme d'un soir ", " Jean de la Lune ". Has appeared in many French films, including : *L'Amant de Bornéo, Le Lit à Colonnes, Les Inconnues dans la Maison, La Maison des Sept Jeunes Filles, Ce n'est pas Moi, Signe Picpus, Adrien, Vingt Cinq Ans de Bonheur, Au Bon-heur des Dames, Lucrèce, Coup de Tête, Mon Amour est Près de Toi, Le Merle Blanc, Lunegarde, Le Millionaire, La Cavalier Noir, Le Roi des Resquilleurs, Une Fille à Papa, Le Capitan, L'Invité de la 11ème Heure, Roger La Honte, L'Ennemi sans Visage, La Revanche de Roger La Honte, Rendezvous à Paris, Les Aventures de Casanova, L'Homme Traqué, On Demande un Ménage, La Kermesse Rouge, Le Diamant de Cent Sous.*

TOBIAS, George. Born New York, July 14, 1901. Ht. 5 ft. 11½ in. ; wt. 185 lb. Long stage career. Debut at Neighbourhood Playhouse, Grand Street, New York ; then with Provincetown Players in " The Hairy Ape ", becoming protégé of the late Louis Wolheim. Later, with Theatre Guild and Theatre Union. Went to Hollywood, 1938. Films (all Warn until 1946) include :—1940 : *Saturday's Children, Torrid Zone, City of Conquest* ; 1941 : *Strawberry Blonde, Sergeant York* ; 1943 : *Yankee Doodle Dandy, Air Force, This Is The Army, Mission to Moscow, Thank Your Lucky Stars* ; 1944 : *Passage to Marseilles,*

Make Your Own Bed, The Mask of Dimitrios, Between Two Worlds ; 1945 : *Objective Burma, Mildred Pearce* ; 1946 : *Nobody Lives Forever, Gallant Bess* (MGM).

TODD, Ann. Born Hartford, Cheshire, Jan. 24, 1909. Ht. 5 ft. 4 in. ; wt. 110 lb. Blonde hair, blue eyes. Educ. Central School of Speech Training, London. Intended to become teacher of elocution and fencing. While still a student, was called on at the last minute to appear as " A Faery Child " in the Arts Theatre production of W. B. Yeats's " The Land of Heart's Desire ", 1928. Decided to become an actress. Notable stage successes include " The Middle Watch ", " Service ", " No More Ladies ", " The Man in Half-Moon Street ", and the title role in " Lottie Dundass " 1943. Made her film debut in *Keepers of Youth* (BIP) 1931. Other films include : *These Charming People, Return of Bulldog Drummond, Men of Yesterday, The Squeaker, South Riding, Poison Pen, Water Gypsies.* 1941 : *Ships With Wings* (Ealing) ; 1946 : *The Seventh Veil* (Ortus-Box), *Perfect Strangers*—U.S. title *Vacation from Marriage* (MGM-Brit), *Gaiety George* (King) ; 1948 : *The Paradine Case* (Selznick) in Hollywood, *Daybreak* (Box), *So Evil My Love* (Hal Wallis-Para), made in Britain.

TOMLINSON, David. Born Henley-on-Thames, May 7, 1917. Ht. 6 ft. 1½ in. ; wt. 175 lb. Brown hair, grey-green eyes. Educ. Tonbridge School. Appeared in amateur productions at Folkestone before playing in touring company as John in " Quiet Wedding ". Was spotted by director Anthony Asquith and made his film debut in same role in *Quiet Wedding* (Soskin) 1941. War service with R.A.F., 1942-5. Other films include :—1941 : *Pimpernel Smith* (Brit-Nat) ; 1945 : *The Way to the Stars* (Two Cities) ; *Journey Together* (R.A.F. Film Unit) ; 1947 : *Master of Bankdam* (Holbein), *Uncle Silas* (Two Cities) ; 1948 : *Broken Journey* (Gains), *Miranda* (Gains).

TONE, Franchot. Born Niagara Falls, New York, Feb. 27, 1908. Ht. 5 ft. 11 in. ; wt. 170 lb. Brown hair, blue eyes. Educ. Cornell University. Was a language teacher before becoming actor. Trained with repertory, and in 1929 joined New York Theatre Guild. Seen by talent scout on New York stage and given first screen role in *The Wiser Sex* (Para) 1932. Other films include : *Gabriel over the White House, Today We Live, Midnight Mary, The Stranger's Return, Stage Mother, Bombshell, Dancing Lady, Moulin Rouge, The World Moves On, Sadie McKee, Straight is the Way, The Girl from Missouri, Reckless, One New York Night, No More Ladies, Mutiny on the Bounty, Dangerous Hour, Suzy, The Gorgeous Hussy, Love on the Run, The King Steps Out, Quality Street, They Gave Him a Gun, Between Two Women, The Bride Wore Red, Man Proof, Love is a Headache, Three Comrades, Three Loves Has Nancy, The Girl Downstairs.* 1940 : *The Trail of the Vigilantes* (Univ) ; 1941 : *Nice Girl* (Univ), *This Woman Is Mine* (Univ), *She Knew All the Answers* (Col) ; 1942 : *The Wife Takes a Flyer* (Col) ; 1943 : *Star Spangled Rhythm* (Para), *Test Pilot No. 5* (MGM), *Five Graves to Cairo* (Para), *His Butler's Sister* (Univ), *True to Life* (Para) ; 1944 : *Phantom Lady* (Univ), *The Hour before the Dawn* (Para), *Dark Waters* (UA), *That Night With You* (UA) ; 1946 : *Because of Him* (Univ) ; 1947 : *Two Men and A Girl* (RKO), *Her Husband's Affairs* (Col), *Amy Comes Across* (Eagle Lion-Hollywood), *Lost Honeymoon* (Eagle Lion-Hollywood), *I Love Trouble* (Col).

TOTO. Real name Antonio de Curtis. Born Naples, 1903. One of the most popular clowns of the modern Italian theatre. Films include : *Fermo con le Mani, Animali Pazzi, S. Giovanni Decollato, L'Allegro Fantasma ;* 1945 : *Il Ratto delle Sabine* (Capitani).

TOTTER, Audrey. Born Joliet, Illinois, Dec. 20. Ht. 5 ft. 3 in. ; wt. 106 lb. Red-blonde hair, blue eyes. Educ. Joliet High School. Appeared in school productions of classical plays. Began her professional stage career in Chicago with a summer theatre company, appearing in " Stage Door ", " Night Must Fall ", " The Late Christopher Bean " and others. Toured for a year in " My Sister Eileen ". For four years played lead in radio serials ; film talent scout who heard her suggested film test, and she made her screen debut in *Main Street After Dark* (MGM) 1944. Other films (all MGM) include—1945 : *The Hidden Eye, Her Highness the Bellboy, Dangerous Partners, The Postman Always Rings Twice, The Sailor Takes a Wife ;* 1946 : *Mr. Griggs Returns, Lady in the Lake ;* 1947 : *The Beginning or the End ?, Tenth Avenue Angel ;* 1948 : *The Unsuspected* (Warn), *High Wall* (MGM).

TRACY, Spencer. Born Milwaukee, Wisconsin, Apr. 5, 1900. Ht. 5 ft. 10 in. ; wt. 170 lb. Brown hair, blue eyes. Educ. Marquette University ; Ripon College, Wisconsin. Tried to enlist in World War I, but was turned down on account of his youth, and returned to school. Later studied medicine, but after college dramatic experience gave up medicine for the stage. Trained at the American Academy of Dramatic Art, and made his professional debut 1922, as one of the robots, in " R.U.R.". Appeared with Ethel Barrymore in " Royal Fandango " on Broadway, 1923. Entered films in 1930 and for fifteen years devoted himself exclusively to the screen. First film : *Up the River* (Fox) 1930. Other films include : *Goldie, Quick Millions, Six Cylinder Love, Sky Devils, Disorderly Conduct, Society Girl, We Humans, She Wanted a Millionaire, Pier 13, Painted Woman, 20,000 Years in Sing Sing, Face in the Sky, Power and Glory, Shanghai Madness, A Man's Castle, The Mad Game, The Show-Off, Looking for Trouble, Bottoms Up, When New York Sleeps, Marie Galante, It's a Small World, Dante's Inferno.* Joined MGM, 1935, when he made *The Murder Man.* Other films—all for MGM—include : *Riffraff, Whipsaw, Fury, San Francisco, Libelled Lady, Captains Courageous, They Gave Him a Gun, Big City, Mannequin, Test Pilot, Boys' Town, Stanley and Livingstone* (20th) 1939, *I Take This Woman.* 1940 : *North West Passage, Edison the Man, Boom Town ;* 1941 : *Men of Boys' Town, Dr. Jekyll and Mr. Hyde ;* 1942 : *Woman of the Year, Tortilla Flat, Keeper of the Flame ;* 1943 : *A Guy Named Joe ;* 1944 : *The Seventh Cross, Thirty Seconds Over Tokyo*—in which he played the role of General Doolittle, who in 1942 commanded the first daylight bombing raid over Tokyo ; 1945 : *Without Love ;* 1946 : *The Sea of Grass ;* 1947 : *Cass Timberlane ;* 1948 : *State of the Union.*

TRAIN, Jack. Born Plymouth, Nov. 28, 1902. Ht. 5 ft. 8 in. Dark brown hair, brown eyes. Educ. Plymouth. Served in Royal Navy in World War I, and became an engineer in Plymouth until Leslie Hore Belisha, then M.P. for Devonport, saw him performing in local concert, and gave him introduction to impresario Archie de Bear which resulted in his professional debut in the revue " Many Happy Returns " at the Duke of York's Theatre, London, 1928. Appeared on stage in " Journey's End " and in " The Chelsea Follies " with Nervo and Knox, later joining them in their act. Made his name in B.B.C. feature " It's That Man Again " with Tommy Handley, impersonating first " Funf ", a burlesque German spy, and then many other characters. His most celebrated ITMA character is " Colonel Chinstrap ". Films include—1942 : *King Arthur Was a Gentleman* (Gains) ; 1943 : *Miss London Ltd.* (Gains) ; 1946 : *Gaiety George* (King) ; 1947 : *What's Yours ?* (Grand Nat), *Colonel Bogey* (John Croydon) in which his voice is heard as " Colonel Chinstrap ".

TRAUBERG, L. Producer. With Kozintsev, made the early talking film *Alone* (1931), the music for which was composed by Shostakovich. Other films include : *The Cloak* (1926), *S.V.D.* (1928), *New Babylon* (1929), *The Youth of Maxim, The Return of Maxim* and *The Viborg Side*—a trilogy about the life of the great Maxim Gorki (1933-7), *Ordinary People* (1943), *Pirogov* (1947-8), the story of the famed Russian surgeon.

TRAVERS, Ben. Writer. Born Hendon, London, 1887. Educ. Charterhouse. Began his career in his father's wine and grocery business in London. Later worked in London publishing house. Served with the R.F.C. in World War I. First play : " The Dippers " based on his own novel. Became famous as writer of farces staged at the Aldwych Theatre, starring Tom Walls and Ralph Lynn. Many of these he adapted for the screen, including : *A Cuckoo in the Nest, Rookery Nook, Thark, Plunder, A Cup of Kindness, A Night Like This, Turkey Time, Dirty Work.* Also wrote the film comedies *Fighting Stock, Stormy Weather.* Wrote stage and screen versions of *Banana Ridge,* appearing himself in the rôle of the Malay servant for more than 400 performances at the Strand Theatre, London, 1938-9. Served with R.A.F. in World War II, 1939-43. Wrote the dialogue for *Uncle Silas.*

TRAVERS, Linden. Real name Florence Lindon-Travers. Born Houghton le Spring, Co. Durham, May 27, 1913. Ht. 5 ft. 5 in. ; wt. 122 lb. Auburn hair, green eyes. Educ. Convent de la Sagesse. Youthful ambition : to be lion tamer. Went straight from school into repertory, first at Newcastle, later at Birmingham. Made her London stage debut as juvenile lead in " Murder in Mayfair ", 1934. Was an overnight success in " No Orchids for Miss Blandish" in 1942, a role she later repeated on the screen. Worked as a V.A.D., then toured R.A.F. Camps for ENSA, 1943-5. First film *Double Alibi* (Warn-Brit), 1936. Other films include : *The Lady Vanishes, Brief Ecstasy, The Terror, Almost a Honeymoon, Candles at Nine, The Stars Look Down ;* 1941 : *The Ghost Train* (Gains), *South American George* (Col-Brit) ; 1942 : *The Missing Millions* (Warn-Brit) ; 1946 : *Beware of Pity* (Two Cities) ; 1947 : *Jassy* (Gains), *Master of Bankdam* (Holbein) ; 1948 : title role in *No Orchids for Miss Blandish* (Alliance).

TREVOR, Claire. Born New York City, Mar. 8, 1909. Ht. 5 ft. 3½ in. ; wt. 112 lb. Blonde hair, hazel eyes. Educ. Public and High Schools at Larch-mont, New York. Trained at American Academy of Dramatic Art, after appearing on the stage at 8 in Maeterlinck's " Blue Bird." Made New York debut, 1932, in " Whistling in the Dark ". While playing on Broadway in " The Party's Over ", was signed for films, appearing first in a series of Warner shorts and later in the feature *Life in the Raw* (20th),

1933. Other films include : *The Mad Game, The Last Trail, Jimmy and Sally, Hold That Girl, White Gold, Dante's Inferno, My Marriage, Navy Wife, Human Cargo, Star for a Night, Career Woman, Second Honeymoon, Big Town Girl, Dead End, The Amazing Mr. Clitterhouse, Stagecoach, I Stole a Million, To Mary with Love* ; 1940 : *Dark Command* (Rep) ; 1941 : *Honky Tonk* (MGM), *Texas* (Col) ; 1942 : *The Adventures of Martin Eden* (Col), *Crossroads* (MGM), *Street of Chance* (Para) ; 1943 : *The Desperadoes* (Col), *Woman of the Town* (UA) ; 1944 : *Farewell My Lovely* (RKO) ; 1945 : *Johnny Angel* (RKO) ; 1946 : *Crack-Up* (RKO) ; 1947 : *Bachelor Girls* (Andrew Stone-UA) ; 1948 : *Born to Kill* (RKO).

TROTTI, Lamar. Writer, producer. Born Atlanta, Georgia, 1900. Educ. University of Georgia. Went into newspaper work immediately after graduation. Appointed film editor " Motion Picture Monthly " in New York, and in 1932 joined Fox Films as a writer. In collaboration with Dudley Nichols wrote screenplay *The Man Who Dared* (1933). Also collaborated on screen plays *You Can't Buy Everything, Hold That Girl,* stories of *Wild Gold, Call It Luck, Bachelor of Arts ;* collaborated on story and screenplay *Can This Be Dixie ?* Other screenplays include : *Life Begins at 40, Steamboat Round the Bend, This is the Life, Gentle Julia, Ramona, The First Baby, The Country Beyond, Pepper, Career Woman, Slave Ship, Wife Doctor and Nurse, In Old Chicago, Alexander's Ragtime Band, Kentucky, The Ox-Bow Incident*—British title *Strange Incident, Immortal Sergeant, Guadalcanal Diary, This is the Life, Wilson*—for which he won the Academy Award 1944 for the best original screenplay, *A Bell for Adano, The Razor's Edge.* 1947, became producer with *Captain from Castile, Mother Wore Tights.*

TROUT, Tom. Born St. Louis, Missouri. Ht. 6 ft. wt. 180 lb. Brown hair, grey eyes. Worked as boiler maker before deciding to try film acting. Saw picture of a talent scout in a magazine and went to Hollywood determined to get an audition ; though without any acting experience read a scene from a script and was given contract. Made film debut in *Between two Women* (MGM) 1945. Other films (all MGM) include 1945 : *Her Highness and the Bell Boy* ; 1946 . *Tenth Avenue Angel* ; 1947 : *Merton of the Movies.*

TUFTS, Sonny. Real name Bowen Charleston Tufts. Born Boston, Massachusetts, July 16. Ht. 6 ft. 3 in. ; wt. 210 lb. Fair hair, blue eyes. Became refrigerator salesman for one of his father's companies while still at school, in 1929. At Yale organized student dance bands and let them to shipping companies for Mediterranean cruises during summer holidays. After having heard Tito Schipa sing during one cruise, became keen on opera, and spent six months in operatic training in France, and two years in America studying music. Made his musical debut in " Who's Who ", in New York, and sang in nightclubs for three years. As a film test, 1942, he burlesqued a Charles Boyer love-scene, and was given a role in *So Proudly We Hail* (Para), 1943. Other films include—1943 : *Government Girl* (RKO) ; 1944 : *I Love a Soldier* (Para), *Bring on the Girls* (Para) ; 1945 : *Here Come the Waves* (Para), *At Miss Susie Slagle's* (Para), *The Virginian* (Para), *Duffy's Tavern* (Para) ; 1946 : *Cross my Heart* (Para), *The Well Groomed Bride* (Para), *Easy Come, Easy Go* (Para) ; 1947 : *Blaze of Noon* (Para), *Swell Guy* (UI).

TURIN, Victor. Director. Born St. Petersburg (now Leningrad), 1897. Started film career as scenario writer. Later became a director for the All-Ukrainian Photo-Cinema Board, where he made his first film, *The Struggle of the Giants.* Had a great influence on the educational and documentary fields of film-making with his best-known film, *Turksib* (first shown in Britain 1930), which he wrote and directed. This " impressionist documentary ", dealing with the building of the railway linking Turkestan and Siberia, is, like Eisenstein's *The Battleship Potemkin,* notable for its use of masses of ordinary people instead of professional crowd players.

TURNER, Lana. Real name Julia Turner. Born Wallace, Idaho, Feb. 8, 1921. Ht. 5 ft. 3 in. ; wt. 110 lb. Blonde hair, grey-green eyes. Educ. Convent of the Immaculate Conception, San Francisco ; Hollywood High School. Went to Hollywood at age of 15, and intended to become dress designer, but was seen by friend of Director Mervyn LeRoy, and instead began screen career at 16. First film : *They Won't Forget* (Warn), 1937. Other films include : *The Great Garrick, Adventures of Marco Polo, Love Finds Andy Hardy, Rich Man Poor Girl, Dramatic School, Calling Dr. Kildare, These Glamour Girls, Every Other Inch a Lady* ; 1940 (all MGM) : *Choose Your Partners, We Who Are Young* ; 1941 : *Ziegfeld Girl, Dr. Jekyll and Mr. Hyde, Honky Tonk, Johnny Eager* ; 1942 : *Somewhere I'll Find You* ; 1943 : *Slightly Dangerous, The Youngest Profession* ; 1944 : *Marriage is a Private Affair, Keep Your Powder Dry* ; 1945 : *Weekend at the Waldorf, The Postman Always Rings Twice* ; 1947 : *Green Dolphin Street, Cass Timberlane ;* 1948 : *Homecoming.*

TWIST, Derek. Director. Born London, May 6, 1905. Educ. Rugby ; Caius College, Cambridge. Began his career in oil business in Singapore. Returned to Britain, 1931, and started his film career in the cutting rooms at Gaumont-British. Was film editor on *Sunshine Susie,* starring the late Renate Muller. Other films include : *Waltz Time, The Passing of the Third Floor Back, Rhodes of Africa, The Thirty-nine Steps* and *The Edge of the World.* Joined the R.A.F. 1939. Later in Air Ministry Public Relations Office, then in R.A.F. Film Unit. Was R.A.F. supervisor and co-producer of *School for Secrets,* the story of British development of Radar. After demobilization, 1946, directed *The End of the River.* 1947 : joined Wessex Films Productions. Associate producer, *Esther Waters.*

USHER, Bob. Stunt man. Real name Robert Edward Usher. Born Ottawa, Oct. 19, 1912. Ht. 5 ft. 8 in. ; wt. 168 lb. Educ. Canada ; U.S.A. Began acting at 9. Youthful ambitions, to be a cowboy, to drive a train, and to be a sailor—achieved all three. Qualified as mechanical engineer. Also was rider on Oklahoma ranch, and fought in the Spanish Civil War. Entered films while visiting Hollywood, in 1933, when he undertook to double for Edward G. Robinson in a dangerous stunt. Recent films in which he has been engaged include : *The Courtneys of Curzon Street, They Made Me a Fugitive, Good Time Girl, An Ideal Husband, Blanche Fury.*

USTINOV, Peter. Actor, writer, director. Born London, Apr. 16, 1921. Educ. Westminster School ; left at 16 and joined the London Theatre Studio to study with Michel St. Denis. Made stage debut 1938 as Waffles in " The Wood Demon " at the Barn

Theatre, Shere, Surrey. Made his London debut at Arts Theatre, 1939 in a sketch written by himself, " The Bishop of Limpopoland ". Has since written and appeared in several of his own revues. Served in army 1942-6. Made his film debut in *Mein Kampf— My Crimes* (ABPC) 1940. Also appeared in *One Of Our Aircraft is Missing* (Brit Nat) 1942. With Eric Ambler wrote *The Way Ahead* (Two Cities), and also appeared as the café proprietor. Directed *School for Secrets ;* co-produced, directed and wrote screenplay of *Vice Versa*.

VALLI, Alida. Born Pola, Italy, 1922. Ht. 5 ft. 4 in. ; wt. 114 lb. Dark auburn hair, blue eyes. Educ. Como Gymnasium ; studied dramatic art at Film Academy, Rome ; was put under contract by Italcine. Made ten films before the suspension of Italian production in 1943. Became one of Italy's leading stars. Early films include : *Assenza Inglustifica, Manon Lescaut, Piccolo Mondo Antico, L'Amante Segreto, Ore 9 Lezione Di Chimica, Catene Invisibili, Le Due Orfanelle, Noi Vivi*. Left the screen during German occupation of Rome ; resumed career in 1945, with *La Vita Ricomincia, Giovanna* and *Il Canto Della Vita* (1946), *Eugénie Grandet, Stasora Nienti di Nueve*. Went to U.S.A. to play leading role in *The Paradine Case* (Selznick) 1948.

VANCE, Dennis. Born Birkenhead, Cheshire, Mar. 18, 1924. Ht. 5 ft. 11½ in. ; wt. 175 lb. Brown hair, grey-green eyes. In 1940, too young to enter Royal Academy of Dramatic Art, joined the Merchant Navy ; transferred later to the Royal Navy, Air Branch. After demobilization set up agency to discover new talent, but was himself spotted by a talent scout, and signed a long-term contract with the Rank Organisation. After six months training with the " Company of Youth " made his film debut in 1948, in *Hamlet* (Two Cities).

VAN DRUTEN, John. Writer. Born London, June 1, 1901. Educ. University College School ; London University. Qualified as a solicitor in 1923, and, till 1926, was lecturer in English Law at University College of Wales. First play, " The Return Half ", 1924. Scored notable success with " Young Woodley ", play of English public school life, Savoy Theatre, London, 1928. Plays include : " After All ", " There's Always Juliet ", " The Distaff Side ", " London Wall ", " Gertie Maude ", " Old Acquaintance ", " The Joyous Season ". Plays filmed include : *Young Woodley, Leave Her to Heaven, Old Acquaintance, The Voice of the Turtle*. Screenplays include : *New Morals for Old, If I Were Free, Night Must Fall, Raffles, Lucky Partners, Johnny Come Lately*.

VASSILIEV, S. Producer. Born 1900. Graduated from the Institute of Screen Art in Leningrad. In 1924, was editor-composer for the Moscow office of the North-Western Film Corporation ; at the same time carried on scientific research work in the State Academy of Art and was assistant secretary to the Association of Revolutionary Cinematographers. Collaborated with G. Vassiliev on the films : *Polar Heroics* (1925), *The Sleeping Beauty* (1929-30), *A Personal Matter* (1930-31) *Chapayev* (1935). *Volochainski Days* (1937), *The Defence of Tzaritsin*, part I and II (1938-9), *The Front* (1943) based on the play by Kornaichuk. Has written a book, " Composition of Cinema Films ", published 1927.

VERA-ELLEN. Real name Vera Rohe. Born Cincinnati, Ohio, Feb. 16. Educ. Norwood High

School. Began her career dancing for social, charitable and service organizations in Kentucky and Ohio. Went to New York as delegate to a convention of American Dancing Teachers and stayed to appear on the stage, in " Very Warm for May ", " Higher and Higher ", " Panama Hattie ", " By Jupiter ", " The Connecticut Yankee ". First film : *Wonder Man* (RKO) 1946. Other films include : *The Kid from Brooklyn* (RKO), *Three Little Girls in Blue* (20th) ; 1947 : *Carnival in Costa Rica* (20th).

VERTOV, Dziga. Director. Born 1896. Entered the cinema industry during the 1917 Revolution and worked on scientific films. His photographic work on chronicle films includes : *Battle of Tzaritsin, Anniversary of the October Revolution*. Vertov later became head of the Cinema Department of the All-Russian Central Executive Committee, and in 1919 formed the " Kinoki " groups for whom he produced twenty-three issues of *Cinema Truth*, a number of scientific chronicles and the first series of the *Cinema Eye*. His best-known films are *Soviet Forward, One-Sixth of the Earth, The Eleventh Year, The Man with the Movie Camera, Symphony of Donbas, Enthusiasm, Three Songs about Lenin, Kirov*. Famous as the creator of the realist film, is still regarded as a leading documentary producer.

VETCHINSKY, Alec. Art director. Born London, Nov. 9, 1905. Gained diploma as architect, then entered films as a " holiday relief " at Gainsborough Studios. Became art director, 1931. Among his outstanding film work is the art direction for *Jack and Jill, Michael and Mary, Sunshine Susie, The Faithful Heart, Love on Wheels, Dr. Syn, Bank Holiday, The Lady Vanishes, Night Train to Munich, Young Mr. Pitt, Kipps, The Lamp Still Burns, The Flemish Farm, Tawny Pipit, Waterloo Road, Don't Take it to Heart, Beware of Pity, Hungry Hill, The October Man*.

VICKERS, Martha. Real name Martha McVicar. Born Ann Arbor, Michigan, May 28, 1925. Ht. 5 ft. 4 in. ; wt. 108 lb. Light brown hair, blue-green eyes. Educ. Chicago, Miami, St. Petersburg (Va.), Detroit, Dallas. Began as a photographic model, and returned to modelling after two successive studios had signed her up, but had not given her much encouragement. Then secured Warner Bros. contract. First film : *The Big Sleep*, 1946. Other films (all Warn) : *The Man I Love ;* 1947 : *The Time the Place and the Girl, That Way with Women, Love and Learn*.

VIDOR, Charles. Director. Born Budapest, July 27, 1900. First World War interrupted his education at the University of Budapest. Before becoming a film director, he was engineer, soldier, sculptor, operatic baritone and fiction writer. Began film career at the UFA studios in Germany, doing odd jobs. Then became an assistant cutter, chief cutter, and assistant director. Assisted in the making of *Frederick the Great* before going to the U.S.A. in 1925. There he was unable to get a job in films and joined a Wagnerian opera company for three years. Reached Hollywood in 1929, and, financed by his own savings, he made *The Bridge*. Outstanding films include : *The Mask of Fu Manchu, Double Door, The Sensation Hunters, Strangers All, The Arizonian, His Family Tree, A Doctor's Diary, The Great Gambini, She's No Lady, New York Town, The Tuttles of Tahiti, The Desperadoes, Cover Girl, Together Again, A Song to Remember, Over 21, Gilda, The Guilt of Janet Ames*.

VIDOR, King. Director. Born Galveston, Texas, Feb. 8, 1894. Educ. Peacock Military Academy, San Antonio, Texas ; Tome College, Port Deposit, Maryland. As a child of 6 was caught in the Galveston floods of 1900 when 8000 people were drowned ; his life was saved when someone dragged him to safety on an upper floor. Began his career as a magazine writer. Then produced and directed three short films in Houston, Texas, which he sold in New York. Went to Hollywood in 1915 ; began there as film extra ; sold several screen stories, joined Universal first as script-clerk, then as scenario writer, and finally as director. Among his early films are the " silents " *Turn in the Road, Jack-Knife Man, Peg o' my Heart* (1923), *Wild Oranges, Wife of the Centaur, His Hour, The Big Parade, La Bohème, Bardeleys the Magnificent, The Crowd, Show People.* Sound films include : *Hallelujah, Billy the Kid, Street Scene, The Champ, Cynara, Strangers Return, Our Daily Bread, Bird of Paradise, Wedding Night, So Red the Rose, The Texas Rangers, Stella Dallas* (produced and directed), *The Citadel* (in Britain for MGM-Brit), *Northwest Passage, Comrade " X ", H.M. Pulham Esq.* (also collaborated on the screenplay), *American Romance* (produced and directed), *Duel in the Sun.*

WAGER, Anthony. Born London, June 24, 1932. Fair hair, blue eyes. Educ. Dollis School ; Christ's College, Finchley. On reading in a London evening paper that a boy was required to play " Young Pip " in *Great Expectations,* he went by himself for an audition, and was chosen from 700 applicants. Had previously organized local children's concert party to entertain in hospitals and camps during World War II, but had no other acting experience. Films include— 1947 : *Great Expectations* (Cineguild), *Hungry Hill* (Two Cities), *Fame Is the Spur* (Boulting-Two Cities).

WALBROOK, Anton. Real name Adolph Wohlbruck. Born Vienna, Nov. 19, 1902. Ht. 6 ft. ; wt. 172 lb. Brown hair, grey eyes. Educ. Vienna ; Berlin. Youthful ambition : to act. At 16 won a scholarship to Max Reinhardt's school in Berlin and became leading actor in Germany, where he also made a number of films. First important screen role was as Johann Strauss in *Walzerkrieg—The Waltz War* (UFA). Other continental films include : *Maskerade, Student of Prague, Gypsy Baron.* Went to Hollywood, 1935, to make English version of *Michael Strogoff*—U.S. title, *The Soldier and the Lady* (RKO). In Britain appeared on the London stage in " Design for Living ", " Watch on the Rhine " and other successful plays. First British film : *Victoria the Great* (Wilcox-RKO) 1937. Other films include : *The Rat, Sixty Glorious Years.* 1940 : *Gaslight* (Brit-Nat), afterwards bought by MGM and re-made as *Murder in Thornton Square, Dangerous Moonlight* (RKO-Brit) ; 1942 : *49th Parallel* —U.S. title *The Invaders* (Ortus) ; 1943 : *The Life and Death of Colonel Blimp* (Archers) ; 1945 : *The Man from Morocco* (ABPC) ; 1948 : *Red Shoes* (Archers).

WALKER, Helen. Born Worcester, Massachusetts, July 17. Ht. 5 ft. 6 in. ; wt. 118 lb. Blonde hair, blue-grey eyes. Educ. local High School. Trained at Boston dramatic school. Understudy to Dorothy McGuire in " Claudia ". While playing in " Jason " was offered a Hollywood contract and made film debut in *Lucky Jordan* (Para) 1942. Other films include : 1944 : *Abroad with Two Yanks* (UA), *The Man in Half Moon Street* (Para) ; 1945 : *Murder He Says* (Para), *Brewster's Millions* (UA) ; 1946 : *Her Adventurous Night* (Univ), *Cluny Brown* (20th), *People Are Funny*

(Para), *Murder in the Music Hall* (Rep) ; 1947 : *The Homestretch* (20th), *Nightmare Alley* (20th).

WALKER, Robert. Born Salt Lake City, Utah, Oct. 13. Ht. 6 ft. ; wt. 145 lb. Brown hair, blue eyes. Educ. San Diego Naval and Military Academy. Trained for a year at American Academy of Dramatic Arts, New York, but became sailor on a cargo boat. Later, after having failed to find opening on Broadway stage became radio actor at Tulsa, Oklahoma. Tried again, in New York and Hollywood, to secure acting roles ; heard by film talent scout on radio. First film : *Bataan* (MGM) 1943. Other films (all MGM) include—1943 : *Madame Curie ;* 1944 : *See Here Private Hargrove, Since You Went Away* (UA), *Thirty Seconds Over Tokyo, Under the Clock ;* 1945 : *Her Highness and the Bellboy, What Next Corporal Hargrove ?, The Sailor Takes a Wife ;* 1946 : *Till the Clouds Roll by ;* 1947 : *The Sea of Grass, The Beginning or the End ?, Song of Love.*

WALLIS, Hal B. Producer. Born Chicago, Illinois, 1899. Educ. Grammar and High Schools, Chicago. Worked at 14 as office boy ; later became commercial traveller. Mother's illness caused the family to move to California, where entered films in 1922 as a cinema manager. Later became publicity director, then studio manager at Warner Bros. Burbank ; appointed executive producer, 1931. In the twelve years following he produced more than 400 outstanding films at Burbank studios including *I am a Fugitive from a Chain Gang, Anthony Adverse, The Story of Louis Pasteur, The Life of Emile Zola, Jezebel, Dodge City, Dark Victory, All This and Heaven Too, The Maltese Falcon, Casablanca, Now Voyager, Watch on The Rhine, This is the Army.* In 1944 formed Hal Wallis Productions, making films for Paramount release including *The Affairs of Susan, You Came Along, Love Letters, Saratoga Trunk, The Strange Love of Martha Ivers, The Perfect Marriage, The Searching Wind, Desert Fury, So Evil my Love* (made in Britain), *I Walk Alone.*

WALLS, Tom. Actor, director, producer. Born Kingsthorpe, Northants, Feb. 18, 1885. Ht. 5 ft. 10½ in. Dark hair, brown eyes. Educ. Northampton County School. Has been engine-driver, jockey, policeman, breeder of prize heifers and bull terriers, and owner and breeder of race-horses—" April the Fifth " won Derby in 1932. Made first stage appearance in Glasgow, in pantomime " Aladdin ", 1905. Next joined " Highwaymen " Concert Party at Brighton. First London appearance was in " Sir Roger de Coverley " in 1907, at Empire Theatre—before it became cinema. With Leslie Henson in 1932 took over the management of the Shaftesbury Theatre—later destroyed by bombing—and appeared there in successful farce, " Tons of Money ". In 1924, at the Aldwych Theatre, London, began the long series of farces (also featuring Ralph Lynn). Among the many of these that were adapted for films, *Rookery Nook* (B and D) 1929, produced by Herbert Wilcox at Elstree, was one of the earliest British sound films. Films as actor and director include : *Tons of Money, Cuckoo in the Nest, Canaries Sometimes Sing, Plunder, A Night Like This, Chance of a Lifetime, Leap Year, Thark, The Blarney Stone, Turkey Time, Stormy Weather, Foreign Affairs, Just Smith.* Acted in and wrote the screenplay *Dirty Work.* Appeared in *On Approval, Me and Marlborough, Pot Luck, For Valour, Dishonour Bright, The Man With 1000 Faces, Strange Boarders, Second Best Bed.* Produced, directed and

ROBERT TAYLOR
(Metro-Goldwyn-Mayer)

appeared in *Crackerjack*. Retired from stage and screen, temporarily, to devote himself to farming, but returned, as a " straight " actor, in *Undercover* (Ealing), 1942. Other recent films include : 1943 : *They Met in the Dark* (Hellman), *The Halfway House* (Ealing) ; 1944 : *Love Story* (Gains) ; 1945 : *Johnny Frenchman* (Ealing) ; 1946 : *This Man is Mine* (Col-Brit) ; 1947 : *Master of Bankdam* (Holbein) ; 1948 : *Spring in Park Lane* (Wilcox-Brit Lion) thereby renewing his association with Herbert Wilcox, begun nearly twenty years previously.

WALSH, Dermot. Born Dublin, Sept. 10, 1924. Ht. 6 ft. ; wt. 154 lb. Dark brown hair, blue-grey eyes. Educ. St. Mary's College, Rathmines. Went straight from college to the Abbey School of Acting and at the same time studied law at the National University, Dublin. Ultimately abandoned law, and joined the Gate Theatre at ten shillings a week, first in " walking-on " roles and later in leading parts. His efforts to enter British films were held up for a year as he could not get a permit to leave Eire until the opportunity came to escort two Irish racehorses to Britain for training. Made his film debut in *Bedelia* (Corfield), 1946. Other films include : 1947 : *Hungry Hill* (Two Cities), *Jassy* (Gains) ; 1948 : *The Mark of Cain* (Two Cities), *High Pavement* (Corfield-Huth).

WALSH, Kay. Born London, 1915. Ht. 5 ft. 4 in. ; wt. 115 lb. Ash-blonde hair, blue eyes. Began stage career as dancer in André Charlot revues, and then in variety (in New York and Berlin) and musical comedy before entering the legitimate theatre. Seen by film talent scout when understudying Frances Day, made film debut in *How's Chances?* (Fox-Brit), 1934. Other films include : *I See Ice, The Mind of Mr. Reeder, Sons of the Sea, All at Sea, The Middle Watch ;* 1940 : *Missing People* (Argyle) ; 1941 : *The Chinese Bungalow* (King) ; 1942 : *In Which We Serve* (Two Cities) ; 1944 : *This Happy Breed* (Cineguild) ; 1947 : *The October Man* (Two Cities), *Vice Versa* (Two Cities) ; 1948 : *Oliver Twist* (Cineguild).

WALTON, William Turner. Composer. Born Oldham, Lancs, 1902. Educ. Oxford, Hon. Mus. D. (Oxon. and Dunelm), Hon. F.R.C.M. First major success as a composer was in 1923, when a string quartet was performed at Salzburg at the Annual Festival of the International Society for Contemporary Music. First film score, *Escape Me Never* (1935). Others include : *As You Like It, Stolen Life, Major Barbara, Next of Kin, The Foreman Went to France, Went the Day Well?, First of the Few, Henry V, Hamlet.*

WANGER, Walter. Producer. Born San Francisco, 1894. Educ. local public schools ; Vevey, Switzerland ; Cascadilla School, Ithaca, New York State ; Dartmouth College, U.S.A. ; Heidelberg University, Germany. Began theatrical career in Britain as assistant to Granville Barker, then in America organized U.S. National Theatre. Began producing his own plays at age of 29, with Nazimova. Served in U.S. Army Air Corps during World War I. Was also attaché to President Woodrow Wilson at American Peace Mission and at Paris Conference. Later joined Jesse Lasky, of Famous Players, as story-buyer and general manager of production in New York, Hollywood, London and Paris. In Britain 1921-3 ; converted Covent Garden Opera House into theatre, and became managing director of a cinema circuit ; also stage producer and producing agent ; in association with Frederick Lonsdale

produced several British and American stage successes. 1923, joined Paramount as general manager. Became producer with Columbia, 1931, and in 1933 transferrred to MGM, for whom he produced *Queen Christina* and *Gabriel Over The White House*. As an independent producer made *The President Vanishes* (1934). Other productions include : *Private Worlds, The Trail of the Lonesome Pine, The Moon's Our Home, Mary Burns Fugitive, Shanghai, Every Night at Eight, Her Master's Voice, Fatal Lady, Big Brown Eyes, The Case Against Mrs. Ames, Spendthrift, Smart Girl, Palm Springs, You Only Live Once, History is Made at Night, Vogues of 1938, I Met My Love Again, Stand In, 52nd Street, Blockade, Algiers, Trade Winds, Stagecoach, Winter Carnival, Eternally Yours, Slightly Honourable, The House Across The Bay, Foreign Correspondent, The Long Voyage Home, Eagle Squadron, Arabian Nights, Salome Where She Danced, Night in Paradise, Scarlet Street, Canyon Passage, A Woman Destroyed, The Secret Beyond the Door.*

WARING, Barbara. Born Kent, Aug. 1, 1912. Trained at Royal Academy of Dramatic Art. Began professional stage career with Coventry Repertory Company. Later appeared in pantomime and sang in cabaret. Stage plays include : " Nine Till Six ", " Duet in Floodlight ", " Pink String and Sealing Wax ". Recent films include : 1942 : *They Flew Alone* (Wilcox-RKO), *Talk About Jacqueline* (Hellman), *In Which We Serve* (Two Cities) ; 1943 : *Asking for Trouble* (Brit Nat), *The Gentle Sex* (Concanen-Two Cities) ; 1944 : *Heaven is Round the Corner* (Brit Nat) ; 1945 : *Twilight Hour* (Brit Nat) ; 1946 : *Hungry Hill* (Two Cities).

WARRACK, Guy. Composer. Has written the music for several documentary films, including : *The Last Shot, A Defeated People, Theirs Is the Glory.* First feature film score : *Daybreak.*

WARRICK, Ruth. Born St. Joseph, Missouri, June 29. Brown hair, blue eyes. Educ. University, Kansas City. Sang on the local radio at 14. While still at college spent three seasons with American summer theatre companies. Later made a name for herself in radio plays, sometimes appearing in as many as twenty different roles in a week. A chance meeting with Orson Welles resulted in a screen test, followed by a rôle in *Citizen Kane* (RKO) 1941. Other films include : 1941 : *Obliging Young Lady* (RKO), *The Corsican Brothers* (UA) ; 1942 : *Journey Into Fear* (RKO) ; 1943 : *Forever and a Day* (RKO), *The Iron Major* (RKO) ; 1944 : *Secret Command* (Col) ; *Mr. Winkle Goes to War* (Col), *Guest in the House* (UA) ; 1945 : *China Sky* (RKO) ; 1946 : *Perilous Holiday* (Col) ; 1947 : *Swell Guy* (UI), *Arch of Triumph* (Enterprise-MGM).

WARTER, Sir Philip. Film company director. Born Folkestone, 1903. Educ. Oratory School, Edgbaston. Married Katherine, daughter of the late John Maxwell, one of the founders of British International Pictures ; is now director Associated British Picture Corporation.

WATT, Harry. Director. Born Glasgow, Oct. 18, 1906. Educ. Edinburgh University. After leaving college in 1929 he sailed to Newfoundland in an open boat. In Canada his first job was selling balloons at Toronto Fair ; later he became waiter. Returning to Britain, became a waiter again, then factory hand, commercial traveller and deck-hand on a cargo boat. Entered films in 1931 with G.P.O. Film Unit, beginning by whitewashing corridors and rising to be assistant director. Was also assistant to Robert Flaherty on *Man of Aran* (GB) 1934. For the G.P.O. Unit co-directed *Night Mail* ; wrote and directed *Six-Thirty Collection, The Saving of Bill Blewett, Big Money, North Sea.* Later directed series of *March of Time* subjects. During World War II wrote and directed for the M.O.I. many propaganda shorts, including : *Squadron 992, Britain at Bay, Dover Front Line.* His *Target for Tonight*, made in 1941, telling the story of a night bombing raid over Germany, made history as the first British propaganda film of feature length to get world-wide distribution. For Crown Film Unit, produced and directed *Britain Can Take It, Christmas Under Fire.* For Army Film Unit, accompanied the Commandos on the Vaagso Raid and later made a film on it. Wrote screenplay and directed *Nine Men.* Directed *Fiddlers Three.* In Australia, directed *The Overlanders, Eureka Stockade.*

WAXMAN, Harry. Lighting cameraman. Born London, 1912. Joined Standard Kine Laboratories in 1926, working under French cameraman Lucien Egrot ; became camera focus assistant to Ernest Palmer, B.I.P. Studio in 1929. Worked at Beaconsfield, Ealing and Worton Hall Studios. Joined Merton Park Studio, 1936, on lighting of documentary films. Served with R.A.F. Film Unit, 1940-6, filming many secret instructional films for the services ; also filmed the liberation of Denmark and rehearsals of D-Day landings. Associate Lighting Cameraman on : *Fame is the Spur.*

WAYNE, John. Real name Marion Michael Morrison. Born Winterest, Iowa, May 28, 1912. Ht. 6 ft. 2 in. ; wt. 198 lb. Brown hair, grey eyes. Educ. Glendale High School ; University of Southern California. Youthful ambition : to be rancher. While studying law at University took holiday job as film property boy, and decided to become a film actor. Was given leading role in his first film, a Western, *The Big Trail* (Fox) 1930. Continued to appear in unspectacular Westerns till Walter Wanger gave him lead in *Stagecoach* (1939). Other important films include : 1940 : *The Long Voyage Home* (Wanger), *Seven Sinners* (Univ) ; 1941 : *Shepherd of the Hills* (Para) ; 1942 : *Lady for a Night* (Rep), *Reap the Wild Wind* (Para), *In Old California* (Rep), *Mademoiselle France* (MGM) ; 1943 : *In Old Oklahoma* (Rep), *A Lady Takes a Chance* (RKO) ; 1944 : *The Fighting Seabees* (Rep), *Tall in the Saddle* (RKO) ; 1945 : *Flame of the Barbary Coast* (Rep), *Back to Bataan* (RKO), *Dakota* (Rep), *They Were Expendable* (MGM) ; 1946 : *Red River* (UA) ; 1947 : *Tycoon* (RKO). Produced and starred in *The Angel and the Badman* (Rep).

WAYNE, Naunton. Born Llanwonno, Glam., June 22, 1901. Ht. 5 ft. 3½ in. Educ. Clifton College. Began his career with electrical corporation in Bristol, but his success in amateur dramatics and local concert parties led him to professional stage career. First professional appearance was at the Pavilion, Barry Island, South Wales, in 1920, with " The Tweenies " concert party. Is well-known as a compere on stage, radio and cabaret. Made his film debut in *The First Mrs. Fraser* (BIP) 1931. Appeared in several others, as a straight actor ; but made first major hit when teamed with Basil Radford in *The Lady Vanishes* (Gains-MGM) 1938, as imperturbable Englishmen, a partnership which they have repeated from time to time. Films include : *Going Gay, For Love of You,*

A Girl Must Live, Night Train to Munich, with Basil Radford. 1940 : *Crooks' Tour* (Brit Nat), with Basil Radford ; 1943 : *Next of Kin* (Ealing) ; 1945 : *Dead of Night* (Ealing), with Basil Radford ; 1946 : *Girl in a Million* (Box), with Basil Radford ; 1947 : *The Calendar* (Gains).

WEBB, Clifton. Born New York, 1894. Ht. 5 ft. 10 in. ; wt. 130 lb. Iron-grey hair, grey eyes. Made his first stage appearance at 7 at Carnegie Hall, New York in " The Brownies " and shortly afterwards as " Oliver Twist ". At 13, was already serious student of singing and painting ; and sang in several operas at Boston in 1911. Next studied dancing and became a popular star in U.S. musical comedy. Appeared on the London stage in " The Fun of the Fayre " in 1921. Played Charles Condomine in " Blithe Spirit " in New York and on tour 1941-4. Made his film debut in *Laura* (20th) 1944, in which he was an overnight success. Other films include : 1946 : *The Dark Corner* (20th), *The Razor's Edge* (20th) ; 1948 : *Julie* (20th).

WEISSMULLER, Johnny. Born Winbar, Pennsylvania. Ht. 6 ft. 3 in. Educ. Chicago University. At Paris Olympic Games in 1924, broke 67 world swimming records. Tested for " Tarzan " while he was holidaying in California when the actor intended for the part had been taken ill. In the long " Tarzan " series Weissmuller has played the title-role more often than any other man. First film : *Tarzan the Ape Man* (MGM) 1932. Others in the series include : *Tarzan and his Mate, Tarzan Escapes, Tarzan Finds a Son, Tarzan's Secret Treasure, Tarzan's New York Adventure* (all MGM). Series continued since 1943 by RKO, including : *Tarzan Triumphs, Tarzan's Desert Mystery, Tarzan and the Amazons, Tarzan and the Leopard Woman, Tarzan and the Huntress, Tarzan and the Mermaids.* 1946 : *Swamp Fire* (Para).

WELLES, Orson. Born Kenosha, Wisconsin, May 6, 1915. Ht. 6 ft. 3½ in. Black hair, black eyes. Educ. Todd School, Woodstock, Illinois. Directed, designed and played leads in school plays. At 17, while in Ireland on walking and sketching tour, joined the Gate Theatre Company, and also appeared as guest actor at the Abbey Theatre. In 1932 toured with Katharine Cornell's company in America, appearing in " Romeo and Juliet ", " Candida ", and " The Barretts of Wimpole Street ". In 1934 formed the Mercury Theatre, New York, also established radio reputation with *March of Time* programme, and in personal narrative versions of literary classics. His radio version of H. G. Wells's " The War of the Worlds " in 1938 caused a nation-wide panic, and led, indirectly, to a Hollywood contract. Was author, producer and star of his first film *Citizen Kane* (RKO) 1941. Other films include : 1942 : *The Magnificent Ambersons* (RKO), *Journey into Fear* (RKO) ; 1944 : *Jane Eyre* (20th) ; 1946 : *To-Morrow is Forever* (RKO), *The Stranger* (RKO) ; 1947 : *The Lady From Shanghai* (Col), *Macbeth* (Rep) ; 1948 : *Cagliostro* (Edward Small) made in Italy.

WELLES, Virginia. Born Wasau, Wisconsin, June 25, 1925. Ht. 5 ft. 2 in. ; wt. 105 lb. Auburn hair, brown eyes. Educ. local public school and college. While studying drama was seen by a talent scout, who arranged a film test, and she made her debut in *Kiss and Tell* (Col) 1945. Other films include : 1946 : *To Each His Own* (Para) ; 1946 : *Ladies' Man* (Para) : 1947 : *Dear Ruth* (Para).

WELLMAN, William A. Director. Born Brookline, Massachusetts. Entered film industry as actor with Douglas Fairbanks Sr. in silent film *The Knickerbocker Buckeroo* 1919. Became property man at Fox Studio, then assistant director. Directed his first film: *The Cat's Pyjamas* (Para) 1926. Silent films include: *Wings* (notable for outstanding trick photography and absence of love story), *Legion of the Condemned*. Sound films include: *Central Airport, Stingaree, Heroes for Sale, Looking for Trouble, Call of the Wild, Small Town Girl, Robin Hood of El Dorado, A Star is Born, Nothing Sacred, Men With Wings, Beau Geste, The Light That Failed, Reaching for the Sun, Pioneer Woman, Roxie Hart* (produced and directed), *The Great Man's Lady, Thunder Birds, Lady of Burlesque, Buffalo Bill, This Man's Navy, Story of G.I. Joe, Gallant Journey* (produced and directed), *Magic Town*.

WHILEY, Manning. Born London, Jan. 23, 1916. Ht. 6 ft. ; wt. 160 lb. Brown hair, brown eyes. Educ. The Hall, Hampstead ; Highgate Grammar School ; Erlanger University, Germany (honours in physics, chemistry, engineering). Abandoned intention of becoming an analytical chemist to study drama with Bruno F. Mackay and Alexander Moissi and afterwards appeared on Nuremberg stage. Returned to Britain, 1933 and joined the Old Vic Company. Made his film debut in 1938 in *Consider Your Verdict*, one of the early films made by the Boulting Brothers, who also gave him an important role in *Pastor Hall*, 1939. Other films include : 1941 : *Old Bill and Son* (Somlo) ; 1947 : *Teheran* (Pendennis) made in Italy, *Uncle Silas* (Two Cities).

WHITE, Barbara. Born Sheerness, Kent, 1923. Ht. 5 ft. 1½ in. ; wt. 112 lb. Brown hair, brown eyes. Educ. Westcliff-on-Sea. A visit to her aunt's dramatic school at Southend made her decide on a stage career. Debut as Miranda in " The Tempest " at Stratford-on-Avon Memorial Theatre in 1941. Toured overseas for ENSA in " The Lady from Edinburgh ". Made first London appearance in a " walking on " role in " Brighton Rock " in 1943, but got her first real chance when as understudy for Mary Llewellyn in the 1944 revival of " Quiet Weekend " she took over the part for a week and was seen by a film executive. Made her film debut in *The Voice Within* (Grand Nat) 1944. Other films include— 1945 : *It Happened one Sunday* (ABPC) ; 1946 : *Quiet Weekend* (ABPC) ; 1947 : *While the Sun Shines* (Internat Screen), *Mine Own Executioner* (Kimmins).

WHITTY, Dame May. Born Liverpool, June 19, 1865. Ht. 5 ft. 4½ in. Grey hair, blue eyes. Educ. privately. Made her first stage appearance at the age of 16 in the chorus of " The Mountain Sylph " at the Court Theatre, Liverpool, and her London debut in 1882 in " Boccaccio " at the Comedy Theatre. Visited America in 1895 with the Lyceum Company. Created Dame Commander, Order of the British Empire, 1918, for her services during World War I. In 1935 played the part of Mrs. Bramson in " Night Must Fall " at the Duchess Theatre, London, afterwards going to America with the play, and where she also appeared in the screen version. First film : *Night Must Fall* (MGM) 1937. Other films include : *The Thirteenth Chair, Marie Walewska, I Met my Love Again, The Lady Vanishes* (in Britain, 1938), *Raffles*. 1940 : *A Bill of Divorcement* (RKO) ; 1941 : *One Night in Lisbon* (Para), *Suspicion* (RKO) ; 1942 : *Mrs. Miniver* (MGM), *Thunder Birds* (20th) ; 1943 : *Forever and a*

Day (RKO), *The Constant Nymph* (Warn), *Flesh and Fantasy* (Univ), *Slightly Dangerous* (MGM), *Lassie Come Home* (MGM), *Madame Curie* (MGM) ; 1944 : *The White Cliffs of Dover* (MGM) ; 1945 : *Devotion* (Warn) ; 1946 : *My Name is Julia Ross* (Col) ; 1947 : *Green Dolphin Street* (MGM), *If Winter Comes* (MGM) ; 1948 : *The Sign of the Ram* (Col).

WHORF, Richard. Actor, director. Born Winthrop, Massachusetts, June 4, 1907. Began his career as an actor with a Boston repertory where he also painted scenery and wrote and produced plays. First appeared in Broadway, 1927, with Miriam Hopkins in " Banshee " ; appeared with the Lunts in " The Taming of the Shrew " 1934 : other plays include : " Three Cornered Moon ", " Amphitryon 38 ", " Idiot's Delight ", " There Shall Be No Night ". Author of two books on stagecraft, " Running the Show ", and " Time to Make-up ". First appeared on screen in : *Midnight* (Univ) 1934. Other films, as actor, include : 1941 : *Blues in the Night* (Warn) ; 1942 : *Yankee Doodle Dandy* (Warn), *Juke Girl* (Warn), *Keeper of the Flame* (MGM) ; 1943 : *Assignment in Brittany* (MGM), *The Cross of Lorraine* (MGM), *The Impostor* (Univ) ; 1944 : *Christmas Holiday* (Univ). Became director : *Blonde Fever* (MGM) 1944. Also directed : *The Hidden Eye, The Sailor Takes a Wife, Till The Clouds Roll By, It Happened in Brooklyn*.

WILCOX, Herbert. Producer, director. Born Cork, 1892. Educ. Brighton. Served in R.F.C. during World War I. Entered film industry in 1919, as film salesman, investing his war gratuity of £117 in formation of his own company, " Astra Films ". A year later in a " glasshouse " studio at Kew, produced and directed his first film, *The Wonderful Story*. Discovered Clive Brook, and starred him in a two-reeler called *Whispering*. Began developing showmanship for which he is now famous when he presented *The Dawn of the World*, a show with biblical background, at Palace Theatre, London, in 1921. Early productions include : *Flames of Passion, Chu Chin Chow, Nell Gwyn, Madame Pompadour, Dawn, The Only Way, Decameron Nights, Scarlet Pimpernel* and *Wolves*. In 1929 built the Imperial Studios, Elstree, the first in Britain to be constructed for sound films. Here he filmed the famous Aldwych farces, with Tom Walls, Ralph Lynn and Robertson Hare. Discovered Anna Neagle, who was then appearing in " Stand Up and Sing " with Jack Buchanan, and starred her with Buchanan in *Good Night Vienna*, 1932, thus beginning the Wilcox-Neagle film partnership which has existed ever since. 1946 joined Sir Alexander Korda, as an independent producer, releasing through British Lion. Produced and directed : *The Flag Lieutenant, The Little Damozel, The Queen's Affair, Bitter Sweet, Nell Gwyn* (1934), *Peg of Old Drury, Limelight, The Three Maxims, The Street Singer*—U.S. title *London Melody, Victoria the Great, Sixty Glorious Years, Nurse Edith Cavell, They Flew Alone, Forever and a Day* (co-directed), *Yellow Canary, I Lived in Grosvenor Square, Piccadilly Incident* (" Daily Mail " award as the best film of 1946), *The Courtneys of Curzon Street, Spring in Park Lane* (directed and co-produced).

WILCOX, Robert. Born Rochester, New York State, May 19, 1910. Ht. 5 ft. 11 in ; wt. 165 lb. Brown hair, blue eyes. Educ. Peddie Preparatory School, New Jersey ; University of Southern California. Worked as concrete mixer on building of Boulder Dam ; became salesman and later secretary for a business in Buffalo. Began his acting career with local Studio Players in " The Petrified Forest ". First film : *Let Them Live* (Univ) 1936. Other films include : *The Stones Cry Out, The Cop, Carnival Queen, Wild and Woolly, Reckless Living, Little Tough Guy, Gambling Ship, Undercover Doctor, Blondie Takes a Vacation.* 1940 : *The Lone Wolf Strikes* (Col), *Island of Doomed Men* (Col), *Dreaming Out Loud* (RKO) ; 1941-5 : Served in U.S. Army. 1946 : *Mysterious Doctor Satan* (Univ), *The Unknown* (Col), *Wild Beauty* (Univ).

WILDE, Cornel. Born New York City, Oct. 13, 1915. Ht. 6 ft. 1 in. ; wt. 174 lb. Brown hair, brown eyes. Educ. public schools, New York ; Columbia University. Went with his father to Budapest in 1916 when his father was recalled there to join Army. Returned to New York, 1920. Later studied art and fencing in Budapest. Was toy salesman in New York department store, commercial artist, advertisement salesman and warden of a boys' club before beginning his stage career with a New York stock company in 1933. Later appeared at the Lyceum Theatre, Manhattan, for forty weeks in " Moon Over Mulberry Street ", and continued stage roles for some years. While appearing as Tybalt in Laurence Olivier's touring company of " Romeo and Juliet " attracted attention of Hollywood. First film : *The Lady With Red Hair* (Warn) 1940. Other films include : 1941 : *High Sierra* (Warn), *Knockout* (Warn), *The Perfect Snob* (20th) ; 1942 : *Manila Calling* (20th), *Life Begins at 8.30* (20th) ; 1943 : *Wintertime* (20th) ; 1945 : *A Song to Remember* (Col), 1001 *Nights* (Col), *Leave Her to Heaven* (20th) ; 1946 : *The Bandit of Sherwood Forest* (Col), *Centennial Summer* (20th) ; 1947 : *The Homestretch* (20th), *Forever Amber* (20th) ; 1948 : *It Had to be You* (Col), *The Walls of Jericho* (20th).

WILDER, Billy. Writer, director. Born Vienna, June 22, 1906. Began his career as " copy boy ", then as sports writer on a Viennese newspaper. Went to Berlin as daily paper crime reporter. Wrote screen story, *People on Sunday,* which UFA made into successful film, directed by Robert Siodmak. Wilder also became a director, first in Berlin, and later in Paris. Went to Hollywood, in 1933, and collaborated on the script of *Champagne Waltz.* First teamed as a writer with Charles Brackett in 1937. Their films together include : *Bluebeard's Eighth Wife, Midnight, What a Life !, Rhythm on the River, Arise My Love, Ninotchka, Hold Back the Dawn.* In collaboration with Raymond Chandler wrote the screenplay *Double Indemnity,* which he also directed. Wrote screenplays and directed : *The Major and the Minor, Five Graves to Cairo, The Lost Weekend, The Emperor Waltz.* Directed *A Foreign Affair.*

WILDER, Thornton Niven. Dramatist and novelist. Born Madison, Wisconsin, Apr. 17, 1897. Educ. schools in California, Ohio and China ; Yale University. (M.A. Princeton ; D.Litt., New York University.) Was first a schoolmaster. First play " The Trumpet Shall Sound " was produced in 1926 at the American Laboratory Theatre. Plays include : " Lucrece ", " Our Town ", " The Merchant of Yonkers ", " The Skin of Our Teeth ". Novels include : " The Cabala ", " The Bridge of San Luis Rey ", " The Woman of Andros ", " Heaven's My Destination ", " The Long Christmas Dinner ". Served 1942-6 with U.S. Army Air Force. Works filmed include : *Our Town, The Bridge of San Luis Rey.*

WILDING, Michael. Born Westcliff-on-Sea, July 23, 1912. Ht. 6 ft. 1 in. ; wt. 162 lb. Brown hair, blue eyes. Taken to Moscow when a month old. Later returned to Britain and was educated at Christ's Hospital, Horsham. In his early youth was a portrait and commercial artist. At 20 lived for a year in Brussels by sketching portraits in cafés and night-clubs. Began his acting career with Watford Repertory Company ; made London debut in " Chase the Ace ", Daly's Theatre, 1933. Later toured Australia and New Zealand in " Victoria Regina". Outstanding London plays include : " Quiet Weekend", " Men in Shadow " (in which he took John Mills' role of " Lew " in 1943) and " While the Sun Shines ". Film debut in *Tilly of Bloomsbury* (Gains) 1940. Other films include—1940 : *Sailors Three* (Ealing) ; 1941 : *Kipps* (20th-Brit), *Ships With Wings* (Ealing), *Cottage to Let* (Gains) ; 1942 : *In Which We Serve* (Two Cities), *Secret Mission* (Hellman), *Undercover* (Ealing) ; 1943 : *Dear Octopus* (Gains) ; 1944 : *English Without Tears* (Two Cities) ; 1946 : *Carnival* (Two Cities), *Piccadilly Incident* (Wilcox-ABPC) ; 1947 : *The Courtneys of Curzon Street* (Wilcox-Brit. Lion), *An Ideal Husband* (LFP) ; 1948 : *Spring in Park Lane* (Wilcox-Brit Lion).

WILLES, Peter. Born Derbyshire, Apr. 30, 1913. Ht. 6 ft. ; wt. 142 lb. Fair hair, blue eyes. Educ. Stowe School ; Munich. Youthful ambition : to be a writer. First became literary agent, and wrote and sold a few short stories. Went to Hollywood " on impulse " and worked as extra for several months, then unexpectedly given featured part in *The Dawn Patrol* (Warn) 1938. Returned to Britain when World War II broke out and served in army ; seriously wounded and captured in Middle East, repatriated 1944. Resumed film career, 1946 in *The Way We Live* (Two Cities) ; 1947 : *The Root of All Evil* (Gains).

WILLIAMS, Bill. Real name William Katt. Born Brooklyn, New York, May 21, 1926. Ht. 6 ft. 1 in ; wt. 190 lb. Blond hair, brown eyes. Educ. Brooklyn Technical High School ; Pratt Institute, Brooklyn. Studied constructional engineering. Is champion swimmer ; was engaged in exhibition swimming when he was offered a job as adagio dancer in St. Louis. In 1935 joined the Municipal Opera Company, St. Louis, afterwards formed his own adagio act. During European tour appeared at the London Palladium for a year, notably at the Royal Command Performance, 1939. Became a " shuttle " air service pilot, then served in U.S. army, but was later discharged on medical grounds. Film debut, 1944, in *Murder in the Blue Room* (Univ). Other films include : 1945 : *West of the Pecos* (RKO), *Thirty Seconds Over Tokyo* (MGM) ; 1946 : *Till The End of Time* (RKO), *Dead Line at Dawn* (RKO).

WILLIAMS, Charles. Composer, music director. Born London, 1893. Conductor of the Queen's Hall Light Orchestra. Has been associated with films since silent days. Recently has worked as music director and conductor on : *English without Tears, The Life and Death of Colonel Blimp, The Silver Fleet, Carnival, Beware of Pity, The Way to the Stars.* Composed and directed the music for : *The Night Has Eyes, Quiet Weekend, While I Live.*

WILLIAMS, Esther. Born Los Angeles, California, Aug. 8. Ht. 5 ft. 7 in. ; wt. 123 lb. Brown hair, hazel eyes. Educ. Los Angeles City College ;

University of Southern California. By 1939 had achieved swimming ambitions and had become Pacific coast champion. Became fashion model. Appeared in Billy Rose's " Aquacade " at New York World Fair, 1939, and was seen by film talent scout. Made film debut in *Andy Hardy's Double Life* (MGM) 1942. Later films (all MGM) include : 1943 : *A Guy Named Joe* ; 1944 : *Bathing Beauty, Ziegfeld Follies* ; 1945 : *Thrill of a Romance, Easy to Wed, The Hoodlum Saint* ; 1946 : *This Time For Keeps* ; 1947 : *Fiesta* ; 1948 : *On an Island with You.*

WILLIAMS, Hugh. Born Bexhill-on-Sea, Sussex, Mar. 6, 1904. Ht. 5 ft. 10 in ; wt. 156 lb. Black hair, blue eyes. Educ. Haileybury College. Began stage career as juvenile lead in " The Charm School ", at Margate, 1921. Next year toured with " Charley's Aunt ", then joined the Liverpool Repertory Company for two years. Went to America to appear in " Journey's End " and while there made his first talkie, *Charley's Aunt* (Col) 1930. Served in army, 1939-45, for a time attached to " Phantom Intelligence ". Films include : *A Night in Montmartre, A Gentleman in Paris, In a Monastery Garden, Whiteface, Down our Street, Insult, Rome Express, After Dark, Bitter Sweet, Sorrell and Son* (1934), *A Woman of the World, Outcast Lady, David Copperfield*—in Hollywood (MGM) 1935, *Lieutenant Darling R.N., The Amateur Gentleman, The Man Behind the Mask, Dark Eyes of London, Wuthering Heights*—in Hollywood (UA) 1939. 1946 : *Girl in a Million* (Box) ; 1947 : *Take My Life* (Cineguild), *An Ideal Husband* (LFP) ; 1948 : *Blind Goddess* (Gains).

WILLIAMS, Ralph Vaughan. Composer. Born Down Ampney, Glos, 1872. Educ. Charterhouse ; Trinity College, Cambridge ; Royal College of Music ; Berlin ; Paris. Mus.Doc. (Cantab), Hon.D.Mus. (Oxon). Awarded the Order of Merit, 1935. In his youth was a leading figure in the revival of British folk-music. At 68, after having composed music for concert-hall, stage, church and home, was persuaded by Muir Mathieson to write his first film score, for *49th Parallel*—U.S. title, *The Invaders* (1941). This was later arranged as a concert suite. Documentary scores include : *Coastal Command, The People's Land, The Stricken Peninsula.* Feature film scores include : *The Flemish Farm, The Loves of Joanna Godden.*

WOOD, Sam. Director, producer. Born Philadelphia, July 10, 1883. Educ. M. Hall Stanton School, Philadelphia. Tried several branches of commerce, including gold-mining and real estate, before becoming interested in film production through business association with producers. Studied directing, acting and film salesmanship ; became assistant director to Cecil B. De Mille, and began directing in 1920. For more than five years directed such stars as Wallace Reid, Gloria Swanson, Rudolph Valentino, Wanda Hawley and Jackie Coogan. Later films include : *One Minute to Play, Rookies, The Barbarian, Stamboul Quest, Hold Your Man, The Late Christopher Bean, Prosperity, Paid, Get Rich Quick Wallingford, The Richest Man in the World, Huddle, Let 'Em Have It, A Night At The Opera, Whipsaw, The Unguarded Hour, A Day at the Races, Madame " X ", Navy Blue and Gold, Lord Jeff, Stablemates, Goodbye Mr. Chips!* (MGM ; made in Britain 1939), *Raffles, Our Town, Kitty Foyle, The Devil and Miss Jones, Kings Row, Saratoga Trunk, Pride of the Yankees, For Whom the Bell Tolls* (produced and directed), *Casanova Brown, Guest Wife, Heartbeat, Ivy.*

WOOLFE, H. Bruce. Production Executive, Children's Entertainment Films. Entered film industry as film salesman before World War I, in which he served in the Army. In 1919 began *Secrets of Nature* series in old Army hut at Elstree, where he also produced the first war documentary, *Armageddon,* followed by *Zeebrugge, Ypres, Mons, The Battles of Coronel and Falkland Islands.* Was the first Film Producers' Representative on the Board of Trade Advisory Committee. Director of G.B. Instructional Ltd. In 1935 was awarded three gold medals and four diplomas for short films shown at the Brussels Film Exhibition. Served on many committees of inquiry. Joined Children's Entertainment Films as member of the Film Production Committee on its formation in 1944. Trade Member on Ministry of Education Committee for the Preparation and Production of Visual Aids. Member of British Film Academy. Hon. President, Association of Specialised Film Producers.

WOOLLEY, Monty. Real name Edgar Montillion Woolley. Born New York, Aug. 17, 1888. Ht. 5 ft. 10 in. ; wt. 180 lb. White hair, blue eyes. Educ. Mackenzie School ; Dobbs Ferry, New York State; Yale (M.A.) ; Harvard (M.A.). Was Assistant Professor of Dramatics at Yale. Served with U.S. Army in World War I. Directed New York stage productions, 1927-35, but did not himself appear on the stage until 1936, in " On Your Toes ". On the stage played Sheridan Whiteside in " The Man Who Came to Dinner " for two years, 1939-41, and later repeated the role in the screen version. Made his film debut in *Live, Love and Learn* (MGM) 1937. Other films include : *Nothing Sacred, Three Comrades* ; 1941 : *The Man Who Came to Dinner* (Warn) ; 1942 : *The Pied Piper* (20th), *The Light of Heart* (20th) ; 1943 : *Holy Matrimony* (20th) ; 1944 : *Irish Eyes Are Smiling* (20th) ; 1945 : *Molly and Me* (20th) ; 1946 : *Night and Day* (Warn) ; 1947 : *The Bishop's Wife* (RKO).

WRIGHT, Dora. Production manager. Born Nov. 22, 1903. Was secretary to London industrial firm before entering films in 1932 as script reader at Gaumont British. Became secretary to scenario department then typist to director Victor Saville. Became Saville's continuity girl on *I Was A Spy* (1933). Promoted to production manager when Saville joined MGM British, 1938. Subsequently became production manager on war-time films made by Crown Film Unit, gathered equipment for *Target for Tonight,* interior scenes of which were filmed in a converted schoolhouse through lack of studio space. Rejoined MGM British in 1947 as production manager at their Elstree studios.

WRIGHT, Teresa. Born New York, Oct. 27, 1919. Ht. 5 ft. 2 in. ; wt. 110 lb. Brown hair, green-blue eyes. Trained for the stage from childhood. Spent two years with the Wharf Theatre, Provincetown, Massachusetts. Toured in " Our Town ". While appearing in the New York production of " Life With Father " was seen by Sam Goldwyn, and signed for important role in *The Little Foxes,* 1941. Other films include : 1942 : *Mrs. Miniver* (MGM) ; 1943 : *Pride of the Yankees* (Goldwyn), *Shadow of a Doubt* (Univ), *Casanova Brown* (RKO) ; 1944 : *Those Endearing Young Charms* (RKO) ; 1946 : *Mrs. Loring's Secret* (Para), *The Best Years of Our Lives* (Goldwyn), *The Trouble With Women* (Para) ; 1947 : *Pursued* (Warn).

DERMOT WALSH
(Gainsborough)

WYER, Reginald H. Director of photography. At 16 was apprenticed for two years to London photographer. Spent three years as projectionist, editor and cameraman with Community Motion Picture Bureau, American firm attached to Y.M.C.A. in Britain. For next fourteen years was director, script-writer, cameraman and editor, making own documentaries, industrial and commercial films, and also did free-lance news-reel work. Decided to devote himself to photography; joined Sydney Box in 1940, worked on government films for Verity Film Company. When Box expanded to feature-film production, Wyer's first assignment was photography of *The Seventh Veil.* Other recent films include : *The Years Between, Girl in a Million, The Upturned Glass, The White Unicorn.*

WYLER, William. Director. Born Mulhouse, France, July 1, 1902. Educ. College of Paris. Entered film industry as European publicity man for American film company. Went to Hollywood, 1920, to become assistant director. Became director in 1928, and made many early westerns, including : *Lazy Lightning, Hard Fists, Desert Dust, Blazing Days, Come Across, The Shakedown.* Directed first-feature films from 1931, including : *A House Divided, The Old Dark House, Tom Brown of Culver, Counsellor at Law, Her First Mate, Glamour, The Good Fairy, The Gay Deception, These Three, Come and Get It, Dodsworth, Dead End, Jezebel, Wuthering Heights, The Westerner, The Little Foxes, Mrs. Miniver.* While in armed forces 1942-5, made training films and documentaries, notably : *Memphis Belle, Glory for Me.* In 1946-7 directed *The Best Years of Our Lives,* which won nine Academy Awards for artistic and technical achievements.

WYMAN, Jane. Real name Sara Jane Fulks. Born St. Joseph, Missouri, Jan. 4, 1914. Blonde hair, brown eyes. Educ. St. Joseph School ; Los Angeles High School ; University of Missouri. Trained as dancer and singer. While still at school appeared in several films as chorus girl. In 1933 became radio singer under name " Jane Durrell ". Returned to Hollywood and won role in : *My Man Godfrey* (Univ) 1936. Other films include : *Cain and Mabel, Smart Blonde, The King and The Chorus Girl, Brother Rat, The Kid From Kokomo.* 1940 : *Flight Angels* (Warn), *My Love Came Back* (Warn) ; 1941 : *Bad Men of Missouri* (Warn), *The Body Disappears* (Warn), *You're In The Army Now* (Warn) ; 1942 : *Larceny Inc., My Favourite Spy* (RKO), *Footlight Serenade* (20th) ; 1943 ; *Princess O'Rourke ;* 1944 : *Crime By Night* (Warn), *Make Your Own Bed* (Warn), *The Dough Girls* (Warn) ; 1945 : *The Lost Weekend* (Para) ; 1946 : *Night and Day* (Warn), *Cheyenne* (Warn) ; 1947 : *The Yearling* (MGM), *Magic Town* (RKO) ; 1948 : *Johnny Belinda* (Warn).

WYNN, Keenan. Born New York, July 27, 1916. Ht. 6 ft. ; wt. 170 lb. Brown hair, blue eyes. Educ. New York. Son of comedian Ed Wynn. Studied dancing in New York and joined Lakewood Summer Theatre for five years. Was a successful comedian in numerous Broadway productions, before making his film debut in, *For Me and My Gal* (MGM) 1942. Other films (all MGM) include : 1942 : *Northwest Rangers ;* 1943 : *Lost Angel ;* 1944 : *See Here Private Hargrove, Since You Went Away* (UA), *Marriage is a Private Affair, Between Two Women, Ziegfeld Follies, Under the Clock* ; 1945 : *Without Love, Weekend at the Waldorf, Easy to Wed, What Next Corporal Hargrove?, No Leave No Love* ; 1946 : *Mr. Griggs Returns, Thrill of Brazil* (Col) ; 1947 :

Song of the Thin Man, The Hucksters ; 1948 : *The Red Mill.*

WYNYARD, Diana. Original name Dorothy Isobel Cox (changed by deed poll, 1936). Born London, Jan. 16, 1906. Ht. 5 ft. 6½ in. ; wt. 126 lb. Brown hair, blue-grey eyes. Educ. Woodford School, Croydon. Voice training with Gwen Lally. Made her stage debut in London in a " walking-on " role in " The Grand Duchess ", Globe Theatre, 1925. Toured with the Hamilton Deane Company, and played with Liverpool Repertory Company, 1927-9. Appeared on the New York stage early in 1932, and the same year made her first film, *Rasputin the Mad Monk* for MGM in Hollywood. Chosen, after world-wide search for suitable type, to play Jane Marryot in *Cavalcade* (Fox) 1933, film version of Noel Coward's stage success. Other Hollywood films include : *Reunion in Vienna, Men Must Fight, Dover Road* and *Over the River.* Returned to Britain in 1934, but appeared only on stage until 1939, when she made *Freedom Radio* (Zampi-Col). Other recent films include : 1940 : *On the Night of the Fire* (Somlo), *Gaslight* (Brit Nat), afterwards bought up by MGM in Hollywood, withdrawn and re-made as *Murder in Thornton Square ;* 1941 : *Kipps* (20th-Brit), *The Prime Minister* (Warn-Brit) ; 1947 : *An Ideal Husband* (LFP).

YOUNG, Frederick A. Director of photography. Born London, 1902. Entered films 1917, and photographed many silent films for Gaumont, Gainsborough and New Era. Films include : *Victoria the Great, Sixty Glorious Years, Goodbye Mr. Chips !, Nurse Cavell* (as lighting cameraman; in Hollywood), *Contraband, 49th Parallel, The Young Mr. Pitt.* Served in army 1942-4 as Chief Cameraman, Army Kinematograph Service. Recent films include : *Caesar and Cleopatra, Bedelia, So Well Remembered, While I Live.* Has also been responsible for European exteriors and backgrounds for Hollywood films.

YOUNG, Gig. Real name Bryon Barr. Born St. Cloud, Minnesota, Nov. 4, 1917. Educ. High School, St. Cloud ; Technical High School, Washington. Worked with car sales company, and in evenings acted with local company, Phil Hayden Players. Decided to try for film career, so played at Pasadena Playhouse and earned money as garage hand and car attendant to pay for dramatic tuition. Made his first professional appearance as Abie in Los Angeles production of " Abie's Irish Rose ". Seen by a casting director, and as a test, appeared in a short : *Here Come the Cavalry* (Warn) 1941. Other films (all Warn) include—1941 : *Dive Bomber ;* 1942 : *One Foot in Heaven, Captains of the Clouds, They Died With Their Boots On, The Man Who Came To Dinner, The Gay Sisters, Air Force, Old Acquaintance.* 1943-6, war service. 1946 : *Escape Me Never ;* 1948 : *The Woman in White.*

YOUNG, Joan. Born 1903. Gained early acting experience by deputizing for other members of the cast in her mother's company at the Woolwich Hippodrome. Has had a long career in music-hall and the legitimate theatre, notably as Mrs. Antrobus in the London production of Thornton Wilder's play, " The Skin of our Teeth " 1943. Appears regularly in B.B.C. drama. Made her film debut in *The Lamp Still Burns* (Two Cities) 1943. Other films include : 1946 : *Strawberry Roan* (Brit Nat), *Caesar and Cleopatra* (Pascal), *School for Secrets* (Two Cities).

YOUNG, Loretta. Real name Gretchen Young. Born Salt Lake City, Utah, Jan. 6, 1913. Ht. 5 ft. 6 in.; wt. 110 lb. Fair auburn hair, blue eyes. Educ. Ramona Convent, Alhambra, California. As a small child appeared in a film with Fanny Ward and the late Theodore Roberts. In her early teens answered a studio " call " intended for her elder sister, Polly Ann Young, and got an important role opposite the late Lon Chaney, in *Laugh Clown Laugh* (MGM) 1928. Since then has appeared continually in films, including : *Scarlet Seas, Girl in the Glass Cage, Fast Life, Careless Age, Forward Pass, Loose Ankles, Right of Way, Road to Paradise, The Squall, Second Floor Mystery, The Ruling Voice, I Like Your Nerve !, Platinum Blonde, Play Girl, Truth About Youth, Beau Ideal, Three Wise Girls, Devil to Pay, Man from Blankley's, Kismet* (1930), *Honourable Mr. Wong, Taxi, Big Business Girl, Callagher, Working Wives, Eight to Five, The Way of Life, Employees Entrance, Weekend Marriage, Life Begins, They Call it Sin, Grand Slam, Heroes for Sale, She Had to Say Yes !, Zoo in Budapest, The Devil's in Love, The Kid's Last Fight, Life of Jimmy Dolan, Midnight Mary, A Man's Castle, The House of Rothschild, Born to be Bad, The White Parade, Caravan* (1934), *Clive of India, Call of the Wild, The Crusades, Shanghai, The Unguarded Hour, Private Number, Ramona, Ladies in Love, Love is News, Cafe Metropole, Love Under Fire, Wife Doctor and Nurse, Second Honeymoon, Four Men and a Prayer, Three Blind Mice, Suez, Kentucky, The Story of Alexander Graham Bell* —British title, *The Modern Miracle*. 1940 : *The Doctor Takes a Wife* (Col), *He Stayed for Breakfast* (Col) ; 1941 : *Lady from Cheyenne* (Univ), *The Men in Her Life* (Col) ; 1942 : *A Night to Remember* (Col) ; 1943 : *China* (Para) ; 1944 : *Ladies Courageous* (Univ), *And Now Tomorrow* (Para) ; 1946 : *The Stranger* (RKO), *Along Came Jones* (RKO), *The Perfect Marriage* (Para) ; 1947 : *The Farmer's Wife* (RKO), *The Bishop's Wife* (RKO).

YOUNG, Robert. Born Chicago, Feb. 22, 1907. Ht. 6 ft. ; wt. 170 lb. Brown hair, brown eyes. Educ. Seattle and Los Angeles public schools ; Lincoln High School, Los Angeles. Began as clerk, first in a bank, later in stockbroker's office, appearing with amateur dramatic societies in the evenings. Joined the Pasadena Community Players when his family moved to California. After nearly fifty productions there he made his film debut, with Helen Hayes in *The Lullaby* (MGM) 1931. Since then has appeared in about a hundred films, including : *The Black Camel, Guilty Generation, Strange Interval, The Wet Parade, New Morals for Old, Unashamed, Kid from Spain, Today We Live, Hell Below, Men Must Fight, Saturday's Millions, Tugboat Annie, Right to Romance, Lazy River, House of Rothschild, Spitfire* (1934), *Paris Interlude, Death on the Diamond, Whom the Gods Destroy, The Band Plays On, The House of Connelly, West Point of the Air, Vagabond Lady, Calm Yourself, Arms and the Girl, The Bride Comes Home, Remember Last Night, Three Wise Guys*. In Britain, played opposite Jessie Matthews in *It's Love Again* (GB) 1936, and also made *Secret Agent* (GB) 1936. U.S. films since then include : *Sworn Enemy, Stowaway, The Longest Night, The Bride Walks Out, Dangerous Number, The Emperor's Candlesticks, I Met Him in Paris, Married Before Breakfast, Navy Blue and Gold, The Bride Wore Red, Romance for Three, Josette, Frou-frou, Three Comrades, Rich Man Poor Girl, The Shining Hour, Bridal Suite, Honolulu, Miracles for Sale, Maisie*. 1940 : *Northwest Passage* (MGM), *The Mortal Storm* (MGM), *Florian* (MGM), *Sporting Blood* (MGM),

Dr. Kildare's Crisis (MGM) ; 1941 : *Western Union* (20th), *The Trial of Mary Dugan* (MGM), *Lady Be Good* (MGM), *Married Bachelor* (MGM), *Highway to Freedom* (MGM), *H. M. Pulham Esq.* (MGM) ; 1942 : *Cairo* (MGM), *Journey for Margaret* (MGM) ; 1943 : *Slightly Dangerous* (MGM), *Sweet Rosie O'Grady* (20th), *Claudia* (20th) ; 1944 : *The Canterville Ghost* (MGM) ; 1945 : *The Enchanted Cottage* (RKO), *Those Endearing Young Charms* (RKO) ; 1946 : *Lady Luck* (RKO), *Claudia and David* (20th), *The Searching Wind* (Para) ; 1947 : *They Won't Believe Me* (RKO), *Crossfire* (RKO) ; 1948 : *Relentless* (Col).

YOUNG, Roland. Born London, Nov. 11, 1887. Ht. 5 ft. 6 in. Dark hair, blue eyes. Educ. Sherborne School ; University College School, London. Trained at Royal Academy of Dramatic Art ; has had long stage career. London stage debut, 1908, in " Find The Woman ". Went to America, 1912, to play Alan Jeffcote in " Hindle Wakes ". Appeared in two silent films in U.S.A. with the late John Barrymore— *Sherlock Holmes* and *Moriarty* (1922), and made his talkie debut in *Unholy Night* (MGM) 1929. First British film was *Wedding Rehearsal* (LFP) 1932. Other films include : *The Bishop Murder Case, Her Private Life, Wise Girls, Madame Satan, The Prodigal, New Moon, Don't Bet on Women, Annabelle's Affairs, One Hour With You, A Woman Commands, William and Mary, Pagan Lady, He Met a French Girl, The White Man, Lovers Courageous, The Guardsman, The Lullaby, This is the Night, Street of Women, The New Yorker, Pleasure Cruise, A Lady's Profession, Blind Adventure, His Double Life, Here is my Heart, David Copperfield, Ruggles of Red Gap, The Unguarded Hour, One Rainy Afternoon, Give Me your Heart, The Man Who Could Work Miracles* (LFP ; made in Britain, 1936), *Gipsy, Call it a Day, King Solomon's Mines* (GB ; made in Britain, 1937) *Ali Baba Goes to Town, Topper, Sailing Along* (GB ; made in Britain, 1938), *The Young in Heart, Topper Takes a Trip, Yes My Darling Daughter*. 1940 : *No No Nanette* (RKO), *The Philadelphia Story* (MGM) ; 1942 : *The Lady Has Plans* (Para), *They All Kissed the Bride* (Col), *Tales of Manhattan* (20th) ; 1943 : *Forever and a Day* (RKO) ; 1944 : *Standing Room Only* (Para) ; 1945 : *And Then There Were None*—British title, *Ten Little Niggers* (20th) ; 1947 : *Bond Street* (World Screen ; made in Britain).

YUTKEVICH, S. Director. Born St. Petersburg (now Leningrad), 1904. Began his career on the stage, appearing in the revue " Good Treatment of Horses " produced by Foregger. Entered films, 1925, first as an actor, then a scenario writer. In 1927 directed his first film, *Lace*, in Moscow, and in 1928-9 directed *Black Sail*, in Leningrad. In 1931 made his first sound film : *The Golden Mountain*. With F. Ermler, co-directed *The Counter Plan*, 1932. The following year he made *Ankara*, for which he took a unit to Turkey for this film dealing with the tenth anniversary of the Turkish Republic. In 1934 set up an experimental film studio in Leningrad. Professor at State Institute of Cinematography, Moscow. Other films include : *Miners* (1936), *Man with the Gun* (1938), *Jacob Sverdlov* (1940), *Schweik* 1943), *Liberated France* (1945), *Hallo Moscow !* (1946), *Festival of Youth*—in colour (1947) *The Kremlin Tower Clock* (1948).

ZANUCK, Darryl Francis. Born Wahoo, Nebraska, Sept. 5, 1902. Ambition from childhood was to make films. Began his career writing stories for the " Rin Tin Tin " dog series. Served with the U.S. Army during World War I. In 1931 was appointed chief executive in charge of Warner Brothers and First National in association with Jack L. Warner. Resigned 1933, and formed 20th Century Productions with Joseph M. Schenck. In 1935 he was appointed Vice President in charge of production 20th Century-Fox Films. In World War II served in the U.S. Army, producing training films. Outstanding productions include : *Clive of India, Lloyd's of London, Stanley and Livingstone, Jesse James, The Grapes of Wrath, Down Argentine Way, How Green Was My Valley, Wilson, Winged Victory, The Purple Heart, The Razor's Edge, Gentleman's Agreement.*

ZETTERLING, Mai. Born Västerås, Sweden, May 25, 1925. Ht. 5 ft. 4 in. ; wt. 98 lb. Fair hair, pale blue eyes. Educ. Eskilstuna and Stockholm. Youthful ambition : to act. Spent three years in Adelaide, Australia, returning to Sweden via London in 1933 to begin training as singer. A scholarship to Sweden's national theatre, Royal Dramatic Theatre, Stockholm, led her later into films. After the showing of the Swedish film *Frenzy* in London, 1946, she made her first British film *Frieda* (Ealing), 1947. In 1948 made *The Bad Lord Byron* (Gains).

ZHELIABUSHKY, V. Director. Entered films, 1916, as one of a group of cameramen who made *The Parade on the Tenth of March in Moscow* free of charge for the Moscow Soviet. For Pathé of France, made *The Funeral of Those Who Fell in the Revolution*. Later filmed Hans Andersen's fairy tales, *The King's New Clothes* and *The Little Match Girl* ; the latter was presented at the Shaftesbury Pavilion, London, the first cinema in Britain to show foreign films. During the revolutionary war with Poland, he made *Polish Brigade* and two other topical films. Has directed many specialist films on industrial subjects, agriculture and education. Other films include : *A Man Child*

Is Born, A New World. Professor at State Institute of Cinematography (Faculty of Cameramen), Moscow.

ZUKOR, Adolph. Born Ricse, Hungary, Jan. 7, 1873. One of the leading pioneers of the film industry, he went to America at the age of 16 and began his career sweeping floors for a New York furrier. Remained in the fur trade till 1902, when his interest in the new " moving pictures " led him to become a film salesman. In 1903 in association with his friend Marcus Loew, he opened a " penny arcade " in New York, to show films, and which became the cornerstone of " Marcus Loew Enterprises ". Created a sensation in 1912 by showing a film with Sarah Bernhardt, *Queen Elizabeth*, the first multiple-reel film ever seen in America. Encouraged by the success of this experiment film Zukor went into film production, and persuaded into films three leading Broadway stars—James O'Neill in *The Count of Monte Cristo*, James K. Hackett in *The Prisoner of Zenda*, and Minnie Maddern Fiske in *Tess of the d'Urbervilles*. The company founded in 1913 for the making of these productions was the basis of Famous Players. Shortly afterwards Zukor signed up Mary Pickford at a salary of $20,000 a year, which was increased to $10,000 a week in 1916, when Zukor merged. his interests with those of Jesse Lasky, as " Famous Players Lasky ". In 1917, after it had absorbed Paramount sales and distribution company, the organization was called " Famous Players Lasky Corporation ", changed in 1927 to " Paramount-Famous Lasky ", in 1930 to " Paramount Publix Corporation " and in 1935 to " Paramount Pictures ", its present title. Adolph Zukor has all the time been its guiding star ; he has been Chairman of the Board since 1935, taking an active part in control of all production.

(See Foreword, " Forty Years in Films " by Adolph Zukor, p. 3).

NOTE—Film titles mentioned in " Who's Who in Films " are given in italics. Dates of films refer to the year of showing in the country of origin, but are not normally given for films shown before 1940.

The name given in brackets after a film title is, as a general rule, that of the production company or unit ; otherwise, that of the distributor. The following abbreviations of British and American companies and units have been used :

ABPC   Associated British Picture Corporation.

ARP   Associated Radio Pictures.

B & D   British and Dominions.

BIF   British Instructional Films.

BIP   British International Pictures.

Brit (in compound names)   British.

Brit Nat   British National.

COI   Central Office of Information.

Col   Columbia.

Gains   Gainsborough.

GB   Gaumont British.

GBI   Gaumont British Instructional.

Grand Nat   Grand National.

Internat Screen   International Screenplays.

Individ   Individual.

LFP   London Film Productions.

MGM   Metro-Goldwyn-Mayer.

Mono   Monogram.

MOI   Ministry of Information.

PRC   Producers' Releasing Corporation.

Rep   Republic.

RKO   R.K.O. Radio.

20th   20th Century-Fox.

UI   Universal-International.

Univ   Universal.

Warn   Warner Brothers.

World Screen   World Screenplays.

Moore Raymond

THEY MADE THE MOVIES!

THESE were the pioneers. These were the men and women who founded the science and the art of the cinema we know and enjoy today.

Some became rich and some died poor—but all deserve to be honoured for all time by those who make, sell, show or see films throughout the world.

Out of a fun-fair novelty has grown a tremendous industry. Out of a slapstick rough-and-tumble has developed a new dramatic art. From a few flickering shadows on a whitewashed wall the film has become one of the most potent influences in the life of civilized man. And all in about seventy years.

First, the technical side. Though Edward Muybridge would have been the last to claim any credit for inventing the moving picture, there is no doubt that his Californian experiment with a galloping horse and twenty-four cameras gave the right people the right ideas about the production of successive images to record an event.

Likewise, George Eastman would never have claimed any credit for the invention of the cinematograph, though it became possible only after he had devised the roll film.

These were only two of the " back room boys " of physics and chemistry who eventually inspired William Friese-Greene to invent the first movie camera. This was followed shortly afterwards by Edison's kinetoscope. Both depended on the fact that the retina of the human eye retains an image of a subject for a fraction of a second after that image disappears, and so a series of stationary pictures can produce an effect of movement.

Then came the men who transformed a toy into a commercial triumph : Stuart Blackton of Sheffield, who went to America and helped Edison with his first films, afterwards becoming one of the most famous of producers ; Louis Lumière, the first man to charge the public for watching his films—flickering, jumpy, yet fascinating pictures of a train, some horses, and a wall falling down ; Robert Paul, inventor of the "theatograph", with which he presented films at the London Alhambra ; Léon Gaumont, whose one-reelers

costing five pounds started the firm that eventually became Gaumont British : Charles Pathé, first to make slow motion films and founder of the first regular newsreel ; George Méliès, the magician who startled everybody with his trick photography ; Will Barker, the commercial traveller who graduated from ordinary photography to the moving picture business in a big way : G. M. Anderson, the actor who turned producer and made the first Westerns, starring Broncho Billy. These were the technical pioneers whose ideas were the small beginnings of the highly intricate and elaborate studio equipment of today.

As for the acting, never has any form of art developed so swiftly from its crude origins to such an important branch of the drama.

The first movie makers shot the simplest of movements—a man walking, a train coming into a station, and so on. Next came the story that could be told by actions only. Criminal dramas such as *The Great Train Robbery* and *The Life of Charles Peace* were the first favourites.

And then comedy. It was the ability to make everyone laugh that caught the world's fancy and turned movies from a mere novelty into one of the greatest of popular entertainments.

Beside the immortal Chaplin many of those early stars look wan and dim, but veteran filmgoers remember with pleasure how much they laughed at the enormous John Bunny and his acidic partner, Flora Finch, and how they shrieked at the frenzied antics of the Keystone Cops, who were never still unless they were asleep.

" Action, action ! " was the slogan. The screen became filled with galloping horsemen led by Broncho Billy or William S. Hart. Then followed Tom Mix, the star who brought the silent Western to perfection, and D. W. Griffith, the first creator of stars and pioneer of the " close-up ".

When the movies began to take acting seriously they discovered Valentino, Francis X. Bushman, Mae Marsh, Gloria Swanson, Pola Negri, Pauline Frederick, Mary Pickford, Douglas Fairbanks, Sr., Lon Chaney, Sr., and Clara Bow in America, and Betty Balfour, Alma Taylor, Violet Hopson and Chrissie White in Britain.

Many of those pioneers are dead now, but their art lives on, developed and improved by their successors who still find that the fundamental principle of acting for the movies is to *move*—all the talk of the " talkies " notwithstanding.

MOORE RAYMOND *has written much for, and about, stage, screen and radio. He is the author of "Smiley" and "Smiley Gets a Gun".*

BIOGRAPHIES OF THE PIONEERS OF FILMS

ANDERSON, G. M. Born Pine Bluff, Ark., U.S.A., 1883. The pioneer of the Westerns began his working life as a newsboy in St. Louis. In 1900 he went on the stage, and later turned to the screen. Realizing the film's commercial possibilities, he and George K. Spoor started the Essanay Company that produced the famous cowboy two-reelers starring Broncho Billy.

ARBUCKLE, Roscoe. Born Kansas City, U.S.A., 1881. Making his stage debut in 1895 and his first film in 1908, " Fatty " Arbuckle was one of the famous funny men of the screen until 1921, when he became involved in a Hollywood tragedy that caused his films to be banned in both America and Britain.

BALFOUR, Betty. Born London, 1903. A brilliant mimic and a great star of the early days, she was one of the few who could never be enticed to go to Hollywood, despite many offers. In 1914 she made her stage debut at the Court Theatre, London, and later became one of C. B. Cochran's stars. In 1920 she made her first screen appearance in *Nothing Else Matters.* Soon came fame with *Squibs, Somebody's Darling, Love Life and Laughter, A Little Bit of Fluff, The Daughter of the Regiment, The Brat.* At one time she was more popular in France than any Hollywood star.

BARKER, Will. Born London. One of the pioneers of the British film industry, he was first of all a commercial traveller keen on photography. Later he became a cameraman, and in 1897 made a film of Queen Victoria's Diamond Jubilee. He founded the Barker Motion Picture Company and produced, among other successes, *Jane Shore* and *Sixty Years a Queen.* In 1920 he was official photographer to the Prince of Wales on his world tour.

BARRYMORE, John. Born Philadelphia, U.S.A., 1882. Cultured, handsome, witty and highly talented, this leading actor of both stage and screen became known as " The Great Profile ". In his youth he studied art, then became a journalist. In 1903 his stage career began in Chicago, and after some years he became America's most celebrated actor. A lover of Shakespeare, he came to London in 1926 and produced " Hamlet ", playing the lead himself. In 1936 he made his

first film, a comedy called *Are You A Mason ?* His greatest achievement on the silent screen was the dual role in *Dr. Jekyll and Mr. Hyde.* He was equally successful in talkies. Among his best films were *Sherlock Holmes, The Beloved Vagabond, The Sea Beast, Moby Dick, A Bill of Divorcement, Grand Hotel, Dinner at Eight, Twentieth Century.* Died 1942.

BLACKTON, Stuart. Born Sheffield, 1875. One of the greatest pioneers of the movies. He went to America in 1885 and later became a reporter in New York. In 1896 he met Edison and, realizing the great future for the moving picture, helped the inventor to make one of his first films by drawing cartoons in front of the camera. He made the first newsreel moving pictures of the Spanish-American war (1897). With Albert E. Smith and William Rock, both Englishmen, he founded the Vitagraph Company. First film: *Raffles the Amateur Cracksman.* For 15 years he was a leading producer in the U.S.A., before returning to England to produce *The Glorious Adventure.* He discovered Victor McLaglen and took him back to America. Among other fine work for the industry, he organized and became president of the Motion Picture Board of Trade.

BOW, Clara. Born Brooklyn New York, 1906. The red-haired " It Girl " played several roles in which she was supposed to have been glimpsed in the nude—but actually wore skin tights. She won a beauty competition while still at school, later went to Hollywood and got a small part in *Beyond the Rainbow* (1922). She was told to cry, and her make-up ran so badly that the scene was severely cut. Thereupon she went in for a business career, but was persuaded to return to the movies in *Down to the Sea in Ships.* This was the beginning of a series of successes including *Dancing Mothers, Eve's Lover, Mantrap, It, Hula, Red Hair, Wild Party, Dangerous Curves, Her Wedding Night, No Limit, Call Her Savage, Hoopla.*

BUNNY, John. Born New York, 1863. The funniest fat man of the silent screen was the son of an English naval officer who emigrated from Penzance to America. He joined a darkie minstrel troupe in 1883 and made many tours before

getting a job in Hollywood in 1910. Soon the miming Falstaff of the films became the most famous star of the day—earning 1000 dollars a week (an enormous salary at that time). He appeared in more than 150 one-reel comedies, nearly always partnered by Flora Finch. In 1912 he visited England and had a tremendous reception. Died 1915.

BUSHMAN, Francis X. Born Norfolk, Va., U.S.A., 1885. One of the richest stars of his time, he worked as a commercial traveller, clerk, schoolteacher, racing cyclist, miner and wrestler before going on the musical comedy stage in New York. In 1911 he joined the Essanay Company and appeared in more than 200 of their films. Then he became a freelance, working for many companies and becoming the most popular star of the day, driving around in a gold-plated car and requiring eighteen secretaries to answer his fan mail. Among his best films were *Ben Hur, Romeo and Juliet, According to Hoyle, The Scarlet Arrow, Once a Gentleman, The Call of the Circus.* He had a small part in *Wilson* (20th) in 1945.

CHANEY, Lon, Sr. Born Colorado Springs, U.S.A., 1883. This master of horrific make-up learned the art of mime from his parents, both deaf mutes. At first ambitious to be a comedian, he went on the musical comedy stage. In 1912 he made his film debut in two-reelers, spending most of his small salary on greasepaint, wigs and other materials for make-up experiments. He first became famous as the cripple in *The Miracle Man* (1930). Then came a series of dramatic roles that rank among screen classics—*The Hunchback of Notre Dame, He Who Gets Slapped, The Unholy Three, Laugh Clown Laugh.* Died 1930.

DRESSLER, Marie. Born Coburg, Canada, 1871. A grand old trouper whose technique was an example for any artist, she had a long stage career before she went into films. She made her first important appearance in 1892 as Cigarette in Ouida's " Under Two Flags ". Hard work plus great talent made her a star of both New York and London (where she went into management at the Aldwych Theatre in 1909). Her first film, in 1914, was the famous *Tillie's Punctured Romance,* starring Charles Chaplin and Mabel Normand. *Anna Christie* (starring

Garbo) brought her screen fame, followed by *Min and Bill, Tugboat Annie, Politics, Emma, Dinner at Eight, Let Us Be Gay*, and others. Won an Academy Award 1930-31, for *Min and Bill*. Died 1934.

EASTMAN, George. Born Waterville, New York, July 12, 1854. By inventing the roll film he made moving pictures possible. Leaving school at 14 years, he became an insurance clerk. At 24, about to go on holiday, he bought a camera and got a photograper to show him how it worked. He cancelled the holiday and stayed at home to study photography. It took him nine years to devise the roll film which made him a millionaire. Died 1932.

EDISON, Thomas Alva. Born Milan, Ohio, U.S.A., 1847. The inventor of the phonograph and the incandescent lamp, the man who applied for nearly 1500 patents in his lifetime, did not invent moving pictures, as is often supposed. In 1891 he invented the kinetoscope— a combined movie camera and projector—and before long became involved in a patent war with W. Friese-Greene, the Englishman who invented the first movie camera. Edison lost. His original kinetoscope is now in the South Kensington Museum, London. Died 1931.

FAIRBANKS, Douglas, Sr. Born Denver, Colorado, U.S.A., 1884. Athletic hero of swashbuckling stories and costume dramas, performer of prodigious feats of agility, husband for 14 years of Mary Pickford ("The World's Sweetheart"), he was one of the most gay and gallant heroes of the screen. He made his stage debut in Denver in 1895, and subsequently became a Broadway star. In 1914 he made his first film, *The Lamb*, exploiting his grin and athletic exuberance. Soon he became one of the most celebrated and wealthiest stars. His best films include *The Mark of Zorro, Robin Hood, The Thief of Bagdad, The Man in the Iron Mask, The Taming of the Shrew, Mr. Robinson Crusoe*. In 1933 he joined up with Korda and made *The Private Life of Don Juan*. Died 1939.

FIELDS, W. C. Born Philadelphia, U.S.A., 1879. Determined to become an actor despite his parents' wishes, he ran away from home at an early age. At first he had to sell papers for a living, but eventually he got into vaudeville as a comic stooge. Meanwhile he practised

juggling and eventually toured the world as a comic juggler. After star part in the " Ziegfeld Follies " for nine years, he got his first film chance in *Sally of the Sawdust* (1925). Before long he became one of the greatest screen laugh-makers. Among his best films were *If I Had a Million, International House, Mrs. Wiggs of the Cabbage Patch, Alice in Wonderland, David Copperfield, Poppy, Never Give a Sucker an Even Break*. Died December 25, 1946.

FINCH, Flora. Born London, 1869. Famous for many years as John Bunny's comedy partner in the early silent days, she began her acting career on the stage with the Shakespearean actor-manager, Ben Greet. She also toured in *The Sign of the Cross* and *The Worst Woman in London*. Her first films were made for Cecil M. Hepworth at Walton. She went to Hollywood and won fame in sour-spinster and nagging-wife roles opposite the fat comedian. After his death she formed her own production company in 1917. Her later films included *The Cat and the Canary, Quality Street, The Scarlet Letter, Come Across*. Died 1940.

FREDERICK, Pauline. Born Boston, U.S.A., 1885. The great dramatic star who was the first lady of the screen for nearly ten years began acting in 1902, when she star :d as a chorus girl in New York. Later she became a leading actress. Then in 1915 she made her screen debut in *The Eternal City*, produced in Rome. Film fame came with *Madame X*, followed by *Zaza, Bella Donna, Smouldering Fires, Devil's Island, The Sacred Flame*. In 1927 she came to London and starred in the stage version of *Madame X*, then made the British film *Mumsie*. Back in Hollywood she appeared in *On Trial, Evidence, The Modern Age, Thank You Mr. Moto*. Died 1938.

FRIESE-GREENE, William. Born Bristol, 1865. He invented the first practical moving picture camera, which he patented in 1889. He gave the first public demonstration on June 26, 1890, to the British Photographic Convention at Chester. Later he became involved in a patents war with Edison, whose kinetoscope was not patented until 1891. The Englishman's claim was eventually supported by the United States Circuit Court. Died 1921.

GAUMONT, Léon. Born Paris, 1864. The British film industry owes a great deal to this Frenchman who, after early moving picture

experiments in Paris, settled in England. In 1902 he started his first studio on a Dulwich cricket ground, making one-reel films for £5, such as *Curfew Shall Not Ring Tonight*. In 1906 he opened in Bishopsgate the first continuous performance cinema. The 45-minute programme included the Olympic Games at Athens—the first newsreel scoop in movie history. In 1910 he demonstrated " talkies "—silent films with gramophone records behind the screen—starring Harry Lauder, George Robey and Clarice Mayne. Later he founded the Gaumont Studios at Lime Grove, Shepherd's Bush, London—subsequently sold to the Ostrer brothers, and now in the Rank Organisation. Died 1946.

GRIFFITH, David Wark. Born Boston, U.S.A., 1895. Began his career on the stage. After seeing his first film in Chicago in 1907, decided to join the film industry. Wrote scripts, acted in early Biograph films, notably *The Eagle's Nest*. Directed his first film, *The Adventures of Dollie*, in 1908. Began the " star " system with Mary Pickford, whom he recognized as someone he could mould into a great screen personality, as distinct from a stage actress. Other stars he discovered include the Gish sisters. He also invented " hazy " photography, when he put layers of chiffon in front of the camera to give a soft effect when photographing Lillian Gish, and is credited with originating the " fade-out ", the " cut-back " and the " close-up ". Best known among his " great " films are *The Birth of a Nation* (1915) and *Intolerance* (1916). With Mary Pickford, Douglas Fairbanks, Sr. and Charles Chaplin, formed United Artists Corporation in 1918. Sold his interests in U.A. in 1938. In 1936 visited Britain, where he was to remake his early success *Broken Blossoms*, but this plan was cancelled and he returned to America.

HARLOW, Jean. Born Kansas City, U.S.A., 1911. Platinum blonde hair, figure, vitality and vituperation—these made her famous on the screen. But it was her acting ability that made her one of the most dynamic stars during her short, brilliant career. A society girl, she went to Hollywood at 19, and secured a contract for a series of Hal Roach comedies. Her disapproving guardian at first opposed her Hollywood career, but later she returned to be an extra in a Clara Bow film. Learning that Howard Hughes sought a star for the talkie version of *Hell's Angels*, she applied for a test and got the part. Then came *China Seas, Dinner at Eight, Blonde Bombshell, Suzy, Libelled Lady, Wife v. Secretary*. Died 1937.

HART, William S. Born Newburgh, New York, 1872. The first of the cowboy heroes who did not simply gallop to and fro across the screen, but knew how to act and give character to each role. After some years at a New York riding academy, he went south and got small parts in Westerns. Director Thomas Ince made him a star. His best films included *Wolves of The Trail, White Oak, Wild Bill Hickock, Tumbleweeds, Sand, The Toll Gate*.

HEPWORTH, Cecil M. Born London, 1874. Pioneer British film producer and director. First experiments in film-making in 1896, in partnership with his cousin, named Wicks. From this partnership was evolved the trademark "Hepwix". In 1899, started filmmaking in garden of his house in Hurst Grove, Walton-on-Thames. Built his first studio there in 1905. This was burnt down, but he built another, part of which still stands. One of his best early films was *Rescued by Rover*, 1905. Directed his first feature film, *Blind Fate*, 1912. Organized one of the earliest film stock companies, which included Chrissie White, Ivy Close, Alma Taylor, Henry Edwards, Violet Hopson, Shayle Gardner, Ralph Forbes, Gerald Ames, Gwynne Herbert, James Carew and Henry Vibart. Last film he directed was *Coming Through the Rye*, 1924. In 1946 was appointed chairman of a Research Committee set up by the British Film Institute for the production of the first official "History of the British Film". 1947, Hon. Member of the British Film Academy.

HOPSON, Violet. Born California, 1891. Her English parents brought her home when she was a few weeks old. She made her stage debut in *The Blue Moon*, appearing later in *The Merry Widow* and other musical comedies. In 1912 she made her first film for the Hepworth Company, and later starred in many racing dramas produced by the Broadwest Company. At that time she was known as the best-dressed British film star. In 1928 she made *Widdecombe Fair*, and since then she has frequently appeared in Herbert Wilcox productions.

INCE, Thomas. Born New York, 1880. His influence in raising the standard of acting on the screen began soon after he directed his first film in 1910. He was responsible for a great many good films, and in all of them he preserved his artistic integrity. Directing the famous William S. Hart, he evolved a special acting technique for the screen and created a new kind of cowboy. Died 1924.

KEARTON, Cherry. Born Yorkshire, 1871. The pioneer of the "Bring-'Em-Back-Alive" type of animal film started his travels in 1912 when he made several adventurous journeys through Central Africa, taking moving pictures that caused a sensation all over the world. Early in World War I he was attached to the Belgian Army and took remarkable pictures under fire. In 1930 he travelled 12,000 miles through Central Africa and, using a native cast, made *Tembi*. Another of his remarkable productions was *Dassan*, a film about penguins on an island off the Cape of Good Hope. Died 1940.

LANGDON, Harry. Born Council Bluffs, Iowa, U.S.A., 1884. This 4 ft. 11 in. moon-faced comic, the son of poor parents, was a newsboy at 10. Later he became an actor in third-rate touring shows, then went into vaudeville, where he found success. His first films were short Mack Sennett comedies, followed by full-length features— *The Strong Man, Tramp Tramp Tramp, Long Pants, The Shrimp, Three's a Crowd*.

LE PRINCE, Louis. Born Metz, France, 1842. One of the very earliest movie makers, his career ended in a mystery that has never been solved. The son of a French Army officer, he was fascinated by photography. Emigrating to America, he began his first moving picture experiments in New York. He came to England and lived in Leeds where, in 1888, he took moving pictures at the rate of twelve a second, and later showed them on a white-washed wall. In 1890 he was seen entering a Paris train at Bourges, and from that moment he disappeared, with his luggage and business papers.

LINDER, Max. Born Bordeaux, France, 1885. France's most famous screen comedian in the early days of films got his first laughs at the Paris Conservatoire, where he won several prizes for comedy. Later he joined the Pathé Company, and this nimble, dapper, light comedian soon became one of the most celebrated film stars in the world. In World War I he was a dispatch rider, and was wounded, gassed and invalided out. In 1916 he went to U.S.A. and joined the Essanay Company, making *Max on a Liner* and *The Little Café*. Later he returned to France to write, direct and star in many films. Died 1925.

LOMBARD, Carole. Born Fort Wayne, Ind., U.S.A., 1909. One of the few big stars who went straight into films without stage experience, she started at the age of eleven with two days' work in a Monte Blue Film, *The Perfect Crime*. Then came the Westerns with Buck Jones and Tom Mix. In 1928 she became one of Mack Sennett's Bathing Beauties. She developed into a dramatic actress, playing in *Power, Dynamite, High Voltage, The Match King, White Woman, Bolero*. Later she took to comedy, both plain and satirical, scoring special success in *Twentieth Century, Nothing Sacred, To Be or Not To Be*. Died 1942 (killed in an aeroplane crash).

LUMIERE, Louis. Born Paris, 1862. The first man to show moving pictures to the paying public opened his cinema in the Boulevard des Capucines on February 2, 1896. He and his brother, Auguste, inspired by Edison's kinetoscope, made their own cameras and projectors—then commercialized them. His earliest films include *The Arrival of a Train at a Country Station, Cavalry Horses Led to be Watered, Breakfast on the Lawn, Bathing in the Mediterranean, The Fall of a Wall*.

MARSH, Mae. Born Madrid, New Mexico, U.S.A., 1895. A great silent star, she was educated in a convent and then became a telephone operator. Her sister Margaret got a part in a film at the old Biograph Company's studios and Mae went to see her make the film. D. W. Griffith spotted her and offered her a contract. She made her screen debut in 1912 in *Escape*. She first became famous in *The Birth of a Nation*, in which she played the tragic sister. Then came *Intolerance, Paddy the Next Best Thing, The Rat*. She retired for 12 years, then returned to the screen in *Over the Hill*. Later she played in *Alice* *in Wonderland, Little Man What Now ?, Black Fury, Tales of Manhattan, Dixie Dugan.*

MELIES, George. Born Paris, 1861. The first "film king", the father of trick photography, was in old age found by a newspaper reporter selling papers and toys in Montparnasse railway station, and spent the last ten years of his life in a home for the aged at Orly founded by himself many years before. A conjurer by profession, in 1895 he experimented with camera magic and discovered many ways of making trick shots with dolls, skeletons and other inanimate objects. For a few years his fantastic films amazed the world. Is often considered the forerunner of Walt Disney. Died 1938.

MIX, Tom. Born El Paso, Texas, U.S.A., 1881. Brought up on his father's ranch, this rough-riding, non-smoking, teetotal cowboy set an example in acting that has been followed by all his successors. At 17 years he fought in the Spanish American war, and later he was a machine-gunner in China during the Boxer rebellion. After having broken in horses for the Boer war he became a Deputy U.S. Marshal in Oklahoma. In 1914 he got his first film job with the Selig Company, and his horsemanship, combined with a natural acting ability, soon made him a star. Many famous actresses played in his films, which included *The Lone Star Ranger, Riders of the Purple Sage, Dick Turpin, Silver Valley, Outlaws of Red River.* In 1925, with his famous horse Tony, he was given a reception by the Lord Mayor of London. Died 1940.

MOORE, Grace. Born Jellico, Tenn., U.S.A., 1901. The first star to make serious music popular on the screen was the daughter of a banker, who gave her every opportunity to study singing with the best teachers. At Washington in 1918 she made her stage debut as Carmen. While studying in Paris, she met Irving Berlin, who persuaded her to appear on Broadway in "The Music Box Revue" of 1923, 1924, and 1925. After appearing in light musicals, she went on the concert platform. In 1928 she made her first appearance at the Metropolitan Opera House as Mimi in "La Bohème" In 1930 she appeared in the film *A Lady's Morals,* based on the life of Jenny Lind. Then, in 1934, came *One Night of Love,* which made

her world-famous. Died 1947 (killed in an aeroplane crash).

MUYBRIDGE, Edward. Real name Edward James Muggeridge, later known as Edweard, and finally as Edward Muybridge. Born Kingston-on-Thames, 1830. The birth of the moving picture idea began with his experiment while he was conducting a geodetic survey in California in 1872. Governor Standford had an argument with some friends about the leg movements of a galloping horse. He lent Muybridge his stables and horses for a test with twenty-four cameras placed at regular intervals and set off by connecting lengths of string as a horse galloped by, thus taking a series of pictures. The result stimulated other minds to work on the idea of successive images to produce moving pictures. Died 1904.

NEGRI, Pola. Born Lipna, Poland, 1899. One of the screen's first passionate beauties, she made her stage debut in Warsaw at the age of sixteen. Skilled as a dancer, she later became a member of the Imperial Russian Ballet. Surprisingly, she became a concert violinist and toured the Continent. In 1917 she started her screen career in *Love and Passion,* directed by Lubitsch. Soon she went to Hollywood and starred in *Forbidden Paradise, The Cheat, Bella Donna, Hotel Imperial, East of Suez.* In 1930 she came to England and starred in *The Woman He Scorned.* Retired in 1933, but returned to the screen in 1943, when she went to Hollywood to play in *Hi Diddle Diddle.*

NORMAND, Mabel. Born Boston, U.S.A., 1894. Charles Chaplin's first co-star began as Mabel Fortescue in a series of short comedies by Vitagraph. Later she became a leading player in Keystone comedies—mostly opposite Chaplin —starting in 1914 with *Mabel's Strange Predicament,* the first film in which he wore his famous comic costume. Many of her later films had Mabel in the cast and title. She made a fortune out of films and was supposed to have spent £20,000 a year on clothes alone. Died 1930.

PATHE, Charles. Born Paris, 1865. The founder of the great film firm of Pathé Frères started his commercial career by charging patrons a franc each to listen to his phonograph at country fairs and such gatherings. Having saved a little money, he invested

it in movie equipment. He was among the first to make slow motion pictures. and the producer of the first very long film, *Les Misérables.* In 1909 founded the Pathé Gazette, the first of the regular newsreels, which was then 400 ft. long. (The average length of a modern newsreel is 1000-1500 ft.)

PAUL, Robert W. Born London, 1870. One of the pioneer inventors and exhibitors, he first took an interest in moving pictures in 1895, when he invented a movie camera. Next year he invented a projector, which he called the "theatograph". For two years at the Alhambra Theatre, London, he presented a programme of moving pictures. Died 1943.

RAIMU, Jules. Born Bandol, France, 1883. One of France's most renowned comedians, he first made his reputation as the principal comic actor on the French stage. Starting as a music-hall extra at Toulon, he knocked about France in small parts until he was twenty-five, when he went to Paris and made a hit in the play "A Man in a Dress Suit". Soon he was as big a star as Guitry. In 1929 he made his film debut, and his many successes include *Un Carnet de Bal, Gribouille, La Femme du Boulanger, The Well-Digger's Daughter.* He was a Chevalier of the Legion of Honour. Died 1946.

SEASTROM, Victor. Born Varmland, Sweden, 1879. One of the Swedes who had a considerable influence on the development of film technique, he was first a stage actor, then a producer, and acquired his own theatre in 1910. Two years later he acted before the camera for the Swedish Biograph Company, and before long he became a director. In 1914 he came to Britain to study technique, and later went to Hollywood, directing and producing for several important companies. Among his best films were *He Who Gets Slapped, The Tower of Lies, The Scarlet Letter, Hell Ship, Wind.*

SEMON, Larry. Born U.S.A., 1890. Son of Zera the Great, magician and acrobat, he had no intention of entering the world of entertainment when he studied at an art school, and later became a cartoonist on a New York newspaper. But an urge to be a funny man sent him to Hollywood, where he made his film debut with Vitagraph. Among his many successes were *The Girl in the Limousine, The Wizard of Oz, Stop Look and Listen, Spuds, Underworld.* Died 1928.

SENNETT, Mack. Born Denville, Quebec, 1884. The man who put Chaplin on the screen was a dancer in musical comedy at the age of seventeen and later got a job with D. W. Griffith in the old Biograph Company. He became a comedy producer and then formed his own company, the Keystone Comedy Company, in 1912. He made stars of Charles Chaplin and Mabel Normand, besides originating the famous Bathing Beauties. His feature films include *Hypnotized, The Bride's Relations, The Old Barn, Mickey, The Extra Girl.*

STILLER, Mauritz. Born Finland, 1883. One of the pioneers, he had an influence on Swedish films that helped to make them so important in the early days. They include *Chains,* and *Bonds That Chafe.* Under him, Victor Seastrom started as a film actor. Stiller went to Hollywood in 1922 and directed *In Self Defence, The Blizzard, Hotel Imperial.* Died 1928.

SWANSON, Gloria. Born Chicago, 1899. One of the great beauties of the screen, she first intended to be an artist, but an offer from the old Essanay Company put her in films. Then she went to Keystone, and later became one of Mack Sennett's Bathing Beauties. Cecil B. De Mille starred her in *The Admirable Crichton,* and later she appeared in *Bluebeard's Eighth Wife, Prodigal Daughters, Zaza, Sadie Thompson, The Trespasser, The Humming Bird.* In 1926 she became her own producer and made *The Loves of Sonya, What a Widow, Tonight or Never, Music in the Air, Father Takes a Wife.*

TAYLOR, Alma. Born London, 1896. One of the most famous British stars in the early days, she made her film debut in 1907 with the Hepworth Company. Soon she partnered Chrissie White as one of the two delightful children in the celebrated series about the Tilly Girls. Later films included *The Cloister and the Hearth, Coming Through the Rye, Alf's Button, Quinney's, South Sea Bubble, The Train of Destiny, Deadlock.* She was the first woman television demonstrator until the B.B.C. gave

up the Baird system in 1935. Later she appeared in the Cicely Court-neidge film *Everybody Dance* (1936).

TURNER, Florence. Born New York, 1888. Probably the first movie actress to be called a film star, she made an early stage debut and soon became well known. In 1902 she appeared with Sir Henry Irving in "Robespierre", when he toured America. In 1907 she joined the Vitagraph Company and was one of the first actresses to make personal appearances. In 1913 she came to London to make her own films, including *The Welsh Singer, The Shepherd Lassie o' Argyle, For Her People, My Old Dutch.* Thereafter she appeared in films in both Britain and America, but never with the same success. Her latest included *The Gilded Highway, Sally in Our Alley, The Kid's Clever, The Law and the Man.*

VALENTINO, Rudolph. Born Italy, 1895. The most sensational romantic actor of the silent screen was the son of an Italian Army doctor. He studied horticulture at Genoa and went to the U.S.A. to be a landscape gardener. He failed —then washed dishes in New York. Later he became a professional dancer and appeared in variety. In 1919 he went to Hollywood and sprang swiftly into fame as the star of *The Four Horsemen of the Apocalypse.* Then followed *The Sheikh, Blood and Sand, Monsieur Beaucaire.* In 1923 he visited London for personal appearances and received a great welcome. His last film, *Son of the Sheikh,* was finished shortly before his death as a result of an appendicitis operation. The public lying-in-state was attended by thousands of hysterical women. Died 1926.

VEIDT, Conrad. Born in Berlin, 1893. Fated for the most part to play spies and other villains, he began as an all-round actor when he made his stage debut in 1913 under Max Reinhardt. After fighting in the German Army during World War I, he went back to the stage, but soon turned to films. His first success was in the startling, surrealistic *The Cabinet of Dr. Caligari.* In 1927 he went to Hollywood to play in *The Laughing Man* and other films. Back in Germany in 1930 he made *The Last Company* and *Congress*

Dances. Then to Britain for *Rome Express, I Was a Spy, Jew Süss, Contraband,* and many more. He became a British citizen in 1939, and later went to Hollywood again. Died 1943.

VON STROHEIM, Erich. Born Vienna, 1885. "The man you love to hate" had a father in the Dragoons and a mother who was lady-in-waiting to Elisabeth, Empress of Austria. In 1902 he became a second lieutenant in the Austrian cavalry. Ending his army career in 1909, he went to America and did all sorts of odd jobs until he got a small part in a touring repertory company. Then came Hollywood, small parts, and his big chance in 1918 when he directed and starred in his own story, *Blind Husbands,* followed by *Foolish Wives, The Merry Widow, Greed, The Wedding March.* When talkies came he left Hollywood for France, where he starred in his own film story, *La Grande Illusion.* Back to Hollywood in 1940, his most important film since then was *Five Graves to Cairo,* in which he played the part of Rommel.

WHITE, Chrissie. Born London, 1894. One of the early British stars, she made her screen debut in 1907 in *For His Little Lady's Sake,* produced by the Hepworth Company. Later she co-starred with Alma Taylor as one of the two Tilly Girls in a series that became highly popular. Then came the Henry Edwards productions—*A Lunatic at Large, Lily of the Alley, The Call of the Sea.* She married her producer and frequently appeared on the stage with him.

WHITE, Pearl. Born Springfield, Miss., U.S.A., 1889. Queen of the silent serials and the most courageous stunt actress in film history, she made her stage debut at the age of six as Little Eva in "Uncle Tom's Cabin". Then she went back to school for some years before joining a circus and learning to be a bareback rider. Later she went on the stage again. Eventually she reached Hollywood and became the old Pathé Company's most famous stunt star, appearing in serials such as *The Perils of Pauline* and *The Exploits of Elaine,* and later in feature films such as *Parisian Nights* and *The Perils of Paris.* Died 1938.

W. J. O'Bryen

IN SEARCH OF

THE STARS OF TOMORROW

WITH the marked growth in the number and importance of British films, the problems of casting and of the creation of sufficient stars to cater for the needs and preferences of the public are amongst the most pressing of all the tasks now facing the British film producer.

It is not too much to say that the only people who can justly be described as "film stars" are those whose personality is by itself sufficient to attract the public into the cinemas. And the number of players, male or female, in British films today who possess this attribute can be counted with ease on the fingers of two hands.

What we have to do, therefore, if we are to retain our hold on the home and Commonwealth markets—let alone capture any part of the American—is to enlarge the number of stars who are able, so to speak, to stand on their own two feet as box-office attractions.

How are we to do this? It is extremely difficult to say. In America, with its vast star system, it is possible for a studio which has made a new film discovery to establish him or her as a star inside two or three films by the simple process of "hanging" the new discovery on an established star and letting the newcomer give proof of ability. But in Britain there are just not sufficient stars on whom to "hang" the new discoveries. Consequently, more often than not, a film has to be made without any established name in it, and the chances are that a large part of the public, hidebound as it is by the star system, will stay away however good the film may be, simply because it has no "star-appeal".

Having no established stars apart from James Mason, Margaret Lockwood, Stewart Granger, Laurence Olivier, Anna Neagle, Ann Todd, Eric Portman, Vivien Leigh, Patricia Roc and one or two others, Britain is forced to make films with players who, however great their acting ability, cannot reasonably be expected, until they have completed a certain number of films, to attract the public except by sheer merit of performance. It is up to the public, therefore, to give British films a chance by judging them on their merits and on the opinions expressed about them both by the critics and by ordinary cinema-goers. In this way our studios can be given the chance of building up a strong star system in Britain such as exists in the United States.

It must also be remembered that in the creation of stars the American film industry is aided by the enormous publicity obtainable through the fan magazines and through the large amount of space available in the national daily press. Once Hollywood has decided to make a star of an unknown player, no pains are spared to make people conscious of the new personality; and the player in turn is expected to co-operate fully with the studio's publicity experts.

Consider Lauren Bacall for instance. When her first film was shown over here, there were queues all round the theatre waiting to see it, although she had never before appeared on the screen either in Britain or in America. Why? Simply because she had been so amply publicized long before the film came to Britain that her name had become a household word although her abilities were unknown. Jane Russell provides another example. It is to be doubted whether even if we had a similar new personality—and I maintain that we have many and better—we should be able to sell her to the public "sight unseen".

How are we to find our new stars? In the first place from the West End stage, and from many first-rate repertory companies throughout the country which provide such an admirable training ground for the beginner. But here there is a difficulty. The centre of the American film industry—Hollywood—is 3000 miles distant from the centre of the American theatre—New York City. Anyone adopting a film career in that country (and most of America's best stars are recruited from the theatre) has virtually to divorce himself from the theatre in order to devote himself to a film career.

In Britain, where most of the studios are within an hour's car ride of the West End theatres, there is a disinclination among the more serious-minded actors to give up the theatre entirely in order to pursue a film career. The stage is the first love of many players, and even the financial inducements offered by the films are more or less negatived by the avarice of the Chancellor of the Exchequer, who sees that film actors and actresses retain very little of their earnings. In many instances, therefore, big stage stars, instead of being lured body and soul into the film business, are prepared only to act in an occasional film here and there, should they be offered a role of sufficient appeal.

W. J. O'BRYEN *has been discovering new talent for stage and screen for many years. He is now a production executive for London Film Productions Ltd.*

EILEEN HERLIE
(London Film Productions)

One has therefore, to look not only to the stage actor but also to the film aspirant who is prepared to go about things the hard way, and to work up from the "extra" ranks through small parts to possible stardom. There have been many examples of such a rise to fame, and there will be many more. But one thing is certain, and that is that this is a heartbreaking existence. For the one who succeeds thousands are disappointed.

But let us, by lining up the talent for our current programme, see how much can be achieved by twelve months of intensive preparation. I speak, of course, only for my own company, London Film Productions. Other studios have, I know, made many valuable discoveries whom I shall mention later. But, so far as we are concerned, I would say that we have done better in our contracts than might have been hoped.

We have engaged such people as Kieron Moore, a young Irish actor who, after a big success on the stage in *Red Roses For Me*, showed tremendous screen promise in his first film *A Man About The House*, which he has since followed up with *Mine Own Executioner* and *Anna Karenina* ; Margaret Johnston, who made a considerable hit in *The Rake's Progress* and is now definitely headed for stardom ; Dulcie Gray, a brilliant stage actress who, with quite a few films behind her, took a leading role in Anthony Kimmins' production of *Mine Own Executioner* ; and Glynis Johns, a potential star if ever there was one, who appears in Oscar Wilde's *An Ideal Husband*. Margaret Leighton, the leading actress of the Old Vic Company, has made her film debut opposite David Niven as Flora MacDonald in *Bonnie Prince Charlie* ; Eileen Herlie, the most sensational stage discovery of many years past, will devote half her time to films for the company and half to the theatre. Others engaged include Hugh Kelly and Iris Russell, two young people who have recently made very successful stage debuts in the West End ; Harriette Johns, a beautiful young girl with much repertory experience ; Ann South, a seventeen-year-old found in a film crowd and given a contract on the strength of a test ; Sheila Manahan, who played so brilliantly in *Happy as Larry*, and Hector Ross.

When these players have appeared on the screen with such established stars as Paulette Goddard, Cary Grant, Ralph Richardson, Orson Welles, Vivien Leigh, David Niven and Michele Morgan, it is reasonable to assume that some if not all of them, will in a short time attain the stature that will enable them to carry films on their own shoulders and so to help other newcomers in their turn. In this way it is hoped to build our stars—which seems to me the only logical system.

A large number of new personalities are likewise being built up by other British companies. Jean Simmons, for instance, who despite her extreme youth and the comparatively small number of films she has made so far has established herself as an outstanding screen personality ; Maxwell Reed is a young man of whom great things are confidently expected ; Sally Ann Howes is similarly a potential star. Ronald Howard has proved that he can stand on his own feet without needing the help of his distinguished father's name. Dennis Price and Dermot Walsh have firmly established themselves. Kathleen Ryan is a new discovery of considerable significance, John McCallum an actor of virility and ability. And there are others, too numerous to mention, who will be heard of more and more during the months to come.

Finally I would suggest that Christine Norden, shared by London Films with M.G.M., who has appeared in several films for this company, is another "one for the book" ; and so, I believe, are John Justin who, after an interruption in his career caused by six years' service in the R.A.F. is now resuming his film career, and Barbara White, a young and already established actress whose beauty and talent leave no reason to doubt her eventual stardom.

The essential factor in star-building is continuity of production. Such continuity has been sadly lacking in British studios until recent years. But cessation of American film imports has given an extra incentive to production, and has thus provided greater opportunity for young British players. When a girl, or a young man, can be assured of appearing in six films or more in fairly quick succession, enabling the taste of success to sweeten the palate of ambition, then perhaps the West End stage may lose some of its lure. Those who benefit will be the cinema-goers of Britain—and of the whole world.

A DIRECTORY OF
SCREENWRITERS' AND ACTORS' AGENTS

ANGLO-AMERICAN ARTISTES LTD.
33-4 Queen's House,
Leicester-square, London, W.C.2
Gerrard 7565-6

BERT AZA LTD.
22 Charing Cross-road, London,
W.C.2
Temple Bar 0222

VIVIENNE BLACK
16 Conduit-street,
London, W.1
Mayfair 6271

MARY BUXTON LTD.
3 Princes House, Jermyn-street,
London, S.W.1
Regent 5555

RITA CAVE
110 Jermyn-street, London,
S.W.1
Abbey 6626
Mayfair 3482

CONNIES LTD.
92 Regent-street, London, W.1
Regent 2531-2

ITALIA CONTI
12 Archer-street, London, W.1
Gerrard 1054

CURTIS BROWN LTD.
6 Henrietta-street, London,
W.C.2
Temple Bar 1873

MRS. T. C. DAGNALL
(A. M. HEATH & CO. LTD.)
Princes House, Jermyn-street,
London, S.W.1
Regent 1347

HERBERT DE LEON LTD.
30 South Audley-street, London,
W.1
Grosvenor 3881-2
Cunningham 8900

DENTON & WARNER'S
140a Shaftesbury-avenue,
London, W.C.2
Temple Bar 5160, 7267

FELIX DE WOLFE AND RICHARD STONE
4-5 William IV-street, London,
W.C.2
Temple Bar 2112-3-4

HARRY DUBENS LTD.
87 Regent-street, London, W.1
Regent 1452-3

ELLISON-BARLOW PRODUC-TIONS LTD.
43 Bedford-street, London,
W.C.2
Temple Bar 3908-9

ESSANAY, LTD.
60-6 Wardour-street, London, W.1
Gerrard 5158-9

FILM CASTING ASSOCIATION
21-2 Poland-street, London,
W.1
Gerrard 7451

FILM RIGHTS LTD.
113-7 Wardour-street, London,
W.1
Gerrard 7151

AIDA FOSTER AGENCY
1011 Finchley-road, London
N.W.11
Speedwell 1179

FOSTER'S AGENCY
Piccadilly House, London, S.W.1
Regent 5367-8

THE AUDREY GARNETT STAGE SCHOOL
277 Malson-road, Cheam,
Surrey
Fairlands 9384

CASSEL GERARD LTD.
16 Conduit-street, London, W.1
Mayfair 9692-3

ERIC GLASS
Piccadilly House, London, S.W.1
Regent 0474, 2170

JOHN GLIDDON LTD.
106 Regent-street, London, W.1
Regent 3970

DEREK GLYNNE, 'G-W' DIRECTION
115 Shaftesbury-avenue, London,
W.C.2
Temple Bar 6916, 2824, 7006

GORDON HARBORD
53 St. Martin's-lane, London,
W.C.2
Temple Bar 8985

GERARD HEATH IN ASSOCIA-TION MONTAGUE LYON AGENCY LTD.
108-11 Jermyn-street, London,
S.W.1
Abbey 2357

HORSFIELD'S AGENCY
Suite 1, Cecil House, 41 Charing
Cross-road, London, W.C.2
Gerrard 3421-2

INTERNATIONAL ARTISTES
Irving House, Irving-street,
London, W.C.2
Whitehall 3046-7

FREDERICK JOACHIM
Remo House, 310 Regent-street,
London, W.1
Langham 3152-3

J. P. PRODUCTIONS & ENTERPRISES
Suite 304, Grand Buildings,
Trafalgar-square, London, W.C.2
Whitehall 0467, 0638

TED KAVANAGH ASSOCIATED LTD.
8 Waterloo-place, London, S.W.1
Whitehall 3036

RAZELLE LAPIN
26 Bassett-road, Kensington,
London, W.10
Ladbroke 2060

ROBERT LAYTON AGENCY
1 Long Acre, London, W.C.2
Temple Bar 9992

JOAN LING LTD.
19 Charing Cross-road, London,
W.C.2
Whitehall 7164

LINNIT & DUNFEE (REPRESENTATION) LTD.
28 Brook-street, London, W.1
Mayfair 0111, 6661

LONDON PLAY CO.
161 New Bond-street, London, W.1
Regent 3782

HARRY LOWE'S AGENCY
Suite 26, Gloucester-mansions,
London, W.C.2
Temple Bar 0376

PATRICK McCROSSAN
20 Sloane-street, London, S.W.1
Sloane 9884-5

AL PARKER LTD.
50 Mount-street, Park-lane,
London, W.1
Grosvenor 4232-3-4-5

ARCHIE PARNELL & CO. LTD.
3 Golden-square, London, W.1
Gerrard 2716-7-8

PEARN, POLLINGER & HIGHAM
39-40 Bedford-street, London, W.C.1

A. D. PETERS
10 Buckingham-street, London, W.C.2
Temple Bar 3792

PRODUCERS' & MANAGERS' AGENCY LTD.
52 Haymarket, London, S.W.1
Whitehall 5961

REEVES & LAMPORT
175 Piccadilly, London, W.1
Regent 2171, 2173

MARION ROSS
40a Greek-street, London, W.1
Gerrard 6182

H. SAXON-SNELL (DIRECTION) LTD.
Panton House, 25 Haymarket, London, S.W.1
Abbey 4413

MYRON SELZNICK (LONDON) LTD.
Byron House, 7-9 St. James's-street, London, S.W.1
Whitehall 9654

CHARLOTTE SHERIDAN LTD.
45 Gerrard-street, London, W.1
Gerrard 2576

AUDREY THACKER
42-3 Cranbourn-street, London, W.C.2
Gerrard 4110

CHARLES L. TUCKER'S ENTERPRISES LTD.
17 Shaftesbury-avenue, London, W.1
Gerrard 6345-6-7-8-9

MARGERY VOSPER LTD.
32 Shaftesbury-avenue, London, W.1
Gerrard 5106-7-8

LIONEL WALLACE AGENCY
Suite 2, 26 Charing Cross-road, London, W.C.2
Temple Bar 2766

A. P. WATT & SON
Hastings House, Norfolk-street, London, W.C.2
Temple Bar 2225

BILL WATTS AGENCY
Piccadilly House, London, S.W.1
Regent 4206, 4150

BETTY WHITE LTD.
33 St. George's-street, Hanover-square, London, W.1
Mayfair 5989

BOX-OFFICE STARS IN BRITAIN

Each year the *Motion Picture Herald* (an American film trade magazine) organizes a poll in which all British exhibitors nominate in order of precedence the ten British stars, and the ten international stars (British included), who have brought most money to their cinemas.

Results for the past three years have been as follows :

British Stars

	1947	1946	1945
1.	James Mason	James Mason	James Mason
2.	Anna Neagle	Margaret Lockwood	Stewart Granger
3.	Margaret Lockwood	Stewart Granger	Margaret Lockwood
4.	John Mills	Michael Redgrave	John Mills
5.	Stewart Granger	Anna Neagle	Phyllis Calvert
6.	Patricia Roc	Phyllis Calvert	Rex Harrison
7.	Michael Wilding	Rex Harrison	Laurence Olivier
8.	Deborah Kerr	John Mills	Anna Neagle
9.	Robert Newton	Robert Donat	George Formby
10.	Trevor Howard	Eric Portman	Eric Portman

International Stars

	1947	1946	1945
1.	Bing Crosby	James Mason	Bing Crosby
2.	James Mason	Bing Crosby	Bette Davis
3.	Anna Neagle	Margaret Lockwood	Greer Garson
4.	Margaret Lockwood	Greer Garson	Humphrey Bogart
5.	Bette Davis	Bette Davis	Bob Hope
6.	John Mills	Stewart Granger	Betty Grable
7.	Alan Ladd	Ingrid Bergman	{ Spencer Tracy { James Mason
8.	Humphrey Bogart	Alan Ladd	Abbott and Costello
9.	Ingrid Bergman	Bob Hope	Stewart Granger
10.	Bob Hope	Van Johnson	Joan Fontaine

ACADEMY AWARDS

STARS, DIRECTORS AND FILMS, 1927-46

THE Academy of Motion Picture Arts and Sciences was founded on May 11, 1927, and consisted then of two hundred and forty members. Today there are more than 12,000 members in all parts of the world. This association is made up of men and women intimately concerned with the production of films, and includes actors, actresses, directors, writers and technicians.

Their annual Awards, or " Oscars " as they are commonly called, are the result of members' votes for outstanding achievements of the year, not only in acting but in direction, writing, production, art and other branches of film-making. When an outstanding performance, production or technical achievement does not come within a recognized category, a " Special Award " is made. The Award takes the form of a gold statuette, usually presented at a large banquet in Hollywood.

If the winners are unable to be present — for example British stars who may not be at liberty to make the journey to Hollywood — presentation is made by deputy, after the official announcement. Thus, Laurence Olivier received his Award for *Henry V* from Ray Milland, who brought it to Britain and presented it to Olivier at Denham during the filming of *Hamlet* in June 1947.

It was Bette Davis who gave the Award its popular name of " Oscar," when she won it for the first time by her performance in *Dangerous* in 1935. She was then married to band leader Harmon Oscar Nelson, and jokingly nicknamed her statuette " Oscar " after her husband's second name—and " Oscar " the Award has remained ever since.

1945-6

ACTOR :
Fredric March in
The Best Years of Our Lives
ACTRESS :
Olivia de Havilland in
To Each His Own
DIRECTOR :
William Wyler for
The Best Years of Our Lives
BEST FILM :
The Best Years of Our Lives
(Goldwyn-RKO)

1944-5

ACTOR :
Ray Milland in
The Lost Weekend
ACTRESS :
Joan Crawford in
Mildred Pierce
DIRECTOR :
Billy Wilder for
The Lost Weekend
BEST FILM :
The Lost Weekend
(Paramount)

1943-4

ACTOR :
Bing Crosby in
Going My Way
ACTRESS :
Ingrid Bergman in
Gaslight
DIRECTOR :
Leo McCarey for
Going My Way
BEST FILM :
Going My Way
(Paramount)

1942-3

ACTOR :
Paul Lukas in
Watch on the Rhine
ACTRESS :
Jennifer Jones in
The Song of Bernadette
DIRECTOR :
Michael Curtiz for
Casablanca
BEST FILM :
Casablanca
(Warner Bros.)

1941-2

ACTOR :
James Cagney in
Yankee Doodle Dandy
ACTRESS :
Greer Garson in
Mrs. Miniver
DIRECTOR :
William Wyler for
Mrs. Miniver
BEST FILM :
Mrs. Miniver
(Metro-Goldwyn-Mayer)

1940-1

ACTOR :
Gary Cooper in
Sergeant York
ACTRESS :
Joan Fontaine in
Suspicion
DIRECTOR :
John Ford for
How Green Was My Valley
BEST FILM :
How Green Was My Valley
(20th-Century Fox)

1939-40

ACTOR :
James Stewart in
The Philadelphia Story
ACTRESS :
Ginger Rogers in
Kitty Foyle
DIRECTOR :
John Ford for
The Grapes of Wrath
BEST FILM :
Rebecca
(Selznick-UA)

1938-9

ACTOR :
Robert Donat in
Goodbye, Mr. Chips !
ACTRESS :
Vivien Leigh in
Gone with the Wind
DIRECTOR :
Victor Fleming for
Gone with the Wind
BEST FILM :
Gone with the Wind
(Selznick-MGM)

INGRID BERGMAN
(*Selznick*)

1937-8

ACTOR :
Spencer Tracy in
Boys Town
ACTRESS :
Bette Davis in
Jezebel
DIRECTOR :
Frank Capra for
You Can't Take It with You
BEST FILM :
You Can't Take It with You
(Columbia)

1936-7

ACTOR :
Spencer Tracy in
Captains Courageous
ACTRESS :
Luise Rainer in
The Good Earth
DIRECTOR :
Leo McCarey for
The Awful Truth
BEST FILM :
The Life of Emil Zola
(Warner Bros.)

1935-6

ACTOR :
Paul Muni in
The Story of Louis Pasteur
ACTRESS :
Luise Rainer in
The Great Ziegfeld
DIRECTOR :
Frank Capra for
Mr. Deeds Goes to Town
BEST FILM :
The Great Ziegfeld
(Metro-Goldwyn-Mayer)

1934-5

ACTOR :
Victor McLaglen in
The Informer
ACTRESS :
Bette Davis in
Dangerous
DIRECTOR :
John Ford for
The Informer
BEST FILM :
Mutiny on the Bounty
(Metro-Goldwyn-Mayer)

1933-4

ACTOR :
Clark Gable in
It Happened One Night
ACTRESS :
Claudette Colbert in
It Happened One Night
DIRECTOR :
Frank Capra for
It Happened One Night
BEST FILM :
It Happened One Night
(Columbia)

1932-3

ACTOR :
Charles Laughton in
The Private Life of Henry VIII
ACTRESS :
Katharine Hepburn in
Morning Glory
DIRECTOR :
Frank Lloyd for
Cavalcade
BEST FILM :
Cavalcade
(Fox)

1931-2

ACTOR :
Fredric March in
Dr. Jekyll and Mr. Hyde
ACTRESS :
Helen Hayes in
The Sin of Madelon Claudet
DIRECTOR :
Frank Borzage for
Bad Girl
BEST FILM :
Grand Hotel
(Metro-Goldwyn-Mayer)

1930-1

ACTOR :
Lionel Barrymore in
A Free Soul
ACTRESS :
Marie Dressler in
Min and Bill
DIRECTOR :
Norman Taurog for
Skippy
BEST FILM :
Cimarron
(Radio)

1929-30

ACTOR :
George Arliss in
Disraeli
ACTRESS :
Norma Shearer in
The Divorcee
DIRECTOR :
Lewis Milestone for
All Quiet on the Western Front
BEST FILM :
All Quiet on the Western Front
(Universal)

1928-9

ACTOR :
Warner Baxter in
In Old Arizona
ACTRESS :
Mary Pickford in
Coquette
DIRECTOR :
Frank Lloyd for
Weary River, Divine Lady, Drag
BEST FILM :
The Broadway Melody
(Metro-Goldwyn-Mayer)

1927-8

ACTOR :
Emil Jannings in
Way of All Flesh, Last Command
ACTRESS :
Janet Gaynor in
*Seventh Heaven, Street Angel,
Sunrise*
DIRECTOR :
Frank Borzage for
Seventh Heaven
Lewis Milestone for
Two Arabian Knights
BEST FILMS :
Wings (Paramount)
Sunrise (Fox)

Among other recipients of Awards have been :
Richard Schweizer, for *Marie Louise* (Swiss) as the best original screenplay of 1944-5 ;
George Bernard Shaw, for *Pygmalion* as the best screenplay of 1937-8 ;
Warner Brothers, for marking an epoch in film history, 1927-8, with *The Jazz Singer*.

THE NATIONAL FILM AWARD BALLOT

THE National Film Award Ballot, organized by the *Daily Mail*, was first held on December 24, 1945. Filmgoers were asked to name their choice for the best film, and the best actor and actress, among all British films generally released between September 3, 1939 and September 3, 1945. The result of this first ballot was declared in 1946, the fiftieth year of the British film industry's existence.

A young Southport schoolteacher, Juliet Brothers, designed the Award—the figure of a woman holding a star high above her head—and the solid silver statuette was executed by the sculptor Rebel Stanton.

Since then the Awards are being made annually for the best film and the best actor and actress appearing in films generally released in the previous year.

Over two million votes were cast in the 1947 poll—excluding more than a quarter of a million ballot papers rejected as invalid in a scrutiny which was as strict as at a Parliamentary election. Ballot papers were accepted at two thousand cinemas and also by post, and a specially-made film trailer was shown explaining how to vote.

1947 AWARD

(covering films September 1945-6)

Best film : *Piccadilly Incident*
(producer and director—Herbert Wilcox ; story—" Florence Tranter " [Anna Neagle])

Actor	Actress
James Mason	Margaret Lockwood
Runners-up	*Runners-up*
Michael Wilding	Anna Neagle
Stewart Granger	Ann Todd
Rex Harrison	Phyllis Calvert
Michael Redgrave	Celia Johnson
Eric Portman	Patricia Roc

1946 AWARD

(covering films September 1939-45)

Best film : *The Way to the Stars*
(producer—Anatole de Grunwald ; director—Anthony Asquith ; story—Anatole de Grunwald and Terence Rattigan)

Actor	Actress
James Mason	Margaret Lockwood
Runners-up	*Runners-up*
John Mills	Phyllis Calvert
Stewart Granger	Patricia Roc
Laurence Olivier	Rosamund John
Robert Donat	Ann Todd
Rex Harrison	Celia Johnson

THE BRITISH FILM ACADEMY

THE British Film Academy is a non-profit-making organization which was founded in 1946 by the film-makers of Great Britain to further the art and technique of the film. Its aim is to stimulate exceptional creative work and to encourage experiment and research in all branches of the industry.

It came into being as the result of a conference of distinguished British film-makers held in the autumn of 1946, when a committee was set up to prepare the Academy's constitution and policy. The chairman of this committee was David Lean ; the remaining members were the Hon. Anthony Asquith, Michael Balcon, Sidney Cole, Thorold Dickinson, Sir Alexander Korda, Frank Launder, Ronald Neame and Harry Watt. Dr. Roger Manvell took office as the first Secretary-General of the Academy in October 1947, when the first official general meeting was attended by nearly a hundred film-makers.

The Academy encourages and assists in the compilation of world film information and statistics. It is building up a library of British film records, books, scripts, designs, musical scores, photographs and other important material; and when this collection has become sufficiently large, it is proposed to promote or advise on the publication of books on the film, exhibitions of British film designs and photography, and concerts of British film music.

In the realm of public relations the Academy is capable of representing the views of the creative film-makers of Britain. It is ready to co-operate with all bodies, both at home and abroad, concerned with the artistic and technical advancement of the film, and with educational organizations for the better appreciation and understanding of the cinema. It supports the study of the film at universities, and encourages research and experimental work—which at a later stage it may itself promote. It intends to make awards of merit for artistic, technical and scientific achievements, and is prepared to assist in the organization of film festivals at home and abroad.

For its members the Academy arranges lectures, debates and private showings of films, and acts as a centre where British film-makers can meet informally to discuss the development of their art among themselves and with distinguished colleagues from abroad.

The affairs of the Academy are supervised by a Council elected from among the members. Membership itself is divided into two categories. Honorary membership is normally reserved for distinguished film veterans, production executives and notable overseas film-makers ; general membership is open to film-makers working on production in British studios or those engaged on professional research in connection with the film.

ESMOND KNIGHT
(Archers)

STARS AND THEIR PUBLIC

H

HAROLD LLOYD
(*Howard Hughes*)

The BERNSTEIN QUESTIONNAIRE

INTRODUCED in 1927 by Sidney L. Bernstein, founder of the Granada group of cinemas in Britain, this questionnaire has two principal objects. They are, to obtain a cross-section of the likes and dislikes of filmgoers in order that they may be provided with the entertainment they most enjoy, and to act as a guide for British and foreign film producers and those engaged in social services.

Five questionnaires were issued between 1927 and 1937. The issue planned for 1940 was cancelled owing to wartime conditions, and it was not until 1946 that it was found possible to issue questionnaire No. 6 to filmgoers attending the Granada cinemas.

Forms were distributed between December 2 and December 31, 1946, and from January 1 to March 31, 1947 the results were analysed to provide the 1946-47 report, which is considered the best gauge of public opinion in Great Britain on stars and films.

The rise in popularity of British films was the most revealing item in the report. The questionnaire asked specifically whether British or American films had improved or deteriorated since 1939. No fewer than ninety-six per cent of the voters declared that British films had improved, against only twenty-six per cent who considered that American films had improved.

Filmgoers were also asked to express an opinion on thirty-six selected films generally released since June 1945. As a result of the votes cast, British films took the three top places as well as the fifth and sixth. *The Way to the Stars* was placed first, seventy-three per cent of the public voting it outstanding, with *The Seventh Veil* and *The Captive Heart* as runners-up with sixty-nine per cent and fifty-six per cent respectively. *The Wicked Lady* and *The Rake's Progress* finished fifth and sixth.

The questionnaire also revealed that James Mason and Margaret Lockwood were the most popular of all film stars; while British-born Alfred Hitchcock was voted the best director. This is the first time since the questionnaire was instituted that stars of British films triumphed over their Hollywood rivals, and the first occasion that a British director finished at the top of the poll.

British male stars took six of the first fifteen places, James Mason alone receiving more than a quarter of all the votes cast, with Stewart Granger second. British-born Ray Milland appeared in third place as the most popular Hollywood star, with Alan Ladd and Bing Crosby as runners-up. In 1937 when the previous questionnaire was issued, the first three places were taken by Gary Cooper, Clark Gable and Charles Laughton.

Similarly, British women stars who have made their names in British films took six of the first fifteen places in the women's list, with two more

British stars who won fame in American films also figuring. Close behind Margaret Lockwood came Ingrid Bergman and Bette Davis. In 1937 the first three places were taken by Norma Shearer, Myrna Loy and Greta Garbo.

Not surprisingly, the voting on stars reveals great changes since the previous Bernstein questionnaire in 1937. Only seven of the first thirty male stars in the 1947 questionnaire results figured in the first thirty in 1937; and only seven of the women stars survive to win places among the first thirty this year. The voting was as follows:

Male

1946-47		1937
James Mason	1	Gary Cooper
Stewart Granger	2	Clark Gable
Ray Milland	3	Charles Laughton
Alan Ladd	4	Robert Taylor
Bing Crosby	5	Ronald Colman
John Mills	6	William Powell
Laurence Olivier	7	Franchot Tone
Humphrey Bogart	8	George Arliss
Spencer Tracy	9	Fredric March
Gary Cooper	10	Robert Donat
Michael Redgrave	11	Leslie Howard
Van Johnson	12	Fred Astaire
Gregory Peck	13	Spencer Tracy
Rex Harrison	14	Herbert Marshall
Cornel Wilde	15	Robert Montgomery
Roy Rogers	16	Wallace Beery
David Niven	17	James Cagney
Tyrone Power	18	Conrad Veidt
Errol Flynn	19	Robert Young
Walter Pidgeon	20	Warner Baxter
Eric Portman	21	Fred MacMurray
Dana Andrews	22	George Raft
John Wayne	23	Victor McLaglen
Paul Henreid	24	Jack Hulbert
Michael Wilding	25	Errol Flynn
Edward G. Robinson	26	John Boles
Robert Donat	27	Bing Crosby
Cary Grant	28	Jack Buchanan
Ronald Colman	29	Will Hay
Dennis Morgan	30	Edward G. Robinson

Comparison with previous questionnaires

	1934	1932	1928
1	George Arliss	Ronald Colman	Ronald Colman
2	Clark Gable	Clive Brook	Richard Dix
3	Wallace Beery	George Arliss	Douglas Fairbanks, Sr.
4	Clive Brook	Robert Montgomery	Adolphe Menjou
5	Robert Montgomery	Maurice Chevalier	Syd Chaplin
6	Ronald Colman	John Boles	Charles Chaplin

Female

1946-47		1937
Margaret Lockwood	1	Norma Shearer
Ingrid Bergman	2	Myrna Loy
Bette Davis	3	Greta Garbo

Phyllis Calvert	4	Ginger Rogers	
Greer Garson	5	Claudette Colbert	
Patricia Roc	6	Shirley Temple	
Vivien Leigh	7	Jessie Matthews	
Jeanne Crain	8	Kay Francis	
Joan Fontaine	9	Merle Oberon	
Dorothy McGuire	10	Loretta Young	
Anna Neagle	11	Jean Arthur	
Barbara Stanwyck	12	Marlene Dietrich	
Betty Grable	13	Gracie Fields	
Ann Todd	14	Elisabeth Bergner	
Claudette Colbert	15	Barbara Stanwyck	
Ida Lupino	16	Madeleine Carroll	
Deanna Durbin	17	Joan Crawford	
Rita Hayworth	18	Ann Harding	
Rosalind Russell	19	Jeanette MacDonald	
Gene Tierney	20	Jean Harlow	
Esther Williams	21	Carole Lombard	
Olivia de Havilland	22	Grace Moore	
Lana Turner	23	Katharine Hepburn	
Jean Kent	24	Sylvia Sidney	
Joan Leslie	25	Irene Dunne	
Loretta Young	26	Miriam Hopkins	
Ginger Rogers	27	Rosalind Russell	
Maureen O'Hara	28	Anna Neagle	
Betty Hutton	29	Janet Gaynor	
Sonja Henie	30	Bette Davis	

Comparison with previous questionnaires

	1934	1932	1928
1	Norma Shearer	Norma Shearer	Dolores del Rio
2	Marie Dressler	Constance Bennett	Betty Balfour
3	Greta Garbo	Marie Dressler	Clara Bow
4	Kay Francis	Ruth Chatterton	Esther Ralston
5	Marlene Dietrich	Janet Gaynor	Vilma Banky
6	Katharine Hepburn	Greta Garbo	Florence Vidor

Asked "Which small-part players would you like to see in star roles?" the public named six British stars in the first ten. The order of voting was:

1	Jean Kent	6	Roland Culver
2	Patricia Roc	7	Joan Davis
3	Glynis Johns	8	Dennis Price
4	Eve Arden	9	Jeanne Crain
5	Jean Simmons	10	Don DeFore

Comparison with previous questionnaire
1937

Male		Female
Arthur Treacher	1	Una Merkel
Eric Blore	2	Patsy Kelly
James Stewart	3	Helen Broderick
Ian Hunter	4	Isabel Jewell
Joseph Calleia	5	Glenda Farrell
Herbert Mundin	6	Betty Furness

Drama was the most popular type of feature film, followed by adventure, crime and films featuring classical music, while horror and cowboy films were considerably disliked. Swing music films attracted only thirty-one per cent support compared with forty-five per cent won by films with classical music—a striking change as against 1937, when light musical films were placed second in order of preference.

In the "shorts" category the results were particularly interesting. Cartoons topped the list, in this order:

1	Cartoons	5	Musicals
2	News Magazines	6	Animal Life
3	Travel	7	Science
4	Sport	8	Social Developments

While films dealing with social developments were "liked very much" by eighteen per cent of the voters, thirty-seven per cent "disliked" this type of film. By contrast, the voting showed that fifty per cent of the audiences put cartoons as their favourite short films, and only ten per cent disliked them.

To the question "What in your opinion are the good and bad points of films?" the results were as follows:

British Films

	Persons replying "Good" Per cent	Persons replying "Bad" Per cent
Acting (stars)	96	4
Choice of story	88	12
Way story is told	81	19
Dialogue	79	21
Acting (small parts)	72	28
Technical side	67	33

American Films

	Per cent	Per cent
Technical side	93	7
Acting (stars)	89	11
Acting (small parts)	77	23
Way story is told	60	40
Choice of story	57	43
Dialogue	56	44

So that the results should be comparable, they were expressed as percentages of the persons replying to each section of the question.

Not only did British directors and producers take nine of the first twelve places—an unprecedented occurrence—but such a well-known director as Frank Capra, who topped the list in 1937, returned to sixteenth, probably because of his absence from Hollywood on war duties. Leo McCarey was voted the most popular American director, achieving third place, doubtless on the strength of *Going My Way* and *The Bells of St. Mary's*. Twenty per cent of the voters who named a director at all, chose Hitchcock.

The voting was as follows:

1946-7		1937
Alfred Hitchcock	1	Frank Capra
Herbert Wilcox	2	Alexander Korda
Leo McCarey	3	W. S. Van Dyke
Anthony Asquith	4	Alfred Hitchcock
Sir Alexander Korda	5	Frank Lloyd
David Lean	6	Cecil B. De Mille
Noel Coward	7	Tom Walls
Gabriel Pascal	8	Ernst Lubitsch
Orson Welles	9	Herbert Wilcox
Frank Capra	10	Mervyn LeRoy
Michael Powell	11	Henry Hathaway
Compton Bennett	12	Victor Saville

Wilcox's rise to second place was due to the popularity of *I Live in Grosvenor Square* and *Piccadilly Incident*. It is also notable that Ernst Lubitsch (eighth in the previous questionnaire) does not appear in the first twenty places.

In drawing up the questionnaire, special effort was made to determine the length and starting time of programme which would be most convenient to the public. The greatest demand was for a three-hour programme (sixty-eight per cent), but opinion differed as to whether the last programme should start at 7, 7.15 or 7.30 p.m.—these three times receiving sixty-eight per cent of the votes between them. About four-fifths of cinemagoers voted for double feature programmes, and the results also indicated that those who prefer a short film outnumber those who want an organ solo by approximately fifty per cent.

The questionnaire showed that ninety-three per cent of the people replying visit the cinema once a week or oftener, while a quarter of the replies came from people who go at least three times a week. The voting was as follows :

	Per cent
More than twice a week	24
Twice a week	40
Once a week	29
Once a fortnight	5
Once a month	2

This question was not asked in previous questionnaires : " If you go to the cinema once a month or more often, which of the following statements best describes your normal cinema-going habits ? "

	Result of voting Per cent
(a) I always go to a particular cinema whatever the film	15
(b) I always go to a particular cinema, but only when I think I will like the film	21
(c) I go to cinemas regularly, choosing the one with the best film	49
(d) I only go to cinemas when there is a film I particularly want to see ...	21

Note : The figures add up to more than 100 per cent because some people ticked more than one alternative. Persons not replying numbered less than one per cent.

Comment : There was apparently a hard core of regular cinemagoers whatever the programme offered, while at the other end of the scale was a floating population only brought to the cinema by films exercising a special appeal. This floating population numbered one in five of those persons filling in the questionnaire.

The critical faculties of filmgoers were tested by the question " What is your opinion of the following films ? " Voters were given the names of thirty-six films and asked to mark them " Outstanding ", " Good ", " Fair " or " Bad ". The list was not composed of the thirty-six most likely to be thought outstanding, hence it omitted some foregone favourites and included other productions of a more unpredictable character. Though placed for purposes of comparison in order of rank below, it must be emphasized that the list is not intended to be a list of the thirty-six best films since the war.

		Out-standing Per cent	Good Per cent	Fair Per cent	Bad Per cent
1	The Way to the Stars *	73	23	4	0
2	The Seventh Veil *	69	26	4	1
3	The Captive Heart *	56	35	8	1
4	The Lost Weekend	55	31	11	3
5	The Wicked Lady *	51	36	10	3
6	The Rake's Progress *	47	41	10	2
	The True Glory	47	40	11	2
8	Spellbound	46	41	11	2
	The Bells of St. Mary's	46	41	11	2
10	Mildred Pierce	45	41	12	2
11	Henry V *	42	25	20	13
12	Valley of Decision	41	45	12	2
13	State Fair	39	43	15	3
14	They Were Sisters *	37	48	13	2
	Brief Encounter *	37	42	17	4
16	The Last Chance	36	41	21	2
17	Leave Her to Heaven	34	44	18	4
18	The Spiral Staircase	33	49	15	3
	Mr. Skeffington	33	45	18	4
	The Picture of Dorian Gray	33	41	20	6
21	I Live in Grosvenor Square *	30	51	17	2
	A Tree Grows in Brooklyn	30	48	19	3
	Wonder Man	30	40	22	8
24	Caravan *	29	49	18	4
25	London Town *	28	41	23	8
26	Perfect Strangers *	27	53	18	2
27	The House on 92nd Street	24	48	23	5
	Dead of Night *	24	47	24	5
29	The Blue Dahlia	23	53	21	3
30	Bedelia *	21	52	24	3
31	Caesar and Cleopatra*	20	38	30	12
32	Saratoga Trunk	19	47	27	7
33	The Road to Utopia	16	51	28	5
34	The Dolly Sisters	15	41	33	11
35	Tonight and Every Night	14	49	32	5
36	The Three Caballeros	12	30	40	18

*—British film. *The True Glory* was an Anglo-American production. *The Last Chance* was made in Switzerland. *The Three Caballeros* was Disney's first combined cartoon and live action film.

James Mason

FILM FANS

*James Mason believes that film fans should
organize into guilds setting a high standard
of good manners. He deplores the behaviour
of some film fans who take part in public
demonstrations of fan worship.*

*We asked James Mason to comment and to
answer several questions on the subject. He believes
that he should not be, as he so often is, quoted out of
context. In expressing the views below, therefore,
he asks us to make it plain that the text belongs
exclusively to Winchester's Screen Encyclopedia,
and may not be reproduced in whole or in part without written permission.*

IT seems to me that fans are splendid so
long as their behaviour is conditioned by
an appreciation of good manners. The very
acts that one takes exception to—that is, the
tearing of clothing, the jumping, the pushing, the
screaming—are all examples of bad manners.
Indeed, I would go so far as to say that the very
habit of autograph-collecting is also strictly a
matter of bad manners. In other words, it is an
example of importunate begging, begging for
something which to young hunters has actually a
market value. And surely begging is only justifiable among the very needy. Club presidents
should explain to their members that, except in
rare instances of highly ambitious young stars,
constant autograph-hunting starts as a nuisance and
becomes in time a persecution which affects the
star's entire life.

An actor like any other type of artist wishes to
lead a normal life. He likes to watch what goes
on around him. He likes to go to a football
match, a dance hall, or a restaurant, and enjoy
the usual privilege of staring around him which
contributes to his enjoyment of these scenes. If
he finds that he can no longer look around without
embarrassment, if he finds that he is always
looking into a row of gaping faces, and if every
movement is accompanied by a constant request
for autographs, he becomes a hunted person. He
has to go into hiding and lead an artificial life
which in time affects both his good humour and
his acting ability.

Unfortunately, the habit of autograph hunting
is encouraged by the old-fashioned producers and
executives of the Hollywood studios. I have
heard them say that they think it is part of the
star's function to be co-operative in the matter of
giving autographs. They do not seem to realize
that the genuine cinemagoers are not autograph
hunters, and they are not the kind of pests who
mob stars in the streets of London and New York.
The fact that the star is mobbed on his or her
arrival in New York or London is no indication
of popularity. Some stars that I could name
have always made a habit of encouraging their
fans by writing " cosy " letters on their fans'
birthdays, and organizing fan receptions wherever
they go. But this habit has never affected the
postponement of a star's decline.

*Question—How does fan worship in the United
States compare with it in Britain?*

The perceptible difference is this, that in London
fan worship is only noticeable on the occasion of
a premiere or some big to-do, like the *Daily
Mail* National Film Award dinner. These
occasions are the scene of a mass exhibitionism
on the part of the fans. But in England the fans
do not habitually bother stars in the streets,
unless they are visitors from other countries.
In the United States, on the other hand, the fans
seem to have a little more courage, or shall we
say, aggressive tendencies when they are on their
own.

Children in America have a greater feeling of
self-importance than they have in England. It is
true that in New York at one time, if not now,
band leaders and other members of the entertainment profession hired posses of teen-agers to
create demonstrations. This resulted in publicity
both for the band leaders and for the teen-agers
themselves. And publicity, unfortunately, is
habit-forming. Once their exploits had been
written up in the press, the teen-agers became as
it were, intoxicated by their own squealing.

*Question—Have you any practical suggestions for
fan club activities? What does your own
group of fan clubs do in this direction?*

I have made a habit or sending photographs to
fans only upon receipt of a subscription to one of
the animal charities. It is obviously a good thing
if the fan clubs themselves can make themselves
useful in a similar way, that is, organize entertainment, whist drives, and so on, so as to collect
money for a specific charity, preferably on a
permanent basis. A good example of this is the
children's ward in a London hospital equipped
by members of the Valentino Association some
years ago.

Question—Do you think that fan clubs serve any constructive purpose in the career of a star?

In a small way they obviously advertise the star and his activities, but in designing his career and choosing his parts, a star would be well advised not to set too much store by the comments of his fans. For the best results he should be guided by his own tastes and instinct, and if he feels that he needs any guidance, that of the professional critics is the most valuable. It is in an effort to do what his fans expect of him that a Hollywood star very often makes the mistake of playing the same parts over and over again.

Question—Do you believe that there should be a close association or personal contact between the stars and their fans—or do you believe that distance lends enchantment?

Oh, very definitely distance lends enchantment.

An actor on both stage and screen strives above all to achieve an illusion. He wishes his audience to identify him with the character that he is portraying. He does not want them to look upon him as a close friend who is just doing a piece of play-acting. His relations and closest friends are rarely fooled ; but if he keeps himself sufficiently remote, the main part of the audience is pleasantly deceived. He should never make the mistake of reducing himself to the status of the boy next door.

The great and glamorous stage actors of the old days wisely kept away from close contact with their public, and, luckily for them, fan magazines were not then in existence. Nowadays, stars are associated more closely with their highly publicized home-life, their exploits in the kitchen or on the tennis court, than with their characterizations on screen or stage.

FANS AS THE STUDIOS SEE THEM

TO the film makers, fans fall roughly into two categories—those who pay to see their idols on the screen, and those afflicted with mass hysteria and gross bad manners, who stay away from the cinemas to mob the stars and annoy the rest of the public.

The paying fans may be hero-worshippers too, but they are sane and sincere. Many of them band themselves together in fan clubs—mostly well-organized bodies which hold social events (if possible with their stars as occasional guests) and run their own magazines. Such genuine fans are of great assistance to the studios, which have special departments to cope with the enormous fan-mail received. All letters are carefully read, as many contain suggestions which indicate the public's changing opinions and preferences. Periodically, digests of correspondence are made for the guidance of production executives in such matters as story selection, casting, teaming and dressing. Fan clubs help the studios by canalizing much of the routine work involved in dealing with requests for autographs and signed photographs.

Some stars raise considerable sums of money for pet charities by inviting grateful autograph hunters to send contributions. For instance, the Red Cross Prisoners of War Fund benefited by Robert Donat's aid. Many fan clubs interest themselves in the endowment of hospital beds. Now and again clubs spring up with the main object of imposing on the good nature and generosity of the stars and getting something for nothing ; but happily these soon die away through their own cupidity.

But what of the other class of fans, whose admiration runs into hysteria ? There are the bicycle squads who trail the stars and pounce upon them at their destination, and others who apparently have no work to do and who wait all day and far into the night to plead for autographs of stars whose films they probably never go to see. These people have been responsible for such disgraceful scenes as took place at the Empire Theatre, Leicester-square, London, in 1947, when mobbing was so violent that Barbara Stanwyck collapsed through exhaustion and Robert Taylor received a black eye. Few stars, indeed, have not suffered from the abandoned attentions of these " admirers".

Film executives escorting Hollywood stars from Southampton dread the arrival at Waterloo, that other battlefield of a modern age. When Sylvia Sidney visited Britain some years ago, studio escorts, police and railway officials were powerless to prevent her from being pushed down between the rails and the platform. In the newspapers next day there were pictures not of a smiling hand-waving star, but of a woman whose eyes were filled with fear.

It is no secret that the authorities dread " personal appearances " of the stars, for extra police, ambulances and first-aid officials are often necessary. Fans are apt to forget that their very voraciousness sometimes defeats their own ends. Often a star is smuggled into or out of a theatre by order of the police, not only to ensure the star's own safety but to prevent accidents among the fans themselves.

A. E. Wilson

THE CRITICS' CIRCLE

WRITING without the aid of any available statistics, I hazard the guess that, apart possibly from the United States, there are more professional film critics employed in Great Britain than in any other country in the world.

Nevertheless, no society exclusively devoted to the interests of film critics exists in this country—in spite of the fact that in smaller countries like Belgium and Czechoslovakia film critics are banded together in specially constituted professional bodies for social and self-protective purposes. However, nearly every journalist who gains his living mainly as a film critic belongs to the Critics' Circle which is, I believe, the largest and most important body of its kind in the world, for its membership is composed of film, dramatic, music and broadcasting critics—a formidable weight of critical authority.

Perhaps I should have placed the dramatic and music critics first. It was the critics of the older arts who founded the Critics' Circle before World War I in the early days when the cinema was a novelty rather than an entertainment commanding the interest of a great public. Hardly a line of genuinely critical writing had been devoted to films. No one in those days ever dreamed that a time would come when the " animated pictures," with their crude knockabout humour, custard-pie throwings, helter-skelter chases and discreet bathing beauty parades, and their jerky, " rainy " dramas of train robberies and persecuted heroines in peril, would be taken so seriously that a large body of intelligent men and women would devote themselves to writing essays and analytical articles about them, and when even the most solemn of the weekly reviews would deem it worth while to give space to such matters.

Certainly the possibility of such a state of affairs could never have entered the minds of the grave and august gentlemen who founded the Circle to serve the interests of the dramatic critics. That was a more leisured and spacious time when those engaged in writing the dramatic notices in the daily and weekly press were allowed the privilege of almost unlimited space and enjoyed a prestige, authority and dignity almost unimaginable in these days of restrictions.

The Critics' Circle, which was evolved from the old Society of Dramatic Critics, was founded in May 1913. At this time many of the giants of the profession were still upholding a great tradition in the daily press, and new plays were accorded notices of a column or a column and a half of

A. E. WILSON *is film and drama critic of "The Star", and has written several books on theatrical subjects.*

closely printed type the morning after the production. There were such notables in the field as William Archer, A. B. Walkley, Sir Owen Seaman, Thomas Catling, E. A. Baughan, J. T. Grein, Dr. J. M. Bulloch, Sir Alfred Robbins, Lord Russell of Liverpool, E. F. Spence, K. C., and H. M. Walbrook. They have all passed on, but of the original members of the Critics' Circle there are still several survivors, among them John Parker, editor of " Who's Who in the Theatre," who is the hon. secretary of the Circle ; S. R. Littlewood, the editor of *The Stage*, who in 1947 celebrated his golden jubilee as a dramatic critic ; Philip Carr, who has lived abroad for many years ; and George Aitchison, long a Brighton editor and now living in retirement. These survivors have seen many changes in the practice of criticism and the functions of the Circle—and none more remarkable, I suppose, than the arrival of the film critic and the creation of an entirely new branch of the profession.

The Circle was founded under the presidency of William Archer, notable for his association with *The World*, the short-lived *Tribune*, and his sturdy pioneering support of the Ibsen drama. He was at that time the dramatic critic of *The Star*. The purpose of the body was clearly defined in the rules :

> The objects of the Critics' Circle (says Rule 1) are (a) to promote the art of criticism and to uphold its integrity in practice ; (b) to foster and safeguard the professional interests of its members and to provide opportunities for social intercourse among them.

There was no mention, of course, in the original set of rules of films or of film critics. Clearly the only sort of critic envisaged was one who concerned himself with the theatre or with music. For the first ten years, indeed, the President was always a dramatic critic. Archer was followed in the chair by J. T. Grein, that gallant champion of advanced and often hopeless causes, with E. F. Spence, G. E. Morrison, Sir Owen Seaman (the editor of *Punch*), A. B. Walkley of *The Times*, and S. R. Littlewood as his successors, and it was not until 1924 that a music critic in the person of Herman Klein became President.

By that time something notable had happened —the arrival of a new body of critics who had begun to occupy space in the press with their writings about the cinema. Many periodicals devoted to the subject were already in existence. They included " trade " papers and gossipy " fan " weeklies and monthlies, but for a long time the dailies ignored the progress and the growing popularity of the film, or at least deemed such matters unworthy of attention. Soon after the first world war, however, some enterprising pioneers—among them Alder Anderson, G. A. Atkinson and A. Jympson Harman of The *Evening News*—had persuaded their editors of the importance of this form of entertainment, and critical notices of new films became a regular feature in nearly every newspaper. The film critics considered themselves in no way inferior to or less important than their professional brethren of the theatre and concert hall and inevitably they desired to join the Circle.

It was a revolutionary idea to some of the old hands, who were not too enthusiastic about such an ambition ; and there was, I remember, a certain amount of opposition when proposals for their membership first came before the Circle.

The thin end of the wedge had already been inserted, however, because some of the dramatic critics—among them E. A. Baughan of the *News Chronicle* (then the *Daily News*)—had also interested themselves in the newer form of entertainment and were writing about films as well as the stage. It was therefore illogical to oppose the entry of members of the rapidly growing body. Opposition was defeated, and in 1925 the Film Section was formed, invigorating the life of the Circle with a new spirit. Many members of the section were young, keen and enthusiastic, and they brought with them fresh subjects for discussion and problems for many animated debates.

I ought to point out, by the way, that membership of the Critics' Circle is an honour and a privilege and not a matter of right. The fact that any person writes what may be classed as criticism for any journal is not necessarily a qualification for membership. There is no question of wholesale admission. For critics— and especially film critics—come and go. Some write for a brief space and thereafter are heard of no more. It is necessary for any would-be member first of all to prove a certain stability, to establish proofs of his ability and responsibility. The rule governing admission to the Circle reads :

> Persons who are and who have been professionally employed in writing dramatic, musical, film or broadcasting criticisms and other writers professionally occupied with these and kindred subjects shall be eligible for membership. *No application for membership shall be considered unless the candidate shall have been professionally so employed regularly and substantially for at least two years immediately preceding such application, unless the Executive Committee decides otherwise*

As the rule denotes, it is within the discretion of the Executive Committee to waive the condition of a two-year qualifying period but the discretion is seldom exercised. Though it is desirable that all qualified critics should be members, the Circle has no desire to rope in everyone merely for the sake of impressing by force of numbers. It aims to set a high standard in the practice of criticism and in the integrity and responsibility of its members, and it is careful in checking the candidate's qualifications, which must be vouched for by two members of the Circle.

Theatrical, music, film or broadcasting press agents, for instance, are not eligible for membership. Any member of the Circle who becomes engaged in paid press agency or publicity work has his membership suspended during such engagement and must surrender his Circle credentials.

There will always be some difference of opinion, I suppose, as to what exactly constitutes film criticism. The question often arises when applications come before the Executive Committee and I have frequently taken part in lively debates on the subject. Clearly the writing of film gossip, however informative or however brightly it may be written, is in no sense criticism and I have known many applications for membership turned down on that account. The fact that there is very often a very thin dividing line between gossip and criticism adds to the difficulty of making a decision.

One matter which has often exercised the minds of the Circle in considering applications for membership is that of the qualifications and functions of those who write for the trade press. There are several very able members among them and there can be no question as to the technical knowledge out of which they write or the quality of their writing. But these critics necessarily view films from a different angle from that of their colleagues of the lay press. They are "spotters" whose chief function is to appraise films for the information and benefit of exhibitors. They are not concerned with matters of art but with salesmanship. They are supposed to provide exhibitors with such information as will guide them in choosing the right films to book.

As one of them, a leading expert in his line, declared in a radio discussion, "I am something in the nature of a tipster. I criticize the film from the manager's point of view. If I don't give him the straight tip I shall probably hear about it from my proprietors." There can be no question that as far as the trade is concerned he is performing a very useful and necessary function, but it is doubtful whether such writings can correctly be described as criticism. Yet that is purely a matter of opinion and the point might involve endless discussion touching upon aesthetics, ethics, and the true function of criticism, and is much too complex to discuss here.

To define what one expects in film criticism is to state the obvious—which I do not propose to do. Every reader, I imagine, has his favourite critic who, apart from whatever pleasure his or her writing may afford, may be relied upon to act as a safe guide to the merits or otherwise of the latest films. The reader attaches himself to this or that critic whose tastes and ideals most nearly correspond to his own. The critic's opinion may be expressed in varying forms from an epigram or a snappy wisecrack (not, to my mind, the fairest form of criticism) to a long and erudite examination of the story and its feasibility, truth to life, improbability, absurdity and what-not, its acting, direction, and technical qualities. Some critics do not attempt to conceal their special likes and dislikes. Others, subduing personal. prejudices, seek to judge the film from the point of view of the average filmgoer. You pay your money and you take your choice among a wide variety.

If the Circle had not previously existed it would have been necessary for the film critics to form one of their own, not so much for its social advantages as for the safeguarding of their own interests. Now and again disputes arise which can be settled only by a display of unity on the part of the critical body. There have been occasions when Hollywood film producers, not seeing eye to eye with the critic and disagreeing with his judgement or the form in which it is expressed, have sought to stifle criticism by imposing a ban. Here the Circle has always gone quickly into action asserting the critic's right to express his honest opinion and upholding the freedom of the Press.

As recently as August 1947, the Circle had cause for satisfaction in the result of the action in which one of its members, Miss E. Arnot Robertson, the author and film critic, was awarded £1500 damages against Metro-Goldwyn-Mayer for alleged libel. The company wrote to the B.B.C. Director of Talks complaining that in her criticisms Miss Arnot Robertson was " completely out of touch with the tastes and entertainment requirements " of the public. In his judgment Mr. Justice Hilbery found there was evidence to support the jury's finding of malice. To allege (he said) that a critic went out of her way to do harm to the industry which supported the art which was the subject matter of her criticisms seemed to him to be capable of being understood in a way which was libellous. The words used in the company's letter to the B.B.C. were in that sense capable of bearing a defamatory meaning.

When one surveys the progress of the film and notes the fact that in many newspapers far more space is devoted to the subject than to drama, the question arises whether the offspring may not some day devour the parent or whether in the course of time the film section may not ambitiously strike out on its own and form a separate body. I see no sign of either happening at present—but you never know. Personally I should prefer all critics to remain in one united body.

According to the current list of the Circle there are about 160 members. This includes men and women engaged by the metropolitan Press or serving the provincial Press in London, country members, foreign and oversea members, honorary members and those temporarily suspended because they are engaged in publicity activities. More than half this number are film critics. Fifty are engaged solely in film criticism ; others combine the function with dramatic criticism. About twenty-five of the film critics are women, the roll being headed by Miss C. A. Lejeune and Miss Dilys Powell, monitresses of the serious Sunday Press. Miss Powell has served as Chairman of the Film Section but so far the Presidency has been held only by men.

There is no definite rule about the matter, but the office of President during the past few years has alternated between representatives of drama, music and films. The first film critic to be elected to the Presidency was A. Jympson Harman in 1942, but such other presidents as E. A. Baughan (who, by the way, began as a music critic), James Agate, P. L. Mannock and myself have combined films with the theatre.

The Circle is highly fortunate in its unpaid officials. It would be hard to find anyone to replace its honorary secretary, John Parker, who is a master of method, accuracy and business-like attention to every detail, and has guided the Circle throughout its existence with a devotion and an energy that has earned the admiration of every member and particularly of every president. And in Milton Deane, who joined the Circle in 1935, the Film Section has an ideal honorary secretary of organizing ability upon whom every film member has learned to rely.

THE MAKING OF FILMS

How a Film is Made: John and Roy Boulting
Where Films Are Made
The Motion Picture Production Code
Five Hundred Famous Films and Their Players
Famous Film Series

KIERON MOORE
(*London Film Productions*)

John and Roy Boulting

HOW A FILM IS MADE

YOU have been sitting in the ease and comfort of a darkened cinema for two or three hours, watching the slow unfolding of a drama or comedy on the screen. . . . What is behind it ?

It is doubtful if the general public have any idea of the intricate web of events leading to the final version of the film they see. The early days of construction might be said to resemble a revolving stage prepared to receive a mammoth and versatile cast on their individual cues. Awaiting the call for their vital contributions shadowy figures gather in the wings from the birth of the idea until its screen maturity.

If the audience should feel inclined to peer beyond the finished article most of its questions would begin from the time the production takes the floor, an event which to the director and producer is already halfway to the realization of their mutual aims.

How, when and where does the film begin ? It begins with an idea. A vague sequence of thought may be set in motion by a thread of conversation in a café or a bar, or an incident in a street or a bus. It may grow out of a play, a short story, or a social problem capable of development in dramatic screen terms.

It then becomes necessary to purchase the story, and either write a skeleton film treatment oneself, or pay an established writer to do so.

By now it is time to obtain the approval of another authority, and the desire and reasons one has for making a film on this particular subject are discussed with a financial executive, preferably an executive with both taste and imagination.

Producer and executive will discuss the terms of production, covering distribution charges, organization and the circumstances controlling the eventual release of the film overseas, not only in the United States but in the Commonwealth, France, Holland, Belgium, the Middle East, Scandinavia and Latin America, and wherever there are potential markets. On the O.K. being given to proceed with the actual production, there is the question of the allocation of studio space for the estimated period of production, and the necessity of obtaining equipment for use during the period of shooting on location for exterior scenes. For reasons of economy, careful planning of both equipment and manpower is required.

The next steps are taken concurrently. The research department goes into action to scour the country for the information required to ensure authenticity. There is hard work for this department in any film, but particularly in a period production such as *Fame Is The Spur*, which entailed careful examination of the conditions in the Welsh mining industry in the early 1900's, the Manchester election fights of the last century, and goodness knows how many period details involving a dusty and diligent penetration of museums and libraries. Finally a dossier of information collected in this way is compiled, providing everyone—producer, director, dress designers, actors, cameramen, art director, and so on—with the material needed.

During this time the director is working on the first film treatment, with or without the aid of a screen writer. An elementary adaptation which embodies characters, situations and settings has been roughly devised. This done, the big three, that is, the writer, director and producer, meet for the first major conference of the production. The casting of the characters is discussed, and the second treatment is begun in which the story is developed into the form of scenes.

Casting follows close on the heels of these developments ; and after a while the principals are selected. Contrary to many notions the producer enlists for this purpose the aid of all the known and trusted agents, and if it becomes necessary he and the director together with their assistants visit different sources of supply in London and the provinces, including repertory theatres and schools of dramatic art. When we made *Brighton Rock*, adapted from the Graham Greene novel, this scheme was put into detailed operation, as in an endeavour to find exactly the type we had in mind for " Rose", a part requiring absolute naivety and extreme youth, we were prepared to give any unknown girl a chance to become a star overnight.

Meanwhile the producer struggles with his own problem of selecting the right technical staff—the art director, cameramen and operators who specialize in the various key functions essential to all film-making. Next comes second treatment, and a quiet but all-important man seldom seen in person on the set steps into the limelight that he will not noticeably share again until the credit titles sweep down the screen—the art director. He is rushed into consultation on matters of setting, locations, colour, and so on. In this second version of the film treatment the dialogue is pruned and perfected into its final form, though at this stage there is a scarcity of camera directions.

The third film treatment is only a step away.

JOHN and ROY BOULTING—*twin brothers, producers and directors—are co-directors of Charter Film Productions Ltd., which they founded in 1937.*

This is finally completed in close consultation with the director, to ensure that in passing through these processes the original idea to which the film owes its life is in no way distorted, while camera directions conform to his own concept.

This is the key treatment from which the film is eventually constructed, containing comprehensive directions and tightened dialogue. The story begins to flow in terms of the cinema rather than words, and all its implications are made ready to appear visually.

At this juncture both cameraman and art director step forward to study the treatment for their individual creations—sketches for detailed scenes, shots for special effects.

A department which is set up to deal only with special effects takes over from there to make a study of the various process shots which the script demands—back projections and glass shots, or hanging miniatures and matte shots, split-screen, and so on. These processes call for great skill and specialized work, and make a considerable contribution to the polish and scope of the finished film.

At this point the dress designer moves into the limelight. She produces sketches which she considers suitable for all players requiring special costumes. These are approved by the producer and director, through whom everything is filtered to preserve a unity of conception. At this juncture, also, the music composer steps in. He is encouraged to understand the mood and setting required, so that his music becomes identified with the production.

Sounds which are comforting to the director begin at this stage to swell in harmony with his hopes for the film. The carpenters' saws and the painters' brushes get to work on the settings, and the property department assembles the furnishings. Meanwhile the art director and his team of assistants and draughtsmen are working on the physical requirements of the sets, and all the trade departments are co-ordinated behind him.

Now the director holds out a hand for the third treatment and takes it away to break it down into a shooting script in which there is a detailed account of camera action. Certain directors, such as Hitchcock, have a thumbnail sketch for every change of camera position in the script. We ourselves do not adopt this method because we believe in drawing inspiration from live creation rather than theory.

The producer busies himself meantime in completing the casting and arranging auditions of small parts and extras. In every instance each player—part or status notwithstanding—is selected by the people who conceived the original idea, so that there is no conflict even in details.

Intensive work is now put in by the assistant director and production manager on the breakdown of the script, involving a complete analysis of the physical requirements of the film. A list is made out comprising the following items—sequences, shooting schedules, sets (studio interiors, lots, locations), costumes and properties, unit, and cast and crowd names and addresses.

In the "dope sheet" (that is, property list) of any film, some of the items listed invite consternation. They may include such things as one large rat, a forced-feeding trolley for use in suffragette scenes, horses' blood and a ripe tomato.

The producer now augments the unit personnel, choosing, in consultation with the heads of each department, suitable assistants—that is, two camera assistants, two cutting-room assistants, and so on. Scenes are selected for the purpose of testing certain players to confirm suitability of casting and to determine aspects of lighting, make-up, dress, colour tones, and the like. These tests take approximately a week, and are made on a small stage in the studio where draughtsmen have prepared a small set. A call then goes out for the "stills" man to ensure a ready supply of routine portraits and publicity pictures of featured players.

During this period a steady drive of output is maintained by the publicity department with the object of stimulating public interest in the unborn film. Publicity is an aspect of the film trade which up to the present has been far too much neglected in this country. The news of daily happenings on the set and production developments is circulated via the press, usually through show columnists and in exceptional instances on the news page, when a story has a universally appealing news twist. Biographies of players and technicians connected with the film are circulated, with articles on the fashions or song hits likely to be popularized by the production. The trade and provincial press is kept regularly informed of progress, and supplied with any publicity stills required. Plans for distribution and poster design are frequently under review. The question of circuit release was discussed likewise in earlier stages during the producer's consultation with the financial executives, as any film costing over £40,000 without a guaranteed release in any of the big British circuits is a great speculation.

Now is the great moment in the life of the film when the production takes the floor and shooting begins.

A new figure steps on the stage with this development. He is the film editor, already familiar with the completed shooting script and conversant with its required rhythm, style and dramatic intention. Incidentally, every week of shooting the producer and composer see a rough assembly of the material already shot. Prints of the previous day's shooting known as "rushes" are shown daily in the studio theatre to the entire unit. The rough assembly, a partly edited form of the film, is a process continuing throughout the shooting schedule under the guidance of the producer.

The schedule, based on the breakdown of the script and subject to snags such as the scarcity of materials, players' indispositions, and so on, is constantly in process of modification. The production manager contends with the time factor.

The relation of the production manager to the film is comparable to that of a supply commander in battle subject to the overriding jurisdiction of his generals, in this case the director and producer. He has to co-ordinate the departments (or forces) at his disposal, and deploy them in accordance with his day-to-day requirements. He must reconcile the frequently conflicting demands of various sections, never allowing them to prejudice the economic or artistic standards for the film laid down by his superior generals.

The battle is nearing completion, shooting is nearly over, and now is the time for special exertions of every conceivable type.

The film has possibly shown signs of falling behind schedule—players' contracts are likely to expire ! Conferences are held to find ways of speeding up the proceedings. The director goes to the producer and says " Why haven't I got this— or that—or the other thing which would solve all my problems ? " And if they are not brothers there is a row. If they are, there is a fight !

As an instance of the tribulations to which a production manager is exposed, take the last days of *Fame is The Spur*. Three hundred players were engaged for the South Wales miners' hall sequence, depicting a massed meeting of pit-workers called to declare a strike. The principal actor was suddenly taken ill. As a result the entire method of shooting had to be re-arranged to provide for this emergency ; and some very quick thinking had to be put in on all sides.

The greatest and most persistent enemy of the entire British film industry next rears its frozen face against a gun-metal sky—the English climate. It can play havoc with the time schedule, frequently involving weeks of delay in shooting.

If the location shooting has been done before the studio period, this involves the post-synchronization of dialogue. This is done without delay while the players retain their sense of atmosphere. Sound recording is frequently impossible in the open because the actors' voices may be lost on the wind, and aeroplanes among other noisy interruptions may interfere continuously —and, in Britain, chirruping sparrows cause more hold-ups than almost anything else !

With the shooting completed, advertisement proofs are available for the publicity campaign, which has gathered momentum since filming began, from a fund of incident and anecdote arising from each day's work.

Now the final stage is begun and all the physical aspects of film-making are welded together. Outstanding work is cleared up, special shots are delivered into the hands of the editor, and various departments concerned with production have their accounts finalized.

The editor is now in command of the field, under the vigilant eye of the director. Montages are compiled, optical shots are made by the laboratories, the title cards are drawn, the music is recorded, and then in a glorious jamboree lasting anything from six to ten days the film is finally " dubbed ", the process of dubbing being that of balancing and merging on to the sound track the dialogue tracks, music tracks, the many sound effects tracks, and so on. When the film has been dubbed it is only a question of the laboratories producing a continuous print of both sound and picture.

At this point the director sometimes falters from his strong purpose and visibly wilts. " It's a bad film ", he declares. " I could have done better ". His ego is momentarily shattered, and this is when the film employment figures may rise as he surrounds himself with benevolent yes-men and has his hand held by the untiring publicity department who by now are convinced of the quality of the goods they have been feverishly selling. This is the time when this department is put on its mettle, as there is a lag in the material available for publicizing.

The number of people employed on a major film in production, particularly a period film, runs into many thousands. Including the floor and studio staffs, any number between seven and ten thousand people may be employed at various times. But at last the film is completed.

The film in spool form now passes to the distribution side, and a delivery date to the public is decided upon. A sneak preview is arranged, and for the first time the director views in complete detachment his monumental epic that grew out of a mere idea.

Ultimately the announcement of a date for the premiere goes forth, and we find you either shaking out the mothballs for the occasion or craning your necks to get a view of someone else's tiara. Perhaps it is the next day and you are queueing with silent persistence in the rain, listening to the street buskers.

In any case there comes the time when you are sitting in the ease and comfort of a darkened cinema . . .

But this is where we came in.

WHERE FILMS ARE MADE

A DIRECTORY OF FILM-MAKERS AT HOME AND ABROAD

Great Britain

ALLIANCE FILM STUDIOS LTD.
Riverside Studios, Crisp-road, Hammersmith, London, W.6. (2 *stages.*) *Telephone :* RIVERSIDE 3012.
Twickenham Studios, The Barons, Twickenham, Middx. (1 *stage.*) *Telephone :* POPESGROVE 7740.

ASSOCIATED BRITISH PICTURE CORPORATION LTD.
B.I.P. Studios, Elstree, Herts. (8 *stages, of which* 4 *are under construction,* 1948.) *Telephone:* ELSTREE 1600.
Welwyn Studios, Welwyn, Herts. (3 *stages.*)
Telephone : WELWYN GARDEN 3241.

BRITISH NATIONAL FILMS LTD.
National Studios, Boreham Wood, Elstree, Herts. (3 *stages.*) *Telephone :* ELSTREE 1644.

BUSHEY FILM STUDIOS LTD.
Bushey Studios, Melbourne-road, Bushey, Herts. (1 *stage.*) *Telephone :* BUSHEY 1621.

CROMWELL FILM CORPORATION LTD.
Southall Studios, 2 Gladstone-road, Southall, Middx. (1 *stage.*) *Telephone :* SOUTHALL 3281.

CROWN FILM UNIT
(Central Office of Information)
Beaconsfield Studios, Station-road, Beaconsfield, Bucks. (1 *stage.*) *Telephone :* BEACONSFIELD 555.

D. & P. STUDIOS, LTD.
Denham Studios, Uxbridge, Middx. (7 *stages.*)
Telephone : DENHAM 2345.
Pinewood Studios, Iver, Bucks. (5 *stages.*)
Telephone : IVER 700

EALING STUDIOS, LTD.
Ealing Studios, Ealing-green, London, W.5. (4 *stages.*) *Telephone :* EALING 6761.

GAINSBOROUGH PICTURES (1928) LTD.
Lime Grove Studios, Shepherd's Bush, London, W.12. (5 *stages.*) *Telephone :* SHEPHERD'S BUSH 1210.

Gainsborough Studios, Poole-street, Islington, London, N.1. (2 *stages.*)
Telephone : CLERKENWELL 1271.

G.H.W. PRODUCTIONS LTD.
(Gordon, Hake, Walker)
The Gate Studios, Boreham Wood, Elstree, Herts. (2 *stages.*) *Telephone :* ELSTREE 2273.

HIGHBURY STUDIOS
Production Facilities (Films) Ltd.,
Highbury Studios, London, N.5. (2 *stages.*)
Telephone : CLISSOLD 3003.

LONDON FILM STUDIOS
Worton Hall, Isleworth, Middx. (1 *silent, 3 sound stages.*) *Telephone :* HOUNSLOW 2323.
Littletown Park, Shepperton, Middx. (1 *recording, 4 sound stages.*) *Telephone :* CHERTSEY 2211.

MERTON PARK STUDIOS LTD.
(in association with Film Producers' Guild, Ltd.)
Merton Park Studios, 269 Kingston-road, London, S.W.19. (2 *stages.*) *Telephone :* LIBERTY 4291.

MGM BRITISH STUDIOS LTD.
MGM Studios, Elstree-way, Boreham Wood, Elstree, Herts. (7 *stages.*) *Telephone :* ELSTREE 2000.

NETTLEFOLD STUDIOS
(Executors of late Archibald Nettlefold)
Nettlefold Studios, Walton-on-Thames, Surrey. (2 *stages.*) *Telephone :* WALTON-ON-THAMES 2414.

WARNER BROS.-FIRST NATIONAL PRODUCTIONS LTD.
Teddington Studios, Broom-road, Teddington, Middx. (2 *stages.*) *Telephone :* KINGSTON 2181.

WEMBLEY FILM STUDIOS LTD. (Fox)
Wembley Studios, Empire-way, Wembley, Middx. (2 *stages.*) *Telephone :* WEMBLEY 3000.

United States of America

AMERICAN FILM CENTER INC.
Director : Donald Slesinger
45 Rockfeller-plaza, New York City 20, N.Y.

BELL & HOWELL COMPANY
President : J. H. McNabb
7100 McCormick-road, Chicago 45, Ill.

BENEDICT BOGEAUS PRODUCTIONS INC.
1040 North Las Palmas-avenue, Hollywood 38, Calif.

J. E. BRULATOUR, INC.
(Distributors of Kodak film stock)
John-street, Fort Lee, N.J.
  J. E. BRULATOUR, INC., OF CALIFORNIA,
  6700 Santa Monica-boulevard, Hollywood, Calif.

CAGNEY PRODUCTIONS, INC.
President : William J. Cagney
Vice Pres. : James Cagney

General Service Studios, 1040 North Las Palmas-avenue, Hollywood 38, Calif.

CALIFORNIA PICTURES CORPORATION
President : Preston Sturges
Vice Pres. : Jules Furthman
  California Studios, 5255 Clinton-street, Hollywood 4, Calif.

CHAPLIN STUDIOS, INC.
President : Charles Chaplin
  1416 North La Brea, Hollywood, Calif.

CINECOLOR CORPORATION
2800 West Olive-avenue, Burbank, Calif.

COLUMBIA PICTURES CORPORATION
President : Harry Cohn
Exec. Vice Pres. : Jack Cohn
  729 Seventh-avenue, New York 19, N.Y.
  Studios :
  1438 North Gower-street, Hollywood 28, Calif.

COMET PRODUCTIONS
President : Mary Pickford
Gen. Manager : Harold Creene.
Co-producers : Charles (Buddy) Rogers and Ralph Cohen
Sam Goldwyn Studios, 1041 North Formosa-avenue,
Los Angeles 46, Calif.

LESTER COWAN PRODUCTIONS
6030 Wilshire-boulevard, Los Angeles 36, Calif.

CROSBY PRODUCTIONS, INC.
President : Bing Crosby
Vice Pres. : Everett Crosby
Hal Roach Studios, Culver City, Calif.

CECIL B. DE MILLE PRODUCTIONS, INC.
President : Cecil B. De Mille
Vice Pres.: Constance A. De Mille
2010 De Mille-drive, Hollywood 27, Calif.

DIANA PRODUCTIONS, INC.
President : Fritz Lang
Exec. Vice Pres. : Walter Wanger
Vice Pres. : Joan Wanger (Joan Bennett)
401 Taft Building, 1680 North Vine-street, Los
Angeles, Calif.
Studios :
Universal-International Studios, Universal City,
California

WALT DISNEY PRODUCTIONS
Chairman : Walt Disney
President : Roy Disney
Burbank, Calif.

E. I. DU PONT DE NEMOURS & CO. (INC.)
Directors : Mary Pickford
Charles (Buddy) Rogers
George Bagnall
Selmar L. Chalif
350 Fifth-avenue, New York 1, N.Y.
6656 Santa Monica-boulevard, Hollywood 38, Calif.

EASTMAN KODAK COMPANY
343 State-street, Rochester 4, N.Y.
6706 Santa Monica-boulevard, Hollywood 38, Calif.

ENTERPRISE PRODUCTIONS, INC.
Chairman : David L. Loew
5255 Clinton-street, Hollywood, Calif.

**FAMOUS PLAYERS CANADIAN
CORPORATION, LTD.**
Directors : Barney Balaban
N. G. Barrow
J. W. DeFarris
George Weltner
Austin Keogh
A. MacCunn
N. S. Robertson
H. P. Robinson
J. J. Fitzgibbons
R. W. Bolstad
Royal Bank Building, Toronto 1, Ontario

FILM INSTITUTE, INC.
President : Lawrence W. Fox, Jr.
630 Ninth-avenue, New York 19, N.Y.

FITZPATRICK PICTURES
(James A. Fitzpatrick)
(Metro-Goldwyn-Mayer Studios), Culver City, Calif.

GENERAL CASTING CORPORATION
1503 Cross Roads of the World, Hollywood 28, Calif.

GENERAL FILM LIBRARY OF CALIFORNIA
1426 North Beachwood-drive, Hollywood, Calif.

SAMUEL GOLDWYN PRODUCTIONS, INC.
1270 Sixth-avenue, New York 20, N.Y.
1041 North Formosa-avenue, Los Angeles 46, Calif.

INTERNATIONAL PICTURES, INC.
Chairman : Leo Spitz
President : William Goetz
Directors : William Goetz
George W. Cohen
Carolyn Gilmore
Leo Spitz
Studios, Universal City, Calif.

WALT LANTZ PRODUCTIONS
(Universal Studios) Universal City, Calif.

JESSE L. LASKY PRODUCTIONS, INC.
RKO Studios, 780 Gower-street, Hollywood, Calif.

SOL LESSER PRODUCTIONS, INC.
9336 West Washington-boulevard, (RKO Pathe
Studios), Culver City, Calif.

LIBERTY FILMS, INC.
President : Frank Capra
Vice Pres. : George Stevens
William Wyler
Samuel J. Briskin
RKO Studios, 780 Gower-street, Hollywood, Calif.

LOEW-LEWIN, INC.
President : David L. Loew
California Studios, 5255 Clinton-street, Hollywood 4,
Calif.

LOEW'S INCORPORATED
President : Nicholas M. Schenck
Vice Pres. : Charles C. Moskowitz
J. Robert Rubin
William F. Rodgers
Edgar J. Mannix
Alexander Lichtman
Howard Dietz
Joseph R. Vogel
Benjamin Thau
Marvin H. Schenck
Executives : Louis B. Mayer
Edgar J. Mannix
Sam Katz
Benjamin Thau
Louis K. Sidney
Alexander Lichtman
J. J. Cohn
J. K. McGuinness
Moe Siegel
J. G. Mayer
1540 Broadway, New York City 19, N.Y.
Studios :
MGM Studios, Washington-boulevard, Culver
City, Calif.

MONOGRAM PICTURES CORPORATION
Chairman : W. Ray Johnston
President : Samuel Broidy
Exec. Dir. : Trem Carr
4376 Sunset-drive, Hollywood 27, Calif.
1560 Broadway, New York 19, N.Y.
Studios :
4376 Sunset-drive, Hollywood 27, Calif.

NERO FILMS, INC.
1041 North Formosa-avenue, Hollywood 46, Calif.

PARAMOUNT PICTURES, INC.
President : Barney Balaban
Chairman : Adolph Zukor
Paramount Building, 1501 Broadway, New York
18, N.Y.
Studios :
Western Studios, 5451 Marathon-street, Hollywood
38, Calif.

PATHE INDUSTRIES, INC.
(Home Office) 625 Madison-avenue, New York 22, N.Y.

PATHE LABORATORIES, INC.
(Home Office) 625 Madison-avenue, New York 22, N.Y.
(Laboratories) Bound Brook, N.J.; 6823 Santa Monica-boulevard, Hollywood, Calif.

PICTORIAL FILMS, INC.
1270 Sixth-avenue, New York 20, N.Y.

P.R.C. PICTURES, INC.
Pathe Building, 625 Madison-avenue, New York 22, N.Y.

P.R.C. STUDIOS, INC.
7324 Santa Monica-boulevard, Los Angeles 46, Calif.

PATHE NEWS
(See RKO Pathe News, Inc.)

MARY PICKFORD COMPANY
9533 Brighton Way, Beverly Hills. Calif.

RADIO CORPORATION OF AMERICA
Chairman : James G. Harbord
President : David Sarnoff
R.C.A. Building, 30 Rockfeller-plaza, New York 20, N.Y.

RADIO-KEITH-ORPHEUM CORPORATION
Chairman : Floyd B. Odlum
Vice Chairman : Ned E. Depinet
1270 Sixth-avenue, New York City 20, N.Y.
Studios :
780 Gower-street, Los Angeles 38, Calif.

RKO PATHE NEWS, INC.
President ; Frederic Ullman Jr.
625 Madison-avenue, New York City, N.Y.

RAINBOW PRODUCTIONS, INC.
President : Leo McCarey
451 North La Cienega, Los Angeles 36, Calif.

J. ARTHUR RANK ORGANISATION, INC.
Chairman : J. Arthur Rank
President : Robert Benjamin
245 West 52nd-street, New York 19, N.Y.

UNITED WORLD PICTURES
(Subsidiary of Universal for documentary films)
President : Matthew Fox
1250 Sixth-avenue, New York 20, N.Y.

REPUBLIC PICTURES CORPORATION
President : Herbert J. Yates
1790 Broadway, New York City 19, N.Y.
Studios :
Republic Studios, 4024 Radford-avenue. North Hollywood, Calif.

HAL ROACH STUDIOS, INC.
8822 West Washington-boulevard, Culver City, Calif.
729 Seventh-avenue, New York 19, N.Y.

HARRY SHERMAN PRODUCTIONS
5255 Clinton-street, Los Angeles 4, Calif.

EDWARD SMALL PRODUCTIONS, INC.
9336 West Washington-boulevard, Culver City, Calif.

HUNT STROMBERG PRODUCTIONS
1040 North Las Palmas-avenue (General Service Studios) Hollywood 38, Calif.

TECHNICOLOR, INC.
President : Dr. Herbert T. Kalmus
15 Broad-street, New York 5, N.Y.

20th CENTURY-FOX FILM CORPORATION
President : Spyros P. Skouras
Vice Pres. : Darryl F. Zanuck
444 West 56th-street, New York City 19, N.Y.
Studios :
Beverly Hills, Calif.

MOVIETONE NEWS, INC.
President : W. C. Michel
460 West 54th-street, New York City, N.Y.

UNITED ARTISTS CORPORATION
President : Edward C. Raftery
729 Seventh-avenue, New York City 19, N.Y.

UNIVERSAL PICTURES COMPANY, INC.
Chairman : J. Cheever Cowdin
President : Nate J. Blumberg
Rockfeller Center, 1250 Sixth-avenue, New York City 20, N.Y.
Studios :
Universal City, Calif.

UNIVERSAL INTERNATIONAL FILMS, INC.
President : Joseph H. Seidelman
1250 Sixth-avenue, New York 20, N.Y.

VANGUARD FILMS, INC.
President : Daniel T. O'Shea
Producers : David O. Selznick
Allan Scott
David Hempsted
9336 Washington-boulevard, Culver City, Calif.
400 Madison-avenue, New York 17, N.Y.
Distribution through :
Selznick Releasing Organization Inc.,
400 Madison-avenue, New York, N.Y.

HAL WALLIS PRODUCTIONS, INC.
5451 Marathon-street, Hollywood, Calif.

WALTER WANGER PRODUCTIONS
(Universal Studio) Universal City, Calif.

WARNER BROS. PICTURES, INC.
President : Harry M. Warner
321 West 44th-street, New York City 18, N.Y.
Studios :
Olive-avenue, Burbank, Calif.

WESTERN ELECTRIC COMPANY, INC.
President : C. G. Stoll
1945 Broadway, New York 7, N.Y.

SOL M. WURTZEL PRODUCTIONS, INC.
1417 North Western-avenue, Hollywood, Calif.

Belgium
PRODUCERS
AGENCIES RÉUNIES VAN DAM—K.H.
86 Boulevard Adolphe Max, Brussels
BELGIQUE CINÉ PUBLICITÉ
64 rue de la Limite, Brussels
BOURGEOIS
27 Boulevard Léopold III, Brussels
C.E.P.
34 rue de l'Ecuyer, Brussels
DEKEUKELEIRE
26 Avenue Jean de Bologne, Brussels
ÉCRAN PUBLICITÉ
30 rue Marché aux Poulets, Brussels
ÉTENDARD FILMS
20 Avenue de France, Antwerp
FLON
29 rue Verte, Brussels
GORDINNE & FILS
18 rue Méan, Liège
HOELEN
110 Chaussée d'Anvers, Kapellen
LUX DISTRIBUTION
42 rue Linée, Brussels
OSTENDE FILMS
Casino de Knocke, Knocke-sur-Mer
PICHONNIER
33 rue de Fossé-aux-Loups, Brussels
PRODUCTION R.D.W.
7 rue Gaucheret, Brussels
PRODUCTION VAN ROY
62 Vanderzypenstraat, Wemmel
PUBLI-CINE
13 rue du Canal, Brussels
ROOTHOOFT
231 rue des Coteaux, Brussels
SOCIÉTÉ BELGE DE PRODUCTION
CINEMATOGRAPHIQUE " BEINAPRO "
92 Avenue Clémenceau, Brussels
VAN PEPERSTRAETE
33 rue Van Elewijck, Wemmel

STUDIOS
ST. CIBELSON
6 rue des Champs, Brussels
ST. CLAUDE MISONNE
49 Avenue de l'Armée, Brussels
ST. SONART
12-14 rue St. Hubert, Woluwé St. Pierre

Czechoslovakia
STUDIOS
BARRANDOV (features and documentaries); Prague-
Barrandov
ZOIN (Cartoons), Zoin

Denmark
PRODUCERS
DANSK FILM CO. A/S, Mynstersvej 1, F.
DANSK KULTURFILM*, Dahlerupsgade 3, K.
FOLK OG VAERN, V.*, Voldgade 117, V.
ILLUSTRA, Gl. Torv 22, K.
MINERVA FILM A/S, Toldbodgade 18, K.
STATENS FILM CENTRAL*, Dahlerupsgade 3, K.
* Government or Government-sponsored producers.

PRODUCERS WITH OWN STUDIOS
ASA, Lyngby
NORDISK FILM CO., Mosedalsvej, Valby
PALLADIUM, Strandparksvej 38, Hellerup
SAGA STUDIO, Annettevej 19, Charlottenlund
TEKNISK FILM KOMPAGNI, Madvigs Alle 3-7, F.
Note: The Post Office and the State Railways occasionally
produce films.

Egypt
STUDIOS
P. BELLENI & E. AVRAMOUSSI
Route des Pyramides, Gizeh, Cairo
SOCIÉTÉ MISR POUR LE THÉÂTRE ET LE
CINÉMA
sh. El Ahram, Gizeh, Cairo
STUDIO IBRAHIM & BADR LAMA
18 sh. Shakour Pasha, Kubbeh-gardens. Cairo
TOGO MIZRAHI & CO.
sh. Abbas, Gizeh, Cairo

France
STUDIOS
CASINO MUNICIPAL DE ROYAN
226 rue Ste. Catherine, Bordeaux, Gironde
PARIS-STUDIOS-CINÉMA
49-50 Quai du Point du Jour, Billancourt, Seine
STUDIOS DE BOULOGNE
68 Avenue J.-B. Clément, Boulogne-sur-Seine
STUDIOS ÉCLAIR
Épinay-sur-Seine, Seine
STUDIO FRANCE
6 rue du Tunnel, Paris 19ème.
STUDIOS FRANCOIS IER
26 bis, rue François Ier., Paris 8ème.
STUDIO DE LA GARENNE
10-12 rue du Château, La Garenne-Colombes,
Seine
STUDIOS DE MARSEILLE
111 rue Jean Mermoz, Marseille
STUDIOS NÉGRIER
22 bis, rue Pasteur, Courbevoie, Seine
STUDIOS DE NEUILLY
42 bis, Boulevard du Château, Neuilly-sur-Seine,
Seine
STUDIOS PATHÉ CINÉMA
6 rue Françoeur, Paris 18ème.
STUDIOS PHOTOSONOR
17 bis, Quai du Président Paul-Doumer, Courbevoie,
Seine
STUDIOS DE LA PLACE CLICHY
15 rue Forest, Place Clichy, Paris
STUDIOS RADIO-CINÉMA
3 Boulevard Aurelle de Paladine, Paris 17ème.
STUDIOS RADIO-CINÉMA DES BUTTES
CHAUMONT
10 rue Carducci, Paris 19ème.
STUDIOS DE ST. MAURICE
7 rue des Réservoirs, St. Maurice, Seine
STUDIOS DE LA VICTORINE
Chemin de St. Augustin, Nice, Alpes-Maritimes

Germany
PRODUCING UNITS

American-licensed
OBJEKTIV FILM, Berlin

British-licensed
STUDIO 45, Berlin
CAMERA-FILM, Hamburg

French-licensed
CIE. CINÉMA CENTRAL, Berlin

Russian-licensed
D.E.F.A. (Deutsche Film Aktiengesellschaft)
Krausenstrasse 38-9, Berlin

STUDIOS
GEISELGASTEIG STUDIOS
JOHANNESTAL, Berlin
NEUBABELSBERG, Berlin
TEMPELHOF STUDIOS, Berlin
AGFA FILM STOCK PLANT, Wolfen

Holland
STUDIOS
CINETONE FILMSTUDIO
Duivendrecht
FILMFABRIEK PROFILTI
Boslaan 3, The Hague
FILMSTUDIO POLYGOON
Koudenhorn 8, Haarlem
N.V. MULTIFILM
Kenaupark 8, Haarlem
PETESO (SMALFILM)
Nw. Duinweg 6, The Hague
TRIOFILM
Vondelstraat 72, Amsterdam

India
PRODUCERS
AURORA FILM CORPORATION
125 Dharamtarla-street, Calcutta
COLUMBIA FILMS OF INDIA LTD.
Humayan Court, Lindsay-street, Calcutta
FAZALBHOY LTD.
1-18 Mount-road, Madras
GEMINI PICTURE CIRCUIT
140 Broadway, Madras
NARAYANAN FILM COMPANY
Mount-road, Madras
NEW THEATRES LTD.
171 Dharamtarla-street, Calcutta
PARAMOUNT FILM COMPANY
Parekh-street, Bombay 4
ROHINI PICTURES LTD., THE
36 Eldams-road, Alwarpet, Madras
SHREE RANJIT MOVIETONE COMPANY
Main-road, Dadar, Bombay
UNIVERSAL PICTURE CORPORATION OF INDIA
Film House, Lamington-road, Bombay
UNIVERSAL PICTURES (INDIA) LTD.
Mount-road, Madras

STUDIOS
BURLINGTON STUDIOS
3 Commercial-road, Darjeeling
NATIONAL STUDIOS LTD.
74-94 Tardeo-road, Bombay
SOUND STUDIO (INDIA) LTD.
16 New Queens-road, Bombay 4

Italy
STUDIOS
CAPITANI-FERT, Rome
CATALUCCI, Rome
CENTRO SPERIMENTALE, Quadraro-Roma
CINECITTA, Quadraro-Roma
F.E.R.T., Turin
I.C.E.T.—MILANO (Industrie Cinematografi e Teatrali),
Via Pestalozzi, Milan
S.A.F.A., Via Mondovi 33, Rome
S.A.F.I.R., Farnesina, Rome
SCALERA FILM, Circonvallazione Appia 110, Rome
SCALERA-VENEZIA, Giudecca, Venice
TIRRENIA, Leghorn
TITANUS, Via della Farnesina, Rome

Mexico
STUDIOS
ESTUDIOS AZTECA
Esq. Calzada Nino Perdido y v. Coyoacan, Mexico City
ESTUDIOS CHURUBUSCO
Rio Churubusco y Calz. de Tlalpan, Mexico City
ESTUDIOS CLASA
(Cinematográfica Latino Americana S.A.)
Calzada de Tlalpan Kilo. 12 y medio, Mexico City
ESTUDIOS CUAUHTEMOC—COAPA
Calzada de Tlalpan, Mexico City
ESTUDIOS Y LABORATORIOS GARCIA MORARA
Av. Coyoacan y Calzada Nino Perdido, Mexico City
MEXICO FILMS
Jorge Stahl, Francisco Montes de Oca 117, Colonia Condesa, Mexico City

Portugal
STUDIOS
COMPANHIA PORTUGUESA DE FILMES
Alameda das Linhas de Torres 156, Lisbon
ESTRELA FILMES, LDA.
Praca D. João da Camara 4-20, Lisbon
FILMES LUMIAR, LDA.
Praça dos Restauradores 13-20, Lisbon
LISBOA FILME, LDA.
Quinta dos Ulmeiros, Alameda das Linhas de Torres 144, Lisbon

Spain
STUDIOS
CHAMARTIN PRODUCCIONES Y DISTRI-BUCIONES CINEMATOGRÁFICAS, S.A.
Avenida Jose Antonio 23, Madrid
CINEMATOGRAFÍA ESPAÑOLA AMERICANA, S.A.
Marques de Valdeiglesias 8, Madrid
ESTUDIOS DE ARANJUEZ, S.A.
Avenida Jose Antonio 31, Madrid
INDUSTRIAS CINEMATOGRÁFICAS ESPAÑO-LAS, S.A.
Alcala 45, Madrid

SALLY ANN HOWES
(*Ealing*)

Sweden

STUDIOS

A/B EUROPA FILM
Kungsgatan 24, Stockholm

A/B SANDREW-ATELJÉERNA
Lästmakaregatan 18, Stockholm

A/B SVENSK FILMINDUSTRI
Filmstaden, Råsunda, Solna

A/B TERRAPRODUKTION
Kungsgatan 65, Stockholm

A/B WIVEFILM
Kungsgatan 18, Stockholm

Switzerland

Production of cultural and educational films has increased enormously in Switzerland in recent years. A great many studios concentrate entirely on the making of documentaries for home schools, where visual education is widely practised, and also for export and exchange with other countries. Inquiries can be sent to the Swiss Film Institute, address—Schweizerische Filmkammer, Länggass-strasse 8, BERNE.

PRODUCERS

AUGUST KERN, Basle

BURLET-FILM G.M.B.H., Zürich 1

CENTRAL-FILM A.G., Zürich 1

CINÉMAS POPULAIRES ROMANDS, Geneva

CINEVOX S.A., Montreux, Vaud

DAHINDEN (JOSEF), Zürich 8

DUVANEL (C.G.), Geneva

FROBENIUS (TONFILM) A.G., Münchenstein, Baselland

GIMMI & CO., Zürich 1

GLORIAFILM A.G., Zürich 6

HANS RUDOLF MEYER, " Tempo ", Zürich 6

PANDORA-FILM A.G., Zürich 1

PAUL SCHMID, Berne

PINSCHEWER FILM, Kollerweg 9, Berne

PRAESENS-FILM A.G., Weinbergstrasse 15, Zürich 1

PRO FILM
Genossenschaft für Film-produktion, Bahnhof-strasse 69a, Zürich 1

PROBST FILM A.G., Zürich 2

ROBERT F. PARLIER D'OLLON, Montreux

SCHWEIZER SCHUL UND VOLKSKINO
Gemeinnütziges Zentralinstitut für Filmwesen, Berne

TURICIA-FILM A.G., Zürich 1

U.S.S.R.

Film production, badly disrupted by the war, is recovering steadily though many studios damaged by enemy action were not in full working order by the end of 1947. When the studios in the western Republics were under fire, studio personnel and equipment were hurriedly evacuated to Central Asia. At Alma Ata and other capital cities, studios which were under construction in 1939 were utilized to ensure continuity of production. By 1947, however, order and cohesion were considerably restored, colour and stereoscopy experiments developed, and the industry regeared to peace-time production.

Leading studios in production in 1947 :

ARMENKINO, Erivan, Ukraine

BAKU STUDIOS, Baku

KIEV STUDIOS, Ukraine

LENFILM, Leningrad

MOSFILM, Moscow

MOSTECHFILM, Moscow

NOVOSIBIRSK STUDIOS, Siberia

*SOYUZDETFILM, Moscow

SVERDLOVSK FILM, Sverdlovsk

TBILISI STUDIOS, Georgia

BALTIC REPUBLICS (STUDIOS)
Estonia and Riga

MINSK STUDIOS, Minsk

Rebuilding in progress (1947) at Alma Ata, Stalinabad, Taskent

* *This studio was turned over to the production of stereoscopic films only, in 1947.*

THE MOTION PICTURE
PRODUCTION CODE

HOLLYWOOD'S Production Code came into existence in 1930 mainly as the result of pressure from the powerful Catholic organization in the United States, the National League of Decency, which had more than sixteen million members at the time. Alarmed by what was considered the low moral tone of many Hollywood films, the League began a campaign to " clean up the screen " and forced the producers to evolve a new morality code.

This was done through the American Motion Picture Association. The Code, consisting of a set of rules concerning sex, manners and morals, was designed to purge the screen of undesirable matters. A special department—the Production Code Administration—was formed to act as liaison between studios and public. The department was maintained by the producing companies at their expense.

As with film censorship in Britain, producers voluntarily submit their films to the rules of the Production Code. There is no law in America which insists on compliance with the Code. Nor does the application of the Code to a film constitute a form of censorship. Censorship rests with the government of each State. A film passed by the Production Code Administration rarely fails, however, to receive State approval.

Normally a Hollywood producer first makes certain that a proposed film meets with the approval of the Production Code Administration. If it does not, he will undoubtedly shelve the project or postpone it until a more suitable time. If the idea is acceptable, a script is submitted. This may be returned for amendment by the P.C.A. or it may receive the seal of approval. The film goes into production only after it has been approved.

The Production Code Administration, contrary to popular supposition, does not take responsibility for the completed film. Its function is solely to see that it does not contravene the Code.

Because of the wide divergences in tastes and morals, as well as in the meanings of words and phrases, British films have frequently been found unacceptable by the American Censorship authorities. To overcome these problems many British producers now submit their scripts to the Hollywood Production Code Administration for guidance and advice before starting a film.

Because American censorship makes no distinction between films for youthful, adolescent or adult audiences it is considered necessary for *all* feature films to be within the comprehension of *all* members of *all* audiences in the United States.

The full text of the Production Code is as follows:
General Principles

1. No picture shall be produced which will lower the moral standards of those who see it. Hence the sympathy of the audience should never be thrown to the side of crime, wrongdoing, evil and sin.
2. Correct standards of life, subject only to the requirements of drama and entertainment, shall be presented.
3. Law, natural or human, shall not be ridiculed, nor shall sympathy be created for its violation.

Particular Applications

I. CRIMES AGAINST THE LAW

These shall never be presented in such a way as to throw sympathy with the crime as against law and justice or to inspire others with a desire for imitation.
1. Murder :
    (a) The technique of murder must be presented in a way that will not inspire imitation.
    (b) Brutal killings are not to be presented in detail.
    (c) Revenge in modern times shall not be justified.
2. Methods of crime should not be explicitly presented :
    (a) Theft, robbery, safe-cracking and dynamiting of trains, mines, buildings, and so on, should not be detailed in method.
    (b) Arson must be subject to the same safeguards.
    (c) The use of firearms should be restricted to essentials.
    (d) Methods of smuggling should not be presented.
3. Illegal drug traffic must never be presented.
4. The use of liquor in American life, when not required by the plot or for proper characterization, will not be shown.

II. SEX

The sanctity of the institution of marriage and the home shall be upheld. Pictures shall not infer that low forms of sex relationship are the accepted or common thing.
1. Adultery, sometimes necessary plot material, must not be explicitly treated, or justified, or presented attractively.
2. Scenes of passion :
    (a) They should not be introduced when not essential to the plot.
    (b) Excessive and lustful kissing, lustful embraces, suggestive postures and gestures, are not to be shown.
    (c) In general, passion should so be treated that these scenes do not stimulate the lower and baser element.
3. Seduction or rape :
    (a) They should never be more than suggested, and only when essential for the plot, and even then never shown by explicit method.
    (b) They are never the proper subject for comedy.
4. Sex perversion or any inference of it is forbidden.
5. White slavery shall not be treated.
6. Miscegenation (sex relationships between the white and black races) is forbidden.
7. Sex hygiene and venereal diseases are not subjects for motion pictures.

8. Scenes of actual child-birth, in fact or in silhouette, are never to be presented.

9. Children's sex organs are never to be exposed.

III. VULGARITY

The treatment of low, disgusting, unpleasant, though not necessarily evil, subjects should be subject always to the dictate of good taste and a regard for the sensibilities of the audience.

IV. OBSCENITY

Obscenity in word, gesture, reference, song, joke, or by suggestion (even when likely to be understood only by part of the audience) is forbidden.

V. PROFANITY

Pointed profanity (this includes the words: God, Lord, Jesus, Christ—unless used reverently—Hell, S.O.B., Damn, Gawd), or every other profane or vulgar expression however used, is forbidden.

VI. COSTUME

1. Complete nudity is never permitted. This includes nudity in fact or in silhouette, or any lecherous or licentious notice thereof by other characters in the picture.

2. Undressing scenes should be avoided, and never used save where essential to the plot.

3. Indecent or undue exposure is forbidden.

4. Dancing costumes intended to permit undue exposure or indecent movements in the dance are forbidden.

VII. DANCES

1. Dances suggesting or representing sexual actions or indecent passion are forbidden.

2. Dances which emphasize indecent movements are to be regarded as obscene.

VIII. RELIGION

1. No film or episode may throw ridicule on any religious faith.

2. Ministers of religion in their character as ministers of religion should not be used as comic characters or as villains.

3. Ceremonies of any definite religion should be carefully and respectfully handled.

IX. LOCATIONS

The treatment of bedrooms must be governed by good taste and delicacy.

X. NATIONAL FEELINGS

1. The use of the flag shall be consistently respectful.

2. The history, institutions, prominent people and citizenry of other nations shall be represented fairly.

XI. TITLES

Salacious, indecent, or obscene titles shall not be used.

XII. REPELLENT SUBJECTS

The following subjects must be treated within the careful limits of good taste:

1. Actual hangings or electrocutions as legal punishment for crime.

2. Third Degree methods.

3. Brutality and possible gruesomeness.

4. Branding of people or animals.

5. Apparent cruelty to children or animals.

6. The sale of women, or a woman selling her virtue.

7. Surgical operations.

Special Regulations re Crime in Motion Pictures

Resolved that the Board of Directors of the Motion Picture Producers and Distributors of America, Incorporated, hereby ratifies, approves, and confirms the interpretations of the Production Code and the practices thereunder, and the resolutions indicating and confirming such interpretations heretofore adopted by the Association of Motion Picture Producers, Incorporated, all effectuating regulations relative to crime in motion pictures, as follows:

1. Details of crime must never be shown and care should be exercised at all times in discussing such details.

2. Action suggestive of wholesale slaughter of human beings, either by criminals, in conflict with police, or as between warring factions of criminals, or in public disorder of any kind, will not be allowed.

3. There must be no suggestion, at any time, of excessive brutality.

4. Because of the increase in the number of films in which murder is frequently committed, action showing the taking of human life, even in the mystery stories, is to be cut to the minimum. These frequent presentations of murder tend to lessen regard for the sacredness of life.

5. Suicide, as a solution of problems occurring in the development of screen drama, is to be discouraged as morally questionable and as bad theatre—unless absolutely necessary for the development of the plot.

6. There must be no display, at any time, of machine guns, sub-machine guns or other weapons generally classified as illegal weapons in the hands of gangsters, or other criminals, and there are to be no off-stage sounds of the repercussion of these guns. This means that even where the machine guns, or other prohibited weapons, are not shown, the effect of shots coming from these guns must be cut to a minimum.

7. There must be no new, unique or trick methods for concealing of guns shown at any time.

8. The flaunting of weapons by gangsters, or other criminals, will not be allowed.

9. All discussions and dialogue on the part of gangsters regarding guns should be cut to the minimum.

10. There must be no scenes, at any time, showing law-enforcing officers dying at the hands of criminals. This includes private detectives and guards for banks, motor trucks, and so on.

11. With special reference to the crime of kidnapping—or illegal abduction—such stories are acceptable under the Code only when the kidnapping or abduction is (a) not the main theme of the story; (b) the person kidnapped is not a child; (c) there are no details of the crime of kidnapping; (d) no profit accrues to the abductors or kidnappers; and (e) where the kidnappers are punished.

   It is understood, and agreed, that the word kidnapping, as used in paragraph 11 of these Regulations, is intended to mean abduction, or illegal detention, in modern times, by criminals for ransom.

12. Pictures dealing with criminal activities, in which minors participate or to which minors are related, shall not be approved if they incite demoralizing imitation on the part of youth.

FIVE HUNDRED
FAMOUS FILMS

A SELECTION OF FILMS AND THEIR PLAYERS 1915-1947

The casts of five hundred outstanding films of Europe and America are given in the following pages, together with the names of the directors of the films, the companies which produced them, the dates of their release and (where the information is available) the sources on which the film scripts were based.

Dates given for American and British films refer to the general release in Great Britain, unless otherwise stated.

Dates given for foreign language films refer to release in the country of origin. For further details of such films readers should consult pages 347-50.

A

Abie's Irish Rose

JEAN HERSHOLT	Solomon Levy
CHARLES ROGERS	Abie Levy
NANCY CARROLL	Rosemary Murphy
J. FARRELL MacDONALD	Patrick Murphy
BERNARD GORCEY	Isaac Cohen
IDA KRAMER	Mrs. Isaac Cohen
NICK COGLEY	Father Whalen
CAMILLUS PRETAL	Rabbi Jacob Samuels
ROSA ROSANOVA	Sarah

PARA   Director : Victor Fleming   1929

Abraham Lincoln

GEORGE BILLINGS	Abraham Lincoln
DANNY HOY	Abraham, aged 7
RUTH CLIFFORD	Ann Rutledge
NELL CRAIG	Mary Todd Lincoln
IRENE HUNT	Nancy Hanks Lincoln
WESTCOTT B. CLARK	Thomas Lincoln
EDDIE BURNS	John McNeil
PAT HARTIGAN	Jack Armstrong
OTIS HARLAN	Denton Offut
LOUISE FAZENDA	Sally
WILLIAM HUMPHREY	Stephen A. Douglas
EDDIE SUTHERLAND	William Scott

WILLIAM MORAN	John Wilkes Booth
WALTER ROGERS	General U. S. Grant
JAMES WELCH	General Robert E. Lee
WILLIS MARKS	Secretary Seward

FIRST NATIONAL   Director : Philip Rosen   1925

Abraham Lincoln

LUCILLE LA VERNE	Midwife
W. L. THORNE	Tom Lincoln
HELEN FREEMAN	Nancy Hanks Lincoln
OTTO HOFFMAN	Offut
WALTER HUSTON	Abraham Lincoln
EDGAR DEERING	Armstrong
UNA MERKEL	Ann Rutledge
RUSSELL SIMPSON	Lincoln's employer
CHARLES CROCKETT	Sheriff
KAY HAMMOND	Mary Todd Lincoln
HELEN WARE	Mrs. Edwards
E. ALYN WARREN	Stephen
JASON ROBARDS	Herndon
GORDON THORPE	Tad Lincoln
IAN KEITH	John Wilkes Booth
CAMERON PRUDHOMME	John Hay
JAMES BRADBURY, SR.	General Scott
JIMMIE EAGLE	Young Soldier
FRED WARREN	General Grant
OSCAR APFEL	Secretary of War Stanton
FRANK CAMPEAU	General Sheridan
HOBART BOSWORTH	General Lee
HENRY B. WALTHALL	Colonel Marshall

UA   Director : D. W. Griffith   1931

Adventure

CLARK GABLE	Harry Patterson
GREER GARSON	Emily Sears
JOAN BLONDELL	Helen Melohn
THOMAS MITCHELL	Mudgin
TOM TULLY	Gus
JOHN QUALEN	Model T
RICHARD HAYDN	Limo
LINA ROMAY	Maria
PHILIP MERIVALE	" Old " Ramon Estado
HARRY DAVENPORT	Dr. Ashlon
TITO RENALDO	" Young " Ramon Estado

MGM   Director : Victor Fleming   1945

Key to Abbreviations of the Names of Film Companies in this Section :

ABPC (*Associated British Picture Corporation*)
ARP (*Associated Radio Pictures*)
B & D (*British & Dominions*)
BIF (*British Instructional Films*)
BIP (*British International Pictures*)
BL (*British Lion*)
BRIT NAT (*British National*)
COI (*Central Office of Information*)
COL (*Columbia*)

GAINS (*Gainsborough*)
GB (*Gaumont British*)
INDIVID (*Individual*)
LFP (*London Film Productions*)
MGM (*Metro-Goldwyn-Mayer*)
MGM-BRIT (*Metro-Goldwyn-Mayer British*)
PARA (*Paramount*)
PARA-BRIT (*Paramount British*)
RKO (*RKO Radio*)

RKO-BRIT (*RKO Radio British*)
SELZNICK (*Selznick ; Selznick-International*)
20TH-FOX (*20th Century Fox*)
20TH-FOX-BRIT (*20th Century-Fox British*)
UA (*United Artists*)
UNIV (*Universal ; Universal-International*)
WARN (*Warner Bros.*)

Algiers

CHARLES BOYER..................Pépé le Moko
SIGRID GURIE.........................Inès
HEDY LAMARR........................Gaby
JOSEPH CALLEIA....................Slimane
ALAN HALE.......................Grand Père
GENE LOCKHART......................Régis
JOHNNY DOWNS.....................Pierrot
STANLEY FIELDS.....................Carlos
MME. NINA KOSHETZ ....Tania
JOAN WOODBURY......................Aicha
CLAUDIA DELL........................Marie
ROBERT GREIG.................Robert Gérig
CHARLES D. BROWN.....................Max
BEN HALL..............................Gil
ARMAND KALIZ....................Sergeant
WALTER KINGSFORD..................Louvain
PAUL HARVEY.......................Janvier
BERT ROACH.........................Bertier
LUANA WALTERS............Native Waitress
WALTER WANGER   Director : John Cromwell   1938
Hollywood version of the French film "Pépé le Moko"

All Quiet on the Western Front

LOUIS WOLHEIM.................Katczinsky
LEW AYRES'....................Paul Baumer
JOHN WRAY....................Himmelstoss
SLIM SUMMERVILLE.................Tjaden
RUSSELL GLEASON....................Muller
WILLIAM BAKEWELL....................Albert
SCOTT KOLK...........................Leer
WALTER BROWNE ROGERS............Behm
BEN ALEXANDER...................Kemmerich
OWEN DAVIS, JR.....................Peter
BERYL MERCER..................Mrs. Baumer
EDWIN MAXWELL...............Mr. Baumer
HAROLD GOODWIN...................Detering
RICHARD ALEXANDER................Westhus
YOLA D'AVRIL.......................Suzanne
ARNOLD LUCY.......................Kantorek
RAYMOND GRIFFITH.........Duval, the *poilu*
RENÉE DAMONDE⎫
POUPÉE ANDRIOT ⎬ ....The French Girls
EDMUND BREESE.................Herr Meyer
HEINIE CONKLIN.................Hammacher
BERTHA MANN.............Sister Libertine
UNIV   Director : Lewis Milestone   1931
From the book by Erich Maria Remarque

All This, and Heaven Too

BETTE DAVIS.........Henriette Deluzy-Desportes
CHARLES BOYER................Duc de Praslin
JEFFREY LYNN..........Henry Martyn Field
BARBARA O'NEIL..........Duchesse de Praslin
VIRGINIA WEIDLER....................Louise
HELEN WESTLEY..............Mme. LeMaire
WALTER HAMPDEN...................Pasquier
HENRY DANIELL.....................Broussais
HARRY DAVENPORT.....................Pierre
GEORGE COULOURIS..............Charpentier
MONTAGU LOVE......Maréchal Sebastiani
JANET BEECHER................Miss Haines
JUNE LOCKHART....................Isabelle
ANN TODD............................Berthe
RICHARD NICHOLS...................Raynald
FRITZ LEIBER................Abbé Gallard
IAN KEITH.........................DeLangle
SIBYL HARRIS................Mlle. Maillard
EDWARD FIELDING.................Dr. Louis
MARY ANDERSON................Rebecca Jay
ANN GILLIS................Emily Schuyler
PEGGY STEWART.............Helen Lexington

VICTOR KILIAN......................Gendarme
MRS. GARDNER CRANE.....Mme. Gauthier
WARN   Director: Anatole Litvak   1941
From the novel by Rachel Field

Aloma of the South Seas

GILDA GREY..........................Aloma
PERCY MARMONT.................Bob Holden
WARNER BAXTER....................Nuitane
WILLIAM POWELL..........Van Templeton
HARRY T. MOREY.................Red Mallory
JULANNE JOHNSTON....................Sylvia
JOSEPH SMILEY.............Andrew Taylor
PARA   Director : A. H. Van Buren   1927
From the play by John B. Hymer and Le Roy Clemens

Amateur Gentleman, The

RICHARD BARTHELMESS.......Barnabas Barty
DOROTHY DUNBAR......Lady Cleone Meredith
GARDNER JAMES............Ronald Barrymore
NIGEL BARRIE...........Sir Mortimer Carnaby
BRANDON HURST......................Peterby
JOHN MILJAN..............Viscount Devenham
EDWARDS DAVIS.................John Barty
BILLIE BENNETT.......Duchess of Camberhurst
HERBERT GRIMWOOD...........Jasper Gaunt
GINO CORRADO............The Prince Regent
SIDNEY DE GRAY.............Captain Chumley
JOHN PETERS.................Captain Slingsby
FIRST NATIONAL   1927
From the novel by Jeffery Farnol

Amateur Gentleman, The

DOUGLAS FAIRBANKS, JR.......Barnabas Barty
ELISSA LANDI............Lady Cleone Meredith
GORDON HARKER...................Natty Bell
BASIL SYDNEY................Louis Chichester
HUGH WILLIAMS........Lord Ronald Meredith
IRENE BROWNE............Lady Hunstanton
ATHOLE STEWART.....Marquess of Camberhurst
CORAL BROWN..............Pauline Darville
MARGARET LOCKWOOD..Georgina Hunstanton
ESME PERCY..................John Townsend
FRANK BERTRAM....................Belcher
GILBERT DAVIS.........The Prince Regent
FRANK PETTINGELL.................John Barty
CRITERION   Director : Thornton Freeland   1936
From the novel by Jeffery Farnol

Amazing Quest of Mr. Ernest Bliss, The

HENRY EDWARDS...................Ernest Bliss
CHRISSIE WHITE..............Frances Clayton
MARY BROUGH.....................Gloria Mott
GERALD AMES.......Dorrington, an adventurer
JAMES ANNAND...................Mr. Crawley
HENRY VIBART.......Sir James Aldroyd, M.D.
DOUGLAS MUNRO.................John Masters
STANLEY TURNBULL................Willie Mott
HEPWORTH   1922
From the novel by E. Phillips Oppenheim

Ambrose Applejohn's Adventure

MATT MOORE..............Ambrose Applejohn
ENID BENNETT..................Poppy Faire
BARBARA LA MARR.............Anna Valeska
ROBERT McKIM......................Borolsky
MATHILDE BRUNDAGE.Mrs. Agatha Whatacombe
EMILY FITZROY..........Mrs. Horace Pengard
OTTO HOFFMAN.............Horace Pengard
THOMAS RICKETTS......................Lush
METRO-GOLDWYN   1924
From the play by Walter Hackett

240

Anna Christie

GRETA GARBO............................Anna
CHARLES BICKFORD.....................Matt
GEORGE F. MARION.....................Chris
MARIE DRESSLER....................Marthy
JAMES T. MACK..............Johnny, the priest
LEE PHELPS............................Larry
MGM Director : Clarence Brown 1930
From the play by Eugene O'Neill

Anna Karenina

GRETA GARBO..................Anna Karenina
FREDRIC MARCH...................Vronsky
FREDDIE BARTHOLOMEW...............Sergei
MAUREEN O'SULLIVAN...............Kitty
MAY ROBSON................Countess Vronsky
BASIL RATHBONE..................Karenin
REGINALD OWEN.......................Stiva
PHOEBE FOSTER.......................Dolly
REGINALD DENNY....................Yashvin
GYLES ISHAM.........................Levin
JOAN MARSH...........................Lili
ETHEL GRIFFIES..............Mme. Kartasoff
HARRY BERESFORD...................Matve
SARAH PADDEN...................Governess
CORA SUE COLLINS....................Tania
MARY FORBES................Princess Sorokino
GUY D'ENNERY......................Butler
BUSTER PHELPS......................Grisha
SIDNEY BRADY............. Vronsky's valet
HARRY ALLEN..........................Cord
ELLA ETHRIDGE.............Anna's maid
SELZNICK Director : Clarence Brown 1935
From the novel by Tolstoy

Annie Laurie

LILLIAN GISH.....................Annie Laurie
NORMAN KERRY............Ian MacDonald
CREIGHTON HALE....................Donald
JOSEPH STRIKER....................Alastair
HOBART BOSWORTH..The MacDonald Chieftain
PATRICIA AVERY.......................Enid
RUSSELL SIMPSON.....................Sandy
BRANDON HURST......The Campbell Chieftain
DAVID TORRENCE.............Robert Laurie
FRANK CURRIER.........Cameron of Lochiel
METRO-GOLDWYN 1928

Anthony Adverse

FREDRIC MARCH............Anthony Adverse
OLIVIA DE HAVILLAND......Angela Guessippi
DONALD WOODS................Vincent Nolte
ANITA LOUISE........................Maria
EDMUND GWENN...........John Bonnyfeather
CLAUDE RAINS....................Don Luis
LOUIS HAYWARD.............Denis Moore
GALE SONDERGAARD....................Faith
STEFFI DUNA........................Neleta
BILLY MAUCH......Anthony Adverse, aged 10
AKIM TAMIROFF.................Carlo Cibo
RALPH MORGAN.....................Debrulle
HENRY O'NEILL................Father Xavier
PEDRO DE CORDOBA..Brother François
GEORGE E. STONE...................Sancho
LUIS ALBERNI..............Tony Guessippi
FRITZ LEIBER......................Ouvrard
JOSEPH CREHAN........Captain Elisha Jorham
RAFAELA OTTIANO ....Signora Bovino
ROLLO LLOYD.............Napoleon Bonaparte
LEONARD MUDIE..............De Bourrienne
MARILYN KNOWLDEN........Florence Udney
MATHILDE COMONT...........Cook Guessippi

EILY MALYON.................Mother Superior
J. CARROL NAISH.............Major Doumet
SCOTTY BECKETT.........Little Boy Anthony
PAUL SOTOFF......................Ferdinando
FRANK REICHER.........Coach Driver to Paris
CLARA BLANDICK.............Mrs. Jorham
ADDISON RICHARDS........Captain Matanaza
WILLIAM RICCIARDI.....Coachman in Leghorn
GRACE STAFFORD......................Lucia
WARN Director : Mervyn LeRoy 1936
From the novel by Hervey Allen

Appointment with Crime

WILLIAM HARTNELL.............Leo Martin
RAYMOND LOVELL...................Loman
ROBERT BEATTY.Inspector Superintendent Rogers
HERBERT LOM.................Gregory Lang
JOYCE HOWARD.................Carol Dane
ALAN WHEATLEY...................Noel Penn
CYRIL SMITH.............Sergeant Weeks
ELSIE WAGSTAFFE..........Mrs. Wilkins
IAN FLEMING.............Governor of Prison
WALLY PATCH.....................Joe Fisher
IAN McLEAN....................Mason (C.I.D.)
HARRY LANE.......................Big Mike
KEN WARRINGTON..................Winckle
PAUL CROFT..........................Dusty
WILFRED HYDE-WHITE..............Cleaner
ALFRED A. HARRIS........Doctor at hospital
HOWARD DOUGLAS.............Mr. Quilp
ALBERT CHEVALIER........Spearman (C.I.D.)
FREDERICK MORANT.........Harry Millerton
JOE CUNNINGHAM.........Chief Prison Officer
JOHN RORKE.............Casson, the butler
ANDERS TIMBERG...............Jerry Winters
VICTOR WESKE.....................Hatchett
JAMES KNIGHT......................Smokey
HARRY TERRY..........................Mick
JOHN CLIFFORD
Man in pepper-throwing sequence
JIMMY RHODES.......................Rusty
ERNEST BUTCHER...............John Brown
ANDRE BELHOMME...................Larry
IVOR BARNARD.................Jonah Crackle
IRIS HUNTER-SYMON...............Cashier
A. G. GUINLE..............Van de Beek
ELIZABETH LONDON.................Peggy
GWENDOLYN GRAY.............Carol's friend
LYN WILLIAMS.......Policeman in Rogers' office
GEORGE STENNING.....................Jeff
BILLY HOWARD......Policeman in A.R.P. shelter
LEON BIJOU..........................Jupp
J. R. ROBERTSON ....Prison Governor
FRANCIS ADAMS.............Prison Priest
BROOKS TURNER.............Chief Warder
MAURICE MAUDE....................Sheriff
EDDIE MAGUIRE.....................Passer-by
PERCY COYTE.....................Hangman
and
Lew Stone and his Band, Elizabeth Webb, Buddy
Featherstonehaugh and his Sextette, Gaston with Helen
BRIT NAT Director : John Harlow 1946

Arsène Lupin

JOHN BARRYMORE.........Duc de Charmerac
LIONEL BARRYMORE.............Guerchard
KAREN MORLEY........................Sonia
JOHN MILJAN.............Prefect of Police
TULLY MARSHALL.............Gourney-Martin
HENRY ARMETTA) ....Sheriff's men
GEORGE DAVIS)
JOHN DAVIDSON.....................Butler

241

JAMES MACK.........................Laurent
MARY JANE IRVING..................Marie
MGM   Director : Jack Conway   1932
From the play by Maurice le Blanc and Francis de
Croisset

Arsenic and Old Lace
CARY GRANT.................Mortimer Brewster
PRISCILLA LANE.................Elaine Harper
RAYMOND MASSEY....... Jonathan Brewster
PETER LORRE......................Dr. Einstein
JACK CARSON.........................O'Hara
JOSEPHINE HULL...............Abby Brewster
JEAN ADAIR............. Martha Brewster
EDWARD EVERETT HORTON.. Mr. Witherspoon
JAMES GLEASON...........Police Lieutenant
GRANT MITCHELL................Rev. Harper
JOHN ALEXANDER.Teddy " Roosevelt " Brewster
CHARLES LANE......................Reporter
EDWARD McNAMARA.................Brophy
EDWARD McWADE.....................Gibbs
WARN   Director : Frank Capra   1945
From the play by Joseph Kesselring

As You Like It
ELISABETH BERGNER................Rosalind
LAURENCE OLIVIER..................Orlando
HENRY AINLEY...............Banished Duke
SOPHIE STEWART.......................Celia
MACKENZIE WARD.............. Touchstone
LEON QUARTERMAINE................Jacques
RICHARD AINLEY.....................Silvius
FELIX AYLMER...............Duke Frederick
AUBREY MATHER......................Corin
FISHER WHITE........................Adam
MOORE MARRIOTT....................Dennis
JOHN LAURIE........................Oliver
LIONEL BRAHAM....................Charles
AUSTIN TREVOR.....................Le Beau
GAVIN GORDON......................Amiens
CYRIL HORROCKS...................1st Lord
ELLIS IRVING......................2nd Lord
LAWRENCE HANRAY...................3rd Lord
JOAN WHITE........................Phoebe
20TH-BRIT   Director : Paul Czinner   1936
From the play by William Shakespeare

Atalante, L'
MICHEL SIMON.................Le Père Jules
DITA PARLO.........................Juliette
JEAN D'ASTE..........................Jean
GILLES MARGARITIS..................Hawker
LOUIS LEFEBVRE.......................Boy
MAURICE GILLES...............Barge Owner
RAYA DILIGENT......................Bargee
GAUMONT (France)   Director : Jean Vigo   1934
(See Foreign Language Films, page 347)

At the Edge of the World
BRIGITTE HELM.....Magda, the Miller's daughter
ALBERT STEINRUCK...............The Miller
WILLIAM DIETERLE*.............John, his son
IMRE RADAY............Michael, his son
CAMILLA VON HOLLAY...........John's wife
ERWIN FABER...................The Stranger
MAX SCHRECK..................The Pedlar
VICTOR JANSON..................The Captain
JEAN BRADIN................The Lieutenant
UFA (Germany)   Director : Karl Grun   1929
* Went to Hollywood 1930, to appear in German
versions of U.S. films. Has remained there as
director (see " Who's Who in Films ").
(See Foreign Language Films, page 347)

Atlantic
FRANKLIN DYALL.................John Rool
(FRITZ KORTNER)   (Heinrich Thomas)
ELLALINE TERRISS................Mrs. Rool
(ELSA WAGNER)   (Anna Thomas)
DONALD CALTHROP..........Pointer, the valet
(GEORG JOHN)   (Vandt)
D. A. CLARKE-SMITH..............Tate Hughes
(HEINRICH SCHROOTH)   (Harry von Schroeder)
HELEN HAYE..................Mrs. Tate Hughes
(JULIA SERDA)   (Clara von Schroeder)
JOAN BARRY...............Betty Tate Hughes
(ELFRIEDE BORODIN)   (Betty von Schroeder)
JOHN STUART.......................Lawrence
(FRANZ LEDERER)   (Peter)
MADELEINE CARROLL...............Monica
(LUCIE MANNHEIM)   (Monica)
FRANCIS LISTER..................The Padre
(THEODOR LOOS)   (Der Pfarrer)
JOHN LONGDEN...................Lanchester
(G. A. KOCH)   (Lersner)
ARTHUR HARDY.................Major Boldy
(HERMANN VALLENTIN)   (Dr. Holtz)
MONTY BANKS.......................Dandy
(WILLY FORST)   (Boldi)
SYDNEY LYNN..........Captain of the Atlantic
(PHILLIPP MANNING)   (Kapitän)
*(Note : The names of the German players and
their parts are given in brackets.)*
BIP   Director : E. A. Dupont   1930
*The world's first bi-lingual all-talkie. From the
play " The Berg " by Ernest Raymond*

Avalanche
LENI RIEFENSTAHL...........Stella Armstrong
SEPPRIST...........................Hanna
ERNST UDET...........Udet, the famous airman
UFA (Germany)   Written and directed   1930
        by Dr. Arnold Fanck
(See Foreign Language Films, page 347)

B

Baby, Be Good !
PRISCILLA LANE................Joyce Winfree
WAYNE MORRIS.................Billy Randolph
JANE BRYAN..........................Kate
EDDIE ALBERT................." Bing " Edwards
JANE WYMAN.....................Claire Terry
RONALD REAGAN...............Dan Crawford
PETER B. GOOD.................Commencement
ARTHUR TREACHER..................Snelling
MORONI OLSEN...................Major Terry
JESSIE BUSLEY.....................Mrs. Brooks
LARRY WILLIAMS...........Harley Harrington
BERTON CHURCHILL...........Mr. Harper
NANA BRYANT....................Mrs. Harper
PAUL HARVEY.............Sterling Randolph
MAYO METHOT.................Girl in bus
ED GARGAN.....................Cab Driver
WARN   Director : Ray Enright   1940

Back Street
CHARLES BOYER.................Walter Saxel
MARGARET SULLAVAN.............Ray Smith
RICHARD CARLSON..............Curt Stanton
FRANK McHUGH.....................Ed Porter
FRANK JENKS.........................Harry
TIM HOLT....................Richard Saxel
PEGGY STEWART................Freda Smith
SAMUEL S. HINDS..................Darren
ESTHER DALE......................Mrs. Smith

242

JOHN McCALLUM
(*Ealing*)

NELL O'DAY....................Elizabeth Saxel
NELLA WALKER..................Corinne Saxel
UNIV   Director : Robert Stevenson   1941
Based on the novel by Fannie Hurst

Bandit of Sherwood Forest, The
CORNEL WILDE......Robert, son of Robin Hood
ANITA LOUISE.............Lady Catherine Maitland
JILL ESMOND................The Queen Mother
EDGAR BUCHANAN..................Friar Tuck
GEORGE MacREADY.........Lord Fitz-Herbert
JOHN ABBOTT...................Will Scarlett
LESLIE DENISON................Alan A-Dale
EVA MOORE..........................Meg
RUSSELL HICKS...................Robin Hood
HENRY DANIELL.......William of Pembroke
MAURICE TAUZIN.............King Henry III
MILES MANDER.................The Sheriff
RAY TEAL......................Little John
IAN WOLFE....................Lord Mortimer
COL Directors: George Sherman and Henry Levin 1946
In Technicolor

Barretts of Wimpole Street, The
NORMA SHEARER............Elizabeth Barrett
CHARLES LAUGHTON..Edward Moulton-Barrett
FREDRIC MARCH...........Robert Browning
MAUREEN O'SULLIVAN.......Henrietta Barrett
KATHARINE ALEXANDER.......Arabel Barrett
UNA O'CONNOR.....................Wilson
IAN WOLFE....................Harry Bevan
MARION CLAYTON.............Bella Hedley
RALPH FORBES.......Captain Surtees Cook
VERNON DOWNING.........Octavius Barrett
NEVILLE CLARKE...........Charles Barrett
MATTHEW SMITH............George Barrett
ROBERT CARLETON............Alfred Barrett
ALLAN CONRAD...............Henry Barrett
PETER HOBBES.............Septimus Barrett
FERDINAND MUNIER............Dr. Chambers
LEO CARROLL.............Dr. Ford-Waterlow
FLUSH..........................Himself
MGM   Director : Sydney Franklin   1934
From the play by Rudolf Besier
Re-issued 1938 and 1945

Battement de Cœur
DANIELLE DARRIEUX.................Arlette
JUNIE ASTOR ....The Ambassador's wife
CLAUDE DAUPHIN........Pierre de Rougemont
ANDRÉ LUGUET ....The Ambassador
SATURNIN FABRE...........The Professor
JEAN TISSIER.......................Roland
CARETTE...........................Yves
CHARLES DÉCHAMPS...........Baron Dvorak
CINE ALLIANCE (France) Director: Henri Decoin 1939
" *Battement de Cœur* " *was bought by the
American producers Robert and Raymond Hakim
and re-made by them as* " *Heartbeat* ", *released
through RKO in 1946*
(*See Foreign Language Films, page* 347)

Beau Brummel
JOHN BARRYMORE......George Bryan Brummel
MARY ASTOR............Lady Margery Alvanley
WILLARD LOUIS........George, Prince of Wales
IRENE RICH..Frederica Charlotte, Duchess of York
ALEC B. FRANCIS..................Mortimer
CARMEL MYERS.......Lady Hester Stanhope
WILLIAM HUMPHREYS.........Lord Alvanley
RICHARD TUCKER............Lord Stanhope
ANDRE BERANGER...............Lord Byron

CLAIRE DE LOREZ.................Lady Manly
MICHAEL DARK..................Lord Manly
TEMPLAR SAXE.............Desmond Wertham
CLARISSA SELWYNNE...........Mrs. Wertham
JAMES A. MARCUS.Snodgrass, an English innkeeper
BETTY BRICE.................Mrs. Snodgrass
ROLAND RUSHTON..............Mr. Abrahams
JOHN J. RICHARDSON.........." Poodle " Byng
WARN   Director : Harry Beaumont   1924

Beau Geste
RONALD COLMAN........Michael (Beau) Geste
NEIL HAMILTON................Digby Geste
RALPH FORBES.................John Geste
ALICE JOYCE.............Lady Patricia Brandon
MARY BRIAN.........................Isobel
NOAH BEERY..............Sergeant Lejaune
NORMAN TREVOR.......Major de Beaujolais
WILLIAM POWELL.................Boldini
VICTOR McLAGLEN.....................Hank
DONALD STUART.......................Buddy
PARA   Director : Herbert Brenon   1927
From the novel by P. C. Wren

Beau Geste
GARY COOPER.....................Beau Geste
RAY MILLAND....................John Geste
ROBERT PRESTON................Digby Geste
HEATHER THATCHER....Lady Patricia Brandon
BRIAN DONLEVY...........Sergeant Markoff
SUSAN HAYWARD..............Isobel Rivers
J. CARROL NAISH ....Rasinoff
ALBERT DEKKER...................Schwartz
BRODERICK CRAWFORD.........Hank Miller
JAMES STEPHENSON..Major Henri de Beaujolais
GEORGE P. HUNTLEY........Augustus Brandon
HARVEY STEPHENS........Lieutenant Martin
DONALD O'CONNOR......Beau Geste, as a child
BILLY COOK............John Geste, as a child
MARTIN SPELLMAN.....Digby Geste, as a child
ANN GILLIS.......Isobel Rivers, as a child
DAVID HOLT.......Augustus Brandon, as a child
PARA   Director : William A. Wellman   1939
From the novel by P. C. Wren

Becky Sharp
MIRIAM HOPKINS.................Becky Sharp
FRANCES DEE.................Amelia Sedley
CEDRIC HARDWICKE........Marquis of Steyne
BILLIE BURKE................Lady Bareacres
ALISON SKIPWORTH..............Miss Crawley
NIGEL BRUCE.................Joseph Sedley
ALAN MOWBRAY..............Rawdon Crawley
COLIN TAPLEY.............William Dobbin
G. P. HUNTLEY, JR..........George Osborne
GEORGE HASSELL.............Sir Pitt Crawley
WILLIAM FAVERSHAM.......Duke of Wellington
CHARLES RICHMAN...........General Tufto
DORIS LLOYD........Duchess of Richmond
LEONARD MUDIE...................Tarquin
BUNNY BEATTY...............Lady Blanche
CHARLES COLEMAN..................Bowles
MAY BEATTY........................Briggs
FINIS BARTON.................Miss Flowery
OLAF HYTTEN.............The Prince Regent
PAULINE GARON....................Fifine
JAMES " HAMBONE " ROBINSON........Page
ELSPETH DUDGEON............Miss Pinkerton
TEMPE PIGOTT.............The Charwoman
OTTOLA NESMITH.........Lady Jane Crawley
RKO-PIONEER   Director : Rouben Mamoulian 1935
Based on the play by Langdon Mitchell, after Thackeray
The first full-length Technicolor feature film

Behold Beatrice

FERNAND LEDOUX................Dr. Mallory
JULES BERRY..................The Ambassador
JACQUES BERTHIER...........Jack Richardson
GÉRARD LANDRY..........Jose de Castrovega
PIZANI........................Alfred
BONVALLET....................Dr. Lemuelson
RENÉE FAURÉ..........................Beatrice
THÉRÈSE DORNY....................Aunt Maud
SUZY PIERSON....................Mrs. Wallace
MARIE CARLOT........................Paula
MARCELLE NAUDIA...........Mme. la Baronne
EMMA LYONEL.......................Mrs. Dent
CIMEP (France)   Director : Jean de Marguenat   1943
From the novel by Pierre Frondaie
(See Foreign Language Films, page 347)

Beloved Rogue, The

JOHN BARRYMORE.............François Villon
CONRAD VEIDT.....................Louis XI
HENRY VICTOR.............Thibault d'Aussigny
MARCELINE DAY.......Charlotte de Vauxcelles
MACK SWAIN.....................Nicholas
SLIM SUMMERVILLE................Jehan
OTTO MATIESEN....................Ilivier
LUCY BEAUMONT....................Mother
LAWSON BUTT............Duke of Burgundy
BERTRAM GRASSBY.........Duke of Orleans
JANE WINTON.......................The Abbess
ROSE DIONE.......................Margot
MARTHA FRANKLIN....................Maid
NIGEL DE BRULIER.................Astrologer
DICK SUTHERLAND................Executioner
UA   1927
Based on the life of François Villon

Beloved Vagabond, The

CARLYLE BLACKWELL......{ Gaston de Mérac
                         Paragot
PHYLLIS TITMUSS...........Joanna Rushworth
OWEN ROUGHWOOD
                 Comte Alphonse de Verneuil
ALFRED WOODS..............Simon Rushworth
EMILIE NICHOL................Mrs. Rushworth
MADGE STUART.....................Blanquette
ALBERT CHASE......................Asticott
MRS. HUBERT WILLIS..........Mrs. Dubosc
HUBERT CARTER................Mr. Dubosc
SYDNEY FAIRBROTHER..........Mrs. Smith
ERNEST HILLIARD.............Major Walters
CAMERON CARR....................Bradshaw
IRENE TRIPOD....................Mme. Boin
ASTRA NATIONAL   1924
From the novel by W. J. Locke

Ben-Hur

RAMON NOVARRO...............Ben-Hur
FRANCIS X. BUSHMAN.............Messala
MAY McAVOY........................Esther
CLAIRE McDOWELL.............Mother of Hur
KATHLEEN KEY......................Tirzah
CARMEL MYERS........................Iras
NIGEL DE BRULIER.................Simonides
MITCHELL LEWIS.............Sheik Ilderim
LEO WHITE.......................Sanballat
FRANK CURRIER......................Arrius
CHARLES BELCHER................Balthasar
BETTY BRONSON....................Madonna
DALE FULLER.......................Amrah
WINTER HALL.......................Joseph
MGM   Director : Fred Niblo   1927
From the novel by General Lew Wallace

A supporting cast of 150,000 appeared in the film which was three years in the making. One year and a half was spent in filming historical sites in Italy, and the remainder of the time in completing the film in California.
Re-issued (with sound effects), May 1931

Best Years of Our Lives, The

MYRNA LOY...................Milly Stephenson
FREDRIC MARCH...............Al Stephenson
DANA ANDREWS...............Fred Derry
TERESA WRIGHT.............Peggy Stephenson
VIRGINIA MAYO...................Marie Derry
CATHY O'DONNELL............Wilma Cameron
HOAGY CARMICHAEL............Butch Engel
HAROLD RUSSELL.............Homer Parrish
GLADYS GEORGE............Hortense Derry
ROMAN BOHNEN.....................Pat Derry
RAY COLLINS.......................Mr. Milton
MINNA GOMBELL..............Mrs. Parrish
WALTER BALDWIN.............Mr. Parrish
STEVE COCHRAN......................Cliff
DOROTHY ADAMS.............Mrs. Cameron
DON BEDDOE...................Mr. Cameron
VICTOR CUTLER....................Woody
MARLENE AAMES.............Luella Parrish
CHARLES HALTON....................Prew
RAY TEAL.......................Mr. Mollett
HOWLAND CHAMBERLIN.............Thorpe
DEAN WHITE........................Novak
ERSKINE SANFORD...................Bullard
MICHAEL HALL.............Rob Stephenson
GOLDWYN   Director : William Wyler   1946
From the novel " Glory for Me " by MacKinlay Kantor

Big Blockade, The
British Civil Service

LESLIE BANKS   MORLAND GRAHAM
Royal Navy and Merchant Navy
WILL HAY   JOHN STUART
          BERNARD MILES
Royal Air Force
JOHN MILLS   MICHAEL RENNIE
PETER DE GREEFF   DAVID EVANS
               Press
QUENTIN REYNOLDS CYRIL CHAMBERLAIN
JOHN BOXER   OWEN REYNOLDS
Russian   MICHAEL REDGRAVE
Dane   LEIF KONOW
               German
ROBERT MORLEY   ALFRED DRAYTON
FRANK CELLIER   AUSTIN TREVOR
MARIUS GORING   ELLIOT MASON
PERCY WALSH   GEORGE MERRITT
JOSS AMBLER   ALBERT LIEVEN
               Quislings
BERNARD REBEL   GEORGE WOODBRIDGE
CHARLES MINOR   LAWRENCE KINGSTON
     Commentary by FRANK OWEN
EALING   Director : Charles Frend   1941
One of the earliest war-reconstruction films, produced with the co-operation of H.M. Government, the Ministry of Economic Warfare, the Royal Navy, the War Office, and the Royal Air Force

Bill of Divorcement, A

JOHN BARRYMORE............Hilary Fairfield
KATHARINE HEPBURN........Sydney Fairfield
BILLIE BURKE...............Margaret Fairfield
DAVID MANNERS................Kit Humphrey

ELIZABETH PATTERSON..........Aunt Hester
PAUL CAVANAGH...............Gray Meredith
HENRY STEPHENSON................Dr. Alliot
RADIO   Director : George Cukor   1933
From the play by Clemence Dane

Bill of Divorcement

MAUREEN O'HARA.............Sydney Fairfield
ADOLPHE MENJOU.............Hilary Fairfield
FAY BAINTER................Margaret Fairfield
HERBERT MARSHALL...........Gray Meredith
DAME MAY WHITTY............Hester Fairfield
PATRIC KNOWLES.................John Storm
C. AUBREY SMITH..................Dr. Alliot
ERNEST COSSART.........Rev. Dr. Pumphrey
KATHRYN COLLIER....................Basset
LAURI BEATTY..........................Susan
RKO   Director : John Farrow   1940
From the play by Clemence Dane

Birth of a Nation, The

HENRY WALTHALL.......Colonel Ben Cameron
MIRIAM COOPER
          Margaret Cameron, the elder sister
MAE MARSH.............Flora, the pet sister
JOSEPHINE CROWELL...........Mrs. Cameron
SPOTTISWOODE AITKEN.........Dr. Cameron
J. A. BERINGER...Wade Cameron, the second son
MAXFIELD STANLEY
          Duke Cameron, the youngest son
JENNIE LEE.....Mammy, their faithful old servant
RALPH LEWIS
     The Hon. Austin Stoneman, Leader of the House
LILLIAN GISH.................Elsie, his daughter
ELMER CLIFTON..............Phil, his elder son
ROBERT HARRON.......Tod, the younger son
WALLACE REID..............Jeff, the blacksmith
MARY ALDEN
     Lydia Brown, Stoneman's mulatto housekeeper
GEORGE SIEGMANN
     Silas Lynch, mulatto Lieutenant Governor
WALTER LONG.............Gus, a renegade negro
JOSEPH HENABERY..........Abraham Lincoln
RAOUL WALSH...............John Wilkes Booth
DONALD CRISP.............General U. S. Grant
HOWARD GAYE.........General Robert E. Lee
WILLIAM DE VAULL
          Nelse, an old-fashioned negro
WILLIAM FREEMAN
          Jake, a black man, faithful unto death
THOMAS WILSON............Stoneman's servant
Supported by a cast of 18,000 people and 3000 horses.
UA   Director : D. W. Griffith   1915
Re-issued in September 1922, and again in May 1931,
for the first time with sound

Bitter Sweet

JEANETTE MacDONALD ....'Sarah Millick
NELSON EDDY....................Carl Linden
GEORGE SANDERS.........Baron von Tranisch
IAN HUNTER..................Lord Shayne
FELIX BRESSART.........................Max
EDWARD ASHLEY.............Harry Daventry
LYNNE CARVER........................Dolly
DIANA LEWIS...........................Jane
CURT BOIS...........................Ernst
FAY HOLDEN...................Mrs. Millick
SIG RUMAN....................Herr Schlick
JANET BEECHER.............Lady Daventry
CHARLES JUDELS...............Herr Wyler
VEDA ANN BORG....................Manon
HERMAN BING................Marketkeeper

GRETA MEYER....................Mama Luden
MGM   Director : W. S. Van Dyke II   1941
From the musical play by Noel Coward
In Technicolor
Re-issued 1946

Blackmail

ANNY ONDRA.....................Alice White
SARA ALLGOOD..................Mrs. White
CHARLES PATON..................Mr. White
JOHN LONGDEN.................Frank Webber
DONALD CALTHROP.....................Tracy
CYRIL RITCHARDS..................The Artist
HANNAH JONES..................The Landlady
HARVEY BRABAN...............Chief Inspector
BIP   Director : Alfred Hitchcock   1929
Begun as a silent film; production was stopped
while the studios were wired for sound, and the
film was re-shot as a talkie, the first in Britain

Blackmail

EDWARD G. ROBINSON.........John R. Ingram
RUTH HUSSEY...................Helen Ingram
GENE LOCKHART.............William Ramey
BOBS WATSON.........................Hank
GUINN WILLIAMS............Moose McCarthy
JOHN WRAY...........................Diggs
ARTHUR HOHL.......................Rawlins
ESTHER DALE.........................Sarah
MGM   Director : H. C. Potter   1939

Blithe Spirit

REX HARRISON............Charles Condomine
CONSTANCE CUMMINGS......Ruth Condomine
KAY HAMMOND.......................Elvira
MARGARET RUTHERFORD........Mme. Arcati
HUGH WAKEFIELD.............Dr. Bradman
JOYCE CAREY.................Mrs. Bradman
JACQUELINE CLARKE.........Edith, the maid
CINEGUILD   Director : David Lean   1945
From the play by Noel Coward
Re-issued 1947

Blood and Sand

RUDOLPH VALENTINO...........Juan Gallardo
LILA LEE............................Carmen
NITA NALDI.......................Doña Sol
GEORGE FIELD....................El Nacional
WALTER LONG......................Plumitas
ROSE ROSANOVA.............Señora Augustus
LEO WHITE.........................Antonio
CHARLES BELCHER.............Don Joselito
JACK WINN..........................Potaje
MARIE MARSTINI.............El Carnacione
GILBERT CLAYTON..................Garabata
HARRY LAMONT.............El Pontelliro
GEORGE PERIOLAT.......Marquise de Guevera
SIDNEY DE GRAY.................Dr. Ruiz
FRED BECKER.......................Don Jose
DORCAS MATHEWS.........Señora Nacional
WILLIAM E. LAWRENCE............Fuentes
PARA   Director : Fred Niblo   1922
From the novel by Vicente Blasco Ibanez

Blood and Sand

TYRONE POWER.......................Juan
LINDA DARNELL............Carmen Espinosa
RITA HAYWORTH.................Doña Sol
NAZIMOVA.............Señora Augustias
ANTHONY QUINN..........Manolo de Palma
J. CARROL NAISH..................Garabato
JOHN CARRADINE..................Nacional

246

ROSAMUND JOHN
(Two Cities)

VAN JOHNSON
(*Metro-Goldwyn-Mayer*)

LYNN BARI......................Encarnacion
LAIRD CREGAR..................Natalio Curro
VICENTE GOMEZ....................Guitarist
WILLIAM MONTAGUE..........Antonio Lopez
GEORGE REEVES.........Captain Pierre Lauren
PEDRO DE CORDOBA........Don Jose Alvarez
FORTUNIO BONANOVA.........Pedro Espinosa
VICTOR KILIAN.......................Priest
MICHAEL MORRIS....................La Pulga
CHARLES STEVENS.............Pablo Gomez
ANN TODD.................Carmen, as a child
CORA SUE COLLINS......Encarnacion, as a child
RUSSELL HICKS.......................Marquis
MAURICE CASS.............El Milquetoast
REX DOWNING.................Juan, as a child
JOHN WALLACE....................Francisco
JACQUELINE DALVA....................Gachi
CULLEN JOHNSON...........Manolo, as a child
LARRY HARRIS..............Pablo, as a child
TED FRYE.................La Pulga, as a child
SCHUYLER STANDISH......Sebastian, as a child
20TH-FOX   Director: 1942
Rouben Mamoulian
Based on the novel by Vicente Blasco Ibanez
In Technicolor
Re-issued 1945

Blue Angel, The
EMIL JANNINGS........Professor Immanuel Rath
MARLENE DIETRICH..............Lola Frolich
KURT GERRON............Kiepert, a magician
ROSA VALETTI.................Guste, his wife
HANS ALBERS......................Mazeppa
EDUARD V. WINTERSTEIN
                    Director of the School
REINHOLD BERNT.................The Clown
HANS ROTH......................The Beadle
CARL HUSZAR-PUFFY.............The Publican
WILHELM DIEGELMANN..........The Captain
UFA (Germany)   Director: 1930
Josef Von Sternberg
From the novel "Professor Unrath" by Heinrich Mann
(See Foreign Language Films, page 347)

Boom Town
CLARK GABLE..............Big John McMasters
SPENCER TRACY..............Square John Sand
CLAUDETTE COLBERT...........Betsy Bartlett
HEDY LAMARR...........Karen Vanmeer
FRANK MORGAN...............Luther Aldrich
LIONEL ATWILL.........Harry Compton
CHILL WILLS...................Harmony Jones
MARION MARTIN....................Whitey
MINNA GOMBELL...........Spanish Eva
JOE YULE...................Ed Murphy
HORACE MURPHY...........Tom Murphy
ROY GORDON....................McCreery
RICHARD LANE.......Assistant District Attorney
CASEY JOHNSON....................Little Jack
BABY QUINTANILLA.................Baby Jack
GEORGE LESSEY....................Judge
SARA HADEN....................Miss Barnes
FRANK ORTH....................Barber
FRANK McGLYNN, SR. ....Deacon
CURT BOIS.......................Ferdie
MGM   Director: Jack Conway   1940

Boys Town
SPENCER TRACY...........Father Flanagan
MICKEY ROONEY.............Whitey Marsh
HENRY HULL....................Dave Morris

LESLIE FENTON....................Dan Farrow
GENE REYNOLDS................Tony Ponessa
EDWARD NORRIS...................Joe Marsh
ADDISON RICHARDS................The Judge
MINOR WATSON...................The Bishop
JONATHAN HALE.............John Hargraves
BOBS WATSON......................Pee Wee
MARTIN SPELLMAN................Skinny
MICKEY RENTSCHLER........Tommy Anderson
FRANKIE THOMAS............Freddie Fuller
JIMMY BUTLER................Paul Furguson
SIDNEY MILLER....................Mo Kahn
ROBERT EMMETT KEANE.............Burton
VICTOR KILIAN.................The Sheriff
MGM   Director: Norman Taurog   1939

Bridge of San Luis Rey, The
LILI DAMITA...........................Camile
ERNEST TORRENCE................Uncle Pio
RAQUEL TORRES......................Pepita
DON ALVARADO....................Manuel
DUNCAN RENALDO...................Esteban
HENRY B. WALTHALL.......Father Juniper
MICHAEL VAVITCH...................Viceroy
EMILY FITZROY....................Marquesa
JANE WINTON.....................Doña Clara
GORDON THORPE....................Jaime
MITCHELL LEWIS.............Captain Alvarado
PAUL ELLIS....................Don Vicente
EUGENIE BESSERER...................Nun
TULLY MARSHALL....................Townsman
MGM   Director: Charles Brabin   1930
From the Pulitzer Prize novel by Thornton Wilder

Bridge of San Luis Rey, The
LYNN BARI..........Micaela (The "Perichole")
AKIM TAMIROFF....................Uncle Pio
FRANCIS LEDERER................ { Manuel
                                { Esteban
NAZIMOVA........................The Marquesa
LOUIS CALHERN..................The Viceroy
BLANCHE YURKA...................The Abbess
DONALD WOODS................Brother Juniper
EMMA DUNN.................Doña Mercedes
BARTON HEPBURN.................Don Rubio
JOAN LORRING......................Pepita
ABNER BIBERMAN....................Maita
MINERVA URECAL.....Servant to Uncle Pio
and
ANTONIO TRIANA AND HIS DANCERS
UA   Director: Rowland V. Lee   1944
From the Pulitzer Prize novel by Thornton Wilder

Brief Encounter
CELIA JOHNSON..................Laura Jesson
TREVOR HOWARD.............Dr. Alec Harvey
CYRIL RAYMOND.................Fred Jesson
VALENTINE DYALL.............Stephen Lynn
STANLEY HOLLOWAY...........Albert Godby
JOYCE CAREY..................Myrtle Bagot
MARGARET BARTON.............Beryl Walters
DENNIS HARKIN...................Stanley
EVERLEY GREGG.............Dolly Messiter
CINEGUILD   Director: David Lean   1946
From the play by Noel Coward

Broadway Melody, The
ANITA PAGE........................Queenie
BESSIE LOVE............................Hank
CHARLES KING.........................Eddie
JED PROUTY....................Uncle Bernie
KENNETH THOMSON.....................Jock

EDWARD DILLON...............Stage Manager
MARY DORAN.........................Blonde
EDDIE KANE....................Zanfield
J. EMMETT BECK.................Babe Hatrick
MARSHALL RUTH....................Stew
DREW DEMAREST.....................Turpe
MGM   Director : Harry Beaumont   1929

Brother Rat
PRISCILLA LANE..............Joyce Winfree
WAYNE MORRIS................Billy Randolph
JOHNNIE DAVIS.......A. Furman Townsend, Jr
JANE BRYAN........................Kate Rice
EDDIE ALBERT.............." Bing " Edwards
RONALD REAGAN..............Dan Crawford
JANE WYMAN.................Claire Adams
HENRY O'NEILL.............Colonel Ramm
GORDON OLIVER.Captain " Lacedrawers " Rogers
LARRY WILLIAMS..........Harley Harrington
WILLIAM TRACEY...........Misto Bottome
JESSIE BUSLEY.....................Mrs. Brooks
OLIN HOWLAND......................Slim
LOUISE BEAVERS.....................Jenny
ISABEL WITHERS....................Nurse
FIRST NATIONAL   Director : William Keighley   1939
From the play by John Monks, Jr., and Fred F. Finklehoffe

Bulldog Drummond
RONALD COLMAN.........Bulldog Drummond
JOAN BENNETT.........................Phyllis
LILYAN TASHMAN.....................Erma
MONTAGU LOVE.......................Peterson
LAWRENCE GRANT..............Dr. Lakington
WILSON BENGE.........................Danny
CLAUDE ALLISTER......................Algy
ADOLPH MILAR...................Marcovitch
CHARLES SELLON....................Travers
TETSU KOMAI........................Chong
UA   Director : F. Richard Jones   1930
From the story by " Sapper "

C

Cabinet of Dr. Caligari, The
CONRAD VEIDT.......................Cesare
WERNER KRAUSS ....Caligari
LIL DAGOVER........................Jane
HANS VON TVARADOVSKI............Francis
FRIEDRICH FEHER.....................Alan
DECLA FILMS (Germany) Director: Robert Wiene 1919
(See Foreign Language Films, page 347)

Cage of Nightingales, A
(La Cage aux Rossignols)
NOEL-NOEL....................Clément Mathieu
MICHELINE FRANCEY.................Martine
GEORGES BISCOT...................Raymond
RENÉ GENIN........................Maxence
RENÉ BLANCARD.....................Rachin
MARGUERITE DUCOURET....Martine's mother
ROGER VINCENT..............The Academician
JEAN MOREL.............The New Director
GEORGES PAULAIS................M. Langlois
RICHARD FRANÇOEUR.........M. de Mazères
ANDRÉ NICOLLE..............M. de La Prade
MARCELLE PRAINCE.....A Patron of the School
MICHEL FRANÇOIS............Eloi Lequérec
ROGER LAUGIER.................Le Petit Krebs
THE BOYS' CHOIR OF THE CROIX DE BOIS
GAUMONT (France)   Director : Jean Dreville 1945
(See Foreign Language Films, page 347)

Camille
NORMA TALMADGE..................Camille
GILBERT ROLAND....................Armand
LILYAN TASHMAN...................Olympe
ROSE DIONE.......................Prudence
HARVEY CLARK....................The Baron
HELEN JEROME EDDY....Camille's maid
ALEC FRANCIS.......................The Duke
ALBERT CONTI.......................Henri
MAURICE COSTELLO..........Armand's father
ETTA LEE.........................Mataloti
FIRST NATIONAL   Director : Fred Niblo   1927
Modernized from the novel " La Dame aux Camélias "
by Dumas

Camille
GRETA GARBO.....................Marguerite
ROBERT TAYLOR....................Armand
LIONEL BARRYMORE..............M. Duval
ELIZABETH ALLAN.................Nichette
JESSIE RALPH.......................Nanine
HENRY DANIELL.........Baron de Varville
LENORE ULRIC.....................Olympe
LAURA HOPE CREWS.............Prudence
REX O'MALLEY.......................Gaston
RUSSELL HARDIE.....................Gustave
E. E. CLIVE.......................Saint Gaudens
MGM   Director : George Cukor   1936
Based on the play and novel " La Dame aux Camélias "
by Dumas

Captain Blood
J. WARREN KERRIGAN.........Captain Blood
JEAN PAIGE.............Arabella Bishop
WILFRID NORTH.............Colonel Bishop
JAMES MORRISON.............Jeremy Pitt
CHARLOTTE MERRIAM.............Mary Traill
BERTRAM GRASSBY.............Don Diego
ALLAN FORREST.........Lord Julian Wade
TEMPLAR SAXE.............Governor Steed
HENRY BARROWS.............Lord Willoughby
OTTO MATIESEN...............Judge Jeffreys
OTIS HARLAN.......................Corliss
JACK CURTIS....................Wolverstone
HENRY HEBERT.............Captain Hobart
ROBERT BOLDER.......Admiral Van der Kuylen
VITAGRAPH   1925
From the novel by Rafael Sabatini

Captain Blood
ERROL FLYNN.....................Peter Blood
LIONEL ATWILL.............Colonel Bishop
ROSS ALEXANDER.................Jeremy Pitt
HENRY STEPHENSON.........Lord Willoughby
HOBART CAVANAUGH.............Dr. Bronson
BESSIE RALPH..................Mrs. Marlow
FRANK McGLYNN..................Rev. Ogle
DAVID TORRENCE.............Andrew Baynes
PEDRO DE CORDOBA.............Don Diego
HARRY GOULDING....................Kent
IVAN SIMPSON...................Prosecutor
DENNIS D. AUBURN.............Lord Gildoy
E. E. CLIVE.............Clerk to the Court
MAUD LESLIE....................Mrs. Baynes
VERNON STEELE.................King James
OLIVIA DE HAVILLAND........Arabella Bishop
BASIL RATHBONE..................Levasseur
GUY KIBBEE.....................Hagthorpe
ROBERT BARRAT..................Wolverstone
DONALD MEEK..................Dr. Whacker
FORRESTER HARVEY.........Honesty Nuthall

HOLMES HERBERT.............Captain Gardner
J. CARROL NAISH....................Cahusac
GEORGE HASSELL.............Governor Steele
LEONARD MUDIE................Baron Jeffreys
STUART CASEY...............Captain Hobart
MARY FORBES....................Mrs. Steed
COLIN KENNY............Lord Chester Dyke
GARDNER JAMES.........................Slave
WARN   Director : Michael Curtiz   1936
From the novel by Rafael Sabatini

Captains Courageous
SPENCER TRACY......................Manuel
FREDDIE BARTHOLOMEW.............Harvey
LIONEL BARRYMORE...................Disko
MELVYN DOUGLAS.................Mr. Cheyne
MICKEY ROONEY.........................Dan
CHARLEY GRAPEWIN............Uncle Salters
JOHN CARRADINE............." Long Jack "
OSCAR O'SHEA......................Cushman
JACK LA RUE..........................Priest
WALTER KINGSFORD...............Dr. Finley
DONALD BRIGGS.........................Tyler
SAM McDANIELS......................" Doc "
BILLY BURRUD.......................Charles
MGM   Director : Victor Fleming   1937
From the novel by Rudyard Kipling

Captive Heart, The
MICHAEL REDGRAVE......Captain Karel Hasek
RACHEL KEMPSON...............Celia Mitchell
FREDERICK LEISTER...........Mr. Mowbray
MERVYN JOHNS.............Private Evans
RACHEL THOMAS...................Mrs. Evans
JACK WARNER...............Corporal Horsfall
GLADYS HENSON.................Mrs. Horsfall
JAMES HARCOURT.....................Doctor
GORDON JACKSON..........Lieutenant Lennox
ELLIOT MASON..................Mrs. Lennox
MARGOT FITZSIMONS..........Elspeth McDougall
DAVID KEIR................Mr. McDougall
DEREK BOND.........'.......Lieutenant Harley
JANE BARRETT.................Caroline Harley
MERIEL FORBES................Beryl Curtiss
ROBERT WYNDHAM
        Lt. Cdr. Robert Marsden, R.N.V.R.
BASIL RADFORD.........Major Ossy Dalrymple
GUY MIDDLETON.........Captain Jim Grayson
JIMMY HANLEY...........Private Matthews
RALPH MICHAEL....Captain Thurston, R.A.M.C.
JACK LAMBERT.........................Padre
KAREL STEPANEK......................Forster
FREDERICK RICHTER......Camp Kommandant
FREDERICK SCHILLER..........German M.O.
                and
Officers and men of the 51st Highland Division and
50th A.A. Brigade
EALING   Director : Basil Dearden   1946
*Made with the co-operation of the War Office and
the British Army of the Rhine*

Carnival
MATHESON LANG..................Silvio Steno
JOSEPH SCHILDKRAUT...........Count Andrea
DOROTHY BOUCHIER..........Simonetta Steno
LILIAN BRAITHWAITE....................Italia
KAY HAMMOND........................Nella
BRIAN BUCHEL........................Lelio
DICKIE EDWARDS.......................Nino
B & D   Director : Herbert Wilcox   1932
From the play by C. M. Hardinge

Catherine the Great
FLORA ROBSON..............Empress Elizabeth
DOUGLAS FAIRBANKS, JR. ...Grand Duke Peter
ELISABETH BERGNER................Catherine
GERALD DU MAURIER...............LeCocq
GRIFFITH JONES................Gregory Orlov
IRENE VANBRUGH.......Princess Anhalt-Zerbst
JOAN GARDINER..................Katushinka
DOROTHY HALE................Countess Olga
DIANA NAPIER..............Countess Vorotzova
LFP   Director : Paul Czinner   1934

Champ, The
WALLACE BEERY.......................Champ
JACKIE COOPER......................Dink
IRENE RICH..........................Linda
ROSCO ATES.........................Sponge
EDWARD BROPHY........................Tim
HALE HAMILTON.......................Tony
JESSE SCOTT.........................Jonah
MARCIA MAE JONES.........Mary Lou
MGM   Director : King Vidor   1932

Champagne Charlie
TOMMY TRINDER
        George Leybourne (Champagne Charlie)
STANLEY HOLLOWAY........The Great Vance
BETTY WARREN...............Bessie Bellwood
JEAN KENT..........Dolly (Bessie's daughter)
ROBERT WYNDHAM
        Duckworth (Chairman of the Mogador)
HARRY FOWLER......................'Orace
DRUSILLA WILLS..............Bessie's dresser
JOAN CAROL..........Cora (Mogador barmaid)
BILLY SHINE..........Mogador Stage Manager
GUY MIDDLETON.................Tipsy Swell
FREDERICK PIPER...................Learoyd
ANDREA MALANDRINOS...............Gatti
PAUL BONIFAS.....................Targetino
AUSTIN TREVOR...................The Duke
PETER DE GREEFF.....Lord Petersfield (his son)
EDDIE PHILLIPS....................Tom Sayers
ERIC BOON.........................Clinker
NORMAN PIERCE
        Landlord of the " Elephant and Castle "
LESLIE CLARKE
        Fred Sanders (Leybourne's brother)
EALING   Director : Cavalcanti   1944

Charley's Aunt
SYD CHAPLIN...Sir Fancourt Babberley (" Babs ")
ETHEL SHANNON.................Elsa Delahay
JAMES E. PAGE......................Spettigue
LUCIEN LITTLEFIELD........Brassett, the Scout
ALEC B. FRANCIS.................Mr. Delahay
PHILLIPS SMALLEY.........Sir Francis Chesney
EULALIE JENSEN......Donna Lucia d'Alvardorez
DAVID JAMES....................Jack Chesney
JIMMIE HARRISON...........Charley Wykeham
MARY AIKEN...........................Amy
PRISCILLA BONNER.....................Kitty
COL   1926
From the farce by Brandon Thomas

Charley's Aunt
FLORA LE BRETON..............Elsa Delahay
HUGH WILLIAMS............Charley Wykeham
CHARLES RUGGLES
        Lord Babberly, who poses as Charley's aunt
DORIS LLOYD.........Donna Lucia d'Alvardorez
JUNE COLLYER.................Amy Spettigue
RODNEY McLENNON.............Kitty Verdun

ESTHER WILLIAMS
(*Metro-Goldwyn-Mayer*)

HALLIWELL HOBBES..........Stephen Spettigue
PHILLIPS SMALLEY.........Sir Francis Chesney
WILSON BENGE.........................Brassett
IDEAL   Director : Al Christie   1931
From the farce by Brandon Thomas

Charley's (American) Aunt
JACK BENNY...........................Babbs
KAY FRANCIS.....................Donna Lucia
JAMES ELLISON...................Jack Chesney
ANNE BAXTER.....................Amy Spettigue
EDMUND GWENN.............Stephen Spettigue
REGINALD OWEN................Mr. Redcliffe
LAIRD CREGAR............Sir Francis Chesney
ARLEEN WHELAN.................Kitty Verdun
RICHARD HAYDN...........Charley Wykeham
ERNEST COSSART.....................Brassett
MORTON LOWRY...............Harley Stafford
LIONEL PAPE.......................Babberly
WILL STANTON.....................Messenger
MONTAGUE SHAW.................Elderly Man
CLAUD ALLISTER)
WILLIAM AUSTIN)..................Spectators
MAURICE CASS.................Octogenarian
20TH-FOX   Director : Archie Mayo   1942
Based on the farce by Brandon Thomas

Chinese Bungalow, The
MATHESON LANG...................Yuan Sing
SHAYLE GARDNER..........Richard Marquess
GEORGE THIRWELL...........Harold Marquis
CLIFFORD McLAGEN...Abdul, the Malay servant
GEORGE BUTLER)
LOUIS MILLER)............Chinese Servants
GENEVIEVE TOWNSEND..............Charlotte
JULIETTE COMPTON....................Sadie
STOLL   1926
From the play by Marion Osmond and James Corbet

Chinese Bungalow, The
MATHESON LANG...................Yuan Sing
JILL ESMOND-MOORE....................Jean
DEREK WILLIAMS.....................Harold
ANNA NEAGLE.......................Charlotte
BALLARD BERKELEY...................Richard
W & F   Director : J. B. Williams   1931
From the play by Marion Osmond and James Corbet

Chocolate Soldier, The
NELSON EDDY.......................Karl Lang
RISE STEVENS...................Maria Lanyi
NIGEL BRUCE..................Bernard Fischer
FLORENCE BATES.................Mme. Helene
DOROTHY GILMORE.....................Magda
NYDIA WESTMAN..................Liesel (maid)
MAX BARWYN.........................Anton
CHARLES JUDELS.................Klementov
MGM   Director : Roy Del Ruth   1942
*Based on " The Guardsman " by Ferenc Molnar,
with music and lyrics from Oscar Straus's " The
Chocolate Soldier "*

Christian, The
RICHARD DIX.....................John Storm
MAE BUSCH......................Glory Quayle
GARETH HUGHES................Brother Paul
PHYLLIS HAVER...................Polly Love
CYRIL CHADWICK............Lord Robert Ure
MAHLON HAMILTON...............Horatio Drake
JOSEPH DOWLING............Father Lampleigh
CLAUDE GILLINGWATER..........Lord Storm
JOHN HERDMAN.................Parson Quayle

BERYL MERCER..........................Liza
ROBERT BOLDER................Rev. Golightly
MILLA DAVENPORT....................Matron
ALICE HESSE..........................Mary
AILEEN PRINGLE.............Lady Robert Ure
ERIC MAYNE.........................Doctor
GOLDWYN   1923
*From the novel by Sir Hall Caine
Richard Dix and other members of the company
came over to Britain to make this film.*

Chu-Chin-Chow
BETTY BLYTHE.......................Zahrat
HERBERT LANGLEY............Abou Hassan
RANDLE AYRTON..................Kasim Baba
JUDD GREEN.......................Ali Baba
EVA MOORE.........................Alcolm
JAMESON THOMAS......................Omar
JEFF BARLOW......................Mustafa
OLAF HYTTEN......................Mukbill
DORA LEVIS.......................Mahbubsh
DACIA..................The Dancing Slave
GRAHAM-WILCOX   Director : Herbert Wilcox   1923
*From the musical play by Oscar Asche and
Frederic Norton
Filmed at UFA Studios, Neubabelsburg, near Berlin*

Cimarron
RICHARD DIX...................Yancey Cravat
IRENE DUNNE...................Sabra Cravat
ESTELLE TAYLOR....................Dixie Lee
NANCE O'NEIL..............Felice Venable
WILLIAM COLLIER, JR. ....The Kid
ROSCO ATES.....................Jess Rickey
GEORGE E. STONE...................Sol Levy
STANLY FIELDS...................Lon Yountis
ROBERT McWADE................Louie Heffner
EDNA MAY OLIVER.........Mrs. Tracy Wyatt
FRANK DARRIEN..................Mr. Bixley
EUGENE JACKSON.....................Isaiah
DOLORES BROWN......Ruby Big Elk (elder)
GLORIA VONIC..........Ruby Big Elk (younger)
OTTO HOFFMAN.............Murch Rankin
WILLIAM ORLAMOND.............Grat Gotch
FRANK BEAL....................Louis Venable
NANCY DOVER...........Donna Cravat (elder)
HELEN PARRISH........Donna Cravat (younger)
DONALD DILLAWAY............" Cim " (elder)
JUNIOR JOHNSON............" Cim " (younger)
DOUGLAS SCOTT............." Cim " (youngest)
REGINALD STREETER..............Yancey, Jr.
LOIS JANE CAMPBELL.............Felice, Jr.
ANN LEE.....................Aunt Cassandra
TYRONE BRERETON...........Sabney Venable
LILLIAN LANE....................Cousin Bella
HENRY ROCQUEMORE........Jouett Goforth
NELL CRAIG............Arminta Greenwood
ROBERT McKENZIE..................Pat Leary
RADIO   Director : Wesley Ruggles   1931
From the story by Edna Ferber

Circonstances Atténuantes
MICHEL SIMON............M. " Le Sentencier "
SUZANNE DANTÈS.......Mme. " Le Sentencier "
ROBERT ARNOUX................The Chauffeur
DORVILLE ...." Le Bouic "
MLLE. LESAFFRE..........Mme. Bouic
ARLETTY...................Marie Qu'a D'Ça
ANDREX..................." Môme de Dieu "
ROBERT OZANNE............" Cinq de Trique "
GEORGES LANNES..........." Coup de Chasse "

ST. OBER............................." Coco "
MICHEL FRANÇOIS.............." La Poupée "
MARIE-JOSÉ.............Mme. " Cinq de Trique "
MILA PARÉLY................." La Panthère "
SOCIÉTÉ FRANÇAISE DE PRODUCTION ET D'ÉDITION 1938
(France)   Director : Jean Boyer
From the novel by Marcel Arnac
(See Foreign Language Films, page 347)

Citizen Kane

JOSEPH COTTEN.............Jedediah Leland
DOROTHY COMINGORE........Susan Alexander
EVERETT SLOANE..............Mr. Bernstein
RAY COLLINS................James W. Gettys
GEORGE COULOURIS......Walter Parks Thatcher
AGNES MOOREHEAD.......Mrs. Kane (mother)
PAUL STEWART.....................Raymond
RUTH WARRICK................Emily Norton
ERSKINE SANFORD..........Herbert Carter
WILLIAM ALLAND.................Thompson
FORTUNIO BONANOVA..............Matiste
GUS SCHILLING...............Head Waiter
PHILIP VAN ZANDT............Mr. Rawlston
GEORGIA BACKUS.............Miss Anderson
HARRY SHANNON...............Kane's father
SONNY BUPP....................Kane III
BUDDY SWAN..................Kane, aged 8
ORSON WELLES...........................Kane
RKO   Director : Orson Welles   1942

City Lights

VIRGINIA CHERRILL.............A Blind Girl
FLORENCE LEE.............Her grandmother
HARRY MYERS.........An Eccentric Millionaire
ALLAN GARCIA...................His butler
HANK MANN.................A Prizefighter
CHARLES CHAPLIN...................A Tramp
Written, produced and
directed by Charles Chaplin   1931
*This film had a special opening run at the Dominion
Theatre, London, in February 1931, where Charles
Chaplin made a personal appearance on the opening
night.*

City of Song

JAN KIEPURA...............Giovanni Gavallone
BETTY STOCKFIELD.............Claire Winter
HUGH WAKEFIELD....The Hon. Roddy Fielding
HEATHER ANGEL......................Carmela
FRANCESCO MALDACEA.................Chi
PHILIP EASTON...................John Barlow
MILES MALLESON............Stage Doorkeeper
STERLING   Director : Carmine Gallone   1930

Coming Through the Rye

ALMA TAYLOR...................Helen Adair
JAMES CAREW.....................Colonel Adair
SHAYLE GARDNER.............Paul Vasher
GWYNNE HERBERT.................Mrs. Adair
EILEEN DENNES.............Sylvia Fleming
HENRY VIBART.................Mr. Tempest
FRANCIS LISTER...............Dick Fellows
RALPH FORBES...............George Tempest
JOHN MacANDREWS.................Simpkins
MARGOT ARMSTRONG...........Alice Adair
NANCY PRICE.................Mrs. Titmouse
CHRISTINE RAYNER...............Jane Peach
HEPWORTH   Director : Cecil M. Hepworth   1924
From the story by Helen Mathers

Congress Dances

LILIAN HARVEY..................Chrystel
CONRAD VEIDT............Prince Metternich

HENRY GARAT............The Czar, Alexander I
GIBB McLAUGHLIN..Bibikoff, the Czar's Adjutant
LIL DAGOVER.....................The Countess
REGINALD PURDELL
                Pepi, secretary to Metternich
DR. PHILIP MANNERING......King of Saxony
HUMBERSTON WRIGHT.....Duke of Wellington
HELEN HAYE.....................The Princess
SPENCER TREVOR.........Finance Minister
TARQUINI D'OR............The Heurige Singer
UFA (Germany)   Director : Erik Charell   1931
(See Foreign Language Films, page 347)

Constant Nymph, The

GEORGE HEINRICH...................Sanger
MARY CLARE........................Linda
MABEL POULTON....................Tessa
DOROTHY BOYD.....................Paulina
BENITA HUME........................Toni
YVONNE THOMAS....................Kate
ERNA STURM........................Susan
IVOR NOVELLO......................Lewis
TONY DE LUNGO...................Roberto
PETER EVAN THOMAS.................Ike
ROBERT GARRISON.................Trigorin
FRANCES DOBLE....................Florence
J. H. ROBERTS................Dr. Churchill
GAINS   Director : Adrian Brunel   1928
*From the novel by Margaret Kennedy, and the play
by her and Basil Dean*

Constant Nymph, The

VICTORIA HOPPER ....Tessa
BRIAN AHERNE....................Lewis Dodd
PEGGY BLYTHE......................Lena
JANE BAXTER........................Toni
JANE CORNELL.......................Kate
BERYL LAVERICK....................Susan
LYN HARDING.......................Sanger
MARY CLARE........................Linda
LEONORA CORBETT..................Florence
TONY DE LUNGO...................Roberto
JIM GERALD.......................Trigorin
ATHOLE STEWART............Charles Churchill
GB   Director : Basil Dean   1934
*From the novel by Margaret Kennedy and the play by her
and Basil Dean. This was the first sound version.*

Constant Nymph, The

CHARLES BOYER..................Lewis Dodd
JOAN FONTAINE.................Tessa Sanger
ALEXIS SMITH.............Florence Creighton
BRENDA MARSHALL.............Tony Sanger
CHARLES COBURN. ....Charles Creighton
DAME MAY WHITTY........Lady Longborough
JEAN MUIR....................Kate Sanger
PETER LORRE................Fritz Bercovy
MONTAGU LOVE.............Albert Sanger
EDWARD CIANNELLI...............Roberto
JOYCE REYNOLDS.............Paula Sanger
DORIS LLOYD.................Miss Hamilton
WARN   Director : Edmund Goulding   1945
*From the novel by Margaret Kennedy, and the play
by her and Basil Dean*

Corn Is Green, The

BETTE DAVIS.......................Miss Moffat
NIGEL BRUCE.......................The Squire
RHYS WILLIAMS.....................Mrs. Jones
ROSALIND IVAN....................Mrs. Watty

MILDRED DUNNOCK............Miss Ronberry
ARTHUR SHIELDS...................Will Davis
GWENYTH HUGHES...............Sarah Pugh
THOMAS LOUDEN.....................Old Tom
BILLY ROY...............................Idwal
BRANDON HURST..............Llewellyn Powell
TONY ELLIS......................Will Hughes
ELLIOTT DARE....................Glyn Thomas
LESLIE VINCENT....................John Owen
ROBERT CHERRY...................Dai Evans
RALPH CATHEY........................Eddie
JOCK WATT.......................The Groom
GENE ROSS......................Gwilym Jones
ROBERT REGENT.................Rhys Norman
JACK OWEN..............................Tudor
JOHN DALL......................Morgan Evans
JOAN LORRING...................Bessie Watty
WARN   Director: Irving Rapper   1946
From the play by Emlyn Williams

Count of Monte Cristo, The

LÉON MATHOT
               Edmond Dantès, Count of Monte Cristo
NELLY CORMON.....................Mercédès
M. GARAT...................Fernand Mondégo
M. COLAS.........................Danglars
ALBERT MAYER......................Villefort
M. DALLEUI.......................Caderousse
FILM D'ART (France)   1917
          Director: Henri Pauctal

*This film was issued as a serial in fifteen episodes
which appeared in the following order: Edmond
Dantès; The State Prisoner; Abbé Faria;
The Secret of Monte Cristo; The Crime at the Inn;
The Vendetta; The Philanthropist; The Grottoes
of Monte Cristo; The Conquest of Paris; Haydée's
Story; Haydée's Revenge; The Day of Reckoning;
The Last Exploits of Caderousse; Villefort's
Punishment; The Triumph of Dantès.
(See Foreign Language Films, page 347)*

Covered Wagon, The

J. WARREN KERRIGAN...........Will Banion
LOIS WILSON...................Molly Wingate
ALAN HALE.....................Sam Woodhull
CHARLES OGLE....................Mr. Wingate
ETHEL WALES...................Mrs. Wingate
ERNEST TORRENCE...................Jackson
TULLY MARSHALL....................Bridger
GUY OLIVER.........................Dunston
JOHNNY FOX.....................Jed Wingate
PARA   Director: James Cruze   1924
From the novel by Emerson Hough

Crime and Punishment

PETER LORRE...................Raskolnikov
EDWARD ARNOLD.............Inspector Porfiry
MARIAN MARSH........................Sonya
TALA BIRELL.......................Antonia
ELISABETH RISDON..........Mrs. Raskolnikov
ROBERT ALLEN......................Dimitri
DOUGLASS DUMBRILLE..............Grilov
GENE LOCKHART......................Lushin
CHARLES WALDRON....The University President
THURSTON HALL...................The Editor
JOHNNY ARTHUR....................The Clerk
MRS. PATRICK CAMPBELL.....The Pawnbroker
COL   Director: Josef Von Sternberg   1936

D

Daddy Long Legs

JANET GAYNOR...................Judy Abbott
WARNER BAXTER..............Jervis Pendleton
UNA MERKEL....................Sally McBride
JOHN ARLEDGE..................Jimmy McBride
ELIZABETH PATTERSON..........Mrs. Lippett
KATHLYN WILLIAMS..........Mrs. Pendleton
SHEILA MANNORS............Gloria Pendleton
CLAUDE GILLINGWATER.................Riggs
LOUISE CLOSSER HALE..........Miss Pritchard
EFFIE ELLSLER..................Mrs. Semple
EDWIN MAXWELL......................Wykoff
KENDALL McCOMAS...........Freddie Perkins
BILLY BARTY..........................Billy
FOX   Director: Alfred Santell   1931
From the novel by Jean Webster

Dance, Fools, Dance

JOAN CRAWFORD......................Bonnie
LESTER VAIL.............................Bob
CLIFF EDWARDS.................Bert Scranton
WILLIAM BAKEWELL..................Rodney
WILLIAM HOLDEN.............Stanley Jordan
CLARK GABLE....................Jake Luva
EARLE FOXE............................Wally
PURNELL PRATT......................Parker
HALE HAMILTON.......................Selby
NATALIE MOOREHEAD...................Della
JOAN MARSH.........................Sylvia
RUSSELL HOPTON.....................Whitey
MGM   Director: Harry Beaumont   1931

Dangerous Moonlight

ANTON WALBROOK..........Stefan Radetzky
SALLY GRAY....................Carole Peters
DERRICK DE MARNEY..........Mike Carroll
KENETH KENT......................De Guise
PERCY PARSONS...................Bill Peters
J. H. ROBERTS.............Resident Physician
CECIL PARKER......................Specialist
GUY MIDDLETON.....................Shorty
JOHN LAURIE..........British Commander
FREDERICK VALK....Polish Bomber Commander
RKO-BRIT   Director: Brian Desmond Hurst   1941
*The film for which Richard Addinsell composed the
" Warsaw Concerto "
Re-issued 1942*

Daniel Deronda

REGINALD FOX.............Daniel Deronda
DOROTHY FANE............Gwendolen Harleth
CLIVE BROOK..............Mallinger Grandcourt
ANN TREVOR..................Mirah Lapidoth
MASTER BRITISH FILMS   1922
From the novel by George Eliot

Dark Angel, The

RONALD COLMAN.................Hilary Trent
VILMA BANKY.....................Kitty Vane
WYNDHAM STANDING.........Gerald Shannon
FRANK ELLIOTT..............Lord Beaumont
HELEN JEROME EDDY...........Miss Pindle
FLORENCE TURNER......................Roma
CHARLES LANE...........Sir Evelyn Vane
FIRST NATIONAL   Director: 1926
          George Fitzmaurice
From the play by Guy Bolton

Dark Angel, The

FREDRIC MARCH	Alan Trent
MERLE OBERON	Kitty Vane
HERBERT MARSHALL	Gerald Shannon
JANET BEECHER	Mrs. Shannon
JOHN HALLIDAY	Sir George Barton
HENRIETTA CROSMAN	Granny Vane
FRIEDA INESCORT	Ann West
CLAUDE ALLISTER	Lawrence Bidley
GEORGE BREAKSTON	Joe
FAY CHALDECOT	Betty
DENIS CHALDECOT	Ginger
DOUGLAS WALTON	Roulston
SARAH EDWARDS	Mrs. Bidley
JOHN MILTERN	Mr. Vane
OLAF HYTTEN	Mills
LAWRENCE GRANT	Mr. Tanner
HELENA BYRNE-GRANT	Hannah
ANN FIELDER	Mrs. Gallop
DAVID TORRENCE	Mr. Shannon
CORA SUE COLLINS	Kitty (child)
JIMMY BAXTER	Alan (child)
JIMMY BUTLER	Gerald (child)
RANDOLPH CONNOLLY	Lawrence (child)

UA   Director : Sidney Franklin   1936
From the play by Guy Bolton

Dark Mirror, The

OLIVIA DE HAVILLAND	Terry Collins / Ruth Collins
LEW AYRES	Dr. Scott Elliott
THOMAS MITCHELL	Detective Stevenson
RICHARD LONG	Rusty
CHARLES EVANS	District Attorney Girard
GARY OWEN	Franklin
LESTER ALLEN	George Benson
LELA BLISS	Mrs. Didriksen
MARTA MITROVICH	Miss Beade
AMELITA WARD	Photo Double

UNIV   Director : Robert Siodmak   1946

Dark Victory

BETTE DAVIS	Judith Traherne
GEORGE BRENT	Dr. Frederick Steele
HUMPHREY BOGART	Michael O'Leary
GERALDINE FITZGERALD	Ann King
RONALD REAGAN	Alec
HENRY TRAVERS	Dr. Parsons
CORA WITHERSPOON	Carrie
DOROTHY PETERSON	Miss Wainwright
VIRGINIA BRISSAC	Martha
CHARLES RICHMAN	Colonel Mantle
HERBERT RAWLINSON	Dr. Carter
LEONARD MUDIE	Dr. Driscoll
FAY HELM	Miss Dodd
LOTTIE WILLIAMS	Lucy

WARN   Director : Edmund Goulding   1939

David Copperfield

W. C. FIELDS	Micawber
LIONEL BARRYMORE	Dan Peggotty
MADGE EVANS	Agnes Wickfield
MAUREEN O'SULLIVAN	Dora Spenlow
EDNA MAY OLIVER	Aunt Betsy Trotwood
LEWIS STONE	Mr. Wickfield
FRANK LAWTON	David, the man
FREDDIE BARTHOLOMEW	David, the child
ELIZABETH ALLAN	Mrs. Copperfield
ROLAND YOUNG	Uriah Heep
HUGH WILLIAMS	Steerforth
BASIL RATHBONE	Mr. Murdstone
ELSA LANCHESTER	Clickett
JEAN CADELL	Mrs. Micawber
LENNOX PAWLE	Mr. Dick
VIOLET KEMBLE COOPER	Jane Murdstone
UNA O'CONNOR	Mrs. Gummidge
HERBERT MUNDIN	Barkis
FLORINE McKINNEY	Little Em'ly, the woman
JESSIE RALPH	Nurse Peggotty
JOHN BUCKLER	Ham
FAY CHALDECOT	Little Em'ly, the child
MARILYN KNOWLDEN	Agnes, the child
HUGH WALPOLE	The Vicar

MGM   Director : George Cukor   1934
*From the novel by Charles Dickens
Re-issued 1940 and 1945*

Dawn Patrol, The

RICHARD BARTHELMESS	Dick Courtney
DOUGLAS FAIRBANKS, Jr.	Douglas Scott
NEIL HAMILTON	Major Brand
WILLIAM JANNEY	Gordon Scott
JAMES FINLAYSON	Field Sergeant
CLYDE COOK	Bott
GARDNER JAMES	Ralph Hollister
EDMOND BREON	Lieutenant Phipps
FRANK McHUGH	Flaherty
JACK ACKROYD / HARRY ALLEN	Mechanics

FIRST NATIONAL   Director : Howard Hawks   1930

Day at the Races, A

GROUCHO MARX	Dr. Hackenbush
CHICO MARX	Tony
HARPO MARX	Stuffy
ALLAN JONES	Gil
MAUREEN O'SULLIVAN	Judy
MARGARET DUMONT	Mrs. Upjohn
LEONARD CEELEY	Whitmore
DOUGLAS DUMBRILLE	Morgan
ESTHER MUIR	" Flo "
SIG RUMAN	Dr. Steinberg
ROBERT MIDDLEMASS	Sheriff
	and
	The Crinoline Choir

MGM   Director : Sam Wood   1937
Re-issued 1947

Day of Wrath
(*Vredens Dag*)

THORKILD ROOSE	Absalon Pedersson
LISBETH MOVIN	Anne, his wife
SIGRID NEIIENDAM	Merete, his mother
PREBEN LERDORFF	Martin, his son by his first wife
OLAF USSING	Laurentius
ANNA SVIERKIER	Herlof's Marthe

FILM-CENTRALEN-PALLADIUM (Denmark)   1943
*Director : Carl Th. Dreyer
Based on the novel " Anne Pedersdotter "
by Wiers Jenssens*
(*See Foreign Language Films, page 347*)

Day Will Dawn, The

RALPH RICHARDSON	Lockwood
DEBORAH KERR	Kari
HUGH WILLIAMS	Colin Metcalfe
GRIFFITH JONES	Gunter
FRANCIS L. SULLIVAN	Wettau
ROLAND CULVER	Naval Attaché
FINLAY CURRIE	Alstad
BERNARD MILES	McAllister
NIALL MACGINNIS	Olaf
ELIZABETH MANN	Gerda

PATRICIA MEDINA....................Ingrid
HENRY OSCAR........................Editor
JOHN WARWICK.....................Milligan
DAVID HORNE........................Evans
HENRY HEWITT................News Editor
ANN FARRER..............Evans' secretary
GEORGE MERRITT......German Trawler Captain
TWO CITIES   Director : Harold French   1942

Dead of Night
MERVYN JOHNS..................Walter Craig
ROLAND CULVER...................Eliot Foley
MARY MERRALL...................Mrs. Foley
GOOGIE WITHERS...............Joan Cortland
FREDERICK VALK............Dr. Van Straaten
ANTONY BAIRD.................Hugh Grainger
SALLY ANN HOWES..............Sally O'Hara
ROBERT WYNDHAM...............Dr. Albury
JUDY KELLY.....................Joyce Grainger
MILES MALLESON...............Hearse Driver
MICHAEL ALLAN..............Jimmy Watson
BARBARA LEAKE...................Mrs. O'Hara
RALPH MICHAEL.................Peter Cortland
ESME PERCY....................Antique Dealer
BASIL RADFORD.................George Parratt
NAUNTON WAYNE..............Larry Potter
PEGGY BRYAN......................Mary Lee
ALLAN JEAYES...............Maurice Olcott
MICHAEL REDGRAVE............Maxwell Frere
ELIZABETH WELCH..................Beulah
HARTLEY POWER................Sylvester Kee
MAGDA KUN..........................Mitzi
GARRY MARSH...................Harry Parker
RENEE GADD......................Mrs. Craig
EALING   1945
Directors of this " omnibus " film were :
Cavalcanti : The " Christmas Party " sequence and
   the " Ventriloquist's Dummy " sequence
Charles Crichton : The " Golfing Story " sequence
Basil Dearden : The " Hearse Driver " sequence
Robert Hamer : The " Haunted Mirror " sequence

Dernier Milliardaire, Le
RENÉE ST.-CYR.................Princess Isabelle
MAX DEARLY........................M. Banco
SINOËL..........................Prime Minister
PAUL OLIVIER...................Chamberlain
MARTHE MELLOT....................Queen
CHARLES REDGIE................Prince Nicolas
MARCEL CARPENTIER......Brown, the detective
RAYMOND CORDY.......................Valet
JOSÉ NOGUÉRO.............Musical Director
AMOS..............................Beggar
PATHE-NATAN (France)   Director : René Clair   1934
(See Foreign Language Films, page 347)

Derrière la Façade
Detectives
LUCIEN BAROUX   JACQUES BAUMER
Tenants.
ANDRÉ LEFAUR   CARETTE
GABY MORLAY   AIMÉ CLARIOND
ELVIRE POPESCO   JACQUES DUMESNIL
MICHEL SIMON   MARCEL SIMON
BETTY STOCKFIELD   ANDREX
ERIC VON STROHEIM   GABRIEL DORZIAT
SIMONE BERRIAU   JULES BERRY
GABY SLYVIA   MARGUERITE MORENO
FRANCINEX (France)   1939
Directors : Yves Mirande and Georges Lacombe
(See Foreign Language Films, page 347)

Disraeli
GEORGE ARLISS
      The Hon. Benjamin Disraeli, M.P.
MRS. GEORGE ARLISS.......Lady Beaconsfield
MARGARET DALE.................Mrs. Travers
LOUISE HUFF
      Clarissa, Duke of Glastonbury's daughter
REGINALD DENNY....Charles, Viscount Deeford
E. J. RATCLIFFE .... Sir Michael Probert,
      Governor of the Bank of England
FRANK LOSEE.....Hugh Myers, a London banker
HENRY CARVILL..........Duke of Glastonbury
GRACE GRISWALD......Duchess of Glastonbury
NOEL TERALE......................Foljambe
FRED J. NICHOLLS.....................Butler
DISTINCTIVE PRODUCTIONS   1922

Disraeli
GEORGE ARLISS......................Disraeli
JOAN BENNETT......................Clarissa
FLORENCE ARLISS...........Lady Beaconsfield
DAVID TORRENCE................Lord Probert
DORIS LLOYD....................Mrs. Travers
ANTHONY BUSHELL......Charles, Lord Deeford
IVAN SIMPSON....................Hugh Myers
MARGARET MANN.............Queen Victoria
GWENDOLEN LOGAN...Duchess of Glastonbury
HENRY CARVILL..........Duke of Glastonbury
NORMAN CANNON...................Foljambe
MICHAEL VISAROFF............Count Bosrinov
CHARLES E. EVANS...................Potter
WARN   Director : Alfred E. Green   1930

Dr. Jekyll and Mr. Hyde
FREDRIC MARCH............{ Dr. Henry Jekyll
                         { Mr. Hyde

MIRIAM HOPKINS.................Ivy Peterson
ROSE HOBART...................Muriel Carew
HOLMES HERBERT.................Dr. Lanyon
HALLIWELL HOBBES....Brigadier-General Carew
EDGAR MORTON.......................Poole
ARNOLD LUCY.......................Utterson
COLONEL MacDONNELL...............Hobson
TEMPE PIGOTT.................Mrs. Hawkins
PARA   Director : Rouben Mamoulian   1932
From the novel by Robert Louis Stevenson

Dr. Jekyll and Mr. Hyde
SPENCER TRACY.............{ Dr. Henry Jekyll
                         { Mr. Hyde
INGRID BERGMAN.................Ivy Peterson
LANA TURNER...................Beatrix Emery
DONALD CRISP.............Sir Charles Emery
IAN HUNTER..................Dr. John Lanyon
BARTON MacLANE...............Sam Higgins
C. AUBREY SMITH.................The Bishop
PETER GODFREY......................Poole
SARA ALLGOOD..................Mrs. Higgins
FREDERIC WORLOCK...............Dr. Heath
WILLIAM TANNEN..............Interne Fenwick
MGM   Director : Victor Fleming   1941
Based on the novel by Robert Louis Stevenson

Don Juan
JOHN BARRYMORE.................Don Juan
MARY ASTOR............Adriana della Varnese
WILLARD LOUIS.....................Pedrillo
ESTELLE TAYLOR................Lucretia Borgia
HELENE COSTELLO........Rena, Adriana's maid
MYRNA LOY...........Maia, Lucretia's maid
JANE WINTON.......................Beatrice

255

JOHN ROCHE.....................Leandro
JUNE MARLOWE.....................Trusia
YVONNE DAY..............Don Juan, aged 5
PHILIPPE DE LACY......Don Juan, aged 10
JOHN GEORGE..................Hunchback
HELENE D'ALGY..............Murderess of Jose
WARNER OLAND.................Cesare Borgia
MONTAGU LOVE......................Donati
JOSEF SWICKARD..........Duke della Varnese
LIONEL BRAHAM...............Duke Margoni
PHYLLIS HAVER....................Imperia
NIGEL DE BRULIER.........Marquis Rinaldo
HEDDA HOPPER.............Marquise Rinaldo
WARN   Director: Alan Crosland   1926
*This was the first feature length film to have a
recorded score and sound effects. It was first
shown by Warners in New York on August 6, 1926*

Don Q, Son of Zorro
DOUGLAS FAIRBANKS, Sr..{ Don Cesar de Vega
                         Zorro, his father
MARY ASTOR................Dolores de Muro
JACK McDONALD............General de Muro
DONALD CRISP.................Don Sebastian
STELLA DE LANTI..................The Queen
WARNER OLAND................The Archduke
JEAN HERSHOLT.................Don Fabrique
ALBERT MacQUARRIE........Colonel Matsado
LOTTIE PICKFORD FORREST.............Lola
CHARLES STEVENS..................Robledo
TOTE DU CROW....................Bernardo
MARTHA FRANKLIN..............The Duenna
ROY COULSON....................Her admirer
ENRIQUE ACOSTA....................Ramon
UA   1926
*From the novel " Don Q's Love Story " by
K. and Hesketh Prichard*

Doomed Battalion, The
TALA BIRELL ....Mari di Mai
LUIS TRENKER.................Florian di Mai
VICTOR VARCONI.........Arthur Franchini
GUSTAV VON SEYFFERTITZ...Austrian General
C. HENRY GORDON............Italian General
GIBSON GOWLAND.................Innerhofer
HENRY ARMETTA....................Angelo
UNIV   Director: Cyril Gardner   1932
From the story by Luis Trenker

Dorothy Vernon of Haddon Hall
MARY PICKFORD.............Dorothy Vernon
ANDERS RANDOLF...........Sir George Vernon
MARC MacDERMOTT......Sir Malcolm Vernon
MME. DAUMERY..................Lady Vernon
ALLAN FORREST...........Sir John Manners
WILFRED LUCAS.............Earl of Rutland
CLARE EAMES..............Queen Elizabeth
ESTELLE TAYLOR..........Mary, Queen of Scots
COLIN KENNY.....................Dawson
COURTENAY FOOTE......Earl of Leicester
LOTTIE PICKFORD FORREST....Jennie Faxton
UA   1925

Double Indemnity
FRED MacMURRAY..............Walter Neff
BARBARA STANWYCK.......Phyllis Dietrichson
EDWARD G. ROBINSON..........Barton Keyes
JEAN HEATHER.............Lola Dietrichson
TOM POWERS.................Mr. Dietrichson
BYRON BARR..................Nino Zaccheti
PARA   Director: Billy Wilder   1944

Down Went McGinty
BRIAN DONLEVY.................Dan McGinty
MURIEL ANGELUS.........Catherine McGinty
AKIM TAMIROFF....................The Boss
ALLYN JOSLYN........................George
WILLIAM DEMAREST............The Politician
LOUIS JEAN HEYDT................Thompson
HARRY ROSENTHAL.......Louie, the bodyguard
ARTHUR HOYT..............Mayor Tillinghast
LIBBY TAYLOR ....Bessy, the coloured maid
THURSTON HALL............Mr. Maxwell
STEFFI DUNA.........................The Girl
DONNIE KERR...........Catherine's boy, aged 4
MARY THOMAS..........Catherine's girl, aged 6
DREW RODDY...........Catherine's boy, aged 9
SHEILA SHELDON.......Catherine's girl, aged 11
PARA   Director: Preston Sturges   1940

Dreyfus
CEDRIC HARDWICKE.................Dreyfus
CHARLES CARSON.........Colonel Picquart
GEORGE MERRITT.......................Zola
SAM LIVESEY........................Labori
BEATRIX THOMPSON.........Lucie Dreyfus
GARRY MARSH.............Major Esterhazy
HENRY CAINE.................Colonel Henry
GEORGE SKILLAN.........Major Paty du Clam
LEONARD SHEPHERD.............Clémenceau
ARTHUR HARDY............General Mercier
ALEXANDER SARNER........Matthieu Dreyfus
FREDERICK LEISTER................Démange
FISHER WHITE....................Pellieux
ABRAHAM SOFAER..................Dubois
LESLIE FRITH.......................Bertillon
VIOLET HOWARD................Marguerite
REGINALD DANCE.......President: Zola Trial
GEORGE ZUCCO....................Cavaignac
NIGEL BARRIE.......................Lauth
RANDLE AYRTON
              President: Dreyfus Court Martial
BIP   Directors: 1931
          F. W. Kraemer and Milton Rosmer
*From the play " The Dreyfus Case " by
Herzog and Rehfisch*

E

Eagle, The
RUDOLPH VALENTINO......Vladimir Dubrovsky
VILMA BANKY.............Mascha Troekouroff
LOUISE DRESSER.................The Czarina
ALBERT CONTI......................Kuschka
JAMES MARCUS.............Kyrilla Troekouroff
GEORGE NICHOLS......................Judge
CARRIE CLARK WARD...........Aunt Aurelia
UA   Director: Clarence Brown   1926

East Lynne
MABEL BALLIN
              Isabel Vane, Mrs. Archibald Carlyle
EDWARD EARLE..............Archibald Carlyle
GLADYS COBURN...............Barbara Hare
HENRY G. SELL...........Francis Levison
GILBERT ROONEY................Richard Hare
HUGO BALLIN   1922
Modernized version of Mrs. Henry Wood's novel

East Lynne
ALMA RUBENS.....................Lady Isabel
EDMUND LOWE.............Archibald Carlyle
LOU TELLEGEN.........Sir Francis Levison
LESLIE FENTON.................Richard Hare

LANA TURNER
(Metro-Goldwyn-Mayer)

MARJORIE DAW..................Barbara Hare
FRANK KEENAN...............Magistrate Hare
LYDIA KNOTT.....................Mrs. Hare
ERIC MAYNE............Earl of Mount Severn
MARTHA MATTOX...........Cornelia Carlyle
BELLE BENNETT.................Afy Hallijohn
PAUL PANZER...................Mr. Hallijohn
HARRY SEYMOUR..................Mr. Dill
RICHARD HEADRICK.................Willie
VIRGINIA MARSHALL............Little Isabel
FOX   1926
From the novel by Mrs. Henry Wood

East Lynne
ANN HARDING.....................Lady Isabel
CONRAD NAGEL...............Robert Carlyle
CLIVE BROOK.................Captain Levison
CECILIA LOFTUS...........Cornelia Carlyle
O. P. HEGGIE.............Lord Mount Severn
DAVID TORRENCE...........Sir Richard Hale
FLORA SHEFFIELD..................Barbara
BERYL MERCER......................Joyce
J. GUNNIS DAVIS....................Dodson
RONALD CROSBY...........William, as a baby
WALLY ALBRIGHT............William, later
FOX   Director : Frank Lloyd   1931
Talkie version of Mrs. Henry Wood's novel

Edison, the Man
SPENCER TRACY...........Thomas A. Edison
RITA JOHNSON.................Mary Stilwell
LYNNE OVERMAN................Bunt Cavatt
CHARLES COBURN...........General Powell
GENE LOCKHART.................Mr. Taggart
HENRY TRAVERS....................Ben Els
FELIX BRESSART...............Michael Simon
PETER GODFREY....................Ashton
GUY D'ENNERY..................Lundstrom
BYRON FOULGER...............Edwin Hall
MILTON PARSONS..........." Acid " Graham
ARTHUR AYLESWORTH............Bigelow
GENE REYNOLDS................Jimmy Price
ADDISON RICHARDS.............Mr. Johnson
GRANT MITCHELL....................Snade
PAUL HURST.......................Sheriff
GEORGE LESSEY...............Toastmaster
JAY WARD...................John Schofield
ANN GILLIS....................Nancy Grey
MGM   Director : Clarence Brown   1940

Elephant Boy
SABU.................Toomai of the Elephants
W. E. HOLLOWAY..................His father
WALTER HUDD......................Petersen
ALLAN JEAYES................Muchua Appa
BRUCE GORDON.................Rham Lahl
D. J. WILLIAMS...................Hunter
HYDE WHIT...................Commissioner
LFP   Directors :   1937
Robert Flaherty and Zoltan Korda
*Based on the story " Toomai of the Elephants " by
Rudyard Kipling*

Enchanted Cottage, The
DOROTHY McGUIRE..................Laura
ROBERT YOUNG.....................Oliver
HERBERT MARSHALL...............Hillgrove
MILDRED NATWICK.............Mrs. Minnett
SPRING BYINGTON............Violet Price
RICHARD GAINES.................Frederick

HILLARY BROOKE..................Beatrice
ALEC ENGLANDER...................Danny
MARY WORTH..................Mrs. Stanton
JOSEPHINE WHITTELL........Canteen Manager
ROBERT CLARKE....................Marine
EDEN NICHOLAS...................Soldier
RKO   Director : John Cromwell   1945
Based on the play by Sir Arthur Wing Pinero

Enfants du Paradis, Les
PIERRE BRASSEUR..........Frédérick Lemaitre
LÉON LARIVE
        Stage Doorkeeper of the " Grand Théâtre "
ARLETTY..........................Garance
MARCEL HERRAND...............Lacenaire
FABIEN LORIS......................Avril
PIERRE RENOIR.....................Jéricho
ÉTIENNE DECROUX..........Anselme Deburau
JEAN-LOUIS BARRAULT......Baptiste Deburau
PIERRE PAULU....Manager of the " Funambules "
MARIA CASARÈS...................Nathalie
JEANNE DUSSOL.................Hairdresser
MARCEL PÉREZ....Director of the " Funambules "
ALBERT REMY...............Scarpia Barigni
JEANNE MARKEN...............Mme. Hermine
GASTON MODOT..................Blind Man
LOUIS SALOU......Le Comte de Montray
JACQUES CASTELOT..............First Dandy
JEAN GOLD..................Second Dandy
GUY FAVIÈRES...............Bank Messenger
PAUL FRANKEUR...........Inspector of Police

Five Years Later
LUCIENNE VIGIER..........First Theatregoer
CYNETTE QUÉRO...........Second Theatregoer
GUSTAVE HAMILTON
        Stage Doorkeeper of the " Grand Théâtre "
ROGNONI....Director of the " Grand Théâtre "
AUGUSTE BOVERIO..............First Author
PAUL DEMANGE.............Second Author
JEAN DIENER...................Third Author
LOUIS FLORENCIE...............Gendarme
MARCELLE MONTHIL..................Marie
ROBERT DHERY....................Célestin
LUCIEN WALTER................Ticket-seller
JEAN-PIERRE DELMON.........Baptiste, Jr.
JEAN LANIER......................Iago
RAPHAËL PATORNI...............Third Dandy
HABIB BENGLIA........Turkish Bath Attendant
S.N. PATHÉ (France)   1945
            Director : Marcel Carné
*Begun during the Occupation of France, the film was
completed, after innumerable production difficulties,
shortly after the Liberation. Many of the cast were
members of the Maquis ; one actor later proved to
have been a collaborator and every scene in which
he had appeared was re-shot*
(*See Foreign Language Films, page 347*)

Escape to Happiness
(American title : *Intermezzo, a Love Story*)
LESLIE HOWARD....................Holger
INGRID BERGMAN...................Anita
EDNA BEST.......................Margit
JOHN HALLIDAY..................Thomas
CECIL KELLAWAY..................Charles
ENID BENNETT......................Greta
ANN TODD.....................Anne Marie
DOUGLAS SCOTT......................Eric
ELEANOR WESSELHOEFT..............Emma
UA   Director : Gregory Ratoff   1939

Esclave Blanche, L'

VIVIANE ROMANCE...................Mireille
JOHN LODGE........................Vedad Bey.
MARCEL DALIO.....................The Sultan
SATURNIN FABRE.................Jemel Pasha
LUCIA FILMS (France)   Director : Marc Sorkin   1938
(See Foreign Language Films, page 347)

Eternal Flame, The

NORMA TALMADGE.......Duchesse de Langeais
ADOLPHE MENJOU.............Duc de Langeais
WEDGWOOD NOWELL..Marquis de Ronquerolles
CONWAY TEARLE.........General de Montriveau
ROSEMARY THEBY..............Mme. de Serizy
KATE LESTER......Princess de Vlamont-Chauvray
THOMAS RICKETTS...........Vidame de Pamier
IRVING CUMMINGS...........Count de Marsay
OTIS HARLAN...................Abbé Conrand
FIRST NATIONAL   Director : Frank Lloyd   1923
From the novel " La Duchesse de Langeais " by
Honoré de Balzac

F

Faithful Heart, The

HERBERT MARSHALL...........Waverley Ango
EDNA BEST..............................Blackie
MIGNON O'DOHERTY.......Miss Gutterscombe
LAWRENCE HANRAY................The Major
ANNE GREY............................Diana
ATHOLE STEWART...............Sir Gilbert
GAINS   Director : Victor Saville   1932
From the play by Monckton Hoffe

Fanny by Gaslight

PHYLLIS CALVERT.....................Fanny
JAMES MASON...............Lord Manderstoke
WILFRED LAWSON...................Chunks
STEWART GRANGER.........Harry Somerford
JEAN KENT.............................Lucy
MARGARETTA SCOTT...................Alicia
NORA SWINBURNE............Mrs. Hopwood
CATHLEEN NESBITT...........Kate Somerford
HELEN HAYE................Mrs. Somerford
JOHN LAURIE...............William Hopwood
STUART LINDSELL..............Clive Seymore
AMY VENESS...................Mrs. Heaviside
ANN WILTON.........................Carver
GUY LE FEUVRE................Dr. Lowenthall
GAINS   Director : Anthony Asquith   1944
From the novel by Michael Sadleir

Femme Disparaît, Une

FRANÇOISE ROSAY.............{ Fanny Helder
⎧ Tona
⎨ Rose Delvé
⎩ Flora Caretti
JEANNE PROVOST...............Mme. Chardin
FLORENCE LYNN.....................Geneviève
CLAUDE DAUPHIN....................Robert
HENRI GUISON.........................Barcy
JEAN NOHAIN..............Police Inspector
DANIEL FILLION.........................Jean
YVA BELLA..........................Séverine
THÉRÈSE DORNY.................Lucie Delvé
ETTORE CELLA.............Giacomo Caretti
SYLVIA STAILE........................Lina
JEAN WORMS...............Professor Chardin
DFG (France)   Director : Jacques Feyder   1942
(See Foreign Language Films, page 347)

Femme du Boulanger, La

RAIMU.............................The Baker
GINETTE LECLERC..................His wife
CHARLES MOULIN...............The Shepherd
FERNAND CHARPIN.............The Marquis
ROBERT VATTIER...................The Curé
ROBERT BASSAC.............The Schoolmaster
BLAVETTE.............................Tonin
DULLAC..............................Casimir
MAFFRE..............................Petugne
JEAN CASTAN.........................Esprit
ALIDA ROUFFE.......................Céleste
MAXIMILIENNE MAX...................Angèle
ODETTE ROGER.......................Miette
CHARBLAY........................The Butcher
MICHEL...........................Barthelmy
MAUPI..............................Barnaba
(France)   Producer and Director :   1938
Marcel Pagnol
(See Foreign Language Films, page 347)

Fifth Form at St. Dominic's

RALPH FORBES.....Oliver Greenfield of the Fifth
MAURICE THOMPSON
Stephen Greenfield, his younger brother
WILLIAM FRESHMAN.......Loman of the Sixth
PERCY FIELD....Horace Wraysford, Oliver's chum
MASTER LEON MORGAN
Bramble, the bully of the Fourth
DOUGLAS PHAIR
Tony Pembury, the Fifth Form cynic
CECIL SUSANDS...........Bullinger of the Sixth
ROY LENNOL...............Simon Wren, a poet
FRANK SLATER.............Raleigh of the Sixth
HUMBERSTON WRIGHT
Dr. Senior, the Headmaster
ROYCE MILTON
Mr. Jellicott, Master of the Fifth Form
CLIFFORD COBB
Mr. Rastle, Master of the Fourth Form
SAM AUSTIN...................Ben Cripps
H. NICHOLLS-BATES.................Jeff Cripps
ROSE ENA..................Mrs. Greenfield
MRS. E. W. ROYCE..............Mrs. O'Grady
PHYLLIS SHANNAW
Nancy Senior, the Headmaster's daughter
GRANGER'S   1921
From the school story by Talbot Baines Reed
Re-issued 1923

Fin du Jour, La

VICTOR FRANCEN....................Marny
LOUIS JOUVET.......................St. Clair
MICHEL SIMON....................Cabrissade
MADELINE OZERAY.................Jeanette
GABRIELLE DORZIAT............Mme. Chabert
ARTHUR DEVÈRE....................Manager
ARQUILLIÈRE.....................M. Lucien
JOFFRE.........................M. Philémon
MME. LHERBAY.............Mme. Philémon
JEAN COQUELIN....................Delormel
PIERRE MAGNIER.............M. Laroche
GRANVAL.........................Deaubonne
JEAN AYME.........................Victor
TONY JACQUOT.....................Pierre
GABY ANDREU.....................Danielle
GASTON MODOT...................Innkeeper
FRANCINEX (France)   Director : Julien Duvivier   1939
(See Foreign Language Films, page 347)

Fire over England

FLORA ROBSON................Queen Elizabeth
LAURENCE OLIVIER............Michael Ingolby
VIVIEN LEIGH.........................Cynthia
LESLIE BANKS..................Earl of Leicester
RAYMOND MASSEY.............Philip of Spain
TAMARA DESNI.........................Elena
MORTON SELTEN.....................Burleigh
HENRY OSCAR.............Spanish Ambassador
LAWRENCE HANRAY.......French Ambassador
ROY RUSSELL..........................Cooper
HOWARD DOUGLAS.................Amberley
CECIL MAINWARING..............Illingworth
FRANCIS DE WOLFE..................Tarleton
GRAHAM CHESWRIGHT............Maddison
GEORGE THIRLWELL.................Gregory
A. CORNEY GRAIN.....................Hatton
HERBERT LOMAS.............Richard Ingolby
ROBERT NEWTON....................Don Pedro
DONALD CALTHROP.............Don Escobal
CHARLES CARSON.............Admiral Valdez
LYN HARDING.....................Sir Richard
ROBERT RENDELL.................Don Miguel
PENDENNIS   Director : William K. Howard   1937
Based on the novel by A. E. W. Mason

First of the Few, The

LESLIE HOWARD.................R. J. Mitchell
DAVID NIVEN..................Geoffrey Crisp
ROSAMUND JOHN...............Diana Mitchell
ROLAND CULVER............Commander Bride
ANNE FIRTH......................Miss Harper
DAVID HORNE......................Mr. Higgins
J. H. ROBERTS............Sir Robert McLean
DERRICK DE MARNEY.Squadron Leader Jefferson
ROSALYN BOULTER..............Mabel Lovesay
HERBERT CAMERON..............MacPherson
GORDON McLEOD..............Major Buchan
TONIE EDGAR BRUCE..........Lady Houston
GEORGE SKILLAN..................Mr. Boyce
ERIK FREUND....................Messerschmitt
F. R. WENDHAUSEN..............Von Straben
JOHN CHANDOS.......................Krantz
VICTOR BEAUMONT.............Von Crantz
SUZANNE CLAIR....................Madeleine
FILIPPO DEL GIUDICE..............Bertorelli
BREFNI O'RORKE.................The Specialist
GERRY WILMOT }............Radio Announcers
JACK PEACH }
" Battle of Britain " pilots and other personnel of
Fighter Command, R.A.F.
LESLIE HOWARD PRODUCTIONS   1942
Director : Leslie Howard

Five Star Final

EDWARD G. ROBINSON..............Randall
H. B. WARNER..............Michael Townsend
MARIAN MARSH.............Jenny Townsend
ANTHONY BUSHELL.............Phillip Weeks
GEORGE E. STONE.............Ziggie Feinstein
FRANCES STARR...........Nancy Townsend
ONA MUNSON.................Kitty Carmody
BORIS KARLOFF.......................Isopod
ROBERT ELLIOTT................Brannegan
ALINE MacMAHON..............Miss Taylor
PURNELL PRATT.......................French
DAVID TORRENCE...............Mr. Weeks
OSCAR APFEL....................Hinchecliffe
GLADYS LLOYD.................Miss Edwards
EVELYN HALL....................Mrs. Weeks
HAROLD WALDRIDGE........Arthur Goldberg
FIRST NATIONAL   Director : Mervyn LeRoy   1932

Foolish Wives

RUDOLPH CHRISTIANS
    Andrew J. Hughes, U.S. Special Envoy to Monaco
MISS DUPONT.....................Helen, his wife
MAUDE GEORGE......Princess Olga Petschnikoff
MAE BUSCH.Her cousin, Princess Vera Petschnikoff
ERICH VON STROHEIM
    Their cousin, Count Sergius Karamzin
DALE FULLER.............Maruschka, a maid
AL EDMUNDSEN.........Pavel Pavlich, a butler
CAESARE GRAVINA
    Caesare Ventucci, a counterfeiter
MALVINA POLO..Marietta, his half-witted daughter
LOUIS K. WEBB.....................Dr. Judd
MRS. KENT....................Dr. Judd's wife
C. J. ALLEN..........Albert I, Prince of Monaco
EDWARD REINACH..Secretary of State of Monaco
VITAGRAPH   Director : Erich von Stroheim   1922

For Whom the Bell Tolls

GARY COOPER...................Robert Jordan
INGRID BERGMAN.......................Maria
AKIM TAMIROFF.........................Pablo
ARTURO DE CORDOVA..............Agustin
JOSEPH CALLEIA.....................El Sordo
KATINA PAXINOU........................Pilar
VLADIMIR SOKOLOFF.................Anselmo
MIKHAIL RASUMNY....................Rafael
FORTUNIO BONANOVA.............Fernando
ERIC FELDARY.........................Andres
VICTOR VARCONI..................Primitivo
LILO YARSON.........................Joaquin
ALEXANDER GRANACH.................Paco
ADIA KUZNETZOFF...................Gustavo
LEONID SNEGOFF.....................Ignacio
LEO BULGAKOV.................General Golz
DUNCAN RENALDO........Lieutenant Berrendo
GEORGE COULOURIS..........André Massart
FRANK PUGLIA..............Captain Gomez
PEDRO DE CORDOBA.....Colonel Miranda
MICHAEL VISAROFF.............Staff Officer
KONSTANTIN SHAYNE............Karkov
MARTIN GARRALAGA..........Captain Mora
JEAN DEL VAL..................The Sniper
JACK MYLONG..................Colonel Duval
FEODOR CHALIAPIN..................Kashkin
PARA   Director : Sam Wood   1944
From the novel by Ernest Hemingway
In Technicolor
Shortened version re-issued 1947

Forever and a Day

C. AUBREY SMITH............Admiral Trimble
RAY MILLAND.............................Bill
ANNA NEAGLE........................Miriam
CLAUDE RAINS.............Ambrose Pomfret
JESSIE MATTHEWS.........Mildred Trimble
CHARLES LAUGHTON.................Butler
IAN HUNTER.............Dexter Pomfret
EDWARD EVERETT HORTON
    Sir Anthony Trimble Pomfret
IDA LUPINO..........................Jennie
BRIAN AHERNE.................Jim Trimble
ROBERT CUMMINGS.............Ned Trimble
MERLE OBERON....................Marjorie
KENT SMITH.................Gates Pomfret
RUTH WARRICK.................Leslie Trimble
RKO   Directors :   1943
    Edmund Goulding, Frank Lloyd,
    Victor Saville, Robert Stevenson
" Omnibus " film, made in Hollywood in aid of the
British Red Cross

49th Parallel
The U-Boat Crew

RICHARD GEORGE.....Kommandant Bernsdorff
ERIC PORTMAN..............Lieutenant Hirth
RAYMOND LOVELL.......Lieutenant Kuhnecke
NIALL MACGINNIS.....................Vogel
PETER MOORE........................Kranz
JOHN CHANDOS...................Lohrmann
BASIL APPLEBY......................Jahner

The Canadians

LAURENCE OLIVIER........Johnnie, the trapper
FINLAY CURRIE...................The Factor
LEY ON..................Nick, the Eskimo
ANTON WALBROOK....................Peter
GLYNIS JOHNS........................Anna
CHARLES VICTOR...................Andreas
FREDERICK PIPER....................David
LESLIE HOWARD........Philip Armstrong Scott
TAWERA MOANA...........George, the Indian
ERIC CLAVERING.......................Art
CHARLES ROLFE.......................Bob
RAYMOND MASSEY................Andy Brock

THEODORE SALT
O. W. FONGER } . United States Customs Officers

ORTUS   Director : Michael Powell   1941

Forty Thousand Horsemen

GRANT TAYLOR.............." Red " Gallagher
BETTY BRYANT..................Julie Rouget
CHIPS RAFFERTY......................Jim
PAT TWOHILL......................Larry
HARVEY ADAMS..................Von Hausen
ERIC RIEMAN...................Von Schiller
JOE VALLI......................." Scotty "
ALBERT C. WINN................Sheik Abu
KENNETH BRAMPTON..........German Officer
JOHN FLEETING.............Captain Gordon
HARRY ABDY...................Paul Rouget
NORMAN MAXWELL...................Ismet
PAT PENNY..................Captain Seidi
CHARLES ZOLI.................Cafe Proprietor
CHARLES TURTIN....................Othman
THEO LIANOS......................Abdul
SERGEANT ROY MANNIX
                        Light Horse Sergeant
EDNA EMMETT, VERA KANDY
IRIS KENNEDY, JOY HART } . Dancing Girls

FAMOUS FEATURE FILMS (Australia)   1941
      Director : Charles Chauvel

*Produced with the co-operation of the Australian
Department of Defence, and officers and men of
the 1st and 2nd Australian Cavalry Divisions*

Four Feathers, The

ROGER LIVESEY......Harry Feversham, as a boy
HARRY HAM........Harry Feversham, as a man
HENRY VIBART..............General Feversham
MARY MASSART.................Ethne Eustace
CYRIL PERCIVAL................Jack Durrance
C. W. CUNDALL............Lieutenant Trench
GWEN WILLIAMS..................Mrs. Adai
ROBERT ENGLISH............Lieutenant Sutch
TONY FRASER...................Abou Fatma
HARRY WORTH...........Major Willoughby
BOBBIE HARWOOD........Lieutenant Castleton
GRAY MURRAY...............Dermod Eustace

STOLL   1922
      From the novel by A. E. W. Mason

Four Feathers, The

RICHARD ARLEN..............Harry Feversham
FAY WRAY.....................Ethne Eustace
CLIVE BROOK.................Captain Durrance
WILLIAM POWELL...........Lieutenant Trench
THEODORE VON ELTZ....Lieutenant Castleton
NOAH BEERY....................Slave Trader
NOBLE JOHNSON.......................Ahmed
HAROLD HIGHTOWER....................Ali
PHILIPPE DE LACY.............Harry, aged 10
GEORGE FAWCETT.........General Feversham

PARA   Directors : Ernest Schoedsack   1930
      Meriam C. Cooper, Lothar Mendes
      From the novel by A. E. W. Mason

Four Feathers, The

JOHN CLEMENTS.............Harry Faversham
RALPH RICHARDSON....Captain John Durrance
C. AUBREY SMITH..........General Burroughs
JUNE DUPREZ.................Ethne Burroughs
ALLAN JEAYES.............General Faversham
JACK ALLEN.............Lieutenant Willoughby
DONALD GRAY.................Peter Burroughs
FREDERICK CULLEY................Dr. Sutton
CLIVE BAXTER.........Young Harry Faversham
ROBERT RENDEL.....................Colonel
ARCHIBALD BATTY...................Adjutant
DEREK ELPHINSTONE.......Lieutenant Parker
HAL WALTERS..........................Joe
NORMAN PIERCE.........Sergeant Brown
HENRY OSCAR.....................Dr. Harraz
JOHN LAURIE...................The Khalifa
AMID TAFTAZANI...........Karaga Pasha

LFP   Director : Zoltan Korda   1939
      From the novel by A. E. W. Mason
      In Technicolor

Four Horsemen of the Apocalypse, The

RUDOLPH VALENTINO........Julio Desnoyers
ALICE TERRY.............Marguerite Laurier
POMEROY CANNON......Madariaga, the centaur
JOSEPH SWICKARD.........Marcelo Desnoyers
BRINSLEY SHAW....................Celendonio
ALAN HALE..............Karl von Hartrott
BRIDGETTA CLARK................Doña Luisa
MABEL VAN BUREN...................Elena
BOWDITCH TURNER................Argensola
NIGEL DE BRULIER.................Tchernoff
JOHN SAINPOLIS.....................Laurier
MARK FENTON.................Senator Lacour
VIRGINIA WARWICK.................Chichi
DEREK GHENT...................Rene Lacour
STUART HOLMES.......Captain von Hartrott
JEAN HERSHOLT.........Professor von Hartrott
HENRY KLAUS.........Heinrich von Hartrott
EDWARD CONNELLY.............Lodgekeeper
GEORGIA WOODTHORPE.............His wife
KATHLEEN KEY................Georgette
WALLACE BEERY.. Lieut. Colonel von Richthofen
JACQUES D'AURAY...........Captain d'Aubrey
CURT REHFELD............Major Blumhardt
Mlle. DOLOREZ.........Mlle. Lucette, the model
" BULL " MONTANA........The French Butcher
ISABEL KEITH.............The German Woman
JACQUES LANOE..............Her husband
NOBLE JOHNSON..................Conquest
HARRY NORTHRUP...............The Count
MINNEHAHA...................The Old Nurse
ARTHUR HOYT.............Lieutenant Schnitz
BEATRICE DOMINGUEZ.................Dancer

METRO-GOLDWYN   Director : Rex Ingram   1922
      From the novel by Vicente Blasco Ibanez

Frankenstein

COLIN CLIVE..................Dr. Frankenstein
MAE CLARKE..........................Elizabeth
JOHN BOLES...............................Victor
BORIS KARLOFF.................The Monster
EDWARD VAN SLOAN...........Dr. Waldman
DWIGHT FRYE.......................The Dwarf
FREDERICK KERR...................The Baron
LIONEL BELMORE............The Burgomaster
UNIV   Director: James Whale   1932

French without Tears

RAY MILLAND....................Alan Howard
ELLEN DREW.......................Diana Lake
DAVID TREE.......................Chris Neilan
GUY MIDDLETON..................Brian Curtis
ROLAND CULVER...........Commander Rogers
JANINE DARCEY....................Jacqueline
JIM GERALD..........................Maingot
KENNETH MORGAN.............Kenneth Lake
PARA   Director: Anthony Asquith   1940
From the play by Terence Rattigan
Re-issued 1943

Frenzy
(*Hets*)

STIG JÄRREL........................Caligula
ALF KJELLIN.................Jan-Erik Widgren
MAI ZETTERLING......................Bertha
OLOF WINNERSTRAND............Headmaster
GÖSTA CEDERLUND....................Pippi
HUGO BJÖRNE.........................Doctor
STIG OLIN..........................Sandman
OLAV RIEGO......................Mr. Widgren
MÄRTA ARBIN...................Mrs. Widgren
JAN MOLANDER.....................Pettersson
ANDERS NYSTRÖM...............Bror Widgren
NILS DAHLGREN.................Police Officer
AKTIEBOLAGET SVENSK FILMINDUSTRI (Sweden)   1944
Director: Alf Sjöberg
(*See Foreign Language Films, page* 347)

Fric-Frac

FERNANDEL..........................Marcel
ARLETTY.............................Loulou
MICHEL SIMON...........................Jo
HÉLÈNE ROBERT.......................Renée
MARCEL VALLÉE...............M. Mercandieu
ANDRÉ GENIN.....................M. Blain
JACQUES VARENNES................Petit Louis
COMPAGNIE COMMERCIALE FRANCAISE
CINEMATOGRAPHIQUE (France)   1939
Director: Maurice Lehmann
Adapted from the play by Edouard Bourdet
(*See Foreign Language Films, page* 347)

Frightened Lady, The

EMLYN WILLIAMS..............Lord Lebanon
CATHLEEN NESBITT..............Lady Lebanon
NORMAN McKINNELL....Chief Inspector Tanner
GORDON HARKER...............Sergeant Totty
CYRIL RAYMOND.............Sergeant Ferraby
BELLE CHRYSTALL.................Aisla Crane
D. A. CLARKE-SMITH...........Dr. Amersham
PERCY PARSONS.......................Gilder
FINLAY CURRIE.......................Brooks
JULIAN ROYCE.......................Kelver
ERIC ROWLAND........................Studd
BL-GAINS   Director: T. Hayes Hunter   1932
From the play "The Case of the Frightened Lady,"
by Edgar Wallace

Front Page, The

ADOLPHE MENJOU................Walter Burns
PAT O'BRIEN...................Hildy Johnson
MARY BRIAN...........................Peggy
EDWARD EVERETT HORTON........Bensinger
WALTER CATLETT....................Murphy
GEORGE E. STONE.............Earl Williams
MAE CLARKE...........................Molly
SLIM SUMMERVILLE...................Pincus
MATT MOORE.........................Kruger
FRANK McHUGH.........................McCue
CLARENCE H. WILSON...Sheriff Hartman
FRED HOWARD.......................Schwartz
PHIL TEAD...........................Wilson
EUGENE STRONG...................Endicott
SPENCER CHARTERS...........Woodenshoes
MAURICE BLACK..............Diamond Louie
EFFIE ELLSLER.................Mrs. Grant
DOROTHEA WOLBERT..................Jenny
JAMES GORDON.................The Mayor
DICK ALEXANDER.....................Jacobi
UA   Director: Howard Hughes   1931

G

Gaslight

ANTON WALBROOK................Paul Mallen
DIANA WYNYARD................Bella Mallen
CATHLEEN CORDELL.................Nancy
ROBERT NEWTON....................Ullswater
FRANK PETTINGELL....................Rough
JIMMY HANLEY.........................Cobb
MINNIE RAYNER..................Elizabeth
MARY HINTON.........Lady Winterbourne
MARIE WHITE...................Alice Barlow
JACK BARTY.........Chairman of the Music-Hall
AUBREY DEXTER.................House Agent
ANGUS MORRISON....................Pianist
and
THE DARMORA BALLET
BRIT NAT   Director: Thorold Dickinson   1940
From the play by Patrick Hamilton
The negatives and print of this film were bought and
withdrawn from circulation by MGM. The film was
re-made and released in 1944 under the title of "The
Murder in Thornton Square"

General Suvorov

N. CHERKASOV.....................Suvorov
M. ASTANGOV...................Arakcheyev
S. KILIGIN.........................Bagration
A. ANTONOV.........................Tyurin
A. YACHNITSKY......................Paul I
G. VOLKONSKY......................Kutuzov
V. AKSENOV.....................Meshchersky
G. KOVROV.........................Prokhor
A. KHANOV.......................Platonitch
MOSFILM (U.S.S.R.)   1941
Directors: V. Pudovkin and M. Doller
(*See Foreign Language Films, page* 347)

Gentle Sex, The

JOAN GATES............Gwen, cockney waitress
JEAN GILLIE.............." Good Time " Dot
JOAN GREENWOOD.......Betty, spoilt only child
JOYCE HOWARD
          Anne, daughter of an Army colonel
ROSAMUND JOHN
          Maggie, member of a Scots family
LILLI PALMER...............Erna, Czech refugee
BARBARA WARING......Joan, ex-dancing teacher
JOHN JUSTIN...................David Sheridan

FREDERICK LEISTER
          Colonel Lawrence, Anne's father
MARY JERROLD.................Mrs. Sheridan
EVERLEY GREGG......Mrs. Simpson, Joan's aunt
ANTHONY BAZELL.......Ted, Dot's boy friend
ELLIOT MASON.....Mrs. Fraser, Maggie's mother
JOHN LAURIE.....................Scots Corporal
ROSALYN BOULTER..Sally, telephonist on gunsite
NOREEN CRAVEN..............Convoy Sergeant
CLIFFORD BUCKTON.............Dock Sergeant
FREDERICK PISLEY...................A Soldier
JAMES SADLER...............Lieutenant Gibson
MERIEL FORBES
         Junior Commander at Convoy Depot
HARRY WELCHMAN
      Captain of Mixed Driving Company
RONALD SHINER......................Racegoer
JIMMY HANLEY.....................A Soldier
MILES MALLESON...............Railway Guard
ROLAND PERTWEE
      Captain of Vehicle Reserve Depot
NICHOLAS STUART..........Canadian Private
FRANK ATKINSON.................Lorry Driver
PETER COTES..............Taffy, David's friend
MAUD DUNHAM....................Mrs. Miller
AMY DALBY.................N.A.A.F.I. Assistant
GRACE ARNOLD.............Café Proprietress
CLAUDE BAILEY...........Embarkation Officer
RICHARD GEORGE........Sea Transport Officer
TWO CITIES-CONCANEN   1943
    Director : Leslie Howard

Gentlemen Prefer Blondes
RUTH TAYLOR.....................Lorelei Lee
ALICE WHITE....................Dorothy Shaw
FORD STERLING...................Gus Eisman
HOLMES HERBERT............Henry Spoffard
MACK SWAIN..................Francis Beekman
EMILY FITZROY..................Mrs. Beekman
TRIXIE FRIGANZA................Mrs. Spoffard
BLANCHE FRIDERICI............Miss Chapman
ED FAUST.........................Robert
EUGENE BORDEN......................Louis
MARGARET SEDDON..........Lorelei's mother
LUKE COSGRAVE..........Lorelei's grandfather
CHESTER CONKLIN....................Judge
YORK SHERWOOD................Mr. Jennings
MILDRED BOYD........................Lulu
PARA   1928
From the story by Anita Loos, and the play by her and John Emerson

Ghost Goes West, The
ROBERT DONAT............{ Murdoch Glourie / Donald Glourie
JEAN PARKER....................Peggy Martin
EUGENE PALLETTE.................Mr. Martin
ELSA LANCHESTER...........Miss Shepperton
RALPH BUNKER.....................Ed Bigelow
PATRICIA HILLIARD................Shepherdess
EVERLEY GREGG.................Mrs. Martin
MORTON SELTEN..................The Glourie
CHILI BOUCHIER...................Cleopatra
MARK DALY.................Murdoch's groom
HERBERT LOMAS......................Fergus
ELLIOT MASON ....Mrs. MacNiff
HAY PETRIE.................The McLaggan
QUENTIN McPHERSON...............Mackaye
LFP   Director : René Clair   1936
From the story by John Buchan

Ghost Train, The
GUY NEWALL....................Teddie Deakin
LOUIS RALPH.....................Saul Hodgkin
JOHN MANNERS.........Charles Murdock
ERNEST VEREBES............Richard Winthrop
ILSE BOIS.......................Miss Bourne
ANNA JENNINGS................Peggy Murdock
AGNES KEROLENKO............Elsie Winthrop
ROSA WALTER....................Julia Price
W & F   Director : C. Bolvary   1928
From the play by Arnold Ridley

Ghost Train, The
JACK HULBERT...................Teddy Deakin
CICELY COURTNEIDGE............Miss Bourne
ANN TODD......................Peggy Murdock
CYRIL RAYMOND.............Richard Winthrop
DONALD CALTHROP.............Saul Hodgkin
ALLAN JEAYES....................Dr. Sterling
ANGELA BADDELEY.................Julie Price
HENRY CAINE....................Herbert Price
TRACEY HOLMES.................Charles Bryant
CAROL COOMBE...................Elsie Bryant
GAINS   Director : Walter Forde   1931
From the play by Arnold Ridley

Gibraltar
VIVIANE ROMANCE...................Mercedes
YVETTE LEBON..........................Maud
ERICH VON STROHEIM...............Marson
ROGER DUCHESNE..............Robert Jackson
ABEL JAQUIN....................Frank Lloyd
JEAN PÉRIER..................Colonel Wilcox
GEORGES FLAMANT.....................Macri
VIGUIER......................Professor Galloway
PASCAL......................Major Rogers
FILMS VICTORIA (France) Director : M. Safra 1938
(See Foreign Language Films, page 347)

Going My Way
BING CROSBY............Father Chuck O'Malley
RISE STEVENS....................Jenny Linden
BARRY FITZGERALD.........Father Fitzgibbon
JAMES BROWN..................Ted Haines, Jr.
JEAN HEATHER...................Carol James
EILY MALYON..................Mrs. Carmody
FRANK McHUGH...............Father Timony
STANLEY CLEMENTS.............Tony Scaponi
PARA   Director : Leo McCarey   1944

Gold Rush, The
CHARLES CHAPLIN.........The Lone Prospector
MACK SWAIN....................Big Jim McKay
TOM MURRAY....................Black Larson
MALCOLM WAITE................Jack Cameron
GEORGIA HALE.............The Girl, Georgia
HENRY BERGMAN ....Hank Curtis
    1926
Written, produced and directed by Charles Chaplin
Re-issued 1943 with sound. Narrative written and spoken by Charles Chaplin, who also composed a new musical score for the film

Golden Boy
BARBARA STANWYCK.............Lorna Moon
ADOLPHE MENJOU.................Tom Moody
WILLIAM HOLDEN..............Joe Bonaparte
LEE J. COBB....................Mr. Bonaparte
JOSEPH CALLEIA.................Eddie Fuseli
SAM LEVENE..........................Siggie

ANN TODD
(*Paramount*)

EDWARD S. BROPHY..............Roxie Lewis
BEATRICE BLINN.......................Anna
WILLIAM H. STRAUSS...............Mr. Carp
DON BEDDOE........................Borneo
COL   Director : Rouben Mamoulian   1939
Based on the play by Clifford Odets

Gone with the Wind
At Tara, the O'Hara Plantation in Georgia
FRED CRANE....................Brent Tarleton
GEORGE REEVES................Stuart Tarleton
VIVIEN LEIGH...................Scarlett O'Hara
HATTIE McDANIEL....................Mammy
EVERETT BROWN....................Big Sam
ZACK WILLIAMS......................Elijah
THOMAS MITCHELL............Gerald O'Hara
OSCAR POLK...........................Pork
BARBARA O'NEIL.................Ellen O'Hara
VICTOR JORY.................Jonas Wilkerson
EVELYN KEYES.................Suellen O'Hara
ANN RUTHERFORD.............Carreen O'Hara
BUTTERFLY McQUEEN..................Prissy
At Twelve Oaks, the nearby Wilkes Plantation
HOWARD HICKMAN..............John Wilkes
ALICIA RHETT....................India Wilkes
LESLIE HOWARD...............Ashley Wilkes
OLIVIA DE HAVILLAND......Melanie Hamilton
RAND BROOKS.............Charles Hamilton
CARROLL NYE.............Frank Kennedy
MARCELLA MARTIN..........Cathleen Calvert
CLARK GABLE....................Rhett Butler
At the Bazaar in Atlanta
LAURA HOPE CREWS.Aunt " Pittypat " Hamilton
HARRY DAVENPORT.................Dr. Meade
LEONA ROBERTS..................Mrs. Meade
JANE DARWELL............Mrs. Merriwether
ALBERT MORIN..................Rene Picard
MARY ANDERSON........Maybelle Merriwether
TERRY SHERO.................Fanny Elsing
WILLIAM McCLAIN.................Old Levi
In Aunt " Pittypat's " Home
EDDIE ANDERSON.................Uncle Peter
Outside " The Examiner " Office
JACKIE MORAN.................Phil Meade
At the Hospital
CLIFF EDWARDS.........Reminiscent Soldier
ONA MUNSON...................Belle Watling
ED CHANDLER.................The Sergeant
GEORGE HACKATHORNE
             A Wounded Soldier in pain
ROSCOE ATES............A Convalescent Soldier
ERIC LINDEN...........An Amputation Case
JOHN ARLEDGE.............A Dying Soldier
During the Evacuation
TOM TYLER..............A Commanding Officer
During the Siege
WILLIAM BAKEWELL.........A Mounted Officer
LEE PHELPS...................The Bartender
Georgia after Sherman
PAUL HURST.................A Yankee Deserter
ERNEST WHITMAN.....The Carpetbagger's friend
WILLIAM STELLIN.........A Returning Veteran
LOUIS JEAN HEYDT.........A Hungry Soldier
ISABEL JEWELL.............Emmy Slattery
During Reconstruction
ROBERT ELLIOTT.............The Yankee Major
GEORGE MEEKER ⎫
WALLIS CLARK   ⎬ ..His poker-playing Captains
IRVING BACON...................The Corporal
ADRIAN MORRIS........A Carpetbagger Orator
J. M. KERRIGAN.............Johnny Gallegher
OLIN HOWLAND........A Yankee Business Man

YAKIMA CANUTT.................A Renegade
BLUE WASHINGTON............His companion
WARD BOND.............Tom, a Yankee Captain
CAMMIE KING.........Bonnie Blue Butler
MICKEY KUHN....................Beau Wilkes
LILLIAN KEMBLE COOPER.......Bonnie's nurse
MGM   Director : Victor Fleming   1942
From the novel by Margaret Mitchell
In Technicolor
Had a special presentation in London, April 1940,
where it ran continuously for four years. The general
release in 1942 did not affect the West End run at
the Ritz, and later at the Rialto
Re-issued 1944 and 1947

Good Earth, The
PAUL MUNI.........................Wang
LUISE RAINER.......................O-lan
WALTER CONNOLLY...................Uncle
TILLY LOSCH........................Lotus
CHARLEY GRAPEWIN..................Father
JESSIE RALPH......................Cuckoo
SOO YONG...........................Aunt
KEYE LUKE.......................Elder Son
ROLAND LUI....................Younger Son
SUZANNA KIM...................Little Fool
CHINGWAH LEE.......................Ching
HAROLD HUBER.....................Cousin
OLAF HYTTEN.........Liu, grain merchant
WILLIAM LAW......................Gateman
MARY WONG....................Little Bride
MGM   Director : Sidney Franklin   1937
Based on the novel by Pearl S. Buck

Goodbye Mr. Chips !
ROBERT DONAT.....................Mr. Chips
GREER GARSON.....................Katherine
                   ⎧   John Colley
                   ⎪ Peter Colley I
TERRY KILBURN.....⎨ Peter Colley II
                   ⎩ Peter Colley III
JOHN MILLS.........Peter Colley, as a young man
PAUL HENREID.......................Staefel
JUDITH FURSE.......................Flora
LYN HARDING.....................Wetherby
MILTON ROSMER..................Chatteris
FREDERICK LEISTER.................Marsham
LOUISE HAMPTON.................Mrs. Wickett
AUSTIN TREVOR......................Ralston
DAVID TREE........................Jackson
EDMOND BREON.............Colonel Morgan
JILL FURSE.................Helen Colley
SCOTT SUNDERLAND.........Sir John Colley
MGM BRIT   Director : Sam Wood   1939
From the novel by James Hilton
Re-issued 1944

Good-Night Vienna
JACK BUCHANAN...Captain Maximilian Schletoff
CLIVE CURRIE...............General Schletoff
WILLIAM KENDALL.....................Ernst
HERBERT CARRICK...................Johann
GIBB McLAUGHLIN...........Max's batman
CLIFFORD HEATHERLEY.............Donelli
O. B. CLARENCE..........The Theatre Manager
AUBREY FITZGERALD.............The Waiter
GINA MALO.........................Frieda
PEGGY CARTWRIGHT................Greta
MURIEL AKED..................The Landlady
JOYCE BLAND.................Countess Helga
ANNA NEAGLE.........................Viki
B & D   Director : Herbert Wilcox   1932

Grand Jeu, Le

FRANÇOISE ROSAY.....................Blanche
PIERRE RICHARD-WILLM.........Pierre Martel
MARIE BELL.........................{ Florence
                             { Irma
CHARLES VANEL......................Clément
GEORGES PITOËFF......................Nicolas
PIERRE LARQUEY.......................Gustin
PIERRE LABRY...............Canteen Attendant
CAMILLE BERT........................Colonel
PIERRE DE GUINGAND.............Captain
ANDRÉ DUBOSC.............Bernard Martel
NESTOR ARIANI........................Aziani
LINÉ CLÉVERS........................Dauville
GÉNO FERNY..................Customs Official
OLGA VELBRIA.......................Aichouch

FILMS OF FRANCE (France) Director: Jacques Feyder 1933
(See Foreign Language Films, page 347)

Grande Illusion, La

JEAN GABIN....................Maréchal
PIERRE FRESNAY..................De Boeldieu
ERICH VON STROHEIM........Von Rauffenstein
MARCEL DALIO.....................Rosenthal
CARETTE...........................The Actor
MODOT...........................The Engineer
JEAN D'ASTE......................The Professor
PECLET...........................A Soldier
DITA PARLO..................The Peasant Girl

REALISATIONS D'ART (France)   1938
Director: Jean Renoir
(See Foreign Language Films, page 347)

Grapes of Wrath, The

HENRY FONDA.....................Tom Joad
JANE DARWELL.....................Ma Joad
JOHN CARRADINE........................Casy
CHARLEY GRAPEWIN..................Grampa
DORRIS BOWDON..............Rose of Sharon
RUSSELL SIMPSON.....................Pa Joad
O. Z. WHITEHEAD........................Al
JOHN QUALEN.........................Muley
EDDIE QUILLAN.......................Connie
ZEFFIE TILBURY......................Granma
FRANK SULLY..........................Noah
FRANK DARIEN...................Uncle John
DARRYL HICKMAN....................Winfield
SHIRLEY MILLS.....................Ruth Joad
ROGER IMHOF........................Thomas
GRANT MITCHELL...................Caretaker
CHARLES D. BROWN..................Wilkie
JOHN ARLEDGE........................Davis
WARD BOND........................Policeman
HARRY TYLER..........................Bert
WILLIAM PAWLEY........................Bill
ARTHUR AYLESWORTH...................Father
CHARLES TANNEN........................Joe
SELMAR JACKSON..........Inspection Officer
CHARLES MIDDLETON...................Leader
EDDIE WALLER.....................Proprietor
PAUL GUILFOYLE.......................Floyd
DAVID HUGHES........................Frank
CLIFF CLARK......................City Man
JOSEPH SAWYER...................Book-keeper
FRANK FAYLEN.........................Tim
ADRIAN MORRIS........................Agent
HOLLIS JEWELL..................Muley's son
ROBERT HOMANS......................Spencer
IRVING BACON........................Driver
KITTY McHUGH.........................Mae

20TH-FOX   Director: John Ford   1940
Based on the novel by John Steinbeck

Great Expectations

JOHN MILLS....................Pip (grown-up)
VALERIE HOBSON.............Estella (grown-up)
BERNARD MILES.................Joe Gargery
FRANCIS L. SULLIVAN...............Jaggers
FINLAY CURRIE.....................Magwitch
MARTITA HUNT................Miss Havisham
ANTHONY WAGER...............Pip, as a boy
JEAN SIMMONS.............Estella, as a girl
ALEC GUINNESS.............Herbert Pocket
IVOR BARNARD.....................Wemmick
FREDA JACKSON..........Mrs. Joe Gargery
TORIN THATCHER...........Bentley Drummle
EILEEN ERSKINE.....................Biddy
HAY PETRIE.................Uncle Pumblechook
GEORGE HAYES....................Compeyson
RICHARD GEORGE...............The Sergeant
EVERLEY GREGG..............Sarah Pocket
JOHN BURCH.....................Mr. Wopsle
GRACE DENBIGH-RUSSELL........Mrs. Wopsle
O. B. CLARENCE.............The Aged Parent
JOHN FORREST..........Pale Young Gentleman

CINEGUILD   Director: David Lean   1946
From the novel by Charles Dickens

Great Gabbo, The

ERICH VON STROHEIM...Gabbo, a ventriloquist
BETTY COMPSON
               Marie, his companion and assistant
DONALD DOUGLAS............Frank, a dancer
MARGIE KANE................Eccentric Dancer

SONO ART-WORLD WIDE   Director: James Cruze   1930
From a story by Ben Hecht

Greed

GIBSON GOWLAND..................McTeague
ZASU PITTS..........................Trina
JEAN HERSHOLT...........Marcus Schouler
CHESTER CONKLIN.................Mr. Sieppe
SYLVIA ASHTON..................Mrs. Sieppe
DALE FULLER.........................Maria
JOAN STANDING......................Selina
AUSTIN JEWELL..............August Sieppe
OSCAR GOTTELL)
                    } ....The Sieppe Twins
OTTO GOTTELL)
TEMPE PIGOTT..............McTeague's mother

METRO-GOLDWYN   1925
Director: Erich von Stroheim
From the novel " McTeague " by Frank Norris

Green for Danger

LEO GENN.........................Mr. Eden
HENRY EDWARDS...................Mr. Purdy
TREVOR HOWARD...................Dr. Barnes
RONALD ADAM.....................Dr. White
JUDY CAMPBELL..................Sister Bates
WENDY THOMPSON................Sister Carter
ROSAMUND JOHN................Nurse Sanson
SALLY GRAY......................Nurse Linley
MEGS JENKINS..................Nurse Woods
JOHN RAE.........................The Porter
MOORE MARRIOTT.............Joseph Higgins
FRANK LING....................Rescue Worker
ALASTAIR SIM.............Inspector Cockrill
GEORGE WOODBRIDGE
               Detective Sergeant Hendricks

INDIVID   Director: Sidney Gilliat   1946

Green Goddess, The

GEORGE ARLISS.........The Rajah of Rukh
ALICE JOYCE..................Lucilla Crespin
DAVID POWELL.............Dr. Basil Traherne

266

HARRY T. MOREY...............Major Crespin
IVAN SIMPSON......................Watkins
WILLIAM WORTHINGTON....:....The High Priest
JETTA GOUDAL....................The Ayah
METRO-GOLDWYN   1924
From the play by William Archer

Green Goddess, The
GEORGE ARLISS................Rajah of Rukh
ALICE JOYCE.........................Lucilla
RALPH FORBES...................Dr. Traherne
H. B. WARNER...............Major Crespin
IVAN SIMPSON......................Watkins
REGGY SHEFFIELD..........'....Lieutenant Carew
BETTY BOYD..........................An Ayah
DAVID TEARLE..................High Priest
NIGEL DE BRULIER...............Temple Priest
WARN   Director : Alfred E. Green   1930
From the play by William Archer

Green Years, The
CHARLES COBURN..............Alexander Gow
TOM DRAKE.....Robert Shannon, as a young man
BEVERLY TYLER.Alison Keith, as a young woman
HUME CRONYN....................Papa Leckie
GLADYS COOPER...............Grandma Leckie
DEAN STOCKWELL....Robert Shannon, as a child
SELENA ROYLE...................Mama Leckie
JESSICA TANDY....................Kate Leckie
RICHARD HAYDN..................Jason Reid
ANDY CLYDE......................Saddler Boag
NORMAN LLOYD..................Adam Leckie
ROBERT NORTH........:......Murdoch Leckie
WALLACE FORD..................Jamie Nigg
EILENE JANSSEN........Alison Keith, as a child
HANK DANIELS......Gavin Blair, as a young man
RICHARD LYON......Gavin Blair, as a child
HENRY O'NEILL...................Canon Roche
HENRY STEPHENSON.................Blakely
NORMA VARDEN...............Mrs. Bosomley
MGM   Director : Victor Saville   1946
From the novel by A. J. Cronin
*A review of this film by a B.B.C. critic, E. Arnot
Robertson, resulted in a court action brought by
the critic against MGM, who claimed that she was
" out of touch " with public taste. Judgment was
given in the High Court, in favour of the critic,
in July 1947.*

Guest in the House
ANNE BAXTER....................Evelyn Heath
RALPH BELLAMY.............Douglas Proctor
ALINE MacMAHON..:.............Aunt Martha
RUTH WARRICK.................Ann Proctor
SCOTT McKAY......................Dan Proctor
JEROME COWAN...................Mr. Hackett
MARIE McDONALD....................Miriam
PERCY KILBRIDE.........John, the butler
MARGARET HAMILTON........Hilda, the maid
CONNIE LAIRD...................Lee Proctor
HUNT STROMBERG   1945
Director : John Brahm
*From the play " Dear Evelyn " by Hagar Wilde
and Dale Eunson*

H

Hatter's Castle
ROBERT NEWTON....................Brodie
DEBORAH KERR........................Mary
BEATRICE VARLEY.............Mrs. Brodie
JAMES MASON.......................Renwick

EMLYN WILLIAMS.....................Dennis
HENRY OSCAR.....................Grierson
ENID STAMP-TAYLOR..................Nancy
ANTHONY BATEMAN..................Angus
JUNE HOLDEN.........................Janet
BREFNI O'RORKE.......................Foyle
GEORGE MERRITT....................Gibson
LAWRENCE HANRAY..............Dr. Lawrie
RODDY HUGHES....................Gordon
CLAUDE BAILEY.....................Paxton
STUART LINDSELL............Lord Winton
MARY HINTON...................Lady Winton
IAN FLEMING...................Sir John Latta
DAVID KEIR..........................Perry
AUBREY MALLALIEU..............Clergyman
PARA-BRIT   Director : Lance Comfort   1942
From the novel by A. J. Cronin
Re-issued 1947

He Who Gets Slapped
LON CHANEY.............He Who Gets Slapped
NORMA SHEARER...................Consuelo
JOHN GILBERT.......................Bezano
TULLY MARSHALL...........Count Mancini
MARC MacDERMOTT...........Beau Regnard
FORD STERLING.....................Tricaud
HARVEY CLARKE....................Briquet
PAULETTE DUVAL.....................Zinida
RUTH KING.........................His wife
BRANDON HURST ⎫
GEORGE DAVIS   ⎬.................Clowns
CLYDE COOK   ⎭
METRO-GOLDWYN   1925
Director : Victor Seastrom
From the play by Leonid Andreyev

Heart of a Nation, The
(*Untel Père et Fils*)
CHARLES BOYER.....................Narrator
LOUIS JOUVET.................{ Pierre Froment
                            { Félix Froment
LUCIEN NAT..................Bernard Froment
RAIMU............................Jules Froment
SUZY PRIM....................Estelle Froment
RENÉE DEVILLERS..........Gabrielle Froment
ROBERT LE VIGAN.............Michel Pierrier
JEAN MERCANTON.............Alain Froment
MICHELE MORGAN.............Marie Froment
HARRY KRIMER................Robert Léonard
PIERRE JORDAN..............Christian Léonard
ANITA GOMBAULT...............Nicole Bienne
DANIEL MENDAILLE........Georges Clémenceau
BISCOT..............................Noblet
COLETTE DARFEUIL....." Moulin Rouge " Girl
FERNAND LEDOUX............Mayor in 1939
PAUL GRAETZ   Director : Julien Duvivier   1940
*Completed three days before the Germans marched
into Paris, the film was destroyed by them with the
exception of one print which producer Paul Graetz
hid, attempted unsuccessfully to smuggle over the
Spanish border, and finally buried in a friendly
farmer's garden. One by one, the cans containing
the print were got out of France, but part was lost.
The film was completed under the same production
and direction in Hollywood, with the original stars,
who had found their way to America*
(*See Foreign Language Films, page 347*)

Heartbeat
GINGER ROGERS......................Arlette
JEAN-PIERRE AUMONT.................Pierre
ADOLPHE MENJOU...............Ambassador

BASIL RATHBONE..............Professor Aristide
EDUARDO CIANNELLI...........Baron Dvorak
MIKHAIL RASUMNY..............Yves Cadubert
MELVILLE COOPER...........Roland Médeville
MONA MARIS..............Ambassador's wife
HENRY STEPHENSON.................Minister
HAKIM   Director: Sam Wood   1946
Re-make of the French film " Battement de Cœur"
(See Foreign Language Films, page 347)

Hearts of the World

ADOLPHE LESTINA.............The Grandfather
JOSEPHINE CROWELL...............The Mother
LILLIAN GISH........The Girl, Marie Stephenson
ROBERT HARRON
       The Boy, Douglas Gordon Hamilton
JACK COSGRAVE..........The Father of the Boy
KATE BRUCE..............The Mother of the Boy
BEN ALEXANDER............The Littlest Brother
M. EMMONS ⎱
F. MARION ⎰ ·········The Boy's Other Brothers
DOROTHY GISH.............The Little Disturber
ROBERT ANDERSON..................M. Cuckoo
GEORGE FAWCETT........The Village Carpenter
GEORGE SIEGMANN. Von Strohm, German Agent
FAY HOLDERNESS...............The Innkeeper
L. LOWY.............A Deaf and Blind Musician
EUGENE POUYET.......................A Poilu
ANNA MAE WALTHALL...A French Peasant Girl
MLLE. YVETTE DUVOISIN............A Refugee
HERBERT SUTCH.............A French Major
MRS. GISH....................Refugee's mother
MRS. HARRON..........Woman with daughter
JESSIE HARRON....................Refugee
MARY HARRON................Wounded Girl
JOHNNY HARRON.............Boy with barrel
COMSTOCK   Director: D. W. Griffith   1918
Re-issued 1925

Heaven Can Wait

GENE TIERNEY.......................Martha
DON AMECHE.............Henry Van Cleve
CHARLES COBURN.............Hugo Van Cleve
MARJORIE MAIN..................Mrs. Strabel
LAIRD CREGAR.................His Excellency
SPRING BYINGTON.........Bertha Van Cleve
ALLYN JOSLYN...............Albert Van Cleve
EUGENE PALLETTE................E. F. Strabel
SIGNE HASSO.....................Mademoiselle
LOUIS CALHERN...........Randolph Van Cleve
HELENE REYNOLDS................Peggy Nash
AUBREY MATHER....................James
MICHAEL AMES.............Jack Van Cleve
LEONARD CAREY.....................Flogdell
CLARENCE MUSE.....................Jasper
DICKIE MOORE.......Henry Van Cleve, aged 15
DICKIE JONES.........Albert Van Cleve, aged 15
TRUDY MARSHALL....................Jane
FRANK ORTH......................Cab Driver
FLORENCE BATES.................Mrs. Craig
CLARA BLANDICK.............Grandmother
ANITA BOLSTER.................Mrs. Cooper
ALFRED HALL..................Mr. Van Cleve
GRACE HAMPTON.........Mrs. Van Cleve
GERALD OLIVER SMITH................Smith
NINO PIPITONE, JR..............Jack, as a boy
CLAIRE DU BREY................Miss Ralston
MAUREEN RODIN-RYAN................Nurse
CHARLES HALTON........Clerk in Brentano's
20TH-FOX   Director: Ernst Lubitsch   1943
Based on the play " Birthday" by Lazlo Bus-Fekete
In Technicolor

Hell's Angels

BEN LYON..................Monte Rutledge
JAMES HALL...................Roy Rutledge
JEAN HARLOW.......................Helen
JOHN DARROW............Karl Arnstedt
LUCIEN PRIVAL.............Baron von Kran
FRANK CLARKE.......Lieutenant von Bruen
ROY WILSON...................." Baldy "
DOUGLAS GILMORE..........Captain Redfield
JANE WINTON.............Baroness von Kranz
EVELYN HALL.............Lady Randolph
WILLIAM B. DAVIDSON............Staff Major
WYNDHAM STANDING
      Squadron Commander, R.F.C.
CARL VON HAARTMAN...Zeppelin Commander
F. SCHUMANN-HEINK...First Officer of Zeppelin
STEPHEN CARR.......................Elliott
PAT SOMERSET.....................Marryat
WILLIAM VON BRINKEN..........Von Richter
HANS JOBY.....................Von Schlieben
UA   Produced and directed by Howard Hughes   1931
This film took nearly three years to make, at a cost
of over £800,000

Hellzapoppin

OLE OLSEN...........................Ole
CHIC JOHNSON......................Chic
MARTHA RAYE.......................Betty
HUGH HERBERT.....................Quimby
JANE FRAZEE.......................Kitty
ROBERT PAIGE......................Jeff
MISCHA AUER.......................Pepi
RICHARD LANE.....................Director
LEWIS HOWARD....................Woody
CLARENCE KOLB.................Mr. Rand
NELLA WALKER..................Mrs. Rand
SHEMP HOWARD....................Louis
ELISHA COOK, JR....................Selby
FRANK DARIEN...................Messenger
KATHERINE JOHNSON.................Lena
GUS SCHILLING.............Orchestra Leader
      with
The Six Hits, Slim & Sam, The Congeroo Dancers,
Olive Hatch Water Ballet
UNIV   Director: H. C. Potter   1942

Henry V

LAURENCE OLIVIER...King Henry V of England
ROBERT NEWTON..............Ancient Pistol
RENEE ASHERSON..........Princess Katharine
LESLIE BANKS....................Chorus
ESMOND KNIGHT.....................Fluellen
LEO GENN.............Constable of France
FELIX AYLMER.......Archbishop of Canterbury
RALPH TRUMAN.......Montjoy, a French Herald
NICHOLAS HANNEN.............Duke of Exeter
HARCOURT WILLIAMS
      King Charles VI of France
ROBERT HELPMANN..............Bishop of Ely
IVY ST. HELIER.........Alice, lady-in-waiting
FREDA JACKSON..............Mistress Quickly
ERNEST THESIGER
      Duke of Berri, the French Ambassador
JIMMY HANLEY
      Williams, soldier in the English Camp
MAX ADRIAN...................The Dauphin
JOHN LAURIE...Jamy, Captain in the English Army
FRANCIS LISTER.............Duke of Orleans
NIALL MACGINNIS
      MacMorris, Captain in the English Army
VALENTINE DYALL.........Duke of Burgundy
GEORGE ROBEY.................Sir John Falstaff

RUSSELL THORNDIKE........Duke of Bourbon
ROY EMERTON............Lieutenant Bardolph
MICHAEL SHEPLEY
    Gower, Captain in the English Army
GRIFFITH JONES...............Earl of Salisbury
MORLAND GRAHAM.....Sir Thomas Erpingham
ARTHUR HAMBLING
    Bates, soldier in the English Camp
BRIAN NISSEN
    Court, soldier in the English Camp
FREDERICK COOPER............Corporal Nym
GERALD CASE............Earl of Westmoreland
MICHAEL WARRE..........Duke of Gloucester
JANET BURNELL........Queen Isabel of France
FRANK TICKLE..........Governor of Harfleur
GEORGE COLE.............................Boy
JONATHAN FIELD...........French Messenger
VERNON GREEVES...............English Herald
ERNEST HARE......................A Priest
TWO CITIES Director : Laurence Olivier 1945
From the play by William Shakespeare
In Technicolor
*The large-scale model of Elizabethan London used
in the film was later exhibited at the London County
Hall*

Here Comes Mr. Jordan

ROBERT MONTGOMERY..........Joe Pendleton
EVELYN KEYES...................Bette Logan
CLAUDE RAINS.....................Mr. Jordan
RITA JOHNSON...............Julia Farnsworth
EDWARD EVERETT HORTON...Messenger 7013
JAMES GLEASON.................Max Corkle
JOHN EMERY.....................Tony Abbott
DONALD MacBRIDE.........Inspector Williams
DON COSTELLO.........................Lefty
HALLIWELL HOBBES....................Sisk
BENNY RUBIN..........................Bugs
COL Director : Alexander Hall 1942
From the play " Heaven Can Wait " by Harry Segall

Hi, Gang !

BEBE DANIELS.................The Liberty Girl
BEN LYON...................Her Other Half
VIC OLIVER........The Nuisance with the Ideas
MOORE MARRIOTT.................Uncle Jerry
GRAHAM MOFFATT.....................Albert
GEORGINA McKINNON...........Mrs. Endicott
MAURICE RHODES..................Little Ben
PERCY PARSONS.................Hergensheimer
DIANA BEAUMONT........... His secretary
JACQUES BROWNE..................Botticelli
MAVIS VILLIERS............... His secretary
FELIX AYLMER...............Lord Amersham
GAINS Director : Marcel Varnel 1941
*A screen version of the famous weekly radio
programme, presented by Bebe Daniels, Ben Lyon
and Vic Oliver for 12 months non-stop, though the
" gang " were bombed out of four studios during
the German air-bombardment of London*

Hindle Wakes

ESTELLE BRODY...........Fanny Hawthorne
HUMBERSTON WRIGHT.......Chris Hawthorne
MARIE AULT................Mrs. Hawthorne
JOHN STUART................Allan Jeffcote
NORMAN McKINNELL.......Nathaniel Jeffcote
IRENE ROOKE.................Mrs. Jeffcote
PEGGY CARLISLE.................Mary Hollins
GRAHAM SOUTTEN...............Mr. Hollins
ARTHUR CHESNEY.........Sir Timothy Farrar

GLADYS JENNINGS..............Beatrice Farrar
JACK ROWAL...............George Ramsbottom
ALF GODDARD..............................Nobby
GAUMONT Director : Maurice Elvey 1927
From the play by Stanley Houghton

Hindle Wakes

BELLE CHRYSTALL...........Jenny Hawthorne
SYBIL THORNDIKE..............Mrs. Hawthorne
NORMAN McKINNELL.............Nat Jeffcote
EDMUND GWENN...........,....Chris Hawthorne
JOHN STUART..................Alan Jeffcote
RUTH PETERSEN.................Mary Hollins
MARY CLARE...................Mrs. Jeffcote
MURIEL ANGELUS...........·..Beatrice Farrar
A. G. POULTON...........Sir Timothy Farrar
LIONEL ROBERTS...................Bob Parker
BOB JOHNSTON...............The Song Plugger
GB Director : Victor Saville 1932
From the play by Stanley Houghton

Hostages
(Les Ôtages)

ANNIE VERNAY...................Annie
SATURNIN FABRE...................Rossignol
LARQUEY...........................Fabien
CHARPIN...........................Beaumont
DORVILLE..........................Rodillar
PIERRE LABRY......................Rameau
HELVETIA FILMS (France)   1939
  Director : Raymond Bernard
(See Foreign Language Films, page 347) .

Hostages

LUISE RAINER............Milada Preissinger
ARTURO DE CORDOVA............Paul Breda
WILLIAM BENDIX..................Janoshik
PAUL LUKAS.....................Rheinhardt
OSCAR HOMOLKA...........Lev Preissinger
KATINA PAXINOU......................Marie
ROLAND VARNO..................Jan Pavel
MIKHAIL RAZUMNY...................Josef
REINHOLD SCHUNZEL...............Daluege
FELIX BASCH................Dr. Wallerstein
ERIC FELDARY.............Peter Lobkowitz
JOHN MYLONG....................Prokosch
PHILIP VAN ZANDT...........Lieutenant Eisner
REX WILLIAMS........Lieutenant Marschmann
HANS CONREID....Lieutenant Glasenapp
MICHAEL VISAROFF..................Solvik
FREDERICK GIERMANN...............Patzer
PARA Director : Frank Tuttle 1944
From the novel by Stefan Heym

How Green Was My Valley

WALTER PIDGEON................Mr. Gruffydd
MAUREEN O'HARA.................Angharad
DONALD CRISP...................Mr. Morgan
ANNA LEE......................Bronwen
RODDY McDOWALL....................Huw
JOHN LODER.........................Ianto
SARA ALLGOOD.................Mrs. Morgan
BARRY FITZGERALD..............Cyfartha
PATRIC KNOWLES....................Ivor
WELSH SINGERS...................Themselves
MORTON LOWRY..................Mr. Jones
ARTHUR SHIELDS................Mr. Parry
ANN TODD.....................Ceinwen
20TH-FOX Director : John Ford 1942
*Based on the novel by Richard Llewellyn
Re-issued 1947*

FRANK SINATRA
(*Metro-Goldwyn-Mayer*)

Human Comedy, The

MICKEY ROONEY..............Homer Macauley
FRANK MORGAN................Willie Grogan
JAMES CRAIG....................Tom Spangler
MARSHA HUNT....................Diana Steed
FAY BAINTER....................Mrs. Macauley
RAY COLLINS...................Mr. Macauley
VAN JOHNSON................Marcus Macauley
DONNA REED....................Bess Macauley
JACKIE "BUTCH" JENKINS...Ulysses Macauley
DOROTHY MORRIS................Mary Arena
JOHN CRAVEN....................Toby George
ANN AYARS.....................Mrs. Sandoval
MARY NASH......................Miss Hicks
HENRY O'NEILL..................Charles Steed
KATHARINE ALEXANDER..........Mrs. Steed
ALAN BAXTER...................Brad Stickman
DARRYL HICKMAN....................Lionel
BARRY NELSON........................Fat
RITA QUIGLEY..................Helen Elliott
CLEM BEVANS......................Henderson
ADELINE DeWALT REYNOLDS......Librarian

MGM   Director : Clarence Brown   1943
From the story by William Saroyan

Hunchback of Notre Dame, The

LON CHANEY........................Quasimodo
PATSY RUTH MILLER...............Esmeralda
NORMAN KERRY........Phœbus de Chateaupers
KATE LESTER............Mme. de Gondelaurier
WINIFRED BRYSON................Fleur de Lys
NIGEL DE BRULIER..............Dom Claude
BRANDON HURST.......................Jehan
ERNEST TORRENCE....................Clopin
TULLY MARSHALL..............King Louis XI
HARRY VON METER..........M. Neufchatel
RAYMOND HATTON.................Gringoire
NICK DE RUIZ..............M. le Torteru
EULALIE JENSEN......................Marie
GLADYS BROCKWELL.............Sister Gudule

UNIV   Director : Wallace Worsley   1924
From the novel by Victor Hugo

Hunchback of Notre Dame, The

CHARLES LAUGHTON
             Quasimodo, the Hunchback
CEDRIC HARDWICKE
         Frollo, the King's High Justice
THOMAS MITCHELL.....Clopin, King of Beggars
MAUREEN O'HARA.....Esmeralda, a gipsy dancer
EDMOND O'BRIEN.............Gringoire, a poet
ALAN MARSHAL...Phœbus, Captain of Archers
WALTER HAMPDEN
         Claude, Archbishop of Notre Dame
HARRY DAVENPORT...Louis XI, King of France
KATHARINE ALEXANDER
         Mme. De Lys, a wealthy widow
GEORGE ZUCCO...................Procurator
FRITZ LEIBER....................A Nobleman
ETIENNE GIRARDOT.......The King's Physician
HELENE WHITNEY.......................Fleur
MINNA GOMBELL..............Queen of Beggars
ARTHUR HOHL......................Olivier
ROD LA ROCQUE...................Phillipo
SPENCER CHARTERS...............Court Clerk

RKO   Director : William Dieterle   1939
From the novel by Victor Hugo

I

I Am a Fugitive

(American title : *I Am a Fugitive from a Chain Gang*)
PAUL MUNI....................James Allen
GLENDA FARRELL....................Marie
HELEN VINSON........................Helen
PRESTON FOSTER.......................Pete
SHEILA TERRY............Allen's secretary
ALLEN JENKINS......................Barney
DAVID LANDAU......................Warden
EDWARD J. McNAMARA.........2nd Warden
BERTON CHURCHILL..................Judge
EDWARD ELLIS.................The Bomber
SALLY BLANE........................Alice
JAMES BELL..........................Red
JOHN WRAY.........................Nordine
HALE HAMILTON.................Rev. Allen
DOUGLASS DUMBRILLE......District Attorney
ROSCOE KARNS.......................Steve
ROBERT WARWICK....................Fuller
NOEL FRANCIS......................Linda

WARN   Director : Mervyn LeRoy   1932

I Lived in Grosvenor Square

ANNA NEAGLE............Lady Patricia Fairfax
REX HARRISON.............Major David Bruce
ROBERT MORLEY.............Duke of Exmoor
DEAN JAGGER.........Sergeant John Patterson
JANE DARWELL...............John's mother
DAME IRENE VANBRUGH......Mrs. Catchpole
PFC. ELLIOTT ARLUCK
          Sergeant Benji Greenbrugh, U.S. Army
EDWARD RIGBY...........Devonshire Innkeeper
R. R. HIGNETT......................Parker
BRENDA BRUCE..........1st Girl in guard's van
AUBREY MALLALIEU..................Bates
MICHAEL SHEPLEY.........Lieutenant Lutyens
JOHN SLATER.................Paratrooper
CHARLES VICTOR.................Taxi Driver
PETER HOBBES.........Paratroop Colonel
GERRY WILMOT......................Narrator
FRANK WEBSTER..............Devon Farmer
WILLIAM MURTON (Lieutenant, R.C.N.)
                         Dakota Pilot
NANCY PRICE.....................Mrs. Wilson
WALTER HUDD........................Vicar
CECIL RAMAGE.......................Trewhewy
PERCY WALSH.......................Merridew
SHEILAGH FRAZER......2nd Girl in guard's van
HELEN LOWRY....................Miss Borrow
RONALD SHINER ⎫
NEVILLE MAPP ⎬............Paratroopers
NORMAN WILLIAMS ⎭
ALVAR LIDDELL...................Announcer
DAVID HORNE..............War Office Major
CYRIL BAKER...............American Pianist
CAPT. ARVID O. DAHL, D.F.C. (U.S.A.A.F.)
                  courtesy appearance
Irene Manning, Carroll Gibbons and his Orchestra
ABPC   Director : Herbert Wilcox   1945

I Married a Witch

FREDRIC MARCH.............Wallace Wooley
VERONICA LAKE..................Jennifer
ROBERT BENCHLEY..........Dr. Dudley White
SUSAN HAYWARD............Estelle Masterson
CECIL KELLAWAY....................Daniel
ELIZABETH PATTERSON..............Margaret
ROBERT WARWICK..............J. B .Masterson
EILY MALYON......................Tabitha
ROBERT GREIG....................Town Crier

271

VIOLA MOORE...........................Martha
MARY FIELD.............................Nancy
NORA CECIL.............................Harriet
EMERY PARNELL.........................Allen
HELEN ST. RAYNER...................Vocalist
ALDRICH BOWKER.........Justice of the Peace
EMMA DUNN..........................His wife
CINEMA GUILD   Director: René Clair   1943

I'll Be Your Sweetheart
MARGARET LOCKWOOD.............Edie Story
VIC OLIVER............................Sam Kahn
MICHAEL RENNIE.................Bob Fielding
PETER GRAVES.....................Jim Knight
MOORE MARRIOTT............George Le Brunn
FREDERICK BURTWELL................Pacey
MAUDIE EDWARDS..................Mrs. Jones
GARRY MARSH.......................Wallace
GEORGE MERRITT............T. P. O'Connor
MURIEL GEORGE..............Mrs. Le Brunn
JONATHAN FIELD.......................Kelly
ELIOT MAKEHAM.................John Friar
ELLA RETFORD.......................Dresser
DAVID CROWLEY...............1st Henchman
ALF GODDARD.................2nd Henchman
JOSS AMBLER..........................Dugan
GAINS   Director: Val Guest   1945

Ils Etaient Neuf Célibataires
SACHA GUITRY..........................Jean
ELVIRE POPESCO....Countess Stacia Batchefskaia
PAULINE CARTON......Clémentine, Stacia's maid
ARNANDY.............M. Renard, Stacia's lawyer
GUSTAVE LIBEAU
          Kequemops (a Belgian film producer)
HENRI CRÉMIEUX.....................Louis
MARGUERITE DEVAL..........Mme. Picaillon
BETTY STOCKFIELD..................Margaret
MARGUERITE MORENO............Consuelo
GENEVIÈVE GUITRY....................Joan
MARGUERITE PIERRY...........Manageress
PRINCESSE CHYLO................Mi-Ha-Ou
          Bachelors
GASTON DUBOSC.....................Antonin
VICTOR BOUCHER...................Alexandre
MAX DEARLY.......................Athanase
ANDRE LEFAUR......................Adolphe
SATURNIN FABRE....................Adhémar
SINOËL.............................Amendé
AIMOS.............................Agenor
GILDES.............................Anatole
MORTON............................Aristide
(France) Producer and Director: Sacha Guitry 1939
     (*See Foreign Language Films*, page 347)

In Which We Serve
NOEL COWARD................Captain "D"
JOHN MILLS..................Shorty Blake
BERNARD MILES.............Walter Hardy
CELIA JOHNSON...........Alix (Mrs. Kinross)
JOYCE CAREY...................Mrs. Hardy
KAY WALSH.....................Freda Lewis
DEREK ELPHINSTONE.........Number One
MICHAEL WILDING..................."Flags"
ROBERT SANSOM..................."Guns"
PHILIP FRIEND...................."Torps"
JAMES DONALD.......................Doctor
BALLARD BERKELEY......Engineer Commander
CHIMMO BRANSON.................."Snotty"
KENNETH CARTEN....Sub-Lieutenant, R.N.V.R.
GEORGE CARNEY.....................Mr. Blake
KATHLEEN HARRISON.............Mrs. Blake
WALLY PATCH....................Uncle Fred

RICHARD ATTENBOROUGH......Young Stoker
PENELOPE DUDLEY WARD...Maureen Fenwick
HUBERT GREGG..........................Pilot
FREDERICK PIPER.................Edgecombe
CAVEN WATSON.......................Brodie
JOHNNIE SCHOFIELD................Coxswain
GEOFFREY HIBBERT. Able Seaman Joey Mackridge
JOHN BOXER.............Able Seaman Hollett
LESLIE DWYER......................Parkinson
WALTER FITZGERALD.......Colonel Lumsden
GERALD CASE...............Captain Jasper Fry
DORA GREGORY...............Mrs. Lemmon
LIONEL GROSE......................Reynolds
NORMAN PIERCE......Mr. Scatterthwaite
ANN STEPHENS.......................Lavinia
DANIEL MASSEY.......................Bobby
JILL STEPHENS.................May Blake
EILEEN PEELE...................Mrs. Farrell
BARBARA WARING.............Mrs. Macadoo
KAY YOUNG.........................Barmaid
JULIET MILLS.................Freda's baby
TWO CITIES   1943
     Directors: Noel Coward and David Lean

Informer, The
VICTOR McLAGLEN.................Gypo Nolan
PRESTON FOSTER.............Dan Gallagher
MARGOT GRAHAME..............Katie Fox
WALLACE FORD.............Frankie McPhillip
UNA O'CONNOR.............Mrs. McPhillip
HEATHER ANGEL..............Mary McPhillip
J. M. KERRIGAN.....................Terry
JOSEPH SAUERS..................Mulholland
NEIL FITZGERALD.........Tommy Connor
DONALD MEEK................Rat Mulligan
D'ARCY CORRIGAN.........The Blind Man
LEO McCABE........................Donahue
GAYLORD PENDLETON.................Daly
FRANCIS FORD.......................Flynn
MAY BOLEY......................Mme. Betty
GRISELDA HARVEY................The Lady
RKO   Director: John Ford   1935

Innocents of Paris
MAURICE CHEVALIER.........Maurice Marny
SYLVIA BEECHER.................Louise Leval
RUSSELL SIMPSON...............Emile Leval
GEORGE FAWCETT...................M. Marny
MRS. GEORGE FAWCETT........Mme. Marny
JOHN MILJAN.....................M. Renard
MARGARET LIVINGSTONE.......Mme. Renard
DAVID DURAND........................Jo-Jo
PARA   Director: Richard Wallace   1930

Iron Mask, The
DOUGLAS FAIRBANKS, SR...........D'Artagnan
MARGUERITE DE LA MOTTE.......Constance
BELLE BENNETT............The Queen Mother
DOROTHY REVIER...........Milady de Winter
VERA LEWIS.................Mme. Peronne
ROLFE SEDAN....................Louis XIII
WILLIAM BAKEWELL....Louis XIV, and his twin
NIGEL DE BRULIER.......Cardinal Richelieu
GORDON THORPE....Young Prince, and his twin
ULRICH HAUPT...................De Rochefort
LON POFF...................Father Joseph
CHARLES STEVENS.................Planchet
HENRY OTTO....................King's valet
LEON BARY.........................Athos
STANLEY J. SANDFORD..............Porthos
GINO CORRADO.....................Aramis
UA   Director: Allan Dwan   1930
     From the novel by Dumas

It's That Man Again

TOMMY HANDLEY
Mayor of " Foaming-at-the-Mouth "
JACK TRAIN............................{ Lefty / Funf
SIDNEY KEITH.....................Sam Scram
HORACE PERCIVAL................{ Alley-Oop / Cecil
DOROTHY SUMMERS..............Mrs. Mopp
DINO GALVANI............................Soso
CLARENCE WRIGHT.................Clarence
LEONARD SHARP......................Claude
GRETA GYNT.....................Stella Ferris
CLAUDE BAILEY.................C. B. Cato
FRANKLIN BENNETT.............Hilary Craven
VERA FRANCES.........................Daisy
RICHARD GEORGE.................Uncle Percy
JEAN KENT............................Kitty
GAINS   Director : Walter Forde   1943
Adapted from the original B.B.C. programme of the
same title

J

Jane Eyre

ORSON WELLES...........Edward Rochester
JOAN FONTAINE.....................Jane Eyre
MARGARET O'BRIEN............Adele Varens
PEGGY ANN GARNER..........Jane, as a child
JOHN SUTTON.......................Dr. Rivers
SARA ALLGOOD........................Bessie
HENRY DANIELL.................Brocklehurst
AGNES MOOREHEAD................Mrs. Reed
AUBREY MATHER................Colonel Dent
EDITH BARRETT...................Mrs. Fairfax
BARBARA EVEREST.............Lady Ingram
HILLARY BROOKE.............Blanche Ingram
ETHEL GRIFFIES.................Grace Poole
MAE MARSH............................Leah
EILY MALYON.................Miss Scatcherd
ERSKINE SANFORD...............Mr. Briggs
JOHN ABBOTT..........................Mason
RONALD HARRIS.........................John
CHARLES IRWIN....................Auctioneer
20TH-FOX   Director : Robert Stevenson   1944
From the novel by Charlotte Brontë
Re-issued 1946

Jazz Singer, The

AL JOLSON... Jakie Rabinowitz, later Jack Robin
MAY McAVOY.......................Mary Dale
WARNER OLAND...........Cantor Rabinowitz
EUGENIE BESSERER............Sara Rabinowitz
CANTOR JOSEF ROSENBLATT...........Himself
OTTO LEDERER..............Moisha Yudelson
BOBBIE GORDON................Jakie, aged 13
RICHARD TUCKER...................Harry Lee
NAT CARR...............................Levi
WILLIAM DEMAREST...........Buster Billings
ANDERS RANDOLF.....................Dillings
WILL WALLING........................Doctor
WARN-VITAPHONE   Director : Alan Crosland   1929
A part-talkie, this was the first film with sound to be
shown in Great Britain—at the Piccadilly Theatre,
London, on September 27, 1928

Jeannie

BARBARA MULLEN............Jeannie McLean
WILFRED LAWSON.............James McLean
GUS MacNAUGHTON.........Angus Whitelaw
PHYLLIS STANLEY..............Mrs. Whitelaw
MICHAEL REDGRAVE..........Stanley Smith

PERCY WALSH...........French Customs Official
PHILIP GODFREY......Restaurant Car Attendant
ALBERT LIEVEN....Count Erich von Wittgenstein
KAY HAMMOND......................Margaret
EDWARD CHAPMAN................Mr. Jansen
HILDA BAILEY.....................Mrs. Jansen
MARJORIE FIELDING............Mrs. Murdoch
GOOGIE WITHERS.................Laundry Girl
also
Frank Cellier, Meinhart Maur, Esme Percy, Rachel
Kempson, Joan Kemp-Welch, Joss Ambler, Katie
Johnson, Lynn Evans, Ian Fleming, Ann Shelton
HELLMAN   Director : Harold French   1941

Jenny Lind

GRACE MOORE.....................Jenny Lind
REGINALD DENNY.................Paul Brandt
WALLACE BEERY.......................Barnum
GUS SHY...............................Olaf
JOBYNA HOWLAND..................Josephine
GILBERT EMERY....................Brougham
GEORGE F. MARION.................Innkeeper
PAUL PORCASI.........................Maretti
GIOVANNI MARTINO...................Zerga
BODIL ROSING.............Innkeeper's wife
JOAN STANDING.........................Louise
MAVIS VILLIERS........................Selma
JUDITH VOSELLI......................Rosatti
MGM   Director : Sidney Franklin   1931

Jew Süss

CONRAD VEIDT.......................Jew Süss
FRANK VOSPER.............Karl Alexander
CEDRIC HARDWICKE.............Rabbi Gabriel
BENITA HUME.................Marie Auguste
SIR GERALD DU MAURIER........Weissensee
PAMELA OSTRER.......................Naemi
MARY CLARE.............Countess Wurben
EVA MOORE............................Jantje
PAUL GRAETZ........................Landauer
HAIDEE WRIGHT.....................Michele
JOAN MAUDE.........Magdalene Sibylle
CAMPBELL GULLAN.................{ Thurn / Taxis
GEORGE MERRITT....................Bilfinger
GIBB McLAUGHLIN.................Pancorbo
DENNIS HOEY........................Dieterle
HENRY HEWITT........................Neuffer
PERCY PARSONS........................Pflug
FRANCIS L. SULLIVAN...........Remchingen
PERCY WALSH...........................Benz
JAMES RAGLAN...............Lord Suffolk
FRANK CELLIER........................Roder
GLENNIS LORIMER.............Chambermaid
DIANA COTTON
Magdalene Sibylle's lady-in-waiting
JANE CORNELL...Marie Auguste's lady-in-waiting
ROBERT NAINBY
Hunting Lodge old Serving-man
HELEN FERRERS.............Countess's mother
HELENA PICKARD......................Teresa
RANDLE AYRTON...............Schoolmaster
MARCELLE ROGEZ...................Graziella
HENRY HALLATT.......................Painter
KYNASTON P. REEVES...................Judge
JOSEPH MARKOVITCH................Seligman
HAY PLUMB.........................Pfaeffle
GRETE HANSEN.................Sophie Fischer
LUCIUS BLAKE.........................Otman
MICKEY BRANTFORD.........Boy in kitchen
FRANK STANMORE....Landlord of Wildbad Inn
STANLEY LATHBURY.....Serving-man at Hirsau

273

SAM LIVESEY.....................Harprecht
WOOLF SILVERBERG........Rabbi of Frankfort
MAURICE AXELRAD............Rabbi of Furth
DOROTHY GIBSON...................Babette
LOIS MEREDITH
.............Lady-in-Waiting to Marie Auguste
CHARLES CASTELLA.............Prison Gaoler
SELMA VAZ DIAS.............Frau Seligman
HUMBERSTON WRIGHT............Bystander
E. A. HILL-MITCHELSON......Recruiting Officer
GWEN CLIFFORD............Hysterical Peasant
BOBBY BLYTHE................Stallholder
LESLIE LAURIER.................Courier
LEWIS BROUGHTON...Official to Karl Alexander
VICTOR FAIRLEY...................Officer
J. R. TOZER....................Gambler
VITTORIO RIETTI....................Rabbi
GB   Director: Lothar Mendes   1935
        From the novel by Lion Feuchtwanger

Johnny Eager

ROBERT TAYLOR................Johnny Eager
LANA TURNER..................Lisbeth Bard
EDWARD ARNOLD........John Benson Farrell
VAN HEFLIN....................Jeff Hartnett
ROBERT STERLING.........Jimmy Courtney
PATRICIA DANE....................Garnet
GLENDA FARRELL..........Mae Blythe
HENRY O'NEILL.................Mr. Verne
DIANA LEWIS.................Judy Sanford
BARRY NELSON.................Lew Rankin
CHARLES DINGLE...................Marco
PAUL STEWART.....................Julio
CY KENDALL.....................Halligan
DON COSTELLO....................Billiken
LOU LUBIN........................Benjy
JOSEPH DOWNING....................Ryan
CONNIE GILCHRIST.....................Peg
ROBIN RAYMOND.................Matilda
LEONA MARICLE................Miss Mines
BYRON SHORES................Officer No. 711
MGM   Director: Mervyn LeRoy   1942
                Re-issued 1946

Jour Se Lève, Le

JEAN GABIN.....................François
JACQUELINE LAURENT.............Françoise
ARLETTY..........................Clara
JULES BERRY...................Valentin
FILM SIGMA (France)   1939
        Director: Marcel Carné
Bought by the American producers Robert and
Raymond Hakim (who bought and re-made
Battement de Cœur), Le Jour Se Lève was
re-made as The Long Night. The only copy in
existence of the original film is preserved in the
British Film Institute.
(See Foreign Language Films, page 347)

Journey for Margaret

ROBERT YOUNG...................John Davis
LARAINE DAY.....................Nora Davis
FAY BAINTER..................Trudy Strauss
NIGEL BRUCE..........Herbert V. Allison
MARGARET O'BRIEN.................Margaret
WILLIAM SEVERN....................Peter
ELISABETH RISDON.............Mrs. Bailey
DORIS LLOYD..................Mrs. Barrie
HALLIWELL HOBBES.............Mr. Barrie
HEATHER THATCHER.............Mrs. Harris
JILL ESMOND.................Susan Fleming

G. P. HUNTLEY, JR.................." Rugged "
LISA GOLM.....................Frau Weber
MGM   Director: W. S. Van Dyke II   1943
        Based on the book by William L. White

Journey's End

COLIN CLIVE.............Captain Stanhope
IAN MacLAREN.............Lieutenant Osborne
DAVID MANNERS.........2/Lieutenant Raleigh
BILLY BEVANS.........2/Lieutenant Trotter
ANTHONY BUSHELL.......2/Lieutenant Hibbert
ROBERT A'DAIR.................Captain Hardy
CHARLES GERRARD.............Private Mason
TOM WHITELEY.........The Sergeant Major
JACK PITCAIRN.............The Colonel
WARNER KLINGER.........German Soldier
TIFFANY   Director: James Whale   1930
        From the play by R. C. Sherriff

Juarez

PAUL MUNI.................Benito Pablo Juarez
BETTE DAVIS.........................Carlota
BRIAN AHERNE....................Maximilian
CLAUDE RAINS.................Napoleon III
JOHN GARFIELD................Porfirio Diaz
DONALD CRISP.........Maréchal Bazaine
JOSEPH CALLEIA.........Alejandro Uradi
GALE SONDERGAARD.....Empress Eugénie
GILBERT ROLAND....Colonel Miguel Lopez
HENRY O'NEILL.........Miguel Miramon
PEDRO DE CORDOBA.........Riva Palacio
MONTAGU LOVE.........Jose de Montares
HARRY DAVENPORT.........Dr. Samuel Basch
WALTER FENNER.............Achille Fould
ALEX LEFTWICH.........Drouyn de Lhuys
GEORGIA CAINE.....Countess Battenberg
ROBERT WARWICK.........Major DuPont
GENNARO CURCI.........Señor de Leon
BILL WILKERSON.........Tomas Mepia
JOHN MILJAN.........Mariano Escobedo
HUGH SOTHERN.............John Bigelow
FRED MALATESTA.................Señor Salas
CARLOS DE VALDEZ.................Tailor
IRVING PICHEL...................Carbajal
FRANK LACKTEEN.................Coachman
WALTER O. STAHL.....Senator del Valle
FRANK REICHER.........Duc de Morny
HOLMES HERBERT.........Marshall Randon
WALTER KINGSFORD.....Prince Metternich
EGON BRECHER.........Baron von Magnus
MONTE BLUE.........Lerdo de Tejada
LOUIS CALHERN...................Le Marc
MANUEL DIAZ.......................Pepe
MICKEY KUHN.........Augustine Iturbide
LILLIAN NICHOLSON.........Josefa Iturbide
NOBLE JOHNSON...................Regules
MARTIN GARRALAGA.................Negroni
VLADIMIR SOKOLOFF.................Camilo
DOUGLAS WOOD.................Mr. Hartman
WARN   Director: William Dieterle   1940

K

Kermesse Héroïque, La

FRANÇOISE ROSAY......The Burgomaster's wife
MICHELINE CHEIREL.................Siska
LYNE CLÉVERS...........The Fishmonger's wife
MARYSE WENDLING.........The Baker's wife
GINETTE GAUBERT........The Innkeeper's wife
MARGARITE DUCOURET.....The Brewer's wife
JEAN MURAT.................Duc D'Olivares
ALERME.....................The Burgomaster

LOUIS JOUVET.....................The Chaplain
BERNARD LANCRET...............Jean Breugal
ALFRED ADAM....................The Butcher
ARTHUR DEVÈRE..............The Fishmonger
MARCEL CARPENTIER..............The Baker
PIERRE LABRY...................The Innkeeper
ALEXANDER D'ARCY..............The Captain
CLAUD ST. VAL.................The Lieutenant
DELPHIN..........................The Dwarf
FILMS SONORES TOBIS (France)   1935
Director : Jacques Feyder
From the novel by Charles Spaak
(See Foreign Language Films, page 347)

King of Jazz

PAUL WHITEMAN AND ORCHESTRA,
JOHN BOLES, LAURA LA PLANTE, JEANETTE
LOFF, GLENN TRYON, MERNA KENNEDY,
KATHRYN CRAWFORD, SLIM SUMMERVILLE,
STANLEY SMITH, BILLY KENT (comedian
dancer), GRACE HAYES (singer), SISTERS G,
RHYTHM BOYS (harmonists), BROX SISTERS
(harmony trio), GEORGE CHILES, JACQUES
CARTIER (voodoo dancer), AL NORMAN (legmania
dancer), FRANK LESLIE, CHARLES IRWIN (M.C.),
JEANIE LANG, PAUL HOWARD (dancer),
MARIAN STATLER AND DON ROSE (rag doll
dancers), TOMMY ATKINS SEXTET AND NELL
O'DAY (adagio dancer), WILBUR HALL (instrumen-
talist), JOHN FULTON, MARKET DANCERS
AND HOLLYWOOD BEAUTIES
   1. " Bridal Veil "—Jeanette Loff, Stanley Smith,
Market Dancers, Hollywood Beauties. Music : " My
Bridal Veil ".
   2. " Bench in the Park "—Paul Whiteman, Jeanette
Loff, Stanley Smith, Rhythm Boys, Brox Sisters, Market
Dancers, and Beauties. Music : "A Bench in the Park ".
   3. " Song of the Dawn "—John Boles, cowboy
chorus, and Paul Whiteman. Song—as title of episode.
   4. "Happy Feet "—Paul Whiteman, Market
Dancers, Rhythm Boys, Sisters G, Al Norman,
Charles Irwin. Song : " I've Got Those Happy Feet ".
   5. " It Happened in Monterey "—John Boles,
Jeanette Loff, George Chiles, Market Dancers and
Sisters G. Music—as title of episode.
   6. " Ragamuffin Romeo "—Jeanie Lang, George
Chiles, Don Rose and Marian Statler. Song : " My
Ragamuffin Romeo ".
   7. " Rhapsody in Blue "—Paul Whiteman, Market
Dancers, Sisters G, Beauties and Jacques Cartier.
Music—as title of episode.
   8. " Melting Pot "—Paul Whiteman, Market
Dancers, Jeanette Loff and George Chiles, Beauties,
Atkins Sextet, and Nell O'Day. Music : National
airs and medley of all numbers in production.
UNIV   Director : John Murray Anderson   1931

King of Kings

H. B. WARNER.................Jesus, the Christ
DOROTHY CUMMING.........Mary, the Mother
ERNEST TORRENCE...........⎫ ⎧.........Peter
JOSEPH SCHILDKRAUT........⎪ ⎪.......Judas
JAMES NEILL................⎪ ⎪.......James
JOSEPH STRIKER.............⎪ ⎪.........John
ROBERT EDESON.............⎪ ⎪.....Matthew
SIDNEY D'ALBROOK..........⎬ The ⎨......Thomas
DAVID IMBODER.............⎪ Twelve ⎪......Andrew
CHARLES BELCHER...........⎪ Disciples ⎪........Philip
CLAYTON PACKARD..........⎪ ⎪.Bartholomew
ROBERT ELLSWORTH.........⎪ ⎪........Simon
CHARLES REQUA.............⎪ ⎪James, the Less
JOHN T. PRINCE............⎭ ⎩....Thaddeus

JACQUELINE LOGAN...........Mary Magdalene
RUDOLPH SCHILDKRAUT
          Caiaphas, High Priest of Israel
SAM DE GRASSE...................The Pharisee
CASSON FERGUSON.................The Scribe
VICTOR VARCONI.................Pontius Pilate
MAJEL COLEMAN.........Procula, wife of Pilate
MONTAGU LOVE.........The Roman Centurion
WILLIAM BOYD...............Simon of Cyrene
M. MOORE.............................Mark
THEODORE KOSLOFF
     Malchus, Captain of the High Priest's Guard
GEORGE SIEGMANN..................Barabbas
JULIA FAYE..........................Martha
JOSEPHINE NORMAN.........Mary of Bethany
KENNETH THOMSON..................Lazarus
ALAN BROOKS........................Satan
MURIEL MacCORMAC...........The Blind Girl
CLARENCE BURTON
          Dysmas, the Repentant Thief
JAMES MASON......Gestas, the Unrepentant Thief
MAY ROBSON.............The Mother of Gestas
DOT FARLEY...........Maidservant of Caiaphas
HECTOR SARNO.........The Galilean Carpenter
LEON HOLMES.................The Imbecile Boy
JACK PADGEN......Captain of the Roman Guard
DE MILLE-PATHE   Director : Cecil B. De Mille   1929

Kipps

MICHAEL REDGRAVE...................Kipps
DIANA WYNYARD.........Helen Walsingham
ARTHUR RISCOE....................Chitterlow
PHYLLIS CALVERT.............Ann Pornick
MAX ADRIAN.................Chester Coote
HELEN HAYE.............Mrs. Walsingham
MICHAEL WILDING........Ronnie Walsingham
LLOYD PEARSON...................Shalford
EDWARD RIGBY.....................Buggins
MACKENZIE WARD...................Pearce
HERMIONE BADDELEY...........Miss Mergle
BETTY ANN DAVIES.................Flo Bates
ARTHUR DENTON.....................Carshot
BETTY JARDINE.....Doris (freckled girl)
FRANK PETTINGELL................Old Kipps
BEATRICE VARLEY...............Mrs. Kipps
PHILIP FROST................Kipps, as a boy
DIANA CALDERWOOD....Ann Pornick, as a girl
GEORGE CARNEY...............Old Pornick
IRENE BROWNE.........Mrs. Bindon-Botting
PETER GRAVES....................Sidney Revel
VISCOUNT CASTLEROSSE.....Man in bath-chair
20TH-BRIT   Director : Carol Reed   1940
From the novel by H. G. Wells

Kissing Cup's Race

VIOLET HOPSON.....The Hon. Constance Medley
GREGORY SCOTT................Lord Hillhoxton
ADELINE HAYDEN-COFFIN....Lady Corrington
ARTHUR WALCOTT......John Wood, the trainer
JOE PLANT (famous flat race jockey)....Bob Doon
CLIVE BROOK.............Lord Rattlington
PHILIP HEWLAND
          Vereker, Lord Rattlington's friend
BROADWEST   1922

Kitty Foyle

GINGER ROGERS...................Kitty Foyle
DENNIS MORGAN...............Wyn Strafford
JAMES CRAIG.......................Mark
EDUARDO CIANNELLI................Giono
ERNEST COSSART......................Pop
GLADYS COOPER.............Mrs. Strafford

275

NAUNTON WAYNE
(*Gainsborough*)

ODETTE MYRTIL.............Delphine Detaille
MARY TREEN......................Pat
KATHARINE STEVENS..................Molly
WALTER KINGSFORD...............Mr. Kennett
CECIL CUNNINGHAM............Grandmother
NELLA WALKER..................Aunt Jessica
EDWARD FIELDING...............Uncle Edgar
KAY LINAKER.....................Wyn's wife
RICHARD NICHOLS.................Wyn's boy
FLORENCE BATES.................Customer
RKO   Director: Sam Wood   1941

L

Lady Eve, The
BARBARA STANWYCK....................Jean
HENRY FONDA........................Charles
CHARLES COBURN......."Colonel" Harrington
EUGENE PALLETTE....................Mr. Pike
WILLIAM DEMAREST..................Muggsy
ERIC BLORE........Sir Alfred McGlennan Keith
MELVILLE COOPER...................Gerald
MARTHA O'DRISCOLL.................Martha
JANET BEECHER....................Mrs. Pike
ROBERT GREIG......................Burrows
DORA CLEMENT.....................Gertrude
LUIS ALBERNI....................Pike's chef
PARA   Director: Preston Sturges   1941

Lady Hamilton
VIVIEN LEIGH............Emma, Lady Hamilton
LAURENCE OLIVIER...............Lord Nelson
ALAN MOWBRAY.........Sir William Hamilton
SARA ALLGOOD............Mrs. Cadogan-Lyon
GLADYS COOPER...................Lady Nelson
HENRY WILCOXON..............Captain Hardy
HEATHER ANGEL...................A Street Girl
HALLIWELL HOBBES...............Rev. Nelson
GILBERT EMERY..................Lord Spencer
MILES MANDER...................Lord Keith
RONALD SINCLAIR....................Josiah
LUIS ALBERNI...............King of Naples
NORMA DRURY................Queen of Naples
KORDA-HOLLYWOOD Director: Alexander Korda 1941

Lady in the Lake
ROBERT MONTGOMERY.........Phillip Marlowe
AUDREY TOTTER...........Adrienne Fromsett
LLOYD NOLAN.............Lieutenant Degarmot
TOM TULLY....................Captain Kane
LEON AMES...................Derace Kingsby
JAYNE MEADOWS...........Mildred Havelend
DICK SIMMONS..................Chris Lavery
MORRIS ANKRUM.............Eugene Grayson
LILA LEEDS......................Receptionist
WILLIAM ROBERTS....................Artist
KATHLEEN LOCKHART..........Mrs. Grayson
ELLAY MORT.............Chrystal Kingsby
MGM   Director: Robert Montgomery   1946
The story of the film was told by means of a
"subjective camera", whereby the audience saw
the action through the eyes of the leading character

Lady Vanishes, The
MARGARET LOCKWOOD........Iris Henderson
MICHAEL REDGRAVE..................Gilbert
PAUL LUKAS.......................Dr. Hartz
DAME MAY WHITTY...............Miss Froy
CECIL PARKER...................Mr. Todhunter
LINDEN TRAVERS............'Mrs.' Todhunter
MARY CLARE.......................Baroness
NAUNTON WAYNE..................Caldicott

BASIL RADFORD.....................Charters
EMIL BOREO.................Hotel Manager
GOOGIE WITHERS.....................Blanche
SALLY STEWART.......................Julie
PHILIP LEAVER..................Signor Doppo
SELMA VAZ DIAS.............Signora Doppo
CATHERINE LACEY..................The Nun
MGM-GAINS   Director: Alfred Hitchcock   1938
Adapted from the novel " The Wheel Spins " by
Ethel Linda White

Last Chance, The
E. G. MORRISON..................Major Telford
JOHN HOY................Lieutenant Halliday
RAY REAGAN.............Sergeant Braddock
LUISA ROSSI........................Tonina
ODEARDO MASINI................An Innkeeper
GIUSEPPE GALEATI.................A Carrier
ROMANO CALO.........................Priest
LEOPOLD BIBERTI.........A Swiss Lieutenant
THERESE GIEHSE................Frau Wittels
ROBERT SCHWARZ............Bernard, her son
PRAESENS FILM (Switzerland)-MGM-INTERNATIONAL 1945
Director: Leopold Lindtberg
(See Foreign Language Films, page 347)

Last Days of Pompeii, The
MARIA CORDA.............Nydia, the blind girl
COUNTESS DE LIGUORO.................Ione
VICTOR VARCONI.....................Glaucus
BERNHARDT GOETZKE...............Arbaces
LIVIA MARIS.........................Julie
EMILE GHIONE......................Calenus
CARL DUSE..........................Burbo
VICTOR EVANGELISTI...............Apecides
GILDO BOCCI.......................Diomed
ITALIA VITALIANI...............Stratonica
SOCIETA ITALIANA GRANDI FILMS (Italy)   1925
From the novel by Lord Lytton
(See Foreign Language Films, page 347)

Last Laugh, The
EMIL JANNINGS..................Hotel Porter
GEORGE JOHN.................Night Watchman
EMILE KURZ.........Porter's housekeeper
MABY DELSCHAFT..............The Daughter
UFA (Germany)   Director: F. W. Murnau   1925
(See Foreign Language Films, page 347)

Laura
GENE TIERNEY........................Laura
DANA ANDREWS............Mark McPherson
CLIFTON WEBB...............Waldo Lydecker
VINCENT PRICE...............Shelby Carpenter
JUDITH ANDERSON.............Anne Treadwell
DOROTHY ADAMS...............Bessie Clary
RALPH DUNN.................Fred Callahan
CY KENDALL.......................Inspector
HAROLD SCHLICKENMAYER ⎫
HARRY STRANG   ⎬......Detectives
LANE CHANDLER   ⎭
20TH-FOX   Director: Otto Preminger   1945
Adapted from the novel by Vera Caspary

Life and Death of Colonel Blimp, The
JAMES McKECHNIE.................Spud Wilson
NEVILLE MAPP.................Stuffy Graves
VINCENT HOLMAN..........Club Porter (1942)
ROGER LIVESEY..................Clive Candy
DAVID HUTCHESON....................Hoppy
SPENCER TREVOR.............Period Blimp
ROLAND CULVER...........Colonel Betteridge

JAMES KNIGHT...............Club Porter (1902)
DEBORAH KERR..............⎰ Edith Hunter
⎱ Barbara Wynne
⎱ Johnny Cannon
DENNIS ARUNDELL.......Café Orchestra Leader
DAVID WARD..........................Kaunitz
JAN VAN LOEWEN............Indignant Citizen
VALENTINE DYALL.............Von Schoborn
ALBERT LIEVEN...................Von Ritter
ERIC MATURIN..............Colonel Goodhead
FRITH BANBURY.............Babyface Fitzroy
ROBERT HARRIS.........Embassy Secretary
ARTHUR WONTNER........Embassy Counsellor
COUNT ZICHY..................Colonel Berg
ANTON WALBROOK..Theo Kretschmar-Schuldorff
JANE MILLICAN................Nurse Erna
URSULA JEANS.............Frau von Kalteneck
PHYLLIS MORRIS.....................Pebble
DIANA MARSHALL....................Sibyl
MURIEL AKED...................Aunt Margaret
JOHN LAURIE........................Murdoch
REGINALD TATE.....................Van Zijl
CAPTAIN W. BARRETT, U.S. ARMY.....The Texan
CORPORAL THOMAS PALMER......The Sergeant
YVONNE ANDRÉE......................The Nun
MARJORIE GRESLEY...............The Matron
FELIX AYLMER...................The Bishop
HELEN DEBROY.................Mrs. Wynne
NORMAN PIERCE...................Mr. Wynne
HARRY WELCHMAN................Major Davis
A. E. MATTHEWS.........President of Tribunal
EDWARD COOPER...............B.B.C. Official
JOAN SWINSTEAD..................Secretary
ARCHERS   Directors: 1943
Michael Powell and Emeric Pressburger
In Technicolor

Life of Émile Zola, The

PAUL MUNI........................Émile Zola
GLORIA HOLDEN..............Alexandrine Zola
JOSEPH SCHILDKRAUT...Captain Alfred Dreyfus
GALE SONDERGAARD...........Lucie Dreyfus
DICKIE MOORE...................Pierre Dreyfus
ROLLA GOURVITCH............Jeanne Dreyfus
DONALD CRISP..................Maître Labori
GRANT MITCHELL.........Georges Clémenceau
JOHN LITEL....................Charpentier
LUMSDEN HARE................Mr. Richards
MARCIA MAE JONES..........Helen Richards
GILBERT EMERY.............Minister of War
HARRY DAVENPORT.........Chief of Staff
RALPH MORGAN............Commander of Paris
WALTER KINGSFORD.........Colonel Sandherr
HENRY O'NEILL.............Colonel Picquart
ROBERT BARRAT.......Major Walsin-Esterhazy
LOUIS CALHERN................Major Dort
ERIN O'BRIEN MOORE.................Nana
MONTAGU LOVE.............M. Cavaignac
ROBERT WARWICK...........Major Henry
FRANK SHERIDAN........M. Van Cassell
MORRIS CARNOVSKY.........Anatole France
VLADIMIR SOKOLOFF............Paul Cézanne
CHARLES RICHMAN..........M. Delagorgue
FIRST NATIONAL   Director: William Dieterle   1937

Lifeboat

TALLULAH BANKHEAD.........Connie Porter
WILLIAM BENDIX.........................Gus
WALTER SLEZAK...................The German
MARY ANDERSON............Alice Mackenzie
JOHN HODIAK........................Kovac
HENRY HULL.......................Ritterhouse

HEATHER ANGEL.................Mrs. Higgins
HUME CRONYN.................Stanley Garrett
CANADA LEE.........................Joe
20TH-FOX   Director: Alfred Hitchcock   1944
From a story by John Steinbeck

Light That Failed, The

RONALD COLMAN.................Dick Heldar
WALTER HUSTON.................Torpenhow
MURIEL ANGELUS.....................Maisie
IDA LUPINO.....................Bessie Broke
DUDLEY DIGGES.................The Nilghai
ERNEST COSSART.....................Beeton
FERIKE BOROS.................Mme. Binat
PEDRO DE CORDOBA...............M. Binat
COLIN TAPLEY......................Gardner
RONALD SINCLAIR..........Dick, as a boy
SARITA WOOTON.............Maisie, as a girl
HALLIWELL HOBBES.................Doctor
CHARLES IRWIN.............Soldier Model
FRANCIS McDONALD...............George
GEORGE REGAS....................Cassavetti
WILFRED ROBERTS...................Barton
PARA   Director: William A. Wellman   1939
Based on the novel by Rudyard Kipling
Re-issued 1946

Lily Christine

CORINNE GRIFFITH.............Lily Christine
COLIN CLIVE..................Rupert Harvey
MARGARET BANNERMAN........Mrs. Abbey
MILES MANDER...................Ambatriadi
JACK TREVOR.................Ivor Summerest
ANNE GREY....................Muriel Harvey
PARA-BRIT   Director: Paul Stein   1932
From the story by Michael Arlen
Lily Christine was given a Royal Premiere in aid of
charity at the Plaza Theatre, London, on April 28,
1932, in the presence of the Prince of Wales and
Prince George

Lion Has Wings, The
Featuring

MERLE OBERON   RALPH RICHARDSON
JUNE DUPREZ   FLORA ROBSON
ROBERT DOUGLAS   ANTHONY BUSHELL
AUSTIN TREVOR   MILTON ROSMER
IAN FLEMING   DERRICK DE MARNEY
Commentary by E. V. H. EMMETT
LFP   Directors: 1939
Michael Powell
Brian Desmond Hurst
Adrian Brunel
This was the first British propaganda film of World
War II. It was sponsored by the Ministry of
Information, and produced in six weeks by
Alexander Korda. It gave an account of how the
war enveloped Europe, and the exploits of the R.A.F.
including shots of the actual participants in the
bombing raid on Kiel Harbour stepping from their
machines on their return to the aerodrome

Little Foxes, The

BETTE DAVIS...................Regina Giddens
HERBERT MARSHALL.........Horace Giddens
TERESA WRIGHT.............Alexandra Giddens
RICHARD CARLSON............David Hewitt
PATRICIA COLLINGE............Birdie Hubbard
DAN DURYEA.................Leo Hubbard
CHARLES DINGLE...............Ben Hubbard
CARL BENTON REID.........Oscar Hubbard
JESSIE GRAYSON.....................Addie

JOSEPH COTTEN
(Selznick)

JEANNE CRAIN
(*20th Century-Fox*)

JOHN MARRIOTT.........................Cal
RUSSELL HICKS.............. William Marshall
LUCIEN LITTLEFIELD..............Manders
VIRGINIA BRISSAC.................Mrs. Hewitt
TERRY NIBERT.........................Julia
ALAN BRIDGE....................Hotel Manager
CHARLES R. MOORE...................Simon
RKO   Director : William Wyler   1942
From the stage play by Lillian Hellman

Little Lord Fauntleroy
MARY   ⎧Cedric Errol, Little Lord Fauntleroy
  PICKFORD   ⎨   " Dearest ", his mother
CLAUDE GILLINGWATER
                    The Earl of Dorincourt
COLIN KENNY.....................Bevis Errol
JOSEPH J. DOWLING......William L. Havisham
KATE PRICE.................Mrs. McGinty
FRED MALATESTA.........Dick, the bootblack
JAMES A. MARCUS............Hobbs, the grocer
ROSE DIONE.........................Minna
FRANCIS MARION....................Her son
EMMETT KING..............Rev. Mordaunt
MME. DE BODAMERE.........Mrs. Higgins
UA   Directors :   1922
    Alfred E. Green and Jack Pickford
From the novel by Frances Hodgson Burnett

Little Mister Jim
JACKIE " BUTCH " JENKINS...Little Jim Tukker
JAMES CRAIG.......... Captain Big Jim Tukker
FRANCES GIFFORD...............Jean Tukker
LUANA PATTEN...............Missey Choosey
SPRING BYINGTON..............Mrs. Starwell
CHINGWAH LEE....................Sui Jen
LAURA LA PLANTE.............Mrs. Glenson
HENRY O'NEILL....................Chaplain
MORRIS ANKRUM.............Colonel Starwell
CELIA TRAVERS.................Miss Martin
RUTH BRADY..................Miss Hall
SHARON McMANUS.....................Elsie
BUZ BUCKLEY........................Ronnie
CAROL NUGENT.......................Clara
JEAN VAN...........................Mary
MGM   Director : Fred Zinnemann   1946

Lives of a Bengal Lancer, The
GARY COOPER............Lieutenant McGregor
FRANCHOT TONE...........Lieutenant Forsythe
RICHARD CROMWELL........Lieutenant Stone
SIR GUY STANDING............Colonel Stone
C. AUBREY SMITH.........Major Hamilton
KATHLEEN BURKE.........Tania Volkanskaya
DOUGLASS DUMBRILLE.....Mohammed Khan
MONTE BLUE.................Hamzulla Khan
AKIM TAMIROFF...............Emir of Gopal
J. CARROL NAISH................Grand Vizier
NOBLE JOHNSON.................Ram Singh
LUMSDEN HARE.......Major General Woodley
JAMESON THOMAS..............Hendrickson
COLIN TAPLEY.............Lieutenant Barrett
PARA   Director : Henry Hathaway   1935
             Re-issued 1946

Loi du Nord, La
MICHELE MORGAN.............Jacqueline Bert
PIERRE RICHARD-WILLM........Robert Shaw
CHARLES VANEL.....Sergeant Dalrymple
JACQUES TERRANE...........Louis Dumontier
ARLETTE MARCHAL................Mrs. Shaw

MAX MICHEL........................Patterson
YOUKA TROUBETSKOI...........Ellis Lowton
FILMS VICTORIA (France)   1939
          Director : Jacques Feyder
    From the novel by Constantin-Weyer
    (See Foreign Language Films, page 347)

London Town
SID FIELD.........................Jerry Sanford
GRETA GYNT.....................Mrs. Barry
PETULA CLARK.........................Peggy
KAY KENDALL........................Patsy
SONNIE HALE.......................Charlie
CLAUDE HULBERT...................Belgrave
MARY CLARE....................Mrs. Gates
TESSIE O'SHEA.......................Herself
JERRY DESMONDE...................George
BERYL DAVIS.........................Paula
" SCOTTY " McHARG..................Bill
W. G. FAY..........................Mike
REGINALD PURDELL.........Stage Manager
ALFIE DEAN.........................Heckler
CHARLES PATON........Novelty Shopkeeper
PAMELA CARROLL..............Street Singer
MARION SAUNDERS...Obbligato to Street Singer
LUCAS HOVINGA......................Dancer
JACK PARNELL......................Drummer
Produced and directed by Wesley Ruggles   1946
                In Technicolor

Looking on the Bright Side
GRACIE FIELDS.........................Graice
JULIAN ROSE...................Oscar Schuliz
RICHARD DOLMAN................Lauret
WYN RICHMOND....................Miss Joy
TONI DE LUNGO...................Delmonico
BETTY SHALE.................Hetty Hunt
BETTINA MONTAHNERS.................Betsy
VIOLA COMPTON...........Sergeant of Police
ARP   Director : Basil Dean   1932

Lost Weekend, The
RAY MILLAND....................Don Birnam
PHILLIP TERRY....................Wick Birnam
JANE WYMAN..............Helen St. James
HOWARD DA SILVA......................Nat
DORIS DOWLING......................Gloria
FRANK FAYLEN.........................Bim
ANITA BOLSTER.................Mrs. Foley
MARY YOUNG.................Mrs. Deveridge
HELEN DICKSON...................Mrs. Frink
E. LAUGHTON.................Mr. Brophy
DAVID CLYDE.........................Dave
LOUIS L. RUSSELL.........Charles St. James
LILLIAN FONTAINE..........Mrs. St. James
PARA   Director : Billy Wilder   1945
    From the novel by Charles R. Jackson

Love on the Dole
DEBORAH KERR........................Sally
CLIFFORD EVANS......................Larry
MARY MERRALL.........Mrs. Hardcastle
GEORGE CARNEY...........Mr. Hardcastle
GEOFFREY HIBBERT.........Harry Hardcastle
JOYCE HOWARD.............Helen Hawkins
FRANK CELLIER.................Sam Grundy
MARTIN WALKER..............Ned Narkey
MARIE O'NEILL.................Mrs. Dobell
IRIS VANDELEUR.................Mrs. Nattle
MARIE AULT........................Mrs. Jike

MARJORIE RHODES.................Mrs. Bull
CHARLES WILLIAMS.............Bill Simmons
COLIN CHANDLER..............Jack Lindsay
JORDAN LAWRENCE...............Sam Hardie
KENNETH GRIFFITHS.............,..Tom Hare
DENNIS WYNDHAM.......................Jim
JOHN SLATER.........................Jackson
BEN WILLIAMS........................Jess
A. BROMLEY DAVENPORT........Pawnbroker
PETER GAWTHORNE.......Police Superintendent
JAMES HARCOURT................Working Man
PHILIP GODFREY...................Charlie Fox
TERRY CONLIN....................Ted Munter
CHARLES GROVES..................Old Man
MURIEL GEORGE.........Landlady at Blackpool
BRIT NAT   Director : John Baxter   1941
From the play by Ronald Gow

Love Parade, The
MAURICE CHEVALIER.....Count Alfred Renard
JEANNETTE MacDONALD........Queen Louise
LUPINO LANE............Jacques, Alfred's Valet
LILLIAN ROTH...Lulu, the Queen's Personal Maid
EDGAR NORTON..........Master of Ceremonies
LIONEL BELMORE..........The Prime Minister
ALBERT ROCCARDI........The Foreign Minister
CARLETON STOCKDALE...........The Admiral
EUGENE PALLETTE.........The Minister of War
E. H. CALVERT.......The Sylvanian Ambassador
ANDRÉ SHÉRON.....................Le Mari
YOLA D'AVRIL......................Paulette
MARGARET FEALLY........1st Lady-in-Waiting
VIRGINIA BRUCE...........2nd Lady-in-Waiting
RUSSELL POWELL..........Afghan Ambassador
WINTER HALL............................Priest
BEN TURPIN................Cross-Eyed Lackey
JEAN HARLOW.........Extra in theatre audience
PARA   Director : Ernst Lubitsch   1929
From the play " The Prince Consort " by Leon
Xanrof and Jules Chancel

Love Story
MARGARET LOCKWOOD................Lissa
STEWART GRANGER......................Kit
PATRICIA ROC...........................Judy
TOM WALLS.............................Tom
REGINALD PURDELL...................Albert
MOIRA LISTER........................Carol
DOROTHY BRAMHALL.................Susie
VINCENT HOLMAN...................Prospero
JOAN REES............................Ariel
WALTER HUDD.........................Ray
BRYAN HERBERT.......................Zed
A. E. MATTHEWS..........Colonel Pitt Smith
JOSEPHINE MIDDLETON........Mrs. Pitt Smith
LAWRENCE HANRAY...........Angus Rossiter
BEATRICE VARLEY.............Miss Rossiter
GAINS   Director : Leslie Arliss   1944

Lydia
MERLE OBERON..............Lydia Macmillan
EDNA MAY OLIVER..................Granny
ALAN MARSHALL....................Richard
JOSEPH COTTEN....................Michael
HANS JARAY.........................Frank
GEORGE REEVES........................Bob
JOHN HALLIDAY.....................Butler
BILLY ROY.........................Johnny
SARA ALLGOOD.............Johnny's mother
FRANK CONLAN.....................Old Ned
KORDA-HOLLYWOOD   Director : Julien Duvivier 1942

M

Madame Curie
GREER GARSON...................Mme. Curie
WALTER PIDGEON...............Pierre Curie
HENRY TRAVERS.................Eugène Curie
ALBERT BASSERMAN.......Professor Jean Perot
ROBERT WALKER.................David LeGros
C. AUBREY SMITH.................Lord Kelvin
DAME MAY WHITTY....Mme. Eugène Curie, Sr.
VICTOR FRANCEN.......President of University
ELSA BASSERMAN................Mme. Perot
REGINALD OWEN................Dr. Becquerel
VAN JOHNSON........................Reporter
MARGARET O'BRIEN....................Irene
MGM   Director : Mervyn LeRoy   1944
From the biography of Mme. Curie written by
her daughter, Eve Curie

Mademoiselle from Armentières
ESTELLE BRODY..Mademoiselle from Armentières
MARIE AULT........................Her Aunt
JOHN STUART.........................John
ALF GODDARD.........................Fred
HUMBERSTON WRIGHT........The Old Soldier
JOHN HAMILTON............The Young Soldier
COLONEL ENGLISH, D.S.O......Albert Raynor
BORIS RANEVSKY..............Liaison Officer
CLIFFORD HEATHERLEY
                    German Intelligence Officer
GABRIEL ROSCA..................M. Branz
SERGEANT L. SMITH, V.C.........The Sergeant
GAUMONT   Director : Maurice Elvey   1927

Madonna of the Seven Moons
PHYLLIS CALVERT
              Madonna (Maddalena and Rosanna)
STEWART GRANGER.....................Nino
PATRICIA ROC.........................Angela
PETER GLENVILLE....................Sandro
JOHN STUART.......................Guiseppe
REGINALD TATE.....................Ackroyd
PETER MURRAY-HILL..................Logan
DULCIE GRAY.........................Nesta
ALAN HAINES........................Evelyn
HILDA BAYLEY....................Mrs. Fiske
EVELYN DARVELL.....................Millie
NANCY PRICE..................Mme. Barucci
JEAN KENT.........................Vittoria
AMY VENESS..........................Tessa
GAINS   Director : Arthur Crabtree   1945
From the novel by Margery Lawrence

Madonna of the Streets
NAZIMOVA....................{ Mary Carlson
                            { Mary Ainsleigh
MILTON SILLS...................John Morton
CLAUDE GILLINGWATER......Lord Patrington
COURTENAY FOOTE.............Dr. Colbeck
TOM KENNEDY................" Bull " Brockins
JOHN T. MURRAY....." Slippery " Eddie Foster
VIVIEN OAKLAND............Lady Sarah Joyce
HAROLD GOODWIN.........Howard Bowman
ROSA GORE.....................Mrs. Elyard
MAY BETH CARR..............Judy Smythe
HERBERT PRIOR.............Nathan Norris
FRED KELSEY.........Detective Griffith
GEORGE IRVING...............Philip Norman
FIRST NATIONAL   1925
From the novel " The Ragged Messenger " by
W. B. Maxwell

Magnificent Ambersons, The
JOSEPH COTTEN........................Eugene
DOLORES COSTELLO....................Isabel
ANNE BAXTER..........................Lucy
TIM HOLT..............................George
AGNES MOOREHEAD...................Fanny
RAY COLLINS...............................Jack
ERSKINE SANFORD.....................Benson
RICHARD BENNETT..........Major Amberson
DON DILLAWAY...............Wilbur Minnafer
MERCURY   Director : Orson Welles   1943
From the novel by Booth Tarkington

Major Barbara
WENDY HILLER.................Major Barbara
REX HARRISON................Adolphus Cusins
ROBERT MORLEY....................Undershaft
ROBERT NEWTON..................Bill Walker
EMLYN WILLIAMS.................Snobby Price
SYBIL THORNDIKE................The General
DEBORAH KERR.....................Jenny Hill
DAVID TREE....................Charles Lomax
PENELOPE DUDLEY WARD...Sarah Undershaft
MARIE LOHR....................Lady Britomart
WALTER HUDD..............Stephen Undershaft
MARIE AULT..................Rummy Mitchens
DONALD CALTHROP.............Peter Shirley
CATHLEEN CORDELL..........Mog Habbijam
TORIN THATCHER.............Todger Fairmile
MILES MALLESON...................Morrison
FELIX AYLMER.........................James
STANLEY HOLLOWAY...............Policeman
S. I. HSIUNG............................Ling
KATHLEEN HARRISON.............Mrs. Price
MARY MORRIS.........................A Girl
PASCAL   Director : Gabriel Pascal   1941
From the play by George Bernard Shaw

Man in Grey, The
MARGARET LOCKWOOD...............Hester
JAMES MASON................Marquis of Rohan
PHYLLIS CALVERT....................Clarissa
STEWART GRANGER...................Rokeby
HELEN HAYE....................Lady Rohan
RAYMOND LOVELL..........The Prince Regent
NORA SWINBURNE............Mrs. Fitzherbert
MARTITA HUNT.................Miss Patchett
JANE GILL-DAVIS.................Lady Marr
AMY VENESS..................Mrs. Armstrong
STUART LINDSELL..................Lawrence
DIANA KING....................Jane Seymour
ANN WILTON.......................Miss Edge
CELIA LAMB...........................Louise
LUPE MAGUIRE..........................Sally
BEATRICE VARLEY.....................Gipsy
HARRY SCOTT...........................Toby
DRUSILLA WILLS........................Cook
GERTRUDE MAESMORE MORRIS
                              Lady Bessborough
HARGRAVE PAWSON...............Lord Craven
JAMES CARSON......................Gervaise
ROY EMMERTON..................Gamekeeper
BABS VALERIE.........................Molly
WALLY KINGSTON................Old Porter
GLYNN ROWLAND..............Lord Mildmay
PATRIC CURWEN.......................Doctor
LOLA HUNT............................Nurse
MARY NAYLOR..................Blennerhassett
RUTH WOODMAN.........................Polly
A. E. MATTHEWS...................Auctioneer

KATHLEEN BOUTALL..................Amelia
GAINS   Director : Leslie Arliss   1943
Based on the novel by Lady Eleanor Smith
Re-issued 1946

Man in the Iron Mask, The
LOUIS HAYWARD.................{ Louis XIV / Philippe
JOAN BENNETT..................Maria Theresa
WARREN WILLIAM.................D'Artagnan
JOSEPH SCHILDKRAUT...............Fouquet
ALAN HALE..........................Porthos
MILES MANDER.......................Aramis
BERT ROACH.........................Athos
WALTER KINGSFORD.................Colbert
MARIAN MARTIN........Mlle. de la Vallière
MONTAGU LOVE.........Spanish Ambassador
DORIS KENYON...................Queen Anne
ALBERT DEKKER................... Louis XIII
WILLIAM BOYLE.......Commandant of Bastille
UA   Director : James Whale   1940
From the novel by Dumas
Re-issued 1944

Man on America's Conscience, The
VAN HEFLIN....................Andrew Johnson
LIONEL BARRYMORE........Thaddeus Stevens
RUTH HUSSEY...................Eliza McCardle
MARJORIE MAIN..................Mrs. Fisher
REGIS TOOMEY.....................McDaniel
J. EDWARD BROMBERG.................Coke
GRANT WITHERS..........Mordecai Milligan
ALEC CRAIG........................Andrews
CHARLES DINGLE........Senator Jim Waters
CARL BENTON REID.....Congressman Hargrave
RUSSELL HICKS.........Lincoln's Emissary
NOAH BEERY, SR....................Sheriff Cass
ROBERT WARWICK............Major Crooks
MONTAGU LOVE.............Chief Justice Chase
LLOYD CORRIGAN...............Mr. Secretary
WILLIAM FARNUM.............Senator Huyler
CHARLES TROWBRIDGE.............Lansbury
LYNNE CARVER.......................Martha
RUSSELL SIMPSON.....................Kirby
MORRIS ANKRUM.............Jefferson Davis
MGM   Director : William Dieterle   1946
Shown in the U.S.A. as "Tennessee Johnson",
1942 ; but exhibition was delayed in Great Britain
because cinema owners felt it was too political

Man Who Came to Dinner, The
BETTE DAVIS....................Maggie Cutler
ANN SHERIDAN...............Lorraine Sheldon
MONTY WOOLLEY.........Sheridan Whiteside
RICHARD TRAVIS..............Bert Jefferson
JIMMY DURANTE.....................Banjo
BILLIE BURKE..........Mrs. Ernest Stanley
REGINALD GARDINER..........Beverly Calton
ELISABETH FRASER.............June Stanley
GRANT MITCHELL..........Mr. Ernest Stanley
GEORGE BARBIER..................Dr. Bradley
MARY WICKES....................Miss Preen
RUSSELL ARMS................Richard Stanley
RUTH VIVIAN........................Harriet
EDWIN STANLEY........................John
BETTY ROADMAN.......................Sarah
WARN   Director : William Keighley   1942
From the play by George S. Kaufman and Moss Hart

Manhandled
GLORIA SWANSON.............Tessie McGuire
TOM MOORE....................Jimmy Hogan

FRANK MORGAN................Arno Riccardi
LILYAN TASHMAN..............Pinkie Doran
PAUL McALLISTER............Paul Garrettson
IAN KEITH......................Robert Brandt
ARTHUR HOUSMAN ...."Chip" Thorndyke
PARA   1925

Manon Lescaut
LYA DE PUTTI.................Manon Lescaut
VLADIMIR GAIDAROW.............Des Grieux
EDUARD ROTHAUSER......Marshal des Grieux
FRITZ GREINER.................Marquis de Bli
HUBERT VON MEYERINCK...The Son of de Bli
FRIDA RICHARD)
EMILIE KURZ   )..............Manon's Aunts
LYDIA POTECHINA..................Susanne
THEODOR LOOS....................Tiberge
SIEGFRIED ARNO......................Lescaut
TRUDE HESTERBERG..................Claire
MARLENE DIETRICH................Micheline
UFA (Germany)   Director: Arthur Robison   1926
*Adapted from the novel by Abbé Prévost and the
opera by Massenet*
(See Foreign Language Films, page 347)

Mare Nostrum
(Our Sea)
UNI APOLON.......................The Triton
ALEX NOVA..............Don Esteban Ferragut
KADA-ABD-EL-KADER.......His son, Ulysses
HUGHIE MACK......................Caragol
ALICE TERRY.................Freya Talberg
ANTONIO MORENO..........Ulysses Ferragut
MLLE. KITHNOU........His wife, Doña Cinta
MICKEY BRANTFORD.......Their son, Esteban
FREDERICK MARIOTTI.........Toni, the Mate
MME. PAQUERETTE.............Dr. Fedelmann
FERNAND MAILLY............Count Kaledine
ANDRE VON ENGLEMAN
                         Submarine Commander
METRO-GOLDWYN   Director: Rex Ingram   1927
Adapted from the novel by Vicente Blasco Ibanez

Marie Louise
JOSIANE..........................Marie Louise
HEINRICH GRETLER...............Mr. Ruegg
MARGRIT WINTER.................Anna Ruegg
ANNE-MARIE BLANC..............Hedi Ruegg
ARMIN SCHWEIZER.............Mr. Banninger
MATHILDE DANEGGER..................Paula
FRED TANNER......................Scheibli
EMIL GERBER..................Schwarzenbach
BERNHARD AMMON.....................André
GERMAINE TOURNIER...........Mme. Fleury
PRAESENS FILM (Switzerland)   1944
          Director: Leopold Lindtberg
(See Foreign Language Films, page 347)

Mata Hari
GRETA GARBO.....................Mata Hari
RAMON NOVARRO....Lieutenant Alexis Rosanoff
LIONEL BARRYMORE..........General Shubin
LEWIS STONE......................Andriani
C. HENRY GORDON..................Dubois
KAREN MORLEY.....................Carlotta
ALEC B. FRANCIS......................Caron
BLANCHE FREDERICI..........Sister Angelica
EDMUND BREESE.....................Warden
HELEN JEROME EDDY........Sister Genevieve
FRANK REICHER................The Cook Spy
MGM   Director: George Fitzmaurice   1932

Matter of Life and Death, A
(American title : *Stairway to Heaven*)
DAVID NIVEN.....................Peter Carter
KIM HUNTER..........................June
ROBERT COOTE.........................Bob
KATHLEEN BYRON..................An Angel
RICHARD ATTENBOROUGH....An English Pilot
BONAR COLLEANO....An American Pilot
JOAN MAUDE..................Chief Recorder
MARIUS GORING.............Conductor 71
ROGER LIVESEY..................Dr. Reeves
ROBERT ATKINS................The Vicar
BOB ROBERTS...................Dr. Gaertler
EDWIN MAX....................Dr. McEwen
BETTY POTTER..................Mrs. Tucker
ABRAHAM SOFAER...............The Judge
RAYMOND MASSEY..........Abraham Farlan
ARCHERS   1946
   Directors: Michael Powell and Emeric Pressburger
In Technicolor
*Chosen for the first Royal Command Film
Performance at the Leicester-square Theatre,
London, on November 1, 1946
Re-issued 1947*

Meet Me in St. Louis
JUDY GARLAND...................Esther Smith
MARGARET O'BRIEN............"Tootie" Smith
MARY ASTOR...............Mrs. Anna Smith
LUCILLE BREMER................Rose Smith
LEON AMES.............Mr. Alonzo Smith
TOM DRAKE......................John Truett
MARJORIE MAIN..............Katie (maid)
HARRY DAVENPORT..................Grandpa
JUNE LOCKHART.............Lucille Ballard
HENRY H. DANIELS, JR......Lon Smith, Jr.
JOAN CARROLL................Agnes Smith
HUGH MARLOWE.............Colonel Darly
ROBERT SULLY...........Warren Sheffield
CHILL WILLS...................Mr. Neely
MGM   Director: Vincente Minelli   1945
In Technicolor

Men of Boys Town
SPENCER TRACY.............Father Flanagan
MICKEY ROONEY...............Whitey Marsh
BOBS WATSON.....................Pee Wee
LARRY NUNN.................Ted Martley
DARRYL HICKMAN....................Flip
HENRY O'NEILL..............Mr. Maitland
MARY NASH..................Mrs. Maitland
LEE J. COBB..................Dave Morris
SIDNEY MILLER...................Mo Kahn
ADDISON RICHARDS............The Judge
LLOYD CORRIGAN.............Roger Gorton
GEORGE LESSEY.............Bradford Stone
ROBERT EMMETT KEANE..............Burton
ARTHUR HOHL.......................Guard
BEN WELDON.................Superintendent
ANN REVERE..................Mrs. Fenely
MGM   Director: Norman Taurog   1941

Men of Two Worlds
The Europeans
ERIC PORTMAN..........District Commissioner
PHYLLIS CALVERT........Dr. Catherine Munro
ARNOLD MARLÉ.............Professor Gollner
CATHLEEN NESBITT...............Mrs. Upjohn
GEORGE COOPE........Conductor of Orchestra
DAVID HORNE..................Concert Agent
CYRIL RAYMOND...........Education Officer

The Africans

ROBERT ADAMS......................Kisenga
ORLANDO MARTINS..................Magole
SAM BLAKE....................Rafti, the Chief
NAPOLEON FLORENT..........Kisenga's father
VIOLA THOMPSON.............Kisenga's mother
ESEZA MAKUMBI...............Saburi, his sister
TUNJI WILLIAMS..............Ali, the dispenser
RUDOLPH EVANS.......Abram, the schoolmaster
URIEL PORTER..............Saidi, the headman
CICELY DALE..................Sarah, his wife
P. ZULAMKAH.................Chief's messenger
JAMES RICH........................Office Clerk
SAMUEL D. LEWIS ⎱
JAMES SMART   ⎰.............. Magole's men
EUSTACE GOMEZ ⎰
Dancers
MAKO BALO, JOE PEREIRA, SLIM HARRIS,
KARI KARI, HENRY VROOM, BERTIE PASUKA
TWO CITIES   Director : Thorold Dickinson   1946
Produced with the co-operation of the Government
of Tanganyika Territory, British East Africa
In Technicolor

Merry Widow, The

MAE MURRAY..........Sally, the Merry Widow
JOHN GILBERT..........................Danilo
ROY D'ARCY................Crown Prince
JOSEPHINE CROWELL............Queen Milena
GEORGE FAWCETT.................King Nikita
TULLY MARSHALL...............Baron Sadoja
COUNT CONTI...............Danilo's Adjutant
SIDNEY BRACY................Danilo's footman
DON RYAN.............Crown Prince's Adjutant
HUGHIE MACK........................Innkeeper
IDA MOORE......................His wife
LUCILLE VON LENT.............Their daughter
DALE FULLER..................Sally's maid
CHARLES MAGELIS.................Flo Epstein
HARVEY KARELS..............Jimmy Watson
EDNA TICHENOR..................Dopey Marie
GERTRUDE BENNETT......Hard-Boiled Virginia
ZALA ZORANA................Frenchie Christine
JACQUELINE GADSDEN.............Madonna
ESTELLE CLARK................French Barber
D'ARCY CORRIGAN.................Horatio
CLARA WALLACKS ⎱
FRANCES PRIMM   ⎰............Hansen Sisters
ZACK WILLIAMS......George Washington White
EDWARD CONNELLY................Ambassador
MEREWYN THAYER..................His wife
LON POFF....................Sadoja's lackey
METRO-GOLDWYN   1926
Director : Erich von Stroheim
From the musical play by Henry W. Savage

Metropolis

ALFRED ABEL..................John Masterman
GUSTAV FROELICH..............Eric, his son
RUDOLF KLEIN-ROGGE...Rotwang, an inventor
FRITZ RASP..............................Slim
THEODOR LOOS...Joseph, secretary to Masterman
HEINRICH GEORGE
Grot, foreman of the Heart-Machine
BRIGITTE HELM........Mary, a girl of the people
UFA (Germany)   Director : Fritz Lang   1926
(*See Foreign Language Films, page* 347)

Métropolitain

GINETTE LECLERC....................Viviane
ALBERT PRÉJEAN........................Pierre
ANDRÉ BRULE........................Zoltini

ANNE LAURENS.....................Suzanne
PIERRE SERGEOL.....................Jackson
MAXIME FABER.....................Cyprien
S.B. FILMS (France)   Director : Maurice Cam   1939
(*See Foreign Language Films, page* 347)

Michael and Mary

EDNA BEST........................Mary Rowe
HERBERT MARSHALL...........Michael Rowe
FRANK LAWTON.......................David
ELIZABETH ALLAN....................Romo
D. A. CLARKE-SMITH....................Price
BEN FIELD........................Tullivant
MARGARET YARDE..............Mrs. Tullivant
SUNDAY WILSHIN.............Violet Cunliffe
GAINS   Adapted and directed by Victor Saville   1932
From the play by A. A. Milne

Michael Strogoff

IVAN MOSJOUKINE............Michael Strogoff
MME. NATALIE KOVANKO.......Nadia Fedoroff
CHAKATOUNY........................Ogareff
MME. BRINDEAU........Marfa, Strogoff's mother
GABRIEL DE GRAVONNE
Jollivet, French correspondent
HENRI DEBAIN.....Blount, English correspondent
MME. DE YZARDUY...................Zangara
DEFAS.....................Pheophar Khan
K. KVANINE....................Basil Fedoroff
PRINCE N. KOUGOUCHEFF.....General Kissoff
E. GAIDAROFF...Alexander II, Emperor of Russia
UNIVERSAL FILM DE FRANCE (France)   1926
Director : Willi Tourjansky
From the novel by Jules Verne
(*See Foreign Language Films, page* 347)

Midsummer Night's Dream, A

JAMES CAGNEY.............Bottom, the weaver
JOE E. BROWN..........................Flute
HUGH HERBERT......................Snout
FRANK McHUGH.......................Quince
VICTOR JORY.......................Oberon
OLIVIA DE HAVILLAND...............Hermia
ROSS ALEXANDER................Demetrius
GRANT MITCHELL...................Egeus
NINI THEILADE....................1st Fairy
VERREE TEASDALE
Hippolyta, Queen of Amazons
DICK POWELL......................Lysander
JEAN MUIR..........................Helena
IAN HUNTER........................Theseus
ANITA LOUISE......................Titania
MICKEY ROONEY.....................Puck
DEWEY ROBINSON.....................Snug
HOBART CAVANAUGH..............Philostrate
OTIS HARLAN...................Starveling
ARTHUR TREACHER..........Ninny's tomb
BILLY BARTY...................Mustard Seed
WARN   Directors :   1935
Max Reinhardt and William Dieterle
From the play by William Shakespeare

Milestones

LEWIS STONE.....................John Rhead
ALICE HOLLISTER............Gertrude Rhead
GERTRUDE ROBINSON............Emily Rhead
HARVEY CLARK....................Sam Sibley
MARY ALDEN......................Rose Sibley
MAY FOSTER....................Nancy Sibley
⎧   Ned Pym
GERALD PRING.......⎨ Young Lord Monkhurst
⎩   Lord Monkhurst

CORREAN KIRKHAM......The Hon. Muriel Pym
LIONEL BELMORE...............Richard Sibley
CARROLL FLEMING.......Thompson, the butler
JACK DONOVAN.......................Webster
BOYD IRWIN..................Arthur Preece
GOLDWYN   Director : Paul Scardon   1922

*From the play by Arnold Bennett and
Edward Knoblock*

Min and Bill

MARIE DRESSLER........................Min
WALLACE BEERY..........................Bill
DOROTHY JORDAN.......................Nancy
MARJORIE RAMBEAU......................Bella
DONALD DILLAWAY.......................Dick
DeWITT JENNINGS.......................Groot
RUSSELL HOPTON..........................Alec
FRANK McGLYNN.............Mr. Southard
GRETTA GOULD................Mrs. Southard
MGM   Director : George Hill   1931

Misérables, Les

M. GABRIEL   Jean Valjean
   GABRIO   M. Madeleine Champmathieu
M. JEAN TOULOUT.....................Javert
M. PAUL JORGE................Mgr. Myriel
M. ROZET...........................Marius
M. G. SAILLARD....................Thénardier
M. CHARLES BADIOLE..............Gavroche
MME. SANDRA MILOWANOFF........ Fantine / Cosette
M. MAILLARD....................Gillenormand
M. PAUL GUIDE.....................Enjolras
MME. CLARA DARCEY-ROCHE...Mlle. Baptistine
MLLE. ANDRÉE ROLANE......Cosette, as a child
MLLE. NIVETTE SAILLARD.............Éponine
MME. RENÉE CARL.............La Thénardier
   And a cast of over 5000 people in 6000 scenes
EUROPEAN (France)   Director : Henri Fescourt 1925

From the novel by Victor Hugo

*The film was released in two parts, " Les Misérables "
and " The Barricades "*

(See Foreign Language Films, page 347)

Misérables, Les

FREDRIC MARCH..................Jean Valjean
CHARLES LAUGHTON.................Javert
CEDRIC HARDWICKE.........Bishop Bienvenue
ROCHELLE HUDSON.................Cosette
FLORENCE ELDRIDGE..............Fantine
JESSIE RALPH.............Mme. Magloire
FRANCES DRAKE....................Éponine
JOHN BEAL.........................Marius
FERDINAND GOTTSCHALK.........Thénardier
JANE KERR...............Mme. Thénardier
MARILYN KNOWLDEN............Little Cosette
JOHN BLEIFER.....................Chenildieu
20TH-FOX   Director : Richard Boleslavsky 1935
From the novel by Victor Hugo

Mission to Moscow

WALTER HUSTON..............Joseph E. Davies
ANN HARDING....................Mrs. Davies
OSCAR HOMOLKA...............Maxim Litvinov
GEORGE TOBIAS.....................Freddie
GENE LOCKHART....................Molotov
ELEANOR PARKER..............Emlen Davies
RICHARD TRAVIS.........Robert Grosjean
HELMUT DANTINE...........Major Kamenev
VICTOR FRANCEN........Prosecutor Vyshinsky

HENRY DANIELL........Joachim von Ribbentrop
FRIEDA INESCORT...............Mme. Litvinov
DUDLEY FIELD MALONE....Winston Churchill
ROMAN BOHNEN.........Nikolai Krestinski
MARIA PALMER................Tanya Litvinov
MORONI OLSEN.......Colonel Philip Faymonville
MINOR WATSON.........Low W. Henderson
VLADMIR SOKOLOFF.........President Kalinin
MAURICE SCHWARTZ...............Dr. Botkin
JEROME COWAN.......................Spendler
KONSTANTIN SHAYNE......Nikolai I. Bukharin
MANNART KIPPEN...............Josef Stalin
KURT KATCH.............Marshal Timoshenko
FELIX BASCH...........Dr. Hjalmar Schacht
FRANK PUGLIA....................Judge Ulrich
DORIS LLOYD................Mrs. Churchill
FRANK REICHER
          Count Werner von der Schulenburg
JOHN ABBOTT................Grigori F. Grinko
DANIEL OCKO............Heinrich Yagoda
IVAN TRISAULT..........Mikhail Tukhachevsky
DAVID HOFFMAN........................Radek
IVAN LEBEDEFF...................Rosengoltz
PETER GOO CHONG.....Ambassador Shigemitzu
LEIGH WHIPPER................Haile Selassie
GEORGE RENEVANT.........Paul Van Zeeland
ALEX CHIRVA......................Pierre Laval
EMILE RAMEAU...........Ignatz Paderewski
WARN   Director : Michael Curtiz   1943

*From the book by Joseph E. Davies, U.S.
Ambassador to Russia 1936-8*

Moby Dick

JOHN BARRYMORE.......................Ahab
JOAN BENNETT.........................Faith
LLOYD HUGHES.........................Derek
WALTER LONG........................Stubbs
VIRGINIA SALE....................Old Maid
JACK CURTIS.......................First Mate
TOM O'BRIEN.......................Starbuck
NIGEL DE BRULIER....................Elijah
NOBLE JOHNSON....................Queequeg
WILLIAM WALLING...............Blacksmith
JOHN INCE.....................Rev. Mapple
WARN   Director : Lloyd Bacon   1931
From the novel by Herman Melville

Modern Times

CHARLES CHAPLIN...................A Tramp
PAULETTE GODDARD..............A Gamine
HENRY BERGMAN...........A Cafe Proprietor
CHESTER CONKLIN..............A Mechanic
STANLEY SANDFORD
HANK MANN   ....The Burglars
LOUIS NATHEUX
ALLEN GARCIA..................The President
Produced and directed by Charles Chaplin   1936
*Chaplin's last " silent " film. It was produced with
sound and music, but without dialogue*

Monsieur Beaucaire

RUDOLPH VALENTINO
         Duc de Chartres (M. Beaucaire)
BEBE DANIELS...............Princess Henriette
LOIS WILSON.......Queen Marie of France
DORIS KENYON.....................Lady Mary
LOWELL SHERMAN....King Louis XV of France
PAULETTE DU VAL..........Mme. Pompadour
JOHN DAVIDSON.....................Richelieu
OSWALD YORKE.....................Miropoix
FLORA FINCH.........Duchesse de Montmorency

BASIL RADFORD
(Gainsborough)

LEWIS WALLER......................François
IAN MacLAREN...............Duke of Winterset
FRANK SHANNON.....................Badger
MAURICE COLBOURNE........John Molyneau
H. COOPER CLIFFE............Beau Nash
DOWNING CLARKE...........Lord Chesterfield
YVONNE HUGHES........Duchesse de Flauhault
HARRY LEE.....................Voltaire
FLORENCE O'DENISHAWN.........Colombine
PARA   1924

*From the novel by Booth Tarkington, and the play
by him and Evelyn Greenleaf Sutherland*

Monsieur Beaucaire

BOB HOPE.......................M. Beaucaire
JOAN CAULFIELD....................Mimi
PATRIC KNOWLES.............Duc de Chandre
MARJORIE REYNOLDS..........Princess Maria
CECIL KELLAWAY..............Duc d'Armand
JOSEPH SCHILDKRAUT........Don Francisco
REGINALD OWEN..............King Louis XV
CONSTANCE COLLIER........The French Queen
HILLARY BROOKE............Mme. Pompadour
FORTUNIO BONANOVA.........Don Carlos
MARY NASH.....................The Duenna
LEONID KINSKEY...................René
HOWARD FREEMAN.......King Philip of Spain
HELEN FREEMAN...........The Spanish Queen
PARA   Director : George Marshall   1946

*Based on the novel by Booth Tarkington
This film was a skit on the celebrated silent film of
1924, starring Rudolph Valentino and Bebe Daniels
(see above)*

Monsieur La Souris

RAIMU...........................M. La Souris
AIMÉ CLARIOND...............Simon Negretti
CHARLES GRANVAL..................Laborde
GILBERT GIL...........................Osting
AIMOS.............................Cupidon
BERGERON.....................Inspector Lognon
PAUL AMIOT..........Superintendent Lucas
PIERRE JOURDAN..................Muller
MICHELINE FRANCEY..........Lucile Boisvin
MARIE CARLOT.......................Dora
LACOMBE PRODUCTIONS (France)   1942
          Director : Édouard Lepage
     (*See Foreign Language Films, page* 347)

Monte Carlo

JACK BUCHANAN........Count Rudolph Falliere
JEANNETTE MacDONALD
                    Countess Vera von Conti
ZASU PITTS...........................Maria
TYLER BROOKE.....................Armand
CLAUDE ALLISTER...Prince Otto von Seibenheim
EDGAR NORTON....Duke Gustav von Seibenheim
JOHN ROCHE..........................Paul
ALBERT CONTI............Master of Ceremony
DONALD NOVIS..................M. Beaucaire
HELEN GARDEN....................Lady Mary
DAVID PERCY.......................Herald
ERIK BEY.....................Lord Winterset
SIDNEY BRACEY....................Hunchback
GERALDINE DVORAK (Garbo " double ")
                         Extra in casino
PARA   Director : Ernst Lubitsch   1930
*From the story " The Blue Coast " by Hans Muller,
and episodes from the play " Monsieur Beaucaire "
by Booth Tarkington and Evelyn Greenleaf Sutherland*

Monte Cristo

JOHN GILBERT
          Edmond Dantès, Count of Monte Cristo
ESTELLE TAYLOR.....................Mercédès
WM. V. MONG.......................Caderousse
ROBERT McKIM..................De Villefort
RALPH CLONINGER..................Fernand
HARRY LONSDALE.............Elder Dantès
AL FILSON........................Morrel
ALBERT PRISCO.....................Danglars
VIRGINIA B. FAIRE..................Haidée
GASTON GLASS.......................Albert
FRANCIS MacDONALD..............Benedetto
GEORGE SIEGMANN..........Luigi Vampa
SPOTTISWOODE AITKEN.................Abbé
RENÉE ADORÉE..........Eugénie Danglars
MAUD GEORGE..............Mme. Danglars
FOX   1923

Moriarty

JOHN BARRYMORE...........Sherlock Holmes
GUSTAV VON SEYFFERTITZ.Professor Moriarty
CAROL DEMPSTER.............Alice Faulkner
ROLAND YOUNG...................Dr. Watson
REGINALD DENNY.............Prince Alexis
DAVID TORRENCE.........Count von Stalburg
PEGGY BAYFIELD...........Rose Faulkner
ANDERS RANDOLF.........James Larrabee
MARGARET KEMP......................Terese
WILLIAM POWELL...............Forman Wells
ROBERT SCHABLE.................Alf Bassick
PERCY KNIGHT...................Sid Jones
ROBERT FISCHER.......................Otto
LUMSDEN HARE.................Dr. Leighton
LOUIS WOLHEIM.....................Craigin
JERRY DEVINE.........................Billy
JOHN WILLARD............Inspector Gregson
HEDDA HOPPER............Madge Larrabee
GOLDWYN   1923

*From William Gillette's play founded on Sir Arthur
Conan Doyle's stories of Sherlock Holmes*

Mort du Cygne, La

YVETTE CHAUVIRE.............Mlle. Beaupré
MIA SLAVENSKA.............Nathalie Karine
JANINE CHARRAT.............Rose Souris
MADY BERRY.......................Célestine
FRANCE ELLYS..................Mme. Souris
SUZANNE GUÉMARD..............Instructress
MAURICETTE CEBRON.........Dance Mistress
CLAIRE GÉRARD...................Mme. Bijou
JACQUELINE QUESSELEC..........Coco Battu
MICHELINE BOURDET..........Clara Bijou
FLORENCE LUCHAIRE.................Flo Flo
CLAUDE MAUD.....................Lamouche
MARGUERITE RAILLY............Mme. Batte
O. BOBOLI..................Mme. Laroche
(France)   1937
     Directors : Jean Benoit-Lévy and Marie Epstein
          From the novel by Paul Morand
     *Bought by MGM and re-made as " Unfinished
                 Dance ", 1947*
     (*See Foreign Language Films, page* 347)

Mr. Deeds Goes to Town

GARY COOPER................Longfellow Deeds
JEAN ARTHUR.................Babe Bennett
GEORGE BANCROFT.................MacWade
LIONEL STANDER.............Cornelius Cobb
DOUGLASS DUMBRILLE...........John Cedar

RAYMOND WALBURN................Walter
H. B. WARNER...................Judge Walker
MARGARET MATZENAUER.....Mme. Pomponi
WARREN HYMER..................Bodyguard
MURIEL EVANS.......................Theresa
RUTH DONNELLY..............Mabel Dawson
SPENCER CHARTERS.................Mal
EMMA DUNN...................Mrs. Meredith
WYRLEY BIRCH....................Psychiatrist
ARTHUR HOYT......................Budington
JOHN WRAY.........................Farmer
JAMESON THOMAS...............Mr. Semple
MAYO METHOT...................Mrs. Semple
GENE MORGAN........................Waiter
WALTER CATLETT.....................Morrow
MARGARET SEDDON............Jane Faulkner
COL   Director : Frank Capra   1936

Mr. Smith Goes to Washington

JEAN ARTHUR......................Saunders
JAMES STEWART............Jefferson Smith
CLAUDE RAINS...........Senator Joseph Paine
EDWARD ARNOLD.................Jim Taylor
GUY KIBBEE...............Governor Hopper
THOMAS MITCHELL.................Diz Moore
EUGENE PALLETTE............Chick McGann
BEULAH BONDI....................Ma Smith
H. B. WARNER...........Senate Majority Leader
HARRY CAREY........President of the Senate
ASTRID ALLWYN..................Susan Paine
RUTH DONNELLY..................Mrs. Hopper
GRANT MITCHELL........Senator MacPherson
PORTER HALL.................Senator Monroe
PIERRE WATKIN........ Senate Minority Leader
CHARLES LANE.......................Nosey
WILLIAM DEMAREST.............Bill Griffith
DICK ELLIOTT......................Carl Cook
BILLY WATSON   ⎫
DELMAR WATSON   ⎪
JOHN RUSSELL   ⎬ ....The Hopper Boys
HARRY WATSON   ⎪
GARY WATSON   ⎪
BABY DUMPLING   ⎭
COL   Director : Frank Capra   1939

Mr. Wu

LON CHANEY.......................Mr. Wu
LOUISE DRESSER...............Mrs. Gregory
RENÉE ADORÉE...................Nang Ping
HOLMES HERBERT...............Mr. Gregory
RALPH FORBES................Basil Gregory
GERTRUDE OLMSTED...........Hilda Gregory
MRS. WONG WING...................Ah Wong
CLAUDE KING......................Mr. Muir
ANNA MAY WONG.................Loo Song
SONNY LOY.......................Little Wu
MGM   Director : William Nigh   1929

Mrs. Miniver

GREER GARSON..................Mrs. Miniver
WALTER PIDGEON...............Clem Miniver
TERESA WRIGHT.................Carol Beldon
DAME MAY WHITTY............Lady Beldon
REGINALD OWEN......................Foley
HENRY TRAVERS.................Mr. Ballard
RICHARD NEY...................Vin Miniver
HENRY WILCOXON....................Vicar
CHRISTOPHER SEVERN..........Toby Miniver
BRENDA FORBES.........Gladys (housemaid)
CLARE SANDARS...............Judy Miniver
MARIE DE BECKER......................Ada

HELMUT DANTINE...............German Flyer
JOHN ABBOTT..........................Fred
CONNIE LEON.........................Simpson
RHYS WILLIAMS......................Horace
MGM   Director : William Wyler   1942
From the novel by Jan Struther

Mrs. Parkington

GREER GARSON...............Susie Parkington
WALTER PIDGEON...Major Augustus Parkington
EDWARD ARNOLD.............Amory Stilham
GLADYS COOPER....Alice, Duchess de Brancourt
TOM DRAKE.......................Ned Talbot
AGNES MOOREHEAD............Aspasia Conti
FRANCES RAFFERTY.............Jane Stilham
PETER LAWFORD.................Lord Thornley
DAN DURYEA...................Jack Stilham
HUGH MARLOWE.................John Marbey
SELENA ROYLE...............Mattie Trounson
FORTUNIO BONANOVA...........Signor Cellini
HUGO HAAS.......................The King
LEE PATRICK......................Madeleine
HARRY CORDING..................Humphrey
CELIA TRAVERS.......................Belle
MARY SERVOSS..................Mrs. Graham
ROD CAMERON......................Al Swann
HELEN FREEMAN...............Helen Stilham
TALA BIRELL..................The Countess
HANS CONRIED....................Mr. Ernst
GERALD OLIVER SMITH................Taylor
MGM   Director : Tay Garnett   1945
Based on the novel by Louis Bromfield

Murder

HERBERT MARSHALL.............Sir John
NORAH BARING.................Diana Baring
PHYLLIS KONSTAM..........Doucie Markham
EDWARD CHAPMAN.............Ted Markham
MILES MANDER.................Gordon Druce
ESME PERCY.....................Handel Fane
DONALD CALTHROP.............Ion Stewart
ESME V. CHAPLIN.......Prosecuting Counsel
AMY BRANDON THOMAS...Defending Counsel
JONSON POWELL.....................Judge
MARIE WRIGHT.................Miss Mitcham
S. J. WARMINGTON..................Bennett
HANNAH JONES.................Mrs. Didsome
The Jury
(In addition to HERBERT MARSHALL)
Foreman : R. E. JEFFREY ; ALAN STAINER,
KENNETH KOVE, GUY PELHAM BOULTON,
VIOLET FAREBROTHER, CLARE GREET,
DRUSILLA WILLS, ROBERT EASTON,
WILLIAM FAZAN, GEORGE SMYTHSON,
ROSS JEFFERSON
BIP   Director : Alfred Hitchcock   1931
From the Clemence Dane thriller " Enter Sir John "

Murder in Thornton Square, The

CHARLES BOYER..............Gregory Anton
INGRID BERGMAN..............Paula Alquist
JOSEPH COTTEN................Brian Cameron
DAME MAY WHITTY...........Miss Thwaites
ANGELA LANSBURY...................Nancy
BARBARA EVEREST.................Elizabeth
EMIL RAMEAU...............Maestro Guardi
EDMUND BREON......General Huddleston
HALLIWELL HOBBES.............Mr. Mufflin
TOM STEVENSON....................Williams
HEATHER THATCHER............Lady Dalroy

LAWRENCE GROSSMITH..........Lord Dalroy
JAKOB GIMPEL........................Pianist
MGM   Director : George Cukor   1944
Based on the play " Gaslight" by Patrick Hamilton.
Originally filmed in Britain under the title
" Gaslight", purchased by MGM, withdrawn from
circulation, and re-made as above

Mutiny on the Bounty
CHARLES LAUGHTON...........Captain Bligh
CLARK GABLE................Fletcher Christian
FRANCHOT TONE................Roger Byam
HERBERT MUNDIN....................Smith
EDDIE QUILLAN.....................Ellison
DUDLEY DIGGES.................." Bacchus "
DONALD CRISP......................Burkitt
HENRY STEPHENSON...........Sir Joseph Banks
FRANCIS LISTER............Captain Nelson
SPRING BYINGTON...............Mrs. Byam
MOVITA............................Tehani
MAMO.............................Maimiti
BYRON RUSSELL....................Quintal
PERCY WARAM.....................Coleman
DAVID TORRENCE................Lord Hood
JOHN HARRINGTON.............Mr. Purcell
DOUGLAS WALTON...................Stewart
IAN WOLFE.........................Maggs
DeWITT JENNINGS...................Fryer
IVAN SIMPSON.....................Morgan
VERNON DOWNING..................Hayward
WILLIAM BAMBRIDGE................Hitihiti
MARION CLAYTON............Mary Ellison
STANLEY FIELDS...................Muspratt
WALLIS CLARK.....................Morrison
CRAUFORD KENT.........Lieutenant Edwards
MGM   Director : Frank Lloyd   1936
Re-issued 1944

N

Nell Gwyn
DOROTHY GISH.....................Nell Gwyn
SYDNEY FAIRBROTHER...........Mrs. Gwyn
EDWARD SORLEY.....................Soldier
JUDD GREEN.........................Sailor
AUBREY FITZGERALD...........Tom Killigrew
RANDLE AYRTON............King Charles II
GIBB McLAUGHLIN..............Duke of York
HILDA COWLEY   )
DORINA SHIRLEY   ) ....Maids of Honour
FRED RAINS.............Earl of Shaftesbury
JOHNNY BUTT................Samuel Pepys
JULIETTE COMPTON.........Lady Castlemaine
TOM COVENTRY....................Innkeeper
BOOTH CONWAY.............King's Messenger
FORRESTER HARVEY.............Charles Hart
DONALD McARDLE........Duke of Monmouth
ROLF LESLIE........................Evelyn
Produced and directed by Herbert Wilcox   1927
Wilcox sold this film to J. D. Williams, an American
who secured distribution in the U.S.A. The profits
of this sale helped to finance studios at Elstree (see
" Associated British Picture Corporation", page 17)

Nell Gwyn
ANNA NEAGLE......................Nell Gwyn
CEDRIC HARDWICKE..............Charles II
JEANNE DE CASALIS....Duchess of Portsmouth
MURIEL GEORGE.......................Meg
HELENA PICKARD...............Mrs. Pepys
DOROTHY ROBINSON.............Mrs. Knipp
ESME PERCY...................Samuel Pepys

MILES MALLESON...................Chiffinch
MOORE MARRIOTT....................Robin
CRAIGHALL SHERRY....................Ben
LAWRENCE ANDERSON....James, Duke of York
B & D   Director : Herbert Wilcox   1935

Night Train to Munich
(American title : *Night Train*)
MARGARET LOCKWOOD........Anna Bomasch
REX HARRISON.....................Gus Bennett
*PAUL VON HERNREID...........Karl Marsen
BASIL RADFORD....................Charters
NAUNTON WAYNE..................Caldicott
JAMES HARCOURT..............Axel Bomasch
FELIX AYLMER..............Dr. Fredericks
WYNDHAM GOLDIE...................Dryton
ROLAND CULVER....................Roberts
ELIOT MAKEHAM....................Schwab
RAYMOND HUNTLEY............Kampenfeldt
AUSTIN TREVOR............Captain Prada
KENETH KENT....................Controller
C. V. FRANCE...........Admiral Hassinger
FREDERICK VALK...........Gestapo Officer
MORLAND GRAHAM................Attendant
20TH-BRIT   Director : Carol Reed   1939
* *Later changed his name to Paul Henreid*

Nous les Gosses
JEAN-PIERRE GEFFROY.................Rozet
GEORGES REYGNIER...................André
JEAN BUQUET....................." Tom Mix "
BERNARD DAYDE.....................Doudou
LOUISE CARLETTI..................Mariette
GILBERT GIL.....................M. Morin
PIERRE LARQUEY.............Le Père Finot
ANDRÉ BRUNOT.....Police Superintendent
ÉMILE GÉNEVOIX............Gros Charles
BUSSIÈRES.........................Gaston
COEDEL..................Père de Laurent
PATHÉ CINEMA (France) Director : Louis Daquin 1941
(See Foreign Language Films, page 347)

Now, Voyager
BETTE DAVIS................Charlotte Vale
PAUL HENREID..............Jerry Durrance
CLAUDE RAINS................Dr. Jaquith
BONITA GRANVILLE.................June Vale
ILKA CHASE........................Lisa Vale
GLADYS COOPER.......Mrs. Henry Windle Vale
JANICE WILSON............Tina Durrance
JOHN LODER................Elliot Livingston
LEE PATRICK................Deb McIntyre
FRANKLIN PANGBORN..........Mr. Thompson
MICHAEL AMES...............Dr. Dan Regan
CHARLES DRAKE.............Leslie Trotter
MARY WICKES.............Dora Pickford
JAMES RENNIE...........Frank McIntyre
DAVID CLYDE....................William
FRANK PUGLIA.....................Manoel
WARN   Director : Irving Rapper   1944
From the novel by Olive Higgins Prouty

Nurse Edith Cavell
ANNA NEAGLE..................Nurse Cavell
EDNA MAY OLIVER........Countess de Mavon
GEORGE SANDERS..........Captain Heinrichs
MAY ROBSON................Mme. Rappard
ZASU PITTS.....................Mme. Moulin
H. B. WARNER............Mr. Hugh Gibson
SOPHIE STEWART............Sister Watkins
MARY HOWARD.............Nurse O'Brien
ROBERT COOTE.....................Bungey

MARTIN KOSLECK......................Pierre
GUI IGNON...........................Cobbler
LIONEL ROYCE............General von Erhardt
JIMMY BUTLER...........................Jean
REX DOWNING.......................François
HENRY BRANDON..........Lieutenant Schultz
FRITZ LEIBER.................Sadi Kirschen
GILBERT EMERY...............Brand Whitlock
LUCIEN PRIVAL............Lieutenant Schmidt
RICHARD DEANE............Lieutenant Wilson
BERT ROACH....................George Moulin
ERNST DEUTSCH.............Public Prosecutor
EGON BRECHER..................Dr. Gunther
WILL KAUFMAN..............Baron von Weser
GUSTAV VON SEYFFERTITZ..President of Court
BODIL ROSING.......................Charlotte
IMPERADIO   Director: Herbert Wilcox   1939
Made in Hollywood

O

Of Mice and Men

BURGESS MEREDITH...................George
BETTY FIELD............................Mae
LON CHANEY, Jr.......................Lennie
CHARLES BICKFORD......................Slim
ROMAN BOHNEN.......................Candy
BOB STEELE............................Curley
NOAH BEERY, Jr.........................Whit
GRANVILLE BATES.....................Carlson
OSCAR O'SHEA........................Jackson
LEIGH WHIPPER.......................Crooks
UA   Director: Lewis Milestone   1939
From the novel by John Steinbeck

Only Way, The

JOHN MARTIN-HARVEY.........Sidney Carton
BEN WEBSTER..........Marquis St. Évremonde
JEAN JAY........................Jeanne Defarge
C. BURTON.....................Jacques Defarge
FISHER WHITE...................Dr. Manette
GORDON McLEOD..............Ernest Defarge
FREDERICK COOPER...........Charles Darnay
MADGE STUART........................Mimi
FRANK STANMORE..............Jarvis Lorry
BETTY FAIRE...................Lucie Manette
J. RAYMOND.........................Jacques
MARY BROUGH....................Miss Pross
GIBB McLAUGHLIN.............Barsad, the spy
HAROLD CARTON......................Stryver
JUDD GREEN.............Prosecuting Counsel
H. IBBERSON.......................The Judge
FRED RAINS............President of the Tribunal
MARTIN CONWAY...........Citizen Prosecutor
MARGARET YARDE......The Vengeance Woman
MICHAEL MARTIN-HARVEY.............No.46
FIRST NATIONAL   1926
From " A Tale of Two Cities " by Charles Dickens

Orphans of the Storm

LILLIAN GISH.................Henriette Girard
DOROTHY GISH.........Louise, the blind girl
JOSEPH SCHILDKRAUT....Chevalier de Vaudrey
MONTE BLUE.........................Danton
FRANK LOSEE.................Count de Linières
CATHERINE EMMETT......Countess de Linières
LESLIE KING...............Jacques Forget-Not
LUCILLE LA VERNE.........Mother Frochard
SHELDON LEWIS.............Jacques Frochard
FRANK PUGLIA...............Pierre Frochard
CREIGHTON HALE......................Picard

LEO KOLMER.....................Louis XVI
MORGAN WALLACE.........Marquis de Praille
SIDNEY HERBERT..................Robespierre
Produced and directed by D. W. Griffith   1923

Our Town

WILLIAM HOLDEN...............George Gibbs
MARTHA SCOTT...................Emily Webb
FAY BAINTER......................Mrs. Gibbs
BEULAH BONDI.....................Mrs. Webb
THOMAS MITCHELL..................Dr. Gibbs
GUY KIBBEE.......................Editor Webb
STUART ERWIN.................Howie Newsome
DORO MERANDE..................Mrs. Soames
RUTH TOBY..................Rebecca Gibbs
DOUGLAS GARDINER............Wally Webb
ARTHUR ALLEN..............Professor Willett
SPENCER CHARTERS...........The Constable
TIM DAVIS.....................Joe Crowell
DIX DAVIS......................Si Crowell
FRANK CRAVEN....................Narrator
UA   Director: Sam Wood   1940
From the Pulitzer Prize play by Thornton Wilder

Our Vines Have Tender Grapes

EDWARD G. ROBINSON.....Martinius Jacobson
MARGARET O'BRIEN...........Selma Jacobson
JAMES CRAIG...............Nels Halverson
FRANCES GIFFORD..............Viola Johnson
AGNES MOOREHEAD...........Bruna Jacobson
MORRIS CARNOVSKY.........Bjorn Bjornson
JACKIE " BUTCH " JENKINS....Arnold Hanson
SARA HADEN.................Mrs. Bjornson
GRETA GRANSTEDT............Mrs. Faraasen
DOROTHY MORRIS...........Ingeborg Jensen
ARTHUR SPACE.................Pete Hanson
ELIZABETH RUSSELL.............Kola Hanson
LOUIS JEAN HEYDT.............Mr. Faraasen
CHARLES MIDDLETON............Kurt Jensen
FRANCIS PIERLOT...................Minister
JOHNNIE BERKES.............Circus Driver
MGM   Director: Roy Rowland   1945
*Based on the book " For Our Vines Have Tender
Grapes " by George Victor Martin*

Outward Bound

LESLIE HOWARD....................Tom Prior
DOUGLAS FAIRBANKS, Jr.............Henry
HELEN CHANDLER......................Ann
BERYL MERCER..................Mrs. Midget
ALISON SKIPWORTH.......Mrs. Cliveden-Banks
LYONEL WATTS............Rev. William Duke
MONTAGU LOVE.................Mrs. Lingley
DUDLEY DIGGES.........Thompson, Examiner
WARN   Director: Robert Milton   1931
From the play by Sutton Vane

Overlanders, The

CHIPS RAFFERTY...............Dan McAlpine
JOHN NUGENT HAYWARD........Bill Parsons
DAPHNE CAMPBELL..............Mary Parsons
JEAN BLUE.......................Mrs. Parsons
HELEN GRIEVE.................Helen Parsons
JOHN FERNSIDE......................Corky
PETER PAGAN.............Sailor (" Sinbad ")
FRANK RANSOME.....................Charlie
STAN TOLHURST.....................Manager
MARSHALL CROSBY...................Minister
JOHN FEGAN.................Police Sergeant
CLYDE COMBO...............Aborigine Jacky
HENRY MURDOCH.............Aborigine Nipper
EALING   Director: Harry Watt   1946
The first British film to be made in Australia

P

Paddy the Next Best Thing

MAE MARSH.................Paddy
LILLIAN DOUGLAS.................Eileen
NINA BOUCICAULT.................Mrs. Blake
MARIE AULT.................Mrs. Adair
MILDRED EVELYN.................Doreen Blake
HAIDEE WRIGHT ⎱
MARIE WRIGHT ⎰ ....The Aunts
DARBY FOSTER.................Lawrence Blake
GEORGE K. ARTHUR.................Jack O'Hara
SIR SIMEON STUART.................General Adair
BERNARD VAUGHAN.................Dr. Adair
TOM COVENTRY.................Micky Doolan
GRAHAM-WILCOX   Director : Graham Cutts   1923

Peg o' My Heart

LAURETTE TAYLOR....Margaret O'Connell (Peg)
MAHLON HAMILTON....Sir Gerald Adair (Jerry)
RUSSELL SIMPSON.................Jim O'Connell
ETHEL GREY TERRY.........Ethel Chichester
NIGEL BARRIE.................Christian Brent
LIONEL BELMORE.................Hawks
VERA LEWIS.................Mrs. Chichester
SIDNA BETH IVINS.........Mrs. Jim O'Connell
D. R. O. HATSWELL.................Alaric Chichester
AILEEN O'MALLEY.................Peg, as a child
FRED HUNTLY.................Butler
METRO-GOLDWYN   Director : King Vidor   1923

Pépé le Moko

JEAN GABIN.................Pépé le Moko
MIREILLE BALLIN.................Gaby
LINE NORO.................Inès
CHARPIN.................Régis
SATURNIN FABRE................."Grand-Père"
GABRIEL GABRIO.................Carlos
LUCAS GRIDOUX.................Slimane
MARCEL DALIO.................L'Arbi
FRÉHEL.................Tania
GILBERT GIL.................Pierrot
ROGER LEGRIS.................Max
PARIS FILM (France)   Director : Julien Duvivier 1937
Based on the novel by Detective Ashelbe
Re-made in Hollywood by Walter Wanger as
" Algiers ", released through UA in 1938
(See Foreign Language Films, page 347)

Peter Pan

BETTY BRONSON.................Peter Pan
ERNEST TORRENCE.................Captain Hook
CYRIL CHADWICK.................Mr. Darling
VIRGINIA BROWN FAIRE.................Tinker Bell
ANNA MAY WONG.................Tiger Lily
ESTHER RALSTON.................Mrs. Darling
GEORGE ALI.................Nana, the dog
MARY BRIAN.................Wendy
PHILIPPE DE LACY.................Michael
JACK MURPHY.................John
PARA   Director : Herbert Brenon   1925
From the play by Sir James Barrie

Phantom Lady

FRANCHOT TONE.................Jack Marlow
ELLA RAINES.................Carol Richman
ALAN CURTIS.................Scott Henderson
AURORA.................Estela Monteiro
THOMAS GOMEZ.................Inspector Burgess
FAY HELM.................Ann Terry
ELISHA COOK, JR..................Cliff
ANDREW TOMBES.................Bartender

REGIS TOOMEY ⎱
JOSEPH CREHAN ⎰ ....Detectives
DORIS LLOYD.................Kettisha
VIRGINIA BRISSAC.................Dr. Chase
MILBURN STONE.................District Attorney
UNIV   Director : Robert Siodmak   1944
Based on the novel by William Irish

Phantom of the Opera, The

LON CHANEY.................The Phantom (Erik)
MARY PHILBIN.................Christine Daae
NORMAN KERRY.................Raoul de Chagny
SNITZ EDWARDS.................Florine Papillon
GIBSON GOWLAND.................Simon
JOHN SAINPOLIS.................Phillippe de Chagny
VIRGINIA PEARSON.................Carlotta
ARTHUR EDMUND CAREW.................The Persian
EDITH YORKE.................Mamma Valerius
ANTON VAVERKA.................The Prompter
BERNARD SIEGEL.................Joseph Buquet
OLIVE ANN ALCORN.................La Sorelli
EDWARD CECIL.................Faust
ALEXANDER BEVANI.................Mephistopheles
JOHN MILJAN.................Valentine
GRACE MARVIN.................Martha
GEORGE B. WILLIAMS....M. Richard, Manager
BRUCE COVINGTON.................M. Monacharmin
CESARE GRAVINA.................Retiring Manager
UNIV   Director : Rupert Julian   1930

Phantom of the Opera, The

NELSON EDDY.................Anatole Garron
SUSANNA FOSTER.................Christine du Bois
CLAUDE RAINS.................Erique Claudin
EDGAR BARRIER.................Raoul Daubert
LEO CARILLO.................Signor Ferretti
JANE FARRAR.................Biancarolli
J. EDWARD BROMBERG.................Amiot
FRITZ FELD.................Lecours
FRANK PUGLIA.................Villeneuve
STEVE GERAY.................Verchères
BARBARA EVEREST.................Aunt
HUME CRONYN.................Gérard
FRITZ LEIBER.................Liszt
NICKI ANDRE.................Lorenzi
GLADYS BLAKE.................Jeanne
ELVIRE CURCI.................Biancarolli's maid
HANS HERBERT.................Marcel
KATE LAWSON.................Landlady
MILES MANDER.................Pleyel
ROSINA GALLI.................Christine's maid
WALTER STAHL.................Doctor
PAUL MARION.................Desjardines
UNIV   Director : Arthur Lubin   1943

Piccadilly Incident

ANNA NEAGLE.................Diana Fraser
MICHAEL WILDING.................Captain Alan Pearson
FRANCES MERCER.................Joan Draper
CORAL BROWNE.................Virginia Pearson
A. E. MATTHEWS.................Sir Charles Pearson
EDWARD RIGBY.................Judd
BRENDA BRUCE.................Sally Benton
LESLIE DWYER.................Sam
MAIRE O'NEILL.................Mrs. Milligan
MICHAEL LAURENCE.................Bill Weston
WILCOX-ABPC   Director : Herbert Wilcox   1946

Picture of Dorian Gray, The

GEORGE SANDERS.................Lord Henry Wotton
HURD HATFIELD.................Dorian Gray
DONNA REED.................Gladys Hallward

ANGELA LANSBURY.................Sibyl Vane
PETER LAWFORD.................David Stone
LOWELL GILMORE...............Basil Hallward
RICHARD FRASER..................James Vane
DOUGLAS WALTON............Allen Campbell
MORTON LOWRY.............Adrian Singleton
MILES MANDER.............Sir Robert Bentley
LYDIA BILBROOK..................Mrs. Vane
MARY FORBES.................. Lady Agatha
ROBERT GREIG.................Sir Thomas
MOYNA MacGILL....................Duchess
BILLY BEVAN..........Malvolio Jones, chairman
RENIE CARSON............Young Frenchwoman
LILLIAN BOND.......................Kate

with

Devi Dja and her Balinese Dancers

MGM Director : Albert Lewin 1945

Based on the novel by Oscar Wilde

Pilgrim, The

CHARLES CHAPLIN.................The Pilgrim
EDNA PURVIANCE....................The Girl
KITTY BRADBURY.................Her mother
MACK SWAIN.......................The Deacon
DASH LOYAL......................The Elder
DINKY DEAR.........................The Boy
MAE WELLS.......................The Mother
SYDNEY CHAPLIN................Her husband
CHUCK REISNER...................The Crook

FIRST NATIONAL 1923

Written and directed by Charles Chaplin

Pimpernel Smith

LESLIE HOWARD........Professor Horatio Smith
FRANCIS L. SULLIVAN.....General von Graum
MARY MORRIS.............Ludmilla Koslowski
HUGH McDERMOTT...........David Maxwell
RAYMOND HUNTLEY..................Marx
MANNING WHILEY.........Bertie Gregson
PETER GAWTHORNE.........Sidimir Koslowski
ALLAN JEAYES.................Dr. Benckendorf
DENNIS ARUNDELL..................Hoffman
JOAN KEMP-WELCH...........Schoolteacher
PHILIP FRIEND......................Spencer
LAWRENCE KITCHEN..........Clarence Elstead
DAVID TOMLINSON....................Steve
BASIL APPLEBY...............Jock MacIntyre
PERCY WALSH.......................Dvorak
SUZANNE CLAIR...................Salesgirl
ROLAND PERTWEE
Sir George Smith (Embassy Official)
CHARLES PATON.....................Steinhof
AUBREY MALLALIEU...................Dean
GEORGE STREET...................Schmidt
ORIEL ROSS.................Lady Willoughby
A. E. MATTHEWS......Earl of Meadowbrook
BRIAN HERBERT.....................Jaromir
ARTHUR HAMBLING.................Jordan
BEN WILLIAMS...................Granbitz
ERNEST BUTCHER.....................Weber

BRIT NAT Director : Leslie Howard 1941

Place of One's Own, A

MARGARET LOCKWOOD.............Annette
JAMES MASON...................Mr. Smedhurst
BARBARA MULLEN.............Mrs. Smedhurst
DENNIS PRICE.....................Dr. Selbie
HELEN HAYE...........Mrs. Manning-Tutthorn
MICHAEL SHEPLEY.....Major Manning-Tutthorn
DULCIE GRAY.......................Sarah
MOORE MARRIOTT...................George
O. B. CLARENCE.....................Perkins

HELEN GOSS..........................Barmaid
EDIE MARTIN..........................Cook
GUS McNAUGHTON............P.C. Hargreaves

GAINS Director : Bernard Knowles 1945

From the novel by Sir Osbert Sitwell

Plainsman, The

GARY COOPER.................Wild Bill Hickok
JEAN ARTHUR...................Calamity Jane
JAMES ELLISON................Buffalo Bill Cody
CHARLES BICKFORD.............John Latimer
HELEN BURGESS.................Louisa Cody
PORTER HALL.....................Jack McCall
PAUL HARVEY....................Yellow Hand
VICTOR VARCONI.............Painted Horse
JOHN MILJAN.........General George A. Custer
FRANK McGLYNN, SR.........Abraham Lincoln
GRANVILLE BATES.................Van Ellyn
FRANK ALBERTSON...........A Young Trooper
PURNELL PRATT...............Captain Wood
FRED KOHLER, SR..............Jake, a teamster
PAT MORIARTY...........Sergeant McGinnis
CHARLES JUDELS.........Tony, the barber
HARRY WOODS..........Quartermaster Sergeant
ANTHONY QUINN...........A Cheyenne Indian
FRANCIS McDONALD.........A River Gambler
GEORGE ERNEST.......................A Boy
GEORGE MacQUARRIE.....General Merritt
GEORGE HAYES.........................Breezy
FUZZY KNIGHT.........................Dave

PARA Director : Cecil B. De Mille 1937

Plough and the Stars, The

BARBARA STANWYCK...........Nora Clitheroe
PRESTON FOSTER.................Jack Clitheroe
UNA O'CONNOR............Maggie Gogan
BARRY FITZGERALD.............Fluther Good
DENIS O'DEA.....................The Covey
EILEEN CROWE.................Bessie Burgess
ARTHUR SHIELDS.............Padraic Pearse
J. M. KERRIGAN................Peter Flynn
BONITA GRANVILLE.........Mollser Gogan
ERIN O'BRIEN MOORE.......Rosie Redmond
F. J. McCORMICK.............Captain Brennan
MORONI OLSEN.........General Connolly
NEIL FITZGERALD.......Lieutenant Langon
CYRIL McLAGLEN...........Corporal Stoddart
BRANDON HURST...............Sergeant Tinley
ROBERT HOMANS.................The Barman

RKO Director : John Ford 1936

From the play by Sean O'Casey

Poil de Carotte

HARRY BAUR......................M. Lepic
ROBERT LYNEN.............Poil de Carotte
CATHERINE FONTENEY...........Mme. Lepic
CHRISTIANE DOR....................Annette
COLETTE SÉGAL...................Mathilde
LOUIS GAUTHIER.................Godfather
SIMONE AUBRY.............Ernestine Lepic
MAXIME FROMIOT...........Félix Lepic
MME. MARTY.......................Honorine

PATHÉ-NATAN (France) 1933

Director : Julien Duvivier

(*See Foreign Language Films, page* 347)

Pontcarral, Colonel d'Empire

PIERRE BLANCHAR.................Pontcarral
ANNIE DUCAUX.....................Garlone
SUZY CARRIER......................Sybille
JEAN MARCHAT......................Rozans
GUILLAUME DE SAX........Fournier Sarloveze

MARCEL DELAÎTRE..................Austerlitz
LUCIEN NAT.....................................Garon
CHARLOTTE LYSES..........Mme. de Mareilhac
LOUVIGNY..................Comte de Mareilhac
CHARLES GRANVAL..........Marquis de Ransac
ALEXANDRE RIGNAULT..............Postman
SIMONE VALÈRE..........Blanche de Mareilhac
PATHÉ CINEMA (France)   1942
           Director : Jean Delannoy
     (See Foreign Language Films, page 347)

Portrait of Maria
(*Maria Candelaria*)
DOLORES DEL RIO...........Maria Candelaria
PEDRO ARMENDARIZ..........Lorenzo Rafael
ALBERTO GALAN...................The Artist
RAFAEL ICARDO....................The Priest
MIGUEL INCLAN................Don Damian
MARGARITA CORTES....................Lupe
JULIO AHUET....................Jose Alfonso
BEATRIZ RAMOS..............Woman Reporter
GUADALUPE DEL CASTILLO.......The Healer
CHURUBUSCO (Mexico)—MGM-INTERNATIONAL   1945
           Director : Emilio Fernandez
     (See Foreign Language Films, page 347)

Pride and Prejudice
Those Living at Meryton Village
EDWARD ASHLEY...............Mr. Wickham
MARTEN LAMONT................Mr. Denny
E. E. CLIVE.................Sir William Lucas
MARJORIE WOOD..................Lady Lucas
MAY BEATTY.....................Mrs. Philips
Those Living at Longbourn
GREER GARSON............Elizabeth Bennet
MAUREEN O'SULLIVAN...........Jane Bennet
ANN RUTHERFORD.............Lydia Bennet
MARSHA HUNT..............Mary Bennet
HEATHER ANGEL..............Kitty Bennet
MARY BOLAND...................Mrs. Bennet
EDMUND GWENN.................Mr. Bennet
Those Living at Netherfield
LAURENCE OLIVIER.................Mr. Darcy
FRIEDA INESCORT................Miss Bingley
BRUCE LESTER..................Mr. Bingley
Those Living at Rosings
EDNA MAY OLIVER...Lady Catherine de Bourgh
GIA KENT..................Anne de Bourgh
MELVILLE COOPER...............Mr. Collins
KAREN MORLEY................Mrs. Collins
MGM   Director : Robert Z. Leonard   1940
     Based on the novel by Jane Austen
              Re-issued 1944

Pride of the Yankees, The
GARY COOPER.....................Lou Gehrig
TERESA WRIGHT.............Eleanor Gehrig
BABE RUTH.......................Babe Ruth
WALTER BRENNAN.................Sam Blake
DAN DURYEA................Hank Hanneman
ELSA JANSSEN.................Mom Gehrig
LUDWIG STOSSEL.................Pop Gehrig
VIRGINIA GILMORE......................Myra
BILL DICKEY.....................Bill Dickey
ERNIE ADAMS................Miller Huggins
PIERRE WATKIN.................Mr. Twitchell
HARRY HARVEY................Joe McCarthy
ROBERT W. MEUSEL.........Robert W. Meusel
MARK KOENIG...................Mark Koenig
BILL STERN......................Bill Stern
ADDISON RICHARDS....................Coach
HARDIE ALBRIGHT.................Van Tuyl

EDWARD FIELDING..............Clinic Doctor
GEORGE LESSEY........Mayor of New Rochelle
EDGAR BARRIER..............:Hospital Doctor
DOUGLAS CROFT..........Lou Gehrig, as a boy
                       with
Veloz and Yolanda and Ray Noble and his Orchestra
RKO   Director : Sam Wood   1943
        From the story by Paul Gallico

Prisoner of Zenda, The
LEWIS STONE...............{ Rudolf Rassendyll
                           King Rudolf
ALICE TERRY..................Princess Flavia
ROBERT EDESON.................Colonel Sapt
STUART HOLMES
                  Duke Michael (Black Michael)
RAMON NOVARRO..........Rupert of Hentzau
BARBARA LA MARR......Antoinette de Mauban
EDWARD CONNELLY.....Marshal von Strakencz
MALCOM McGREGOR
                  Count Fritz von Tarlenheim
LOIS LEE....................Countess Helga
THURSTON FAIRFAX..................Bersonin
AL JENNINGS......................De Gautet
F. G. BECKER....................Detchard
SNITZ EDWARDS......................Josef
HARRY JONES.......................Hans
PARA   Director : Rex Ingram   1923
     From Edward Rose's stage version of the novel by
                   Anthony Hope

Prisoner of Zenda, The
RONALD COLMAN..........{ Rudolf Rassendyll
                         King Rudolf V
MADELEINE CARROLL..........Princess Flavia
DOUGLAS FAIRBANKS, Jr....Rupert of Hentzau
MARY ASTOR............Antoinette de Mauban
C. AUBREY SMITH.................Colonel Zapt
RAYMOND MASSEY..............Black Michael
DAVID NIVEN.............Fritz von Tarlenheim
MONTAGU LOVE...................Detchard
WILLIAM VON BRINCKEN...........Kraftstein
PHILIP SLEEMAN................Lanengram
ELEANOR WESSELHOEFT................Cook
FLORENCE ROBERTS.................Duenna
TORBEN MEYER........Black Michael's butler
LAWRENCE GRANT..........Marshal Strakencz
IAN MACLAREN....................Cardinal
RALPH FAULKNER.................Bersonin
BYRON FOULGER............Master Johann
HOWARD LANG......................Josef
BEN WEBSTER........British Ambassador
EVELYN DERESFORD...British Ambassador's wife
BOYD IRWIN..........Master of Ceremonies
EMMETT KING..........Lord High Chamberlain
AL SHEAN..............Orchestra Leader
CHARLES HALTON..........Passport Officer
OTTO FRIES.................Luggage Officer
SPENCER CHARTERS...................Porter
ALEXANDER D'ARCY.............De Gautet
HENRY ROQUERMORE..........Man at station
LILLIAN HERMER................Wife at station
PAT SOMERSET
LESLIE SKETCHLEY }.....Two Guards at lodge
SELZNICK   Director : John Cromwell   1938
     From Edward Rose's stage version of the novel by
                   Anthony Hope

Private Life of Helen of Troy, The
MARIA CORDA........................Helen
LEWIS STONE....................Menelaus
RICARDO CORTEZ.....................Paris

TERESA WRIGHT
(Paramount)

GEORGE FAWCETT....................Eteoneus
ALICE WHITE.........................Adraste
GEORGE ELLIOTT...................Telemachus
TOM O'BRIEN..........................Ulysses
BERT SPROTTE......................Achilles
MARIO CARILLO..........................Ajax
CHARLES PUFFY........Malapokitoratoreadetos
GEORGE KOTSONAROS................Hector
CONSTANTINE ROMANOFF............Aeneas
EMILO BORGATO.....................Sarpedon
ALICE ADAIR........................Aphrodite
HELEN FAIRWEATHER.................Athena
VIRGINIA THOMAS.......................Hera
FIRST NATIONAL   Director: Alexander Korda 1929

Private Life of Henry VIII, The
CHARLES LAUGHTON...............Henry VIII
ROBERT DONAT...............Thomas Culpeper
LADY TREE.................Henry's old nurse
BINNIE BARNES............Katheryn Howard
ELSA LANCHESTER............Ann of Cleves
MERLE OBERON....................Anne Boleyn
FRANKLIN DYALL....................Cromwell
MILES MANDER..................Wriothesly
WENDY BARRIE...............Jane Seymour
CLAUD ALLISTER.....................Cornell
JOHN LODER................Thomas Peynell
EVERLEY GREGG...........Katherine Parr
LAWRENCE HANRAY.................Cranmer
WILLIAM AUSTIN.............Duke of Cleves
JOHN TURNBULL....................Holbein
FREDERICK CULLY...........Duke of Norfolk
JUDY KELLY...............Lady Rochford
GIBB McLAUGHLIN........French Executioner
SAM LIVESEY   English Executioner
LFP   Director: Alexander Korda 1933

Professor Mamlock
S. MEZHINSKI................Professor Mamlock
E. NIKITINA............Frau Professor Mamlock
O. ZHAKOV.....................Rolf Mamlock
V. CHESNOKOV.................Dr. Hellpach
N. SHATERNIKOVA.........Fraülein Dr. Inge
P. KIRILLOV..........................Ernst
T. GURETSKAYA....................Aenne
N. FAUSEK..................Mother Wendt
Y. TOLUBEYEV......................Fritz
B. SVETLOV...................Dr. Karlsen
I. ZONNE....................Dr. Wagner
M. TAGIANOSOVA...........Sister Jadwiga
V. KISELEV.......Bernard Seidl (journalist)
C. BUDAROV..........................Willi
A. ZARZHITSKAYA...................Hilde
S. RYABINKIN.......................Peter
V. MERKURIEV......................Krause
V. TASKIN....................Von Rettwitz
Y. MALIUTIN..................The Colonel
BORIS SCHILCHTING..Police Investigator Keppke
G. SAMOILOV.....................Adjutant
P. SUKHANOV................Storm Trooper
M. SHELKOVSKY...............1st Detective
B. FEODOSIEV..........2nd Detective Agitator
LENFILMS (U.S.S.R.)   Directors: 1939
          Adolf Minkin and
          Herbert Rappoport
     From the play by Friedrich Wolf
   (See Foreign Language Films, page 347)

Pygmalion
LESLIE HOWARD..............Professor Higgins
WENDY HILLER.........................Eliza

WILFRED LAWSON...................Doolittle
MARIE LOHR....................Mrs. Higgins
SCOTT SUNDERLAND........Colonel Pickering
JEAN CADELL....................Mrs. Pearce
DAVID TREE.........................Freddy
ESME PERCY..........Count Aristid Karpathy
VIOLET VANBRUGH............Ambassadress
IRIS HOEY   )   (Ysabel
VIOLA TREE   ).. Social Reporters ..(Perfide
IRENE BROWNE.....................Duchess
O. B. CLARENCE....................A Vicar
WALLY PATCH...............1st Bystander
F. H. MALTBY...............2nd Bystander
GEORGE MOZART................3rd Bystander
IVOR BARNARD............Sarcastic Bystander
PASCAL   Directors: 1938
     Gabriel Pascal, Anthony Asquith
               Leslie Howard
   From the play by George Bernard Shaw

Q

Quai des Brumes, Le
JEAN GABIN....................Jean (a deserter)
MICHELE MORGAN.....................Nelly
MICHEL SIMON...........Zabel, Nelly's guardian
PIERRE BRASSEUR......................Lucien
DELMONT...........................Panama
AIMOS.........................." Quart-Vittel "
ROBERT LE VIGAN...................The Artist
RENÉ GENIN.......................The Doctor
JENNY BURNAY..............Lucien's friend
ROGER LEGRIS...................The Waiter
PÉREZ......................The Chauffeur
WALTER................Lucien's associate
CINÉ ALLIANCE (France)   1937
        Director: Marcel Carné
   (See Foreign Language Films, page 347)

Quiet Wedding
MARGARET LOCKWOOD..........Janet Royd
DEREK FARR...............Dallas Chaytor
MARJORIE FIELDING
                Mildred Royd, Janet's mother
A. E. MATTHEWS.....Arthur Royd, Janet's father
ATHENE SEYLER....................Aunt Mary
JEAN CADELL...................Aunt Florence
MARGARETTA SCOTT......Marcia, Janet's sister
DAVID TOMLINSON)   (John
SIDNEY KING   ).....Janet's brothers (Denys
PEGGY ASHCROFT.................Flower Lisle
FRANK CELLIER.....Mr. Chaytor, Dallas's father
ROLAND CULVER............Boofy Ponsonby
MICHAEL SHEPLEY..........Marcia's husband
MURIEL PAVLOW....................Miranda
SOSKIN-PARA   Director: Anthony Asquith   1941
   Based on the play by Esther McCracken

Quo Vadis ?
EMIL JANNINGS........................Nero
LILIAN HALL-DAVIS...................Lygia
BRUTO CASTELLANI....................Ursus
ANDRÉE HABAY.....................Petronius
RINA DE LIGUORO...................Eunice
ALPHONSE FRYLAND..................Vinicius
ELENA DI SANGRO..................Poppaea
     Supported by a cast of 20,000 people
(Italy)   Director: Enrico Guazzoni   1926
   From the novel by Henryk Sienkiewicz
   (See Foreign Language Films, page 347)

R

Raffles

RONALD COLMAN..................Raffles
KAY FRANCIS......................Gwen
BRAMWELL FLETCHER..............Bunny
FRANCES DADE.....................Ethel
DAVID TORRENCE................McKenzie
ALISON SKIPWORTH............Lady Melrose
FREDERICK KERR..............Lord Melrose
JOHN ROGERS...................Crawshaw
WILSON BENGE.................Barraclough
UA   Director : George Fitzmaurice   1930
*From the short stories of E. W. Hornung, and the
play by him and Eugene W. Presbrey*

Rain

JOAN CRAWFORD.............Sadie Thompson
WALTER HUSTON............Alfred Davidson
WILLIAM GARGAN...........Sergeant O'Hara
GUY KIBBEE....................Joe Horn
WALTER CATLETT.........Quartermaster Bates
BEULAH BONDI..............Mrs. Davidson
MATT MOORE................Dr. MacPhail
KENDALL LEE..............Mrs. MacPhail
BEN KENDRICKS..................Griggs
FREDERIC HOWARD...............Hodgson
UA   1933
*From the play by John Colton and C. Randolph,
adapted from the story " Rain " by Somerset
Maugham (see also " Sadie Thompson ")*

Rains Came, The

MYRNA LOY.............Lady Edwina Esketh
TYRONE POWER.............Major Rama Safti
GEORGE BRENT................Tom Ransome
BRENDA JOYCE................Fern Simon
NIGEL BRUCE...........Lord Albert Esketh
MARIA OUSPENSKAYA.............Maharani
JOSEPH SCHILDKRAUT...........Mr. Bannerjee
MARY NASH..................Miss McDaid
JANE DARWELL.....Aunt Phoebe (Mrs. Smiley)
MARJORIE RAMBEAU.............Mrs. Simon
HENRY TRAVERS..........Rev. Homer Smiley
H. B. WARNER..................Maharajah
LAURA HOPE CREWS.....Lily Hoggett-Egburry
WILLIAM ROYLE..........Raschid Ali Khan
MONTAGUE SHAW.............General Keith
HARRY HAYDEN..........Rev. Elmer Simon
HERBERT EVANS....................Bates
ABNER BIBERMAN.........John, the Baptist
MARA ALEXANDER.........Mrs. Bannerjee
WILLIAM EDMUNDS................Mr. Das
20TH-FOX   Director : Clarence Brown   1940
Based on the novel by Louis Bromfield

Rake's Progress, The
(American title : *Notorious Gentleman*)
REX HARRISON.............Vivian Kenway
LILLI PALMER.............Rikki Krausner
GODFREY TEARLE..........Colonel Kenway
GRIFFITH JONES............Sandy Duncan
MARGARET JOHNSTON......Jennifer Calthrop
GUY MIDDLETON..................Fogroy
JEAN KENT...................Jill Duncan
MARIE LOHR.................Lady Parks
GARRY MARSH.............Sir Hubert Parks
DAVID HORNE...........Sir John Brookley
JOHN SALEW....................Burgess
ALAN WHEATLEY.................Edwards
BREFNI O'RORKE.................Bromhead

JOAN MAUDE.....................Alice
OLGA LINDO........Woman in palais-de-danse
PATRICIA LAFFAN............Miss Fernandez
HOWARD MARION-CRAWFORD
                          Coldstream Guardsman
CHARLES VICTOR.................Old Sweat
DAVID WALLBRIDGE.........Vivian, as a boy
JOHN DODSWORTH..........Team Manager
EMRYS JONES....................Bateson
JACK VYVYAN...........Fred (mechanic)
FREDERICK BURTWELL...........Magistrate
GEORGE CROSS.................Policeman
INDIVID   Director : Sidney Gilliat   1945
From the story by Val Valentine

Ramona

DOLORES DEL RIO...............Ramona
WARNER BAXTER...............Alessandro
ROLAND DREW....................Felipe
VERA LEWIS...............Señora Moreno
MICHAEL VISAROFF..........Juan Canito
JOHN T. PRINCE........Father Salvierderra
MATHILDE COMONT.................Marda
CARLOS AMOR...........A Sheep Herder
JESS CAVIN................Bandit Leader
JEAN..........................The Dog
UA   1928

Rat, The

IVOR NOVELLO... Pierre Boucheron (" The Rat ")
MAE MARSH................Odile Étrange
ISABEL JEANS........Zélie de Chaumet
ROBERT SCHOLTZ.............Herman Stetz
ESME FITZGIBBONS.........Madeleine Sornay
HUGH BROOK......................Paul
JAMES LINDSAY.........Detective Caillard
MARIE AULT..................Mère Colline
IRIS GREY.......................Rose
JULIE SUEDO..................Mou-Mou
GAINS   Director : Graham Cutts   1926
From the play by Ivor Novello and Constance Collier

Rebecca

LAURENCE OLIVIER.........Maxim de Winter
JOAN FONTAINE.............Mrs. de Winter
GEORGE SANDERS...........Jack Favell
JUDITH ANDERSON...........Mrs. Danvers
NIGEL BRUCE...........Major Giles Lacy
C. AUBREY SMITH..........Colonel Julyan
REGINALD DENNY..........Frank Crawley
GLADYS COOPER..........Beatrice Lacy
PHILIP WINTER..................Robert
EDWARD FIELDING.................Frith
FLORENCE BATES.......Mrs. Van Hopper
MELVILLE COOPER.................Coroner
LEO G. CARROLL..............Dr. Baker
FORRESTER HARVEY.............Chalcroft
LUMSDEN HARE....................Tabbs
LEONARD CAREY....................Ben
SELZNICK   Director : Alfred Hitchcock   1940
*From the novel by Daphne du Maurier
Re-issued 1944*

Rebecca of Sunnybrook Farm

MARIAN NIXON..................Rebecca
RALPH BELLAMY...............Dr. Ladd
MAE MARSH...................Aunt Jane
LOUISE CLOSSER HALE......Aunt Miranda
ALPHONSE ETHIER.............Mr. Cobb
SARAH PADDEN.............Mrs. Cobb
ALAN HALE...............Mr. Simpson

EULA GUY.........................Mrs. Simpson
CHARLOTTE HENRY...............Emma Jane
CLAIRE McDOWELL...............Mrs. Randall
RONALD HARRIS.............Jack-o'-Lantern
WILLIS MARKS.........................Jacob
LUCILLE WARD....................Pig Woman
TOMMY CONLON.................John Randall
WALLY ALBRIGHT...............Billy Randall
FOX   Director: Alfred Santell   1932
From the novel by Kate Wiggin
A silent version was made with Mary Pickford in
the title role

Rembrandt
CHARLES LAUGHTON......Rembrandt van Rijn
GERTRUDE LAWRENCE..........Geertje Dirx
ELSA LANCHESTER..........Hendrickje Stoffels
EDWARD CHAPMAN..................Fabrizius
JOHN BRYNING................Titus van Rijn
RICHARD GOFE...............Titus, as a child
MEINHART MAUR.......................Ornia
WALTER HUDD.................Banning Cocq
JOHN CLEMENTS..............Govaert Flink
HENRY HEWITT......................Jan Six
GEORGE MERRITT..........Churchwarden
JOHN TURNBULL....................Minister
SAM LIVESEY......................Auctioneer
LAWRENCE HANRAY...............Hertsbeeke
ABRAHAM SOFAER..........Dr. Menasseh
WILLIAM FAGAN.................Burgomaster
RAYMOND HUNTLEY..................Ludvig
LEWIS BROUGHTON }
FREDERICK BURTWELL } ..... Saskia's brothers
BARONESS BARANY.......Waitress at inn
MARIUS GORING.........Baron Leivens
ALLAN JEAYES.....................Dr. Tulp
BASIL GILL........................Adriaen
HERBERT LOMAS.....Miller Harman van Rijn
GERTRUDE MUSGROVE............Agelintje
QUENTIN McPHERSON.............An Official
JACK LIVESEY....................Journeyman
BARRY LIVESEY...................A Peasant
EDMUND WILLARD.............Van Zeeland
ROGER WELLESLEY.....Burgomaster's secretary
BYRON WEBBER }
BELLENDEN POWELL } .... Court Members
CHARLES PATON }
HECTOR ABBAS } ....Burghers at auction
LEONARD SHARPE }
JERROLD ROBERT SHAW }
HENRY HEWITT } ..Museum Directors
GEORGE PUGHE }
LFP   Director: Alexander Korda   1936

Retour à l'Aube
DANIELLE DARRIEUX.................Anita
PIERRE DUX.......................Karl Ammer
JACQUES DUMESNIL.................Keith
PIERRE MINGAND....................Osten
SAMSON FAINSILBER.................Weber
DELAITRE.............Police Superintendent
FLORENCIE...................P.C. Ivrogne
NUMES FILS....................The Solicitor
THÉRÈSE DORNY.................The Couturier
MARCELLE BARY........Cloakroom Attendant
AMY COLIN.............The Elegant Woman
RAYMOND CORDY.....................Pali
COMPAGNIE COMMERCIALE FRANCAISE
CINÉMATOGRAPHIQUE (France)   1939
Director: Henri Decoin
From the novel by Vicki Baum
(See Foreign Language Films, page 347)

Return of the Rat, The
IVOR NOVELLO.......................Pierre
ISABEL JEANS.......................Zélie
MABEL POULTON....................Lisette
GORDON HARKER....................Morel
BERNARD NEDELL....................Henri
MARIE AULT.............Mère Colline
HARRY TERRY........................Alf
SCOTCH KELLY........................Bill
GLADYS FRAZIN....................Yvonne
GAINS   Director: Graham Cutts   1930

Rhapsody in Blue
ROBERT ALDA.................George Gershwin
JOAN LESLIE...................Julie Adams
ALEXIS SMITH.................Christine Gilbert
CHARLES COBURN...........Max Dreyfus
JULIE BISHOP.................Lee Gershwin
ALBERT BASSERMAN.........Professor Frank
MORRIS CARNOVSKY...........Mr. Gershwin
ROSEMARY DE CAMP.........Mrs. Gershwin
HERBERT RUDLEY...............Ira Gershwin
EDDIE MARR.............Buddy de Sylva
OSCAR LORAINE....................Ravel
ERNEST GOLM...................Otto Kahn
MARTIN NOBLE.............Jascha Heifetz
HUGO KIRCHHOFFER.........Walter Damrosch
WILL WRIGHT...................Rachmaninoff
as themselves
AL JOLSON   OSCAR LEVANT
PAUL WHITEMAN   GEORGE WHITE
HAZEL SCOTT   ANNE BROWN
TOM PATRICOLA   JOHN B. HUGHES
THE WARNER CHORAL SINGERS
WARN   Director: Irving Rapper   1945
Based on the life story of George Gershwin

Rio Rita
BEBE DANIELS...................Rita Ferguson
JOHN BOLES...........Captain Jim Stewart
DOROTHY LEE.......................Dolly
BERT WHEELER................Chick Bean
ROBERT WOOLSEY.....................Lovett
SAM NELSON.......................McGinn
SAM BLUM........................Café Owner
DON ALVARADO...........Roberto Ferguson
GEORGE RENEVANT.................Ravenoff
EVA ROSITA.......................Carmen
NICK DE RUIZ.....................Padrone
TINY SANDFORD...................Davalos
HELEN KAISER.................Mrs. Bean
FRED BURNS.......................Wilkins
RADIO   1930

Robin Hood
DOUGLAS FAIRBANKS, SR.
The Earl of Huntingdon, afterwards Robin Hood
WALLACE BEERY......Richard the Lion-Hearted
SAM DE GRASSE.................Prince John
ENID BENNETT.....Lady Marian Fitzwalter
PAUL DICKEY............Sir Guy of Gisbourne
WILLIAM LOWERY The High Sheriff of Nottingham
ROY COULSON.................The King's Jester
BILLIE BENNETT... Lady Marian's serving-woman
MERRILL McCORMICK }
WILSON BENGE   } Henchmen to Prince John
WILLARD LOUIS.....................Friar Tuck
ALAN HALE.........................Little John
MAINE GEARY...................Will Scarlett
LLOYD TALMAN.................Alan-a-Dale
UA   Produced and directed   1924
by Douglas Fairbanks, Sr.

Rogue Song, The
LAWRENCE TIBBETT....................Yegor
CATHERINE DALE OWEN........Princess Vera
NANCE O'NEIL................Princess Alexandra
JUDITH VOSSELLI............Countess Tatiana
ULRICH HAUPT...................Prince Serge
ELSA ALSEN....................Yegor's mother
FLORENCE LAKE........................Nadja
LIONEL BELMORE....................Ossman
WALLACE MacDONALD...............Hassan
KATE PRICE........................Petrovna
H. A. MORGAN........................Frolov
BURR MACINTOSH.............Count Peter
JAMES BRADBURY, Jr................Azamat
STAN LAUREL........................Ali-Bek
OLIVER HARDY....................Murza-Bek
MGM   Director: Lionel Barrymore   1930
From the musical play " Gipsy Love " by Basil Hood
and Franz Lehar

Roi S'Amuse, Le
VICTOR FRANCEN....Jean IV, King of Ruritania
RAIMU............................M. Bourdier
ELVIRE POPESCO...............Thérèse Marnix
GABY MORLAY..................Mme. Bourdier
HÉLÈNE ROBERT.............Hélène Bourdier
PHILIPPE HERSENT
                    Marquis de Chamarande's son
DUVALLES.............................Blond
(France)   Director: Pierre Colombier   1938
(See Foreign Language Films, page 347)

Romeo and Juliet
NORMA SHEARER......................Juliet
LESLIE HOWARD......................Romeo
JOHN BARRYMORE...................Mercutio
EDNA MAY OLIVER.....................Nurse
BASIL RATHBONE.....................Tybalt
C. AUBREY SMITH..............Lord Capulet
ANDY DEVINE........................Peter
RALPH FORBES........................Paris
REGINALD DENNY...................Benvolio
MAURICE MURPHY................Balthasar
CONWAY TEARLE..............Prince of Verona
HENRY KOLKER.................Friar Laurence
ROBERT WARWICK.............Lord Montague
VIRGINIA HAMMOND.........Lady Montague
VIOLET KEMBLE COOPER.......Lady Capulet
MGM   Director: George Cukor   1937
From the play by William Shakespeare

Romola
LILLIAN GISH........................Romola
DOROTHY GISH........................Tessa
RONALD COLMAN..........Carlo Bucellini
WILLIAM POWELL................Tito Melema
CHARLES LANE..................Baldassarre
HERBERT GRIMWOOD.............Savonarola
BONAVENTURA IBANEZ.........Bardo Bardi
FRANK PUGLIA........................Spini
AMELIA SUMMERVILLE...............Brigida
ANGELO SCATIGNA..................Bratti
EDULILO MUZZI.......................Nello
TINA RIVALI..................Monna Ghita
METRO-GOLDWYN   1925
From the novel by George Eliot

Rupert of Hentzau
ELAINE HAMMERSTEIN..........Queen Flavia
BERT LYTELL·······{Rudolph Rassendyll
                    King Rudolph of Ruritania
LEW CODY..................Rupert of Hentzau

CLAIRE WINDSOR.........Helga von Tarlenheim
HOBART BOSWORTH.............Colonel Sapt
BRYANT WASHBURN......Fritz von Tarlenheim
MARJORIE DAW....................Rosa Holf
ELMO LINCOLN..........Simon, the woodsman
IRVING CUMMINGS...............Bernenstein
MITCHELL LEWIS......................Bauer
ADOLPHE MENJOU.......Count Rischenheim
JOSEPHINE CROWELL.............Mother Holf
NIGEL DE BRULIER....Herbert, Simon's brother
GERTRUDE ASTOR......................Paula
METRO-GOLDWYN   1925
From the novel by Anthony Hope

S
Sabotage
SYLVIA SIDNEY....................Mrs. Verloc
OSCAR HOMOLKA.................Her husband
DESMOND TESTER.................Her brother
JOHN LODER..............................Ted
JOYCE BARBOUR.......................Renée
MATTHEW BOULTON............Superintendent
S. J. WARMINGTON...............Hollingshead
WILLIAM DEWHURST...............Professor
GB   Director: Alfred Hitchcock   1936
From the novel by Joseph Conrad

Sadie Thompson
GLORIA SWANSON.............Sadie Thompson
LIONEL BARRYMORE..........Oliver Hamilton
BLANCHE FRIDERICI...........Mrs. Hamilton
CHARLES LANE...................Dr. McPhail
FLORENCE MIDGLEY.............Mrs. McPhail
JAMES A. MARCUS.........Joe Horn, the trader
SOPHIA ARTEGA....................Ameena
WILL STANTON.............Quartermaster Bates
RAOUL WALSH..........Sergeant Tim O'Hara
UA   Director: Raoul Walsh   1928
From the story by Somerset Maugham
(See " Rain ")

Safety Last
HAROLD LLOYD....................The Boy
MILDRED DAVIS...................The Girl
BILL STROTHER.....................The Pal
NOAH YOUNG........................The Law
WESTCOTT B. CLARKE.........The Floorwalker
MICKEY DANIELS....................The Kid
ANNA TOWNSEND................The Grandma
HAL ROACH   1923

Saint Joan, the Maid
SIMONE GENÉVOIS.................Joan of Arc
JEAN DEBUCOURT.The Dauphin, later Charles VII
PHILIPPE HÉRIAT.............Sir Giles de Rais
CHOURA MILENA...........Isabeau de Paule
DANIEL MENDAILLE.........Lord John Talbot
PIERRE DOUVAN.............Bishop Cauchon
            and a cast of 20,000 other players
RAPID FILMS (France)   1930
            Director: Marco de Gastyne

Sally
COLLEEN MOORE.......................Sally
LLOYD HUGHES...............Blair Farquar
LEON ERROL...........Duke of Checkergovinia
DAN MASON....................Pops Shendorf
JOHN T. MURRAY..................Otis Hooper
EVA NOVAK....................Rosie Lafferty
RAY HALLOR..................Jimmy Spelvin

CARLO SCHIPA...............Sascha Commuski
MYRTLE STEDMAN.............Mrs. Ten Brock
E. H. CALVERT.................Richard Farquar
LOUISE BEAUDET.............Mme. Julie du Fey
FIRST NATIONAL   Director: Alfred E. Green   1925
*From the Ziegfeld musical comedy by Guy Bolton
and Jerome Kern*

Sally
MARILYN MILLER.......................Sally
ALEXANDER GRAY...............Blair Farquar
JOE E. BROWN.........Connie (the Grand Duke)
T. ROY BARNES...................Otis Hooper
PERT KELTON.................Rosie, his friend
FORD STERLING...............Pops Shendorff
MAUDE TURNER GORDON....Mrs. Ten Brock
NORA LANE...............Marcia, her daughter
E. J. RATCLIFFE......John Farquar, Blair's father
JACK DUFFY.....................The Old Roué
FIRST NATIONAL   Director: John Francis Dillon   1930
*From the Ziegfeld musical comedy by Guy Bolton
and Jerome Kern*

Sally Bishop
MARIE DORO....................Sally Bishop
HENRY AINLEY....................John Traill
MAIE HANBURY.............Mrs. Durlacher
DALLAS CAIRNS...............Mr. Durlacher
FLORENCE TURNER...................Janet
A. BROMLEY DAVENPORT.......The Landlord
SYDNEY FAIRBROTHER.........The Landlady
STELLA ST. AUDRIE..............Mrs. Bishop
MLLE. VALIA.................Miss Standish Rowe
HUMBERSTON WRIGHT.............The Judge
MARY DIBLEY...................Mrs. Priestley
GEORGE TURNER.....................Arthur
BUNTY FOSSE....................The Child
STOLL   Director: Maurice Elvey   1924
From the novel by E. Temple Thurston

Sally in Our Alley
GRACIE FIELDS...................Sally Winch
IAN HUNTER.......................George Miles
FLORENCE DESMOND............Florrie Small
FRED GROVES.......................Alf Cope
GIBB McLAUGHLIN.................Jim Sears
BEN FIELD.........................Sam Bilson
IVOR BARNARD.....................Tod Small
RENEE MACREADY.................Lady Daphne
BARBARA GOTT....................Mrs. Pool
FLORENCE HARWOOD.............Mrs. Kemp
HELEN FERRERS...........Duchess of Wexford
ARP   Director: Maurice Elvey   1932
From the play " The Likes of 'Er " by Charles McEvoy

Salome
NAZIMOVA...........................Salome
ROSE DIONE.........................Herodias
MITCHELL LEWIS.....................Herod
NIGEL DE BRULIER.................Jokanaan
EARL SCHENCK................Young Syrian
ARTHUR JASMINA.....................A Page
FREDERICK PETERS....Naaman, the executioner
LUIS DUMAR.......................Tigellinus
UA   1923
From the play by Oscar Wilde

San Demetrio, London
On board M.V. " San Demetrio "
WALTER FITZGERALD
                Chief Engineer Charles Pollard
ARTHUR YOUNG.........Captain George Waite

RALPH MICHAEL...........2nd Officer Hawkins
NEVILLE MAPP.............3rd Engineer Willey
BARRY LETTS.............Apprentice John Jones
MICHAEL ALLEN...........Cadet Roy Housden
FREDERICK PIPER........Bo'sun W. E. Fletcher
HERBERT CAMERON.........Pumpman Davies
JOHN OWERS........................Steward
GORDON JACKSON.....Messboy John Jamieson
ROBERT BEATTY.............." Yank " Preston
CHARLES VICTOR   ⎫
JAMES McKECHNIE   ⎪
JOHN COYLE   ⎬.............Deckhands
DUNCAN MacINTYRE   ⎪
REX HOLT   ⎭
MERVYN JOHNS.........Greaser John Boyle
On board H.M.S. " Jervis Bay "
LAWRENCE O'MADDEN
                Captain E. S. F. Fegen, V.C., R.N.
JAMES DONALD........Gunnery Control Officer
JAMES SADLER..........Officer of the Watch
PETER MILLER STREET..........Midshipman
Other Characters
NIGEL CLARKE
            R. J. E. Dodds (shipping manager)
JAMES KNIGHT
            Captain Smith (S.S. " Gloucester City ")
DAVID HORNE.............Mr. Justice Langton
DIANA DECKER.....................Shopgirl
EALING   Director: Charles Frend   1944
*From the official account by F. Tennyson Jesse of the
epic of the tanker " San Demetrio," which, on fire
and crippled after enemy action in the Atlantic, was
brought back to port by the remnant of her crew*

Scaramouche
RAMON NOVARRO........Andre-Louis Moreau
ALICE TERRY..............Aline de Kercadiou
LEWIS STONE.........Marquis de la Tour d'Azyr
LLOYD INGRAHAM........Quintin de Kercadiou
JULIA SWAYNE GORDON
                Countess Thérèse de Plougastel
WILLIAM HUMPHREY...Chevalier de Chabrillane
OTTO MATIESEN............Phillipe de Vilmorin
GEORGE SIEGMANN....Georges Jacques Danton
BOWDITCH TURNER...............Le Chapelier
JAMES MARCUS...............Challfau Binet
EDITH ALLEN.....................Climène Binet
LYDIA YEAMANS TITUS............Mme. Binet
JOHN GEORGE.....................Polichinelle
NELSON McDOWELL..............Rhodomont
DE GARCIA FUERBURG.Maximilien Robespierre
ROY COULSON...............Jean Paul Marat
EDWIN ARGUS.....................Louis XVI
CLOTILDE DELANO..........Marie Antoinette
WILLARD LEE HALL......The King's Lieutenant
NAPOLEON BONAPARTE
                A Lieutenant of Artillery
LORIMER JOHNSTON.........Count Dupuye
EDWARD CONNELLY.....A Minister to the King
HOWARD GAYE...............Viscount d'Albert
J. EDWIN BROWN.................M. Benoit
CARRIE CLARK WARD..........Mme. Benoit
EDWARD COXEN.....................Jacques
METRO-GOLDWYN   Director: Rex Ingram   1924
*From the novel by Rafael Sabatini
Re-issued 1929*

Scarface
PAUL MUNI...................Tony Camonte
ANN DVORAK........................Cesca
KAREN MORLEY.....................Poppy
OSGOOD PERKINS.....................Lovo

BORIS KARLOFF......................Gaffney
C. HENRY GORDON.................Guarino
GEORGE RAFT.......................Rinaldo
PURNELL PRATT.....................Publisher
VINCE BARNETT......................Angelo
INES PALANGE................Mrs. Camonte
HARRY J. VEJAR....................Costillo
EDWIN MAXWELL..........Chief of Detectives
TULLY MARSHALL............Managing Editor
HENRY ARMETTA......................Pietro
HOWARD HUGHES   Director : Howard Hawks   1932

Scarlet Pimpernel, The
LESLIE HOWARD............Sir Percy.Blakeney
MERLE OBERON................Lady Blakeney
RAYMOND MASSEY.................Chauvelin
NIGEL BRUCE.............The Prince of Wales
BRAMWELL FLETCHER..............The Priest
ANTHONY BUSHELL.......Sir Andrew Ffoulkes
JOAN GARDNER...........Suzanne de Tournay
WALTER RILLA.............Armand St. Just
MABEL TERRY-LEWIS......Countess de Tournay
O. B. CLARENCE.........Count de Tournay
ERNEST MILTON..................Robespierre
EDMUND BREON........Colonel Winterbottom
MELVILLE COOPER....................Romney
GIBB McLAUGHLIN................The Barber
MORELAND GRAHAM................Treadle
JOHN TURNBULL.................Jellyband
GERTRUDE MUSGROVE
                Jellyband's daughter, Sally
ALLAN JEAYES.................Lord Grenville
A. BROMLEY DAVENPORT
                French Innkeeper (Brogard)
WILLIAM FRESHMAN............Lord Hastings
HINDLE EDGAR...................Lord Wilmot
LFP   Director : Harold Young   1935
From the novel by Baroness Orczy

School for Danger
CAPTAIN HARRY REE, D.S.O., O.B.E., Croix de
   Guerre, Médaille de Résistance..............Felix
JACQUELINE NEARNE, M.B.E..............Cat
WING COMMANDER EDWARD BAIRD
                Henri Pickard
C.O.I.-R.A.F. FILM UNIT   1947
      Director : Wing Commander Edward Baird
*A documentary film, in which the players were
members of the French Resistance and of the
organization built up in Great Britain to assist
resistance in all Occupied Countries*

School for Secrets
The Boffins
RALPH RICHARDSON.....Professor Heatherville
RAYMOND HUNTLEY....Professor Laxton-Jones
JOHN LAURIE.......................Dr. McVitie
ERNEST JAY........................Dr. Dainty
DAVID TOMLINSON............Mr. Watlington
FINLAY CURRIE.....Sir Duncan Wilson Wills
NORMAN WEBB.................Dr. Wainwright
MICHAEL HORDERN
                Lieutenant Commander Lowther
The Wives
PAMELA MATTHEWS..........Mrs. Watlington
JOAN HAYTHORNE..........Mrs. Laxton-Jones
JOAN YOUNG....................Mrs. McVitie
ANN WILTON....................Mrs. Dainty
The R.A.F.
RICHARD ATTENBOROUGH.......Jack Arnold

DAVID HUTCHESON...Squadron Leader Sowerby
PATRICK WADDINGTON
                Group Captain Aspinall
CYRIL SMITH.............Flight Sergeant Cox
HUGH DEMPSTER......Squadron Leader Slatter
JAMES HAYTER.................Warrant Officer
D. BRADLEY-SMITH.....Air Vice Marshal Cotter
ROBIN BAILEY..................Billeting Officer
KENNETH BUCKLEY...Squadron Leader Buckley
PAUL CARPENTER.....Flight Lieutenant Argylle
ANTHONY DAWSON....Flight Lieutenant Norton
ROBERT LONG.............Flying Officer Davies
RICHARD MANTELL..........Air Vice Marshal
MURRAY MATHESON...Wing Commander Allan
ANTHONY WICKHAM......Flying Officer Ogden

The W.A.A.F.
PEGGY EVANS..................Daphne Adams
INGRID FORREST.........Penelope Birkenshaw
GERALDINE KEYES...........Phyllis Hammond
VIDA HOPE.............W.A.A.F. Flight Sergeant
SONIA ELVERSON.............W.A.A.F. Teller

The Raiding Party
ROBERT WYNDHAM....................Major
ANDREW BLACKETT.................Captain
WILLIAM OWEN.............Paratroop Sergeant
TONY ARPINO...................1st Commando
PETER MARCH..................2nd Commando
BOB ELSON.....................3rd Commando
ROGER KEYES..................4th Commando
TREVENING HILL...............5th Commando
EDWARD HODGE...............6th Commando

The Germans
JOSEPH ALMAS...............Dr. Klemmerhahn
ARTHUR RIECK...........Lieutenant Hense
ERNST URBACH.....................1st Sentry
KARL MOREL......................2nd Sentry

The Civilians
MARJORIE RHODES...............Mrs. Arnold
EDWARD LEXY............Sir Desmond Prosser
HUGH PRYSE.............Sir Nicholas Hathaway
O. B. CLARENCE...................Old Retainer
AUBREY MALLALIEU........1st Club Member
DESMOND ROBERTS.........2nd Club Member
GUY BELMORE...............3rd Club Member
ALVAR LIDDELL.............B.B.C. Announcer
                and
         The Dagenham Girl Pipers
TWO CITIES   Director : Peter Ustinov   1946
*Made with the co-operation of the Air Ministry,
Admiralty, War Office, Technical Research
Department, Malvern College, and R.A.F.
Farnborough*

Sea Beast, The
JOHN BARRYMORE................Ahab Ceeley
DOLORES COSTELLO.............Esther Harper
GEORGE O'HARA................Derek Ceeley
MIKE DONLIN.......................Flask
SAM BAKER.......................Queequeg
GEORGE BURRELL.....................Perth
SAM ALLEN.....................Sea Captain
FRANK NELSON.......................Stubbs
MATHILDE COMONT.....................Mula
JAMES BARROWS.............Rev. Harper
VADIN URANOFF............Pip, the half-wit
SO-JIN..........................Fedallah
FRANK HAGNEY....................Daggoo
WARN   Director : Millard Webb   1926
From the novel " Moby Dick " by Herman Melville

299

JEAN KENT
(*Gainsborough*)

Sea Hawk, The

MILTON SILLS.......{ Sir Oliver Tressilian / Sakr-el-Bahr, the Sea Hawk
ENID BENNETT............Rosamund Godolphin
LLOYD HUGHES........Master Lionel Tressilian
WALLACE MacDONALD.Master Peter Godolphin
MARC MacDERMOTT........Sir John Killigrew
WALLACE BEERY..................Jasper Leigh
FRANK CURRIER..................Asad-ed-Din
MME. MEDEA RADZINA.......Fenzileh, his wife
WILLIAM COLLIER, JR.........Marzak, her son
LIONEL BELMORE.........Justice Anthony Baine
FRED DE SILVA...........Ali, Asad's lieutenant
HECTOR V. SARNO..................Tsamanni
ALBERT PRISCOE.......................Yusuf
GEORGE E. ROMAINE......Spanish Commander
CHRISTINE MONTT.........The Infanta of Spain
EDWARDS DAVIS.......Chief Justice of England
HENRY BARROWS.......................Bishop
Supported by a cast of 3320 performers
FIRST NATIONAL   1925
From the novel by Rafael Sabatini

Sea Hawk, The

ERROL FLYNN.................Geoffrey Thorpe
BRENDA MARSHALL...............Dana Maria
CLAUDE RAINS.........Don Jose de Cordoba
DONALD CRISP..............Sir John Burleson
FLORA ROBSON.........Queen Elizabeth
ALAN HALE.........................Carl Pitt
HENRY DANIELL...........Lord Wolfingham
UNA O'CONNOR..................Miss Latham
JAMES STEPHENSON....................Abbott
GILBERT ROLAND..............Captain Lapez
WILLIAM LUNDIGAN............Danny Logan
JULIEN MITCHELL................Oliver Scott
MONTAGU LOVE..............King Philip II
J. M. KERRIGAN..................Eli Matson
DAVID BRUCE....................Martin Burke
CLIFFORD BROOKE...........William Tuttle
CLYDE COOK..................Walter Boggs
FRITZ LEIBER....................Inquisitor
ELLIS IRVING...................Monty Preston
FRANCIS MacDONALD.................Kroner
PEDRO DE CORDOBA........Captain Mendoza
IAN KEITH.........................Peralta
JACK LA RUE..............Lieutenant Ortega
HALLIWELL HOBBES..............Astronomer
ALEC CRAIG....................Chartmaker
VICTOR VARCONI...........General Aguirre
ROBERT WARWICK.................Frobisher
HARRY CORDING................Slave Master
WARN   Director : Michael Curtiz   1940

Secret Agent

MADELEINE CARROLL..................Elsa
JOHN GIELGUD....................Ashenden
PETER LORRE.................." The General "
ROBERT YOUNG.......................Marvin
PERCY MARMONT....................Caypor
FLORENCE KAHN.................Mrs. Caypor
LILLI PALMER.........................Lilli
CHARLES CARSON...................." R "
GB   Director : Alfred Hitchcock   1936
From the novel " Ashenden " by Somerset Maugham

Sergeant York

GARY COOPER..................Alvin C. York
WALTER BRENNAN..........Pastor Rosier Pile
JOAN LESLIE...............Gracie Williams
GEORGE TOBIAS..............." Pusher " Rose
STANLEY RIDGES................Major Buxton

MARGARET WYCHERLY..........Mother York
WARD BOND.......................Ike Botkin
NOAH BEERY, JR................Buck Lipscomb
JUNE LOCKHART.................Rosie York
DICKIE MOORE.................George York
CLEM BEVANS.......................Zeke
HOWARD DA SILVA.....................Lem
CHARLES TROWBRIDGE...........Cordell Hull
HARVEY STEPHENS..........Captain Danforth
DAVID BRUCE.....................Bert Thomas
CHARLES ESMOND.............German Major
JOSEPH SAWYER................Sergeant Early
PAT FLAHERTY.........Sergeant Harry Parsons
ROBERT PORTERFIELD..........Zeb Andrews
ERVILLE ALDERSON............Nate Tomkins
WARN   Director : Howard Hawks   1942

Service for Ladies

LESLIE HOWARD..................Max Tracey
GEORGE GROSSMITH.........." Mr. Westland "
BENITA HUME................Countess Ricardi
ELIZABETH ALLAN...........Sylvia Robertson
MORTON SELTEN..............Mr. Robertson
CYRIL RITCHARD.................Breslmayer
BEN FIELD....................Sir William Carter
ANNIE ESMOND...................The Duchess
PARA   Director : Alexander Korda   1932

Seven Keys to Baldpate

DOUGLAS MACLEAN...William Hallowell Magee
EDITH ROBERTS..................Mary Norton
ANDERS RANDOLF..........Thomas Norton
CRAUFORD KENT...................Hal Bentley
NED SPARKS.........................Bland
WILLIAM ORLAMOND...........The Hermit
BETTY FRANCISCO..............Chicago Molly
MAYM KELSO..................Mrs. Rhodes
FRED KELSEY..................Chief of Police
PARA   1926
*From the novel by Earl Derr Biggers, and the
comedy by George M. Cohan*

Seven Keys to Baldpate

RICHARD DIX..................William Magee
MIRIAM SEEGAR..................Mary Norton
CRAUFORD KENT...................Hal Bentley
MARGARET LIVINGSTON.......Myra Thornbill
JOSEPH ALLEN......................Peters
LUCIEN LITTLEFIELD..........Thomas Hayden
DEWITT JENNINGS.........Mayor Cargan
CARTLETON MACY.................Kennedy
NELLA WALKER................Mrs. Rhodes
JOE HERBERT.........................Max
ALAN ROSCOE.......................Bland
HARVEY CLARK...............Lija Quimby
EDITH YORKE....................Mrs. Quimby
RADIO   1931
First talkie version of the silent film (above)

Seventh Heaven

JANET GAYNOR........................Diane
CHARLES FARRELL....................Chico
BEN BARD.........................Brissac
DAVID BUTLER.......................Gobin
ALBERT GRAN.........................Boul
GLADYS BROCKWELL...................Nana
EMILE CHAUTARD............Père Chevillon
GEORGE STONE..................Sewer Rat
JESSIE HASLETT................Aunt Valent
LILLIAN WEST....................Arlette
MARIE MOSQUINI.................Mrs. Gobin
FOX   Director : Frank Borzage   1928
From the play by John Golden

301

Seventh Veil, The

JAMES MASON........................Nicholas
ANN TODD..........................Francesca
HERBERT LOM.......................Dr. Larsen
HUGH McDERMOTT................Peter Gay
ALBERT LIEVEN...............Maxwell Leyden
YVONNE OWEN.................Susan Brook
DAVID HORNE....................Dr. Kendal
MANNING WHILEY................Dr. Irving
GRACE ALLARDYCE....................Nurse
ERNEST DAVIES.........................Parker
JOHN SLATER..........................James
ARNOLD GOLDSBOROUGH, MUIR MATHIESON .... Conductors
ORTUS-BOX Director: Compton Bennett 1945

Shadow of a Doubt

TERESA WRIGHT................Young Charlie
JOSEPH COTTEN.................Uncle Charlie
MACDONALD CAREY..............Jack Graham
HENRY TRAVERS...............Joseph Newton
PATRICIA COLLINGE...........Emma Newton
HUME CRONYN................Herbie Hawkins
WALLACE FORD................Fred Saunders
EDNA MAY WONACOTT..........Ann Newton
CHARLES BATES.................Roger Newton
IRVING BACON.................Station Master
CLARENCE MUSE...............Pullman Porter
JANET SHAW..........................Louise
ESTELLE JEWELL.....................Catherine
UNIV Director: Alfred Hitchcock 1943

Sheik, The

AGNES AYRES...................Diano Mayo
RUDOLPH VALENTINO.Sheik Ahmed Ben Hassan
WALTER LONG..........................Omair
ADOLPHE MENJOU.......Raoul de Saint Hubert
LUCIEN LITTLEFIELD....................Gaston
GEORGE WAGGNER....................Youssef
PATSY RUTH MILLER...............Slave Girl
F. R. BUTLER.................Sir Aubrey Mayo
PARA 1923

From the novel by E. M. Hull

Ships with Wings

JOHN CLEMENTS...............Lieutenant Stacey
LESLIE BANKS..........Vice Admiral Weatherby
JANE BAXTER..................Celia Weatherby
ANN TODD.......................Kay Gordon
BASIL SYDNEY.................Captain Fairfax
EDWARD CHAPMAN..............Papadopolos
HUGH WILLIAMS......................Wagner
FRANK PETTINGELL...................Fields
MICHAEL WILDING...........Lieutenant Grant
MICHAEL RENNIE...........Lieutenant Maxwell
CECIL PARKER............German Air Marshal
JOHN STUART...............Commander Hood
FRANK CELLIER..............General Scarappa
MORLAND GRAHAM............C.P.O. Marsden
CHARLES VICTOR...................MacDermot
HUGH BURDEN.......Sub Lieutenant Weatherby
BETTY MARSDEN..........................Jean
GEORGE MERRITT.........Surgeon Commander
JOHN LAURIE.......Lieutenant Commander Reid
CHARLES STUART....................Von Rittau
and
H.M.S. "Ark Royal"
EALING Director: Sergei Nolbandov 1941

This film was inspired by the work of the Air Branch, R.N., and dedicated to H.M.S. "Ark Royal", in which many of the scenes were shot. Production was frequently delayed by naval action—notably the Battle of Matapan.

Shop Around the Corner, The

MARGARET SULLAVAN...........Klara Novak
JAMES STEWART..................Alfred Kralik
FRANK MORGAN..............Hugo Matuschek
JOSEPH SCHILDKRAUT..........Ferencz Vadas
SARA HADEN..............................Flora
FELIX BRESSART.......................Pirovitch
WILLIAM TRACY...................Pepi Katona
INEZ COURTNEY..........................Ilona
SARAH EDWARDS............Woman Customer
EDWIN MAXWELL........................Doctor
CHARLES HALTON....................Detective
CHARLES SMITH..........................Rudy
MGM Director: Ernst Lubitsch 1940

Show Boat

LAURA LA PLANTE..................Magnolia
JOSEPH SCHILDKRAUT................Ravenal
ALMA RUBENS.............................Julie
EMILY FITZROY...............Parthenia Hawks
OTIS HARLAN..............Captain Andy Hawks
ELISE BARTLETT..........................Ellie
JACK MacDONALD..........................Pilot
NEELY EDWARDS.....................Schultzy
JANE LA VERNE.......... Magnolia, as a child; Kim
GERTRUDE HOWARD..................Queenie
RALPH YEARSLEY..................The Killer
GEORGE CHESEBRO......................Steve
HARRY HOLDEN..........................Means
MAX ASHER.........................Utility Man
JIM COLEMAN........................Stagehand
CARL HERLINGER...................Wheelsman
UNIV Director: Harry Pollard 1929

From the story by Edna Ferber

Sign of the Cross, The

FREDRIC MARCH..............Marcus Superbus
ELISSA LANDI...........................Mercia
CLAUDETTE COLBERT.................Poppaea
CHARLES LAUGHTON......................Nero
IAN KEITH............................Tigellinus
VIVIAN TOBIN............................Dacia
HARRY BERESFORD......................Favius
FERDINAND GOTTSCHALK............Glabrio
ARTHUR HOHL............................Titus
JOYZELLE JOYNER.....................Ancaria
TOMMY CONLON....................Stephanus
NAT PENDLETON..........................Strabo
CLARENCE BURTON...................Servilius
PARA Director: Cecil B. DeMille 1932

From the play by Wilson Barrett

Re-issued 1945 *with a modern prologue*:

ARTHUR SHIELDS................James Costello
STANLEY RIDGES.................Thomas Lloyd
JAMES MILLICAN.........Captain Kevin Driscoll
TOM TULLY...........................Hoboken
OLIVER THORNDIKE
Lieutenant Robert Hammond
WILLIAM FORREST........Colonel Hugh Mason

Since You Went Away

CLAUDETTE COLBERT.............Anne Hilton
JENNIFER JONES........Jane, her elder daughter
SHIRLEY TEMPLE
Bridget (Brig), her younger daughter
JOSEPH COTTEN
Lieutenant Anthony Willett, U.S.N.R.
MONTY WOOLLEY.............Colonel Smollett
ROBERT WALKER
Corporal William G. Smollett II, his grandson
LIONEL BARRYMORE...........The Clergyman

HATTIE McDANIEL.....................Sidelia
ALBERT BASSERMAN
        Dr. Sigmund Gottlied Golden
LLOYD CORRIGAN..............Mr. Mahoney
KEENAN WYNN............Lieutenant Solomon
AGNES MOOREHEAD..........Emily Hawkins
GORDON OLIVER..............A Marine Officer
CRAIG STEVENS..............Danny Williams
JACKIE MORAN..............Johnny Mahoney
NAZIMOVA...........Zosia Koslowska (a welder)
GUY MADISON...........Harold Smith (a sailor)
JANE DEVLIN..................Gladys Brown
ANN GILLIS................Becky Anderson
SELZNICK   Director : John Cromwell   1945

Singing Fool, The

AL JOLSON.......................Al
BETTY BRONSON..................Grace
JOSEPHINE DUNN..................Molly
REED HOWES.................John Perry
EDWARD MARTINDEL...............Marcus
ARTHUR HOUSMAN............Blackie Joe
DAVID LEE.....................Sonny Boy
R. E. O'CONNOR.............Cafe Manager
WARN   Director : Lloyd Bacon   1929

Sixty Glorious Years

ANNA NEAGLE.................Queen Victoria
ANTON WALBROOK...............Prince Albert
C. AUBREY SMITH........Duke of Wellington
WALTER RILLA......Prince Ernest of Saxe-Gotha
CHARLES CARSON.............Sir Robert Peel
GRETA WEGNENER............Baroness Lehzen
FELIX AYLMER...............Lord Palmerston
LEWIS CASSON...............Lord John Russell
PAMELA STANDISH.........The Princess Royal
GORDON McLEOD................John Brown
STUART ROBERTSON...............Mr. Anson
OLAF OLSEN...Frederic William, Prince of Prussia
HENRY HALLETT
        The Rt. Hon. Joseph Chamberlain
WYNDHAM GOLDIE..The Rt. Hon. A. J. Balfour
MALCOLM KEEN..The Rt. Hon. W. E. Gladstone
FREDERICK LEISTER
        The Rt. Hon. H. H. Asquith
DERRICK DE MARNEY
        The Rt. Hon. Benjamin Disraeli
MARIE WRIGHT.....................Maggie
JOYCE BLAND............Florence Nightingale
FRANK CELLIER.................Lord Derby
HARDY BRABAN.................Lord Salisbury
AUBREY DEXTER.....H.R.H. the Prince of Wales
LAIDMAN BROWNE...........General Gordon
WILCOX-RKO   Director : Herbert Wilcox   1938

Smilin' Through

NORMA TALMADGE........Kathleen Moonyen
WYNDHAM STANDING..........John Carteret
HARRISON FORD.............{ Kenneth Wayne
                  { Jeremiah Wayne
ALEC B. FRANCIS..................Dr. Owen
GLENN HUNTER..............Willie Ainley
GRACE GRISWALD.....................Ellen
MIRIAM BATTISTA..Little Mary, Moonyen's sister
EUGENE LOCKHART............Village Rector
FIRST NATIONAL   1922

Smilin' Through

JEANETTE MacDONALD.......{ Kathleen
                   { Moonyean Clare
BRIAN AHERNE................Sir John Carteret
GENE RAYMOND.............{ Kenneth Wayne
                 { Jeremy Wayne

IAN HUNTER.................Rev. Owen Harding
FRANCES ROBINSON.....................Ellen
PATRICK O'MOORE.....................Willie
ERIC LONSDALE..............Charles (batman)
JACKIE HORNER..........Kathleen, as a child
DAVID CLYDE.....................Sexton
FRANCES CARSON...................Dowager
RUTH RICKABY........................Woman
MGM   Director : Frank Borzage   1942
Re-issued 1946
In Technicolor

Son of the Sheik

RUDOLPH VALENTINO { Sheik Ahmed Ben Hassan,
                        { Ahmed, his son
VILMA BANKY............Yasmin, a dancing girl
GEORGE FAWCETT.....................André
MONTAGU LOVE......................Ghabah
KARL DANE......................Ramadah
WILLIAM DONOVAN.....................S'rir
AGNES AYRES...........Wife of the Sheik
BULL MONTANA.........................Ali
BYNUNSKY HYMAN..............The Pincher
ERWIN CONNELLY...............The Zouave
CHARLES REQUA.....................Pierre
UA   1926
From the novel " The Sons of the Sheik " by
E. M. Hull

Song of Bernadette, The

JENNIFER JONES...........Bernadette Soubirous
WILLIAM EYTHE...............Antoine Nicolau
CHARLES BICKFORD...............Peyramale
VINCENT PRICE...................Vital Dutour
LEE J. COBB....................Dr. Douzous
GLADYS COOPER...Sister Marie Theresa Vauzous
ANNE REVERE...............Louise Soubirous
ROMAN BOHNEN.............François Soubirous
MARY ANDERSON.............Jeanne Abadie
PATRICIA MORISON.........Empress Eugénie
AUBREY MATHER....................Lacade
CHARLES DINGLE...................Jacomet
EDITH BARRETT..........Croisine Bouhouhorts
SIG RUMAN.................Louis Bouriette
BLANCHE YURKA.......Aunt Bernarde Casterot
ERMADEAN WALTERS.........Marie Soubirous
MARCEL DALIO.....................Callet
PEDRO DE CORDOBA.........Dr. Le Crampe
JEROME COWAN............Emperor Napoleon
CHARLES WALDRON.........Bishop of Tarbes
MORONI OLSEN.....................Chaplain
NANA BRYANT......Convent Mother Superior
MANART KIPPEN..........Charles Bouhouhorts
MERRILL RODIN.............Jean Soubirous
NINO PIPITONE, JR............Justin Soubirous
JOHN MAXWELL HAYES........Father Pomian
JEAN DEL VAL...................Estrade
NESTOR PAIVA......................Baker
TALA BIRELL....................Mme. Bruat
EULA MORGAN.............Mme. Nicolau
ALAN NAPIER...................Psychiatrist
DOROTHY SHEARER...........Mother Superior
FRANK REICHER.................Dr. St. Cyr
CHARLES LA TORRE................Duran
NINO PIPITONE, SR...........Mayor's secretary
EDWIN STANLEY................Mr. Jones
LIONEL BRAHAM...........Baron Massey
IAN WOLFE.........Minister of Interior
ANDRE CHARLOT....................Bishop
20TH-FOX   Director : Henry King   1944
From the book by Franz Werfel

Sorrell and Son

H. B. WARNER	Stephen Sorrell
ANNA Q. NILSSON	Dora Sorrell
NILS ASTHER	Christopher Sorrell
MICKY McBAN	Christopher, as a child
ALICE JOYCE	Fanny Garland
CARMEL MYERS	Florence Palfrey
LOUIS WOLHEIM	Sergeant Major Buck
NORMAN TREVOR	Thomas Roland
PAUL McALLISTER	Dr. Orange
MARY NOLAN	Molly Roland

UA   Director : Herbert Brenon   1928

From the novel by Warwick Deeping

Sorrell and Son

H. B. WARNER	Sorrell
PETER PENROSE	Kit, as a boy
HUGH WILLIAMS	Kit, as a man
WINIFRED SHOTTER	Molly
MARGOT GRAHAME	Dora
DONALD CALTHROP	Dr. Orange
WALLY PATCH	Buck
EVELYN ROBERTS	Roland
HOPE DAVY	Ethel
LOUIS HAYWARD	Duncan
RUBY MILLAR	Mrs. Palfrey

B & D   Director : Herbert Wilcox   1934

H. B. Warner came to Britain to play his original role in the talkie version of Warwick Deeping's novel

Southerner, The

ZACHARY SCOTT	Sam
BETTY FIELD	Nona
BEULAH BONDI	Granny
BUNNY SUNSHINE	Daisy
JAY GILPIN	Jot
PERCY KILBRIDE	Harmie
BLANCHE YURKA	Ma
CHARLES KEMPER	Tim
J. CARROL NAISH	Devers
NORMAN LLOYD	Finlay
JACK NORWORTH	Doctor
NESTOR PAIVA	Bartender
ESTELLE TAYLOR	Lizzie
DOROTHY GRANGER	Party Girl
NOREEN ROTH	Becky

UA   Director : Jean Renoir   1945

Spellbound

INGRID BERGMAN	Dr. Constance Peterson
GREGORY PECK	J.B.
HARRY ACKER	Attendant
DONALD CURTIS	Harry

SELZNICK   Director : Alfred Hitchcock   1945

Spiral Staircase, The

DOROTHY McGUIRE	Helen
GEORGE BRENT	Professor Warren
ETHEL BARRYMORE	Mrs. Warren
KENT SMITH	Dr. Parry
RHONDA FLEMING	Blanche
GORDON OLIVER	Steve Warren
ELSA LANCHESTER	Mrs. Oates
SARA ALLGOOD	Nurse Barker
RHYS WILLIAMS	Mr. Oates
JAMES BELL	Constable

RKO   Director : Robert Siodmak   1946

Based on the novel " Some Must Watch " by Ethel Lina White

Spirit of the People

(*American title : Abe Lincoln in Illinois*)

RAYMOND MASSEY	Abraham Lincoln
GENE LOCKHART	Stephen Douglas
RUTH GORDON	Mary Todd Lincoln
MARY HOWARD	Ann Rutledge
DOROTHY TREE	Elizabeth Edwards
HARVEY STEPHENS	Ninian Edwards
MINOR WATSON	Joshua Speed
ALAN BAXTER	Billy Herndon
HOWARD DA SILVA	Jack Armstrong
ALDRICH BOWKER	Jude Bowling Green
MAURICE MURPHY	John McNeil
LOUIS JEAN HEYDT	Mentor Graham
CLEM BEVANS	Ben Mattling
HARLAN BRIGGS	Denton Offut
ELISABETH RISDON	Sarah Lincoln
CHARLES MIDDLETON	Tom Lincoln
HERBERT RUDLEY	Seth Gale
ROGER IMHOF	Mr. Crimmin
ANDY CLYDE	Stage Driver

RKO   Director : John Cromwell   1940

Based on the play by Robert E. Sherwood

Squibs

BETTY BALFOUR	" Squibs ' Hopkins
FRED GROVES	P.C. Charles Lee
HUGH E. WRIGHT	Sam Hopkins
CRONIN WILSON	Bully Dawson
AMBROSE MANNING	Ex-Inspector Robert Lee
TOM MORRIS	Gus Holly
WILLIAM MATTHEWS	Peters
LESLIE STEWARD	Jim Wall
ANNETTE BENSON	Ivy Hopkins
FAIRY EMLYN	Mrs. Wall
MARY BROUGH	Mrs. Lee

WELSH-PEARSON   1922

Suggested by Clifford Seyler's one act play

Stagecoach

CLAIRE TREVOR	Dallas
JOHN WAYNE	Ringo Kid
ANDY DEVINE	Buck
JOHN CARRADINE	Hatfield
THOMAS MITCHELL	Doc Boone
GEORGE BANCROFT	Curly Wilcox
LOUISE PLATT	Lucy Mallory
DONALD MEEK	Mr. Peacock
BERTON CHURCHILL	Mr. Gatewood
TIM HOLT	Cavalry Lieutenant
CHRIS MARTIN	Chris
ELVIRA RIOS	Yakeema
FRANCIS FORD	Sergeant Billy Pickett
MARGA ANN DAIGHTON	Mrs. Pickett
FLORENCE LAKE	Nancy
WALTER McGRAIL	Captain Sickle
PAUL McVEY	Express Agent
BRENDA FOWLER	Mrs. Gatewood
CHIEF BIG TREE	Indian Scout
YAKIMA CANUTT	Cavalry Scout
CHIEF WHITE HORSE	Indian Leader
BRYANT WASHBURN	Cavalry Captain
DUKE LEE	Lordsburg Sheriff
TOM TYLER	Luke Plummer
JOE RICKSON	Ike Plummer
CORNELIUS KEEFE	Captain Whitney
HARRY TENBROOK	Telegrapher
NORA CECIL	Boone's landlady
JACK PENNOCK	Bartender
LOU MASON	Sheriff

MARY KATHLEEN WALKER
Lucy's baby (2½ days old)
KENT ODELL...................Billy Pickett, Jr.
WILLIAM HOPPER............Cavalry Sergeant
ED BRADY.......................Saloonkeeper
VESTER PEGG..................Hank Plummer
UA   Director: John Ford   1939

Stage Door Canteen
CHERYL WALKER.......................Eileen
WILLIAM TERRY..........." Dakota " Ed. Smith
MARJORIE RIORDAN.....................Jean
LON McCALLISTER................." California "
MARGARET EARLY....................Ella Sue
MICHAEL HARRISON................." Texas "
DOROTHEA KENT.....................Mamie
FRED BRADY......................." Jersey "
MARION SHOCKLEY....................Lillian
PATRICK O'MOORE..............The Australian
with
The Stars of the Stage Door Canteen, and
Six Famous Bands
SOL LESSER   Director: Frank Borzage   1943

Stanley and Livingstone
SPENCER TRACY.............Henry M. Stanley
NANCY KELLY....................Eve Kingsley
RICHARD GREENE..................Gareth Tyce
CEDRIC HARDWICKE.....Dr. David Livingstone
WALTER BRENNAN..................Jeff Slocum
CHARLES COBURN....................Lord Tyce
HENRY HULL........James Gordon Bennett, Jr.
HENRY TRAVERS...............John Kingsley
MILES MANDER..............Sir John Gresham
DAVID TORRENCE................Mr. Cranston
PAUL STANTON...............Captain Webb
HOLMES HERBERT.........Frederick Holcomb
MONTAGUE SHAW...........Sir Oliver French
BRANDON HURST..........Sir Henry Forrester
HASSAN SAID.......................Hassan
PAUL HARVEY.................Colonel Grimes
RUSSELL HICKS ⎫
FRANK DAE   ⎭..........Commissioners
JOSEPH CREHAN....................Morehead
ROBERT MIDDLEMASS.............Carmichael
FRANK JAQUET.......................Senator
CLARENCE DERWENT........Sir Francis Vane
20TH-FOX   Director: Henry King   1939
Re-issued 1947

Stars Look Down, The
MICHAEL REDGRAVE...........David Fenwick
MARGARET LOCKWOOD.........Jenny Sunley
EMLYN WILLIAMS.................Joe Gowlan
NANCY PRICE................Martha Fenwick
EDWARD RIGBY..............Robert Fenwick
ALLAN JEAYES................Richard Barras
CECIL PARKER..........Stanley Millington
LINDEN TRAVERS.........Laura Millington
MILTON ROSMER.........Harry Nugent, M.P.
GEORGE CARNEY........." Slogger " Gowlan
IVOR BARNARD........................Wept
OLGA LINDO...................Mrs. Sunley
DESMOND TESTER.............Hughie Fenwick
DAVID MARKHAM.............Arthur Barras
AUBREY MALLALIEU.................Hudspeth
KYNASTON P. REEVES................Strother
GRAFTON-GRAND NATIONAL   1940
Director: Carol Reed
From the novel by A. J. Cronin

State Fair
JEANNE CRAIN.....................Margy Frake
DANA ANDREWS...................Pat Gilbert
DICK HAYMES.....................Wayne Frake
VIVIAN BLAINE........................Emily
CHARLES WINNINGER.............Abel Frake
FAY BAINTER..................Melissa Frake
DONALD MEEK...................Hippenstahl
FRANK McHUGH.......................McGee
PERCY KILBRIDE.....................Miller
HENRY MORGAN.....................Barker
JANE NIGH.........................Eleanor
WILLIAM MARSHALL...................Marty
PHIL BROWN.....................Harry Ware
JOSEPHINE WITTELL............Mrs. Metcalfe
20TH-FOX   Director: Walter Lang   1945
In Technicolor

Stella Dallas
RONALD COLMAN.,.........Stephen Dallas
BELLE BENNETT...................Stella Dallas
ALICE JOYCE...................Helen Morrison
JEAN HERSHOLT.....................Ed. Munn
LOIS MORAN.....................Laurel Dallas
DOUGLAS FAIRBANKS, JR....Richard Grosvenor
VERA LEWIS........................Miss Tibbits
BEATRIX PRYOR.............Mrs. Grosvenor
MAURICE MURPHY ⎫
JACK MURPHY   ⎬....Sons of Helen Morrison,
NEWTON HALL   ⎭   as children
CHARLES HATTEN ⎫
ROBERT GILLETTE ⎬....Sons of Helen Morrison,
WINSTON MILLER ⎭   ten years later
UA   Director: Henry King   1926

Story of Louis Pasteur, The
PAUL MUNI.......................Louis Pasteur
JOSEPHINE HUTCHINSON.......Marie Pasteur
ANITA LOUISE...................Annette Pasteur
DONALD WOODS..............Dr. Jean Martel
FRITZ LEIBER...................Dr. Charbonnet
HENRY O'NEILL.................Dr. Emile Roux
PORTER HALL..................Dr. Rossignol
RAYMOND BROWN................Dr. Radisse
AKIM TAMIROFF.................Dr. Zaranoff
HALLIWELL HOBBES.............Dr. Lister
FRANK REICHER..................Dr. Pfeiffer
DICKIE MOORE...............Joseph Meister
RUTH ROBINSON..................Mrs. Meister
WALTER KINGSFORD.................Emperor
HERBERT CORTHELL..........President Thiers
IPHIGENIE CASTIGLIONI...............Empress
WARN   Director: William Dieterle   1936

Strange Incident
(American title: The Ox-Bow Incident)
HENRY FONDA.......................Gil Carter
DANA ANDREWS........................Martin
MARY BETH HUGHES.............Rose Mapen
ANTHONY QUINN......................Mexican
WILLIAM EYTHE.......................Gerald
HENRY MORGAN....................Art Croft
JANE DARWELL....................Ma Grier
MATT BRIGGS...........Judge Daniel Tyler
HARRY DAVENPORT............Arthur Davies
FRANK CONROY.............Major Tetley
MARC LAWRENCE....................Farnley
PAUL HURST....................Monty Smith
VICTOR KILIAN........................Darby
CHRIS-PIN MARTIN....................Pancho
TED NORTH..........................Joyce

305

CORNEL WILDE
(*20th Century-Fox*)

GEORGE MEEKER..................Mr. Swanson
ALMIRA SESSIONS.............Miss Swanson
MARGARET HAMILTON............Mrs. Larch
DICK RICH.............................Mapes
FRANCIS FORD.....................Old Man
STANLEY ANDREWS..................Bartlett
BILLY BENEDICT.....................Greene
RONDO HATTON..................Gabe Hart
PAUL BURNS........................Winder
LEIGH WHIPPER.......................Sparks
GEORGE CHANDLER.,.........Jimmy Carnes
GEORGE LLOYD......................Moore
20TH-FOX   Director : William A. Wellman 1943
*From the novel " The Ox-Bow Incident " by
Walter Van Tilburg Clark
First shown in Britain 1945*

Student Prince, The
RAMON NOVARRO........Prince Karl Heinrich
NORMA SHEARER......................Kathi
JEAN HERSHOLT.................Dr. Juttner
GUSTAVE VON SEYFFERTITZ....King Karl VII
PHILLIPE DE LACY..............Heir Apparent
EDGAR NORTON........................Lutz
BOBBY MACK.....................Kellermann
EDWARD CONNELLY..........Court Marshal
OTIS HARLAN......................Old Ruder
JOHN S. PETERS.....................Student
MGM   Director : Ernst Lubitsch   1927
*From the play by W. Meyer-Foerste, and the operetta
by Dorothy Donnelly and Sigmund Romberg*

Sullivan's Travels
JOEL McCREA.................John L. Sullivan
VERONICA LAKE....................The Girl
ROBERT WARWICK...............Mr. LeBrand
WILLIAM DEMAREST..............Mr. Jones
FRANKLIN PANGBORN...........Mr. Casalsis
PORTER HALL....................Mr. Hadrian
BYRON FOULGER.................Mr. Valdelle
MARGARET HAYES...................Secretary
ROBERT GREIG........................Butler
ERIC BLORE...........................Valet
PARA   Director : Preston Sturges   1942

Sunday Dinner for a Soldier
ANNE BAXTER...........................Tessa
JOHN HODIAK.....................Eric Moore
CHARLES WINNINGER...........Grandfather
ANNE REVERE.........................Agatha
CONNIE MARSHALL......................Mary
CHILL WILLS......................Mr. York
ROBERT BAILEY...........Kenneth Normand
BOBBY DRISCOLL........................Jeep
JANE DARWELL..................Mrs. Dobson
BILLY CUMMINGS...................Michael
MARIETTA CANTY..................Samanthy
BARBARA SEARS.............W.A.C. Lieutenant
LARRY THOMPSON⎱
BERNIE SELL   ⎰........Military Policemen
CHESTER CONKLIN..............Photographer
20TH-FOX   Director : Lloyd Bacon   1945
Based on a story by Martha Cheavens

Sunny Side Up
JANET GAYNOR....................Molly Carr
CHARLES FARRELL..............Jack Cromwell
SHARON LYNN.....................Jane Worth
FRANK RICHARDSON...........Eddie Rafferty
EL BRENDEL......................Eric Swenson
MARJORIE WHITE.................Bee Nichols

JOE BROWN...........................Joe Vitto
MARY FORBES.................Mrs. Cromwell
ALAN PAULL..........................Raoul
PETER GAWTHORNE....................Lake
FOX   Director : David Butler   1930

Sunshine Susie
RENATE MULLER.............Sunshine Susie
JACK HULBERT.................Herr Hasel
OWEN NARES...................Herr Arvay
MORRIS HARVEY.....................Klapper
SYBIL GROVE...................The Secretary
GLADYS HAMER......................A Servant
GAINS   Director : Victor Saville   1932
*Adapted from the German musical comedy " The
Private Secretary "*

Suspicion
CARY GRANT.........................Johnnie
JOAN FONTAINE........................Lina
CEDRIC HARDWICKE........General McLaidlaw
NIGEL BRUCE..........................Beaky
DAME MAY WHITTY.........Mrs. McLaidlaw
ISABEL JEANS.................Mrs. Newsham
HEATHER ANGEL.................Ethel (maid)
AURIOL LEE...................Isobel Sedbusk
REGINALD SHEFFIELD.......Reggie Wetherby
LEO G. CARROLL.........Captain Melbeck
RKO   Director : Alfred Hitchcock   1942

Svengali
JOHN BARRYMORE..................Svengali
MARIAN MARSH.......................Trilby
BRAMWELL FLETCHER...........Little Billee
DONALD CRISP....................The Laird
LUMSDEN HARE........................Taffy
CARMEL MYERS.......................Honori
LUIS ALBERNI........................Gecko
FERIKE BOROS........................Marta
ADRIENNE D'AMBRICOURT.....Mme. Vinard
YOLA D'AVRIL..........................Maid
PAUL PORCASI...........Concert Manager
WARN   Director : Archie Mayo   1931
From the novel " Trilby " by George Du Maurier

Symphonie Pastorale, La
MICHÈLE MORGAN..................Gertrude
PIERRE BLANCHAR................The Pastor
LINE NORO..........................Amélie
LOUVIGNY.........................Casteran
JEAN DESAILLY.....................Jacques
ANDRÉE CLÉMENT.....................Piette
ROSINE LUGUET...................Charlotte
FILMS GIBE (France)   Director : Jean Delannoy 1946
From a story by André Gide
(*See Foreign Language Films, page 347*)

T

Tale of Two Cities, A
RONALD COLMAN...............Sydney Carton
ELIZABETH ALLAN..............Lucie Manette
EDNA MAY OLIVER.............Miss Pross
REGINALD OWEN....................Stryver
BASIL RATHBONE.......Marquis St. Évremonde
BLANCHE YURKA...........Mme. De Farge
HENRY B. WALTHALL...........Dr. Manette
DONALD WOODS.............Charles Darnay
WALTER CATLETT.....................Barsad
FRITZ LEIBER.......................Gaspard

H. B. WARNER........................Gabelle
MITCHELL LEWIS...............Ernest De Farge
CLAUDE GILLINGWATER.........Jarvis Lorry
BILLY BEVAN....................Jerry Cruncher
ISABEL JEWELL....................Seamstress
LUCILLE LA VERNE.............The Vengeance
TULLY MARSHALL..................Woodcutter
FAY CHALDECOTT.............Lucie, the child
EILY MALYON..................Mrs. Cruncher
E. E. CLIVE.............Judge in Old Bailey
LAWRENCE GRANT...............Prosecutor
ROBERT WARWICK..........Judge at Tribunal
RALF HAROLDE....................Prosecutor
JOHN DAVIDSON.....................Morveau
TOM RICKETTS...................Tellson, Jr.
DONALD HAINES...:.........Jerry Cruncher, Jr.
BARLOWE BORLAND..............Jacques 116
MGM   Director : Jack Conway   1936
From the novel by Charles Dickens
Re-issued 1947

Tarakanova

PIERRE RICHARD-WILLM........Count Orloff
ANNIE VERNAY.............Princess Tarakanova
SUZY PRIM..................Empress Catherine
ROGER KARL...................Prince Radziwill
ABEL JAQUIN.........................Nikolsk;
RENÉ BERGERON.....................Inquisitor
JANINE MERREY..............Waiting-woman
NERO FILMS (France)   Director : Fédor Ozep   1938
(See Foreign Language Films, page 347)

Tarzan, the Ape Man

JOHNNY WEISSMULLER...............Tarzan
NEIL HAMILTON.........................Holt
MAUREEN O'SULLIVAN..................Jane
C. AUBREY SMITH................Mr. Porter
DORIS LLOYD....................Mrs. Cutten
FORRESTER HARVEY................Beamish
CURTIS NERO.........................Riano
MGM   Director : W. S. Van Dyke   1932
From the novel by Edgar Rice Burroughs
In this film Johnny Weissmuller made his debut as
Tarzan
(See Film Series, page 321)

Tell England

CARL HARBORD....................Edgar Doe
TONY BRUCE.....................Rupert Ray
DENNIS HOEY......................The Padre
C. M. HALLARD.................The Colonel
FREDERICK LLOYD.............Captain Hardy
GERALD RAWLINSON........Lieutenant Doon
LIONEL HEDGES.................Private Sims
SAM WILKINSON................Private Booth
WALLY PATCH.............Sergeant Instructor
HUBERT HARBEN....................Mr. Ray
FAY COMPTON....................Mrs. Doe
BIF   Directors :   1931
Anthony Asquith and Geoffrey Barkas
From the book by Ernest Raymond
This film took more than a year to make, and had
a cast of 8000.   The Gallipoli landing scenes were
filmed at Malta, where the naval scenes were also
taken with the help of the Mediterranean Fleet.

Tess of the D'Urbervilles

BLANCHE SWEET........................Tess
CONRAD NAGEL..................Angel Clare
STUART HOLMES.........Alec d'Urberville
GEORGE FAWCETT..........John Durbeyfield

VICTORY BATEMAN............Joan Durbeyfield
COURTENAY FOOTE.....................Dick
JOSEPH J. DOWLING................The Priest
METRO-GOLDWYN   1925
From the novel by Thomas Hardy

Tess of the Storm Country

MARY PICKFORD.............Tessibel Skinner
LLOYD HUGHES................Frederick Graves
GLORIA HOPE...................Teola Graves
DAVID TORRENCE................Elias Graves
FORREST ROBINSON.......,....Daddy Skinner
JEAN HERSHOLT....................Don Lotta
DANNY HOY...................Ezra Longman
ROBERT RUSSELL................Dan Jordan
GUS SAVILLE...............Old Man Longman
MME. DE BODAMERE............Mrs. Longman
UA   1923

They Were Sisters

PHYLLIS CALVERT........................Lucy
JAMES MASON......................Geoffrey
HUGH SINCLAIR........................Terry
ANNE CRAWFORD.......................Vera
PETER MURRAY-HILL................William
DULCIE GRAY....................Charlotte
BARRIE LIVESEY......................Brian
PAMELA KELLINO..................Margaret
ANN STEPHENS......................Judith
HELEN STEPHENS....................Sarah
JOHN GILPIN......................Stephen
BRIAN NISSEN.........................John
DAVID HORNE....................Mr. Field
BREFNI O'RORKE..................Coroner
ROLAND PERTWEE.'.......Sir Hamish Nair
AMY VENESS....................Mrs. Purley
THORLEY WALTERS.................Channing
JOSS AMBLER....................Blakemore
ROY RUSSELL....................Lethbridge
EDIE MARTIN.........................Cook
DORA SEVENING.....................Janet
HELEN GOSS........................Webster
GAINS   Director : Arthur Crabtree   1945

Thief of Bagdad, The

DOUGLAS FAIRBANKS, SR...The Thief of Bagdad
SNITZ EDWARDS..............His Evil Associate
CHARLES BELCHER.............The Holy Man
JULANNE JOHNSTON............The Princess
ANNA MAY WONG...........The Mongol Slave
WINTER-BLOSSOM.....The Slave of the Lute
BRANDON HURST...................The Caliph
TOTO DU CROW..............His Soothsayer
SO-JIN...................The Mongol Prince
K. NAMBU...................His Counsellor
SADAKICHI HARTMANN....His Court Magician
NOBLE JOHNSON.........The Indian Prince
M. COMONT.................The Persian Prince
CHARLES STEVENS.................His Awaker
SAM BAKER......................The Sworder
UA   Director : Raoul Walsh   1925

Thief of Bagdad, The

CONRAD VEIDT........................Jaffar
SABU................................Abu
JUNE DUPREZ....................Princess
JOHN JUSTIN........................Ahmad
REX INGRAM.........................Djinni
MILES MALLESON.....................Sultan
MORTON SELTEN.................The Old King

MAY MORRIS..........................Halima
BRUCE WINSTON................The Merchant
HAY PETRIE...........................Astrologer
ADELAIDE HALL... ....Singer
ROY MERTON...........................Jailer
ALLAN JEAYES.................The Storyteller
ALEXANDER KORDA   1940
Directors : Ludwig Berger and Michael Powell
In Technicolor

*Begun at Denham Studios, England, in 1939, this
was completed in Hollywood. " Old Bagdad "
was reconstructed in a suitable spot in the Mohave
Desert, as the original plan to take the unit to the
area of Bagdad itself was forestalled by the outbreak of war. Conrad Veidt never returned, and
died in Hollywood in 1943. Sabu remained,
became a U.S. citizen, and served in the U.S. Air
Corps.*

Things to Come
RAYMOND MASSEY.............(John Cabal
                            (Oswald Cabal
EDWARD CHAPMAN.....(Pipper Passworthy
                    (Raymond Passworthy
RALPH RICHARDSON.................The Boss
MARGARETTA SCOTT................(Roxana
                                (Rowena
CEDRIC HARDWICKE...........Theotocopulos
MAURICE BRADDELL..............Dr. Harding
SOPHIE STEWART................Mrs. Cabal
DERRICK DE MARNEY........Richard Gordon
ANN TODD.....................Mary Gordon
PEARL ARGYLE................Katherine Cabal
KENNETH VILLIERS.......Maurice Passworthy
IVAN BRANDT...................Modern Mitani
ANNE McLAREN..................The Child
JOHN CLEMENTS................The Airman
LFP   Director : William Cameron Menzies 1936
*Adapted for the screen by H. G. Wells from his
novel " The Shape of Things to Come "*

39 Steps, The
ROBERT DONAT................Richard Hannay
MADELEINE CARROLL...............Pamela
LUCIE MANNHEIM..................Miss Smith
GODFREY TEARLE.........Professor Jordan
PEGGY ASHCROFT..............Crofter's wife
JOHN LAURIE.........................Crofter
HELEN HAYE.....................Mrs. Jordan
FRANK CELLIER...................The Sheriff
WYLIE WATSON.....................Memory
GB   Director : Alfred Hitchcock   1935
From the novel by John Buchan

This Happy Breed
ROBERT NEWTON............ ...Frank Gibbons
CELIA JOHNSON.................Ethel Gibbons
JOHN MILLS..................Billy Mitchell
KAY WALSH................Queenie Gibbons
STANLEY HOLLOWAY..........Bob Mitchell
AMY VENESS.....................Mrs. Flint
ALISON LEGGATT................Aunt Sylvia
EILEEN ERSKINE..........................Vi
JOHN BLYTHE...........................Reg
GUY VERNEY................. ...Sam Leadbitter
MERLE TOTTENHAM.....................Edie
BETTY FLEETWOOD...................Phyllis
CINEGUILD   Director : David Lean   1944
*From the play by Noel Coward
In Technicolor*

This Is the Army
GEORGE MURPHY..................Jerry Jones
JOAN LESLIE......................Eileen Dibble
GEORGE TOBIAS..............Maxie Twardofsky
ALAN HALE...............Sergeant McGhee
CHARLES BUTTERWORTH........Eddie Dibble
DOLORES COSTELLO.............Mrs. Davidson
UNA MERKEL.......................Rose Dibble
STANLEY RIDGES...............Major Davidson
ROSEMARY DE CAMP..................Ethel
RUTH DONNELLY................Mrs. O'Brien
DOROTHY PETERSON.............Mrs. Nelson
FRANCES LANGFORD............Café Singer
GERTRUDE NIESEN....................Singer
KATE SMITH.....................Kate Smith
ILKA GRUNING................Mrs. Twardofsky
CAPTAIN RONALD REAGAN.......Johnny Jones
SERGEANT JOE LOUIS..................Joe Louis
T/SERGEANT TOM D'ANDREA...........Tommy
SERGEANT JULIE OSHINS........Ollie Twardofsky
SERGEANT ROBERT SHANLEY.......Ted Nelson
CORPORAL HERBERT ANDERSON.Danny Davidson
WARN   Director : Michael Curtiz   1944
Based on the Irving Berlin stage show

Three Musketeers, The
DOUGLAS FAIRBANKS, SR..........D'Artagnan
LEON BARRY........) The   (......Athos
GEORGE SEIGMANN.) Three (....Porthos
EUGENE PALLETTE..) Musketeers (.....Aramis
BOYD IRWIN. De Rochefort, the Cardinal's henchman
THOMAS HOLDING
               George Villiers, Duke of Buckingham
SIDNEY FRANKLIN.................Bonacieux
CHARLES BELCHER...............Bernajoux
CHARLES STEVENS .Planchet, D'Artagnan's lackey
NIGEL DE BRULIER..........Cardinal Richelieu
WILLIS ROBARDS.............Captain de Tréville
LON POFF......................Father Joseph
MARY MACLAREN...The Queen, Anne of Austria
MARGUERITE DE LA MOTTE
                          Constance Bonacieux
BARBARA LA MARR.........Milady de Winter
WALT WHITMAN...........D'Artagnan's father
ADOLPHE MENJOU...Louis XIII, King of France
UA   Director : Fred Niblo   1922
From the novel by Dumas

Three Musketeers, The
M. AIMÉ SIMON-GIRAUD...........D'Artagnan
M. HENRI ROLLAN..) The   (......Athos
M. MARTINELLI.....) Three (......Porthos
M. P. DE GUINGAND) Musketeers (.....Aramis
MLLE. PIERRETTE MADD...Constance Bonacieux
M. DESJARDINS.....................De Tréville
M. JOFFRE.......................Bonacieux
M. GASTON JACQUET.................De Winter
M. CHARLES DULLIN.............Father Joseph
M. PAUL HUBERT....................Felton
M. ARMAND-BERNARD.................Planchet
M. MARCEL VALLÉE...............Mousqueton
M. CHARLIER...............D'Artagnan's father
MLLE. ALTEM....................Doña Estefania
M. DE MAX.................Cardinal Richelieu
M. RIEFFLER.......................Louis XIII
MLLE. C. MERELLI...........Milady de Winter
M. HENRI BAUDIN.................De Rochefort
MLLE. JEANNE DESCLOS...............The Queen
MME. JOFFRE..................Mother Superior
GAUMONT (France) *From the novel by Dumas* 1922
(See Foreign Language Films, page 347)

Three Musketeers, The

WALTER ABEL	D'Artagnan
PAUL LUKAS	Athos
MARGOT GRAHAME	Milady de Winter
HEATHER ANGEL	Constance
IAN KEITH	De Rochefort
MORONI OLSEN	Porthos
ONSLOW STEVENS	Aramis
ROSAMUND PINCHOT	Queen Anne
JOHN QUALEN	Planchet
RALPH FORBES	Duke of Buckingham
MURRAY KINNELL	Bernajou
LUMSDEN HARE	De Tréville
MILES MANDER	King Louis XIII
NIGEL DE BRULIER	Cardinal Richelieu
WADE BOTELER	Peylerand
STANLEY BLYSTONE	Villand
RALPH FAULKNER	Jussac

RKO   *From the novel by Dumas*   1935

Three Musketeers, The

DON AMECHE	D'Artagnan
RITZ BROTHERS	Three Lackeys
BINNIE BARNES	Milady de Winter
LIONEL ATWILL	De Rochefort
GLORIA STUART	Queen
PAULINE MOORE	Lady Constance
JOSEPH SCHILDKRAUT	King
JOHN CARRADINE	Naveau
MILES MANDER	Cardinal Richelieu
DOUGLASS DUMBRILLE	Athos
JOHN KING	Aramis
RUSSELL HICKS	Porthos
GREGORY GAYE	Vitroy
LESTER MATTHEWS	Duke of Buckingham
EGON BRECHER	Landlord
MORONI OLSEN	Bailiff
GEORGES RENAVENT	Captain Fageon
MONTAGUE SHAW	Ship Captain
JEAN PARRY	} Guards
FREDRIK VOGEDING	

20TH-FOX   Director: Allan Dwan   1939
From the novel by Dumas
Re-issued 1944 as " The Singing Musketeer "

Through the Back Door

MARY PICKFORD	Jeanne Bodamere
GERTRUDE ASTOR	Hortense Reeves
WILFRED LUCAS	Elton Reeves
HELEN RAYMOND	Marie
C. NORMAN HAMMOND	Jacques Lanvain
ELINOR FAIR	Margaret Brewster
ADOLPHE MENJOU	James Brewster
PEACHES JACKSON	Conrad
DOREEN TURNER	Constant
JOHN HARRON	Billy Boy
GEORGE DROMGOLD	Chauffeur

UA   1922

Thunder Rock

MICHAEL REDGRAVE	David Charleston
BARBARA MULLEN	Ellen Kirby
JAMES MASON	Streeter
LILLI PALMER	Melanie
FINLAY CURRIE	Captain Joshua
FREDERICK VALK	Dr. Kurtz
SYBILLA BINDER	Anne Marie
FREDERICK COOPER	Briggs
JEAN SHEPEARD	Mrs. Briggs
BARRY MORSE	Robert
GEORGE CARNEY	Harry
MILES MALLESON	Chairman of Directors

BRYAN HERBERT	Flanning
JAMES PIRRIE	New Pilot
A. E. MATTHEWS	Mr. Kirby
OLIVE SLOANE	Woman Director
TOMMY DUGGAN	} Office Clerks
TONY QUINN	
HAROLD ANSTRUTHER	British Consul
ALFRED SANGSTER	Director

CHARTER   Director: Roy Boulting   1943
Re-issued 1947

Tilly of Bloomsbury

EDNA BEST	Tilly
TOM REYNOLDS	Samuel Stillbottle
CAMPBELL GULLAN	Percy
VERA LENNOX	Amelia
LEONARD PAGDEN	Lucius Welwyn
GEORGETTE ESMOND	Martha, his wife
HELEN HAYE	Lady Adela Mainwaring
FRED LEWIS	Abel Mainwaring
HENRY KENDALL	Richard
ISABEL JEANS	Sylvia
LOTTIE BLACKFORD	Mrs. Banks

SAMUELSON   1922
From the play of the same name, and the novel
" Happy Go Lucky " by Ian Hay

To Be or Not To Be

CAROLE LOMBARD	Maria Tura
JACK BENNY	Joseph Tura
ROBERT STACK	Lieutenant Stanislav Sobinski
FELIX BRESSART	Greenberg
LIONEL ATWILL	Rawitch
STANLEY RIDGES	Professor Siletsky
SIG RUMAN	Colonel Ehrhardt
TOM DUGAN	Bronski
CHARLES HALTON	Producer Dobosh
GEORGE LYNN	Actor-Adjutant

KORDA-HOLLYWOOD   1942
Director: Ernst Lubitsch

Tol'able David

RICHARD BARTHELMESS	David Kinemon
WARNER RICHMOND	Allan Kinemon
EDMUND GURNEY	Hunter Kinemon
LAWRENCE EDDINGER	Senator Gault
FORREST ROBINSON	Grandpa Hatburn
ERNEST TORRENCE	Luke Hatburn
WALTER P. LEWIS	Iscah Hatburn
RALPH YEARSLEY	Saul Hatburn
HARRY HALLAM	The Doctor
MARION ABBOTT	Mother Kinemon
PATTERSON DIAL	Rose Kinemon
GLADYS HULETTE	Esther Hatburn
LASSIE	Racket

INSPIRATION   Director: Henry King   1923
From the short story by Joseph Hergesheimer

Tol'able David

RICHARD CROMWELL	David Kinemon
NOAH BEERY	Luke
JOAN PEERS	Esther Hatburn
GEORGE DRUYEA	Alan Kinemon
HENRY B. WALTHALL	Amos Hatburn
EDMUND BREESE	Hunter Kinemon
BARBARA BEDFORD	Rose Kinemon
HELEN WARE	Mrs. Kinemon
HARLON E. KNIGHT	Iska
PETER RICHMOND	Buzzard
JAMES BRADBURY, SR.	Galt
RICHARD CARLYLE	Doctor

UA   Director: John Blystone   1931
Sound version of the film of 1923

Tom Brown's School Days

CEDRIC HARDWICKE	Dr. Arnold
FREDDIE BARTHOLOMEW	East
JIMMY LYDON	Tom Brown
JOSEPHINE HUTCHINSON	Mrs. Arnold
BILLY HALOP	Flashman
POLLY MORAN	Sally
HUGHIE GREEN	Walker
ERNEST COSSART	Squire Brown
ALEC CRAIG	Old Thomas
GALE STORM	Effie
BARLOWE BORLAND	Old Grimey
FORRESTER HARVEY	Coachman
LEONARD WILLEY	Farmer Jenkins
IAN FULTON	Old Brooke
CHARLES SMITH	Digges
DICK CHANDLER	Tadpole
PAUL MATTHEWS	Leyton
JOHN COLLUM	Sidney
HARRY DUFF	Westcott

RKO　　Director : Robert Stevenson　　1940
From the novel by Thomas Hughes

Tom Sawyer

JACKIE COOGAN	Tom Sawyer
JUNIOR DURKIN	Huckleberry Finn
MITZI GREEN	Becky Thatcher
LUCIEN LITTLEFIELD	The Teacher
TULLY MARSHALL	Muff Potter
CLARA BLANDICK	Aunt Polly
MARY JANE IRVING	Mary Sawyer
ETHEL WALES	Mrs. Harper
JACKIE SEARL	Sid Sawyer
DICK WINSLOW	Joe Harper
CHARLES STEVENS	Injun Joe
JANE DARWELL	Widow Douglass
CHARLES SELLON	The Minister

PARA　　Director : John Cromwell　　1931
From the story by Mark Twain

Torrent, The

RICARDO CORTEZ	Don Rafael Brull
GRETA GARBO	Leonora Moreno
GERTRUDE OLMSTED	Remedios
EDWARD CONNELLY	Pedro Moreno
LUCY BEAUMONT	Doña Pepa Moreno
LUCIEN LITTLEFIELD	Cupido
MARTHA MATTOX	Doña Bernarda Brull
TULLY MARSHALL	Don Andres

COSMOPOLITAN　　1926

Trader Horn

HARRY CAREY	Trader Horn
EDWINA BOOTH	Nina T
DUNCAN RENALDO	Peru
OLIVE GOLDEN	The Missionary

MGM　　Director : W. S. Van Dyke　　1931
From the book by Aloysius Horn and Ethelreda Lewis
Most of the film was made in the heart of Africa, where more than two years were spent filming jungle scenes and animals.

Tree Grows in Brooklyn, A

DOROTHY McGUIRE	Katie
JOAN BLONDELL	Aunt Sissy
JAMES DUNN	Johnny Nolan
LLOYD NOLAN	McShane
PEGGY ANN GARNER	Francie Nolan
TED DONALDSON	Neeley Nolan
JAMES GLEASON	McGarrity
RUTH NELSON	Miss McDonough
JOHN ALEXANDER	Steve Edwards

B. S. PULLY	Christmas Tree Vendor
FERIKE BOROS	Grandma Rommely
LILIAN BRONSON	Librarian
CHARLES HALTON	Mr. Barker
PETER CUSANELLI	Barber

20TH-FOX　　Director : Elia Kazan　　1945
From the novel by Betty Smith

Trelawney of the Wells

NORMA SHEARER	Rose Trelawney
OWEN MOORE	Tom Wrench
GWEN LEE	Avonia
LEE MORAN	Colpoys
ROY D'ARCY	Gadd
VIRGINIA PEARSON	Mrs. Telfer
WILLIAM HUMPHREY	Mr. Telfer
EFFIE ELLSLER	Mrs. Mossop
RALPH FORBES	Arthur Gower
O. P. HEGGIE	Vice Chancellor Sir William Gower
ANDREE TOURNEUR	Clara Defoenix
CYRIL CHADWICK	Captain Defoenix
MARGARET SEDDON	Miss Trafalgar Gower

MGM　　Director : Sidney Franklin　　1929
From the play by Sir Arthur Wing Pinero

Trial of Mary Dugan, The

NORMA SHEARER	Mary Dugan
LEWIS STONE	Edward West
H. B. WARNER	District Attorney
RAYMOND HACKETT	Jimmy Dugan
LILYAN TASHMAN	Dagmar Lorne
OLIVE TELL	Mrs. Edgar Rice
ADRIENNE D'AMBRICOURT	Marie Ducrot
DeWITT JENNINGS	Police Inspector Hunt
WILFRED NORTH	Judge Nash
LANDERS STEVENS	Dr. Welcome
MARY DORNE	Pauline Agguero
MYRA HAMPTON	May Harris
WESTCOTT CLARK	Police Captain Price
CHARLES MOORE	James Madison
CLAUD ALLISTER	Henry Plaisted

MGM　　Director : Bayard Veiller　　1929
From the play by Bayard Veiller

Trial of Mary Dugan, The

ROBERT YOUNG	Jimmie Blake
LARAINE DAY	Mary Dugan
TOM CONWAY	Edgar Wayne
FRIEDA INESCORT	Gertrude Wayne
JOHN LITEL	Mr. West
MARSHA HUNT	Agatha Hall
MARJORIE MAIN	Mrs. Collins
HENRY O'NEILL	Galwey
SARA HADEN	Miss Matthews
FRANCIS PIERLOT	John Masters
ADDISON RICHARDS	Captain Gregory Price
PIERRE WATKIN	Judge Nash
ALMA KRUGER	Dr. Saunders

MGM　　Director : Norman Z. McLeod　　1941
From the play by Bayard Veiller

Triumph of the Rat, The

IVOR NOVELLO	Pierre Boucheron
ISABEL JEANS	Zélie de Chaumet
NINA VANNA	Comtesse Madeleine de l'Orme
MARIE AULT	Mère Colline
LEWIN MANNERING	Comte Henry Mercereau
MRS. HAYDEN COFFIN	Duchesse de l'Orme
JULIE SUEDO	Mou-Mou
CHARLES DORMER	René Duval
GABRIEL ROSCA	The Apache

GAINS　　Director : Graham Cutts　　1927

Triumph of the Scarlet Pimpernel, The

MATHESON LANG............Sir Percy Blakeney
MARJORIE HUME.............Lady Blakeney
NELSON KEYS....................Robespierre
HADDON MASON.....................Tallien
JULIETTE COMPTON.........Theresia Cabbarus
DOUGLAS PAYNE.....................Rateau
HAROLD HUTH..............Fouquier Tinville
B & D   Director: T. Hayes Hunter   1929
From a story by Baroness Orczy

Turn of the Tide, The

JOHN GARRICK..................Marney Lunn
SAM LIVESEY.....................Henry Lunn
NIALL MACGINNIS................John Lunn
JOAN MAUDE......................Amy Lunn
J. FISHER WHITE..............Isaac Fosdyck
GERALDINE FITZGERALD.......Ruth Fosdyck
WILFRED LAWSON..............Luke Fosdyck
MOORE MARRIOTT............Tindal Fosdyck
BRIT NAT   Director: Norman Walker   1935

*This story of life in a Yorkshire fishing village
was one of the early films produced by J. Arthur
Rank, and won an award at the International Film
Exhibition at Venice*

Turning Point, The

MIKHAIL DERZHAVIN
   Colonel-General Muravyev (Commander in Chief
                 of the Front)
PAVEL ANDRIEVSKY
        Colonel General Vinogradov
A. ABRIKOSOV......Lieutenant General Krivenko
YURI TOLUBEYEV
     Major-General Lavrov (Member of War Council)
ALEXEI ZRAZHEVSKY
    Lieutenant-General Panteleyev (Engineer Corps)
STEPHAN RAKHMANIN
     Major General in charge of reconnaissance
NIKOLAI KORN
     Major General in charge of operations
MARK BERNES..." Minutka ", Commander's driver
VASSILI MAREV..........Lieutenant Feodorov
PAVEL VOLKOV.......................Stepan
LENFILMS (U.S.S.R.) Director: Frederick Ermler 1946
*Produced with the co-operation of the Army Staff
of the Leningrad Front*
(See Foreign Language Films, page 347)

21 Days

VIVIEN LEIGH......................Wanda
LAURENCE OLIVIER...................Larry
LESLIE BANKS.......................Keith
FRANCIS L. SULLIVAN...............Mander
DAVID HORNE.......................Beavis
WILLIAM DEWHURST........Lord Chief Justice
FREDERICK LLOYD...................Swinton
ROBERT NEWTON.....................Tolley
ESME PERCY........................Wallen
ELLIOT MASON.................Frau Grunlick
ARTHUR YOUNG......................Asher
HAY PETRIE.........................Evan
MEINHART MAUR....................Grunlick
MORRIS HARVEY..................Pawnbroker
LAWRENCE HANRAY.................Solicitor
FRED GROVES.......................Barnes
AUBREY MALLALIEU...............Magistrate
LFP   Director: Basil Dean   1940
*Based on the story by John Galsworthy, "The First
and the Last"*
Made in 1937

2000 Women

PHYLLIS CALVERT............Freda Thompson
FLORA ROBSON...............Miss Manningford
PATRICIA ROC...............Rosemary Brown
RENEE HOUSTON................Maud Wright
REGINALD PURDELL..............Alec Harvey
ANNE CRAWFORD.............Margaret Long
JEAN KENT..................Bridie Johnson
JAMES McKECHNIE.............Jimmy Moore
BOB ARDEN..................Dave Kennedy
CARL JAFFE................Sergeant Hentzner
MURIEL AKED................Miss Meredith
KATHLEEN BOUTALL...........Mrs. Hadfield
HILDA CAMPBELL-RUSSELL.Mrs. Hope Latimer
CHRISTINA FORBES............Frau Holweg
THORA HIRD................Mrs. Burtshaw
DULCIE GRAY...............Nellie Skinner
JOAN INGRAM..............Mrs. Tatmarsh
BETTY JARDINE.................Teresa King
CHRISTIANE DE MAURIN.............Annette
GUY LE FEUVRE...................M. Boper
PAUL SHERIDAN................French Officer
GAINS   Director: Frank Launder   1944
*Based on the experience of civilian women interned
in Vittel Camp, France, during World War II*

Two Worlds

Austrian Officers
C. M. HALLARD................The Colonel
GUS SHARLAND....................The Major
JACK TREVOR....................The Captain
JOHN LONGDEN.................The Lieutenant
JOHN ST. JOHN.................The Officer
JOHN HARLOW...................Corporal
JOHN McMAHON..................A Soldier
Russian Officers
GEORGES MAKAROFF..............The Colonel
BORIS RAVENSKY.................The Ensign
ANDREW ENGELMANN.........The Lieutenant
Theatre Players
CONSTANCE CARPENTER...............Mizzi
MEINHARD-JUENGER }........Comedy Singers
TEDDY HILL   }
Jewish People
RANDLE AYRTON.........Simon Goldscheider
NORAH BARING.....................Esther
DONALD CALTHROP..................Mendel
MIRJAM ELIAS.....................Singer
BIP   Director: A. E. Dupont   1931
The first tri-lingual talkie

U

Uncle Tom's Cabin

MARGARITA FISCHER...............Eliza
JAMES B. LOWE.................Uncle Tom
ARTHUR EDMUND CAREWE....George Harris
GEORGE SIEGMANN.............Simon Legree
EULALIE JENSEN...................Cassey
MONA RAY.........................Topsy
VIRGINIA GREY......................Eva
LASSIE LOU AHERN.............Little Harry
LUCIEN LITTLEFIELD..........Lawyer Marks
ADOLPH MILAR..................Mr. Haley
GORDON RUSSELL...................Loker
GERTRUDE HOWARD............Aunt Chloe
JACK MOWER..................Mr. Shelby
VIVIEN OAKLAND..............Mrs. Shelby
JOHN ROCHE...............Augustine St. Clare
AILEEN MANNING............Aunt Ophelia
SEYMOUR "SKIPPER" ZELLIF......Mr. Harris
C. E. ANDERSON..................Johnson
UNIV   Director: Harry Pollard   1928

BARBARA WHITE
(*Associated British Picture Corporation*)

Underworld
(Les Bas Fonds)

JEAN GABIN.........................Pépel
LOUIS JOUVET......................The Baron
SUZY PRIM.........................Vassilissa
VLADIMIR SOKOLOFF................Kosvylev
JUNIE ASTOR.......................Natasha

ALBATROS (France)   Director : Jean Renoir   1937
From the story by Maxim Gorki
(See Foreign Language Films, page 347)

Up in Arms

DANNY KAYE.......................Danny Weems
DINAH SHORE......................Virginia
DANA ANDREWS.....................Joe
CONSTANCE DOWLING.........Mary Morgan
LOUIS CALHERN...........Colonel Ashley
GEORGE MATHEWS..................Blackie
BENNY BAKER......................Butterball
ELISHA COOK, JR....................Info Jones
LYLE TALBOT............Sergeant Gelsey
WALTER CATLETT.........Major Brock
GEORGE MEEKER)
RICHARD POWERS) ....Ashley's aides
MARGARET DUMONT.........Mrs. Willoughby
DONALD DICKSON...........Singer at dock
CHARLES ARNT.............Mr. Higginbotham
CHARLES HALTON..........Dr. Freyheisen
TOM DUGAN........................Pitchman
SIG ARNO.........................Waiter
HARRY HAYDEN.............Dr. Weavermacher
CHARLES D. BROWN..........Mr. Campbell
MAURICE CASS.....................Dr. Jones
FRED ESSLER.....................Headwaiter
RUDOLF FRIML, JR................Band Leader
and
The Goldwyn Girls

RKO   Director : Elliott Nugent   1944
In Technicolor

V

Vanity Fair

MABEL BALLIN..................Rebecca Sharp
HOBART BOSWORTH..............Lord Steyne
GEORGE WALSH..............Rawdon Crawley
EARLE FOXE............Captain William Dobbin
HARRISON FORD...............George Osborne
ELEANOR BOARDMAN..........Amelia Sedley
WILLARD LOUIS.............Joseph Sedley
LAURA LA VARNIE...........Miss Crawley
WILLIAM HUMPHREYS.........Mr. Sedley
ROBERT MACK...........Sir Pitt Crawley
TEMPE PIGOTT.............Mrs. Sedley
JAMES MARCUS.............Old Osborne
DORCAS MATTHEWS.............Lady Jane
EUGENE ACKER.....................Max
EDDIE JONES......................Fritz
ROSE GORE...............Jemima Pinkerton
MRS. A. NEWTON...........Miss Pinkerton
LAURA POLLARD..............Mrs. Tinker
SADIE GORDON...............Miss Firkins
GEORGIA SHERART..........Miss Briggs
PAT CALHOUN..................Mr. Quill
LEO WHITE........................Isadore
B. HYMAN.......................Mr. Moss
OTTO LEDERER..................Mr. Bloom
FRANK HAYES..................Mr. Wenham
JOHN McKINNON..........Captain Macmurdo
LES BATES.......................Mr. Sharp

KATHLEEN CHAMBERS............Mrs. Sharp
OTTO MATIESEN....................Napoleon
HUGO BALLIN   1923
From the novel by W. M. Thackeray
See also " Becky Sharp " the first full-length
Technicolor film, 1935

Victoria the Great

ANNA NEAGLE.................Queen Victoria
ANTON WALBROOK.........The Prince Consort
WALTER RILLA..................Prince Ernest
MARY MORRIS..............Duchess of Kent
H. B. WARNER..............Lord Melbourne
GRETA WEGNENER...........Baroness Lehzen
C. V. FRANCE.........Archbishop of Canterbury
CHARLES CARSON.............Sir Robert Peel
HUBERT HARBEN...........Lord Conyngham
FELIX AYLMER...................Palmerston
ARTHUR YOUNG...................Gladstone
DERRICK DE MARNEY........Disraeli (young)
HUGH MILLAR...............Disraeli (old)
PAUL LEYSSAK.....................Stockmar
PERCY PARSONS..........President Lincoln
LEWIS CASSON
Archbishop of Canterbury (Jubilee)
HENRY HALLETT..........Joseph Chamberlain
GORDON McLEOD................John Brown
WYNDHAM GOLDIE............Cecil Rhodes
TOM HESSLEWOOD...........Sir Francis Grant
MILES MALLESON.................Physician
WILCOX-RKO   Director : Herbert Wilcox   1937

Virtuous Isidore, The

FERNANDEL........................Isidore
FRANÇOISE ROSAY..............Mme. Husson
COLLETTE DARFEUIL.............Her maid
MARCEL SIMON...................The Mayor
MARCEL CARPENTIER..........Chief Fireman
MADY BERRY......................A Gossip
SIMONE BOURLAY............Isidore's mother
MARGUERITE PIERRY..........The Courtesan
FILMS ORMUZD (France)   1933
Director : Bernard Deschamps
From the story " Le Rosier de Madame Husson "
by Guy de Maupassant
(See Foreign Language Films, page 347)

Vortex, The

IVOR NOVELLO..........Nicky Lancaster
WILLETTE KERSHAW
Florence Lancaster, his mother
SIMEON STUART...... David Lancaster, his father
FRANCES DOBLE..........Bunty Mainwaring
ALAN HOLLIS.................Tom Veryan
KINSEY PEILE..........Pauncefort Quentin
JULIE SUEDO...................The Dancer
DOROTHY FANE...........Helen Saville
GAINS   1928
From the play by Noel Coward

W

Wake Island

BRIAN DONLEVY.................Major Caton
ROBERT PRESTON..................Joe Doyle
MACDONALD CAREY. Lieutenant Bruce Cameron
ALBERT DEKKER..............Shad McCloskey
BARBARA BRITTON..........Sally Cameron
WILLIAM BENDIX.........." Smacksie " Randall
MIKHAIL RASUMNY..........Ivan Probenski
WALTER ABEL............Commander Reynolds
DAMIAN O'FLYNN..........Captain Patrick

BILL GOODWIN.................Sergeant Higbee
PHILLIP TERRY.................Private Warren
DON CASTLE.................Private Bill Cunkel
ROD CAMERON..................Captain Lewis
FRANK ALBERTSON.............Johnny Rudd
PARA   Director : John Farrow   1943
Produced with the co-operation of the U.S.
Marine Corps

Waltz Dream, The
JACOB TIEDKE
        Eberhard XXIII, Duke of Flausenburg
MADY CHRISTIANS....Princess Alix, his daughter
CARL BECKERSACHE
        Peter Ferdinand, Archduke of Austria
WILLY FRITSCH
        Lieutenant Nicholas, his aide-de-camp
JULIUS FALKENSTEIN
        Count Rockoff, Lord Chamberlain of Flausenburg
MATHILDE SUSSIN
        Countess Cockeritz, maid-of-honour to the Princess
XENIA DESNI
        Franzi, conductor of a Viennese ladies' orchestra
UFA (Germany)   Director : Ludwig Berger   1926
From the opera by Oscar Straus
(See Foreign Language Films, page 347)

Wandering Jew, The
MATHESON LANG...................Matathias
HUTIN BRITTON.........................Judith
WINIFRED IZARD........................Rachel
FLORENCE SAUNDERS....................Joanne
HUBERT CARTER...................The Ruler
LIONEL D'ARAGON..................Raymond
MALVINA LONGFELLOW..............Gianella
SHAYLE GARDNER.....................Pietro
LEWIS GILBERT.........................Mario
ISOBEL ELSOM..........................Olalla
GORDON HOPKIRK..............Olalla's lover
HECTOR ABBAS......................Zapportas
LOUISE CONTI..........................Maria
FRED RAYNHAM...........Grand Inquisitor
JERROLD ROBERTSHAW...............Texada
STOLL   1923
From the play by E. Temple Thurston

Wandering Jew, The
CONRAD VEIDT.......... { The Wandering Jew / The Unknown Knight / Matteos Dattadios
MARIE NEY...........................Judith
CICELY OATES........................Rachael
BASIL GILL.....................Pontius Pilate
ANNE GREY........Jeanne de Beaudricourt
BERTRAM WALLIS....................Boemund
HECTOR ABBAS......................Issachar
DENNIS HOEY.................De Beaudricourt
JACK LIVESEY........................Godfrey
TAKASE..............................Phirous
JOAN MAUDE........................Gianella
JOHN STUART................Pietro Morelli
ARNOLD LUCY...............Andrea Michalotti
PEGGY ASHCROFT............Olalla Quintana
FRANCIS L. SULLIVAN.........Juan de Texeda
FELIX AYLMER.........................Ferera
IVOR BARNARD.........................Castro
ABRAHAM SOFAER...................Zapportas
STAFFORD HILLIARD.....................Juan
ROBERT GILBERT.....................1st Monk
CONWAY DIXON......................2nd Monk
GB   Director : Maurice Elvey   1933
From the play by E. Temple Thurston

War Against Mrs. Hadley, The
EDWARD ARNOLD................Elliott Fulton
FAY BAINTER...................Stella Hadley
RICHARD NEY...............Theodore Hadley
JEAN ROGERS..................Patricia Hadley
SARA ALLGOOD........Mrs. Michael Fitzpatrick
SPRING BYINGTON..............Cecelia Talbot
VAN JOHNSON...............Michael Fitzpatrick
ISOBEL ELSOM..............Mrs. Laura Winters
FRANCES RAFFERTY.....................Sally
DOROTHY MORRIS.......................Millie
HALLIWELL HOBBES...................Bennett
CONNIE GILCHRIST......................Cook
HORACE McNALLY......................Peters
MILES MANDER........Dr. Leonard V. Meecham
"RAGS" RAGLAND....................Louie
MARK DANIELS..........................Bob
CARL SWITZER.................Messenger Boy
MGM   Director : Harold S. Bucquet   1942

Waterloo Bridge
MAE CLARKE...........................Myra
KENT DOUGLASS..........................Roy
DORIS LLOYD...........................Kitty
FREDERICK KERR...........Major Wetherby
ENID BENNETT..................Mrs. Wetherby
ETHEL GRIFFIES..................Mrs. Hobley
RITA CARLISLE...................The Cockney
UNIV   Director : James Whale   1932
Based on the play by Robert E. Sherwood

Waterloo Bridge
VIVIEN LEIGH..........................Myra
ROBERT TAYLOR...................Roy Cronin
LUCILE WATSON.........Lady Margaret Cronin
VIRGINIA FIELD........................Kitty
MARIA OUSPENSKAYA......Mme. Olga Kirowa
C. AUBREY SMITH.................The Duke
JANET SHAW........................Maureen
JANET WALDO...........................Elsa
STEFFI DUNA..........................Lydia
VIRGINIA CARROLL....................Sylvia
LEDA NICOVA...........................Marie
FLORENCE BAKER.....................Beatrice
MARGERY MANNING....................Mary
FRANCES MacINERNEY.................Violet
ELEANOR STEWART....................Grace
MGM   Director : Mervyn LeRoy   1940
Based on the play by Robert E. Sherwood

Waterloo Road
JOHN MILLS.......................Jim Colter
STEWART GRANGER.................Ted Purvis
ALISTAIR SIM...............Dr. Montgomery
JOY SHELTON.....................Tillie Colter
BEATRICE VARLEY................Mrs. Colter
ALISON LEGGATT.......................Ruby
ARTHUR DENTON........................Fred
VERA FRANCES.........................Vera
LESLIE BRADLEY................Mike Duggan
BEN WILLIAMS...............Corporal Lewis
GEORGE CARNEY.................Tom Mason
ANNA KONSTAM..........................May
DENNIS HARKIN.........................Alf
JEAN KENT............................Toni
JOHNNY SCHOFIELD..................Landlord
FRANK ATKINSON....................Barman
WYLIE WATSON.....................Tattooist
MIKE JOHNSON.......................Mugsy
DAVE CROWLEY.............."Baked Beans"
JOHN BOXER........................Policeman
GEORGE MERRITT.............A.R.P. Warden

WALLACE LUPINO................Tillie's uncle
AMY DALBY......................Tillie's aunt
NELLIE BOWMAN................Tillie's mother
GAINS   Director : Sidney Gilliat   1945

Way of All Flesh, The
EMIL JANNINGS...............August Schilling
BELLE BENNETT.................Mrs. Schilling
PHYLLIS HAVER...............The Temptress
DONALD KEITH..................August Junior
PHILIPPE DE LACY....August Junior, as a child
FRED KOHLER.....................The Tough
PARA   Director : Victor Fleming   1928

Way to the Stars, The
(American title : *Johnny in the Clouds*)
MICHAEL REDGRAVE...........David Archdale
JOHN MILLS..............Peter Penrose
ROSAMUND JOHN...............Miss Todd
DOUGLASS MONTGOMERY.......Johnny Hollis
RENEE ASHERSON..............Iris Winterton
STANLEY HOLLOWAY.............Mr. Palmer
BASIL RADFORD.................Tiny Williams
FELIX AYLMER..........Rev. Charles Moss
BONAR COLLEANO, JR..............Joe Frizelli
JOYCE CAREY....................Miss Winterton
TREVOR HOWARD......Squadron Leader Carter
TYRON NICHOL..........Colonel Rogers
WILLIAM OWEN.............." Nobby " Clarke
GRANT MILLER.............Wally Hecker
JEAN SIMMONS.....................A Singer
JOHNNIE SCHOFIELD................Jones
CHARLES VICTOR.............Corporal Fitter
DAVID TOMLINSON..........." Prune " Parsons
HARTLEY POWER...............Colonel Page
VIDA HOPE.........................Elsie
HUGH DEMPSTER............." Tinker " Bell
CHARLES FARRELL..........American Orderly
ANTHONY DAWSON............Bertie Steen
BILL LOGAN.....................Radio Operator
JOHN HOWARD.................Shelter Officer
MURRAY MATHESON.............Joe Lawson
JOHN McLAREN............" Cheerio " Chester
JACQUELINE CLARKE...............A Waitress
ALF GODDARD..................P.T. Instructor
CAVAN WATSON.............R.A.F. Corporal
SYDNEY BENSON.....................Fred
PETER COTES...................Aircraftman
IAN WARNER McGILVRAY........Little Peter
ANN WILTON...................Schoolmistress
TWO CITIES   Director : Anthony Asquith   1945
Awarded a silver star as the best British film of the
war years 1939-45, by the " Daily Mail " National
Film Award Ballot, 1946
Re-issued 1946

We Dive at Dawn
JOHN MILLS............Lieutenant Taylor, R.N.
LOUIS BRADFIELD.....Lieutenant Brace, R.N.R.
RONALD MILLAR..Lieutenant Johnson, R.N.V.R.
JACK WATLING.........Lieutenant Gordon, R.N.
REGINALD PURDELL...Chief Petty Officer Dabbs
CAVEN WATSON......Chief Petty Officer Duncan
NIALL MACGINNIS...Petty Officer Mike Corrigan
ERIC PORTMAN.........Leading Seaman Hobson
LESLIE WESTON.....Leading Seaman Tug Wilson
NORMAN WILLIAMS................" Canada "
LIONEL CROSE......................" Spud "
DAVID PEEL....................." Oxford "
PHILIP GODFREY................." Flunkey "
ROBERT WILTON................." Pincher "
GAINS   Director : Anthony Asquith   1943

Welcome Stranger
BING CROSBY..................Dr. Jim Pearson
BARRY FITZGERALD........Dr. Joseph McRory
JOAN CAULFIELD.................Trudy Mason
ELIZABETH PATTERSON...........Mrs. Gilley
FRANK FAYLEN...................Bill Walters
WANDA HENDRIX...............Emily Walters
ROBERT SHAYNE..............Roy Chesley
CHARLES DINGLE............Mr. Chesley, Sr.
PERCY KILBRIDE................Nat Dorkas
LARRY YOUNG......................Dr. Jenks
ELLIOTT NUGENT..........Medical Examiner
PARA   Director : Elliott Nugent   1946

Westerner, The
GARY COOPER....................Cole Harden
WALTER BRENNAN.........Judge Roy Bean
FRED STONE.................Caliphet Mathews
DORIS DAVENPORT......Jane-Ellen Mathews
FORREST TUCKER...............Wade Harper
LILIAN BOND................Lily Langtrey
PAUL HURST..................Chickenfoot
CHILL WILLS...................Southeast
CHARLES HALTON..............Mort Borrow
TOM TYLER.....................King Evans
LUPITA TOVAR....................Teresita
DANA ANDREWS..................Bart Cobble
JUAN RIVERO....................Juan Gomez
ROGER GRAY.................1st Homesteader
ARTHUR AYLESWORTH.......2nd Homesteader
TREVOR BURDETTE..............Shad Wilkins
NEW REALM   Director : William Tyler   1940

What Price Glory ?
VICTOR McLAGEN..............Captain Flagg
EDMUND LOWE.................Sergeant Quirt
DOLORES DEL RIO................Charmaine
WILLIAM V. MONG............" Cognac Pete "
PHYLLIS HAVER.........." Shanghai Mabel "
ELENA JURADO........Carmen of the Philippines
LESLIE FENTON...............Lieutenant Moore
BARRY NORTON.............Private Lewisohn
SAMMY COHEN...............Private Pipinsky
TED McNAMARA................Private Kiper
AUGUST TOLLAIRE...............French Mayo
FOX   1928

White Cargo
LESLIE FABER..........................Weston
GYPSY RHOUMA..................Tondelayo
JOHN HAMILTON....................Ashley
MAURICE EVANS....................Langford
SEBASTIAN SMITH.................The Doctor
HUMBERSTON WRIGHT........The Missionary
HENRI DE VRIES..................The Skipper
GEORGE TURNER...................The Mate
TOM HELMORE....................Worthing
Directors : J. B. Williams and A. W. Barnes   1930
Based on the novel " Hell's Playground " by
Vera Simonton, and the play by Leon Gordon

White Cargo
HEDY LAMARR...................Tondelayo
WALTER PIDGEON...........Harry Witzel
FRANK MORGAN...............The Doctor
RICHARD CARLSON..............Langford
REGINALD OWEN...................Skipper
HENRY O'NEILL..............Rev. Roberts
BRAMWELL FLETCHER..........Wilbur Ashley
CLYDE COOK........................Ted
LEIGH WHIPPER....................Jim Fish

OSCAR POLK.........................Umeela
DARBY JONES.............Doctor's houseboy
RICHARD AINLEY................Worthing
MGM   Director : Richard Thorpe   1943
*Based on the novel " Hell's Playground " by
Vera Simonton, and the play by Leon Gordon*
Re-issued 1947

White Hell of Pitz Palu, The
GUSTAV DIESSEL............Dr. Johannes Krafft
LENI RIEFENSTAHL....................Maria
ERNST PETERSEN.......................Hans
OTTO SPRING.......................Christian
ERNST UDET.....................The Aviator
SOKOL (Germany)   1930
Directors : Dr. Arnold Fanck and G. W. Pabst
*Pitz Palu is a summit 12,835 feet high in the Bernina
Alps, Switzerland.   The director and cast faced
storms, avalanches and other dangers while the film
was being made.*
(See Foreign Language Films, page 347)

White Sister, The
LILLIAN GISH..............Angela Chiaromonte
RONALD COLMAN......Captain Giovanni Severi
GAIL KANE...................Marchesa di Mola
J. BARNEY SHERRY..........Mgr. Saracinesca
CHARLES LANE..........Prince Chiaromonte
JULIETTE LA VIOLETTE........Mme. Bernard
S. SERENA...........Professor Ugo Severi
RAMON IBANEZ................Count del Ferice
ALFREDO MARTINELLI......Alfredo del Ferice
CARLONI TALLI................Mother Superior
ANTONIO BARDA.............Alfredo's tutor
GUISEPPE PAVONI.................Archbishop
INSPIRATION   Director : Henry King   1924

Whoopee
EDDIE CANTOR................Henry Williams
ELEANOR HUNT.................Sally Morgan
PAUL GREGORY.......................Wanenis
JOHN RUTHERFORD.........Sheriff Bob Wells
ETHEL SHUTTA..................Mary Custa
SPENCER CHARTERS.......Jerome Underwood
CHIEF CAUPOLICAN.................Black Eagle
ALBERT HACKETT.........Chester Underwood
WILL H. PHILBRICK.........Andy McNab
WALTER LAW...................Judd Morgan
MARILYN MORGAN.......Harriett Underwood
UA   Director : Thornton Freeland   1931
*From the musical comedy by William Anthony
McGuire
In Technicolor*

Wicked Lady, The
JAMES MASON..........Captain Jerry Jackson
MARGARET LOCKWOOD.......Barbara Worth
PATRICIA ROC.....................Caroline
GRIFFITH JONES.............Sir Ralph Skelton
FELIX AYLMER.......................Hogarth
MICHAEL RENNIE................Kit Locksby
ENID STAMP-TAYLOR.....Henrietta Kingsclere
JEAN KENT........................Doxy
GAINS   Director : Leslie Arliss   1946
*From the novel " The Life and Death of the
Wicked Lady Skelton " by Magdalen King-Hall*

Wilson
ALEXANDER KNOX...........Woodrow Wilson
CHARLES COBURN......Professor Henry Holmes
GERALDINE FITZGERALD........Edith Wilson

THOMAS MITCHELL...........Joseph Tumulty
RUTH NELSON................Ellen Wilson
CEDRIC HARDWICKE
                    Senator Henry Cabot Lodge
VINCENT PRICE............Senator G. McAdoo
WILLIAM EYTHE.................George Felton
MARY ANDERSON..............Eleanor Wilson
RUTH FORD...................Margaret Wilson
SIDNEY BLACKMER..........Josephus Daniels
MADELEINE FORBES.............Jessie Wilson
STANLEY RIDGES.............Admiral Grayson
EDDIE FOY, Jr.....................Eddie Foy
CHARLES HALTON................Colonel House
THURSTON HALL..... Senator E. H. Jones
J. M. KERRIGAN..............Edward Sullivan
JAMES RENNIE.................Jim Beeker
KATHERINE LOCKE..............Helen Bones
STANLEY LOGAN.........Secretary Lansing
MARCEL DALIO...................Clémenceau
EDWIN MAXWELL.......William Jennings Bryan
CLIFFORD BROOKE.............Lloyd George
TONIO SELWART.................Von Bernstorff
JOHN INCE...................Senator Watson
CHARLES MILLER............Senator Bromfield
ANNE O'NEAL.........................Jennie
ARTHUR LOFT...................Secretary Lane
RUSSELL GAIGE.................Secretary Colby
JAMESSON SHADE.............Secretary Payne
REGINALD SHEFFIELD........Secretary Baker
ROBERT MIDDLEMASS......Secretary Garrison
MATT MOORE...............Secretary Burleson
GEORGE ANDERSON........Secretary Houston
ROBERT BARRON.........Secretary Meredith
PAUL EVERTON.................Judge Westcott
ARTHUR SPACE.............Francis Sayre
GEORGE MacCREADY..............McCombs
ROY ROBERTS.....................Ike Hoover
FRANK ORTH.......................Smith
DEWEY ROBINSON....................Worker
FRANCIS X. BUSHMAN.........Barney Baruch
CY KENDALL..........Charles F. Murphy
20TH-FOX   Director : Henry King   1945
In Technicolor

Wings of the Morning
Prologue 1889
D. J. WILLIAMS............Mairik (Gipsy King)
ANNABELLA.................Marie, his daughter
LESLIE BANKS...............Earl of Clontarf
PAT NOONAN...................Police Sergeant
PHILIP FROST.........Valentine (as a boy)
HERMIONE DARNBOROUGH.....Gipsy Dancer
Modern Story 1936
ANNABELLA..................Maria (alias Mario)
HENRY FONDA..................Kerry Gilfallen
HARRY TATE...................Paddy (butler)
IRENE VANBRUGH.....................Marie
STEWART ROME........Valentine (old man)
HELEN HAYE.......................Jenepher
EDWARD UNDERDOWN...........Don Diego
EMMANUELO........Don Frasco (Spanish jockey)
MARK DALY...............Jimmy (a groom)
SAM LIVESEY......................Angelo
NICHOLAS NADEJINE..................Benito
STEVE DONOGHUE...................Himself
                        and
JOHN McCORMACK, the world-famous tenor
20th-FOX-BRIT   Director : Harold Schuster   1937
*The first full-length Technicolor film made in Britain
Re-issued 1940 and 1945*

Winterset

BURGESS MEREDITH......................Mio
MARGO................................Miriamne
EDUARDO CIANNELLI..................Trock
JOHN CARRADINE.....................Romagna
EDWARD ELLIS....................Judge Grant
PAUL GUILFOYLE.......................Garth
MAURICE MOSCOVITCH...............Esdras
STANLEY RIDGES.....................Shadow
WILLARD ROBERTSON...............Policeman
MISCHA AUER..........................Radical
MYRON McCORMICK....................Carr
HELEN JEROME EDDY..........Mrs. Romagna
BARBARA PEPPER......................Girl
ALEC CRAIG..........................Hobo
FERNANDA ELISCU.....................Piny
GEORGE HUMBERT.....................Lucia
MURRAY ALPER.......................Louie
PAUL FIX.............................Joe
RKO   Director : Alfred Santell   1936
From the play by Maxwell Anderson

Wizard of Oz, The

JUDY GARLAND.....................Dorothy
FRANK MORGAN............Professor Marvel
RAY BOLGER..................The Straw Man
BERT LAHR..............The Cowardly Lion
JACK HALEY................The Tin Man
BILLIE BURKE........................Glinda
MARGARET HAMILTON..........Miss Gulch
CHARLEY GRAPEWIN.............Uncle Henry
PAT WALSHE.........................Nikko
CLARA BLANDICK..................Auntie Em
TOTO...............................Toto
with
THE SINGER MIDGETS as The Munchkins
MGM   Director : Victor Fleming   1940
In Technicolor
Re-issued 1945

Woman in the Window, The

EDWARD G. ROBINSON........Richard Wanley
JOAN BENNETT.....................Alice Reed
RAYMOND MASSEY.............Frank Lalor
EDMOND BREON................Dr. Barkstane
ARTHUR LOFT...................Claud Mazard
DAN DURYEA.......Heidt, the blackmailer
THOMAS E. JACKSON........Inspector Jackson
DOROTHY PETERSON............Mrs. Wanley
CAROL CAMERON.............Elsie Wanley
BOBBY BLAKE.................Dickie Wanley
RKO   Director : Fritz Lang   1945

Woman of Paris, A

EDNA PURVIANCE.............Marie St. Clair
ADOLPHE MENJOU................Pierre Revel
CARL MILLER...................John Millet
LYDIA KNOTT.....................His mother
CHARLES FRENCH.................His father
CLARENCE GELDERT...........Marie's father
BETTY MORRISSEY.....................Fifi
MALVINA POLO.....................Paulette
UA   Director : Charles Chaplin   1924

Woman to Woman

BETTY COMPSON.....................Deloryse
CLIVE BROOK.............{David Compton
                        {David Anson-Pond
JOSEPHINE EARLE..........Mrs. Anson-Pond
MARIE AULT......................Henrietta
M. PETER......................Little Davy
Produced and directed by Graham Cutts   1924
From the play by Michael Morton

Woman to Woman

BETTY COMPSON.......................Lola
GEORGE BARRAUD....................David
JULIETTE COMPTON..................Vesta
WINTER HALL..................Dr. Garvin
MARGUERITE CHAMBERS...........Florence
GEORGE BILLINGS.................Little David
BURLINGTON-GAINS   1930
          Director : Victor Saville
From the play by Michael Morton

Woman's Face, A

JOAN CRAWFORD.................Anna Holm
MELVYN DOUGLAS..........Dr. Gustaf Segert
CONRAD VEIDT.................Torsten Barring
OSA MASSEN......................Vera Segert
REGINALD OWEN..............Bernard Dalvik
ALBERT BASSERMAN....Consul Magnus Barring
MARJORIE MAIN.........Emma Kristiansdotter
DONALD MEEK..............Herman Rundvik
CONNIE GILCHRIST............Christina Dalvik
RICHARD NICHOLS................Lars-Erik
CHARLES QUIGLEY.....................Eric
GWILI ANDRE........................Gusta
CLIFFORD BROOKE.................Wickman
GEORGE ZUCCO..........Defence Attorney
HENRY KOLKER.......................Judge
ROBERT WARWICK }
GILBERT EMERY } ....Associate Judges
HENRY DANIELL..........Public Prosecutor
SARAH PADDEN................Police Matron
WILLIAM FARNUM..........Court Attendant
MGM   Director : George Cukor   1941

Wuthering Heights

MERLE OBERON.......................Cathy
LAURENCE OLIVIER................Heathcliff
DAVID NIVEN........................Edgar
FLORA ROBSON....................Ellen Dean
DONALD CRISP.................Dr. Kenneth
GERALDINE FITZGERALD............Isabella
HUGH WILLIAMS.....................Hindley
LEO G. CARROLL....................Joseph
CECIL HUMPHREYS.............Judge Linton
MILES MANDER..................Lockwood
ROMAINE CALLENDER................Robert
CECIL KELLAWAY...................Earnshaw
REX DOWNING............Heathcliff, as a child
SARITA WOOTON..........Cathy, as a child
DOUGLAS SCOTT.........Hindley, as a child
MME. ALICE EHLERS.........Harpsichordist
UA   Director : William Wyler   1939
From the novel by Emily Brontë
Re-issued 1944

Y

Yankee at the Court of King Arthur, A

HARRY C. MYERS................The Yankee
PAULINE STARK.....................Sandy
ROSEMARY THEBY.......Queen Morgan le Fay
CHARLES CLARY...............King Arthur
GEORGE SIEGMANN.............Sir Sagramore
CHARLES GORDON.........The Page, Clarence
WILFRED McDONALD............Sir Launcelot
FOX   1922
From the novel by Mark Twain

Young Mr. Lincoln

HENRY FONDA:............Abraham Lincoln
ALICE BRADY....................Abigail Clay
MARJORIE WEAVER...............Mary Todd

ARLEEN WHELAN................Hannah Clay
EDDIE COLLINS..........................Efe
PAULINE MOORE...............Ann Rutledge
RICHARD CROMWELL..............Matt Clay
DONALD MEEK..................John Fielder
DORRIS BOWDON.................Carrie Sue.
EDDIE QUILLAN..................Adam Clay
SPENCER CHARTERS......Judge Herbert A. Bell
WARD BOND....................Palmer Cass
MILBURN STONE...........Stephen A. Douglas
CLIFF CLARK...................Sheriff Billings
ROBERT LOWERY.......................Juror
CHARLES TANNEN..........Ninian Edwards
FRANCIS FORD...................Frank Ford
FRED KOHLER, Jr............." Scrub " White
FAY LINAKER.................Mrs. Edwards
RUSSELL SIMPSON................Woolridge
CLARENCE HUMMEL WILSON......Dr. Mason
EDWIN MAXWELL..............John T. Stuart
CHARLES HALTON.................Hawthorne
ROBERT HOMANS...................Mr. Clay
JACK KELLY...............Matt Clay, as a boy
DICKIE JONES.............Adam Clay, as a boy
HARRY TYLER........................Barber
20TH-FOX   Director : John Ford   1939

Young Mr. Pitt, The

ROBERT DONAT.........⎰The Earl of Chatham
                        ⎱William Pitt
ROBERT MORLEY............Charles James Fox
PHYLLIS CALVERT..............Eleanor Eden
JOHN MILLS.............William Wilberforce
RAYMOND LOVELL.................George III
MAX ADRIAN.......................Sheridan
FELIX AYLMER....................Lord North
ALBERT LIEVEN.....................Talleyrand
STEPHEN HAGGARD...............Lord Nelson
GEOFFREY ATKINS........William Pitt, as a boy
JEAN CADELL....................Mrs. Sparry
AGNES LAUGHLAN............Queen Charlotte
IAN McLEAN.........................Dundas
A. BROMLEY DAVENPORT.....Sir Evan Nepean
JOHN SALEW.........................Smith
HERBERT LOM.....................Napoleon
STUART LINDSELL..............Earl Spencer
HENRY HEWITT...................Addington
FREDERICK CULLEY.......Sir William Farquhar
FRANK PETTINGELL................Coachman
LESLIE BRADLEY............Gentleman Jackson
ROY EMMERTON..................Dan Mendoza
HUGH McDERMOTT................Mr. Melvill
ALFRED SANGSTER..............Lord Grenville
20TH-FOX BRIT   Director : Carol Reed   1941

Young Tom Edison

MICKEY ROONEY..................Tom Edison
FAY BAINTER...........Mrs. Samuel Edison
GEORGE BANCROFT............Samuel Edison
VIRGINIA WEIDLER...........Tannie Edison
EUGENE PALLETTE.................Mr. Nelson
VICTOR KILIAN...................Mr. Dingle
BOBBIE JORDAN...................Joe Dingle
J. M. KERRIGAN...............Mr. McCarney

LLOYD CORRIGAN.................Dr. Pender
JOHN KELLOG....................Bill Edison
CLEM BEVANS..................Mr. Waddell
EILY MALYON...................Schoolteacher
HARRY SHANNON...........Captain Brackett
MGM   Director : Norman Taurog   1940

Young Woodley

MADELEINE CARROLL........Laura Simmons
SAM LIVESEY....................Mr. Simmons
FRANK LAWTON............Young Woodley
AUBREY MATHER.................Mr. Woodley
BILLY MILTON......................Vining
GERALD RAWLINSON..................Milner
JOHN TEED........................Ainger
TONY HALFPENNY.....................Cope
RENEE RAY....................The Shopgirl
BIP   Director : Thomas Bentley   1931
From the play by John van Druten

Z

Zéro de Conduite

JEAN D'ASTE......Mr. Huguet (junior master)
ROBERT LE FLON................." Sourpuss "
DU VERON...................The Vice Principal
DELPHIN........................The Principal
MME. ÉMILE...............Mother Haricot
LARIVE....................Maths. Master
LOUIS LEFEBVRE....................Caussat
GILBERT PRUCHON.....................Colin
COCO GOLSTEIN.....................Druel
GÉRARD DE BÉDARIEUX.............Tabart
LOUIS DE GONZAGUE-FRICK......The Prefect
RAYA DILIGENT......................Fireman
ARGUI-FILM (France)   Director : Jean Vigo   1933
(See Foreign Language Films, page 347)

Ziegfeld Girl

JAMES STEWART.................Gilbert Young
JUDY GARLAND...............Susan Gallagher
HEDY LAMARR..................Sandra Kolter
LANA TURNER...................Sheila Regan
TONY MARTIN..................Frank Merton
JACKIE COOPER..................Jerry Regan
IAN HUNTER...................Geoffrey Collis
CHARLES WINNINGER........" Pop " Gallagher
EDWARD EVERETT HORTON.......Noble Sage
PHILIP DORN...................Franz Kolter
PAUL KELLY....................John Slayton
EVE ARDEN.....................Patsy Dixon
DAN DAILEY, Jr.................Jimmy Walters
AL SHEAN..........................Al
FAY HOLDEN.....................Mrs. Regan
FELIX BRESSART....................Mischa
ROSE HOBART...................Mrs. Merton
BERNARD NEDELL.............Nick Capalini
ED McNAMARA..................Mr. Regan
MAE BUSCH.........................Jenny
RENIE RIANO........................Annie
JOSEPHINE WHITTELL................Perkins
SERGIO ORTA...................Native Dancer
MGM   Director : Robert Z. Leonard   1941

TYRONE POWER
(20th Century-Fox)

FAMOUS FILM SERIES

The Astaire-Rogers Films
(RKO)
Featuring
FRED ASTAIRE
and
GINGER ROGERS

Flying Down to Rio	1933
The Gay Divorce	1934
Roberta	1935
Top Hat	1935
Follow the Fleet	1936
Swing Time	1936
Shall We Dance	1937
Carefree	1938
The Story of Vernon and Irene Castle	1939

Blondie
(Columbia)
Featuring
PENNY SINGLETON
    as Blondie
ARTHUR LAKE as Dagwood
LARRY SIMMS
 as Alexander (the little boy)
    and
DAISY, the dog

Blondie	1938
Blondie Meets the Boss	1939
Blondie Takes a Vacation	1939
Blondie Brings Up Baby	1939
Blondie on a Budget	1940
Blondie Has Servant Trouble	1940
Blondie Plays Cupid	1940
Blondie Goes Latin	1941
Blondie in Society	1941
Blondie Goes to College	1942
Blondie for Victory	1942
Blondie's Blessed Event	1942
The Boss Said No	1942
A Bundle of Trouble	1942
Leave It to Blondie	1945
Life with Blondie	1946
Blondie's Lucky Day	1946
Blondie Knows Best	1946
Blondie's Big Moment	1943
Henpecked	1947
Blondie in the Dough	1947
Blondie's Holiday	1947
Blondie's Anniversary	1948

Rita Hayworth, Glenn Ford, Larry Parks and Janet Blair all appeared in *Blondie* films early in their careers.

Crime Doctor
(Columbia)
Featuring
WARNER BAXTER

Crime Doctor	1943
The Strangest Case	1943
The Doctor's Courage	1945
The Doctor's Warning	1945
The Doctor's Man Hunt	1946
The Millerson Case	1947

Disney Features
(Walt Disney Productions)

Snow White and the Seven Dwarfs	1938
Re-issued 1946	
Pinocchio	1940
Re-issued 1946	
The Reluctant Dragon	1941
Dumbo	1942
Fantasia	1942
Bambi	1942
Saludos Amigos	1943
The Three Caballeros	1945

The following live characters were introduced in a Disney film for the first time : Aurora Miranda, Carmen Molina, Dora Luz, and The Disney Girls.

Make Mine Music   1946
In which was heard the music of Sergei Prokofiev and other modern composers. Among the performers who recorded the sound were Benny Goodman and his orchestra, Nelson Eddy, the Andrew Sisters, Dinah Shore, Sterling Holloway, Andy Russell, Jerry Colonna, the Ken Darby Chorus, the Pied Pipers, and the King's Men. Riabouchinska and Lichine appeared in the ballet sequence of combined live action and animation.

Song of the South   1947
First live action feature. A musical drama of the Old South, based on " The Immortal Tales of Brer Rabbit " by Joel Chandler Harris.
JAMES BASKETT
    as Uncle Remus
BOBBY DRISCOLL as Johnny
LUANA PATTEN   as Ginny
RUTH WARRICK
   as Johnny's Mother
ERIC ROLF
   as Newspaper Editor

HATTIE McDANIEL
    as Tempy
LUCILE WATSON
    as Mis' Doshy
GLENN LEEDY   as Toby

Dr. Gillespie
(MGM)
Featuring
LIONEL BARRYMORE
 as Dr. Gillespie

Calling Dr. Gillespie	1942
Dr. Gillespie's New Assistant	1943
Crazy to Kill	1943
Three Men in White	1944
Between Two Women	1945
Cynthia's Secret	1947

Dr. Kildare
(MGM)
Featuring
LEW AYRES
 as Dr. Kildare

Young Dr. Kildare	1939
Calling Dr. Kildare	1939
The Secret of Dr. Kildare	1940
Dr. Kildare's Strange Case	1940
Dr. Kildare Goes Home	1941
Dr. Kildare's Crisis	1941
My Life Is Yours	1941
Mary Names the Day	1941
The Doctor and the Debutante	1942

The Falcon
(RKO)
Featuring
GEORGE SANDERS

Falcon Takes Over	1942
Falcon's Brother	1942

Featuring
TOM CONWAY

Falcon Strikes Back	1943
Falcon In Danger	1943
Falcon and the Co-Eds	1943
Falcon Out West	1944
Falcon in Hollywood	1944
Falcon in Mexico	1945
Falcon in San Francisco	1945
Falcon's Alibi	1947
Falcon's Adventure	1947

The Hardy Family
(MGM)
Featuring
MICKEY ROONEY
    as Andy Hardy
LEWIS STONE
    as Judge Hardy
FAY HOLDEN
    as Mrs. Hardy
SARA HADEN
    as Aunt Milly

A Family Affair	1937
You're Only Young Once	1938
Judge Hardy's Children	1938
Love Finds Andy Hardy	1938
Out West with the Hardys	1939
The Hardys Ride High	1939
Andy Hardy Gets Spring Fever	1939
Judge Hardy and Son	1940
Andy Hardy Meets Debutante	1940
Andy Hardy's Private Secretary	1941
Life Begins for Andy Hardy	1941
The Courtship of Andy Hardy	1942
Andy Hardy's Double Life	1943
Andy Hardy's Blonde Trouble	1944
Love Laughs at Andy Hardy	1947

The Jones Family
(20th Century-Fox)
Featuring
JED PROUTY as John Jones
SPRING BYINGTON as Mrs. John Jones
KEN HOWE as Jack Jones
GEORGE ERNEST as Roger Jones

Young As You Feel	1931
Business and Pleasure	1932
Every Saturday Night	1936
Educating Father	1936
Back to Nature	1936
Off to the Races	1937
Borrowing Trouble	1937
Hot Water	1937
Love on a Budget	1938
Trip to Paris	1938
Safety in Numbers	1938
Down on the Farm	1938
Everybody's Baby	1939
Quick Millions	1939
The Jones Family in Hollywood	1939
Too Busy to Work	1939
On Their Own	1940

Maisie
(MGM)
Featuring
ANN SOTHERN

Maisie	1939
Congo Maisie	1940
Gold Rush Maisie	1941
Maisie Was a Lady	1941
Cash and Carry	1941
She Got Her Man	1942
The Girl in Overalls	1943
You Can't Do That to Me	1944
Up She Goes	1946
Undercover Girl	1947

The " Road " Series
(Paramount)
Featuring
BING CROSBY, BOB HOPE
and DOROTHY LAMOUR

Road to Singapore Re-issued 1944	1940
Road to Zanzibar Re-issued 1944	1941
Road to Morocco	1942
Road to Utopia	1945
Road to Rio	1947

Tarzan
(RKO)
Featuring
JOHNNY WEISSMULLER as Tarzan
BRENDA JOYCE as Jane
JOHNNY SHEFFIELD as Boy

Seven different producing organizations have filmed this series ; the present producer (1947) is Sol Lesser, who releases through RKO. There have been ten Tarzans (including Buster Crabbe, Herman Brix and Glenn Morris) and nine Janes since the original production, *Tarzan of the Apes* (1918), starring Elmo Lincoln and Enid Markey ; Edgar Rice Burroughs, author of " Tarzan of the Apes," produced two of the series. Johnny Weissmuller made his debut as Tarzan in *Tarzan the Ape Man* (1932). Films in the series since then are :

Tarzan, the Fearless	1933
Tarzan and His Mate	1934
Tarzan Escapes	1936
Tarzan's Revenge	1938
Tarzan and the Green Goddess	1938
Tarzan Finds a Son !	1939
Tarzan's Secret Treasure	1941
Tarzan's New York Adventure	1942
Tarzan Triumphs	1943
Tarzan's Desert Mystery	1944
Tarzan and the Amazons	1945
Tarzan and the Leopard Woman	1946
Tarzan and the Huntress	1947
Tarzan and the Mermaids	1948

The Thin Man
(MGM)
Featuring
WILLIAM POWELL as Nick Charles
MYRNA LOY as Nora
and
ASTA, the dog

The Thin Man	1934
After the Thin Man	1936
Another Thin Man	1939
Shadow of the Thin Man	1941
The Thin Man Goes Home	1944
Song of the Thin Man	1947

FILM MUSIC

CONTEMPORARY TRENDS IN FILM MUSIC : Muir Mathieson
NOTABLE FILM MUSIC : compiled by John Huntley
BRITISH FILM MUSIC OF 1947 : compiled by John Huntley

TREVOR HOWARD
(*Individual*)

Muir Mathieson

CONTEMPORARY TRENDS IN
FILM MUSIC

FOR ten or fifteen years I have been engaged in planning and fitting music to films. During this period the studios of the world have been effecting great progress towards a satisfactory combination of the visual and aural arts of the cinema ; greater developments lie ahead as the film moves from the experimental to the more mature stage as a medium of expression and entertainment. In this country we have attempted to attract more and more of our finest contemporary musicians to the film world so that their knowledge and integrity may enhance the worthwhile qualities of the films for which they compose. In the recording, we employ such orchestras as the Philharmonia and the London Symphony Orchestra to do full justice to the finished scores.

About five years of confusion and indecision followed the coming of the talkies before music began to settle down to its rightful place. The turning point was roughly 1935. Not that first-class film music did not exist before then ; after all, Saint-Saens had composed for a film in France as early as 1907, while many other notable accompaniments to silent and early talking films were evolved. But the situation became more or less stabilized about 1935. Max Steiner scored *The Informer*, and thus established himself as one of Hollywood's leading composers—a position he still holds today. In this country, Arthur Bliss composed his famous *Things to Come* music, while William Walton also started on his film career with music for the Elisabeth Bergner film *Escape Me Never*. Documentary also settled down about this period with Walter Leigh's *Song of Ceylon* and the entry of Benjamin Britten into the G.P.O. Film Unit. On the Continent, Honegger's *L'Idée* and Georges Auric's *A Nous la Liberté* were being screened and praised wherever good filmcraft was noted.

After ten years of steady development, we can now look at the film scores of 1946 and 1947 and the plans being made for 1948, and note the fact that enthusiasm on behalf of contemporary musicians has not diminished. There is William Walton for example. Walton's name is famous wherever British contemporary music is listened to and discussed. To the Proms' audiences his *Façade* suite is always a highlight of the season, conducted in many instances by the composer himself. His comedy overture *Portsmouth Point*, the Violin Concerto, the Concerto for Viola and Orchestra, and his Symphony receive regular performances in the concert halls of the world and have all been recorded.

Walton entered the film world in 1935 with *Escape Me Never* ; this was followed a year later by music for the Shakespearean production *As You Like It*. Then in 1939 he wrote for *Stolen Life*, a second Elisabeth Bergner film. 1941 produced music for the Shaw film *Major Barbara*, followed by *Next of Kin*, *The Foreman Went to France* and *Went the Day Well?* at Ealing Studios in 1942, as well as *The First of the Few* at Denham. From this Leslie Howard production came the " Spitfire Prelude and Fugue ", available on a gramophone record and frequently heard in the concert hall. His music for Laurence Olivier's *Henry V* is now a classic of film music history, and it is most appropriate that Walton should have written for Olivier's *Hamlet*. Here is further evidence of the composer's complete grasp of the technical requirements of the screen, combined with a masterly understanding of the emotional impact of music when properly used in films.

Ralph Vaughan Williams was " doing his bit " by driving a cart round the village and countryside, collecting scrap metal and old bones, when I went to see him in 1940 to ask him to write his first film score. That was for *49th Parallel*. Since then, he has composed for a number of other films, including the documentaries *Coastal Command*, *Stricken Peninsula* and *The People's Land*, as well as three further features—*The Flemish Farm*, *The Loves of Joanna Godden*, and, in 1947, *Scott of the Antarctic*. This " grand old man " of English music was born in 1872 before anyone had ever heard of films, let alone talkies ; incidentally, it is interesting to work out from that how old this " youngster " was when he did his first work for the films—a point that goes to show his tremendous adaptability and willingness to try anything new. His music is broad and expansive, full of the open air, and particularly successful in subjects such as the *Antarctic* film.

Apart from the music itself, a number of purely technical problems have had to be solved, while others are still being discovered and investigated.

MUIR MATHIESON *has conducted or directed the music of many outstanding British films, and has been responsible for introducing into films the music of many outstanding British composers.*

We are beginning to learn that the transition from music to speech, for example, is of the greatest importance to the flow of the sound track. Where music coincides with dialogue, very great care is needed to avoid those disheartening effects in the cinema when the music seems to be in competition with the speech and the audience gets the feeling that the speech is fighting a losing battle. The quality of the dialogue and its level must be considered in relation to orchestral volume.

If the dynamic level and tone colour can be kept constant between dialogue and music, ugly clashes and uncomfortably discordant effects can be avoided. By considering the musical pitch of the voices on the sound track, the composer can arrange to score his music so that it comes above or below the frequency line of the speech. In this way, we create a musical sandwich, with the orchestra restricting itself to the upper register of the flutes and violins, for example, while the bass comes from the bassoons, percussion and double basses. In the sandwich is the speech, which proceeds, unimpaired by the music, at a different pitch.

In our title music (the equivalent of the operatic overture) we try to avoid the seemingly inevitable crash of sound that normally precedes a feature film. Although the principle of getting the audience's attention by a fanfare of trumpets or loud burst of sound from the orchestra still stands today as it did for Rossini and countless other operatic and symphonic writers, at least once in a while there comes a film that can be treated differently. On such occasions, a solo voice may be used most effectively to back the "credit" titles, as in *Men of Two Worlds* with music by Arthur Bliss.

Today, instead of leaving the musical accompaniment for the censor's certificate and the renter's titles to the mercy of the cinema projectionist's choice of gramophone records, we start our overture music to allow for the orchestra on the sound track being heard right from the word "go". Although a censor's card has not been allocated at the time when the music is recorded, we allow so much additional track to fill in the space that will be occupied by this film strip when the film is shown. Similarly, with the gong that announces "J. Arthur Rank Presents" we now build the two great bangs into the score itself so that every available second of screen time can be utilized in creating the atmosphere of the story to follow.

The cartoon film, especially the items produced by Walt Disney, offers the closest collaboration between music and the visual art to be found in the cinema. The cartoon animators deal more closely in the fundamentals of the film than the makers of the "live" film. Cartoon-making concerns the mechanics of the cinema plus the closest attention to the rhythms of the moving film strip. Music is an indispensable factor to the existence of a cartoon, as anyone will realize who has seen a *Mickey Mouse* without a sound track. Because of the need for strong steady rhythms, popular music (especially jazz) is very well suited to the cartoon technique ; even so, there have been some very interesting experiments with more serious forms of music in films like *Make Mine Music* and *Fantasia*. Much remains to be done in this direction although, as *Fantasia* showed, the quality of interpretation of the classics varies considerably, depending on one's own ideas of what Beethoven's Sixth Symphony and Bach's Toccata and Fugue should look like in Technicolor.

A cartoon score is designed to fit the film exactly. For a "live" film, the music is timed to the nearest second and sometimes to the nearest third of a second. For cartoons, every movement is planned to synchronize exactly with the rhythm of the music, so that each cell unit in the assembly of the animation has its counterpart in the score— and that means timing to single frames or one twenty-fourth of a second. The normal practice is, therefore, to work out the main line of the story, select suitable music items and then synchronize *the film to the music* ; in *Fantasia*, the whole of the visual film naturally had to be fitted to the music. Now that the David Hand cartoon unit is operating in Britain, it may be that before long we shall be seeing home-produced films of this type and have the opportunity of noting how our composers will deal with this specialized kind of cinema entertainment.

The training of new composers and film conductors has become an important facet of our work. In 1947 we introduced a scheme whereby two final-year students from the Royal College of Music and two from the Royal Academy of Music are attached to the studios for three days a week in order that they may specialize in the use of music in films at the time of their college training. One from each establishment is a composer and one a potential film music director. In this respect, we have received every assistance from the colleges who have now the opportunity to show their interest in this the youngest and probably most vigorous offspring of one of the oldest arts.

As our music develops and explores the vast possibilities still open to it, so the composers of all countries are continually approaching the film in a new light, firm in the belief that, as Ralph Vaughan Williams once put it, " The film contains potentialities for the combination of all the arts such as Wagner never dreamt of."

NOTABLE FILM MUSIC

compiled by JOHN HUNTLEY

Film	Music by	Country	Date
ACCIAIO	Georges Malipiero	Italy	1933
À NOUS LA LIBERTÉ	Georges Auric	France	1931
ADVENTURES OF ROBIN HOOD	Erich Wolfgang Korngold	U.S.A.	1938
ALEXANDER NEVSKY	Sergei Prokofiev	U.S.S.R.	1939
ANTHONY ADVERSE	Erich Wolfgang Korngold	U.S.A.	1936
ARRAH-NA-POUGH	Walter Cleveland Simon	U.S.A.	1911
ASSASSINATION DU DUC DE GUISE, L'	Saint-Saens	France	1907
AS YOU LIKE IT	William Walton	Britain	1936
BATTLESHIP "POTEMKIN"	Edmund Meisel	U.S.S.R.	1925
BELLE ET LA BÊTE, LA	Georges Auric	France	1946
BELLS, THE	Gustav Holst	Britain	1931
BERLIN	Edmund Meisel	Germany	1927
BEST YEARS OF OUR LIVES, THE	Hugo Friedhofer	U.S.A.	1946
BIRTH OF A NATION, THE	Karl Breil	U.S.A.	1914
BLACKMAIL	Hubert Bath	Britain	1929
BLUE ANGEL, THE	Friedrich Hollaender	Germany	1930
BURMA VICTORY	Alan Rawsthorne	Britain	1945
CAPTIVE HEART, THE	Alan Rawsthorne	Britain	1946
CARNET DE BAL, UN	Maurice Jaubert	France	1937
CITIZEN KANE	Bernard Herrmann	U.S.A.	1942
CITY, THE	Aaron Copland	U.S.A.	1939
COAL FACE	Benjamin Britten	Britain	1936
COASTAL COMMAND	Ralph Vaughan Williams	Britain	1942
DANGEROUS MOONLIGHT	Richard Addinsell	Britain	1941
DEAD OF NIGHT	Georges Auric	Britain	1945
DEFEATED PEOPLE, A	Guy Warrack	Britain	1945
DERNIER MILLIARDAIRE, LE	Maurice Jaubert	France	1934
DESERT VICTORY	William Alwyn	Britain	1943
DEVOTION	Erich Wolfgang Korngold	U.S.A.	1946
DON JUAN	William Axt (incidental music)	U.S.A.	1926
ENTRÉE DES ARTISTES	Georges Auric	France	1939
ESCAPE ME NEVER	William Walton	Britain	1935
ÉTERNEL RETOUR, L'	Georges Auric	France	1944
FARREBIQUE	Henri Sauguet	France	1946
FEMME DU BOULANGER, LA	Vincent Scotto	France	1938
FIN DU JOUR, LA	Maurice Jaubert	France	1939
FIRE OVER ENGLAND	Richard Addinsell	Britain	1937
FIRST OF THE FEW, THE	William Walton	Britain	1942
FLEMISH FARM, THE	Ralph Vaughan Williams	Britain	1943
FLESH AND FANTASY	Alexander Tansman	U.S.A.	1944
FOREMAN WENT TO FRANCE, THE	William Walton	Britain	1942
49th PARALLEL	Ralph Vaughan Williams	Britain	1941
FOUR FEATHERS, THE	Miklos Rozsa	Britain	1938
FRENCHMAN'S CREEK	Victor Young	U.S.A.	1945
GOLDEN MOUNTAINS	Dmitri Shostakovitch	U.S.S.R.	1931
GOODBYE, MR. CHIPS !	Richard Addinsell	Britain	1939
GUEST IN THE HOUSE	Werner Janssen	U.S.A.	1945
HALFWAY HOUSE	Lord Berners	Britain	1944
HENRY V	William Walton	Britain	1945
HOTEL RESERVE	Lennox Berkeley	Britain	1944

JOHN HUNTLEY *is author of* " British Film Music " (1947) *and British correspondent of the American* publication " Film Music Notes ".

327

Film	Music by	Country	Date
IDÉE, L'	Arthur Honegger	France	1934
I MARRIED A WITCH	Franz Waxman	U.S.A.	1942
INFORMER, THE	Max Steiner	U.S.A.	1935
INHUMAINE, L'	Darius Milhaud	France	1924
INSTRUMENTS OF THE ORCHESTRA	Benjamin Britten	Britain	1946
IVAN THE TERRIBLE	Sergei Prokofiev	U.S.S.R.	1946
JOUR SE LÈVE, LE	Maurice Jaubert	France	1940
JUNGLE BOOK, THE	Miklos Rozsa	U.S.A.	1942
KEYS OF THE KINGDOM	Alfred Newman	U.S.A.	1945
LOST HORIZON	Dmitri Tiomkin	U.S.A.	1937
LOST WEEKEND, THE	Miklos Rozsa	U.S.A.	1945
LOVE FROM A STRANGER	Benjamin Britten	Britain	1937
LOVE ON THE DOLE	Richard Addinsell	Britain	1941
MADAME CURIE	Herbert Stothart	U.S.A.	1943
MAINTENANCE COMMAND	Gordon Jacob	Britain	1944
MAJOR BARBARA	William Walton	Britain	1941
MALTA, G.C.	Arnold Bax	Britain	1942
MAN OF ARAN	John Greenwood	Britain	1934
MASK OF DIMITRIOS, THE	Adolph Deutsch	U.S.A.	1944
MAXIM'S RETURN	Dmitri Shostakovitch	U.S.S.R.	1936
MAYERLING	Arthur Honegger	France	1937
MEMPHIS BELLE, THE	Gail Kubik	U.S.A.	1944
MEN OF TWO WORLDS	Arthur Bliss	Britain	1946
MERCHANT SEAMEN	Constant Lambert	Britain	1941
MUTINY ON THE BOUNTY	Bronislau Kaper	U.S.A.	1935
NEW BABYLON	Dmitri Shostakovitch	U.S.S.R.	1929
NEW EARTH	Hanns Eisler	Holland	1934
NEXT OF KIN	William Walton	Britain	1942
NIGHT MAIL	Benjamin Britten	Britain	1936
NIGHT MUST FALL	Edward Ward	U.S.A.	1939
NONE BUT THE LONELY HEART	Hanns Eisler	U.S.A.	1944
NORTH STAR	Aaron Copland	U.S.A.	1943
NOW, VOYAGER	Max Steiner	U.S.A.	1942
OCTOBER	Edmund Meisel	U.S.S.R.	1928
ONE TENTH OF A NATION	Roy Harris	U.S.A.	1940
OF MICE AND MEN	Aaron Copland	U.S.A.	1940
OPEN CITY	Renzo Rosselini	Italy	1945
OUR TOWN	Aaron Copland	U.S.A.	1940
OVERLANDERS, THE	John Ireland	Britain	1946
PAYS DU SCALP	Maurice Jaubert	France	1929
PINOCCHIO	Leigh Harline	U.S.A.	1940
PLOW THAT BROKE THE PLAINS, THE	Virgil Thompson	U.S.A.	1936
PRAGUE CASTLE	Ferdei Bartos	Czecho-slovakia	1932
PRIDE AND PREJUDICE	Herbert Stothart	U.S.A.	1940
PYGMALION	Arthur Honegger	Britain	1938
QUAI DES BRUMES, LE	Maurice Jaubert	France	1938
QUATORZE JUILLET, LE	Maurice Jaubert	France	1932
RAIN	Lou Lichtveld	Holland	1929
RAKE'S PROGRESS, THE	William Alwyn	Britain	1945
RISING TIDE	Clarence Raybould	Britain	1933
RIVER, THE	Virgil Thompson	U.S.A.	1938
SAN FRANCISCO	Bronislau Kaper	U.S.A.	1936
SEVENTH CROSS, THE	Roy Webb	U.S.A.	1944
SEVENTH VEIL, THE	Benjamin Frankel	Britain	1945
SINCE YOU WENT AWAY	Max Steiner	U.S.A.	1944
SONG OF BERNADETTE, THE	Alfred Newman	U.S.A.	1944
SONG OF CEYLON	Walter Leigh	Britain	1934
SONG OF LIFE	Hanns Eisler	France	1930

Film	Music by	Country	Date
SOUTH RIDING	Miklos Rozsa	Britain	1938
SPANISH EARTH	Marc Blitzstein and Virgil Thompson	U.S.A.	1937
SPECTRE OF THE ROSE	George Antheil	U.S.A.	1946
SPELLBOUND	Miklos Rozsa	U.S.A.	1945
STAGECOACH	Richard Hageman	U.S.A.	1939
STOLEN LIFE	William Walton	Britain	1939
TABU	Hugo Riesenfeld	U.S.A.	1931
TARGET FOR TONIGHT	Leighton Lucas	Britain	1941
THINGS TO COME	Arthur Bliss	Britain	1935
TUNISIAN VICTORY	William Alwyn and Dmitri Tiomkin	Britain and U.S.A.	1944
TURN OF THE TIDE, THE	Arthur Benjamin	Britain	1935
VICTORIA THE GREAT	Anthony Collins	Britain	1937
VOLGA-VOLGA	I. O. Dunayevsky	U.S.S.R.	1938
WAR IS HELL	Hanns Eisler	Germany	1931
WAY TO THE STARS, THE	Nicholas Brodzsky	Britain	1945
WENT THE DAY WELL?	William Walton	Britain	1942
WESTERN APPROACHES	Clifton Parker	Britain	1945
WINGS OF THE MORNING	Arthur Benjamin	Britain	1937
WIZARD OF OZ, THE	Herbert Stothart	U.S.A.	1939
YOUR FREEDOM IS AT STAKE	Kaj Rosenberg	Denmark	1945
ZÉRO DE CONDUITE	Maurice Jaubert	France	1933

OUTSTANDING BRITISH FILM MUSIC OF 1947-8

Film	Music by	Film	Music by
Against the Wind	Leslie Bridgewater	Mark of Cain	Bernard Stevens
Anna Karenina	Constant Lambert	Master of Bankdam	Arthur Benjamin
Black Narcissus	Brian Easdale	Mine Own Executioner	Benjamin Frankel
Blanche Fury	Clifton Parker	Miranda	Temple Abady
Bonnie Prince Charlie	Ian Whyte	My Brother Jonathan	Hans May
Brighton Rock	Hans May	Nicholas Nickleby	Lord Berners
Broken Journey	John Greenwood	Night Beat	Benjamin Frankel
Brothers, The	Cedric Thorpe Davie	October Man	William Alwyn
Captain Boycott	William Alwyn	Odd Man Out	William Alwyn
Corridor of Mirrors	Georges Auric	One Night with You	Bixio
Dancing with Crime	Benjamin Frankel	Red Shoes	Brian Easdale
Daughters of Darkness	William Alwyn	Root of All Evil	Bretton Byrd
Daybreak	Guy Warrack	Saraband for Dead Lovers	Alan Rawsthorne
Dear Murderer	Benjamin Frankel	Scott of the Antarctic	Ralph Vaughan Williams
End of the River	Lambert Williamson	Silver Darlings	Clifton Parker
Fame is the Spur	John Wooldridge	Snowbound	Cedric Thorpe Davie
First Gentleman, The	Lennox Berkeley	So Evil My Love	William Alwyn
Frieda	John Greenwood	Take My Life	William Alwyn
Good Time Girl	Lambert Williamson	They Made Me a Fugitive	Marius François Galliard
Great Expectations	Walter Goehr	They Walk Alone	William Alwyn
Hamlet	William Walton	Things Happen at Night	George Melachrino
Hills of Donegal	Percival Mackey	This Was a Woman	Mischa Spoliansky
Holiday Camp	Bob Busby	Uncle Silas	Alan Rawsthorne
Hue and Cry	Georges Auric	Upturned Glass, The	Bernard Stevens
Hungry Hill	John Greenwood	Vice Versa	Anthony Hopkins
Ideal Husband, An	Arthur Benjamin	When the Bough Breaks	Clifton Parker
It Always Rains on Sundays	Georges Auric	While I Live	Charles Williams
Jassy	Henry Geehl	White Cradle Inn	Bernard Grun
Loves of Joanna Godden,	Ralph Vaughan Williams	White Unicorn, The	Bretton Byrd
Man About the House, A	Nicholas Brodzsky	Woman in the Hall, The	Temple Abady
Man Within, The	Clifton Parker		

MARK STEVENS
(*20th Century-Fox*)

THE DOCUMENTARY FILM

SUSAN HAYWARD
(RKO-Radio)

H. Bruce Woolfe

DOCUMENTARY
AT THE CROSSROADS

THE form of film known as documentary goes back a good deal further than is generally supposed. The first I can remember was Ponting's record of *Scott's Journey to the Antarctic*. This was drawing large crowds to the Polytechnic in London when World War I broke out. Later Lowell Thomas presented *With Allenby in Palestine*. It may be that these films cannot properly be described as documentaries because they were accompanied by lectures from their producers, but they were in the true spirit of documentary and the lectures were given only because sound films were then unknown.

Following these came such war films as *Armageddon, Zeebrugge, Ypres* and *Mons*. These were documentaries inasmuch as they were true records of events, although some of the events included were reconstructed in the same way that scenes were re-enacted in the documentaries of World War II.

In America, Robert Flaherty created a sensation when he produced *Nanook of the North* in 1922, and *Moana of the South Seas* a few years later. In 1929, Grierson brought out *Drifters*. The number of documentaries was increased by the work of Basil Wright with *Song of Ceylon* and others, Rotha with *Shipyard* and *Face of Britain*, and Cavalcanti with *Rien que les Heures*. All these films, and others, built up a reputation for British documentaries at home and abroad which was not transient but which persisted. These films were made because the producers had something to express. They believed in their subjects and consequently they were successful.

When World War II broke out the tradition was continued and the reputation enhanced. *Target for Tonight, Western Approaches, Theirs is the Glory* and other films were successful wherever shown. During the war, however, another school of documentary came into being. The Government needed propaganda and the Ministry of Information was prepared to pay for it. A number of companies started production in order to meet these requirements. They were naturally quite willing to accept Government orders for which they were paid with Government money, but they had to make their films according

to their briefs whether they believed in them or not. Business concerns also came into the market, and, largely owing to the influence of the Excess Profits Tax, a number of films were made showing the working of industrial enterprises. As a result, films dealing with food, coal, munitions and various social questions were produced.

During the war entertainment was so scarce that anything that was flashed on the screen could command an audience—but at what cost nobody knows. What we *do* know is that audiences gradually began to dislike these films until a certain resentment grew up against them in the public mind. This resentment found expression in the 1946-7 Bernstein Questionnaire in which the type of film occupying first place in public " dislike " was the film concerned with Social Developments.

Another pointer to the decline of British documentaries is the fact that at the Brussels Festival in 1935 British documentary exhibits gained several awards. In 1947, at the same Festival, British documentaries were not even in the running.

Is there a conclusion to be drawn from the success of the earlier productions which were not sponsored in the usually accepted meaning of that word, and the non-success in the public eye of those that are ? I believe there is. In the old days, producers made their films with a real sincerity. Nowadays they have to express not what they feel but what somebody else imposes on them. They might or might not feel sincerely about what they attempt to express, but unless a director or producer feels sincerely about the subject he is presenting as a documentary film, he had better leave it alone.

The post-war public has decided it has little use for documentaries. Obviously there has got to be a change if the British documentary is to regain the prestige it has lost. If documentary films are to achieve their purpose—and they have a great purpose to achieve—they must be widely shown in the cinemas in order to reach a great number of people. And to be shown in the cinemas they must be of interest to their audiences.

How can this interest be regained ? War, which has provided some of our finest documentary films, is no longer a subject for film making. Social questions worked out in terms of documentaries are dull and are not wanted. Industrial documentaries are played out. What remains ?

H. BRUCE WOOLFE *is a pioneer of British documentary films and was producer of " Armageddon", "Zeebrugge", " Ypres", " Mons " and " The Battle of the Falkland Islands". He is now on the staff of Children's Entertainment Films as a production executive.*

The recent success of *The Overlanders* shows that the story-documentary can draw an audience. This type of film is not easy to handle. Recently a body of eight or nine documentarians got together to discuss this matter and to seek for suitable suggestions for story-documentaries. A considerable number of ideas were sent in, but it was found, after several meetings and much discussion, that only one of these ideas was practicable.

This means that our documentary producers have got to do some hard thinking if the national reputation for this class of film is to be retained. Times have changed ; so has the public's taste. While the earlier documentaries succeeded because of their sincerity and originality, I believe that if the modern style is pursued any further there will soon be a slump in documentaries. Modern audiences are not deeply interested in films of mechanical progress or sociological questions. They would probably be more interested if they could see films of the type of Robert Flaherty's *Nanook*, which someone had the inspiration to re-issue, in 1947, with great success.

There are many difficulties in the path of documentary producers. Costs have mounted considerably and the risks of production have correspondingly increased. Conditions of the market are all in favour of the feature producer and against the shorter film. And the fact remains that the modern type of documentary is not wanted.

Is there not a connection between these two facts ? If the documentary film were more interesting, would not the market be more accommodating ? I believe this is so and am convinced that if documentary concerned itself less with propaganda and more with human interest there would soon be a different story to tell. If the new Films Act is framed in such a way that a fairer method of marketing specialized films can be adopted, and producers take up seriously the development of the story-documentary, we could soon be in a fair way to regain the prestige we have lost.

In the meantime, it is obvious that documentary has reached the crossroads of its history. It is up to the producers to choose the right road.

BRITISH DOCUMENTARY PRODUCERS

(Members of the Association of Specialised Film Producers Ltd.)

A—35 *mm. production ;* B—16 *mm. production ;* C—*cartoon, diagram and film strip ;* D—*studio, equipment and allied facilities.* EP—*Executive Producer.*

ANGLO-SCOTTISH PICTURES LTD. (A)
Bernard Davies (EP),
London Film Studio, Shepperton, Middx
Chertsey 2211, ext. 121

BIRMINGHAM COMMERCIAL FILMS LTD. (B)
Harold Juggins (EP),
8 Lozells-road, Birmingham, 19
Northern 3090

BRITISH FILMS LTD. (A, D)
K. L. Lockstone (managing director),
199 Piccadilly, London, W.1
Regent 2828

BRITISH INDUSTRIAL FILMS LTD. (A, B, C, D)
John Curthoys (EP),
Chenil Galleries, King's-road, London, S.W.3
Flaxman 0941

BRITISH INSTRUCTIONAL FILMS LTD. (A, B, C, D)
A. Russell Borland (EP),
Film House, Wardour-street, London, W.1
Gerrard 4341

B. M. PRODUCTIONS LTD. (A)
Bernard Mainwaring (EP),
12 Quadrant Arcade, Regent-street, London, W.1
Regent 3063

BYRON PICTURES LTD. (A)
W. de Lane Lea (EP),
7-9 St. James's-street, London, W.1
Abbey 3515

CHELSEA COLOUR FILMS LTD. (B)
H. R. Dance (EP),
Willing House, 356 Gray's Inn-road, London, W.C.1
Terminus 7522

CITIZEN FILMS LTD. (A)
Herbert Marshall (EP),
The Studio, 10A Randolph-avenue, Maida Vale, London, W.9
Cunningham 0643

CONCORD PRODUCTIONS LTD. (A)
J. Gardner Lewis (EP),
199 Piccadilly, London, W.1
Regent 2828

DIAGRAM FILMS LTD. (A, C)
Miss W. B. A. Woolfe (EP),
28-30 Little Russell-street, London, W.C.1
Holborn 5249

FILM CENTRE LTD. (A, C, D)
Edgar H. Anstey (EP),
34, Soho-square, London, W.1
Gerrard 4253

FILMS OF GREAT BRITAIN LTD. (A)
Andrew Buchanan (EP),
Park Studios, Putney Park-lane, London, S.W.15
Putney 6274/4052

FILM PRODUCERS GUILD LTD. (A)
E. P. L. Pelly (EP),
Guild House, Upper St. Martin's-lane, London, W.C.2
Temple Bar 5420

FOSTER FILMS LTD. (A)
R. V. Foster (EP),
14 St. Mary Abbots-place, London, W.14
Sloane 2600
COMMUNICATIONS TO :
53, Leith Mansions, Grantully-road, London, W.9
Cunningham 2680

FURNEAUX-WEBER LTD. (B)
Rupert Furneaux (EP),
A, Willing House, 356 Gray's
Inn-road, London, W.C.1
Terminus 7530

G-B ANIMATION LTD. (A, B, C, D)
David Hand (EP),
Moor Hall, Cookham, Berks
Bourne End 810

G-B INSTRUCTIONAL LTD. (A, B, C, D)
I. H. Cremieu-Javal (EP),
80–82 Regent-street, London, W.1
Regent 7222

G-B SCREEN SERVICES LTD. (A)
E. Pearl (EP),
128 Finchley-road, London, N.W.3
Hampstead 4424

G.W.H. PRODUCTIONS LTD. (A, D)
J. B. Sloan (EP),
The Gate Studios, Station-road, Boreham Wood, Herts
Elstree 2080

GREENPARK PRODUCTIONS LTD. (A)
Paul Fletcher (EP),
Guild House, Upper St. Martin's-lane, London, W.C.2
Temple Bar 5420

HARVEY HARRISON FILMS LTD. (A)
Harvey Harrison (EP),
8 Harley-place, London, W.1
Langham 1260

INTERNATIONAL REALIST LTD. (A)
Basil Wright (EP),
9 Great Chapel-street, London, W.1
Gerrard 8395

MERTON PARK STUDIOS LTD. (A, C, D)
F. A. Hoare (EP),
269 Kingston-road, Merton Park, London, S.W.19
Liberty 4291

NATIONAL INTEREST PICTURE PRODUCTIONS LTD. (A, C)
A. E. C. Hopkins (EP),
21 Soho-square, London, W.1
Gerrard 5843

PATHE PICTURES LTD. (A, B, C, D)
Howard Thomas (EP),
103–9 Wardour-street, London, W.1
Gerrard 5701

S. PRESBURY & CO. LTD. (A)
J. E. Presbury (EP),
Gloucester House, 19 Charing Cross-road, London, W.C.2
Whitehall 3601

PUBLICITY FILMS LTD. (A, B)
E. W. Beckett (EP),
Guild House, Upper St. Martin's-lane, London, W.C.2
Temple Bar 5420

PUBLIC RELATIONSHIP FILMS LTD. (A, C)
Dr. Richard Massingham (EP),
29 Whitehall, London, S.W.1
Whitehall 4000

SCIENCE FILMS LTD. (A, C)
W. E. Woolfe (EP),
28–30 Little Russell-street, London, W.C.1

Holborn 5249
COMMUNICATIONS TO :
The Studio, College Slip, Bromley, Kent
Ravensbourne 5150

SELWYN FILM SERVICES LTD. (A)
C. A. Radley (EP),
19 Lexham-mews, London, W.8
Western 4969

SIGNAL FILMS LTD. (C)
G. A. Holdsworth, D.S.O., O.B.E. (EP),
Wallace Centre, 5 Berwick-street, London, W.1
Gerrard 2639

THIS MODERN AGE LTD. (A)
S. Nolbandov (EP),
18 Old Burlington-street, London, W.1
Regent 0613

TRIDENT FILMS LTD. (A)
Mrs. Rosanne Brownrigg (EP),
77 Dean-street, London, W.1
Gerrard 1458–9

UNITED MOTION PICTURES (LONDON) LTD. (B)
E. C. Davey (EP),
24 Denmark-street, London, W.C.2
Temple Bar 2025

VERITY FILMS LTD. (A)
A. T. Burlinson (EP),
Guild House, Upper St. Martin's-lane, London, W.C.2
Temple Bar 5420

WALLACE PRODUCTIONS LTD. (A)
A. V. Curtice (EP),
8 Berwick-street, London, W.1
Gerrard 2639

R. E. Tritton

THE GOVERNMENT'S
FILM DEPARTMENT
IN WAR AND PEACE

THE origins of the Government's information films and of the school of British documentary films which has been called "Britain's essential contribution to the film" are one and the same. Both began in 1929 when the Empire Marketing Board appointed John Grierson to make films of a factual nature about the Empire's people and their occupations.

When the Empire Marketing Board was dissolved in 1934, the film unit belonging to it was transferred to the General Post Office. This G.P.O. film unit (now known as the Crown Film Unit) was in its turn transferred to the Ministry of Information when this was formed at the beginning of the war.

Thus the documentary film has been closely allied to the Government Information Service since its very early beginnings. The relationship still holds firm and today the Government is the biggest sponsor of factual films in the country.

During the war the films sponsored by the Ministry of Information played an important part in the dissemination of information about the progress of the war, both at home and abroad. Today the same thing holds good, and the film is being used as a medium of education and information more than ever before. Let us see how the work of the Films Division of the Central Office of Information today differs from the work of the Films Division of the Ministry of Information in the war years.

Throughout the war the public at home and, to a lesser extent, the world overseas, had to be kept informed of new developments in the national situation, and people had to be trained to unfamiliar work in the shortest possible time. To help in this, the Films Division of the Ministry of Information made films either through the Crown Unit or through the independent documentary film units on a very wide variety of subjects. The films ranged from such ten-reel feature films as *Western Approaches*, which was distributed very widely throughout the whole world, to one-minute trailers carrying some particular exhortation to the people of this country. During the war the M. of I. produced in this way more than 700 different films of varying types and lengths.

The method of operation was for the Films Division, M. of I., to commission films in consultation with Public Relations Offices of the various Government departments, allotting the films to those units best able to carry out the particular type of work in hand. The Government department concerned was kept fully in the picture, but did not play the full role of sponsorship which it now does under the Central Office of Information. The M. of I. in the war had the right to initiate and see through to their conclusion any films on any subjects thought to be within the charter of the Ministry. There was little planning ahead because the changing conditions of the war made it impossible, and there was little difficulty over money, but the shortage of manpower was a very serious problem.

Much of the raw material of films made by the Government during the war originated with the Service Film Units. *Desert Victory*, *The True Glory* and *Burma Victory* are examples of such films.

In addition to films made for information in this country, both on strictly war subjects and on matters connected with the home front, films were made by the Colonial Film Unit, which was under the control of the Ministry of Information. Primarily devised for the West African native, these films were simple in technique and designed to educate and interest an unsophisticated audience.

The British Council during the war also played its part in the projection overseas by means of films of the British way of life.

The M. of I. during the war used all the methods of distribution available at home and abroad. At home, varying systems of distribution through the cinemas of the country were operated in conjunction with the Cinematograph Exhibitors' Association. The system at the end of the war was for twelve one-reel films a year to be distributed free through all the cinemas of the country. That plan still holds good. In addition to this arrangement, films were distributed through the normal commercial channels on their merits, many of them having wide distribution and bringing considerable revenue to the Exchequer.

There was and always will be, however, a large number of information films which for various reasons are not suitable for showing in the public cinema. To bring these films to their right audiences, a wide system of non-theatrical

R. E. TRITTON *is Director of the Films Division, Central Office of Information.*

distribution by means of mobile projection vans and the Central Film Library was started.

Towards the end of the war there were 140 mobile projection units. Their bases were the regional offices of the Ministry of Information throughout the country. These mobile units brought the specialist films to the specialist audience. Thus, if the Ministry of Agriculture wished a film about some aspect of dairy farming brought to the notice of dairy farmers, the film was shown by the projection vans to groups of farmers collected locally with the help of the regional officer of the Ministry of Agriculture. This system covered a very wide field and was notably successful.

The Central Film Library, which operates from London, is a lending library of 16 mm. films made primarily by the Government for purposes of information. It supplies any reasonable request free of charge and its borrowers include universities, hospitals, youth hostels, clubs, women's institutes, and many other organizations of this type.

Oversea distribution during the war was limited by obvious difficulties. In those countries which could be reached, official British films were shown widely and successfully, both commercially and non-theatrically. In America particularly, the work of the Films Division of the British Information Services was most effective. Such films as *Desert Victory* have brought in hundreds of thousands of dollars to the Exchequer, and even in 1947 *Western Approaches* broke box-office records in New York, Philadelphia and Los Angeles—a satisfactory state of affairs for the British taxpayer.

So much for the wartime work in the days of the Ministry of Information. Now to turn to the post-war system.

Production is similar in method, but has two fundamental differences. First, the Central Office of Information is not theoretically a policy-making body. This prohibits the Films Division from embarking upon projects on its own initiative. All films now have to be sponsored by a Government department or one of the two committees controlling the Home and Overseas Information Services of the Government. The second fundamental change is in the nature of the programme. During the war the main target for all films was the home audience. Such films as were used overseas (and some were very successful) were by-products of the home market. Almost no films other than British Council subjects were made specifically for audiences overseas. This was changed after the war: the Foreign Office, the Overseas Information Department of the Board of Trade, and the British Council now sponsor films through the Films Division of the Central Office of Information for oversea use. Some thirty per cent. of the total output is now aimed at the foreign market.

It should be emphasized that films made by the Government are objective and are not concerned with party politics or the policies of any particular group. The work of the Home Departments —Health, Education, Agriculture, and so on— goes on at a slightly higher rate than during the war years. Education has a very ambitious film programme ahead, partly through official channels and partly through the trade.

The distribution machinery is also the same at home. The three channels are used—the theatres, the mobile vans and the Central Film Library. At the moment the accent is on the production and export drive, and a large percentage of the 140 mobile vans still available is engaged on factory shows.

Oversea distribution has been increased considerably. All European British Embassies and Legations are being staffed with Films Officers and equipped with a basic library of films for non-theatrical use. Contracts have been made both in this country and in countries all over the world for the commercial showing of British films overseas.

Everything is being done not only to maintain the high standards of film-making and distribution set by the Films Division of the Ministry of Information during the war, but to raise to even greater efficiency the dissemination of British information all over the world by means of the film.

OUTSTANDING WAR DOCUMENTARIES

Britain Can Take It
(Overseas title : **London Can Take It**)
Crown Film Unit, 1940.
Burma Victory
British Army Film Unit, 1945.
Producer : Lieutenant-Colonel David Macdonald.
Director : Captain Roy Boulting. From material taken by British, Indian and American combat cameramen of S.E.A.C.
Close Quarters
Crown Film Unit, 1943.
Director : Jack Lee.
Coastal Command
Crown Film Unit, 1942.
Director : Jack Holmes.
Defeated People, A
Crown Film Unit, 1946.
Director : Humphrey Jennings.
Desert Victory
Army Film and Photographic Unit, and R.A.F. Film Production Unit, 1943.
Producer : Major David Macdonald.
Director : Captain Roy Boulting.
Fires Were Started
Crown Film Unit, 1943.
Director : Humphrey Jennings.
Journey Together
R.A.F. Film Production Unit, 1945.
Director : Flight Lieutenant John Boulting.
Left of the Line
British and Canadian Army Film Units, 1944.
Listen to Britain
Crown Film Unit, 1942.
Director : Humphrey Jennings.
Malta G.C.
Army Film Unit, and Crown Film Unit, 1943.

Next of Kin
Ealing, 1942.
Director : Thorold Dickinson.
Nine Hundred, The
Photographed by Combat Camera Units of the Mediterranean Allied Air Forces, R.A.F. and British Army Film Units, 1945.
Silent Village, The
Crown Film Unit, 1943.
Director : Humphrey Jennings.
Target for Tonight
Crown Film Unit, 1941.
Director : Harry Watt.
Today and Tomorrow
World Wide Pictures, 1945.
Director : Robin Carruthers.
True Glory, The
British and American Service Film Units, 1945.
British team headed by Carol Reed, American team by Captain Garson Kanin.
True Story of Lili Marlene, The
Crown Film Unit, 1944.
Director : Humphrey Jennings.
Tunisian Victory
British and American Service Film Units, 1944.
British team headed by Major Hugh Stewart and Captain Roy Boulting, American team by Captain Frank Capra.
We Sail at Midnight
Crown Film Unit, 1943.
Director : Julian Spiro.
Western Approaches
Crown Film Unit, 1944.
Director : Pat Jackson.
World of Plenty
Paul Rotha Productions, 1943.

RECENT C.O.I. RELEASES

A selection showing the variety of government-sponsored films

All Eyes on Britain
Data Film Unit, 1947.
Director : Blayden Peake. For Economic Information Committee.
Balance, The
Films of Fact, 1947.
Director : J. B. Holmes. For Board of Trade.
Breeding for Milk
Crown Film Unit, 1947.
Director : Jack Gowers. For Ministry of Agriculture.
Children Learning by Experience
Realist Film Unit, 1947.
Director : Margaret Thomson. For Ministry of Education.
Children on Trial
Crown Film Unit, 1946.
Director : Jack Lee. For Home Office.
Country Policeman
Merlin Films, 1947.
Director : Gilbert Gunn. For Scottish Home Department.
Cumberland Story, The
Crown Film Unit, 1947.
Director : Humphrey Jennings. For Ministry of Fuel and Power.
Cyprus is an Island
Greenpark, 1946.
Director : Ralph Keene. For Ministry of Information.

Downlands
Greenpark, 1947.
Directors : Charles de Latour and Humphrey Swingler. For Ministry of Agriculture & Fisheries.
Here is the Gold Coast
Director : John Page. For Colonial Office.
Instruments of the Orchestra
Crown Film Unit, 1946.
Director : Muir Mathieson. For Ministry of Education.
Thousand Million a Year, A
Anglo-Scottish Pictures, 1947.
For Customs and Excise Department.
University of Flying
Horizon Film Unit, 1947.
Director : Max Munden. For Ministry of Supply.
World is Rich, The
Films of Fact, 1947.
Producer : Paul Rotha.
Associate Director : Michael Orram. For Ministry of Food.
Your Children and You
Realist Film Unit, 1946.
Director : Brian Smith. For Ministry of Health in co-operation with the Central Council for Health Education.

ANNE BAXTER
(20th Century-Fox)

"THE MARCH OF TIME"

*T*HE *March of Time* has a unique place in the history of the cinema. These twenty-minute films were the first screen productions which aimed at mixing the topicality of the newsreel with the creative purpose of the documentary.

The story of *The March of Time* is the sequel to the attempt of two young Yale graduates in New York to make the essential news facts of the world comprehensive and yet concise enough to remain in the mind of the man in the street. These two young men, Henry R. Luce and Briton Hadden, were cub reporters in 1922. Their idea was to bring out a publication devoted entirely to significant news of the week, sifted and set out as a story. The next year—1923—they brought out the magazine *Time*.

In 1934, the vice-president of *Time*, Roy Larsen, met Louis de Rochemont, a young American who had been doing experimental documentary film work for the U.S. Government, and who had later tried a new type of film called *The March of the Years*. This set out to reconstruct aspects of the history of man, but had failed commercially. De Rochemont and Larsen formed the first editorial board of *The March of Time*, bringing out their first film in America in 1934.

Its immediate success brought about the opening of *The March of Time* offices in Paris and London in 1935. Richard de Rochemont, brother of producer Louis, came over from New York to head this new venture. The first issue of *The March of Time* played in 417 theatres. In 1947 the series was appearing regularly in thirty-eight countries, in over 12,000 cinemas; and French, German-Swiss, Spanish, Flemish, Norwegian, and Portuguese voices spoke the commentaries in their own languages. An innovation introduced at the end of 1947 is to have an American voice for U.S. distribution, and an English voice for distribution in Britain.

The first issues dealt with three or four subjects each month. Now each issue is devoted to one subject, for it was soon realized that behind most news is a long story.

All over the world men who are making present-day history face *The March of Time*'s cameras. Whether they be statesmen, scientists, workmen or peasants, their actions and their words are recorded for history, a testimony for future generations as well as for audiences of today.

In 1943 Louis de Rochemont left *The March of Time* to become a feature producer for 20th Century-Fox, and Richard de Rochemont became producer of *The March of Time*. The organization in New York today employs over a hundred people, and film coverage for stories all over the world is obtained by eight production units.

FIRST YEAR, 1935-6

No.
1 (Oct.) *S.S. ' Mohawk ' Disaster*
Tokyo
Max Buchsbaum
Moscow (Russia : Stalin)
Croix de Feu
2 (Nov.) *East of Suez* (Palestine)
Sudden Death
New York (Speakeasies)
Trans-Pacific (Air Line)
3 (Dec.) *Father Coughlin*
Pennsylvania
Cambridge, Mass. (Magic Camera)
Pacific Ocean (American Naval Manœuvres)
4 (Jan.) *U.S.A.* (Townsend Pension Scheme)
The Northwest (Duck Shooting)
Japan—China
5 (Feb.) *South Pacific* (Students become weather observers on desert island)
New York City (Strike Breaking)
London (Shipping Story)
6 (Mar.) *Tennessee Valley* (American Congress, public damming and electrical works)
U.S.A. (Hartman's Dental Solution)
Moscow
7 (Apr.) *C.C.C. Camps*
French Guiana
England (Britain's " Hollywood ")
8 (May) *America's Army of National Defence*
France (Deibler, Executioner)
Geneva (League of Nations)

SECOND YEAR, 1936-7

No.
1 (June) *Austria* (Hapsburgs)
U.S.A. (Dog Trials)
France (Peasantry and Politics)
2 (July) *U.S.A.* (Juvenile Crime)
Angola La !
England (Aviation)
3 (Aug.) *U.S.A.* (Presidential Elections and Unemployment Relief)
Albania
England (Football Pools)
4 (Sept.) *New England* (Fisheries)
U.S.A. (Jockey Club)
England (Tithe War)
5 (Oct.) *Ireland's New Deal*
U.S.A. (The Lunatic Fringe)
Washington (The Presidency)
6 (Nov.) *U.S.A.* (College Football)
New Orleans (Canadian Waterways)
Belgium (Rex Rally)
7 (Dec.) *Princeton, N.J.* (Veterans of Future Wars)
U.S.A. (Arson)
England (Food and Physical Training)
8 (Jan.) *U.S. Labour Front* (Lewis)
Texas Centenary
The Far East (Chiang Kai-Shek)
9 (Feb.) *U.S.A.* (Battle for Clean Milk)
U.S.A. (Winter Vacations)
British Empire (Coronation)

10 (Mar.) *U.S.A. (Enemies of Alcohol)*
          U.S.A. (Trailer-Caravans)
          Black Areas
11 (Apr.) *Father of the Turks*
          Conquering Cancer
          Birth of Swing
12 (May) *Salt Lake City*
          Amateur Sleuths
          Land of Cotton

THIRD YEAR, 1937-8

No.
1 (June) *Child Labour*
          Federal Theatres (Uncle Sam, Impresario)
          D.O.R.A. (Defence of the Realm Act)
2 (July) *Dogs for Sale*
          Railroad Renaissance
          Scotland's Highland Problems
3 (Aug.) *Poland and War*
          Girls and Work
          U.S. Dust Bowl
4 (Sept.) *War in China*
          Passamaquoddy
5 (Oct.) *Junk and War*
          Hollywood
          Fiorello La Guardia
6 (Nov.) *Youth in Camps*
          Oxford
          Rehearsal for War
7 (Dec.) *The Spoils System*
          Amoskeag
          America's Gibraltar
8 (Jan.) *New Schools for Old*
          Tips and Waiters
          Alaska's Salmon War
9 (Feb.) *U.S. Secret Service*
          Britain's Noblemen
          Ships, Strikes and Seamen
10 (Mar.) *Finland*
          Pests of 1938
          The Human Heart
11 (Apr.) *French Wine*
          Babies Wanted
          Ulster v. Eire
12 (May) *Inside Nazi Germany*

FOURTH YEAR, 1938-9

No.
1 (June) *Old Dixie's New Boom*
          Hire Purchase
          Russians in Exile
2 (July) *Crime and Prisons*
          Nazi Conquest No. 1
3 (Aug.) *Brain Trust Island*
          Czechoslovakia
4 (Sept.) *One Million Missing*
          America's Laugh Industry
          Britons on Holiday
5 (Oct.) *Racketeers v. Housewives*
          Man at the Wheel
6 (Nov.) *G-Men of the Sea*
          Britain and Peace
7 (Nov.) *Inside the Maginot Line*
8 (Dec.) *U.S. Firefighters*
          Father Divine's Deal
9 (Jan.) *The Refugee—Today and Tomorrow*
10 (Feb.) *Men of Medicine*
11 (Feb.) *Uncle Sam—The Good Neighbour*
12 (Mar.) *Mexico's New Crisis*
          Youth Prepares
13 (Apr.) *Mediterranean—Background for War*

FIFTH YEAR, 1939-40

No.
1 (May) *America Thinks It Over*
2 (June) *Japan—Master of the Orient*
3 (July) *Britain—Peace and Propaganda*
4 (Aug.) *The Movies March On !*
5 (Oct.) *New World Metropolis*
6 (Oct.) *Battle Fleets of Britain*
7 (Nov.) *Soldiers with Wings*
8 (Jan.) *Newsfronts of War, 1940*
9 (Jan.) *Uncle Sam the Farmer*
10 (Feb.) *Crisis in the Pacific*
11 (Mar.) *Vatican City*
12 (Apr.) *Canada at War*
13 (May) *Dixie, U.S.A.*

SIXTH YEAR, 1940-1

No.
1 (June) *The Philippines, 1898-1946*
2 (July) *America's Youth*
3 (Aug.) *U.S. Navy, 1940*
4 (Sept.) *Gateways to Panama*
5 (Oct.) *Britain's R.A.F.*
6 (Nov.) *On Foreign Newsfronts*
7 (Dec.) *The Dutch East Indies*
8 (Jan.) *Mexico*
9 (Feb.) *America Prepares*
10 (Mar.) *America Speaks Her Mind*
11 (Apr.) *Labour and Defence, U.S.A.*
12 (May) *Americans All !*
13 (June) *Australia at War*

SEVENTH YEAR, 1941-2

No.
1 (June) *Crisis in the Atlantic*
2 (July) *G-Men Combat Saboteurs*
3 (Aug.) *China Fights Back*
4 (Sept.) *Peace by Adolf Hitler*
5 (Oct.) *Thumbs Up Texas*
6 (Nov.) *Men of Norway*
7 (Dec.) *Sailors with Wings*
8 (Jan.) *Main Street, U.S.A.*
Special (Feb.) *Battlefields of the Pacific*
9 (Mar.) *America at War*
10 (Mar.) *The Argentine Question*
11 (Apr.) *New England's Eight Million Yankees*
12 (May) *America's New Army*
13 (June) *Far East Command*

EIGHTH YEAR, 1942-3

No.
1 (July) *India in Crisis*
2 (Aug.) *India at War*
3 (Sept.) *Men in Washington*
4 (Oct.) *Men of the U.S. Navy*
5 (Nov.) *G-Men at War*
6 (Dec.) *The Fighting French*
7 (Jan.) *Prelude to Victory*
8 (Feb.) *Mr. and Mrs. America*
9 (Mar.) *The Navy and the Nation*
10 (Apr.) *The New Canada*
11 (May) *Inside Fascist Spain*
12 (May) *Food and War*
13 (June) *Union of South Africa*

NINTH YEAR, 1943-4

No.
1 (Aug.)   *Preparation for Invasion*
2 (Oct.)   *Show Business at War*
3 (Oct.)   *Bill Jack v. Adolf Hitler*
4 (Nov.)   *. . . And Then Japan*
5 (Dec.)   *Airways to Peace*
6 (Jan.)   *Europe's Crossroads*
7 (Feb.)   *Naval Log of Victory*
8 (Mar.)   *Up Beat in Music*
9 (Apr.)   *Sweden's Middle Road*
10 (May)   *South American Front*
11 (June) *The Irish Question*
12 (July) *Underground Report*
13 (Aug.) *Backdoor to Tokyo*

TENTH YEAR, 1944-5

No.
1 (Sept.) *British Imperialism, 1944*
2 (Sept.) *Racial Problems*
3 (Oct.)   *What To Do with Germany*
4 (Nov.)   *Strategy of Liberation*
5 (Dec.)   *Post-War Jobs*
6 (Jan.)   *Uncle Sam—Mariner ?*
7 (Feb.)   *Inside China Today*
8 (Mar.)   *Report on Italy*
9 (Apr.)   *The Unknown Battle*
10 (May)   *Profile of Britain*
11 (June) *The Returning Veteran*
12 (Oct.) *Teen Age Girls*
13 (Nov.) *Palestine Problem*

ELEVENTH YEAR, 1945-6

No.
1 (Dec.)   *Pacific Frontiers*
2 (Jan.)   *Battle for Beauty*
3 (Feb.)   *The Philippines, 1946*
4 (Mar.)   *Justice Comes to Germany*
5 (Apr.)   *Challenge to Hollywood*
           (Round the British Studios)
6 (May)   *Report on Greece*
7 (June)   *New York's Night Club Boom*
8 (July)   *Life with Baby*
9 (Aug.)   *Wanted—More Homes*
10 (Sept.) *Tomorrow's Mexico*
11 (Oct.) *Problem Drinkers*
12 (Nov.) *Atomic Power*
13 (Dec.) *Is Everybody Happy ?*

TWELFTH YEAR, 1946-7

No.
1 (Dec.)   *The New France*
2 (Dec.)   *World Food Problem*
3 (Feb.)   *The Soviet's Neighbour—Czechoslovakia*
4 (Feb.)   *The American Cop*
5 (Apr.)   *Nobody's Children*
6 (June)   *Germany—Handle with Care*
7 (June)   *Storm Over Britain*
8 (July)   *U.S. Teachers Crisis*
9 (Aug.)   *The Russians Nobody Knows*
10 (Sept.) *Fashion Means Business*
11 (Oct.) *Your Doctors Today*
12 (Nov.) *"T" Men in Action*
13 (Dec.) *Trouble in Turkey*

"THIS MODERN AGE"

PRODUCED by the Rank Organisation, *This Modern Age* is the counterpart of America's *The March of Time*.

Early in 1946, two men, Sergei Nolbandov and George Ivan Smith, planned Britain's first film news magazine, and the first issue, *Homes for All*, was shown in September 1946.

Produced at the rate of one a month, *This Modern Age* presents an impartial review of the problems, movements, developments and crises—industrial, political and human—of the world.

By the end of 1947 some fifty expert technicians and a permanent team of script writers specializing in this form of screen journalism had been assigned exclusively to the production of these films. It is symbolical of this modern age that many of the unit production managers are women.

FIRST YEAR, 1946

No.
1 (Sept.) *Homes for All*
           Modern planning in town and country.
2 (Nov.)   *Scotland Yard*
           An authentic record of the Yard at work.
3 (Dec.)   *Tomorrow by Air*
           History of British aviation from 1909.

SECOND YEAR, 1947

No.
4 (Jan.)   *Fabrics of the Future*
           Review of the textile industries.
5 (Feb.)   *Thoroughbreds for the World*
           The influence of British bloodstock in the breeding of thoroughbreds.
6 (Mar.)   *Palestine*
           The development of Palestine.
7 (Apr.)   *Coal Crisis*
           The importance of coal to Britain's economic future.
8 (May)   *Sudan Dispute*
           The problem of joint administration in Egypt and the Sudan.
9 (June)   *Development Areas*
           The former depressed areas of Britain.
10 (July) *The Rape of the Earth*
           The story of soil erosion.
11 (Aug.) *Antarctic Whale Hunt*
           The story of *Balaena*, the first whale ship to carry aircraft.
12 (Sept.) *Jamaica*
           A review of life and problems today in Jamaica and the West Indies.
13 (Oct.) *Food Crisis*
           Britain's agriculture and its relation to the world food situation.
14 (Nov.) *Report on the Ruhr*
           The Ruhr under British Occupation.
15 (Dec.) *Land Short of People*
           The industrial development of Australia.

BARBARA STANWYCK
(*Warner*)

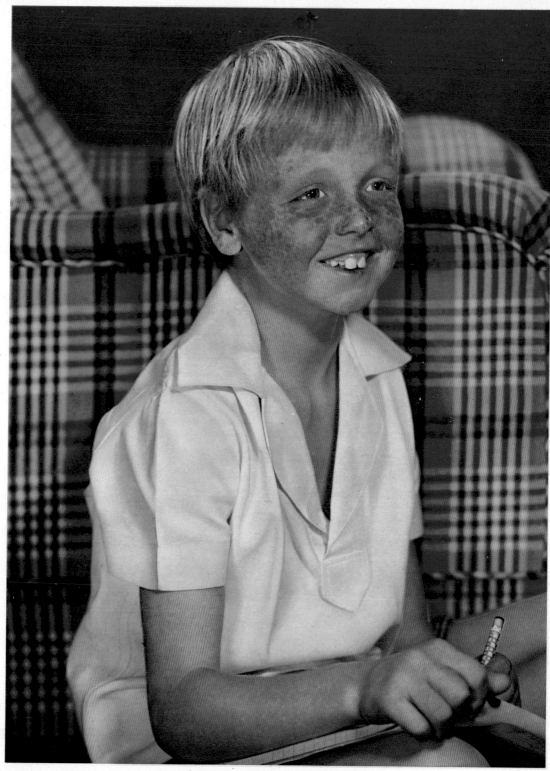

JACKIE "BUTCH" JENKINS
(Metro-Goldwyn-Mayer)

THE "SPECIALIZED" CINEMA

M

RICHARD ATTENBOROUGH
(*Gainsborough*)

C. A. Lejeune

THE "SPECIALIZED" CINEMA

THE "specialized" cinema—by which I mean more particularly the theatre that specializes in showing foreign films other than American—is a comparatively new institution in this country. Roughly speaking, it came in with the talkies.

Before that time of course there had been hundreds of foreign films shown in England. The Continental market supplied a large number of the "shorts" used in the early days of moving pictures. Some of the most impressive of the early feature films came from France and Italy. *Les Misérables, Cabiria* and *Quo Vadis* made a sensation over here before D. W. Griffith had even thought of *The Birth of A Nation*.

Anyone who went to the pictures in the early 1920's will remember the fine series of films that came to us from Sweden—among others, *Thy Soul Shall Bear Witness* and *Love's Crucible, A Lover in Pawn* and *The Atonement of Gösta Berling*. It was this last film—incidentally the last great work of the Swedish national cinema we were to see in this country for more than twenty years—that introduced a handsome young woman called Greta Garbo, of whom great things were hoped.

The Swedish import was never abundant, but it was good. It borrowed heavily from literature, as did the smaller Danish import that came across the North Sea about the same time, but it had a beautiful quality, purely visual, of architecture and lighting. It came too early in the cinema, however, to win or hold any sort of real recognition in this country. The movie was still exclusively a popular form of entertainment ; the group feeling, the experimentalist feeling, the student enthusiasm for new ideas and new technique that was to come later, had not yet invaded it.

The great German revival of the middle 'twenties attracted far more attention. It is impossible to think of those days when we saw, one after another in a great rich pageant, *The Golem, The Street, Destiny, Warning Shadows, Dr. Mabuse, Siegfried, The Student of Prague, The Cabinet of Dr. Caligari, Cinderella, The Waltz Dream*, and a hundred others, without a sense of high excitement. This was the golden age of the German cinema, a time when a generation was creeping out of the shadows of the first world war into a new and full existence ; a time of artistic abundance, almost of profligacy, when each artist was aflame to help another artist, and every craftsman felt himself a brother-craftsman.

C. A. LEJEUNE, *one of the best known of British writers on the cinema, is film critic of "The Observer" and London film correspondent of the " New York Times ".*

The German films of these few years will always be remembered as the works of an extraordinary renaissance. Wordsworth has a word for it :

> *Bliss was it in that dawn to be alive,*
> *But to be young was very heaven.*

During these last doomed years before the onrush of talkies, the more curious and discerning filmgoer had also begun to be intrigued by the work of two other countries—France and Russia. He had, of course, seen French films from his childhood, without always knowing they were French—mainly trick films, serials, historical romances. But now, all of a sudden, a number of films turned up from France that were quite startling in their imagination and force. A man named René Clair made a fantasy called *Paris qui Dort*, and later an even better fantasy called *The Italian Straw Hat* ; Abel Gance made *J'Accuse* ; Jacques Feyder, a Belgian by birth, made *L'Atlantide, Crainquebille, Les Nouveaux Messieurs*, and the superb *Thérèse Raquin* ; Vokoff made *Kean* ; documentary films came into vogue ; there was a movement of experiment in the air, and the fashionable word was " avant-garde ".

It would be fond to pretend that the influence of French films in the 'twenties on the British cinema was deeply marked : it was not. The films were not widely shown, and there was no organized body of literate opinion in those days ready to seek them out. The sudden startling onslaught of the first Soviet films in the very late 'twenties was a different matter. There was a political audience waiting for them ; their astounding force and fervour of expression was met with a corresponding force and fervour of appreciation ; the very obstacles set in the way of their public exhibition were enough to forge them fast in private esteem.

Potemkin, The End of St. Petersburg, The Ghost That Never Returns, Turksib, Giant Harvest, and all the others of that period, were great films and remain unforgettable. I suppose in all there could not have been more than a couple of dozen of them imported into England before the talkies tore the existing fabric of the cinema to pieces, but their number was quite incommensurate with their influence. It is one of the small ironies of scientific progress that this tremendous development in film-making should have taken place at the precise moment when the coming of sound made it invalid ; that we were just beginning to appreciate a new and lively form of silent cinema when the silent cinema drew its last quiet breath.

So far as general commercial distribution was concerned, the arrival of the talkies killed the foreign film stone dead. There was a moment, when some of the daintier rosebuds of the Hollywood screen opened their lips for the first time and talked, that the American film was within an inch of being regarded in this country as a foreign import. It is still a matter for argument whether it might not have been better so. The fact that Britain and the United States use the same syntax and share to a great extent a common vocabulary does not mean that the two countries are one in matters of tradition, taste and understanding.

The British Consul in America who advised a Hollywood cameraman on his way to London never to forget that " though you may *think* you talk the same language as the English, you are really going to a foreign country " showed a great deal of practical wisdom. But ever since the first perilous days of the talkies it has been Hollywood's policy to smooth out the differences of speech between the English-speaking peoples. By achieving with great patience and skill a kind of cosmopolitan screen language, they have retained their cosmopolitan screen market. The average British filmgoer never thinks of an American feature as a foreign film.

But as soon as talkies became general, the Continental film, far closer to us geographically than the products of Hollywood, was unmistakably recognized as an alien. It was foreign on two counts : the people in it talked a language most of us did not understand, and the screen was cluttered up with sub-titles, devices now archaic and remote. The ordinary commercial exhibitor, once talkies were the rule, would as soon offer his patrons a Continental film as he would offer them gas lighting and hard wood seats. There was only one thing to be done by the minority who wanted to show Continental films and the minority who wanted to see them, and that was to organize one or two little theatres solely for that purpose. And so the specialized cinemas came into being.

There are not more than a handful of them in Great Britain even now, but they have the solid backing of over a hundred Film Societies, and both their influence and their public are constantly growing. The importance of a theatre like the Academy, the Rialto, the Curzon or Studio One in London, the Cosmo in Glasgow, is out of all proportion to its small annual programme and its limited seating capacity. Whether it rains or snows, whether the news is good or bad, whether the film is fresh or old, whether the critics have been kind or cool, these theatres have queues for the box-office every night. Their mailing-lists multiply like the greenfly ; their telephones are constantly ringing ; their customers come from places as far away as Aberdeen or Bournemouth, and make their visit something of a pilgrimage.

The people who go to these specialized theatres are intelligent and they talk ; they are literate and they write ; thanks to their good sense, their conversation, their ardour and their contacts, a film like *Les Enfants du Paradis* or *Symphonie Pastorale*, *Le Jour se Lève* or *Un Carnet de Bal*, *Frenzy* or *Day of Wrath*, is heralded throughout the country by a kind of mysterious grape-vine.

The specialized theatre movement will grow. It is bound to grow because it is needed. With an entertainment medium as vast, as cosmopolitan, as heterogeneous as the cinema, catering for so many people of so many races, ages, tastes, and levels of education, it is impossible to contrive one common programme that will please everybody. It is palpably far wiser, less fretting, and more expedient to give up the struggle for a compromise, and boldly arrange the available material into distinct programmes, each of which will have a character and appeal of its own, each of which should please one class of customer. The B.B.C. has done something to meet the same problem by creating the Third Programme. The cinema will find its burdens far more manageable by encouraging specialized theatres.

When we look back at the wealth of material that has come to us from Continental studios in the past, when we consider how much poorer we should have been emotionally, intellectually, and artistically if we had missed seeing the great films from Sweden, France, Germany and Russia, we realize how mean and narrow our film experience will be unless we can keep it constantly refreshed with the best films that can be found in all the countries where films are made. Every nation has something to give to the understanding of the one, the real, the common art. Because the modern film deals in speech, because speech as well as manner varies from country to country, because getting the sense of a foreign idiom involves an effort uncongenial to the relaxed or unpractised mind, the Continental film is inappropriate in an average, mixed cinema programme.

But there are a great number of people in this country who feel that they too are ill-at-ease and out of place with an average, mixed cinema programme. You cannot cajole them ; you cannot force them ; they are of that kind, and nothing will change them. It is for such people that the specialized theatre is precisely designed, and it is at such a theatre, among such people, that the imaginatively daring film of any nationality will get its point across most cleanly.

These people are well-mannered and house-trained ; they are regular customers, and come back again and again with uncompromising loyalty. It does not take much to make them happy. No leopard-skin seats, no pink and amber lights, no Mighty Wurlitzer, no variety turns, no competition nights, no jollying along from frenzied shorts designed to save them from the frightful doom of thought : just a good film, British, American, French, Swedish, German, Danish, Russian ; a management in which they can have confidence, and usherettes soft-footed and as near as can be dumb ; a quiet house, a friendly audience, and the mettle of the game. That is all they ask, and that is what the specialized cinema can give them.

FOREIGN LANGUAGE FILMS
SHOWN IN GREAT BRITAIN

CINEMAS SPECIALIZING IN FOREIGN LANGUAGE FILMS

London

ACADEMY, 165 Oxford-street, W.1

CARLTON, 30a Tottenham Court-road, W.1

* CLASSIC, 98 Baker-street, W.1

* CLASSIC, Brighton-road, South Croydon, Surrey

* CLASSIC, Belle Vue-road, Hendon, N.W.4

* CLASSIC, Upper Tooting-road, S.W.17

CURZON, Curzon-street, W.1

* EMBASSY, 87 Notting Hill-gate, W.11

EVERYMAN, Holly Bush-vale, Hampstead, N.W.3

* GLOBE, Upper Richmond-road, Putney, S.W.15

RIALTO, 3 Coventry-street, W.1

* ROXY, Westbourne-grove, W.2

STUDIO ONE, 225 Oxford-street, W.1

* TATLER, Charing Cross-road, W.C.2

† TORCH THEATRE, 37 Wilton-place, S.W.1

* VOGUE, 30 Stoke Newington High-street, N.16

intermittently † *members only*

Provinces

BEDFORD : PICTUREDROME (Sundays only)

BRADFORD : CIVIC PLAYHOUSE, Chapel-street, Leeds-road

BRISTOL : ACADEMY

CAMBRIDGE : ARTS, Market-passage
 NEW

EDINBURGH : GATEWAY, Elm-row, Leith-walk

GLASGOW : COSMO, Rose-street

LEEDS : TATLER, Boar-lane

MANCHESTER : GAIETY, Peter-street

OXFORD : SCALA, 57 Walton-street
 SUPER, Magdalen-street

Note : Years given in the column headed "Shown" are those in which the films were publicly shown in Great Britain. Some films, though available to Film Societies, have not been publicly shown.

AUSTRIA

	Made	Shown
Burghtheater	1936	1937
Episode	1935	1937
Ernte	1936	1937
Hands of Orlac	1924	1929
Hortobagy	1936	1945
Liebesmelodie	1936	1936
Liebelei	1933	1934
Maria Baskirtseff (Tagebuch) ..	1936	1936
Maskerade	1934	1935
Spiegel, Der	1937	1938
Sylvia und Ihr Chauffeur ..	1936	1936
Tales from the Vienna Woods ..	1937	1937

CZECHOSLOVAKIA

	Made	Shown
Extase	1933	1938
Janosik	1936	1936
Reka (Young Love)	1933	1935

A Czechoslovak Film Festival was held in Great Britain in 1947 at the New Gallery, London, May 2-9, and at the Cosmo Cinema, Glasgow, May 12-17. Feature films shown publicly included :

	Made
Men without Wings ..	1945-6
Stolen Frontier	1945-6
Warning, The	1945-6
Warriors of Faith (in colour)	1945-6

also the puppet film—

Hurvinek and Spejbl ..	1945-6

Other Czech films shown (to Film Societies) during the Festival were :

	Made
Slavik	1945-6
(The Violin and the Dream : Oxford University Film Society)	
Unruly Teacher, The ..	1945-6
(Cambridge University Film Society)	

DENMARK

	Made	Shown
Day of Wrath (Vredens Dag) ..	1943	1946
Fredlos	1936	1936
Invisible Army, The	1945	1946
Red Meadows, The	1945	1946

EGYPT

	Made	Shown
Wedad, the Slave	1935	1936

(First and last Egyptian film to be presented in Britain. Box-office returns at Studio One, London, where it was shown, were £15 for one week.)

FRANCE

	Made	Shown
A Nous la Liberté	1931	1932
Accord Final	1939	1940
Amok	1934	1940
Atalante, L'	1934	1946
Au Service de la France ..	1937	1939
		1944
Battement de Cœur	1939	1940
(Re-made by RKO as		1945
Heartbeat, 1946)		
Beethoven	1939	1939
Behold Beatrice	1943	1947
Belle Equipe, La	1937	1938
Bête Humaine, La	1939	1939
		1941
		1946
Bois Sacré, Le	1940	1946
Boule de Suif	1946	1947
Cage of Nightingales, A		
(La Cage aux Rossignols) ..	1945	1946
Carnet de Bal, Un	1937	1937
		1938
		1943
Carrefour	1932	1939
(Re-made by MGM as		
Crossroads, 1942)		
Ces Messieurs de la Santé ..	1935	1935
Charlemagne	1934	1934
Charrette Fantôme, La ..	1939	1940
Ciel Est à Vous, Le	1943-4	1946
Circonstances Atténuantes ..	1938	1941
		1944
Count of Monte Cristo, The ..	1917-9	1922
Crazy Ray, The	1923	1925
(Paris Qui Dort)		
Crainquebille	1934	1935
Crime et Châtiment	1935	1936
		1937
Dernier Milliardaire, Le ..	1934	1934
		1945
Derrière la Façade	1939	1943
		1945
Disparus de St. Agil, Les ..	1938	1939
		1947
Domino	1946	1947
Drame de Shanghai, Le ..	—	1939
Education de Prince	—	1942
Enfants du Paradis, Les ..	1945	1946
Entrée des Artistes	1938	1938
		1939
		1942
Epervier, L'	1940	1940
Esclave Blanche, L'	1938	1942
Femme Disparaît, Une ..	1942	1946
Femme du Boulanger, La ..	1938	1939
		1942
		1946
Fin du Jour, La	1939	1943
		1946
Fric-Frac	1939	1946
Gens de Voyage	1937	1939
		1942

	Made	Shown
Gibraltar	1938	1939
		1943
		1944
Grand Jeu, Le	1933	1946
Grande Illusion, La	1938	1938
Gribouille	1937	1938
Heart of a Nation, The		
(Untel Père et Fils)	1940	1943
Hostages (Les Otages)	1939	1939
		1940
		1945
Homme Qui Cherche la Vérité, L' ..	1939	1944
Hôtel du Nord	1938	1939
		1940
		1944
Ignace	1929	1939
		1942
Ils Etaient Neuf Célibataires	1939	1940
Italian Straw Hat, The ..	1928	1931
J'Accuse (Silent)	1919	1920
J'Accuse (Sound)	1938	1938
J'Etais une Aventurière ..	1939	1939
Joueur d'Echecs, Le	1938	1939
Jour Se Lève, Le	1939	1940
		1944
(Bought by Hakim Brothers of		1946
Hollywood, and withdrawn from		
circulation. Sole existing copy		
procured by B.F.I. in 1946 for		
preservation. Re-made by RKO		
as The Long Night, 1947)		
Katia	1938	1938
		1943
Kean	1922	1924
Kermesse Héroïque, La	1935	1935
		1936
		1937
		1938
Lac aux Dames	1935	1935
Loi du Nord, La	1939	1947
Mademoiselle Ma Mère ..	1937	1938
		1941
Marseillaise, La	1937	1939
		1940
Maternelle, La	1932	1933
Mayerling	1937	1941
		1944
Métropolitain	1939	1946
Michael Strogoff	1926	1926
Million, Le	1931	1931
Misérables, Les (Silent) ..	1925	1926
Misérables, Les (Sound) ..	1933	1936
Monsieur La Souris	1942	1947
Mort du Cygne, La	1937	1945
(Bought by MGM, and re-made		1946
as Unfinished Dance, 1947)		
Naples au Baiser de Feu ..	1937	1939
		1941
		1946
Nous les Gosses	1941	1945
Nous les Jeunes	1938	1940
		1944
		1946
Nouveaux Messieurs, Les ..	1928	1940
Panique	1946	1947
Passion de Jeanne d'Arc, La ..	1928	1930
Pépé le Moko	1937	1937
(Re-made in Hollywood as Algiers,		
1938)		
Perles de la Couronne, Les ..	1937	1938
Pièges	1938	1945

FRANCE—continued

	Made	Shown
Poil de Carotte	1933	1933
		1947
Pontcarral, Colonel d'Empire ..	1942	1947
Prison Without Bars	1938	1939
(An English version was made at Denham, 1939)		
Prisons de Femmes	1939	1940
Quai des Brumes, Le	1937	1939
Quatorze Juillet	1932	1933
Remontons les Champs Elysées	1938	1939
Remous	1934	1935
Rien Que les Heures	1926	—
(Documentary. Director— Cavalcanti)		
Retour à l'Aube	1939	1939
		1941
Rois du Sport, Les	1937	1939
		1942
Roi S'Amuse, Le	1938	1938
Roman d'un Tricheur, Le ..	1937	1940
Sérénade	1940	1940
Sous les Toits de Paris	1930	1930
Symphonie Pastorale, La ..	1946	1946
(Won three awards at Cannes Film Festival, 1946)		1947
Tarakanova	1938	1943
		1944
Thérèse Raquin	1927	1928
Three Musketeers, The	1922	1922
Tragédie Impériale	1938	1940
Trois de St. Cyr	1939	1939
Trois Valses	1938	1939
Un de la Légion	1936	1939
Underworld (Les Bas Fonds) ..	1937	1938
		1944
Virtuous Isidore, The ..	1933	1933
		1944
Voleur de Femmes, Le	1940	1940
Well-Digger's Daughter, The (La Fille du Puisatier) ..	1945	1947
Yeux Noirs, Les	1939	1939
Zéro de Conduite	1933	1946

GERMANY

	Made	Shown
Ammenkoenig, Der	1936	1937
At the Edge of The World	1929	1938
Avalanche (Storm over Mont Blanc)	1930	1931
Berlin (Documentary)..	1927	1932
Blue Angel, The	1930	1931
Blue Light	1932	1932
Brothers Karamazov	1931	1935
Cabinet of Dr. Caligari, The ..	1919	1924
Cinderella	1923	1927
Congress Dances	1931	1932
Destiny	1921	1924
Emil and the Detectives	1931	1933
		1934
		1936
		1945
Golem, The	1920	1923
Joyless Street	1925	—
Kameradschaft	1931	1933
Last Laugh, The	1925	1925
Letzte Rose	1932	1936
Love of Jeanne Ney, The ..	1927	1928
" M "	1931	1932
Mädchen in Uniform	1931	1932

	Made	Shown
Manon Lescaut	1926	1927
Metropolis	1926	1927
Musik im Blut	1935	1935
Old and Young King, The ..	1935	1935
Regine	1937	1937
Reifende Jugend	1936	1936
Schimmelreiter, Der	1935	1936
Siegfried	1923	1928
Street, The	1923	1928
Student of Prague, The	1926	1936
Testament of Dr. Mabuse, The ..	1933	1934
Träumende Munde	1932	1932
Vaudeville (Variety)	1925	1926
Waltz Dream, The	1926	1927
War Is Hell	1932	1932
Warning Shadows	1922	1924
Waxworks	1924	1931
Westfront 1918	1930	1932
White Hell of Pitz Palu, The	1930	1931

HOLLAND

	Made	Shown
Dood Wasser	1934	1935

ITALY

	Made	Shown
Barber of Seville, The	1946	1947
Last Days of Pompeii, The ..	1925	1926
Open City	1944	1947
Quo Vadis	1926	1926

MEXICO

	Made	Shown
Portrait of Maria (Maria Candelaria)	1945	1946

PALESTINE

	Made	Shown
Land of Promise	1936	1937
This Is the Land	1935	1936

POLAND

	Made	Shown
Mamele	1939	1940

SPAIN

	Made	Shown
Days of Hope (Sierra de Teruel : Espoir) ..	1937	1945
Spanish Earth	1937	1937

Days of Hope was produced by André Malraux and Edouard Corniglion-Molinier, who helped to form the air squadron attached to the International Brigade. The film was completed during Occupation of France, hidden by one of Pathé's Paris staff, and released in France after the Liberation in 1944.

SWEDEN

	Made	Shown
Atonement of Gösta Berling, The ..	1923	1924
Frenzy (Hets)	1944	1946
Intermezzo	1936	1937
Lover in Pawn, A (The Outlaw and his Wife)	1917	1921
Love's Crucible (Mortal Clay) ..	1921	1922
Thy Soul Shall Bear Witness (The Stroke of Midnight)	1920	1921

SWITZERLAND

	Made	Shown
Last Chance, The		
(Multi-lingual film. A story of refugees escaping to Switzerland, speaking in their own languages)	1945	1946
Marie Louise	1944	1945

U.S.S.R.

	Made	Shown
Adventures in Bokhara ..	1943	1944
Alexander Nevsky (Warrior of Russia)	1939	1941
Artomov and Sons	1941	1946
Baltic Deputy	1937	1943
Battle for the Ukraine	1943	1944
Battleship "Potemkin"		
(Seeds of Freedom) ..	1926	1945
Bed and Sofa	1927	1933
		1934
Chapayev	1934	1941
Cherevichki (Christmas Slippers) ..	1928	1946
Childhood of Maxim Gorki, The ..	1938	1942
		1943
		1945
Defeat of the Germans Near Moscow,		
The	1942	1942
Drive to the West	1944	1944
End of St. Petersburg, The ..	1927	1930
General Line, The	1929	—
General Suvorov	1941	1941
		1944
Ghost That Never Returns, The ..	1928	—
Girl No. 217	1944	1945
Hallo Moscow !	1945	1946
In the Rear of the Enemy	1941	1941
Innocent Though Guilty	1945	1946
Ivan the Terrible	1944	1946
Jacob Sverdlov	1940	1944
Kharkov Trials, The	1944	1944
Kutuzov 1812	1944	1945
Land of Toys (Children's film) ..	1937	1944
Lenin in 1918	1939	1940
		1946
Lenin in October	1938	1939
		1941
Lermontov	1944	1945

	Made	Shown
Little Hunchback Horse		
(Children's film ; in colour) ..	1941	1943
Lone White Sail (Children's film) ..	1937	1943
Magic Fish, The (Children's film) ..	1937	1942
Magic Seed	1941	1945
Masquerade		
(Based on the poem by Lermontov)	1941	1943
May Day Parade in Moscow, 1946		
(In Agfa colour)	—	1947
Military Secret	1945	1946
Mongolia	1946	1946
		1946
Mother	1926	—
My Universities	1940	1942
		1944
New Babylon	1929	—
New Gulliver, The ..		
(Children's puppet film) ..	1938	1943
New Teacher, The	1939	1941
		1944
October (Ten Days that Shook the		
World)	1927	—
One Day of War in the Soviet Union	1942	1943
Peter the Great	1937	1946
Pt. I only		1939
Professor Mamlock	1939	1939
(First shown by film society in March, 1939. Banned by British Board of Film Censors. Licensed by L.C.C. and shown at Academy Cinema, London, in July, 1939, and also in 1944)		1944
Rainbow	1944	1944
Russian Guerrillas	1942	1943
Shors	1939	1941
Spring Song	1940	1944
Stone Flower, The	1946	1947
Storm over Asia	1928	—
Story of Stalingrad, The	1943	1943
Tanya	1940	1944
Turksib	1929	1930
Turning Point, The	1946	1946
Ural Front, The	1943	1946
Victory Parade in Moscow	—	1945
Volga-Volga	1938	1945
Vow, The	1945-6	1947
We from Kronstadt	1936	1947
Zoya	1944	1945

PATRICIA PLUNKETT
(*Ealing*)

A DIRECTORY OF
THE FILM SOCIETIES
OF GREAT BRITAIN

ENGLAND

ARCHITECTURAL ASSOCIATION FILM GROUP
(16 mm.)
Miss M. C. Miller, Students' Common Room, Architectural Association School of Architecture, 34, Bedford-square, London, W.C.1

A.S.E. FILM SOCIETY (16 mm.) (F)
E. N. Lee, Admiralty Establishment, Lythe Hill House, Haslemere, Surrey

BARNET FILM CLUB (16 mm.) (F)
A. C. Robb, 30 Lovelace-road, East Barnet, Herts

B.B.C. & REGENT-ST. POLYTECHNIC FILM SOCIETY (F)
C. McKenna, The Polytechnic, 309 Regent-street, London, W. 1

BECKENHAM FILM SOCIETY (16 mm.)
Wilson Midgley, Larchmont, Crab-hill, Beckenham, Kent

BILLINGHAM FILM SOCIETY
P. H. Sykes, 6 Crooks Barn-lane, Norton-on-Tees, Co. Durham

BIRMINGHAM (CITY OF) EDUCATION COMMITTEE
T. W. Rumsby, M.A., George Dixon Grammar School Birmingham 17

BIRMINGHAM FILM SOCIETY
Mrs. Knight, 8 Highfield-road, Birmingham

BIRMINGHAM GRAMMAR SCHOOL
T. W. Rumsby, M.A., George Dixon Grammar School, Birmingham 17

BOURNEMOUTH FILM SOCIETY (F)
Miss Margaret Jolliffe, 64b Wellington-road, Bournemouth, Hants

BOURNVILLE FILM SOCIETY (F)
J. Bartlett, c/o Council Office, Cadbury Bros., Bournville, Birmingham

BRADFORD CIVIC PLAYHOUSE (F)
M. Hancock, The Bradford Civic Playhouse, Chapel-street, Leeds-road, Bradford

BRADFORD FILM INSTITUTE SOCIETY (F)
Mrs. L. Sutcliffe, "Delafield", North-avenue, Wakefield

BRIDGWATER ARTS CENTRE FILM SOCIETY
(16 mm.) (F)
Mrs. J. Rees, The Spinneys, Durleigh-road, Bridgwater, Somerset

CAMBRIDGE UNIVERSITY FILM SOCIETY (F)
Ernest Richards, Pembroke College, Cambridge

CARLISLE W.E.A. FILM SOCIETY (F)
A. Worley, "Westgarth", Brisco, Carlisle

CATTERICK CAMP FILM SOCIETY (16 mm.) (F)
Sgt. J. W. Jennings, Catterick Education Centre, Hipswell Lodge, Catterick Camp, Yorks

CHELTENHAM COLLEGE FILM SOCIETY (F)
Henry Johnston, The College, Cheltenham

CHELTENHAM FILM SOCIETY (F)
J. H. Langley, 8 Albert-road, Pittville, Cheltenham

CHESTER FILM SOCIETY (F)
R. R. Zanker, 37 Overleigh-road, Chester

CHRIST'S HOSPITAL FILM SOCIETY (F)
John H. Edwards, Northgate, Christ's Hospital, Horsham, Sussex

DARLINGTON FILM SOCIETY (F)
W. F. Houghton, M.A., Education Office, North Lodge, Darlington

DRAKE HALL TRAINING COLLEGE FILM SOCIETY (16 mm.) (F)
F. A. Edwards, Drake Hall Training College, nr. Stafford

ETON COLLEGE FILM SOCIETY (F)
P. S. H. Lawrence, The River House, Eton, Windsor, Berks

EXETER CINEMA SOCIETY (F)
E. Keen, 6 College-road, Exeter, Devon

FARNBOROUGH & R.A.E. FILM SOCIETY (F)
J. Humphries, 17 Pinehurst Cottage, Farnborough, Hants

GATESHEAD FILM CLUB (16 mm.) (F)
H. D. Carpenter, 12 Oaklands, Newcastle-on-Tyne

GOLDSMITH'S COLLEGE FILM SOCIETY
(16 mm.) (F)
Alan Brebner, Goldsmith's College, London, S.E.14

HEREFORD FILM SOCIETY (F)
J. S. Ransome, 132 St. Owen-street, Hereford

HIGHBURY LITTLE THEATRE
Basil W. Harley, Sheffield-road, Sutton Coldfield, Warwicks

HITCHIN FILM CLUB (16 mm.)
Miss E. D. Wright, 35 Hermitage-road, Hitchin, Herts

HULL & DISTRICT FILM SOCIETY (F)
A. Leaper 22 Barrington-avenue, Hull

KEIGHLEY GIRLS' GRAMMAR SCHOOL FILM CLUB (F)
Miss D. V. Scott, Keighley Girls' Grammar School, Keighley, Yorks

LEAMINGTON SPA FILM SOCIETY (F)
H. Chesterfield, 23 Parade, Leamington

LEEDS ARTS CENTRE FILM CLUB (16 mm.) (F)
Miss M. J. Dunning, 21 Hird-street, Leeds 11

LEEDS FILM SOCIETY (F)
E. Bradbury, Flat 8, 19 Cromer-terrace, Leeds 2

(F) *Member of the Federation of English and Welsh Film Societies*

LEICESTER FILM SOCIETY (F)
J. R. Cottrill, 22 Eastfield-road, Western Park, Leicester

LEIGH, ATHERTON & TYDESLEY DISTRICT FILM SOCIETY (16 mm.) (F)
James C. Fletcher, Hindles Cottage, Atherton, Manchester

LETCHWORTH FILM SOCIETY (F)
R. G. Hodder, Burcott Broadway, Letchworth, Herts

LINCOLN W.E.A. FILM SOCIETY (16 mm.)
Arthur Bartlett, Stamp End, Lincoln

MACCLESFIELD FILM SOCIETY (16 mm.) (F)
Rev. H. L. Lismer Short, M.A., 124 Buxton-road, Macclesfield

MANCHESTER & DISTRICT FILM SOCIETY (F)
Mervyn Reeves, 8 Burlington-road, Manchester 20

MANCHESTER & SALFORD FILM SOCIETY (F)
J. R. Peters, 24 Westray-road, Manchester 13.
R. Cordwell, 185 Ansdell-road, Blackpool

MARLBOROUGH COLLEGE FILM SOCIETY
M. O. Marshall, Marlborough College, Marlborough, Wilts.

MEDWAY FILM GUILD (16 mm.) (F)
J. E. Brown, c/o Medway School of Art, Rochester, Kent

MERSEYSIDE FILM INSTITUTE SOCIETY (F)
T. F. Wilson, " Casita ", Ashbourne-avenue, Blundell-sands, Liverpool 23

NEW LONDON FILM SOCIETY
Miss Olwen Vaughan, Le Petit Club Francais, 4 St. James's-place, London, S.W.1

NORTH STAFFORDSHIRE FILM SOCIETY (F)
R. S. Miles, 30 Chell Green-avenue, Tunstall, Stoke-on-Trent

NORTHAMPTON FILM SOCIETY (F)
J. H. Thornton, 39 The Headlands, Northampton

NORWICH FILM SOCIETY (F)
G. Cockshott, 13 Bracondale, Norwich

NOTTINGHAM & DISTRICT FILM SOCIETY (F)
H. F. Darking, 23 Bilbie-street, Nottingham

OLDHAM FILM SOCIETY (F)
C. Brown, 36 Shawhall Bank-road, Greenfield, nr. Oldham, Lancs

OXFORD FILM SOCIETY
E. E. Bowtell, "North Winds", Blandford-avenue, Oxford

OXFORD UNIVERSITY FILM SOCIETY (16 mm.) (F)
Peter Ericsson, New College, Oxford

PERCIVAL GUILDHOUSE FILM SOCIETY (16 mm.)
M. W. Beresford, Percival Guildhouse, Rugby

PIERS PLOWMAN FILM SOCIETY CLUB (16 mm.)
W. Croome, c/o The Club, Holyrood-terrace, Worcester-road, Malvern

PLANET FILM SOCIETY (16 mm.)
Roger Dale, 48 Langbourne-mansions, London, N.6

PORT TALBOT FILM SOCIETY (F)
C. Clark, Claremont Bungalow, Baglan, Port Talbot

PRESTON FILM SOCIETY (F)
D. H. N. Cowley, 18a Garstang-road, Fulwood, Preston, Lancs

R.A.F. STATION, SCAMPTON, FILM SOCIETY (F)
F/Lt. Pine, Officers' Mess, R.A.F. Station, Scampton, Lincs

READING & DISTRICT FILM SOCIETY (F)
Aubrey W. Thorpe, "Trevilley", 12 Finch-road, Earley, nr. Reading, Berks

ST. ALBANS FILM SOCIETY (16 mm.) (F)
C. Swinson, 26 Woodstock-road, St. Albans, Herts

S.A.M.A. FILM GROUP (16 mm.) (F)
A. J. H. Watkins, 40 Sunnyside-road, Worcester

SHEFFIELD FILM SOCIETY (F)
M. D. Jeeps, Vernon House, 11-15 Broomhall-road, Sheffield 10

SIDMOUTH FILM SOCIETY (F)
H. Clare, Grand Cinema, Sidmouth, Devon

SLOUGH SCIENTIFIC FILM SOCIETY (16 mm.) (F)
A. D. Purvis, 62 Sussex-place, Slough, Bucks

SOUTHAMPTON FILM SOCIETY (F)
Mrs. Constance Sewell, 5 Highfield Lodge, Highfield-lane, Southampton

SOUTHEND FILM SOCIETY (F)
P. Finch, 70 Parkanaur-avenue, Thorpe Bay, Essex

SOUTHPORT FILM SOCIETY
Miss F. Falkner, 5 Cambridge-road, Southport, Lancs.

SPENNYMOOR FILM SOCIETY (F)
Miss D. Scott, The Settlement, King-street, Spennymoor, Co., Durham

THE TRIANGLE FILM SOCIETY (16 mm.) (F)
Sir James Knott Youth Centre, Church-way, North Shields

TONBRIDGE SCHOOL FILM SOCIETY (F)
Major E. H. J. Eames, Hill Side, Tonbridge, Kent

TOPSHAM FILM CLUB (16 mm.) (F)
Mrs. A. E. James, The School House, Topsham, Devon

TYNESIDE CITIZENS' THEATRE (F)
Geoffrey Branson, People's Theatre, Rye-hill, Newcastle-on-Tyne 1

UNITY THEATRE FILM GROUP (16 mm.)
J. W. Oswald, Unity Theatre, Goldington-street, London, N.W.1

WATFORD FILM SOCIETY (F)
Mrs. K. Cooper, 31 Devereux-drive, Watford, Herts

WELWYN GARDEN CITY FILM SOCIETY (16 mm.) (F)
Miss Joyce Bamber, 128 Parkway, Welwyn Garden City, Herts

WEST BOROUGH SOCIAL CENTRE (MAIDSTONE) (16 mm.)
Miss M. Hobday, 78 Cobtree Estate, Chatham-road, nr. Maidstone, Kent

WEST LONDON FILM SOCIETY (F)
H. E. Norris, 88 Eastcote-avenue, Greenford, Mddx

WEST SURREY FILM SOCIETY (F)
J. W. Penycote, c/o "Surrey Advertiser", Martyr-road, Guildford, Surrey

WALES

ABERGAVENNY FILM SOCIETY (F)
L. K. Harrington, West End Studios, Frogmore-street, Abergavenny, Mon

CARMARTHEN ARTS CLUB FILM SOCIETY (16 mm.) (F)
E. John, M.A., Myrddin-crescent, Carmarthen, Wales

SWANSEA FILM SOCIETY (F)
W. N. Davies, Carwedd, Glebe-road, Loughor, Swansea, Glam

THE NEW FILM SOCIETY, COLWYN BAY (F)
J. F. Marshall, "Woodlands", Rosemary-avenue, Nant-y-Glyn-road, Colwyn Bay

TREDEGAR FILM SOCIETY (F)
Edgar Williams, Iddlesleigh, Tredegar, Mon

IRELAND

BELFAST FILM INSTITUTE SOCIETY
A. A. K. Arnold, 6 College Green House, College Green, Belfast, N. Ireland

IRISH FILM SOCIETY (DUBLIN, WATERFORD & PORTAOIGHISE)
C. V. Whelan, 5 North Earl-street, Dublin

PORTADOWN FILM SOCIETY (F)
Mrs. S. Stevenson, Windsor Lodge, Portadown, N. Ireland

SCOTLAND

ABERDEEN FILM SOCIETY (SF)
Mrs. A. C. Hendry, 7 Queen's-terrace, Aberdeen

AYRSHIRE FILM SOCIETY
A. J. Nelson, 6 Hilary-crescent, Ayr

DUNDEE & ST. ANDREWS FILM SOCIETY (SF)
J. Gordon Colquhoun, 48 Farington-street, Dundee

DUNFERMLINE & WEST FIFE FILM SOCIETY (SF)
J. S. M. Condon, 56 Keir-street, Cowdenbeath

EDINBURGH FILM GUILD (SF)
H. Forsyth Hardy, Film House, 6-8 Hill-street, Edinburgh 2

EDINBURGH UNIVERSITY FILM SOCIETY (16 mm.) (SF)
J. W. S. McKerral, 5 Ravelstone-terrace, Edinburgh 4

GLASGOW FILM SOCIETY (SF)
C. A. Oakley, Cosmo Cinema, Rose-street, Glasgow

INVERNESS FILM SOCIETY (SF)
R. R. MacEwen, c/o Stewart Rule & Co., Old National Bank Buildings, Inverness

PERTH FILM SOCIETY (SF)
Dr. J. Kelman, 26 Viewlands-terrace, Perth

(SF) *Member of the Federation of Scottish Film Societies*

Principal distributors of foreign language films in Great Britain are :

A.B.F.D., 169 Oxford-street, London, W.1

Anglo-Continental Films, 55 Porchester-terrace, London, W.2

Avon Distributors, J. Fairfax Jones, 2 The Gables, Vale of Health, London, N.W.3

British Lion Film Corporation, 76 Wardour-street, London, W.1

Butcher's Film Service Ltd., 175, Wardour-street London, W.1

Carlyle Pictures Ltd., 191 Wardour-street, London, W.1

Délégation de la Cinématographie Française, 27 Queen Anne-street, London, W.1

Exclusive Films Ltd., 113 Wardour-street, London, W.1

Film Sales Ltd., 191 Wardour-street, London, W.1

Film Traders Ltd., 167 Oxford-street, London, W.1

General Film Distributors (Foreign Film Dept.), 127-33 Wardour-street, London, W.1

Wallace Heaton, 127 New Bond-street, London, W.1

International Films Ltd., 167 Wardour-street, London, W.1

Metro-Goldwyn-Mayer, 16 mm. Dept., 1 Belgrave place, London, S.W.1

National Film Board of Canada, 8 Long Acre, London, W.C.2

National Film Library, 4 Great Russell-street, London, W.C.1

New Realm Pictures Ltd., Queens House, Leicester-square, London, W.C.2

Piccadilly Cinematograph Film Productions Ltd., 101 Wardour-street, London, W.1

Soviet Film Agency, 5 Kensington Palace-gardens, London, W.8

Studio One Distributors, 225 Oxford-street, London, W.1

United Curzon Corporation Ltd., Miss Hart, Room 7, Customs Chambers, St. Dunstan's-hill, London, E.C.3

Workers' Film Association, Transport House, Smith-square, London, S.W.1

Zionist Federation, 67 Great Russell-street, London, W.C.1

Note: *Many short films made in their respective countries are available from the Belgian, Danish and Polish Embassies.*

JOAN GREENWOOD
(Gainsborough)

THE CINE SOCIETIES

OF GREAT BRITAIN

Compiled by Dr. H. MANDIWALL, F.R.P.S., M.B.K.S.

WITH a few brushes and tubes of paint an artist can go and perhaps paint a masterpiece. But the artist in cine photography has to convey his message through the medium of a mechanical device of high precision involving many scientific and technical problems, so that it is essential to pool resources and to be in constant touch with other enthusiasts. Hence the rise of the amateur society which gradually adapted itself to the needs of the cine photographer, and today consists, generally speaking, of two kinds—(1) producing societies, and (2) exhibiting societies.

Producing Societies are of two kinds :

(*a*) Societies (and these probably have the largest membership) that are interested in producing films for amusement and entertainment only.

(*b*) Societies interested in serious productions of a more erudite character, mainly educational and instructional. Research dealing with practical features in moving picture technique is undertaken, the results of which are utilized for their own film productions.

DR. MANDIWALL *is a Fellow of the Royal Photographic Society and a leading figure in British amateur cine photography.*

Exhibiting Societies are similarly divided :

(*a*) Societies that hire films from film libraries and exhibit them for the amusement and entertainment of their members.

(*b*) Societies that do not concern themselves with entertainment, but meet for purposes of study. In these societies, films dealing with the technique of film production in all its phases are exhibited and subsequently discussed.

It will thus be seen that societies exist to suit all tastes. There is equal scope for the beginner or the expert, the light-hearted or the serious student.

Most of the societies are represented in the Federation of Cinematograph Societies which exists to foster the art of cine photography and to assist its members with advice and practical help. Its resources enable it to draw on the best expert opinion, professional and amateur. Lectures are arranged, films are judged and criticized, inter-society competitions fixed, and influence exerted in many directions in the world of cine photography.

The Federation will be glad to advise those wishing to join a society.

Central Organizations

BRITISH AMATEUR CINEMATOGRAPHERS' CENTRAL COUNCIL
L. M. Froude, F.C.A., c/o 4 Great Russell-street, London, W.C.1

BRITISH FILM INSTITUTE
4 Great Russell-street, London, W.C.1

FEDERATION OF CINEMATOGRAPH SOCIETIES
H. Mandiwall, M.B., B.S., L.D.S., F.R.P.S., M.B.K.S., c/o 16 Princes-gate, London, S.W.7

INSTITUTE OF AMATEUR CINEMATOGRAPHERS
L. M. Froude, F.C.A., Hill End, Woodcote-side, Epsom, Surrey

ROYAL PHOTOGRAPHIC SOCIETY, KINE SECTION
T. S. Lutas, F.R.P.S., c/o 16 Princes-gate, London, S.W.7

Local and Other Societies

BEACONSFIELD BAPTIST CHURCH F.S.
F. P. Girling, Pine Close, Gaviots-way, Gerrards Cross

BECKENHAM C.S.
S. H. Davis, BM/GMRR, London, W.C.1

BELFAST Y.M.C.A. C.C.
E. Silver, c/o Y.M.C.A., Wellington-place, Belfast

BIRMINGHAM P.S. (CINE SECTION)
Waterloo House, 20 Waterloo-street, Birmingham 2
F. G. Ratcliff, A.R.P.S., 33 New Summer-street, Birmingham 19

BOURNVILLE C.C. (CINE SECTION)
Camera Club Room, Dining Hall Block (N.W. Corner), Bournville Works, Birmingham
W. J. Perry, 159 Woodlands Park-road, Bournville, Birmingham 30

BRADFORD CINE CIRCLE
Cambridge House Annexe, Horton-lane, Bradford
A. C. Whitehead, The Towers, Clayton, Bradford

BRISTOL C.C.
5 Marsh-street, Bristol
W. J. Green, 19 Parkstone-avenue, Horfield, Bristol 7

BROMEDGE DRAMATIC & C.C.
Mrs. R. Wareing, 1 High Leigh-road, Bromedge, Lymm, Ches.

CARDIFF A.C.S.
Royal Hotel, Cardiff
F. H. Kidd, 82 Pencisely-road, Cardiff

CINEMA CLUB
3 Rodborough-road, London, N.W.11

CINEPHOTO PLAYS
Miss J. E. Crawley, 57 Nicander-road, Liverpool

CORNISH C.S.
Rev. F. E. Coward, St. Mary's Hall, Truro, Cornwall

CROUCH END A.C.S.
R. T. Southon, 8 Victoria-parade, Muswell-hill, London, N.W.10

DUNDEE C.S.
J. R. L. Halley, The Ridge, Craigie, Dundee

EASTBOURNE C. & C.C. (CINE SECTION)
J. Godchaux Abrahams, M.B.E., Edgeland House, 25 Silverdale-road, Eastbourne

ECCLES AMATEUR CINE GROUP
E. Collier, 9 Glendale-road, Eccles, Lancs.

EDINBURGH C.S.
J. Douglas, 23 Corstorphine Bank-drive, Edinburgh

EVERYMAN SOCIETY
Miss S. Erulkar, 75 Oakwood-court, London, W.14

FINCHLEY A.C.S.
Miss K. Lunnis, 16 Chalcot-crescent, Regents-park, London, N.W.1

HALIFAX C.C.
Britannic Buildings, Central-street, Halifax
C. H. Horner, Green Hayes, Halifax

HAMPTON C.C.
J. E. Roberts, 2 New-street, Oswestry, Salop

HARPENDEN P. & C.S. (CINE SECTION)
Friends' Meeting House, Southdown-road, Harpenden, Herts
H. A. Bell, 8 Bloomfield-road, Harpenden, Herts

HEBDEN BRIDGE LITERARY & SCIENTIFIC SOCIETY (CINE SECTION)
Kenneth T. Crabtree, Hilton-street, Hebden Bridge, Yorks

HOUNSLOW P.S. (CINE SECTION)
H. Mandiwall, M.B., B.S., L.D.S., F.R.P.S., M.B.K.S., 234 Staines-road, Hounslow, Middx

HYDE C.S.
G. Wain, F.R.P.S., 170 Dowson-road, Hyde, Ches.

ISLE OF WIGHT A.C.S.
R. E. Hannam, 1 Queens Cottages, Old-road, Cowes, I.O.W.

KINGSTON C.C.
W. J. Kelsey, 24 Sandhurst-avenue, Surbiton, Surrey

KODAK WORKS P.S. (CINE SECTION)
R. W. Harris, Kodak Works, Wealdstone, Harrow, Middx

LEDBURY AMATEUR DRAMATIC & CINE SOCIETY
L. J. Somers Smith, Newbury-park, Ledbury, Herefords.

LEEDS C.C. (CINE SECTION)
H. Bryce Thomson, 2 Belmont-avenue, Leeds 2

LONDON A.F.C.
Miss M. Jasper, 99 Cambridge-street, London, S.W.1

LONDON COUNTY COUNCIL STAFF C.C.
J. Wilkinson, Room 517, County Hall, London, S.E.1

MANCHESTER Y.M.C.A. C.S.
P. Wilson, 35a, Greenleach-lane, Worsley, Manchester

MELBOURNE (DERBY) P.S. (CINE SECTION)
F. S. Tivey, 15 Windsor-avenue, Melbourne, Derby

METROPOLITAN-VICKERS A.C. & P.S.
M. V. Club, Moss-road, Stretford, Manchester
C. Bramwell, 12 Leyburn-avenue, Stretford, Manchester

NEWCASTLE & DISTRICT AMATEUR CINE-MATOGRAPHERS ASSOCIATION
I. B. Milne, 72 Queens-road, Monkseaton, Whitley Bay, Northumberland

NEWPORT & DISTRICT A.F.S.
Albany Chambers, Skinner-street, Newport, Mon
Frank E. Johns, 128 Stow Hill, Newport, Mon

NORTH KENT C.C.
A. Stanton, 42 Springhead-road, Erith, Kent

NORTHAMPTON C.C. (BRANCH OF PHOT. SECTION OF NORTHAMPTON NATURAL HISTORY SOCIETY)
32 Bridge-street, Northampton
N. A. Pearce, Normanhurst, St. George's-avenue, Northampton

OLDHAM LYCEUM C.C.
W. Rothwell Heywood, 73 Queens-road, Oldham, Lancs

OLDHAM P.S. (CINE SECTION)
George Schofield, 122 Eric-street, Clarksfield, Oldham, Lancs

OSWESTRY C.S.
Miss R. D. Brindley, 1 Stanley-place, Oswestry, Salop

PLANET FILM SOCIETY
H. Roger Dale, 48 Lanbourne-mansions, Highgate, London, N.6

REDDITCH C. & P.C.
H. J. Paramore, B.Sc., M.I.B.E., F.I.F.M., Oak Tree, Evesham-road, Astwood-bank, Redditch, Worcs

ROMFORD & DISTRICT C.S.
L. A. Aves, 5 Allandale-road, Romford, Essex

SALFORD C.S.
H. G. Percival, 97 Ashton-lane, Sale, Manchester

SHEFFIELD P.S. (CINE GROUP)
11-13 Midland Bank Chambers, 10 Charles-street, Sheffield 1
D. J. D. Wood, 21 Moorbank-road, Sandygate, Sheffield 10

SHROPSHIRE P.S. (CINE SECTION)
11 St. Alkmunds-square, Shrewsbury
C. D. Ide, Penn House, Ebnal-road, Shrewsbury

SOUTHALL & DISTRICT P.S.
R. G. Hurren, 82 Ranelagh-road, Southall, Middx.

STOKE-ON-TRENT C.S.
H. T. Morfey, 6 Edward-avenue, Newcastle, Staffs.

SUMMIT PRODUCTIONS
J. Huntley, 15 Ruskin-avenue, Kew, Surrey

SUTTON C.C.
P. Hickman, 128 Banstead-road, Carshalton, Surrey

SUTTON COLDFIELD C.S.
E. Summer, 26 Fredrick-road, Sutton Coldfield, Warwick

TORBAY C.S.
S. T. Stevens, 12 Round Hill-road, Torquay, Devon

VENTURERS F.S.
F. J. Ind, 39 Swaby-road, Wandsworth, London, S.W.18

WANSTEAD & WOODFORD C.C.
Men's Club, High-road, Woodford Green, Essex
S. F. Martin, 134 Malford-grove, Snaresbrook, Essex

WEST LONDON C.S.
A. F. Shave, 77a Adelaide-grove, London, W.12

WHITEHALL C.S.
Harry Walden, A.R.P.S., 3 Copse-avenue, West Wickham, Kent

WIMBLEDON C.C.
Miss D. M. Sheppard, 35 Denmark-avenue, Wimbledon, London, S.W.19

WISBECH P.S. (CINE SECTION)
Walter H. Seath, 124 Ramnoth-road, Wisbech

WORKERS' FILM ASSOCIATION LTD.
Transport House, Smith-square, London, S.W.1
Alderman Joseph Reeves, 9 Broadhurst-gardens, Reigate, Surrey

F. D. Russell-Roberts

THE PROGRESS OF THE 16 MM. FILM

SOMETHING like a revolution has quietly occurred in the film world since the end of the war. Although it has taken place without any fuss or publicity, it is almost as far-reaching as though the railways had suddenly put out extensions from their main lines to all the villages in the country.

What has happened is that the villager, instead of having to arrange a bus or train journey to the nearest town in order to see good films, can now see them in his own local hall, brilliantly projected and with sound as good as he will hear anywhere. The high class entertainment hitherto available only in the cinemas in the larger towns has been brought practically to his doorstep.

This has been made possible by the rapid development and perfection of the 16 mm. film and its projecting apparatus. 16 mm. films are not new. As every ex-Service man and woman knows, they have been used extensively for purposes of training and entertainment. The need for showing films at short notice and often under the most primitive conditions has resulted in so much improvement in all the necessary equipment that the presentation of a modern 16 mm. show is now comparable in quality with that of its big brother in the ordinary cinemas.

Mobile film units consist of a van with storage space devised so that every item necessary for a complete show can be swiftly packed or unpacked. Screen, projector, sound equipment, cables, projection booth and disc apparatus can all be unpacked and in working order in a matter of minutes. Regular circuits are under the control of the same men who have so successfully organized the circuits of larger cinemas in the towns.

An ever-increasing number of films is being made available, and most of the large producing companies prepare 16 mm. versions of their best films. From these films and an extensive range of interesting and informative shorts, a large selection of films has been built up, and exhibitors have acquired much valuable experience in the presentation of 16 mm. mobile exhibitions.

As in all new movements, there have been some abuses. A small proportion of men have concerned themselves solely with quick profits. These men, aptly called the pirates of the trade, have done the movement some harm, but they are being steadily eliminated as the regular and experienced exhibitor acquires growing control of this new development.

Experience of 16 mm. film has shown that it can succeed where a well-planned unit has carefully chosen its exhibition centres, and has had regard to the opinions of the villagers. It can succeed also where the small exhibitor goes out himself and puts on his show with the minimum of assistance, either from his wife and family or from some helper in each village.

The presentation of 16 mm. film cannot, however, at this stage cope with the overheads incurred by comfortably placed owner-managers who tackle the job from expensive headquarters. The progress of mobile 16 mm. projection must depend on the hard work of the exhibitor who has a lively sense of his responsibilities and an intention to build for the future.

It would be difficult to imagine a worse winter than that of 1946-7, with its rain and floods, its frost and snow, its blocked roads and general lack of warmth in which to promote a new venture. Yet 16 mm. survived and defeated the weather, and if it could hold its own in that winter, nothing should deter its future activities. But it is obvious that the exhibitor will have to consider the needs of the public he serves. The word " serves " is important, because this new development offers great opportunity of social service in the more remote parts of the country.

Most villagers are conservative in their tastes, have very definite ideas of what films they like, and demand comfortable seats and a warm hall as do their urban relatives. There are often local difficulties in the way of attending on a particular day or at a particular hour, and occasionally after the novelty has worn off there is a tendency to give up going to the travelling shows.

For these reasons it is foolish to expect a film show to succeed automatically in the first few weeks of exhibition. The exhibitor must win over the villagers to his shows. He must be human, must pander to their tastes, and must show that he is there to serve and bring entertainment to them regularly, regardless of weather, and not just to take his customers' money and then disappear into the night.

There are still many in the trade and among the general public who do not believe in the future of 16 mm. films. Undoubtedly 16 mm. has its battles to fight. But the mobile narrow gauge film show spells progress, and progress cannot be arrested. Whatever the evil-wishers to the new development may say, it will ultimately play an important part in the leisure activities of our time.

The Kinematograph Renters' Society and the Cinematograph Exhibitors' Association have had the whole question under discussion ; their

F. D. RUSSELL-ROBERTS *is manager of Metro-Goldwyn-Mayer's 16 mm. department in London.*

recommendations have been wise and helpful, but it is obvious that the 16 mm. film will have to acquire the strength to stand on its own feet. Yet it is important that the associations should lead the progress of 16 mm. rather than content themselves by placing restrictions on its abuse.

Why, I wonder, does the prejudice against 16 mm. films exist—as certainly it does ? After all, 16 mm. is merely a width of film. It is *film* just as much as 35 mm. and there should be no reason why it should be governed by a different set of regulations. Once 16 mm. is accepted as part of the legitimate film trade then it should be governed by the same rules as those established for the commercial cinema, so far as these are practicable to the peculiar characteristics of the mobile show.

There is a vast field open to the non-theatrical exhibition of 16 mm. films which, under wise guidance, cannot harm the normal cinema and may do much to promote the appreciation of films in general. I refer to such institutions as boarding schools, where cinema attendance is not normally allowed ; to organizations which, under the guidance of the churches, Youth Movements and similar bodies, can remove young people from the dangers of the street ; to hospitals ; and to prisons and similar institutions.

The development of this class of film exhibition depends largely on the adequate supply of efficient projectors at a reasonable price. There are now at least half a dozen companies manufacturing projectors, and despite industrial difficulties today these projectors will become available in increasing numbers in the near future. I look forward with confidence to the time when all institutions and schools will have 16 mm. projectors for entertainment and recreation.

THE NATIONAL FILM LIBRARY

THE National Film Library is run by a committee responsible to the British Film Institute, which was founded in 1933 as a result of a commission on educational and cultural films and its publication " The Film in National Life ".

The committee consists of a chairman, and representatives of the Association of Directors and Secretaries for Education, the Ministry of Education, the British Kinematograph Society, the British Museum, the Historical Association, the Imperial Institute, the Central Office of Information, the Royal Photographic Society, the Royal Society of Arts, the Science Museum, the Government Cinematograph Adviser, and the governors of the Institute.

The British Film Institute is financed partly by membership subscriptions, and partly by grants from the Sunday Cinematograph Fund administered by the Privy Council. In 1938 the Film Library was voted a non-recurrent grant of £3000 from the Privy Council.

The choice of films is undertaken by a selection committee, and current films are selected monthly. The aims of the National Film Library are :

(1) To make the collection representative of the art of the film, from its pioneer stage in 1896.

(2) To provide historians of the future with raw material.

(3) To record contemporary life and habits so that a social history will be given to posterity.

The films are preserved in vaults at Aston Clinton near Aylesbury, where the temperature is thermostatically controlled and the humidity of the air checked for the better preservation of the celluloid. The present one-story vaults contain thirteen million feet of stock, and the rate of intake has now compelled the Committee to search for a new twelve-acre site.

The National Film Library committee and the governors of the British Film Institute consider that their policy should be as follows :

(1) To preserve and maintain the collection in as good a condition as possible.

(2) To acquire more films for preservation.

(3) To develop a film lending library or loan section for use in promoting film appreciation.

The Library now has nearly 4000 films of varying dates from 1896. The films are acquired by various means : feature films and newsreels are given by the trade, but short films, documentaries, and research films—which are not usually profitable to their owners—have often to be bought. During 1946, 116 full length films and 200 newsreels were acquired, and, in 1947, 321 films and 156 newsreel items.

A *bona-fide* student may visit the Library by previous arrangement and see a film through a movieola, a projection machine for one person, and the committee hope to be able to extend the lending service of the Library. Films lent out totalled 2639 in 1946 and 3375 in 1947.

The address of the National Film Library is 4 Great Russell-street, London, W.C.1.

PEGGY ANN GARNER
(*20th Century-Fox*)

CHILDREN AT THE CINEMA

CHILDREN AT THE CINEMA: Mary Field, M.A.

CHILDREN'S ENTERTAINMENT FILMS

FILMS AS AN AID TO TEACHING: Renée Marcousé, Licencié Art et Archéologie, Ph.D.

THE BERNSTEIN CHILDREN'S QUESTIONNAIRE

ROY ROGERS AND TRIGGER
(*Republic*)

Mary Field

CHILDREN AT THE CINEMA

IN May 1944, Mr. J. Arthur Rank set up the Children's Entertainment section of G.B. Instructional Ltd. The purpose of the section is to provide films of a good and formative kind to be shown at the Gaumont Junior and Odeon National Cinema Clubs for Boys and Girls. These clubs meet every Saturday morning, and Mr. Rank is chairman of both groups. His avowed purpose is to show the club members not merely films that are innocuous but films that are " good " for them, in the same sense that first class children's books are " good " for their readers.

The films are not limited in their showing to the Gaumont and Odeon groups. They are eventually available for children's performances in other cinemas, while as 16 mm. film they can be used in schools, youth clubs and other recreational centres. They are shown also throughout chains of children's cinema clubs in Canada and in New Zealand.

The initial problem facing C.E.F. was " What is a children's entertainment film ? " Many educational films had been made for young people in this country, but none had been produced to entertain them. Indeed, practically the only country to make any films for the amusement of children, before 1945, was Russia. Nothing was known in Great Britain of the reaction of children to films made primarily for their entertainment, since no such films existed on which any research could be based. A great deal of work had been undertaken on the *effect* of the cinema on the child, but this was all carried out with adult films and so was of very little value for the purpose of this new experiment.

It was therefore resolved to work on the principle of trial and error. The first terms of reference were to produce one reel of film a week for the club programmes, but this was soon modified since reasonably suitable short films for children were not so rare as suitable features or serials. Also it proved almost impossible to condense a logical and exciting film story into the brief space of the ten minutes taken up by a single reel.

Children's films of all types were made during 1944-5 and exhibited to the clubs as quickly as possible. Stories lasting ten, twenty and thirty minutes were produced, nature films were made, a cartoon was achieved and a children's cine-magazine was started, called *Our Magazine*, which appeared once every four weeks. But although

these efforts were received very critically by adults —both film experts and educationists—even the weakest effort was accepted by child audiences with interest and pleasure. The new type of entertainment, though by no means perfect, proved quickly acceptable to those for whom it was intended.

Criticism of the films by the clubs came through three channels, the managers who are expert in recording the reactions of an audience, the committees of children who help to run the clubs, and individual club members. Large numbers of reports of films are regularly received and sorted. On the whole, letters of unqualified approval are discounted. The letters giving reasoned criticism prove the most helpful guides to the children's reactions to a film. The policy of production has been largely based on those critical letters and, feeling their way carefully forward, the group of film technicians in charge of the job at C.E.F. progressed from making forty-six reels of film in 1944-45 to sixty-seven reels in 1946 and touched the one hundred mark in 1947. So, too, the type of production has become more ambitious and has embraced coloured cartoons, a serial, a series of slapstick comedies and full-length feature films.

In so short a time it is, of course, not possible to collect enough material on which to base definitive statements about children's entertainment films. Certain very clear tendencies, however, in the reactions of children to films made especially for their entertainment are already apparent. The children who attend are from seven to fourteen years. But the type of audience aimed at in the films is usually the extrovert group of eight to eleven, though the seven-year-olds also enjoy these pictures, even if their special interest in fantasy seldom has exclusive consideration. The older group of over-elevens usually leave the clubs at any time between the ages of eleven and fourteen when they feel the need for adolescent entertainment.

The children's natural taste in films appears to be good. They will applaud very beautiful camera movements and enjoy good singing. A film with the commentary in rhymed couplets provoked two children, at least, to record their views on it in excellent heroic verse. Not infrequently also a film is commended for its photography or because the actors in it " spoke so nicely ".

It appears that films made for adults, however " suitable " they may be deemed for children, seldom interest a young audience in their story. The children follow the action with their eyes but

MARY FIELD *has been Director of Production, Children's Entertainment Films, since its inception in* 1944 *and has long worked with Gaumont-British Instructional Films.*

their brains are not engaged in the development of the plot. For this reason when a Western is being shown most of the children cheer and applaud the riding and the chasing. But the moment action is replaced on the screen by dialogue, however essential that dialogue may be to the theme of the film, the attention of the audience wanders. Its members begin to talk and fidget. From this, some observers have deduced that children do not like talking films or that they cannot both look and listen at the same time.

This is not true. When a children's film is being shown, children listen enthralled to the dialogue, *so long as it is relevant to the plot*, and retain a great deal of it to repeat afterwards. They show, too, a remarkable memory for the names of quite minor characters. When the film is within the range of their understanding, children make a highly intelligent audience.

Indeed so logical are children when they watch a film that more care has to be taken to tie up loose ends in a children's screen story than is always necessary in an adult film. A typical criticism— " This is a silly film. The schoolmaster said the race was three lengths of the baths, and they finished up the end they started ! "—shows the exact attention to detail demanded of those who undertake to produce films for children.

To engage the interest of the under-elevens, it is almost essential that children of the same age shall appear upon the screen. For just as adults like to identify themselves with the characters of the story, so children demand the same pleasure, though they can identify themselves at times with an animal hero. Once this identification has taken place, care must be taken not to shock or grieve the child audience. *Bambi* for instance was unbearably sad to many young children, who wept copiously, to the surprise of their escorts who thought the film " so suitable because it is all about animals ". In a children's film no lasting sorrow occurs to any character that members of the audience may imagine to be themselves, nor are there close-ups of a violent or disturbing nature, though a general " free-for-all " fight that takes place all over the screen is too diffused in its interest to disturb any ordinarily sensitive child.

While the majority of most child audiences enjoy action and activity in films there is a minority which likes a quieter form of entertainment. The noisy majority have tended to mislead organizers of child entertainment, who have thought that Westerns and thrilling serials were the only fare to offer when planning their programmes. But letters show that the slapstick fantasy *The Voyage of Peter Joe*, a series of complete episodes without the suspense of the serial, has proved one of the most popular films of the week-to-week type ever shown in the clubs. " It is a pity it had to end so soon " was a little girl's view of this non-violent picture. " There were tears at the last episode," wrote a manager. In the same way the various items that go to make up *Our Magazine* all attract praise. Cricket

matches or animal items are very popular. Visits to museums or art exhibitions make a special appeal to some and hold the attention of all.

One section of child audiences which has been persistently overlooked is the girls. Possibly the reason why more boys than girls go to special children's cinema shows is not that the girls stay at home to help mother but that they have less inducement to go to the cinema. Girls are less interested in chases, wild riding, jungle thrills and motor racing. Perhaps, too, they get tired of the inferior part played by heroines in most films of action. We have learned that for children's films it is best to include a girl as well as a boy to hold the interest. Moreover the girl should play an active and useful part in the story.

In *Here We Come Gathering* the heroine actually slapped the hero's face (while he was yet unregenerate) and, after a shocked gasp of surprise, the boy section of the audience " took it ". *The Little Ballerina* is definitely a film for girls though there is a boy's part in it, but most of the stories, like *Bush Christmas*, have the interest fairly divided between both sexes.

Directing a film for children is not an easy job. The greater part of the audience goes to the adult cinema with its parents and is accustomed to good slick film production. Yet ordinary competent direction does not entirely meet the needs of the young filmgoer. Children are more curious and inquisitive than grown-ups. They want to know more and see more. So the child's film must have more close-ups than the ordinary production ; we must know what is in the lost wallet, what was the coin the hero nobly spurned. Children are also more interested in the backgrounds of their films than the ordinary cinemagoer. For this reason they tend to dislike quick cutting and prefer a scene to be held long enough for them to take it in and understand it. But that does not mean that they like their films to move slowly ; on the contrary they like a good steady pace to be kept up. So a special technique of production involving quick action with slow cutting has had to be evolved and perfected.

The content of a children's film is a bone of contention. Many people criticizing children's films forget that their primary purpose is entertainment, and demand more instruction which properly belongs to school. Yet we must not forget that to the unformed mind nearly everything is interesting, and that good entertainment is always educative in the wider sense. So in selecting its stories C.E.F. chooses almost always a documentary background. *Jean's Plan* is set against the background of the canals of southern England ; *The Boy Who Stopped Niagara* has as an essential character the great Falls themselves ; *Dusty Bates* pursues his thrilling adventures in the docks and warehouses of the Port of London ; *Circus Boy* takes us inside the Big Top ; and *Bush Christmas* makes the mountains of New South Wales a thrilling reality.

More ambitious in purpose, *The Little Ballerina*

introduces its audience indirectly to another art than that of the cinema and shows children to whom ballet is the great thrilling reality of life, as thrilling as football or dirt-track racing. The *Magic Globe* series is disguised geography, the *Tales of the Woodlands* are a version of nature study.

The underlying purpose of such films is that they shall prove beneficial to the children who see them. The first films produced were definitely " moral " in tone. The children had no objection since most of them are incurable moralists themselves, demanding that right shall triumph, though a small minority query why " the ' goodies ' must always win."

Adult critics however were uniformly against the *expressed* moral, and policy was adjusted to the *implied* moral—to moral education which as defined by Sir Michael Sadleir is, above all, contact with good example. So, in the stories of the children's films, honesty, truth, kindness and co-operation are practised by characters who are not superhuman but have enough faults to be normal and natural. The bad characters in these films are never such as to arouse sympathy but are rather devised so that they provoke ridicule. There is no glory or glamour in being the villain of a children's film. Indeed villains are no longer regarded as essential.

The early productions of C.E.F. did indeed follow the pattern of the Westerns while changing their content, but they were essentially conflicts between good and bad. Gradually becoming more confident, the scenario writers have been able to discard this formula, replacing it by the film of achievement—for example *The Little Ballerina*, *Circus Boy* and *Fortune Lane*. The next step is to the film of fantasy, always difficult to achieve, and so gradually to the films of great life stories, the finest moral education of all.

The reactions of a London Club audience to *The Boy Who Stopped Niagara* were exceedingly interesting. This three-reel fantasy, with a dash of René Clair and a touch of Marx Brothers fooling, but concerned with a little girl and boy, was something entirely new and strange to the child filmgoers. It was outside their experience. They could not understand it. Now usually when they do not understand an adult film they lose all interest and begin to talk and play. But this film held their interest. It was about children, and must, therefore, be worth following. It deserved a mental effort.

So, for half an hour, a thousand children sat puzzled and absorbed, too occupied to laugh much, but so identified with the action on the screen that anxious advice was called out to the actors from the auditorium. After the mental effort of watching the film, the audience gave vent to its feeling of relaxation by shouting and whistling at the main titles of the next film to an abnormal degree. What they needed was the lights up and a few minutes in which to discuss and adjust their ideas and curiosity about the strange film they had followed with such ready intelligence. Here was no passive audience.

C.E.F. does not itself produce films but initiates and supervises production. Fourteen or fifteen companies produced films for it in 1947. By this means there is a refreshing variety of approach and direction, while a steady development and improvement in the films is maintained and experiment and variety encouraged. The staff of C.E.F. itself is small. It consists of only seven principals including a research worker. But in this way the films sponsored by the group retain a singleness of purpose.

C.E.F.'s policy is to have films produced in various parts of the British Commonwealth. But the imposition of the seventy-five per cent *ad valorem* duty on films from overseas—including those from Commonwealth countries—has meant the modification of the 1948 programme.

C.E.F. does not work alone. It has the help and advice of the Advisory Council on Children's Entertainment Films. This council of seventeen members, representing Government departments and national bodies interested in the leisure hours of children, meets regularly once a month, discusses stories, advises on treatments, sees rushes, and passes finished films. Working as a body the Advisory Council also contributes to the continuity of policy shown in the development of children's films.

What is the real value of making special entertainment films for children ? Firstly, children are quick to copy things they see done on the screen, and good behaviour and good manners shown regularly week by week must have an effect, producing a general background of ethical experience against which parents, clergy and teachers can work in detail. Secondly the chief harm done to children by the adult cinema is not so much bad example, which is usually outside their understanding and experience, but the inculcation of the habit of letting the eye alone be entertained. Meanwhile the mind remains passive, so producing the unintelligent, unreasoning adult filmgoer. It is useless, however, to try to train children and adolescents to appreciate films when the good films they are shown are outside the range of their understanding. By producing well-made films within the scope of child experience, an audience of intelligent filmgoers is being built up —filmgoers who can later learn to appreciate well-made adult films and so make first class productions worth while to the film industry.

Yet, above all, emphasis must be laid on the " E " of C.E.F. To entertain children, to make them laugh the kind, happy laugh of release is an important piece of educative and social work.

NICKY YARDLEY in *Bush Christmas*
(*GB Instructional*)

CHILDREN'S ENTERTAINMENT FILMS

The structure of the organization responsible for the making and distribution of children's entertainment films in Great Britain is as follows :

CHILDREN'S ENTERTAINMENT FILMS, G.B. INSTRUCTIONAL LTD.
17 Oxendon Street, Haymarket, London, S.W.1
Telephone : Whitehall 2826

ADVISORY COUNCIL
Chairman :
LADY ALLEN OF HURTWOOD
(Chairman of the Nursery School Association)

MISS R. S. ADDIS
The National Council for Mental Health

OLIVER BELL, M.A., J.P.
British Film Institute

MISS D. D. CHILCOT
Library Association

W. H. C. DAVEY
Home Office

MRS. WALTER ELLIOT, C.B.E.
National Association of Girls Clubs and Mixed Clubs

Rev. BENJAMIN GREGORY, D.Litt.
Christian Cinema Council

Alderman MRS. E. J. GREGORY, O.B.E., J.P.
Association of Education Committees

W. GRIFFITH, M.A.
National School of Teachers

H. FORSYTH HARDY
Scottish Office

RANDAL KEANE, M.A.
National Association of Boys Clubs

FREDA, COUNTESS OF LISTOWEL
National Federation of Women's Institutes

MRS. R. MARCOUSÉ
Ministry of Education (as observer)

DEREK McCULLOCH, O.B.E.
British Broadcasting Corporation

MRS. E. M. WYKES
National Union of Townswomen's Guilds

Representing the Committee on Children's Cinema
Clubs :
LORD ABERDARE
A. E. MORGAN, M.A., LL.D.

FILM PRODUCTION EXECUTIVE COMMITTEE
MISS MARY FIELD, M.A.
H. BRUCE WOOLFE
E. McQUAID
(Controller, Odeon National Cinema Club)
VICTOR P. POWELL
(Controller, Gaumont British Junior Club)

STAFF
MARY FIELD, M.A....................Director
H. BRUCE WOOLFE..........Production Adviser
MARY CATHCART BORER, B.Sc..Scenario Editor
PATRICIA LATHAM.....Assistant Scenario Editor
W. D'ARCY...................Production Manager
ALEX F. PRIMROSE...........Business Manager
MARTHA McCULLOCH...............Research

FILMS PRODUCED 1945-7
Features

Jean's Plan
Adventure. How a young girl's ingenuity foils jewel thieves. With Vivian Pickles, Billie Brooks, and Tony Hellman.

Escape from Norway
Adventure. The resistance of Norwegian fisherfolk to the German occupation. (English commentary)

Bush Christmas
Adventure. In the Blue Mountains of New South Wales, five children recapture some stolen horses. With Helen Grieve, Nicky and Michael Yardley, Morris Unicomb, and Neza Saunders.

The Boy Who Stopped Niagara
Fantasy. A boy dreams that at the pull of a switch he stops Niagara Falls. (Made in Canada.)

Circus Boy
Comedy Adventure. A schoolboy lives with a circus for a month. With James Kenny, and Florence and George Stephenson.

The Little Ballerina
Drama. Featuring the first screen appearance of Margot Fonteyn and the Sadler's Wells Ballet. With Yvonne Marsh, Marian Chapman, Doreen Richards, and Anthony Newley.

Stage Frights
Comedy. Fun and games behind the scenes at a theatre. With Mark Daly and Graham Moffatt.

The Secret Tunnel
Adventure. How two boys solve the mystery of a stolen Rembrandt. With Anthony Wager and Ivor Bowyer.

The Frozen Falls*
Adventure. The story of a secret formula hidden in a lead mine. With Ray Jackson, Peter Scott, Michael Dean, and Tony Richardson.

The Elephant and the Skipping Rope
Fantasy. How an elephant teaches a little girl to skip. (English version, with commentary, of a Russian children's film.)

Fortune Lane
Comedy Adventure. The story of a boy who wants to be a railwayman. With Douglas Barr, Brian Weske, and Angela Glynne.

* First film to use the independent frame method, a development of back projection, perfected by David Rawnsley of the Rank Research Department.

Short Stories

Tom's Ride
How a boy " earned " a bicycle. (1 *reel*)

Sports Day
With Jean Simmons. (2 *reels*)

Trouble at Townshend
London children in the country. With Petula Clark. (2 *reels*)

Here We Come Gathering
Life on a Kentish fruit farm. (2 *reels*)

The House Goblin
A Swedish folk story told in verse. (1 *reel*)

Series

The Voyage of Peter Joe
A series of six adventures, with Brian Peck, Mark Daly, Graham Moffatt, and Knox Crichton. This series is a revival of custard-pie slapstick comedy, with stories written by Marriott Edgar. (*Each 2 reels*).

1. *A Smashing Job*
   Peter Joe, Nobby and Albert do a job of furniture removing.

2. *Ghostesses*
   They discover a ghost.

3. *All's Fair*
   They find a children's theatre at a fairground.

4. *The Soldier's Cottage*
   They help to build a " prefab ".

5. *The Laundry*
   The boys come to the rescue when the laundry girls go on strike.

6. *Stamp Ramp*
   Adventures with a stamp collector.

Club Magazine (Monthly)
A collection of short news items about the activities of the members of various clubs, and general interest items likely to appeal to children—toy-making, model aeroplane clubs, a visit to a farm, and so on. (1 *reel each*)

Community Singing Films (colour)
These songs are conducted and arranged by Leslie Woodgate for children's community singing. The sound is set against coloured cartoons. (1 *reel each*)

   Heave Away, My Johnny

   The Wraggle Taggle Gypsies

   Dashing Away with the Smoothing Iron

   One More River

   Oh, No John !

   Bound for the Rio Grande

Serial

Dusty Bates (5 episodes)
This serial, consisting of five two-reel instalments, is the first of its kind to be made in England. It is the story of a young stowaway who, with the son and daughter of the ship's captain, brings to justice a dangerous gang of jewel thieves.

Travel

Portuguese Harvest
A boy among the grape pickers in the Douro Valley. (1 *reel*)

Magic Globe Series
Two English children are transported by magic to a foreign country and taken sightseeing by children of the country in which they find themselves. The countries served are : Canada (2), Czechoslovakia, Lapland, Poland. (1 *reel each*)

Nature

Sally Sparrow
Adventures of a sparrow at the London Zoo, with a commentary in rhymed couplets.

Secrets of Nature
Re-edited, with new commentaries for children. (500-650 *feet each*)
On the Beach
A Visit to the Swans
A Visit to the Farne Islands
A Home of the Seabirds
Birds of the Marshes
A Lonely Family
Ravens at Home
Under the Hedge
All about Sand-flies
Under the Rocks
Fishy Looks
Story of a Butterfly

Tales of the Woodland
Nature stories written by Enid Blyton. (1 *reel each*)
A Home in the Stream (Otter)
Rabbits, Rabbits !
Hide and Seek (Camouflage and Nature)
All Kinds of Houses (Birds' Nests)
Sleepy Heads (Hibernation)
A Tadpole Tale (Life of a Frog)

Cartoons
(Black and White)

Robbie Finds a Gun
Robbie, a rabbit, gets into trouble with his catapult. (1 *reel*)

(Colour)

Squirrel War (Serial : 3 episodes)
Who Robbed the Robins ?

Interest

Tale of a Trawler
Pen Pictures from Rhodesia
Behind the Scenes at the Zoo

Renée Marcousé

FILMS AS AN AID TO TEACHING

TWO committees, set up in London in 1946, provide proof of the growing importance of visual education. The National Committee for Visual Aids in Education, representing the teachers and education authorities, is the policy committee. The Committee for the Production and Preparation of Visual Aids in Education, set up by the Minister of Education, is the technical committee on which are representatives of the National Committee, certain Government departments, and the film industry. It is responsible for the execution of the programme presented by the other committee and provides consumers and producers with an opportunity to discuss mutual problems of distribution, apparatus and material.

This attempt to co-ordinate the needs of the schools and the interests of the industry will, it is hoped, end an unsatisfactory situation which existed up to 1946. Work in visual education had already started before the last war, and in 1940, according to a survey made by the British Film Institute, there were some 1700 projectors in schools and other education centres in England and Wales. Four hundred of these were sound projectors, the rest silent. In 1934, Gaumont British Instructional began their educational film programme, and made over 200 films in the course of five years. A few other commercial firms produced educational films on a much more limited scale. Most commercial producers were unwilling to make educational films until sufficient projectors were in the schools to guarantee an adequate financial return, and education authorities were often unwilling to provide equipment until suitable films were available.

The extensive use made of visual material both in the Forces and for civilian audiences brought recognition of its value, and in 1944 the Minister of Education began an experimental programme of Visual Units. These units are designed to show the relative educational values of the sound and silent film, the film strip, the wall panel and model. The two committees were set up to solve educational and technical problems and to co-ordinate the work and requirements of teacher and producer.

The appreciation of the merits of visual education is but one of the developments which have taken place in teaching in recent years, and which have called for a new approach on the part of the

MRS. R. MARCOUSÉ, *Licencié Art et Archéologie, Ph.D., is secretary of the Committee for the Production and Preparation of Visual Aids in Education, and observer for the Ministry of Education on the advisory council of Children's Entertainment Films.*

teacher. The child is no longer relegated to the desk, and activities which require initiative and self expression are encouraged. Visual education has therefore a valuable contribution to make. Children taught almost exclusively by the written or spoken word have also to learn by looking. This demands training in observation, and appreciation by the teacher of the nature of the new material and of its effect on the child.

Visual teaching is not merely the illustration of a verbal lesson nor a verbal interpretation by the teacher of the films and photographs. This would imply neglect and misunderstanding of the specific contribution of the media. Visual material has the power to stir the imagination and to rouse the curiosity. But it is for the teacher to make use of these impressions, to verify them, and by encouraging the child to express what he has experienced make him aware of what he has seen. The role of the teacher is as important in visual as in verbal teaching, and the worth of the material depends on the use he makes of it.

Some teachers in the past, unable to get suitable films for the classroom, made their own. This happened in Scotland, where great interest in this medium was shown before the war and where many teachers' groups were already doing active work. But not every teacher is a potential producer, and although the content was adequate, the film frequently was quite unimpressive. To present a simple fact in impressive visual form calls for the experienced artist-producer rather than the amateur, and the educational film should be a work of art if it is to be effective as a teaching medium.

Some material from *Turksib*, one of the great silent films made in Russia, which was re-edited by the Dartington Hall Film Unit and made available to schools under the title of *The Nomads*, may well illustrate this point. The nomadic tribe is seen crossing the desert in search of new pastureland. The sequence which never failed to hold the interest of the junior group was the sudden swift drama of the sandstorm—the swirling sand, the bag of wool split open, the struggle to get the camel's head down, crouching figures almost hidden by the sand, a skeleton, and then the sun shining and the long line of camels continuing on its way. The photography, the arrangement of the material, the implication of each scene, all combine to intensify an experience shown on the screen.

This film was used in a junior school with a class of ten year olds. It produced an intense activity on the part of the children in the form of maps, drawings, poems, paintings, written descriptions of the nomad's life, and a fairy story. I quote one of these poems by a boy of ten :

A SANDSTORM

In the distance we could see
The black clouds coming nearer
Oh Lord, it is a sandstorm
Alas, the day it darkens
As if the night comes on
Yet it's only morning
Oh, how we all are scorning—
And the storm is upon us at last.

With the storm, there comes grim death
We close our eyes in terror
The camels are uneasy
And we hear the horses whinny,
The terror-stricken cattle
Cower up together
The blinding sand comes higher
Just like a raging fire—
Then all is peaceful and calm at last.

The language of the poem expresses rhythm and feeling, and shows how deeply the child had been moved and how intense his interest had been in the subject. The psychological situation thus created is singularly favourable. Teacher and child have shared in a common experience. The child is eager to be led deeper into the details of the subject. Such effects can be achieved only if educational films have the quality of a work of art.

The film is only one medium of visual education, and the still photograph, the wall chart and film strip are as important in the classroom. Each fulfils a different purpose, and the co-operation of teacher and producer is again required to ensure that each subject is presented in its proper medium.

At present the film strip is in great demand. It is easy to handle, inexpensive, and requires little storing space. The teacher, moreover, gives the required commentary and can control the movement of the image on the screen. Many teachers prepare their own film strips and this adds to the interest and usefulness of the medium.

A well-prepared film strip, however, is not just a series of disconnected pictures or drawings : the theme or argument is brought out in the arrangement of the material. Some excellent film strips were made for instructional purposes in the Services in which skilful use was made of colour, diagram, cartoon and picture.

The still picture has one great advantage over other visual aids. It permits each child to make his observations in his own time, provided he is allowed to do so. This medium has already a long tradition in the classroom, but it is used for the most part as an illustration to a verbal lesson. Older children in particular have often lost the habit of looking, and require training in observation. Here, as with other visual media, the teacher has an essential part to play, and by means of carefully prepared questions can make the child aware of what is otherwise taken for granted. Some pictures rouse little interest in a class when the children are given an opportunity to look at them. Yet the same pictures lead to lively discussion and general class activity when the question method is used and the children are obliged to study the material.

There is still much research required in the use of visual material in the teaching of specific subjects such as English or Modern Languages. Selections from the silent and out-of-date film *Lorna Doone* produced surprising results with a class whose reading ability was below the average. The children's interest was aroused by the film. They read the original text, discussed the interpretation given in the film and were incited to read on to discover what happened.

The still picture can also be used to increase the child's vocabulary and awake his appreciation of the quality of words. It requires training and practice to describe a picture adequately and to put impressions into words. A class will produce a great variety of expressions for the same picture and it is for the teacher to explain why some are preferable to others. Here, as with other visual aids, discrimination is required in the selection of outstanding material. The child who said in his description of a South Carolinian Negro, " his grey fluffy hair almost like the little wire springs from a watch," was expressing the qualities inherent in the picture. Results of this kind depend not on the number of pictures shown, but on their quality and on the use that is made of them.

Mention should also be made of the role of film strip and still picture in relation to the film. It is not always possible or desirable to show all aspects of a topic on the screen, and frequently the related media are required to give more detailed information. The subject matter of a single film will often provide material for a whole series of film strips, wall charts or still pictures on different aspects of the topic.

The need for further research in visual education has been realized by the newly formed committees, and a thorough inquiry is being undertaken by the Foundation of Educational Research. Guidance is required on the use of the material and evidence of the effect of each medium on different age groups.

What should be achieved by film, film strip or picture in the teaching of different topics ? What visual material is appropriate for the education of handicapped or backward children ? In particular we have little knowledge of the effect of films on the younger age groups. In spite of the extensive use made of visual aids in Germany and America before 1939, insufficient scientific research has been carried out on questions such as these. It is hoped that the work now being undertaken will provide some of the evidence required and contribute to the knowledge of teacher and producer alike.

The BERNSTEIN QUESTIONNAIRE FOR CHILDREN

IN 1947, for the first time in British film history, child audiences were invited to answer a questionnaire about their likes and dislikes at the cinema. The questions were similar to those addressed to adult patrons of the Granada cinemas.

The questionnaire was designed with the collaboration of a Harley-street psychologist, education authorities, and public opinion survey experts, and was addressed to 50,000 children between seven and fifteen years who attend the Saturday morning matinees first introduced by Sidney Bernstein in 1927.

One outstanding conclusion is that although children (boys and girls) voted Roy Rogers their favourite star, they did not like cowboy films, which were placed seventh in the children's order of preference. More popular films were Historical (1), Comedy (2), Cartoon (3), Thriller (4), Serial (5) and Adventure (6).

The children's favourite stars were (in order of preference) :

1 Roy Rogers
2 James Mason
3 Bing Crosby
4 Stewart Granger
5 Margaret Lockwood
6 Gene Autry
7 George Formby
8 Alan Ladd
9 Tarzan (Johnny Weissmuller)
10 John Wayne.

This voting shows that children's decisions are largely influenced by the stars and films they see at ordinary performances as well as at their special matinees.

Here are other details of the likes and dislikes of cinema-going children :

Favourite Films : *Black Arrow* and *Flash Gordon Conquers the Universe*. These are both children's serials and came first and third in order of preference. *Lassie Come Home* was second. Also popular with the girls—although it came nowhere with the boys—was *The Bells of St. Mary's*.

Love Scenes : 19 per cent of the boys and 66 per cent of the girls liked love scenes. Rather oddly, one in four of the seven-year-old boys liked them, while the eleven-year-old boys liked them least.

Films About Animals and Children : Overwhelmingly popular with both sexes, although with girls interest tends to wane as they grow older.

Disney Characters : Both boys and girls rated Donald Duck top favourite, with Mickey Mouse and Pluto runners-up.

Newsreels : These were liked by 76 per cent of the boys but only 61 per cent of the girls. Interest increases as children grow older.

Singing : Three in four liked community singing, and most children enjoyed the singing competitions which are a feature of the children's matinees.

Question : *What kind of films do you like best, which next best and so on?*

	ALL REPLIES	BOYS	GIRLS
1	Historical	Historical	Historical
2	Comedy	Comedy	Comedy
3	Cartoon	Cartoon	Cartoon
4	Thriller	Serial	Thriller
5	Serial	Thriller	Serial
6	Adventure	Adventure	Adventure
7	Cowboy	Cowboy	Cowboy

Comment : Historical films led the list by a handsome margin. Age differences were negligible. The low position of cowboy films was odd in view of the popularity of Roy Rogers and other cowboy stars.

Question : *Who are your favourite film stars?*

ALL REPLIES

1	Roy Rogers	11	Abbott and Costello
2	James Mason	12	Errol Flynn
3	Bing Crosby	13	Shirley Temple
4	Stewart Granger	14	Bill Boyd
5	Margaret Lockwood	15	Johnny M. Brown
6	Gene Autry	16	Humphrey Bogart
7	George Formby	17	Margaret O'Brien
8	Alan Ladd	18	The Three Stooges
9	Tarzan (Johnny Weissmuller)	19	Cornel Wilde
10	John Wayne	20	Betty Grable

21 Bob Hope

BOYS		GIRLS
Roy Rogers	1	Roy Rogers
James Mason	2	Margaret Lockwood
Bing Crosby	3	James Mason
Stewart Granger	4	Stewart Granger
Gene Autry	5	Bing Crosby
George Formby	6	Shirley Temple
Tarzan (Johnny Weissmuller)	7	Margaret O'Brien
Alan Ladd	8	Gene Autry
Abbott and Costello }	9	Cornel Wilde
Errol Flynn }	10	Betty Grable
John Wayne	11	John Wayne
Margaret Lockwood	12	Alan Ladd
Bill Boyd	13	{ George Formby
Johnny M. Brown	14	{ Humphrey Bogart
Humphrey Bogart	15	{ Abbott and Costello
The Three Stooges	16	{ The Three Stooges
Bob Hope	17	{ Bob Hope
Betty Grable	18	Errol Flynn
Cornel Wilde }	19	{ Johnny M. Brown
Shirley Temple }	20	{ Tarzan (Johnny Weissmuller)
Margaret O'Brien	21	Bill Boyd

Comment : Roy Rogers was the most popular star by an overwhelming majority. He received more than six times as many votes as the next star on the list---the preponderance being more marked in the boys' votes. Girls placed Margaret Lockwood, Shirley Temple, Cornel Wilde and Betty Grable relatively much higher than boys did, and gave negligible support to George Formby and " Tarzan " who were comparatively popular with boys.

Question : *Do you like newsreels ?*

	ALL REPLIES	BOYS	GIRLS	
Yes	71	76	61	per cent
No	28	23	38	per cent
No reply	1	1	1	per cent

Age Analysis :

BOTH SEXES

	Under 8	8	9	10	11	12	13	14 and over	
Yes	63	70	70	72	71	74	78	74	per cent
No	36	29	29	27	28	25	22	25	per cent
No reply	1	1	1	1	1	1	0	1	per cent

BOYS

	Under 8	8	9	10	11	12	13	14 and over	
Yes	65	76	76	77	77	81	85	86	per cent
No	33	24	23	22	22	18	15	12	per cent
No reply	2	0	1	1	1	1	0	2	per cent

GIRLS

	Under 8	8	9	10	11	12	13	14 and over	
Yes	56	60	56	64	61	64	68	58	per cent
No	43	39	43	35	39	35	32	42	per cent
No reply	1	1	1	1	0	1	0	0	per cent

Comment : Newsreels were more popular with boys than with girls, and in both cases interest increased with age

Question : *Do you like films with animals in them ?*

	ALL REPLIES	BOYS	GIRLS	
Yes	93	95	90	per cent
No	6	4	9	per cent
No reply	1	1	1	per cent

Age Analysis :

BOYS

	Under 8	8	9	10	11	12	13	14 and over	
Yes	95	94	95	95	94	95	93	92	per cent
No	3	5	4	4	5	4	6	6	per cent
No reply	2	1	1	1	1	1	1	2	per cent

GIRLS

	Under 8	8	9	10	11	12	13	14 and over	
Yes	93	90	90	90	87	91	89	85	per cent
No	6	9	9	10	12	8	10	13	per cent
No reply	1	1	1	0	1	1	1	2	per cent

Comment: Animal films were universally popular, but there was a tendency for popularity to decline with increased age, particularly with girls.

Question : *Do you dislike films in which people are hurt ?*

	ALL REPLIES	BOYS	GIRLS
Yes	46	43	51
No	53	56	48
No reply	1	1	1

Age Analysis :

BOTH SEXES

	Under 8	8	9	10	11	12	13	14 and over	
Yes	53	53	45	45	46	42	35	40	per cent
No	46	46	54	54	53	57	64	60	per cent
No reply	1	1	1	1	1	1	1	0	per cent

BOYS

	Under 8	8	9	10	11	12	13	14 and over	
Yes	52	53	42	40	43	38	28	35	per cent
No	47	46	57	59	56	61	72	65	per cent
No reply	1	1	1	1	1	1	0	0	per cent

GIRLS

	Under 8	8	9	10	11	12	13	14 and over	
Yes	55	53	51	55	52	49	46	47	per cent
No	44	46	49	45	47	51	53	53	per cent
No reply	1	1	0	0	1	0	1	0	per cent

Comment : Less than half the children objected to films in which people are hurt. In interpreting this fact it must be remembered that the question can be taken to apply to " slapstick " or " knockabout " comedies and to films in which the villain gets his deserts.

Boys displayed greater indifference than girls, but the age analysis showed that while girls grew more sensitive to cruelty as they grew older, boys became more indifferent, the proportion disliking such films falling from one-half to one-third. Further light was thrown on this fact by the replies to the next question.

Question : *Do you feel that you want to look away or go on watching when someone is getting hurt on the screen ?*

	ALL REPLIES	BOYS	GIRLS
Look away	43	36	55
Go on looking	56	63	44
No reply	1	1	1

Age Analysis :

BOTH SEXES

	Under 8	8	9	10	11	12	13	14 and over	
Look away	57	45	47	44	38	35	29	26	per cent
Go on looking	42	54	52	55	61	64	70	74	per cent
No reply	1	1	1	1	1	1	1	0	per cent

BOYS

	Under 8	8	9	10	11	12	13	14 and over	
Look away	51	46	40	35	30	28	19	20	per cent
Go on looking	48	53	59	64	69	71	80	80	per cent
No reply	1	1	1	1	1	1	1	0	per cent

GIRLS

	Under 8	8	9	10	11	12	13	14 and over	
Look away	66	66	61	58	52	44	44	36	per cent
Go on looking	32	33	38	41	47	55	56	64	per cent
No reply	2	1	1	1	1	1	0	0	per cent

Comment : It was difficult to interpret the overall figures of those children who said they wanted to go on looking (56 per cent), since it was obvious that they would not wish to lose the thread of the action. (Some children made notes to this effect on the questionnaire.)

Question : *Which film did you enjoy most out of all the films you ever saw ?*

ALL REPLIES

	per cent
Black Arrow	8.4
Lassie Come Home	3.4
Flash Gordon Conquers the Universe	2.8
Smoky	2.2
Courage of Lassie	1.6
Don Winslow of the Navy	1.4
The Bells of St. Mary's	1.3
	21.1
Other films	78.9
Total	100

Question : *Why did you like the film so much ?*

	per cent
" Because it was exciting "	16
" Because it had animals in it "	12.6
" Because it was in colour "	9.6
" Because there was fighting in it "	7.2
" Because it was funny "	7.1
" Because my favourite star was in it "	5.3
" Because there was music in it "	2.6
All other replies	39.6

Comment : No answers were suggested to the children, and 60 per cent of their spontaneous replies fell into seven clearly marked categories, as above. While the exact meaning attached by the child to the word " exciting " may be disputed, it seems clear that it is some kind of suspense which is sought. It is also noteworthy that colour and music were, of themselves, reasons for liking a film.

Age Analysis :

BOTH SEXES

	Under 8	8	9	10	11	12	13	14 and over	
Colour	9	9	9	10	9	10	10	13	per cent
Animals	15	11	14	14	13	10	11	9	per cent
Fighting	7	10	7	7	8	6	6	4	per cent
Exciting	12	15	16	17	16	19	16	14	per cent
Fav. star	3	3	4	6	7	7	6	10	per cent
Funny	8	10	6	8	6	6	7	8	per cent
Music	2	3	3	2	3	3	3	3	per cent
Other reasons	44	39	41	36	38	39	41	39	per cent

BOYS

Under 8	8	9	10	11	12	13	14 and over
Animals	Exciting	Exciting	Exciting	Exciting	Exciting	Exciting	Exciting
Exciting	Fighting	Animals	Animals	Animals	Animals	Colour	Colour
Fighting	Animals	Fighting	Fighting	Fighting	Fighting	Animals	Animals
Colour	Funny	Colour	Colour	Funny	Colour	Fighting	Fav. star
Funny	Colour	Funny	Funny	Colour	Funny	Funny	Funny
Fav. star	Fav. star	Fav. star	Fav. star	Fav. star	Fav. star	Fav. star	Fighting
Music	Music	Music	Music	Music	Music	Music	Music
No love	No love	No love	No love	No love	No love	No love	No love

GIRLS

Under 8	8	9	10	11	12	13	14 and over
Colour	Colour	Animals	Exciting	Colour	Exciting	Exciting	Colour
Animals	Exciting	Colour	Colour	Exciting	Colour	Animals	Exciting
Funny	Funny	Exciting	Animals	Animals	Animals	Colour	Fav. star
Exciting	Animals	Fav. star	Fav. star	Fav. star	Fav. star	Fav. star	Funny
Music	Fav. star	Funny	Funny	Funny	Funny	Funny	Music
Fighting	Music	Music	Fighting	Music	Music	Music	Animals
Fav. star	Fighting	Fighting	Music	Fighting	Fighting	Fighting	Fighting
No love	No love	No love	No love	No love	No love	No love	No love

Question : *Do you like love scenes in films ?*

	ALL REPLIES	BOYS	GIRLS	
Yes	37	19	66	per cent
No	62	80	33	per cent
No reply	1	1	1	per cent

Age Analysis :

BOTH SEXES

	Under 8	8	9	10	11	12	13	14 and over	
Yes	41	39	34	35	34	40	36	40	per cent
No	58	60	65	64	65	59	63	60	per cent
No reply	1	1	1	1	1	1	1	0	per cent

BOYS

	Under 8	8	9	10	11	12	13	14 and over	
Yes	26	23	18	16	14	18	16	28	per cent
No	73	76	81	83	85	82	83	72	per cent
No reply	1	1	1	1	1	0	1	0	per cent

GIRLS

	Under 8	8	9	10	11	12	13	14 and over	
Yes	68	67	67	64	65	69	63	58	per cent
No	31	32	32	36	34	30	37	42	per cent
No reply	1	1	1	0	1	1	0	0	per cent

Comment : As might be expected, a much larger proportion of girls than of boys expressed an interest in love scenes but it was perhaps unexpected to find that as many as one-quarter of the seven-year-old boys expressed such an interest. The interest of boys declined up to eleven years old, then rose again, while girls' interest declined fairly uniformly with increased age.

MARGARET O'BRIEN
(*Metro-Goldwyn-Mayer*)

CLAUDE JARMAN, Jr.
(*Metro-Goldwyn-Mayer*)

Question : *Do you like Walt Disney films ?*

	ALL REPLIES	BOYS	GIRLS	
Yes	96	96	96	per cent
No	4	4	4	per cent

Question : *If you do like Disney films, which characters do you like best, which next best, and so on ?*

	ALL REPLIES	BOYS	GIRLS
1	Donald Duck	Donald Duck	Donald Duck
2	Mickey Mouse	Mickey Mouse	Mickey Mouse
3	Pluto	Pluto	Minnie Mouse
4	Donald Duck's Nephews	Goofy	Pluto
5	Goofy	Donald Duck's Nephews	Donald Duck's Nephews
6	Minnie Mouse	Minnie Mouse	Goofy
7	Horace Horsecollar	Horace Horsecollar	Horace Horsecollar

Question : *Do you like films with children in them ?*

	ALL REPLIES	BOYS	GIRLS	
Yes	92	89	97	per cent
No	7	10	2	per cent
No Reply	1	1	1	per cent

Age Analysis :

BOYS

	Under 8	8	9	10	11	12	13	14 and over	
Yes	90	85	89	90	89	89	87	89	per cent
No	7	13	10	9	10	10	12	9	per cent
No reply	3	2	1	1	1	1	1	2	per cent

GIRLS

	Under 8	8	9	10	11	12	13	14 and over	
Yes	95	98	95	98	98	98	97	96	per cent
No	4	1	4	1	1	1	3	0	per cent
No reply	1	1	1	1	1	1	0	4	per cent

Comment: Films with children in them were universally popular, but slightly less so with boys than with girls.

Question : *Do you like community singing ?*

	ALL REPLIES	BOYS	GIRLS	
Yes	78	74	86	per cent
No	21	26	13	per cent
No reply	1	0	1	per cent

Age Analysis :

BOTH SEXES

	Under 8	8	9	10	11	12	13	14 and over	
Yes	81	77	79	79	78	77	77	78	per cent
No	18	22	20	20	21	22	22	22	per cent
No reply	1	1	1	1	1	1	1	0	per cent

BOYS

	Under 8	8	9	10	11	12	13	14 and over	
Yes	78	72	76	74	72	72	74	72	per cent
No	21	28	24	26	27	28	25	28	per cent
No reply	1	1	0	0	1	0	1	0	per cent

GIRLS

	Under 8	8	9	10	11	12	13	14 and over	
Yes	89	89	88	88	88	84	81	87	per cent
No	10	10	11	12	12	16	19	13	per cent
No reply	1	1	1	0	0	0	0	0	per cent

Comment : Community singing appealed to four children out of five, and more strongly to girls than boys. With girls it declined in appeal up to thirteen years old, then rose.

Question : *Do you like stage competitions ? If you do like stage competitions, fill in your three favourite kinds.*

ALL REPLIES	per cent	BOYS	per cent	GIRLS	per cent
Singing	37	Intelligence Quiz	32	Singing	48
Intelligence Quiz	30	Singing	30	Tap dancing	42
Tap dancing	26	Tap dancing	16	Intelligence Quiz	28
Musical Bumps	9	Clowning	9	Musical Bumps	10
Clowning	8	Musical Bumps	8	Acrobats }	8
Acrobats	7	Conjuring	7	Piano playing }	
Piano playing }		Acrobats }	6	Clowning }	7
Conjuring }	6	Piano playing }		Spelling Bee }	
Spelling Bee }		Spelling Bee }	5	Conjuring }	5
Tug-of-War }	4	Tug-of-War }		Acting }	
Acting }		Acting	4	Tug-of-War	4

Age Analysis :

SINGING

	Under 8	8	9	10	11	12	13	14 and over	
Boys	35	30	30	27	28	34	33	26	per cent
Girls	51	49	49	50	50	43	43	42	per cent

INTELLIGENCE QUIZ

	Under 8	8	9	10	11	12	13	14 and over	
Boys	18	20	29	29	37	39	45	55	per cent
Girls	16	21	27	29	35	32	40	29	per cent

TAP DANCING

	Under 8	8	9	10	11	12	13	14 and over	
Boys	23	19	16	13	13	16	15	15	per cent
Girls	50	48	46	42	36	39	35	33	per cent

Comment : Singing was popular with all ages and both sexes. Tap dancing appealed chiefly to girls, especially the youngest, and intelligence quizzes to boys, chiefly the oldest.

Question : *Do you like Saturday morning shows better than shows for grown-ups ?*

	ALL REPLIES	BOYS	GIRLS	
Yes	91	93	90	per cent
No	8	6	9	per cent
No reply	1	1	1	per cent

Age Analysis :

BOTH SEXES

	Under 8	8	9	10	11	12	13	14 and over	
Yes	97	96	95	93	90	87	92	74	per cent
No	2	3	4	6	9	12	17	25	per cent
No reply	1	1	1	1	1	1	1	1	per cent

BOYS

	Under 8	8	9	10	11	12	13	14 and over	
Yes	97	98	95	94	92	89	83	68	per cent
No	2	2	3	5	7	10	16	32	per cent
No reply	1	0	2	1	1	1	1	0	per cent

GIRLS

	Under 8	8	9	10	11	12	13	14 and over	
Yes	98	95	94	81	88	85	81	83	per cent
No	2	4	5	7	11	14	18	16	per cent
No reply	0	1	1	2	1	1	1	1	per cent

Comment : Although children's matinées were remarkably popular, they declined in appeal with increased age, and most rapidly with boys.

Question : *Can you think of anything which would make your Saturday morning shows better than they are ?*

	ALL REPLIES	BOYS	GIRLS	
More stage shows	25	23	28	per cent
Less noise	14	13	14	per cent
Sell ice-cream	5	6	5	per cent
More cowboy films	4	4	4	per cent
More cartoon films	4	3	4	per cent
More animal films	3	3	2	per cent
The shows are perfect	17	18	15	per cent
No suggestions	22	24	20	per cent

Comment : The term " stage shows " was used to cover all suggestions made by children involving live performances —for example, acrobats, conjurors and bands—as opposed to films. The demand for stage shows was marked, especially from girls, and rose with increased age. Similarly, the noise and shouting troubled the older children more. The remark " the shows are perfect " was offered spontaneously by 17 per cent of the children. It was the very young who tended to find the shows satisfying. Boys on the whole did not offer any idea more often than girls.

Note : The percentages do not add to 100 per cent, since many children made more than one suggestion.

JOHN HOWARD DAVIES
("*Oliver Twist*"—Cineguild)

GLOSSARY AND INDEX

A GLOSSARY OF
TECHNICAL TERMS AND ABBREVIATIONS

A.B.C. : Associated British Cinemas.

A.B.P.C. : Associated British Picture Corporation.

A.C.T. : Association of Cine Technicians.

Animation : Photography of inanimate objects in such a manner that upon the screen they appear to have the power of voluntary motion.

A.S.F.P. : Association of Short Film Producers.

Back Projection : A device by which a previously shot sequence of scenery is projected on to a screen behind the players, and re-shot with them in the foreground to suggest that they are actually in the scene.

Black and White : The positive print of a film supplied for showing in the cinema.

Blimp : A soundproof cover on the film camera to absorb the noise which would otherwise interfere with the sound track.

Blow-up : A film enlarged to 35 mm. from 16 mm.

B.B.F.C. : British Board of Film Censors.

B.F.I. : British Film Institute.

B.F.P.A. : British Film Producers Association.

B.K.S. : British Kinematograph Society.

Caption : A sub-title ; words appearing on the screen to assist the audience to follow a silent or foreign film.

C.E.A. : Cinematograph Exhibitors' Association.

Cinemicrography : The cinematography of microscopic objects.

Clapper Board : A blackboard bearing chalked scene and "take" numbers, and a hinged piece of wood. At the beginning and end of each "take," the board is held up to be photographed by the visual or mute film camera, and the hinged wood is brought down smartly to strike the frame of the board, making a noise to mark the beginning of the film in the sound camera. This enables the editor to synchronize the mute or visual film with its corresponding sound track.

Clapper Boy : The boy with the clapper board.

Close-up : A shot taken with the camera close to the subject—often used to give the face of the player in detail and filling the screen.

Combined M and E Track : Often the music and effects tracks are recorded separately ; when they are perfected they are "mixed" carefully for balance of volume to make one sound track.

Combined Print : A print of the film in which the visual or mute film is combined or "married" to the sound track, on the same reel of film.

Continuity : The smooth flowing of the film from one shot to another.

Continuity Girl : The girl in charge of continuity. While the film is being shot, this girl attends to details of scenery, clothes, and so on, so that no discrepancies arise from the elapse of time between "takes", which would spoil the illusion of continuous action. For instance, an actor smoking the stub of a cigarette in the opening of a scene must be careful not to be seen smoking a longer one later on, when the story of the film provides no break.

Crane Shot : A high angle shot taken with the camera suspended over the scene from a special kind of crane.

Credit Titles : The announcements normally appearing at the beginning of a film, giving the names of the chief people who made the film and the players who took part in it.

Cut-outs : Scenes rejected from the film by the editor. Some may be saved for use as "library" shots in later films and stored, others may be discarded.

Cutter : An assistant to the editor.

Cutting Copy : The collection of "rushes"—the first prints from the original negative, on which the editor and his staff of cutters work to make the "rough cut".

Director : The creative controller of the film throughout. He is in charge of the interpretation of the script.

Dissolve (or *mix*) : The gradual merging of one shot into the next. While the first shot gradually disappears, the second shot appears to emerge out of it. A dissolve can be made either by the camera or in the laboratory.

Distribution : The method by which the completed film is marketed, and so ultimately shown to the public or other intended audience.

There are two types of distribution— theatrical, where the film is handled by the commercial cinema, and non-theatrical, where the film (usually 16 mm.) is shown to non-commercial audiences, for example, schoolchildren, villagers, or specialists seeing technical films.

Dolly : A hand-propelled vehicle on which the camera is mounted for "tracking shots" (those where the camera itself moves bodily for an appreciable distance).

Dope (or *continuity sheet*) : A detailed description of the scenes actually shot. The term is also applied to a description of a film taken down after its final assembly.

Double Exposure : Exposure of the same film twice or more, producing two or more images, one over the other. This process is used in films where the actor plays a dual role.

Double-headed: A film with the visuals on one mute film, and the sound track on another reel. Such a film can be shown on any projector with double spool boxes. One roll of film passes the picture illuminant, and the other roll passes the sound head.

Dubbing : The process of adding sound or sounds, whether already on a sound track or newly created ; for example, a commentary in a sound studio on to a reel of film.

Dupe (duplicating) Negative : From the original negative a large but limited number of prints can be made. It is therefore usually necessary to make duplicating negatives to get an adequate number of prints.

Dupe (duplicating) Print : The positive prints made directly from the original negative on either lavender or fine-grain stock, from which the duplicating negatives are struck.

Editola (or movieola) : A projection machine used for convenience in the cutting-room. It shows the film through a small round window, and can take one sound track. It can be stopped, reversed, and restarted by a handle, so that the person working it may easily locate or repeat any particular part of the film.

Editor : The person responsible for supervising the cutting of a film from both the aesthetic and technical aspects.

Effects Track : It is customary for the sound track of a film to be built up gradually of several separate tracks. Music may be on one, voices on another, and " effects "—such as the sound of a door shutting or the splash of an oar—on another.

Extras (or supers) : Men and women who have non-speaking parts in crowd or background scenes.

Fade-in : The gradual appearance of the image from darkness. The beginning of a film or of a sequence is usually introduced in this way.

Fade-out : The reverse process from the fade-in, by which scenes disappear gradually. It is usually employed for ending a sequence or a film.

F.P.G. : Film Producers' Guild.

F.D.F.U. : Federation of Documentary Film Units.

Fine-grain Stock : The film stock which is used for printing the positive film for dupe negatives from the original negative.

Flash-back : A device by which shots or sequences of film are introduced to action in the past or memory of it. This was notably employed in *Cavalcade* (made in 1932), where old newsreel material was used, and in *In Which We Serve*, which was told entirely in flash-back.

Floor : The flat expanse of studio space on which the sets are built and the film is enacted and shot. (In Hollywood the word " stage " is used.)

Flam : An abbreviation of " inflammable ", used to denote film on a cellulose nitrate base, which is highly inflammable, and whose use is consequently subject to many safety regulations. The 35 mm. commercial films are usually " flam " because this base gives the best photographic quality.

Frame : One of the many succeeding pictures which make up a film, made by one exposure of the original negative film in the camera. Sometimes in faulty projection one sees the divisions between the frames on the screen, and parts of two adjacent frames are projected. This possibility was exploited for comic effect in *Hellzapoppin*.

Insert : A cine-photograph of an object, such as a map or diagram, which is inserted as a sequence in a film.

K.R.S. : Kinematograph Renters' Society.

Lap Dissolve : The same as " dissolve ".

Lavender : A film stock, of this colour, used for making duplicating positives from the original negative of a film.

Leader : The extra length of a film at the beginning, which is not part of the film to be projected on the screen. It is provided to allow the projectionist sufficient length to thread in the projector before starting the projection of the film itself. This leader bears numbers and markings to guide the projectionist, so that a correct opening or follow-on may be made.

Library Shots : Parts of previously shot film material incorporated in a new film. Such sequences of film as are likely to be of value are kept carefully classified in special film libraries. If someone making a film requires a shot, say of Nigeria, he pays a library so much for the use of such a shot in order to save the cost of making one specially. Sometimes the library shot may also be chosen not for economy but for its association or historical value, for example, newsreels of the Coronation.

Lip Synching : An abbreviation of " lip synchronization ", a complicated technical process by which a sound track is " translated ". The speech is re-recorded in the language required, but in order to harmonize the sounds heard with the lip movements seen on the screen, the translator chooses words which are as similar as possible, phonetically and in length, to those of the original version.

Location, to be on : To be making a film away from the studio on sites specially suited to the subject of the film.

Long Shot : A shot of a person, object or scene taken at a distance.

Lot, the : The outdoor space at a studio on which exterior scenes are frequently filmed.

M and E Track : See *Combined M and E Track*.

Married Print : See *Combined Print*.

Medium Shot (or *Mid Shot*) : A shot taken with the camera focused on the middle distance of the scene, so that the shot is half way between a long shot and a close-up.

Mix : See *Dissolve*.

Montage : The generally accepted meaning is a series of quick dissolves from one subject to another to indicate a sequence of events or to dramatize a situation. A classic example is the " Odessa Steps " sequence in *Potemkin*, directed by Sergei Eisenstein.

Motion, Accelerated : The reverse of slow motion described below. This device can be used for comic effect.

Motion, Slow : A method of showing a movement so that it appears slower than normal. This is used extensively in scientific research, in the analysis of movements in athletics, and for comic effect.

Motion, Stop : A method of making a film of a movement that is naturally slow so that it will appear to take place rapidly. Some of the best-known stop motion photography appears in the Gaumont British Instructional *Secrets of Nature* series.

Movieola : See *Editola*.

Mute : The roll of film on which only the visuals are printed, and no sound.

N.A.T.K.E. : National Association of Theatrical and Kinematograph Employees.

Negative : The light sensitive film stock that is exposed in the camera and subsequently processed.

Number Board : The same as " clapper board ".

Opticals : Transition devices, such as fades and mixes.

Panning : The movement of the camera on its axis, either vertically or horizontally. (From the word " panorama ")

Positive : The print made from a negative.

Producer : The term can denote the person financially responsible for the film, but it usually refers to the person who guides the whole film from the artistic and technical point of view, and who has the final word in any important decision.

Reel : A 35 mm. reel will take 1000 ft. of film and a 16 mm. one will take 400, 800, or 1600 ft. of film, but the term is loosely used and must not be taken as an exact measure.

Renter : One dealing with film sales and distribution and linking the producer and the cinema.

Reversal : Changing of a film from negative to positive, or vice versa, by chemical means.

Rough Cut : The film when roughly assembled for the first screening to all concerned for criticism.

Running Shot : A shot made with the camera moving along bodily on tracks.

Rushes : The rapidly processed film which is rushed through the laboratories after a day's shooting, and shown to all concerned for criticism.

S.F.A. : Scientific Film Association.

Scenario : A term for a shooting script.

Set : The background, reconstructed on the floor or on the lot, against which the film is enacted.

Shooting Script : The final draft of the film on paper with full directions. All the scenes are broken down into shots, each of which represents a change of camera angle.

S.M.P.E. : Society of Motion Picture Engineers.

Split-screen : A device by which part of a frame is shot with the other part masked, and then that part exposed to make some special trick or effect.

Still : A photograph of a scene from a film, sometimes enlarged from a cine negative.

Sub-titles : Words appearing alone on the screen, with no visuals showing simultaneously. See *Superimposed Titles*.

Superimposed Titles. This term may denote :
(*a*) Words appearing at the base of the visuals of a silent or foreign language film, and popularly called " sub-titles ".
(*b*) Words appearing against a decorative background, for example, main titles or credits at the opening of a film.

Take : One shot of a particular scene. Several " takes " are usually made as the director or his associates attempt to achieve the perfect interpretation.

Titles : A term loosely used to denote any lettering on the screen, particularly at the beginning of a film.

Tracking Shot : A shot taken with the camera moving bodily along.

Treatment : The script of a film up to all but the final stage, which is called the " shooting script ".

Vaults : The fireproof space in which films are stored.

Visuals : The pictures making up a film.

Wipe : A transition device by which one scene is wiped off the screen by the succeeding one.

—

GENERAL INDEX

383

INDEX TO ADVERTISERS

Northern Transport Agency (London) Ltd
Gerrard Street
London W.1.

Northern Transport Travel Bureau
15 Charles II Street
London S.W.1

A CHALLENGE TO OLD STANDARDS

Accepted ideas of screen brightness and definition have been left far behind with the introduction of the Ross " Streemlite " arc lamp and projector equipment. Quite independent tests of the truly remarkable arc lamp show it to be capable of a much higher light output than any other lamp in its class—a claim we are prepared to substantiate by tests in any cinema in the country.

On every other count too, Ross equipment has received the acclamation and recognition of every progressive Exhibitor who has witnessed its performance. These equipments coupled to RCA Sound Systems afford the highest standard in sound and picture presentation. Either of the Ross distributors will be pleased to arrange for an early demonstration of this superb product of Britain's leading optical company.

ROSS LONDON

Co-distributors of all Ross Cinematograph equipment :—

PATHE EQUIPMENT LTD.
111 WARDOUR STREET
LONDON, W.1

RCA PHOTOPHONE LTD.
43 BERKELEY SQUARE
LONDON, W.1

GLAMOUR *maxfactorized*

DEBORAH KERR
MGM *Star* of
"IF WINTER COMES"

It's so easy to be *maxfactorized*
. . . so exciting and thrilling, too.
Just try this famous *Max Factor
Hollywood* Make-up in the correct
shades which are individually prescribed to enliven,
enhance, and harmonize
perfectly with the natural
colourings of your hair,
eyes, and complexion…and
you will be transformed, as
if by magic, into a vision
of irresistible loveliness.

COLOUR HARMONY MAKE-UP

created by

MAX FACTOR
'Cosmetics' of
the Stars' are
obtainable
from your local
Chemist, Hair-
dresser & Store

Max Factor
HOLLYWOOD & LONDON

PICTURES *and*

BRITISH NATIONAL
PICTURES

Pathe Pictures Ltd
Distributors of

ASSOCIATED BRITISH
PICTURES *and*
BRITISH NATIONAL
PICTURES

athe PICTURES LTD.

Lester Ferguson

Moira Lister

Annette Simmonds

Rita Cave

Personal Service

for

Producers and

Artistes

Alan Wheatley

Lizbeth Webb

Freddie Bartholomew

110 JERMYN STREET, LONDON, S.W.1

Telephone : Abbey 6626

391

Several "Everest"-made full-length features recently completed in record time provide convincing testimony of how this unique reflex camera is helping cut British Film production costs by giving perfectly exposed and composed shots at every first "take".

Vinten "EVEREST" STUDIO CAMERAS

W. VINTEN LTD., NORTH CIRCULAR ROAD, CRICKLEWOOD, LONDON, N.W.2

ASSOCIATED BRITISH
PICTURE CORPORATION LIMITED

Architect's Plan of **NEW ELSTREE STUDIOS**

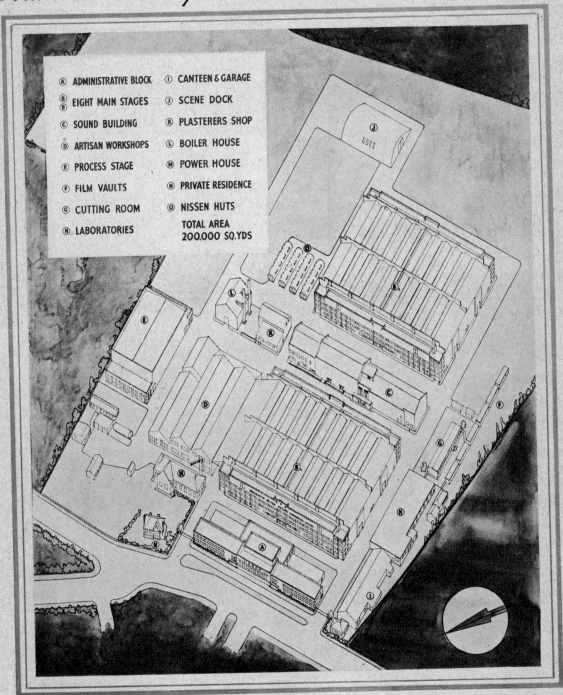

- Ⓐ ADMINISTRATIVE BLOCK
- Ⓑ EIGHT MAIN STAGES
- Ⓒ SOUND BUILDING
- Ⓓ ARTISAN WORKSHOPS
- Ⓔ PROCESS STAGE
- Ⓕ FILM VAULTS
- Ⓖ CUTTING ROOM
- Ⓗ LABORATORIES
- Ⓘ CANTEEN & GARAGE
- Ⓙ SCENE DOCK
- Ⓚ PLASTERERS SHOP
- Ⓛ BOILER HOUSE
- Ⓜ POWER HOUSE
- Ⓝ PRIVATE RESIDENCE
- Ⓞ NISSEN HUTS

TOTAL AREA
200,000 SQ.YDS

394

curtains
made from
GLASS

THE ILLUSTRATION SHOWS TYGLASS CURTAINS

in the Central Properties Department of the J. Arthur Rank Organisation at Denham

TYGLASS is woven glass and has the appearance of and handles like silk.

It is fireproof, moth and vermin proof, mould proof and is not affected by humidity.

Made in various woven and printed designs or dyed, the lustrous colours never fade

and its pristine beauty is restored by dry cleaning.

For draperies there is nothing so lasting as Tyglass, produced by the makers of Tyga Tested Textiles.

FOTHERGILL AND HARVEY LIMITED
Thirty Seven Peter Street, Manchester 2

DISCOVERY OF BRITAIN

Yes, it's Britain's turn to be discovered! Cinema audiences in most countries are getting a good look at British folk, maybe for the first time, as a result of the much increased showing of British films abroad.

It seems they're glad to know us. The way we walk, talk, dress—where we work, what we play, the way we live. These are the commonplaces of life, but they are what men and women have in common. Sometimes they emerge from a nation's literature, sometimes they take a hundred years to find their way across land and sea and other barriers.

Good films, being invitations to friendly voyages of discovery, are helping in this urgent task of wiping out the 'blind spots,' the ignorance and insularity and the silly fears which follow from all these. Once there was talk of 'a far-away country' and 'people of whom we know nothing.' But such phrases need to be erased from every language. Films are one of the best means, ready to hand, of taking the blinkers off the human race and of spreading this knowledge and understanding of which we are all in such need.

J . ARTHUR RANK ORGANISATION LIMITED

We have an unusually wide experience of electrical installation work in the film world. We have carried out complete installations for hundreds of cinemas — including some of the largest and best known — and a number of important British film studios. We are proud of this record and welcome opportunities to add to it.

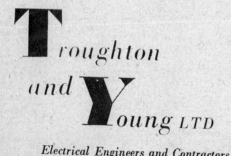

Troughton and Young LTD

Electrical Engineers and Contractors

143 KNIGHTSBRIDGE · S.W.1

Telephone: KENSINGTON 8881 *(10 lines)*

"The more I use it — the better I like it!"

Says Elizabeth Craig, famous cookery expert

G.5429

"House Proud" PLANNED KITCHEN FURNITURE

Sold only by
Approved "House Proud" Distributors

1. KITCHEN CABINET No. 618. Heavy gauge aluminium. Top cupboard fitted two shelves, bottom cupboard fitted one shelf, two lined drawers. Vitreous enamel working top. Chrome plated, recessed handles, stove enamelled in pastel shades. Ht. 72 in., Wth. 42 in., Depth of working top 18 in. Fixed Retail Selling Price £39 19 6

2. SINK UNIT No. 602. Stainless Sheffield steel one-piece top. Aluminium body fitted lined drawer and large cupboard with one shelf. Chrome plated, recessed handles. Stove enamelled in pastel shades. Ht. 36 in., Wth. 42 in., Dth. 18 in. Fixed Retail Selling Price 30 Gns.

3. KITCHEN DRESSER No. 377. Heavy gauge aluminium. Fitted five drawers and large cupboard with one shelf. Vitreous enamel working top. Stove enamelled in pastel shades. Size: 30 in. wide, 15 in. deep, 33 in. high. Fixed Retail Selling Price £16 15 6

4. KITCHEN DRESSER No. 378. Heavy gauge aluminium. Fitted eight drawers. Vitreous enamel working top. Stove enamelled in pastel shades. Size: 30 in. wide, 15 in. deep, 33 in. high. Fixed Retail Selling Price £18 15 0

5. WALL CUPBOARD No. 379. Constructed of heavy gauge aluminium and fitted one shelf. Stove enamelled in pastel shades. Size: 30 in. wide, 9 in. deep, 24 in. high. Fixed Retail Selling Price £7 17 6

VERNONS INDUSTRIES LTD. LIVERPOOL

Daily Mail
FILM
AWARD
ANNUAL
1 9 4 8

This is a book that no film enthusiast can afford to miss. It is a feast of good entertainment ; a valuable source of reference ; and a worthy tribute to Britain's high achievement in the world of films.

- A triumphant year of British film-making is placed on permanent record in a book that will delight all filmgoers.

- Produced by the House of Winchester in conjunction with the *Daily Mail*, this Annual gives the stories, cast lists and production details of the fifty-six films eligible for the 1948 National Film Award.

- Here the reader may recapture the enjoyment of such outstanding British films as *Odd Man Out*, *Frieda*, *Jassy*, *Great Expectations*, *Holiday Camp*, *Mine Own Executioner*, and *The October Man*. Each story is vividly illustrated with " stills " from the film, and there are large portrait photographs of the stars.

- In addition, there is an illustrated article by Norah Alexander, the well-known film critic, on the growth of the British film industry, and Cecil Wilson has reviewed the work of the *Daily Mail* Film Award Department.

There are 192 pages and more than 400 illustrations.
Crown quarto.   Price : 10*s*. 6*d*. net.

WINCHESTER PUBLICATIONS
16 MADDOX STREET   LONDON, W.1.   LIMITED
Telephone : MAYfair 1064

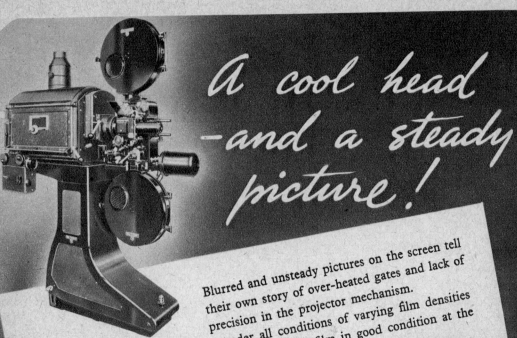

A cool head
—and a steady
picture!

Blurred and unsteady pictures on the screen tell their own story of over-heated gates and lack of precision in the projector mechanism.

To maintain a bright picture under all conditions of varying film densities and foggy atmospheres and yet still present the film in good condition at the gate is only one of the benefits enjoyed by Walturdaw users. This distinguishing feature of the Walturdaw V and the extra precision which we put into every other part of it will need only a moment's consideration to convince you of the obvious operating advantages and improved screen results which must follow the installation of such a first-class sound and vision equipment. Why not ask for a demonstration today?

An exclusive feature of the Walturdaw Five is its removable water-cooled gate shown here.

WALTURDAW
CINEMA SUPPLY CO. LTD., 46 GERRARD ST., W.1
Telephone: GERRARD 1067

BIRMINGHAM · LEEDS · LIVERPOOL · MANCHESTER · NEWCASTLE · CARDIFF · DUBLIN · GLASGOW

4 OUTSTANDING WINCHESTER BOOKS

★ **THE QUEEN ELIZABETH**

This magnificent book about a great ship has been warmly praised by the reviewers. Two typical opinions are : " Lovers of the sea and admirers of ships . . . all over the world will be eager to possess this unique record of British shipping and ship-building genius." (*The Shipping World.*) " A big and handsome volume befitting a big and handsome ship . . . a splendid instance of the printer's art and crafts-manship." (*The Journal of Commerce and Shipping Telegraph.*)
Designed and edited by Clarence Winchester. Demy quarto. 160 pp. Twelve colour plates, a colour sectional diagram, and 102 half-tone illustrations. *Price: 42s. net.*

★ **THE VISUAL LIBRARY**

These volumes provide a new approach to the problems of learning. They make brilliant use of the strip-cartoon technique to provide readers of all ages with easily assimilated knowledge of the world around them. The first title in the series is *Insect Life*, which will be followed by volumes on medicine and the human body, wonders of world engineering, and other scientific, industrial and educational subjects. $8\frac{3}{4} \times 7\frac{1}{4}$ inches. 76 pp. *Price: 6s. 6d. net each volume.*

★ **THEY ALSO SERVE** by DOROTHEA ST. HILL BOURNE

The dramatic and fascinating story of the mascots of the Empire's Fighting Services of World War II, told by the Organizing Secretary of the Allied Forces Mascot Club. This is probably the most remarkable book about animals ever published. It contains scores of stories of animal courage and devotion from all over the world. Demy octavo. 236 pp. 83 half-tone illustrations. *Price: 15s. net.*

★ **THE PERMANENT WAY** by HORACE GREENLEAF *and* G. TYERS

A superbly illustrated book which tells how British railroads are built, maintained and operated. It includes fascinating chapters on the great railway pioneers and their daring feats of railway construction. It is not a textbook, and, though primarily addressed to railway enthusiasts, is of wide general interest. Crown quarto. 256 pp. Four colour plates and 78 photogravure illustrations. *Price: 21s. net.*

WINCHESTER PUBLICATIONS LIMITED
16 MADDOX STREET, LONDON, W.1

403

A Book for Screen Enthusiasts

The sparkling text is lavishly illustrated. There are fifty-one reproductions in half-tone of photographs showing famous stars and directors in the studio or on location, and many unusual shots of film technicians at work on the production of films.

FROM
SCRIPT TO SCREEN

by

BRUCE WOODHOUSE

THIS fascinating book takes the reader behind the scenes of a film studio and explains the vast and complicated organization that is employed in the making of modern entertainment films. The author describes the work of all studio departments, from that of the studio guards to that of the Press and publicity officers. Shooting on the floor and on location, sound recording, film editing, and acting for the films are some of the aspects of the technique of film-making which are comprehensively explained in these pages. Among the valuable Appendices is one containing a director's shooting script of a vivid sequence from the outstanding British film, *Mine Own Executioner*.

The author, who has long been connected with the making of films, has written an informative and amusing book which is sure of a warm welcome from the vast number of those who love the cinema.

With a Foreword by   12s. 6d. net.
SIR ALEXANDER KORDA

WINCHESTER PUBLICATIONS LTD.
16 MADDOX STREET, LONDON, W.1

Telephone : MAYfair 1064